# Psychosocial Treatment of Chronic Mental Patients

MILIEU VERSUS SOCIAL-LEARNING PROGRAMS

Gordon L. Paul and Robert J. Lentz

Harvard University Press, Cambridge, Massachusetts and London, England   1977

Copyright © 1977 by the President and Fellows of Harvard College
All rights reserved
Printed in the United States of America

Library of Congress Cataloging in Publication Data
Paul, Gordon L
　　Psychosocial treatment of chronic mental patients.

　　Bibliography: p.
　　Includes indexes.
　　1. Psychiatric hospital care. 2. Milieu therapy.
3. Behavior modification. 4. Token economy (Psychology)
5. Schizophrenia. I. Lentz, Robert J., 1943-　　joint
author. II. Title.
RC439.P28　　616.8'914　　77-10868
ISBN 0-674-72112-8

# Preface

This book represents the culmination of work that began at the end of 1965 when I became a consultant to public mental hospitals in Illinois. During the first year of consulting it became obvious that the chronically institutionalized population was the largest and most difficult problem to contend with, both locally and nationally. It also became clear that the usual one day per week of typical consultant activities was not going to be able to improve total institutional effectiveness, much less directly help the severely disabled people who constituted the majority of institutional residents. Similarly, staff training efforts seemed equally futile in the long run; the administrative structure existing in mental institutions failed to support the attempts of institutional staff to try out different procedures, and it was impractical to train professional or nonprofessional institutional staff in the usual way, in isolation from the total program context. Of greater concern was the fact that the empirical effectiveness of nearly all institutional practices was unknown.

Over the following year I reviewed the empirical status of the chronic patient, analyzed changes in functioning necessary for these people to return successfully to the community, and conducted a search of the literature to determine whether any approach had even suggestive empirical promise for helping the chronically institutionalized population. Working in collaboration with a number of other consultants and institutional staff, I made plans to conduct a comparative evaluation of the effectiveness of both the existing and the most promising total treatment programs and submitted a grant proposal to seek federal funding for support of the research component of ongoing treatment programs, which was finally awarded in the summer of 1968. Because of the delays in funding, I was not only the principal investigator and project director but the only staff member remaining by the time the funding finally arrived. Nevertheless, with the extraordinary efforts of Illinois Department of Mental Health administrative personnel and the first senior staff employed, the comparative project finally began in the fall of 1968.

The comparative project involved three ongoing groups of the most severely debilitated chronic mental patients ever subjected to systematic study, initially equated on all dimensions that had empirical relevance. Two adjacent clinical units at a regional mental health center were established to house two different psychosocial treatment programs—the most promising developed on the basis of previous empirical findings—with the same staff conducting both programs. Continuous assessments of staff, patients, and program operations on both psychosocial units were maintained through a period of nearly four and a half years of ongoing clinical operations, and assessments were obtained every six months on equated hospital comparisons. As patients were released to the community, replacements were admitted, and original group equivalency was maintained. All patients successfully achieving release from the institutions were systematically followed up for at least a year and a half after the close of the intramural psychosocial programs. Thus, data were collected continuously for six years. The data analysis, literature reviews, interpretations, and reports in the present book spanned two and a half years, overlapping the final follow-up period. The major outcome of the comparative project was that a clear treatment of choice emerged for the chronically institutionalized, with comparative cause-effect documentation of the absolute level of the effectiveness of a treatment program for the first time.

Documented contributions to improving institutional practices related to assessment procedures, staffing, training, staff utilization, administrative practices, aftercare procedures, and a variety of other factors of importance to the effective operation of programs in mental institutions are included in this book as well. Since the design and instrumentation of the comparative project are offered as a model for future research, the seemingly obsessive detail and complex statistical analyses of interest to research workers and academicians are included. However, the book is written so that institutional administrators, program directors, professional clinicians, and preprofessional staff can gain an understanding of operations and findings of interest by selectively following the recommended summaries and parts of chapters.

Those who want to gain a maximum understanding of the comparative project, findings, and recommendations should read the entire book. That is admittedly difficult to do, given the time limitations of most academicians, clinicians, researchers, and administrators. Therefore, some further guidance may help. Chapter 1 presents the historical and current extent of the problem posed by the chronically institutionalized mental patient, along with the empirical and theoretical analysis that provided the rational focus for the comparative project. Chapter 2 summarizes the historical findings for promising treatment programs, which formed the basis for the development of the psychosocial programs in the comparative project. Chapter 3 provides the rationale and overview of the comparative project. Those with little time can read just the summaries of chapters 1 and 2 and all of chapter 3. The guide to the remainder of the volume in chapter 3, combined with the contents, should help each reader locate areas of individual interest for more detailed perusal. It would likely help to read the chapter summaries and part summaries in order, even if other reading is more selective. No content summaries are provided for the concluding chapters in part 9; the recommendations on treatment practices in chapter 42 and the analyses and recommendations related to legal and ethical practices in chapter 43 cannot be adequately considered out of context.

Gordon L. Paul

# Acknowledgments

A project as complex as the one covered in this book, spanning a period of about ten years from its germinal stage to completion, is obviously not a one-man operation. No list of names could accurately represent the many people who assisted in the conduct of the comparative project or adequately represent the contribution of those involved. A list of the junior staff of the psychosocial units and the clinical and support staff at the center and other locales, without whom no project would have existed, would run several pages. The many professional colleagues who helped through informal discussions also are too numerous to list, although those who have made direct contributions are noted in chapters 3, 4, 5, and 10. Elaine Cumming and Alan Kraft reviewed the milieu therapy program proposal, helping to ensure its representativeness. The residents of mental institutions who were the focus of the entire operation have been disguised in presentation for their own benefit. To all of the above, I express my personal gratitude, with apologies to others whom I missed.

Some have made such special contributions that specific acknowledgment will be made here. The project was supported in part by Public Health Service grant MH 15553 from the National Institute of Mental Health. However, if it had not been for the individual efforts of James T. Cumisky and Howard R. Davis within NIMH, the project would have foundered on several occasions for lack of funds resulting from unanticipated political and bureaucratic events and delays. Similarly, Peter K. Levison, research and program adviser in the Illinois Department of Mental Health and Developmental Disabilities, was often instrumental in providing emergency assistance and in seeking supplemental funding sources to allow a continuation of the operations. A special debt of gratitude goes to Lewis Kurke, who served as the regional director and acting superintendent of the center during the entire intramural period of operation, not only for assistance in implementing changes and overcoming bureaucratic barriers in the state system but for establishing and supporting an administrative organization and social environment that allowed the project to operate. Estil L. Ellis, the business manager and assistant superintendent of the center over the entire period, was invaluable in maintaining the day-to-day operations and keeping in touch with key persons in intermediary and central-office positions within the state systems. Glen Minks, Charles Crouch, Frank McGarry, and the staff of the Management Information Service were particularly helpful in providing ongoing computer processing of massive amounts of data for clinical and research utilization. Larry Barnett, the center pharmacist, was crucial in maintaining special drug conditions in specific studies and throughout the project, as well as providing assistance in cost-effectiveness determinations. Flor-de-Lisa Crisostomo served as a helpful and cooperative consulting physician throughout the intramural period of operations, ensuring careful and controlled drug conditions, as well as maintaining the physical health of psychosocial residents.

Every member of the research and treatment senior staff noted in chapters 4 and 37 made invaluable contributions to both the specification of procedures and the implementation of the ongoing project. The personal relationships that evolved with staff members over our time together were significant factors in maintaining my own continued effort and in many cases served to form the basis for strong, lifelong friendships. During their tenure, each senior staff person truly became a member of the group, whose individual contributions became a part of the whole project. Many of their ideas, and often their words, are incorporated in the psychosocial treatment manuals (chapters 6-8), appendixes, and elsewhere in this report of the project. Titus McInnis and Beverly L. Holly served, respectively, as program director and program supervisor for the psychosocial units throughout the entire intramural operation of the project and thus deserve special acknowledgment. Without them, the day-to-day clinical operations would not have functioned in the manner described.

In addition to those noted above who contributed directly to the conduct of the project, several others made unique contributions to the analysis, interpretation, and production of this book. J. B. (Dean) Orris developed the Stereotypy/Variability scores used in some analyses. Nearly all the complex statistical analyses on which our findings are based were ably handled by Marco J. Mariotto, Joel P. Redfield, and Mark H. Licht. A special note of gratitude goes to these men for their conceptual and technical effort and to Lloyd G. Humphreys, Maurice Tatsuoka, and Robert Linn for their frequent consultation on unique and difficult problems of data analysis. Al L. Porterfield and Christopher T. Power assisted in final hand checking and data analyses, retrieval of institutional data, literature searches, and a variety of professional tasks—often under considerable time pressure. Phil Berck and Stan Warburton similarly handled the many complex figures, without which the findings would be much less easily interpreted. Production of this book was supported in part by a grant from the Joyce Foundation, William Ramsey, executive director.

My personal gratitude is extended to Karen Price, Melody Kopisch, and Nancy Kendall, who served as research observers and data analysts through the writing of this book, and to Ilena Shelite, who served as executive secretary and administrative assistant for most of the project, including the production of this book. The observers were crucial members of the larger observational staff who obtained assessments with such extraordinary reliability and validity, and all four remained with the project through no less than seven occasions in which delays in the notification of funding went to the very day on which they would be laid off. Ilena Shelite's competence, efficiency, and devotion are responsible for the completion of this book now, rather than a year or two later. Her prior efficiency resulted in the immediate retrieval of necessary information when needed. She also typed the entire manuscript, translating from my handwriting, and set the book in print. Appreciation is also expressed to Kathryn Engel, Robert Cherney, Deborah Devick, Lisa Klairmont, Barbara Meyer, and Shirley Paceley for assistance with proofreading and indexing. Finally, I must acknowledge the understanding and support I received from my wife, Joan, and my children, Dennis, Dana, and Joni, for the period in which my time with them was limited to one or two brief evenings a week—with a firm vow not to let it happen again.

A final note should be made about the authorship of this book. As I noted above, it could not have been written without the contribution of the people mentioned. Many of the ideas and some of the words of senior staff will be found in various parts of it without specific acknowledgment, since they had become incorporated within the total cooperatively determined procedures. Our original plan had been for Titus McInnis to be one of the coauthors of this book and for David W. Doty and Dale E. Theobald to contribute to some chapters. Unfortunately, a funding crisis, which resulted in a decision to terminate the psychosocial unit, included their layoff. Since all three obtained new positions at some distance from the performance site, time pressures precluded their direct contribution to the volume, but each has provided many of the ideas in it through his prior work. Although I wrote over 99% of this book, Bob Lentz is appropriately listed as the coauthor because of his contribution to the overall project and the production of this book. He was a member of the clinical senior staff group almost from the beginning of the project, with responsibility for supervision of all research staff and the day-to-day monitoring of data collection, reduction, and analysis through the entire project. He also supervised, coordinated, and organized the massive data analyses, conducted literature searches and interpretations, and participated in detailed discussions and reviews of the organization and interpretations to be included in the book. Thus, the ideas and content in it reflect our shared effort and mutually agreed upon recommendations. We hope this effort will result in improved institutional practices.

Gordon L. Paul

# Contents

**PART 1: BACKGROUND AND OVERVIEW**

1. The Chronically Institutionalized Mental Patient    1
   *Historical and Current Status 1*
   *An Interactional Frame of Reference 2*
   *Summary 6*

2. Milieu and Social-Learning Approaches to Treatment    7
   *The Milieu Approach 7*
   *The Social-Learning Approach 9*
   *"Bridging the Gap" 10*
   *Summary 11*

3. Design and Overview of the Comparative Project    13
   *The Rationale for Design and Treatment 13*
   *The Overall Design 15*
   *A Guide to the Remainder of the Book 18*

**PART 2: PROGRAMS, POPULATIONS, AND PROCEDURES**

4. The Treatment Setting, Organization, and Staffing    19
   *The Geographical Zone 19*
   *The Regional State Hospital 20*
   *The Regional Mental Health Center 22*
   *The Psychosocial Units 25*
   *Summary 29*

5. The Treatment Programs and Their Assessment    31
   *General Content 31*
   *Differential Nature of Interactions Among Programs 33*
   *Methods of Assessing Program Operation 33*
   *Actual Differences in Staff Performance Among Programs 36*
   *Summary 40*

6. The Orientation and Common Procedures Manual    42
   *Common Assumptions of Psychosocial Treatment Programs 42*
   *Common Objectives and Areas of Focus 42*
   *Common Operational Procedures and Attitudes 43*
   *Appendix 47*

7. The Milieu Therapy Manual    49
   *Basic Principles and Concepts 49*
   *The Therapeutic Community 51*
   *Procedural Rules for Staff 53*
   *Program Content 54*
   *Appendix 62*

8. The Social-Learning Program Manual    74
   *Basic Principles and Concepts 74*
   *The Token Economy 76*
   *Procedural Rules for Staff 78*
   *Program Content 79*
   *Appendix 86*

9. The Clinical Staff and Their Assessment    102
   *Methods of Assessing Characteristics, Attitudes, and Orientations of Clinical Staff 102*
   *Selection Procedures, Clinical Staff Characteristics, and Turnover 103*
   *Opinions About Mental Patients 106*
   *Preferences on the Nature of Treatment and Technique Utilization 108*
   *Summary 111*

10. Nonprofessional Clinical Staff Training    113
    *Two Approaches to Training Psychosocial Staff 113*
    *Differential Outcomes Associated With the Two Training Approaches 115*
    *Summary 117*

11. Methods of Assessing Patient Behavior    119
    *Relatively Stable Personal-Social Characteristics 120*
    *Level of Functioning Over Institutions 120*
    *Continuous Objective Assessment Within Psychosocial Programs 121*
    *Release and Community Stay 126*

12. The Chronically Institutionalized Population    127
    *Selection of Patients and Group Equation 128*
    *Summary 132*

## PART 3: THE FIRST SIX MONTHS ON THE PSYCHOSOCIAL UNITS: PROGRAM INTRODUCTION AND RAPID RESPONSE

13. Notable Events and Overview of the First Six Months     133

14. Differential Effectiveness of Milieu and Social-Learning Programs After Program Introduction     138
*Changes in Global Functioning 138*
*Changes in Maladaptive Behavior 138*
*Changes in Adaptive Behavior 141*
*Summary and Individual Improvement Rates 143*

15. Other Ongoing Resident Activity After Program Introduction     148
*Comparative Characteristics of Large Community Meetings 148*
*Differential Utilization of Resources 150*
*Time Spent In Programs and With Other People 152*
*Variability of Resident Activity 152*
*Summary 155*

16. Staff Attitudes and Performance Before and After Program Introduction     157
*Opinions About Mental Patients 157*
*Attitudes Toward and Interpretations of Treatment Programs 157*
*Performance in Psychosocial Programs 162*
*Summary 172*

17. Summary of Findings for the First Six Months     175

## PART 4: THE NEXT TWO YEARS ON THE PSYCHOSOCIAL UNITS: VARIABILITY AND PEAK RESPONSE

18. Notable Events and Overview of the Next Two Years     177

19. Differential Effectiveness of the Milieu and Social-Learning Programs During the Next Two Years     182
*Changes in Global Functioning 182*
*Changes in Maladaptive Behavior 182*
*Changes in Adaptive Behavior 188*
*Summary and Individual Improvement Rates 194*

20. Other Ongoing Resident Activity During the Next Two Years     204
*Comparative Characteristics of Large Community Meetings 204*
*Differential Utilization of Resources 208*
*Time Spent In Programs and With Other People 210*
*Variability of Resident Activity 211*
*Summary 215*

21. Staff Attitudes and Performance During the Next Two Years     217
*Opinions About Mental Patients 217*
*Attitudes Toward and Interpretations of Treatment Programs 218*
*Performance in Psychosocial Programs 226*
*Summary 236*

22. Summary of Findings for the Next Two Years     239

## PART 5: THE NEXT YEAR AND A HALF ON THE PSYCHOSOCIAL UNITS: DECLINE OF EFFECTIVENESS AND SEARCH FOR CAUSE

23. Notable Events and Overview of the Next Year and a Half     243

24. Differential Effectiveness of the Milieu and Social-Learning Programs During the Next Year and a Half     249
*Changes in Global Functioning 249*
*Changes in Maladaptive Behavior 249*
*Changes in Adaptive Behavior 257*
*Summary and Individual Improvement Rates 261*

25. Other Ongoing Resident Activity During the Next Year and a Half     268
*Comparative Characteristics of Large Community Meetings 268*
*Differential Utilization of Resources 271*
*Time Spent In Programs and With Other People 274*
*Variability of Resident Activity 275*
*Summary 279*

26. Staff Attitudes and Performance During the Next Year and a Half     282
*Opinions About Mental Patients 282*
*Attitudes Toward and Interpretations of Treatment Programs 283*
*Performance in Psychosocial Programs 289*
*Summary 298*

27. Summary of Findings for the Next Year and a Half     301

## PART 6: THE LAST SIX MONTHS ON THE PSYCHOSOCIAL UNITS: ATTEMPTS TO REGAIN THE PEAK

28. Notable Events and Overview of the Last Six Months     305

29. Differential Effectiveness of the Milieu
and Social-Learning Programs During the
Last Six Months     309
*Changes in Global Functioning 309*
*Changes in Maladaptive Behavior 309*
*Changes in Adaptive Behavior 315*
*Summary and Individual Improvement
  Rates 319*

30. Other Ongoing Resident Activity During
the Last Six Months     327
*Comparative Characteristics of Large
  Community Meetings 327*
*Differential Utilization of Resources 331*
*Time Spent In Programs and With Other
  People 333*
*Variability of Resident Activity 335*
*Summary 340*

31. Staff Attitudes and Performance During
the Last Six Months     345
*Opinions About Mental Patients 345*
*Attitudes Toward and Interpretations of
  Treatment Programs 346*
*Performance in Psychosocial Programs 350*
*Summary 361*

32. Summary of Findings for the Last
Six Months     364

PART 7: PSYCHOSOCIAL VERSUS
HOSPITAL GROUPS: INTRAMURAL
FUNCTIONING AND COMMUNITY
PLACEMENT

33. An Overview of Hospital Comparisons,
Community Placement, and Termination
of the Psychosocial Units     369

34. Comparative Intramural Change of the
Psychosocial and Hospital Groups     373
*The Inpatient Assessment Battery (IAB) 373*
*Some Minor Paradoxes on the IAB 377*
*A Comment on Psychotropic Drugs 379*
*Summary and Predictability of IAB
  Improvement 380*

35. Comparative Release Rates     384
*Effectiveness in Achieving Significant
  Release 384*
*Efficiency in Achieving Significant
  Release 385*
*Relationship to Intramural Functioning and
  Predictability of Significant Release 386*
*Summary of Comparative Release 387*

36. Summary of Findings From Programs and
Placement     388

PART 8: A YEAR AND A HALF AFTER:
COMMUNITY FOLLOW-UP WITH
SOCIAL-LEARNING PRINCIPLES

37. Notable Events and Overview of the
Follow-up Period     391

38. Follow-up Consultation to Community
Facilities and Resulting Programs     394
*Nonspecific Characteristics of Psychosocial
  Aftercare Consultation 394*
*Two Modes of Follow-up 395*
*Actual Staff Performance in Community
  Facilities 398*
*Summary 405*

39. Postrelease Levels of Functioning in
the Community     406
*Changes in Functioning for Released
  Residents 406*
*Changes in Functioning in Different
  Community Facilities 408*
*Summary 411*

40. Practical Outcome of the Psychosocial
and Hospital Programs With Social-Learning
Follow-up     412
*Comparative Release Rates With Continuing
  Community Stay 412*
*Comparative Effectiveness and Efficiency
  of Achieving Continuing Community
  Stay 413*
*Comparative Cost-Effectiveness of
  Programs 415*
*Summary 418*

41. Summary of Findings From Community
Follow-up     420

PART 9: CONCLUSIONS AND
RECOMMENDATIONS

42. Current Status of the Milieu and Social-
Learning Approaches     423
*Comparative Effectiveness 423*
*Differential Areas of Success 423*
*Representativeness of Intramural Programs
  and Findings 432*
*Factors Related to Release and Community
  Stay 439*

43. Concluding Comments on Institutional
Research and Treatment     443
*Ethical Issues and Legal Trends Related
  to the Recommendations 443*
*Further Considerations for Improving
  Institutional Practices 463*
*Providing the Best Treatment While
  Extending Knowledge 467*

APPENDIXES

A. Instruments for Assessing Staff Attitudes
and Orientation                              469

B. Revised Fine Costs That Replace "Token
Costs" in Chapter 8                          478

C. Examples of Detailed Procedural Memos
Recommended                                  479

Notes            488
References       502
Author Index     515
Subject Index    520

# Psychosocial Treatment
of Chronic Mental Patients

PART 1
# Background and Overview

## 1. The Chronically Institutionalized Mental Patient

### HISTORICAL AND CURRENT STATUS

A review of the status of the chronically institutionalized mental patient in 1967 documented the failure of long-stay patients to participate in the upsurge in discharge rates that had been occurring since 1955 (Paul, 1969a). At that time, the total resident population in public mental hospitals had consistently decreased, in spite of increased yearly admissions, suggesting a renewed effectiveness of institutional treatment programs. The basis of that encouraging trend appeared to lie in a number of progressive changes. These changes included the introduction of psychotropic drugs, a return to "moral treatment" with open-door philosophies, unit decentralization, and increased focus on community crisis care and intervention (Bellak, 1964; Gilligan, 1965; Pasamanick et al., 1967).

But there was a hidden feature of these increasing release rates: fewer than a third of resident beds appeared to be involved (Glass, 1965). Jones and Sidebotham (1962) went so far as to state that each hospital had actually become "two hospitals"—one an acute, short-term, rapid turnover facility and the other a large, custodial facility with a static population. The chronic population in the United States still constituted approximately two-thirds of the resident population with prospects being for even greater increases since the proportion of first-admission functional psychotics who never left the hospital, combined with readmissions who became long-term, was still running from 20% to 75% (Hassall et al., 1965; Hogarty & Gross, 1966; Person, 1965; Peterson & Olsen, 1964; Ullmann, 1967). Additionally, the probability of release and community stay after two years' residence in a mental hospital was still reported to be about 6% without change in this century (Gurel, 1966; Hassall et al., 1965; Kramer et al., 1961; Morgan & Johnson, 1957; Ullmann, 1967). Even more disheartening were the conclusions of literature reviewers that no treatment had been shown to have any long-term effect on discharge and community stay of the chronic population (Fairweather & Simon, 1963; Gurel, 1966; Piotrowski & Efron, 1966; Sanders et al., 1967; Vitale, 1964a).

Since the mid-1960s, given primary impetus from the community mental health ideology incorporated in the 1963 Community Mental Health Centers Act (Public Law 88-164), the decline in resident hospital beds has continued at an accelerated pace, with admissions also declining since 1971 (Taube & Meyer, 1975). The decline in the resident population was initially met with enthusiasm (Tyce & Rynearsen, 1966) and taken as evidence for the effectiveness of community-based treatment (Cochran, 1974). Serious questions have been raised, however, concerning the practical operations involved in the increased emphasis on alternatives to hospitalization and short-stay, rapid turnover facilities that have contributed to the decline in the resident population. The early promise of some active intervention procedures has not been fulfilled on long-term follow-ups (e.g., Davis et al., 1972), and the level of functioning in the community of even acute patients released from institutional programs has been marginal at best (Erickson, 1975). Additionally, the trend to short stays and rapid turnover has been accompanied by an increase in readmission and multiple admission rates to the extent that current institutional operations are described as a revolving door. The extent of increases in readmissions is such that a recent review of the literature set an expected one-year recidivism rate at 40-50% of releases (Anthony et al., 1972), with the most recent available data on functional psychoses reporting that more than 72% of the institutional admissions are readmissions (Taube, 1974).

Data also suggest that new mental health centers show similar patterns to public mental hospitals, with multiple admissions and readmissions systematically increasing the longer a center has been in operation (Rutledge & Binner, 1970) and that the length of stay increases with increasing readmissions (Kraft et al., 1967). Chu and Trotter (1974), in fact, suggest that what has been done for mental patients in the "new movement" is not different or more effective than what was previously accomplished in mental hospitals. They argue that beds have simply been moved to different locations. Even reports that yield favorable conclusions for active short-stay facilities with first admissions, combined with aggressive precare and aftercare, indicate a continuing build-up of chronically institutionalized mental patients who "silt into the care system year after year and utilize enormous resources" (Smith et al., 1974). Thus, irrespective of the relative effectiveness or ineffectiveness of the recent overall community emphases, reports continue to indicate that there are growing numbers of long-stay, chronically institutionalized patients.

Chronically institutionalized mental patients, themselves, have been increasingly involved in the accelerated reduction in resident beds since the review of status in the mid-1960s. This is especially evident in more "progressive" states such as Illinois, California, and New York, where inpatient beds were reduced as much as 58% between 1967 and 1973 (Taube, 1975). Nearly all of the reductions in the chronic population can be attributed to the aggressive placement of long-stay mental patients in private extended-care facilities, such as foster homes, nursing homes, or other board and care facilities (Mendel, 1974; Rieder, 1974). The greatest relative proportions of these placements have involved movement of geriatric patients to nursing homes for continued custodial care, as is evident in reductions of more than 78% and 84% of resident mental patients over the age of sixty-five, respectively, in California and Illinois between 1967 and 1973 (Taube, 1975). However, such administrative releases have also involved the younger long-stay patient. Unfortunately, since few, if any, preparations have typically been made for continuing rehabilitation efforts in such placements, several critics indicate that patients are simply being shuffled to "back wards" in the community (e.g., Lamb & Goertzel, 1971; Reich, 1973)—essentially being declared incurable by default, since existing institutional programs have not made a significant impact on their functioning.

Anthony et al. (1972) report 30% to 40% recidivism rates one to two years after placement in community extended-care facilities for chronically institutionalized patients released from mental hospitals, even though the level of functioning required to remain in extended-care placements would be expected to be lower than that for releases functioning independently. Professional follow-up of such placements is notably lacking; however, the most recent reports indicate that "more than half" of patients "turned-out" of mental institutions "wound up back in the institutions" within a year (Rieder, 1974). Rieder presents statistics indicating that after a decade of increasing discharges, nearly half of the resident patients remaining in state mental hospitals are still those who have been institutionalized five years or more, while more than 72% of the resident population are those who have been hospitalized a year and a half or more. Additionally, in hospitals where attempts at extended-care placement have been carried out, half of the resident population remaining after active placements were patients who were so severely debilitated that they were not accepted for placement and had essentially zero probability of release (e.g., Lamb, 1968; Stewart et al., 1968).

Thus, the problem of the chronically institutionalized mental patient does not appear to have lessened since completion of the 1967 review (Paul, 1969a). Reviewers still conclude that no specific treatment has been shown to have any long-term effect on discharge and community stay of the chronic population (Anthony et al., 1972; Erickson, 1975; Mendel, 1974; Rieder, 1974). Higher functioning patients have often been shifted to other locales than the hospital—and essentially declared to be untreatable—while the large residual population remaining hospitalized appears to be shifting to an even more severely debilitated group with little hope of change through traditional hospital practices.

## AN INTERACTIONAL FRAME OF REFERENCE

At the time of Paul's earlier review (1969a), hundreds of prognostic studies had been undertaken relating individual patient characteristics to institutional outcome, usually defined as length of hospitalization or early release (e.g., Becker, 1956, 1959; Peretz et al., 1964; Sherman et al., 1964; Vaillant, 1966; Zubin et al., 1961). Even though the majority of such studies were retrospective in nature and lacked cross-validation and demonstration of reliability of measurement, considerable agreement existed concerning significant factors such as age, sex, marital status, education, socioeconomic class, and, most importantly, the presence of withdrawn, ineffective prehospital adjustment. A sampling of recent prognostic studies found continuing consistency (e.g., Bromet et al., 1971; Bromet et al., 1974; Depue & Dubicki, 1974; Eisenthal et al., 1972; Hamlin & Ward, 1973; Mednick, 1973; Rosenblatt, 1974). However, the degree of overlap between patients possessing negative prognostic indicators who do or do not become long-stay chronic hospital residents, combined with the fact that the majority of prognostic studies have been conducted in traditional hospital settings, precludes assignment of the major accountable variance to patient characteristics alone. This is particularly apparent in prognostic studies involving both traditional hospital programs and experimental treatments (see Sanders et al., 1967).

On the other hand, numerous writers have described the features of the mental hospital itself as appearing to produce the "typical institutionalization syndrome" of dependence, apathy, troublesome behavior, withdrawal, lack of responsibility, etc., in addition to the problems that may have led to hospitalization (e.g., Bockoven, 1963; Goffman, 1961; Kahne, 1959; Lehrman, 1961a; Sommer & Osmond, 1961; Ullmann, 1967). Honigfeld and Gillis (1967) found that time-in-hospital was linearly related to decreases in patient functioning when other variables were partialed out of the relationship. Several studies have found that the longer a person remains in the traditional mental hospital, the poorer are his chances of release or community stay (Anthony & Buell, 1973; Buell & Anthony, 1973; Dunham & Weinberg, 1960; Kramer et al., 1956; Lorei & Gurel, 1973; Malzberg, 1958; Odegard, 1961; Wanklin et al., 1956; Wing & Brown, 1970).

Several writers have summarized the authority structure of the traditional mental hospital, which—based upon a disease model interpretation of behavior problems and deviancy—appears to have established conditions fostering a custodial-caretaking philosophy for those patients who do not immediately respond to treatment efforts (Ellsworth, 1968; Fowlkes, 1975; Ludwig, 1971; Rosenhan, 1973; Ullmann, 1967; Ullmann & Krasner, 1975; Wing & Brown, 1970). The primary mode through which these conditions seem to operate has been described as the *aide culture*, reflecting the operational rules that appear to develop among the attendants and aides working in traditional hospital settings. The goal of the psychiatric aide in a traditional setting is "the discharge of his duties, as he sees them, with the least effort" (Ullmann, 1967, p. 25). "The aide had as his objectives the safety and protection of his patients. His other objectives were establishing the conditions which the physician wanted and which were appropriate for medical patients: cleanliness, cooperation, quiet, and docility" (p. 23). Since treatment is traditionally viewed as the job of professionals, the nonprofessional staff come to view their role only as caretaking.

Although the caretaker view of the traditional aide's role tends to increase staff-patient activities that are patterned after the care of physically disabled patients—doing things for patients and instructing them to follow prescribed procedures—the medical authority structure of the traditional mental hospital appears to foster staff activities other than patient contact. Ullmann and Krasner (1975) describe this situation: "In a large psychiatric hospital ... the people most intimately involved with patients, trainees and attendants, being on the lowest level of the hierarchy, report to people whose job is to supervise them ... The effects are to denigrate interacting with patients; advancement and authority are negatively associated with interaction with patients. The supervisor makes his decisions on the basis of acts that he can see, acts that are visible, and those are rarely interactions with patients" (p. 197). Thus, the traditional mental hospital structure appears to encourage aide-level staff to spend their time ensuring that cleanliness is maintained and doing paperwork and drug charts—visible activities—rather than interacting with patients.

Gruenberg (1967,1974), Gruenberg et al. (1969,1970), and Zusman (1966) have focused upon the problem of the chronically institutionalized mental patient, referring to the complex of dysfunctional behaviors often seen in long-stay patients as a "social breakdown syndrome." These authors offer a theoretical explanation for the development of the hard-core patient group in terms of an interaction between patient characteristics and traditional hospital environments such as those characterized by the aide culture. Entertaining an interactional view suggests that much of the failure of past treatment attempts with the hard-core hospitalized group may lie with the restrictive view that the basis of their behavioral excesses and deficits was to be found entirely in the patients themselves. In contrast, if the environment plays a major role in the development and, more importantly, the maintenance of such problems, the long-stay mental patient might be helped if this environment is changed. Since the goal of mental health facilities, on both economic and humanitarian grounds, is not merely to improve patient functioning within institutions but to release these people to greater independence in the community, the interaction between patient behavior and the postrelease environment would also be an important consideration in any attempt to bring about change.

Many theorists using a social interactional view have pointed to the complexity of the patient-environment relationship in determining both the definition of deviance and hospitalization or rehospitalization (Becker, 1963; Clum, 1975a,1975b; Ferster, 1965; Goffman, 1961; Parsons, 1957; Paul, 1967a; Peterson, 1968; Rosenblatt & Mayer, 1974; Szasz, 1963; Ullmann, 1967; Ullmann & Krasner, 1975).

Basically, this formulation views the labeling of a particular individual or act as deviant, and the resulting social action of hospitalization or rehospitalization, not as an inherent characteristic of the person or his behavior but the application by others of sanctions for behavior that was upsetting to them. Thus, the factors determining community stay for a released mental patient might be expected to reflect both the person's behavior in important areas and the degree of distress imposed upon significant others in his postrelease environment, interacting with the expectations, tolerance, and support offered.

The social interactional formulation gained considerable empirical support from follow-up studies of released mental patients that Paul (1969a) reviewed earlier. Even though the majority of these investigations, like the prognostic studies, were retrospective and correlational and lacked demonstrated reliability of measurement and cross-validation, considerable consistency was obtained over the earlier studies, and it continued to appear in later reports. Although length or frequency of hospital stay (the longer or more frequent the stay, the greater the readmission rate) is still the most consistent factor identified in follow-up studies (Arthur et al., 1968; Cunningham et al., 1969; Lehrman, 1961b; Lorei & Gurel, 1973; Mendel & Rapport, 1969; Michaux et al., 1969; Rawls, 1971; Rosenblatt & Mayer, 1973, 1974; Strauss & Carpenter, 1974; Zolik et al., 1971) several other factors continue to appear with regularity.

The occurrence of bizarre behavior on the part of the patient in the community was also identified as a major reason for rehospitalization in a series of papers from the Ohio State University Psychiatric Hospital acute patient follow-up program (see Pasamanick et al., 1967; Davis et al., 1972) and in numerous other reports (e.g., Arthur et al., 1968; Brown et al., 1958; Forsyth & Fairweather, 1961; Greenblatt et al., 1965; Lorei, 1967; Sanders et al., 1967; Wing, 1965). Additionally, the type of living arrangements (alone, parental or conjugal family, relatives, boardinghouse, or other extended-care facility) and employment have been related to community stay in many reports (e.g., Arthur et al., 1968; Brown et al., 1958; Cropley & Gazan, 1969; Cunningham et al., 1969; Forsyth & Fairweather, 1961; Johnson et al., 1971; Lorei, 1967; Lorei & Gurel, 1973; Mendel & Rapport, 1969; Nameche, 1967; Rawls, 1971; Sherman et al., 1964; Strauss & Carpenter, 1974; Vitale & Steinbach, 1965; Wohl, 1964; Zolik et al., 1971).

Support and clarification of these factors was found in the series of studies carried out by Freeman and Simmons (1963). Early retrospective surveys in which rehospitalization and performance were found to relate to the type of household to which patients were released were taken as support for family tolerance for deviance as the major factor in posthospitalization outcome. Tolerance for deviance in these early studies meant "the continued acceptance of the former patient by his family members, even when he fails to perform in instrumental roles." However, later prospective studies, which assessed the patient's behavior as well as attitudes of significant others, produced results more in keeping with other reports and with an interactional view of postrelease community stay. In essence, social class and significant others' expectations of performance levels were significantly related to patients' performance but not to rehospitalization. Four other areas were related to whether patients were rehospitalized or remained in the community for at least a year: work, social participation, the occurrence of bizarre behavior, and the degree to which patients presented management problems for families. Although work and social participation were significantly related to community tenure, there was more overlap between success and failure groups in these areas, which led Freeman and Simmons to recast their position on the tolerance for deviance hypothesis because their original definition of deviance was restricted to instrumental role deviance. However, work, management problems, and bizarre behavior were all interrelated; all posed the general problem of distress for significant others. Thus, the patients' behavior, the degree of distress imposed, and tolerance and support of significant others may all be viewed as important to community tenure.

Prior to final formulation of the comparative project, Miller (1965, 1967) had presented the most comprehensive analysis and summary of interacting factors and characteristics associated with community stay and rehospitalization in a retrospective study of over a thousand patients released to a California Bureau of Social Work. In addition to replicating others' findings with regard to significantly better prognosis for lower age, shorter hospitalization, higher social class, and the currently married, Miller found marriage to be a positive factor only in the absence of marital conflict. Sex, religion, race, place of residence (urban-rural), and official diagnosis were unrelated to success. Unlike Freeman and Simmons, Miller found that patients returning to conjugal homes were rehospitalized less than those returning to parental homes (although patients returning to other relatives did as well as those returning to spouses, and those living alone did as poorly "adult-children"). The suggested basis for this reversal was that inclusion of Veterans Administration patients with pensions in the Freeman and Simmons sample increased the tolerance of deviant behavior for parents but reduced it for wives.

Except for the reversal on parental homes and conjugal homes, even stronger relationships were found for the factors identified earlier. Employment status was significantly related for males in all living conditions and for females living alone or with relatives; for wives returned to their conjugal home, employment status was unrelated but performance of household responsibilities was related—performance of instrumental roles in which financial support by self or spouse was obtained was highly related to community stay. Those experiencing close social relationships regardless of sex or type of family were more likely to remain in the community, and isolates were more likely to return. Finally, the occurrence of bizarre behavior on the part of the released patient was the most consistent variable related to rehospitalization across all living conditions (excluding length of hospitalization).

Miller, however, found a curvilinear relationship between the severity of distressing behaviors and the reactions of family and community members. Relatively mild behavior, such as "always appeared nervous," "often appeared in a daze," or "drinks too much," although out of the ordinary, was tolerated and was not associated with rehospitalization. Severe deviations that might distress nearly anyone, such as "couldn't dress or take care of self," "made no sense when they talked," "hurt someone else," "forgot to do important things," etc., were highly associated with rehospitalization and were independent of living arrangements. A middle-range group of deviant behaviors, such as "said they heard voices," "got into debt with foolish buying," or "do not want to talk or be with anyone," was associated with tolerance of deviance; if significant others were distressed, rehospitalization occurred, but if significant others were not overly distressed, community stay continued.

Miller (1965) appropriately pointed out that care must be taken not to overestimate the explanatory power of data from follow-up studies. First, since the studies are necessarily correlational, specific causality remains a "strengthened hypothesis." Second, the prognostic value of such findings was quite limited in the traditional setting because hospital release without rehospitalization was a statistically rare event; it was especially so with the long-stay mental hospital patient. In Miller's sample of 546 patients released after two or more years of hospitalization, only thirty-nine (7%) were not rehospitalized during the five-year follow-up period. The more recent movement to place chronic patients in community extended-care facilities suggests lower rehospitalization rates than those reported by Miller (Anthony et al., 1972; Rieder, 1974). However, the lower rehospitalization rates are more likely a function of the increased tolerance of the extended-care facilities, which benefit financially by retaining ex-patients, since decreases in level of functioning after placement have been reported (Ellsworth, 1968; Epstein & Simon, 1968; Lamb & Goertzel, 1972). When rehospitalization does occur from such community placements—at rates reported to range from 30% to over 50% in less than two years—the occurrence of extreme bizarre behavior appears to be the primary factor.

The follow-up studies, in combination with the social interactional view of treatment environments, suggested a psychosocial approach to change in conditions for the chronically institutionalized and a demarcation of target areas for attempted rehabilitation for long-stay mental patients. The psychosocial approach reflects assumptions similar to those described by Ullmann (1967) for a sociopsychological model but without specific ones regarding the particular principles involved. Thus, the *psycho-* component of *psychosocial approach* reflects the fact that the particular excesses or deficits in motoric, emotional, or cognitive and ideational behavior of the long-stay mental patient are those that are traditionally referred to as psychological rather than physical or biological (Paul, 1974). The *-social* component similarly reflects the importance of the social environment as the context in which most of the relevant behavior occurs, appropriateness or inappropriateness of behavior is defined, and changes from custodial conditions might be expected to produce changes in behavior (Paul, 1974; Ullmann, 1967).

Based upon the analysis of follow-up studies, any psychosocial approach that might result in returning the chronically institutionalized mental patient to the community with tenure—with hope of even a minimally independent existence—seemed to necessitate a specific focus of efforts. The target areas of focus were identified as "(a) *resocialization*, including the development of self-maintenance, interpersonal interaction, and communications skills; (b) *instrumental role performance*, including the provision of 'salable' vocational skills, and 'housekeeping' skills; (c) *reduction or elimination of extreme bizarre behavior*, including appropriate changes in frequency, intensity, or timing of individual acts or mannerisms consensually identified as distressing; (d) *provision of at least one supportive 'roommate' in the community*, including either a spouse, relative, parent, or friend" (Paul, 1969a, p. 84).

Additionally, both the psychosocial approach and the follow-up studies that focused on the long-stay patient suggested that continuity of care would be most important in the period immediately following release, since the great majority of released chronic patients were, and continue to be, rehospitalized within the first several months, regardless of discharge target site (Anthony & Buell, 1973; Anthony et al., 1972; Brown et al., 1958; Cunningham et al., 1969; Fairweather et al., 1969; Vitale, 1964; Vitale & Steinbach, 1965; Wohl, 1964).

## SUMMARY

The hard core refractory group of chronically institutionalized mental patients have been identified as one of the most difficult problems confronting the mental health field. After nearly a decade of active community-focused treatment procedures and considerable movement of patient populations, no change in the centrality of this problem has occurred. The problem posed by the chronically hospitalized mental patient seems to result from an interaction of patient characteristics and traditional hospital environments, although the bulk of the evidence suggests that ineffective treatment techniques combined with traditional hospital environments may contribute more weight than patient characteristics.

Analysis of the findings of follow-up studies suggests that the likelihood of a patient's remaining in the community after institutional release is a joint function of patient behavior, environmental factors, and the interaction between the two. Considerable agreement on these factors, from both empirical studies and social-interaction theory, indicates that a psychosocial approach offers promise. However, these factors further suggest that necessary target areas of focus are resocialization, instrumental role performance, extreme bizarre behavior, and community social support.

# 2. Milieu and Social-Learning Approaches to Treatment

Recent reviewers still conclude that no specific treatment has been shown to have a lasting effect on release and community stay of the chronically institutionalized mental patient. Prior to the initiation of the comparative project reported in this book, a review of the literature was undertaken to determine if even suggestive evidence offered promise for changing the usual custodial environment along the lines suggested by the areas for rehabilitation defined in chapter 1. Since that review formed the basis for the treatment programs that were included in the comparative evaluation project, it is summarized here to provide the reader with some developmental perspective.[1]

Since instrumental role performance seemed to be an essential target and vocational retraining necessitates a change from the traditional custodial environment by introducing trainers or sending patients to trainers, vocational rehabilitation programs were considered promising. But in a summary of the results of all vocational rehabilitation efforts with hospitalized mental patients in projects supported by the United States Vocational Rehabilitation Administration, Crisswell (1967) reported that no matter what retraining procedures had been tried, 59% to 80% returned to the hospital, and two-thirds of those who did not were maintained only by continued professional contact. Neff and Koltuv (1967) reported similar results in a massive effort in a five-year research and demonstration project, including several different approaches to vocational training, with auxiliary individual and group psychotherapy available, and adequate control groups and statistical analyses. While a "quite moderate" increase in vocational success was obtained for experimental clients, there were no differences in rehospitalization or personal and social adjustment. It thus appeared that an attempt to increase instrumental role performance alone was not a very promising approach.

On the other hand, there were encouraging trends, which often included work and vocational training as part of broader environmental changes with custodial patients. Two that focused upon resocialization and the reduction of extreme bizarre behavior had been derived from totally different backgrounds: milieu therapy or the therapeutic community, derived from a return to moral treatment philosophy in the applied setting, and social-learning therapy, derived from basic laboratory research on the principles of learning, motivation, and social interaction. Both trends emphasized a psychosocial focus.

## THE MILIEU APPROACH

Although the milieu therapy approach was becoming better articulated (e.g., Artiss, 1962; Cumming & Cumming, 1962; Edelson, 1967; Jones, 1953; Kraft, 1966; Wilmer, 1958), no well-controlled studies had yet evaluated the effectiveness of specifically defined therapeutic communities with the hard-core chronic mental patient. However, a large literature existed on this approach, which is characterized by increased social interaction and group activities, expectancies, and group pressure directed toward normal functioning, more informal patient status, goal-directed communication, freedom of movement, and treatment of patients as responsible people rather than as custodial cases. Gilligan (1965) had reviewed the positive reports of improved behavior following the early "total push" projects, which included both somatic and milieu treatments. Since those early projects, numerous reports had appeared in which within-hospital improvements in socialization and bizarre behavior were observed in small groups of patients following the introduction of special milieu therapy programs (e.g., Barrett et al., 1957; Martin, 1950; D. H. Miller & Clancy, 1952; Rashkis, & Smarr, 1957). Other special milieu therapy programs had been reported as resulting in moderate though increased discharge rates for chronic patient groups in comparison to status prior to the introduction of special programs (e.g., Bartholow & Tunakan, 1967; Brooks, 1960; Ellsworth et al., 1958; D. H. Miller, 1954). Similar improvements in discharge rates of chronic patients had been reported for entire hospitals following a change to a therapeutic community operation (e.g., Clark, 1965; Clark & Oram, 1966; Cumming & Cumming, 1962; Ellsworth & Stokes, 1963; Galioni, 1960; Wing, 1965).

A few studies, more or less approaching adequate experimental design, had compared a special milieu therapy program to the traditional custodial treatment provided in large mental hospitals. Galioni et al. (1953) reported an intensive eighteen-month milieu program with a chronic population in which prior release rates had been less than 2%. At the completion of the project, the release rate for the experimental group was two and a half times that of controls (40 of 214 versus 15 of 223). However, after an eighteen-month follow-up the net-release rates between the two groups did not differ because of rehospitalization rates. Moderate within-hospital improvement with chronic patients had been reported by Appleby et al. (1960), although results were difficult to interpret since "control patients" improved as well and were housed within the same ward. In a pioneering project of the Dutchess County Unit of Hudson River State Hospital, Kasius (1966) had found moderate within-hospital improvement for a group of hard-core chronic patients in the new unit in comparison to a similar group in the parent hospital; however, after five years of operation, 73% of the males and 60% of the females in residence were still chronic patients who had been transferred to the unit at its inception (Bennett, 1966).

In contrast, four projects with smaller groups of patients had found significantly better release rates for long-stay patients undergoing variations of milieu therapy in contrast to usual custodial care. The first series of studies were summarized by Wing (1965); however, the patients involved were selected from moderately handicapped long-stay patients who were prejudged to have rehabilitation potential. More impressive, because of the unselected use of hard-core chronic patients with equated experimental and control groups, was the study by Ellsworth (1964). He looked at 142 male functional psychotics with at least five years' continuous hospitalization who were assigned to a milieu therapy unit or to regular chronic wards at the Fort Meade Veterans Administration hospital. Following thirty months of treatment, the milieu program resulted in a 59% release rate compared to 25% on regular wards. Additionally, on twelve-month follow-ups, 87% of milieu versus 64% of controls had not been rehospitalized. Although more than two-thirds of these patients were discharged to sheltered-care facilities, perhaps accounting for the very low rehospitalization rates, Ellsworth's results were most promising controlled findings.

The third project had been conducted at Philadelphia State Hospital and reported by Sanders et al. (1967). Three milieu programs, varying in the degree of social interaction required, were conducted for a twelve-month period, along with a control treatment consisting of the usual hospital program and a thirty-six-month follow-up. A total of 278 patients were involved, ranging in age from nineteen to seventy-two years and with a length of hospitalization from one to thirty-six years; unfortunately, like the Wing studies, subjects were selected from better-adjusted chronic patients on clinical evaluation of ability to leave the hospital within twelve months, resulting in an unusually high release rate for all groups during the study period. Within-hospital improvements were found in socialization for the milieu patients, and significant differences in release rate were found over the entire period (78% for the milieu program demanding most activity versus 58% for controls); however, when rehospitalizations due to the occurrence of bizarre behavior were taken into account, the net-release rates over the four-year period varied from 27% to 38% and did not differ between groups. Older patients with a greater length of hospitalization showed the greatest comparative response to the milieu programs.

The fourth project had been conducted by Gellman and Soloff at Chicago State Hospital (summarized in Neff & Koltuv, 1967). Three groups of hard-core chronic patients were involved, none of whom was exposed to a total therapeutic community. All continued to reside at the hospital, but two groups were bused daily to another location where they were exposed to one of two variants of milieu therapy—one emphasizing vocational training at a sheltered workshop and the other emphasizing social and recreational activities at a mental health center. Although results were modest and characterized by high readmission rates, both groups exposed to three to six hours per day of milieu programs for nine to twelve months showed higher discharge rates than patients continuing the regular hospital programs; there were no significant differences between the two groups.

Several authors had reported a failure of milieu therapy to have a positive impact on long-stay mental patients (e.g., Durell et al., 1965; Greenblatt et al., 1965; Kraft et al., 1967; Rapaport, 1960; Wilensky & Herz, 1966). However, those negative reports providing adequate descriptive data appear to have violated some of the basic tenets of the milieu therapy approach (see Cumming & Cumming, 1962); specifically, group interaction was given less emphasis than individual, psychoanalytically oriented psychotherapy, and the patient role appeared to have remained unmodified.

Thus, before the current comparative project was initiated, the general milieu therapy literature was characterized by a paucity of evidence and a plethora of equivocal results; however, the bulk of evidence suggested that when the principles of milieu therapy were applied to long-stay chronic mental patients, resocialization frequently resulted, and, to a lesser extent, there was some reduction of extreme bizarre behavior. The few controlled studies offered the promise of greater release rates than previously obtained with traditional treatment alternatives, although an adequate test of a well-articulated milieu therapy program had not yet appeared. The greatest weakness appeared to lie in a failure to systematically include specific focus on instrumental role training, elimination of bizarre behavior, and provision for community support and follow-up within milieu programs.

## THE SOCIAL-LEARNING APPROACH

The second promising approach for rehabilitating the chronic mental patient was termed *social-learning therapy*, a systematic extension of principles and techniques derived from basic research on learning to the clinical alteration of behavior—especially the principles of instrumental and associative learning, along with appropriate types and schedules of reinforcement. Although a social-learning approach shares much in common with milieu therapy, there are differences in the form of greater emphasis on response-contingent consequences rather than group pressure and encouragement as basic vehicles of change. Also, because of the differing historical bases from which the two approaches were derived, social-learning therapy had been characterized by more systematic control of physical and social interchanges. Like milieu therapy, no well-controlled studies had yet appeared evaluating the effectiveness of a total social-learning program for returning the chronic mental patient to the community. However, since this approach had grown from basic laboratory research, a large number of controlled investigations underlay the broader extensions and applications.

Many examples of the extrapolation and testing of principles and techniques of social influence and learning to the treatment context had been summarized in recent books by Franks (1969), Goldstein et al. (1966), Krasner and Ullmann (1965), and Paul (1966). Ullmann and Krasner (1965) had discussed the major principles and techniques and presented several reports indicating highly encouraging results in the treatment of chronic hospital patients. In one comprehensive controlled study, Meichenbaum (1966a) had demonstrated remarkable changes in schizophrenic patients' pathognomic verbalizations and level of abstraction through the systematic application of social and token contingencies—in most cases, training patients to surpass even the normal population after eight sessions. Additional controlled experimental studies involving the contingent manipulation of reinforcement schedules through social attention and interest had effectively modified such modal problems of institutionalization and bizarre behavior as the expression of affect (Salzinger & Pisoni, 1958; Weiss et al., 1963), sick and healthy talk (Ullmann et al., 1965), and delusions (Rickard et al., 1960; Rickard & Dinoff, 1962). Similar effects of systematic learning procedures had been shown on increasing social behavior (King et al., 1960; Ullmann et al., 1961), perception (Ullmann et al., 1963), abstraction level (Little, 1966; Meichenbaum, 1966b), and common associations (Sommer et al., 1962; Ullmann et al., 1964).

Wagner and Paul (1970), in a pilot project with nineteen incontinent male patients averaging twenty-five years of continuous hospitalization, had reduced the number of soilings per day from an average of 19.5 to 3.5 in seventeen weeks of treatment, using only contingent materials and social reinforcement through an understaffed group of aides. Several studies by Ayllon and colleagues (e.g., Ayllon, 1963; Ayllon & Haughton, 1964; Ayllon & Michael, 1959) had investigated the utility of instrumental procedures for instituting change in the behavior of chronic mental patients by identifying specific behaviors, recording their frequency of occurrence, and then reducing, increasing, and again reducing their frequency as a consequence of contingent token or social reinforcement. A wide range of bizarre verbal, motoric, and interpersonal behaviors characteristic of chronically institutionalized patients responded to such controlled contingencies. Thus, although none of these studies involved total treatment programs, the effectiveness of extended social-learning procedures for changing specified bizarre behavior and increasing instrumental role performance within the hospital setting had been well documented.

The extension of social-learning procedures to a systematic treatment program in a ward or unit was relatively recent and, at the initiation of the comparative project, still in its first stages even though many service programs for chronic patients had been initiated on the basis of the rather limited literature (see Davison, 1969; Krasner & Atthowe, 1968). Ayllon and his colleagues were responsible for formulating the initial procedures for extending the use of learning principles to complete ward programs. He called the basic approach *token economy*, since actual tokens, such as special cards or chips, were vested with reward value to mediate control of behavior much in the way that money does in a natural economy.

Ayllon and Azrin (1965) had reported several studies conducted at Anna State Hospital within a closed-ward token economy. That report established the ability of a token-economy program to change chronic psychotic behavior within a highly controlled ward; however, the program was directed at the development of procedures and testing of principles rather than at testing overall therapeutic outcome.[2] Atthowe and Krasner (1968) reported the results of a token-economy program undertaken with a chronic brain-damaged and geriatric ward at Menlo Park Veterans Administration Hospital, which replicated Ayllon and Azrin's findings. Dramatic results for increased in-hospital adjustment were seen in increased social responsiveness, attendance at group activities, number of passes, and responsible self-maintenance. Even though the nature of the population precluded hospital release as a major goal of the program, the release rate more than doubled during the first year of operation in comparison to a baseline period with the same staff.

Another token-economy program with therapeutic goals had been in operation at Patton State Hospital with two open wards of chronic patients (Bruce, 1966). Although the service orientation of the Patton program did not provide an adequate design to evaluate the effectiveness of the program, the impression of the hospital administration, supplemented with anecdotal evidence, had been quite favorable (Gericke, 1965). Controlled studies within the Patton program replicated the findings of Ayllon and Azrin and Atthowe and Krasner on the effectiveness of contingent social and token reinforcement for changing behavior characteristic of chronically institutionalized patients (Schaefer, 1966). Particularly encouraging were the results of a controlled study by Schaefer and Martin (1966). Highly significant decreases in apathy and corresponding increases in responsibility and activity were obtained through the token economy over a three-month period with twenty chronic patients compared to an equated group not receiving the token treatment.

Finally, Steffy et al. (1966) had reported a token-economy program at Lakeshore Psychiatric Hospital with a female population of chronic schizophrenics and mental defectives. Like the other token programs, the main focus of the project was on increasing adaptive behavior within the hospital and did not include a control sample for evaluating effectiveness in terms of release. Steffy had, however, included a continuing assessment battery. The results of the Anna State, Patton State, and Menlo Veterans Administration programs were replicated in Steffy's program; there was effective within-hospital change for such bizarre behaviors as refusal to eat, withdrawal, violent acts, delusional and incoherent talk, mutism, inappropriate affect, and meaningless, repetitious activities.

At the time of the initial review of the literature, no negative reports had appeared concerning the effectiveness of token-economy programs, even though twenty-two institutions had such programs in varying stages of development with chronic mental patients (Krasner & Atthowe, 1968). At least two well-planned programs had been abandoned after early starts, however, Hughes (1965) had attempted to establish a token-economy program on a service basis without external support at Anna State Hospital, and Hallsten and Fletcher (1966), after winning the Francis F. Gerty Award for their proposal, had attempted to establish a program at Galesburg State Research Hospital. In both instances, the programs were abandoned because of administrative obstruction that prevented adequate training, control, and retention of staff.[3] Similar verbal reports had been obtained regarding both milieu therapy and token-economy programs in several parts of the country.

Thus, before the current comparative project was initiated, the literature on social-learning procedures with the chronic mental hospital population had established its efficacy for improving socialization, reducing extreme bizarre behavior, and improving instrumental role performance individually, within the institution. The bulk of the evidence further suggested that a comprehensive social-learning program focused upon returning the chronic patient to the community could be quite successful. Like milieu therapy, the greatest weakness to date had been the failure to include provision for community support and follow-up.

"BRIDGING THE GAP"

One last research program was noted in the initial preparatory review because it shared some characteristics of both milieu and learning approaches, and contributed evidence on the problem of rehospitalization. Fairweather (1964) first reported the results of a program that was focused upon resocialization and instrumental role performance, involved the establishment of problem-solving patient groups and the use of group pressure, and combined these with a step system in which responsibilities, passes, and funds were contingent upon appropriate behavior. A traditional ward program served as a control, and staff were equated by switching midway through the experimental period. A total of 195 patients were randomly assigned to the two wards. Because the patients were previously housed in Veterans Administration open wards, none posed the severe disability problems seen in state hospital back wards or in the Atthowe and Krasner study conducted at the same hospital, although about half of the patients had accumulated two or more years in mental hospitals. Highly significant differences were obtained in favor of improved within-hospital performance for the experimental program. However, significant effects were found between the two staff groups, indicating that transfers, attention, and bizarre behavior were more a function of the staff involved than of treatment programs. Although the experimental program resulted in more early releases, no systematic aftercare was included; by the time of a six-month postrelease follow-up, rehospitalizations were sufficient that no difference in net release existed between the experimental and control groups. Like previous follow-up studies, supportive living situations were more related to community stay than were treatment programs in the institution, and the institutional treatment made no specific contribution in helping those released adjust to the community.

Fairweather et al. (1969) had recently completed an extension of the earlier program, which had not yet been published at the time of the initial preparatory review. The extension compared the follow-up status of patients released from the experimental treatment program in two different ways. One group was released to the community with the regularly available extramural care, such as outpatient care, home care, etc. The other group was released to a community lodge supported by the mental health facilitiy where the patients continued to function as a family, providing mutual support for one another. The lodge group was initially followed by professional staff, with contact gradually reduced until the group became completely autonomous. By the end of six months, 65% of the lodge group had been in the community over three-quarters of the time, compared to 24% of the control group. Similarly, 50% of the lodge group had been employed over three-quarters of the time compared to 3% of the control group. Significant differences between the two groups continued for the thirty-month study period. Although the number of patients to leave the lodge for less protected living arrangements was negligible, Fairweather noted that the cost of maintaining a patient in the lodge with employment was approximately 27% of the hospital cost.

Although Fairweather was not the first to find that groups of chronic patients could be moved to hospital extensions in the community successfully and at lower cost (e.g., Berrington, 1966; Vitale & Steinbach, 1965; Wing, 1965), the finding that released patients could be taught to live together in mutual support after a declining-contact period of professional direction seemed most important. Pasamanick et al. (1967) had similarly found that new hospitalizations could be prevented by providing drugs, advice, and reassurance to patients and relatives in their homes on a declining-contact basis.

Combining these two findings suggested a promising addition to the attempt at community return of the long-term hospital patient that had not been systematically dealt with by either the milieu or social-learning approaches—namely, the provision of supportive roommates in the community for those who have either undesirable relatives or none at all. By providing declining contact in the living situation from the time of release, support of the released patient by significant others might be taught and maintained; when no appropriate significant others exist before release, patients might be taught to be significant others themselves, released as a family and similarly treated in the community.

## SUMMARY

The literature at the time of the comparative project suggested that both milieu and social-learning approaches offered considerable promise, but neither had yet been systematically evaluated for specific effectiveness in the treatment of the chronically institutionalized mental patient. The evidence did suggest that both milieu and social-learning approaches might be effective in resocialization, and the social-learning approach appeared to be quite effective in reducing or eliminating bizarre behavior and increasing instrumental role performance. Although neither milieu nor social-learning programs had included direct provision for aftercare and community social support, recent research results offered direct suggestions for bridging the gap from institution to community by training groups to live together in mutual support, starting in the institution and extending maintenance into the community on a declining-contact basis.

An additional feature that appeared necessary to all focal areas of rehabilitation with the chronic mental patient was the inclusion of clear and explicit steps that successively approximate normal behavior through which patients progress. Although this feature was not a typical part of milieu therapy with acute patients, it had been a major part of Fairweather's (1964) program, and identifiable steps related to increased levels of responsibility and functioning had been common to the more promising programs with chronic patients —both milieu (Cumming & Cumming, 1962; Ellsworth, 1964) and social-learning (Atthowe & Krasner, 1968; Steffy et al., 1966).

Because of the paucity of well-controlled investigations in the institutional treatment area, it appeared that the major hope for the chronic mental patient lay in outcome studies following sound and rigorous experimental principles. On the basis of the evidence, both milieu and social-learning approaches seemed sufficiently promising to undertake a controlled comparative study to determine overall and differential degress of success in the chronic population.

# 3. Design and Overview of the Comparative Project

## THE RATIONALE FOR DESIGN AND TREATMENT

The relative effectiveness of nearly any institutional treatment program for individual patient problems or for given patient groups remains largely unknown. Even ruling out comparative studies, there is a near absence of sound evaluation of treatment programs in mental hospitals and mental health centers (Fairweather, 1967) and almost a complete absence of objective data on activities within extended-care facilities (Lamb & Goertzel, 1971). Large-scale drug evaluations, especially those of the National Institute of Mental Health and Veterans Administration cooperative studies, have often used more sophisticated research designs. However, even the most comprehensive comparative studies (e.g., May, 1968) have not included sufficient description or documentation of the institutional treatment program or staff component to provide evidence of specific effectiveness or the nature of those components in need of change. The Veterans Administration Psychiatric Evaluation Project, as with most other systems evaluations, provided correlates of more and less effective institutions of a demographic nature, such as size and staffing, but could not provide research evidence of clinical utility regarding the effectiveness of staff functioning (Gurel, 1970; Ullmann, 1967).

There are two reasons for the lack of progress in firm comparative knowledge on institutional treatment programs: the absence of solid evidence of either effective or ineffective treatment procedures for given problems or populations and the failure to transfer knowledge obtained from special research studies to day-to-day clinical work with continuing evaluation. The absence of solid evidence is itself only partially a result of practical problems in applied research (see Paul, 1967b); it is more a function of the failure to apply rigorous experimental design and procedure. Except for the greater number and complexity of variables involved, methodological principles for comparative treatment evaluation are no different from those of any other scientific research—whether the treatments to be evaluated are individual outpatient procedures (Paul, 1967a) or inpatient programs (Paul, 1969b). In all instances, cause-effect relationships are sought between sets of variables and behavioral events or changes. Similarly, the only way that such relationships can be established for a set of independent variables (such as a treatment program) is for that set to be manipulated systematically alone somewhere in the design. The failure to transfer knowledge to day-to-day clinical work with continued evaluation also stems from practical problems, because of the absence of appropriate assessment procedures to provide objective research data and practical, individual monitoring of relevant variables in ongoing clinical work at the same time.

Paul (1969b) has argued that the possibility of clinical work approaching the status of an applied science will depend upon empirically derived answers to the question: "What treatment, by *whom*, is most effective for *this* individual with *that* specific problem, under *which* set of circumstances, and how does it come about?" Although no single investigation can answer this question, posing it provides a framework for delineating the aspect of the question for which a given study seeks answers and the classes of variables that must be considered. Except for the final part, which refers to the theoretical concepts and principles that best account for specific changes obtained, this clinical-research question summarizes the domains and classes of variables that must be at least described and/or controlled, if not actively manipulated, in either evaluative research or maximally useful ongoing system monitoring, irrespective of the theoretical predilections of the evaluator or investigator.[1] Thus, no matter what the theoretical stance, the data to be taken into account must include the domains of clients (or patients or residents), the individuals or groups to be changed; therapists (or change agents or behavior modifiers), the people or groups responsible for producing or maintaining the change; and time.

Within each domain, specific classes of variables must also be considered. Within the client domain these classes include (1) the problem behaviors that are distressing to the client or significant others and result in the client's entry to treatment—more specifically, the number and nature (excess or deficit) of distressing or maladaptive motoric, physiological and emotional, or cognitive and ideational activities that are the focus of therapeutic efforts; (2) the relatively stable personal-social characteristics of the client that may interact with treatment procedures as either assets or liabilities or may be significant in defining appropriate role behavior and thereby interact with specification of problem behaviors; and (3) the physical-social life environment of the client that may provide intercurrent life experiences that interact positively or negatively with changes in problem behaviors and that set the time or place for the identification or occurrence of problem behaviors.

Similarly within the broad therapist domain, specific classes of variables must be reliably described, manipulated, or controlled, including (1) the specific therapeutic techniques through which change in problem behaviors is attempted —that is, the number and nature of specific procedures, whether discrete events or a complex series of actions and strategies; (2) the relatively stable personal-social characteristics of therapists (and of the group if more than one change agent is working with certain clients) that may interact positively or negatively with the effectiveness of specific techniques for certain clients, problem behaviors, or settings; and (3) the physical-social treatment environment in which therapeutic techniques are applied that may interact with variables in other classes.

The third major domain, time, serves to further specify the set of circumstances for other classes of variables and to determine the focus and nature of assessment within and between periods related to treatment, depending upon the nature of the questions asked.

In institutional treatment programs, the client domain by tradition becomes the patient domain; the variables included in the physical-social environment classes are largely encompassed as a subset of the therapist domain; and the time domain first focuses assessment within the institution, and is related later to assessments in outside physical-social environments if details of cause-effect relationships are to be retained.

In view of the knowledge that existed on treatment of the chronically institutionalized mental patient, the aspect of the question for which cause-effect information appeared especially ready took the form of "What treatment ... is most effective ... with that specific problem ...?" Other aspects should then, ideally, be controlled in the design—at least described or measured to provide comparative data across studies and a basis for strengthened hypotheses from correlational data (see Paul, 1967a, 1969b, for elaboration). Because of the complexity of the variables involved, the only way in which a treatment program could be "systematically manipulated alone somewhere in the design" was through a partial factorial design, such as that demonstrated in individual extramural treatment evaluation (Paul, 1966, 1967b). This meant that a minimum of three groups had to be involved. Either two groups had to receive two different treatment programs that would be comparatively evaluated or one had to receive a to-be-evaluated treatment program while the other received an attention-placebo treatment. In either instance, both groups had to be involved with the same treatment staff, or cause-effect relationships could not be established for treatment programs. The third group would serve as the necessary comparison for the state of affairs in the absence of the programs to be evaluated. Hence, all groups had to be drawn from the same population and assessed by the same criteria over the same time periods.

Rather than posing these experimental design requirements for establishing comparative cause-effect relationships as a "classical experimental straight jacket," in opposition to continuous systems monitoring (Guttentag, 1973) or individual functional analyses (Sidman, 1960), the question and delineation of classes of variables suggest a complementary strategy for improving institutional treatment. The strategy retains the well-designed partial factorial comparative outcome study to establish cause-effect relationships for given treatment procedures for specified problems in highly controlled, small-sample research under actual clinical treatment conditions. Continuous systems monitoring and analysis could then ensure continued effectiveness of previously established procedures in day-to-day clinical work or, through large-scale, multiple-institution evaluation, extend the basic findings from the highly controlled comparative study over variants of patients, problems, staff, and settings. Individual functional analysis is unquestionably the most rigorous method for determining the specific functional relationships and parameters of treatment procedures for the individual case. Similarly replicated within-subject time-series and time-samples designs, particularly multiple baseline and reversal designs, are exceptionally useful both before and after comparative partial-factorial studies for determining probable mechanisms of change, establishing that change does or does not come about, and extending findings over variants of patients, problems, staff, and settings. Strategically, continuous systems monitoring, when aided by time-series analyses (see Glass et al., 1975), within-subject designs (see Kazdin, 1973), and lower-level group designs (see Paul, 1969b), could also be exceptionally useful in the evaluation of systematic modifications to the basic procedures found most effective from highly controlled comparative studies, without the time and expense of a complete replication of partial-factorial designs. Partial-factorial designs with appropriate comparison groups are, however, the only means of clearly establishing solid data on comparative effectiveness (see Kazdin, 1973; Paul, 1969b).

Thus, with the above convictions concerning the nature of treatment evaluation and the accumulation of scientific and clinical knowledge, the problem of the chronically institutionalized mental patient was attacked through a partial-factorial design to evaluate the comparative effectiveness of ongoing clinical programs developed on the basis of previous empirical findings. Those findings suggested that a psychosocial orientation was the most promising, and either milieu or social-learning variants of procedural technology were more likely to be effective than any other alternatives.

The long-term goal of the work reported here is to improve institutional treatment practices in general and to significantly reduce the number of those individuals who become or remain chronic residents of mental institutions. The comparative project was designed to accomplish the following aims:

1. To articulate and evaluate the comparative effectiveness of the two most promising therapeutic programs—milieu therapy and social-learning therapy—for returning the chronic mental patient to the community. Effectiveness in relationship to each other and to traditional hospital treatment, when all include systematic aftercare services.

2. To identify the limits of change that can be accomplished with the overall programs within staffing restrictions characteristic of public mental hospitals.

3. To explore the systematic effects of both programs on differential areas of success.

4. To explore the prognostic value of patient characteristics and functioning for release and community stay, as well as postrelease environmental factors.

5. To demonstrate a feasible model for investigating institutional treatment outcome under actual clinical conditions, providing more rigorous design, controls, and procedures than had been previously accomplished.

The general absence of sound knowledge on institutional practices, as well as unanticipated and uncontrolled events, resulted in numerous additional hypotheses that were generated and evaluated over the course of the project.

## THE OVERALL DESIGN

The project design implemented involved three groups of chronically institutionalized psychotic patients drawn from four state hospitals in central Illinois. Two identical, adjacent units were established at a mental health center to house psychosocial programs—milieu therapy at one and social-learning therapy at the other—both staffed by the same personnel at a level equal to that existing in a comparison state hospital. Twenty-eight beds were maintained on the continued treatment service of the comparison state hospital. Initially three equated patient groups of twenty-eight each were formed; two were transferred to the center units to receive one or the other of the psychosocial programs, while the third was sent to the state hospital (or remained there) to receive the usual hospital programs. Intensive aftercare, on a declining-contact schedule, was provided for twenty-six weeks postrelease for patients in all groups and as needed thereafter. Rehospitalization, when necessary, was to the place of release. As patients were released into the community from each study group or died, new patients were admitted from the original chronically hospitalized resident pool, maintaining the initial equivalency of groups.

Continuous intramural assessments were obtained on staff and patients of the psychosocial programs through objective behavioral observations with sample assessments of the hospital staff and programs. Patients in all three groups were assessed through structured interviews and standardized rating scales before entry to the project, at six-month intervals, and prior to release. Patients who were released were also assessed in the community at six-month intervals. Relevant personal-social characteristics of staff and patients were evaluated, with psychosocial staff providing data on attitudes and opinions about patients and treatment programs at six-month intervals. The comparative efficacy of the psychosocial programs was evaluated by comparing changes in specific components and overall level of functioning, release, and community stay rates and in the number of patients served with each other and with the comparison group undergoing the usual hospital programs. Identical criteria for entry and release were maintained for all three groups. The original plan called for psychosocial programs to be conducted on a closed-research basis for three years, with a minimum two-year follow-up on each patient released to the community. Aftercare consultation was to be shifted from psychosocial staff to regular extramural community staff after the initial six months declining-contact was accomplished.

Changes in plans were instituted over the period of the project because of uncontrolled external factors. In fact, the design actually implemented and described above reflects a change from original plans as a result of a four-month delay in initial notification of federal research funding. The major impact of the delay was a change in the nature of the patient population that was available for treatment. The first plan focused on the "garden-variety" chronic mental patient, typical of those found on the back wards of public mental hospitals throughout the nation. Because only about 6% of these patients ever achieved release with relatively independent functioning under traditional hospital procedures (Paul, 1969a), this population was the one for whom psychosocial programs offered major promise and for whom the comparative project and programs were initially designed. The design had planned to restrict the point of origin of study patients to two equivalent geographic regions, each of which would provide a comparison group at the state hospital to allow a comparative evaluation of the aftercare consultation performed by the regular Department of Mental Health extramural community staff. Because more than three hundred patients from the specified areas in the comparison hospital met selection criteria, such crossing of factors within the design would have been feasible.

Unfortunately, the delay in notification of federal funding precluded further restrictions of an ongoing effort to empty the back wards of the hospital through placement of acceptable chronic patients in private extended-care facilities in the community. The result was that not enough chronically institutionalized patients who met specific age and length of hospitalization criteria (18 to 55 years old, with two or more years of hospitalization) remained in the comparison hospital to form equated groups with the restricted geographical point of origin. Additionally, the only patients remaining were those who were so debilitated or so bizarre that they had been rejected for shelter-care placement. Thus, the design actually implemented involved the three groups, rather than four, with the patient population being the most severely debilitated of any group previously subjected to systematic study—now having a zero probability of release to relatively independent functioning.

In addition to the change in the nature of the population available for treatment, the delay in notification of funding resulted in the loss of professional assistance for the project. A research associate who had been in training under state support for over a year to function as program director took another position, and two coinvestigators and a milieu trainer undertook other commitments during the four-month period, which removed them from participation in the comparative project because of other demands on their time.[2] Thus, approximately twenty-four professional man-months were lost at the beginning of the project, leaving only the principal investigator-project director as the total staff until notification of federal funding finally arrived—over a month past the starting date of the approved grant. The personnel losses were compounded through inability to select, recruit, and train project staff, with resulting delays in developing training manuals and research protocols, opening and equipping the physical plant to house the psychosocial programs, and assessing and transferring study patients. Since the project director carried a full university load, all of these procedures had to be completed during the summer, and the six-month assessments at all locations had to be established to coincide with breaks in academic requirements to allow time for the project director and assessors, who were also graduate students in clinical psychology, to coordinate them.

Several other changes in original plans were required over the total project period as a result of uncontrolled external events and procedural changes initiated on the basis of findings from substudies of specific psychosocial procedures during the project. (Each change is detailed separately in this book.)

The final overall design and timing of procedures implemented over the six-year project period are presented in figure 3.1. The total intramural treatment period actually covered nearly four and one-half years rather than the three initially planned. Because of the initial delay the first six month assessment occurred after only fourteen weeks of full operation of the psychosocial programs. However, as originally planned, all patients were assessed, equated groups were formed, and patients were transferred to study locations with the post-transfer assessment documenting continued equation. A baseline for both psychosocial groups was then instituted concurrent with the establishment of continuous objective assessments of staff, residents, and programs to determine the equality and nature of staff and resident functioning before introduction of the differential treatment procedures. The objective assessments were continued throughout the intramural treatment period on both milieu and social-learning units, with the same staff conducting both psychosocial programs.

The six-month assessments reflect the continuing assessment of all patients on the same instruments according to schedule. Even

Figure 3.1. Final overall design of the comparative project

| | Treatment group | | | | Analyses in book | | |
|---|---|---|---|---|---|---|---|
| Procedures | Hospital comparison | Milieu therapy | Social-learning | Anniversary assessment | Psychosocial comparisons | Three group comparisons |
| Pretransfer assessment and equation | x | | | 0 | | Chapter 12 |
| Transfer, orientation, habituation | | x | x | | | |
| Posttransfer assessment | x | x Baseline 1 x | | | Part 3 | |
| Differential treatment | | Continuous objective assessment of staff, residents, & programs | | | The first six months | |
| 1st "six-month" assessment | x | x | x | 1 | | |
| Continuing differential treatment | | | | | | |
| 2nd six-month assessment | x | x | x | 2 | | |
| Continuing differential treatment | | | | | | |
| 3rd six-month assessment | x | x | x | 3 | Part 4 | |
| Continuing differential treatment | | | | | The next two years | |
| 4th six-month assessment | x | x | x | 4 | | Part 7 |
| Continuing differential treatment | | | | | | Intramural functioning |
| 5th six-month assessment | x | x | x | 5 | | and |
| Continuing differential treatment | | | | | Part 5 | community placement |
| 6th six-month assessment | x | x | x | 6 | The next year and a half | |
| Continuing differential treatment | | | | | | |
| 7th six-month assessment | x | x | x | 7 | | |
| Continuing differential treatment | | | | | | |
| 8th six-month assessment | x | Baseline 2 | x | 8 | Part 6 | |
| Return to baseline | | | | | The last six months | |
| Differential treatment | | | | | | |
| 9th six-month assessment | x | x | x | 9 Prerelease | | |
| Community placement | | x | x | | | |
| Social-learning aftercare of releases | x | | x | 6 month follow-up | | |
| 6 month follow-up of releases | x | | x | | Part 8 | |
| Social-learning aftercare of releases | x | | x | 1 year follow-up | A year and a half after | |
| 12 month follow-up of releases | x | | x | | | |
| Social-learning aftercare faded | | | x | | | |
| 18 month follow-up of releases | x | | x | 1½ year follow-up | | |

Note. x indicates the identical assessment over groups on components of the Inpatient Assessment Battery. Continuous objective assessments of staff and residents were maintained in psychosocial programs from the start of baseline 1 through community placement, with the same staff conducting both programs. All aftercare was conducted by psychosocial staff. The equation at anniversary assessment 0 was maintained for all replacements before anniversary 9, maintaining twenty-eight patients per group.

though the nature of the patient population actually treated made release to relatively independent functioning with self-support almost impossible, that release criterion was maintained through the eighth anniversary assessment for all three treatment groups and through the ninth anniversary assessment for psychosocial groups. Some psychosocial residents did, in fact, achieve significant release to relatively independent functioning and received the declining-contact aftercare for two years as originally planned—but the psychosocial staff remained responsible for aftercare consultation. Patients who did not achieve release to relatively independent functioning were again evaluated for community placement in extended-care facilities (all had previously been rejected for such placement before project entry). Community follow-up for these patients was restricted to approximately a year and a half declining-contact aftercare consultation, rather than two years, because of funding restrictions and numerous external events that interfered with an unambiguous evaluation of different modes of aftercare consultation.

## A GUIDE TO THE REMAINDER OF THE BOOK

As indicated in figure 3.1, comparative analyses of the psychosocial programs over time are presented in separate sections of this book that are based upon the occurrence of notable procedural changes or uncontrolled external events that affected either staff or residents. Parts 3 and 4 cover the period of nearly two and a half years through the fifth anniversary assessment, during which specific procedures were carried out according to plan, suffering mainly from delays in availability of services and supplies. Part 5 covers a period of a year and a half following an externally imposed change in one treatment procedure that was discovered to have had adverse effects on both psychosocial programs and the manner in which the basis for the problem was investigated. Part 6 covers the last six months of intramural operation, during which baseline procedures were reintroduced, followed by a twenty-week period of differential psychosocial treatment in which procedural changes designed to overcome adverse effects of the earlier externally imposed change in procedure were evaluated. Part 7 covers all intramural comparisons between milieu, social-learning, and hospital programs, as well as community placement procedures and comparative release rates. Part 8 details the nature of community placements, aftercare consultation, in-community functioning, and overall practical outcome in terms of comparative release and community stay rates, with cost-effectiveness analyses.

Parts 3 through 8 thus cover the empirical results of the comparative project. Because these results and events related to them are likely to be of differential interest to readers from a variety of backgrounds, the overview chapter within each part not only details notable events and procedural changes relevant to the empirical findings reported but provides a guide to particular chapters and parts of chapters that might be of particular interest to preprofessional staff, research workers, program directors, professional clinicians, etc. Chapters within each part may be understood without reference to other empirical chapters for specific areas of study.

Part 2 consists of a procedures section that describes the physical-social environment in which the project and treatment programs were conducted (chapter 4), comparing the general content and specific therapeutic techniques of the three treatment approaches and the means of assessing actual staff performance (chapter 5), as well as presenting the psychosocial treatment manuals used to define the treatment programs and to train psychosocial staff (chapters 6-8). The manner of assessing relatively stable personal-social characteristics of staff and characteristics of the staff groups (chapter 9) and psychosocial staff training procedures (chapter 10) are also included, as are methods of assessing problem behaviors and relatively stable personal-social characteristics of patients (chapter 11) and the nature and equation of patient groups (chapter 12).

Each of the sections presenting empirical findings (parts 3-8) concludes with a brief summary chapter. Part 9 relates the major findings and experiences from the six-year comparative project to other empirical findings and practices, with recommendations for future institutional research and treatment.

# PART 2
# Programs, Populations, and Procedures

## 4. The Treatment Setting, Organization, and Staffing

### THE GEOGRAPHICAL ZONE

The project was conducted within Mental Health Zone VI (now region 3-b) of Illinois, one of eight geographic districts originally created by legislation in 1961. As detailed by Reidy (1964), the Illinois zone system emphasized the community mental health ideology and the major recommendations contained in the final report of the congressional Joint Commission on Mental Illness and Health (1961) and incorporated in the 1963 Community Mental Health Centers Act (Public Law 88-164). In fact, under the progressive leadership of the first (Francis J. Gerty) and second (Harold M. Visotsky) directors of the Illinois Department of Mental Health, implementation of the system was already underway by the time the national program was announced.

Through decentralization of responsibilities to regional areas, comprehensive mental health services were planned to include community resources, as well as direct services through Department of Mental Health facilities. Departmental facilities were to include newly constructed mental health centers designed to serve as the zone center for overall coordination and development of services and to provide direct inpatient and outpatient care. State hospitals had previously been the primary facilities; they were described in 1963 as simply "warehousing" patients because of shortages, overcrowding, and old buildings in disrepair (Reidy, 1964). A large construction and renovation program, plus an increase in staffing levels, was planned to upgrade existing state hospitals for inclusion in the regionalized treatment system as backup facilities to provide treatment and rehabilitation of more refractory and difficult-to-manage patients (see Glass, 1974).

Each zone director was to be given maximum flexibility for developing appropriate service networks and approaches as required by the particular population of the region. Lewis Kurke was appointed zone director for Mental Health Zone VI in 1965 shortly after preliminary arrangements had begun for a controlled treatment evaluation for chronically institutionalized mental patients. He remained in that position for the entire intramural period of the project until the psychosocial units were terminated. At the time of his appointment, zone VI consisted of eighteen counties in the east-central section of the state with a combined population (1960 census) of 816,812 persons covering 11,749 square miles. Six communities within the zone had 1960 populations ranging from 27,000 to 78,000, while five ranged from 10,000 to 23,000; the rate of population increase in the zone was greater than that of the state as a whole. A large part of the area was used for agriculture, although the population centers were primarily devoted to light and heavy manufacturing, as well as service industries. Smaller communities focused more on farm marketing. Four population centers also contained universities, including the University of Illinois at Urbana-Champaign.

Under the new regional system the zone director assumed direct line authority over all Department of Mental Health facilities in the region, with responsibility for organization and development of community networks and facilities as well. The zone director was responsible to the department director. An existing state hospital in the northernmost county of the zone and a newly constructed mental health center in a west-central county were to serve as the basic Department of Mental Health resources for regional services to adolescents and adults. Community resources were to provide the first level of immediately accessible services, with the zone being further divided into six subzone geographical areas to facilitate planning and community organization. Eventually each of the six subzones would be the responsibility of a team of extramural community staff, typically consisting of an administrator (nurse or social worker), six community workers (nurses, social workers, or other B.A.- or M.A.-level staff), and a clerk-typist, plus trainees receiving practicum credit from universities in the region. While subzone extramural staff were hired at differing times, five of the six teams were in operation when the project started in 1968.

In keeping with the community-oriented focus of the region, the primary task of the subzone extramural staff was always defined to be in community organization efforts. However, their initial task was two-fold, to provide direct services through precare activities to prevent hospitalization in either the regional center or hospital and placement and aftercare activities to return geriatric and chronically institutionalized patients to their local communities from the regional hospital. As originally planned, the subzone extramural staff would have been in a unique position to monitor released patients from all project groups through their ongoing aftercare operations and to provide assistance in prerelease job and home finding. In fact, the original project design limited study patients to those originating in two adjacent subzone regions to provide equation of extramural staff. However, the delay in notification of funding and related changes in composition of the patient population in the regional hospital resulted in broadening the point of patient origin to the full zone. Additionally the original plan to transfer released project patients to the ongoing aftercare operations of subzone extramural staff, following completion of the first six months of declining-contact aftercare, was precluded because subzone staff eventually worked themselves out of direct service altogether to focus only on community organization efforts (see Illustrative Cases, chapter 19).

The original plan for Department of Mental Health facilities in zone VI thus called for local community resources to provide first-level services and for the center to provide second-level intensive treatment services for the entire zone on a short-term basis; patients requiring prolonged hospital services were to be transferred to the regional hospital. Although the original comparative treatment evaluation for chronically institutionalized patients had been planned within the regional hospital, by 1967 the success of subzone precare activities was sufficient that, combined with funding problems, originally planned center units were not all required for provision of second-level services. Therefore the traditional state hospital comparison group was housed in the regional hospital and the psychosocial programs were located in the regional center, with all study patients being drawn from the chronically institutionalized population who originated within the original eighteen counties of zone VI.[1]

## THE REGIONAL STATE HOSPITAL

The regional hospital in which the hospital comparison group resided was a large mental institution, typical of most other state hospitals built around the turn of the century and later modernized. It was located in the outskirts of a community of about 28,000 (1960) on a wide expanse of land liberally planted with mature trees. Although the architecture still retained the "medieval character" described for the hospital in 1965 (Peterson, 1968), by 1967 the reconstruction and renovation promised by the Department of Mental Health had resulted in a reduction of the 122 buildings that once composed the hospital to 55 separate modernized buildings.

The physical plant and facilities of the regional hospital were a source of pride to the hospital administration by 1967. In a document prepared for the federal grant application, the hospital administration described the institution in this way:

> The facilities generally are those needed to adequately serve a full complement of of standard diagnostic and treatment programs, as well as to furnish patients with the necessities of a secure and comfortable living. Examples are the Medical and Surgical Building, Diagnostic Building, Power Plant, Mechanical Building, Administration Building, Store, Central Dietary Facility, Laundry, Chapel, Auditorium, and Library. Facilities for clinical laboratory work, x-ray, neurology and EEG examination, Dental Service, Pharmacy, Pathological study, record keeping, staff conferences, and professional study are good. Facilities for recreational, occupational, and industrial assignment are quite adequate, except for a gymnasium which is scheduled to be built within the next year. Spacious playground areas are available for games, sports, and other outdoor recreational pursuits approximately 8 months of the year. Indoor facilities exist in 3 or 4 areas, including those for dancing, shows, bowling, and more sedentary endeavors. There is a separate, well-equipped building for art-related activities. There is also a fairly well-stocked patients' library.
>
> Occupational therapy facilities are especially plentiful. There is a two-story building devoted solely to this purpose, where activities such as woodworking, plastics, pottery, weaving, pattern-making, etc. can be followed. Educational therapy opportunities also exist for both basic skills and training in business machine operation. A wide range of industrial therapy assignments is possible. These include the laundry, food service, clothing service, greenhouse, commissary, messenger service, and housekeeping. Training facilities are also available in mechanical trades, such as a carpenter

shop, tin shop, paint shop, etc. and the hospital has active vocational rehabilitation and industrial therapy departments.

Thus, the renewed physical plant was exceptionally good by customary state hospital standards, providing facilities for the hospital operation to be nearly totally self-contained, including housing for the superintendent and several staff on the hospital grounds. Office space for the staff located in a central administration building or on separate floors or wings of buildings housing patients, was more than adequate; only nursing stations were located in patient areas.

Along with the renovated physical plant, the conditions of over 30% overcrowding, which existed as late as 1963 (Reidy, 1964), had been removed by the latter half of 1967 because of the aggressive placement of geriatric and chronically institutionalized patients in community extended-care-facilities and the reduction of admissions resulting from the early efforts of subzone community staff. Nevertheless, approximately 2,500 resident patients still remained, with the great majority of patients still consisting of chronically institutionalized patients, both geriatric and nongeriatric. Staffing of the regional hospital had also been improved through the addition of numerous professional staff and hospital participation in training and residency programs of colleges and universities, as well as the National Institute of Mental Health hospital improvement program. However, even with such improvements and approval of an expanded staffing plan, the actual overall staff-to-patient ratio at the time the final project application was submitted was just under 0.63 (FTE/ADPL), even including unpaid trainees.[2]

By the actual starting date of the project in the fall of 1968, the total resident population had been further reduced to about 1,800 patients (see chapter 12). Over the intramural treatment period of the project, the population was finally reduced to fewer than 1,000 through a combination of reduced admissions, continued placement of geriatric patients in private shelter-care or nursing homes, and transfer of large numbers of out-of-zone patients to other hospitals. The compositon of the patient population and staff-to-patient ratios also changed as the hospital became a facility for the developmentally disabled; however, as described below, the changes had relatively little effect upon the conditions of treatment for the patients in the hospital comparison group.

The administrative organization of the regional hospital followed traditional lines (Rappaport et al., 1971; Schulberg & Baker, 1975; Ullmann, 1967), with the major organizational breakdown for patient care being based upon sex, age, and nature of disorder. The superintendent (Gabriel Misevic) and assistant superintendent and clinical director (Vincas Janevicious) remained constant from the time preliminary arrangements to conduct a controlled evaluation of the treatment of chronic patients were undertaken as part of consultation to the regional hospital through completion of the intramural treatment period of the project. Although several changes in organizational charts and the nature and wording of reports occurred over the latter period, which lasted for about seven and a half years, the basic characteristics remained remarkably constant, without change from those in 1965 (Peterson, 1968), particularly for the wards on which patients in the hospital comparison group resided.

Authority clearly rested in the superintendent, with day-to-day directives carried out by the assistant superintendent and clinical director. The two primary administrative sections were the Acute-Intensive Treatment Service and the Continued Treatment Service each with a director and an assistant or associate director. Further subdivisions of major services included geriatric, child and adolescent, and medical-surgical services at the time the project began. The majority of wards within these services were segregated by sex. Although several reorganizations in major service units occurred over the intramural treatment period, the acute/chronic organization remained as primary patient care divisions. In all instances, physicians were directors and assistant or associate directors of each patient service unit. Each ward within a service unit had a physician in charge, followed in authority by a registered nurse and then a licensed practical nurse or charge aide. While medical authority was maintained in decision making, line authority over staff was within professional disciplines or service classifications, with about fifty separate departments or sections, each having its own director and chain of command. Each department or section was responsible for its own training, although the nursing service provided a separate training division for all staff within its area of responsibility (aides, attendants, and nurses).

Although the number and placement of wards within the Continued Treatment Service (for a time called the Residential Unit Division) varied over time, the above organizational structure characterized each separate variation for the wards on which patients in the hospital comparison group were housed. The only notable difference was that six full-time social workers assigned to the Continued Treatment Service from the Social Work Department, supplemented by up to thirty trainees, were assigned according to subzone areas to work in collaboration with subzone extramural staff. Two of the social workers (Barbara Tucker and Virginia Savoy) later served as hospital liaisons to the project to monitor treatment programs, release criteria, and within-hospital movement of project patients in the hospital comparison group. Over the entire intramural treatment period of nearly four and a half years, patients in the hospital comparison group were spread over as many as twelve different wards at one time, with ward size ranging from sixteen to eighty-four beds (the mean was forty-nine). Over half of the wards were closed, and all were segregated by sex. Staff-to-patient ratios on the Continued Treatment Service over the intramural treatment period are compared with those on the psychosocial units in table 4.1.

Overall the patients in the hospital comparison group were residents of one of the best hospitals operating under traditional state hospital organization, without the conditions of overcrowding, poor physical plant, and serious understaffing that are typical of most other state mental institutions.

## THE REGIONAL MENTAL HEALTH CENTER

The regional center in which the psychosocial units were housed was officially opened in fall 1966. The center is located about two miles northeast of the largest industrial city in the zone on gently sloping ground, which covered just over eighty-nine acres. Like other new centers in the state (Reidy, 1964), the architecture of the regional center followed a modernistic, horizontal scheme with ceiling-to-floor windows throughout. The physical plant consists of 240,000 square feet under a single roof, largely on one floor, surrounded by a service drive, with parking on three sides. Although the entire physical plant was housed under one roof, the center appeared to consist of twelve separate buildings separated by exterior and interior courts and connected by ten-foot-wide corridors. Four twenty-eight-bed residential treatment units—each offering 12,000 square feet of living, recreational, educational, and office space—extended to the east and to the west from north-south corridors, providing eight self-contained units for intramural residential treatment. The south projection of the building contained the visitor entrances from landscaped malls on either side to lobby-waiting rooms and related public spaces. Offices for all zone administrative staff, business offices, management information services with data-processing equipment, and a staff library were located here, along with seminar and conference rooms for use in training, business, and community meetings.

The middle sections between residential units contained offices and conference rooms, some of which were used by subzone extramural staff and project research staff, as well as record rooms and data storage space. Security offices, physicians' offices and examining rooms, a central audiovisual aids department, and a pharmacy were also located within this area. All centerwide facilities for occupational and recreational use of staff, residents, and the community were located in the interior court, including a gymnasium; swimming pool; music, sewing, and arts and crafts rooms; a small barber-beauty shop; a home-living kitchen and dining group; small auditorium; library; and classrooms. All facilities were readily accessible from residential units by means of the main corridors or from outside by means of side entrances, which did not disturb the residential units. The extreme north end of the center, straddling the two main corridors, contained all mechanical equipment and maintenance offices, the receiving area and storerooms, the central food preparation area, a snack bar, and a cafeteria. The cafeteria was used largely by administrative, research, maintenance, extramural staff, and guests since intramural residents and treatment staff had dining facilities on each residential unit.

The physical plant of the center thus reflected the community mental health ideology underlying the zone concept. Only 40% of total space was constructed for residential treatment, with the self-contained residential units built in accordance with the moral treatment philosophy (Bockoven, 1963) to include the majority of staff and resident activities, including staff offices, in the same area. While a few central facilities were available for use in training intramural residents, the majority of the center physical plant was devoted to extramural and community services. This focus was emphasized even more by the absence of support staff to operate any of the centerwide facilities, partially because of funding difficulties and partially because of administrative philosophy. In addition, several aspects of center operation expressly encouraged the residential units to be dependent upon the external community for goods and services that they could not provide themselves.

The original plan for use of the residential units at the center had been for six units each to provide services to the six subzones, with two units to be reserved for special projects. Actual use of the units varied over time. The center had officially opened in the fall of 1966; a year later, one residential unit had been in operation for about six months and another had just opened. The major focus of operations

Table 4.1. Actual staff-to-resident (patient) ratios.

| Project period[a] | Psychosocial programs | | | | Hospital comparison | |
|---|---|---|---|---|---|---|
| | On-the-floor only | | Total staff | | Total staff continued treatment | |
| | Staff-to-resident ratio | %nonprofessional staff | Staff-to-resident ratio | %nonprofessional staff | Staff-to-patient ratio | %nonprofessional staff |
| First | 0.428 | 81.3% | 0.505 | 79.6% | 0.529 | 78.0% |
| Second | .446 | 82.1% | .523 | 80.3% | .533 | 79.6% |
| Third | .446 | 82.1% | .523 | 80.3% | .536 | 80.4% |
| Fourth | .472 | 83.1% | .567 | 78.7% | .548 | 78.8% |
| Fifth | .500 | 84.2% | .581 | 81.6% | .563 | 79.4% |
| Sixth | .509 | 84.5% | .610 | 79.0% | .554 | 81.2% |
| Seventh | .509 | 84.5% | .592 | 81.4% | .519 | 82.7% |
| Eighth | .490 | 83.7% | .585 | 79.3% | .595 | 83.7% |
| Ninth | .500 | 84.0% | .603 | 78.4% | .633 | 84.3% |
| Average | .478 | 83.3% | .566 | 79.8% | .557 | 80.9% |

Note. Table entries are the ratio of average treatment staff full-time equivalent to average daily patient load. See note 9.
a. Each period is 6 months.

to that time had been on extramural work within the zone, using the center simply as a base for operations. The work during this period had been sufficiently successful in developing local alternatives to hospitalization that the zone director determined that all six units would not be needed for service to subzone areas and offered two adjacent units for use in the comparative project.

By the actual start of the project, the center had been open for nearly two years but was operating only one residential treatment unit, with a very high staffing level but a nominal number of intramural residents receiving treatment. In fact, when project units were opened, the fifty-six psychosocial residents were nearly triple the number of residents previously receiving treatment in the center at any one time. Concurrent with opening of the psychosocial units, two residential units (one for males, one for females) were opened to provide treatment for adolescents in the zone. One unit continued to provide services to the local subzone surrounding the center, as originally planned. However, intramural services for adults in the remaining five subzones were handled by a single residential unit, which was seldom at capacity. Ultimately one residential unit was opened to serve mildly retarded adolescents, and the remaining unit was put on semipermanent loan to the Department of Corrections to use for partial day or night programming with young parolees. The psychosocial units thus accounted for more intramural residents than any other unit in the center and a more severely debilitated population than the majority of intramural center staff had ever seen before—especially those staff who had been employed for the two years during which the great majority of people about the building were not residents.

The administrative organization of the intramural services of the regional center reflected as complete a decentralization of authority to a goal-oriented unit system as is likely to be feasible (see Schulberg & Baker, 1975). A superintendent did not exist from the opening of the center through termination of the intramural psychosocial treatment programs nearly six and a half years later. Instead the zone director functioned as an acting superintendent. Responsibility for day-to-day management of the facility and line authority over center staff was delegated to the business manager and assistant superintendent (Estil L. Ellis), who, like other staff with line authority, was not a physician. Only one to two physicians or psychiatrists, in addition to the zone director, were on the center staff at any time during the intramural project period. Physicians functioned in a consultative role to residential units throughout the center, providing management of psychotropic drugs, physical examinations, treatment of minor physical problems, accidents, and emergencies, and diagnostic and referral services for more severe physical problems. Independent line authority was decentralized to individual unit directors, appointed by the acting superintendent. Once a director was established for a residential treatment unit, or a set of units—as in the case of adolescent and psychosocial programs—total authority and responsibility for all aspects of staffing, treatment programming, training, etc., was vested in that person and unit to develop and carry out the targeted goal. Because appointments were made on a competency basis rather than on the basis of professional disciplines, unit directors were variously psychologists, nurses, social workers, and educators. Line authority was similarly program oriented within independent units without any organization along professional disciplines.

A few people mistakenly viewed the organization as a laissez-faire approach to administration by the acting superintendent. In fact, however, the administrative actions of the acting superintendent appeared to be purposeful and discriminative. For example, to encourage interunit communication and development of ways to use community resources, as well as to prevent the center from expending funds on nontreatment staff, no centralized staff were provided to run the center's off-unit facilities and services. The coordination instead was left to the unit staffs themselves to determine. On the other hand, staffing plans, program evaluations, and community-linkage contacts were regularly monitored by the zone director with explicit approval, disapproval, or instructions for change provided. Similarly, the majority of services that tend to foster self-contained institutions were excluded from the center, to be provided on contractual basis in the local community (e.g., linen services, housekeeping, medical and dental work, lab work) or by the residents (e.g., clothing, laundry). The absence of public transportation, however, restricted the extent to which maximum use of community resources was possible.

When decisions involving broad changes requiring rapid implementation were made, a favorite administrative tactic of the zone director and acting superintendent appeared to be a public announcement that the change was in effect as of a specific date. A short time later an assistant or associate would help those responsible work out the manner of implementation and provide necessary support for doing so. This approach was frequent in extramural operations but was used only once in the intramural operations. That occasion occurred just prior to the opening of the psychosocial units, when the large increases in intramural staff for both adolescent units and psychosocial units made a significant impact on support staff at the center. An announcement was made that all staff- and resident-related functions (except food service, pharmacy, engineering and maintenance, management information service, medical consultation, security, and fire inspection) were decentralized to the units. Thus, auxiliary staff (educators, vocational training staff, clerical staff) and support functions (medical and clinical records, personnel and timekeeping, printing, coordination and supervision of center facilities, public aid and social security investigations, etc.) were also decentralized to the individual units. The business manager and assistant superintendent was ready with a few additional staff positions and additional office space for each unit to aid in implementation. This method of running the center thus seemed to reflect satisfaction with operations rather than laissez-faire administration.

A strong open-unit philosophy was followed within the center, to the extent that the psychosocial units were the only ones with locked doors. All units except the adolescent units were coeducational, all operated on a first-name basis between residents and staff, and none allowed uniforms for either residents or staff. While each residential unit independently established its own programs, all adolescent units operated on some variant of a token-economy or incentive system, while all other units used milieu therapy. The psychosocial units thus were housed in an institution that provided relatively meager facilities and services for intramural treatment by usual standards. Nevertheless, the administrative organization and social environment of the center provided about as compatible a psychological environment for the psychosocial programs as could be found in any current institutional setting.

## THE PSYCHOSOCIAL UNITS

The psychosocial programs were located in the first and second westward projecting residential units of the center, with the milieu therapy program on one (unit A) and the social-learning program on the other (unit B). The units were thus adjacent, separated by an open courtyard-activity area. Except for the color of the walls, the two units were identical in every respect. Each had a rectangular, double-corridor design, with front and rear entrances at the end of each 10 x 60 foot corridor. Offices and work rooms for clinical staff and secretaries were located on the outside edge of each corridor, to the front of the units. On one side, immediately after a large work room, was a laundry and linen room, equipped with a washer and dryer for use by residents. A small serving kitchen was next, from which food prepared in a central kitchen was served. A refrigerator, stove, sink, and small cabinets were also included to allow some resident training in cooking and housekeeping. An L-shaped dining area was immediately adjacent to the kitchen, furnished with seven four-place tables and chairs for dining or activity use during noneating hours. The dining L looked out upon a small, enclosed, exterior court with one leg of the L connecting the two corridors. Residents' bedrooms were located on the outside edge of each corridor for the remainder of the length of the units. As used in the psychosocial programs, fourteen residents occupied bedrooms on each side, ranging from a six-bed 12 x 21 foot dormitory through 12 x 8 foot private rooms. Males were assigned rooms on one side of each unit and females on the other, with a bathing area containing one tub and three showers for each sex at the rear end of each corridor. Each room had one lavatory, access to interconnecting toilets, mirrors, and wardrobes. Bedside stands and chairs were included in the private rooms.

The major resident activity area consisted of about 3,200 square feet of space bounded on the sides by bedrooms and at the rear by a 12 x 12 foot classroom-lounge and a 12 x 7 foot TV room. The classroom-lounge was equipped with tables, chairs, a piano, and a chalkboard for use as an informal gathering place, meetings, and a quiet reading-writing room during nonclass hours. To the front of this activity area, between the corridors, was a staff work area bounded by a small office and drug room on one side with a first-aid treatment room and canteen storage room on the other. Medical records and personal effects of on-duty staff were stored in the small office, while the central work area contained clipboards with schedules, resident data, etc.; it was generally the focal point from which staff embarked for other areas. Low counters with open passageways connected the rooms to either side of the staff work area, with storage space under the counters. In the center of the open activity area was a 31 x 21 foot activity pit, three steps below floor level and surrounded by waist-high storage cabinets. Between the activity pit and the staff work area was a 20 x 20 foot open living room, furnished with several sofas, endtables, and easy chairs. Between the activity pit, classroom-lounge, and TV room was an open 900-square-foot area furnished with a few chairs and a gaming table. Three seclusion rooms with high windows were located between the staff work area and the enclosed exterior court, bounded on each side by public restrooms.

The residential units were well designed to promote high rates of resident-resident and staff-resident interaction, with staff offices being directly on the units and focal areas being both open and compact. The design promoted interaction to the extent that off-unit classrooms had to be used because sufficient separation of classes working in different areas could not be obtained within the units. The layout of units also made it possible for a staff member to view all resident areas, except the dining and kitchen areas, from the staff work area. The rectangular design also made controlled access possible to specific areas, although no mechanical turnstyles were used. In fact, the only mechanical device used at all for programmatic purposes was a timer on the TV set. All other areas in which controlled access was desired relied upon staff to encourage interpersonal contact; the TV timer merely insured staff contact through resident request.

The administrative organization and staffing of the project was geared to accomplish three specific goals: (1) to allow findings from the project to be potentially applicable to institution in public mental hospitals and/or mental health centers by establishing the number and educational level of clinical and treatment staff to be representative of those in existence elsewhere; (2) to assess the differential effectiveness of milieu and social-learning programs without a confounding of staff characteristics by having the same staff conduct both programs, equating staff time and focus in each through counterbalanced rotation; and (3) to ensure that resident, staff, and program functioning were objectively and validly assessed and evaluated in ways that left as few questions as possible about significant events that transpired by structuring documentation into the work of clinical staff and by maintaining a research staff whose only job was data collection, reduction, and analysis. Implementation of the goals, of course, had to occur within the confines of bureaucratic reality and the frequent uncontrolled events of the outside world. Although three distinct changes in organization and staffing plans occurred over the intramural period of the project, the basic character of staffing and administrative organization remained constant.

The principal investigator and project director (Gordon L. Paul), a consulting clinical psychologist from the University of Illinois, was responsible for all aspects of the project and maintained final authority over clinical, research, and personnel operations. All other staff were functionally organized as treatment staff (on-the-floor clinical staff and auxiliary staff) or research staff. Research staff regularly consisted of at least two half-time graduate research assistants and six technician-level professional observers, plus data reduction and processing staff.[3] Two secretaries regularly processed clinical data and handled the usual secretarial and stenographic work, but they worked on the treatment units and, administratively, reported to the program director. One secretary (Ilena Shelite) became responsible for coordination and supervision of all clinical forms and processing during the intramural period and ultimately functioned as an administrative assistant to the project director after the units were terminated. The first staff reorganization, required by the total decentralization of center services, added an M.A.-level psychologist position to administer the storage and processing of research data. Therefore a research supervisor (Robert J. Lentz), also a clinical psychologist, joined the project within the first six months of operation to become responsible for the day-to-day monitoring of data collection and reduction for all staff, residents, patients, and programs. The research supervisor also assumed responsiblity for research personnel action, supervision, and training, with line authority over all research staff. To ensure validity of research assessments, the research supervisor joined the clinical senior staff group with one day per week clinical responsibilities being assumed from intern psychologists to maintain original clinical staffing levels. The project director then regularly spent one day per week at the center with research staff and administration and one day there with treatment staff and administration.

The program director of the treatment staff (Titus McInnis), also a clinical psychologist, was responsible for the day-to-day operation of both psychosocial programs, including all personnel action, supervision, training, and direct clinical work. The program director had line authority over all treatment staff. The program supervisor (Beverly L. Holly), a registered nurse, was responsible for direct supervision and scheduling of on-the-floor clinical staff and direct clinical work, as well as provision and coordination of all medical services. The program supervisor had direct line authority over all on-the-floor clinical staff beyond the program director. Two intern clinical psychologists were responsible for on-the-floor clinical work along side nonprofessional staff, serving as models, trainers, and supervisors as well as behavioral analysts. The intern positions, by design, were filled by a succession of M.A.-level psychologists who each worked thirteen months, allowing one month overlap for training of new interns.[4] The liaison coordinator (successively, Kay M. Davidson and Paula D. Griffith), a B.A.-level psychologist, was responsible for the usual social-work services, including all outside contacts with relatives and community agencies, legal agencies, etc., as well as coordination and direct clinical work in prerelease planning groups and aftercare. The liaison coordinator was assigned only half-time for these duties, functioning as an administrative assistant to the project director the balance of the time. One part-time social worker trainee (Kathryn Craighead) was assigned to the liaison coordinator for a brief period; otherwise no unpaid professional trainees were involved in resident contact.

The above staff (program director, program supervisor, psychologists, liaison coordinator), totaling 4.5 full-time equivalents, constituted the original professional staff who had on-the-floor clinical responsibilities for the operation of both psychosocial programs; they were known collectively as the clinical senior staff. While the specific composition of this group changed as a function of staff reorganizations, a total of 4.5 full-time equivalents were maintained to cover the same duties throughout the intramural period. Each of the positions maintained responsibility for leading specific resident groups and monitoring individual residents in both treatment programs. The clinical senior staff were thus responsible for handling all clinical administration and coordination of services both inside and outside the center, all relations with clinical personnel (selection, hiring, training, supervision, promotion, morale—and, occasionally, firing), conduct of the treatment programs, and direct clinical work with residents. Although each senior staff position had specific areas of responsibility, the focus for all staff in the project was on cross-training and competency criteria rather than on professional or position identification. Therefore, with the exception of medical services, all senior clinical staff were cross-trained so that a minimum of two people had competency in each area of functioning at any time, and all had expertise in the direct clinical application of both psychosocial programs, sharing supervision of lower-level staff. Although specific lines of authority and responsibility were clear, all staff were encouraged to approach whomever they felt most appropriate or most comfortable with ideas or problems, including the project director, without rigid application of the chain of command. In fact, the senior staff largely functioned as a cooperative group for continuous identification and solution of ongoing problems of staff, residents, and programs, with weekly meetings of the senior clinical staff group and the project director maintaining "touch with reality."[5]

Clinical junior staff, or change agents, constituted the bulk of the on-the-floor treatment staff, with responsibility for constant application of both psychosocial programs and resident care twenty-four hours per day, seven days per week. Licensed practical nurses were required for coverage of medical problems, drugs, and first aid and generally to assist the program supervisor with medical services. The great majority of the junior staff, however, had no prior training at all beyond high school or high school equivalency nor did the practical nurses have training beyond that related to physical nursing. Junior staff were at the aide level, although numerous position titles were used—institution worker, psychiatric aide, nursing assistant, licensed practical nurse—until a career series of personnel classification ultimately was approved; at that time all junior staff were reclassified as mental health technicians or supervisors.

All junior staff received the same content training in both psychosocial programs and were assigned to semipermanent shifts (8:00 A.M.-4:30 P.M.; 4:00 P.M.-12:30 A.M.; 12:00 A.M.-8:30 A.M.). Similar to the senior staff, all junior staff were also cross-trained to perform all functions, although each was assigned specific responsibilities on a daily basis. Each shift had a supervisor of the day designated on a daily basis to be responsible for carrying out programs and making decisions required in the absence of senior staff. Authority structure within the junior staff group, beyond the supervisor of the day, was essentially horizontal, with each change agent being expected to assist and/or supervise every other change agent on an individual competency basis.[6] Only the practical nurses were originally assigned to be supervisor of the day because each shift was required to have them on duty, and the personnel code required them to receive a higher salary. However, training of new staff was always assigned on the basis of individual staff competency. As differential promotions of staff occurred, the supervisor of the day was ultimately assigned completely on the basis of competency criteria.

Although the change agents were obviously on the the bottom of the treatment staff hierarchy with regard to pay, prior training, and ultimate responsibility, the organization and operation of the psychosocial programs made every attempt to develop and appreciate their contribution. The structure of the programs, in fact, specified procedures sufficiently that change agents had the information on which to make decisions without waiting for approval of supervisors, and they were required to do so. In addition to clear employment of a competency criterion for assignment of specific responsibilities and promotions, junior staff were similarly encouraged to share ideas beyond their regular required levels of operation with any other staff member in the organization, and frequently they were asked to develop specific proposals. Opportunity was provided for communication within and between shifts through scheduled staff meetings at the overlap of every shift change. Senior staff always attended the night-day and day-evening overlap meetings, and the project director always attended these meetings once a week on his clinical day. Additionally, elected representatives from each shift met weekly with the program director and program supervisor, and off-hour coverage of evenings, nights, and weekends was scheduled by senior staff at least once a week on an intermittent basis. All staff were on a first-name basis with one another as well as with residents, both in person and in written communications. The only exception was the project director, who was typically referred to as "Dr." by residents and junior staff to maintain a slightly greater distance such that more authority was implied on the few occasions that he directly intervened to solve problems.

The clinical staffing of each psychosocial unit typically consisted of a day shift of three change agents (one of whom was an intern psychologist) during weekdays and two change agents on weekends; an evening shift of two change agents, plus a supervisor who moved between units; and a night shift of two change agents. Although the original staffing plan for the combined programs called for the 4.5 professional staff and 21 change agents, the decentralization of center services at the beginning of the project removed the program supervisor from some planned activities and required access to a practical nurse every day on all shifts. Therefore, to provide the typical on-the-floor staffing, a reorganized plan increased the ultimate clinical compliment of change agent positions to 25, of whom six were practical nurses. In practice, actual staff-to-resident ratios were considerably below the staffing plans for change agents. Equation of staff time between programs was accomplished by a counterbalanced rotation of day-shift staff every half-day (e.g., A.M.-Unit A, P.M.-Unit B, A.M.-Unit B) and evening- and night-shift staff every other day. Total equation of both time-in-programs and focus within programs occurred for individual staff every six weeks, including days off. Equation of time for the program director and program supervisor was accomplished through regularly scheduled group meetings in each program and scheduled rounds, while the liaison coordinator similarly had scheduled rounds and group meetings within each intramural program; however, aftercare contact was determined by the number of released residents in the community.

Auxiliary treatment staff from the outset of the project were to include a total of 6.1 full-time equivalent positions to serve both programs. These positions included three educators to provide direct classroom instruction for residents (three periods in each program, five days per week); three rehabilitation counselors to provide vocational training, coordinate and evaluate extramural vocational training, and assist in job finding and follow-up for released residents; and a consulting physician a half-day per week to prescribe and monitor drugs and treat patients with physical problems directly or through referral to a local general hospital. Of the auxiliary staff, only the consulting physician (F. V. Crisostomo) functioned according to the original plan for the intramural period. All the other auxiliary staff positions were involved in the first two of the three reorganizations in staffing. Upon the initial decentralization of center services, the three educator and rehabilitation positions were reassigned directly to the psychosocial staff—but the positions were vacant. These positions were assigned to the program director for supervision and coordination as auxiliary treatment staff.

Since the original delay in notification of funding resulted in the loss of extramural vocational training facilities, the first reorganized staffing plan called for the three educators and two counselors or vocational trainers to be supervised directly by the third rehabilitation position, functioning as an educational-vocational coordinator. The three educators were hired at the beginning of the project, including one with an M.A. in special education (Margaret Maynard) and two high-school graduates with some prior experience in adult education (Mayrose White and Leota Walker) to conduct specified classes. The rehabilitation positions proved exceptionally difficult to fill. Only one degreed rehabilitation counselor (Carl Miller), in fact, was ever employed—the positions and functions being filled variously by M.A.-level psychologists, social workers, educators, or registered nurses. For over two years, only one of the rehabilitation counselor positions was filled, and that by three different people. Since the decentralized services required psychosocial staff to develop and supervise resident vocational training positions within the center, only that function was actually covered with replacements. Upon the abrupt termination of the third person in a rehabilitation position, auxiliary staff were reorganized by moving the special educator (with a known track record) into the coordinator position and promoting the most effective change agent into the educator position.[7] The two additional rehabilitation positions were then filled, but all three professional auxiliary staff were officially added to the clinical senior staff group with full training on the floor and participation in policy decisions. The 4.5 full-time equivalent positions for on-the-floor clinical staff were, however, maintained as the on-unit work replaced time for intern psychologists to work on other duties that did not directly involve the current project.

The final reorganization of staff occurred toward the end of the intramural treatment period when additional staff were added in preparation for an expansion of the psychosocial operations. Over the last six months of the period, the research supervisor terminated on-the-floor clinical work to devote full time as director of an expanded research design, while other senior staff continued with clinical duties. The intern psychologists and added auxiliary staff for the expanded design were all added to the clinical senior staff group for planning purposes, maintaining the 4.5 full-time equivalent positions.[8]

In summary, treatment staffing of the psychosocial units was originally established to be comparable to that existing in public mental hospitals. Total decentralization of center services resulted in a required addition to the staffing plan. The final staffing plan called for an on-the-floor clinical and administrative complement of 29.5 full-time equivalent positions, of which 4.5 were professional level (one Ph.D, two M.A., one R.N., and one-half B.A.), while the remaining 25 were nonprofessional (six practical nurses and nineteen high-school equivalent). The total treatment and administrative staff called for by the final staffing plan, beyond the on-the-floor clinical staff, included 3.3 full-time equivalent professional positions (0.2 Ph.D for the project director, 0.1 M.D. for the consulting physician, and 3 auxiliary M.A.-R.N. level rehabilitation positions), and three nonprofessional positions (3 auxiliary educators at high-school equivalency), for an overall total of 35.8 full-time equivalent of which 78.2% were nonprofessional.

The above staffing plan to conduct both milieu and social-learning programs with twenty-eight residents in each, plus coverage of aftercare services, reflected a considerably lower staff-to-resident ratio than those existing in most reported milieu or token-economy programs (e.g., Gelfand, 1972; Hollander et al., 1973; Milby et al., 1975; Singh & DiScipio, 1972). It also showed a considerably lower staff-to-resident ratio for the psychosocial programs than that most recently reported to exist in public mental hospitals throughout the United States (Meyer, 1975). However, the actual staff-to-resident ratios existing over the intramural treatment period of the project, presented in table 4.1, show that the full staffing plan was never implemented over a full six-month period during the project.[9] The high turnover in change-agent staff, combined with hiring freezes and personnel regulations that prevented overlap training of replacements, were the primary reasons the programs remained chronically understaffed. In fact, the only way in which staffing of the psychosocial units was maintained as high as it was over the last third of the intramural period was through participation in several federal assistance programs for the unemployed. Nevertheless, comparison of the actual staff-to-resident ratios existing in the psychosocial programs with those existing for the chronic wards of the comparison state hospital over the same time periods show both the staffing ratios and the proportion of nonprofessional staff to have been approximately equal over the entire intramural treatment period. Comparison of parallel figures for the entire state during the period covered by the ninth six-month period in table 4.1 (from Witkin, 1974, table 1, p. 18) shows that a higher staff-to-patient ratio (0.720) with a lower proportion of nonprofessional personnel (64.2%) existed over the entire state than those with which psychosocial programs and chronic wards of the regional hospital were operating.

## SUMMARY

There were clear differences between the psychosocial and comparison hospital physical environments and administrative organizations. The hospital housing the comparison group and the mental health center housing the milieu and social-learning groups were both adult treatment facilities of the Department of Mental Health within the same geographical zone. The zone itself represented a relatively new regionalization of mental health services under a single director, following the community-oriented focus of the progressive Illinois zone system, covering a large area of east-central Illinois, with both urban and rural areas.

The regional hospital was a large mental institution, typical in size and architecture to most other state hospitals built around the turn of the century, and later modernized. Reconstruction, renovation, and a rapidly reducing patient population—all the result of the implementation of the zone system master plan—had resulted in a physical plant and facilities that were exceptionally good by customary standards, and more facilities were available than existed in the regional center. The administrative organization of the regional hospital retained a traditional character throughout the intramural treatment period of the project, with acute-chronic service units remaining primary patient care divisions through several changes in organizational charts. The authority structure was also traditional; physicians held all administrative positions from superintendent to clinical director to directors, assistant and associate directors of sections or service units, to individual wards. While medical authority was maintained in decision making, line authority over staff was oriented within professional disciplines or service classifications, with about fifty departments each having a separate director and chain of command. By the time the project started, the patients in the hospital comparison group were residing in one of the best of hospitals operating under traditional medical organization, without the conditions of overcrowding, poor physical plant, and serious understaffing that characterize most other state mental institutions.

The regional center was a new facility that had been open for only two years at the time the project got underway. The physical plant was under a single roof, with 40% of space devoted to eight residential treatment units—each having room for twenty-eight beds in addition to office, work, and activity space—with the major part of the building devoted to offices and community-oriented support staff and facilities. The intramural services of the center were totally decentralized to residential unit directors by the zone director, who also served as acting superintendent. Day-to-day management of the center was delegated to the nonmedical business manager. The acting superintendent—the only physician in an administrative position—set general policy along community-oriented moral treatment lines, with all remaining functions being the responsibility of each decentralized program. Although the center was new, few facilities and services existed for intramural treatment outside the residential units themselves. The administrative organization and social environment of the center was actively nonhospital, providing as compatible a psychological environment for the psychosocial programs as would be likely in any current institutional setting.

The psychosocial programs were housed in adjacent residential units of the center and were identical in every respect, except for the color of paint on the walls. The administrative organization provided clear lines of responsibility from the project director—a consulting clinical psychologist—through research and treatment staff. While the treatment staff had a clear chain of command from the program director to the program supervisor to nonprofessional change agents, all staff operations emphasized cross-training and competency criteria rather than profession or position identification. A small group of professional staff—clinical senior staff—largely functioned as a cooperative group for continuous identification and solution of ongoing problems of staff, residents, and programs with continuing responsibility for all administrative, clinical, supervisory, and personnel actions for both milieu and social-learning programs, including those of auxiliary staff. The bulk of treatment staff were nonprofessional change agents—clinical junior staff—who received all of their clinical training within the project. Emphasis on cross-training and competency criteria also existed for junior staff, with legitimate decision making required as a part of functioning. Both junior staff and senior staff worked on the floor with residents—all on a first name basis—equating time and focus between milieu and social-learning programs by counterbalanced rotation.

While treatment staffing of the psychosocial units was originally established to be comparable to that existing in public mental hospitals, the actual full staffing plan was not implemented for a full six-month period during the intramural operation of the project. However, the same hiring freezes and personnel regulations that contributed to the staff shortages in psychosocial programs also were in effect at the regional hospital. Actual staffing ratios and proportions of nonprofessional staff remained approximately equal between the psychosocial units and the regional hospital over the entire intramural project period. Thus, differences in staff functioning between psychosocial programs and traditional hospital programs reflect different utilization of staff.

# 5. The Treatment Programs and Their Assessment

## GENERAL CONTENT

The milieu and social-learning programs were conducted at the regional center in identical, adjacent, closed, coed twenty-eight bed units by the same staff. The hospital comparison group was housed over the continued treatment service of the regional hospital, where wards were segregated by sex and averaged forty-nine beds (range sixteen to eighty-four); over half were closed. Staffing ratios were approximately equal, although the organization of staff (professional disciplines versus functional program responsibilities) led to considerably different staff utilization.

Both psychosocial programs were constructed around the common objectives and areas of treatment focus that had been identified from the literature reviewed in chapter 1 as crucial targets for rehabilitation of the severely disabled chronic mental patient: resocialization (development of self-maintenance, interpersonal interaction, and communication skills), instrumental role performance (provision of prevocational, vocational, and housekeeping skills), reduction or elimination of extreme bizarre behaviors (changes in frequency, intensity, or timing of individual distressing acts or mannerisms), and provision of support in the postrelease community (at least one supportive significant other, be it family or friend—preferably a roommate). Consistent with the underlying experimental-behavioral rationale summarized earlier, both milieu and social-learning programs emphasized an explicit nondisease, reeducative model, with several common operational procedures and attitudes being detailed in one of the staff training manuals.[1]

The common procedures for the programs were those that appeared promising from previous literature. Specifically, both programs shared procedures that: emphasized a resident rather than a patient status; communicated that residents were responsible people; emphasized expectation of movement with gradual increases in responsibility required; encouraged social interaction with a range of opportunities to acquire social skills; stressed clarity of communication with focus on action rather than explanation; provided training and opportunity to practice vocational and housekeeping skills; reacquainted residents with the outside world; and specified areas for change in concrete terms for each individual.

To ensure coverage of these objectives, detailed schedules for residents and staff provided common content, exposure, and focus upon rehabilitation targets in both psychosocial programs. Morning and evening routines and mealtimes were scheduled, with programmatic interactions and assessments focused upon training in resocialization. Three to four periods per day of informal interaction, when recreational facilities were open, centered upon assessment and training in social skills. Two activity periods during each weekday used physical exercise, arts and crafts, and practical-skills training as means to activate residents and as training to focus on external stimuli, while three periods of formal classes each weekday focused upon functional arithmetic, reading, writing, speaking, homemaking, and grooming. Small and large group meetings during weekdays and evenings were scheduled for practice in problem identification and solution, as well as social-skills training. While weekend schedules differed from weekday ones, the same training focus was maintained in both psychosocial programs as during weekdays, including specific periods for training housekeeping skills. A step system increased the responsibilities of residents in each program, with higher levels of performance, more time in prevocational and vocational training, and greater exposure to the outside world being gradually introduced as residents demonstrated competence in lower-level behaviors.

Hospital programs in which the hospital comparison group participated varied somewhat because patients were spread over as many as twelve wards and were segregated by sex. So that outcome comparisons could be made with representative traditional procedures in the absence of psychosocial programs, project staff made no intrusion (beyond assessment) in usual programs in operation at the hospital. The six-month assessments were collected on schedule by the project staff, with continuous weekly monitoring of the placement of comparison patients and the ward schedules in which they were placed by liaison workers at the hospital and a regionwide computer monitoring system.

With minor modifications, the major treatment modalities of the wards on which the hospital comparison group resided were listed as follows by the physician in charge of each ward: "(1) chemotherapy; (2) industrial therapy; (3) recreational and activity therapy, including (a) social activities, (b) physical activities; (4) individual or group therapy; (5) ward meetings." Occasionally, "milieu therapy" was listed in place of the last two treatments, with a specific meeting designated as "milieu therapy." By the second year of project operation, management by objectives had been introduced at the hospital, and Paul's original review of the literature (1969a) had been published, including the targets of rehabilitation and operational and structural recommendations held in common for psychosocial programs. A review of the annual or semiannual program descriptions and evaluations from the hospital found a decidedly "popular" cast to appear from that time on, including reference to step levels, resocialization goals, recommendations to mix sexes, etc. Attempts to introduce change in hospital programs were evident from time to time in the written evaluations of program deficits. An occasional new ward psychiatrist complained of the continual transfer of staff from one ward to another by the nursing division and the lack of coordination and communication between disciplines and shifts. However, the latter "troublemakers" seldom remained at the hospital, and the majority of physicians in charge continued to see program deficits as residing only in shortages of staff and equipment.

In spite of the change in wording used to describe programs, continued monitoring found no change in actual schedules or operations for the wards on which the hospital comparison group resided over the entire intramural period of the project. In fact, operations appeared to remain quite similar to those described for these wards a year before the project began (Wagner & Paul, 1970) and to the description of the operations of the same hospital from informal observations three years before that (Peterson, 1968). Actual schedules for the hospital comparison group wards—even three years after management by objectives had been introduced—still showed that activities and meetings were scheduled on only a quarter of the wards, classes and activities on a quarter, and half the wards had no scheduled events except arising time, bedtime and meals.

Differences in program content for members of hospital, milieu and social-learning groups over a usual seven-day week of sixteen-hour days, presented in table 5.1, were considerable for both scheduled and actual treatment time. Even though more resources were available in the hospital than in the center, the scheduled time for use in active treatment in the hospital was negligible. Particularly notable is the discrepancy in time spent in drug administration, which highlights other differences in the reeducative versus medical orientations between the psychosocial and hospital programs. In addition to clear differences in terminology (residents vs. patients; change agents vs. nursing aides, attendants, nurses, and doctors; units vs. wards; center vs. hospital; drugs vs. medication), and authority structure (first name basis vs. use of professional titles; street clothes for staff and residents vs. white

Table 5.1. Weekly program scheduled for average resident (patient).

| Program content | Hospital comparison | | Milieu therapy | Social-learning |
|---|---|---|---|---|
| Classes, meetings, focused activities[a] | 4.9% | ( 2.9%) | 58.9% | 58.9% |
| Meals [a] | 18.8% | | 14.7% | 14.7% |
| A.M. and P.M. routines[a] | 6.3% | | 11.6% | 11.6% |
| Unstructured time | 63.8% | (65.8%) | 11.6% | 11.6% |
| Drug administration | 6.3% | | 3.1% | 3.1% |
| Total formal treatment | 4.9% | ( 2.9%) | 85.2% | 85.2% |

Note. Figures in parentheses show discrepancy in incidence observed in a one-week sample from those defined in daily schedules.
a. "Meals" and "A.M. and P.M. routines" included as formal treatment for psychosocial programs since self-care and self-maintenance training were regularly carried out. "Classes, meetings, focused activities" included as formal treatment for all programs.

uniforms for staff and institutional uniforms for patients; decisions made by any responsible staff member based upon detailed resident behavior vs. hierarchical decisions by nurse and physician based upon aide description of patient behavior), the fact that more time was scheduled for the administration of drugs than for any formal interactive treatment certainly suggests that—in spite of the changed words for describing hospital programs—the disease-model characteristics of custodial institutions still characterized the regional hospital programs.

## DIFFERENTIAL NATURE OF INTERACTIONS AMONG PROGRAMS

While the supporting organizational structure and content of programs provides the opportunity for treatment to occur with a focus on particular objectives, the specific treatment techniques in institutional programs functionally reduce to the interpersonal interaction component of staff behavior with regard to residents (patients)—operationally, the nature, frequency, and content of verbal and nonverbal interactions. Although both psychosocial programs were constructed to share common objectives, content, and operational focus, the principles and treatment procedures were constructed to differ systematically.

The detailed manuals that defined the milieu and social-learning programs required different approaches to construction because of the differing historical roots of the programs. Since the social-learning program was based upon the extension of principles and techniques derived from controlled laboratory investigations, well-established, operational principles already existed. Therefore, the principles and techniques of instrumental and associative learning and the basic features of token economies were extended to a comprehensive, integrated program. Unlike laboratory-derived principles of learning, milieu therapies were derived from work in applied settings with primary focus upon stated attitudes rather than principles and procedures. Therefore, specific principles of milieu therapy were deduced and made concrete, based upon a thorough review of the descriptive reports of earlier programs, consultation with major practitioners, empirical principles of social psychology, and prior personal experience. Procedures were then developed based on the principles. Thus, both psychosocial programs were exactly parallel in degree of description of operation, clarity, and specificity of operating principles and specific staff behavior x resident behavior x setting interactions. A continuing book of procedural memos was maintained to further specify procedures to questions that arose. [2]

The major focus of staff interactions for bringing about therapeutic change in the chronically institutionalized resident differed considerably. The major vehicle for the milieu program was the therapeutic community structure, with interactional focus on communication of expectancies, group cohesiveness, group pressure, controlled crisis resolution, and group problem solving. The social-learning program used the token-economy structure, with interactional focus on individual prompts, response-contingent consequences, social and material reinforcement, and individual associative learning. All staff were required to master each component of interaction in both programs before they were allowed to operate independently. The interactional focus of hospital programs was not specified, with training being concerned primarily with physical care and drug administration. Since hospital staff were often transferred from one ward to another, informal familiarization with schedules and specific problem patients was the most that could be expected. However, the authority structure, program content, and mode of training in the comparison hospital all set conditions conducive to operation of the aide culture in staff-patient interactions.

## METHODS OF ASSESSING PROGRAM OPERATION

### Usual Clinical Records

A traditional mode of monitoring staff behavior in institutional programs is through the required written records on drug charts, progress notes in the medical record, daily census sheets, etc. Ullmann (1967) summarized findings that show how such traditional monitoring of written criteria may actually provide incentives for staff not to interact with patients, instead spending time doing paperwork, a public record of their activity. These traditional clinical records were regularly completed by staff in all three treatment programs. In the regional hospital these records were the only systematic monitoring by hospital staff of the treatment programs.

In addition to the traditional clinical records, both psychosocial programs included an extensive Clinical Frequencies Recording System for detailing resident behavior on thirty-five forms within each program each day. The system (described in detail in chapter 11) provided objective assessment of resident behavior for both clinical programming and comparative evaluation. It also provided hour-by-hour monitoring of staff performance since each focused activity and/or each resident was specifically assigned to be the responsibility of a given position, and each position was assigned daily to a specific staff member. Clinical frequency forms were time-place-situation specific, detailed staff action as well as resident behavior, and identified each staff member by a coded identification number. Therefore, a moment-to-moment permanent record of staff performance in interaction with residents was automatically maintained such that appropriate credit for errorless performance—or identification of errors for corrective feedback—was monitored daily by the supervisor of the day, senior staff, and change agents. Thus, by placing the focus of required paperwork in the context of the desired staff behavior, with detailed specification and training, written records became an integral part of the accurate application and monitoring of the psychosocial programs rather than a bureaucratic exercise that took staff away from the residents.

*The Staff-Resident Interaction Chronograph (SRIC)*

The nature, frequency, and content of staff-resident interactions define the specific treatment techniques applied in institutional programs. Therefore, staff behavior was continuously time sampled on both psychosocial units by a staff of trained observers who objectively coded the presence or absence of discrete instances of staff activity in functional relationship to resident behavior on the SRIC. The SRIC categories for coding behavior were determined through rational generation and selection (Goldberg & Hase, 1967; Loevinger, 1965) to provide complete coverage of staff behavior as related to functional classes of resident behavior. The goal was to provide objective information on staff performance in sufficient detail that monitoring of individual staff could provide feedback on their performance with time-place-situation specificity, while concurrently providing summary data, through computer summarization, on the entire staff group to determine the reliability and differentiation of the actual operations of the psychosocial programs. The differentiation was particularly important since the same staff conducted both psychosocial programs.

The categories for coding observations form a 5 x 21 SRIC matrix in which the five columns represent classes of resident (or patient) behavior (table 5.2). The twenty-one rows represent classes of staff behavior (table 5.3). A single SRIC observation consisted of ten sequential one-minute periods (timed with stopwatch) during which all behavior of a single staff member was recorded in functional relationship to the behavior of residents present. Within each minute, each instance of staff contact (or lack of contact) was entered in one or more cells of the matrix by recording the initials of the resident involved—or of the group when staff behavior was directed to more than one resident. All entires in the SRIC matrix, except Neutral column entries, reflected the staff response to the class of resident behavior presented. Neutral column entries reflected staff-initiated interactions, with the exception of the last three classes of staff behavior shown in table 5.3. Announce and Attend/Record/Observe categories did not involve interaction but coded staff activities determined by other job requirements and were always recorded as Neutral with regard to resident behavior. Ignore/No Response staff activity recorded in the Neutral resident column had special meaning since it reflected job-irrelevant activity

Table 5.2. Classification of resident behavior to which staff response is functionally related on the Staff-Resident Interaction Chronograph (SRIC).

| Classification | Major characteristic of resident (patient) activity |
| --- | --- |
| Appropriate | Performs correct behavior of the right strength and intensity as required by time-place-circumstance (e.g., normal conversation, reading in class or recreation periods, "straight" response to request) |
| Inappropriate Failure | Fails to perform a behavior required by time-place-circumstance or performs a behavior inappropriate in the specific time-place-circumstance (e.g., sleeping in class, touching another's genitals in public, no response to request) |
| Inappropriate Crazy | Performs a behavior inappropriate or bizarre regardless of time-place-circumstance (e.g., verbalized delusions, incoherent speech, physical intrusion, self-injury) |
| Request | Questions; asks for help, information, favors; makes other straight requests of staff |
| Neutral | Absence of behavior specifically appropriate, inappropriate, or request, used to record staff-initiated behavior determined by circumstances other than specific resident behavior (e.g., schedule-determined announcement, greeting) |

Note. The descriptions are not sufficiently detailed for use in training observers or making observations. Detailed training materials, manuals, recording forms, normative and validity data, and computer programs for data reduction required to use the SRIC are available in Paul (in press).

Table 5.3. Classification of staff behavior on the Staff-Resident Interaction Chronograph (SRIC).

| Classification | Major characteristic of staff activity |
| --- | --- |
| Positive Verbal | Praise, compliments, positive feedback, verbal positive reinforcement |
| Negative Verbal | Reprimands, discouragement, derogatory remarks, negative feedback |
| Positive Nonverbal | Smiles, friendly gestures, positive intonation in utterance, positive physical contact |
| Negative Nonverbal | Frowns, grimaces, bristles, negative intonation in utterance, negative gestures |
| Positive Nonsocial | Gives physical or material goods, admits to services |
| Negative Nonsocial | Removes physical or material goods, withholds admittance to services |
| Positive Statement | Statements of expectations, encouragement, urging, persuasion *before the behavior occurs* |
| Negative Statement | Statements of negative expectations and prohibitions *before the behavior occurs* |
| Positive Prompt | Statements of expectations or requirements with explicit reference to positive individual consequences |
| Negative Prompt | Statements of expectations or requirements with explicit reference to negative individual consequences |
| Positive Group Reference | Statements with positive allusion or reference to a group to which the individual belongs |
| Negative Group Reference | Statements with negative allusion or reference to a group to which the individual belongs |
| Reflect/Clarify | Statements of problem existence, restatements of problem or opinion, questioning metacommunications |
| Suggest Alternatives | Statements proposing possible courses of action or interpretations of behavior |
| Instruct/Demonstrate | Statements of specific instruction or advice, physical demonstrations and modeling |
| Doing With | Engages in a specific shared activity with resident (e.g., games, conversation) |
| Doing For | Provides a specific service without resident's assistance (e.g., feeding, tying shoes) |
| Physical Force | Pulls, shoves, drags, pushes, restrains |
| Ignore/No Response | Stops attending, turns and leaves, fails to acknowledge action or communication |
| Announce | Announces scheduled events, activities, or other information |
| Attend/Record/Observe | Attends to residents without interaction; engages in job-relevant paperwork or discussions with staff |

Note. See note to Table 5.2.

to the exclusion of residents (e.g., sleeping on duty, working on crossword puzzles or chatting with another staff member without attention to residents). Ignore/No Response under other columns reflected a response to resident behavior and was treated as interaction.

A single SRIC observation was summarized by adding the frequency of entries within each cell of the ten 5 x 21 matrixes, plus calculating the frequency of occurrence of four sequences that represented functionally related but temporally discontiguous staff-resident interactions. The sequences assessed the frequency with which the same inappropriate resident behavior that received a prompt continued, and staff then ignored or staff responded with some other action; and the same inappropriate resident behavior that received a positive statement or negative feedback continued, and staff then ignored or staff continued to provide additional positive statements and/or negative feedback. Each SRIC observation also coded the specific time and activity involved, as well as the code number of the staff member and the number of residents present. Computer summarization within each treatment program then provided average hourly rates of staff activity within each of the ninety-seven separate cells of the SRIC matrix, plus sequences, number of residents present, and proportions of residents contacted. Since each psychosocial program specified particular programmatic procedures, the computer summaries also coded the absolute and proportional number of errors in staff activity within milieu and social-learning programs.

The same staff of professional observers made SRIC observations and observations of resident behavior on the Time Sample Behavioral Checklist (TSBC). (Details of observer training and the manner of ensuring valid, reliable, nonreactive data collection and reduction for both TSBC and SRIC are presented in chapter 11.) Observational schedules during the entire intramural period of the psychosocial programs, from the start of the first baseline through termination, were maintained to provide coverage of waking hours using 100 to 150 SRICs per week for each psychosocial program. Observers were present on the floor approximately 50% of the time, through application of both TSBC and SRIC. The schedules of observation over the milieu and social-learning programs systematically sampled staff positions and the beginning, middle, and end of functional program periods such that full equation of observations with equal weighting for actual time spent occurred every two weeks. Since staff time in each position was assigned to provide total equation of staff members in each functional period and position over programs every six weeks, SRIC observations recorded each staff member with equal weighting of contact in each program over six-week periods. However, for consistency in analyses and presentation, average hourly staff activity on the SRIC was summarized for all staff actually working over standard time blocks, consisting of four-week periods between each anniversary assessment, plus a two-week period overlapping the six-month anniversary assessments (see figure 3.1). Separate blocks were summarized for baseline conditions.

## ACTUAL DIFFERENCES IN STAFF PERFORMANCE AMONG PROGRAMS

Staff performance in the psychosocial programs was continuously assessed with details of differentiation between programs and within programs. To provide a descriptive comparison of the actual differences in staff behavior between psychosocial and hospital programs, SRIC data were summarized for psychosocial programs over the entire intramural period of nearly four and a half years for comparison with a full one-week sample of SRIC observations obtained in hospital programs.[3] Unlike the psychosocial data, the sample of hospital staff is likely to overestimate the total amount of interaction because of suggestive evidence of reactivity (observers on occasion heard some hospital staff tell others "get busy, they're coming" when the key went in the door) and the choice to observe whatever staff member was engaged with residents to provide the best picture of the nature of interactions in hospital programs.

Differences in how staff spent their time are shown in table 5.4, where average hourly instances of staff activity and percentage of total activity are presented for psychosocial and hospital programs relative to the class of resident (patient) behavior to which staff responded. Staff activity under psychosocial baseline conditions is also presented for comparison, since instructions to staff during baseline conditions were modeled after descriptions of the aide culture—although the existence of the more active schedule (table 5.1) during baseline conditions clearly differentiated psychosocial baselines from traditional hospital programs.

The most obvious difference in actual staff behavior between programs presented in table 5.4 is in the total amount of staff activity. Even under baseline conditions, psychosocial staff performed nearly 35% more instances of activity per hour than hospital staff, while operational psychosocial programs over the entire intramural period averaged nearly 91% and 142% more activity per hour, respectively,

Table 5.4. Nature of resident (patient) behavior to which staff responded.

| Resident behavior | Average instances per hour | | | | % of staff activity | | | |
|---|---|---|---|---|---|---|---|---|
| | Hospital | Psy-Soc baseline | Milieu | Social-learning | Hospital | Psy-Soc baseline | Milieu | Social-learning |
| Appropriate | 41.86 | 59.31 | 107.78 | 168.85 | 25.6% | 26.8% | 27.1% | 53.9% |
| Inappropriate Failure | 25.05 | 54.66 | 184.46 | 60.33 | 15.2% | 24.7% | 46.4% | 19.2% |
| Inappropriate Crazy | 1.94 | 13.89 | 17.39 | 2.25 | 1.2% | 6.3% | 4.4% | 0.7% |
| Request | 6.97 | 8.89 | 4.51 | 1.73 | 4.2% | 4.0% | 1.1% | 0.6% |
| Neutral | | | | | | | | |
|   Interaction | 26.74 | 26.53 | 34.76 | 31.56 | 16.3% | 12.0% | 8.7% | 10.1% |
|   No interaction | 47.22 | 49.25 | 48.70 | 48.74 | 28.7% | 22.3% | 12.2% | 15.5% |
|   Ignore | 14.69 | 8.81 | 0.08 | 0.06 | 8.9% | 4.0% | 0 | 0 |
| Total staff activity | 164.47 | 221.34 | 397.67 | 313.51 | 100% | 100% | 100% | 100% |

for social-learning and milieu programs. The only class of staff activity that was performed at higher rates by hospital staff than by psychosocial staff was "ignore-neutral" job-irrelevant activity. By far, the greatest proportion of staff activity in hospital programs (54%) was not in response to resident behavior but fell into the Neutral category. In fact, nearly 38% of all staff activity in hospital programs did not involve interactions with residents at all, nearly 9% consisted of ignore-neutral job-irrelevant activity and nearly 29% consisted of paperwork, discussions with other staff, drug preparations, and observing residents without interacting.

Psychosocial staff under baseline conditions were similar to traditional hospital programs in showing the highest proportion of activity to be not in response to resident behavior (38%) with notable instances of job-irrelevant activities. In contrast, the great majority of staff activity in the social-learning program was focused upon appropriate resident behavior, while the major proportion of staff activity in the milieu program was focused upon resident failures. Job-irrelevant behavior averaged only eight and six instances every hundred waking hours, respectively, for milieu and social-learning programs. The effect of having full activity schedules for residents on psychosocial units is apparent in comparisons of staff activities during the psychosocial baseline with traditional hospital programs on appropriate and inappropriate behavior. The presence of active schedules provided more opportunities for residents to perform both appropriate and inappropriate behavior, which is reflected in the higher rates of staff activity in response to these classes of resident behavior during psychosocial baselines than in hospital programs.

There were considerable differences in the attention received by an individual resident between programs because of the differing activity levels and program structure. The average staff member in the hospital programs was responsible for 19.8 patients during a week's observation. In contrast, psychosocial staff were each responsible for 22.6 residents during the original baseline; but with improvements in resident functioning and fulfillment of the staff complement by the second baseline, each staff member was responsible for only an average of 18.2 residents over all baseline weeks. The extent to which program structure influences staff responsibility is most apparent in comparisons of milieu and social-learning programs, where exact equation of residents, staff, and staff time was maintained, but the differing program structures resulted in each staff member's being responsible for an average of 17.1 residents in the milieu program and an average of 15.5 in the social-learning program. Thus, even though staff-to-patient ratios were equal, the program structure resulted in differences over conditions in the number of residents for whom each staff member was responsible, as well as differences in the amount of staff activity.

The effect of the differences on the attention an individual resident received is shown in table 5.5. The "average contacts per hour" column shows extreme differences between the number of contacts residents received in the psychosocial programs compared to either the psychosocial baseline conditions or the hospital programs. Additionally, the resident in the hospital programs received a considerably greater proportion of contacts only as a member of the patient group, rather than as an individualized, personal contact. In fact, the "probability of contact" figures in table 5.5 show an individual patient in the hospital programs to have less than a 25% chance of

Table 5.5. Amount of staff attention residents received.

| Focus of attention resident received | Probability of contact in 10 min. | | | Average contacts per hour | | | | Average interaction per contact | | | |
|---|---|---|---|---|---|---|---|---|---|---|---|
| | Hospital | Psy-Soc baseline | Milieu | Social-learning | Hospital | Psy-Soc baseline | Milieu | Social-learning | Hospital | Psy-Soc baseline | Milieu | Social-learning |
| As individual | 0.245 | 0.388 | 0.612 | 0.694 | 1.47 | 2.22 | 3.68 | 4.17 | 1.49 | 2.54 | 4.50 | 3.66 |
| As part of group | .132 | .088 | .064 | .037 | .79 | .55 | .38 | .22 | .80 | .82 | .48 | .23 |
| Total | .377 | .476 | .676 | .731 | 2.26 | 2.77 | 4.06 | 4.39 | 2.29 | 3.36 | 4.98 | 3.89 |

receiving an individual, personalized contact from a staff member during a ten minute observation even when hospital staff were doing their best. In contrast, over the entire intramural period, milieu and social-learning residents were much more likely to receive an individual, personalized contact from a staff member than not during any ten-minute period during waking hours.

Table 5.5 shows even greater differentiation between conditions in the amount of interaction—instances of discrete verbal content or other staff behavior directed to the individual— within contacts. The net effect on the total amount of attention received from staff (contacts x interactions) by an individual resident or patient was that residents under psychosocial baseline conditions received nearly 80% more attention that hospital patients. The amount of staff attention the residents in psychosocial programs received was greater than that of hospital patients by a factor of 3.30 in the social-learning program and 3.91 in the milieu program. It is clear that the manner in which available staff are utilized makes tremendous differences in the amount of attention residents received.

Differences in the nature of staff activity among the programs are shown in table 5.6, which summarizes the average hourly rates and relative proportions of each of the twenty-one classes of staff behavior from SRIC observations. The relative comparability of the absolute rates of Attend/Record/Observe shows that all staff under all conditions devoted about equal amounts of activity to job-relevant duties not involving direct resident contact. However, the lower rates of staff interactions with

Table 5.6. Average hourly rates of staff activities.

| Nature of staff activity | Average instances per hour | | | | % of all staff interactions | | | |
|---|---|---|---|---|---|---|---|---|
| | Hospital | Psy-Soc baseline | Milieu | Social-learning | Hospital | Psy-Soc baseline | Milieu | Social-learning |
| Positive Verbal | 0.73 | 3.65 | 42.47 | 46.93 | 0.7% | 2.2% | 12.2% | 17.7% |
| Negative Verbal | 1.26 | 3.53 | 27.96 | 0.83 | 1.2% | 2.2% | 8.0% | 0.3% |
| Positive Nonverbal | 41.34 | 49.60 | 114.73 | 90.87 | 40.3% | 30.4% | 32.9% | 34.3% |
| Negative Nonverbal | 2.88 | 2.91 | 3.80 | 0.43 | 2.8% | 1.8% | 1.1% | 0.2% |
| Positive Nonsocial | | 3.34 | 1.40 | 36.99 | | 2.0% | 0.4% | 14.0% |
| Negative Nonsocial | | 0.03 | 0.48 | 1.67 | | | 0.1% | 0.6% |
| Positive Statement | 0.32 | 2.00 | 49.05 | 1.04 | 0.3% | 1.2% | 14.1% | 0.4% |
| Negative Statement | 0.15 | 0.11 | 0.01 | 0.02 | 0.1% | 0.1% | | |
| Positive Prompt | 0.08 | 0.02 | 0.02 | 19.81 | 0.1% | | | 7.5% |
| Negative Prompt | | 0.01 | 0.06 | 12.66 | | | | 4.8% |
| Positive Group Reference | | 0.02 | 36.48 | 0.32 | | | 10.5% | 0.1% |
| Negative Group Reference | | | 9.97 | 0.01 | | | 2.9% | |
| Reflect/Clarify | 10.43 | 23.53 | 32.59 | 12.35 | 10.2% | 14.4% | 9.3% | 4.7% |
| Suggest Alternatives | 0.07 | 0.02 | 2.19 | 0.49 | 0.1% | | 0.6% | 0.2% |
| Instruct/Demonstrate | 15.73 | 20.17 | 8.64 | 10.97 | 15.3% | 12.4% | 2.5% | 4.1% |
| Doing With | 13.92 | 18.51 | 17.25 | 24.33 | 13.6% | 11.3% | 4.9% | 9.2% |
| Doing For | 13.17 | 1.98 | 1.08 | 0.83 | 12.8% | 1.2% | 0.3% | 0.3% |
| Physical Force | 0.07 | 0.52 | 0.12 | 0.30 | 0.1% | 0.3% | | 0.1% |
| Ignore/No Response | 17.10 | 42.14 | 0.65 | 3.90 | 16.7%[a] | 25.8%[a] | 0.2%[a] | 1.5%[a] |
| Announce | 0.09 | 1.84 | 3.14 | 1.87 | (0.1%) | (0.8%) | (0.9%) | (0.6%) |
| Attend/Record/Observe | 47.13 | 47.41 | 45.56 | 46.87 | (28.7%) | (21.4%) | (13.1%) | (14.9%) |
| Total Interactions | 102.56 | 163.28 | 348.89 | 264.71 | 114%[a] | 105%[a] | 100%[a] | 100%[a] |
| Total Activity | 164.47 | 221.34 | 397.67 | 313.51 | (160%) | (136%) | (114%) | (118%) |

Note. Empty cells signify less than 0.0045 instances per hour.
a. "Ignore-neutral" included in percentage figures but not in total interactions.

patients in the hospital programs are evident in the greater proportion of activity accounted for by such noninteractive behaviors.

Even though hospital staff were considerably less active than psychosocial staff, the extent to which conditions supporting the aide culture affected actual staff behavior is evident in the few classes of behavior that did occur at higher absolute frequencies in hospital programs. The absolute incidence of Doing For not only occurred at relatively high rates but at higher rates in hospital programs than in all psychosocial conditions, reflecting the custodial-caretaking philosophy of the medical model as distinct from the psychosocial expectations that residents could do things for themselves. Ignore/No Response and Instruct/Demonstrate also occurred at higher absolute rates in the hospital programs than in either psychosocial program, indicating the extent to which hospital staff tended to ignore all patient behavior—including appropriate behavior—and to simply tell patients what to do when things needed to be done. This tendency is also evident in the exceptionally low levels of Announce, reflecting only nine announcements every hundred waking hours; even the few scheduled events (meals, bedtime, etc.) tended to be handled by instruction rather than by announcements (e.g., "Line up at the door for lunch" rather than "Time for lunch"). The only other staff behavior to occur with higher absolute frequency in hospital programs was Negative Statements. While the absolute incidence of these was only fifteen instances per hundred waking hours, such behaviors are particularly derogatory to patients (e.g., "Don't put beans in your nose" when beans were not being put in anyone's nose) and a reflection of the apparent lower position of patients.

While all of the above behaviors clearly show the actual performance of the hospital staff to be similar to descriptions of the aide culture, the relatively high frequency of Positive Nonverbal and Doing With indicate the presence of friendly social interactions and shared activities. However, such positive social behaviors in the hospital programs were not differentiated on the basis of patient behavior; less than 48% were contingent on appropriate patient behavior, and the remainder were staff initiated or contingent upon inappropriate patient behavior. The same six classes of behavior accounted for the majority of staff activity in psychosocial baseline conditions and hospital programs (Positive Nonverbal, Reflect/Clarify, Instruct/Demonstrate, Doing With, Ignore/No Response, Attend/Record/Observe). The major area in which psychosocial baseline conditions did not approach hospital programs was Doing For even during baselines, psychosocial staff let residents perform activities themselves. Because of the higher activity levels of psychosocial staff, Positive Nonverbals accounted for a relatively higher proportion of staff-patient interactions in hospital programs, while Ignore/No Response occurred with higher frequency and accounted for a greater proportion of staff-resident interactions during psychosocial baselines. Overall, however, the nature of staff performance during psychosocial baselines was considerably closer to hospital programs than to either of the psychosocial programs.

Details of absolute and differential staff performance between milieu and social-learning programs are analyzed and presented in later chapters, along with their relationships to changes over time in resident behavior. For current comparisons, we shall note that all seven classes of staff behavior differentially specified in the Milieu manual occurred at higher absolute frequencies than in the social-learning program, traditional hospital programs, or psychosocial baseline conditions (Negative Verbal, Positive Nonverbal, Positive Statements, Positive Group Reference, Negative Group Reference, Reflect/Clarify, Suggest Alternatives). These staff behaviors also accounted for a greater proportion of all staff-resident interactions in the milieu program, except for Positive Nonverbals and Reflect/Clarify, which proportionally accounted for more staff-patient interactions in hospital programs because of the low incidence of total interactions. Similarly, the majority of classes of staff behavior differentially specified in the social-learning manual occurred at higher absolute frequencies and accounted for a greater proportion of interactions than in the milieu program, traditional hospital programs, or psychosocial baseline conditions (Positive Verbal, Positive Nonsocial, Negative Nonsocial, Positive Prompt, Negative Prompt, Positive Nonverbal and Doing With when contingent on appropriate behavior). Instruct/Demonstrate and Ignore/No Response were also differentially specified for social-learning versus milieu application but still occurred at lower rates than either traditional hospital programs or psychosocial baseline conditions.

## SUMMARY

Clear differences existed between the psychosocial and hospital programs on nearly every dimension, and there were systematic similarities and differences documented between the milieu and social-learning programs. Both psychosocial programs shared common objectives that are best described as a non-disease, reeducative model of treatment, with supporting organizational structure and highly specified program content emphasizing active treatment and expectation of change. In spite of changes in wording to describe programs for the hospital comparison group, the traditional hospital programs still epitomized a disease model of treatment. The supporting organizational and authority structure of the hospital continued to emphasize chemotherapy, with negligible program content for the long-stay patient—remaining characteristic of custodial institutions without expectations of patient movement, despite some obvious attempts to change that situation.

Psychosocial programs systematically differed in the particular treatment techniques defined, although both were highly specified with operating principles and procedures defining appropriate resident behavior x staff behavior x setting interactions. In contrast, the traditional hospital programs had no defined operating principles and procedures. However, a comparison of a full-week sample of staff behavior obtained through objective observational assessment on the SRIC found actual hospital staff behavior to be reminiscent of that of the aide culture previously described in custodial institutions. Comparisons were also made with the actual staff behavior of psychosocial baseline conditions and psychosocial programs over the entire intramural period, with clear differences existing in the amount and nature of staff behavior.

While psychosocial and hospital programs all provided routine progress notes, drug charts, etc., as means of assessing staff performance, these written notations were the only regular means by which the hospital supervisory staff monitored its treatment programs. Both psychosocial programs, in contrast, provided moment-to-moment monitoring of staff performance through an extensive Clinical Frequencies Recording System maintained by the clinical staff themselves. Additionally, the SRIC provided continuous objective assessment of actual staff behavior by trained observers throughout the intramural period for psychosocial programs.

# 6. The Orientation and Common Procedures Manual

People are usually placed in a mental institution not because they are ill or have broken laws but because they have acted in ways that disturb themselves or other people. They typically have upset relatives or people in the community by behaving in socially unacceptable ways. Once people are admitted to a hospital because of their disturbing behavior, they face the problem of adjusting to the environment of the institution itself. If they refuse to accept the hospital routine, they may become labeled as severely disturbed or called problem patients. Thus, in most treatment programs, adjustment to the hospital and just getting along on a daily basis mean people must passively accept what is going on around them. In most current community psychiatric units and other short-term treatment facilities, the program focus is correctly upon rapid return to the community; frequently, however, the patient is released so quickly, often only after administration of drugs, that the disturbing behaviors or conditions in which they occur are not changed. Therefore, many people continue to return, often repeatedly, to mental institutions. Eventually many of those who repeatedly return to institutions or who never leave lose whatever appropriate social and vocational skills they had prior to admission. Thus, two primary problem groups have developed: those who have become chronically institutionalized and those who are in danger of becoming chronically institutionalized.

## COMMON ASSUMPTIONS OF PSYCHOSOCIAL TREATMENT PROGRAMS

As opposed to many mental hospital programs, we do not consider the people we are treating to be ill. We prefer to think of them as either having learned inappropriate behaviors or as having failed to learn or forgotten behavior needed for getting along outside an institution. We assume, furthermore, that each person is capable of being returned to an independent and productive life in the outside community if he or she can modify the inappropriate behaviors that have been learned and learn the appropriate ones necessary to functioning in a normal world. The two treatment programs that best manifest these two assumptions and that operate on the principle of respecting these people as human beings are the two programs that constitute the psychosocial rehabilitation programs.

## COMMON OBJECTIVES AND AREAS OF FOCUS

To reeducate people and to provide them with the skills necessary for functioning in the community, it is important to know exactly what we expect the residents to do. It is just as important that residents know what is expected of them. In other words, what do we want them to learn? For our purposes, we can spell out four major areas of focus for residents in both treatment programs.

1. *Resocialization.* First, each person must be able to perform the normal, daily habits of self-care, i.e., those things that all adults are expected to do for themselves in our society. This includes getting out of bed when they are supposed to without constant prodding, making their beds, and keeping their rooms in order. Also, grooming habits, such as shaving, combing one's hair, and bathing regularly, are very important because of the impression appearance makes on other people and because it affects the way people think of themselves. We expect each resident to be neatly dressed, with buttons buttoned, zippers zipped, wearing appropriate clothing, etc. We want the residents to be able to eat with appropriate table manners and to get their own food from the cafeteria. We also expect them to either do their own laundry or make arrangements to have someone else perform this service.

---

This chapter comprises the staff training manual that details the common procedures of the psychosocial programs to preprofessional staff. The style and format of the original manual have been retained.

Another area that we often take for granted is that of getting along with other people: how to carry on a conversation, how to act appropriately in a group of people, how to participate in recreation. We hope to teach our residents these kinds of interpersonal skills. Also, the ability to use methods of communication, such as reading and writing, is necessary for living in the outside community.

2. *Instrumental role performance.* Since many residents may have never learned, or lost, vocational and/or housekeeping skills, we assess and provide instruction in these areas so that when they return to the community, they can assume the responsibilities of being part of a household once again. Whether their role is to be that of major financial support of the family or that of the person responsible for maintaining the home, or both, our residents must be able to contribute to whatever community living arrangements to which they return. Thus, we provide instruction in such basic home management skills as how to shop for groceries and personal items, how to cook, how to budget money, use banking facilities, do dishes, set tables, mop floors, etc.

Certain behaviors are necessary to succeed in employment in addition to the minimal skills needed to perform the job. We not only conduct regular vocational assessment and training but expect our residents to learn such additional work behaviors as getting along with coworkers, staying on the job, and producing an acceptable quality and quantity of work. Since all instrumental roles require movement between places, we also ensure that our residents can drive or use public transportation.

3. *Reduction or elimination of extreme bizarre behaviors.* Because we assume that our residents were institutionalized for behaving in ways disturbing to themselves or others, one of our major common objectives is the modification of these disturbing behaviors. Bizarre or crazy behavior can be described as unpredictable, unusual acts that most people have trouble understanding and that are distressing to them. We want to change the frequency (how often), the intensity (strength), and the timing (when) of these actions and behaviors that make them undesirable. Some of the more common problem behaviors we want to eliminate or reduce because they distress people are talking or responding to things that do not exist; threats of injury to one's self or others; talking in ways that do not make sense to others; talking or mumbling to oneself; giggling, smiling, or making faces with no apparent stimulus or reason; avoiding other people; failing to respond to things that occur around them; crying or shaking without apparent reason; being too noisy or active. Further distressing actions, such as creating fire hazards, destroying property, hitting other people, soiling oneself, and inappropriate public displays of sexual behavior are also target behaviors to change. In general, any behavior that interferes with the rights of others or interrupts desirable activities is not allowed to continue in either program because it is not tolerated in the outside community.

4. *Support in the postrelease community.* Studies have indicated that residents who return to a positive home and work situation upon release from an institution are more likely to stay in the community. A common objective of both treatment programs, therefore, is to make provisions for each resident to return to such an environment in the community upon release. This means teaching residents' families how to handle problems that may arise or, in the case of those residents having no family to which they can return, teaching residents themselves in groups of two or three to live and work together in the community.

## COMMON OPERATIONAL PROCEDURES AND ATTITUDES

There are certain procedures and attitudes common to both programs that should effect changes in the desired directions.

1. Consistent with our view that the people we treat are not sick, we emphasize a *resident rather than patient status.* Residents are here to learn new skills or relearn forgotten skills rather than to be "cured." Further, since we want to reduce and eliminate the differences between those we treat and ourselves and guide them toward normal behavior, we approach the residents from their entry into a treatment program with the understanding that they will be in the program for a limited period of time.

To decrease the hospital like atmosphere and the differences between staff and residents that typically exist in traditional treatment programs, there is an emphasis on informal dress of staff, open channels of communications, and broad, but clear, authority structure. Also, staff eat the meal that falls on their shift with the residents to provide models of appropriate behavior for the residents and to show the residents that the staff members are like themselves.

Open communication between staff and residents and among staff members is strongly encouraged. We must be prepared to respond to the residents at all times and consider what they say as important. Staff members are expected to act immediately on every legitimate written or verbal request of a resident, whether by carrying it through themselves or by assigning it to someone else for follow-up. Because every staff person is responsible for retraining the residents and for providing information to fellow staff members, all staff, regardless of position, should feel comfortable in seeking out any other staff member to communicate ideas. This is not to say, however, that at all times each staff person is equal in authority. Each staff member does have a daily schedule specifying responsibilities for that day. While only one staff person is responsible for specific procedures on any given occasion, nearly all staff members participate in all procedures at different times. Authority is based not upon professional titles but upon the competency of each individual and the responsibilities for which each staff member is accountable.

2. Since we feel that the residents are responsible adults, this attitude is emphasized through consistent communications. *Posted rules* communicate that residents are expected to follow certain minimal rules of group living and to do their share in participating in self-care, work, recreational, and social activities. Because we are teaching behaviors to the residents, what we teach is specified in a list of the ten basic unit rules that every resident is expected to know and to follow. This list is also a statement of what we hope each resident will accomplish. In general, residents on both units are expected to care for themselves and for their appearance; to perform their own housekeeping chores and to share in those of the unit; to respect, in terms of their behavior, the rights of others; to be cooperative; to attend and to engage in activities; to acquire the skills and habits that will allow them to function after they leave; to return to the community; and not to act crazy. (For a list of the ten basic rules, refer to the appendix following this section of the training manual.) The responsibility for successfully meeting the stated expectations resides with the residents themselves. This is in keeping with our assumption that the residents can be responsible adults capable of meeting these expectations.

3. A primary part of each treatment program is a *step system*, which gradually increases the expectations placed on the residents in terms of both relative degrees of independence and relative levels of responsibility. The step system serves a dual purpose: it makes clear to the residents that as they act more appropriately they assume more responsibility and gain more privileges, and it ensures that the residents make systematic progress toward acquiring behaviors necessary for functioning in the community. Once the residents thoroughly familiarize themselves with the four step levels, they are able to determine, for themselves, how much further they have to go to attain the program goals and to be released. It is always emphasized that our overriding expectation is to see the residents return to the community; the step system allows the residents to gradually move from the lower entrance level to higher levels and eventually to release in small enough steps so that they don't become overwhelmed.

In order to move up from step 1, where all activities are supervised, the residents must begin to make approximations to most of the behaviors we expect them to acquire for living in the outside community. They must attend classes, regularly care for themselves, take part in the maintenance of the unit, begin to interact appropriately with other residents and staff, and not blatantly violate any of the basic unit rules. Because the residents in step 1 will be expected only to begin demonstrating these skills, their pass privileges will be limited to the center, and they must be accompanied by another person on these passes.

As the residents move through the step levels, the skills they demonstrate in each previous step must be carried through to the higher steps. In other words, the system is accumulative, so that step 2 residents must meet the requirements of step 1 in addition to meeting increased expectancies and responsibilities. At step 2, more "straight" and cooperative interaction is required of the residents, who must also assume individual work assignments within the center for three hours a day. They must perform acceptable work on the assignment. They will also be expected to accompany a step 1 resident on a center pass as well as to take two unaccompanied center passes and one accompanied downtown pass. Furthermore, they must have no more than mild infractions of the basic unit rules on record while at step 2. The residents will spend a minimum of two weeks on step 2 during which time they will be able to take center passes alone and also go downtown if accompanied.

At step 3, where the residents must demonstrate the stated expected behaviors for a minimum of three weeks, they will be able to go downtown alone and take accompanied overnight passes. They will be expected to spend a full day on an individual work assignment, to demonstrate the ability to read and write, to demonstrate housekeeping skills, and to serve as a model to other residents in most areas of behavior.

By the time the residents reach step 4, they will have acquired most of the terminal behaviors the programs have established as goals. Step 4 residents should be able to serve as models to other residents in all areas of behavior, to demonstrate useful vocational skills, and to take three overnight unaccompanied passes. They are also expected to consider seriously their release by participating in a prerelease planning group and by preparing, with assistance, a reasonable release plan within one month after their entry to step 4. We expect the residents to fulfill all requirements for step 4 and to be released to the community three months after they have reached step 4. Once in the community, the residents participate, at a minimum, in a twenty-six-week follow-up program with six-monthly visits for two years to be conducted by the unit staff while they are living independently with supportive others. (For a detailed listing of the step level requirements and privileges, refer to the appendix for this portion of the manual.) In summary, the step level system, by gradually and specifically increasing the expectations and responsibilities required of each resident, will provide the residents with a clearly stated means of determining where they are and where they have to go within the overall framework of each treatment program.

4. Since we want to avoid training the residents further in being institutionalized and because our emphasis is on situations similar to those they will meet after release, we expose them to *normal social interactions* and to the practical skills that are relevant to appropriate functioning in the community. Both treatment programs encourage social interactions and skills and provide a variety of activities as well as large and small group meetings. Further, our programs include classes that teach self-care skills, housekeeping, money management, use of community facilities, etc., as well as the basic reading, writing, and math skills. Through large and small group meetings and activities, the residents have the opportunity to acquire additional routine, but nonetheless important, skills, such as how to catch a bus, how to fill out a job application, how to act during an interview, how to make telephone calls from a pay phone, etc. These group meetings also focus on interpersonal skills; for instance, there is training on how to talk with other people and how to make a positive impression.

The residents have scheduled informal interaction periods, as well as classes and meetings. Games, television, crafts materials, and other recreational equipment are available during the informal interaction periods. Thus, the residents are able to engage in activities with other people on an informal basis, much as they would during leisure time in their own homes. Physical activities and more structured project-making periods are also included in the schedules of each program. The purpose of these classes, meetings, periods of activity, and opportunities for interaction is to provide the residents with the means to relearn and practice newly learned skills and techniques that they need to get along in the outside community.

5. Both treatment programs emphasize *clarity of communication* through concrete instruction in appropriate behavior and focus on utilitarian action rather than on explanation. Appropriate communication with residents and other staff is essential to fulfilling the objectives of the treatment programs. We expect all staff to use what is termed *descriptive language* in all forms of communication. In brief, descriptive language is terminology that specifies what is going on at a given time and does not make inferences as to why it is going on. Descriptive language describes action and does not depend on the personal interpretation and judgment of the observer. It is language that describes the current environment and does not look into something within the individual for an explanation. It is language that allows exact replication, i.e., when a person describes what particular behaviors a resident is performing at a particular time, any other person knows exactly what was going on, in terms of those specific behaviors, if descriptive language is used.

There are several important reasons for using descriptive language in these treatment programs. First of all, going back to one of our original assumptions, we do not consider our residents to be sick; we therefore avoid attaching labels or giving names to classes of behaviors as if these labels explained everything about the person who behaves in those ways. We want to avoid putting our residents into a particular categorical box. Rather, we concentrate our efforts on changing particular and specific behaviors, and therefore we expect the behavior of the residents to be described in specific terms so that we can change exactly what needs to be changed. For example, if someone refers to a resident as being aggressive, we have very little idea as to what that resident did to earn that label. It is far easier instead to determine what happened if the person said the resident had hit another resident or that the resident pushed someone to the floor. A second reason for the use of descriptive language is that we keep accurate records of what the residents and staff are doing. These records serve the residents by establishing a clear picture of behavior through frequent and steady observations; they provide information on the progress each resident is making and can be, therefore, rewarding to the change agents by demonstrating that there has been progress. The actions and behaviors of change agents themselves are recorded to ensure that the programs are being properly applied and to aid each staff member in the future training of other change agents. Behavior of both residents and staff is recorded in the same way and at the same times on both units. To be effective, the records must be written in terminology that is not ambiguous, inferential, or subject to personal interpretation; that is, the records must be written in descriptive language.

6. Both treatment programs provide opportunities to practice *vocational and housekeeping skills,* with feedback and training in marketable skills when needed. All residents, at some time in the treatment program, are evaluated to determine their work skills and in what areas they have the most potential for succeeding at a job.

Once residents enter step 2, they are assigned as an assistant on a job within the center. They are evaluated daily by their supervisor on the job or by a unit staff person on their basic work behaviors, such as the quality of their work, how they get along with their coworkers, whether they arrive at their job on time, etc. The residents may have several different assignments and thus be exposed to a variety of jobs. It may be that such training within the center is not all that the residents need or want, or perhaps some residents will return to the community to run their own home and may need to acquire only housekeeping skills. In that case, the resident spends time in learning practical home economics, such as cooking, shopping, etc., and is assigned to work that requires application of those skills. If the residents seek further training, they may have the opportunity to go to a public vocational training center for intensive and longer-term specialized training. The training center provides us with the same kind of information with which supervisors within the center provide us, i.e., the quality and quantity of work, how they get along with coworkers, etc.

7. Each treatment program *reacquaints residents with the outside world* by exposing them to the community through trips and passes and bringing in community volunteers. Many residents have lost all contact or concern for what is going on in the world. The programs reinstitute this contact to ensure that residents can adapt and function adequately in the community. Initially each resident is provided with noninstitutional clothing rather than uniforms through trips or passes with a specified sum of money provided to spend. The canteen on each unit is supplied with items to operate similar to a general store. Our residents must be able to function in the community and must know how to use the resources of the community if they are to be permanently released from the center.

8. Each treatment program specifies *unique areas for change in concrete terms* for each individual. Through the preassessment battery given to each resident, through the existing records, and through daily assessment instruments used on each unit, the staff is able to determine the behaviors that each resident should acquire and those that should be eliminated. The target behaviors so defined are communicated to each individual in descriptive terms so that the residents know at all times what behaviors they need to change and in what direction such changes will lead them. It is therefore essential that staff use descriptive terminology in filling out the daily assessment forms to eliminate the need for any translation.

9. Both treatment programs prepare residents and significant others to live in mutually supportive ways in the community through *prerelease training and scheduled aftercare.* Once the residents have reached step 4, they attend small group meetings that focus on the practical problems they may meet upon return to the outside community. In addition, the families are trained in handling problems that may arise. How to deal with the people in their home situations in a positive manner is heavily emphasized. Following release, a staff member visits the homes of former residents on a declining-contact basis. Any staff member who has a positive relationship with a particular resident may be called upon to handle the postrelease visits. The follow-up consists of a minimum of four weekly, five biweekly, and three monthly home visits for a total of twenty-six weeks, with long-term follow-up every six months for two years. During these visits, reassurance and concrete advice on problems and practical matters are provided.

The extramural subzone staffs are also involved with prerelease planning and job and home finding for all residents in their area, as well as long-term follow-ups.

10. In both treatment programs, when no family exists, the residents are prepared to live in mutually supportive ways in the community through prerelease training and scheduled aftercare by training in groups of two and three as a family to provide support for one another. Because it is important for successful independent living to have a roommate who can offer support when problems arise and because there will be residents on our units who have no family to which they can return, the treatment programs provide training to residents who may live together. The prerelease training focuses on the same areas mentioned above and also involves discussions of the special problems that arise when three men or three women live together. The aftercare is conducted on the identical basis that was previously stated.

Although there are objectives and procedures common to both treatment programs, the ways in which these objectives are met involve specific techniques, operations, and procedures that differ for each unit. These are described in the following manuals.

APPENDIX

A. Ten Basic Rules

As a resident of the rehabilitation unit, you are expected to:
1. Care for yourself and present a desirable appearance.
2. Perform your own housekeeping chores and to share in those of the unit.
3. Think, talk, and act straight (in ways which make sense to others).
4. Show gentlemanly or ladylike behavior.
5. Show respect for the rights of others, for yourself, and for property.
6. Interact cooperatively and actively with residents, staff, and others.
7. Attend and participate in all scheduled activities (be where you're supposed to be).
8. Acquire and demonstrate work habits and skills that will provide for an income after you leave.
9. Move through the four step levels of the program and return permanently to the outside community.
10. *NOT* act "crazy"!!!

B. Step Level Requirements and Privileges

*Minimal Expectations for Step 1 Performance*

1. Attend and participate in most scheduled unit activities, including six hours of daily supervised large and small groups.
2. Regularly care for self, i.e., get up on time, present a desirable appearance, bathe, eat without assistance.
3. Take part in maintenance of unit, i.e., make bed, clean up area, help in general upkeep.
4. Initiate and respond to conversation.
5. Respond to requests.
6. Take at least one accompanied center pass.
7. No blatant violations of the basic unit rules.

Eligibility for step 2 will be considered after a resident has met expectations for step 1 for a minimum of one week.

*Privileges Accompanying Step 1*

1. Accompanied center passes.

*Minimal Expectations for Step 2 Performance*

1. All things required at step 1.
2. Assume half-day individual assignments with at least acceptable ratings.
3. Be cooperative and active with other residents and staff during most free time, informal interaction, and recreation periods.
4. Engage in "straight" conversations with other residents and staff.
5. Take at least two unaccompanied center passes and one accompanied downtown pass.
6. Accompany a resident on step 1 on a center pass at least once.
7. No more than mild infractions of the basic unit rules.

Eligibility for step 3 will be considered when a resident has met the expectations for step 2 for a minimum of two weeks.

*Privileges Accompanying Step 2*

1. May accompany residents on step 1 on center passes.
2. May take unaccompanied center passes.
3. May take accompanied downtown passes.

*Minimal Expectations for Step 3 Performance*

1. All things required at step 2.
2. Assume full-day individual assignment in center with at least acceptable ratings.
3. Demonstrate ability to read and write.
4. Demonstrate housekeeping skills.
5. Serve as model to other residents in most areas of behavior.
6. Take at least three downtown passes and one accompanied overnight pass.
7. Accompany a resident at step 2 on a downtown pass at least once.
8. No violations of basic unit rules.

Eligibility for step 4 will be considered when a resident has met the expectations for step 3 for a minimum of three weeks.

*Privileges Accompanying Step 3*

1. May accompany residents on step 1 on center passes.
2. May accompany residents on step 2 on downtown passes.
3. May take unaccompanied center passes.
4. May take unaccompanied downtown passes.
5. May take accompanied overnight passes.

*Minimal Expectations for Step 4 Performance*

1. All things required at step 3.
2. Full-day individual assignments at center with at least acceptable ratings.
3. Serve as model to residents in all areas of behavior.
4. Demonstrate useful vocational skills.
5. Participate in prerelease planning group.
6. Prepare reasonable release plan within one month after entry to step 4.

7. Take at least three unaccompanied overnight passes.
8. Be released for independent living within three months after entry to step 4.

*Privileges Accompanying Step 4*

1. May accompany residents on step 1 on center passes.
2. May accompany residents on step 2 on downtown passes.
3. May accompany residents on step 3 on overnight passes.
4. May take unaccompanied center passes.
5. May take unaccompanied downtown passes.
6. May take unaccompanied overnight passes.

*Postrelease Requirements*

1. Independent living with supporting others.
2. Cooperate in twenty-six-week follow-up by unit staff.

# 7. The Milieu Therapy Manual

The principles and procedures in this program have grown from applied research in institutional settings. While working with residents on the milieu unit and administering the milieu therapy program, we assume that a basic set of principles is valid. This means that we think about the resident's behavior and methods of changing it according to these principles, and we consistently apply these principles and procedures in all our dealings with residents on the milieu unit.

## BASIC PRINCIPLES AND CONCEPTS

### Law of Expectancy

While there are many laws of milieu or environmental influence and many situational principles, a few are so basic that we must always keep them in mind. Three major laws of situational determination form the basis for most of our principles and procedures. The first is the *law of expectancy*. It states that the frequency of occurrence of an action, behavior, or response is a function of the expectation communicated at the time of or prior to its occurrence. Behaviors for which consistent positive expectations are communicated in a specific situation will increase in frequency and continue to occur; behaviors that do not receive consistent communication of positive expectation or that receive communication of negative expectations that they will not occur in a specific situation will decrease in frequency and eventually cease to occur.

An *expectancy* or expectation is a state or quality of regarding a particular event (action, behavior, response, or environmental change) as likely or reasonable to happen or occur. *Communication* refers to the transmission or imparting of information. The law of expectancy requires that expectations be clearly communicated to change or maintain behavior. For a specific expectancy to be transmitted, the communication must be explicit. Communication of expectancies may occur in a number of ways. A *written statement* of expected behavior, in the form of explicit rules or laws, is one of the most common forms of communicating expectancies. However, since it is impossible to anticipate all behaviors in all situational contexts, written communications have limited utility for changing or maintaining specific behaviors at specific times. Therefore, the most flexible means of communicating expectancies is through precise concrete verbal descriptions regarding expected behavior.

*Positive statements* are verbalizations before a behavior has occurred that communicate that a given behavior is appropriate to a given situation and is expected to occur. Positive statements consist of sentences transmitting information that certain actions, behaviors, or responses can and should occur, increase in frequency, or increase in intensity (suggestion, persuasion, urging, encouragement, or straightforward statements of expected behavior). When verbalizations communicating that a behavior is appropriate to the situation and is expected to occur are transmitted at the time the behavior is occurring, or after it has occurred, the statements are called *positive feedback*. Positive feedback consists of utterances, clauses, or sentences transmitting information that given actions, behaviors, or responses that are occurring or have already occurred are appropriate and expected, therefore carrying the implication that the same behavior will be expected in the future (praise, compliments, or straightforward statements of the appropriateness of performed behavior). Conversely, *negative feedback* refers to verbalizations communicating that a behavior is undesirable, inappropriate to the situation, and not expected to occur. Like positive feedback, negative feedback is delivered at the time the behavior is occurring or after it has occurred. Negative feedback, thus, consists of utterances, clauses, or sentences that transmit information that certain actions, behaviors, or responses

---

This chapter comprises the staff training manual that details the procedures of the milieu program to preprofessional staff. The style and format of the original manual have been retained.

that are occurring or have already occurred are inappropriate and *not* expected, therefore carrying the implication that the same behavior should stop and will not be expected in the future (reprimands, discouragement, or straightforward statements of the inappropriateness of performed behavior and negative expectation of its future occurrence).

The meaning of the content of given actions, especially of written or verbal statements, is often drastically changed by the timing, the context, or the verbal or nonverbal behavior accompanying the action or statement. *Metacommunication* refers to these events, which serve as messages about a communication that may qualify the content, thereby confirming the content, subtly altering it, or completely reversing it. Metacommunications may, in fact, communicate expectancies more strongly than the content of a statement. It is essential for clear communication of expectancies for both metacommunications and explicit content to be consistent. For this reason, *negative statements* (verbalizations before a behavior has occurred, which communicate that a behavior is inappropriate and not expected to occur) as distinct from negative feedback (occurring during or after a behavior has occurred) are not to be used, since the timing and context of such statements would metacommunicate an expectancy for the behavior to occur—just the opposite of the explicit content. For example, "You shouldn't put beans in your ear" is a negative statement if delivered at a time and in a context when the person had never participated in that behavior—metacommunicating "I expect you to put beans in your ear." On the other hand, if time and context were appropriate (the person was, in fact, putting beans in his or her ear), the verbal statement would be negative feedback with consistent metacommunication of "I don't expect you to put beans in your ear."

Consistent and genuine nonverbal metacommunications are especially crucial to communication of expectancies through positive statements and positive and negative feedback. For example, "You're really doing a good job" (positive feedback content) delivered in a monotone or sarcastically, without smiles or friendly gestures, will not communicate that the behavior is appropriate and expected but rather metacommunicate the opposite, or at least confuse the message. Similarly, "Wouldn't you like to play cards?" (positive statement content) yelled across the unit by a staff member who is talking on the phone and making no attempt to join the residents or get cards for them metacommunicates "You're not expected to play cards" rather than encourages them to do so.

Many undesirable or inappropriate behaviors result if metacommunications replace explicit verbal communications. An expectancy for clear communication from residents must also be established. Such an expectancy may best be established through *interpretation* of metacommunications; verbally translate and describe the message conveyed by a resident's behavior. Continually require nonverbal messages to be translated into verbal ones.

*Provision of opportunity* to perform is the final major way in which positive and negative expectancies are communicated. When a certain behavior is expected, the opportunity for performance of the behavior is clearly provided; on the other hand, if the behavior is not expected or is prohibited, no explicit steps are made to provide the opportunity to act, or steps may be taken to remove the opportunity. For example, if a parent always dresses a child, the parent is communicating that he or she does not expect the child to dress itself through the failure to provide the opportunity, and the likely result is that the child will live up to the communicated expectations.

Thus, we have two major principles for increasing and maintaining appropriate behaviors: provide appropriate positive statements prior to the time of the behavior and positive feedback at the time of the behavior and afterward, and provide the opportunity for the behavior to occur. We have three major principles for decreasing and eliminating inappropriate behaviors: provide negative feedback at the time of the behavior or afterward, remove the opportunity for the behavior to occur, and interpret the metacommunicative aspect of the behavior.

*Law of Involvement*

The second major law of milieu or environmental influence is the *law of involvement*. This law states that the acquisition and maintenance of new or different actions and behaviors is a function of the degree of personal participation in overcoming challenges—people must "do it themselves." A *challenge* or *crisis* is a situation in which the expected or necessary behavior is not immediately available. For example, if driving a car is an expected behavior, but the skills are not there (the person doesn't know how), a mild crisis or challenge exists. In order to learn people cannot merely watch others but must involve themselves in resolving this challenge through personal experience—by doing it themselves.

*Decision making* and *problem solution* are classes of behavior that are especially dependent upon the law of involvement. These classes of behavior are also particularly important because they are involved in nearly every aspect of normal living. In almost everything we do as adults, we are choosing between alternatives—making decisions—whether in choosing which clothes to wear in the morning, whether to turn right or left at an intersection, or whether to watch the news or a movie on TV; decisions cannot be made without involvement. When the possible alternatives for decisions are either conflicting or unclear, a problem exists, and hence a challenge or crisis. Therefore, practice in problem solution or controlled crisis resolution is one of the most effective principles to follow in milieu treatment. Staff members must always be on guard lest they provide solutions to problems or make decisions for the resident; the residents must do it themselves.

An important principle derived from the law of involvement and the law of expectancy may be phrased "experience speaks louder than words." For example, if a resident group is told that they have responsibility for a decision (a positive statement) but the decision is either made for them or overruled, the experience will more strongly communicate expectancies and control future behavior than the verbal statement. Therefore, extreme care must be taken in giving responsibility for decisions that can be legitimately made and in follow-through of decisions, even when they may appear incorrect. The experience of success or failure resulting from following through on a decision provides feedback that will help clarify future expectancies. However, just as others may communicate expectancies for an individual and deprive or provide opportunities to perform, people themselves may set expectancies of being incapable or of being the kind of person who behaves in particular ways. If people don't try, they don't perform the desired act and therefore confirm that they are the sort of person who behaves in a particular manner. When past expectancies have been such that people have experienced many failures in attempting to follow through on their own decisions, they may come to think of themselves as failures. Therefore, it is essential that each person successfully perform behaviors that have been considered failures in the past. This means that the environment should be organized to provide a good chance for success, using positive statements to encourage behavior that probably will succeed—gradually increasing challenges and complexity of crises as they succeed at lesser ones.

*Group Cohesiveness*

The third major law of milieu or environmental influence is that of *group cohesiveness*, which states that the occurrence or nonoccurrence of an action or behavior is dependent upon a sense of belonging to a collective—being a member of a group. *Social pressure* is a major source of motivation for adults—both through communicating expectancies and by applying sanctions. The group to which a person belongs provides the support and encouragement to perform specific behaviors, and it also controls the most important consequences. Being held in esteem and approved by the group is the most powerful reward; disapproval by the group and, ultimately, expulsion from it is the most powerful penalty.

All people belong to many groups at many different levels, e.g., the city group by virtue of being in the same geographical area, the church group, the neighborhood group, etc. The peer group is the most important one in terms of its cohesiveness and the social control of the behaviors of its members. This results from a greater sense of belonging, greater time spent together, and greater in-group interaction as a result of smaller size (most effective size being two to twelve group members). Group cohesiveness is strengthened both by continuity of membership, in which more time is spent in in-group interaction, and through competition with other groups, which develops a we versus they orientation. The operation of the law of group cohesiveness may easily be seen in reference to cliques in high schools and delinquent gangs in which the social pressure of the peer group often leads to behavior on the part of group members that runs counter to approved behavior of society in general and may even lead to behavior that has disastrous consequences for the individual. Because of the law of group cohesiveness, we must be very careful to develop group solidarity and to ensure that the locus of control of expectations and consequences remains as much as possible with specific peer groups.

THE THERAPEUTIC COMMUNITY

The major operations for bringing about therapeutic change in the milieu program lie in communicated expectancies, resident involvement, and group pressure. The major vehicle for implementing the principles described earlier is the therapeutic community, an entire unit organized as a collective or miniature community in which the residents are considered the participants and the managers of their own affairs within the structure of the step system and the ten basic unit rules for group living. Beyond the fixed requirements of the basic unit rules and the step system, major regulations are purposely left fluid to provide problems or controlled crises for the residents to solve. Because each of us on the treatment staff might differ in our focus on specific appropriate behaviors, time periods are scheduled for feedback and recording of behavior. In the appendix at the end of this section of the manual a complete list of behaviors to be recorded and areas of focus at specific times may be found.

*The Community Group*

While specific procedural principles of staff behavior define the interactions within the program, the two organizational features that play the major role in the therapeutic community are the community group and the living groups. The community group consists of all residents on the unit and all staff assigned to the unit at any given time. The living groups consist of three heterosexual subgroups within the community, each composed of nine or ten residents, along with staff members assigned to each group.

The living groups are responsible for the content and performance of their own activities and for the individual behavior of their members; the community group is responsible for the regulation, legislation, and solution of problems that affect the entire unit. Problems and decisions within the basic structure of the community are first directed to the living groups, who may report to the community group and refer suggestions and problems to the community group. In nearly all instances, decisions within living groups are acted upon on the basis of discussion and majority vote. Within the community group, decisions are acted upon on the basis of discussion and majority vote, but with each living group and the staff group (staff members present) having one vote. An executive council, consisting of two elected members from each living group, is given responsibility for identification of decisions to be made and for drawing up proposals to be presented to the community group if the entire group cannot reach decisions.

The use of such governmental and group organization has a number of distinct advantages. Expectancies for responsible behavior are clearly communicated, both in concrete verbal terms and through provision of the opportunity for problem solving, decision making, and social interaction. Since social or group pressure is the primary motivational factor, the provision of such a group organization with the power to make important decisions ensures that the opinions of the group are meaningful to the resident members; it also ensures that the residents take part in problem solving, decision making, and communicating expectancies to one another.

*The Living Groups*

The living groups form the basic frame of reference for the identification of problems, encouragement of change, and source of group pressure. In addition to spending scheduled activities together, the members are encouraged to eat, work, take passes, and spend informal interaction and free periods together.

Living groups are responsible for routine unit tasks such as housekeeping. Further, it is the responsibility of the group to propose their members for passes, to be approved or disapproved by the community group. Similarly, it is a living group responsibility to nominate its members for higher-step status to the community group and the decision of the total community regarding such advancement. Staff function in these areas is to ensure correct interpretation of the requirements of the unit rules and step level requirements.

The only time a staff member personally invokes sanctions or consequences for behavior of residents is upon the occurrence of those blatant and destructive inappropriate behaviors that cannot be tolerated because of their effect on others (see the list of intolerable behavior at the end of this manual). When those behaviors occur, negative feedback is given immediately along with *expulsion* from the group (the resident is physically removed from the group and from the opportunity of performing prohibited behaviors). Expulsion may be instituted by placing a resident in an expulsion room where the opportunity to perform the inappropriate behavior no longer exists or by removing the resident from group interaction or membership in some other means determined by the group. All other inappropriate behaviors are handled by negative feedback, positive statements for appropriate behavior, and referral of the problem to the resident's living group for a decision on handling. Similarly, living group members are given the responsibility for encouraging their own group members to meet expectations. Living groups report to the community group on such problems and their resolution. If the living group does not handle such problems adequately, the community group has responsibility for dealing with the problem.

After the initial assignment of residents to living groups, changes in group composition, as well as such matters as eating and sleeping arrangements, are subject to change through discussion and vote in the community meeting. As members of living groups are released, the groups are encouraged to remain intact, with the released members being replaced by new residents. The arrival of a new resident and his or her introduction into the program is also the responsibility of the living group.

*Scheduled Activities*

On the milieu unit each living group is assigned a daily schedule, which, for step 1 residents on weekdays, includes six hours of scheduled classes and activities, about three hours of informal interaction periods, about two hours for meals, one to three hours for small and large group meetings, a half-hour of canteen time, and about one hour of free time. When residents advance to step 2, the activities (except for the community meeting) give way to three hours of individual assignments, and at step 3 to six hours.

On weekends, one to two hours are designated as housekeeping periods, about three and a half hours scheduled for meals, a half-hour of canteen time, one and a half hours for free time, an hour to an hour and a half for activities, and three to five hours for informal interaction periods.

While members of living groups are all on step 1, the entire group is assigned to attend scheduled group activities. As residents move up through step levels, they are encouraged to take individual assignments as subgroups when possible and as consistent with individual training needs and capabilities. Even when the majority of members of a living group might be on full-time individual assignment, living group membership is maintained.

While group membership provides the major vehicle for therapeutic change, the organization of the unit is also structured to provide opportunity for individual practice in decision making. Thus, material goods, activities, and privileges are provided free to the residents but in restricted quantities and times: a choice between alternatives is required at nearly all times.

With this general orientation we now turn to specific procedural rules to be followed on the milieu unit.

## PROCEDURAL RULES FOR STAFF

1. *Always use positive statements and feedback.* Be sure to verbalize expected behavior in concrete terms at least at scheduled times, and elsewhere when the occasion permits—suggest, persuade, encourage before the behavior occurs. Let the residents know clearly what they should be doing, and attempt to get them to do it. At all times provide positive feedback. When residents perform desirable behavior, compliment and praise. When they do not, reassure them that they can. Compliment and praise the person and encourage the behavior; persuade them to try. State what needs to be done; suggest how it can be carried out. Clarify communications by verbally stating nonverbal language; interpret. Never allow yourself or coworkers to interact mechanically or condescendingly or to use jargon; keep your communication explicit and metacommunications concordant.

2. *Never ignore undesirable behavior.* To combat the residents' own expectation of failure, care must be taken to see that they are never ignored, punished, or rejected for a failure. Rather, reassurance of their own worth and positive feedback for trying new behaviors should be the rule; be "for the deviant" but "against the deviant behavior." Respond to all resident communications. Never let undesirable behavior go by; provide negative feedback, discourage, reprimand, tell them that members of the unit do not act in that manner. Specify the undesirable behavior and refer to the unit rules for expected behavior. However, except for intolerable behavior leading to group expulsion, do not invoke other sanctions or consequences. Rather, provide negative feedback and encourage appropriate behavior. Refer to the fact that undesirable behavior must be referred to the living group for a decision on what to do if it continues. Interpret the metacommunication of undesirable behavior, especially with regard to the communication to the living group. Never leave a resident who is performing inappropriate behavior (unless you must attend to something else, in which case a minimum of seventy seconds must be devoted to the inappropriate behavior if it doesn't change).

3. *Maximize resident responsibility, decision-making, and problem solving.* Never do anything for the residents that they can possibly do for themselves or that another living group member could assist them in doing. Provide problems to solve by clarifying what needs to be done, but never solve a problem or make a decision for a resident—always delegate. If the residents request a decision or problem solution, reflect it back to them (e.g., "How could you handle it?") if it is an individual problem. Refer it to the living group or community group if the problem involves other people. If the residents are unable to come up with a decision following reflection, help them clarify alternatives, e.g., "What alternatives are available?" If the residents are unable to clarify, staff may suggest two or more reasonable alternatives from which residents may choose, one of which should be to form a committee to solve the problem in appropriate circumstances. This is as far as a staff member should ever go; staff should never make the decision. Similarly, staff should vote in either living groups or community meetings only after resident votes are in. Delegate responsibility to living group members for other members of the group; enlist the aid of members in encouraging and persuading appropriate behavior.

4. *Foster cohesiveness within living groups.* Always encourage group activities even at times when the group isn't scheduled together: suggest accompanied passes within the living group, encourage interaction between members

during free time and informal interaction. Develop competitiveness between living groups; always take the opportunity to compare the group performance of living groups, e.g., "Living group A now has fewer members at step 1 than any other group." During recreation periods shared by two groups, have the groups function as teams in competition. Take every opportunity to refer to living group membership—use the terms *your group*, *our group*, and *we* versus *they*. Immediately refer problems of a member or member's behavior to the living group for resolution first; let the living group itself refer problems to the community group if necessary. Always emphasize the responsibility of the group for its members, and of members for the group. If a resident lacks skills, elicit suggestions from the group on how the member could gain them. Encourage group members to share information on problem solution and to assist each other. Refer to the group as a unit.

5. *Always record occurrence of positive statements, negative feedback and resident's behavior.* Recordings must be made immediately to maintain accuracy and prevent loss of data through forgetting. These data must reflect real events. Always list your staff number on recording forms.

## PROGRAM CONTENT

Following the outline of a daily schedule that provides details of timing for functional periods (see appendix), discussion of the content of each of the major activities yields a descriptive picture of the specific procedures implemented on the milieu unit.

1. *Morning routine.* Residents sleep in one of four types of rooms, all fully equipped with draperies, bedside stand, and chair: six-bed, four-bed, two-bed, or one-bed. Residents have free choice in selecting their sleeping area; however, since some areas are more desirable than others, a problem often arises regarding who sleeps where. The solution to this problem is the responsibility of the community group for deciding an equitable basis for room assignment, based upon a guiding principle of assignment by living groups. The living groups are then responsible for deciding who sleeps where. These assignments and solutions change from time to time.

All residents are expected to get up in the morning, this is not to be decided upon by the residents. However, since one of the three living groups has responsibility for breakfast preparation each morning (see the section on meals below), lights on for that group is a half-hour earlier than lights on for members of the other two groups. As the assigned change agent goes to the rooms to turn on the lights, the residents should be awakened with individual positive statements, referring to group membership, shaking if necessary—e.g., "Time for members of group A to get up—let's go, George, you have to get up now." Five minutes after the lights have been turned on, the change agent returns to the room to record whether residents are up for later announcement (by groups rather than individuals) in the community meeting, providing positive feedback for those who are up. Those who are not out of bed are given positive statements and negative feedback, and persuaded to get up at that time—e.g., "Gee, Harold, you really let your living group down by not being up on time this morning. You should get up now and start preparing for appearance check," enlisting the aid of other members of his group to help encourage him.

Once the residents are awakened, they have about a half-hour to dress, groom themselves, make their beds, and pick up their rooms before starting breakfast preparation, or breakfast. During this period, some residents may require staff assistance. For example, a change agent may have to instruct and encourage a resident to shave, by reflecting "How could you go about it?" and by encouraging other group members to help. During this period the change agent casually goes from room to room encouraging and persuading residents to complete dressing and grooming and to have the bed made and room in order. Appearance is checked and recorded no earlier than twenty minutes after lights on. Bed and area is recorded after appearance—as always, providing positive and negative feedback, persuading those who have not yet met the terminal behavior expected (see "Expected Behavior" in appendix) to perform at least one more component behavior at that time—praising and complimenting the individuals for their attempts. Appearance is also recorded and encouraged before lunch and dinner, with feedback in front of the wall mirrors in the common living area.

This schedule is in effect seven days a week, except Saturday and Sunday, when breakfast is not served and the earliest lights on is a half-hour later than on weekdays and late sleeping privileges of up to two more hours are available to all three living groups on the basis of majority vote the night before; therefore, one or more living groups may be sleeping in. After lights on for late sleepers, the above procedures, in the same order, are carried out in the half-hour after lights on.

2. *Meals.* Monday through Friday, breakfast, lunch, and dinner periods are scheduled on the unit with thirty minutes allotted for serving and eating. However, since seating space is available for only twenty-six to twenty-eight people, while up to thirty-five staff and residents may be there for a meal, not all people can eat

at the same time. Additionally, preparation, serving, and cleanup for each meal is the responsibility of specific living groups on a rotating schedule, with the half-hour before the meal allotted for preparation, and the half-hour after the meal for cleanup. The determination of which living groups eat in what order and the schedule of dietary responsibility by living groups again provide problems that are the responsibility of the community group to solve. Therefore, the schedule for dietary responsibility and the manner in which living groups eat within the allotted time must be worked out by the community group.

The same procedure is followed for all three meals. A half-hour before mealtime, the change agent assigned to the living group with dietary responsibility convenes the living group in the dining area—as always, with positive statements delegating responsibility for encouraging promptness of lax group members to the group itself. The assignment of tasks (e.g., pickup of food cart, setting tables, serving, scraping dishes, etc.) is the responsibility of the living group—likely to be worked out during the living group business meeting on Tuesday evening. Initially, however, the change agent reflects the problem to the group for solution. If, after ten minutes of silence or discussion, during which the change agent encourages participation with positive statements and questioning for task requirements, job assignments are not made, the change agent defines the problem and suggests alternatives, e.g., "Doesn't it seem we have these jobs to do [lists tasks]? Now, we could all do everything at the same time, or we could assign two group members to pick up the food cart, three to set the table, etc. Which should we do?" If members choose the latter alternative, the change agent reflects the problem of assignments back to them—in any case, giving positive feedback for making decisions, and following through the group decision, even if it appears to be a poor one. The various means and success of the different groups in handling this task can later form a basis for comparative discussion in the community meeting.

At the specified time, the assigned change agent rings the meal bell and announces "Time for breakfast (lunch, dinner)" throughout the unit. Staff encourage members of their living groups to attend the meal with positive statements, delegating responsibility for encouraging promptness of lax group members to other group members. Any problems that arise regarding promptness are solved by referral to the living group—later to the community group if there are difficulties for the entire unit. The specified change agent records attendance at meals as residents go through the serving line. All staff eat with members of their assigned living groups, and senior staff who are not assigned to particular living groups circulate on different days among all three living groups. During meals, staff freely interact with residents at all times, providing negative feedback on inappropriate mealtime behavior and positive statements and feedback on appropriate mealtime behavior (see "Expected Behavior" in appendix for criteria), as always, referring to group membership. As residents leave the dining area, the assigned change agent records the appropriateness of mealtime behavior for later announcements by living group performance in the community meeting.

On Saturday and Sunday, the dinner procedure is identical to that on weekdays. However, a single brunch period is substituted for breakfast and lunch. Residents may prepare snacks in the unit kitchen on weekends; again, the schedule for the living groups is the responsibility of the community group. Coffee is always available for residents during free periods, informal interaction periods, and any activity scheduled on the unit; however, it is the responsibility of the community group to work out the manner of handling the preparation, disbursement, and timing by living groups.

3. *Community meeting.* The community meeting is the first scheduled meeting of the day Monday through Friday and is the most important meeting in the milieu program. It is here that decisions about matters affecting the unit as a whole are made by the community group. During this meeting residents and staff may bring up any topic they wish for discussion. Since this meeting is so important, it is attended by all residents and by all staff available at the time. The meeting begins by the specified change agent's announcing the meeting throughout the unit and recording all those in attendance. All change agents encourage attendance of their living group members by positive statements with living group reference. Residents not at the meeting are persuaded to attend by other members of their living group.

The first part of each meeting consists of a staff report on the residents' activities during the previous evening and night (or weekend). Anything notable that happened, both good and bad, is reported for individuals by name. Additionally, a summary of specific desirable behaviors (i.e., appearance, getting up on time, attendance at scheduled activities, etc.) by living groups is announced from the previous day (or weekend) to increase group competition. One day per week the performance of residents on individual assignments is also summarized in the group. Throughout these reports, all staff freely give positive and negative feedback and problem identification with reference to living groups. At the end of the staff report, a summary statement comparing living groups is made, praising the group with the best performance and reassuring and encouraging the other groups.

The remainder of the meeting focuses upon the identification, discussion, and solution of problems brought up in the staff report. However, in one meeting the residents vote on status changes (step 1 to step 4). Candidates for status changes are chosen by the living groups the previous night at the weekly living group business and promotion proposal meeting, and such candidates are nominated for status change at the following community meeting. In one meeting residents vote on passes. Candidates for passes (off-center and weekend) are chosen by the living groups the previous night at the weekly living group pass meeting, and they are nominated for passes at the following community meeting. It is the responsibility of the living group representative and the nominees to present plans and their basis and the responsibility of all staff to ensure clarity within the requirements of the step system and basic unit rules before a vote is taken. Clarity is ensured by reflecting and questioning with regard to fixed requirements. All voting within the community meeting is based upon the majority (i.e., three of four) vote, with each living group and the staff group holding one group vote. The group vote, in each case, is based upon the majority within the group, with staff always voting last.

Following voting on status changes and passes and after staff reports on other days, any topic germane to an individual, living group, or community group is brought up by anyone. The entire meeting can simply be a conversational period if that is what the residents want; residents may bring up personal problems for group discussion; the behavior of any resident or staff member may be brought up for discussion by any resident or staff member; the organization or reorganization of living groups can be brought up for discussion and voting; on-unit responsibilities can be divided or redivided; the manner and scheduling of unit housekeeping and dietary responsibilities can be changed on group vote; rotation of living groups through unit activities and classes, sleeping quarters, weekend housekeeping, etc., can be discussed and changed; officers can be elected to represent the unit; complaints can be discussed and recommendations made and voted upon; special activities such as parties, picnics, and money-making activities can be proposed and organized by residents.

In general, all procedural rules are to be continually followed by staff. As a group, staff should be particularly alert to remember several important areas of focus in the community meeting.

Share only legitimate authority with the residents. There are obviously some changes that cannot be made by residents in the community meeting. Reorganization of the timing and content of most of the daily schedule, requirements of the step system, and the ten basic rules, for example, are not subject to change by residents. Staff should remind residents of such limits if it appears that they do not know them or have forgotten them. It is important that residents' votes be for decisions that can be carried out. For example, on Fridays when passes are voted on, it is the duty of staff to point out the limitations on passes. A step 1 resident, for example, cannot be awarded a weekend pass, and voting on such a pass cannot be allowed in the community meeting. Residents are to be queried about whether all necessary requirements have been met before voting.

Staff must respond quickly to decisions made during the community meeting. If residents are to be shown that their decisions really mean something, then staff must respond to them when it is appropriate. Delays in implementing the decisions must be explained to the residents. Resident decisions must be honored, even if they are not (in staff opinion) the best decisions.

Responsibility for decision making lies with the residents. One of the possible problems in the community meeting is staff impatience. Sometimes silence is all that residents offer. In this case, after ten minutes of silence, staff either propose a problem in need of a decision or question the meaning communicated by the silence. Sometimes the residents just fail to come to grips with a problem and offer no solutions. In this case staff suggest two or more possible solutions for the residents' consideration. However, if the residents continue to fail to deal adequately with group concerns (in the opinion of staff), it is necessary for staff to wait until they do or to suggest referral to resident committees or the executive council. It is the residents, not the staff, who need practice in managing their affairs. It does no good for staff to jump in and do things for the residents. The staff point out the reality of situations to residents, at times suggest alternatives, express their own opinions, and vote, but they do not take over the decision-making process. If decisions are not made, allow the resulting chaos to prevail; it provides the pressure for problem solution the following day.

At the end of the community meeting, staff make a point of providing feedback to members of their living group about the desirability of participation, and the specified change agent records resident participation.

4. *Informal interaction.* All residents are scheduled for three to four informal interaction periods each day (five on Sunday). During the scheduled time all of the recreational facilities

within the unit are available for the residents to use. Staff focus is upon the encouragement and recording of appropriate interaction. Certain activities go on in designated areas of the unit. For purposes of clarification, the procedures and staff responsibilities are listed by areas.

*Activity pit* (the sunken area in the center of the unit). All residents may freely enter and use materials in the activity pit, although usage times by living groups might be established by the community group if problems arise. A change agent is assigned to record entrance to the activity pit, usage of materials there, and to encourage activities, interaction, and desirable behavior for residents. Writing tables, arts and crafts materials, a radio and a record player, cards and other recreational materials are available. In general, games requiring a partner and the use of any constructive materials or equipment (paints, etc.) are specifically encouraged. All materials may be checked out on request—therefore, requiring decisions. Any problems that arise because residents request more materials than are available are referred to the community group for resolution.

Appropriate social interaction, especially within living groups, is the focus of positive statements and feedback during these periods. This includes such behaviors as a resident's responding to a staff request, responding courteously and appropriately to conversation from another resident or staff, initiating an appropriate conversation with another resident or staff, playing a game appropriately with another resident or staff, or cooperating with or helping another resident perform a constructive activity. At the end of each hour or when the scheduled informal interaction period is over (if less than an hour), the change agent assigned to the pit records the occurrence of such interaction. At other times, change agents encourage and persuade appropriate behaviors, give instructions on the use of equipment, and are available as partners for residents.

*TV room.* During informal interaction residents may use the TV room freely, unless the community group determines another schedule. The change agent assigned to cover the TV room records the presence of residents every hour on the form to be kept in the room. Which programs the residents watch is determined by a group decision of those in the TV room. Since more residents are likely to desire to watch TV than there are seats available at any time, a problem may again exist, which is referred to the community group for a decision on the preference schedule of any particular living group member at any time. During informal interaction, residents in the TV room are encouraged by positive statements to contribute to discussions constructively and appropriately, especially those with regard to the program to be watched.

*Classroom-lounge.* The large room at the end of the unit functions both as an informal gathering place and as a quiet reading room or writing room during informal interaction periods. Unless problems arise that lead to the community group's formulating different regulations, residents may enter or leave the classroom-lounge at any time during informal interaction periods, with the assigned change agent being sure to record use of the room. The piano is located in the lounge, and appropriate interaction, such as playing duets and group singing, is encouraged. Also, residents who have checked out record players or radios play them in the lounge, if in doing so they do not interfere with constructive or appropriate activities of other residents. If they do the problem is immediately referred to the resident involved for solution. Writing tables are also available, as well as comfortable lounge chairs for reading. The same kinds of appropriate social interaction listed above are encouraged and persuaded. Reading and letter writing are also encouraged by positive statements. At the end of each hour, the change agent records appropriate participation and provides feedback and further encouragement to residents in the classroom-lounge. If the job of the change agent in recording and interacting with residents in this situation presents difficulty because of free access in residents coming and going, the change agent may introduce this problem to the community meeting for solution.

*Common living area.* When no meeting on the unit is scheduled, the common living area is open to all residents, again on a free-choice basis. No equipment is available in this area, although residents may use or consume canteen items or items checked out from other stations here. Appropriate behavior as elsewhere designated for social interaction is the focus of attention in this area. Residents not engaging in appropriate behaviors are encouraged by staff to use facilities in the other areas during informal interaction periods.

*Nondesignated areas.* In general, residents are discouraged from spending time in their rooms or from sitting alone in the chairs along the two side walls. Residents spending informal interaction periods in these areas are recorded and at least once every hour are approached with negative feedback on these activities, with attempts to persuade and encourage other informal interaction. Coffee in the dining area is generally available to residents during informal interaction periods, dependent upon the regulations developed by the community group for handling these activities.

5. *Activity periods.* All residents in step 1 are assigned to meet with their living group for two group activity periods each weekday

morning. The procedure for encouraging and recording attendance to these unit activity periods is identical to that described for the community meeting. These activity periods are conducted on the unit, in the center, or downtown. They include crafts, gym, shopping trips, training in practical skills, and other activities as suggested by the staff or living group members. Initially the staff schedule specific activities. However, when possible, the place and content of the activity periods are decided upon by the living groups themselves. In these instances the staff member may suggest the alternatives but require the decision to be made by a majority vote of the living group. Among alternatives are the joint participation of two living groups as teams in competition. If difficulties arise in the use of available facilities, they can be resolved, first by discussion and resolution between the living groups involved and second, if resolution cannot be reached, by referral to the community group for scheduling of possible time periods. Whatever activity is selected by the living groups, staff members continually encourage participation with positive statements and feedback and record resident participation at the end of each activity period.

6. *Class periods.* Each Monday through Friday afternoon all residents in steps 1 and 2 are assigned to three forty-five-minute periods for activities and classes conducted by staff educators. During each of these time periods, three separate classes are conducted, with each of the three living groups assigned to one of the three classes during each time period. Some classes are conducted on the unit itself, using the classroom-lounge, activity pit, open living room, or bedrooms, while some classes are conducted in other places in the center. The content of these classes includes instruction in communication skills—reading, writing, and speaking—elementary mathematics, and practical home economics and grooming. Since the residents are assigned and attend these classes in the stable and cohesive living groups, the level of needed training and performance within each class is likely to vary a great deal. Staff members encourage higher-functioning residents with positive statements to assist the lower-functioning residents within their living group to participate in the training.

The procedure for encouraging and recording attendance at center activities and classes is the same as that described for the community meeting. As soon as the living group has convened, the change agent escorts them to the place in which the class is held and, on arrival, records attendance. During the class period, the responsibility for providing information and instructional content lies with the educator. Change agents do not interfere with the educator except to ensure that the educator communicates positive expectations to the residents and does not violate procedural rules of the program.

The major role of the change agent during these periods is to persuade and encourage participation on the part of the residents through the use of positive statements and positive and negative feedback, always referring as much as possible to group performance and group membership. At the end of the class period, participation is recorded and feedback given to the group as a whole. Some residents reach step 3 and still need training in the academic areas. In those cases, the resident is scheduled to attend classes with the living group as part of the individual assignment; however, the residents attend on their own rather than being escorted with the living group to the class area.

7. *Small groups.* In addition to regularly scheduled activities of living groups and the total community group, four other small group meetings are included in the program. Two of these meetings are actually living group meetings, which are described below (see "Advancement Through Step Levels" and "Passes"). When residents progress to step 4, they are assigned to the prerelease planning group, in addition to the regular living group. The group meets daily for a half-hour during weekdays under the leadership of the liaison coordinator. This group focuses on training and planning for release, as well as discussion of practical problems that might be encountered after release. Whenever possible, family members of residents in the prerelease group meet with the group. The liaison coordinator is responsible for announcing, encouraging, and recording attendance at this meeting, following the procedures described for the community meeting. Similarly, the procedural rules for encouraging and recording problem solving and participation are the same as those described for activities and classes.

The fourth small group meeting is that of the executive council, attended one evening each week by two elected representatives from each living group. This group has the responsibility for identifying decisions to be made by the community group, for initiating suggestions and recommendations for program changes, and for drawing up proposals to be presented to the community group if it has been unable to reach decisions. One of the first tasks of the executive council, whenever new members enter, is the election of officers (chairman, to conduct the meetings; recorder, to transcribe and report activities; and vice-chairman, to serve in place of the chairman when necessary). The offices and tasks of the executive council are subject to change on proposal to the community group and majority group vote. A change agent is assigned to monitor the executive council and to be on call for attendance at the request of the members. Staff procedures described earlier (reflect, clarify, present alternatives) are followed, along with positive statements for participation and problem solving.

8. *Canteen time.* The canteen, located in the work area of the unit, is open every evening and is announced throughout the unit. Items available include cigarettes, candies, cosmetics, grooming aids, soaps, use of a safety deposit box, and inexpensive clothing. In addition various items are available for overnight checkout, including privacy screens and writing tables. Coupons worth ten cents at the center cafeteria or snack bar are also available.

The use of the canteen is limited to twenty minutes for each living group. Since not all living groups can be first, the order of usage of the canteen provides another problem for the community group to resolve. Items within the canteen are priced in terms of credits. Although all items are free to the residents, each resident is limited to obtaining items worth three credits each day (except Tuesday when an extra credit is allowed to purchase grooming items) to provide realistic limits that require them to practice decision making. Smaller items are on display with the accompanying credit price list located on the nearby counter in the work area. Other items are on display in the storage room, and living groups are encouraged to look at these items as well.

When residents wish to save up credits for more expensive items, they may do so by requesting that their credits for the evening be kept on account. If they fail to make the request, the credits for that evening are lost. Similarly, members of a living group may pool credits for more expensive items, on discussion, decision, and mutual request of the residents involved. A mail-order catalog is available in the canteen from which residents may order items on a limited basis. If a resident or living group indicates interest in a particular item, the staff determine the item's cost (in credits) and availability. This information is given to the resident or living group at canteen time the following evening. An item may be ordered when half of the necessary credits are available, either on account or through pooling, and picked up when the remainder of credits is available. The change agent assigned to the canteen each evening is responsible for handling and recording all transactions, being sure to reflect and clarify but not to make decisions for the residents. Other change agents are responsible for announcing and encouraging each living group to use the canteen.

If the residents have items that they would like to deposit in the canteen safety deposit box, they may have access to a box for a week's period during breaks between classes, free times, informal interactions, and canteen periods if they request to reserve a box during the Monday night canteen when a resident may either request it for another week or discontinue use of the box.

Residents are permitted to sign up for money (if they have a trust fund) or snack bar coupons any night of the week during canteen time. The coupons can be received immediately although the snack bar is open only on designated nights of the week. Money cannot be obtained until the following day and only on Monday through Friday, since it must be obtained from the business office. Residents are permitted up to two dollars per week in coupons except when taking other types of passes.

Gifts received from visitors may be food, clothing, or other nonperishable items. Food is placed in the unit kitchen for dietary workers to provide at meals in normal portions. Clothing is marked and placed in storage for the resident's use. Other nonperishable items remain in the resident's possession unless there are living group or community decisions to the contrary.

9. *Housekeeping and odd jobs.* Monday through Friday, most unit housekeeping (dusting, sweeping, emptying ash trays, etc.) is handled by residents on individual assignments. On Saturday and Sunday, major cleaning is done during three housekeeping periods. During these housekeeping periods, all other activities and facilities are closed. All three living groups are expected to take part in housekeeping, with specific areas assigned as the responsibility of each living group. Assignments are made first on the basis of decisions made by all residents present at the beginning of the housekeeping period. If this procedure poses problems for the residents, they are encouraged to bring it up in community meeting for resolution (likely alternatives being a rotating schedule of living groups to areas; each living group responsible for specific areas on a permanent basis, rotation of responsibility for the entire unit over living groups).

In any case, the staff follow the usual procedures with regard to announcement of the activity and encourage participation through positive statements and reflection to living group members. The task assignment within areas and living groups is the responsibility of the living group, with staff providing reflection, clarification, and suggested choice of alternatives. At the end of the period, participation is recorded with feedback to groups.

Other odd jobs, such as running errands or carrying messages, may come up from time to time. The living groups are expected to provide a resident to perform such odd jobs during free periods on any day. Which living group is responsible for providing such assistance at any given time is a problem to be solved by the community group, and which member of a living group who is chosen is a problem to be solved by the living group. When no janitorial assistants are available on individual assignments, daily housekeeping can be handled as odd jobs.

10. *Free periods.* During scheduled free periods and when no assignment is scheduled, residents may use all the unit facilities but those in the pit. The TV room, classroom-lounge, and common living area are all available. The major distinction between scheduled informal interaction and free time is that no extra efforts are made to encourage in-group interaction or social participation—rather, residents are allowed to do essentially as they choose. Interaction is not recorded by change agents during these periods, but the use of facilities is recorded. Staff are available to interact with residents during these periods, continuing positive and negative statements and feedback regarding desirable and undesirable behaviors. Extra living group meetings are called as needed during free periods.

11. *Weekend activity period (gym).* Since staff coverage is usually short on weekends, residents not on passes are scheduled for only one activity period. Except that the activities are restricted to physical ones (gym or outdoor games) and that only attendance is recorded, this period follows the procedure for the regular activity periods.

12. *Bedtime routine and bathing.* Each evening, one hour before scheduled lights out the announcement is made that rooms are open for bedtime preparation. Unit activities are expected to cease at this time, except that on Friday and Saturday evenings the TV room and classroom-lounge may remain open an additional three and a half hours. Residents are expected to take at least three baths or showers a week during the bedtime preparation period Sunday through Friday. There is time during this hour for eighteen residents to bathe each weekday, with residents having twenty minutes to shampoo their hair (if necessary) and to clean themselves thoroughly. Bathing is scheduled by living groups and members within living groups are structured by the staff, but any changes in the schedule deemed necessary by the residents can be instituted by a decision of the residents themselves during living group and community meetings.

Staff use suggestion, persuasion, encouragement, and verbal instruction in getting residents to bathe on time and properly. The residents' living group is enlisted to share major responsibility for such encouragement and instruction. Positive feedback is given for good performance.

Failure to bathe properly or on time results in negative feedback, discouragement, or a reprimand from the staff, and such problems are referred to the resident's living group for further handling.

Residents are to be in bed by lights off. Staff start encouraging preparation an hour earlier and enlist the aid of other living group members a half-hour before lights out if some residents are lagging. Living groups may decide that their group in one-bed or two-bed rooms will keep lights on for an additional half-hour, as long as all members in the one-bed and two-bed rooms do the same.

It is the responsibility of the residents to decide which, if any, living groups stay up later on Friday and Saturday nights, the decision is made by majority vote at the time for regular lights out. Except for those living groups who elect to stay up later, residents are required to be in bed by the regular scheduled lights out time.

One change agent is assigned to supervise and record the use of each large bathroom during bedtime preparation. At lights out one staff member checks each room on the women's side and turns off lights. Another staff member has similar duties on the men's side. If some living groups elect to stay up later on Friday and Saturday nights, this checking is repeated at the later bedtime for these groups.

13. *Advancement through step levels.* The procedure for moving up in the step level system begins at the weekly living group business and promotion meeting. Announcement, encouragement, and recording of attendance for these meetings is handled in the manner described under "Community Meeting" with each of the three living groups meeting at the same time but in different areas of the unit. Staff members may attend these meetings to help focus the task, through positive statements and clarification. However, it is expected that they will be run by the residents. During these meetings all problems that the living group must resolve may be introduced, discussed, and decisions made, with staff following procedures described in the community meeting section. The one task that must always be included is a review of step level requirements, identification of living group members who have met requirements for advancing in the system, and nomination for advancement through majority vote and recording. Staff encourage advancement with positive statements and positive and negative feedback referring to the expectations for advancement and the comparative standing of the group with other living groups. When a living group is meeting alone, staff remain on call to provide information or clarification. Each living group nominates members at the community meeting the morning after for discussion and vote on advancement.

Residents approved for advancement are scheduled, with other members of their living group, for an appointment with the liaison coordinator and rehabilitation counselor for consideration of individual assignments. New schedules and advancements become effective the Monday following approval by the community group.

14. *Individual assignments.* All residents in step 2 are required to work on individual assignments for three hours per day, typically from 9:00 A.M. to 12:00 noon, Monday through Friday. Residents in steps 3 and 4 are required to work on individual assignments six hours per day, typically from 9:00-12:00 A.M. and 1:00-4:00 P.M., Monday through Friday. These individual assignments are selected to provide work experiences for the resident, both in terms of giving added responsibility and of reactivating old work skills or teaching new ones. Jobs are developed on the unit itself, such as janitorial assistant, laundry assistant, etc. Jobs are also developed within the various departments of the center, such as clerical assistant, carpenter's assistant, etc. Job assignments are made on the basis of each resident's needs, in cooperation with the rehabilitation counselor, liaison coordinator, and unit supervisor. The rehabilitation counselor is responsible for maintaining daily ratings of job performance on residents in steps 2, 3, and 4. Except for the first week on a new assignment, residents must maintain at least an average satisfactory rating to stay on the step level and job; during the first week the last day must be satisfactory.

Staff encourage residents to attend during the first week of a new assignment, but thereafter attendance is the responsibility of the resident and the living group. Whenever possible, residents are given individual assignments in subgroups of two or three from their living groups. In any case, feedback on performance is given by living group identification and residents' names once per week in the community meeting.

15. *Passes.* To expose residents to the outside world and prepare them for release, passes both within the center and downtown are not only encouraged but required for residents to move up through the step levels. Passes also serve as opportunities for residents to engage in cooperative behavior with living group members and to function in a semisupervisory fashion when they accompany residents who are not yet eligible to take unaccompanied passes.

In addition to the motivation provided by positive statements, group pressure, and meeting the requirements of various step levels, passes are encouraged by making a portion of the residents' funds contingent upon their taking a pass. Each resident with a trust fund may draw up to thirty dollars a month in connection with passes.

Three kinds of passes are available to residents: center passes, downtown passes, and overnight passes. The number and kinds of passes a resident must take to fulfill the requirements of a step level are listed under "Step Level Requirements and Privileges." In general, early passes are encouraged when accompanied by either higher- or lower-level residents, staff, or relatives to ensure gradual exposure to the outside community. Below is an outline of the times passes are taken, maximum lengths of time per type of pass, and maximum amounts of money a resident can draw in connection with a particular type of pass.

Times passes may be taken:

1. Center passes (up to 3 hours)
   6:00-9:00 P.M. daily, except when scheduled for a meeting
   9:00-11:00 A.M. Saturday and Sunday
   1:00-4:00 P.M. Saturday and Sunday

2. Downtown
   A. 4 hours + $2.00 maximum
   5:00-9:00 P.M. daily, except when scheduled for a meeting
   Between 5:00 P.M. & 12:00 midnight Friday
   Between 8:00 A.M. & 12:00 midnight Saturday
   Between 8:00 A.M. & 9:00 P.M. Sunday
   B. 4-8 hours + $4.00 maximum
   Between 5:00 P.M. & 12:00 midnight Friday
   Between 8:00 A.M. & 12:00 midnight Saturday
   Between 8:00 A.M. & 9:00 P.M. Sunday

3. Overnight
   A. 24 hours + $12.00 maximum
   Between 5:00 P.M. Friday & 9:00 P.M. Sunday
   B. 48 hours + $15.00 maximum
   Between 5:00 P.M. Friday & 9:00 P.M. Sunday

A resident is allowed to take up to thirty dollars a month in spending money with any combination of passes and center coupons from the canteen.

A resident may take center passes during the specified time periods by placing a request with the staff member assigned and signing the pass sheet, indicating time out, destination, and time of return. Downtown and overnight passes require prior approval since funds frequently have to be arranged.

All residents are scheduled for a weekly evening living group pass meeting, with the three living groups meeting at the same time in different parts of the unit. These meetings follow the procedures described above for the weekly living group business and promotion meeting, except the focus is on passes. The requirements and availability of downtown and overnight passes are reviewed, including eligibility, step level requirements, etc. Residents are encouraged to discuss any downtown or overnight pass desired during the following Friday through Thursday. The residents then request a pass and specific amount of money, indicating the desired time out, destination, time in, and the individual within the living group, if any, accompanying. The living group then votes on whether the resident should be nominated for the pass or passes requested, and the staff member records necessary information on the appropriate form for those residents nominated. Those nominated are presented in the community meeting the next morning for discussion and voting on passes. Residents meeting requirements and approved by majority vote have passes approved. Those meeting requirements for requested passes are announced the following morning during community meeting.

APPENDIX

The following pages contain detailed schedules and recording times for residents, summary lists of resident expected behavior and intolerable behavior, and change agent schedules. Copies of each recording form regularly completed by treatment staff are also available (Paul, in press). Details of staff activities each day may be seen by referring to these materials and the major content area covered above, keeping in mind that day shift change agents and psychologists switch units daily at the noon hour, while evening and night shifts alternate between units every other day. In addition to the activities detailed above, all shifts overlap a half-hour, during which staff reports are made. Each staff member is given specific responsibilities regarding activities, recording forms, living groups, and residents on a daily basis. Night shift personnel are assigned specific summarizing duties for keeping continuous records.

A. Milieu Unit Resident Schedule

Monday-Friday

*5:55-7:00 A.M. Arise, dress, groom, make bed, room in order*

5:55   Lights on for dietary living group
6:00   Getting up for dietary living group recorded
6:15   Appearance for dietary living group recorded
6:22   Area neat, bed made for dietary living group recorded
6:25   Lights on for remaining living groups
6:30   Getting up for remaining living groups recorded
6:45   Appearance for remaining living groups recorded
6:50   Area neat, bed made for remaining living groups recorded

6:30-7:00 Breakfast preparation by dietary living group

*7:00-8:00 A.M. Breakfast & breakfast cleanup*

7:00-7:30 Breakfast (appropriateness of meal behavior recorded)
7:30-8:00 Breakfast cleanup by dietary living group

*8:15-9:00 A.M. Community meeting*

8:15   Attendance recorded
8:55   Participation recorded

*9:00-12:00 A.M. Step 1 residents*
*9:00-9:45 A.M. Unit activity period 1 (Living group A, B, or C)*

9:00   Attendance recorded
9:40   Participation recorded

*10:00-10:30 A.M. Informal Interaction*

Individual assignment interviews
Individual appointments
10:25   Informal interaction recorded

*10:30-11:30 A.M. Unit activity period 2 (Living group A, B, or C)*

10:30   Attendance recorded
11:25   Participation recorded

*11:30-12:00 Noon Informal interaction & lunch preparation*

11:30   Appearance of dietary group recorded
11:40   Appearance of other living groups recorded
11:55   Informal interaction recorded

*9:00-12:00 A.M. Step 2, 3, & 4 residents: individual assignments*

*12:00-1:00 P.M. Lunch*

    12:00-12:30 Lunch (appropriateness of meal behavior recorded)
    12:30- 1:00 Lunch cleanup

*1:00-4:00 P.M. Step 1 & 2 residents*
*1:15-4:00 P.M. Classes*

    1:15-2:00 Period 1 (Living group A,B,&C)
    1:15      Attendance recorded
    1:55      Participation recorded

    2:10-2:55 Period 2 (Living group A,B,&C)
    2:10      Attendance recorded
    2:55      Participation recorded

    3:05-3:50 Period 3 (Living group A,B,&C)
    3:05      Attendance recorded
    3:50      Participation recorded

*1:00-4:00 P.M. Step 3 & 4 residents: individual assignments*

*4:00-5:00 P.M. Step 1, 2, & 3 residents*
*4:00-5:00 P.M. Free time & dinner preparation*

    4:25      Appearance for dietary group recorded
    4:40      Appearance for other living groups recorded
    4:30-5:00 Dinner preparation by dietary living group

*4:00-4:30 P.M. Step 4 residents: Prerelease small group*

*5:00-6:00 P.M. Dinner*

    5:00-5:30 Dinner (appropriateness of meal behavior recorded)
    5:30-6:00 Dinner cleanup

*6:00-9:00 P.M. Passes*

*6:00-7:00 P.M. Canteen & free time*

*7:00-8:00 P.M. Meetings or informal interaction*

    Informal interaction: Monday, Wednesday, Friday
    7:55      Informal interaction recorded

    Weekly living group business meeting & promotion proposals: Tuesday
    7:00      Attendance recorded

    Weekly living group pass meeting: Thursday
    7:00      Attendance recorded

*8:00-9:00 P.M. Meetings or informal interaction*

    Weekly executive council: Tuesday
    8:00      Attendance of executive council recorded
    8:55      Informal interaction for all but executive council recorded

*9:00-10:00 P.M. Bedtime preparation*

    Baths or showers recorded as completed (as scheduled 3 times per week)

*10:00 P.M. Regular lights out*

*10:30 P.M. Late lights out*

*11:30 P.M.-12:30 A.M. Late bed preparation (Friday only)*

*12:30 A.M. Late lights out (Friday only)*

Saturday & Sunday

*6:30-7:00 A.M. Arise, dress, groom, make bed, room in order (except late sleeping living groups)*

    6:30      Lights on for all but late-sleeping living groups
    6:35      Getting up for regular rising living groups recorded
    6:55      Appearance for regular rising living groups recorded
    7:00      Bed made, area neat for regular rising living groups recorded

*Late sleeping living groups*

    8:30 A.M. Latest rising time for late-sleeping living groups
    Getting up recorded 5 minutes after lights on
    Appearance recorded 25 minutes after lights on
    Bed made, area clean recorded 30 minutes after lights on

*7:00-9:00 A.M. Free time, may prepare snacks*

*9:00-12:00 Noon Passes*

*9:05-10:00 A.M. Housekeeping*

    9:45      Participation recorded

*10:00-11:00 A.M.*

> *Saturday Housekeeping*
> 10:45 Participation recorded
>
> *Sunday Informal interaction*
> 10:55 Informal interaction recorded

*11:00-11:30 A.M. Free period & brunch preparation*

> 11:00 Appearance of dietary group recorded
> 11:10 Appearance of other living groups recorded

*11:30 A.M.-1:00 P.M. Brunch*

> 11:30-12:30 Brunch (appropriateness of meal behavior recorded)
> 12:30- 1:00 Brunch cleanup

*1:00-4:00 P.M. Passes*

*1:00-2:00 P.M.*

> *Saturday Free time*
>
> *Sunday Informal interaction*
> 1:55 Informal interaction recorded

*2:00-3:00 P.M.*

> *Saturday Gym*
> 2:50 Attendance recorded
>
> *Sunday Free time*

*3:00-4:00 P.M. Informal interaction*

> 3:55 Informal interaction recorded

*4:00-5:00 P.M. Free time & dinner preparation*

> 4:25 Appearance of dietary group recorded
> 4:30-5:00 Dinner preparation by dietary living group
> 4:40 Appearance of remaining living groups recorded

*5:00-6:00 P.M. Dinner*

> 5:00-5:30 Dinner (appropriateness of meal behavior recorded)
> 5:30-6:00 Dinner cleanup

*6:00-9:00 P.M. Passes*

*6:00-7:00 P.M. Canteen & free time*

*7:00-9:00 P.M. Informal interaction*

> 7:55 Informal interaction recorded
> 8:55 Informal interaction recorded

*9:00-10:00 P.M. Bedtime preparation*

> Baths or showers recorded as completed

*10:00 P.M. Regular lights out*

*10:30 P.M. Late lights out*

*11:30 P.M.-12:30 A.M. Late bed preparation (Saturday only)*

*12:30 A.M. Late lights out (Saturday only)*

B. Expected Behavior

  I. Self-Maintenance

    A. Getting up on time: recorded each morning

    B. Appearance: recorded 3 times per day

1. Proper use of makeup
2. Clean fingernails
3. Hair combed
4. Teeth brushed
5. All appropriate clothing on
6. Clothing buttoned, zipped, tucked
7. Clothing clean and neat
8. Body clean
9. No odor
10. Shaven
11. Hair cut appropriately (males)

    C. Bed made, area clean: recorded each morning

1. Nothing on floor or bed
2. Sheets tucked in
3. Blanket straight and neat
4. Pillow straight and neat
5. Bedding not soiled
6. Furniture in appropriate places
7. Everything put away properly
8. Drawers and closets neat

    D. Appropriate mealtime behavior: recorded each meal

1. Return tray properly
2. No stealing and grabbing
3. Clean clothing, face, and hands
4. Courteous table manners
5. Proper use of utensils
6. Proper use of hands
7. No sloppiness

8. No gulping
9. Appropriate interaction

E. Bathing (at least 3 times per week)

1. Obtain and return soap and towel
2. Exchange clothes
3. Soap and rinse head area (face, neck, ears)
4. Soap and rinse upper half of body (shoulders, back, armpits, arms, hands, chest)
5. Soap and rinse lower half of body (crotch, legs, feet)
6. Clean tub or shower stall
7. Finish within 20 minutes

II. Communication Skills

A. Attend classes: attendance recorded at each of three classes per weekday (with living group)

B. Participate in classes: participation recorded in each of three classes per weekday

III. Interpersonal Skills

A. Informal interaction: recorded three or four times per day

1. Responding to requests
2. Responding courteously and appropriately to conversation
3. Initiating courteous and appropriate conversation
4. Cooperative interaction with other residents and with staff (doing things together)
5. Helping another resident perform a constructive activity

B. Attend small group meetings: attendance recorded as scheduled

C. Participate in small group meetings: participation recorded as scheduled

D. Attend community meetings: attendance recorded five times per week

E. Participate in community meetings: participation recorded five times per week

F. Attend unit activity periods: attendance recorded at each of two periods per weekday

G. Participate in unit activity periods: recorded at each of two periods per weekday

H. Attend weekly living group meetings: recorded twice a week

I. Attend and participate in unit recreational activities: recorded once each weekend

IV. Work and Housekeeping Skills

A. Take part in maintenance of unit

1. Odd jobs: recorded as requested
2. Housekeeping periods: recorded three times per weekend

B. Individual assignments: performance recorded each day by job supervisor

C. Intolerable Behavior

A resident who performs an intolerable behavior is expelled from the community (sent to the expulsion room), to be released after a specified period of quiet activity, and is subject to whatever sanctions the living group or the community group might impose. Intolerable behaviors are:

1. Acts that are offensive or interfere with rights or desirable activities of others (for example, creating a fire hazard, stealing, excessive swearing, damaging people or things, making excessive noise, publicly displaying inappropriate sexual behavior, spitting, etc.).
2. Absence or leave without prior explanation and approval.

D. Milieu Unit Change Agent Schedules:

Monday-Friday Morning (0800-1300)

*Change Agent 1*

At 0800
Staff report & in-service training.

*Change Agent 2*

At 0800
Staff report & in-service training.

*Change Agent 3 (psychologist will sub)*

At 0800
Staff report & in-service training.

*Programs, Populations, and Procedures* 66

| *Change Agent 1* | *Change Agent 2* | *Change Agent 3 (Psychologist will sub)* |
|---|---|---|
| At 0815<br>Announce community meeting.<br>Record attendance (A32).*<br>Provide feedback, encourage attendance, take part in meeting. | At 0815<br>Record inappropriate time on unit (A9).<br>Prepare drugs: units A & B. | At 0815<br>After attendance at community meeting is recorded, encourage attendance.<br>Keep log of votes & decisions. |
| At 0855<br>Complete recording of participation in community meeting (A32). | | |
| At 0900<br>Announce activity period 1: groups A, B, & C.<br>Encourage attendance; vote on activity.<br>Record positive statements & negative feedback (A32). | At 0900<br>Record attendance (A32); encourage attendance; vote on activity.<br>Record positive statements & negative feedback (A32). | At 0900<br>Record inappropriate time on unit (A9).<br>Encourage attendance; vote on activity.<br>Record positive statements & negative feedback (A32). |
| At 0940<br>Complete recording of participation in activity period 1 by group A (A32). | At 0940<br>Complete recording of participation in activity period 1 by group B (A32). | At 0940<br>Complete recording of participation in activity period 1 by group C (A32). |
| 0945-1000<br>Take break. | 0945-1000<br>Take break. | 0945-1000<br>Take break. |
| At 1000<br>Record use of pit & pit activities (A5,A6,A7).<br>Provide & record positive statements & negative feedback for informal interaction in pit (A33). | At 1000<br>Announce informal interaction.<br>Record use of all areas except pit (A2,A3,A4,A8,A9,A10).<br>Provide & record positive statements & negative feedback for informal interaction in all areas except pit (A33). | At 1000<br>Assist where needed. |
| At 1025 (Pit)<br>Complete recording of interaction (A33). | At 1025<br>Complete recording of interaction (A33). | |
| At 1030<br>Announce activity period 2 for group A.<br>Record attendance (A32), encourage attendance, vote on activity.<br>Record positive statements & negative feedback (A32). | At 1030<br>Announce activity period 2 for group B.<br>Record attendance (A32), encourage attendance, vote on activity.<br>Record positive statements & negative feedback (A32). | At 1030<br>Announce activity period 2 for group C.<br>Record attendance (A32), encourage attendance; vote on activity.<br>Record positive statements & Negative feedback (A32). |
| At 1125<br>Complete recording of participation in activity period 2 by group A (A32). | At 1125<br>Complete recording of participation in activity period 2 by group B (A32). | At 1125<br>Complete recording of participation in activity period 2 by group C (A32). |
| At 1130<br>Distribute drugs to dietary group. | At 1130<br>Announce appearance check for dietary group.<br>Record appearance (A29), provide feedback, persuade one improvement. | At 1130<br>Announce informal interaction.<br>Record use of pit (A5,A6,A7) and all other areas (A2,A3,A4, A8,A10) used for informal interaction.<br>Provide and record positive statements & negative feedback for informal interaction (A33). |
| By 1140<br>Start lunch preparation. Note: in event of short staff, give supervision of dietary group to dietary worker. | At 1140<br>Announce appearance check for remaining groups.<br>Record appearance (A29), provide feedback, persuade one improvement.<br>Distribute drugs from cart by mirror at time of appearance check. | |
| | | At 1155<br>Complete recording of interaction (A33). |

*Numbers in parentheses refer to the specific form used (see Paul, in press).

| Change Agent 1 | Change Agent 2 | Change Agent 3 (Psychologist will sub) |
|---|---|---|
| At 1200<br>Announce lunch. Record attendance (A1). | At 1200<br>Eat (try to be first in line). Interact with residents. | At 1200<br>Eat (try to be first in line). Interact with residents. |
| At 1202<br>Give form A1 to dietary worker to record extra portions.<br>Record appropriateness of mealtime behavior (A31). | | |
| At 1215<br>Give form A31 to change agent 2.<br>Eat, interact with residents. | At 1215<br>Record appropriateness of mealtime behavior (A31). | At 1215<br>Interact with residents. |
| At 1230<br>Lunch cleanup, dietary workers supervise. | | At 1230 (Psychologist)<br>Record use of free time activities (A2,A3,A4,A7,A8,A10).<br>Interact with residents during free time.<br>Handle expulsion room. |
| 1230-1300<br>Take break. | 1230-1300<br>Take break. | 1230-1300<br>Take break. |

Monday-Friday Afternoons (1300-1630)

| Change Agent 1 | Change Agent 2 | Change Agent 3 |
|---|---|---|
| At 1315: Period 1 class<br>Announce class A for living group A.<br>Record attendance (A32), encourage attendance, record positive statements & negative feedback (A32). | At 1315: Period 1 class<br>Announce class B for living group B.<br>Record attendance (A32), encourage attendance, record positive statements & negative feedback (A32). | At 1315: Period 1 class<br>Announce class C for living group C.<br>Record attendance (A32), encourage attendance, record positive statements & negative feedback (A32). |
| At 1400<br>Complete recording of class A participation (A32). | At 1400<br>Complete recording of class B participation (A32). | At 1400<br>Complete recording of class C participation (A32). |
| At 1410: Period 2 class<br>Announce class C for living group A.<br>Record attendance (A32), encourage attendance, record positive statements & negative feedback (A32). | At 1410: Period 2 class<br>Announce class A for living group B.<br>Record attendance (A32), encourage attendance, record positive statements & negative feedback (A32). | At 1410: Period 2 class<br>Announce class B for living group C.<br>Record attendance (A32), encourage attendance, record positive statements & negative feedback (A32). |
| At 1455<br>Complete recording of class C participation (A32). | At 1455<br>Complete recording of class A participation (A32). | At 1455<br>Complete recording of class B participation (A32). |
| At 1505: Period 3 class<br>Announce class B for living group A.<br>Record attendance (A32), encourage attendance, record positive statements & negative feedback (A32). | At 1505: Period 3 class<br>Announce class C for living group B.<br>Record attendance (A32), encourage attendance, record positive statements & negative feedback (A32). | At 1505: Period 3 class<br>Announce class A for living group C.<br>Record attendance (A32), encourage attendance, record positive statements & negative feedback (A32). |
| At 1550<br>Complete recording of class B participation (A32). | At 1550<br>Complete recording of class C participation (A32). | At 1550<br>Complete recording of class A participation (A32). |
| At 1555 (Free time for residents)<br>Record use of TV, lounge (A2,A3,A4). | At 1555 (Free time for residents)<br>Record use of living room (A8), chairs (A10), bedroom (A8), and nondesignated areas. | |
| At 1600<br>Staff report & in-service training. | At 1600<br>Staff report & in-service training. | At 1600<br>Staff report & in-service training. |

Monday-Friday Evening (1600-2430)

| Change Agent 1 | Change Agent 2 |
|---|---|
| At 1600<br>Staff report & in-service training. | At 1600<br>Staff report & inservice training. |
| | At 1615<br>Prepare drugs. |

*Change Agent 1*

At 1625
　Announce appearance check for dietary group, record appearance (A29), provide feedback, persuade improvement.

At 1630
　Start dinner preparation. Note: In event only one change agent is on duty, give supervision of dietary group to dietary worker.

At 1700
　Announce dinner, record attendance (A1).

At 1702
　Give clipboard, form A1 to dietary worker to record extra portions.
　Record appropriateness of mealtime behavior (A31).

At 1715
　Give form A31 to change agent 2.
　Eat, interact with residents.

At 1730
　Start dinner cleanup.

At 1800
　Announce canteen time.
　Dispense items and record for each resident who receives or checks out items (A18). (Monday A21).
　After canteen announce free time.

At 1900
　Sign out residents taking passes. Record (A26). (M, W, F: Pit)
　Record pit entrance and use of pit activities (A5, A6, A7).
　Provide & record positive statements & negative feedback for informal interaction in pit (A33).

At 1900 (Tuesday)
　Announce weekly group business & promotion proposals meetings.
　Assist all three groups.
　After meeting announce free time.

At 1900 (Thursday)
　Record attendance (A32) at group meetings.
　Assist all three groups.
　After meeting record use of free time activities (A2, A3, A4, A5, A8, A10).

At 1955 (M, W, F)
　Record informal interaction (A33).

At 2000
　Record use of pit activities (A5, A6, A7).
　Provide & record positive statements & negative feedback for informal interaction in pit (A33).

At 2000 (Tuesday)
　Announce weekly executive council meeting.
　Record attendance (A32).
　Assist as needed.

At 2055
　Record interaction (A33).

At 2100
　Announce bedtime preparation. Supervise bathrooms.
　Record & persuade scheduled bathers (A20).

*Change Agent 2*

By 1630
　Distribute drugs to dietary group.

At 1640
　Announce appearance check for remaining groups, record appearance (A29).
　Provide feedback, persuade one improvement.
　Distribute drugs from cart by mirror at time of appearance check.

At 1700
　Eat (try to be first in line).
　Interact with residents.

At 1715
　Record appropriateness of mealtime behavior (A31).

At 1730
　Record use of free time activities, interact with residents (A2, A3, A4, A7, A8, A10).

At 1800
　Assist as needed.
　After canteen, record use of free time activities (A2, A3, A4, A7, A8, A10).
　Interact with residents.

At 1900 (M, W, F)
　Announce informal interaction.
　Record use of all areas except pit (A2, A3, A4, A8, A10).
　Provide & record positive statements & negative feedback for informal interaction in all areas except pit (A33).

At 1900 (Tuesday)
　Record attendance (A32) at group meetings.
　Assist all three groups.
　After meeting record use of free time activities (A2, A3, A4, A7, A8, A10).

At 1900 (Thursday)
　Announce weekly group pass meetings.
　Assist all three groups.
　After meeting announce free time.

At 1955 (M, W, F)
　Record informal interaction (A33).

At 2000
　Announce informal interaction.
　Record use of all areas except pit (A2, A3, A4, A8, A10).
　Provide & record positive statements & negative feedback for informal interaction in all areas except pit (A33).

At 2000 (Tuesday)
　Record use of all informal interaction areas including pit (A2, A3, A4, A5, A6, A7, A8, A10).

At 2055
　Record interaction (A33).

At 2100
　Admit & record residents returning from passes (A26, A27).
　Prepare drugs.

At 2130
　Persuade residents to prepare for bed.
　(Friday only) Take vote & record late-sleeping groups for Saturday (A13).

## Change Agent 1

At 2200
Record use of free time activities (Friday) (A2, A3, A4, A7, A8, A10).
Assist change agent 2.

At 2230
Turn off & record late lights (A13).

At 2300
Record use of free time activities (Friday) (A2, A3, A4, A7, A8, A10).

At 2400
Staff report & in-service training.
Give & record report

**Monday-Friday Night (0000-0830)**

At 0000
Staff report & in-service training.

At 0030 (Friday only)
Late lights out (males).

0030-0555
Prepare drugs, drug inventory, cards, & orders; other duties as required.

At 0555
Awaken dietary living group.

At 0600
Record getting up (A30), provide feedback about getting up and persuade to get up. Provide positive statements regarding appearance and bed and area (dietary group).

No earlier than 0615
Record appearance (A29), provide feedback, persuade one improvement (dietary group).

At 0622
Record bed and area (A30), provide feedback, persuade one improvement (dietary group).

By 0630
Distribute drugs to dietary group.

At 0630
Start breakfast preparation. Take dietary group to kitchen; supervise breakfast preparation.

At 0650
Turn breakfast preparation over to dietary worker and residents. Record bed and area (A30), provide feedback, persuade one improvement.

At 0700
Announce breakfast, record attendance (A1).

At 0702
Give clipboard to dietary worker to record extra portions (A1).

## Change Agent 2

By 2145
Distribute drugs.

At 2155
Take vote & record late lights (A13).
Turn off lights.
Persuade dallying residents to go to bed.
Take vote & record late bed (Friday) (A13).

By 2200
Complete medical treatments.

At 2230
Admit & record residents returning from passes (Friday) (A26, A27).
Assist change agent 1.

At 2335
Announce late-bed preparation (Friday)

At 2400
Staff report & in-service training.

At 0000
Staff report & in-service training.

At 0030 (Friday only)
Late lights out (females).

0030-0555
Summarize data sheets.
Check drug preparation for living groups not on dietary; other duties as required.

At 0530
Call & check time; set clocks in secretarial area & kitchen.

At 0555
Assist change agent 1.

From 0600 to 0625
Assist change agent 1 with positive statements and negative feedback, keeping residents in rooms, drugs, etc.

At 0625
Awaken remaining living groups.

At 0630
Record getting up (A30), provide feedback about getting up, and persuade to get up. Provide positive statements regarding appearance and bed and area.

No earlier than 0645
Record appearance for remaining living groups (A29), provide feedback, persuade one improvement.

At 0700
Eat (try to be first in line).
Interact with residents.

## Change Agent 1

At 0702
  Give clipboard to dietary worker to record extra portions (A1).
  Record appropriateness of mealtime behavior (A31).

At 0715
  Give record, A31, to change agent 2.
  Eat, interact with residents.

At 0730
  Start breakfast cleanup. Note: if only one change agent on duty, give supervision to dietary worker.

At 0800
  Staff report & in-service training in community meeting. Give and record report.

Weekend Mornings (0800-1300)

At 0800
  Staff report & in-service training.

At 0825
  Awaken late sleeping living groups.

By 0830
  Record getting up (A30), provide feedback, persuade late sleepers to get up.

By 0850
  Record appearance for late sleepers (A29), provide feedback, persuade one improvement.

By 0855
  Record bed & area for late sleepers (A30), provide feedback, persuade one improvement.

At 0905 (Housekeeping)
  Announce housekeeping period; take & record vote on areas of responsibility for living groups (A34).

At 0945
  Record participation in housekeeping (A34).

At 1000 (Housekeeping): Saturday only
  Announce housekeeping period; take & record vote on areas of responsibility for living groups (A34).

At 1045: Saturday only
  Record participation in housekeeping (A34).

At 1000 (Informal interaction): Sunday only
  Announce informal interaction; record use of all areas except pit (A2, A3, A4, A8, A10). Provide & record positive statements & negative feedback in all areas except pit (A33).

At 1055: Sunday only
  Record interaction (A33).

At 1100 (Free time for residents)
  Record use of free time activities (A2, A3, A4, A7, A8, A10).

By 1110
  Start brunch preparation. Note: if only one change agent on duty give supervision of dietary group to dietary worker.

At 1130
  Announce brunch, record attendance (A1).

## Change Agent 2

At 0715
  Record appropriateness of mealtime behavior (A31).

At 0730
  Distribute drugs to all residents except dietary group.

At 0750
  Record use of free time activities (A2, A3, A4, A7, A8, A10).

At 0800
  Staff report & in-service training in community meeting.

At 0800
  Staff report & in-service training.
  Prepare drugs.

At 0830
  Announce availability of snacks; record snacks prepared (A16).

By 0900
  Distribute drugs to late sleepers.

At 0905 (Housekeeping)
  Assist all three living groups as needed during housekeeping, providing positive statements & positive and negative feedback. Record (A2, A3, A4, A5, A6, A7, A8, A9, A10).

At 1000 (Housekeeping): Saturday only
  Assist all three living groups as needed during housekeeping, providing positive statements & positive and negative feedback. Record (A2, A3, A4, A5, A6, A7, A8, A9, A10).

At 1000 (Informal interaction): Sunday only
  Record inappropriate time on unit (A9).
  Record use of pit and pit activities (A5, A6, A7), provide & record positive statements & negative feedback for interaction in pit (A33).

At 1055: Sunday only
  Record interaction (A33).

At 1100
  Announce appearance check starting with dietary group, record appearance (A29), provide feedback, persuade one improvement. Distribute drugs to dietary and other two groups.

At 1110
  Continue appearance check with nondietary groups, record appearance (A29), provide feedback, persuade one improvement. Distribute drugs.

At 1130
  Eat (try to be first in line).
  Interact with residents.

*Change Agent 1*

At 1132
  Give clipboard to dietary worker to record extra portions & entry (A1).
  Record appropriateness of meal behavior (A31).

At 1200
  Eat, interact with residents.

At 1225
  Announce last call for brunch, record attendance (A1).

At 1230
  Start brunch cleanup (finish by 1300).

*Weekend Afternoons (1300-1630)*

At 1300 (Free time): Saturday only
  Record use of free time activities, (A2, A3, A4, A7, A8, A10).
  Interact with residents.

At 1300 (Informal interaction): Sunday only
  Announce informal interaction. Record use of all areas except pit (A2, A3, A4, A8, A10). Provide & record positive statements & negative feedback in all areas except pit (A33).

At 1355: Sunday only
  Record interaction (A33).

At 1400 (Gym): Saturday only
  Announce gym.
  Accompany & supervise in gym.

At 1450: Saturday only
  Record attendance (A32).

At 1400: Sunday only
  Record use of free time activities (A2, A3, A4, A7, A8, A10).
  Interact with residents.

At 1500 (Informal interaction)
  Announce informal interaction. Record use of all areas except pit (A2, A3, A4, A8, A10).
  Provide & record positive statements & negative feedback in all areas except pit (A33).

At 1555
  Record interaction (A33).

At 1600
  Report & in-service training.
  Give & record report.

*Weekend Evenings (1600-2430)*

At 1600
  Staff report & in-service training.

At 1625
  Announce appearance check for dietary group.
  Record appearance (A29), provide feedback, persuade improvement.

At 1630
  Start dinner preparation. Note: If only one change agent on duty give supervision of dietary group to dietary worker.

*Change Agent 2*

At 1155
  Record use of free time activities (A2, A3, A4, A7, A8, A10).

At 1200
  Record appropriate mealtime behavior (A31). (Finish by 1245).

At 1255
  Record brunch participation for dietary group (A34).

At 1300 (Free time): Saturday only
  Interact with residents during free time. Assist change agent 1 as needed.

At 1300 (Informal interaction): Sunday only
  Record use of pit and pit activities (A5, A6, A7). Provide and record positive statements & negative feedback for interaction in pit (A33).

At 1355: Sunday only
  Record interaction (A33)

At 1400 (Gym): Saturday only
  Record inappropriate time on unit (A9).
  Accompany & assist change agent 1 in gym.

At 1400: Sunday only
  Interact with residents during free time.
  Assist change agent 1 as needed.
  Check unit for lights out; make list & give to project secretary.

At 1500 (Informal interaction)
  Record use of pit and pit activities (A5, A6, A7).
  Provide & record positive statements & negative feedback for interaction in pit (A33).

At 1555
  Record interaction (A33).
  Record use of free time activities (A2, A3, A4, A7, A8, A10).

At 1600
  Report & in-service training.

At 1600
  Staff report & in-service training.

At 1615
  Prepare drugs.

By 1630
  Distribute drugs to dietary group.

*Programs, Populations, and Procedures* 72

*Change Agent 1*

At 1700
    Announce dinner, record attendance (A1).

At 1702
    Give form A1 to dietary worker to record extra portions.
    Record appropriateness of mealtime behavior (A31).

At 1715
    Give record sheet, A31, to change agent 2.
    Eat, interact with residents.

At 1730
    Start dinner cleanup.

At 1800
    Announce canteen time.
    Dispense items and record for each resident who receives or checks out items (A18).
    After canteen announce free time.
    Prepare drugs.

At 1900
    Sign out residents taking passes. Record (A26).
    Record pit entrance and use of pit activities (A5, A6, A7). Provide and record positive statements & negative feedback for informal interaction in pit (A33).
    Serve coffee to residents.

At 1955
    Record informal interaction (A33).

At 2000
    Record pit entrance and use of pit activities (A5, A6, A7). Provide and record positive statements & negative feedback for informal interaction in pit (A33).
    Serve coffee to residents.

At 2055
    Record informal interaction (A33).

At 2100
    Announce bedtime preparation. Supervise bathrooms.
    Record & persuade scheduled bathers (A20).

At 2200
    Record use of free time activities (A2, A3, A4, A7, A8, A10) (Saturday).
    Assist change agent 2. Pick up soap from shower rooms.

At 2230
    Turn off & record late lights (A13).

At 2300
    Record use of free time activities (A2, A3, A4, A7, A8, A10) (Saturday).

*Change Agent 2*

At 1640
    Announce appearance check for remaining groups.
    Record appearance (A29), provide feedback, persuade one improvement.
    Distribute drugs from cart by mirror at time of appearance check.

At 1700
    Eat (try to be first in line).
    Interact with residents.

At 1715
    Record appropriateness of mealtime behavior (A31).

At 1730
    Record use of free time activities (A2, A3, A4, A7, A8, A10).
    Interact with residents.

At 1800
    Assist change agent 1 as needed.
    After canteen, record use of free time activities (A2, A3, A4, A7, A8, A10).
    Interact with residents.

At 1900
    Announce informal interaction. Record use of all areas except pit (A2, A3, A4, A8, A10).
    Provide & record positive statements & negative feedback for informal interaction in all areas except pit (A33).

At 1955
    Record informal interaction (A33).

At 2000
    Announce informal interaction.
    Record use of all areas expect pit (A2, A3, A4, A8, A10). Provide & record positive statements & negative feedback for informal interaction in all areas except pit (A33).

At 2055
    Record informal interaction (A33).

At 2100
    Admit & record residents returning from passes (A26, A27).
    Assist change agent 1 with showers.

At 2130
    Persuade residents to prepare for bed. Take vote & record late-sleeping groups for Sunday (Saturday only) (A13).

At 2145
    Distribute drugs.

At 2155
    Take vote & record late lights (A13).
    Turn off lights.
    Persuade dallying residents to go to bed.
    Take vote & record late bed (A13) (Saturday).

By 2200
    Complete medical treatments.

At 2230
    Admit & record residents returning from passes (A26, A27) (Saturday).
    Assist change agent 1.

*Change Agent 1*

At 2400
    Staff report & in-service training.
    Give & record report.

Weekend Nights (0000-0830)

At 0000
    Staff report & in-service training.

At 0030 (Saturday only)
    Assist change agent 2.

0030-0630
    Summarize data sheets & other duties as required.

At 0630
    Awaken all but late sleeping living groups.

At 0635
    Record getting up (A30), provide feedback, persuade to get up.

By 0655
    Record appearance (A29), provide feedback, persuade one improvement.

By 0700
    Record bed & area (A30), provide feedback, persuade one improvement.

At 0700
    Announce availability of free time activities, record use (A2, A3, A4, A7, A8, A10).
    Prepare special medical meals.

At 0800
    Staff report & in-service training.
    Give & record report.

*Change Agent 2*

At 2335
    Announce late bed preparation (Saturday).

At 2400
    Staff report & in-service training.

At 0000
    Staff report & inservice training.

At 0030 (Saturday only)
    Turn off & record late bed lights (A13).

0030-0630
    Prepare drugs, inventory, cards & orders; other duties as required.

At 0630
    Assist change agent 1 as needed.

At 0635
    Assist change agent 1 as needed.

At 0700
    Distribute drugs to regular risers.
    Interact with residents during free time. Handle late sleepers arising before 0800.

At 0750
    Record use of free time activities (A2, A3, A4, A7, A8, A10).

At 0800
    Staff report & in-service training.

# 8. The Social-Learning Program Manual

The principles and procedures in this program have grown from basic research on learning. While working with residents on the social-learning unit and administering the social-learning program, we assume that a basic set of principles is valid. This means that we view the resident's behavior and methods of changing it according to these principles, and we consistently apply these principles and procedures in all our dealings with residents on the social-learning unit.

BASIC PRINCIPLES AND CONCEPTS

*Law of Effect*

While there are many laws of learning and many detailed principles, a few are so basic that we must always keep them in mind. Two major laws of learning form the basis for most of our principles and procedures. The first is the *law of effect*. It states that the frequency of occurrence of an action, behavior, or response is a function of the effect or consequence that results. Behaviors that result in a positive effect or outcome for the person who performs them will increase in frequency and continue to occur; behaviors that do not result in a positive effect or outcome for the person performing them or that result in a negative effect or outcome will decrease in frequency and eventually cease to occur.

When a behavior increases in frequency as a function of stimulus events that follow its occurrence (consequences), *reinforcement* is said to have occurred: the behavior has been reinforced or strengthened. The stimulus events (objects, actions, environmental changes) that serve to strengthen the behavior that they follow are called *reinforcers*. Positive reinforcers are objects or events that increase the frequency of the behavior that precedes their occurrence (subjectively pleasant, desirable, and rewarding objects or events). Negative reinforcers are objects or events that increase the frequency of the behavior that precedes their termination (subjectively unpleasant, undesirable, and aversive objects or events).

Thus, we have two major principles for increasing or strengthening appropriate behaviors: *positive reinforcement* (arrange for positive reinforcers to occur as a consequence of the behavior) and *negative reinforcement* (arrange for negative reinforcers to be avoided or taken away as a consequence of the behavior). We also have three major principles for decreasing or weakening inappropriate behaviors: *aversion* (arrange for negative reinforcers to occur as a consequence of the behavior), *response cost* (arrange for positive reinforcers to be avoided or taken away as a consequence of the behavior), and *extinction* (a way of weakening inappropriate behavior that is already under reinforcement control; by arranging for neutral consequences to occur rather than reinforcing consequences following occurrence of the behavior, the behavior will gradually extinguish by occurring less frequently if no favorable consequences result).

*Association by Contiguity*

The second major law is that of *association by contiguity*, which states that stimulus events (objects, actions, environmental changes) that are contiguous or occur together will come to be associated, function in similar ways, or mean the same thing. Thus, new reinforcers may be developed through pairing an existing reinforcer several times with another stimulus event. This means that timing is very important since two events to be associated must occur immediately and simultaneously on several occasions to ensure success. Similarly, the association between a target behavior (response) and a reinforcer must be immediate at early stages of learning, i.e., immediate reinforcement, or the wrong behavior may be reinforced. Because of association by contiguity, we must also be very careful in applying negative reinforcers to

---

This chapter comprises the staff training manual that details the procedures of the social-learning program to preprofessional staff. The style and format of the original manual have been retained.

decrease inappropriate behavior, since the change agent may become an aversive stimulus for some residents if he or she is frequently associated with negative reinforcers.

Reinforcers that are necessary to sustain life (e.g., food, water, sleep) are called *primary reinforcers* because no learning is needed for them to become effective. Primary reinforcers are very important because most people will eventually respond to them, no matter how initially unresponsive they may be. However, primary reinforcers are somewhat difficult to use in changing behavior for two reasons. First of all, the effectiveness of most primary reinforcers is highly dependent upon the extent to which a person has recently received the reinforcer; e.g., for most people who have just eaten a large meal (they are satiated), food will not be an effective reinforcer, but if food has not been obtained for a long time (the person is deprived), food will probably be very effective. Second, and more important, it is very hard to apply primary reinforcers with the right timing—that is, immediately upon the occurrence of the behavior to be reinforced.

A *discriminative stimulus* sets the time and place when a behavior will have reinforcing consequences, for example, the green traffic light that indicates it is safe to cross a street. Through pairing with primary reinforcers, discriminative stimuli may themselves become effective as reinforcers through association by contiguity. When this occurs, they may be called *secondary* or *acquired reinforcers*. An acquired reinforcer that has been associated with many different reinforcing stimuli may become effective in a wide variety of situations independent of specific satiation and deprivation conditions; it may then be called a *generalized reinforcer*. Two important examples of stimuli that are likely to serve as acquired generalized reinforcers are social attention and money. A child's crying will have pleasant consequences only if some adult such as a parent is around to take heed and feed or change it. The parent's attention, therefore, first sets the time and place where the crying has a pleasant consequence; eventually attention may become reinforcing in itself. The parent's attention will then be likely to increase other behaviors in new situations; e.g., when the parent takes the child to the potty chair and smiles and hugs the child for urinating in the potty, the child will more likely repeat that act than the act of soiling its diapers because of the approving attention from its parent. Thus, in this example, the parent's attention changes from discriminative stimulus to acquired reinforcer to generalized reinforcer. Other probable social reinforcers include a smile, a pat on the back, and praise; they indicate that the presence of other people is likely to result in the person's acts leading to pleasant consequences.

The most widely known secondary (and generalized) reinforcer is money. If people have money, they often can obtain what they ask for; without money, they can ask, but in vain. Money sets the time and place where the act of asking has reinforcing consequences. People may learn the value of money for food, candy, toys, or the like and still work for money (that is, increase the behavior that earns money as a consequence) in new situations and even work to obtain money for things that they have not yet decided to buy. This is a real advantage of generalized reinforcers; usually they can be administered immediately, and they are not dependent upon specific states of deprivation or satiation for their effectiveness.

Acquired reinforcers such as money or the attention of others will become ineffective or stop functioning as reinforcers if they are not backed up. That is, if money becomes worthless (like confederate money or chips from a bankrupt gambling casino), the person quickly stops working for it. Money is nothing but a token (a sign or symbol representing other stimuli): when it is no longer useful, it is no longer an effective reinforcer. The things that make it meaningful are called *backup reinforcers*.

While no learning is required for a primary reinforcer to become effective, secondary reinforcers must develop (acquire) their effectiveness through association by contiguity. Thus, each individual will have certain stimulus events functioning as reinforcers, dependent upon his or her unique learning history. For each person, some behaviors occur more frequently than others. If a high-frequency behavior is made contingent upon performance of a low-frequency behavior, the low-frequency behavior is likely to increase. If kissing another is a high-frequency behavior for someone and treating them to meals in expensive restaurants is a low-frequency behavior, the number of expensive meals bought will likely increase if followed by kissing. That is, "allowing a high frequency behavior to occur" may be used to reinforce other behavior. This is the Premack principle, so named for the psychologist who formulated it.

*Developing New Behaviors*

Application of reinforcing consequences is used to change existing behaviors. Several additional principles and procedures are especially useful in developing new behaviors, ones that a person is not already performing. Basic to developing any new terminal or target behavior is the fact that almost any behavior can be broken down into components—smaller segments of behavior that are parts of the whole target behavior.

*Shaping* by the method of successive approximations is an effective means of developing a new behavior. In shaping, instead of waiting for the complete target behavior to occur before reinforcing consequences are brought to bear, first, a component of the target behavior is reinforced, then closer and closer movement in the direction approximating the target behavior, and finally, only the target behavior itself. When a particular target behavior consists of a series of separate acts that must succeed each other like links in a chain, a special method of shaping called *chaining*, is employed. In developing a new behavior through chaining, reinforcement is initially applied to either the first or the last act in the series of component behaviors, then only to a combination of that act and the next in the series, then only to the combination of that act and the next two in the series—gradually lengthening the chain until the entire series of acts constituting the new behavior is performed and reinforcement occurs.

Shaping would be an extraordinarily time-consuming procedure for developing new behavior if we had to wait for component behaviors to occur. A more efficient way to instigate desirable behavior is through *prompting* —providing instructional information concerning the behavior, including specifying the consequences that will result. The instructional component of a prompt may be provided through physical guidance (e.g., physically assist the person in performance of the response), demonstration or modeling (e.g., have the learner observe another person perform the response), or written or verbal means.

Modeling is often the most efficient means of prompting complex behavior, since the learner can see another person perform the target behavior and be reinforced for it—thus providing all instructional information in detail and a demonstration of the resulting consequence. Physical prompts (guidance) may be most efficient for instigating (priming) motor behavior in nonverbal persons or in training detailed components of motor skills, such as writing. In physical prompts, the specification of consequences may not always be obvious to the learner; therefore, verbal specification of consequences should usually be included. In general, if the learner is verbal, verbal prompts are likely to be the most efficient means of instigating new behavior because both instructional information and specification of consequences are included in a single statement. Verbal prompts nearly always take the form of "If ..., then ...," or "Because ..., therefore ...," statements, with the first clause specifying the behavior and the second one specifying the consequence—*positive prompts* if the consequence is positive, *negative prompts* if it is negative. For example, "If you go to class now, you'll earn a token for being on time" (positive prompt); "If you continue to raise your voice, you won't be able to go on a pass" (negative prompt); "Because you didn't clean your fingernails, you won't be able to work in the kitchen" (negative prompt).

The development of new behaviors through shaping and chaining may be hastened by prompting an existing response that has a component relation to the target behavior, reinforcing the component when it occurs, and then prompting and reinforcing variations of the component or a combination of components (in the case of chaining) in the direction of the total target behavior. For very small component behaviors in which verbal specification of consequences is difficult or may have the potential of sounding mechanical, *simple instruction* followed by immediate reinforcement may be used in shaping or chaining. For example, in teaching components of taking a shower, an instruction-reinforcement sequence might be: "George, take this washcloth in your right hand" (he does); "Good, now put it under the water" (he does); "Fine—keep up the good work by rubbing the washcloth on the soap," etc. For our purposes, it should be clear that prompts always include a specification of consequences, while simple instructions do not. Prompts are usually preferable to instructions. As the learner becomes more proficient in performing a target behavior, prompts and instructions can be gradually faded out (reduced in frequency, intensity, and specificity) so that the person comes to respond to more naturally occurring discriminative stimuli.

## THE TOKEN ECONOMY

The major operations for bringing about therapeutic change in the social-learning program lie in response-contingent consequences for the occurrence or nonoccurrence of adaptive behavior. These consequences consist of both material and social reinforcements administered by the treatment staff. The major vehicle for implementing the principles is the *token economy*, which refers to the fact that colored strips of plastic, called *tokens*, are used as a medium of exchange much as money operates in the outside world. The tokens gain value as generalized reinforcers because their exchange is required for such primary and secondary reinforcers as the material goods and privileges the residents desire. In the fully operative token economy almost every behavior of the resident either gains or costs tokens. Therefore, by providing tokens for adaptive behaviors and withholding them or instituting token costs for nonadaptive behaviors, the resident is gradually trained to successively closer approximations of the behaviors necessary for functioning in the outside community.

*Tokens as Reinforcers*

The use of tokens as the major vehicle for reinforcement has a number of distinct advantages. Tokens, by definition, become generalized reinforcers because a wide range of both primary and secondary reinforcers can be obtained with tokens. Therefore, in working with a group of residents, we are much more likely to have a common medium of exchange, a common generalized reinforcer, which allows the residents freedom to choose their own backup reinforcers rather than having the staff attempt to determine the reinforcers unique to each resident. While it would be impossible to distribute many primary and secondary reinforcers in the ongoing treatment environment, we can immediately reinforce appropriate behavior with tokens. This is true for two reasons: (1) tokens should have consistent reinforcing power (they are relatively resistant to satiation since they can be exchanged for many different backup reinforcers and can be saved for spending at a later time), and (2) tokens can be carried and disbursed more easily than most of the backup reinforcers. However, the effectiveness of tokens as generalized reinforcers is dependent upon backup reinforcers being available only upon the exchange of tokens; therefore, in the fully operating token economy it is necessary that the availability of all possible backup reinforcers be well controlled.

Our basic medium of exchange is the one-token value represented by a token of a specified color (the color may change from time to time or for specific residents). One token is the unit of value indicated on the token cost sheet (see appendix). However, just as money has different values, we also have tokens of other colors whose value is equivalent to that of five tokens; these tokens of higher value are used primarily with residents on step 2 and above who are on individual assignments and are receiving tokens in a lump sum on "payday." Tokens of any value are disbursed only at scheduled times and only for specific behaviors. This is for two reasons. First, each of us on the treatment staff probably differs in our willingness to withhold or to pay tokens for a specific behavior, and second, we must prevent either "inflation" or "depression" from entering into the unit's economy.

*Tokens and Scheduled Activities*

On the social-learning unit each resident is assigned a daily schedule, which, for step 1 residents on weekdays, includes six hours of scheduled classes and activities, about three hours of informal interaction periods, about two hours for meals, one to two hours for small and large group meetings, one hour of canteen time, and about one hour of free time. As residents advance to step 2 the activities give way to three hours of individual assignments; at steps 3 and 4, activities and classes give way to six hours of individual assignments. On weekends, one to two hours are designated as housekeeping periods, about three and a half hours scheduled for meals, one hour of canteen time, one and a half hours for free time, one to one and a half hours for activities, and three to five hours for informal interaction. For each of these periods, the means of disbursing or collecting tokens and of using social reinforcement and extinction procedures are detailed below.

For scheduled activities and classes one token is disbursed immediately for punctual attendance, and one token is given at the end of the period for participation. No resident should ever miss tokens that have been earned, and none should ever receive tokens that have not been earned. In a similar fashion, no resident must ever be allowed to obtain privileges or material goods for which there are token charges without paying those tokens.

Shaping is included in the token economy in two ways. Tokens disbursed for appearance, maintenance of bed and area, appropriate mealtime behavior, and taking showers shape behavior toward required performance levels with tokens themselves, i.e., the criterion for receiving a token gradually shifts upward. A second method of shaping is used for participation within specified segments of informal interaction periods, activities and classes. During these periods a *shaping chip* is immediately administered to bridge the time gap until token disbursement. These shaping chips have the same appearance as tokens except they are another color. They have no value once the period is ended and the token has been exchanged for them; they merely serve to bridge the time gap between a resident's performance and the receipt of a token for appropriate behavior at the end of the period. For example, each time residents perform their assigned task during a class, they receive a shaping chip. At the end of that period they turn in the shaping chips to the change agent in exchange for a token. During scheduled free periods, no tokens are disbursed, but social reinforcement is maintained. Social reinforcement must always be included along with token exchange and, when warranted, on all other occasions of resident contact. In the appendix at the end of this manual appears a complete list of token costs and those backup reinforcers for which residents may spend tokens. As indicated in the remaining parts of the manual, the time and amounts of token disbursement are completely specified. These lists are also posted on the unit and contained in a manual that is given to the residents upon their entrance into the treatment program.

The token-economy system has been carefully developed in such a way that residents performing very minimal levels of behavior do not receive many reinforcers. As residents move up through the step levels, they gradually earn more tokens, thereby acquiring access to more reinforcers in all areas. When the residents are ready for step 4, they essentially buy themselves out of the token system by purchasing a credit card, which allows them free access to all reinforcers as long as they are meeting the requirements of the step level. Additionally, by scheduling token payments for certain events on a weekly basis, residents on steps 2-4 are introduced to delayed reinforcement and the necessity for planning ahead, much as they will operate in the outside community.

Residents are not forced to do anything, with the exception of not performing blatant violations of unit rules. Rather, after the residents' initial sampling of available backup reinforcers, regular programmed consequences and their free choice within the token system guide them in the direction of more appropriate behavior. For the most part, inappropriate behavior is handled by a complete absence of reinforcement, either through failure to earn tokens or through failure to gain favorable attention from staff members; appropriate behavior always receives social reinforcement and token reinforcement. Blatant and destructive inappropriate behaviors that cannot be tolerated because of their effect on others result in *response costs* in the form of token charges and a procedure we term *time out* (see list in appendix). The time-out procedure means that the resident is physically removed from the opportunity of receiving positive reinforcers or from the opportunity of avoiding negative reinforcers. Time out may be instituted by placing a resident in a time-out room where positive reinforcers are not available or by requiring correction of the effects of inappropriate behavior that prevents avoidance of negative reinforcers as well as losing the opportunity to receive positive reinforcers. With this general orientation we may now turn to specific procedural rules to be followed on the social-learning unit.

## PROCEDURAL RULES FOR STAFF

1. *Always reinforce desirable behavior immediately.* Be sure that tokens are given to residents at the scheduled times when their behavior warrants it; they should never miss tokens they have earned. During the activities, classes, and informal interaction periods, scan all residents assigned to you to determine who is participating as required; then disburse shaping chips at scheduled points throughout the period or as residents meet their participation targets. At all times socially reinforce (i.e., touch, praise, compliment, smile, appropriately attend to) behavior at the time it occurs, sounding as sincere and enthusiastic as possible. Talk to residents freely when they are talking "straight." Never allow yourself or co-workers to interact mechanically or condescendingly or to use jargon; such behavior minimizes your reinforcing power.

2. *Never reinforce undesirable behavior.* Be sure that tokens are not given to those who fail to meet criteria; rather, specify the reason why a token was not earned, and prompt for the next opportunity—for example, "You don't earn your appearance token this morning, Herman, because your hair is all tangled. If you comb the tangles out of your hair by noon and otherwise look as good as you do now, you'll probably earn your appearance token then." Be sure to avoid inadvertent social reinforcement. In general, unless an inappropriate behavior is one that would incur a response cost or time out if it were to continue, do not attend to inappropriate behavior; ignore the behavior and walk away. If inappropriate behavior occurs that would incur a response cost or a time-out procedure if it were to continue, prompt for its termination and for incompatible behavior. If it terminates, reinforce; if it doesn't, apply the appropriate response cost or time-out procedure. If inappropriate behavior occurs that would result in failure to earn a token if it were to continue, prompt for its termination and for incompatible behavior. If it terminates, reinforce; if it doesn't, ignore it until it does. Only one such prompt may be made for a given behavior in each scheduled period for either type of inappropriate behavior. Do not talk or attend to residents at all if they are not talking straight. Be sure that goods and privileges are obtained only on exchange of tokens.

3. *Pair social stimuli and behavioral specification with reinforcement.* When tokens or shaping chips are given out, always specify the behavioral criterion for which they are earned, and always include verbal compliments and praise and/or positive nonverbal interaction (smiles, pleasant tone, gentle touch, eye contact, etc.) as a regular part of the procedure—e.g., "You did a really good job smoothing the sheets and putting things away this morning, George; here is your token for keeping your room in order." When social reinforcement is given without token exchange, always make the behavioral criterion a part of the statement, e.g., "I'm glad to see you take an interest in

knitting, Jean." Specification should always identify the resident's behavior in the resident's own language, not in jargon. Whenever possible token exchange and reinforcement should take place in front of other residents. When response costs are imposed, not only is the behavior specified to the resident, but the resident's name, the response cost, and the behavior responsible for the response cost are subject to community discussion until the response cost is paid off. Again, never allow your nonverbal behavior to be different from your verbal behavior or from the consequences the resident deserves.

4. *Shape desirable behavior and use prompts and instructions.* When the residents are not yet performing a complete target behavior on their own, reinforce specified approximations of the final behavior. Performance criteria are systematically increased as residents successfully meet or exceed the targets assigned them. In all instances, prompt or instruct once for the approximation and then reinforce while prompting the next requirement, e.g., "Your room is a mess, Minerva; you'll have to at least pick your blanket up from the floor to earn your token" (she does); "That's good, Minerva; here is your bed and area token for today. Tomorrow, you should have your blankets off the floor again and have your sheets tucked in to earn your bed and area token." For scheduled activities, each activity should be announced throughout the unit. Residents who do not respond to announcements may be prompted once for each activity each day—e.g., "It's time for you to go to ... Come now or you won't receive your attendance token." This prompt may be faded as the resident responds to the announcement and, eventually, the time. However, before the prompt fades, the resident must be exposed to and sample the activity and associated reinforcers.

For inappropriate behavior, the resident should be prompted not more than once during any time period that the behavior is incorrect. Specify the behavior, refer to the unit rule being violated, inform the resident of the consequence if the behavior continues, and follow by a prompt for an incompatible adaptive behavior if possible. For example, "George, you're not showing gentlemanly behavior when you eat mashed potatoes with your hands. If you keep doing that, you won't receive your token for good meal behavior. Try using your fork like this, and you'll probably earn your token." For behaviors that would incur a response cost or time-out procedure (see appendix) prompt only once as above if you can anticipate its occurrence. Then if the behavior occurs, inform the resident of the response cost and firmly and matter-of-factly escort him or her to the time-out room.

Prompts and instructions should also be used in response to any straight request or statements of a problem by a resident. Always give information and advice in terms of the consequences to the resident.

5. *Always record token exchange, chips, behavior, and relevant criteria.* Recordings must be made immediately to maintain accuracy and prevent loss of data through forgetting. These data must reflect real events. Always list your staff number on recording forms.

## PROGRAM CONTENT

Following the outline of a daily schedule that provides details of timing for functional periods (see appendix), discussion of the content of each of the major activities yields a descriptive picture of the specific procedures to be implemented on the social-learning unit.

1. *Morning routine.* Residents sleep in one of four types of rooms: six-bed dorms having no draperies, no chairs, and no bedside tables; four-bed dorms and two-bed dorms having draperies but no other accessories; and single rooms, fully equipped with draperies, chairs, and bedside tables. The six-bed dorms are free, while rooms with more privacy and accessories are available only by weekly token rental. Greater privacy and/or accessories require proportionally higher rents. Rental costs are specified and posted (see appendix); however, rental rates may be reduced for the more expensive accommodations when competition for them does not exist. Any resident wishing to rent a particular room (or other space) may force out an occupant previously assigned by paying the full rental cost. In addition to having more privacy and accessories, residents renting sleeping quarters are awakened later than those in the free dorm. Lights are turned on in the rented rooms thirty-five minutes later than lights on in the free dorms. As the assigned change agent goes to the rooms to turn on the lights, the residents are awakened with a single announcement, such as "time to get up," shaking them if necessary. Five minutes after the lights have been turned on, the change agent returns to the room to disburse and record tokens for being out of bed, specifying the basis for the token, and praising those who are. To residents not out of bed, the change agent specifies the basis for the absence of a token, prompts for arising the next day, and prompts for arising immediately so that they do not miss the next token.

Once the residents are awakened, they have about a half-hour to dress, groom themselves, make their beds, and pick up their rooms before breakfast preparation or early breakfast. During this period, some residents may require individual staff assistance. For example, a change agent may have to shape and chain shaving behavior with a resident who is unable to shave himself. The change agent in this instance places the razor in the resident's hand and puts the resident's hand to his face, then reinforces the behavior. Such step-by-step procedures involving specific prompts followed by social reinforcement for the behavior and eventual fading of the prompts require that the change agent be able to break a terminal behavior into its specific components. Such shaping does not mean that the change agent performs the behavior for the resident, but rather that the staff member assists the resident in performing the behavior for himself, and fades the assistance.

Appearance tokens are disbursed and recorded no earlier than twenty minutes after lights on. The change agent assigned this responsibility gives these tokens in front of a mirror on the basis of specific criteria (see appendix). The residents' appearance may not initially meet all requirements for terminal appearance, but they are still given a token accompanied by praise and specification for those which they meet, followed by a prompt for the next higher criteria to be met for the next appearance token. Criteria are rank ordered in terms of difficulty, beginning with the easiest to correct immediately. Residents should always be prompted to correct their easiest failure to earn a token at the next appearance check. Appearance tokens are also disbursed before early lunch and early dinner in front of the wall mirrors in the common living area. It is very important that change agents record the criteria met for the appearance token and those prompted for the next so that they consistently apply shaping principles. At the time morning appearance tokens are disbursed, residents are prompted regarding the bed and area token, which is disbursed and recorded following that for appearance. Disbursement of bed and area tokens, shaping with "meet or exceed" criteria, and successive prompting are identical to that described above for appearance tokens—as always, pairing social reinforcement with disbursal of tokens. The bed and area check is always finished before early breakfast.

This schedule is in effect seven days a week, except Saturday and Sunday, when some residents may purchase late sleeping privileges the night before. Names of late sleepers are indicated on the daily bed recording form, along with the time they are to get up (the latest being two hours after regular lights on in rented rooms). Tokens for getting up on time, appearance, and bed and area are disbursed to late sleepers in the same order as above during the half-hour after waking time. All residents except those in step 4 receive these tokens. Step 4 residents receive only social reinforcement and recording of terminal behavior (since they possess "credit cards").

2. *Meals.* Monday through Friday, breakfast, lunch, and dinner periods are scheduled on the unit with forty minutes allotted for serving and eating. However, since seating space is available for only twenty-six to twenty-eight people, while up to thirty-five staff and residents may be there for a meal, not all people can eat at the same time. Therefore, meal entrance is staggered with early meal and regular meal periods. The early meal period in each instance lasts thirty minutes, during which staff, residents working as dietary assistants (at regular meal rate), step 4 residents, and lower-step residents purchasing the higher-cost early meals may eat. The regular meal period starts twenty minutes after the early meal period and lasts only twenty minutes, during which residents purchasing the lower-cost regular meals may eat.

The same procedure is followed for all three meals. At the specified time, the change agent assigned rings the meal bell and announces "Time for early breakfast (lunch, dinner)" throughout the unit. Early meal tokens are collected and recorded as people line up at the serving kitchen. No one is allowed to enter the line for early meal without paying the appropriate number of tokens, and no one is allowed to purchase an early meal after five minutes have elapsed from the time early meal is announced. Twenty minutes after the early meal announcement, the regular meal is announced in the same way. Regular meal tokens are then collected and recorded as residents line up at the serving kitchen. No one is allowed to enter the regular meal line without paying the appropriate number of tokens within the five-minute period following announcement. During the initial serving or at any other time during the scheduled meal period after the serving line is completed, residents may purchase extra helpings, which are also recorded. All staff interact freely with residents during meals as long as they are talking "straight" and use social reinforcement for appropriate mealtime behavior. A single prompt and shaping with social reinforcement is used for inappropriate mealtime behavior—referring to the token consequence and thereafter totally ignoring if the inappropriate behavior does not terminate. As residents leave the dining area, the assigned change agent disburses and records tokens for appropriate mealtime behavior—as always, specifying criteria, socially reinforcing, and prompting for higher criteria when terminal behavior is not achieved. The criteria for appropriate mealtime behavior are rank ordered for difficulty (see appendix) and should be prompted in order from easiest to most difficult for any resident not meeting all criteria. Initially, early meal residents are prompted to leave at the end of their thirty-minute period and regular meal residents at the end of their twenty-minute period. After a resident has spent one week in the program, the prompt is faded, and a single announcement is made. Those who do not leave at the scheduled time do not receive the appropriate mealtime behavior token.

Monday through Friday, food pickup, meal preparation, serving, and cleanup are handled by residents on individual assignments (see below) as dietary assistants, under the supervision of the dietary personnel. When no residents at step 2 or above are assigned as dietary assistants and on weekends, these tasks are handled by residents as odd jobs, at one token per hour, plus early meals at the regular meal rate. A half-hour before the early meal period, the assigned change agent announces the availability of "temporary dietary jobs for one token an hour" and records and instructs residents who volunteer. If enough residents do not volunteer, specific residents may be prompted. In either case, tokens are disbursed and recorded at the beginning of the regular meal period for the first hour and on completion of the job for the second hour. (This job is very attractive for those who haven't earned enough tokens to eat.) On Saturday and Sunday, the dinner procedure is identical to that on weekdays. However, a single brunch period without differential charge for time of eating is substituted for breakfast and lunch. Brunch is announced and tokens collected and recorded in the same manner as early meals, except the line is open for entry for a full hour. A last call for brunch with individual prompts following the regular meal procedure is given at the end of the hour. On Saturday and Sunday residents who are up may purchase and prepare snacks in the unit kitchen. Coffee is always available and may be purchased (with tokens only) by residents during free periods, informal interaction periods, and any activity scheduled on the unit (at the discretion of the supervising staff member regarding feasibility).

3. *Class periods.* Each Monday through Friday morning, all residents in steps 1 and 2 are assigned to three forty-five minute periods for activities and classes conducted by staff educators. During each of these time periods, three separate classes are conducted. Each resident in step 1 and 2 is assigned to a class no larger than ten, to be attended in a group that is supervised by one of the unit staff members. Some classes are conducted on the unit itself using the classroom-lounge, activity pit, open living room, or bedrooms, while some classes are conducted in other places in the center. The content of these classes includes instruction in communications skills—reading, writing, and speaking—elementary mathematics, and practical home economics and grooming. Since residents are assigned to classes within each period on the basis of needed training, the composition of each class group during each period may vary. Staff members have a specified place on the unit at which they pick up and leave their groups at the beginning and end of each period.

For each of these periods the residents receive one token for attending and one token for participating. At the beginning of each scheduled period the staff member announces the period and the class and calls the names of the residents assigned to that period and class. For the first three days on a new schedule, residents who do not come in response to the announcement are individually prompted. Attendance tokens are disbursed and recorded as each resident arrives, including social reinforcement and behavioral specification. As soon as a class group convenes, the change agent escorts them to the place in which the class is held. During the class period, the responsibility for providing information and instructional content lies with the educator. Change agents do not interfere with the educator except to ensure that the educator does not inadvertently reinforce inappropriate behavior or violate procedural rules of the program.

The major role of the change agent during class periods is to shape and reinforce participation on the part of the residents through both social reinforcement and shaping chips. The shaping chips are used in three ways, but always with the purpose of bridging the gap between actual participative behavior and the receipt of the participation token at the end of the class period. First, the chips may be used on the basis of a gradually increasing criterion for attentiveness and participation just as tokens are used to shape appearance. Second, as a resident's participation increases in quality, the chips are used to reinforce continuous participation and attentiveness by disbursement and recording of a chip each time that a resident involves himself or herself in an appropriate verbal interaction, and, finally, by disbursement and recording of shaping chips every ten minutes for sustained attentive and participative behavior when the situation calls for it, such as in reading silently or continuous conversation. Five minutes before the end of a class participation period, shaping chips are exchanged for a token, as always, socially reinforcing and specifying the basis for receipt of the token. Both the behavior for receiving the chips and the target behavior are specified on the recording form to raise the criterion for token receipt gradually; to receive a participation token, the residents must meet or better their previous level for shaping chips, and, after the final level is reached, meet or exceed the number, up to continuous participation. At the end of the first period the residents are returned to the unit and the groups reformed for the second period, etc., until the end of period three.

Some residents reach step 3 and still need training in the academic areas. In those cases, class assignments in academic areas where they still need improvement are made as individual assignments instead of additional work assignments. In these instances the residents attend on their own and do not receive tokens during the activity or class period itself, but rather receive credit for individual assignment tokens to be paid at the weekly payday.

4. *Informal interaction.* All residents are scheduled for three to four informal interaction periods each day (five on Sunday). During the scheduled time all of the recreational facilities within the unit are available for the residents to use. Shaping chips (exchangeable for a participation token) are used to reinforce appropriate interaction. Certain activities go on in designated areas of the unit. For purposes of clarification, the procedures and staff responsibilities are listed by areas.

*Activity pit* (the sunken area in the center of the unit). One entrance to the pit is screened off, and residents wishing to use the materials in the pit are required to pay admission as they enter and to enter only on the hour. A change agent is assigned to admit and record the payment of the residents as they enter and to keep records of all token exchanges occurring within the pit. Writing tables, arts and crafts materials, radios and record players, cards, and other recreational materials are available. In general, games requiring a partner are free of charge, as is the use of any constructive materials or equipment (paints, etc.). Games that do not require a partner are rented at one token per hour. The radio and record player cost one token per half-hour and are rented without the resident's having to enter the pit. These are to be used in the lounge or the common living area. If these areas are full, however, residents may rent time in their rooms to play them.

Shaping chips are used to immediately reinforce the occurrence of appropriate social interaction during these periods. This includes such behaviors as a resident's responding to a staff request, responding courteously and appropriately to conversation from another resident or staff, initiating an appropriate conversation with another resident or staff, playing a game appropriately with another resident or staff, or cooperating with or helping another resident perform a constructive activity. Chips are exchanged for tokens at the end of each hour or when the scheduled informal interaction period is over (if less than an hour). The change agent assigned to the pit records such exchanges, ushers those residents out of the pit who do not wish to pay for another hour, and collects the tokens of those wishing to pay for another hour, if the schedule permits. While in the pit the staff member socially reinforces appropriate behaviors, is available as a partner for the residents, prompts the residents as to what alternative activities are available, and gives instructions as to how to use the equipment.

*TV room.* Residents purchase TV time at the rate of one token per hour or any fraction thereof. They may purchase time for the hour or the half-hour. The change agent assigned to supervising the TV room records all token payments and exchanges on the form to be kept in the room. Which programs the residents watch is determined by a group decision. During informal interaction, shaping chips are given to residents who contribute to such decisions constructively and appropriately. Any appropriate conversation occurring in the room is also reinforced with shaping chips. At the end of the hour, the change agent requests that residents who wish to watch another hour pay their tokens and that those who do not leave the room.

*Classroom-lounge.* The large room at the end of the unit functions both as an informal gathering place and as a quiet reading or writing room during informal interaction periods. Residents are charged one token per hour or any fraction of an hour and may enter the room on the hour or the half-hour. The piano located in the lounge may be rented at the rate of one token per half-hour. Appropriate interaction resulting from a resident's playing the piano (group singing) is reinforced with shaping chips. Also, residents who have rented record players or radios play them in the lounge, if in doing so they do not interfere with constructive or appropriate activities of other residents. Writing tables are available, as well as comfortable lounge chairs for reading. The same kinds of behaviors as previously listed are reinforced with shaping chips. Reading and letter writing are also reinforced. At the end of the hour, shaping chips are exchanged for tokens. The designated change agent records all transactions, requests payment from those residents wishing to remain or enter, and ushers out those not wishing to pay.

*Common living area.* When no meeting on the unit is scheduled, the common living area is free of charge during informal interaction. No equipment is available in this area, although residents may use or consume canteen purchases or items rented from other stations in this area. The appropriate behaviors designated elsewhere to receive shaping chips are reinforced.

Staff prompt residents to use the facilities of the other areas if the residents are not engaging in appropriate behaviors.

*Nondesignated areas.* Residents may rent time in their rooms during informal interaction at the rate of two tokens per hour or less. The staff member records payment and is responsible for informing the residents when their time has elapsed. It costs one token per hour to sit in the chairs placed by the wall. The residents may purchase coffee during informal interaction periods, without additional charge for being in the dining area.

5. *Small groups.* Residents meet in small reeducative therapy groups to develop skills in identifying specific problems and applying learning principles to those problems. The focus is on individual and interpersonal problem behaviors of the members in the groups as they are demonstrated in the center and the community setting. Groups provide opportunities for residents to receive help concerning their own problems from both staff and other residents. In addition, they learn to identify problems others are having and to offer solutions. The small group reeducative procedures used have been described in detail by Paul and Shannon (*Journal of Abnormal Psychology*, 1966, *71*, 124-135) and by Lazarus (in G. M. Gazda, ed., *Theories and Methods of Group Psychotherapy and Counseling* [Springfield: Thomas, 1969]).

There are four regular therapy groups, each consisting of seven members. These groups are heterogeneous as to level of functioning and include both sexes. Leaders of these groups are the two psychologists, the unit director, and the unit supervisor, each of whom meet continually with the same group.

When the residents progress to step 4, they are assigned to a new group (prerelease group) that focuses on training and planning for release as well as discussion of practical problems that might be encountered after release. Whenever possible, family members of residents in the prerelease group meet with this group. The liaison coordinator leads the prerelease group.

The four regular groups each meet two times per week on Monday through Thursday mornings. The prerelease group meets at least two to four times per week, depending upon the availability of the liaison coordinator, for a minimum of two and a half hours per week. Since group leaders regularly alternate their morning unit assignments, group meetings also alternate, with two groups regularly meeting on Monday and Wednesday one week and Tuesday and Thursday the following week. The other two groups alternate on a reverse schedule so that only two groups are meeting during any single informal interaction period.

Since at least fourteen residents meet in small groups during this informal interaction period, only one change agent is assigned to supervise informal interaction for the remainder of the residents (see the informal interaction section of the manual) during the times the small groups meet. The other change agents are free to attend the group meetings if they wish to develop skills in leading such groups.

The procedure for announcing and prompting attendance, disbursement of attendance tokens, shaping chips, and participation tokens follows that described under "Class periods" except the group leader is responsible for these activities.

6. *Community meeting.* Every Friday during the last period of the morning, all staff and residents attend a unit community meeting. Announcement, prompts, and attendance tokens for this meeting are identical to those described for class periods. This meeting is conducted by the unit director or unit supervisor, but all staff are encouraged to take an active part. During this meeting, approved passes are announced and residents taking these socially reinforced. Also, job openings are described, and the performance of residents on individual assignments is summarized. Similarly, residents advancing in step level or about to be released are announced and socially reinforced for their accomplishments. New residents on the unit are formally introduced during the first meeting following their arrival. The remainder of the meeting is devoted to presentations of any program changes, or clarification, discussion, and solution of problems that affect the entire unit (staff and residents); anything about which members have questions or concern may be discussed. Similarly, any news of interest to the entire unit is discussed. In general, all staff are free to offer problem solutions, suggestions, and recommendations, verbalizing the basis for them in terms of the immediate or ultimate consequences for residents. Social reinforcement and prompting is freely used in this period. Although shaping chips are not used during this meeting, participation tokens are disbursed at the end of the meeting.

7. *Activity periods.* All residents in step 1 are assigned to two supervised group activity periods each weekday afternoon. Like the morning classes these afternoon activities are assigned specifically to change agents in groups no larger than ten. All reinforcement and shaping procedures described for the class periods are followed for the unit activity periods; however, no additional educators are involved. Rather, the unit activity periods are conducted by the change agents themselves, sometimes combining two groups and two change agents. These activity periods are conducted on the unit, in the center, and downtown. They include crafts, gym, shopping trips,

training in practical skills, and other activities as suggested by the staff or residents. The major purpose is to involve step 1 residents in active behavior.

8. *Canteen time.* The canteen, located in the work area of the unit, is open every evening and is announced throughout the unit. During the first week in the program residents receive an individual prompt. The items that can be purchased with tokens include cigarettes, candies, cosmetics, grooming aids, soaps, inexpensive clothing, and use of a safety deposit box and token bank. In addition various items are available for overnight rental, including privacy screens, chairs, bedside stands, and writing tables. The smaller items are on display with the accompanying price list located on the nearby counter in the work area. Other items are on display in the storage rooms, and residents are exposed to these items as well.

In addition a mail-order catalog is available in the canteen from which residents may order items on a limited basis. When a resident indicates interest in a particular item, the staff determine the item's cost (in tokens) and availability. This information is given to the resident at canteen time the following evening. If residents order an item, they pay half the cost at the time the order is placed and the other half when the item is received. During canteen time a resident may also purchase coupons for one token each. The coupons can then be exchanged for items at the cafeteria or snack bar at the rate of ten cents per coupon.

On Monday evenings the last ten minutes of canteen time is spent in collecting rent for bedrooms for that Monday through the next Sunday nights. If any residents wish to move up to a more private or better furnished room, they indicate their desire at this time. In the event that the better rooms are all taken at that time, the residents are encouraged to either rent a screen to allow for more privacy in their present rooms until the more private room is available or to bid in competition with the room's current occupants. In the process of renting rooms, priority is always given to the residents at the highest step and in descending order of steps thereafter.

9. *Housekeeping and odd jobs.* Monday through Friday most unit housekeeping (dusting, sweeping, emptying ash trays, etc.) is handled by residents on individual assignments. On Saturday and Sunday major cleaning is done during three housekeeping periods. The change agents assigned to these periods announce the housekeeping period, during which all other activities are closed. All residents are then instructed in specific jobs and areas and supervised by the change agent, with tokens disbursed and recorded at the end of the period for participation.

Other odd jobs, such as running errands or carrying messages, are announced as the need arises during free periods on any day. These tasks pay one token, to be recorded and disbursed along with the resident's name and "odd job" on completion. These are limited and are never used for "make work" to provide tokens for residents who have not earned enough tokens. When no janitorial assistants are available on individual assignments, daily housekeeping duties are handled as odd jobs.

10. *Free periods.* During scheduled free periods and when no assignment is scheduled, residents may use all the unit facilities but those in the pit. The TV room, classroom-lounge, and common living area are all available. The major distinction between scheduled informal interaction and free time is that no shaping chips are given during free time so the residents cannot earn tokens at these times. Residents are, however, required to pay for goods and services at the usual rate. Change agents are assigned areas of responsibility so that token payments can be recorded at each station. Social reinforcement and prompts toward adaptive behavior are maintained, and staff are available for interaction with residents even though no shaping chips are given.

11. *Weekend activity period (gym).* Since staff coverage is usually short on weekends, residents not on passes are scheduled for only one activity period. Except that the activities are restricted to physical ones (gym or outdoor games) and that only attendance tokens are disbursed, this period follows the procedure for the regular activity periods.

12. *Bedtime routine and bathing.* Each evening, one hour before scheduled lights out, the announcement is made that rooms are open for bedtime preparation, and all other areas except the open living room are closed (except on Friday and Saturday evenings when the TV room and classroom-lounge may remain open an additional three and a half hours). During the bedtime preparation period, Sunday through Friday, eighteen residents per night are scheduled to take showers or baths, so that each resident is assigned three shower times per week. The shower schedule is announced, and residents are prompted once, five minutes before their bathing time. It is only when the residents are scheduled to bathe that they earn a token for doing so. They have twenty minutes in the shower area, during which they shampoo their hair (if necessary) and soap their bodies entirely. Change agents sometimes have to shape residents to take thorough showers and give tokens accordingly. On Saturdays, the same time period is set aside for residents wishing to take extra baths. The charge at these times is one token per bath or shower.

Unless the residents purchase a later bedtime,

they are to be in bed by lights off. Residents are prompted once, a half-hour before lights off, to start preparing for bed if they have not done so—socially reinforcing those who are. It costs one token per half-hour or any fraction thereof for a resident to be out of bed or have lights on in the room after lights out. Similarly, it costs one token per half-hour or any fraction thereof to be out of the room in the living area, Sunday through Thursday. The cost for staying up past lights out on Friday and Saturday is one token per hour up to two and a half hours, to be paid at the time for regular lights out.

Because bathing time is so tightly scheduled, one change agent is assigned to supervise each large bathroom during bedtime preparation. At lights out, one change agent checks each room on the women's side, turns off lights, collects and records tokens paid for late-bedtime privileges, and prompts dallying residents, e.g., "Unless you want to pay for staying up later, you should be in bed." Another change agent has similar duties on the men's side. On Friday and Saturday nights at lights out, tokens are collected and recorded for sleeping late the following morning.

During sleeping hours, at 11:30 P.M., 1:00 A.M., 3:00 A.M., and 5:00 A.M., residents who have soiled during the daytime or night at any time in the past week are awakened and escorted to the restroom. These residents are all sleeping in the free dorms. The procedure is to turn on the lights in the dorm and, without taking care to be quiet, to rouse the residents—stating the basis for the trip as a consequence for previous soiling. Other residents who complain of the lights or noise are prompted regarding the advantages of renting a more private room.

13. *Advancement through step levels.* The procedure for moving up in the step level system begins at the weekly group information and promotion sign-up meeting. Announcement, prompting, and attendance tokens for this meeting are handled in the same manner decribed under class periods. At this meeting, the assigned change agent reviews the minimal requirements for the step levels (see appendix for list of minimal step level requirements) and discusses the advantages of advancement in terms of consequences, i.e., the higher the residents advance, the more tokens they can earn and therefore the more goods and services they can purchase; more pass privileges are allowed with each higher step and the residents are closer to release with each move up. The change agent also reiterates that each resident is expected to advance through the system and then invites discussion of these points and asks if any residents feel that they are qualified to proceed to the next level. The question of a particular resident's making a step level advancement is open for discussion by the group, with staff's making sure that the discussion focuses only on behaviors that are relevant to a resident's advancement. It is also appropriate for staff to prompt the resident who has met the requirements but has not requested advancement, socially reinforcing both appropriate discussion and the accomplishment that qualifies for advancement—always focusing upon the individual's behavior as the determining factor. Each resident wishing to move up to the next step level then requests advancement by paying the required number of tokens and signing the request form. At each request, the resident is "buying" an interview with the liaison coordinator and rehabilitation counselor for consideration of individual assignments. New schedules and step level advancements are announced during the Friday community meeting following the request and become effective the next Monday.

14. *Individual assignments.* All residents in step 2 are required to work on individual assignments for three hours per day, typically from 1:00 to 4:00 P.M., Monday through Friday. Residents in steps 3 and 4 are required to work on individual assignments six hours per day, typically 8:00-11:00 A.M. and 1:00-4:00 P.M., Monday through Friday—the major variation being for dietary assistants, whose working hours necessarily fall around meals. Assignments are selected to provide work experiences for the resident, both in terms of giving added responsibility and in terms of reactivating old work skills or teaching new ones. Jobs are developed on the unit itself, such as janitorial assistant, dietary assistant, etc. Jobs are also developed within the various departments of the center, such as clerical assistant, carpenter's assistant, etc. Job assignments are made on the basis of each resident's needs in cooperation with the rehabilitation counselor, liaison coordinator and unit supervisor. The rehabilitation counselor is responsible for maintaining daily ratings of job performance on residents in steps 2, 3, and 4. Except for the first week on a new assignment, residents must maintain at least an average satisfactory rating to stay on the step level and job; during the first week the last day must be satisfactory.

Residents are prompted for attendance during the first week of a new assignment; thereafter, attendance is the total responsibility of the resident. Instead of disbursing tokens immediately, individual assignment tokens are delayed to a weekly payday on the unit each Monday at 12:00 noon. At this time, the residents are paid an hourly rate exceeding that available on step 1 for satisfactory performance, with increases for more than fifteen hours per week and bonuses for good and excellent performance. As always, at the time of disbursement, the basis of payment is specified and socially reinforced.

15. *Passes.* To expose residents to the outside world and prepare them for release, passes both within the center and downtown are not only encouraged but required for residents to move up through the step levels. Passes also serve as opportunities for residents to engage in cooperative behavior and to function in a semi-supervisory fashion when they accompany residents who are not yet eligible to take unaccompanied passes.

In addition to meeting the requirements of various step levels, passes are encouraged by making a portion of the residents' funds contingent upon their taking a pass. While it is true that a resident has to spend tokens for the privilege of taking a pass, each resident with a trust fund may also draw up to thirty dollars a month in connection with passes.

Three kinds of passes are available to residents: center passes, downtown passes, and overnight passes. The number and kinds of passes a resident takes to fulfill the requirements of a step level are listed under "Step Level Requirements and Privileges." The costs of passes (in tokens) are listed on the token cost sheet. In general, passes are cheaper when accompanied by either higher- or lower-level residents, staff, or relatives to encourage exposure to the outside community. Below is an outline of the times passes may be taken, maximum lengths of time per type of pass, and maximum amounts of money a resident may draw in connection with a particular type of pass.

Times passes may be taken:

1. Center passes (up to 3 hours)
   6:00-9:00 P.M. daily, except when scheduled for a meeting
   9:00 A.M.-12:00 noon Saturday and Sunday
   1:00-4:00 P.M. Saturday and Sunday

2. Downtown
   A. 4 hours + $2.00 maximum
      5:00-9:00 P.M. daily, except when scheduled for a meeting
      Between 5:00 P.M. & 12:00 midnight Friday
      Between 8:00 A.M. & 12:00 midnight Saturday
      Between 8:00 A.M. & 9:00 P.M. Sunday
   B. 4-8 hours + $4.00 maximum
      Between 5:00 P.M. & 12:00 midnight Friday
      Between 8:00 A.M. & 12:00 midnight Saturday
      Between 8:00 A.M. & 9:00 P.M. Sunday

3. Overnight
   A. 24 hours + $12.00 maximum
      Between 5:00 P.M. Friday & 9:00 P.M. Sunday
   B. 48 hours + $15.00 maximum
      Between 5:00 P.M. Friday & 9:00 P.M. Sunday

A resident is allowed to take up to thirty dollars a month in spending money with any combination of passes and token exchange.

A resident may take center passes during the specified time periods by paying the tokens to the specified change agent and signing the pass sheet, indicating time out, destination, and time of return. Downtown and overnight passes require prior approval, since funds frequently have to be arranged.

All residents are scheduled for a weekly evening information and pass sign-up meeting, conducted by a change agent. Announcement, prompting, and attendance tokens for this meeting are handled in the same manner as for class periods. During this meeting, information on the requirements and availability of downtown and overnight passes is presented—including eligibility, requirements, costs, etc. Residents are invited to sign up for any downtown or overnight pass desired during the following Friday through Thursday at this time—prompting residents who are eligible in terms of the consequences in moving up step levels, and obtaining money, socially reinforcing appropriate discussion and questions. The residents then request a pass and specific amount of money by signing up on the appropriate form, indicating the desired time out, destination, time in, and the individual, if any, accompanying. Half of the cost of the pass is collected and recorded at the time of signup, with the remainder collected and recorded at the time of departure. Those meeting requirements for requested passes are announced in the next community meeting.

## APPENDIX

The following pages contain detailed schedules and token disbursement times for residents at each step level, summary lists of ways to earn tokens, token costs, and change agent schedules. Copies of each recording form regularly completed by treatment staff are also available (Paul, in press). Details of staff activities each day may be seen by referring to these materials and the major content areas covered above, keeping in mind that day shift change agents and psychologists switch units daily at the noon hour, while evening and night shifts alternate between units every other day. In addition to the activities detailed above, all shifts overlap a half-hour, during which staff reports are made. Each staff member is given specific responsibilities regarding activities, recording forms, and residents on a daily basis. Night shift personnel are assigned specific summarizing duties for keeping continuous records.

A. Social-Learning Unit Resident Schedule

Monday-Friday

*5:55-7:00 A.M. Arise, dress, groom, make bed, room in order*

- 5:55 Lights on in free dormitories
- 6:00 Getting-up token distributed to residents in free dormitories
- 6:15 Personal appearance token distributed to residents in free dormitories
- 6:22 Area neat, bed made token distributed to residents in free dormitories
- 6:30 Lights on for residents in rented rooms
- 6:35 Getting-up token distributed to residents in rented rooms
- 6:45 Personal appearance token distributed to residents in rented rooms
- 6:50 Area neat, bed made token distributed to residents in rented rooms

*7:00-8:00 A.M. Breakfast*

7:00-7:30 Early breakfast
- 7:05 Latest entry to early breakfast
- 7:30 Latest appropriate meal behavior token distributed to residents purchasing early breakfast

7:20-7:40 Regular breakfast
- 7:25 Latest entry to regular breakfast
- 7:40 Latest appropriate meal behavior token distributed to residents purchasing regular breakfast

7:30-8:00 Breakfast cleanup

*8:00-11:00 A.M. Step 1 and 2 residents*
*8:15-11:00 A.M. Classes*

8:15-9:00 Period 1 (class A, B, or C)
- 8:15 Token given for attending period 1 class
- 8:55 Chips exchanged for participation token

9:10-9:55 Period 2 (class A, B, or C)
- 9:10 Token given for attending period 2 class
- 9:50 Chips exchanged for participation token

10:05-10:50 Period 3 (class A, B, or C)
- 10:05 Token given for attending period 3 class
- 10:45 Chips exchanged for participation token

*8:00-11:00 A.M. Step 3 and 4 residents: individual assignments*

*11:00 A.M.-12:00 noon Meetings or informal interaction*

*2 days a week, Monday-Thursday*
Small group meeting (group A, B, C, or D)

- 11:00 Token given for attending small group meeting
- 11:50 Chips exchanged for participation token

*2 days a week, Monday-Thursday*
Informal interaction (when no meeting is scheduled)

- 11:50 Chips exchanged for interaction token

*Friday Community meeting*

- 11:00 Token given for attending community meeting
- 11:45 Participation token given for community meeting

*12:00 Noon Personal appearance token distributed ("payday" for step 2 and 3 residents)*

*12:20-1:00 P.M. Lunch*

12:20-12:50 Early lunch
- 12:25 Latest entry to early lunch
- 12:50 Latest appropriate meal behavior token distributed to residents purchasing early lunch

12:40-1:00 Regular lunch
- 12:45 Latest entry to regular lunch
- 1:00 Latest appropriate meal behavior token distributed to residents purchasing regular lunch

12:50 Begin lunch cleanup

*1:00-4:00 P.M. Step 1 residents*

*1:00-1:45 P.M. Informal interaction*

Individual assignment interviews
Individual appointments
- 1:40 Chips exchanged for interaction token

*1:45-4:00 P.M. Unit activities*

1:50-2:45 Activity period 1 (activity group A, B, C, or D)
1:50 Token given for attending activity 1
2:40 Chips exchanged for participation token

3:00-3:50 Activity period 2 (activity group A, B, C, or D)
3:00 Token given for attending activity 2
3:45 Chips exchanged for participation token

*1:00-4:00 P.M. Step 2, 3, and 4 residents: inidivdual assignments*

*4:00-5:00 P.M. Free time and dinner prepaation*

4:30-5:00 Dinner preparation
4:40 Personal appearance token distributed

*5:00-6:00 P.M. Dinner*

5:00-5:30 Early dinner
5:05 Latest entry to early dinner
5:30 Latest appropriate meal behavior token distributed to residents purchasing early dinner

5:20-5:40 Regular dinner
5:25 Latest entry to regular dinner
5:40 Latest appropriate meal behavior token distributed to residents purchasing regular dinner

5:30 Begin dinner cleanup

*6:00-9:00 P.M. Passes*

*6:00-7:00 P.M. Canteen and free time*

*7:00-8:00 P.M. Meetings or informal interaction*

Informal interaction: Monday, Wednesday, Friday
7:55 Chips exchanged for interaction token

Weekly group information and promotion sign-up: Tuesday
7:00 Token given for attendance

Weekly group information and pass sign-up: Thursday
7:00 Token given for attendance

*8:00-9:00 P.M. Informal interaction or committee meetings*

8:55 Chips exchanged for interaction token

*9:00-10:00 P.M. Bedtime preparation*

Token given when bath or shower is completed (as scheduled 3 times per week)

*10:00 P.M. Regular lights out*

*10:30 P.M. Late lights out*

*11:30 P.M.-12:30 A.M. Late bed preparation (Friday only)*

*12:30 A.M. Late lights out (Friday only)*

Saturday and Sunday

*5:55-7:00 A.M. Arise, dress, groom, make bed, room in order (except late sleepers)*

5:55 Lights on in free dormitories
6:00 Getting-up token distributed to residents in free dormitories
6:15 Personal appearance token distributed to residents in free dormitories
6:22 Area neat, bed made token distributed to residents in free dormitories
6:30 Lights on in rented rooms
6:35 Getting-up token distributed to residents in rented rooms
6:45 Personal appearance token distributed to regular risers in rented rooms
6:50 Area neat, bed made token distributed to regular risers in rented rooms

*Late Sleepers*

8:30 A.M. Latest arising time for late sleepers
Getting up token distributed 5 minutes after lights on
Appearance token for late sleepers distributed 25 minutes after lights on
Area clean, bed made token distributed 30 minutes after lights on

*8:30-9:00 A.M. Free time, may purchase and prepare snacks*

*9:00-12:00 Noon Passes*

*9:05-10:00 A.M.*

*Saturday Housekeeping*
9:45 Token for performing housekeeping assignment given

*Sunday Informal interaction*
9:55    Chips exchanged for interaction token

*10:00-11:00 A.M. Housekeeping*

10:45    Token for performing house-keeping assignment given

*11:00-11:30 A.M. Free period and brunch preparation*

11:05    Personal appearance token distributed

*11:30 A.M.-1:00 P.M. Brunch*

12:30    Latest entry to brunch
12:45    Latest appropriate meal behavior token distributed

*1:00-4:00 P.M. Passes*

*1:00-2:00 P.M.*

*Saturday Free time*

*Sunday Informal interaction*
1:55    Chips exchanged for interaction token

*2:00-3:00 P.M.*

*Saturday Informal interaction*
2:55    Chips exchanged for interaction token

*Sunday Free time*

*3:00-4:00 P.M.*

*Saturday Gym*
3:50    Token given for attendance at gym

*Sunday Informal interaction*
3:55    Chips exchanged for interaction token

*4:00-5:00 P.M. Free time and dinner preparation*

4:30-5:00 Dinner preparation
4:40    Personal appearance token distributed

*5:00-6:00 P.M. Dinner*

5:00-5:30 Early dinner
5:05    Latest entry to early dinner
5:30    Latest appropriate meal behavior token given to residents purchasing early dinner

5:20-5:40 Regular dinner
5:25    Latest entry to regular dinner
5:40    Latest appropriate meal behavior token given to residents purchasing regular dinner

5:30    Begin dinner cleanup

*6:00-9:00 P.M. Passes*

*6:00-7:00 P.M. Canteen & free time*

*7:00-9:00 P.M. Informal interaction*

7:55    Chips exchanged for interaction token
8:55    Chips exchanged for interaction token

*9:00-10:00 P.M. Bedtime preparation*

Token given when bath or shower completed (as scheduled, Sunday only)

*10:00 P.M. Regular lights out*

*10:30 P.M. Late lights out*

*11:30 P.M.-12:30 A.M. Late bed preparation (Saturday only)*

*12:30 A.M. Late lights out (Saturday only)*

B. Ways to earn tokens

I. Self-maintenance

A. Getting up on time: 1 token each morning

B. Appearance: 1 token 3 times per day

1. Proper use of makeup
2. Clean fingernails
3. Hair combed
4. Teeth brushed
5. All appropriate clothing on
6. Clothing buttoned, zipped, tucked
7. Clothing clean and neat
8. Body clean
9. No odor
10. Shaven
11. Hair cut appropriately (males)

C. Bed made, area clean: 1 token each morning

1. Nothing on floor or bed
2. Sheets tucked in
3. Blanket straight and neat
4. Pillow straight and neat
5. Bedding not soiled

6. Furniture in appropriate places
7. Everything put away properly
8. Drawers and closets neat

D. Appropriate mealtime behavior: 1 token each meal

1. Return tray properly
2. No stealing and grabbing
3. Clean clothing, face, and hands
4. Courteous table manners
5. Proper use of utensils
6. Proper use of hands
7. No sloppiness
8. No gulping
9. Appropriate interaction

E. Bathing: 1 token 3 times per week

1. Obtain and return soap and towel
2. Exchange clothes
3. Soap and rinse head area (face, neck, ears)
4. Soap and rinse upper half of body (shoulders, back, armpits, arms, hands, chest)
5. Soap and rinse lower half of body (crotch, legs, feet)
6. Clean tub or shower stall
7. Finish within 20 minutes

II. Communication Skills

A. Attend classes: 1 token for each of 3 classes per weekday
B. Participate in classes: 1 token for each of 3 classes per weekday

III. Interpersonal Skills

A. Informal interaction: 1 token 3 or 4 times per day

1. Responding to requests
2. Responding courteously and appropriately to conversation
3. Initiating courteous and appropriate conversation
4. Cooperative interaction with other residents and with staff (doing things together)
5. Helping another resident perform a constructive activity

B. Attend small group meetings: 1 token 2 times per week

C. Participate in small group meetings: 1 token 2 times per week

D. Attend community meeting: 1 token once a week

E. Participate in community meeting: 1 token once a week

F. Attend unit activity periods: 1 token for each of 2 periods per weekday

G. Participate in unit activity periods: 1 token for each of 2 periods per weekday

H. Attend weekly informational meetings: 1 token twice a week

I. Attend and participate in unit recreational activities: 1 token each weekend

IV. Work and Housekeeping Skills

A. Take part in maintenance of unit

1. Odd jobs: 1 token per hour as requested
2. Housekeeping periods: 1 token per each of 3 periods on weekends

B. Individual assignments: 2 tokens per hour up to 15 hours; 3 tokens per hour each hour thereafter; bonus paid at rate of ½ per day for each day of good job performance rating and 3 tokens per week if all days were rated good, 1 token per each day of excellent job performance rating, and 7 tokens per week if all days were rated excellent.

C. Token Costs

I. Meals (Pay before each meal)

A. Weekdays
1. Regular breakfast 3
Early breakfast 4
Extra food (per helping) 1

2. Regular lunch 6
Early lunch 8
Extra food (per helping) 1

3. Regular dinner 5
Early dinner 7
Extra food (per helping) 1

B. Weekends
1. Brunch 8
Extra food (per helping) 1

    2. Regular dinner 5
       Early dinner 7
       Extra food (per helping) 1

II. Sleeping Quarters (Rent weekly)

   A. Rooms (per week)
      1. 6-bed dormitory 0
      2. 4-bed dormitory (drapes) 10
      3. 2-bed room (drapes) 16
      4. 1-bed room (fully equipped) 22

   B. Room accessories (per night)
      1. Bedside stand 1
      2. Chair 1
      3. Screen 1

III. Passes (during regular pass hours)

   A. Center passes (up to 3 hours) (pay at departure; 6-9 P.M. weekdays, all day Saturday and Sunday)
      1. Accompanied or unaccompanied 3
      2. If accompanying a lower step level resident 2

   B. Downtown passes (pay half at sign-up, remainder at departure; 5-9 P.M. Sunday-Thursday, 5-12 P.M. Friday, 8 A.M.-12 P.M. Saturday and Sunday)
      1. Up to 4 hours + $2.00 maximum
         A. Accompanied 6
         B. Unaccompanied 10
         C. If accompanying lower step level resident 6

      2. 4-8 hours + $4.00 maximum
         A. Accompanied 12
         B. Unaccompanied 15
         C. If accompanying lower step level resident 12

      3. 8-16 hours + $8.00 maximum
         A. Accompanied 18
         B. Unaccompanied 20
         C. If accompanying lower step level resident 18

   C. Overnight passes (pay half at sign-up, remainder at departure; 5 P.M. Friday-9 P.M. Sunday)
      1. 24 hours + $12.00 maximum
         A. Accompanied 25
         B. Unaccompanied 30

      2. 48 hours + $14.00 maximum
         A. Accompanied 40
         B. Unaccompanied 50

IV. Recreational activities (pay at time of use; double at other times)

   A. TV (during free time and informal interaction—per hour) 1
   B. Classroom-lounge (during free time and informal interaction—per hour) 1
      1. Piano (per ½ hour) 1
   C. Pit (during informal interaction—per hour) 1
      1. Games requiring partner 0
      2. Solitary games (during free time and informal interaction—per hour) 1
      3. Constructive equipment 0
      4. Radio, record player (during free time and informal interaction—per ½ hour) 1
      (To be played in lounge or common living area)

V. Time privileges (pay at time of use, except C)

   A. Staying up between 10:00-10:30 P.M. on weekdays
      1. Lights on or out of bed in room 1
      2. In living area 2
   B. Up after 10:00 P.M. on Friday and Saturday (per hour to 12:30 A.M.) 1
   C. Sleep-in time on weekends (to be paid night before—per hour to 8:30 A.M.) 1

VI. Privacy (pay at time of use)

   A. Unscheduled time in room
      1. Time in room during free time (per hour or fraction of hour) 1
      2. Time in room during scheduled activities (per hour or fraction of hour) 2
   B. Unscheduled time on unit during scheduled activities (except time out—per hour) 2

VII. Sign-up for advancement to higher step levels (pay at time of sign-up)

   A. From step 1 to step 2 1
   B. From step 2 to step 3 2
   C. From step 3 to step 4 (credit card) 100

VIII. Miscellaneous (pay at time obtained)

   A. Resident requested appointment with staff (per 5 minutes) 1
   B. Telephone (per 3 minutes) 1
   C. Extra baths (per bath or shower) 1
   D. Hiring laundry service (per load) 1
   E. Haircut or beauty shop (per visit) 1
   F. Resident requested drugs (per pill) 1
   G. Use of unit bank (per transaction) 1
   H. Safety deposit box (per week) 1

I. Sitting in chairs placed by walls (per hour)   1

IX. Canteen: Items as priced on display (pay at purchase time)

X. Use of kitchen facilities (pay at time of use)
   A. Coffee (when a resident is scheduled to be on unit—per cup)   1
   B. Kitchen snacks when scheduled (per item)   1

XI. Fines: A resident who has been fined can purchase nothing but regular lunch until the fine has been paid in full. The resident will also be sent to time out to be released after a specified period of quiet activity. (See appendix B and chapter 28 for revised fine costs.)

A. Intolerable acts that are offensive or interfere with rights or desirable activities of others (for example, creating a fire hazard, excessive swearing, damaging people or things, making excessive noise, publicly displaying inappropriate sexual behavior, spitting, etc.—per incident)   25

B. Use of goods or facilities without paying required tokens: double usual charges as fine

C. Absence or leave without prior explanation and approval (per ½ hour)   5

D. Stealing: Resident will turn over all tokens in possession and will be placed on a special system + 25 token fine

D. Social-Learning Unit Change Agent Schedule:

Monday-Friday Morning (0800-1300)

*Change Agent 1*

At 0800
   Staff report & in-service training.

At 0815: Period 1 class
   Announce class C.
   Record & disburse attendance tokens (B32).*
   Record & disburse shaping chips during class hour (B32).

At 0900
   Complete exchange of shaping chips for participation tokens. Record (B32).

At 0910: Period 2 class
   Announce class A.
   Record & disburse attendance tokens (B32).
   Record & disburse shaping chips during class hour (B32).

At 0955
   Complete exchange of shaping chips for participation tokens. Record (B32).

At 1005: Period 3 class
   Announce class A.
   Record & disburse attendance tokens (B32).
   Record & disburse shaping chips during class hour (B32).

At 1050
   Complete exchange of shaping chips for participation tokens. Record (B32).

*Change Agent 2*

At 0800
   Staff report & in-service training.

At 0815: Period 1 class
   Announce class B.
   Record & disburse attendance tokens (B32).
   Record & disburse shaping chips during class hour (B32).

At 0900
   Complete exchange of shaping chips for participation tokens. Record (B32).

At 0910: Period 2 class
   Announce class B.
   Record & disburse attendance tokens (B32).
   Record & disburse shaping chips during class hour (B32).

At 0955
   Complete exchange of shaping chips for participation tokens. Record (B32).

At 1005: Period 3 class
   Announce class B.
   Record & disburse attendance tokens (B32).
   Record & disburse shaping chips during class hour (B32).

At 1050
   Complete exchange of shaping chips for participation tokens. Record (B32).

At 1055 (Friday)
   Ask for volunteers to set up pit for community meeting.

*Change Agent 3 (psychologist will sub)*

At 0800
   Staff report & in-service training.

At 0815: Period 1 class
   Announce class A.
   Record & disburse attendance tokens (B32).
   Record & disburse shaping chips during class hour (B32).

At 0900
   Complete exchange of shaping chips for participation tokens. Record (B32).

At 0910: Period 2 class
   Announce class C.
   Record & disburse attendance tokens (B32).
   Record & disburse shaping chips during class hour (B32).

At 0955
   Complete exchange of shaping chips for participation tokens. Record (B32).

At 1005: Period 3 class
   Announce class C.
   Record & disburse attendance tokens (B32).
   Record & disburse shaping chips during class hour (B32).

At 1050
   Complete exchange of shaping chips for participation tokens. Record (B32).

---

*Numbers in parentheses refer to the specific form used (see Paul, in press).

## The Social-Learning Program Manual

| Change Agent 1 | Change Agent 2 | Change Agent 3 (Psychologist will sub) |
|---|---|---|
| At 1100<br>Announce informal interaction (M-Th). Announce availability of activities, collect & record tokens for TV, lounge, living room (B2,B3,B4,B5,B6,B7,B8, B10).<br>Record & disburse shaping chips (M-Th) (B33).<br>Announce community meeting (Fri).<br>Disburse & record attendance tokens (B32). | At 1100<br>Assist change agent 1 as needed. | At 1100<br>Small group meetings (M-T-W-Th).<br>Record & disburse shaping chips (B32).<br>Community meeting, keep log (Friday). |
| At 1155<br>Complete exchange of shaping chips for interaction tokens (M-Th). Record (B33).<br>Complete recording and disbursement of participation tokens for community meeting (Fri) (B32). | At 1155<br>Announce availability of dietary jobs at 1 token/hour, send volunteers to dietary worker.<br>Record (B22). | At 1155<br>Complete exchange of shaping chips for participation tokens (M-Th).<br>Record (B32). |
| At 1200<br>Announce appearance check. Disburse and record appearance tokens (B29).<br>Record & prompt for next check (B29).<br>Tell residents to pick up drugs.<br>Catch up on recording if necessary. | At 1200<br>Disburse drugs (do not announce).<br>Take care of tests for diabetics. Monday: send step 2 and step 3 residents to change agent 3 for pay.<br>Catch up on recording if necessary. | At 1200<br>Payday. Disburse and record tokens for step 2 and 3 residents (M) (B19). |
| At 1220<br>Eat lunch, interact with residents.<br>Record meal behavior (B31).<br>Disburse tokens for appropriate meal behavior (B31).<br>Prompt for next meal, record (B31). | At 1220<br>Announce early lunch.<br>Collect tokens & record (B1).<br>Give form B1 to dietary worker.<br>Eat lunch, interact with residents.<br>Assist with meal behavior. | |
| At 1240<br>Announce regular lunch.<br>Collect tokens & record (B1). | | 1240-1300 (Psychologist)<br>Record meal behavior (B31).<br>Disburse tokens for appropriate meal behavior (B31).<br>Prompt for next meal, record (B31). |
| | At 1242<br>Announce free time for residents.<br>Collect & record tokens for use of TV, lounge, small living room, bedroom, etc. (B2,B3,B4,B7,B8,B10).<br>Handle medical meals. | |
| 1245-1315<br>Take break. | 1245-1315<br>Take break. | |

Monday-Friday Afternoons (1300-1630)

| Change Agent 1 | Change Agent 2 | Change Agent 3 |
|---|---|---|
| At 1300<br>Collect & record pit entrance & activities (B5,B6,B7).<br>Disburse and record shaping chips for informal interaction in pit (B33). | At 1300<br>Announce informal interaction.<br>Collect & record tokens for all areas except pit (B2,B3,B4,B8, B10).<br>Disburse and record shaping chips for informal interaction. | At 1300<br>Assist where needed. |
| At 1340 (Pit)<br>Complete exchange of shaping chips for interaction tokens, record (B33). | At 1340<br>Complete exchange of shaping chips for interaction tokens, record (B33). | |
| At 1350<br>Announce activity 1 (a).<br>Record & disburse attendance tokens (B32).<br>Record & disburse shaping chips during activity (B32). | At 1350<br>Announce activity 1 (b).<br>Record & disburse attendance tokens (B32).<br>Record & disburse shaping chips during activity (B32). | At 1350<br>Announce activity 1 (c).<br>Record & disburse attendance tokens (B32).<br>Record & disburse shaping chips during activity (B32). |
| At 1445<br>Complete exchange of shaping chips for participation tokens, record (B32). | At 1445<br>Complete exchange of shaping chips for participation tokens, record (B32). | At 1445<br>Complete exchange of shaping chips for participation tokens, record (B32). |

*Programs, Populations, and Procedures*  94

*Change Agent 1*

1445-1500
Take break.

At 1500
Announce activity 2 (a).
Record & disburse attendance tokens (B32).
Record & disburse shaping chips (B32).

At 1540
Complete exchange of shaping chips for participation tokens, record (B32).

At 1550 (Free time for residents)
Collect & record tokens for TV, lounge (B2, B3, B4).

At 1600
Staff report & in-service training.

*Change Agent 2*

1445-1500
Take break

At 1500
Announce activity 2 (b).
Record & disburse attendance tokens (B32).
Record & disburse shaping chips (B32).

At 1540
Complete exchange of shaping chips for participation tokens, record (B32).

At 1550 (Free time for residents)
Collect & record tokens for living room, chairs, bedroom, & nondesignated areas (B7, B8, B10).

At 1600
Staff report & in-service training.

*Change Agent 3 (Psychologist will sub)*

1445-1500
Take break.

At 1500
Announce activity 2 (c).
Record & disburse attendance tokens (B32).
Record & disburse shaping chips (B32).

At 1540
Complete exchange of shaping chips for participation tokens, record (B32).

At 1600
Staff report & in-service training.

Monday-Friday Evening (1600-2430)

*Change Agent 1*

At 1600
Staff report & in-service training.

At 1615
Prepare drugs.

At 1635
Check for tokens for medical meals.

At 1640
Distribute drugs. Do not announce. Note: when only one change agent on duty, place drugs by mirror.

At 1700
Eat (try to be first in line).
Interact with residents.

At 1720
Announce regular dinner.
Collect tokens & record (B1). Give form B1 to dietary worker to collect & record extra portions.

At 1722
Record meal behavior (B31).
Disburse tokens for appropriate meal behavior.
Record & prompt for next meal (B31).
By 1730, finish early dinner residents.
By 1740, finish regular dinner residents.

At 1800
Announce canteen time.
Sell items and record for each resident who buys or rents items (B17, B18; Monday-B21).
After canteen announce free time.

*Change Agent 2*

At 1600
Staff report & in-service training.

At 1630
Announce availability of dietary jobs at 1 token/hour, send volunteers to dietary worker, record (B22). Give appearance token to volunteers (B29).

At 1640
Announce appearance check.
Disburse & record appearance tokens (B29).
Prompt & record for next check (B29).
Tell resident to go pick up drugs.

At 1700
Announce early dinner. (Wait until change agent 1 is through disbursing drugs to be first in line.)
Collect tokens & record (B1). Give form B1 to dietary worker to collect & record extra portions.

1702-1720
Record meal behavior (B31).
Disburse tokens for appropriate meal behavior.
Record & prompt for next meal (B31).
Give form B31 to change agent 1.

At 1720
Eat.
Interact with residents.

At 1725
Serve medical meals.

At 1740
Collect & record tokens for free time activities (B2, B3, B4, B7, B8, B10).

At 1800
Assist as needed.
After canteen collect and record tokens for free time activities (B2, B3, B4, B7, B8, B10).
Prepare drugs.

*Change Agent 1*

At 1900
 Collect tokens and record for residents taking center passes (B26).
 Collect & record pit entrance & activity tokens (B5, B6, B7).
 Disburse & record shaping chips for informal interaction in pit (B33).
 Serve coffee to residents.

At 1900 (Tuesday)
 Announce group information and promotion sign-up meeting.
 Conduct meeting and collect advancement requests and tokens when appropriate (B24).
 After meeting announce free time.
 Serve coffee to residents.

At 1900 (Thursday)
 Disburse & record attendance tokens for information and pass meeting (B32).
 Assist change agent 2 with meeting.
 Collect & record tokens for free time activities (B2, B3, B4, B7, B8, B10).

At 1955 (M, W, F)
 Exchange shaping chips for interaction tokens in pit, record (B33).

At 2000
 Collect & record pit entrance & activity tokens (B5, B6, B7).
 Disburse & record shaping chips for informal interaction in pit (B33).
 Serve coffee to residents.

At 2055
 Exchange shaping chips for interaction tokens in pit, record (B33).

At 2100
 Announce bedtime preparation.
 Supervise bathrooms.
 Disburse & record bathing tokens (B20).

At 2200
 Collect & record free time activity tokens (Friday) (B2, B3, B4, B7, B8, B10, B11).
 Assist change agent 2.

At 2230
 Turn off late lights.

At 2300
 Collect & record free time activity tokens (Friday) (B2, B3, B4, B7, B8, B10, B11).

At 2330
 Escort soilers to bathroom (female).

At 2400
 Staff report & in-service training.
 Give & record report.

Monday-Friday Night (0000-0830)

At 0000
 Staff report & in-service training.

*Change Agent 2*

At 1900 (M, W, F)
 Announce informal interaction.
 Collect & record tokens for all areas but pit (B2, B3, B4, B8, B10, B11).
 Disburse & record shaping chips for informal interaction outside pit (B33).

At 1900 (Tuesday)
 Disburse & record attendance tokens for group meeting (B32).
 Assist change agent 1 with meeting.
 Collect & record tokens for free time activities (B2, B3, B4, B7, B8, B10).

At 1900 (Thursday)
 Announce information and pass sign-up meeting.
 Conduct meeting and collect pass requests and tokens when appropriate (B27).
 After meeting announce free time.
 Serve coffee to residents.

At 1955 (M, W, F)
 Exchange shaping chips for interaction tokens, record (B33).

At 2000
 Announce informal interaction.
 Collect & record tokens for all areas but pit (B2, B3, B4, B8, B10, B11).
 Disburse & record shaping chips for informal interaction (B33).

At 2055
 Exchange shaping chips for interaction tokens, record (B33).

At 2100
 Admit & record residents returning from passes (B26, B27).
 Prepare drugs.
 Assist change agent 1 with showers.

At 2130
 Prompt residents who are not preparing for bed.
 (Friday only) Collect & record late sleepers for Saturday (B13).

By 2145
 Distribute drugs.

At 2155
 Turn off lights.
 Prompt dallying residents.
 Collect & record late light tokens (B13).
 Collect & record late bed tokens (Friday) (B13).

By 2200
 Complete medical treatments.

At 2230
 Record residents returning from passes (Friday) (B26).
 Assist change agent 1.

At 2330
 Escort soilers to bathroom (male).

At 2335
 Announce late bed preparation (Friday).

At 2400
 Staff report & in-service training.

At 0000
 Staff report & in-service training.

## Change Agent 1

At 0030 (Friday only)
Late lights out (males).

At 0100
Escort soilers to bathroom (males); other duties as required.

At 0200
Prepare drugs, drug inventory, cards, & orders.

At 0300
Escort soilers to bathroom (males); other duties as required.

At 0400
Prepare drugs; drug inventory, cards, & orders.

At 0500
Escort soilers to bathroom (males); other duties as required.

At 0555
Awaken free bed dorm & dietary workers.

At 0600
Record & disburse getting up tokens; free bed dorm & dietary (B30). Prompt for rising so appearance token is not missed (do not record prompt).

At 0615
Assist change agent 2 as needed.

By 0630
Finish bed & area check; free bed dorms.
Record & disburse bed & area tokens; dietary assistants (B30).
Record & prompt for next bed & area token (B30).
Distribute drugs to dietary assistants.

At 0650
Distribute drugs to all but dietary assistants.

By 0700
Distribute drugs to others.

At 0700
Eat (try to be first in line).
Interact with residents.

At 0720
Announce regular breakfast.
Collect & record tokens for regular breakfast (B1).

## Change Agent 2

At 0030 (Friday only)
Late lights out (females).

At 0100
Escort soilers to bathroom (females); other duties as required.

At 0200
Summarize data sheets.

At 0300
Escort soilers to bathroom (females); other duties as required.

At 0400
Summarize data sheets.

At 0500
Escort soilers to bathroom (females); other duties as required.

No earlier than 0615
Start appearance check in free bed dorms.
Record & disburse appearance tokens, dietary (B29).
Prompt for next appearance and record prompt (B29).
Prompt for bed & area, same prompt from day before (do not record prompt).

At 0630
Awaken residents in rented rooms.

At 0635
Record & disburse getting-up tokens in rented rooms (B30). Prompt for rising so appearance token is not missed (do not record prompt).

No earlier than 0645
Start appearance check in rented rooms.
Record & disburse appearance tokens to all except dietary assistants (B29).
Record & prompt for next appearance check (B29).
Prompt for bed & area; same prompt as day before (do not record prompt).

By 0700
Finish bed & area check in rented rooms.
Record & disburse bed & area tokens to all except dietary assistants (B30).
Record & prompt for next bed & area token (B30).

At 0700
Announce early breakfast (wait until change agent 1 is through distributing drugs to be first in line).
Collect & record tokens for early breakfast (B1).

0702-0722
Give form B1 to dietary worker to record & collect tokens for extra portions.
Record meal behavior (B31).
Record & disburse tokens for appropriate meal behavior (B31). Record & prompt for next meal (B31).
Get food just before regular meal is announced.

At 0722
Give form B31 to change agent 1.
Eat, interact with residents.

## Change Agent 1

0722-0740
Give form B1 to dietary worker to record & collect tokens for extra portions.
Record meal behavior (B31).
Record & disburse tokens for appropriate meal behavior (B31).
Record & prompt for next meal (B31).
By 0730, finish early residents.
By 0740, finish regular residents.

At 0800
Staff report & in-service training.
Give and record report

### Weekend Mornings (0800-1300)

At 0800
Staff report & in-service training.

At 0815
Announce odd jobs, snack preparation, record (B22).

At 0825
Awaken late sleepers.

By 0830
Record & disburse getting up tokens to late sleepers (B30). Prompt for rising, so appearance token is not missed.

By 0850
Record & disburse appearance tokens to late sleepers (B29).
Record & prompt for next appearance check (B29).
(Prompt as day before for bed & area.)

By 0855
Record & disburse bed & area tokens to late sleepers (B30).
Record & prompt for next bed & area token (B30).

At 0905 (Housekeeping): Saturday only
Announce housekeeping period, request volunteers for housekeeping at 1 token/hour; assign jobs & supervise. Record (B2, B3, B4, B5, B6, B7, B8, B9, B10).

At 0905 (Informal interaction): Sunday only
Announce informal interaction.
Collect & record tokens for all areas except pit (B2, B3, B4, B8, B10).
Record & disburse shaping chips (B33).

At 0955 Sunday only
Exchange chips for interaction tokens, record (B33).

At 1000 (Housekeeping)
Announce housekeeping period, request volunteers for housekeeping at 1 token/hour; assign jobs & supervise. Record (B2, B3, B4, B5, B6, B7, B8, B9, B10).

At 1100 (Free time for residents)
Collect & record tokens for free time activities (B2, B3, B4, B8, B10, B11).
Announce availability of dietary jobs at 1 token/hour, send volunteers to dietary worker, record (B34).

At 1105
Announce appearance check.
Disburse & record appearance tokens (B29).
Prompt for next check, tell residents to pick up drugs.

## Change Agent 2

At 0740
Collect & record tokens for free time activities (B2, B3, B4, B7, B8, B10).
Serve medical meals.

At 0800
Staff report & in-service training.

At 0800
Staff report & in-service training.
Prepare drugs.

At 0830
Announce availability of snacks.
Collect & record snacks purchased (B16).

By 0900
Distribute drugs to late sleepers.

At 0905 (Housekeeping): Saturday only
Record job assignments (B34).

At 0945 Saturday only
Disburse & record participation in housekeeping tokens (B34).

At 0905 (Informal interaction): Sunday only
Collect & record pit entrance and activities (B5, B6, B7).
Record & disburse shaping chips in pit (B33).

At 0955 Sunday only
Exchange chips for interaction tokens, record (B33).

At 1000 (Housekeeping)
Record job assignments (B34).

At 1045
Disburse & record participation in housekeeping tokens (B34).

At 1105
Disburse drugs (do not announce).
Do clinitest.

*Change Agent 1*

At 1130
    Announce brunch, collect tokens & record (B1).
    Give clipboard to dietary worker to collect & record extra portions & entry to line.

At 1133
    Record meal behavior (B31).
    Disburse tokens for appropriate meal behavior (B31).
    Record & prompt for next meal (B31).

At 1200
    Eat, interact with residents.

At 1225
    Announce last call for brunch, collect & record tokens for meal entry (B1).
    Interact with residents in living area.

At 1255
    Record & disburse tokens for 2d hour's work to dietary assistants (B34).

Weekend Afternoons (1300-1630)

At 1300 (Free time): Saturday only
    Collect & record tokens for all free time activities (B2, B3, B4, B7, B8, B10, B11).
    Interact with residents.

At 1300 (Informal interaction): Sunday only
    Announce informal interaction.
    Collect & record tokens for all areas except pit (B2, B3, B4, B8, B10).
    Record & disburse shaping chips (B33).

At 1355 Sunday only
    Exchange chips for interaction tokens, record (B33).

At 1400 (Informal interaction): Saturday only
    Announce informal interaction.
    Collect & record tokens for all areas except pit (B2, B3, B4, B8, B10).
    Record & disburse shaping chips (B33).

At 1455 Saturday only
    Exchange chips for interaction tokens, record (B33).

At 1400 (Free time): Sunday only
    Collect & record tokens for all free time activities (B2, B3, B4, B7, B8, B10, B11).
    Interact with residents.

At 1500 (Gym): Saturday only
    Announce gym; accompany & supervise in gym.

At 1550 Saturday only
    Disburse & record attendance tokens (B32).

At 1500 (Informal interaction): Sunday only
    Announce informal interaction.
    Collect & record tokens for all areas except pit (B2, B3, B4, B8, B10).
    Record & disburse shaping chips (B33).

At 1555 Sunday only
    Exchange chips for interaction tokens, record (B33).

At 1600
    Staff report & in-service training.
    Give and record report.

*Change Agent 2*

At 1130
    Eat (try to be first in line).
    Interact with residents.

At 1155
    Collect & record tokens for free time activities (B2, B3, B4, B8, B10, B11).

At 1200
    Record meal behavior (B31).
    Disburse tokens for appropriate meal behavior (B31).
    Record & prompt for next meal (B31).
    Record & disburse tokens for 1st hour's work to dietary assistants (B34).
    (Finish by 1245).

At 1300 (Free time): Saturday only
    Interact with residents.
    Assist change agent 1 as needed.

At 1300 (Informal interaction): Sunday only
    Collect & record pit entrance and activities (B5, B6, B7).
    Record & disburse shaping chips in pit (B33).

At 1355 Sunday only
    Exchange chips for interaction tokens, record (B33).

At 1400 (Informal interaction): Saturday only
    Collect & record pit entrance and activities (B5, B6, B7).
    Record & disburse shaping chips in pit (B33).

At 1455 Saturday only
    Exchange chips for interaction tokens, record (B33).

At 1400 (Free time): Sunday only
    Interact with residents.
    Assist change agent 1 as needed.
    Check unit for lights out; make list and give to project secretary.

At 1500 (Gym): Saturday only
    Collect & record tokens for inappropriate time on unit (B9).
    Accompany & assist change agent 1 in gym.

At 1500 (Informal interaction): Sunday only
    Collect & record pit entrance and activities (B5, B6, B7).
    Record & disburse shaping chips in pit (B33).

At 1555
    Collect & record tokens for all free time activities (B2, B3, B4, B7, B8, B10, B11).

At 1600
    Staff report & in-service training.

Weekend Evenings (1600-2430)

*Change Agent 1*

At 1600
    Staff report & in-service training.

At 1615
    Prepare drugs.

At 1630
    Give drugs to dietary volunteers.

At 1635
    Check for medical meal tokens.

At 1640
    Distribute drugs, do not announce.

At 1700
    Eat (try to be first in line).
    Interact with residents.

At 1720
    Announce regular dinner.
    Collect tokens & record (B1). Give form B1 to dietary worker to collect & record extra portions.

At 1722
    Record meal behavior (B31).
    Disburse tokens for appropriate meal behavior.
    Record & prompt for next meal (B31).
    By 1730, finish early dinner residents.
    By 1740, finish regular dinner residents.

At 1800
    Announce canteen time.
    Sell items & record for each resident who buys or rents items (B18).
    After canteen announce free time.
    Prepare drugs.

At 1900
    Collect tokens & record for residents taking center passes (B26).
    Collect & record pit entrance & activities tokens (B5, B6, B7).
    Disburse & record shaping chips for informal interaction in pit (B33).
    Serve coffee to residents.

At 1955
    Exchange shaping chips for interaction tokens in pit, record (B33).

At 2000
    Collect & record pit entrance & activities tokens (B5, B6, B7).
    Disburse and record shaping chips for informal interaction in pit (B33).

At 2055
    Exchange shaping chips for interaction tokens in pit, record (B33).

*Change Agent 2*

At 1600
    Staff report & in-service training.

At 1630
    Announce availability of dietary jobs at 1 token/hour, send volunteers to dietary worker, record (B34). Give appearance tokens to volunteers, record (B29).

At 1640
    Announce appearance check.
    Disburse & record appearance tokens.
    Prompt & record for next check (B29).
    Tell resident to pick up drugs.

At 1700
    Record & disburse tokens for 1st hour's work to dietary assistants (B34).
    Announce early dinner. (Wait until change agent 1 is through disbursing drugs to be first in line.)
    Collect tokens & record (B1). Give form B1 to dietary worker to collect & record extra portions.

1702-1720
    Record meal behavior (B31).
    Disburse tokens for appropriate meal behavior.
    Record & prompt for next meal (B31).
    Give form B31 to change agent 1.

At 1720
    Eat.
    Interact with residents.

At 1740
    Collect & record tokens for free time activities (B2, B3, B4, B7, B8, B10).

At 1755
    Record & disburse tokens for 2nd hour's work to dietary assistants (B34).

At 1800
    Assist change agent 1 as needed.
    After canteen collect & record tokens for free time activities (B2, B3, B4, B7, B8, B10).

At 1900
    Announce informal interaction.
    Collect & record tokens for all areas but pit (B2, B3, B4, B8, B10, B11).
    Disburse & record shaping chips for informal interaction (B33).

At 1955
    Exchange shaping chips for interaction tokens, record (B33).

At 2000
    Announce informal interaction.
    Collect & record tokens for all areas but pit (B2, B3, B4, B8, B10, B11).
    Disburse and record shaping chips for informal interaction (B33).

At 2055
    Exchange shaping chips for interaction tokens, record (B33).

*Change Agent 1*

At 2100
    Announce bedtime preparation.
    Collect & record extra bathing tokens (B20).
    Supervise bathrooms.

At 2200
    Collect & record free time tokens (Saturday) (B2, B3, B4, B8, B10, B11). Assist change agent 2. Pick up soap from shower rooms.

At 2230
    Turn off late lights.

At 2300
    Collect & record free time tokens (B2, B3, B4, B8, B10, B11) (Saturday).

At 2330
    Escort soilers to bathroom (female).

At 2400
    Staff report & in-service training.
    Give & record report.

Weekend Nights (0000-0830)

At 0000
    Staff report & in-service training.

At 0030 (Saturday only)
    Late lights out (females).

At 0100
    Escort soilers to bathroom (females); other duties as required.

At 0200
    Summarize data sheets.

At 0300
    Escort soilers to bathroom (females); other duties as required.

At 0400
    Summarize data sheets.

At 0500
    Escort soilers to bathroom (females); other duties as required.

At 0555
    Awaken free bed dorm.

At 0600
    Record & disburse getting-up tokens; free bed dorm (B30). Prompt for rising so appearance token is not missed (do not record prompt).

At 0615
    Assist change agent 2 as needed.

By 0630
    Finish bed & area check in free bed dorms.
    Record & disburse bed & area tokens (B30).
    Record & prompt for next bed & area token (B30).

*Change Agent 2*

At 2100
    Admit & record residents returning from passes (B26, B27).
    Assist change agent 1 with showers.

At 2130
    Prompt residents who are not preparing for bed.
    Collect & record late sleepers for Sunday (Saturday only) (B13).

By 2145
    Distribute drugs.

At 2155
    Turn off lights. Prompt dallying residents.
    Collect & record late bed tokens (B13).

By 2200
    Complete medical treatments.

At 2230
    Admit & record residents returning from passes (Saturday) (B26, B27).
    Assist change agent 1.

At 2330
    Escort soilers to bathroom (male).

At 2355
    Announce late bed preparation (Saturday).

At 2400
    Staff report & in-service training.

At 0000
    Staff report & inservice training.

At 0030 (Saturday only)
    Late lights out (males).

At 0100
    Escort soilers to bathroom (males); other duties as required.

At 0200
    Prepare drugs, inventory, cards, & orders.

At 0300
    Escort soilers to bathroom (males); other duties as required.

At 0400
    Prepare drugs, inventory, cards, & orders.

At 0500
    Escort soilers to bathroom (males); other duties as required.

At 0555
    Assist change agent 1 as needed.

At 0615
    Start appearance check of residents in free bed dorms.
    Record & disburse appearance tokens (B29).
    Prompt for next appearance and record prompt (B29).
    Prompt for bed & area, same prompt from day before (do not record prompt).

At 0630
    Awaken residents in rented rooms.

*Change Agent 1*

At 0645
 Start appearance check in rented rooms.
 Record & disburse appearance tokens to all regular risers (B29).
 Record & prompt for next appearance check (B29).
 Prompt as day before bed & area (do not record prompt).

At 0700
 Announce availability of all free time activities; collect & record tokens for all areas excluding pit (B2, B3, B4, B8, B10, B11).
 Prepare special medical meals.

At 0800
 Staff report & in-service training.

*Change Agent 2*

At 0635
 Record & disburse getting-up tokens in rented rooms (B30). Prompt for rising so appearance token is not missed (do not record prompt).

By 0700
 Finish bed & area check in rented rooms.
 Record & disburse bed & area tokens to all regular risers (B30).
 Record & prompt for next bed & area token (B30).

At 0700
 Handle late sleepers arising before 0800.

At 0750
 Collect & record tokens for free time activities, excluding pit (B2, B3, B4, B8, B10, B11).

At 0800
 Staff report & in-service training.

# 9. The Clinical Staff and Their Assessment

The performance of the clinical staff in the implementation of the milieu and social-learning programs was continuously assessed by objective observations. These assessments document the nature of treatment techniques actually applied by staff in the conduct of the psychosocial programs and show differences between psychosocial programs, psychosocial baseline conditions, and a sample of staff performance in traditional hospital programs (see chapter 5). Relatively stable personal-social characteristics of clinical staff are also important to allow comparisons of staff across different treatment settings in the event that such characteristics of individual staff, or of the aggregate staff group, might moderate the application or effectiveness of specific treatment techniques.

In addition to the usual demographic characteristics (e.g., age, sex), the major personality dimensions of extroversion-introversion and emotionality-stability appear sufficiently robust as to be potentially important descriptive characteristics of individual staff or aggregate staff groups (Peterson, 1965). In addition the attitudes, opinions, and beliefs held by clinical staff about mental patients, mental illness, and approaches to treatment have been widely assumed to mediate the nature of staff behavior. While some relationships have been found between measures of these staff characteristics and measures of institutional treatment effectiveness, other possible sources of influence have been present in studies finding such relationships to the extent that no cause-effect conclusions are possible (Edelson & Paul, 1976). However, the potential importance of attitudes and orientations of clinical staff is sufficient that their assessment as more specific personal-social characteristics is warranted.

## METHODS OF ASSESSING CHARACTERISTICS, ATTITUDES AND ORIENTATIONS OF CLINICAL STAFF

All personal-social characteristics of project clinical staff were assessed by paper-and-pencil instruments since the majority of characteristics were either biographical or cognitive-interpretative, and—unlike residents—all staff should function at a high enough level to employ self-report measures. With the exception of biographical data, all staff were informed that there were no right or wrong answers. Each was also assured that none of the instruments would be used for anything other than description of the staff group and that no individual would be personally identified in any presentation of data. The data obtained follow.

*Biographical Data.* Upon entry to employment each staff member provided information on his or her age, sex, race, education, prior institutional treatment experience, marital status, and number of children.

*Pittsburgh Scale of Social-Extroversion-Introversion and Emotionality* (Bendig, 1962). Upon entry to employment, each staff member also completed the Bendig scales, consisting of sixty items in a true-false format, yielding an Extroversion score ranging from 0 to 30 and an Emotionality score ranging from 0 to 30. The fifteen Minnesota Multiphasic Personality Inventory (MMPI) L-scale items were also included in the questionnaire to provide a check on validity of reports.

*Opinions About Mental Illness Scale* (Cohen & Struening, 1962). Attitudes, opinions, and beliefs (see Fishbein & Ajzen, 1975) about mental patients were assessed on the Opinions About Mental Illness Scale (OMI) upon entry to employment and on completion of academic training for each staff member and at every anniversary assessment (see figure 3.1). As originally constructed, the OMI consists of fifty-one items rated on six-point Likert-type scales ("strongly agree"-"strongly disagree"), yielding five factor scores labeled with regard to mental illness or mental patients as Authoritarianism, Benevolence, Mental Hygiene Ideology, Social Restrictiveness, and Interpersonal Etiology. Since the operating assumptions of the psychosocial programs were largely unrepresented in the original scale items, a sixth score was added consisting of the sum of nine additional items (see appendix A) that focused on the attitudes implicit in the

Orientation and Common Procedures Manual. The sixth score was descriptively labeled Social-Learning Ideology.

All analyses and presentation of OMI data were based upon transformations of the raw factor scores. All within-score analyses between groups or over time were computed on standardized scores (mean=50, SD=10), based upon the within-score mean and variance of all staff at all assessments. This standardization provided a common metric for all six scores, allowing the most sensitive test of differential change or pattern differences (interactions involving scores). Between-score differences, all graphic presentations, and comparisons of pattern similarities were based upon sten score transformations according to Struening and Cohen's (1963) standardization norms (mean=4.5, SD=2) to facilitate comparisons with other staff groups. Since no sten-norms existed for Social-Learning Ideology, its scores were entered as 10 x % of total points endorsed for analyses involving sten scores. Group means were first determined for raw scale scores and then sten transformed to capitalize on the greater discriminality of raw scores (see Cohen & Struening, 1963). A psychosocial ideal was provided by the project director to reflect the pattern and level of the most desirable endorsement of OMI items with regard to the assumptions underlying both psychosocial programs.

*Therapist Orientation Sheet* (Paul, 1966). Attitudes toward and interpretations of the treatment programs and techniques were assessed on the Therapist Orientation Sheet (TOS) upon entry to employment, on completion of academic training for each staff member, and at every anniversary assessment for all clinical staff employed (see figure 3.1). The TOS includes an attitude section, consisting of twenty-four five-point bipolar items relating to the nature of treatment (e.g., activity, relationship, goals), and a technique section, consisting of twenty therapeutic techniques rated on five-point scales regarding level of utilization from "never" to "almost always." For use with institutional treatment programs and nonprofessional therapists, a supplementary sheet was included to provide further clarification of the descriptive adjectives employed. Usual TOS administration instructs staff members to complete all items according to their personal beliefs or preferences. However, when the TOS was administered to psychosocial staff after completion of training, the responses were obtained under each of three instructional sets: one set for each of the psychosocial programs—reflecting staff interpretations of the nature of each program (attitude items) and appropriate use of techniques in each program (technique items) inferred from their training and experience—and one set under usual instructions, reflecting preferred nature of treatment (attitude items) and use of techniques (technique items). Two preliminary items were added to the TOS for each administration after completion of training. They requested staff to choose which of the two psychosocial programs each believed to be "most effective" and "most enjoyable."

For analyses of institutional programs, five pattern differentiation scores were derived within both attitude and technique sections. Each score consists of the mean of items with similarity of relative ratings between milieu and social-learning programs, determined by the project director's rating of the ideal level of endorsement for each item that reflected the assumptions underlying each program or the specified distribution of technique utilization, as presented in the respective treatment manuals. For example, score T-1 equals the mean of technique items receiving "5" ideal ratings for the milieu program and "3" ideal ratings for the social-learning program, while score A-3 equals the mean of attitude items receiving "5" ideal ratings in both programs. (The entire TOS as employed in the project, including the items and scoring format for each pattern differentiation score, is in appendix A.) Interitem correlations within pattern differentiation scores on a sample of eleven senior staff and forty-two junior staff ranged from r=0.38 to r=0.97 (mdn. r=0.74).

## SELECTION PROCEDURES, CLINICAL STAFF CHARACTERISTICS, AND TURNOVER

Selection and recruitment of psychosocial senior staff was nearly always by means of informal requests for nominations from known professionals and personal acquaintances. Formal letters of recommendation and transcripts were regularly evaluated, plus interviews and on-site visits varying from three hours to two days, during which all senior staff and all available junior staff were given the opportunity for mutual evaluation of a candidate. The first group of senior staff were evaluated and recruited by the project director; all later additions and replacements required consensus of continuing senior staff, taking junior staff opinions into account. The same characteristics used for selecting junior staff were included in evaluating clinical senior staff in addition to an evaluation of professional competence. Once a mutual agreement was reached for a candidate to join the psychosocial programs, the lengthy process of application to the state personnel department began so that the new employee would be placed on the payroll. This process required completion of appropriate tests and evaluations to be placed upon an eligible list, determining which position description would allow the desired candidate to be reached, and requesting the eligible list, interviewing the people on it, and obtaining waivers from those with higher civil service points—occasionally reclassifying a position to circumvent an aggressive political patronage candidate—and, finally, processing papers to establish the desired candidate on payroll. The whole process required about three months and untold staff hours.[1] The majority of professional staff came from current students or recent graduates of universities within the zone.

Junior staff were selected from applicants who met high-school equivalency and civil-service requirements for aide-level jobs at the center. Applications were usually initiated by newspaper advertisements or by a friend already on the staff who knew an opening would be forthcoming. Selection was based upon half-hour interviews by two senior staff who judged applicants to demonstrate average or above-average intelligence, appearance and interpersonal skills that would provide positive models for residents, absence of anxiety regarding description of specific job conditions (work under close monitoring in two specified programs, presence of bizarre and violent behavior on the part of residents, frequent presence of incontinence, etc.), and absence of strong attitudinal convictions counter to treatment philosophy. After the programs were operating, qualified applicants were also given a tour of the units and informally evaluated by the current junior staff. The local community from which applicants were drawn was largely industrial and chronically suffered from high unemployment rates. Even at minimum salary levels there were usually seven applicants for every opening. Therefore, the large majority of junior staff came from the unemployed ranks of the lower-to-middle socioeconomic levels.

The characteristics of psychosocial staff at

Table 9.1. Characteristics of clinical staff.

|  | Hospital staff:[a] Sample assessment | | Psychosocial staff:[b] Start of period | | End of period | |
| --- | --- | --- | --- | --- | --- | --- |
| Variable | Jr. staff (N=40) | All staff (N=43) | Jr. staff (N=19) | All staff (N=24) | Jr. staff (N=25) | All staff[c] (N=36) |
| Age |  |  |  |  |  |  |
| Mean years | 42.6 | 41.7 | 23.9 | 24.7 | 28.2 | 29.2 |
| S.D. | 14.11 | 14.09 | 8.43 | 7.82 | 8.84 | 8.66 |
| Sex (% female) | 57.5% | 55.8% | 84.2% | 75.0% | 68.0% | 58.3% |
| Race (% black) | n.a. | n.a. | 21.1% | 20.8% | 36.0% | 27.7% |
| Education |  |  |  |  |  |  |
| Mean years | 11.1 | 11.3 | 12.6 | 13.7 | 12.2 | 14.1 |
| S.D. | 1.40 | 1.55 | 1.18 | 2.64 | 1.28 | 3.24 |
| Institutional experience |  |  |  |  |  |  |
| Mean years | 8.8 | 8.7 | d | e | 2.0 | 2.0 |
| S.D. | 6.73 | 6.75 |  |  | 1.31 | 1.40 |
| Marital status (% married) | 67.5% | 67.4% | 52.6% | 58.3% | 52.0% | 52.8% |
| Parental status (% with children) | 72.5% | 69.8% | 42.1% | 37.5% | 56.0% | 44.4% |
| Extroversion |  |  |  |  |  |  |
| Mean | 19.6 | 19.5 | 21.4 | 21.0 | 18.7 | 18.2 |
| S.D. | 5.65 | 5.93 | 4.69 | 4.89 | 4.55 | 4.35 |
| Emotionality |  |  |  |  |  |  |
| Mean | 10.2 | 10.1 | 10.3 | 10.0 | 10.5 | 10.2 |
| S.D. | 6.05 | 5.87 | 5.61 | 5.13 | 4.75 | 5.25 |
| L-scale |  |  |  |  |  |  |
| Mean | 4.4 | 4.2 | 3.8 | 3.5 | 3.8 | 3.3 |
| S.D. | 2.69 | 2.67 | 2.07 | 1.96 | 2.33 | 2.33 |

a. Consists of 66% of clinical staff working directly with the hospital comparison group during a one-week sample (no data obtained for psychologists, physicians, social workers, etc.).
b. Consists of all clinical staff employed during each assessment, including professional staff with any resident contact. Only four staff at the end were also present at the beginning.
c. Includes expanded professional staff in preparation for broadening operations to prechronic patients, eight of whom filled only two positions for the current psychosocial program.
d. Only 12% with any prior contact.
e. Only 24% with any prior contact.

the beginning and end of the intramural period and those of the hospital staff directly treating the comparison group during a one-week sample are presented in table 9.1 for comparative purposes. While all psychosocial clinical staff provided data, only 66% of hospital staff sampled did so. Some failed to return the completed questionnaires; however, the majority of missing data from hospital staff resulted from the differential utilization of professional staff, as *not a single* psychologist or physician entered any of the hospital wards during the entire ten day period during which data were collected. Thus, nonprofessional staff characteristics are presented separately in table 9.1. Of the psychosocial junior staff, the majority were female, about half being women with children who had just reached school or day-care age, a quarter were recent high-school graduates entering full-time employment for the first time, and a quarter had been working or seeking work for several years. The increases in age and experience from the beginning to the end of the intramural period were partially the result of continuing staff, while increases in age and the percentage of males, parents, and blacks were largely the result of center participation in federal assistance programs for the unemployed. However, the only changes in psychosocial staff characteristics that were statistically significant over the entire period of nearly four and a half years were age, experience, and Extroversion.

The psychosocial group was significantly younger, less experienced, and more highly educated (largely because of practical nurses on the junior staff) than the hospital staff who were actually in contact with patients during the one week sample ($p$'s $< 0.01$). It is likely that the educational differences would have been equalized or reversed for total staff had the professional hospital staff been available. Significantly fewer psychosocial staff had children than hospital staff, and a significantly greater proportion of junior staff were female ($p < 0.05$) at the beginning of the project; however, the sex difference in group composition had dropped below significance by the sixth anniversary assessment ($p$'s $> 0.20$). Racial composition was not compared because those data could not be obtained from hospital staff. Marital status, Extroversion, Emotionality, and L-scale scores did not differ significantly between hospital and psychosocial staff at any time during the intramural period nor did differences obtained in the proportion of staff falling into specific personality types. Using Paul's (1969c) cutting points on the Bendig scales, all psychosocial staff employed and the hospital sample found the majority of staff to be stable-extroverts (53.0%-psychosocial, 53.5%-hospital) and the next largest subgroup to be stable-introverts (28.9%-psychosocial, 27.9%-hospital), with relatively few being emotional-extroverts (9.6%-psychosocial, 9.3%-hospital) or emotional-introverts (8.4%-psychosocial, 9.3%-hospital).

Staff turnover was also considerably greater in psychosocial programs than in the regional hospital. According to the personnel officer's estimate (no data were available) the six-month turnover (number of terminations per average number employed) among nonprofessional treatment staff at the regional hospital ran about 12% during the project, until the career series with higher salaries became effective, when turnover was estimated to be about 9% every six months. Turnover in hospital professional staff was said to be negligible. In contrast, turnover among psychosocial professional staff averaged 26.5% per six-month period, largely the result of the planned turnover of interns each year. Psychosocial junior staff turnover ranged from a high of 48.7% during the third six months of operation to a low of 12.2% during the six months immediately following implemtnation of the career series, for an average turnover of 26.7% every six months. Over the entire intramural period, seventy-eight junior staff were hired to fill the clinical complement of twenty-five positions. Of the seventy-eight initially hired, five left before completing training to work with residents and fifty-three terminated as change agents after completion of training. Over the entire period, only an average of 22.4 change agent positions were actually filled. Staff turnover on the psychosocial units was thus about average for that found in both general and psychiatric hospitals, while estimated turnover at the regional hospital was much less than average (see Denman & Ryder, 1971; McCloskey, 1974; Tuchi & Carr, 1971).

While turnover is unquestionably costly in staff time, relatively high turnover may actually contribute positively to program operation since training of new employees regularly requires experienced staff to review details of appropriate procedures (Tuchi & Carr, 1971). Conditions within the psychosocial units appear to have included several features that have been empirically associated with high staff turnover rates, as well as several that have been associated with low rates (see Porter & Steers, 1973). Characteristics of the psychosocial units that have typically been associated with high job satisfaction and low turnover rates appear to be equity within psychosocial staff for merit salary increases and promotions, personal recognition and feedback with very high "personal consideration" in supervisory style, small working-unit size, good peer-group identity and interaction (to the extent that terminating staff continued to maintain social contacts if they were in the area), high levels of responsibility with variability in tasks, high role clarity, and a relative absence of extremes in personality characteristics. On the other hand, several characteristics have been associated with low job satisfaction and high turnover rates: inequity in work load and pay levels compared to those of other units in the center (psychosocial units had lower staff-to-resident ratios and higher expectations for interaction levels and responsibility, and they worked with more severely debilitated and more dangerous residents, while receiving much lower pay), little community recognition because of the project's attempts to avoid publicity, younger staff, staff with low levels of tenure in current or previous jobs, and potential family conflicts, especially regarding changing roles of women (approximately 30% of junior staff received brief counseling from senior staff members at one time or another; the most frequent problems related to husbands' less-than-positive reactions to staff wives' movements toward greater personal independence in thinking and action).

Thus, the morale problems of psychosocial junior staff, as well as turnover rates, appear to have been about average for active mental health units. The primary difference may have been that senior staff put more emphasis on the identification and resolution of the basis of morale problems. In fact, the stated reasons of terminating junior staff for leaving were considerably different from those of parallel staff elsewhere (see Denman & Ryder, 1971; Porter & Steers, 1973). The majority of terminating junior staff (38.4%) stated external bases for leaving (illness, pregnancy, family leaving area, drafted). In spite of the low level of functioning of residents and their high levels of assaultiveness, only 3.8% of terminating staff reported emotional reactions to residents or programs as a basis for leaving. Although high levels of performance were required, only 7.7% were dismissed for poor performance. While low salaries were of concern, only 9.6% of terminating junior staff left for higher paying jobs outside the mental health field, while 13.5% left for better paying jobs within the field—some within psychosocial units or other units in the center. A particularly impressive figure is that the remainder of terminating junior staff (26.9%) left to continue their education. It thus appears that work in the psychosocial programs had some significant impact on the staff as well as on residents; however, the low proportion of staff terminating for jobs outside of the mental health field was most likely a function of the poor economy in general and the high unemployment rates in the local area in particular.

## OPINIONS ABOUT MENTAL PATIENTS

Average scores on the Opinions About Mental Illness Scale (OMI) at the beginning and end of the intramural period for junior staff alone and all clinical staff combined are presented in figure 9.1 for comparison with the sample of hospital staff who were treating the comparison group. As detailed in later chapters, certain OMI scores appeared to be very responsive to changes in resident behavior. Although psychosocial staff working at the end of the intramural period showed no significant change in level of Authoritarianism, Interpersonal Etiology, or Social-Learning Ideology from those of the original clinical staff employed before the arrival of residents, the differences in the remaining three scores from the beginning to the end of the intramural period were significant. At both the

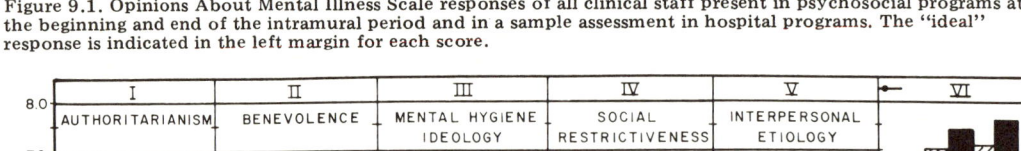

Figure 9.1. Opinions About Mental Illness Scale responses of all clinical staff present in psychosocial programs at the beginning and end of the intramural period and in a sample assessment in hospital programs. The "ideal" response is indicated in the left margin for each score.

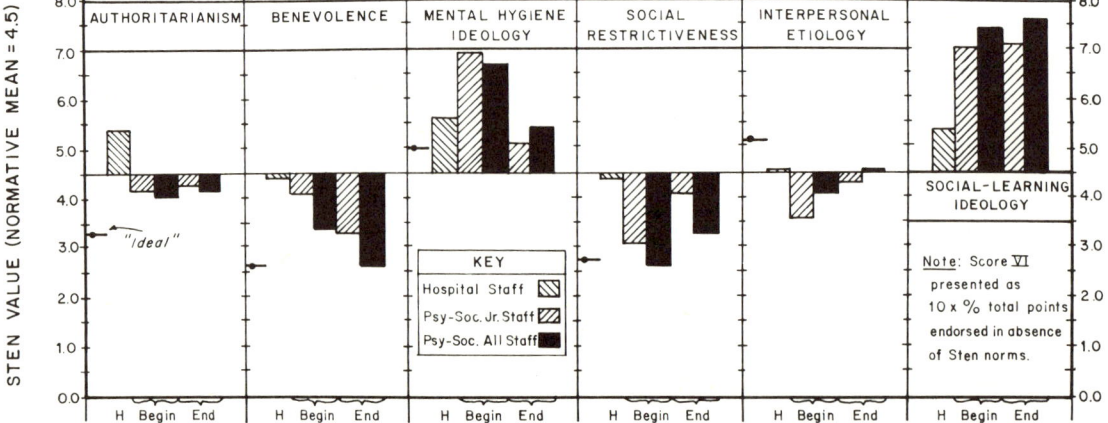

beginning and end of the intramural period, as well as at intervening assessments, psychosocial senior staff were significantly lower than junior staff on both Benevolence and Social Restrictiveness and higher on Social-Learning Ideology (p's < 0.05), without differences on Authoritarianism, Mental Hygiene Ideology, or Interpersonal Etiology (p's > 0.20).[2]

Significant differential patterns of OMI scores were found between hospital staff and any combination of psychosocial staff on all analyses (p's < 0.01). On all occasions, hospital staff scored significantly higher on Authoritarianism and Social Restrictiveness and significantly lower on Social-Learning Ideology than either psychosocial junior staff alone or all clinical staff combined (p's < 0.05). Interpersonal Etiology did not differ between hospital and psychosocial staff on any analysis (p's > 0.20), while Benevolence and Mental Hygiene Ideology differed over analyses as a result of changes in psychosocial staff. Mental Hygiene Ideology scores of psychosocial staff were significantly higher than the hospital group at the end of original training (p's < 0.05) but did not differ at the end of the intramural period (p's > 0.20) after psychosocial staff had lowered scores in the direction of ideal assumptions underlying the psychosocial programs. While Benevolence scores of all psychosocial clinical staff combined were significantly lower than the hospital sample on all occasions (p's < 0.05), junior staff alone did not differ from the hospital staff prior to the original arrival of residents (p > 0.20).

Comparisons among individual OMI scores found Mental Hygiene Ideology for hospital staff to be significantly higher than Benevolence, Social Restrictiveness, and Interpersonal Etiology; no other differences between scores were significant.[3] In contrast, the Social-Learning Ideology score maintained its exceptionally high level of endorsement at all times for psychosocial staff. All psychosocial clinical staff combined regularly produced Mental Hygiene Ideology scores that were significantly higher than all remaining scores, while Authoritarianism and Interpersonal Etiology were regularly higher than Benevolence and Social Restrictiveness, without other differences among OMI scores. Less discrimination was obtained for psychosocial junior staff alone—excluding the uniformly high levels of Social-Learning Ideology. At the first assessment, before the arrival of the residents, Mental Hygiene Ideology was significantly higher than all remaining scores, without further differentiation for junior staff alone. By the end of the intramural period, Authoritarianism, Benevolence, Social Restrictiveness and Interpersonal Etiology still did not differ, but Mental Hygiene Ideology was significantly higher than Benevolence for junior staff alone.

The overall profile of OMI scores for either the hospital sample or for psychosocial staff did not produce a good match to any of the occupational clusters reported in Cohen and Struening's (1963) normative groups. Although the hospital group was similar to Cohen and Struening's "aides" on Authoritarianism, Benevolence, and Interpersonal Etiology, their Social Restrictiveness scores fell closer to "physicians and dentists" in the normative groups, while Mental Hygiene Ideology was much higher than the normative "aide" group, equaling the average score for "psychiatrists." For psychosocial staff, Authoritarianism was lower than the normative "aide" group and higher than "psychologists" or "psychiatrists," falling closest to "office clerical." Benevolence scores of junior staff at the beginning of the intramural period were similar to those of normative "psychologists," but all other psychosocial staff scores fell below all other occupation groups in the normative samples, except "engineering, housekeeping, and kitchen personnel." The remaining three OMI scores for psychosocial staff showed a profile similar in shape to Cohen and Struening's "psychologists," "social workers," "clergy," and "psychiatrists," with relatively higher scores on Mental Hygiene Ideology and Interpersonal Etiology and lower socres on Social Restrictiveness. However, Social Restrictiveness moved from low scores of about the level of the normative "psychiatrists" to mid-range levels more similar to "special services" and "physical medicine and rehabilitation" normative groups. Interpersonal Etiology remained largely within the range of normative "aides" and "white-collar" workers. Psychosocial Mental Hygiene Ideology started above the highest normative occupational group, "psychologists and social workers," and ended at the level of the second highest normative groups—"psychiatrists" and "clergy." Overall, comparisons of the pattern and level of scores show the psychosocial junior staff and senior staff to have been closer to each other and to the ideals underlying the psychosocial programs than to any other occupational group.

An examination of intercorrelations among OMI scores found considerably different patterning for hospital staff than for psychosocial staff.[4] For hospital staff, Authoritarianism appeared to be the major influencing score, being significantly correlated (r's in the ± 0.40s to ± 0.60s) in the positive direction with Social Restrictiveness and Interpersonal Etiology and in the negative direction with Mental Hygiene Ideology and Social-Learning Ideology. Mental Hygiene Ideology was similarly negatively correlated with Social Restrictiveness (r=-0.55) and positively correlated with Benevolence (r=0.42), while Social Restrictiveness was positively related to Interpersonal Etiology (r=0.43). The psychosocial staff at the beginning of the intramural period replicated only two intercorrelations found for hospital staff: the positive relationship between Authoritarianism and Social Restrictiveness (r=0.43) and the positive relationship between Mental Hygiene Ideology and Benevolence (r=0.40). The only other significant relationships within the original psychosocial group reflected the influence of Social-Learning Ideology, which was negatively related to Social Restrictiveness (r=-0.87) and Benevolence (r=-0.42) and positively related to Interpersonal Etiology (r=0.47). At the end of the intramural period, OMI scores for psychosocial staff still showed Authoritarianism and Social Restrictiveness to be positively related, while both were negatively related to Mental Hygiene Ideology and Social-Learning Ideology. In general, interrelationships among OMI scores for the hospital sample appear similar to those obtained for other hospital treatment staff (see Edelson & Paul, 1976), with Authoritarianism providing the major influence, while Social-Learning Ideology appeared to retain the primary influence for psychosocial staff.

The predictability of OMI scores from individual staff characteristics found only sex and education to yield significant relationships for psychosocial staff at the beginning of the intramural period. Females tended to score higher on Benevolence (r=0.58) and Mental Hygiene Ideology (r=0.48). Relationships with education for the psychosocial group largely represent senior staff-junior staff differences. Staff with higher education tended to score lower on Benevolence (r=-0.72) and Social Restrictiveness (r=-0.51) and higher on Social-Learning Ideology (r=0.58). Education and experience were the only significant predictors of OMI scores at the end of the intramural period, again reflecting differences between junior staff and senior staff on the same three scores. In contrast to psychosocial staff, the OMI scores of the hospital staff were predictable from more individual staff characteristics but at generally lower levels (r's in the ± 0.30s and ± 0.40s). Thus, older hospital staff tended to score higher on Social Restrictiveness and lower on Social-Learning Ideology, while females and those with more institutional experience tended to score higher on Benevolence and lower on Interpersonal Etiology. Married hospital staff tended to score higher on Social-Learning Ideology, and higher levels of education were related to lower scores on Authoritarianism, Social Restrictiveness, and Interpersonal Etiology. Personality variables were not significantly related to OMI scores for either psychosocial or hospital staff. Thus, although all significant relationships were in keeping with those of prior literature (see Edelson & Paul, 1976), OMI scores of hospital staff were related to more individual characteristics than those of psychosocial staff, where educational level showed the primary relationships.

## PREFERENCES ON THE NATURE OF TREATMENT AND TECHNIQUE UTILIZATION

Average preferred attitude and preferred technique pattern differentiation scores on the Therapist Orientation Sheet (TOS) at the beginning and end of the intramural period are presented in figure 9.2 for comparison with the sample of hospital staff who were directly treating the comparison group. Although, as detailed in later chapters, several significant changes occurred in the TOS scores of psychosocial staff during the period, the pattern remained the same. No differences approached significance between the TOS scores of psychosocial staff from the beginning to the end of the treatment period. Additionally, no differences between the psychosocial junior staff and senior staff approached significance, and no consistent differences were obtained between professional and nonprofessional psychosocial staff at any time during the intramural treatment period.[5]

The preferred attitude scores in figure 9.2 reveal clear differences between hospital staff and psychosocial staff in their personal preferences regarding the nature of treatment (p's < 0.01). Similarities occurred only on TOS scores A-2 and A-5, reflecting preferences of both groups of staff for therapeutic relationships at about the midpoint of the "structured-unstructured," "nonpermissive-permissive" dimension (A-2) and a slight preference for clients (patients, residents) being "usually comfortable" with "affective-learning" (A-5). Other preferences for nature of treatment were at opposite ends of the continuum and significantly different (F's > 80.53, p's < 0.01). Thus, psychosocial staff preferred a more "active-formal" activity structure, with "personal, change-oriented" therapeutic relationships focusing upon "current behavior with rational planning." In contrast, hospital staff preferred a "passive-informal" activity structure with "impersonal" therapeutic relationships in which change was relatively "unimportant" and focus was more on "historical behavior with spontaneous actions." Preferred attitude scores were differentiated by staff, with all psychosocial staff scores in figure 9.2 being significantly different except A-1 versus A-4. Differences among hospital staff scores were also significant, except A-1 versus A-3 and A-2 versus A-5. Both staff groups clearly indicated preferences for the nature of treatment programs to be essentially as they existed through the support of the differing administrative structures and the differing program schedules in which they worked. Hospital staff preferred the medical-custodial approach and psychosocial staff preferred the reeducative-active treatment approach.

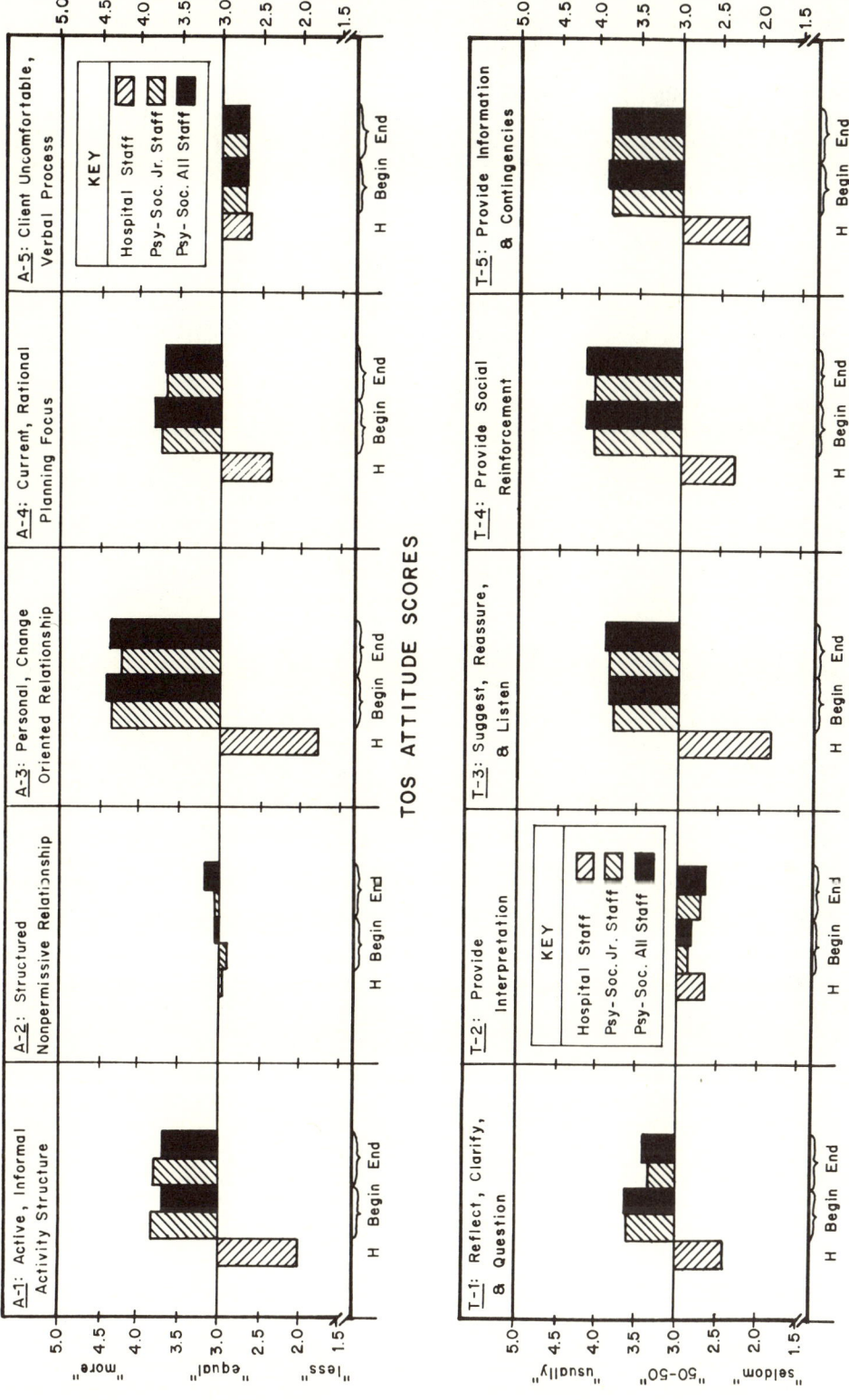

Figure 9.2. Therapist Orientation Sheet preferred responses of all clinical staff present in psychosocial programs at the beginning and end of the intramural period and in a sample assessment in hospital programs.

Examination of intercorrelations among TOS preferred attitude scores found no significant relationships within either hospital staff or psychosocial staff at the beginning of the intramural period, although a few significant intercorrelations were found for psychosocial staff at the end. However, Extroversion scores of hospital staff were significantly negatively related to A-3 (r=-0.33) and A-4 (r=-0.52), indicating a tendency for more extroverted hospital staff to prefer more impersonal relationships without planning or focus on changing patients. OMI scores were not significantly related to TOS preferred attitude scores within the hospital sample. Within the original psychosocial staff, in contrast, several TOS preferred-attitude scores were related to individual staff characteristics and OMI scores (r's in the ± 0.40s and ± 0.50s). Higher A-1 scores, reflecting a preference for an even more active, informal activity structure, tended to be given by psychosocial staff with lower educational levels and those who scored relatively higher on OMI Social Restrictiveness and relatively lower on Social-Learning Ideology. Higher A-2 scores, reflecting a preference for relatively more structured, nonpermissive relationships tended to be given by staff who were older, more highly educated, married, with lower OMI Benevolence scores—all characteristics of senior staff. Higher A-3 scores, reflecting a preference for a personal, change-oriented relationship, tended to be given by psychosocial staff who scored higher on OMI Mental Hygiene Ideology and Interpersonal Etiology. A-4 scores were related only to race and educational level, indicating a tendency for white staff and more highly educated staff to prefer a greater emphasis on current behavior and rational planning. Finally, higher A-5 scores, reflecting a belief in the need for some resident discomfort and verbal-conceptual learning, tended to be given by black staff, more introverted staff, and staff scoring relatively lower on Mental Hygiene Ideology. Over time, TOS preferred-attitude scores of psychosocial staff continued to show little clustering and became less related to individual staff characteristics but continued to show relationships with OMI scores. Thus, the nature of treatment preferred by psychosocial staff not only differed from that preferred by the sample of hospital staff but showed greater consistency with other attitudinal measures.

The preferred technique scores in figure 9.2 also reveal clear differences between hospital staff and psychosocial staff in the preference for utilization of specific therapeutic techniques (p's < 0.01). Preferred techniques were differentiated within staff groups in nearly opposite directions. Psychosocial staff preferred high levels of T-3, T-4, and T-5, which were significantly higher than T-1, while T-2 was significantly lower than all other scores. In contrast, T-2 was the highest preferred technique score for hospital staff, while T-3 was significantly lower than all other scores. T-5 was also significantly lower than T-2 for the hospital sample, while none of the remaining differences between scores was significant. Even though T-2 was the highest preferred technique for hospital staff and the lowest for psychosocial staff, it was the only one on which the staff groups did not differ significantly, reflecting relatively little preference for use of interpretation. All other scores differed significantly (F's > 30.67, p's < 0.01), essentially reflecting a preference by the hospital staff to use any treatment technique seldom. Thus, the extreme differences in activity level actually observed in the operation of psychosocial programs and traditional hospital programs (chapter 5) were directly reflected in the stated preferences of the respective staff groups; psychosocial staff preferred to use many techniques at high levels of interaction with differentiation among procedures, least preferring direct interpretation, and hospital staff indicated preference for few techniques at low levels of interaction without much differentiation among procedures, most preferring direct interpretation.

Examination of intercorrelations among TOS preferred technique scores found a three-score cluster for the sample of hospital staff, involving T-1, T-2, and T-3, the highest relationship being between T-1 and T-2 (r=0.66), while the remaining correlations were lower (r's in the 0.30s). T-3 and T-5 were also significantly correlated for hospital staff (r=0.37). Thus, hospital staff who endorsed relatively higher preferences for use of reflection, clarification, and questioning also tended to prefer more use of interpretation and suggestion, reassurance, and listening. Advice and contingency management also tended to be preferred by hospital staff who liked more use of suggestion, reassurance, and listening. At the beginning of the intramural treatment period, psychosocial staff showed a three-score cluster among T-3, T-4, and T-5 (r's in the 0.50s and 0.60s), reflecting a tendency for the same staff to prefer higher utilization rates of suggestion, reassurance, listening, social reinforcement and advice, and contingency management. T-1 was also significantly related to T-2 (r=0.69), T-3 (r=0.64) and T-5 (r=0.42). No other significant relationships were found for T-2 and T-4. The extent and nature of clustering among preferred technique scores for psychosocial staff changed over time; however, differences in patterning were regularly obtained from that found for hospital staff.

Several significant relationships were found between preferred technique scores and individual characteristics for hospital staff, although only one OMI score was related to preferred techniques (r's in the ± 0.30s and ± 0.40s). These relationships showed a tendency for hospital staff who preferred relatively higher use of suggestion, reassurance, and listening (T-3) to be younger, male, and to have less institutional experience. Hospital staff who indicated relatively higher preference for use of advice and contingency management (T-5) tended to be younger, more highly educated, and to score lower on OMI Social Restrictiveness. TOS scores T-1 and T-4 were unrelated to staff characteristics, but T-2 was related to parental status, indicating a tendency for hospital staff with children to prefer relatively greater use of interpretation. In contrast to hospital staff, few individual psychosocial staff characteristics were related to preferred technique scores, but several OMI scores were. Race was the most frequent individual staff characteristic to be related to preferred technique scores at the beginning of the intramural period (r's in the -0.40s), showing a tendency for white staff to prefer higher rates of T-3, T-4, and T-5. T-4 was also negatively related to Emotionality (r=-0.48), reflecting a tendency for less emotional staff to prefer higher levels of social reinforcement.

Only preference for use of reflection, clarification, and questioning (T-1) was unrelated to OMI scores for psychosocial staff at the beginning of the intramural period. All other preferred technique scores were significantly related to at least one OMI score (r's in the ± 0.40s and ± 0.50s). Staff preferring greater use of interpretation (T-2) tended to score lower on Mental Hygiene Ideology and Interpersonal Etiology, while staff preferring greater use of suggestion, reassurance, and listening (T-3) tended also to score higher on Social-Learning Ideology. Higher preference for social reinforcement (T-4) was associated with higher scores on Social-Learning Ideology and lower scores on Social Restrictiveness, while higher preferences for use of advice and contingency management (T-5) were associated with lower OMI Benevolence. The relationships changed somewhat over time for psychosocial staff but continued to show little predictability of TOS preferred technique scores from individual characteristics and several relationships to OMI scores. Thus, the treatment techniques preferred by psychosocial staff not only differed in level and pattern from those of hospital staff but showed differential relationships to other variables as well.

## SUMMARY

Methods of assessing relatively stable personal-social characteristics of clinical staff included biographical data, personality variables, and instrumentation for six-month assessments of attitudes, opinions, and beliefs regarding mental patients and treatment programs. The manner of selecting psychosocial clinical staff was described, and the characteristics of psychosocial staff and turnover were compared to those of hospital staff providing treatment for the hospital comparison group. Although the staffing levels in psychosocial and hospital settings were approximately equal, the differing utilization of staff suggested by the different administrative structures was further emphasized on comparison of a one-week sample of hospital staff with psychosocial staff. Nearly all direct patient contact in traditional hospital programs was the responsibility of nonprofessional staff, although professional staff retained decision-making authority. In contrast, all psychosocial senior staff also had on-the-floor responsibilities, even though the structure of the programs gave major decision-making responsibility to nonprofessional staff as well.

The large majority of nonprofessional psychosocial staff came from the unemployed ranks of the lower-to-middle socioeconomic levels. Comparisons of psychosocial staff with the hospital staff in contact with the comparison group found several differences. Psychosocial staff were younger, less experienced, and slightly more highly educated and had fewer children than the sample of hospital staff. Females constituted a larger proportion of the psychosocial staff. No differences were found between groups in marital status or personality variables. The turnover of psychosocial staff was high, averaging about the same level as that reported elsewhere for general and psychiatric hospitals, while the staff turnover rate at the regional hospital was estimated to be less than half that found for psychosocial staff and elsewhere.

Comparisons of psychosocial staff and the sample of hospital staff on OMI scores found clearly different patterns to exist on attitudes, opinions, and beliefs about mental patients, with neither group matching previous occupational patterns. Considerably different patterning of OMI scores was found as well, with Authoritarianism being the strongest influence among hospital staff and Social-Learning Ideology being the strongest influence among psychosocial staff. OMI scores were related to more individual staff characteristics within the hospital group than within the psychosocial group.

Comparisons of psychosocial staff and the sample of hospital staff on preferred TOS scores found remarkable differences between groups. In general, both groups of staff reported preference for the nature of treatment programs to be just like the ones supported by the differing administrative structures and differing program schedules for hospital and psychosocial programs. Hospital staff indicated preference for a medical-custodial approach, while psychosocial staff indicated preference for a reeducative-active treatment approach. The extreme differences in actual performance of psychosocial and hospital staff were also reflected in stated preferences for technique utilization on the TOS. Hospital staff indicated preference for use of few techniques, all at low levels of interaction without much difference among procedures, but most preferring the use of direct interpretation. Psychosocial staff indicated preference for use of interpretation at the same absolute level as hospital staff, but as the least-preferred technique. Rather, psychosocial staff liked to use many techniques at high levels of interaction, with differentiation among procedures. Differential patterning and predictability of TOS scores was found as well.

Thus, although staffing levels were approximately equal between the traditional state hospital programs and psychosocial programs, nearly every other relevant dimension showed extreme differences, including the administrative structure and utilization of staff, the level and specificity of staff activity, and the attitudinal orientation and composition of the treatment staff. Differences in treatment effectiveness between psychosocial and traditional hospital programs could therefore be related to any or all of the above differences. However, since the same psychosocial staff conducted both milieu and social-learning programs within the same physical-social settings, differences between psychosocial programs can be related to the differing programs themselves.

# 10. Nonprofessional Clinical Staff Training

The use of nonprofessional mental health workers was initially given major impetus because of economics and professional manpower shortages (see Arnhoff et al., 1969). Although nonprofessional personnel have sometimes been used as cheaper substitutes for professionals, often they have served in innovative functions and roles that have expanded services to areas where none existed before (e.g., Guerney, 1969; Sobey, 1970; Rappaport et al., 1971). Such use of nonprofessional personnel has by no means been accompanied by professional consensus (e.g., Moore & Stewart, 1972), with one writer (Marler, 1971) even asserting that each of the arguments for their use is either "fallacious, illogical or injurious."

Whatever the arguments for the use of nonprofessionals elsewhere, there should be little question of the therapeutic potential represented by the large number of aide-level nonprofessional staff in public mental institutions (Ellsworth & Ellsworth, 1970). At last report (Witkin, 1974), over 72% of all inpatient staff in public mental institutions in the United States were nonprofessionals, representing a vast reservoir of talent—if staff were maximally utilized. Ellsworth's excellent review (1968), combined with recent summaries of institutional practices that appear to support the custodial aide culture for chronically institutionalized populations, point to organizational and operational practices that hinder the therapeutic utilization of nonprofessional institutional staff. The majority of these practices appeared to be present in the regional hospital, while attempts to avoid them were made in the psychosocial programs.

The organizational structure and setting can only provide the opportunity for maximum utilization of nonprofessional staff. After establishing the structure, determining the population to be served and the nature and direction of changes desired, specifying treatment procedures, and selecting the available population of potential change agents, the primary operations determining the therapeutic utility of nonprofessional staff will be those involving training and maintenance of their performance. The majority of staff training in mental institutions until recent years has been conducted by a separate training division, in which the content of training focused upon theoretical concepts of classification, abnormal psychology, treatment philosophy, etc., with job-specific training handled informally after the formal training period was completed (e.g., Cuadra & Reed, 1957). More recently, many institutions have integrated academic and clinical training by placing trainees in both formal academic classroom sessions and in ward assignments concurrently, but with content still separated (e.g., Distefano & Pryer, 1970). This approach was used for nonprofessional staff of the regional hospital, but with training in ward assignments still being informal. With the growing popularity of behavioral treatment programs, recent reports of institutional staff training have shown a decrease in general theoretical content to a more specific job-behavior focus of training, with both integrated academic and clinical exposure (e.g., Liberman, 1968), and formal academic training followed by separate clinical training (e.g., Panyan et al., 1970).

## TWO APPROACHES TO TRAINING PSYCHOSOCIAL STAFF

All academic and on-the-job training of psychosocial staff took place within the psychosocial units and was the total responsibility of the psychosocial staff. The original group of change agents had to be trained in both milieu and social-learning procedures, as well as in all other job functions, before the residents arrived. Later additions and replacements to the junior staff occurred after programs were operating and senior staff had other ongoing responsibilities. Therefore, although the same content was used for training initial and later change agents, two different modes of training were required. The initial group of junior staff was trained in a sequential/professional mode, in which academic instruction was completed before on-the-job clinical training began, with all training conducted by the professional staff. Later change agents were trained in an integrated/technical mode, in which abbreviated academic instruction by professional staff was integrated with on-the-job clinical observation, then followed by on-the-job training conducted by experienced change agents.[1] Because of the turnover in junior staff, over 73% of all junior staff were trained in the integrated/technical mode.

*Academic Training.* A formal academic training period was required for both modes, with successful completion of a paper-and-pencil test demonstrating conceptual knowledge of principles and procedures being required before trainees were allowed to receive on-the-job training in interaction with residents. The academic training period covered a total of twenty-seven working days for the initial group and eighteen working days for later trainees.[2] Those in the initial group all received training at the same time, before the existence of ongoing treatment programs. Later trainees were trained in the presence of ongoing programs, either individually or in groups of two, three, or four. For the sequential/professional mode, all instructors were professional staff and devoted the majority of their time to training, without ongoing clinical responsibilities. Instructors for the integrated/technical mode included senior staff and experienced change agents who carried full clinical duties in addition to training the junior staff additions and replacements.

The major reduction in time devoted to the academic training period between the initial group and later change agents occurred in areas not specifically related to the resident population and psychosocial treatment programs. A general orientation and familiarization with facilities conducted by nonproject personnel was reduced from three days for the initial group to one day for later trainees.[3] Focus on physical medicine, first aid, nursing, and drug procedures was reduced from five full days for the initial group to two hours for later trainees; the remainder of training in nursing procedures was deferred to on-the-job training after shift assignments were undertaken. Pretesting and completion of required personnel forms and post-testing and feedback required a half-day each for all trainees. The final major time reduction occurred in coverage of specific orientation to the project and treatment units (project structure, overview of the problems of the chronically institutionalized resident population, goals of the treatment programs, and an introduction to the principles and requirements of research) and in coverage of clinical theory and procedures not directly related to the job (models of deviancy, history of institutional treatment, and overview of treatment programs for different and similar populations).[4] For the initial group, a half-day was devoted to specific orientation and one and a half days to clinical theory and procedures not directly related to the job. For the later additions and replacements, these two areas of content were reduced to one two-hour lecture-discussion session with the project director, plus integration of content into discussions as elaboration or contrast to specific job-related principles and procedures by senior staff.

The majority of academic training time for all change agents (sixteen days) focused on the resident population to be served and on the particular treatment programs and procedures to be applied. The materials for training consisted of the three manuals that presented the assumptions and procedures of both treatment programs, supplemented by the appendixes that detailed daily resident and staff schedules and appropriate and inappropriate resident behaviors, and thirty-five Clinical Frequency Recording System forms for each treatment unit. The forms were structured not only to monitor the performance of residents in particular functional periods but to specify successive levels of achievement by residents, which determined the focus of interaction by staff in concrete terms. Thus, the staff were required to fully understand programmatic behavior to properly complete recording forms.

The sequential/professional training procedures instituted for the original group of change agents during the academic period involved classroom reading, lectures, large and small group discussions, films, and role playing. Two days were spent in field trips for observation of the institutional population at the regional hospital, one day on the Orientation and Common Procedures Manual, four days each on the Milieu and Social-Learning Manuals, and five days on discrimination training between programs and on Clinical Frequency recording forms. Instructors related previously covered material to the section of focus by the Socratic method. Role-playing procedures were used extensively in training on procedural rules and on detailed coverage of functional periods; instructors demonstrated appropriate and inappropriate procedures with other instructors playing the role of residents. Trainees then role played the procedures themselves, received feedback, and again role played until they followed appropriate procedures. For discrimination training and recording practice, trainees divided into small groups and role played specific procedures within functional periods, first for one treatment program and then the other. Instructors provided setting events, monitored performance, modeled appropriate staff behavior, and provided feedback. After small group review and rehearsal, discussion in the large group related any problems or solutions that had come up.

The integrated/technical training procedures instituted for later change agents during the academic period involved one day on the Orientation and Common Procedures Manual, and five days each on the Milieu Manual, the Social-Learning Manual, and recording practice and discrimination training. Observation of ongoing programs, staff, and residents was integrated throughout, and only one instructor at a time met with trainees; instructors were rotated within sections of each manual as each instructor's other duties allowed. Each manual was assigned in sections for individual study, discussion with an instructor, observation of staff and residents in the ongoing treatment programs, and discussion of the practices with the experienced change agents who were observed. During each discussion period with senior staff instructors, previously covered principles and procedures were reviewed, contrasted, and related to new content. During the five days devoted to review and discrimination training, trainees were assigned to an experienced change agent who explained recording procedures. Trainees reviewed each functional period in the manual and then accompanied an experienced change agent working that functional period, first on one unit and then the other, concurrently making practice recordings. The experienced change agent compared recordings at the end of each functional period and discussed the procedures with the trainee. A senior staff instructor finally met with the trainee after practice recordings of the same functional period were made on both units for a review of the principles, procedures, observations, and recordings and how they differed between programs.

*On-the-job Training.* Upon completion of the academic training period all trainees were required to pass a test on principles and procedures before being given regular assignments for on-the-job training. For the initial group of change agents, on-the-job training was completely conducted by the senior staff and the project director. For additions and replacements, on-the-job training was conducted by experienced junior staff from the ranks of earlier trainees, with certification checks performed by senior staff.

On-the-job training followed common procedures for all change agents. Trainees were each assigned a training form that listed the functional activity periods within the two treatment programs. For each duty, the trainee first observed an assigned instructor perform the activity on a minimum of three occasions, followed by a discussion session concerning the interactions and events that occurred. The trainee then performed the particular functional activity under total supervision on a minimum of six occasions until he or she demonstrated errorless performance. Total supervision of that activity was then reduced to 30-50% monitoring of trainee performance by assigned instructors. Finally, after the trainee had demonstrated adequate performance regularly under partial supervision, a formal check resulted in certification of the change agent to perform the activity on the particular unit without supervision. Instructors, whether senior staff or experienced junior staff, were assigned on a daily basis. For trainees entering the project after the initial group, senior staff conducted the certification checks after junior staff instructors indicated that trainees were ready.

Although trainees progressed at different rates, by the end of the sixth week of on-the-job training, all were performing duties with residents, with the majority of duties being supervised at the 30-50% level. By the end of the eighteenth week of on-the-job training, every trainee was operating independently as certified clinical change agents, without specific supervision. However, usual monitoring of all staff at all times still included intermittent appearance of senior staff, regular appearance of research observers, and a half-hour daily group session at the time of shift changes for continuing in-service training through distribution of written memos and clarification of procedures as questions arose. Continuous monitoring and appraisal of staff performance was maintained through the Clinical Frequencies Recording System and through objective observations on the Staff-Resident Interaction Chronograph. The observations were obtained on all staff in contact with residents, whether trainees or certified change agents, with individual feedback on performance every other week.

## DIFFERENTIAL OUTCOMES ASSOCIATED WITH THE TWO TRAINING APPROACHES

Attitudinal changes associated with the program-specific training procedures and relative changes between the two approaches to training were examined by Paul and McInnis (1974). Comparisons of the expanded Opinions About Mental Illness Scale (OMI) and preferred attitude and technique scores of the Therapist Orientation Sheet (TOS) were made from original entry to employment to completion of the academic training period for the original trainees who received the sequential/professional mode and for an equal number of consecutive additions or replacements who received the integrated/technical mode of training. Overall and differential changes were found for attitudes, opinions, and beliefs about mental patients and treatment procedures. In addition, the traditional/sequential mode of instruction, which used extensive classroom time with professional level instructors, resulted in better performance on the academic test on content of training than did abbreviated classroom instruction integrated with clinical observation.

The majority of attitudinal changes were found on the OMI scores. Large increases were obtained on Social-Learning Ideology for both groups, while Authoritarianism did not change for either. Later trainees who received abbreviated academic training integrated with observation of residents produced decreases on Benevolence and increases on Interpersonal Etiology, while the initial group who received the more traditional classroom approach to academic training changed slightly in opposite directions. Although both groups increased Mental Hygiene Ideology and decreased Social Restrictiveness, the amount of change was much larger for the initial group of trainees who had not had much exposure to the chronically institutionalized population. At the end of the academic training period, the initial group who had received more extensive classroom instruction and less resident exposure was significantly higher on Mental Hygiene Ideology and lower on Social Restrictiveness and Interpersonal Etiology than the later trainees who received opposite emphasis during the academic period. The changes on OMI scores as a result of job-specific training within a nondisease, reeducative model were quite similar to changes found in previous studies that combined clinical experience of trainees with academic instruction (see Edelson & Paul, 1976; Paul & McInnis, 1974). Changes in Benevolence and Social Restrictiveness appeared to be partially a function of exposure to the particular resident population, which was considerably more severely debilitated than those of previous studies.

Unlike OMI changes, neither approach to training was associated with significant changes in TOS attitude scores reflecting the preferred nature of treatment programs. Differential changes obtained in TOS preferred technique scores resulted in equalizing the two training groups at the end of the academic training period, where differences had existed previously (see figure 9.2 for the resulting pattern). However, both TOS and OMI scores of nonprofessional trainees showed considerable similarity to those of the senior staff by the end of academic training, if not at initial selection. Paul and McInnis noted that the underlying attitudes and beliefs of senior staff appeared to be conveyed to junior staff trainees, who either found them compatible or tended to change in that direction. Given the role of senior staff as sources of both social and job-related reinforcers and models of standards for the new group that nonprofessional trainees were entering, these data were quite consistent with predictions from functional theories of attitude change. Agreement with senior staff could be viewed as serving "instrumental-social adjustment" and "knowledge-object appraisal" functions (Kiesler et al., 1969, pp. 302-342). In fact, the similarity of trainee attitudes at the end of the academic training period significantly predicted academic test performance, while neither changes in attitude scores nor academic performance were predictable from demographic or personality variables, and little predictability of academic performance was obtained from absolute scores after training. Paul and McInnis hypothesized that these findings might reflect added effort expended in mastery of content for those trainees who became more similar to senior staff in attitudes and beliefs as a function of the greater value of senior staff approval or disapproval for them.

On-the-floor performance during and after the on-the-job portion of training was evaluated by Paul, et al. (1973) for a continuing subsample of the junior staff trainees examined by Paul and McInnis (1974). Objective data on quality of performance were compared from SRIC observations of each trainee during a six-week period of on-the-job training when they were still receiving moment-to-moment supervision on 30-50% of duties and during a later six-week period when each was functioning as a certified clinical change agent after completion of on-the-job training.[5] In contrast to the superior performance on the academic test of principles and procedures for the initial group who received extended classroom instruction in the sequential/professional mode, on-the-floor performance was clearly superior at the same point in training in both milieu and social-learning programs for later trainees who received the integrated/technical mode of training. Of major importance was the finding that junior staff maintained an equally good level of performance in both treatment programs after they were certified and no longer under the direct supervision of their respective instructors, whether on-the-job training had been conducted by senior staff or experienced junior staff.

The differences in the relative superiority of conceptual understanding for trainees receiving the sequential/professional approach, while more rapid acquisition of on-the-job interactional skills was obtained for trainees receiving the integrated/technical approach, have also been reported in other behavioral training programs for aide-level personnel (e.g., Gardner, 1972; Martin, 1972). There is a recurring theme in the literature indicating greater satisfaction and preference for on-the-job training with integrated academic content rather than the more traditional didactic-sequential procedure (e.g., Bensberg et al., 1964; Batman, 1968; Krieger, 1970). After comparing the relative ease with which a practical on-the-job training orientation increased interaction rates with the difficulties encountered by another aide training program, which emphasized formal didactic training, Ellsworth (1968) went so far as to state that formalized classroom training was both undesirable and unnecessary. Paul et al. (1973) noted that Ellsworth's extreme position was not warranted because differences in his approach and that of the other training program were more likely a function of a specific behavioral focus versus a general theoretical focus. In fact, on-the-floor performance in both psychosocial programs was significantly predicted from the academic test within both training groups, even though the range was restricted by the requirement that all trainees pass the academic test at a high level of understanding before undertaking on-the-job training. Thus, it seems more likely that increased focus on classroom instruction by professional staff does result in increased understanding of principles and procedures; however, given minimal understanding, the integration of clinical observation with academic content, followed by practicum training by those performing the same functions, results in more rapid acquisition and performance of duties at a high level of skill.

Although the academic test predicted on-the-floor performance of junior staff during and after on-the-job training, OMI scores did not, even though differences in OMI scores had been found at the end of the academic training period. As with previous literature (Cuadra & Reed, 1957; Butterfield & Warren, 1962; McClelland & Rhodes, 1969), demographic, personality, and attitudinal data provided little or no overall predictability of the quality of on-the-floor performance. Only TOS preferred technique T-2 (preference for use of interpretation) consistently predicted the quality of on-the-floor performance, showing poorer performance by trainees who preferred high levels of interpretation. The relationship of attitudinal similarity to senior staff, which had been found to predict academic performance, also predicted on-the-floor performance but only when senior staff were providing immediate on-the-job supervision. Additionally, Extroversion was found to be highly predictive of good performance by female junior staff when they were directly supervised by senior staff but predictive of poorer performance after moment-to-moment supervision was faded. Thus, the differential social reinforcement value of specific feedback by senior staff appeared to be differentially operative on the basis of attitudinal similarity, while the reversal of performance by extreme extroverts without direct supervision suggested that continued excellence of performance might be more a function of compliance than of identification for those extreme scores (see Kelman, 1958). Overall, however, the best predictor of the quality of ultimate on-the-floor performance was actual on-the-floor performance during training under the same conditions.

Although junior staff trained by the integrated/technical mode showed superior performance at the same point in training to those trained by the sequential/professional mode, both groups maintained their quality of on-the-floor performance after moment-to-moment supervision was faded. In fact, nonprofessional change agents continued to improve their quality of performance over time after certification, offering strong testimony to the fact that clear specification of desired activities with continuing feedback will maintain staff performance (e.g., Bricker et al., 1972; Ellsworth, 1973; Pommer & Streedbeck, 1974; Wallace et al., 1973; Quilitch, 1975). When combined with highly specific staff behavior x resident behavior x setting specification and training, continuing assessment and feedback, and meaningful consequences, continuing improvements (rather than declines) were obtained for both programs. While comparative data are not yet available on the relative quality of psychosocial staff performance in relation to other programs, the quantity of staff-resident interaction resulting from both approaches to training with continuing maintenance operations was far above that reported elsewhere, even for the lowest interaction rate ever obtained in the psychosocial programs (see Dailey et al., 1974; Liberman et al., 1974; Paul et al., 1973).

## SUMMARY

Although many professionals have not accepted the use of nonprofessional mental health workers, the therapeutic potential of these institutional staff—at least with long-stay populations—leaves little room for argument. The organizational and administrative structure of the psychosocial programs was designed to provide maximum utilization of nonprofessional staff, and the specificity of programs and monitoring procedures were geared to maintain staff performance. Training then constitutes the primary operations by which the therapeutic utility of staff will or will not be realized.

Although all training—both academic and on-the-job for milieu and social-learning programs—was the responsibility of psychosocial staff themselves and covered the same content, two different modes of training were required because of the absence of residents and ongoing programs before the intramural period began. Therefore, the first group of junior staff received a sequential/professional mode of training in which professional staff first covered academic content and then supervised on-the-job clinical training after the arrival of residents. All later junior staff received an integrated/technical mode of training in which abbreviated academic coverage by professional staff was integrated with clinical observation, followed by on-the-job training conducted by experienced junior staff. Both modes of psychosocial training emphasized job-related behavior rather than general orientation, concrete functions rather than abstract theory, modeling and feedback rather than totally didactic presentation, and specified programs and staff behavior x resident behavior x setting interactions. This approach contrasted with the nonprofessional training in the regional hospital, which was conducted by a separate training division, focusing upon didactic presentation of general materials and theory, with only informal training occurring in on-ward procedures.

Attitudinal changes were associated with the behavior-specific training, and differential patterns of change were found for the two approaches. Trainee attitudes tended toward those of instructors, and attitudinal similarity was related both to academic performance and quality of on-the-floor performance. Although neither attitudinal data nor demographic variables were predictive of staff performance, some relationships were obtained with preferred techniques and personality variables. The sequential/professional mode of training was associated with higher academic test performance, and the integrated/technical mode of training led to better on-the-floor performance at the same point in training. Junior staff maintained their high levels of on-the-floor performance after moment-to-moment supervision was faded upon completion of on-the-job training, with performance in each psychosocial program being predictable from the academic test of understanding of principles and procedures and from on-the-floor performance during training.

The success of the procedures for monitoring and maintaining the amount and quality of actual performance of nonprofessional psychosocial staff was evident in continuing increases, rather than declines, in performance over time after completion of training. The combined procedures thus unquestionably maximized the potential of the nonprofessional staff.

# 11. Methods of Assessing Patient Behavior

In clinical practice and research, assessment procedures must be chosen according to specific aims, since different purposes require different classes and levels of assessment (Cronbach & Gleser, 1965; Gleser, 1968). The main reason for assessing patient behavior in the comparative project was to provide unambiguous identification and equation of patient groups and evaluation of comparative effectiveness of the three treatment programs on improving the level of functioning and achieving institutional release with community stay. Another was to identify differential areas of success or failure in changing identified targets of rehabilitation through the milieu and social-learning programs, as well as to examine process characteristics of patient behavior within each program for descriptive purposes.

The necessity for standardized objective assessment needs little documentation. However, to maintain validity for the identified purposes, practical and clinical considerations become paramount in selection of assessment procedures from those meeting minimum scientific requirements of reliability, sensitivity to change—when applicable—and the lowest possible level of inference entering into the data base. Many traditional approaches to assessment are clinically or practically inapplicable for use with severely disabled chronic patients because of their low level of functioning, apathy, uncooperativeness, or troublesome behavior. The most desirable form of assessment—exhaustive time sampling of all relevant classes of behavior and continuous frequency counts of situationally defined appropriate and inappropriate behavior—was practically restricted before the start of the current project because of the absence of generalizable instruments and trained observers. The instrumentation was developed and applied within the psychosocial programs during the project, providing the additional advantage of clinical utility in day-to-day operations. However, standardized rating scales with a constant time-limited observational base provided the best compromise for assessing patient functioning over different institutions and groups. Although such global measures are not adequate for treatment programming or for assessing specific improvement for most patient groups (Paul, 1969b, 1974), the extent of bizarre behavior and deficits within the hard-core chronic population makes such global measures meaningful for assessing overall effectiveness (see Lentz et al., 1971). Additionally, several relatively stable personal-social characteristics of institutionalized patients had been found to have some limited prognostic value in earlier research. Therefore, archival data were also used to provide descriptive information for definition of the patient groups and for examination of possible overall or differential predictability of patient response to treatment.

Thus, the data base on which evaluations were made included multiple sources for multiple purposes. Archival data and standardized scales provided information on relatively stable personal-social characteristics for describing and equating the patient groups and for examining possible bases for differential response to treatments. Standardized rating scales—using both professional raters in standardized settings and ratings of day-to-day behavior by clinical staff with the most patient contact—provided assessment of overall level of functioning over situations, behaviors, and instruments for describing and equating patient groups from the several institutions and for evaluating differential improvement across milieu, social-learning and comparison hospital groups during and after treatment. Discrete observational assessments and frequency recordings by both clinical staff and professional observers provided continuous assessment of resident behavior within the psychosocial programs for objective evaluation of global functioning, differential areas of success and failure, comparative description of ongoing individual and group processes, and moment-to-moment individual clinical response. Finally, archival data provided the data base for determining comparative efficiency and effectiveness of the three treatment approaches in achieving release from the institution with continuing community stay.

## RELATIVELY STABLE PERSONAL-SOCIAL CHARACTERISTICS

Data on relatively stable personal-social characteristics were obtained on each patient prior to project entry from two sources.

*Biographical Data Sheet.*[1] Trained record readers transcribed archival data from medical records to obtain demographic information on age; sex; race; marital status; nature of symptom onset (gradual-sudden, presence of precipitating factors); months continuous and accumulated hospitalization; educational, vocational, and economic data quantified via the Hollingshead Two-Factor Socioeconomic Index (Hollingshead & Redlich, 1958); diagnosis; previous somatic treatment (chemotherapy, electroconvulsive shock, insulin shock, and other medical procedures); current psychotropic drugs; presence of living relatives; and geographical subregion at the time of hospitalization. Agreement exceeded 99% on all variables in overlapping samples of ten records for each pair of record readers.

*Process-Reactive Status.* The Ullmann-Giovannoni Process-Reactive Scale (Ullmann & Giovannoni, 1964) was administered concurrently with the initial MSBS (described below) to provide descriptive data on premorbid history because archival data were inadequate for more widely used instruments (Garmezy, 1970). Items on which patients failed to respond were scored zero. Average intraclass interrater reliability exceeded $r=0.98$ on all ratings.

*Nature of Analyses and Presentation.* The relatively stable personal-social characteristics were used for prescreening and equation of original groups of patients (chapter 12). Replacements were equated on all variables by substituting scores of new patients for those they replaced and retesting groups on anniversary assessment 0 data, retaining the original criteria for equation. Predictability of patient improvement or differential response on the basis of these individual characteristics are reported within the later outcome chapters.

## LEVEL OF FUNCTIONING OVER INSTITUTIONS

The full Inpatient Assessment Battery (IAB) was obtained on each patient in all groups before transfer, after transfer, and at each anniversary assessment (see figure 3.1). For patients achieving release and/or rehospitalization, the full battery was also obtained during the week preceding release or following rehospitalization. Three instruments were used in the IAB.

*Minimum Social Behavior Scale (MSBS).* The MSBS was developed for assessing low-level behavior in chronic populations (Farina et al., 1957). It consists of thirty-two items rated on the basis of a ten to fifteen minute structured interview, standardized for setting as well as interview-provided stimuli. Each item is rated "present" or "absent," yielding a potential range of zero to thirty-two, with higher scores indicating higher levels of functioning. Ratings were always completed by professional-level (B.A. and M.A.) project staff, who underwent a minimum of two hours training on the conduct and scoring of MSBS interviews before patient contact.[2] All pre-transfer interviews included two staff—one interviewing and rating while the other only rated—cross-sectionally overlapped for assessing reliability, with each patient's score derived as the average of the two raters (see Lentz et al., 1971). Thereafter, raters were cross-sectionally overlapped each time a new interviewer-rater was included in assessments, equating specific raters over all three treatment groups. Graduate students in clinical psychology who were to become interns or research assistants were used as interviewer-raters to provide equal unfamiliarity with all patients. Raters who had demonstrated reliability on both level and order worked independently on their second assessment periods. Average intraclass reliability among raters exceeded $r=0.98$ at every assessment on the MSBS.

*Inpatient Scale of Minimal Functioning (ISMF).* The ISMF is a ward-rating scale developed for assessing low-level functioning and troublesome behavior in chronic populations (Paul et al., 1976). It consists of twenty-two items concerning the presence, absence, or frequency of occurrence of specific behaviors within the institutional setting during the week prior to the rating. The items are those of the Social Breakdown Syndrome Gradient Index (Gruenberg et al., 1966), weighted according to the severity or adaptiveness of each behavior, summed over two raters and items, yielding a potential range of zero to sixty, with higher scores indicating higher levels of functioning. Questionnaires were administered to one day shift and one evening shift aide-level staff member having most contact with the patient to be rated, with day shift ratings being returned before forms were distributed to the evening shift. The time interval covered by ISMF ratings was always identical for patients in each treatment group at each anniversary assessment and included the time during which MSBS ratings were obtained. Average intraclass interrater reliabilities on the ISMF over pre-post transfer assessments on the original eighty-four patients (anniversary assessment 0), corrected by the Spearman-Brown formula for summing over raters, was $r=0.86$. (Reliabilities at other assessments varied and are reported in relevant chapters.)

*Nurses Observational Scale for Inpatient Evaluation (NOSIE-30).* The NOSIE-30 is a ward-rating scale developed for assessing higher levels of functioning than either the MSBS or ISMF (Honigfeld, 1966). It consists of thirty items, each rated on five-point scales on the frequency of occurrence ("never" to "always") of specific behaviors during the three days prior to the rating. A Total Assets Score, based upon the sum of two raters, yields a potential range of 0 to 208, generally covering upper ranges of level of functioning, with higher scores indicating higher levels of functioning.[3] The same two aide-level staff (one day shift, one evening shift) who completed ISMF ratings also completed NOSIE-30 ratings at each assessment, with the time interval for the rating including that during which MSBS ratings were obtained. Average intraclass interrater reliabilities on the NOSIE-30 over pre-post transfer assessments on the original eighty-four patients (anniversary assessment 0), corrected by the Spearman-Brown formula for summing over raters, was $r=0.95$. (Reliabilities at other assessments varied and are reported in relevant chapters.)

*Nature of Analyses and Presentation.* Two-way (treatment groups x trials) repeated measures analyses of variance (ANOVAs) conducted on each component of the IAB from pretransfer to posttransfer assessments found the original group equation to be maintained, without significant change or interactions on any instrument (all p's > 0.20), while each score was stable over individual patients (all r's > 0.70). Therefore, all anniversary assessment 0 scores were computed as the average of pretransfer and posttransfer scores to provide the most stable assessment of functioning before introduction of psychosocial programs (pretreatment) for each patient in all groups (chapter 12).

Before additional analyses were carried out, every score was standardized within each instrument (mean=50, SD=10), based upon the mean and variance of all patients at every assessment from the pretransfer assessment to the last intramural assessment, to provide a common metric.[4] While comparative analyses were conducted on each IAB component separately (with summary findings noted in appropriate chapters) principle components analyses yielded such consistency that the primary, and most meaningful, assessment of overall functioning was obtained through analysis of a single combined factor score. Specifically, the standardized scores on MSBS, ISMF, and NOSIE-30 for all patients present were entered into principle components analyses at every anniversary assessment from 0 through 9. Each of the analyses yielded a single large principle component accounting for approximately 80% of the variance, with exceptional agreement among principle components solutions (all coefficients of congruence > 0.90). Over time periods, root mean square loadings on the principle component were equal to 0.89 for each instrument, indicating that a simple linear combination of standardized scores provides an internally consistent measure of overall functioning, combining different data sources for maximum validity. Therefore, a standardizd overall IAB Functioning Score was computed for each patient at each assessment by averaging the standardized scores from each component instrument. The factor score then served as the primary dependent variable for evaluating level of functioning over different institutions.

Original group equation and initial level of IAB Functioning at anniversary assessment 0 are presented in chapter 12. All comparative analyses of within- and between-group change over the entire intramural period on IAB Functioning for psychosocial and hospital groups are presented in chapter 34. These analyses are presented for original equated groups throughout the entire intramural period, while correlational analyses over time were computed on all patients present, including replacements.[5]

Improvement status ("worse," "no change," "improved") was determined for each patient at various times for purposes of prediction and clinical exposition. To provide a means of classification independent of the level from which change was assessed for each patient, the standard error of measurement for the IAB Functioning Score was determined from the average reliability of components at anniversary assessment 0 ($r=0.9496$). Cutoffs were then established for the degree of increase or decrease required for significance with a two-sided test at $p < 0.05$ (1.96 times the standard error of measurement). Thus, each patient was classified as "worse" or "improved" if his or her score at a second point exceeded the first by ±2.9 on IAB Functioning. While the improvement classification loses discriminability of degree, it does allow an objective classification of change with clinical meaning, which does not require equation at the initial point.[6] (Comparative improvement rates and predictability of IAB improvement are presented in chapter 34, and the predictability of release and community stay from IAB Functioning and improvement are presented in chapter 35.)

## CONTINUOUS OBJECTIVE ASSESSMENT WITHIN PSYCHOSOCIAL PROGRAMS

Continuous assessments within the psychosocial programs were maintained from the start of the original baseline through termination of the psychosocial units and community placement on three sets of assessment procedures.

*The Clinical Frequencies Recording System.*[7] The occurrence of specific discrete behaviors for each resident within the psychosocial programs was immediately recorded by clinical staff members on one of thirty-five parallel forms on each unit. The forms were structured to be time-place-situation specific with particular staff members responsible for specific forms according to their scheduled duties within each program. The incidence of utilization of all facilities, services, and consumable items were regularly recorded on one of twenty-three forms—including the time of use, the number and nature of resources used, and, for facilities and services, the number of half-hour periods or portion thereof in which utilization occurred. Similarly, the number of periods in which residents were not "where they were supposed to be, when they were supposed to be" were regularly recorded on the inappropriate time sheet, while each incidence of intolerable behavior was recorded with complete descriptive specification as to nature (e.g., "physical assault," "fire setting"), circumstances, and consequences on a separate form for each resident. All of the clinical frequency forms also provided details of tokens spent and token costs for residents of the social-learning program and of expenditures of canteen credits for residents of the milieu program.

The remaining clinical frequency forms provided for monitoring of resident responsiveness within programs in each functional period and a continuous record of tokens earned for social-learning residents. Staff recorded the presence or absence of terminal-level performance (i.e., performance indistinguishable from normal) for each discrete target behavior specified in the treatment manuals under "Program Content," "Ways to Earn Tokens," or "Expected Behavior." Additionally the structure of the forms and daily replacement by night shift change agents provided continuous recording of successive levels of achievement below terminal levels, specified component subtargets of appropriate behavior, and detailed the staff focus of programmatic procedures such that moment-to-moment and day-to-day continuity was automatically maintained. For example, the appearance form provided for specification of each of the eleven criteria detailed for appearance in the appendixes of the treatment manuals for each of the three daily appearance checks. Residents meeting terminal level performance on all criteria on a single check received appropriate programmatic interaction and were recorded as achieving terminal-level appearance on that appearance check (and receiving a terminal-level token in the social-learning program). For residents not achieving terminal-level appearance, discrete components at the terminal level were recorded, plus the specific component behavior that was prompted or encouraged (and the receipt or nonreceipt of a shaping token in the social-learning program). By reference to the detailed record of the previous appearance check, staff could immediately determine the prior level of achievement, the identified subtarget, the discrete behavior of focus, and—for social-learning residents—the criterion for receiving a token.

The clinical frequency recording forms were an integral part of the accurate application of the psychosocial programs themselves and provided for ongoing objective specification of situationally defined appropriate and inappropriate behaviors in enough detail for day-to-day use in clinical programming. Night shift change agents regularly replaced forms (following detailed instructional manuals) to ensure that all required forms with appropriate codes and prior resident data were in place for the next day. Night shift change agents also summarized the daily frequency recordings into total frequencies for two classes of inappropriate behavior, nineteen classes of facilities and services utilization, and four classes of consumables utilization. Appropriate behavior within programs was summarized for the total frequency of terminal-level performance in twenty-two classes of behavior. Each of the daily total frequencies was also cumulatively summed each Monday through Sunday by night shift change agents so that clinical staff could instantly determine the performance of any resident within a current one-week period, from a ten-minute period through a week's performance.

The weekly totals were independently calculated by a project secretary as a double check on accuracy. As in all aspects of psychosocial operations, each summary form was also identified as the work of a specific staff member so that appropriate credit for errorless performance, or corrective feedback, could be given. In addition to summaries for total frequencies, night shift change agents also accounted for recordings missed for each resident from a form kept for that purpose. Senior clinical staff, and later a secretary, concurrently computed weekly denominators, specifying the number of opportunities each resident had to earn a terminal-level frequency recording within each class of behavior. The denominators were based upon each resident's schedule, including weekends and holidays, corrected for missed recordings because of illness, passes, etc. The weekly frequency of opportunities for each resident to use facilities, services, and commodities or to perform an intolerable behavior or an inappropriate time was determined by computer.

To ensure reliability of clinical frequency recordings and data reduction, staff were trained to 100% accuracy of performance within each functional period and within each program—including appropriate recordings—before being allowed to work independently in that activity. Thereafter, regular reliability samples on each class of behavior were conducted between senior and junior clinical staff within each six-month period. (Obtained reliabilities are reported within relevant chapters.) The supervisor-of-the-day was further responsible for a daily visual check, followed by summarization by staff other than those who made the recordings, with a double check by a secretary. The weekly summaries and denominators were then keypunched and verified by project operators with a computer list and error check before further analyses. The entire system was used for clinical programming and monitoring, although comparisons of resident functioning beyond a week were not monitored until late in the project in an effort to prevent staff reactivity from knowledge of incoming results. However, the Clinical Frequency Recording System also provided objective data for comparative evaluation.

Clinical frequency index scores for objective assessment of functioning for each resident were calculated weekly by computer to provide assessment of specific areas of resident responsiveness within programs for comparative evaluation. A Total Inappropriate Behavior Index, consisting of the ratio of total instances of Intolerable Behavior and instances when a resident was not "where he was supposed to be, when he was supposed to be" to total opportunities to perform, provides a direct assessment of grossly inappropriate response to minimal expectations for appropriate behavior. The total incidence per week of dangerous and aggressive acts recorded for Intolerable Behavior was also analyzed separately; in particular, assaultiveness was discovered to be an especially difficult problem with the current population. A Total Appropriate Behavior Index, consisting of the ratio of all terminal-level frequencies for all appropriate classes of behavior to the opportunity to perform, provided an overall assessment of weekly adaptive responses within programs.

Three component index scores for adaptive behavior were regularly calculated to provide direct assessment of treatment targets that had been identified as crucial for the rehabilitation of chronically institutionalized patients. Two specific index scores provided assessment of the resocialization target: Self-Care Index, consisting of the proportion of terminal-level performance over six classes of self-maintenance activities (e.g., personal appearance, meal behavior, bathing) relative to the opportunities to demonstrate each class of behavior, and an Interpersonal Skills Index, consisting of the proportion of terminal-level performance over six classes of interpersonal interaction and communication skills (e.g., informal interaction, normal participation in meetings) relative to the opportunities to demonstrate such skills. The instrumental role performance rehabilitation target was directly assessed by an Instrumental Role Index, consisting of the proportion of terminal-level performances over twelve classes of instrumental role behavior—primarily "on task" in classes and job training positions and "on time" at scheduled meetings, activities, and work—relative to the opportunities to perform each class of behavior.

Clinical frequency index scores for objective description of ongoing activities were also calculated weekly by computer to provide process information on resident behavior within the psychosocial programs. These scores include a Utilization of Consumables Index and a Facilities' and Services' Utilization Index, reflecting, respectively, the ratio of use of the four classes of consumables (e.g., meals, canteen items) and the nineteen classes of facilities and services (e.g., TV, time with staff, off-unit facilities) relative to their scheduled availability. Additionally, a Stereotypy/Variability Score for facilities and services utilization was calculated for each resident to provide a descriptive picture of the range of facilities and services used. This score consists of the ratio of the total facilities and services used, squared $[(\Sigma x)^2]$, to the sum of squared incidence of use of each individual facility or service $[\Sigma x^2]$—thus providing an index independent of the total rate of use, with a possible range from 1.00 (reflecting stereotypy, with a single facility or service accounting for all utilization) to 19 (reflecting all facilities and services used with equal frequency).

Thus, each clinical frequency index score—whether indexing level of adaptive or maladaptive functioning or ongoing process characteristics—provided objective data on the weekly performance of residents, based upon their actual behavior, which was continuously recorded over twenty-four hours per day, seven days per week. For consistency in analysis and presentation, average weekly scores were computed and filed within standard time blocks for the entire intramural period, which consisted of four-week blocks between each anniversary assessment, plus a two-week block overlapping the six-month anniversary assessments (see figure 3.1). Separate blocks were summarized for baseline conditions.

*The Time-Sample Behavioral Checklist (TSBC).*[8] All concurrent resident behavior within psychosocial programs was continuously time sampled each waking hour through objective coding of the presence or absence of discrete behaviors on the TSBC by a staff of trained professional observers. The categories for coding behavior were extended from those originally presented by Schaefer and Martin (1966) through rational generation and selection of items (Goldberg & Hase, 1967; Loevinger, 1965). The goal of item selection was to provide complete coverage of resident behavior in sufficient detail to allow individual problem identification and weekly monitoring in clinical work but with higher level scores summed over time and situations providing objective assessment of functioning for overall evaluation of individual and comparative effectiveness of treatment.

Each observation specified the time and activity during which the observation occurred, plus three codes to indicate the basis for the absence of a resident from a scheduled observation. Each observation then consisted of two-seconds' focus upon the identified individual, following which the presence or absence of sixty-nine specific behavioral characteristics during the instant of observation were coded within seven categories, recording the resident's physical location (seventeen classes, e.g., bedroom, hallway), position (six classes, e.g., walking, lying down), awake-asleep status (two classes: eyes open or eyes closed), facial expression (six classes, e.g., smiling with apparent stimulus, neutral with no apparent stimulus), social orientation (four classes, e.g., alone, with staff), engagement in normal elective appropriate behaviors (seventeen classes, e.g., talking normally to others, personal grooming, writing), and performance of crazy behaviors (seventeen classes, e.g., talking to self, posturing). Schedules provided for a discrete observation of each resident every waking hour, systematically sampling the beginning, middle, and end of each functional period within both psychosocial programs. Complete equation of observational settings with equal numbers of observations in functional periods on the milieu and social-learning unit occurred within each one-week period. Within each set of observations, the order in which residents present were observed was determined by a table of random numbers, and observers were counterbalanced over schedules. Prior to either clinical or research use, all TSBC data were computer scored to provide weekly indexes of the relative frequency of specific classes of behavior per observation for each resident.

The same staff of professional observers made TSBC observations and observations of staff-resident interactions on the SRIC. To ensure reliability and validity of observational data, each observer was trained to a criterion of 100% agreement in full-day checks on each instrument prior to being allowed to collect data independently on that instrument. Thereafter, regular and unpredictable full-day reliability samples were obtained, cross-sectionally overlapping all observers on each instrument every six months. (Obtained reliabilities for the weekly TSBC scores used in analyses are reported in relevant chapters.) The usual number of observers was six, but over the entire project period a total of twenty-one female observers were employed, drawn from the same population as junior clinical staff. All twenty-one achieved criterion on the TSBC, but only nineteen accomplished training criteria on the SRIC. Ongoing analyses of level and pattern of data collected by individual observers were also obtained each time a new observer became certified to ensure that individual drift did not occur. Observers were reinforced for accuracy rather than outcome on both SRIC and TSBC observations, with daily visual checks being maintained by the chief observer and spot checks by senior research staff. The summarization and collation of raw observations for keypunching was done by someone other than the one who made the specific observations. Project operators keypunched and verified each observation, and a computer list and error check were maintained for each weekly computer run.

In addition to the above efforts to ensure reliability of data collection and reduction, continuing efforts were employed to ensure maximum representativeness of the behaviors observed. Observers were initially trained and continuously monitored to be nonreactive. Through use of both SRIC and TSBC, observers were present on the floor on an average schedule of ten minutes on, ten minutes off, with the specific time of arrival being unpredictable. During on-the-floor coverage neither verbal nor nonverbal interactions were allowed with either staff or residents, and observers were not allowed to interact with residents or be seen interacting by residents at other times. Continuous monitoring indicated that both staff and residents habituated to the presence of observers, or a new observer, within three days, and a substudy found staff to be nonreactive to the presence or absence of observers (Hagen et al., 1975). Separate substudies have also established that these data collection procedures and training system have resulted in the absence of bias in TSBC observations as a function of familiarity with residents being observed or the "typicality" of behavior (Redfield & Paul, 1976), with TSBC data showing excellent convergent, discriminative, and predictive validity (Lentz, 1975; Montgomery et al., 1974; Mariotto & Paul, 1974, 1975; Paden et al., 1974; Paul et al., 1976; Paul et al., 1972; Theobald & Paul, 1976).

The TSBC was developed to provide objective

assessment of concurrent, clinically relevant behavior in sufficient detail for use in week-to-week clinical programming and individual monitoring of residents. However, such clinical use was purposively not employed until late in the project in an effort to prevent staff reactivity from knowledge of incoming results. Even late in the project TSBC data were used only for problem identification and monitoring for research purposes to allow evaluation of ongoing psychosocial programs in clinical application based only upon the data recorded by clinical staff. The higher-level TSBC index scores were derived to provide continuous objective data on concurrent clinically relevant behavior for comparative evaluation.

TSBC index scores for objective assessment of functioning for each resident provided weekly computer-scored assessment of the relative frequency of concurrent resident behavior per observation. The TSBC Total Inappropriate Behavior Index provides an overall assessment of concurrent, clinically inappropriate (crazy) behavior—a proportional score that reflects the observed incidence of any one of twenty-four classes of bizarre, maladaptive behaviors—thus directly assessing one of the target areas identified as crucial for rehabilitation of chronically institutionalized patients. The TSBC Total Appropriate Behavior Index assesses concurrent, clinically appropriate behavior, reflecting the relative frequency of any one of twenty-seven classes of normal behavior, including facial expressions (e.g., smiling with apparent stimulus), positions (e.g., sitting, walking), and elective activities (e.g., grooming, writing).

Component index scores were also derived for inappropriate behavior to allow assessment of possible differential effectiveness of psychosocial programs with conceptually different classes of clinically maladaptive crazy behavior. The behaviors entering these component scores were based upon the higher-order factors found in earlier studies of rating-data (Lorr et al., 1967). The Schizophrenic Disorganization Index reflects the relative frequency of occurrence of nine classes of bizarre motoric behaviors (e.g., rocking, repetitive movements, blank staring). The Cognitive Distortion Index reflects the relative frequency of occurrence of six classes of bizarre verbal and facial expressions indicative of thought disorder (e.g., delusions and hallucinations, incoherent speech, smiling without apparent stimulus), while the Hostile-Belligerence Index reflects the relative frequency of occurrence of six classes of high-intensity aggressive behaviors (e.g., screaming, cursing, verbal intrusion).

TSBC index scores for objective description of ongoing activities were also calculated weekly by computer to provide process information on resident behavior within the different psychosocial programs. These scores included the relative proportion of observations on which each resident was awake, with Eyes Open, and With Others, rather than alone. Four Stereotypy/Variability scores were also regularly computed, following the format described above for clinical frequencies, providing a descriptive picture of the range of concurrent crazy and appropriate behaviors performed, the range of other people with whom time was spent, and the range of physical locations frequented by each resident.

Thus, each TSBC index score—whether reflecting level of adaptive or maladaptive functioning, or ongoing process characteristics—provided objective data on the weekly concurrent behavior of residents, based upon their actual behavior as observed in continuous two-second hourly time samples every waking hour, seven days per week. For consistency in analysis and presentation, the average weekly TSBC scores were computed and filed within the same four-week and two-week standard time blocks described above for Clinical Frequencies.

*The Group Activity Index (GAI).* Specific characteristics of the unitwide community meetings were recorded weekly to provide additional process information on differential structure within the psychosocial meetings. Since the social-learning program scheduled a unitwide community meeting only on Fridays, the full community meeting each Friday was observed in both programs, with the professional observers coding frequency and time data on a GAI form taken directly from the definitions of MacDonald (1964). One GAI observer coded frequency data for each resident present on the total instances of "straight speech" (i.e., appropriate initiation, response, or continuing conversation on a single topic); the target of communication as staff, residents, or the group as a whole; and the total instances of active interferences (disrupting discussions, whispering or crazy talk, walking about, entering late or leaving early). A second observer recorded the total length of meeting time in seconds and the number of seconds during which there was complete silence in the meeting.[9]

Since the length of meetings and number of members present varied between programs and over time, GAI data were summarized by computer only for total meeting characteristics rather than by individuals, transforming the total frequency of straight speeches and interferences to a standard meeting length of forty-five minutes. The remainder of the scores were summarized and analyzed as proportions of actual speeches or meeting times. Thus, each GAI score provided objective data on the comparative characteristics of unitwide meetings each week, based upon the actual behavior observed for staff and residents in each psychosocial program. For consistency in analysis and presentation, the weekly GAI scores were computed and summarized within the same four-week and two-week standard time blocks as Clinical Frequencies and TSBCs.

*Analysis and Presentation of Continuous Objective Data.* Before analyses were carried out, every index score for assessment of functioning from Clinical Frequencies and TSBC at the original baseline and successive anniversary assessment weeks was standardized (mean=50, SD=10), based upon the mean and variance of all residents over each of the assessment weeks to provide a common metric. Principle components analyses at every anniversary assessment 0-9 on the Total Appropriate and Total Inappropriate Indexes from both Clinical Frequencies and TSBC found a large first principle component to account for approximately 70% of the variance. Over time periods, root mean square loadings ranged from ±0.80 to ±0.92 for each of the four total index scores, indicating that a simple linear combination of the standardized total scores would also provide an internally consistent measure of overall functioning from continuous objective data, averaging over data sources for maximum validity. Therefore, an objective Global Functioning Factor Score was computed for each resident at each anniversary assessment by averaging the standardized Total Appropriate Behavior Indexes and the (reflected) Total Inappropriate Behavior Indexes from Clinical Frequencies and TSBC.

The standardized Global Functioning Factor Score also allowed the determination of objective improvement status at various times for prediction and clinical exposition. Parallel to the improvement classification derived for IAB Functioning, the standard error of measurement for objective Global Functioning was determined from the average reliability of components over anniversary assessment 0 (baseline) through anniversary assessment 1 ($r=0.970$). Cutoffs were then established for the degree of increase or decrease required for significance with a two-tailed test (1.96 times the standard error of measurement). Thus, each individual resident was classified as objectively "worse" or "improved" if his or her Global Functioning Factor Score at a second point exceeded the first by ±3.19.[10]

The extent to which milieu and social-learning groups were equated on objective measures of functioning before introduction of programmatic procedures is presented in chapter 12. All remaining analyses of continuous objective data for milieu and social-learning programs are presented within time intervals marked by procedural changes or other notable events. In these chapters, all graphs of continuously assessed behavior over standard time blocks (with the exception of the GAI) and all statistical analyses over anniversary assessment periods are presented for original equated groups, while correlational analyses over time with unitwide means (including the GAI) were computed on all residents present.[11]

RELEASE AND COMMUNITY STAY

Release and community stay evaluations were adapted from Gurel (1966) and Ullmann (1967). "Significant release" required that a resident not only be released from the mental institution (center or hospital) but remain continuously in the community without return to psychiatric or correctional facilities for a minimum of ninety consecutive days before being considered a release. "Continued significant release" required that an individual have achieved a significant release and remain in the community at each follow-up without return to psychiatric or correctional facilities. Efficiency was assessed by counting "project weeks in institution" rather than days because of the chronicity of the population and the fact that criteria for release were maintained at independent functioning (requiring self-support and independent living arrangements) through anniversary 8, and changed to community placement (allowing board and care living arrangements) thereafter. "Project weeks in institution" were determined as the number of weeks from entry to one of the project treatment groups (standardized as the week following the original psychosocial baseline for all original groups) to the start of a significant release or to the time of a particular assessment or transfer to another group for those not released. Project weeks were cumulative for reinstitutionalization to the original treatment group. Length of community stay was determined by counting days in community from the start of a significant release to the time of the follow-up assessment.[12]

# 12. The Chronically Institutionalized Population

Preliminary arrangements for a controlled treatment evaluation for chronically institutionalized mental patients began as part of the principal investigator's consultation to the regional state hospital three years before the actual start of the comparative project. At that time, the state hospital had maintained an average daily patient load of over 3,200 resident patients for several years. Consistent with national trends over two-thirds of these patients were chronically institutionalized, nearly half of whom were geriatric (most of these had grown old within the institution rather than being admitted after becoming aged). Therefore, by establishing selection criteria—age range of eighteen to fifty-five years, two or more years' hospitalization, functional psychotic diagnosis (schizophrenia), without debilitating physical conditions, indications of organicity, or homocidal history—nearly two-thirds of the mental hospital beds were filled by patients who currently were, or once were, members of the targeted population, but with restriction to those who would not be excluded from the labor force by age or physical condition alone.

Over the next two years, the extramural subzone staff of the Department of Mental Health engaged in an effort to move residents out of the state hospitals by placing acceptable patients in private extended-care board and room facilities, with a resulting reduction of nearly 22% of the average daily patient load in the state hospital for the region. Concurrently a grant application was submitted to request funding for a comparative treatment evaluation to be conducted entirely within the state hospital. However, before the starting date of the evaluation, space in the mental health center was offered for use in the comparative evaluation of treatment procedures, since funding problems and successful hospital prevention precluded use of all units for second-level services. Because of time-consuming bureaucratic problems and because the center facilities were much more convenient and provided for additional control in evaluation, a change in site and design was requested of the granting agency. Additionally, for further control and convenience, the patient population was to be restricted to those whose point of origin had been from one of two subzones adjacent to the center so that a restricted number of subzone community staff could handle aftercare and follow-up of hospital and psychosocial groups.

A review committee from the federal granting agency visited the center and concluded that because of the proposed changes in the plan of operation, a new proposal was required, with more explicit detail on all aspects of procedure. Several interlocking time-limiting factors put constraints upon the starting dates for a new application: a concurrent grant with an outside job training agency; focus of community placement activities of the subzone extramural staff; academic duties of investigators, which dictated the timing of preparations, staff selection and training, and patient selection and anniversary assessment operations; limited state funds for supporting a research associate who had been in training for the project for a year; and the fact that space in the center had to be occupied with patients within thirteen months or it would be lost to another agency. Finally agreements were reached to establish a starting date nine months later, with early notification of availability of funds in seven months, to allow preparatory work and hiring to proceed. An extension of normal deadlines for submission was granted to allow the new application to be prepared over the six weeks following the site visit. At the time the new application was prepared, even with the 22% reduction in patient load at the regional state hospital, approximately 1,200 of the 2,500 resident patients were nongeriatric patients in Continued Treatment Service (chronic wards), and 300 from the specified subzone areas met selection criteria for the target population.

A four-month delay in notification of funding not only had several immediate and long-lasting effects on project operations (see chapters 3 and 13), but ultimately changed the nature of the patient population available for treatment. When funding was not assured at the promised date, the state hospital, in collaboration with subzone extramural staff, went ahead with plans to transfer all acceptable chronic patients to private extended-care facilities, which resulted in an additional reduction of over 28% in patient load by the time notification of funding allowed actual patient selection to be undertaken.

Although over half of the approximately 1,800 resident patients remaining in the regional state hospital were still chronically institutionalized, the success of the subzone extramural staff in making community placements in the geographic region had been so great that there were not enough long-stay patients in the hospital who met selection criteria from the targeted subzone areas to form equated groups as originally planned. Additionally the only patients remaining in the state hospital and three more hospitals that also housed chronic patients who originated in the geographic region were those who were functioning at such a low level of self-care or who demonstrated such excesses in bizarre behavior that they had been rejected for extended-care community placement. This was clearly a different population from the average chronic psychiatric population for whom the project was originally designed. The geographical area of origin was thus expanded to include the entire eighteen counties of the region (six subzones rather than two), and "subzone of origin" became an additional equation variable.

## SELECTION OF PATIENTS AND GROUP EQUATION

Following the discovery of population attrition at the regional state hospital, the central records of the Department of Mental Health were searched to identify the location of patients who met selection criteria (eighteen to fifty-five years old, two or more years' hospitalization, primary diagnosis of schizophrenia, point of origin within the geographical zone) and still remained hospitalized. A total of 158 patients originating in five of the six subzones that had operational subzone community staff were located over the four state hospitals nearest to the center, including the regional hospital. Administrative arrangements were negotiated at each hospital for access to patients, staff, records, and working space. Complete biographical data, process-reactive ratings, and assessments on the Inpatient Assessment Battery (IAB) were completed on 137 patients—enough to form the original equated groups—within a week and a half of the first hospital visits. All data were scored over a two-week period and three groups of twenty-eight patients each were equated (all $p > 0.20$) on all descriptive, and IAB variables by random assignment from stratified blocks on NOSIE-30 scores, within sexes. The groups were then randomly assigned to the hospital(as the state hospital comparison group) or to the center (for milieu therapy or social-learning treatment).

*Descriptive Characteristics.* The relatively stable personal-social descriptive characteristics of the three original equated groups (presented in table 12.1) reveal the excellent equation of the three groups, as well as the chronic nature of the patients to be treated. Not only had these patients been rejected for community placement, but an even greater proportion had previously received electroconvulsive and insulin shock treatments than the total group of rejected patients who still remained hospitalized (see Lentz et al., 1971). The study patients had also been hospitalized longer than the total group of rejected patients from which they were selected, having spent approximately seventeen years—on the average, nearly two-thirds of their adult lives—in a mental institution.

Study patients were representative of the total hard-core residual group in other characteristics, being low in socioeconomic status, well within the process range of the process-reactive continuum, with initial symptom onset being intermediate rather than sudden, without original precipitants being identified for the majority. Fewer than 15% of the patients had experienced marriage that had not ended in divorce, and the great majority were maintained on psychotropic drugs. Diagnosis was equated to the extent that all patients had previously been labeled schizophrenic and nonorganic. Further investigation of diagnoses were not undertaken because of their notorious unreliability and lack of concurrent or predictive validity and a scientific preference for equation on actual functioning rather than labels. Although equation was also obtained on the presence of living relatives and geographical subregion of origin, these variables were only to ensure equality of resources over the three groups if release were to occur. However, the probability of release was obviously low, since the characteristics of the patient group clearly revealed them to be the most recalcitrant residual group of people with whom mental hospitals had ever attempted to cope.

Intercorrelations among descriptive characteristics, which might potentially relate to treatment responsiveness (all variables in table 12.1 except diagnosis, previous chemotherapy, living relatives, and subregion of origin) yielded eighteen significant correlations over all patients combined. Of these, none were significantly different among the three groups, further attesting to the comparability of equated groups prior to introduction of treatment programs.[1] All of the correlations were comparable to those found earlier by Lentz et al. (1971)

Table 12.1. Personal-social characteristics of original groups of patients before introduction of programs.

| Variable | Social-learning (N=28) | Milieu therapy (N=28) | Hospital comparison (N=28) | Total (N=84) |
|---|---|---|---|---|
| Age | | | | |
| Mean years | 45.3 | 44.8 | 44.4 | 44.8 |
| S.D. | 9.71 | 9.39 | 10.43 | 9.74 |
| Sex (% female) | 50.0% | 50.0% | 50.0% | 50.0% |
| Race (% black) | 14.3% | 7.1% | 17.9% | 13.1% |
| Socioeconomic status[a] | | | | |
| Mean | 62.1 | 63.3 | 60.6 | 62.0 |
| S.D. | 9.67 | 10.64 | 13.57 | 11.46 |
| Process-reactive status[b] | | | | |
| Mean | 7.54 | 8.21 | 8.54 | 8.06 |
| S.D. | 4.213 | 4.109 | 4.305 | 4.227 |
| Marital status (% never married or divorced) | 82.1% | 89.3% | 85.7% | 85.7% |
| Original symptom onset | | | | |
| Mean onset[c] | 1.57 | 1.71 | 1.71 | 1.67 |
| S.D. | .634 | .659 | .659 | .646 |
| Precipitants identified | 21.4% | 35.7% | 21.4% | 26.2% |
| Duration hospitalization | | | | |
| Mean mos. current | 173.3 | 169.5 | 172.2 | 171.7 |
| S.D. | 121.18 | 110.03 | 120.54 | 115.95 |
| Mean mos. total | 199.1 | 201.8 | 209.5 | 203.5 |
| S.D. | 110.53 | 115.86 | 108.88 | 110.53 |
| Hospital diagnosis | | | | |
| Schizophrenic | 100.0% | 100.0% | 100.0% | 100.0% |
| Organic | 0.0% | 0.0% | 0.0% | 0.0% |
| Previous somatic treatment | | | | |
| Chemotherapy | 100.0% | 100.0% | 100.0% | 100.0% |
| Electroconvulsive shock | 50.0% | 46.4% | 39.3% | 45.2% |
| Insulin shock | 28.6% | 28.6% | 32.1% | 29.8% |
| Other | 14.3% | 25.0% | 7.1% | 15.4% |
| Current psychotropic drugs | 89.3% | 96.4% | 89.3% | 91.7% |
| Living relatives on record | 96.4% | 85.7% | 85.7% | 89.3% |
| Geographical subregion at hospitalization | | | | |
| Mean | 5.6 | 5.6 | 5.8 | 5.6 |
| S.D. | 2.73 | 2.24 | 2.71 | 2.55 |

Note. All means, variances, and frequencies equated at $p > 0.25$ appropriate statistical tests (Bartlett, ANOVA, chi-square, Fisher exact probability).
a. A higher index indicates a lower status.
b. Process $\leq 12$.
c. Gradual (1) to sudden (3).

within the residual group of chronically institutionalized patients remaining in east-central Illinois state hospitals. Only two sex differences appeared, indicating that females tended to have been married more than males (r=-0.34) and were of relatively higher socioeconomic status (r=-0.40). Two small but significant correlations (in the 0.20s) with race indicated a tendency for black patients to be of lower socioeconomic status and younger than white patients. The only other significant correlation (r=0.25) with socioeconomic status indicated a tendency for patients of relatively lower status to have received more "other" medical treatment. Age was correlated only with length of hospitalization, for both most recent hospitalization (r=0.55) and total hospitalization (r=0.65), as would be expected in a group who had been hospitalized nearly two-thirds of their adult lives. Similarly, the part-whole correlation between length of total hospitalization and length of current hospitalization was strong (r=0.87).

The remaining significant relationships among demographic variables were in agreement with prior investigations of hospitalized mental patients and notable only in the fact that significant correlations existed at all within the restricted range. Thus, correlations (in the 0.20s) with the process-reactive score—even though the entire population was "process"—found the "more-process" patients to tend toward more gradual onset of initial symptomatology, longer lengths of hospitalization, more prior medical treatment, and more unsuccessful or absent marriages than the "less-process" patients. Similarly, low, but significant, correlations (in the 0.20s) found the presence of identified precipitating factors to be associated with relatively shorter total hospitalization and with prior electroconvulsive shock treatment, while prior insulin shock treatment was associated with longer current hospitalization. Significant positive correlations (in the 0.20s) were found between "other" medical treatments and both prior electroconvulsive and insulin shock treatments, while prior shock treatments correlated 0.46, reflecting the extent to which hospitals had unsuccessfully attempted to cope, repeatedly, with the same individuals.

*Level of Functioning.* IAB scores at anniversary assessment 0 for the original equated groups (presented in table 12.2) reveal the excellent equation on overall functioning before the introduction of the psychosocial programs.[2] The average level of functioning reflected on each component of the IAB was at, or slightly below, the level of the total residual chronic group from which study patients were selected (Lentz et al., 1971; Paul et al., 1976).

Comparisons of the level of functioning of the current patient groups with those reported by others on component instruments of the IAB found the current group to be more severely disabled than any other patient group previously subjected to systematic study.[3] Even on survey and instrument development samples, the only other institutionalized patients who scored lower than the current group on any measure were chronically regressed geriatric patients permanently residing on locked nursing wards. In general, the overall level of functioning of the current study patients before the introduction of programs was more similar to older, chronic, geriatric patient groups who averaged from twenty-five years to several decades of hospitalization than to younger chronic patients who were more similar in demographic characteristics. Like geriatric patients, over a third were mute or incontinent, and the great majority were totally deficient in social and self-care skills. However, unlike geriatric patients, the majority of patients selected to participate in the comparative project also demonstrated extreme bizarre behaviors.

A better picture of the actual behavior of study patients upon entry to the project is shown in table 12.3, where the data are presented from continuous objective assessments of the psychosocial groups during the baseline week before introduction of programmatic procedures.[4] Even though all group equation had been based only upon the original assessments of personal-social characteristics and IAB Functioning, table 12.3 shows excellent pretreatment equation on all components of actual behavior of psychosocial groups as well. All means were well equated; the only differences in variance were atrributed to two social-learning residents who showed deviantly high incidence of Cognitive Distortion for the group, two milieu residents who showed deviantly high levels of Interpersonal Skills for the group, and more clustering about the group mean on Self-Care skills in the milieu group than in the social-learning group.

Table 12.2. Level of functioning of original groups of patients before introduction of programs: Inpatient Assessment Battery (IAB).

| Score | Social-learning (N=28) | Milieu therapy (N=28) | Hospital comparison (N=28) | Total (N=84) |
|---|---|---|---|---|
| IAB Factor Score | | | | |
| Mean | 49.15 | 49.65 | 50.44 | 49.74 |
| S.D. | 6.950 | 6.606 | 5.422 | 6.305 |
| Component instruments | | | | |
| NOSIE-30[a] | | | | |
| Mean | 131.68 | 127.07 | 136.57 | 131.77 |
| S.D. | 28.624 | 28.029 | 21.962 | 26.348 |
| ISMF[b] | | | | |
| Mean | 48.41 | 49.11 | 48.84 | 48.79 |
| S.D. | 4.836 | 5.103 | 5.279 | 5.023 |
| MSBS[c] | | | | |
| Mean | 22.95 | 24.07 | 24.16 | 23.73 |
| S.D. | 5.156 | 4.820 | 3.880 | 4.627 |

Note. All means and variances equated at $p > 0.25$ by Bartlett's test and ANOVA.
a. Nurses Observational Scale for Inpatient Evaluation.
b. Inpatient Scale of Minimal Functioning.
c. Minimal Social Behavior Scale.

Table 12.3. Level of functioning of psychosocial treatment groups before introduction of programs: continuous objective assessments from TSBC and Clinical Frequencies.

| Objective index | Social-learning (N=28) Mean | S.D. | Milieu therapy (N=28) Mean | S.D. | Total (N=56) Mean | S.D. |
|---|---|---|---|---|---|---|
| Global Functioning Factor Score | 42.60 | 6.616 | 43.90 | 7.033 | 43.25 | 6.797 |
| Maladaptive behavior | | | | | | |
| Total Inappropriate Clinical Frequencies | 0.1886 | 0.10328 | 0.1914 | 0.11218 | 0.1900 | 0.10685 |
| Inappropriate Concurrent Behavior (TSBC) | .9260 | .52865 | .8497 | .39714 | .8879 | .46487 |
| Schizophrenic Disorganization Index | .6219 | .41759 | .5918 | .36562 | .6068 | .38918 |
| Cognitive Distortion Index | .2495 | .21873 | .2221 | .12440 | .2358 | .17685 |
| Hostile-Belligerence Index | .0036 | .01440 | .0032 | .01221 | .0034 | .01323 |
| Adaptive behavior | | | | | | |
| Total Appropriate Concurrent Behavior (TSBC) | 2.4471 | 0.46725 | 2.5217 | 0.52260 | 2.4844 | 0.49261 |
| Total Appropriate Clinical Frequencies | .1885 | .12859 | .2560 | .13359 | .2223 | .13430 |
| Interpersonal Skills Index | .0366 | .06582 | .1001 | .12939 | .0684 | .10664 |
| Instrumental Role Performance Index | .3757 | .27094 | .5338 | .27029 | .4547 | .27976 |
| Self-Care Index | .1287 | .08632 | .1260 | .05147 | .1274 | .07043 |

Note. All means equated at $p > 0.25$ by $t$-test and two-way ANOVA. Component variances differ significantly at $p < 0.05$ for Cognitive Distortion, Interpersonal Skills, and Self-Care.

The extent to which the targets of rehabilitation identified from the literature for chronically institutionalized mental patients pointed to severe behavioral excesses and deficits for these patients is clear from table 12.3. Inappropriate Concurrent Behavior from the TSBC shows the average resident over both groups performed a clinically inappropriate (crazy) behavior on approximately 90% of the two-second observations taken each waking hour prior to introduction of programs; reduction or elimination of such extreme bizarre behaviors was clearly required. The highest frequency class of clinically inappropriate behaviors was bizarre motoric behaviors (e.g., repetitive movements, blank staring, etc.) reflected in the Schizophrenic Disorganization Index. Bizarre verbal and facial behaviors (e.g., delusions and hallucinations, incoherent speech, etc.) reflected in the Cognitive Distortion Index were considerably less frequent than bizarre motoric behaviors but still occurred nearly a quarter of the time. Although the absolute incidence of Hostile-Belligerence was low, any occurrence of such high-intensity aggressive behaviors is clinically disruptive. A further indication of the extent of maladaptive behavior present before the introduction of the programs is reflected in the Total Inappropriate Clinical Frequencies, which shows the average resident to have given a gross inappropriate response to minimal expectations on nearly 20% of the opportunities to perform.

The severe deficits of these patients are also evident in the adaptive behavior indexes in table 12.3. Although the average resident was performing about two and a half concurrent, clinically appropriate behaviors in each two-second observation (TSBC Total Appropriate Behavior), normal performance of social and instrumental behavior (Total Appropriate Clinical Frequencies) occurred on only 22% of opportunities. The majority of normal performance of adaptive behavior was accounted for by being "on task" and "on time" for scheduled classes and activities (Instrumental Role Performance), but even these highest-frequency adaptive behaviors occurred less than half the time. The need for resocialization was particularly evident in the severe deficits in interpersonal interaction and communication skills reflected in the Interpersonal Skills Index—showing a failure of adaptive performance over 93% of the time—and in the Self-Care Index—reflecting a failure of appropriate self-maintenance activities over 87% of the time. While no previous observational studies have provided directly comparable data on institutionalized mental patients, the current population was clearly more severely disabled than any reported previously (e.g., Aumack, 1969; Harmatz et al., 1975; Hunter et al., 1962; Liberman et al., 1974).

Correlations of descriptive characteristics and level of functioning—indexed by the overall IAB Factor Score and the objective Global Functioning Factor Score—were calculated for descriptive characteristics that might relate to treatment responsiveness (all variables in table 12.1 except diagnosis, previous chemotherapy, living relatives, and subzone of origin). Five significant correlations were obtained with IAB Functioning for all patients combined over all three groups. As previously found by Lentz et al. (1971) in the larger hard-core population, the strongest relationship ($r=0.38$) was with the process-reactive score, even when mutes were excluded from the correlation. Although the entire population was "process," the "more-process" patients still tended toward lower levels of IAB Functioning. Low but significant correlations (in the 0.20s) also found that relatively lower levels of functioning were associated with the absence of identified precipitating factors on initial hospitalization, more gradual onset of initial symptomatology, prior insulin shock, and relatively longer lengths of total hospitalization. Only age correlated with objective Global Functioning ($r=0.26$), indicating a slight tendency for older residents in both psychosocial programs to function at higher levels than younger residents. IAB Functioning and objective Global Functioning Scores were correlated at $r=0.61$ at the pretreatment assessment.

None of the correlations between descriptive variables and IAB Functioning were significantly different among the three groups nor were correlations between descriptive variables and objective Global Functioning significantly different between milieu and social-learning groups, further indicating the comparability of equated groups.

## SUMMARY

The delay in the original notification of funding, combined with a maximum push of community and hospital staff to move patients into the community, resulted in a different study population from that in the original plan. The chronically institutionalized patients who remained hospitalized were those functioning at such a low level of self-care or demonstrating such excesses of bizarre behavior that they had been rejected for community placement. Prior to the introduction of differential treatment procedures, the three groups of the most severely debilitated chronically institutionalized adults ever subjected to systematic study were essentially identical on level and nature of functioning and on every characteristic of potential importance to treatment responsiveness.

# PART 3

# The First Six Months on the Psychosocial Units: Program Introduction and Rapid Response

## 13. Notable Events and Overview of the First Six Months

The most notable event of the first six months was that the project actually started; the programs were introduced according to prescribed procedures, and all required assessments were maintained. Although the delays had resulted in a multitude of changes in the original plans, several preliminary steps had been accomplished before the arrival of the residents.

An incredible amount of bureaucratic regulations and practices had been negotiated to shorten the typical three- to nine-month lag in introducing changes in procedures of a variety of state agencies and code departments to allow the project to operate at all. Even procedures that were allowed within the existing regulations had needed changes to accomplish actions that were required in two weeks rather than the typical six weeks to three months. Before the arrival of residents, necessary review committees, cost sharing and indirect cost agreements, etc., had been established within the center and between the center and federal agencies. Minimum supplementary funding had been obtained to replace some of the funds lost from the delay in notification. The physical plants of two psychosocial units had been opened and equipped to a minimal operating level, and administrative contact was established for working relationships between the psychosocial units and eight divisions within the center and ten agencies, divisions, and departments outside it. Approval for new job classifications, position descriptions, selection criteria, and certification of training programs had been obtained, and the initial minimum group of clinical, research, and auxiliary personnel needed for operation had been recruited, selected, processed, and trained. A reliable social worker at the state hospital had also been enlisted to monitor patient movement, thus ensuring that the same release criteria were maintained over all groups (independent self-support and an identified significant other over this period).

Additional accomplishments before the arrival of the residents included the development and printing of necessary clinical and research manuals and forms. Instrumentation and coding procedures for the Inpatient Assessment Battery and staff attitude, opinion, and descriptive assessments were prepared, and assessors were trained in their use. Instruments and forms for continuous objective assessment of staff and resident behavior had been developed and printed, and staff were trained in their use; however, the final formats were not established until pretesting during the orientation and exposure periods after the arrival of the residents, and summary and keypunch forms and computer programs were not completed until several months later. Treatment manuals and staff and resident schedules with equation of focus and staff time over programs had also been developed and printed, but the details of the timing of functional periods were not made final until they had been tested during orientation and exposure periods. All chronically institutionalized mental patients from the geographic area who met other selection criteria and still remained in one of the four state hospitals after having been rejected for shelter-care placement had been located, screened, and assessed. The assessments had been hand scored, and the three equated groups had been formed, and the legal aspects of transfer papers, medical records, informed consent from relatives and guardians, etc., had been completed.

The transfer of patients to the study locations was accomplished over a two-week period. For patients transferred to the psychosocial units, a common transfer and orientation procedure was followed at each of the state hospitals. Two days before transfer, each patient—even if completely disorganized or lying mute and incontinent on the floor—was briefly interviewed (ten to fifteen minutes) by two staff members (one senior, one junior) from the psychosocial programs, and the impending transfer to the center was described as a pleasant change where the patient would learn how to get along in the normal community again. The staff members described the center, attempting to relate it to the patient's previous experience. The date of the transfer was set, and attempts were made to ease any anxiety engendered by reassurance and provision of additional information. The patients were then transported to the center by automobile in groups of four by the same staff who had interviewed them two days earlier. The trip itself was viewed as a therapeutic opportunity in which staff pointed out landmarks, described the new facility in detail, described patient and staff roles, attempted to engage the patients in conversation, and mentioned the possibility of future release. Four patients were transferred to each psychosocial unit every other day. The study patients assigned to the state hospital group who were not already at the study location were informed of the move in the usual way and transferred in the routine manner over the same two-week period.

Additional patients who were not part of the three equated groups were also transferred to the state hospital to allow a controlled evaluation of the therapeutic versus routine transfer procedures employed. Equated subgroups of patients transferred by the therapeutic procedure and patients not transferred at all showed no change in functioning, while routine transfer patients declined temporarily and then returned to pretransfer levels of functioning after exposure to the new location for a few weeks. Thus, the therapeutic transfer procedures prevented a slight, temporary decrement in patient functioning, which occurred as a result of routine transfer procedures. (Details of the substudy have been published in Lentz & Paul [1971].)

Common orientation procedures were followed on both psychosocial units for the first two weeks after the completion of the transfers. The residents were introduced to staff and to each other and were shown the layout of the unit and center facilities through group meetings and tours. Clothing and medical and legal needs were assessed, and several small groups were taken downtown to try to provide each resident with a minimum amount of street clothing. The educators and the rehabilitation counselor conducted individual assessment sessions to determine current strengths and weaknesses in practical, academic, and vocational areas. Verbal descriptions and group tours were used in an attempt to familiarize residents with the daily schedules they would be expected to follow once the programs began.

Since nearly all residents were indigent and a majority did not exist legally (being committed, incompetent, and without a legal conservator), senior staff—the liaison coordinator in particular—began a never-ending job of meetings and correspondence with public aid, vocational rehabilitation, and Social Security, as well as a variety of legal agencies and other resources, in an attempt to obtain funds for residents' personal use and training. Neither state funds nor other sources were adequate during the initial orientation nor at any time during the intramural period to provide the minimum amounts of cash specified in the treatment manuals or to provide adequate minimum street clothing for residents. Therefore, active solicitations of donations of clothes and cash became a regular part of operations.

Common exposure procedures were introduced on both psychosocial units during the week following the two weeks of orientation. Residents' daily schedules were introduced, with the resident groups (all on step 1) being required to follow schedules to familiarize themselves with the routine, activities, and facilities available (see Ayllon & Azrin, 1968). The final minute-by-minute aspects of all staff and resident schedules were then established on the basis of empirical practicality during this period. Additionally, practice exercises and reliability checks on all forms and continuous assessment instruments and observers were completed during the exposure period. By the end of the week, all schedules, forms, and data collection procedures had been established.

Baseline conditions were then set up for one week on both psychosocial units to provide a common base for assessing resident functioning in both psychosocial groups after familiarization with schedules and facilities but before the introduction of programmatic procedures. The expectations were communicated to residents of both units by posted rules and group meetings in which they were told that they were no longer to be coerced into any particular activity because they could be responsible for their own behavior. All specific expectations of treatment programs were explained, and all schedules continued in operation.

Staff were given general instructions not to employ regular procedures of either treatment program during baseline but to attempt to maintain a positive atmosphere. Their approach was to make sure that residents were informed of what they were supposed to do and where they were supposed to be. Their major concern was to see that units were clean, beds made, residents dressed, and drugs given at appropriate times. When a task needed to be done, residents were first told to do it; if they did not, the task could be offered to "good workers." If all the procedures were unsuccessful, staff were to do the task themselves. Although staff were instructed to be pleasant, they were also told to think of themselves first and to ignore any resident behavior that did not interest them. Bothersome resident behavior could be ignored, or the resident could be instructed to stop. Assaults were to be dealt with by traditional means (drugs, restraints, tepid baths, physical separation, or instruction). Any questions from residents concerning the change in procedure were to be answered by simply stating that the doctor made the decision and the staff member did not know why. In general, instructions to staff were typical of those of the mental hospital aide culture.

All continuous objective assessments of both staff and resident functioning were started at the beginning of baseline conditions and were maintained throughout the remainder of the intramural period. Thus, a common base for assessing change between psychosocial programs, with the same staff, physical plant, and program schedules, existed before the introduction of programmatic procedures. Components of the Inpatient Assessment Battery (IAB) were also readministered to residents of both psychosocial groups and the state hospital comparison group at the end of the baseline week. An analysis of the data found no significant overall or differential change in functioning for any of the three groups as a result of transfer, new physical plant, or any other factors. Thus, a reliable and stable pretreatment assessment was established on the IAB over the current period for all three groups, while the continuously assessed objective measures of functioning on the psychosocial units demonstrated that they provided a stable, representative pretreatment base for assessing change when the programmatic procedures began.

The introduction of the psychosocial programs followed immediately upon the completion of the baseline week. During the first week of program introduction, the core therapeutic modalities (token economy on the social-learning unit and therapeutic community and living groups on the milieu therapy unit) were initiated following required exposure procedures to assure some familiarity with the principles for residents in each program. During the following three weeks, residents were no longer required to participate. Rather, the remaining principles and procedures of the two differential programs were gradually introduced, with total reliance upon these principles and procedures as the motivating factors. This was also the primary period of intensive on-the-job training for the initial group of junior staff. Both programs were completely operational by the end of the fourth week after baseline. Because of the initial delays, only twelve weeks remained before the first scheduled six-month anniversary assessment. Thus, the first "six months" of operation actually involved a total of only eighteen weeks of operation of the psychosocial programs (including the two-week assessment period), of which only partial programs had been operating over the first four-week block.

Differences from the structure or procedures detailed in the program manuals during the first eighteen weeks of operation were almost totally caused by the absence of funds. The limited budget of the center and the lack of familiarity with the consumption levels of large groups of residents (only a token number of residents had been in the center before this period) resulted in a much lower availability of consumables, facilities, and services than those set out in the manuals. In fact, no off-unit facilities and services were available at all because there were no staff or volunteers to operate them. Neither public transportation nor vans or buses were available to make use of downtown training opportunities. The original delay in notification of funding had resulted in the loss of outside sources for vocational evaluation and training. In fact, the training facilities were never reinstated throughout the entire intramural period because of a shortage of psychosocial staff to handle paperwork and transportation and the unwillingness of the outside training center to modify its routine after the departure of the original director, with whom arrangements had been made. Also, neither canteen coupons nor money was available to pay residents who attained higher step-level status for work in job training within the center. This shortage was a joint result of an absence of funds and conflicting regulations that prevented residents from receiving state funds.

On-unit consumables were similarly restricted during the first six months; neither coffee nor snacks were available at times other than regular meals and a few informal interaction periods—and then only coffee could be obtained through the serving kitchen. Canteen items were similarly restricted to cigarettes and candy bars, because the major grooming supplies were not available. Only two credits rather than three were available during baseline on both units and on the milieu unit for canteen purchases during the first six months. Weekend activity schedules had not been changed to reflect the schedule shown in the manuals since psychosocial programs had to fit schedules to the availability of the gymnasium on weekends: half of each unit had the weekend off-unit activity on Saturday and the other half on Sunday.

All other programmatic structure and procedures during the first eighteen weeks of program operation followed those stated in the treatment manuals, with the exception of a special Christmas program. Holiday schedules always followed weekend schedules, but with group meetings and informal interaction substituted for off-unit activities and housekeeping periods. Christmas day was the only time when program structures were not followed; both token exchanges and living group responsibilities were removed, but programmatic social interactions were maintained. On Christmas outside groups (such as carolers) were allowed on the units. A special contingency program was instituted during this period, in which residents with exceptionally high accumulated token fines were prompted to terminate specific intolerable behaviors for the three days preceding Christmas, with the consequence being a proportional payoff on the fine, which would allow the unrestricted status for the Christmas program. The usual restrictions in token spending were maintained during the last sixteen weeks of the period for social-learning residents with fines, including accumulated fines of more than thirty tokens resulting in the loss of regular beds, with nights being spent in a time out room. No overcorrection procedures were used for dealing with intolerable behavior in the social-learning program over the first six months, and the length of time out for all applications and time out and expulsion for all intolerable behavior, including assaults, was the remainder of the forty-five-minute functional period, with a minimum stay of twenty minutes. Medical meal procedures (appendix C) were instituted shortly after the introduction of the programs, following one resident's twenty-one-day hunger strike.

The use of psychotropic drugs during the first six months was the subject of systematic study. Nearly 92% of the psychosocial residents had been on continuous low-dosage psychotropic drugs at the time of transfer. A review of the literature found no firm evidence that such drug practice was beneficial; instead, it suggested that the drugs might lead to dangerous side effects and possibly reduced efficiency in the acquisition and transfer of learning from drug to nondrug states. Therefore, a triple-blind withdrawal study was undertaken concurrent with the introduction of programmatic procedures. After two equated subgroups of residents were formed within each program, based upon their assessed performance during baseline, all received coded drugs in different forms. One subgroup in each program received placebos, and the other received the same drug and dosage as they had previously, but in a different form. Following continuous monitoring through the first anniversary assessment—in which residents, clinical staff administering drugs, and observers recording resident functioning were not aware that a drug study was being carried out—absolutely no evidence at all was obtained for any beneficial effects of continuing maintenance chemotherapy. (Details of the study and its results, including considerable methodological improvements over other withdrawal studies, are published in Paul et al. [1972].) Thus, fewer than 50% of the residents in either program received active psychotropic drugs after the introduction of programs, and there were no differences at the first anniversary assessment between those who were and those who were not receiving drugs.

Staffing of the psychosocial programs remained considerably below the necessary clinical complement over the first six months because of the decentralization of center activities and the required increase of staff becoming known only after original training had begun. Thus, by the time baseline conditions were instituted, only 77% of the clinical complement was filled, including the liaison coordinator who spent only half-time in clinical contact. By the first anniversary assessment, only 84% of the complement was filled, and only 69% of staff present at the first anniversary assessment were continuous from those working during baseline conditions—reflecting the high turnover and added training burden that existed during this period. Of auxiliary staff, only the three educators and one rehabilitation counselor position had been filled. However, none of the demographic characteristics of the staff group (age, education, experience, sex, race, marital or parental status, extroversion, or emotionality) changed significantly ($p$'s $> 0.20$) from those of the original staff group present before arrival of residents.

The remaining chapters of part 3 report the results of the first six months of operation on the psychosocial units for both staff and residents. The objective outcome data on differential effectiveness from continuous assessments of resident behavior are presented in chapter 14, which details the statistical analyses for overall resident behavior for the interested research worker. The professional clinician or program director can obtain details of results by skipping the sections subtitled "Statistical evaluation." Preprofessional staff and others with little time should be able to obtain a good understanding of the outcome during this period by inspecting tables and figures and reading the summary and individual-improvement rates section at the end of chapter 14.

The descriptive characteristics of other ongoing resident activities are reported in chapter 15. Characteristics of the large group meetings, the use of available resources, time spent awake and with others, and the relative variability of several classes of resident behavior are analyzed and described to provide a picture of the effects on resident behaviors that had no specific good or bad connotation beforehand. Relationships that emerged between these characteristics and the level of resident functioning are reported in the text. Details of the statistical analyses are not reported, but the research worker should be able to follow the analyses given in the chapter notes, with the results incorporated in the text. Each section of chapter 15 ends with a detailed content summary. Preprofessional staff should also be able to obtain a good understanding of other resident behavior by inspecting the tables and figures and reading the summary of chapter 15.

All staff data are reported in chapter 16, including changes in staff opinions about mental patients, and staff attitudes, preferences, and interpretations of the nature and techniques of the milieu and social-learning programs. Details of actual staff performance during baseline conditions and after the introduction of programmatic procedures are also presented in this chapter, providing objective data on the reliability and differentiation of treatment conditions, how staff spent their time, and the amount and nature of attention residents actually received. Details of the statistical analyses are not reported, but the nature of analyses is referred to in notes for the interested research worker, and the results are incorporated in the text. Each section of chapter 16 ends with a detailed content summary for preprofessional staff and others short on time. The figures and tables in chapter 16 are sufficiently complex that some study and reference to in-text explanations would likely save time.

Finally, the major conclusions and results at the end of the first six months on the psychosocial units are briefly summarized in chapter 17.

# 14. Differential Effectiveness of Milieu and Social-Learning Programs After Program Introduction

## CHANGES IN GLOBAL FUNCTIONING[1]

Raw changes in total appropriate and inappropriate functioning from before the program introduction through the first anniversary assessment are presented in figure 14.1, which shows an exceptionally rapid response to both programs over the four weeks during which successive aspects of treatment procedures were introduced. Continued rapid improvement was particularly apparent in both appropriate and inappropriate concurrent behavior (TSBC) over the first four weeks when the programs were completely operational. During the remaining two and a half months, through the first anniversary assessment period, improvement occurred at a much slower rate, with the trends suggesting stability or perhaps even a slight decrement from the early response of milieu residents.

*Statistical evaluation.* Overall changes from the baseline period to the first anniversary assessment were evaluated by a two-way repeated measures ANOVA on the standardized Global Functioning Score (milieu vs. social-learning programs; baseline vs. anniversary 1). This analysis found a significant time main effect ($F=235.02$, $df=1/54$, $p < 0.01$). and a significant program x time interaction ($F=10.96$, $df=1/54$, $p < 0.01$). Partitioning of simple effects found that a significant improvement in Global Functioning occurred for both the milieu program (mean change from 43.90 to 51.44, $F=72.32$, $df=1/54$, $p < 0.01$) and the social-learning program (mean change from 42.60 to 54.29, $F=173.83$, $df=1/54, p < 0.01$). Since the two groups did not differ in Global Functioning before the different treatment programs began, the program x time interaction reflects a significantly greater improvement for the social-learning program than for milieu therapy, even though both programs produced improvement.

## CHANGES IN MALADAPTIVE BEHAVIOR

The changes in Global Functioning clearly show significant improvement for residents in both treatment programs, with the social-learning program providing additional gains over those obtained by milieu therapy. Clinically the reduction in overall maladaptive behavior during this brief time period was remarkable. The reduction in Total Inappropriate Clinical Frequencies (figure 14.1) reflects an average change from approximately 19% grossly inappropriate response to minimal expectations for appropriate behavior to about 9% for milieu residents and less than 1% for social-learning residents. Perhaps even more notable is the reduction in concurrent, clinically inappropriate (crazy) behavior reflected in TSBC Total Inappropriate Behavior (figure 14.1), which directly reflects one of the most important target areas for rehabilitation of the chronic population. Before the treatment procedures began, the average resident on both treatment units had performed a crazy behavior on approximately 90% of the two-second observations taken every waking hour. By the time of the first anniversary assessment, the relative frequency of clinically maladaptive behavior had been reduced by about half for those in both programs. Of greater clinical interest are the changes in components of TSBC Total Inappropriate Behavior (figure 14.2), which suggest further differential responsiveness to the two treatment programs.

*Statistical evaluation.* To statistically evaluate a possible differential change in maladaptive behavior over this time period, standardized scores for Total Inappropriate Clinical Frequencies and TSBC Schizophrenic Disorganization, Cognitive Distortion and Hostile-Belligerence indexes were entered into a three-way repeated-measures ANOVA (milieu vs. social-learning programs; baseline vs. anniversary 1; scores).[2] As expected from the primary analysis on Global Functioning, the time main effect for maladaptive behavior was significant in the overall analysis ($F=87.21$, $df=1/54$, $p < 0.01$), as were the score main effect ($F=3.55$, $df=3/162$, $p < 0.05$) and the score x time interaction ($F=5.71$, $df=3/162$, $p < 0.01$).

Of more interest are the results of selective partitioning of simple effects and a priori tests of individual components. Tests of within-group

## Differential Effectiveness of the Programs 139

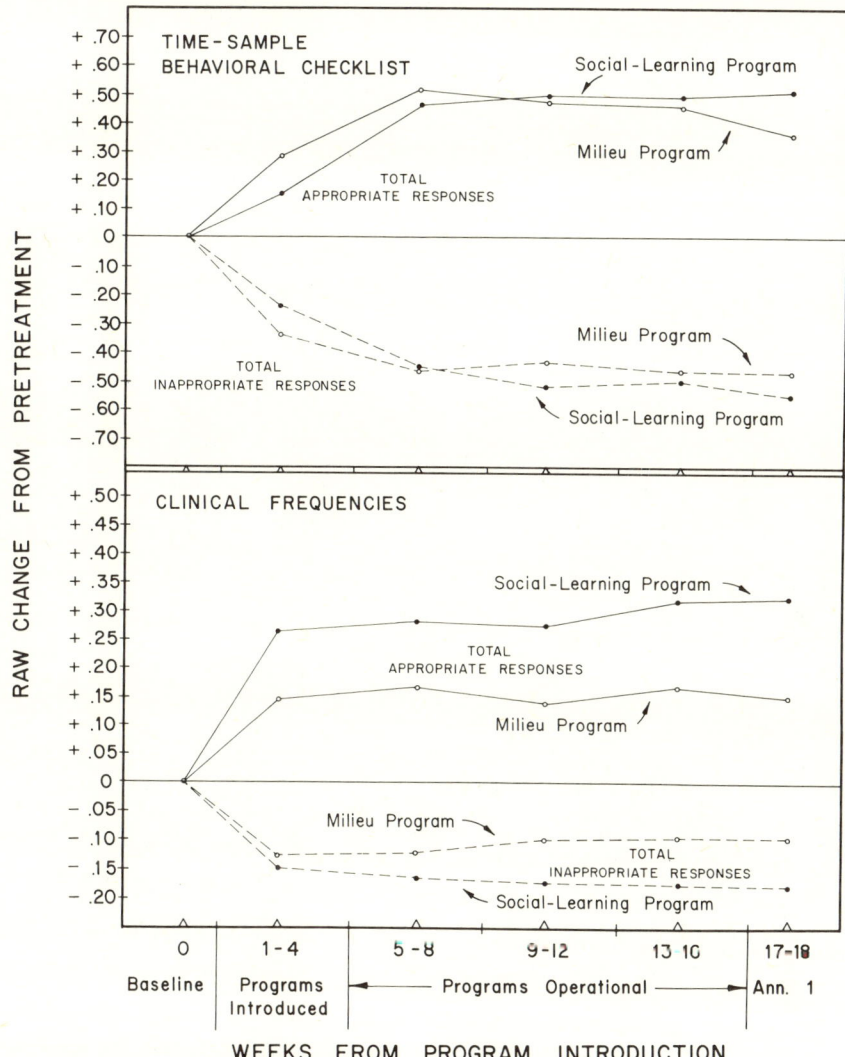

Figure 14.1. Overall changes in concurrent behavior (TSBC) and responsiveness within programs (Clinical Frequencies).

change on each score found significant reductions on all four maladaptive behavior indexes for the milieu program (all F's > 7.67, df=1/54, p < 0.01). Parallel tests for the social-learning program found significant reductions in Schizophrenic Disorganization, Cognitive Distortion, and Total Inappropriate Clinical Frequencies (all F's > 44.25, df=1/54, p < 0.01), but the reduction in Hostile-Belligerence was not statistically significant (F < 1). The simple interaction between the treatment programs and change over time were significant for Cognitive Distortion (F=6.78, df=1/54, p < 0.05) and Total Inappropriate Clinical Frequencies (F=16.93, df=1/54, p < 0.01), indicating greater improvement for social-learning than milieu residents in both instances. The differential change was sufficient that residents in the social-learning program were significantly lower than milieu residents in absolute level by the first anniversary assessment (F=5.23, df=1/54, p < 0.05).

*Descriptive interpretation.* Both treatment programs significantly reduced Schizophrenic Disorganization, without differential effectiveness between them. The change (figure 14.2) took place rapidly upon the introduction of the treatment programs and was relatively stable for the last two and a half months of this period. On an absolute level, the behaviors entering the Schizophrenic Disorganization Index—primarily bizarre overt motor behaviors (e.g., rocking, repetitive movements, blank staring, etc.)—were the highest frequency maladaptive clinical behaviors observed among residents before the programs started. The average resident on both units performed one of these bizarre behaviors on approximately 61% of the two-second observations each waking hour. However, these high-frequency bizarre

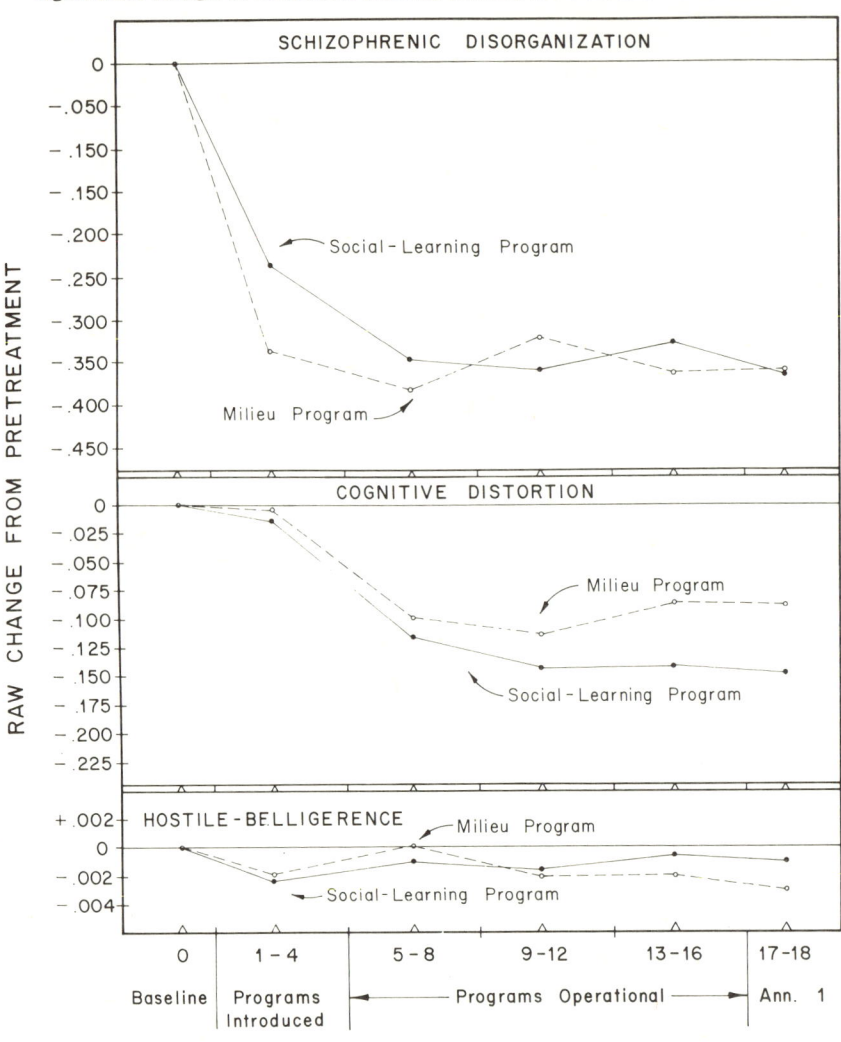

Figure 14.2. Changes in component clinically maladaptive behaviors from the TSBC.

motoric behaviors were rapidly reduced by nearly two-thirds, to an average incidence of about 24% within this relatively brief exposure to treatment.

Both treatment programs produced significant reductions in gross inappropriate response to minimal expectations ("Clinical Frequencies," figure 14.1), and in "Cognitive Distortion" (figure 14.2), but the social-learning program was differentially even more effective than the milieu program was. The average incidence of Inappropriate Clinical Frequencies was reduced, respectively, to about 9% and less than 1% of opportunities to perform in the milieu and social-learning programs. On an absolute level, the behaviors entering into the Cognitive Distortion Index—primarily bizarre verbal and facial behaviors indicative of thought disorder (e.g., delusions, hallucinations, incoherent speech, smiling without stimulus, etc.)—were less frequent than those of the Schizophrenic Disorganization Index, occurring on approximately 24% of observations before the introduction of programs. By the time of the first anniversary assessment, the social-learning program had reduced Cognitive Distortion by over half of the initial level to about 10% occurrence, while the reduction achieved through the milieu program resulted in an absolute average occurrence of just over 13% by the end of the period.

The Hostile-Belligerence Index (figure 14.2) was the primary source of the significant ANOVA effects involving scores, since absolute level and change were considerably smaller for both programs than for the other classes of maladaptive behavior. On an absolute level, the behaviors entering the Hostile-Belligerence

Index occurred on an average of just over 0.3% of observations before the introduction of programs. The incidence was reduced in both programs by the time of the first anniversary assessment to zero in the milieu program and to 0.25% of observations in the social-learning program. The differences were not statistically significant. Even though the incidence of Hostile-Belligerence was low on an absolute basis, the nature of these behaviors—high-intensity aggressive behaviors (e.g., screaming, cursing, verbal intrusion, etc.)—is such that any occurrence is disruptive clinically. However, low-rate, high-intensity behaviors are much less adequately assessed by time sampling than are the behaviors entering into other TSBC indexes.

A better assessment of dangerous and aggressive acts at the treatment unit level, especially physical assault, was available in recorded clinical frequencies of intolerable behavior, each occurrence of which required a special report to be logged by clinical staff. The change in the average weekly incidence of Intolerable Behavior differed significantly between treatment programs from baseline to the first anniversary assessment (chi-square= 10.33, df=1, p < 0.01).[3] This difference was a result of a significant decrease in incidence of Intolerable Behavior on the social-learning unit (from 32 to 6, chi-square=16.45, df=1, p < 0.01), while the milieu unit did not differ significantly from the social-learning unit at baseline (p > 0.10) and did not change significantly over this time period (from 21 to 23, chi-square < 1). The differences between programs in the incidence of Intolerable Behavior during the first anniversary assessment period were statistically significant (chi-square= 8.83, df=1, p < 0.01).

## CHANGES IN ADAPTIVE BEHAVIOR

The changes in components of maladaptive behavior clearly show dramatic and significant reductions in Schizophrenic Disorganization for residents of both treatment programs. While the milieu therapy program also produced major and significant reductions in grossly inappropriate responses to minimal behavioral expectations and in dysfunctional cognitive behaviors, the social-learning program produced even greater ones. The frequency of observed instances of time-sampled Hostile-Belligerence was low to start with, and then decreased slightly, without differences between programs; however, the total incidence of aggressive Intolerable Behavior was reduced only in the social-learning program. Thus, one of the areas identified as essential for rehabilitation of the chronically institutionalized population had shown dramatic and differential improvement, even by the first anniversary assessment period.

Both concurrent behavior (TSBC) and responsiveness within programs (Clinical Frequencies) reflected rapid improvement, with Clinical Frequencies suggesting further differential effectiveness between the milieu and social-learning programs (figure 14.1). On an absolute level, the TSBC Total Appropriate Index found that residents on both treatment units were performing about two and a half appropriate behaviors on the average observation. By the time of the first anniversary assessment, the average social-learning resident had shown an increase of one appropriate behavior on approximately 51% of observations, and the average milieu resident had shown an increase of one appropriate behavior on about 36% of observations. The increase in Total Appropriate Clinical Frequencies reflects an average change from approximately 22% terminal-level performance (i.e., not distinguishable from normal) of social and instrumental behaviors to more than double the initial level for social-learning residents (nearly 51%) and to about 40% for milieu therapy residents. Of greater clinical interest are the changes in the components of adaptive clinical frequencies, which directly reflect the other identified target areas for rehabilitation. These indexes, presented in figure 14.3, suggest further differential responsiveness to the two treatment programs over all three components of social and instrumental behavior.

*Statistical evaluation.* In order to evaluate differential change in adaptive behavior over this time period, standardized scores for TSBC Total Appropriate Behavior and Clinical Frequencies for Instrumental Role Performance, Interpersonal Skills and Self-Care Indexes were entered into a three-way repeated-measures ANOVA (milieu vs. social-learning programs; baseline vs. anniversary 1; scores). As expected from the primary analysis on Global Functioning, the time main effect for adaptive behavior was significant in the overall analysis ($F=104.55$, df=1/54, $p < 0.01$), as were the scores main effect ($F=35.22$, df=3/162, $p < 0.01$) and interactions of programs x time ($F=9.82$, df=1/54, $p < 0.01$), programs x scores ($F=3.40$, df=3/162, $p < 0.05$), and time x scores ($F=5.94$, df=3/162, $p < 0.01$).

Of more interest are the results of a selective partitioning of simple effects and a priori tests of individual components. Tests of the within-groups change on each score found significant increases on all four adaptive behavior indexes for both the milieu (all F's > 4.69, df=1/54, $p < 0.05$) and the social-learning program (all F's > 20.47, df=1/54, $p < 0.01$). The simple interactions between treatment programs and change over time were significant

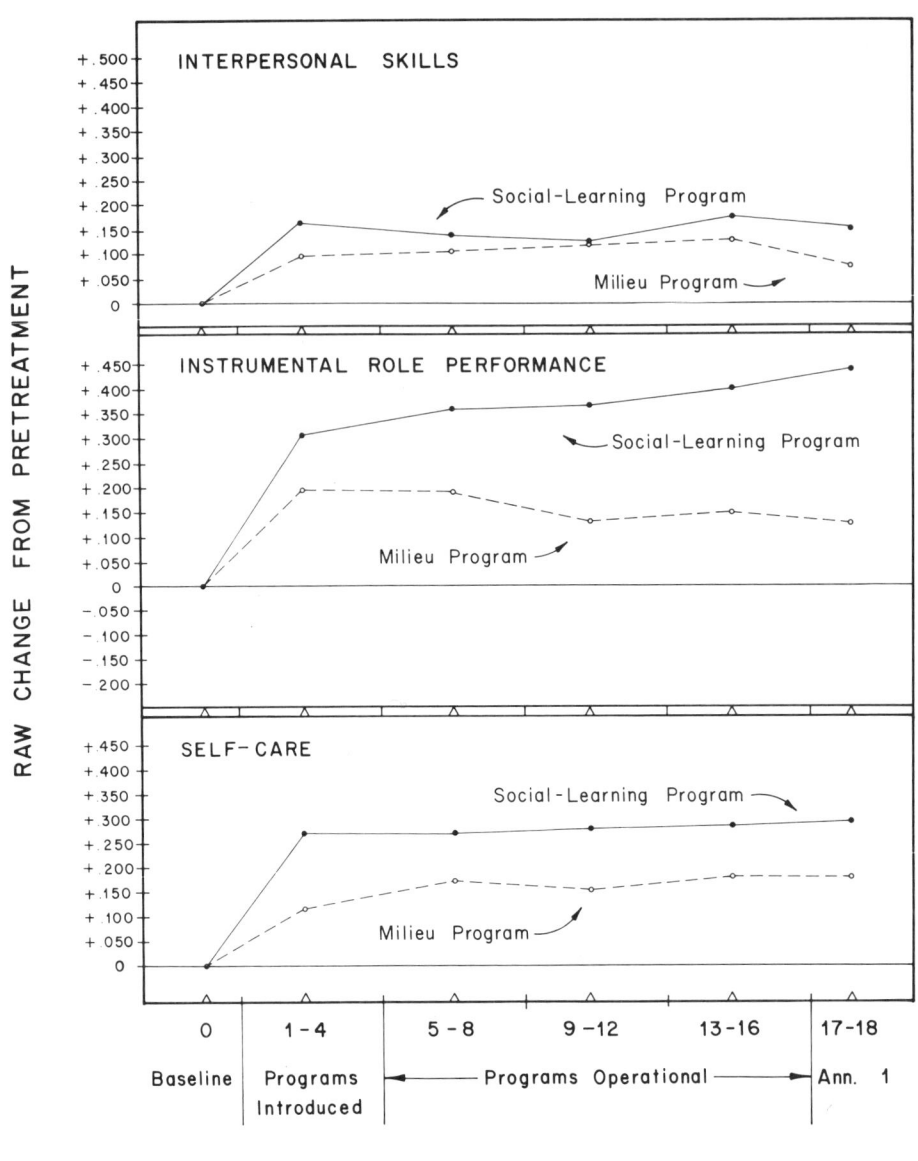

Figure 14.3. Changes in component adaptive behavior from Clinical Frequencies.

for Instrumental Role Performance (F=12.75, df=1/54, p < 0.01) and for Self-Care (F=6.64, df=1/54, p < 0.05), indicating greater improvement for social-learning than for milieu residents in both instances. The differential change was sufficient that residents in the social-learning program were significantly higher than milieu residents in absolute level by the first anniversary assessment (F=6.20, df=1/54, p < 0.05).

*Descriptive interpretation.* Thus, both treatment programs significantly increased concurrent appropriate behavior, without differential effectiveness between them. The change (figure 14.1, TSBC) took place rapidly, resulting in an increased incidence of appropriate concurrent behavior in both programs, although the trend over the last two and a half months of the period suggested there was a tendency for differences in improvement rates. Both treatment programs also produced significant increases in Interpersonal Skills, without differential effectiveness (figure 14.3). This index was the primary source of the significant ANOVA effects involving scores, since absolute level and change were considerably smaller for both programs than for other classes of adaptive behavior. On an absolute level, the behaviors entering the Interpersonal Skills Index—relative frequencies of interpersonal interaction and communications skills—reflect the greatest deficits of all areas for residents in the study. Before the introduction of the programs, the average resident demonstrated terminal-level performance (i.e., normal) of these social skills on only 7% of the available opportunities. While residents in both programs showed significant increases, approximately doubling the initial rate, the average over programs for incidence of normal interpersonal skills performance was still only about 18% of available opportunities at the first anniversary assessment.

Both treatment programs produced significant increases in Self-Care and Instrumental Role Performance (figure 14.3), but the social-learning program was differentially even more effective than the milieu program with these classes of adaptive behavior. Self-Care showed rapid change during the program introduction, with more gradual change after that. The behaviors entering the Self-Care Index—relative frequencies of terminal-level performance of self-maintenance activities (e.g., personal appearance, meal behavior, bathing, maintenance of personal living area, etc.)—directly reflect another component of the resocialization target area for rehabilitation. On an absolute level, normal performance of self-care activities was also exceptionally low before the introduction of the treatment programs, occurring, on the average, on fewer than 13% of opportunities. By the time of the first anniversary assessment, milieu residents had increased Self-Care to an average 30% terminal performance, and social-learning residents had improved even more, to an average of over 42% terminal performance—more than tripling the initial level.

Residents of both programs were initially less deficient in Instrumental Role Performance, the third rehabilitation target, than in either Interpersonal Skills or Self-Care, averaging about 45% normal performance over the two groups before the start of the programs. However, a greater disparity in responsiveness to the two programs is apparent in figure 14.3 for Instrumental Role Performance. Residents of both treatment programs showed the rapid initial improvement made in other areas of functioning, but milieu residents failed to continue to improve, and social-learning residents demonstrated steady gains. Thus, the behaviors entering the Instrumental Role Index—primarily "on task" in classes and low-level jobs and "on time" at scheduled work, activities, and meetings—appear to be especially responsive to the social-learning principles, reaching about 81% average terminal-level performance by the first assessment period. Milieu residents also showed significant gains in Instrumental Role Performance but had apparently stabilized at an average of about 66% terminal-level performance by the first anniversary assessment.

## SUMMARY AND INDIVIDUAL IMPROVEMENT RATES

Dramatic and significant improvement in Global Functioning occurred for both treatment programs, with the social-learning program producing even greater improvement than the milieu therapy program did. Parallel findings were obtained on an analysis of components of both maladaptive and adaptive behavior. Both programs were equally effective in producing rapid and major reductions in the highest-frequency bizarre clinical behaviors—Schizophrenic Disorganization—and significant increases in the most deficient area of performance—Interpersonal Skills. Both programs also were equally effective in increasing residents' appropriate concurrent behavior. While significant and dramatic improvements in the majority of other areas of behavior were obtained by those in both programs, the social-learning program was differentially even more effective in reducing Total Inappropriate Clinical Frequencies and Cognitive Distortion and in increasing Self-Care and Instrumental Role Performance. Only the social-learning program, however, significantly reduced the incidence of aggressive Intolerable Behavior.

Since clinical workers are more often concerned with percentage improvement of individual cases than with parametric group differences, the Global Functioning Factor Scores were further evaluated on the basis of individually significant change to provide an indication of the extent of individual resident response. Improvement rates presented in table 14.1 disclose exceptionally high rates of individual improvement over this period for both treatment programs, with the social-learning program affecting more residents than the milieu program did. Particularly striking is the finding of significant improvement in objectively and continuously assessed behavior for every resident in the social-learning program. The possible predictability of responsiveness from the fourteen demographic variables (see table 12.1) and the initial level of functioning was assessed within the milieu program, where a quarter of residents showed no change. Significant correlations showed a tendency only for improved residents within the milieu program to be more likely female than male (r=0.41) and to have been hospitalized a relatively shorter time (r=-0.39).[4]

While none of the residents in either program had improved sufficiently to obtain release to independent functioning (the requirement for discharge during this period), 15% of those in both programs had improved so rapidly, with stable increases in functioning, that they were promoted and maintained their status at higher step levels within the programs. Another 7% of

Table 14.1. Objective improvement rates in overall functioning from program entry to first anniversary assessment for original equated groups (N=28 each).

| Treatment program | Condition at first "six-month" assessment | | |
|---|---|---|---|
| | Worse[a] | No change | Improved[a] |
| Social-learning | 0% | 0% | 100% |
| Milieu therapy | 0% | 25% | 75% |

a. "Improved" and "worse" classification based upon individual change from entry exceeding 1.96 times the standard error of measurement on the standardized Global Functioning Factor Score. Fisher exact probability (two-sided)=0.01.

milieu and 11% of social-learning residents were promoted but failed to maintain their functioning to meet the stringent requirements to stay at the higher levels; they were consequently demoted back to step 1.

The responsiveness to both treatment programs, and the differential responsiveness to the social-learning program, during only eighteen weeks of active treatment procedures was truly remarkable. Given the severely debilitated nature of the residents, even the 75% figure of those significantly improved for the least effective psychosocial program was surprising. But even with such significant improvement, the residents were still functioning at minimal levels at best—still demonstrating bizarre clinical behaviors 38% of the time (down from 90%) and demonstrating normal social and instrumental behavior only 40% and 51% of the time, respectively, for the milieu and social-learning groups (up from only 22%). The individual improvements obtained during this period in the social-learning program ranged from a reduction in incontinence of six incidents per day to one incident per week in a man who was still mute, through a change from total apathy and lack of communication to functioning indistinguishable from the normal population. The range of improvements during this period in the milieu therapy program was equally broad, except that 25% of the milieu residents showed no significant change at all during the period.

*A Few Illustrations.* A few case descriptions may help to illustrate both the range in the rate of change obtained during the first eighteen weeks of treatment for improved residents and the behavior reflected in the TSBC and Clinical Frequencies.

*Jess W. (social-learning)* was a forty-eight-year-old, single ex-farmer who had been hospitalized continuously for about six years since his admission to a state hospital. Jess was not representative of the lower-functioning members of the population in the study, but he was clearly typical of large numbers of long-term institutionalized residents encountered in state hospitals: apathetic, inactive, only minimally conversational and cooperative. Jess's behavior at the state hospital before transfer was reported to lack a demonstration of any self-care, instrumental role, or interpersonal skills. Aides described Jess as "always" sitting and sleeping unless otherwise directed, and he frequently refused to perform even simple self-care tasks expected of everyone on the ward. While his bizarre behavior was infrequent, he was reported to be "rather mute," never initiating a conversation, never attempting to be friendly, and avoiding other people.

The accuracy of the state hospital descriptions was apparent on Jess's entry to the social-learning program. During the week before the programs began, he sat alone for hours, staring at his shoes, neither speaking nor responding, with no interest in activities. This extreme apathy and inactivity was largely responsible for his TSBC Total Inappropriate Index of 0.54, since objective observations found him engaging in blank staring 27% of the time, and his eyes were closed an additional 24% of the time. His responsiveness within the treatment program was also low on an absolute level before the introduction of specific procedures. His Interpersonal Skills Index was 0, reflecting a complete absence of normal social interaction or participation in activities or meetings. While high for the group of residents as a whole, his Self-Care Index of 0.21 reflected that he never cleaned his personal living area appropriately, never demonstrated adequate meal behavior, and presented an acceptable appearance on only 14% of the opportunities. The majority of his positive self-care behaviors came from the fact that he did arise on time every morning. His Instrumental Role Performance Index of 0.46 was slightly above average for the group, largely attributable to the fact that he attended classes on time at every scheduled announcement and attended meetings on time on 50% of occasions. However, he failed to attend activities or scheduled jobs.

Jess's progress during the period exemplifies the general improvements in resident behavior from before the introduction of the procedures to the first anniversary assessment in the social-learning program. By eight weeks after program introduction, Jess had demonstrated rapid and significant gains. His concurrent, clinically inappropriate behavior had reduced to 0.30, reflecting reductions in blank staring to 16% and reductions in "eyes closed" to 13%. His interpersonal skills were still low but had improved from 0 to 5% normal social interaction. His Self-Care Index had dramatically improved to 0.69 reflecting 100% terminal-level performance for cleaning his personal living area and bathing, in addition to arising on time. Additionally he passed 76% of his appearance checks perfectly, and his meal behavior was indistinguishable from normal 32% of the time. Similar rates of improvement were seen in Instrumental Role Performance, which had increased to 0.94; he appeared for all scheduled classes and meetings and performed in class totally appropriately 83% of the time.

By the first anniversary assessment, eighteen weeks after the introduction of the social-learning procedures, all areas of functioning showed even further improvement. His concurrent clinically inappropriate behavior had been reduced by over half the initial level to 0.21, with blank staring now occurring less than 9% of the time, and his eyes closed on only 13% of observations. His Interpersonal Skills had improved to 20% normal social interaction—still low on an absolute level but a dramatic increase from the zero level before program introduction. Self-Care improved further to 0.81, maintaining his perfect performance in the areas of self-maintenance he had achieved by the eighth week, while further improving meal behavior to 42% performance indistinguishable from normal and improving appearance to 95%. His Instrumental Role Performance was maintained at the level achieved by the eighth week. Because of these improvements, without any increases in inappropriate behavior, Jess both qualified for and requested promotion to step 2. Thus, by the first anniversary assessment, Jess had progressed from a rather typical chronic patient, characterized by extreme deficits in social behavior and apathetic withdrawal, to participation and improved skills indistinguishable from those of normal people the majority of the time.

Cass L. (milieu program) was a fifty-four-year-old, single, former odd-jobber who had been continuously hospitalized for about five years. Like Jess W., Cass was initially less severely disabled than the majority of the other residents in the program, but he was clearly representative of large numbers of long-term institutionalized residents in state hospitals. Withdrawal and apathy were the major features reflected in his TSBC Total Inappropriate Index of 0.94 during the week before the introduction of the treatment program. His clinically inappropriate behaviors were about average incidence for the group, reflecting high occurrence of lying down during scheduled activities (35%), as well as blank staring, pacing, shaking, and grimacing without external stimulation when he was not lying down. In spite of the incidence of clinically inappropriate behavior, Cass's social and instrumental behavior—while low in absolute terms—were among the highest of all residents in the study at program entry, showing normal performance on Total Appropriate Clinical Frequencies on 42% of the occasions. The major source of his high Appropriate Index was his Instrumental Role Performance of 0.88, which reflected that he attended and participated in most classes, activities, and jobs, even at program entry. Cass was also high for the group on Self-Care, with an index of 0.20, reflecting that he regularly got up on time and bathed appropriately; however, before the program began, he never presented an acceptable personal appearance or maintained his personal living area at normal levels. Interpersonal Skills deficits were indicated in an index of 0.16; while above the group mean, this index reflects that he was engaging in normal interpersonal interaction or communication on only 16% of the available opportunities.

Cass's progress during the current period was the most outstanding of all residents in the milieu program. Primarily because of his relatively higher appropriate behavior, Cass was immediately elected a group leader upon the introduction of the living groups. Before eight weeks had elapsed, his clinically inappropriate concurrent behavior had dropped from 0.94 to 0.07, with no single bizarre behavior occurring more than once. Withdrawal, his major concurrent clinical feature, had dropped to less than a quarter of the level of occurrence before program entry. His progress in the reduction of clinically inappropriate behavior continued, though more slowly, through the first anniversary assessment. Cass became quite active within the milieu program, guiding and encouraging his living group and the community group toward progress and performance. The areas of his own adaptive performance at program entry continued without loss, and his deficit areas drastically improved to the extent that his Total Appropriate Clinical Frequencies reflected performance indistinguishable from normal on 98% of opportunities by the first anniversary assessment. This performance showed nearly a complete removal of deficits in all areas, with Self-Care, Interpersonal Skills, and Instrumental Role behaviors improving, respectively, to 98%, 97%, and 100% terminal-level performance. Thus, Cass had progressed from a rather typical chronic patient showing nearly continuous withdrawal, apathy, and inappropriate clinical behavior, and considerable deficits in social and instrumental behavior, to functioning indistinguishable from that of the average person. This rapid improvement was such that he had achieved step 4 promotion within the program, was engaged in job training thirty hours per week, and was preparing discharge plans by the first anniversary assessment.

Sam F. *(milieu program)* was a laborer who had spent more than seventeen years in state hospitals since his last admission at the age of thirty. His functioning before program entry was more typical of that of the majority of other residents in the program who did not show actively disruptive behavior. His initial TSBC Total Inappropriate Index of 1.40 indicated that he was performing more than one clinically inappropriate behavior on every objective observation. The content of this behavior was similar to that of Cass L.—standing alone or lying down, blank staring, talking to himself, and grimacing without external stimulus—but at higher rates of occurrence. However, unlike Cass, Sam showed more severe deficiencies in social and instrumental behavior, reflected by a Total Appropriate Clinical Frequency Index of 0.23—right at the mean for the group. His Instrumental Role Performance of 0.48 was also at the group mean, as were his absolute level of Self-Care and Interpersonal Skills. Before program introduction, Sam never adequately maintained his personal living area or his appearance, and he did not eat appropriately on any occasion. His Interpersonal Skills were similarly deficit; he performed normal social interaction on only 2% of the opportunities.

Sam's progress during the period was similar to the improvements shown by the majority of other residents in the milieu program. The greatest improvements occurred immediately in his levels of inappropriate behavior. Within eight weeks of the program introduction Sam's concurrent clinically inappropriate behavior had dropped from an average of 1.4 incidents on every observation to a single incidence on fewer than 17% of observations—about an eighth the frequency of the initial level. All areas of his clinically inappropriate behavior had improved, and "talking to self" had completely dropped out. His improvements in social and instrumental deficits were less dramatic. His Interpersonal Skills had improved but only to a level of normal social interaction on about 12% of opportunities to perform; he made no improvements at all in Self-Care. By the first anniversary assessment, Sam still failed to eat appropriately or to show adequate maintenance of his appearance or his personal living area on a single occasion. Nevertheless, there were signs that he would improve further. His Instrumental Role Performance had increased to 0.71 by the first anniversary assessment, reflecting his attendance at classes and activities in more than three-quarters of scheduled periods. Thus, Sam had improved from a severely debilitated and apathetic chronic patient—typical of the nonassaultive residents of the current group—to a point in which his clinically inappropriate behaviors were a rarity. While there were important improvements in his appropriate behavior by the time of the first anniversary assessment, even doubling initial levels still left Sam a severely debilitated man who could in no way survive outside an institution.

Bobbi F. *(social-learning)* was a fifty-two-year-old former housewife who had been hospitalized over fourteen years by the time of her transfer to the social-learning program. Her behavior upon entry to the program was representative of that of the large group of other residents in the project who had come from the locked wards of state hospitals—frequently spending most of her time in the canvas-restrained tubs of hydrotherapy. Her initial TSBC Inappropriate Index of 1.30 reflected high levels of active, clinically bizarre behavior across all three indexes of Schizophrenic Disorganization, Cognitive Distortion, and Hostile-Belligerence. For a full week before the program began, she ran around nude, walked on furniture, and physically attacked both staff and residents. During one early week, she accounted for twenty-three incidents of assault within a seven-day period. Her Cognitive Distortion Index reflected delusional or hallucinatory statements on 30% of observations, such as shouting "There is a vampire on the wall" and "They are going to kill Princess Grace." Her adaptive behavior was completely deficient, with a Total Appropriate Clinical Frequency Index of only 0.04, reflecting a complete absence of bathing, maintenance of personal living area and appearance, and appropriate meal behavior. She further showed a complete absence of appropriate social interaction and class participation—attending class only 20% of the time.

Bobbi's response to the introduction of the social-learning procedures was particularly dramatic and impressive following the severe disruption she demonstrated earlier—but typical of the response of other agitated and aggressive residents in the program. The most obvious improvement was a great reduction in her disruptive and intolerable behavior from 23 incidents before the program introduction to weekly averages of 5 by the eighth week and 0.5 by the first anniversary assessment. Such change was similarly reflected on the Hostile-Belligerence Index, which reduced and stabilized at essentially zero from the eighth week of treatment on. Her concurrent, clinically inappropriate behavior similarly reduced to less than a third of the initial level within eight weeks. By the first anniversary assessment, a single occurrence of bizarre behavior was occurring on only 45% of observations. Her delusional verbalizations in particular had nearly stopped by the end of the period, and Cognitive Distortion was occurring on only 5% of objective observations. Similarly her agitation, running, etc., had been reduced to the extent that her entire Schizophrenic Disorganization Index had dropped to 0.28 (one-third the initial rate) within eighteen weeks of the program introduction.

With the reduction in bizarre and aggressive behavior, Bobbi concurrently showed major gains in areas of deficient adaptive behaviors. Her Instrumental Role Performance showed over a sixfold increase, to the point where she was attending 60% of classes on time and participating appropriately in 47% of them. Her Interpersonal Skills had improved from zero to 12% normal social interaction, and her Self-Care had improved to 8%—largely reflecting successful training in bathing. She still was completely deficient in normal performance of all other areas of self-care. Thus, Bobbi reflects the nature of improvement obtained for residents representative of the most severely deficient and actively disturbed patients in any institution. Her rapid and significant improvements were obvious by the eighth week of the program, and this progress was either held or bettered by the first anniversary assessment eighteen weeks following the introduction of the social-learning program. Unquestionably the levels of her disturbance and deficiency at the first anniversary assessment still required institutional control for her survival, but great strides toward normalization had clearly occurred for Bobbi and other residents similar to her.

# 15. Other Ongoing Resident Activity After Program Introduction

## COMPARATIVE CHARACTERISTICS OF LARGE COMMUNITY MEETINGS

The differential characteristics of the large community meetings were examined via the Group Activity Index (GAI) obtained at the Friday meetings within each program.[1] Productive characteristics of the community meetings from before the program introduction through the first anniversary assessment are presented in figure 15.1, which shows the near absence of productive activity in either community meeting during the baseline week. At that time, fewer than twenty-five instances of straight speech (i.e., appropriate initiation, response, or continuing normal conversation on a single topic) occurred in either program by staff and residents combined over the forty-five minutes of the community meeting. Upon the introduction of programmatic procedures, straight speech immediately increased, with further gains throughout the period and without significant differences between programs.[2] The average number of straight speeches in the community meetings covaried with mean changes in Global Functioning of the units over the same time period (r=0.72), tending to parallel increases in all adaptive components of resident behavior (r's in the 0.60s & 0.70s) and to increase with decreases in all maladaptive components of resident behavior (r's in the -0.60s & -0.70s). By the first anniversary assessment, both community meetings averaged over 160 instances of normal, task-oriented talk.

Differences in the structure and use of the community meetings are apparent on examination of the proportion of straight speeches that were made by residents rather than staff. While between-program differences were not statistically significant over the few standard time blocks involved, there was a decline in the proportion of the total straight speeches that were contributed by social-learning residents to a steady 40% during the last three blocks (figure 15.1). The introduction of milieu procedures, in contrast, resulted in an immediate increase in the proportion of straight speeches contributed by the residents, paralleling the election of another resident as group leader. Although the proportion of their straight speeches declined after the initial increase, the last three blocks reflect a steady rate of 50% to 60% of normal, task-oriented talk to be contributed by residents, the majority being by the group leader.

Additional differences in the structure of community meetings were apparent in the target of resident speeches. Resident speeches within the social-learning community meetings were regularly directed to staff (84%) with few speeches directed to individual residents (10%), without significant variability over the entire period. Milieu residents, on the other hand, directed 100% of their straight speeches to staff before the introduction of therapeutic community procedures. When the program began and another resident was elected community leader, the focus of straight resident speeches moved largely to individual residents (62%) with considerably fewer to staff (25%). Both of the differences between the programs were significant ($p < 0.05$) and did not vary through anniversary assessment 1. Straight resident speeches directed to the group as a whole immediately increased upon the introduction of milieu therapy procedures and remained at a constant level of about 13%. Social-learning residents gradually increased the proportion of speeches directed to the group as a whole, ending the period at about 13%. Thus, while the total number of normal, task-oriented conversations increased in community meetings within both programs, the differing structure and purpose of the meetings was apparent in greater resident-resident interactions within the milieu meetings and greater staff-resident interactions in the social-learning meetings.

Similar changes were also apparent in the nonproductive characteristics of community meetings, presented in figure 15.2. About half of the meeting time in both programs was spent in total silence before the introduction of programmatic procedures. By the time of the first anniversary assessment, time spent silent

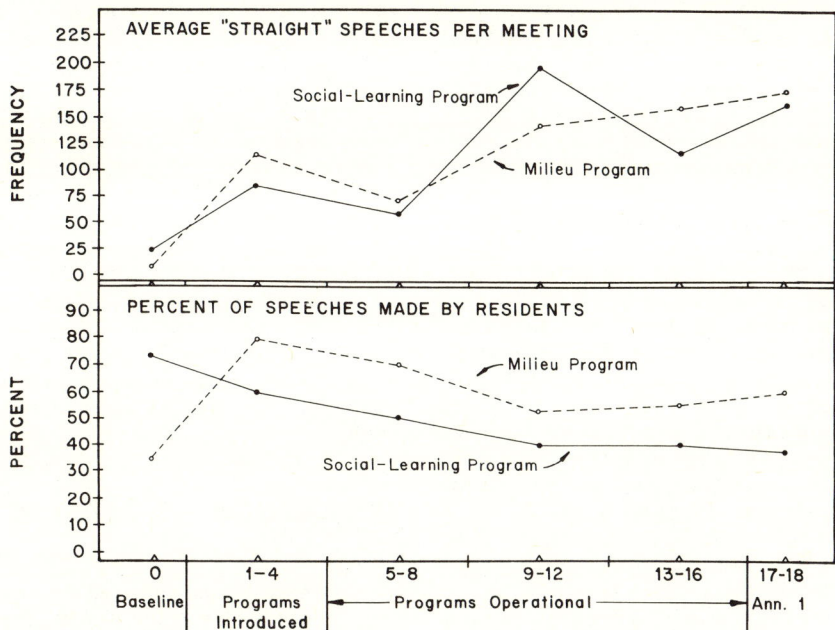

Figure 15.1. Productive characteristics of large community meetings.

had reduced to about a quarter of community meeting time, without differences between the programs over the period. The proportion of community meetings spent in silence covaried with mean changes in Intolerable Behavior (r=0.62) and in the Cognitive Distortion Index (r=0.79) over the same time periods and changed in opposite directions to mean concurrent appropriate behavior (r=-0.68).

Significant differences in structure were apparent in the active interferences with ongoing community meeting functions (disrupting discussions, whispering, or crazy talk, walking about, entering late or leaving early). The ratio

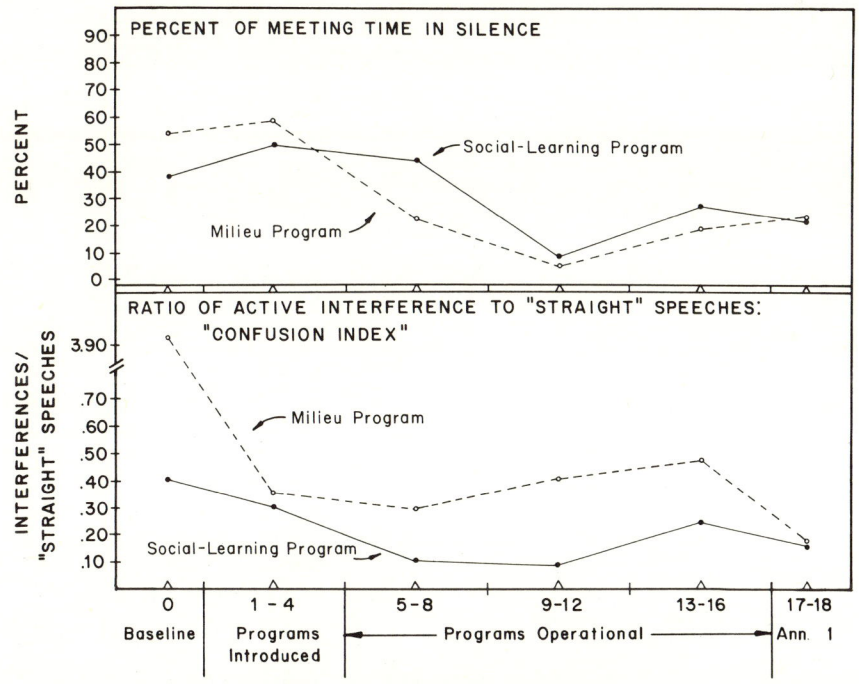

Figure 15.2. Nonproductive characteristics of large community meetings.

WEEKS FROM PROGRAM INTRODUCTION

of active interferences to straight speeches, presented in figure 15.2, provides an inverse index of productivity, or conversely, something of a "confusion index." The total lack of productivity of the therapeutic community meeting before the milieu procedures began is clearly apparent in a rate of interruptions (primarily entering late, leaving early, and walking around) nearly four times the number of straight speeches. While the introduction of the therapeutic community structure immediately decreased interferences, the relative nonproductive confusion in community meetings remained higher in the milieu program than in the social-learning program throughout the period ($p < 0.05$). Mean interferences in community meetings did not vary significantly with any other class of behavior on a unitwide basis for the milieu program but did vary conversely with average Intolerable Behavior ($r=-0.83$) for the social-learning program—probably as a result of disruptive residents receiving time out, which removed them from the meeting after one major interference.

Thus, the community meetings in both programs showed increases in task-oriented, normal talk and decreases in the amount of time with complete group silence, paralleling other improvements in resident functioning. The differential structure and purpose of the community meetings was apparent. The social-learning meeting focused primarily on communication of information and clarification, discussion, and solution of problems affecting the entire unit. This structure resulted in a greater proportion of staff-initiated discussion, more resident communications being directed to staff than to other residents, and an overall meeting with less confusion and relatively more on-task behavior than at milieu community meetings. In contrast, the community meetings within the milieu program focused more on resident-initiated and -required decision making under the direction of the resident group leader, with only guidance from staff. This structure produced a greater proportion of resident-to-resident communication and an overall meeting in which the pressure to manage their own affairs resulted in less immediate on-task behavior and more confusion during the meetings than in the social-learning program —exactly the results that milieu principles require.

## DIFFERENTIAL UTILIZATION OF RESOURCES

The relative use of facilities and services and consumables from before the program introduction through the first anniversary assessment is presented in figure 15.3.[3] Although off-unit facilities and services were not available during this period, all on-unit facilities and services (e.g., TV, lounge, laundry, radio, time with staff, etc.) and the majority of consumable items (regular meals, coffee, and limited snacks and canteen items) were equally accessible to residents of both programs. The utilization indexes in figure 15.3 reflect that

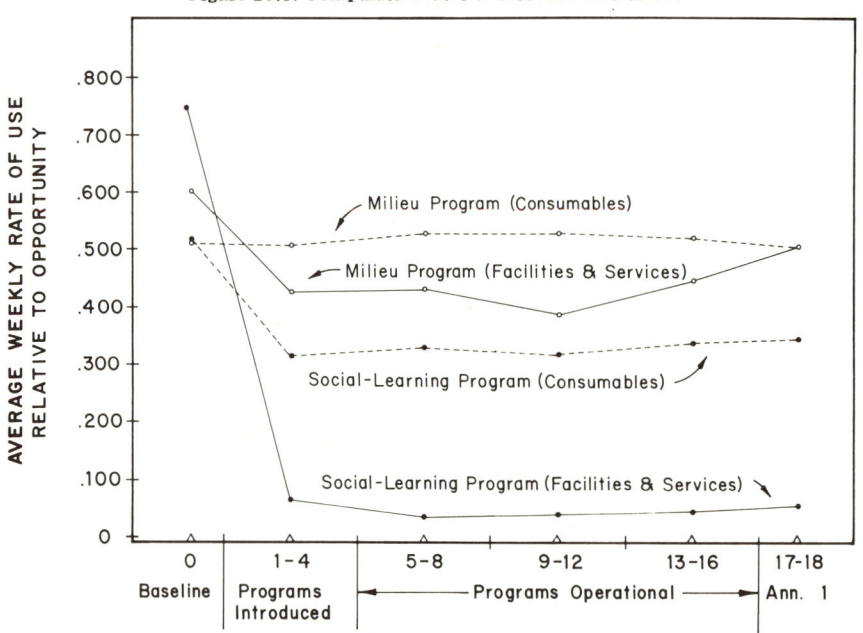

Figure 15.3. Comparative rates of resource utilization.

consumables were used on an average of 51% of opportunities and facilities and services on an average of 68% of opportunities by all residents before the introduction of programmatic procedures, without differences between groups (p > 0.10).

Clear differences were apparent immediately after the treatment procedures began. Upon the introduction of the token-economy structure, residents in the social-learning program immediately reduced their use of consumables and facilities and services (F's > 31.12, df=1/54, p < 0.01), with a greater reduction in facilities' and services' utilization than in consumables (F=15.99, df=1/54, p < 0.01). In contrast, milieu residents showed no change at all in their utilization of consumables, even though the living groups took over the responsibility for the majority of service. There was also a slight but nonsignificant reduction in their use of facilities and services. Over the entire period, the reductions in utilization rates within the social-learning program were significantly greater than those within the milieu program (F's > 15.59, df=1/54, p < 0.01). By the first anniversary assessment, milieu utilization rates of 51% of opportunities had been maintained at a significantly higher level than social-learning rates of 35% for consumables and 6% for facilities and services (F's > 15.32, df=1/54, p < 0.01).

Further differences resulting from the differential program structure were apparent from the change in functioning within programs as related to the change in resource utilization. Within both programs, the unitwide utilization of facilities and services changed in opposite directions to the average level of adaptive behaviors (r's in the -0.80s & -0.90s). The level of unitwide utilization of consumables showed the same pattern within the social-learning program to a significantly greater degree than within the milieu program, where relationships were in the opposite directions but were largely nonsignificant. The major basis for such relationships lies in the high rates of resource utilization before the programmatic procedures began at the same time that the lowest levels of functioning and highest rates of maladaptive behavior occurred. The relationships provide clear evidence that merely providing material goods in the absence of structured programs did not help the severely debilitated mental patient.

An examination of individual resident characteristics associated with utilization rates during the first anniversary assessment found that residents within both programs were similar with regard to use of consumables. Those who were using more consumables tended to be higher in Global Functioning and to have higher levels of both concurrent appropriate behavior and appropriate responsiveness within programs (r's in the 0.70s & 0.80s), without differences between the groups. Similarly, residents of both programs with higher rates of clinically bizarre concurrent behavior tended to use fewer consumables (r=-0.55). However, milieu residents using fewer consumables tended to be those still showing gross inappropriate response to minimal expectations (r=-0.74) to a significantly greater degree than social-learning residents did (r=-0.30). Differential relationships were apparent between programs by the first anniversary assessment with regard to the use of facilities and services. Significant correlations within the social-learning program were obtained between both adaptive (r's in the 0.30s & 0.40s) and maladaptive (r's in the -0.30s & -0.40s) measures of functioning and utilization of facilities and services. None of these correlations were significant within the milieu program (r's in the ± 0.10s & ± 0.20s), but milieu correlations were significantly lower than social-learning correlations. Social-learning residents who made greater use of facilities and services tended to be functioning at higher levels by the first anniversary assessment, while milieu residents were not.

In summary, even though there was equal access for residents in both programs, milieu residents continued to use resources at about the same rate as before program introduction. Social-learning residents reduced their resource utilization immediately upon the introduction of programmatic procedures and used fewer resources than milieu residents did through the first anniversary assessment. As soon as resource utilization was contingent upon token expenditure in the social-learning program, residents chose to use tokens more for consumables than for facilities and services, reflecting the greater value of consumable items as backup reinforcers for this population. By the time of the first anniversary assessment, higher-functioning residents in both programs were using relatively more consumables than lower-functioning residents were. However, facilities' and services' utilization was related to current functioning only in the social-learning program—reflecting the greater token-earning power of the residents who had improved more. The use of facilities and services in the milieu program, where all resources were free, was unrelated to the level of current functioning or maladaptive behavior. Even though milieu residents used significantly more resources than social-learning residents did after the programs were introduced, the latter showed significantly greater improvement over the current time period. These findings, combined with the fact that unitwide resource utilization changed in opposite directions to average resident functioning, indicates that the quantity of resources available was not as important as how those available were used.

## TIME SPENT IN PROGRAMS AND WITH OTHER PEOPLE

Given the social focus of the treatment programs, potential responsiveness required that residents at least be awake and in contact with other people before the programmatic procedures could have an effect. Possible differences in these ongoing characteristics between programs were examined by TSBC indexes for "eyes open" and "with others."[4] Before the introduction of programmatic procedures, residents in both programs did not differ on either class of behavior ($p > 0.20$). They were found, on the average, to be awake on 80% of observations during waking hours and to be in the presence of other people on only 66% of observations. The relatively large amount of time spent alone before program introduction is indicative of active avoidance, since the physical structure of the units encouraged at least sitting in the presence of others.

Immediately upon the introduction of the psychosocial programs, both resident groups significantly increased the average time awake and time spent with others (F's > 22.84, df=1/54, $p < 0.01$), without significant differences between groups. Stable levels were maintained for both classes of behavior, with the average resident being awake on 89% of observations during the first anniversary assessment. Time with others had increased to 90% for social-learning residents and 83% for milieu residents, but the differences were not statistically significant ($p > 0.10$). Over both programs, mean changes in Global Functioning and adaptive components of resident behavior covaried with unitwide increases in time awake (r's in the 0.60s & 0.70s) and time with others (r's in the 0.80s & 0.90s). Similarly, decreases in most mean maladaptive components corresponded with unitwide increases in time awake (r's in the -0.60s & -0.70s) and time with others (r's in the -0.80s & -0.90s), without differences between programs. Thus, both groups had equal access to procedures of the respective programs, and both programs had increased "time in" and with others corresponding to improvements in other areas.

An examination of individual resident characteristics found only one differential relationship between programs by the first anniversary assessment for "awake" and "with-others" status. Milieu residents who were more often asleep during waking hours tended to be those who were still showing gross inappropriate response to minimal expectations ($r=-0.52$); no such relationship existed for social-learning residents ($r=0.17$). No other significant differences were found between programs, with overall correlations showing residents with "eyes open" a greater proportion of the time also tending to show more adaptive behavior (r's in the 0.30s & 0.40s) and less maladaptive behavior (r's in the -0.50s & -0.60s). The only significant correlations between "with others" and measures of functioning found residents over both programs with higher proportions of time in the presence of other people to tend toward a lower incidence of Intolerable Behavior ($r=-0.40$) and higher rates of Instrumental Role Performance ($r=0.37$). These relationships suggest that unpleasant residents who failed to carry out responsibilities might have been avoided by other residents by the time of the first anniversary assessment.

Summarizing "time awake" and "with others," residents in both programs showed immediate increases once programmatic procedures began, paralleling other improvements in their functioning. The increased levels of time awake and with others remained relatively stable through the first anniversary assessment, without differences between programs. By the time of the first anniversary assessment, higher-functioning residents in both programs tended to be those who were awake a greater proportion of the time, with only one differential relationship existing between programs. Residents spending greater proportions of time with other people tended toward a lower incidence of Intolerable Behavior and higher rates of Instrumental Role Performance, without differences between programs. Overall, therefore, both programs had increased "time in" and with others corresponding to other improvements, and both groups had equal access to procedures of the respective programs.

## VARIABILITY OF RESIDENT ACTIVITY

The last group of descriptive characteristics of ongoing resident behavior to be examined is the individual variability within specific classes of activity. Earlier analyses provided an evaluation of differential amount and level of each class of behavior. Stereotypy/Variability scores provide a descriptive picture of the range of activity within each class for individual residents, independent of total amount.[5] Average Stereotypy/Variability scores for five classes of behavior before the introduction of treatment programs and during the first anniversary assessment are presented in table 15.1. None of the scores differed between groups before the introduction of programmatic procedures (p's > 0.20).

The variability of concurrent clinically bizarre, crazy behaviors (from the TSBC) did

Table 15.1. Relative Stereotypy/Variability of resident activity.

| Treatment program | Assessment period | Crazy behaviors | | Appropriate behaviors | | Social contacts | | Resource utilization | | Physical location | |
|---|---|---|---|---|---|---|---|---|---|---|---|
| | | Mean | S.D. | Mean | S.D. | Mean | S.D. | Mean | S.D. | Mean | S.D. |
| Social-learning | Baseline | 4.41 | 1.631 | 3.85 | 1.390 | 1.89 | 0.217 | 2.86 | 0.635 | 3.02 | 1.507 |
| | Anniversary 1 | 2.88 | 1.284 | 3.35 | 1.072 | 2.25 | .380 | 1.93 | .841 | 3.85 | 1.055 |
| Milieu therapy | Baseline | 4.04 | 1.478 | 3.61 | 1.015 | 1.90 | .245 | 2.68 | .462 | 3.51 | 1.044 |
| | Anniversary 1 | 3.85 | 1.794 | 3.13 | 1.058 | 2.39 | .262 | 3.05 | .513 | 6.12 | 1.606 |
| Total | Baseline | 4.23 | 1.567 | 3.73 | 1.223 | 1.90 | .231 | 2.78 | .563 | 3.26 | 1.320 |
| | Anniversary 1 | 3.37 | 1.635 | 3.24 | 1.070 | 2.32 | .333 | 2.49 | .892 | 4.99 | 1.768 |

Note. Table entries are Stereotypy/Variability scores. A score of 1 represents complete stereotypy (all incidence of activity of a single type); higher scores reflect greater variability, with maximum possible scores (crazy behavior=17, appropriate behavior=17, social contact=3, resource utilization=19, physical location=17) indicating equal incidence of all types of activity.

not change significantly after the introduction of milieu therapy procedures or at any other time through the first anniversary assessment. In contrast, the variability in individual crazy behaviors in the social-learning program showed a gradual reduction through the first anniversary assessment, paralleling (r=0.83) mean changes in Cognitive Distortion. By the time of the first anniversary assessment, the reduction in variability of crazy behavior for social-learning residents was significant itself and significantly greater than the change for milieu residents (F's > 9.55, df=1/54, p < 0.01). Thus, both milieu and social-learning programs had dramatically reduced the amount of clinically bizarre concurrent behavior, but residents in the milieu program were still performing as wide a range of crazy behaviors though at a lower level. Social-learning residents had reduced both the amount and the range of different types of crazy behaviors performed, particularly dropping out those bizarre behaviors indicative of thought disorder.

The variability of concurrent appropriate behaviors (from the TSBC) dropped significantly upon the introduction of treatment procedures in both programs (F=10.32, df=1/54, p < 0.01) and remained stable through the first anniversary assessment, without differences between programs. Both treatment programs had significantly increased the incidence of concurrent appropriate behavior over this period. Therefore, these findings indicate that individual residents in both programs had reduced the range of different appropriate behaviors performed and greatly increased the rate of performance of others.

Residents in both programs increased the proportion of time spent with other people over the current period. The Stereotypy/Variability scores for social contacts (table 15.1) show that the range of people with whom residents spent time (i.e., other residents, staff, outsiders) also increased. The increases were significant (F=66.13, df=1/54, p < 0.01) and occurred immediately after baseline. The variability of social contacts remained stable through the first anniversary assessment, without differences between programs. Thus, both programs produced increases in the amount of time spent with other people and the range of people with whom time was spent, without differences between groups.

The variability of resource utilization (table 15.1) showed significant changes in opposite directions between programs (F=36.88, df=1/54, p < 0.01). The Stereotypy/Variability score reflects the range of variability in types of facilities and services used. While the average facilities' and services' utilization rates had changed in opposite directions to adaptive functioning in both programs, differential effects were apparent for variability of facilities and services. For the social-learning program, unitwide changes in the range of facilities and services also changed in the opposite direction to the average level of most adaptive behaviors (r's in the -0.80s & -0.90s) and covaried with the average level of most maladaptive behaviors (r's in the 0.80s & 0.90s). Correlations between unitwide means in the variability of facilities and services and mean levels of functioning for the milieu program were nearly mirror images of those for the social-learning program—covarying with most adaptive behaviors (r's in the 0.70s & 0.80s) and changing in opposite directions to most maladaptive behaviors (r's in the -0.70s & -0.80s). Thus, social-learning residents not only reduced their total use of facilities and services, but reduced the number of different types they used as well (F=38.39, df=1/54, p < 0.01). In contrast, milieu residents had maintained the utilization rate that had existed before the program introduction but increased the range of facilities and services they each used (F=6.08, df=1/54, p < 0.05).

The Stereotypy/Variability scores for physical location provide an index of the relative amount of movement of individual residents within the geographical areas of the units (e.g., corridor, lounge, dining area, common living area, etc.). Means presented in table 15.1 reflect significant increases in the range of locations frequented by residents in both programs following the introduction of programmatic procedures (F's > 7.13, df=1/54, p < 0.01), with the increase of milieu residents being significantly greater than that of social-learning residents (F=16.16, df=1/54, p < 0.01). Residents on both units increased the variability of locations frequented as soon as the treatment programs were introduced. However, social-learning residents then remained relatively stable to the end of the period, paralleling increases in mean level of functioning (r's in the ± 0.80s & ± 0.90s). Milieu residents continued to increase the variability of locations throughout the period, with mean location variability paralleling changes in functioning to a lesser degree (r's in the ± 0.60s & ± 0.70s). Thus, individual residents within the milieu program showed considerably greater movement across different locations within the unit than did social-learning residents. An inspection of the specific locations frequented found social-learning residents spending more time in locations where regular token disbursements occurred and milieu residents tending to spread across all available locations to a greater degree.

An examination of the intercorrelations among all five Stereotypy/Variability scores during the first anniversary assessment found only one significant relationship overall and within both programs. The variabilities of social contacts and of concurrent appropriate behavior were significantly related (r=0.44), without differences between units. This correlation shows a tendency for residents who performed a greater range of appropriate behaviors also to spend time with a greater range of other people (i.e., staff, residents, and outsiders). Although correlations between units were not significantly different, the variability of location utilization did correlate significantly with the variability of social contacts (r=0.38) and the variability of facilities' and services' utilization (r=0.66) only within the social-learning program. The variability of location utilization was correlated with the variability of appropriate behavior (r=0.38) only within the milieu program. Thus, stereotypy or variability of activities was not a consistent personal attribute of residents in either program.

Residents showing greater variability in social contacts tended to be performing higher levels of adaptive behavior and less maladaptive behavior (r's in the ± 0.20s & ± 0.30s), without differences between units. Similarly, residents showing greater variability in the range of concurrent appropriate behaviors tended to be those with higher levels of functioning and less maladaptive behavior (r's in the ± 0.50s & ± 0.60s), although one significant differential relationship was found between programs. Within the milieu program, residents showing greater variability in the range of concurrent appropriate behaviors tended to have less gross inappropriate response to minimal expectations (r=-0.59), while no such relationship existed within the social-learning program (r=-0.02).

Although no significant differences occurred between the units in the correlations of the variability of crazy behavior with levels of functioning, there was a suggestive pattern. Within the social-learning program, the only significant relationships obtained with variability of crazy behavior were with the level of Cognitive Distortion (r=0.58) and Total Inappropriate Clinical Frequencies (r=0.59). Within the milieu program, these relationships were not significant, but nearly all other relationships with measures of functioning were, indicating greater variability in the range of bizarre acts to be associated with lower levels of adaptive behavior and higher levels of maladaptive behavior (r's in the ± 0.30s & ± 0.40s). Similarly, while correlations were not significantly different, the variability of location utilization was negatively related to concurrent bizarre behavior only within the social-learning program (r=-0.48) and to Interpersonal Skills only within the milieu program (r=-0.37). Differential characteristics of behavioral variability as a result of the differing program structures are, therefore, suggested. However, over both programs, residents showing a greater range of location utilization were those who tended not to be in contact with other people (r=0.57) and tended not to be awake as frequently (r=-0.28). The variability of facilities and services utilization was not related to level of functioning within either program.

Thus, the relative variability of resident activity also reflected differential patterns of within-program processes. Residents in both programs reduced the range of concurrent appropriate behaviors, while increasing the amount of appropriate behavior performed. They also increased the range of the class of people with whom they spent time and increased the amount of time they spent with other people. Process differences were apparent in the remaining three Stereotypy/Variability scores. Although both programs had produced significant reductions in the amount of clinically bizarre, crazy behavior, milieu residents continued to perform the same range of specific types of bizarre behaviors, while social-learning residents reduced the range as well as the amount. The variability of facilities and services used by residents changed in opposite directions, with social-learning residents reducing not only the amount of resource utilization but the range as well. Milieu residents, in contrast, did not change their rate of resource utilization but increased the range of facilities and services they used. Finally, residents in both programs increased the range of geographical locations frequented within the units, but milieu residents increased theirs considerably more than social-learning residents. Although the stereotypy/variability of activities was not a consistent personal attribute, residents functioning at relatively higher levels tended to show greater variability in the range of concurrent appropriate behaviors and social contacts and less variability in the range of bizarre behaviors. The programs had produced some differential relationships with the variability of bizarre behavior as well. The range of facilities and services used was not related to functioning within either program, but the range of locations frequented was differentially related to functioning between programs; those who tended to be alone and asleep more often used a greater number of locations more frequently.

## SUMMARY

In addition to the data on comparative effectiveness described in chapter 14, there were differences in the characteristics of other ongoing resident activity once the psychosocial programs were introduced. Paralleling improvements in resident functioning, the unitwide community meetings showed increases in task-oriented normal talk and decreases in time silent. The different structure and purpose of community meetings was apparent in greater proportions of staff rather than resident speech, greater proportions of resident speech directed to staff rather than other residents, and overall meetings with less confusion and more on-task behavior within the social-learning program than within the milieu program.

Similar differences resulting from program structure were seen in comparative utilization of resources. As soon as resources were contingent upon token expenditures, social-learning residents dramatically reduced their rate of utilization, which remained at a significantly lower rate than did that of milieu residents. Milieu residents, for whom resource utilization required only decision making, continued at the same levels as before program introduction. Social-learning residents showed a greater reduction in the use of facilities and services than in the use of consumables, reflecting the greater value of consumable items as backup reinforcers for this population. Although higher-functioning residents within both programs tended to use more consumables than did lower-functioning residents, the use of facilities and services was related to current functioning only within the social-learning program. Over the entire period, unitwide resource utilization changed in opposite directions to average resident functioning. Since social-learning residents also improved more than milieu residents did—while using significantly fewer facilities, services, and consumables—it is clear that how available resources were used was more important than the quantity of resources that were obtained.

Immediately upon the introduction of programmatic procedures, both milieu and social-learning residents increased the amount of time awake during waking hours and the amount of time spent in the presence of other people. These increases were relatively stable without differences between programs through the first anniversary assessment. By the time of the assessment, higher-functioning residents in both programs tended to be those who were awake a greater proportion of the time. Residents spending relatively more time with others tended to be those with higher rates of instrumental role performance and lower rates of intolerable behavior (i.e., nonaversive people). Overall, both programs had increased "time in" and time with others such that residents of both groups had equal access to the procedures of the respective programs.

Changes in the variability of ongoing resident activity also showed emerging differences in the day-to-day processes within the psychosocial programs. Residents in both programs had increased the amount of concurrent appropriate behavior and the amount of time spent with others. While changes in variability of the latter activities did not differ between programs, the increases in appropriate behavior were accompanied by decreases in the range of different appropriate behaviors performed. In contrast, the increases in time spent with other people were accompanied by increases in the range of people with whom time was spent (staff, other residents, outsiders). Although residents in both programs had reduced the amount of clinically bizarre, crazy behaviors, there were significant differences in variability. Milieu residents continued to perform the same range of bizarre behaviors throughout the period, reducing the amount. Social-learning residents significantly reduced both the total amount of bizarre behavior, and restricted the range of crazy behaviors performed.

There were also differences in the variability of resource utilization. Milieu residents maintained a constant level of use but increased the range of facilities and services they used. Social-learning residents not only reduced their utilization rate but restricted the range of facilities and services as well, reflecting greater discrimination in selection. The variability of physical locations frequented within the units increased for both programs but increased more for milieu residents than for social-learning residents. Milieu residents showed considerably greater movement across different physical locations, while social-learning residents tended to restrict their movement to fewer locations where regular token disbursements occurred.

Some differential relationships were obtained between variability scores and level of functioning between programs, though relatively higher-functioning residents within programs tended to show greater variability in appropriate behavior and social contacts and less variability in the range of bizarre behaviors. Similarly residents using a greater range of locations tended to be those who were more frequently alone and asleep. However, the stereotypy/variability of resident activities was not a consistent individual attribute, and the variability of resource utilization was unrelated to functioning in either program.

Thus, analyses of the characteristics of other ongoing resident activity following program introduction provide a descriptive picture in keeping with the differential program structures and additional support that outcome data were influenced only by programmatic procedures.

# 16. Staff Attitudes and Performance Before and After Program Introduction

## OPINIONS ABOUT MENTAL PATIENTS

Average sten scores on the Opinions About Mental Illness Scale (OMI) for junior staff alone and all clinical staff combined at the end of academic training (before the arrival of the residents) and at the first anniversary assessment are presented in figure 16.1, which reveals the essential parallelism of the staff group from the beginning to the end of the current period, even though only 69% of staff were continuous over both points in time.[1] Although a slight reduction is suggested in Social Restrictiveness over this period of rapid improvement in resident behavior, no significant overall or differential change occurred on any score for either continuing staff or the staff groups employed at the beginning and end of the period (p's > 0.20).[2] Rather, Mental Hygiene Ideology and Social-Learning Ideology continued to show the exceptionally high levels of endorsement that had resulted from original training, while the other four scores remained at or below original pretraining levels. At the first anniversary assessment, all differences among individual OMI scores shown in figure 16.1 were significant, except for Authoritarianism and Interpersonal Etiology.[3]

The extent to which the overall level and pattern of staff OMI scores approached the ideal assumptions underlying both psychosocial programs may be seen by comparing staff means with the ideal responses indicated in the margins of figure 16.1 for each score. The pattern of the six staff scores was significantly related to the ideal at the beginning of the period (r=0.84) and did not change significantly by the first anniversary assessment (r=0.90).[4] Although the level of endorsement over all six staff scores combined moved closer to ideal assumptions between posttraining and the first anniversary assessment, this change was not statistically significant ($D^2$=11.43 & 9.17, respectively, p > 0.10).[5] The major deviation from the desired level of endorsement at both assessments was a Mental Hygiene Ideology score that was too high—reflecting an overendorsement of welfare and positive motivation items and an underendorsement of potential dangerousness.

An examination of the intercorrelations among OMI scores at the first anniversary assessment still found Authoritarianism and Social Restrictiveness to be positively related (r=0.71), even though both were low in absolute level. Mental Hygiene Ideology was positively related to Benevolence (r=0.40) and negatively related to Social Restrictiveness (r=-0.39). No other interrelationships were significant. The only individual staff characteristics that were related to OMI scores at the first anniversary assessment were education and Extroversion. Higher levels of education were related to lower scores on Benevolence (r=-0.66) and higher scores on Social-Learning Ideology (r=0.39), reflecting the significant differences between junior and senior staff on these scores. More-extroverted staff tended to score higher on both Authoritarianism (r=0.53) and Social Restrictiveness (r=0.44), while none of remaining staff characteristics (age, sex, race, marital or parental status, experience, Emotionality) were related to OMI scores. Thus, OMI scores tended to be less clustered and less predictable from individual characteristics after active involvement in treatment than before treatment began.

In summary, the attitudes, opinions, and beliefs about mental patients held by the psychosocial staff were not changed significantly by exposure to the chronic population during the first six months, nor were the staff attitudes to which residents were exposed different from the beginning to the end of the period. The pattern of staff OMI scores remained close to the ideals underlying the psychosocial programs, with a tendency for Mental Hygiene Ideology, Authoritarianism, and Benevolence to be higher than desired and Social Restrictiveness to become lower than desired—even though the last three scores were already below those of typical mental hospital staff.

## ATTITUDES TOWARD AND INTERPRETATIONS OF TREATMENT PROGRAMS

In contrast to the absence of change in staff opinions about mental patients over the first

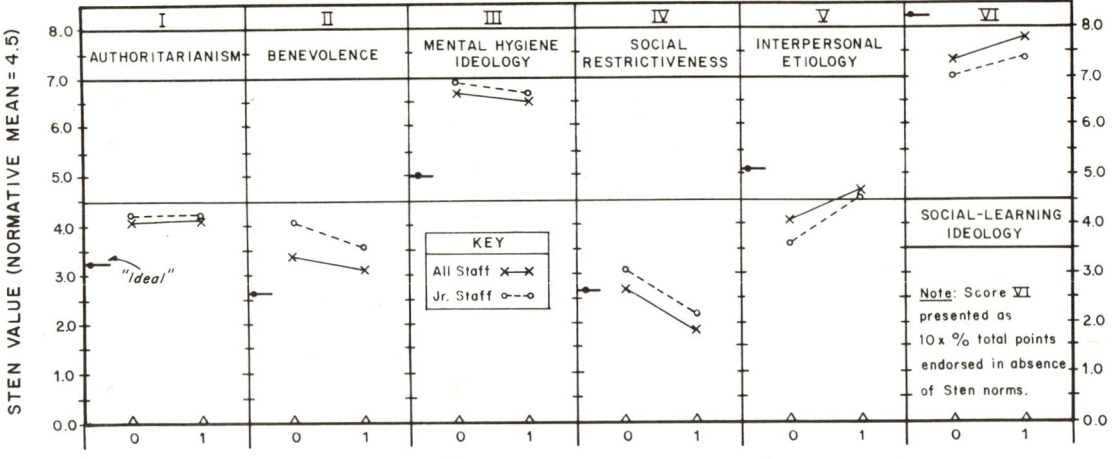

Figure 16.1. Opinions About Mental Illness Scale responses by all psychosocial staff present during the first six months. The "ideal" response is indicated in the left margin for each score.

period of exposure, some opinions about the programs themselves showed dramatic shifts by the first anniversary assessment. Upon completion of academic training but before work with the severely debilitated population, 79% of clinical staff expressed no differential opinions to the preliminary questions on the Therapist Orientation Sheet (TOS) about which of the two psychosocial programs they believed to be most effective and most enjoyable. Of those who did express opinions, each psychosocial program received "most effective" choices by 50% of staff, and the milieu program was chosen as "most enjoyable" by 75%. By the time of the first anniversary assessment, following the rapid and differential change by residents within the two programs, 100% of clinical staff expressed opinions—96% believing the social-learning program to be the more effective (an accurate judgment well in advance of any comparative data analysis) and 69% choosing the social-learning program as the more enjoyable in which to work, reversing the earlier preference for the milieu program.

Average pattern differentiation scores on the TOS for all clinical staff working at the end of original academic training and at the first anniversary assessment are presented in figure 16.2.[6] Since the same staff conducted both programs, scores are plotted for responses obtained under each of three instructional orientations by the same staff: one set for each of the psychosocial programs—reflecting staff interpretations of the nature of the programs (attitude scores) and relative use of techniques (technique scores) inferred from their training and experience—and one set for their own personal beliefs or preferences as change agents. In general, relatively few changes occurred in either preferences or interpretations compared to the shifts in opinions about the comparative effectiveness and relative enjoyability of programs.

The preferred-attitude scores in figure 16.2 reveal the essential parallelism of the staff group from the beginning to the end of the period in their personal preferences about the nature of treatment. Continuing staff showed no significant overall or differential change in preferred TOS attitude scores ($p > 0.10$); however, the total staff employed at the beginning and end of the period showed a significant reduction on A-5 ($p < 0.01$), without changes in other scores ($F$'s $< 1$).[7] This change reflects even less endorsement of a need for client discomfort and verbal-conceptual learning during treatment by the end of the period, moving more toward the "usually comfortable," "nonverbal-affective learning" end of the continuum. However, the pattern over all five scores remained constant, with all differences between preferred-attitude scores shown in figure 16.2 being significant at the first anniversary assessment, except for A-1 and A-4.

The extent to which the overall level and pattern of preferred-attitude scores approached the ideal assumptions underlying each psychosocial program may be seen by comparing preferred staff means with the ideal responses for the nature of each program (figure 16.2). The pattern of the five preferred-attitude scores was significantly related to the milieu ideal on both assessments, without significant change from the beginning to the end of the period ($r$'s=0.98 & 0.91, respectively). The pattern was less related ($p < 0.10$) to the social-learning ideal at posttraining, with the degree of relationship failing to achieve statistical significance at either assessment ($r$'s=0.67 & 0.74, respectively). The overall level of preferred attitude scores

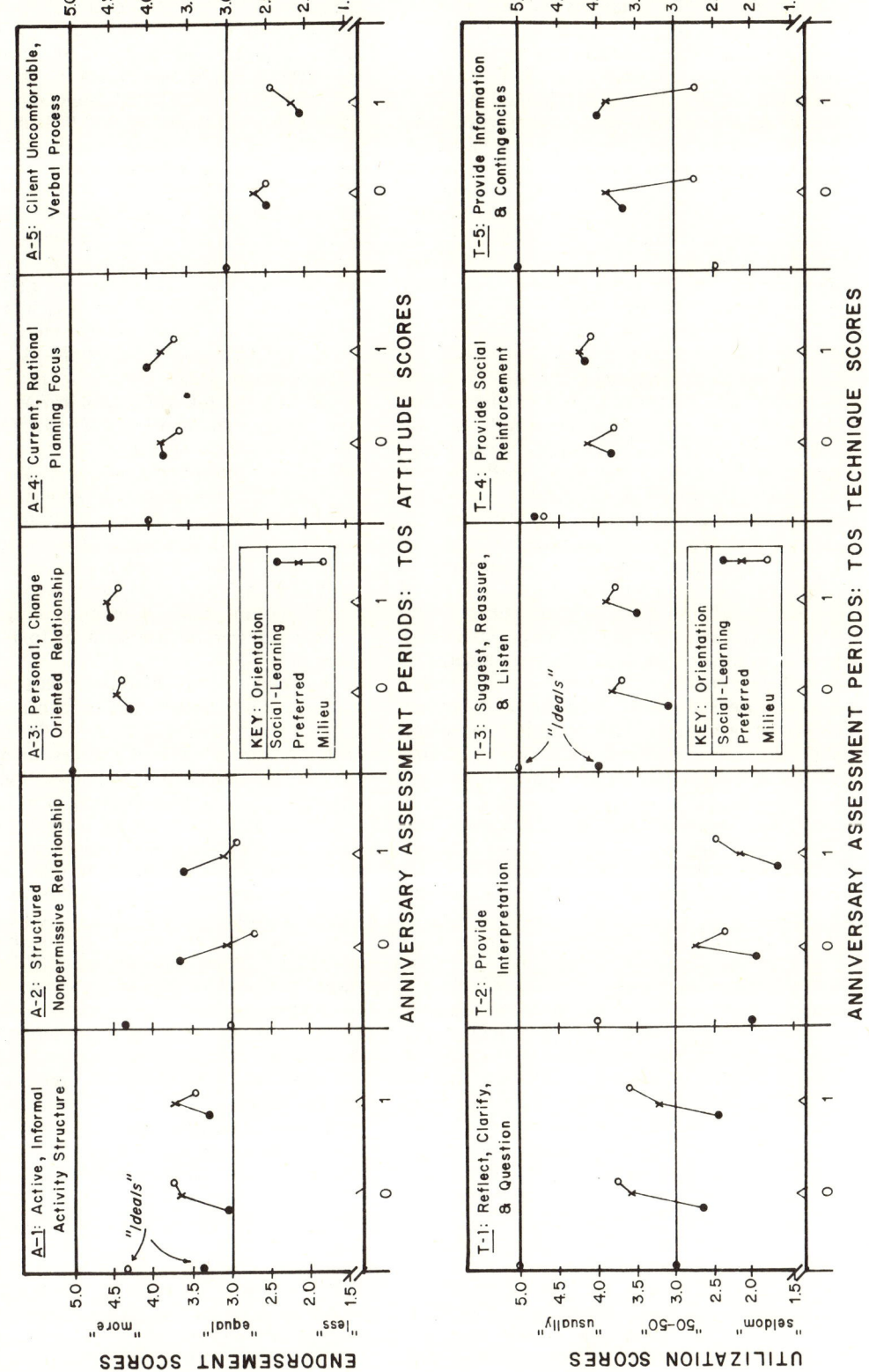

Figure 16.2. Therapist Orientation Sheet responses under three response sets by all psychosocial staff present during the first six months. "Ideal" responses are indicated in the left margin for each orientation for each score.

was closer to the milieu ideal than the social-learning ideal at posttraining ($D^2$=0.80 & 2.10, respectively, p=0.063) and at the first anniversary assessment ($D^2$=1.36 & 2.63, respectively, p=0.063), although the reduction in A-5 at the first anniversary assessment resulted in greater deviations from either ideal (p=0.063). Thus, the nature of treatment characteristics preferred by staff tended to be closer to the ideal milieu program, primarily as a function of preferences for therapeutic relationships which were at the midpoint of the "structured-unstructured," "nonpermissive-permissive" dimension (A-2), since the "ideals" for A-3, A-4, and A-5 are identical and the preferred response to A-1 was midway between the two ideals.

An examination of the intercorrelations among TOS preferred attitude scores at the first anniversary assessment found A-5 to be positively related to A-2 (r=0.44) and negatively so to A-3 (r=-0.56), while A-3 was also related to A-4 (r=0.45). TOS preferred scores on A-2 and A-5 were also significantly related to several individual staff characteristics and OMI scores (r's in the 0.40s & 0.50s). Specifically, higher A-2 and A-5 preferred TOS scores (reflecting greater preference for structured-nonpermissive relationships and relatively greater belief in the need for some client discomfort and verbal-conceptual learning) tended to be given by staff who were males and more highly educated with lower scores on OMI Benevolence and Mental Hygiene Ideology—all of which were more characteristic of senior staff. Higher A-1 scores, reflecting a greater preference for an active informal structure of activities, tended to be given by staff who were single and had less education and higher OMI Benevolence scores (r's in the 0.40s)—all of which were more characteristic of junior staff. A-3 was related only to age (r=-0.39), reflecting a tendency for younger staff to prefer relatively more personal, change-oriented therapeutic relationships. A-4 was related only to OMI Social-Learning Ideology (r=0.45), reflecting a tendency for staff with relatively higher endorsement of Social-Learning Ideology to have a greater preference for the focus of treatment to be on current topics with rational planning. Thus, while more clustering among preferred-TOS attitude scores occurred after treatment began, like OMI scores, preferences for the nature of treatment were less predictable from individual staff characteristics than they had been at the beginning of the period.

The attitude scores for each psychosocial orientation in figure 16.2 also reveal the essential parallelism of the staff group from the beginning to the end of the period in their interpretation of the nature of each treatment program. Both continuing staff and total staff groups consistently produced different patterns of attitude scores in their interpretation of the nature of the milieu and social-learning programs, with differential change between posttraining and the first anniversary assessments (p's < 0.01).[8] A-2 and A-3 did not change significantly for either orientation (p's > 0.20); A-4 showed a significant increase over both orientations combined (p < 0.05); and A-1 and A-5 changed differentially between orientations (p < 0.01). The differential changes on A-1 reflected an increase for the social-learning orientation and a decrease for the milieu orientation, and A-5 reflected a greater reduction for the social-learning orientation than for the milieu orientation. However, the pattern over all five scores remained constant in the interpretation of the nature of treatment programs within the respective orientations. All comparisons between TOS attitude scores shown in figure 16.2 within the social-learning orientation were significantly different from one another, as were all scores within the milieu orientation, except A-1 and A-4. At the first anniversary assessment, differences between orientations were not significant for A-1 and A-3 (p > 0.10), but the social-learning scores were significantly higher than the milieu scores for A-2 (p < 0.01) and A-4 (p < 0.05), while the lower social-learning score on A-5 approached significance relative to the milieu score (p < 0.10).

A comparison of the relative pattern of staff attitude scores under each psychosocial orientation to the ideal response for the nature of each program in figure 16.2 shows the directionality to be parallel but with deviations in the absolute level of endorsement. The extent to which the staff interpretations of the nature of each program approached the ideal was apparent in significant relationships over the five TOS attitude scores at both assessments for the milieu orientation (r's=0.99 & 0.95, respectively) and for the social-learning orientation (r's=0.96 & 0.88, respectively). These relationships did not differ significantly between orientations or over assessments. Similarly the overall level of staff responses under the two orientations compared to their respective ideals did not change significantly over assessments for the milieu ($D^2$'s=1.20 & 1.54, respectively) or social-learning orientation ($D^2$'s=1.29 & 1.62, respectively), and the relative deviations from ideals did not differ significantly between orientations. Thus, even with changes during the period and staff preferences being closer to the milieu ideal than the social-learning, the nature of programs was interpreted differentially, with staff interpretations remaining close to the ideals underlying each program.

The preferred technique scores in figure 16.2 also show the essential consistency in pattern among treatment procedures that staff preferred to use over both assessments. Both continuing staff and all staff employed at both assessment periods showed differential change among scores over time (p < 0.01). Preferred technique scores T-3, T-4, and T-5 did not differ among themselves, and they did not change between assessments. Low T-2 scores, reflecting a dislike for the use of interpretation, became significantly lower by the first anniversary assessment (p < 0.01) and remained the least-preferred technique at both assessments. Similarly while preference for the use of reflection, clarification, and questioning (T-1) approached a significant reduction (p < 0.10), it remained significantly above T-2 and significantly below T-3, T-4, and T-5 on both assessments.

In contrast to the closer approximation of preferred attitude scores to the milieu ideal, preferred technique scores were more closely related to the social-learning ideal. The pattern of the five preferred technique scores was significantly related to the social-learning ideal on both assessments, without significant change from the beginning to the end of the period (r's=0.92 & 0.94, respectively), while remaining unrelated to the milieu ideal at both assessments (r's=0.05 & 0.02, respectively). Similarly the overall level of preferred technique scores deviated more from the milieu ideal than from the social-learning ideal at both the posttraining assessment ($D^2$'s=6.93 & 2.71, respectively, p=0.063) and the first anniversary assessment ($D^2$'s=9.60 & 1.66, respectively, p=0.063). Parallel to the earlier findings about changes in the program that the majority of staff found most enjoyable, the change in preferred techniques over the period moved further in level from the milieu ideal and closer to the social learning ideal (p < 0.01). However, the absolute deviation in level of technique scores, particularly for T-4 and T-5, remained considerably below the social-learning ideal.

An examination of the intercorrelations among TOS preferred-technique scores at the first anniversary assessment found less clustering among preferred techniques than had existed before participation in the psychosocial programs. In fact, only two significant correlations were obtained: T-1 was positively correlated with both T-2 (r=0.61) and T-3 (r=0.60). Additionally these three preferred technique scores were all negatively related to OMI scores 2 and 3 (r's in the -0.40s & -0.50s), reflecting a tendency for staff preferring relatively higher use of reflection, clarification, and questioning, interpretation, and suggestion, reassurance, and listening to score relatively lower on Benevolence and Mental Hygiene Ideology. However, none of the individual staff characteristics were related to the three preferred-technique scores. Preferred technique score T-5 was also negatively related to OMI Benevolence and to education and marital status (r's in the ± 0.40s). These relationships showed a tendency for staff preferring relatively greater use of advice and contingency management to be married and have more education and lower Benevolence scores—all more characteristic of senior staff. T-4 was related only to age (r=-0.45), reflecting a tendency for younger staff to prefer a relatively greater use of social reinforcement. In general, however, the preference for specific therapeutic techniques remained relatively unrelated to individual staff characteristics.

The technique scores for each psychosocial orientation in figure 16.2 show a consistent patterning of staff interpretations of the appropriateness of the relative use of different techniques within each program. Both continuing staff and total staff groups produced different patterns of technique scores for the two programs at both assessments, with differential change between posttraining and first anniversary assessments (p's < 0.01). Scores T-1, T-4, and T-5 did not change significantly for either program orientation (p's > 0.20), while T-2 and T-3 showed differential change (p's < 0.01). The differential change on T-2 reflects a decrease for the social-learning orientation and an increase for the milieu orientation and T-3 reflects a greater increase for the social-learning than for the milieu orientation. However, the pattern over all five scores remained constant in the staff interpretation of the appropriateness of the relative use of techniques within the respective orientations. With the exception of T-4 and T-5, all comparisons between TOS technique scores shown in figure 16.2 within the social-learning orientation were significantly different from one another. Within the milieu orientation, T-1, T-3, and T-4 did not differ among themselves but were significantly higher than T-5. T-2 was significantly lower than all other technique scores within both orientations. At the first anniversary assessment, the differences between orientations were not significant for T-3 and T-4 (p > 0.20), but milieu scores were significantly higher than social-learning scores on T-1 and T-2 and significantly lower on T-5 (p's < 0.01).

The differences between orientations for technique scores show relative staff interpretations in the direction of the ideal response for the utilization of each group of techniques in figure 16.2, but with considerable differences in the absolute level of utilization inferred. The extent to which the staff interpretations of the appropriate pattern of technique utilization approached the ideal for the social-learning program was apparent in significant relationships over the five TOS technique scores at both assessments, without differences between them (r's=0.99). The pattern of endorsement of relative utilization of techniques for the milieu program was not significantly related to the milieu ideal at either assessment (r=0.72 & 0.73, respectively), with the lower relationship approaching significance in comparison to that within the social-learning orientation ($p < 0.10$). The major basis for the lower relationship to the milieu ideal was the T-2 score, which was endorsed by staff at a much lower level than desired relative to other scores.

The overall level of staff responses under the two orientations compared to their respective ideals became closer, but not significantly, over assessments for both the social-learning ($D^2$'s= 3.53 & 1.96, respectively) and the milieu orientation ($D^2$'s=6.56 & 5.88, respectively). The relative deviations from ideals did not differ significantly between orientations at either assessment. The largest deviations from ideal levels within both orientations resulted from utilization endorsements by staff which were lower than desired. Thus, while staff interpretations of the appropriateness of the relative use of different techniques were differentiated in desired directions between programs, the pattern of endorsement was closer to the ideal within the social-learning program. However, interpretations differed from desired levels of utilization for both programs—primarily in lower utilization endorsements where large differences occurred.

In summary, the attitudes and interpretations held by psychosocial staff regarding treatment programs showed some changes during the first eighteen weeks of program operation. Following the dramatic and differential improvement in residents during this period, all staff expressed opinions on the differences between programs as most effective and most enjoyable, while few had had differential opinions previously. Before the program introduction, there had been no differences in opinions about effectiveness, and the milieu program had been judged more enjoyable; after the first anniversary assessment, most staff believed the social-learning program was more effective and more enjoyable.

Preferred-TOS attitude scores, reflecting staff preferences for the nature of treatment programs, remained constant in their order of endorsement. The lowest score moved even lower—primarily as a result of new staff rather than changes in continuing staff—reflecting a greater preference for residents being "usually comfortable" in a "nonverbal-affective learning process." The nature of treatment characteristics preferred by staff tended to be closer to the ideal milieu program than to the ideal social-learning program, without change over the period. While more clustering among preferred attitude scores occurred after involvement in in the psychosocial programs, preferences for the nature of treatment were less predictable from individual staff characteristics than they had been previously. While some differential changes occurred in the level of endorsement of TOS attitude scores for each program orientation, the pattern of scores remained constant within each orientation over the current period. The nature of the programs was interpreted differentially, with staff interpretations remaining close to the ideals underlying each program over both assessment periods.

Preferred TOS technique scores, reflecting staff preferences for the use of differential treatment procedures, also remained constant in their order of endorsement. The least-preferred techniques moved even lower, reflecting a dislike for the use of interpretation by both continuing and new staff. In contrast to the closer approximation of staff preferences to the milieu ideal for the nature of treatment, preferred techniques were more closely related to the social-learning ideal, without change over the period. Also in contrast to preferred attitude scores, preferred technique scores showed less clustering after the psychosocial programs had begun, but did remain relatively unrelated to individual staff characteristics as well. While some differential changes also occurred in the interpretation of appropriate technique utilization for each program, the pattern of TOS technique scores remained constant within each orientation over the period. Staff interpretations of the relative use of different techniques were differentiated in desired directions between the milieu and social-learning programs. However, the pattern of interpretation was closer to the ideal within the social-learning program, with the major misinterpretation within the milieu orientation being in the endorsement of the use of interpretation at a much lower level than desired relative to other techniques.

Overall, while staff opinions were responsive to the differential resident improvement over the period about which program was the more effective and the more enjoyable, interpretations and preferences on the nature of treatment programs and the relative utilization of techniques were remarkably constant in their major characteristics. Over both time periods, staff interpretations of both nature and techniques were well differentiated in appropriate directions within and between psychosocial orientations, with staff preferences remaining much closer to either psychosocial orientation than to those of mental hospital staff.

## PERFORMANCE IN PSYCHOSOCIAL PROGRAMS

The OMI and TOS data provide information concerning staff attitudes, opinions, and beliefs about the residents and treatment programs. In contrast, the Staff-Resident Interaction Chronograph (SRIC) provides objective data on what staff actually did—how they spent their time and the nature of their contacts with residents—in general, the reliability and differentiation of the psychosocial programs as they actually operated.[9]

How staff spent their time during the current period is shown in figure 16.3, where total instances of activity and percentages of staff activity relative to the class of resident behavior in each program are plotted from baseline conditions (before the introduction of the programs) through the first anniversary assessment. An inspection of the staff activity during baseline conditions presented in figure 16.3 shows the essential identity of focus of staff behavior over the two units before the two programs were introduced. Slightly over 145 instances of activity were performed per hour by the average staff member on each unit during baseline conditions. Like the traditional hospital program, the greatest proportion of staff activity during baseline (44%) was not in response to resident behavior but was staff initiated. In fact, 38% of their activity did not involve interactions with residents at all; over 1% consisted of "ignore-neutral" job-irrelevant activity and about 37% consisted of announcements, relevant paperwork, and observing residents without interacting. About 21% and 19% of the activity involved staff interactions in response to inappropriate resident behavior ("crazy" and "failure," respectively), while 13% and 3%, respectively, involved staff

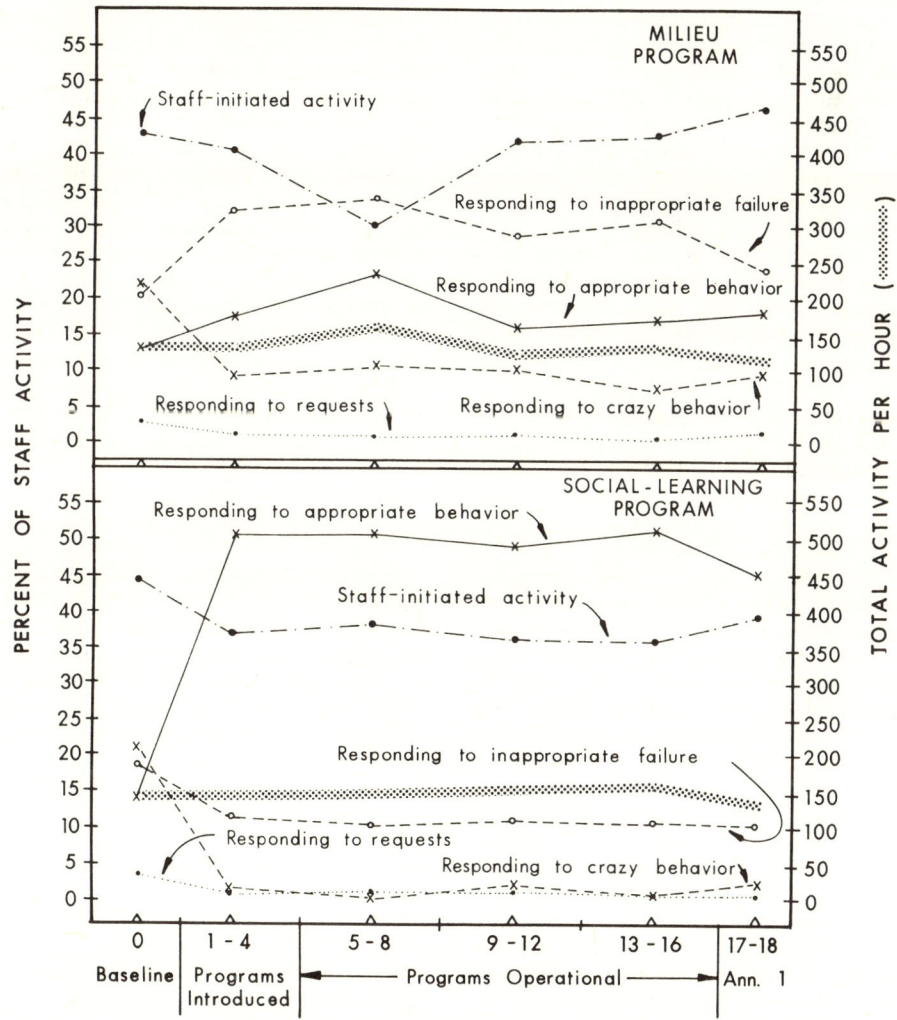

Figure 16.3. How staff spent their time during baseline conditions and the first eighteen weeks after introduction of programs. Average total activity per hour is indicated by the shaded line and scale in the right margin.

interactions in response to appropriate resident behavior and requests.

Figure 16.3 shows relatively little change in the total instances of staff activity in either program throughout the period once procedures began, but there were clear and differential changes in the focus of activity. The introduction of social-learning procedures immediately resulted in an increase in response to appropriate resident behavior to a stable rate of about 50% of all staff activity, with a concurrent stable reduction in the relative proportion of all other areas of focus. This increase reflects the operation of shaping procedures that attend to appropriate components and approximations to terminal-level behaviors of residents rather than awaiting completely normal behaviors. While 37% of staff activity in the social-learning program was not in response to resident behavior (down from 44% during baseline), only 28% of it did not involve interactions with residents, and only 0.3% consisted of irrelevant activity. Changes in the relative focus of staff activity in the social-learning program directly paralleled changes in resident Global Functioning over the entire period, with the proportion of staff activity focused upon appropriate behavior covarying with changes in resident functioning (r=0.92), while all other proportions varied in opposite directions to resident functioning (r's=-0.80s & -0.90s).

The introduction of milieu therapy procedures similarly resulted in a stable reduction in the relative proportion of staff activity in response to resident requests and crazy behavior, which varied in opposite directions to the functioning of milieu residents (r's in the -0.90s). However, the proportions of staff interactions focused upon resident requests and crazy behavior were still significantly above those in the social-learning program.[10] The proportion of staff activity involving interactions in response to appropriate resident behavior and failures also increased upon the introduction of milieu therapy procedures and then decreased slightly, with levels still remaining above those existing earlier. The staff focus on resident failures was significantly higher in the milieu program than in the social-learning program and covaried with resident functioning over the entire period (r=0.84). Staff focus on appropriate behavior was significantly lower than in the social-learning program and was not significantly related to change in resident functioning in the milieu program. Thus, the relative staff focus on appropriate resident behavior versus resident failures not only differed significantly between programs but was differentially related to resident improvement within programs—exactly in keeping with the expectations of the respective program manuals.

Figure 16.3 also shows a decrease in the proportion of staff-initiated activity upon the introduction of milieu procedures, followed by an increase to the level existing under baseline conditions. However, the relative level of staff-initiated activity after the introduction of milieu procedures did not differ significantly from that in the social-learning program over the entire period and was unrelated to changes in resident functioning. Over the first eighteen weeks of the milieu program, 40% of staff activity was not in response to resident behavior (down from 44% during baseline), but only 33% of staff activity did not involve interactions with residents and only 0.5% consisted of irrelevant activity. Thus, in both programs, staff maintained the same level of activity but changed focus in ways that decreased irrelevant activities and increased the proportion of activity involving resident interaction.

The attention received by an individual resident within the psychosocial programs changed considerably once programmatic procedures were introduced, even though the number of residents, staffing ratios, and total staff activity remained essentially constant. The structure of the treatment programs (which divided staff responsibilities for resident subgroups during functional time periods), combined with improved resident functioning (which allowed more individual assignments), resulted in a reduction of the number of residents for whom an individual staff member was typically responsible. With the same total staff and resident population, the average number of residents for whom each staff member was responsible was reduced from 22.6 during baseline to an average of 17.3 in the milieu program and 13.9 in the social-learning program over the remainder of the period. The net effect for the average individual resident of the change in focus of staff activity, and the smaller functional groups for whom staff became responsible, is shown in table 16.1.

The introduction of programmatic procedures resulted in the individual resident's receiving contact from staff at a level over 23% higher than the baseline rate in the milieu program and more than double the baseline rate in the social-learning program. An inspection of the "average contacts per hour" in table 16.1 shows that the number of contacts only as a part of a group actually reduced after the implementation of programs, such that the proportion of contacts that were personalized to the individual increased in both milieu (81% to 93%) and social-learning (78% to 97%) programs. Thus, even though milieu residents spent more time in integrated groups, staff contact was still personalized to the individuals within each group. The "probability of contact" figures in table 16.1 show that an individual resident in the milieu program had nearly a 40%

Table 16.1. Amount of staff attention psychosocial residents received before introduction of programs (baseline) and during first eighteen weeks after program introduction.

| Focus of attention resident received | Probability of contact in 10 min. | | | | Average contacts per hour | | | | Average interactions per contact | | | |
|---|---|---|---|---|---|---|---|---|---|---|---|---|
| | Milieu | | Social-learning | | Milieu | | Social-learning | | Milieu | | Social-learning | |
| | Baseline | Program | Baseline | Program | Baseline | Program | Baseline | Program | Baseline | Program | Baseline | Program |
| As individual | 0.273 | 0.386 | 0.198 | 0.546 | 1.64 | 2.32 | 1.19 | 3.28 | 1.56 | 1.89 | 2.05 | 2.26 |
| As part of group | .064 | .030 | .056 | .018 | .38 | .18 | .34 | .11 | .36 | .14 | .58 | .07 |
| Total | .337 | .416 | .254 | .564 | 2.02 | 2.50 | 1.53 | 3.39 | 1.92 | 2.03 | 2.63 | 2.33 |

chance of receiving a personalized, individual contact from a staff member during the average ten-minute period during waking hours over the first eighteen weeks of program operation. The probability of contact for an individual social-learning resident increased to nearly 55%, that is, during the first eighteen weeks of program operation, a resident was more likely to receive a personalized, individual contact from a staff member than not during a ten-minute period.

Table 16.1 also reveals that the average interactions within each individual contact also increased in both programs. Thus, the introduction of programmatic procedures resulted in the individual resident's receiving more personalized contacts, and the amount of interaction within each contact—instances of discrete verbal content or other staff behavior directed to the resident—also increased slightly. The net effect on the total amount of attention received from staff (contacts x interactions) was a 31% increase for milieu residents and a 96% increase for social-learning residents, with the average social-learning resident receiving nearly 55% more total attention from staff than the average milieu resident received during the first eighteen weeks of program operation. Thus, the number of staff and residents were constant over time, and the same staff were equated in time spent on each unit; however, the introduction of procedures resulted in increased attention for individual residents in both groups, with the social-learning program providing more individual staff attention than the milieu program did, where pressure from other members of the resident groups was encouraged.

How well staff equated their performance during baseline conditions is shown in the average hourly rates of staff activity presented in table 16.2. While SRIC summary tables, such as 16.2, seem complex, the main body of each table simply reproduces the 5 x 21 SRIC matrix for each unit so that the reader can examine the average hourly instances of specific staff behavior in relationship to the class of resident behavior to which staff activities were directed. The "+", "o", and "-" designations within each cell indicate the appropriateness of each staff activity as defined in the respective treatment manuals for the milieu and social-learning programs. All cells with these designations represent staff-resident interactions, with the exception of the last three classes of staff behavior (Ignore/No Response; Announce; Attend/Record/Observe) under the Neutral column. Ignore/No Response under other columns reflects an active withdrawal or withholding of other staff response and is considered interaction. The six columns on the right of each table provide a summary of the average hourly instances of each class of staff behavior ("total staff behavior"), the relative distribution of interactive staff behavior ("% of interactions"), and the distribution of total programmatic errors by class of staff activity ("% of all staff error"). Similarly, the three rows at the bottom provide a summary of the average hourly instances of staff activity according to the class of resident behavior to which staff responded and the proportion of those instances that were appropriate programmatic interactions within the respective treatment programs.

Since programmatic procedures were not in operation under baseline conditions, the designations of appropriateness within cells and "correct interactions" and "error" in the summary rows and columns of table 16.2 provide a means of comparing how staff performance during baseline would have fit the respective programs had the programs been in effect. While the distributions of staff interactions during baseline conditions were not desirable from the principles of either psychosocial program, the total error rates presented show that 75.9% of staff interactions during baseline would have been totally inappropriate by milieu standards, while only 12% would have been so by social-learning standards. The basis for the difference lies primarily in the active ignoring of inappropriate resident behavior, which, in isolation, would have been appropriate by rules of the social-learning program but an error by rules of the milieu program. In fact, about 92% of the errors by either program standards would have been attributable to staff's inappropriately ignoring residents.

In general, however, staff did an excellent job of equating their performance over the two units during baseline conditions. Both total interactions and total activity were functionally identical between units. Additionally the instances of specific staff behavior were distributed in similar order for both level and proportion over units, with the most frequent staff interaction being Ignore/No Response, followed by Instruct/Demonstrate. About 8% to 9% of staff interactions during baseline were Positive Nonverbal and Doing With, reflecting a fairly high degree of friendly interaction and shared activity. Doing For was the only other staff interaction that occurred regularly during baseline. No negative responses to resident behavior occurred with any regularity at all.

A comparison to the distribution of staff interactions during the sample of the traditional hospital programs found that the same five highest-frequency classes of staff interactions during the original psychosocial baseline were also the highest for traditional hospital staff, but with differences in the relative distribution. Hospital staff showed considerably higher rates of Positive Nonverbal and lower rates of Ignore/

No Response; the most frequent response of hospital staff to any resident behavior (including inappropriate behavior) was to smile, while psychosocial staff ignored. Hospital staff also showed a higher proportion of total activity in the "Ignore-Neutral" cell (8.9% vs. 1.5%), reflecting attention to irrelevant activities to the total exclusion of residents. Attend/Record/Observe was the second most frequent of all activities during the psychosocial baseline and the most frequent for hospital staff. Hospital staff further differed from the baseline performance of psychosocial staff in performing higher rates of Reflect/Clarify and both Negative Verbal and Negative Nonverbal. Thus, the actual staff behavior on psychosocial units during baseline documents the equality of conditions to which residents in the milieu and social-learning groups were exposed; however, the original baseline conditions only partially replicated the distribution of staff behavior later observed in the traditional hospital comparison group, but was closer to traditional hospital procedures than to either of the desired psychosocial programs.

How well staff differentiated their performance of the psychosocial programs during the eighteen weeks after the introduction of programmatic procedures is shown in the average hourly rates of staff activity presented in table 16.3. All of the figures in the table reflect immediate changes to stable levels of performance over the eighteen-week period, with the exception of three classes of staff behavior in the milieu program. Positive Nonverbals, Positive Statements, and Positive Group References in the milieu program all increased over the first eight weeks of the program and decreased thereafter—still remaining well above original baseline levels (accounting for the temporary increase in percentage response to "inappropriate failure" and "appropriate behavior" in figure 16.3). However, even these three classes of staff behavior remained stable as a percentage of total interactions over the entire period.

Table 16.3 shows that staff not only changed their behavior drastically from baseline conditions but differentiated between psychosocial programs exceptionally well in their actual performance. In fact, differences in the average hourly rate between programs were significant over the period for fifteen of the twenty-one classes of total staff behavior. Four of the six classes of activity where staff did not perform at different rates after the programs began were activities for which differential procedures were not required—being totally appropriate for both (Announce, Attend/Record/Observe), totally inappropriate for both (Negative Statement), or differentially allowable for both (Physical Force). Doing For was differentially allowable but did not differ between programs—remaining at a low rate of just over one instance per hour over the entire eighteen weeks. Negative Nonsocial was differentially appropriate for the social-learning program as a consequence for inappropriate behavior and differentially allowable for the milieu program as a response to specified crazy resident behaviors; however, the rates did not differ between programs—remaining at an exceptionally low average of only thirty-two instances of removing physical or material goods or withholding admittance to services every hundred waking hours, even in the social-learning program. Parallel differences were obtained between the programs on evaluation of the relative percentage of interactions accounted for by each class of staff behavior. Only Instruct/Demonstrate yielded different results—showing significantly higher total instances for staff in the social-learning program but no significant difference between programs in the percentage of total interactions.

All differences in staff performance between programs during the first eighteen weeks were in keeping with the differential requirements specified in the treatment manuals. Six of the seven classes of staff behavior that were performed at significantly higher rates in the milieu program than in the social-learning program were differentially specified in the Milieu Manual. The six classes included milieu procedures that were to be applied at all times across all classes of resident behavior (Positive Statement, Positive Group Reference, Reflect/Clarify, Suggest Alternatives) or that specified the nature of content for responding to inappropriate resident behavior (Negative Verbal, Negative Group Reference). Staff not only performed these classes of behavior at a significantly higher rate in the milieu program, but on an absolute level over 52% of all staff-resident interactions in the milieu program were accounted for by these milieu-specific verbal communications. Two classes of staff behavior (Positive Verbal, Positive Nonverbal) were performed at lower rates in the milieu program than in the social-learning program but still occurred at relatively high levels as required by the Milieu Manual. When these behaviors are taken into account, table 16.3 shows that nearly 74% of all staff-resident interactions in the milieu program involved specific procedures detailed for milieu therapy.

One class of staff behavior was performed at a significantly higher rate in the milieu program (Negative Nonverbal), which was not differentially specified, in that nonverbal metacommunications should be consistent with verbal content in both programs. An analysis of SRIC sequences provides a possible explanation for the differential findings for the incidence of Negative Nonverbals. One requirement of the

Table 16.2. Average hourly rate of staff activity on psychosocial units before introduction of programmatic procedures.

| Staff behavior | Resident behavior to which staff responded ||||||||||||| Total staff behavior || % of interactions || % of all staff error[c] ||
| | Appropriate || Inappropriate Failure || Inappropriate Crazy || Request || Neutral || | | | | | | |
| | Milieu | S.Lrng | Milieu | S.Lrng | Milieu | S.Lrng | Milieu | S.Lrng | Milieu | S.Lrng | Milieu | S.Lrng | Milieu | S.Lrng | Milieu | S.Lrng |
|---|---|---|---|---|---|---|---|---|---|---|---|---|---|---|---|---|
| Positive Verbal | 0.12[+] | 0.54[+] | - | - | - | 0.06[-] | 0.12[o] | 0.12[o] | 0.12[o] | 0.30[o] | 0.36 | 0.90 | 0.4% | 1.0% | | 0.6% |
| Negative Verbal | - | - | 0.12[+] | 0.06[o] | 0.18[+] | 0.36[-] | 0.06[-] | 0.12[o] | - | - | 0.36 | 0.54 | 0.4% | 0.6% | 0.1% | 1.1% |
| Positive Nonverbal | 4.08[+] | 4.38[+] | 0.18[o] | 0.36[o] | o | 0.12[o] | 1.38[o] | 1.62[o] | 1.56[o] | 1.62[o] | 7.20 | 8.10 | 8.0% | 9.0% | 0.1% | 1.1% |
| Negative Nonverbal | 0.06[-] | - | o | 0.42[o] | 0.30[o] | 0.72[o] | o | 0.06[o] | - | - | 0.36 | 1.20 | 0.4% | 1.3% | 0.1% | 0.6% |
| Positive Nonsocial | - | + | - | - | - | - | 0.48[o] | 0.36[o] | 0.06[o] | 0.48[o] | 0.54 | 0.84 | 0.6% | 0.9% | | |
| Negative Nonsocial | - | - | 0.06[-] | + | o | 0.06[+] | - | - | - | - | 0.06 | 0.06 | 0.1% | 0.1% | 0.1% | |
| Positive Statement | + | o | + | - | + | 0.06[-] | + | o | 0.06[+] | o | 0.06 | 0.12 | 0.1% | 0.1% | | 1.1% |
| Negative Statement | - | - | - | 0.06[-] | - | 0.06[-] | - | - | - | - | | 0.06 | | 0.1% | | 0.6% |
| Positive Prompt | - | + | - | + | - | 0.06[+] | - | + | - | + | | 0.06 | | 0.1% | | |
| Negative Prompt | - | - | - | - | - | - | - | o | - | - | | | | | | |
| Positive Gp. Reference | + | o | + | - | + | - | + | o | + | o | | | | | | |
| Negative Gr Reference | - | - | + | o | + | o | + | - | o | - | | | | | | |
| Reflect/Clarify | 0.12[+] | o | 0.12[+] | 0.06[o] | 0.06[+] | 0.06[o] | 0.18[+] | 0.54[o] | 0.24[+] | o | 0.72 | 0.12 | 0.8% | 0.1% | | |
| Suggest Alternatives | + | o | + | 0.06[o] | + | - | + | o | + | o | | 0.06 | | 0.1% | | |
| Instruct/Demonstrate | 1.50[o] | 1.14[+] | 4.32[-] | 3.96[o] | 0.78[o] | 1.80[o] | 0.60[o] | 0.42[o] | 3.48[o] | 4.86[o] | 10.68 | 12.30 | 11.9% | 13.7% | 6.4% | |
| Doing With | 5.46[+] | 6.36[+] | 0.18[o] | - | - | - | 0.48[o] | 0.42[o] | 1.02[+] | 1.38[+] | 6.96 | 8.16 | 7.8% | 9.1% | | |
| Doing For | - | o | 0.36[-] | 0.30[-] | 0.06[-] | 0.06[-] | 0.96[o] | 1.20[o] | 0.24[-] | 0.36[o] | 1.62 | 1.92 | 1.8% | 2.1% | 1.0% | 3.4% |
| Physical Force | - | - | - | o | - | 0.18[o] | - | - | - | - | | 0.24 | | 0.3% | | |
| Ignore/No Response | 7.44[-] | 7.44[-] | 23.94[-] | 21.12[+] | 29.22[-] | 26.10[+] | - | - | 2.16[-] | 2.16[-] | 62.76 | 57.12 | 70.1%[a] | 63.7%[a] | 92.4% | 92.0% |
| Announce | b | b | b | b | b | b | b | b | 0.42[+] | 1.98[+] | 0.42 | 1.98 | (0.3%) | (1.4%) | b | b |
| Attend/Record/Observe | b | b | b | b | b | b | b | b | 53.28[+] | 51.54[+] | 53.28 | 51.54 | (36.6%) | (35.5%) | b | b |
| Total interactions | 18.78 | 20.16 | 29.10 | 26.46 | 30.60 | 29.70 | 4.26 | 4.32 | 6.78 | 9.00 | 89.52 | 89.64 | 102%[a] | 102%[a] | 75.9% | 12.0% |
| % correct interactions[c] | 60.1% | 61.6% | 1.4% | 98.6% | 4.3% | 98.8% | 98.6% | 97.2% | 64.6%[a] | 76.0%[a] | 24.1% | 88.0% | b | b | 0.0% | 0.0% |
| Total activity | b | b | b | b | b | b | b | b | 62.64 | 64.68 | 145.38 | 145.32 | (162%) | (162%) | b | b |

Note. If programmatic procedures had been in effect: + = specifically programmed staff behavior; - = programmatic error. Empty cells signify less than 0.0045 instances per hour. o = allowable staff choice; 
a. "Ignore-neutral" included in percentage figures, but not in total interactions.
b. Irrelevant cells.
c. If programmatic procedures had been in effect.

Table 16.3. Average hourly rate of staff activity on psychosocial units after introduction of programs.

| | Resident behavior to which staff responded | | | | | | | | | | | Total staff behavior | | % of interactions | | % of all staff error | |
|---|---|---|---|---|---|---|---|---|---|---|---|---|---|---|---|---|---|
| | Appropriate | | Inappropriate Failure | | Inappropriate Crazy | | Request | | Neutral | | | | | | | | |
| Staff behavior | Milieu | S.Lrng | Milieu | S.Lrng | Milieu | S.Lrng | Milieu | S.Lrng | Milieu | S.Lrng | | Milieu | S.Lrng | Milieu | S.Lrng | Milieu | S.Lrng |
| Positive Verbal | 6.16+ | 16.40+ | 0.07- | 0.03- | 0.01- | 0.01- | - | o | 0.12o | 0.11o | | 6.36 | 16.55 | 7.3% | 15.1% | 1.0% | 2.3% |
| Negative Verbal | 0.01- | 0.05- | 3.35+ | 0.52+ | 3.62+ | 0.06o | 0.02- | - | 0.03- | 0.08- | | 7.03 | 0.71 | 8.0% | 0.6% | 0.7% | 7.4% |
| Positive Nonverbal | 9.59+ | 25.60+ | 1.62o | 0.33o | 0.19o | - | 0.06o | 0.02o | 0.77o | 1.79o | | 12.23 | 27.74 | 13.9% | 25.3% | 0.1% | 21.1% |
| Negative Nonverbal | 0.01- | 0.36- | 1.54o | 0.39o | 1.75o | 0.03o | o | 0.01o | - | 0.01- | | 3.30 | 0.80 | 3.8% | 0.7% | 1.2% | 3.4% |
| Positive Nonsocial | 0.09- | 19.57+ | 0.01- | 0.05- | - | 0.01- | 0.09o | 0.01o | o | o | | 0.19 | 19.64 | 0.2% | 17.9% | 0.5% | 5.7% |
| Negative Nonsocial | - | 0.08- | 0.04- | 0.19+ | 0.08o | 0.03+ | - | - | - | 0.02- | | 0.12 | 0.32 | 0.1% | 0.3% | 0.6% | 4.6% |
| Positive Statement | 0.46+ | o | 15.16+ | 0.07- | 2.54+ | 0.01- | 0.02+ | o | 0.32+ | 0.02+ | | 18.50 | 0.10 | 21.1% | 0.1% | 0.5% | 1.7% |
| Negative Statement | - | - | 0.02- | - | 0.01- | - | - | - | 0.02- | - | | 0.05 | | 0.1% | | | 1.1% |
| Positive Prompt | 0.02- | 1.36+ | 0.03- | 6.57+ | - | 0.07+ | - | - | - | 0.54+ | | 0.05 | 8.54 | 0.1% | 7.8% | 0.6% | |
| Negative Prompt | - | 0.01- | 0.02- | 3.63+ | 0.02- | + | - | - | - | 0.02- | | 0.04 | 3.66 | | 3.3% | 0.5% | |
| Positive Gp. Reference | 2.61+ | o | 5.63+ | 0.02- | 0.83+ | - | 0.02+ | o | 1.07+ | 0.03o | | 10.16 | 0.05 | 11.6% | 0.1% | 0.6% | |
| Negative Gp. Reference | - | - | 2.50+ | o | 1.34+ | o | 0.02+ | - | 0.03o | - | | 3.89 | | 4.4% | 0.6% | | |
| Reflect/Clarify | 0.17+ | 0.07o | 3.60+ | 0.45o | 0.54+ | 0.03o | 0.13+ | 0.01o | 0.58+ | 0.06o | | 5.02 | 0.62 | 5.7% | 0.4% | | |
| Suggest Alternatives | 0.01+ | 0.01o | 0.72+ | 0.34o | 0.06+ | - | 0.01+ | o | 0.54+ | 0.14o | | 1.34 | 0.49 | 1.5% | 9.2% | 60.2% | 7.4% |
| Instruct/Demonstrate | 0.91o | 2.86+ | 5.05+ | 3.48o | 0.44+ | 0.08o | 0.10o | 0.11o | 2.17o | 3.52o | | 8.67 | 10.05 | 9.9% | 14.9% | 2.3% | 6.3% |
| Doing With | 4.48+ | 9.36+ | 0.12- | 0.11- | 0.07- | 0.02- | 0.35- | 0.43- | 3.34+ | 6.40+ | | 8.36 | 16.32 | 9.5% | 0.9% | 10.8% | 0.6% |
| Doing For | 0.24o | 0.23o | 0.10- | 0.09- | 0.02- | 0.02- | 0.31o | 0.18o | 0.57- | 0.52o | | 1.22 | 1.04 | 1.4% | 0.1% | 0.1% | 38.3% |
| Physical Force | - | 0.01- | 0.04o | 0.05o | 0.05o | 0.01o | - | - | 0.01- | - | | 0.10 | 0.07 | 0.1% | 3.0%a | 21.5% | b |
| Ignore/No Response | 0.06- | 0.17- | 0.30- | 1.49+ | 0.71- | 1.17+ | 0.02- | b | 0.71- | 0.50- | | 1.80 | 3.33 | 2.1%a | (0.8%) | b | b |
| Announce | b | b | b | b | b | b | b | b | 1.79+ | 1.15+ | | 1.79 | 1.15 | (1.4%) | (27.1%) | b | b |
| Attend/Record/Observe | b | b | b | b | b | b | b | b | 40.43+ | 41.35+ | | 40.43 | 41.35 | (30.9%) | | | |
| Total interactions | 24.82 | 76.14 | 39.92 | 17.81 | 12.26 | 1.55 | 1.15 | 0.77 | 9.57 | 13.26 | | 87.72 | 109.53 | 100%a | 100%a | 9.6% | 1.6% |
| % correct interactions | 98.3% | 99.1% | 85.6% | 97.9% | 93.3% | 95.5% | 96.5% | 100% | 86.0% | 95.2%a | | 90.4% | 98.4% | b | b | 0.0% | 0.0% |
| Total activity | b | b | b | b | b | b | b | b | 52.50 | 56.26 | | 130.65 | 152.53 | (149%) | (139%) | b | b |

Note. + = specifically programmed staff behavior; o = allowable staff choice; - = programmatic error. Empty cells signify less than 0.0045 instances per hour.
a. "Ignore-neutral" included in percentage figures, but not in total interactions.
b. Irrelevant cells.

milieu program was that undesirable behavior was never to be ignored. SRIC sequences revealed that staff averaged over nineteen instances of positive statements and negative feedback per hour in response to inappropriate resident behavior in the milieu program during this period but that these procedures were effective in terminating inappropriate behavior only 75% of the time. On the average, the same resident inappropriate behavior continued to occur on 4.93 occasions per hour after having received positive statements and negative feedback, and staff properly continued to provide additional positive statements and negative feedback on 4.92 occasions—i.e., slipups occurred only once every hundred hours. Thus, staff were quite reliable in application of continued programmatic interactions for inappropriate resident behavior, but it seems probable that the continuing focus on inappropriate resident behavior resulted in more instances of negative affect for staff. The higher incidence of frowns, grimaces, negative intonations, etc. (Negative Nonverbal) shown in the milieu program (table 16.3) than in the social-learning program may reflect a genuine communication of higher rates of negative affect experienced as a result of the continuing focus on inappropriate resident behavior. This interpretation is also consistent with the greater proportion of staff who reported the social-learning program to be the more enjoyable at the first anniversary assessment.

The three classes of staff behavior that accounted for the highest proportion of interactions in the social-learning program consisted of positive social and nonsocial behaviors (Positive Verbal, Positive Nonverbal, Positive Nonsocial), while the fourth highest consisted of shared social activity (Doing With). Staff not only performed these behaviors at a signifcantly higher rate in the social-learning program than in the milieu program, but in a highly consistent, contingent manner. An inspection of the within-cell distribution of these staff behaviors in the social-learning program (table 16.3) reveals that 96% of the positive behaviors and 57% of shared activities were contingent upon appropriate resident behavior rather than being staff initiated. Thus, on an absolute level, nearly 65% of all staff-resident interactions were accounted for by positive social and material reinforcement contingent upon appropriate resident behavior. The four remaining classes of staff behavior that were performed at significantly higher rates in the social-learning program than in the milieu program were those that were differentially specified by the respective manuals for dealing with inappropriate resident behavior and/or initiating new or different resident behaviors (Positive Prompt, Negative Prompt, Instruct/Demonstrate, Ignore/No Response).

Particularly striking is the low rate of Ignore/No Response, even when it was appropriate to use in the social-learning program, in comparison to the high rate during baseline. Part of the low rate of active ignoring was a result of the success of positive reinforcement procedures in reducing the frequency of inappropriate resident behaviors and part was from staff application of other appropriate procedures. However, one condition in the social-learning program required Ignore/No Response as the only appropriate staff behavior: if an inappropriate resident behavior that would not incur a response cost was prompted (for termination and incompatible behavior), but continued to occur. Analyses of SRIC sequences found an additional basis for low rates of Ignore/No Response to lie in the success of prompts in changing behavior. Specifically staff averaged over ten prompts per hour for inappropriate behavior during this period, and the prompts were effective in terminating the inappropriate behavior more than 94% of the time. In fact, a prompted inappropriate behavior continued, on the average, on only fifty-eight occasions every hundred hours, and staff properly ignored that behavior on all but one occasion. Thus, staff were quite reliable in active ignoring when it was required, but the success of other procedures resulted in a restricted number of instances in which Ignore/No Response was the only appropriate staff behavior.

Actual staff performance during the first eighteen weeks clearly differentiated between programs on the basis of requirements specified in the respective treatment manuals. Table 16.3 also shows that the within-program accuracy in staff performance was exceptional, with over 90% of staff-resident interactions in the milieu program following procedures and a remarkable 98.4% of staff-resident interactions in the social-learning program doing the same. The distribution of errors shown in table 16.3 reveals that the majority of staff errors in the social-learning program consisted of inappropriate Ignore/No Response and Negative Nonverbals. However, the exceptionally low total instances of errors in the social-learning program —averaging only 1.75 instances per hour—were such that these highest rate errors reflect only sixty-seven and thirty-seven instances of error, respectively, every hundred waking hours.[11] Only 5.7% of the errors consisted of the misapplication of milieu therapy procedures in the social-learning program, and 0.5% consisted of activities that were inappropriate at any time. The remainder of social-learning errors (93.8%) consisted of misapplication of social-learning procedures; however, even these occurred at a remarkably low rate of less than 1.5% of all staff-resident interactions. In contrast, errors in the milieu program not only occurred at a higher rate of 9.6% of all interactions (8.39 instances per hour), but 83.3% of them resulted from misapplication of social-learning procedures in the milieu program; 9.1% and 7.6% of the errors, respectively, consisted of activities that were inappropriate at any time and misapplication of milieu procedures. As shown in table 16.3, the majority of milieu errors consisted of inappropriate Instruct/Demonstrate for resident failures.

Actual staff performance was, thus, well differentiated between programs. Although the accuracy of performance was exceptional in both, it was better in the social-learning program. In addition, the distribution of relative proportions of staff-resident interactions clearly followed the procedures in the social-learning manual and reflected the ideal distribution of technique utilization from the TOS (figure 16.2). While the actual staff performance in the milieu program was well differentiated in appropriate classes of behavior from the social-learning program and was accurate on an absolute level, Instruct/Demonstrate did occur at too high a rate, reflecting a spillover of procedures from one program to the other. The distribution of relative proportions of staff-resident interaction was therefore not as close to the ideal distribution specified in the milieu therapy manual and on the TOS (figure 16.2) as that of the social-learning program.

The other primary deviations in actual performance from an ideal distribution in the milieu program were lower rates of Reflect/Clarify and Suggest Alternatives than desired (table 16.3). While these classes of procedures were performed at a higher rate in the milieu program than in the social-learning program, the absolute level was lower than that specified by the treatment manual and lower than the TOS ideals that primarily covered these procedures (T-1 & T-2, figure 16.2) Additionally although the relative proportions of Positive Verbals, Positive Nonverbals, Positive Statements, and Positive Group References in the milieu program were all appropriately differentiated, the decline in absolute instances of the last three classes of staff behavior in the last half of the period was of concern because of a tendency for the staff-resident interactions of the milieu program to become too negative. The relatively low absolute rate of Positive Nonverbals, especially when responding to residents' failures, also reflected a tendency for junior staff to apply milieu procedures in a more mechanical fashion than desired, without genuine nonverbal metacommunication of affect. While this difficulty was relatively infrequent on an absolute level, a focus on genuineness of interactions was always a component of staff feedback during this period. In general, then, while milieu procedures were accurately differentiated from social-learning procedures, the actual rates of utilization did, in fact, correspond to the staff interpretations reflected on the TOS (figure 16.2), which involved appropriate differentiation in relative levels between programs but endorsements of specific absolute rates of utilization that were lower than the ideal for the milieu program.

An examination of the relationships between average instances of each class of staff behavior and unitwide levels of resident functioning over standard time blocks of the present period primarily reflected the major changes from baseline to the operation of programs because of the relative stability of staff behavior after the programs were introduced. Thus, significant relationships (r's in the $\pm 0.80$s & $\pm 0.90$s) were obtained between changes in staff behavior and changes in unitwide functioning in expected directions within each program. Resident functioning increased with increases in total Positive Verbals, with percentage correct interactions, and with decreases in Ignore/No Response for both programs. Increases in resident functioning within the social-learning program were associated with increases in staff use of Positive Nonsocials, Positive Prompts, and Doing With, while increases in resident functioning within the milieu program were associated with increases in staff use of Negative Verbals, Positive Statements, and Positive Group References. These correlations were often significantly different between programs and related to changes in adaptive and maladaptive resident behaviors in both concurrent behavior (TSBC) and responsiveness within programs (Clinical Frequencies), as well as the overall measures of Global Functioning. Other changes in staff behavior were related only to changes in resident responsiveness within programs. Within the milieu program, increases in Negative Group References and Negative Nonverbals were related only to decreases in Inappropriate Clinical Frequencies. Similarly within the social-learning program, increases in Positive Nonverbals and Negative Prompts were associated only with increases in Appropriate Clinical Frequencies and decreases in Inappropriate Clinical Frequencies. Thus, the changes in staff performance from baseline to the introduction of the programs were in keeping with prescribed programmatic procedures and were differentially related to improvements in resident functioning over the current period.

In summary, objective data from the SRIC document the equality of conditions to which residents in the milieu and social-learning groups were exposed before the introduction of the programs. The focus of staff activity, the rate of activity and staff-resident interactions, and the distribution of specific staff behavior were all functionally identical on the psychosocial units under original baseline conditions.

While original baseline conditions only partially replicated the distribution of staff activities later observed in the traditional hospital programs, staff behavior and resident experience under psychosocial baseline conditions were much closer to traditional hospital programs than to that in either of the psychosocial programs. The introduction of programmatic procedures did not change the total level of staff activity in either program but resulted in clear and stable differences in the focus of staff activities. In both programs, the change in focus of activities resulted in less staff irrelevant behavior and a lower proportion of staff activities devoted to announcements, relevant paperwork, and observing residents without interacting, with corresponding increases in the proportion of activities involving staff-resident interactions.

Even though the number of residents, total staff activity, and staffing ratios essentially remained constant over time—with the same staff equated in time spent in each program—the changes in the focus of staff activity once the program procedures began resulted in drastic changes in the attention the residents received. Both programs resulted in major increases in the number of contacts and the total attention received by an individual resident, with more staff-to-resident attention being apparent in the social-learning program. Even though the milieu program focus on instigating resident-to-resident interaction within groups resulted in a lower level of staff-to-resident attention than in the social-learning program, even contacts within groups were clearly personalized such that milieu residents still received considerably more direct staff attention than during baseline conditions or than that which patients received in the traditional hospital program.

The actual differentiation of staff performance in the psychosocial programs after the introduction of programmatic procedures was remarkable. Both the focus of staff activity and the rate of performance of specific classes of of staff behavior during the first eighteen weeks of operation were in keeping with the differential requirements specified in the treatment manuals. Additionally improvements in resident functioning over the entire period were differentially related in expected directions to changes in the focus of staff activities and to changes in the specific classes of staff-resident interaction within each program.

When working in the milieu program, staff performed all milieu-specific interactions at a significantly higher rate than they did when working in the social-learning program, with 90.4% of all staff-resident interactions being appropriate on an absolute level. The specific distribution of the relative proportions of staff-resident interactions in the milieu program was not as close to the ideal distributions specified in the Milieu Manual as could be desired. Rather, actual staff behavior deviated from ideal levels in the same manner that staff interpretations of the appropriate level of technique utilization deviated from the ideal on the TOS—primarily in absolute rates that were lower than desired, especially for classes of behavior involving interpretation. Of the actual errors in the milieu program, the great majority consisted of applying social-learning procedures, primarily in providing specific instruction rather than encouragement or reflection.

When working in the social-learning program, staff not only performed social-learning specific procedures at a significantly higher rate than they did when working in the milieu program, but 98.4% of all staff-resident interactions in the social-learning program were appropriate on an absolute level. Additionally the distribution of relative proportions of staff-resident interactions in the social-learning program clearly followed those specified in the treatment manual and the ideal distribution of technique utilization from the TOS. While errors in the social-learning program were nearly nonexistent, proportionally fewer instances consisted of a misapplication of milieu procedures. Thus, while staff did a better job of reproducing all aspects of the ideal social-learning program, the absolute level of accuracy in the actual performance of both programs was exceptional, with clear and reliable differentiation being maintained throughout the period.

SUMMARY

The staff attitudes, opinions, and beliefs about mental patients did not change significantly from the original posttraining assessment to the first anniversary assessment. OMI scores tended to be less clustered and less predictable from individual staff characteristics after active involvement in treatment than before. However, the pattern and level of OMI scores remained close to the ideals underlying the psychosocial programs and different from those of typical mental hospital staff. Thus, the opinions about mental patients to which residents were exposed did not differ from before original baseline conditions through the first eighteen weeks of operation of the psychosocial programs, nor did exposure to the chronic population or staff turnover produce changes in these opinions for the staff group as a whole.

In contrast to the absence of change in opinions about patients, opinions and interpretations of treatment programs showed some changes.

The most dramatic shift occurred on opinions about psychosocial programs as relatively "most effective" and "most enjoyable." Before the implementation of programs, few staff expressed opinions; those who did divided evenly on probable effectiveness, and judged the milieu program to be "more enjoyable" by a ratio of three to one. Following the dramatic and differential improvement in resident behavior, all staff expressed opinions; most believed that the social-learning program was both more effective and more enjoyable by the first anniversary assessment.

Preferred TOS attitude scores—reflecting staff preference for the nature of treatment programs—showed some change over the current period but remained constant in the order of endorsement. While more clustering occurred among preferred attitude scores after the psychosocial programs began, such preferences became less predictable from individual staff characteristics. The nature of treatment characteristics preferred by staff tended to be closer to the ideal milieu program than to the ideal social-learning program. Although some differential changes occurred in the level of endorsement of TOS attitude scores for each program orientation—reflecting staff interpretation of the nature of each psychosocial program—the pattern of scores remained constant within each orientation, and the nature of the programs was interpreted differentially, with interpretations remaining close to the ideals underlying each program.

Preferred TOS technique scores—reflecting staff preferences for the use of different treatment procedures—also showed some change but remained constant in the order of endorsement. These scores, unlike preferred attitude scores, showed less clustering after involvement in the psychosocial programs but remained relatively unpredictable from individual staff characteristics. In contrast to the closer approximation of staff preferences for the nature of treatment to the milieu ideal, preferred techniques were more closely related to the social-learning ideal. Although some differential changes occurred in the level of endorsement of TOS technique scores for each program orientation—reflecting staff interpretation of appropriate technique utilization within each psychosocial program—the pattern of scores also remained constant within each orientation, and the relative use of different techniques were interpreted differentially in desired directions between milieu and social-learning orientations. The pattern of interpretation of technique utilization was close to the ideal only within the social-learning orientation, with misinterpretations within the milieu orientation occurring at lower levels of endorsement than desired, particularly for the use of interpretation as a treatment technique.

Over both assessments, however, staff interpretations of the nature of programs and relative utilization of techniques were remarkably consistent in their major characteristics and well differentiated in appropriate directions within and between the programs. Staff preferences remained much closer to either psychosocial program than to those of typical mental hospital staff.

More important for determining the actual operation and differentiation of treatment conditions within and between programs is the objective data from the SRIC. The equality of conditions to which residents in the psychosocial groups were exposed before the introduction of the programs was well documented. Original baseline conditions showed the two groups to have received essentially identical treatment programs, with equalities of all characteristics, including the specific focus of staff activity, the rate of activity and staff-resident interactions, and the distribution of specific staff behaviors. Original baseline conditions were much closer to conditions that were later observed in the traditional hospital programs than to either of the psychosocial programs as they operated during the first eighteen weeks following the introduction of the programs.

The total level of staff activity did not change over the current period, but the introduction of programmatic procedures resulted in clear and stable differences in the focus and content of staff activities. In both programs, the change in focus resulted in less irrelevant behavior and increases in the proportion of activities involving staff-resident interactions. Even though the number of residents, total staff activity, and staffing ratios essentially remained constant—with the same staff equated in time and focus of work in each program—the changes in structure and focus resulted in dramatic increases in the attention residents received. While both programs resulted in an increased amount of contact and total attention received by an individual resident, the social-learning program resulted in even more staff attention being received by individual residents than those in the milieu program. While the group focus and the encouragement of more resident-to-resident attention within groups in the milieu program resulted in lower levels of resident attention received directly from staff than in the social-learning program, the contacts within the groups were clearly personalized to the extent that milieu residents still received more direct, individual attention from staff than they did in baseline conditions or than that which existed in the traditional hospital programs.

The actual differentiation of the two psychosocial programs after the introduction of programmatic procedures by the same staff was remarkable. Not only the focus of staff activity but the rate of performance of specific classes of staff behavior and the resident behavior x staff behavior match during the first eighteen weeks of operation were in keeping with the differential requirements specified in the treatment manuals. Improvements in resident functioning from before the introduction of the programs through the first anniversary assessment were also differentially related in expected directions to changes in the focus of staff activities and to changes in specific classes of staff-resident interaction within each program. Specified milieu procedures were performed at differentially higher rates when staff worked in the milieu program, and specified social-learning procedures were performed at differentially higher rates when staff worked in the social-learning program. On an absolute level, 90.4% of all staff-resident interactions in the milieu program were correct, with the majority of errors resulting from an inappropriate spillover of social-learning procedures. On an absolute level, 98.4% of all staff-resident interactions in the social-learning program were correct, with total errors being nearly nonexistent and the spillover of milieu procedures being infinitesimal.

The distribution of the relative proportions of specific staff behaviors actually performed in each program paralleled the utilization endorsements for TOS technique scores. Thus, while milieu procedures were performed at significantly higher rates within the milieu program, the relative distribution deviated from ideal levels, primarily in absolute rates that were lower than desired for some classes of behavior, especially those involving interpretatation. Social-learning procedures were not only performed at significantly higher rates within the social-learning program, but the distribution of relative proportions of staff-resident interactions in the social-learning program clearly followed those specified in the treatment manual and the ideal distribution on the TOS. Staff therefore did a better job of carrying out all aspects of the ideal social-learning program, but the absolute level of accuracy in actual performance of both programs was exceptional, and clear and reliable differentiation was maintained throughout the period.

These analyses of staff attitudes and performance in the first six months provide some interesting information on staff. More important, however, is the clear documentation of the equivalency of conditions during initial baseline and the differentiation of treatment programs according to prescribed procedures during the first eighteen weeks of operation. The documentation, combined with the overall equivalency of all other possible sources of influence, including psychotropic drugs, clearly establishes that the differential outcome during this period was a consequence of the differential treatment procedures applied within the milieu therapy and social-learning programs.

# 17. Summary of Findings for the First Six Months

All of the necessary preparations for starting the psychosocial programs were finally accomplished after considerable delays resulting from the late notification of funding and the decentralization of center operations. Patients were assessed in state hospitals, equated groups were formed, and transfer, orientation, and habituation procedures were carried out. An equated baseline week on the psychosocial units documented the absence of effects of new staff, physical plants, and transfer procedures on residents before the introduction of the programs. Even though the delays resulted in a severe shortage of clinical staff, the differential procedures of the milieu therapy and social-learning programs were introduced over a four-week period. Thereafter the programs continued to be carried out according to the procedures of the respective manuals, with the only differences from specified conditions being an absence of off-unit facilities and services and lower levels of consumables and material goods than specified because of shortages of funds. A systematic drug-withdrawal study over the period found that maintenance psychotropic drugs neither helped nor hindered residents or their response to programs by the first anniversary assessment.

As a result of the initial delays, the first "six-month" assessment actually occurred after only eighteen weeks of program operation, with full programs operating for only fourteen weeks by the first anniversary assessment. In spite of the short time period, shortage of staff, and lower levels of facilities, services, and commodities, the outcome data reported in chapter 14 showed a dramatic and differential improvement for residents following the introduction of psychosocial programs. The continuous objective assessments of hour-by-hour behavior found that every resident in the social-learning program showed significant improvement in overall functioning, no matter how disturbed they were initially and without regard to any individual characteristics. Three-quarters of the residents in the milieu program also showed significant improvement, with better response by females and residents with relatively shorter lengths of hospitalization.

Improvement was obtained in components of both adaptive and maladaptive behavior in both programs, but with differential effectiveness being apparent, even after only eighteen weeks of differential treatment. Both psychosocial programs were equally effective in producing rapid and major reductions in the highest-frequency clinically bizarre motor behaviors over this period. Both programs had also brought about dramatic reductions in grossly inappropriate resident responses to minimal expectations and in clinically bizarre verbal and facial expressions indicative of thought disorder, but the social-learning program was even more effective than the milieu program with these classes of behaviors. The social-learning program significantly reduced the incidence of dangerous and aggressive acts, but milieu procedures had no effect at all on such aggression. Thus, by the first anniversary assessment, both programs had resulted in significant improvement in components of one crucial target of rehabilitation for the severely disabled chronic population—reduction or elimination of extreme bizarre behaviors—but the social-learning program was more effective.

Both programs were also equally effective in producing dramatic increases in appropriate concurrent behavior and significant increases in the most deficient area of resident performance—interpersonal skills. Although both programs also produced significant increases in the remaining component of the resocialization target of rehabilitation—resident self-care—and in instrumental role performance, the social-learning program was even more effective than the milieu program in producing improvements in these classes of resident behavior. Thus, the two remaining identified targets that are crucial for the rehabilitation of the seriously disabled chronic mental patient showed improvement in response to psychosocial programs, with the social-learning program yielding even greater improvements than the milieu program did.

The characteristics of other ongoing resident activity during baseline and the first eighteen weeks following program introduction, reported in chapter 15, provide a descriptive picture in keeping with the different program structures. Unitwide community meetings showed changes paralleling improvements in resident functioning and reflected the different structure of the therapeutic community meeting in the milieu program and the informational meeting in the social-learning program. Comparative use of resources similarly reflected the differing program structures and provided clear evidence that how available resources were used was more important than how many were obtained. Resident time spent awake and with other people increased equally in both programs, with indications that aversive people—even within the severely disturbed population—tended to be avoided by others. Several changes in the variability of ongoing resident activity showed emerging differences in the day-to-day processes between the psychosocial programs as well. While all of these differences are interesting in their own right, as a whole these characteristics support the differing program structures and procedures as the basis for the differential improvements reported in chapter 14.

The details of staff attitudes and performance, reported in chapter 16, showed there were no changes in attitudes, opinions, and beliefs about mental patients after exposure to such severely debilitated resident groups. Psychosocial staff remained close to the ideals underlying the psychosocial programs, as they had at the end of training, and continued to differ from typical mental hospital staff. Opinions and interpretations of the treatment programs shifted in response to differential experience with resident changes in the two programs. A few slight changes occurred in staff preferences for the nature of treatment programs and for the use of different treatment procedures; however, the order of endorsement remained stable, with the preferred nature of the program being closer to the ideal milieu program but preferred techniques being closer to the ideal social-learning program. The nature of the programs were differentially interpreted by staff, with interpretations remaining close to the ideals underlying each program over both assessments of the period. Staff interpretations of the appropriateness of relative use of techniques were close to the ideal only for the social-learning program, with some techniques being underendorsed for the milieu program. Staff interpretations of the relative use of techniques did remain well differentiated between programs, however, and much closer to either psychosocial program than to those of typical mental hospital staff.

The moment-to-moment continuous objective assessments of staff behavior, also reported in chapter 16, provided documentation that the original baseline conditions gave psychosocial residents essentially identical experiences that were much closer to traditional hospital conditions than to either psychosocial program. Even though the same staff equated time and focus of work on each unit, the introduction of programmatic procedures resulted in clear and stable differences in the focus and content of staff activities and dramatic increases in the amount of attention residents received—even though total staff activity did not change. The actual differentiation of the two psychosocial programs over the first eighteen weeks of operation was remarkable. The rate of performance of specific staff behaviors and resident behavior-by-staff behavior match precisely followed the differential requirements specified in the treatment manuals, with the relative distribution of actual staff-resident interaction paralleling staff's endorsed levels of technique utilization. Thus, although staff did a better job of carrying out the ideal social-learning program, the two programs were exceptionally well differentiated over the first eighteen weeks. Even including the four weeks before the full programmatic procedures were introduced, 90.4% of all staff-resident interactions in the milieu program were correct on an absolute level, and 98.4% in the social-learning program followed prescribed procedures.

The clear documentation of the equivalency of baseline conditions and appropriate differentiation of treatment programs during the first eighteen weeks of operation clearly establishes that the differential outcome of this period was a function of the specified procedures. By the first anniversary assessment, the most severely debilitated chronically institutionalized adults for whom systematic treatment efforts have ever been studied showed truly remarkable response to both psychosocial programs. The social-learning program was more effective with the majority of component behaviors and, overall, with all rehabilitation targets. Even with such dramatic improvements, however, the residents in both programs were still functioning at minimal levels and required institutional control for their survival.

PART 4

# The Next Two Years on the Psychosocial Units: Variability and Peak Response

## 18. Notable Events and Overview of the Next Two Years

The most notable event of the next two years was the day-to-day, week-to-week maintenance of prescribed programs and all required assessments, with continuing focus upon the identification and resolution of needs and problems of residents and staff. The majority of backlogged administrative details resulting from the earlier delays in notification of funding and the decentralization of center support services were completed during this period, although negotiation of red tape to maintain operations was a continuous job. Early in the period, the development and printing of summary and keypunch forms for all data were completed, with the regular triple-check data reduction system, keypunching, verification, and computer summarization of over 5,000 IBM cards per week instituted. This system provided regular empirical data for feedback and correction of performance to staff. The backlog of data from the first six months was also summarized and filed over the period. Institution of a regional management information service allowed the incorporation of a computer reporting system, which provided information on patients in the hospital comparison group a week in advance of any anticipated transfer or release, thus, providing an additional check, independent of the hospital liaison, for monitoring in-hospital placement and appropriate criteria and assessments in the event of discharge.

Regular procedures were established for the continuation of medical and legal services to psychosocial residents, with the backlog of physical, dental, and visual exams completed, and work on restitution of legal rights continuing throughout the entire two years. Continuing work with relatives, Social Security, public aid, and other agencies resulted in 60% of psychosocial residents finally receiving contributions to provide minimal funds for personal use and training, while solicitations of donations of clothing and cash continued, with most cash contributions coming from psychosocial staff themselves. Additional operating funds were also obtained to provide adequate food and consumables to the units and to stock canteens; plans to film operations were eliminated in lieu of the latter. Conflicting regulations were ultimately negotiated during the period to provide canteen coupons and to allow training funds for higher step level residents without the state's immediately confiscating resident funds for payment of past treatment expenses. Continuing administrative work during the period was required to maintain operations in spite of alternating hiring freezes, and there were no fewer than four increases in salaries or fringe benefits, which required supplemental funds. Even with continuing staff shortages, multiple community contacts were established to seek sources of significant others for residents upon release and volunteers to aid in the transition between the institution and the community. The identification and resolution of both staff and resident problems was an ongoing process, with response to several notable events affecting ongoing operations. By the last six months of the period, all operations were occurring exactly as prescribed in spite of continuing shortages of staff and funds, with administrative and communication networks functioning smoothly.

Several notable events involving individual residents were logged during the next two years. Some of the events had obvious effects that were immediately apparent and resulted in changes in focus or procedure, while others had no obvious immediate impact. The accidental death of a social-learning resident during the first week of the period had a major and obvious impact on both staff and residents. The resident, who was in good health and responding well to treatment, apparently inhaled a piece of bacon during breakfast one morning, although the original cause of death was thought to be acute coronary occlusion. In spite of rapid staff response with first aid and multiple attempts to aid him by psychosocial staff, ambulance attendants, and consulting physicians, he was pronounced dead in less than twenty-five minutes from the time of his initial difficulty, with a postmortem examination determining the cause of death as "asphyxiation due to inhaled food." The public nature of his death and attempts at resuscitation in the presence of other residents, with resulting feelings of helplessness, resulted in a dramatic sense of grief, loss, and low morale for both staff and residents. Several staff and residents attended his funeral, and discussions concerning his death, the meaning of death, and related associations were brought up by residents in meetings in both programs for several weeks. Temporary deleterious effects were apparent in reduced functioning and increased assaultiveness on both units. Attempts to counteract such effects were made by increasing emphasis upon both more stringent control of inappropriate resident behavior and particularly focusing upon genuine positive social interactions. A little over six months after the death, a social-learning resident was discovered to suffer from advanced terminal cancer. She was transferred to a medical hospital where she died three weeks later. No major effects were apparent on either staff or residents from her death, perhaps because of the distance in both time and place and the prior discussions of death.

Additional notable events during the next two years included the first releases of improved residents to independent functioning from both programs and the replacement of residents who were released and those who died with new residents, who were equated with the original pretreatment functioning of those they replaced. Both releases and replacements had mixed effects on residents. Staff received a morale boost by seeing successful releases, but had mixed feelings concerning replacements who were functioning at the low, pretreatment levels of those who were released. Before the end of the current period, one of the released milieu residents had failed at community functioning and was returned to the program. Upon her return, she caused sufficient disturbance that an all-day community meeting was held to determine how to deal with her disruptive behavior; the result was a special program using heightened drugs, overnight expulsion, and several other restrictions, which were lifted following three days without occurrence of the specified disruptive behaviors. Three similar special programs also occurred for another milieu resident during the two-year period. Two special programs were instituted in the social-learning program to control especially disruptive residents but without resident participation in developing the programs.

Remaining notable extraneous and uncontrolled events, which were unrelated to program operations during the next two years, included a bomb threat and a resident kidnapping. The bomb threat occurred about midway through the period and did not involve the psychosocial units in the center. However, when an unidentified person called to state that a bomb had been placed at another location in the center, the resulting activity by police, security, and the implementation of emergency disaster procedures resulted in a disruption of routines for a day and a new topic of conversation for a few days afterward. The resident kidnapping occurred just after the fourth anniversary assessment and involved a well-laid plan by two eighty-year-old women who successfully took the fifty-year-old son of one of them—a resident in the milieu program—out of the center during an accompanied pass, hid him for two days, and then moved him to his mother's home some fifty miles away so she could care for him. Staff located the resident in two days, but nearly a week passed before his mother decided he was too difficult and attempted to rehospitalize him, at which time he returned to the milieu program, no worse off.

Changes in structure or procedure of psychosocial programs included occasional changes in meeting times from one hour to another or one night to another to accommodate the availability of off-unit facilities. These changes were always equated between units and were inconsequential except for the weekend activity schedule, which was finally changed to reflect the schedules shown in the manuals during the last six months of the period. All other changes in structure or procedure during the period involved the ultimate introduction of facilities, services, and commodities specified in the program manuals as funds became available and bureaucratic lag was overcome or changes in details of procedures for dealing with assaultive resident behavior and protecting staff and residents from assaults.

Holiday schedules, the special Christmas program, and the manner of dealing with all inappropriate and intolerable behaviors, except assaults, over the next two years remained identical in both programs to the original ones (chapter 13). Midway through the first six months of the period, however, it became obvious that the minimum stay in time-out or expulsion rooms (twenty minutes) was not sufficient to prevent the increasing levels of physical assault in the milieu program, and time out and the fine procedure in the social-learning program was inadequate for handling a few assaultive residents who had physically injured staff or residents severely, despite maximum attempts at control by drugs. In fact, time out appeared to be functioning as a way for some residents to avoid contact with people and work, since they would simply commit a minimum violation with the obvious intent of going to a time-out room to sleep. "Time out" thus appeared to be functioning as a positive reinforcer with more potency than the loss of other reinforcers that occurred as a result of time-out status for some residents.

Procedures were therefore instituted to remove the positive aspects of being in time out through an intermittent and unpredictable tooting of an aerosol air horn or a spray of water mist through a high window to prevent chronic offenders in time out from sleeping. One time-out room was equipped with a room heater and vaporizer, in a protected enclosure, which could be turned on to provide aversive heat-humidity conditions for residents who still found time out to be a positive experience (see Paul et al., 1962). The aversiveness resulting from these conditions was no worse than normal conditions that existed in state hospitals without air conditioning in the summer months in central Illinois, to which all residents had been exposed. None of these changes involved expulsion rooms, since the milieu principles were based upon residents being expelled from the living group.

The continuing increases in assaults on staff and residents in the milieu program and the occasional severely damaging attacks by those in the social-learning program resulted in additional morale problems for both residents and staff. Since the majority of junior staff were female and unable to handle physically larger residents and residents were unable or unwilling to assist, male senior staff were spending extraordinary amounts of time on the units during off-hours for protection. Finally, in desperation, the therapeutic community proposed and passed a resolution that the length of expulsion time as a consequence for assault be increased from the remainder of one functional period to a maximum of seventy-two hours. After clearance from appropriate review committees, this length of time was instituted in both programs shortly after the second anniversary assessment and remained in effect for a little over three months. Then, as a result of concerns about the need for a three-day period of control, staff and residents in the milieu program voted to reduce the time to a maximum of forty-eight hours. The length of time in time out or expulsion as a consequence for physical assaults then remained constant until just before the fifth anniversary assessment when a statewide policy directive from the central office of the Department of Mental Health placed a maximum length of time at two hours for such procedures. Concurrent with the change from seventy-two to forty-eight hours as a consequence for assaults, several other procedures were instituted to protect staff and residents and to increase safety, security, and morale. Tear-gas cartridges were placed on each unit, and staff were trained in their use and in self-defense; however, the tear gas was sufficiently deviant from the philosophy of the programs that staff found it unpleasant, and its use was discontinued after a single application. Part-time male student workers were employed to study on each unit during off-hours when male staff were not on duty (one on each unit at $1.50 per hour), to be available to assist female staff in the event of an assault, and transceivers were installed to allow contact of security officers for assistance when needed.[1]

The continued work on community contacts and clearances of necessary regulations resulted in the recruitment and training of community volunteers to make off-unit and downtown facilities and services available, which had been previously restricted because of shortages of staff and funds. Volunteers were assigned to off-unit activity areas (snack bar, movies, sewing room, etc.) to make these facilities and services available during evenings and weekends, starting midway between the second and third anniversary assessments. Volunteers were also available to accompany residents on center and downtown passes. A month later, a van became available, which, combined with assistance from community volunteers, allowed a group trip for about a third of the residents on each unit each week to introduce them to community facilities and training. These trips occurred during the regularly scheduled activity periods, with social-learning residents earning attendance through individually contracted targets established in small groups, and milieu residents attending according to the "living group of the week." "Living group of the week" status was determined on the basis of the best total group performance during the previous week on some specific criterion of functioning (e.g., appearance), with the criterion established by community vote before seeing the data on performance.

After nearly seven months with off-unit facilities open by volunteers, few residents in either program were making use of them—having apparently habituated to remaining on the residential units. Therefore, a special sampling-exposure substudy was carried out for twenty-two weeks toward the end of the period in an attempt to increase resident utilization of off-unit facilities. The procedure involved a week of refamiliarization tours during daytime activity periods, followed by weekly alternations between regular announcements of availability and sampling exposure. The sampling-exposure procedures involved escorting eligible residents to the available activity areas and providing exposure, sampling, or participation in the activity before requesting a decision on off-unit passes (for results, see Curran et al., 1973). The procedures were effective in increasing off-unit facilities utilization by milieu residents but made no impact at all on social-learning residents.

During the last third of the two-year period,

the remaining components of treatment programs that had been delayed because of a lack of funds and conflicting regulations were instituted as described in the treatment manuals. Limited funds to pay higher step level residents cash for work in training positions were obtained and instituted. Canteen coupons, commodities, and grooming supplies were finally obtained, and individual kits with private grooming materials were provided for each resident, with credits increased accordingly in the milieu program. Sufficient coffee and snacks were finally obtained to provide them regularly during informal interaction periods and other activities. Individual exposure to potential training positions for residents on step 1 who had already gained maximum benefit from activity periods was also instituted during this period. Thus, although the lag between initiation of requests or proposals for some components of operations took as long as eighteen months to get through the bureaucracy, by the last six months of the current period the only items still not received were locks for the cabinets. All other materials, commodities, facilities, and services, as well as staff-resident interactions, were as detailed in the treatment manuals.

The use of psychotropic drugs over the current two-year period followed the recommendations presented by Paul et al (1972), in which conscious use of high-dosage "chemical straightjackets" was attempted to control violent residents when other procedures were not available. However, after analyzing the results of the study over the first six months of the period, maintenance psychotropic drugs were gradually reduced between the second and third anniversary assessments to a point where fewer than 25% of residents in either program were on them. After longer periods of expulsion or time out were instituted, drugs became the last resort for controlling aggressive residents, with high dosages systematically and gradually reduced at a rate to allow residents so treated to perform all new behaviors acquired on higher drug dosages at each lower dosage level.[2] Drug usage remained at these low levels until the fifth anniversary assessment, at which time staff responded to the reduction in the length of time for time out and expulsion. Staff reaction was the preparatory placement of about half the residents in each program on maintenance drugs, since few residents had shown any increase in assaultiveness at the time drugs were changed.

Staffing of the psychosocial programs remained below the necessary clinical complement for the entire period of the next two years as a result of continuing high turnover among junior staff, with state freezes in hiring and personnel policies that prevented necessary overlap for training junior staff. Over the first year of the period, only 81% to 84% of the clinical complement was present, even including the liaison coordinator and the research-supervisor, who each spent less than 25% time in clinical contact on the floor. At the fourth and fifth anniversary assessments, 94% and 97% of the clinical complement were working, still including the "part-time" clinical staff. The turnover and training burden remained high, with continuing staff from the previous six months being 77%, 56%, 66%, and 77%, respectively, for anniversary assessments 2, 3, 4, and 5. Only 23% of staff employed at the fifth anniversary assessment were continuous from the first anniversary assessment. Auxiliary positions also remained understaffed. Only one (of three allotted) rehabilitation counselor position had ever been filled, and that position had been filled twice and was again vacated unexpectedly during the last quarter of the period. Therefore, the one educator with a degree was moved into that position to provide coordination of training positions until rehabilitation counselors could be found, and the best preprofessional change agent was promoted to the classroom-educator position. Nevertheless, other than significantly increasing average experience from 0.23 to 0.96 years ($p < 0.05$), none of the characteristics of the staff group (age, education, sex, race, marital or parental status, Extroversion or Emotionality) changed significantly ($p$'s $> 0.20$) over the two-year period, nor did the characteristics change from those of the original staff group present before the arrival of the residents.

The remaining chapters of part 4 report the results of the next two years' operation of the psychosocial units for both staff and residents, with changes in behavior related to the above notable events when relationships occurred. The objective outcome data on resident functioning, reported in chapter 19, present details of statistical analyses for the research worker; however, the professional clinician or program director can obtain details of results by skipping the statistical sections. Preprofessional staff and others with little extra time can obtain an understanding and clinical idea of the outcome over this period by inspecting tables and figures, and reading the summary and individual improvement rates section. The illustrative cases at the end of the section also provide details on the follow-up procedures for released residents.

The changes in characteristics of large group meetings, the use of available resources, time spent awake and with others, and the relative variability of several classes of resident behavior within each psychosocial program are compared in chapter 20, along with the relationships of these characteristics to resident functioning and other notable events. All staff data are reported in chapter 21, including changes in attitudes, opinions, preferences, and interpretations, as well as details of actual staff performance, providing objective data on the reliability and differentiation of treatment programs and the nature of attention received by residents. As in part 3 details of the statistical analyses are not reported in chapters 20 and 21 but are referenced, with results incorporated in text for the interested research worker. Each section of these two chapters ends with a detailed content summary, and each chapter ends with a summary section, from which preprofessional staff and others short on time should be able to obtain a good understanding of findings, combined with study of the tables and figures. The major conclusions and results at the end of the next two years on the psychosocial units are briefly summarized in chapter 22.

# 19. Differential Effectiveness of the Milieu and Social-Learning Programs During the Next Two Years

## CHANGES IN GLOBAL FUNCTIONING[1]

Raw changes in total appropriate and inappropriate functioning from the first through fifth anniversary assessment periods—plotted relative to functioning before program introduction—are presented in figure 19.1, which shows considerable variability in the response to both programs over the two-year period. Starting with the significant improvements obtained by the first anniversary assessment, a decline in functioning is suggested for both programs during the six months immediately following the first assessment period and the death of a resident—particularly in appropriate and inappropriate concurrent behavior (TSBC). Thereafter, the trends for milieu residents, while variable, appear to remain relatively stable in the degree of improvement maintained, except for appropriate concurrent behavior (TSBC), which reflects several valleys and peaks. The superiority of response to the social-learning program in total appropriate and inappropriate behavior appears to have been maintained, with further improvements gradually occurring—particularly for appropriate behavior—over the remainder of the period through the fifth anniversary assessment.

*Statistical evaluation.* Overall changes during this two-year period were evaluated by a two-way repeated measures ANOVA on the standardized Global Functioning Factor Score (milieu vs. social-learning programs; anniversary assessments 1, 2, 3, 4, 5). This analysis found significant main effects for programs ($F=5.55$, $df=1/54$, $p < 0.05$) and for time ($F=3.50$, $df=4/216$, $p < 0.01$), without a significant program x time interaction ($F < 1$). Additional two-way ANOVAs with partitioning of simple effects were carried out on successive pairs of anniversary assessment periods to clarify the findings. The source of the significant time main effect was found to lie in a significant decrease in Global Functioning for both programs from the first to the second anniversary assessments (mean change over programs from 52.86 to 51.45; $F=5.49$, $df=1/54$, $p < 0.05$) and a significant increase for both programs from the fourth to the fifth anniversary assessments (mean change from 51.69 to 53.24; $F=6.40$, $df=1/54$, $p < 0.05$). The significant program main effect was found to occur consistently over all anniversary assessment periods after the first (all $F$'s $> 4.81$, $df=1/54$, $p < 0.05$), indicating that a significantly greater absolute level of Global Functioning of residents in the social-learning program was maintained throughout the period. Over the entire period from anniversary assessment 1 to 5, residents in the social-learning program showed significant additional improvement in Global Functioning (mean change from 54.29 to 56.64; $F=6.48$, $df=1/54$, $p < 0.05$), while those in the milieu program showed neither additional improvement nor decline (mean change from 51.44 to 50.84; $F < 1$).

Comparisons of change from baseline to successive anniversary assessment periods, nevertheless, found the milieu program to show significant improvement in Global Functioning from before program introduction to each assessment period (all $F$'s $> 16.92$, $df=1/54$, $p < 0.01$). However, the social-learning program not only showed significant improvement in Global Functioning from pretreatment to each assessment period (all $F$'s $> 64.64$, $df=1/54$, $p < 0.01$) but significantly greater improvement than the milieu program did at each point (all $F$'s $> 7.69$, $df=1/54$, $p < 0.01$). The relatively greater improvement for the social-learning program resulted in absolute differences in Global Functioning that were substantial by the fifth assessment period (means of 56.64 vs. 50.84, respectively, for social-learning and milieu groups; $F=11.72$, $df=1/54$, $p < 0.01$).

## CHANGES IN MALADAPTIVE BEHAVIOR

The changes in Global Functioning clearly show significant improvement from before program entry to each point during the next two years for both treatment programs. The social-learning program not only maintained greater improvement than that obtained by milieu therapy but provided additional gains

*Differential Effectiveness of the Programs* 183

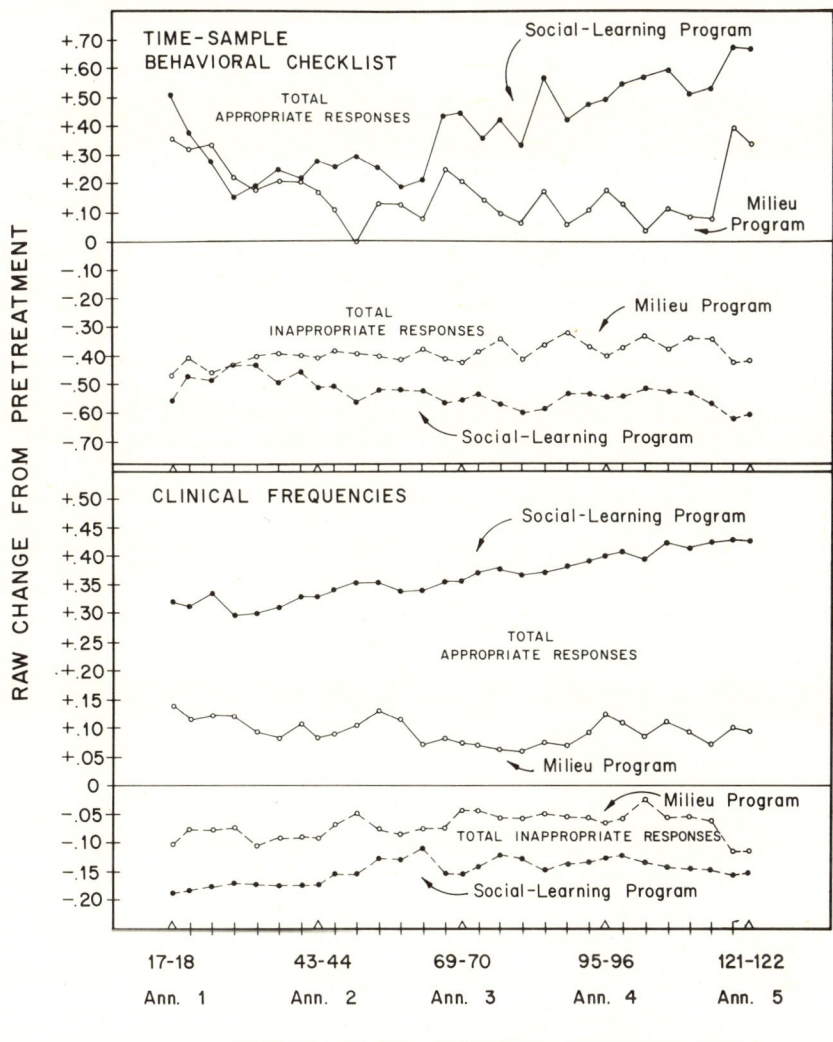

Figure 19.1. Overall changes in concurrent behavior (TSBC) and responsiveness within programs (Clinical Frequencies) during the next two years.

over the next two years. However, residents in both programs showed significant decreases in Global Functioning during the six months following the first assessment period and significant increases during the six months preceding the fifth assessment period. These changes, plus the variability apparent over time and classes of behavior in figure 19.1, suggest that analyses of the components of functioning are particularly important for the current time period.

From a clinical perspective, Total Inappropriate Clinical Frequencies (figure 19.1) ranged from an average of less than 8% to greater than 16% grossly inappropriate response to minimal expectations for appropriate behavior for milieu residents during this time period. The parallel range for social-learning residents averaged less than 1% to greater than 7%—both

maintaining improvement from the 19% rate before the program introduction but with temporary increases at various times during the two-years. Similarly, clinically inappropriate, crazy behavior (reflected in TSBC Total Inappropriate Behavior, figure 19.1) was maintained well below the 90% rate of performance of crazy behavior every waking hour that occurred before the introduction of the specific treatment procedures. Since the TSBC index reflects one of the most important target areas for rehabilitation of the chronic population, changes in such inappropriate behavior are particularly worthy of monitoring. During this period, the relative frequency of clinically maladaptive behavior in the social-learning program increased from about 38%, during the first anniversary assessment, to a high of about 49% four months later, and then showed a fairly regular downward trend to about 33% during the fifth anniversary assessment—nearly one-third the pretreatment level. The relative frequency of clinically maladaptive behavior in the milieu program ranged from a low of 38% to a high of about 52%, with several peaks and valleys, finishing the period with about a 43% rate of occurrence during the fifth anniversary assessment—still about half the rate of clinically maladaptive behavior occurring before program entry but at a greater absolute level than the reduction achieved by the first anniversary assessment. Of greater interest are the changes in components of TSBC Total Inappropriate Behavior. These indexes, presented in figure 19.2, suggest the possibility of additional differential responsiveness to the two treatment programs.

*Statistical evaluation.* To statistically evaluate changes in maladaptive behavior over this two-year period, standardized scores for Total Inappropriate Clinical Frequencies and TSBC Schizophrenic Disorganization, Cognitive Distortion, and Hostile-Belligerence Indexes were entered into a three-way repeated measures ANOVA (milieu vs. social-learning programs; anniversary assessments 1, 2, 3, 4, 5; scores). As expected from the primary analyses on Global Functioning, the program main effect for maladaptive behavior was significant in the overall analysis ($F=4.17$, $df=1/54$, $p < 0.05$), as were the program x scores interaction ($F=2.82$, $df=3/162$, $p < 0.05$) and the time x scores interaction ($F=1.92$, $df=12/648$, $p < 0.05$). Both the scores main effect and the three-way interaction of programs x time x scores approached significance ($p < 0.07$). Additional three-way ANOVAs with partitioning of simple effects and a priori tests of individual

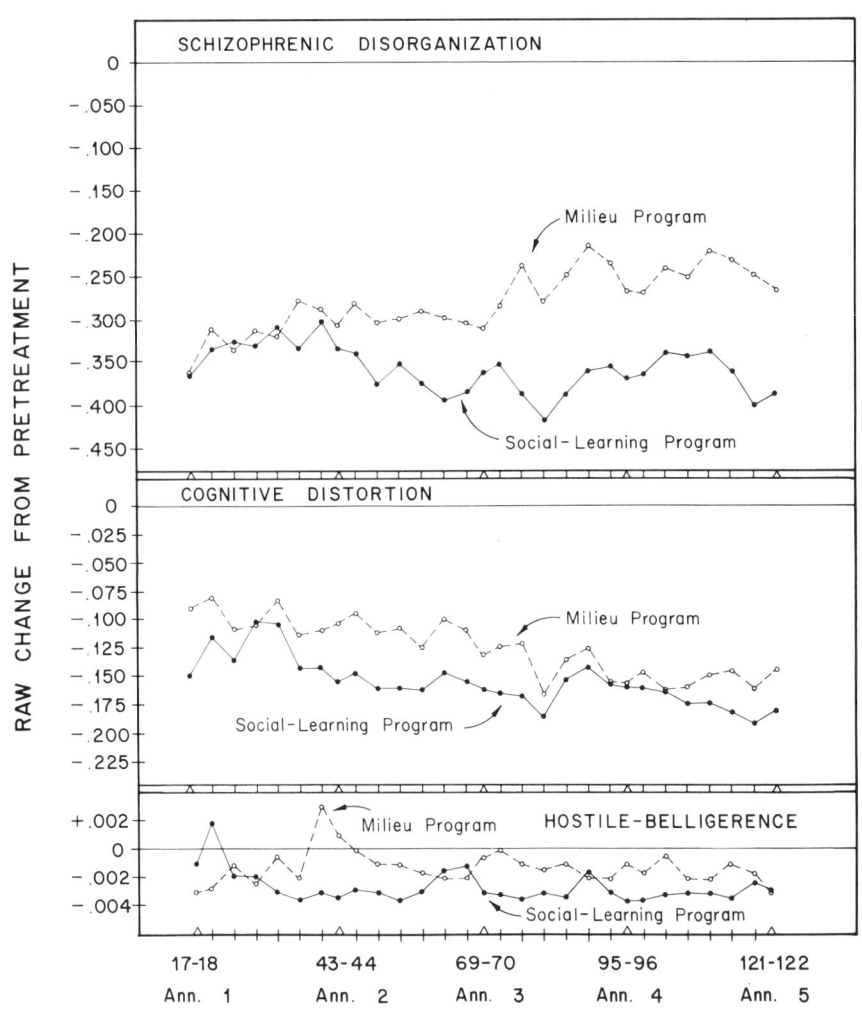

Figure 19.2. Changes in component clinically maladaptive behaviors from the TSBC during the next two years.

components were carried out on successive anniversary assessment periods to clarify these findings.[2] As previously found for Global Functioning, the main effects and interactions involving programs, time, and scores for maladaptive behavior were largely attributable to changes occurring between the first and second or fourth and fifth anniversary assessments, or the overall change from the beginning to the end of the two-year period.

The only significant within-groups change on Total Inappropriate Clinical Frequencies during the entire period (see figure 19.1) was a significant reduction for milieu residents from the fourth to fifth anniversary assessment (F=7.72, df=1/54, p < 0.01). The reduction in Total Inappropriate Clinical Frequencies for social-learning residents at the same time approached significance (F=3.51, df=1/54, p < 0.10), while none of the simple interactions between treatment programs and change over time were significant (all p > 0.10). However, the absolute level of Total Inappropriate Clinical Frequencies remained significantly lower for social-learning residents than for milieu residents at the time of the fifth anniversary assessment (F=4.08, df=1/54, p < 0.05). Significant between-groups changes from the first to second anniversary assessment periods were totally attributable to differential change in Hostile-Belligerence (figure 19.2). The simple interaction between programs and changes over time for that period was significant (F=18.35, df=1/54, p < 0.01), reflecting a reduction in Hostile-Belligerence for social-learning residents and an increase for milieu residents. The within group change for milieu residents was also significant (F=7.05, df=1/54, p < 0.05). No other changes within or between programs approached significance between pairs of successive anniversary assessment periods in any of the four maladaptive behavior indexes (all p > 0.10).

While none of the changes within successive pairs of anniversary assessments were significant for Cognitive Distortion (figure 19.2), both treatment programs showed an overall reduction from the first anniversary assessment to the end of the two-year period (F=12.91, df=1/54, p < 0.01). The within group change was significant for milieu residents (F=5.25, df=1/54, p < 0.05), without significant differences occurring between programs (F < 1). In contrast, Schizophrenic Disorganization (figure 19.2) did reflect significant differential change over the two-year period (F=4.82, df=1/54, p < 0.05), with social-learning residents further reducing Schizophrenic Disorganization slightly, while milieu residents showed an increase that approached significance (F=3.64, df=1/54, p < 0.10). Tests of within-groups change on each score from the pretreatment baseline to the fifth anniversary assessment found significant reductions in Schizophrenic Disorganization, Cognitive Distortion, and Total Inappropriate Clinical Frequencies for both milieu (all F's > 12.20, df=1/54, p < 0.01) and social-learning programs (all F's > 24.76, df=1/54, p < 0.01), without significant change for either program in Hostile-Belligerence (p's > 0.10).

*Descriptive interpretation.* Thus, in contrast to the rapid and relatively smooth changes in maladaptive behavior obtained immediately upon the introduction of the treatment programs, changes over the next two years showed considerable variability and differentiation between classes of maladaptive behavior. Both programs had produced significant reductions in gross inappropriate response to minimal expectations by the first anniversary assessment, with the social-learning program being differentially even more effective with this class of maladaptive behavior (Inappropriate Clinical Frequencies, figure 19.1). By the end of the period, the status of Inappropriate Clinical Frequencies was essentially unchanged, with the average incidence of these frequencies occurring, respectively, at about 8% and 3% of opportunities to perform in the milieu and social-learning programs—down from about 19% before the introduction of the programs. The only significant change between anniversary assessments during this period was a significant reduction in Inappropriate Clinical Frequencies for milieu residents from the fourth to the fifth anniversary assessment. However, the point-to-point plots of Inappropriate Clinical Frequencies in figure 19.1 reveal trends that span a sufficient range to indicate significant change over some time points. Two such trends are apparent for the milieu program: an overall increase from a low during the third four-week block preceding anniversary assessment 2 to a peak during assessment 3, and an overall decrease from a peak during the second four-week block after anniversary assessment 4 to a low during assessment 5. Only one well-demarcated trend approached a significant range for the social-learning program: an increase from a low during anniversary assessment 2 to a peak during the second four-week block preceding assessment 3.

The possible association of notable events recorded in the research log to trends in resident behavior was examined. Unfortunately no clear isolated events could be related to the start and stop of most trends for Inappropriate Clinical Frequencies. The major factor associated in time with the initial increases in both programs was active concern and attempts to deal with assaultive behavior and protection of staff. Increased length of time out and expulsion as a consequence for assaultive behavior was introduced in both programs during the second block after anniversary assessment 2 (as a result of a milieu community decision). The termination of the increase or stabilization of Inappropriate Clinical Frequencies was immediately preceded by the start of male part-time student workers and the introduction of transceivers to contact security officers for assistance in the event of physical assault. The only event that coincided with the beginning of the downward trend in Inappropriate Clinical Frequencies in the milieu program was the termination of special sampling-exposure procedures to increase utilization of off-unit facilities. This change removed one opportunity per day every other week to fail in response to a minimal expectation (respond to an announcement to join the group) for residents of both programs. Since the milieu residents, on the average, more often failed to meet such expectations than social-learning residents did, they may have shown greater differential response to the removal of an opportunity for failure. Overall, however, the major outcome for the two-year period for Inappropriate Clinical Frequencies was the maintenance of the improvement achieved earlier, with the social-learning program still showing greater effectiveness for this class of maladaptive behavior.

Both programs had significantly reduced Schizophrenic Disorganization by the first anniversary assessment, without differential effectiveness. While residents in both programs maintained significant improvement from pretreatment over the current two-year period, differential responsiveness was obtained during the period, with the social-learning program showing slight additional reductions and the milieu program losing some ground (figure 19.2). On an absolute level, the behaviors entering the Schizophrenic Disorganization Index—primarily bizarre overt motoric behaviors (e.g., rocking, repetitive movements, blank staring, etc.)—had been the highest-frequency maladaptive clinical behaviors occuring before the introduction of the treatment programs for the chronic population. By the end of the two-year period, the average resident was performing one of these bizarre behaviors during a two-second observation each waking hour, at a rate of just over 32% and 24%, respectively, for milieu and social-learning programs—down from approximately 61% prior to program introduction. Figure 19.2 reveals two trends for milieu residents and one for social-learning residents, which span a sufficient range to indicate significant change over some time points within the two-year period for Schizophrenic Disorganization. Both trends for milieu residents were increases, from anniversary assessment 1 to the second four-week block preceding anniversary assessment 2, and from anniversary assessment 3 to the second four-week block preceding anniversary assessment 4. The trend for the social-learning residents was a decrease from a peak immediately preceding anniversary assessment 2 to a low during the third four-week block following anniversary assessment 3.

The only notable specific event associated in time with the initial increase in Schizophrenic Disorganization in the milieu program was the death of the resident in the social-learning program (which was discussed in meetings in both programs). Although the increase was not statistically significant for the social-learning program residents, a parallel increase is apparent in figure 19.2. Additionally the increases in Cognitive Distortion in both programs and in Hostile-Belligerence for the social-learning program during the four-week block immediately following anniversary assessment 1, while not statistically significant, coincide with the resident's death and suggest overall temporary deleterious effects. Clinically these changes certainly agree with the felt loss and distress that was apparent at the time for both staff and residents. The decline in Schizophrenic Disorganization in the social-learning program and stabilization in the milieu program was concurrent with active attempts to tighten up on assaultive behavior. Several other aspects of programs were introduced during the period of this downward trend, including volunteers from the community to accompany residents on passes (third block after assessment 2), the weekly group trip to expose residents to the community (fourth block after assessment 2), and the start of part-time student workers and other assistance for dealing with assaultive behavior (block preceding assessment 3). A bomb threat at the institution, with ensuing activity by police, security officers, and emergency procedures, coincided with the start of the second upward trend in Schizophrenic Disorganization in the milieu program, as did the return of a released resident.

Although none of the increases were statistically significant, it is worthy of note that the increase occurring during the third block preceding anniversary assessment 4 in both Schizophrenic Disorganization and Cognitive Distortion for both treatment programs coincided with the start of sampling-exposure procedures to expose residents to off-unit facilities. The temporary increases in concurrent, clinically maladaptive behavior, particularly in the presence of increased adaptive responses (figures 19.1 & 19.3), are suggestive of mild stress reactions with ensuing extinction upon exposure to unfamiliar surroundings. Overall, however, the major outcome for the two-year period for Schizophrenic Disorganization was a differential response to the two programs, with residents in the milieu program maintaining improvement but with some loss, while the social-learning program was more effective in maintaining improvement for this class of clinically bizarre motoric behaviors.

Both programs had also significantly reduced Cognitive Distortion by the first anniversary assessment, with the social-learning program producing even greater reductions than the milieu program did. Over the next two years, initial reductions in Cognitive Distortion were not only maintained but reduced further by both milieu and social-learning procedures (figure 19.2). The reduction for milieu residents was sufficient that programs were not differentially effective for this class of behavior by the end of the period. On an absolute level, the behaviors entering into the Cognitive Distortion Index—primarily bizarre verbal and facial behaviors indicative of thought disorder (e.g., delusions, hallucinations, incoherent speech, smiling without a stimulus, etc.)—had been less frequent than those of the Schizophrenic Disorganization Index before introduction of treatment procedures, occurring on approximately 24% of observations. By the fifth assessment period, the incidence of Cognitive Distortion had been reduced by over two-thirds in both treatment programs, to between 7% and 8% occurrence.

Figure 19.2 also shows a downward trend for Cognitive Distortion in both treatment programs from a peak at the third block before anniversary assessment 2 to a low during the third block after assessment 3. It parallels the downward trend in Schizophrenic Disorganization for the social-learning program and is associated with the same events in time, except that it appears to have started earlier. The only specific events concurrent with the start of this trend were the release and replacement of improved residents in both programs—perhaps showing the residents that it was true that they could leave the institution. However, the major outcome for the two-year period for Cognitive Distortion was a further reduction of this class of clinically bizarre verbal and facial expressions, without differential effectiveness of the two programs.

The Hostile-Belligerence Index had shown a reduction from an average level of just over 0.3% of observations before the introduction of the programs to zero and 0.25%, respectively, for milieu and social-learning programs by the first anniversary assessment; the differences were not statistically significant. By the end of the current two-year period, both programs averaged only about 0.1% occurrence, without differences between them. The nature of behaviors entering into the Hostile-Belligerence Index—high-intensity aggressive behaviors (e.g., screaming, cursing, verbal intrusion, etc.)—are such that they are less adequately assessed by time sampling since any occurrence is clinically disruptive.

Even with time sampling problems, figure 19.2 shows a significant peak above original baseline for both programs during the first six months of the period. The social-learning peak was concurrent with the death of a resident, followed by an immediate reduction. The reduction in Hostile-Belligerence in the social-learning program corresponded in time with the application of procedures designed to remove positive characteristics of time out; in the milieu program, it was concurrent with the increase in expulsion time. Throughout the majority of the two-year period, however, Hostile-Belligerence varied non-significantly below the original low absolute level.

A better assessment of dangerous and aggressive acts, without the problems of time sampling high-intensity and low-frequency behaviors, especially for physical assault, was available at the treatment unit level in the recorded clinical frequency of each occurrence of Intolerable Behavior. By the first anniversary assessment, the social-learning program had reduced the average number of weekly incidents of Intolerable Behavior from thirty-two to six, while the milieu program had not changed the incidence. During the current time period, the average weekly incidence of Intolerable Behavior did differ significantly between programs over all anniversary assessments (chi-square=10.67, df=4, $p < 0.05$). Significant differential change between programs from pretreatment, where the incidence of Intolerable Behavior did not differ, was obtained at each anniversary assessment (all chi-squares $> 10.33$, df=1, $p < 0.01$), with the social-learning program showing a significantly lower incidence than the milieu program did at each point (all chi-squares $> 8.83$, df=1, $p < 0.01$).[3] From the beginning to the end of the current period, the social-learning program maintained the reduced incidence of Intolerable Behavior achieved by the first anniversary assessment (change from 6 to 11.25; chi-square=1.05, df=1, $p > 0.30$), with the reduction from the pretreatment baseline itself being significant (chi-square=9.02, df=1, $p < 0.01$). In contrast, the milieu program showed an increased incidence of Intolerable Behavior over the two-year period (change from 23 to 60.5), which was itself significant (chi-square=15.96, df=1, $p < 0.01$) and, further reflected a significant increase from pretreatment baseline (chi-square=18.19, df=1, $p < 0.01$).

An examination of the point-to-point weekly incidence of Intolerable Behavior on the milieu unit found the significant increase to occur first during the six-month period after the first anniversary assessment (chi-square=12.64, df=1, $p < 0.01$), paralleling the increase noted earlier in Hostile-Belligerence. However, further trends were apparent for the milieu program, which seemed clearly related to other notable events from the research log. Specifically the increase during the first six months was abrupt, occurring between the third and fourth blocks after anniversary assessment 1 (chi-square=5.24, df=1, $p < 0.05$), coinciding with the first release and replacement of residents. This change suggests that such releases and replacements were disruptive to the residents and that the milieu procedures were not sufficient to prevent physical aggression under such conditions. This hypothesis receives further support from the fact that the incidence of Intolerable Behavior was again significantly reduced to the pretreatment level in the milieu program (chi-square=14.40, df=1, $p < 0.01$) immediately after the introduction of extended expulsion time as a consequence of assaultive behavior and again significantly increased immediately following a reduction of expulsion time (chi-square=4.40, df=1, $p < 0.05$). A further increase occurred following the bomb threat, after expulsion time had already been reduced (chi-square=4.15, df=1, $p < 0.05$). Thus, the major outcome for the two-year period on aggression and assaultive behavior was an increased incidence for the milieu program, which appeared to be related to the nature of consequences for assaultive behavior. The social-learning program maintained differential effectiveness in reducing Intolerable Behavior and still showed a significant improvement from pretreatment.

## CHANGES IN ADAPTIVE BEHAVIOR

The changes in components of maladaptive behavior clearly show greater differentiation between programs. While variability was apparent at different times, both programs essentially maintained the significant reductions achieved earlier in grossly inappropriate responses to minimal behavioral expectations, with the social-learning program still showing greater reductions than the milieu program did. Both programs also maintained significant improvement from before program introduction in Schizophrenic Disorganization; however, they were differentially effective for this class of clinically bizarre motoric behaviors. The social-learning program produced slight additional reductions in Schizophrenic Disorganization, while the milieu program showed slight increases from the reduction obtained by the first anniversary assessment. The frequency of observed instances of time-sampled Hostile-Belligerence remained low, with the exception of variation during the first six months of the period, without differences between programs. However, the total incidence of aggressive Intolerable Behavior was maintained at a significantly reduced level only by social-learning procedures, with such behavior actually increasing in the milieu program. Dysfunctional cognitive behaviors, on the other hand, were further reduced during the two-year period by both programs, without differential effectiveness. Thus, by the end of the next two years, both programs had demonstrated continued significant effects on maladaptive behavior, being equally effective in reducing dysfunctional cognitive behavior. However, therapeutic community procedures were significantly less effective in controlling dangerous and aggressive acts. Overall, the social-learning program demonstrated clear superiority to the milieu program in one of the critical target areas essential for rehabilitation of the chronically institutionalized population: elimination or reduction of extreme bizarre maladaptive behaviors.

Turning to an examination of adaptive behavioral components of functioning, further differentiation between social-learning and milieu procedures is suggested in both concurrent behavior (TSBC) and responsiveness within programs (Clinical Frequencies). Considerable variability is apparent in concurrent appropriate behavior. On an absolute level, the TSBC Total Appropriate Index (figure 19.1) found that social-learning residents were performing about 2.96 appropriate behaviors on the average observation during the first anniversary assessment (up 0.51 from pretreatment baseline). They then showed a steady decrease to a low of 2.59 appropriate behaviors during the third four-week block after assessment 1, followed by an overall, erratic increase to 3.11 during the fifth anniversary assessment. The TSBC Total Appropriate Index for milieu residents found that about 2.88 appropriate behaviors were performed on the average observation during the first anniversary assessment (up 0.36 from pretreatment baseline). Milieu residents then showed an extended decrease in concurrent appropriate behavior through the second four-week block after assessment 2—actually performing slightly below the pretreatment level during this block. Milieu residents again increased concurrent appropriate behavior with erratic peaks and valleys over the next year and a half and dramatically increased just before the fifth anniversary assessment, ending the period at about the same level of concurrent appropriate behavior as was obtained during the first anniversary assessment.

In contrast to concurrent appropriate behavior, Total Appropriate Clinical Frequencies (figure 19.1) showed a steady increase over the entire period for social-learning residents. The increase reflects an average change from about 51% terminal-level performance of social and instrumental behaviors during the first anniversary assessment to over 61% during the fifth anniversary assessment—an increase approximately tripling the initial level before program introduction. Milieu residents, in contrast, showed some variability in Appropriate Clinical Frequencies, reflecting a slight change from about 40% terminal-level performance during anniversary assessment 1 to about 35% during assessment 5—about one and a half times the initial level before the program introduction. Of greater clinical interest are the changes in components of adaptive Clinical Frequencies, which reflect the other identified target areas for rehabilitation of the chronically institutionalized resident. These indexes, presented in figure 19.3, suggest continued differential responsiveness to the two treatment programs over all three components of social and instrumental behavior.

*Statistical evaluation.* To statistically evaluate possible differential change in adaptive behavior over this time period, standardized scores for TSBC Total Appropriate Behavior and Clinical Frequencies for Instrumental Role Performance, Interpersonal Skills, and Self-Care Indexes were entered into a three-way repeated measures ANOVA (milieu vs. social-learning programs; anniversary assessments 1, 2, 3, 4, 5; scores). As expected from the primary analysis on Global Functioning, the overall analyses of adaptive behavior found significant main effects for both programs (F=5.05, df=1/54, p < 0.05) and time (F=4.94, df=4/216, p < 0.01), as well as a significant programs x time interaction (F=4.58, df=4/216, p < 0.01). Additionally, although the score's main effect was not significant (p > 0.20), all three interactions involving scores were: programs x scores (F=3.38,

Figure 19.3. Changes in component adaptive behavior from Clinical Frequencies during the next two years.

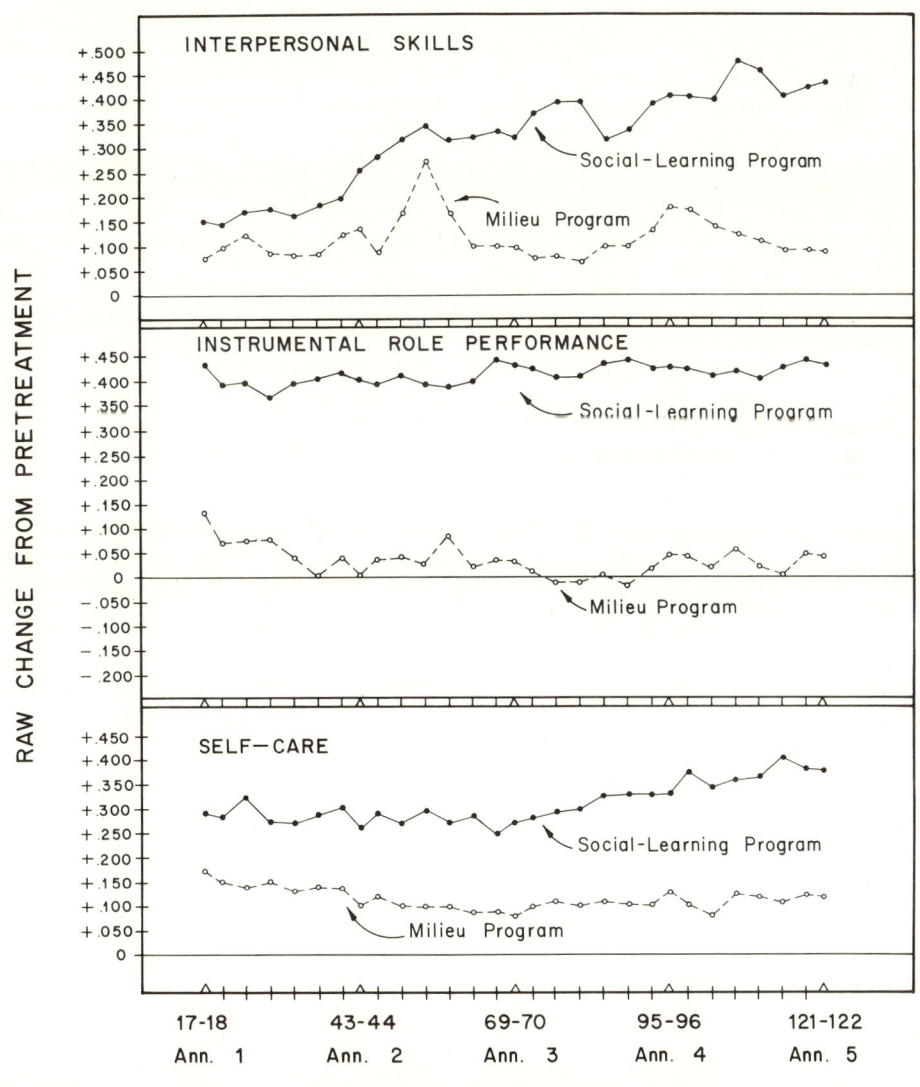

df=3/162, p < 0.05), time x scores, and programs x time x scores (F=12.96 and 4.03, respectively; df=12/648, p < 0.01). Additional three-way ANOVAs with partitioning of simple effects and a priori tests of individual components were carried out on successive anniversary assessment periods to clarify the findings.[2] Unlike the results obtained for Global Functioning and maladaptive behavior, differential changes involving programs, time, and component scores were found throughout the two-year period for adaptive behavior.

The overall reduction in concurrent appropriate behavior between anniversary assessments 1 and 2 (TSBC Total Appropriate Index, figure 19.1) was significant within groups for both milieu (F=5.66, df=1/54, p < 0.05) and social-learning programs (F=9.14, df=1/54, p < 0.01), as was the overall increase between anniversary assessments 4 and 5 (milieu F=4.99; social-learning F=7.31; df=1/54, p < 0.05 & 0.01, respectively). In neither instance did the simple program x time interaction approach significance (F's < 1). No other TSBC changes within the current period approached significance for milieu residents, with the overall change from anniversary assessment 1 to 5 indicating neither gains nor losses at the end of the period for concurrent appropriate behavior (F < 1). Social-learning residents, on the other hand, showed an additional significant within-groups increase from anniversary assessment 2 to 3 (F=5.60, df=1/54, p < 0.05), which approached significantly greater change than that attained by milieu residents over the same six months (F=3.71, df=1/54, p < 0.10). The differential increase in TSBC Appropriate Behavior from the beginning to the end of the current period for social-learning residents versus milieu residents approached statistical significance (F=3.71, df=1/54, p < 0.10), as did the within-group increase for the social-learning program itself (F=3.59, df=1/54, p < 0.10).

The only differential response between programs on Instrumental Role Performance (figure 19.3) during the current period occurred from anniversary assessment 1 to 2 (F=4.34, df=1/54, p < 0.05), which was attributable to a significant reduction within the milieu program, almost to pretreatment levels (F=6.52, df=1/54, p < 0.05). Thereafter, no significant changes occurred within or between programs during the entire two-year period (all F's < 1). On an absolute level, the social-learning program maintained the exceptional improvement in Instrumental Role Performance obtained earlier (F < 1) and at a level significantly above that of the milieu program at every assessment period (all F's > 5.26, df=1/54, p < 0.05).

During the current period, the milieu program also showed a significant within-groups decrease in Self-Care (figure 19.3) between anniversary assessments 1 and 2 (F=6.52, df=1/54, p < 0.05). The decrease approached significance in comparison to change by the social-learning program over the same six months (F=3.05, df=1/54, p < 0.10). Both milieu and social-learning programs produced significant within-group increases in Self-Care between anniversary assessments 3 and 4 (F=5.63 and 4.77, respectively; df=1/54, p < 0.05), without differential change during the period (F < 1). However, in addition to maintaining superiority in Self-Care at every anniversary assessment during the two year period (all F's > 7.50, df=1/54, p < 0.01), the social-learning program showed further additional gains relative to the milieu program over the entire period (F=10.48, df-1/54, p < 0.01).

Interpersonal Skills showed a pattern of change different from all other components of adaptive behavior over the next two years (figure 19.3). The overall increase in Interpersonal Skills for the social-learning program was statistically significant (F=65.00, df=1/54, p < 0.01) and differentially greater than that of the milieu program (F=59.93, df=1/54, p < 0.01). From the beginning to the end of the current period, the milieu group simply maintained the level of improvement gained earlier (F < 1), although there were several significant changes within the two years. In addition to the significant differential change obtained by the end of the period, simple programs x time interactions were also obtained between anniversary assessments 2 and 3 (F=13.55, df=1/54, p < 0.01) and between assessments 4 and 5 (F=24.85, df=1/54, p < 0.01)—in both instances reflecting significantly greater increases for social-learning residents than for milieu residents. Social-learning residents, in fact, showed consistent increases in Interpersonal Skills throughout the entire period (all F's > 5.08, df=1/54, p < 0.05). Milieu residents also showed significant within-group increases from anniversary assessments 1 to 2 (F=4.64, df=1/54, p < 0.05) and 3 to 4 (F=12.91, df=1/54, p < 0.01), which were not significantly different from the parallel increases shown by social-learning residents (p > 0.25). However, milieu residents demonstrated significant declines in Interpersonal Skills during the six months following both peak responses (F=12.73, df=1/54, p < 0.01). The greater improvement obtained by social-learning residents during this period was sufficient that they were significantly higher in Interpersonal Skills, on an absolute level, from the second anniversary assessment through the rest of the period, with the level achieved by the fifth anniversary assessment being more than two and a half times that of the milieu residents (F=21.24, df=1/54, p < 0.01).

Both programs showed overall improvement in adaptive behavior from before program entry to the end of the current period ($F=67.66$, $df=1/54$, $p < 0.01$). However, tests of the within-groups change from pretreatment baseline to anniversary assessment 5 found the milieu program to have maintained significant improvement on TSBC Total Appropriate Behavior and on Self-Care ($F=8.57$ and $7.77$, respectively, $df=1/54$, $p < 0.01$) to approach statistical significance for improvement in Interpersonal Skills ($F=3.61$, $df=1/54$, $p < 0.10$) and to show significant improvement in Instrumental Role Performance no longer ($F < 1$). By contrast, parallel tests of within-groups change found the social-learning program to have maintained or increased improvement from before program entry on all four indexes of adaptive behavior (all $F$'s $> 29.47$, $df=1/54$, $p < 0.01$). Additionally the social-learning program was found to have differentially produced significantly greater improvement than the milieu program from pretreatment baseline on all four indexes of adaptive behavior (all $F$'s $> 7.51$, $df=1/54$, $p < 0.01$).

*Descriptive interpretation.* Thus, changes in adaptive behavior over the next two years found the initial superiority of the social-learning program to gain even further over improvements of the milieu program. However, greater differentiation among components of adaptive behavior also occurred, with considerable variability existing within concurrent appropriate behavior (figure 19.1, TSBC). Both programs had produced significant increases in concurrent appropriate behavior by the first anniversary assessment, without differential effectiveness between them. By the end of the current two-year period, the milieu program still showed significant gains over the level of concurrent appropriate behavior before the introduction of specific treatment procedures but neither additional gains nor losses from the improvement obtained by the first anniversary assessment. In contrast, the social-learning program showed sufficient additional gains over the next two years that improvement in concurrent appropriate behavior from before introduction of specific treatment procedures was not only significant but significantly greater than that of the milieu program.

There was an overall decline in functioning during the first six months of the current period and an increase in functioning during the last six months for both Global Functioning and some components of maladaptive behavior. The same pattern was also significant for concurrent appropriate behavior in both treatment programs (figure 19.1, TSBC). Additionally the increase in concurrent appropriate behavior for the social-learning program during the second six months of the current period was also significant. An inspection of the point-to-point plots of TSBC Total Appropriate Behavior in figure 19.1 also reveals additional trends, which span a sufficient range to indicate significant change over some time points within the time frame. Such additional trends are apparent in the increases for both programs immediately before anniversary assessment 3, in the peak between assessments 3 and 4, and in the overall increase following the low point during the second block preceding assessment 4 for the social-learning program.

As with the increases in clinically maladaptive behavior during the same period, the only specific event associated with the start of the downward trend in concurrent appropriate behavior at the beginning of the present period was the death of a resident. The overall pattern of changes in resident behavior immediately following the death appear largely in the concurrent activities of residents rather than in their responsiveness within treatment programs —showing increases in both bizarre motoric behavior and dysfunctional cognitive behavior and major decreases in appropriate concurrent activities. This pattern is clinically suggestive of an agitated grief reaction at the group level, in which program requirements prohibited major withdrawal from functional activities. However, the felt distress was still apparent in the depression of normal elective activities (such as reading, engaging in group activities, playing games, etc.) and in the increase in clinically significant crazy behaviors, which, in part, are potentially indicative of stress-produced arousal (see Paul & Bernstein, 1973).

The termination of the downward trend in concurrent appropriate behavior during the third block before anniversary assessment 2 in both programs (figure 19.1, TSBC) coincided with parallel changes in the improved direction for Cognitive Distortion (figure 19.2). The only notable events occurring at this time were the first releases of residents in both programs and the introduction of their replacements. These events certainly provided a positive change in stimuli for staff and perhaps enough validation to residents that it was possible to leave the institution that their attention was somewhat redirected.

While social-learning residents maintained concurrent appropriate behavior after the reversal, milieu residents showed another reduction immediately following anniversary assessment 2 (figure 19.1, TSBC). The only notable event associated with the beginning of the reduction was the institution of extended expulsion time as a consequence for assaultive behavior. Although the extension had been instituted as a result of a milieu community decision and clearly reduced assaultive behavior and Schizophrenic Disorganization, the content of milieu community meetings reflected considerable guilt and concern about the severity of their decision. The immediate increases in concurrent adaptive behavior for milieu residents after the low point was associated with both the start of community volunteers to accompany residents on passes and the institution of a special program by the community to control an especially destructive and abusive resident. The weekly group trip to the outside community began during the next block, and the next low point for the milieu residents was associated with a community decision to reduce the length of expulsion time for assaultive behavior.

The dramatic increase in concurrent appropriate behavior in both programs immediately before anniversary assessment 3 occurred at the same time that Inappropriate Clinical Frequencies stabilized. The point of increase corresponded with the start of male student workers and the introduction of transceivers to contact security officers for assistance with physical assaults. While the trend did not achieve statistical significance, the decrease in concurrent behavior for milieu residents immediately following anniversary assessment 3 (figure 19.1, TSBC) was associated with both the readmission of a previously released resident and the bomb threat to the institution. The reversal of this trend in both programs (third block preceding assessment 4) coincided with the beginning of the special sampling-exposure procedures to off-unit facilities. Since Schizophrenic Disorganization and Cognitive Distortion also increased at this time, the change in environmental stimulation may have sufficiently increased resident arousal that all concurrent activities—clinically adaptive and clinically maladaptive—were temporarily performed at a higher rate.

The gradual significant increase in concurrent adaptive behavior for social-learning residents over the last seven months of the period began at the same time that money was made available to pay residents in both programs for job training on higher step levels. At the same time, more individualized assignments were introduced for step 1 residents in both programs to provide exposure to available job-training positions. The major increase in concurrent adaptive behavior in both programs at the end of this period was preceded by the introduction of commodities and materials that had been held up for months. Specifically sufficient coffee and other consumables were obtained to make them available during informal interaction periods, and individual kits containing private grooming materials finally arrived. Additionally weekend activity schedules were changed just before the increase to allow all residents within each program to stay together with both staff members rather than dividing groups.

Overall, the major feature of concurrent appropriate behavior for the two-year period was the demonstration of the exceptional sensitivity of this class of behavior to both subtle and not-so-subtle environmental and psychological influences—even (or especially) for such low-functioning, chronically institutionalized residents. The major result for milieu residents was the end-of-period maintenance of the level of improvement they had achieved earlier. On the other hand, social-learning residents had shown sufficient additional improvement by the end of the period that their overall increase in concurrent appropriate behavior from before the introduction of specific treatment procedures was significantly greater than that of the milieu residents.

Much less sensitivity to moment-to-moment influences was apparent in the components of adaptive responsiveness within treatment programs, with only Interpersonal Skills showing major variability (figure 19.3). Both programs had increased Interpersonal Skills by the first anniversary assessment, without differential effectiveness. While, by the end of the next two years, the milieu program had essentially maintained the level of improvement attained earlier, the social-learning program had produced significantly greater improvements. On an absolute level, the behaviors entering the Interpersonal Skills Index—relative frequencies of interpersonal interaction and communications skills—reflected the greatest deficits of all areas of functioning before the introduction of specific treatment procedures. By the end of the period, the average milieu resident had approximately doubled the initial rate of terminal-level performance of these social skills but was still performing normal Interpersonal Skills on only about 19% of available opportunities. In contrast, the average social-learning resident had shown sufficient additional improvement that normal social skills were being performed on nearly 48% of available opportunities—more than two and a half times the rate achieved by milieu residents.

Figure 19.3 shows the several significant trends in Interpersonal Skills within the two-year period. While the overall upward movement for the social-learning program was significant over every six-month period, the milieu program showed parallel increases only during the first and third six-month intervals. The increase in performance of Interpersonal Skills during the first six months is especially noteworthy, since this was the only increase in functioning obtained in any class of behavior during the period following the death of a social-learning resident. The major increase in this period, however, did not occur until the release and replacement of residents in both programs and showed a major upward trend immediately following the extended time of time out and expulsion for assaultive behavior. The upward trend continued to the peak in both programs after anniversary assessment 2 when community volunteers started, and the special program for controlling the exceptionally disruptive milieu resident was instituted.

The relative stability of Interpersonal Skills for social-learning residents and the significant downward trend for milieu residents following the peak was a unique change in trend—not occurring in any other class of behavior. The only notable event occurring at that time was the introduction of the group trips to the local community, which staff had hoped would increase social communication by providing novel stimulation. Although the trips may have borne no causal relationship at all to the changes in trends of Interpersonal Skills, the clinical impression was that although staff appreciated the novelty, residents communicated less—being a bit overwhelmed by the community, with the ratio of trained staff (rather than volunteers) being too low to efficiently make use of the new experience. Many residents, however, worked to go on the trips, probably because they usually stopped for refreshments. The start of the significant upward trend in Interpersonal Skills in the middle of the third six-month period coincided with the introduction of special sampling-exposure procedures to expose residents to off-unit facilities within the institution. The peak for the milieu residents during anniversary assessment 4 also coincided with another special program to control an exceptionally disruptive resident. No notable events were logged that coincide with the beginning of the decline for milieu residents in the last six months of the period.

Overall the major outcome of the next two years for the Interpersonal Skills of milieu residents—like concurrent appropriate behavior—was the end-of-period maintenance of the level of improvement they had achieved earlier. Concurrently the Interpersonal Skills of social-learning residents demonstrated significant regular gains, differentially better than those of milieu residents over the entire period. The gains reflect a marked improvement in one of the major components of the resocialization target for rehabilitation.

Both programs had also significantly increased Self-Care by the first anniversary assessment, with the social-learning program producing even greater improvements than the milieu program did. During the next two years (figure 19.3), milieu residents showed a slight but significant decrease in Self-Care during the first six months (paralleling declines in functioning noted for other behavioral classes) and a slight but significant increase during the third six months. The resulting end-of-period outcome for milieu residents was essentially maintenance of the improvements achieved earlier. In contrast, social-learning residents not only maintained earlier improvements in Self-Care, and superiority to milieu residents, but showed additional significant differential gains over the entire period. The behaviors entering the Self-Care Index—relative frequencies of terminal-level performance of self-maintenance activities (e.g., personal appearance, meal behavior, bathing, maintenance of personal living area, etc.)—reflect the other component of the resocialization target for rehabilitation. On an absolute level, normal performance of Self-Care activities had also been exceptionally low before the treatment programs had begun. By the beginning of the current period, the average milieu resident had doubled the initial rate of less than 13% terminal performance of Self-Care, and the average social-learning resident had more than tripled it. By the end of the current period, milieu residents still averaged over 25% and social-learning residents had further improved Self-Care to nearly 50% of opportunities not distinguishable from normal—nearly four times the initial rate of performance.

Residents of both programs initially had been less deficient in Instrumental Role Performance than in other areas, averaging about 45% normal performance over the two groups before the introduction of the programs. While residents in both programs had shown significant improvements in Instrumental Role Performance by the first anniversary assessment, milieu residents had already stabilized at about a 66% level of terminal performance. In contrast, social-learning residents had continued steady improvement to a truly remarkable 81% level of terminal performance. Over the entire two-year period (figure 19.3), the only significant change for either program was a significant reduction in Instrumental Role Performance for milieu residents during the first six months (paralleling similar reductions in other classes of behavior). The milieu residents never regained their loss such that their program failed to produce significant improvement relative to their status before the program introduction for the remainder of the two-year period. In contrast, the social-learning program maintained the high levels of improvement achieved earlier throughout the entire two-year period, remaining significantly higher than the milieu program at every point. Thus, the outcome by the end of the current period leaves no doubt that the behaviors entering the Instrumental Role Index—primarily "on task" in classes and job training and "on time" at scheduled work, activities, and meetings—were not responsive to milieu therapy procedures but were especially responsive to social-learning procedures. Thus, superiority was evident for the social-learning program in the third major target area for rehabilitation of the chronic population.

## SUMMARY AND INDIVIDUAL IMPROVEMENT RATES

The group analyses clearly show additional differentiation of the treatment programs over the next two years. Both programs showed decreases in Global Functioning during the first six months of the period (apparently associated with the impact of the death of a resident) and increases during the last six months (apparently associated with improved procedures for controlling assaultive behavior and protecting staff and with the long-delayed availability of a number of positive materials and supplies). However, although the Global Functioning of milieu residents continued to maintain improvement from before introduction of programs, no further overall gains were achieved during the next two years. The Global Functioning of social-learning residents started the period showing even greater improvement than milieu residents and improved significantly more during the next two years, demonstrating clear overall superiority by the end of the period.

Although both programs had demonstrated continued significant effects on maladaptive behaviors, the social-learning program showed its clear superiority to the milieu program in the reduction or elimination of extreme bizarre behaviors—one of the crucial target areas for the rehabilitation of the severely disabled chronic population. Changes in the highest frequency bizarre clinical behaviors—Schizophrenic Disorganization—still showed significant reductions from pretreatment for both programs, but the social-learning program was differentially more effective in maintaining the reduction of these behaviors. Hostile-Belligerence remained low, without significant differences at the end of the next two years; however, the total incidence of aggressive Intolerable Behavior was significantly maintained at a reduced level only by social-learning procedures. In fact, therapeutic community procedures were largely ineffective in controlling dangerous and aggressive acts, which significantly increased over the next two years. Both programs essentially maintained the reductions achieved earlier in grossly inappropriate responses to minimal behavioral expectations, with the social-learning program consistently showing greater reductions than the milieu program— although this class of maladaptive behavior was at a relatively low frequency for both groups during the two-year period. The only area of maladaptive behavior in which therapeutic community procedures resulted in additional improvement over the period was with dysfunctional cognitive behavior. Both programs demonstrated continued significant reductions on bizarre cognitive behavior, to the point that significant improvement from pretreatment was substantial and did not differ between groups.

Similarly while both programs had exhibited continued significant effects on overall adaptive behavior, several differential effects were evident over the next two years. Although concurrent appropriate behavior was found to be particularly sensitive to environmental and psychological influences in both programs, milieu residents ended the period with the same level of improvement shown at the beginning of the period, while social-learning residents continued to improve to the point that significant differential improvement was evident. The classes of adaptive behavior assessing components of the resocialization and instrumental role targets of rehabilitation also showed major and significant differentiation of program effectiveness over the next two years. Residents in the milieu program maintained earlier improvements in Interpersonal Skills and Self-Care but lost those in Instrumental Role Performance—to the degree that their performance was no better than it was before the programs began. In contrast, residents in the social-learning program maintained the dramatic and significant improvement in Instrumental Role Performance throughout the entire two-year period, without a single waiver. Additionally further differential increases were obtained over the next two years in both components of resocialization, Self-Care and Interpersonal Skills, and they were even more dramatic than those that had occurred immediately on program introduction. At the end of the two years, social-learning residents demonstrated a significantly greater improvement in all four classes of adaptive behaviors than those in the milieu program.

Since clinical workers are more often concerned with percentage improvement of individual cases than with parametric group differences, the Global Functioning Factor Scores were further evaluated on the basis of individually significant change to provide an indication of the extent of individual resident response. Improvement rates presented in table 19.1 disclose that an additional half of the social-learning residents showed still further significant individual improvement during the next two years, over the dramatic improvement obtained by the first anniversary assessment. A quarter of the milieu residents showed additional improvement; however some residents in both programs showed declines in functioning.

Possible differential predictability of respon-

Table 19.1. Objective rates of additional change in overall functioning at fifth anniversary assessment for original equated groups (N=28 each).

| Treatment program | Additional change from condition on first "six-month" assessment | | |
|---|---|---|---|
| | Worse[a] | No change | Improved[a] |
| Social-learning | 14.3% | 35.7% | 50.0% |
| Milieu therapy | 25.0% | 50.0% | 25.0% |

a. "Improved" and "worse" classifications based upon individual change from assessment 1 exceeding 1.96 times the standard error of measurement on the standardized Global Functioning Factor Score. Chi-square = 3.818, $p < 0.10$.

siveness over the period from demographic and level of functioning variables was examined by correlational analyses.[4] Only one significant differential prediction was found for the milieu program, indicating that improvement during the two years was more related to shorter length of current hospitalization for the milieu group ($r=-0.49$) than for the social-learning group ($r=0.15$). No significant predictors of individual change over the two years were obtained for the two programs combined or for the social-learning program alone. Thus, neither overall nor differential predictability was obtained from any of the remaining demographic variables (age, sex, race, socioeconomic status, process-reactive status, marital status, nature of symptom onset, identified precipitants on initial hospitalization, total length of hospitalization, prior electroconvulsive or insulin shock, or other medical treatments), nor level of functioning at program entry or at the beginning of the period, nor drug status at any time during the period.

Similarly an examination of the possible predictability of individual resident change within the period found no overall or differential predictors for the decreases in functioning during the first six months or for the improvement within the social-learning group during the last six months. The only significant overall prediction of improvement during the last six months was attributable to milieu residents; those who improved tended not to have received IST ($r=-0.47$). No such relationship was obtained for social-learning residents ($r=-0.03$). Additionally improvement during the last six months was more related to shorter length of current and total hospitalization for the milieu group (r's=-0.43 & -0.42, respectively) than for the social-learning group (r's=0.22 & 0.26, respectively). Improvement between anniversary assessments 2 and 3 was related to shorter lengths of current and total hospitalization over both groups (r's=-0.38 & -0.32, respectively), without differences between the programs. The only significant differential predictor of change in the latter period was for improving social-learning residents who tended not to have received other medical treatments ($r=-0.52$) more than improving milieu residents had ($r=0.03$). Improvement between anniversary assessments 3 and 4 was related to lower levels of functioning at anniversary assessment 3 ($r=-0.29$) and to more process scores on the Process-Reactive Scale ($r=-0.38$), without differences between the groups.

In general, the correlational analyses reflect an absence of consistent overall or differential predictability of improvement within the period from demographic, level of functioning, and drug variables, with the exception of a tendency for a relatively shorter length of hospitalization to be related to improvement for milieu residents. The only other notable relationship with improvement was a correlation between change from anniversary assessments 2 to 3 and Intolerable Behavior during anniversary assessment 3. This correlation was significant over all residents ($r=-0.43$), without differences between groups, indicating a tendency for residents who changed for the worse or failed to improve within that period to perform higher rates of dangerous and aggressive acts. This time period was also the one in which the length of time out and expulsion as a consequence for physical assaults was changed. The relatively greater influence of aggressive and assaultive behavior immediately following the change was also apparent in a significant increase in the relationship of individual Intolerable Behavior to Global Functioning from original baseline ($r=-0.25$) to the third anniversary assessment ($r=-0.52$) and a significant decrease to the fifth anniversary assessment ($r=-0.41$). However, with the exception of Intolerable Behavior, resident characteristics contributed relatively little to changes in functioning during the period.

The extent to which changes during the next two years affected comparative status is shown in table 19.2, which presents the individual improvement rates from program entry. While a full quarter of the milieu residents showed significant declines over the two-year period, only one had declined to a point of functioning at a lower level than at program entry. The net effect for milieu residents was the same "three-quarters significantly improved" as had been

Table 19.2. Objective improvement rates in overall functioning from program entry to fifth anniversary assessment for original equated groups (N=28 each).

| Treatment program | Condition at fifth six-month assessment | | |
|---|---|---|---|
| | Worse[a] | No change | Improved[a] |
| Social-learning | 0.0% | 7.1% | 92.9% |
| Milieu therapy | 3.6% | 21.4% | 75.0% |

a. "Improved" and "worse" classifications based upon individual change from entry exceeding 1.96 times the standard error of measurement on the standardized Global Functioning Factor Score. Fisher exact probability =0.064, "improved" versus "no change" and "worse."

obtained at the first anniversary assessment—essentially reflecting the maintenance of previous gains. The few declines in the social-learning program resulted in two residents showing no improvement from pretreatment and none becoming worse. The net improvement rate of over 90% also reflected the remarkable gains for the social-learning program residents. Differential predictability of improvement from demographic, drug, and level of functioning data found that milieu residents who showed improvement at the end of the period were more likely to be female than male (r=0.41) and to have a relatively shorter period of current hospitalization (r=-0.47). These correlations differed significantly from the nonsignificant correlations within the social-learning group and were the same variables that had been related to improvement for the milieu group at the first anniversary assessment. None of the demographic, drug, or level of functioning variables were significantly related to improvement over both groups combined or within the social-learning group alone. Thus, the improvement of milieu residents was partly a function of sex and length of hospitalization, but the exceptional level of improvement obtained by the social-learning group was not related to resident characteristics or behavior.

During the current period, 11% of the milieu residents and 25% of the social-learning residents had improved sufficiently, with stable increases in functioning, to have been promoted and maintained status at higher step levels within the program—undergoing vocational training at the fifth anniversary assessment. Another 11% of the milieu and 18% of the social-learning residents had achieved promotions during the period but failed to maintain functioning to meet the stringent requirements to stay at higher step levels; they were consequently demoted to step 1. While there was considerable activity during the period in the milieu program, relatively fewer residents were contributing to the activity (table 19.1). For example, four residents accounted for a total of eighteen separate promotions and consequent demotions.

Even with significant improvement for three-quarters of the milieu residents, given the severely debilitated levels at which they started, the majority were still functioning at minimal levels at the end of the period. As a group, they still demonstrated bizarre clinical behaviors 43% of the time and normal social and instrumental behavior only 35% of the time. The gains achieved in the social-learning program during this period seem all the more remarkable in comparison to the gains achieved in the milieu program, as well as the level at which they started. Fully 25% of the social-learning residents were functionally indistinguishable from other "normal" people by the fifth anniversary assessment. Even so, as a total group, they were also functioning only slightly above minimum survival levels—still demonstrating bizarre clinical behavior, on the average, a little less than a third of the time and normal social and instrumental behavior over all areas, on the average, about 61% of the time.

Nevertheless, residents in both programs improved to the extent that they achieved significant releases to relatively independent functioning (the requirement for discharge during this period)—one each for the milieu and social-learning programs. A second significant release occurred for the milieu program; however, she failed at community adjustment and was readmitted to the program during the period. Two more social-learning residents had behaviorally improved to be eligible for release but no external employment was available—thereby failing to meet a requirement for release during this period.

*A Few Illustrations.* Since the achievement of significant release to relatively independent functioning for any of the residents from these severely debilitated groups is notable, brief case descriptions of significant releases during the current period illustrate both the nature of improvements and that of aftercare problems. The majority of plans and agreements for vocational training, training of residents and significant others to live together in mutually supportive ways, and the takeover of aftercare and followup by regular extramural staff of the

Department of Mental Health never came to pass. Therefore, these problems are also described below.

*Cass L. (milieu program)* had shown the most outstanding response of all residents in the milieu program after the initial introduction of programmatic procedures (see illustrative cases, chapter 14) and was the first resident to achieve release to relatively independent living with self-support after only thirty weeks of treatment. Cass's rapid response to treatment had resulted in regular promotion through the step levels such that he achieved step 4 status after only sixteen weeks.

Upon promotion to step 4, Cass was scheduled for the prescribed six hours per day in vocational training because he had graduated from all classes. Vocational training for Cass, and all other psychosocial residents, was limited to unskilled job training within the center under the supervision of the auxiliary rehabilitation counselor, since the outside training facilities were never available (see chapter 13). Primary vocational training thus focused upon personal and interpersonal factors (appropriate appearance, clothing, social and interpersonal relationships with supervisors and coworkers) and scheduling factors (determining where and when, promptness, etc.), which would be necessary in any unskilled or semiskilled job. A functional job analysis was performed on each available training position, and direct training in specific job tasks was provided, with daily checks on performance (e.g., Ayllon & Azrin, 1968). While his janitorial training position in the center did directly apply to the employment Cass obtained, this was not the usual case. The high unemployment rate in the geographic region surrounding the center, combined with the limited range of training positions available, typically required psychosocial staff to perform a job analysis and provide specific instructions in postrelease employment positions for each released resident. Cass responded well to the job training position, regularly receiving superior ratings in all three classes of performance.

Concurrent with the increase to six hours per day in the center job upon promotion to step 4, Cass also began the scheduled two and a half hours per week meetings with the liaison coordinator in the prerelease planning group. Cass was the first resident in the program to achieve step 4 status, and he was the only member of the group for the first few weeks. The scheduled work on release plans and potential problems that might be encountered continued, focusing on budgeting and money management, use of public transportation, and use of a telephone, since these were skills in which he was still deficient. Continued work on his current personal or interpersonal problems or deficits was also a regular emphasis of the prerelease group. Cass carried out all assigned tasks on his scheduled passes without difficulty, and his performance on the job required little additional work in the prerelease group—the only major focus being on continuation of appropriate bathing and clothing selection. Training and practice in completion of job applications and job interviews were also given before his regularly scheduled job-hunting trips.

The particular clinical focus in the prerelease group meetings was on the circumstances surrounding the previous psychotic episodes or conditions that had led to hospitalization in an attempt to provide alternative, preventative modes of dealing with such circumstances. Unfortunately the length of time that had elapsed since initial hospitalization was so long for most residents that only inadequate descriptions from medical records were available. For Cass, the primary circumstances surrounding his initial hospitalization appeared to involve the stimulus deprivation he experienced after being out of work and without social contacts for an extended period, with resulting delusional thinking and visual and auditory hallucinations. Focus was, therefore, placed upon ways Cass could arrange conditions for ensuring regular activities and social contacts to prevent such problems from reoccurring after release, since none were now in evidence after his rapid response to the milieu program.

The conditions for ensuring stimulus input and supportive social contacts were the very basis for the planned work with families, and the plan to release residents in small groups of two to three to be significant others for each other (chapter 6). The plan was never implemented for Cass, however, or for any other of the residents of psychosocial programs. In Cass's case, and others where family members did still exist, the family members typically wanted no part of a relative who had been institutionalized for so long and frequently would not agree to any contact, much less consider joint living arrangements. Cass's relatives were willing to accept an occasional visit but did not want him to live in the same town because of the embarrassment caused by his previous role as the "village looney." Given the severe disability levels of the resident group, same-sex pairs within programs did not progress at a rate that would allow them to be roommates and both obtain jobs at the same time.

Because of these difficulties, three different levels of significant others were established. Level 1 was that originally specified: a full-time roommate who could be trained to live in mutual support. At the second level was someone who lived in the same building or worked at the same location as the ex-resident, who could have daily contact and would agree to socialize a minimum of two hours per week. The third—and minimum level—was a volunteer who would agree to at least two hours per week social contact, plus six-month postrelease interviews. Even though psychosocial staff spent many hours contacting groups and receiving statements of interest, adequate significant others were never obtained for Cass or for any other released psychosocial resident.

What at first appeared to be an ideal solution to the significant-others problem for Cass occurred when he was accepted for employment with an industrial maintenance company. His immediate supervisor expressed sufficient personal interest in Cass at the time he was hired that the supervisor was asked if he would be willing to serve as a level-two significant other. Even though the supervisor was only able to come in for a brief meeting with the prerelease group (which was held on evenings or weekends if necessary to accommodate significant others) and to complete the prerelease expectancy interview, psychosocial staff were delighted that two of the three requirements for release had been met.

The remaining requirement before release was for adequate living arrangements that would be close to public transportation, could be financed within the income anticipated, and were either close to low-priced restaurants or included cooking privileges. A boardinghouse would have been an ideal living arrangement, in the absence of a supportive roommate, but few existed in the entire area except for private board and care facilities, in which the great majority of residents received public assistance and did not work. These facilities were rejected for Cass and others who were to attempt self-support. Finally, rather than lose the job and significant other, Cass arranged to rent a room at the YMCA on a temporary basis until more appropriate arrangements could be found.

At the time of release, Cass had changed dramatically from the rather typical chronic patient who had entered the milieu program showing nearly continuous withdrawal, apathy, and clinically inappropriate behavior with serious deficits in social skills. Over the last four weeks in residence, Cass performed all adaptive behaviors at a terminal level (i.e., indistinguishable from normal) on 90% to 100% of opportunities, and his inappropriate behavior was almost nonexistent—showing instances of inappropriate withdrawal on less than 1% of hourly observations. His Inpatient Assessment Battery showed significant improvement (from 55.7 to 65.4), and he was not only functionally indistinguishable from other "normal" people but actually appeared slightly more social than the majority of noninstitutionalized men in the community of his previous and anticipated socioeconomic level.

Unlike the smooth response to the intramural program, the course of Cass's aftercare was erratic, and problems arose from a variety of sources, including the absence of reliable significant others, community biases regarding former mental patients, lack of consistency by regular staff of the Department of Mental Health, and problems common to any unskilled laborer in times of high unemployment. During the prerelease expectancy interview, Cass verbalized reasonable and appropriate plans in all areas of functioning and had adequate plans to avoid isolation. The expectancy interview with the job supervisor who had agreed to serve as a significant other, however, revealed stereotyped thinking, with expectations that Cass would occasionally hallucinate, talk to himself, be apathetic, and have trouble at night; the supervisor's biases came about primarily as a result of having previously employed former mental patients from other programs who had shown such behaviors. Nevertheless, the first two months out went quite smoothly, with weekly follow-up meetings providing assistance with a few practical problems. Cass saved money in addition to meeting his regular expenses. The job went well, and the significant other occasionally attended a movie with Cass, although they obviously did not maintain social contact outside the job situation.

The first aftercare crisis occurred for Cass at the beginning of his third month out, when he was fired from his job—concurrently losing his significant other—as a result of an incident that later was determined to be based primarily upon biases regarding mental patients. Another former mental patient at Cass's plant had an episode of crazy screaming, and blamed the incident on Cass. Later information clarified Cass's innocence; but by that time, the news that a "crazy man" was working had spread with usual elaborations—to the extent that Cass had already been fired to placate the office staff who were upset, even though they had never met him. Cass was unemployed for only two weeks before being hired by the same maintenance firm with whom he had his original training position, and he remained in that job beyond the end of the first six months follow-up. However, because of the loss of his significant other, assistance with job hunting, home hunting, and the introduction and eventual discharge of a second significant other (at the third level), fading of aftercare contact to the minimum schedule of once per month did not occur until the sixth month.

The original design and agreements called for the transfer of aftercare and follow-up procedures to regular subzone extramural staff of the Department of Mental Health after psychosocial staff had completed the first six months of declining-contact aftercare. Prior practice had been for subzone extramural staff to provide regular monthly follow-up contact for all released patients for an indefinite period, with such aftercare having been their primary activity for the previous two years. During that period, the majority of the work of the subzone staff had consisted of identifying patients in state hospitals who could be placed with relatives or in extended-care facilities rather than attempts at releases to self-support. Two workers had been identified in each of the six subzones as project contacts so they could be trained to use specific assessment instruments and a compatible conceptual approach.

For a variety of reasons, the total transfer of aftercare and follow-up to regular extramural subzone staff for Cass, or the majority of other released residents never came about. One of the major reasons for the failure was that the habitual style of aftercare by many subzone staff was limited to answering questions—often incorrectly—that might be posed by residents or others, but only during regular working hours; obtaining drug prescriptions and delivering drugs; arranging contacts for ex-patients with other agencies; and transporting ex-patients from one place to another if transportation was not readily available. This mode of operation was obviously not what "aftercare" or "follow-up" meant to psychosocial staff, and it was not geared to maintain relative independence; in fact, it appeared to foster sick-role concepts among ex-residents. Therefore, supervisory relationships were established with the regular extramural staff who were supposed to provide the direct service. This arrangement was seldom totally adequate, since the supervisory psychosocial staff had no direct line authority for subzone staff and subzone staff understandably tended to identify with the mode of operation of their coworkers. A few subzone staff did work exceptionally hard, particularly in job and home finding, and attempted to apply psychosocial concepts and procedures in their contacts with ex-residents. However, an 80% turnover per year in the subzone staff working on aftercare allowed little continuity in training to occur.

These problems became more difficult over time as the role of regular extramural staff was shifted, by administrative policy, from providing direct service to community organization in which local community clinics within the subregions were gradually given the responsibility for all aftercare. The shifts in activity occurred at different rates in different subregions. Within two years, however, the extramural staff were no longer providing aftercare. Concurrently with the shifts in responsibility, even the competent extramural staff experienced conflicting demands. The local clinics that were to take over aftercare responsibilities tended to operate on a traditional model where ex-patients in the community were assigned to come to the clinics, most of which were open only during usual working hours, where "drugs and questions" were provided. Thus, psychosocial staff eventually took over all aftercare through the completion of the project, when all contacts were gradually transferred to local clinics (chapter 37).

Subzone staff did not start aftercare with Cass until some time after the scheduled transfer. Before the six-month follow-up, there was an opening in a boardinghouse, and Cass moved there from the YMCA. When the second significant other failed to follow through on minimum social contacts, the operator of the boarding home agreed to serve as a significant other (level two). Thus, Cass's circumstances looked reasonably stable; he had a continuing job, a living arrangement that provided social contacts, and a significant other on the premises. However, a more severe crisis than the first occurred just after the six-month assessment; Cass's significant other forged a check on Cass's account for $850. Five days later Cass was discharged from his job for "appearing distracted and working too slow"—quite possibly a result of the stress and loss of money. Cass returned to the YMCA and, with the assistance of project staff, began a four-month search to find work. During this period of relative inactivity and absence of social contact, Cass reported hearing voices occasionally and spent some sleepless nights rummaging around his room. Psychosocial staff continued to visit him at least every other week during this period, helping him plan schedules for job hunting and socialization and providing him with psychotropic drugs temporarily.

Throughout this period, Cass was able to manage financially and did obtain a new significant other, and a job as a dishwasher after the four-month period, just before the end of his first year out. The psychotropic drugs were faded, and transfer to regular subzone extramural staff attempted. Once back at work with social contact, Cass did quite well. Extramural staff reported no clinical problems on visits of once to twice per month over a period of three months. Cass quit his dishwashing job after three months, and the subzone staff member who was supposed to be conducting aftercare then arranged heavy doses of psychotropic drugs and proposed placement in a board and care facility. At this point, psychosocial staff established the supervisory relationship with extramural staff and attempted weekly instruction of the extramural staff member. Cass obtained another job as a dishwasher, drugs were again faded, and follow-up contacts with a new subregion extramural staff member were once again occurring only once a month over the last six months of scheduled follow-up.

By the time of the twenty-four-month follow-up, Cass had been employed as a dishwasher for over six months and had friends at the YMCA whom he reported "going out" with two or three times per week, in addition to participating in group discussions. His primary sources of pleasure were the group discussions, shopping downtown about once a week, and reading books, magazines, and newspapers. Although a new level-three significant other (the fifth) had just been established, Cass reported he had three friends with whom he could talk over personal problems if the need arose. In general, after several crisis periods, he appeared to have stabilized at about the level of the majority of men in the local area of similar socioeconomic status and continued to be indistinguishable from them. Throughout the two-year follow-up, Cass had remained financially independent, even during the period of unemployment. On the final, formal, follow-up interview, Cass reported that he was "comfortable enough" with his situation, felt that he had benefited from treatment, and preferred his current life to that of an institution. Psychosocial staff maintained informal contact with Cass through the termination of the project, occasionally providing him advice and assistance after subzone extramural staff no longer were making direct contacts. The last significant other also failed to function adequately, and Cass continued to move from job to job a couple of times a year, but he maintained consistent living arrangements at the YMCA and was financially stable. At the time of termination of the project, Cass had maintained self-support for over five years since his release, and there was no indication that he would need reinstitutionalization in the future.

*Kate G. (milieu program)* was the second significant release from the milieu program during this period. Like Cass L., her initial response to the intramural program was rapid and relatively without incident. Upon entry to the milieu program, Kate was a fifty-three-year-old divorced housewife and mother of five children who had never worked outside the home. According to hospital records, during her most recent hospitalization, over nine years earlier, Kate had received "chemotherapy, electroconvulsive therapy, insulin shock therapy, and occupational/activity therapy with minimal effect on her behavior." She had three previous hospitalizations of three months to two years, with attempts at discharge lasting fewer than six months in each instance.

Like Cass L., Kate was less severely disabled than the majority of other residents in the project before entry into the program, demonstrating one of the highest levels of concurrent appropriate behavior in the program. However, her self-care skills, except bathing, were notably deficient; she failed to present an acceptable personal appearance, maintain her personal living area, or demonstrate normal meal behavior on a single occasion before the program began. No individual crazy behaviors exceeded 10% of hourly observations before the introduction of the program, but several clinically inappropriate behaviors occurred with regularity, including blank staring, pacing, stereotypic rocking, grimacing without stimulus, lying down on the floor, and sleeping instead of attending scheduled activities. Although Kate's Interpersonal Skills were also among the highest of all residents, 60% of her interactions were inappropriate, being characterized by hospital staff as "demanding, immature, and manipulative."

When the therapeutic community procedures were introduced, Kate was immediately elected not only a "living group leader" but a "community group leader" as well. She responded rapidly to milieu procedures, to the extent that her steady and gradual improvements had brought nearly all areas of her functioning to levels indistinguishable from normal ones on 90% to 100% of observations by the first anniversary assessment, with stability thereafter. She graduated from all three classes, and her performance in job training within the center dietary department went so well that she was encouraged by her supervisor to apply for a regular position. The only difficulties Kate experienced at all during her intramural treatment were problems with money management on passes, which became the focus of work in the prerelease group. In addition to the usual prerelease planning content, particular emphasis was placed upon means of avoiding circumstances similar to those that had been associated with Kate's prior psychotic episodes—excessive use of alcohol and lack of sleep concurrent with sexual escapades with men she met in bars.

Even with Kate's exceptional personal appearance and interpersonal skills, after a few weeks on step 4, she continued to experience many disappointments in trying to find a job as soon as the prospective employers learned of her history of hospitalization. Against the advice of psychosocial staff, Kate elected to conceal her history of hospitalization and finally obtained a job as a motel maid in a town some fifty miles from the center. Since she had a brother in the same town, he was reluctantly engaged as a significant other (level three), although he was opposed to Kate's being considered for release and refused to come to the center for prerelease planning. As much preparation as possible was accomplished with the brother by telephone, and the prerelease expectancy interview was conducted in the efficiency apartment that Kate had obtained. Thus, thirty-three weeks after the introduction of milieu procedures, Kate had dramatically improved from the disheveled, obnoxious patient who entered the program showing a wide range of bizarre behaviors, to a pleasant, attractive, middle-aged woman. Her Inpatient Assessment Battery showed significant improvement (from 55.7 to 65.7), and she had maintained the high level of normal behavior achieved by the first anniversary assessment through the time of release. The prerelease expectancy interview indicated she had appropriate plans in all areas, and she was aware of conditions to avoid and how to avoid them. Although the brother's significant-other expectancy interview was largely congruent with Kate's, the lack of opportunity for adequate training was apparent in his expectations for her to be socially isolated and upset around other people.

Upon release, fifteen aftercare contacts were made during the first two months, primarily providing practical advice on transportation, mode of socializing, and helping Kate perform a functional analysis of the job. Thereafter, the minimum declining-contact schedule was followed, fading to one contact per month for the last three months of the intensive follow-up period. During this period, both Kate and her brother reported things were going "just beautifully," that there were no problems at all, and no help was needed. She was reported to have established new friends and had the liaison coordinator over for coffee to meet a few of them. The transfer of follow-up to extramural staff did not occur on schedule because the subzone worker had left, and the position had not been filled. The liaison worker therefore continued to make monthly visits for two more months, with continued reports and apparent evidence of excellent functioning with a well-established social network having been developed.

One week after the last such report the situation exploded. The brother called requesting immediate rehospitalization for Kate because she was "manic, hostile, and had blown all her money." Investigation of the specific circumstances revealed that Kate had, indeed, been duped by a "get rich quick" pyramid sales scheme and had given her savings to fast-talking salesmen. While the problem was one to cause distress, it did not appear to warrant the extreme reaction that was apparent for both Kate and her brother. In fact, when senior staff investigated the company and reported the situation, it turned out that no fewer than three junior staff were also in the process of being swindled by the same group. It was finally exposed that both Kate and the brother had been duping the aftercare worker over the earlier follow-up period. The brother and his wife had been regularly providing excess alcohol to Kate and using threats to "send her back" if she did not do exactly as they demanded. Thus, not only was Kate being supplied with alcohol, against aftercare plans, but worries and concerns as a result of attempting to hide her prior patient status had been withheld from discussions with the aftercare staff for fear of her brother's retaliation.

Although intensive crisis intervention was attempted, following fifteen contacts, Kate was admitted to the psychiatric unit of the local hospital after thirty-six weeks in the community. Psychosocial staff attempted, unsuccessfully, to establish a program of treatment in the local psychiatric ward, and she was readmitted to the milieu program three weeks later. Upon readmission, Kate was heavily drugged and had returned to her loud, demanding, assaultive interactions—at one point, displaying over three times the level of inappropriate clinical behavior and a third the level of appropriate behavior that had existed before original program entry. Three months passed before she approached the level of improvement achieved earlier; however, she again achieved promotion to step 4 by the fifth anniversary assessment.

Kate eventually achieved release once again, after the current period. She functioned well for seven months and then experienced another crisis episode, precipitated by excessive drinking and the inappropriate purchase of an automobile, which depleted her savings. Although she was not rehospitalized, staff coverage-using social-learning rather than milieu principles—was sufficient that the six-week period of intervention was counted as "in-institution" days for data analysis. Thereafter, a reasonable level-three significant other was finally obtained and declining contact was achieved. Kate remained self-supporting without further difficulty, working as a waitress, through the end of the project nearly two years later.

The lessons learned from the aftercare experiences with Cass and Kate were applied to the last significant release to relatively independent functioning from the milieu program, which occurred after the fifth anniversary assessment. By more actively pressing for details of any difficulty, with continued reassurance of personal support, as well as maintaining direct contact by psychosocial staff, crises were prevented, and there was a relatively smooth transition to completely independent functioning. The last such significant release from the milieu program had maintained independent functioning and self-support in the community for over three years at project termination.

*Thelma N. (social-learning)* was the only social-learning resident to achieve significant release during the current period, although two more residents had behaviorally improved to a level qualifying for release by the fifth anniversary assessment. The even tighter job situation delayed release longer than the three months on step 4 stated as a program requirement, but the residents were not demoted since neither residents nor staff could control the outside economy.

Upon entry to the social-learning program, Thelma was a forty-two-year-old single woman who had spent over half her adult life continuously committed to a mental institution. Although she reportedly had worked as a part-time waitress in her sister's restaurant during high school, she had never worked for compensation beyond periods of a few months when she had served as a paid companion to two elderly women. The majority of her time before hospitalization had been spent as a live-in housekeeper/babysitter, without compensation, in her sister's home. Thelma's behavior was quite similar to Kate G's before entry into the program, demonstrating one of the highest levels of concurrent appropriate behavior of all residents in the project but with extreme deficits in Self-Care, particularly appearance, and a variety of low-frequency crazy mannerisms. Thelma's Interpersonal Skills were much lower than Kate's, with 100% of her interactions being inappropriate before the introduction of the social-learning program. The nature of her social interaction accurately reflected her interpersonal aversiveness, which was described by hospital staff as low-frequency, high-intensity "nagging, tattling, complaining, and lying," concurrent with marked stammering and facial grimaces.

Thelma's response to the social-learning program was remarkable. She (and another female resident) progressed steadily through the step levels, graduating from all classes and achieving promotion to step 4 only eleven weeks after the introduction of programmatic procedures. All areas of functioning—including Interpersonal Skills—became indistinguishable from normal on 90% to 100% of all hourly observations by the time of her promotion to step 4, with inappropriate behaviors reduced and maintained at or near zero. The content of prerelease groups followed that described for Cass L., but social-learning principles were employed. Thelma's performance in job training within the center dietary department went well, with occasional problems caused by her continued "complaints and exaggerations." The primary clinical focus of prerelease group meetings for Thelma was on alternative means of verbalizing concerns and ways of establishing social interactions to allow friendships to develop. Practice in pacing speech to overcome stammers and grimaces was provided in the context of role playing job interviews. There was further work on money management and initiation of social contacts through structured tasks on passes, which Thelma handled without incident.

Unfortunately the other resident who had paralleled Thelma's progress to step 4 experienced a traumatic sexual incident on her first accompanied overnight pass, with her functioning deteriorating thereafter, to the extent that she was lost as a potential release partner for Thelma. Thelma's relatives were not only unwilling to become involved as significant others, but refused to visit and even made attempts through contacting the state's attorney general to try to establish "24-hour supervision in an institution for the rest of her life." The difficulty in obtaining employment and a significant other continued for over four months before Thelma found a job as a live-in domestic/sitter for a divorced professional saleswoman, who agreed to serve as a significant other (level two).

Thus, Thelma was released only thirty weeks after the introduction of social-learning procedures, having dramatically improved from the obnoxious, disheveled patient who had entered the program to a pleasant, socially appropriate woman. Her Inpatient Assessment Battery showed significant improvement (from 58 to 66), and she continued to demonstrate the high levels of normal behavior achieved at the time of her promotion to step 4 for the entire period of over four months up to release. The prerelease expectancy interviews revealed appropriate plans and congruence between Thelma and her significant other, even though only two conjoint sessions of prerelease planning had been available for training.

Upon release, the regular weekly to biweekly declining contacts were made during the first two months, with the only notable problem being an alcoholic grandmother who, unbeknown to psychosocial staff, also lived in the home. The grandmother resented Thelma's presence; however, after a stormy argument with the daughter—who also tended to abuse alcohol—the grandmother had moved out, and Thelma was instructed to "keep the door locked" to prevent the grandmother's return. No job analysis was conducted initially because the employer preferred to do that herself. At the end of the second month, the employer was "cool and uncommunicative" to the liaison coordinator, and later called the program director to state that the situation was not "working out." After several contacts, including psychosocial psychologists, problems in mutual communication were identified: Thelma was "nervous" about the potential threat of the grandmother, but rather than verbalizing that concern, she attempted to distract herself by "chattering" to the employer; the employer was not pleased with the way that Thelma vacuumed and dusted and found her "chattering" to be an irritant, but had not told Thelma her objections. A job analysis was then performed, and specific modes of open communication were recommended to Thelma and her employer, both for communication to each other and to the liaison coordinator.

After two weeks, the procedures appeared to have improved the situation, although the continued threat of a visit by the grandmother maintained a potentially explosive situation. One month after the initial communication of problems, the grandmother did make an appearance, and, contrary to her employer's orders, Thelma responded to the grandmother's threats by letting her in the house. Thelma was immediately fired by her employer, who was intoxicated at the time, thus losing both her job and significant other. After nine days of intensive job hunting, with minimal assistance from staff, Thelma obtained a position as a dishwasher at a nearby university. She independently found a sleeping room with kitchen privileges in the home of an elderly woman, who later consented to serve as a significant other (level two). The arrangements proved satisfactory, and Thelma gradually developed a circle of friends from whom she gained normal social supports.

The remaining period of declining contact was completed with once per month visits and an occasional telephone contact. Transfer to regular extramural staff was completed during her second six months out with brief contacts averaging once per month; however, Thelma functionally rejected the regular subzone staff, accepting no contacts at all during her third six months out. Rather, she tended to contact the attorney who had helped her with a family inheritance or to make occasional telephone contact with psychosocial staff when she wished advice. The six-month postrelease interviews were regularly held on schedule. Thelma's dishwashing job was seasonal—terminating at the end of the academic year—and she independently found other employment with a window-washing firm and eventually as a waitress.

By the time of the twenty-four-month follow-up, Thelma had enlisted her own friend as a significant other and was exceptionally active socially—regularly attending club meetings, movies, parties, and going out or having friends in almost daily. She reported more than four close friends and was considerably satisfied with nearly all her activities. Her only concern was the realistic one of job stability in times of high unemployment. However, informal reports through Thelma's self-selected significant other and her attorney indicated no additional problems beyond those common to the unskilled labor force, even after termination of formal follow-up. At the time of termination of the project, Thelma had maintained self-support for over five years since her release, with no suggestion of any need for reinstitutionalization in the future.

Lessons learned from the earlier aftercare experiences were applied to the additional significant releases from the social-learning program, which did not occur until after the fifth assessment. The job situation remained the primary practical problem with both men who were later released. Jess W. (see illustrative cases, chapter 14) improved further and was eventually released. He had one job change, but early and continuing open communication with his first employer, who was also serving as his significant other, prevented the change from being a crisis. Jess's aftercare proceeded quite smoothly, and he became totally independent of all mental health staff after obtaining a driver's license and an automobile—remaining in the community and fully employed for over three years at project termination. The remaining significant release from the social-learning program required more attention than Jess because of less stable jobs and limits on transportation; however, he too had remained self-supporting for nearly three years upon termination of the project, remaining indistinguishable from others of similar socioeconomic level. While the independent releases from the social-learning program were all functioning at higher levels in the community than those of the milieu program, the fact that all were where they were offered significant hope for the other long-stay patients.

# 20. Other Ongoing Resident Activity During the Next Two Years

## COMPARATIVE CHARACTERISTICS OF LARGE COMMUNITY MEETINGS

Productive characteristics of the large community meetings from the first through the fifth anniversary assessment periods—obtained from the Group Activity Index (GAI) in Friday meetings—are plotted in figure 20.1, which shows considerable variability in average straight speeches (i.e., appropriate initiation, response, or continuing normal conversation on a single topic) per meeting in both programs over the two-year period.[1] The straight speeches within the milieu community meetings ranged from a peak of 243 instances per 45-minute meeting immediately after the first anniversary assessment, to a low of 130, after the third assessment—ending the period with a sudden drop to 134 instances per meeting during the fifth assessment. Within the social-learning community meetings, average straight speeches ranged from a peak of 206 instances per meeting immediately after the first anniversary assessment to a low of 105 before the fourth assessment—ending the period with a sudden increase to 177 during the fifth assessment. Unlike the results immediately after the introduction of programmatic procedures, milieu community meetings averaged significantly more straight speeches than social-learning community meetings did over the entire period ($p < 0.01$).[2] However, the amount of normal, task-oriented talk in both sets of community meetings continued at a rate greater than five times that existing before the programmatic procedures had begun.

The relationships between average straight speeches and unitwide measures of functioning also differed from those obtained immediately after introduction of programs. The absolute level of straight speeches in community meetings did not covary with the mean changes in Global Functioning over standard time blocks. In fact, the only overall relationship that was significant for community meetings in both programs over the period was a tendency for straight speeches to vary in the opposite direction to the unitwide incidence of Intolerable Behavior within both programs ($r=-0.40$). Unitwide Total Appropriate Clinical Frequencies correlated significantly with the average straight speeches in community meetings over time but in opposite directions within programs. Straight speeches in milieu community meetings were positively correlated with Appropriate Clinical Frequencies over time ($r=0.37$), primarily reflecting a parallel decrease in both over the first six months of the period and an increase in both between the third and fourth anniversary assessments. Straight speeches in social-learning community meetings were negatively correlated with Appropriate Clinical Frequencies over time ($r=-0.39$), primarily reflecting the relative stability of straight speeches, except for the decline during the middle of the two-year period, while Appropriate Clinical Frequencies regularly increased over the entire period.

The majority of important trends in the amount of normal, task-oriented talk during community meetings in both programs were related to notable events recorded in the research log. The highest number of total straight speeches in both programs during the first block after the first anniversary assessment corresponded with the death of a resident. Although the tone of the meetings immediately following the death was subdued, the straight speech of both staff and residents occurred at a high rate as they discussed the circumstances and meaning of death. The remainder of the first six months showed reductions in the amount of straight speeches by both staff and residents, with a slight increase at the time of the first releases and replacements in both programs.

The increase in straight speeches during the first three months after the second anniversary assessment corresponded with the increase in expulsion time and time out as a consequence for assaultive behavior. The decline that began between the second and third anniversary assessments corresponded with the introduction of community volunteers and the weekly group trips to the outside community. It also paralleled stability or declines in unitwide Interpersonal

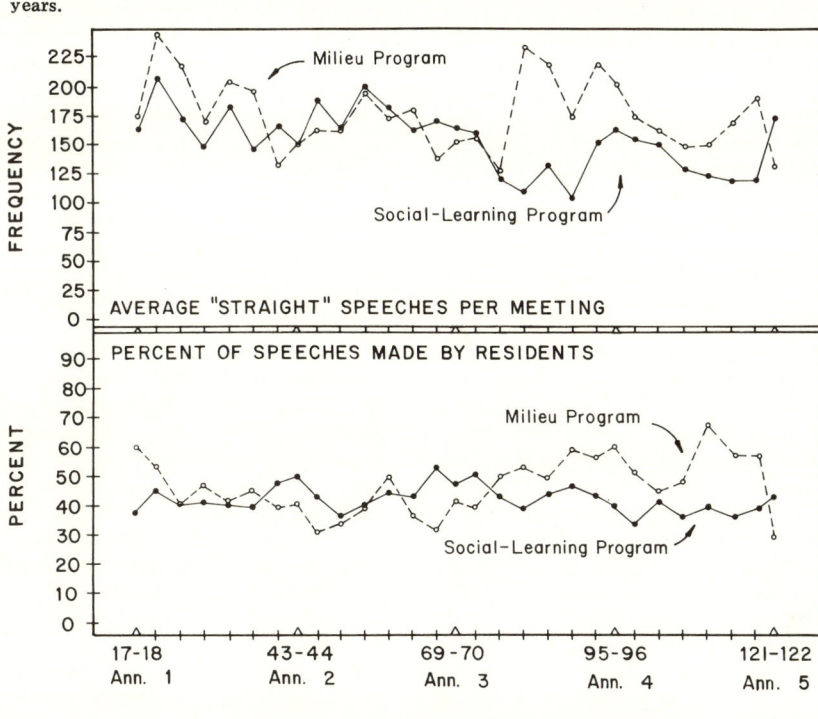

Figure 20.1. Productive characteristics of large community meetings during the next two years.

Skills that began at the same time. These changes further support the suggestion that the trips failed to provide the desired stimulus for conversation, since the ratio of trained staff to volunteers was too low to make the new experience effective.

The downward trend in straight speech in social-learning meetings continued until the block before the fourth anniversary assessment. The increase that occurred at that time in both sets of meetings corresponded with money becoming available to pay residents on higher step levels for job training and the introduction of more individualized assignments to provide exposure to available job training positions for step 1 residents. In contrast to the declines in normal communication following the introduction of volunteers and group trips, these programmatic changes appeared to provide a stimulus for increased conversation. The increase in straight speeches in milieu community meetings just before the fifth anniversary assessment corresponded with the availability of additional commodities and materials. Residents were obviously interested in these goods and spent considerable task-oriented discussion in determining procedural details for handling them.

The most dramatic differential change in average straight speeches between programs is apparent in the marked increase shown in figure 20.1 for milieu community meetings between the third and fourth anniversary assessments. No notable events were recorded in the research log that would account for this increase. However, an inspection of the individual GAIs and notes of milieu community meetings found the source of this increase to have been caused by a single resident—specifically, the milieu resident who had been released and then readmitted (Kate G., chapter 19). Upon her readmission, just after the third anniversary assessment, she was hyperactive and intense but relatively straight in her speech during community meetings—attempting to regain her previous position of community group leader. During the low point following the third anniversary assessment, she alone accounted for nearly 50% of resident straight talk, while other residents, including the group leader, reduced their contributions. The large increase in total straight speeches appeared to be a result of Kate's change in strategy, where she continued to talk at the same rate during meetings, but gave up campaigning, and started pressuring the current group leader and staff to take action. The result was that staff nearly doubled their rate of speech, and the resident group leader nearly quadrupled her rate in response to Kate's change of focus.

The reversals between programs in the amount of straight speech in the community meetings during the fifth anniversary assessment appeared to result from the drastic reduction in the length of time for time out and expulsion as a consequence for assaultive behavior that occurred immediately before that assessment period. Although the change in procedure—the result of a statewide policy directive—did not produce significant changes in resident functioning until the next four-week block, its effects on staff and residents were clearly and differentially apparent in community meetings. Only one milieu resident had shown major increases in assaultiveness during the fifth anniversary assessment, but staff and resident concern was clear. Staff initiation of discussions on resident responsibility and the manner of handling assaultive behavior increased in both programs. However, the social-learning program had other means of controlling assaultiveness as a part of regular procedures, while the milieu program did not. Therefore, social-learning community meetings focused upon communication of the changed procedures and reiteration of the other consequences, resulting in an increase in normal, task-oriented talk for both staff and residents. Since expulsion was the only regular programmatic consequence for assaultiveness in the milieu program, the community meetings focused upon the crisis of how to deal with the problem. Thus, staff increased their rate of speech because of their realistic concern over personal safety, but residents drastically reduced their straight speech to the extent that total task-oriented talk in the meeting was reduced.

Parallel differences in the structure and use of community meetings are also apparent on an examination of the proportion of straight speeches that were made by residents rather than staff in figure 20.1. As with the time periods before the first anniversary assessment, social-learning residents varied nonsignificantly around a 40% contribution of total straight speeches, with only one notable trend during the entire two years: a peak of 53% contribution in the block before the third anniversary assessment and a low of 35% after the next one. In contrast, milieu residents showed considerable variability over the period, with a peak of 68% contribution of total straight speeches before the fifth anniversary assessment and a low of 29% during it. The trends in proportion of speech contributed by milieu residents largely paralleled the total amount of straight speech in the community meetings. The proportion of straight speeches contributed by milieu residents was significantly higher for the entire period than that of social-learning residents ($p < 0.05$), largely because of the differences in the last half of the two-year period.

The differences in the target of resident speeches during community meetings, which became apparent after the introduction of programs, were maintained throughout the next two years. Straight resident speeches within the social-learning community meetings were regularly directed to staff (81%), with few speeches to individual residents (13%) or the group as a whole (6%). Until the community meetings during the fifth anniversary assessment, milieu residents continued to direct the majority of their straight speeches to other individual residents (56%), with considerably fewer to staff (35%) and the group as a whole (8%). All of these differences between programs were significant ($p < 0.05$). The dramatic reduction in the total amount of resident straight speech during the fifth anniversary assessment was accompanied by a reversal of the target to whom the speeches were directed. During these meetings, the majority of milieu resident speech was directed to staff (66%) rather than other residents (27%), reflecting attempts to offer suggestions and seek guidance for ways to deal with assaultiveness after expulsion time had been reduced.

Thus while considerable variability occurred over the period, the community meetings in both groups maintained much higher levels of normal, task-oriented conversations than those existing before the program introduction. The differing structure and purpose of community meetings was also apparent; the milieu community meetings generally showed higher amounts of straight speech with a greater proportion of resident activity and more resident-resident interactions, while social-learning community meetings consisted of greater proportions of staff-resident interactions.

Nonproductive characteristics of community meetings over the next two years are presented in figure 20.2. The time spent in total silence varied nonsignificantly around 20% of meeting time for both programs, without significant differences between them ($p > 0.20$). The proportion of community meetings spent in silence was unrelated to specific changes in unitwide functioning, remaining well below the level of complete silence that existed before the introduction of programmatic procedures throughout the period. However, even the 20% time in total silence reflects the continuing lack of enthusiasm of the resident population for the large group meetings.

Significant differences in structure and atmosphere between programs continued to be apparent in the active interferences with ongoing community meeting functions (disrupting discussions, whispering or crazy talk, walking about, entering late or leaving early). The ratio of active interferences to straight speeches, presented in Figure 20.2, shows that the

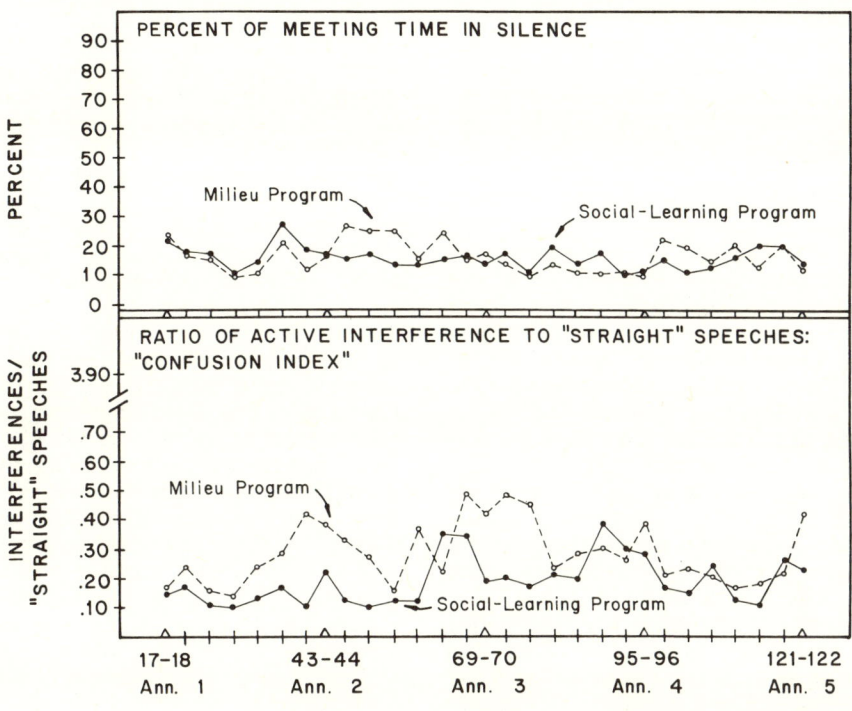

Figure 20.2. Nonproductive characteristics of large community meetings during the next two years.

relative amount of nonproductive confusion in community meetings remained below that existing before the treatment programs had begun. Both the absolute number of interferences and the amount of confusion during meetings were significantly higher within the milieu community meetings than within the social-learning community meetings over the two-year period ($p < 0.01$).

Although within-program changes in interferences during meetings were not correlated with other unitwide measures of functioning over time, the differences between units in Clinical Frequencies were reflected in community meeting interferences (r's in the ± 0.50s & ± 0.60s). These relationships showed that interferences in community meetings covaried over time with the unitwide differences in inappropriate and intolerable behavior and changed in opposite directions to appropriate responsiveness in other settings. Particularly notable are the decreases in confusion following the increase in time of expulsion and time out after the second anniversary assessment and the corresponding increases in confusion before the third anniversary assessment when the times were reduced. An increase in nonproductive confusion in milieu community meetings was also apparent during the fifth anniversary assessment—again, reflecting the disturbance of the group about the reduction of expulsion time.

Thus, over the entire two-year period, community meetings in both programs maintained higher levels of normal task-oriented talk and lower levels of confusion and time with complete group silence than before the programs had been introduced. The productivity of community meetings thus paralleled the overall level of improvement in residents. However, the specific characteristics of community meetings—with the exception of interferences, which paralleled Clinical Frequencies—were more a function of program structure, specific events, and resulting focal topics of meetings than of the level of functioning shown in other areas. Although community meetings did not differ in the amount of time silent between groups, the therapeutic community structure of the milieu program clearly resulted in more activity by residents than the social-learning program did. The milieu community meetings were not only characterized by greater amounts of resident straight speech and more resident-resident interactions but by more interferences and overall confusion as well. The social-learning community meetings, with the differing focus, maintained higher levels of talk by staff, more resident-to-staff interactions, and an overall meeting with less confusion and more immediate on-task behavior than at the milieu community meetings. However, the immediate concern of both staff and residents to the reduction in expulsion time at the end of the period was apparent in milieu community meetings. The meetings reflected increases in interferences and decreases in resident straight speech, with the majority of resident speech directed to staff for the first time since the introduction of the milieu therapy procedures.

## DIFFERENTIAL UTILIZATION OF RESOURCES

The relative use of facilities and services and of consumables from the first through the fifth anniversary assessment is presented in figure 20.3.[3] Although there was equal access to resources for residents in both programs, the differing structures had produced differences in resource utilization immediately upon the introduction of programmatic procedures. The utilization rates in figure 20.3 reveal that social-learning residents continued to use facilities and services and consumables at significantly lower rates than before program introduction (F's > 25.63, df=1/54, $p < 0.01$) without significant change at any time during the two-year period ($p > 0.15$). They also continued to use consumables at a higher rate than facilities and services (F's > 12.38, df= 1/54, $p < 0.01$), reflecting the relatively greater potency of consumable items (meals, coffee, snacks, canteen items) as backup reinforcers compared to facilities and services (e.g., TV, lounge, radio, time with staff, etc.).

Milieu residents continued to use both consumables and facilities and services at significantly higher rates than social-learning residents did throughout the period (F's > 8.42, df=1/54, $p < 0.01$), and they showed no differences between the use of consumables and use of facilities and services ($p > 0.15$). The utilization of consumables by milieu residents did not differ from rates existing before the introduction of programmatic procedures, and they did not change significantly at any time during the current period ($p > 0.20$). In contrast to the use of consumables, the milieu group did change significantly in its use of facilities and services during the period. The trends in milieu facilities and services utilization shown in figure 20.3 indicate a decrease from the second to the third anniversary assessment, followed by an increase to the fourth assessment, and another decrease to the fifth assessment, all of which were significant (F's > 4.86, df=1/54, $p < 0.05$). By the fifth anniversary assessment, milieu residents were using facilities and services at significantly lower rates than they had before the introduction of programmatic procedures or at the first anniversary assessment (F's > 7.74, df=1/54, $p < 0.01$).

Even though neither group showed significant change in the use of consumables over the next two years, the minor changes tended to covary with some unitwide measures of functioning within each program. Average rates of use of consumables tended to covary with concurrent appropriate behavior in the social-

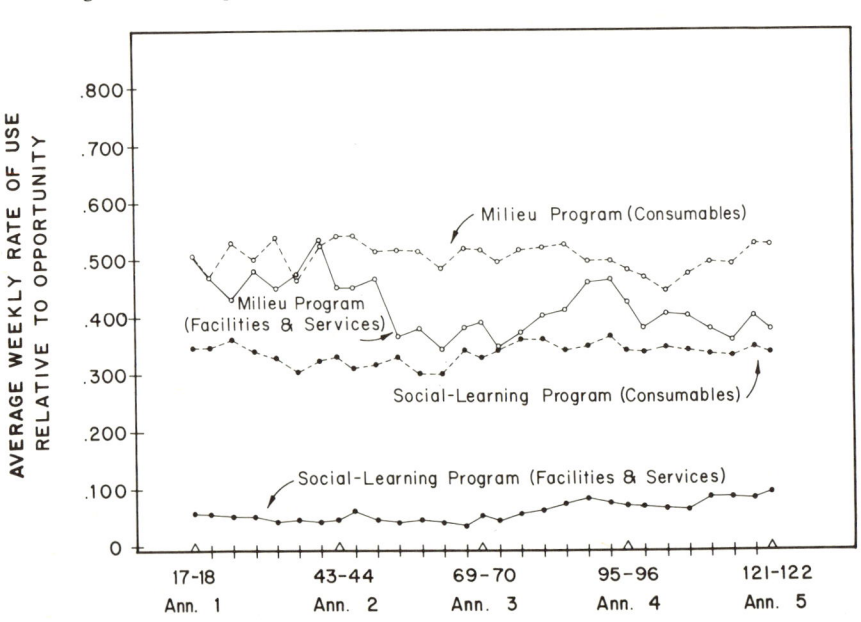

Figure 20.3. Comparative rates of resource utilization during the next two years.

learning program (r=0.40) and to vary in the opposite direction to unitwide concurrent bizarre behavior (r=-0.43) and gross inappropriate response to minimal expectations (r=-0.41) in the milieu program. Although the change in the rate of utilization of consumables was not statistically significant, the upward trend for the milieu program at the end of the period was concurrent with the increased availability of consumable items at that time. The differences between the units were reflected in overall correlations of mean consumables' utilization with unitwide measures of functioning. Negative correlations with most adaptive behaviors and positive correlations with most maladaptive behaviors (r's from ± 0.42 to ± 0.96) reflected the greater improvement of social-learning residents concurrent with lower rates of consumables' utilization relative to milieu residents. These relationships indicated that merely providing material goods was not as important as the manner in which they were provided.

The differences resulting from the two program structures were also apparent in the pattern of change in facilities' and services' utilization over time. Even though social-learning residents did not significantly change their level of facilities' and services' utilization during the period, their pattern of change covaried with unitwide levels of concurrent adaptive behavior (r=0.72), Self-Care (r=0.84) and Interpersonal Skills (r=0.43) to a significantly greater degree than for milieu residents. The only significant unitwide change in adaptive behavior that covaried with facilities' and services' utilization for milieu residents was Self-Care (r=0.42), although Schizophrenic Disorganization tended to change concurrently in opposite directions (r=-0.40). The significant reduction in facilities' and services' utilization after the second anniversary assessment paralleled the increase in expulsion time, suggesting that the expulsion of more active milieu residents was responsible for the decrease in resource utilization. The increase in facilities' and services' utilization before the fourth anniversary assessment—shown in figure 20.3 for both programs—coincided with the introduction of special sampling-exposure procedures to expose residents to off-unit facilities within the institution. Although these procedures had resulted in significant increases only for milieu residents, those that did occur for social-learning residents paralleled changes in adaptive behavior and were maintained when special procedures stopped. In contrast, milieu residents did not maintain the higher levels of facilities' and services' utilization after the termination of the sampling-exposure procedures. Overall correlations of mean facilities' and services' utilization with unitwide measures of functioning over time (r's from ± 0.38 to ± 0.94) also reflected the greater improvement of social-learning residents concurrent with lower rates of resource utilization relative to those of milieu residents. As with consumables' utilization, these correlations indicated that the quantity of resources used was not as important as how they were obtained.

An examination of individual resident characteristics associated with utilization rates during the fifth anniversary assessment found differential relationships existing between programs. Although residents using more consumables tended to be higher functioning in both programs, by the fifth anniversary assessment these relationships were significantly stronger within the social-learning program (r's in the 0.80s & 0.90s) than within the milieu program (r's in the 0.40s to 0.60s). Facilities and services also tended to be used more by social-learning residents who were performing all adaptive behaviors at higher levels (r's in the 0.60s & 0.70s) and bizarre behaviors at lower levels (r=-0.53), while facilities' and services' utilization was totally unrelated to levels of functioning within the milieu program (p > 0.10).

In summary, even though residents in both programs had equal access to resources, the patterns of utilization that had been established immediately upon the introduction of programmatic procedures were maintained throughout the next two years. Social-learning residents continued to use significantly fewer resources than they had before the program introduction and fewer resources than milieu residents used, and there were no significant changes in utilization rates at any time during the period. They also continued to use consumables at a higher rate than they used facilities and services, reflecting the greater value of consumable items as backup reinforcers for this population. Milieu residents did not change their rate of utilization of consumables significantly at any time during the period, continuing at about the same rate of use as before the program introduction. Thus, even though milieu residents were largely responsible for serving consumables, no changes in use occurred. Facilities' and services' utilization by milieu residents, however, changed significantly during the period—showing reductions concurrent with longer expulsion times for more active assaultive residents and increases concurrent with special sampling-exposure procedures to off-unit facilities—ending the period at lower utilization rates than had existed at the beginning.

By the time of the fifth anniversary assessment, higher-functioning residents in both programs were still using relatively more consumables than lower-functioning residents were, but the relationships were stronger within the social-learning group. Facilities' and services' utilization was related to level of functioning only within the social-learning group, where tokens were required for access. Within the milieu program, with facilities and services free, no relationship existed with level of functioning or maladaptive behavior. Throughout the entire period, social-learning residents continued to show greater improvement concurrent with lower rates of resource utilization than milieu residents did—again providing evidence that how available resources were used was more important than how many resources were obtained.

## TIME SPENT IN PROGRAMS AND WITH OTHER PEOPLE

Possible differences between programs in the amount of time in which residents were awake and in contact with other people were examined via TSBC indexes for "eyes open" and "with others."[4] By the time of the first anniversary assessment, the average resident had increased the average time awake from 80% to 89% of observations, without differences between groups. Over the next two years, the average time awake remained quite stable, without differences over time or between programs at any point during the period ($p > 15$). At the end of the two years, the average resident was awake on 91% of observations over both programs, remaining at a significantly higher level than before program introduction throughout the period ($F=22.08$, $df=1/54$, $p < 0.01$).

The amount of time spent with other people had also significantly increased upon the introduction of programs, from 66% of observations to 90% for social-learning residents and 83% for milieu residents. Over the two years, time with others showed significant decreases between the first and second anniversary assessments and the third and fourth assessments, and a significant increase between the fourth and fifth assessments ($F$'s $> 5.89$, $df=1/54$, $p < 0.05$). Although none of the changes in time with others were differentially significant between programs (including the low of 73% for milieu residents at assessment 2 and the low of 76% for social-learning residents at assessment 4), the end-of-the-period rate of 83% within both programs reflected a decrease approaching significance over the entire two-year period for social-learning residents ($F=3.78$, $df=1/54$, $p < 0.06$). Over both groups, unitwide changes in time spent with others paralleled mean changes in Global Functioning and most adaptive components of resident behavior ($r$'s in the 0.60s to 0.80s) and varied in the opposite direction to mean changes in most maladaptive behaviors ($r$'s in the -0.50s & -0.60s), without significant differences between the programs. Throughout the period, time with others remained significantly greater than before program introduction for both groups ($F=54.50$, $df=1/54$, $p < 0.01$). Thus, both programs had equal access to procedures of the respective programs during the current period, maintaining increases in "time in," while time with others largely corresponded to improvements in other areas.

An examination of individual resident characteristics found no significant differential relationships between programs for "awake" and "with others" status by the fifth anniversary assessment. Rather, overall correlations found residents in both programs who had "eyes open" a greater proportion of time and spent more time with other people to tend toward higher levels of Global Functioning and concurrent appropriate behavior ($r$'s in the 0.40s & 0.50s) and lower levels of inappropriate behavior ($r$'s in the -0.30s to -0.60s). Also, during the fifth anniversary assessment—following staff-initiated increases in the use of psychotropic drugs in response to reductions in consequences for assaultiveness—residents in both programs who were receiving drugs were found to be asleep during waking hours to a significantly greater degree than those not receiving drugs ($r=-0.42$). Significant differential relationships were found between programs, however, when awake and with others status were correlated with individual improvement. Improvement status was significantly correlated with "eyes open" ($r=0.52$) and "with others" ($r=0.58$) only within the social-learning group. Thus, while both groups were equally exposed to procedures of the respective treatment programs during the next two years, the amount of such exposure was related to improvement only for the social-learning program.

Summarizing "time awake" and "with others," residents in both programs maintained the increased proportion of time awake that had been established from the introduction of the programs. The average time awake remained stable throughout the next two years, without significant differences over time or between programs at any point during the period. Time spent with other people was also maintained at a significantly higher level than that existing before the program introduction. However, time with others increased and decreased significantly during the period, paralleling improvements in resident functioning. By the time of the fifth anniversary assessment, the proportion of time spent with others was identical across programs. Higher-functioning residents in both programs tended to be those who were awake a greater proportion of the time and who spent more time with other people, without differences between groups. Residents who were receiving psychotropic drugs tended to spend more time asleep during waking hours in both programs than those who were not receiving them. However, while residents within both programs maintained equal increases in "time in," and increases in time with others corresponding to other improvements, the access to procedures of the respective treatment programs was significantly related to individual improvement in functioning only within the social-learning group.

## VARIABILITY OF RESIDENT ACTIVITY

The individual variability of ongoing resident activity—as distinct from the individual amount and level of behavior—is the last group of descriptive characteristics to be examined. The average Stereotypy/Variability scores for five classes of behavior during the current period are presented in table 20.1, providing a descriptive picture of the individual range of activity within each class, independent of amount.[5] While none of the scores differed between groups before the program introduction, there were several differences by the time of the first anniversary assessment.

The variability of concurrent, clinically bizarre, "crazy" behaviors (from the TSBC) had not changed for milieu residents but had significantly reduced for social-learning residents by the first anniversary assessment. The reduced range of specific crazy behaviors performed by social-learning residents was stable over the next two years, without significant changes at any time ($p > 0.10$). The variability of individual crazy behaviors of milieu residents showed a significant decrease from a peak during the second anniversary assessment to a low during the third assessment ($F=20.61$, $df=1/54$, $p < 0.01$), paralleling the time of increased expulsion for assaultiveness, without other significant changes during the period ($p > 0.10$). This change for milieu residents was such that both programs showed significant reductions in the variability of crazy behavior from before the introduction of programs to the third anniversary assessment onward ($F$'s $> 16.30$, $df=1/54$, $p < 0.01$). While milieu residents showed greater variability of crazy behavior than social-learning residents at every point during the two-year period ($r=0.65$), differences in mean variability were not significant after the third anniversary assessment ($p > 0.20$).

Although the variability of crazy behavior for social-learning residents did not change significantly during the period, the minor variations that occurred tended to parallel only the unitwide level of Cognitive Distortion ($r=0.53$), without significant relationships to other changes in functioning. In contrast, the variability of crazy behavior for milieu residents covaried not only with the unitwide level of Cognitive Distortion ($r=0.73$) but with average Global Functioning ($r=0.45$). Additionally changes over time for the milieu group tended to be in opposite directions to Intolerable Behavior ($r=-0.61$) and Schizophrenic Disorganization ($r=-0.52$). Thus, although the social-learning program had produced significantly greater reductions in clinically bizarre behavior, by the end of the period both programs had reduced the range of specific crazy behaviors that individual residents were performing.

The variability of concurrent appropriate behaviors (from the TSBC) had dropped significantly in both programs and remained stable through the first anniversary assessment. Over the next two years, social-learning residents significantly increased the variability of concurrent appropriate behavior ($F=29.45$, $df=1/54$, $p < 0.01$), with increases being significantly greater than those of milieu residents between the first and second anniversary assessments, the fourth and fifth assessments, and over the entire period ($F$'s $> 7.70$, $df=1/54$, $p < 0.01$). Milieu residents approached significant change in the variability of concurrent appropriate behavior only between the second and third anniversary assessments ($p < 0.10$) during the time of increased length of expulsion.

Parallel to these events were changes in the average variability of concurrent appropriate behavior over time for the milieu group, which tended to be in the opposite directions to unitwide Intolerable Behavior ($r=-0.38$). In contrast, changes in the variability of concurrent appropriate behavior for the social-learning group covaried with the majority of appropriate Clinical Frequencies ($r$'s in the 0.40s & 0.60s) and tended to change in the opposite direction to unitwide clinically bizarre behavior ($r=-0.59$). The changes were such that the individual variability of concurrent appropriate behavior was significantly greater for social-learning residents than for milieu residents at all points after the second anniversary assessment ($F$'s $> 6.18$, $df=1/54$, $p < 0.05$). In fact, milieu residents no longer differed from the individual variability that had existed before the program introduction ($p > 0.10$), while social-learning residents showed significantly greater individual variability in concurrent appropriate behavior than had existed before the program introduction ($F=8.50$, $df=1/54$, $p < 0.01$). Thus, although the incidence of concurrent appropriate behavior was significantly higher than that existing before treatment programs began for both groups, by the end of the next two years, milieu residents had increased the amount of appropriate behavior performed, but the range of specific behaviors remained the same. Social-learning residents had increased not only the amount of concurrent appropriate behavior more than milieu residents had but the range as well.

Table 20.1. Relative Stereotypy/Variability of resident activity.

| Treatment program | Assessment period | Crazy behaviors | | Appropriate behaviors | | Social contacts | | Resource utilization | | Physical location | |
|---|---|---|---|---|---|---|---|---|---|---|---|
| | | Mean | S.D. | Mean | S.D. | Mean | S.D. | Mean | S.D. | Mean | S.D. |
| Social-learning | Baseline | 4.41 | 1.631 | 3.85 | 1.390 | 1.89 | 0.217 | 2.86 | 0.635 | 3.02 | 1.507 |
| | Anniversary 1 | 2.88 | 1.284 | 3.35 | 1.072 | 2.25 | .380 | 1.93 | .841 | 3.85 | 1.055 |
| | Anniversary 2 | 2.82 | 0.978 | 4.00 | 1.437 | 2.36 | .343 | 1.67 | .829 | 4.43 | 1.306 |
| | Anniversary 3 | 2.50 | 1.281 | 4.30 | 1.651 | 2.31 | .348 | 1.84 | .811 | 5.09 | 1.325 |
| | Anniversary 4 | 2.84 | 1.740 | 4.05 | 1.331 | 2.43 | .295 | 1.76 | .642 | 4.72 | 1.017 |
| | Anniversary 5 | 3.01 | 1.775 | 4.72 | 1.540 | 2.43 | .321 | 1.93 | .702 | 4.93 | 1.189 |
| Milieu therapy | Baseline | 4.04 | 1.478 | 3.61 | 1.015 | 1.90 | .245 | 2.68 | .462 | 3.51 | 1.044 |
| | Anniversary 1 | 3.85 | 1.794 | 3.13 | 1.058 | 2.39 | .262 | 3.05 | .513 | 6.12 | 1.606 |
| | Anniversary 2 | 4.20 | 1.648 | 3.01 | 1.180 | 2.59 | .268 | 3.08 | .514 | 6.16 | 1.624 |
| | Anniversary 3 | 2.85 | 1.456 | 3.26 | 1.112 | 2.53 | .352 | 2.84 | .599 | 6.20 | 1.373 |
| | Anniversary 4 | 3.21 | 1.400 | 3.17 | 1.120 | 2.61 | .306 | 2.76 | .307 | 5.65 | 1.071 |
| | Anniversary 5 | 3.28 | 1.375 | 3.14 | 1.169 | 2.46 | .361 | 2.77 | .474 | 5.95 | 1.425 |
| Total | Baseline | 4.23 | 1.567 | 3.73 | 1.223 | 1.90 | .231 | 2.78 | .563 | 3.26 | 1.320 |
| | Anniversary 1 | 3.37 | 1.635 | 3.24 | 1.070 | 2.32 | .333 | 2.49 | .892 | 4.99 | 1.768 |
| | Anniversary 2 | 3.51 | 1.520 | 3.50 | 1.404 | 2.47 | .329 | 2.38 | .992 | 5.30 | 1.709 |
| | Anniversary 3 | 2.68 | 1.383 | 3.78 | 1.504 | 2.42 | .368 | 2.34 | .872 | 5.64 | 1.458 |
| | Anniversary 4 | 3.02 | 1.590 | 3.61 | 1.306 | 2.52 | .314 | 2.26 | .711 | 5.18 | 1.143 |
| | Anniversary 5 | 3.15 | 1.594 | 3.93 | 1.580 | 2.45 | .342 | 2.35 | .731 | 5.44 | 1.407 |

Note. Table entries are Stereotypy/Variability scores. A score of 1 represents complete stereotypy (all incidence of activity of a single type); higher scores reflect greater variability, with maximum possible scores (crazy behavior=17, appropriate behavior=17, social contact=3, resource utilization=19, physical location=17) indicating equal incidence of all types of activity.

The Stereotypy/Variability scores for social contacts had increased in both programs, indicating a greater range of people with whom residents spent time (i.e., other residents, staff, outsiders) by the first anniversary assessment. Additional significant increases in the variability of social contacts over both programs occurred from the first to the second anniversary assessment and the third to the fourth assessment, with a significant loss for the milieu program between the fourth and fifth assessment. The reduction within the milieu program occurred abruptly at the end of the period, concurrent with the reduction in resident contributions to the large community meeting. However, the overall increase in variability of social contacts from the beginning to the end of the next two years was significant over both programs ($F=4.51$, $df=1/54$, $p < 0.05$), without differences between groups.

Differential relationships over time were found between the programs for variability of social contacts during the current period. On the social-learning unit, mean changes in the range of social contacts covaried significantly with the unitwide performance of Self-Care ($r=0.38$) and Interpersonal Skills ($r=0.43$), suggesting that a wider range of people was sought out as the resident group improved in those classes of functioning. However, the range of social contacts within both units also covaried with gross inappropriate response to minimal expectations ($r=0.51$) and varied negatively within the milieu program with concurrent appropriate behavior ($r=-0.72$), Self-Care ($r=-0.46$), and Instrumental Role Performance ($r=-0.40$).

Some portion of these apparently paradoxical relationships could be attributed to visiting significant others (outsiders). Visiting relatives were few in number (fewer than five residents in either program regularly received visits from relatives), but those who came regularly tended to infantilize residents; there were documented increases in inappropriate behavior and decreases in level of functioning following these occasions. However, the primary source of outsiders contributing to the range of social contacts was community volunteers. In spite of instructions to the contrary, volunteers tended to initiate more contact with residents who were functioning at lower levels and appeared to them to need more help. Thus, the range of social contacts within the social-learning program reflects both initiations by higher-functioning residents with a broader range of people and initiations of relatives and volunteers to lower-functioning residents. The range of social contacts within the milieu program reflects almost totally the initiations of relatives and volunteers.

The variability of resource utilization had changed in opposite directions between programs by the first anniversary assessment, with milieu residents increasing the range of facilities and services used, while social-learning residents decreased the range. Over the next two years, no significant changes occurred at any time within or between programs ($p > 0.20$). Rather, milieu residents continued to show greater variability in the use of facilities and services than social-learning residents did throughout the period ($F=62.98$, $df=1/54$, $p < 0.01$). However, a gradual downward trend for milieu residents over the entire period was such that, by the fifth anniversary assessment, no significant difference was obtained from the range of facilities and services used before the program introduction ($F < 1$). The reduced range of facilities and services of the social-learning group remained at significantly lower levels than the pretreatment baseline throughout the period ($F's > 43.57$, $df=1/54$, $p < 0.01$). Thus, by the end of the next two years, milieu residents were using facilities and services at a lower rate than they had before program introduction but used essentially the same range as before. Social-learning residents had reduced the rate of utilization significantly more than milieu residents had, and the variety of different facilities and services used by individual residents as well.

The Stereotypy/Variability scores for physical location had increased significantly in both groups after the introduction of programmatic procedures, with milieu residents increasing even more than social-learning residents. Over the next two years, these scores—providing an index of the relative amount of movement of individual residents within geographical areas of the units (e.g., corridors, lounge, dining area, common living area, etc.)—did not change significantly for milieu residents ($p > 0.20$). Social-learning residents, however, showed steady increases in the range of physical locations used through the third anniversary assessment ($F=13.70$, $df=1/54$, $p < 0.01$) with stability thereafter, largely paralleling changes in Inappropriate Clinical Frequencies during the period ($r=0.66$). Throughout the entire two years, milieu residents continued to show greater individual variability than social-learning residents in locations used ($F's > 7.86$, $df=1/54$, $p < 0.01$), but both groups maintained higher location variability than they had before the programmatic procedures had been introduced ($F=65.21$, $df=1/54$, $p < 0.01$).

An examination of the intercorrelations among all five Stereotypy/Variability scores during the fifth anniversary assessment found few significant correlations, none of which replicated over programs. Three intercorrelations were only significant within the milieu group: the variabilities of social contacts and of concurrent appropriate behaviors (r=0.64) and the variability of locations with the variability of crazy behavior (r=0.44) and with the variability of facilities and services used (r=0.53). Two correlations were only significant within the social-learning group: the variability of concurrent appropriate behavior was positively correlated with the variability of facilities and services used (r=0.40) and negatively correlated with the variability of crazy behavior (r=-0.39). These correlations reflect completely different patterns, with a tendency for milieu residents who performed a greater range of concurrent appropriate behavior also to spend time with a greater range of other people. Milieu residents who were observed in wider ranges of physical locations on the unit also tended to perform a greater number of different types of crazy behaviors and to use a wider range of facilities and services. In contrast, social-learning residents performing a greater range of concurrent appropriate behaviors tended to perform fewer types of crazy behaviors and to use a wider range of facilities and services. Thus, different patterns of relationships existed between programs, and the stereotypy or variability of activities was not a consistent personal attribute of residents in either program.

Similar to relationships found earlier, residents showing greater variability in social contacts tended to be performing higher levels of adaptive behavior (r's in the 0.20s & 0.30s) during the fifth anniversary assessment, without differences between programs. Similarly, residents exhibiting greater variability in the range of concurrent appropriate behaviors still tended to be those with higher levels of functioning and less maladaptive behavior (r's in the ± 0.40s to ± 0.70s), but without differences between programs. In contrast to earlier findings, no differential patterning of relationships with the variability of crazy behavior was apparent during the fifth anniversary assessment. Rather, the variability of crazy behavior was not at all related to the level of maladaptive behavior in either program but was negatively related to all measures of adaptive behavior (r's in the -0.30s & -0.40s), without differences between the groups.

The variability of locations frequented was not related to a single measure of functioning within the social-learning program and was related to only one measure within the milieu program, which showed a tendency for milieu residents performing lower levels of Interpersonal Skills to use a wider range of locations (r=0.46). However, there was a slight tendency over both programs for residents using a wider range of locations to be those who were less often with other people (r=-0.29). Significant differential relationships between programs were found for the variability of facilities and services used. Social-learning residents using a greater range of facilities and services tended to be those performing higher levels of all adaptive behaviors (r's in the 0.40s to 0.60s) and lower levels of Inappropriate Clinical Frequencies (r=-0.41). All of these correlations were significantly greater than zero-level relationships within the milieu group.

Thus, the relative variability of individual resident activity continued to reflect differential patterns of within-program processes over the next two years. Residents in both programs continued to increase the range of class of people with whom they spent time during the period, primarily because of the presence of community volunteers who provided more opportunities to spend time with outsiders. The pattern of change over the next two years differed between groups, suggesting that outsiders were sought out by higher-functioning social-learning residents, while lower-functioning residents in both programs tended to be sought out by outsiders. The reduced range of bizarre crazy behavior for social-learning residents was maintained throughout the current period. Milieu residents reduced the variability of crazy behavior for the first time during the period in which increased expulsion time for assaultive behavior was in effect. Although the social-learning program had produced significantly greater reductions in the amount of clinically bizarre behavior, by the end of the two years, both programs had reduced the range of specific crazy behaviors that individual residents were performing as well.

Social-learning residents showed increases in the variability of concurrent appropriate behavior over the next two years, paralleling significantly greater increases in functioning over milieu residents. The incidence of concurrent appropriate behavior had remained significantly higher than that existing before the introduction of programs for both groups. By the end of the period, milieu residents had increased the amount of appropriate behavior, but the range of specific behaviors performed remained the same. In contrast, social-learning residents had increased both the amount and the range of specific appropriate behaviors performed. No significant changes occurred in the variability of resource utilization over the next two years. Social-learning residents continued to use a significantly reduced range of facilities and services—below their own level before program introduction and below that of milieu residents. By the end of the period, individual milieu residents were using essentially the same range of resources as they had before the introduction of programmatic procedures. Finally, social-learning residents continued to increase the variability of physical locations frequented within the unit. Although both groups maintained higher location variability than that existing before the introduction of programs, milieu residents remained stable and at higher levels than were social-learning residents in the individual variability in locations used throughout the two-year period.

By the end of the period, the stereotypy/variability of activities was still not a consistent personal attribute, and differential patterning of relationships was apparent within the programs. However, over both programs, residents functioning at relatively higher levels tended to show greater variability in the range of concurrent appropriate behaviors and social contacts and less variability in the range of bizarre behaviors. Differential relationships were obtained between levels of functioning and the remaining stereotypy/variability scores. Higher-functioning social-learning residents tended to show greater variability in resource utilization. No such relationships existed for milieu residents. Location variability, in contrast, was unrelated to functioning within the social-learning group, but milieu residents using a greater range of locations tended to be those performing lower levels of Interpersonal Skills. There was still a slight tendency for residents using a greater number of locations to be asleep more during waking hours, suggesting that the range of locations somewhat reflected out-of-the-way places.

## SUMMARY

In addition to the data on comparative effectiveness described in chapter 19, there were differences in the characteristics of other ongoing resident activity during the next two years. Residents at the unitwide community meetings in both programs maintained higher levels of normal task-oriented talk and lower levels of confusion and time silent than before the introduction of programs, paralleling the overall level of improvement. However, with the exception of group interferences, which paralleled clinical frequencies, the characteristics of community meetings were more related to program structure and focal topics of meetings than of resident functioning in other areas. The amount of time spent silent remained at reduced levels for both groups throughout the next two years, without differences between programs. The milieu program, nevertheless, clearly produced more activity during community meetings than the social-learning program did. The differential structure and purpose of community meetings was apparent in greater proportions of resident rather than staff speech, more resident-resident rather than resident-staff interactions, and more interferences and confusion in milieu than in social-learning meetings. However, the last milieu community meetings of the period showed increases in interferences and decreases in resident speech, with the majority of resident speech directed to staff for the first time since introduction of the therapeutic community structure—reflecting the concerns of both staff and residents to the reduction of expulsion time for consequating assaultive behavior.

Comparative utilization of resources also continued to show differences resulting from program structures. Throughout the next two years, social-learning residents continued to use significantly fewer resources than before program introduction and significantly fewer resources than milieu residents did, without change at any point. The greater value of consumable items as backup reinforcers for this population continued to be apparent in significantly greater utilization of consumables than of facilities and services by the social-learning group. In contrast, milieu residents, for whom resource utilization required only decision making, showed no difference between utilization of consumables versus facilities and services. Milieu residents used consumables at the same rate as before the program introduction, without change during the two years. However, they reduced their use of facilities and services by the end of the period, significantly increased it during the period corresponding with special sampling exposure to off-unit facilities, and decreased it during the period concurrent with longer expulsion times for more active, assaultive residents. By the end of the period, higher-functioning residents in both programs were using more consumables than lower-functioning residents were, with relationships being stronger within the social-learning group. Facilities' and services' utilization was related to functioning only within the social-learning program. However, parallel to findings immediately after the program introduction, social-learning residents continued to show greater improvements with less use of facilities, services, and consumables—again providing clear evidence that how available resources were used was more important than how many were obtained.

Throughout the next two years, residents in both groups maintained the increased proportion of time awake that had been established upon the introduction of programs, without differences over time or between groups. Time spent with other people was also maintained at a significantly higher level than that existing before the introduction of programmatic procedures. However, time with others increased and decreased significantly during the period, paralleling improvements in resident functioning within each program. By the end of the two-year period, the time spent with other people was identical across programs, with higher-functioning residents in both groups tending to be those who spent more time with others and who were awake a greater proportion of the time. The only relationship of the increase in psychotropic drug use at the fifth anniversary assessment to resident functioning was found here; residents receiving psychotropic drugs spent more time asleep during waking hours in both programs. Overall residents within both programs maintained equal increases in "time in," and in time with others corresponding to other improvements. However, the access to procedures of the respective programs was significantly related to individual improvement during the next two years only within the social-learning group.

Changes in the variability of ongoing resident activity also continued to show differences in the day-to-day processes within the psychosocial programs. The introduction of community volunteers contributed to continuing increases in the range of people (i.e., staff, other residents, outsiders) with whom time was spent. Both groups increased the variability of social contacts equally; the pattern of change suggested that lower-functioning residents tended to be sought out for contact in both programs and that higher-functioning residents within the social-learning program initiated a broader range of contacts themselves. The variability of clinically bizarre crazy behavior of milieu residents was reduced for the first time during the period in which increased expulsion time was in effect. Social-learning residents maintained their earlier reduction in the variability of crazy behavior. Thus, by the end of the next two years, the social-learning program had produced significantly greater reductions in the amount of clinically bizarre behavior, but both programs had equally reduced the range of different crazy behaviors that individual residents were performing.

The incidence of concurrent appropriate behavior remained significantly higher than that existing before the introduction of programs for both groups. By the end of the next two years, milieu residents had increased the amount but not the range of specific appropriate behavior. Social-learning residents, in contrast, increased both the amount and the individual range of specific behavior over the next two years to a significantly greater degree than did milieu residents. No significant changes in the variability of resource utilization occurred over the next two years. Rather, social-learning residents continued to use a significantly reduced level and range of facilities and services, below their own level before program introduction and below that of milieu residents. By the end of the next two years, individual milieu residents were still using the same range of resources as they had before the introduction of the program. The variability of physical locations frequented increased over the period for social-learning residents but remained stable for milieu residents. Both groups continued to show greater location variability than before the introduction of programs, with milieu residents showing higher levels of location variability than social-learning residents did throughout the two years.

By the end of the period, higher-functioning residents within both programs tended to show greater variability in the range of concurrent appropriate behaviors and social contacts and less variability in the range of bizarre behaviors. Higher-functioning social-learning residents also tended to show greater variability in the range of facilities and services used, while no relationship to functioning existed for milieu residents. There was a slight tendency in both programs for residents using a greater range of locations to be those who slept more during waking hours, but location variability was related to functioning only within the milieu program. That relationship showed residents with lower Interpersonal Skills tended toward use of a greater range of locations. Differential patterning of interrelationships among stereotypy/variability scores was apparent between programs. The stereotypy/variability of resident activities was still not a consistent individual attribute within either program.

Thus, analyses of the characteristics of other ongoing resident activity during the next two years provide a descriptive picture that continues to be in keeping with the differential program structures and additional support that outcome data were primarily a function of programmatic procedures and identified events.

# 21. Staff Attitudes and Performance During the Next Two Years

## OPINIONS ABOUT MENTAL PATIENTS

Average sten scores on the Opinions About Mental Illness Scale (OMI) for junior staff alone and all clinical staff combined from the first through fifth anniversary assessments are presented in figure 21.1.[1] Original scores at the end of academic training are also plotted for comparative purposes. Although a reduction in Social Restrictiveness had occurred over the period of rapid resident improvement through the first anniversary assessment, none of the OMI changes were significant immediately after the introduction of the programs. Over the next two years, the only significant overall or differential change among OMI scores occurred between the first and second anniversary assessments for continuing staff.[2] The significant differential change among scores ($p < 0.05$) during this period was totally attributable to a significant decrease in Mental Hygiene Ideology and a significant increase in Social Restrictiveness ($p$'s $< 0.05$); no significant change occurred for the remaining four scores ($p$'s $> 0.20$).

Figure 21.1 shows that the change in Social Restrictiveness essentially represented a return to the original posttraining level, while the reduction in Mental Hygiene Ideology indicated movement away from the exceptionally high level of endorsement that had existed earlier toward a more desirable level compared to the ideal assumptions underlying the psychosocial programs. Over the entire two-year period, Social-Learning Ideology continued to show the exceptionally high levels of endorsement that had been obtained at the end of original staff training. Even with the changes between the first and second anniversary assessments and with only 23% of staff continuing over the period, OMI scores showed no significant overall or differential change at the end of the next two years from the levels that had existed at the beginning of the period or from those existing before the residents arrived ($p$'s $> 0.10$). By the fifth anniversary assessment, the order among individual OMI scores shown in figure 21.1 remained constant, but differences between scores were no longer significant between Authoritarianism and Benevolence or between Benevolence and Social Restrictiveness.[3] As at the first anniversary assessment, Authoritarianism and Interpersonal Etiology also did not differ significantly, but differences between all remaining scores were significant.

Comparison of the staff means with the ideal responses indicated in the margins of figure 21.1 for each score shows that the pattern of the six staff scores remained parallel to the ideal assumptions underlying both programs. In fact, the changes resulted in the pattern's moving significantly closer to the ideal ($p < 0.01$) from the first ($r=0.90$) to the second anniversary assessment ($r=0.97$), without additional significant change through the fifth one ($r=0.94$).[4] The level of endorsement over all six staff scores combined also moved closer to ideal assumptions from the first to the second anniversary assessment ($D^2=9.17$ & $5.63$, respectively, $p=0.063$) without additional change through the fifth assessment ($D^2=6.63$, $p > 0.10$).[5] Thus, the only significant changes that occurred over the next two years resulted in both pattern and level of staff OMI responses moving closer to ideal assumptions, primarily through more desirable (realistic) levels of endorsement of items reflecting potential dangerousness of residents and "welfare" attitudes. These changes occurred during the first six months of the current period, following the first decrease in functioning of both resident groups, considerable concern over increases in assaultiveness in the milieu group, and the first releases and replacements of residents. Since there was considerable variability in resident functioning over the remainder of the next two years, in the absence of prior change in staff OMI scores, the changes that were apparent at the second anniversary assessment suggest that the differential experience with changed resident behavior had more effect on staff attitudes than staff attitudes had on resident behavior.

An examination of the intercorrelations among OMI scores at the fifth anniversary assessment found even less clustering than had

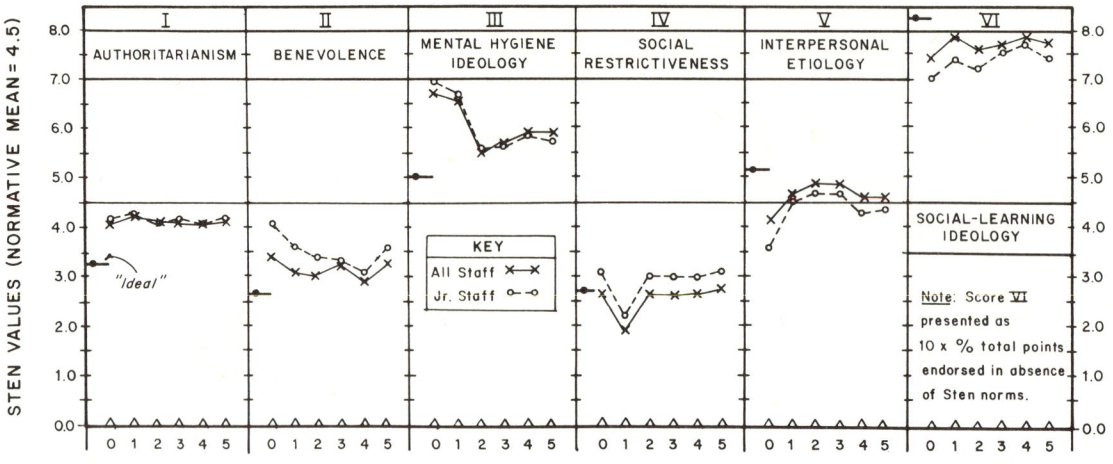

Figure 21.1. Opinions About Mental Illness Scale responses by all psychosocial staff present during the next two years. The ideal response is indicated in the left margin for each score.

existed at the first one. The only intercorrelations remaining significant at the end of the next two years involved Social Restrictiveness, which was still positively related to Authoritarianism (r=0.47) and negatively related to Mental Hygiene Ideology (r=-0.52). Even less predictability from individual staff characteristics was obtained, with the only significant relationships being with education and race. More highly educated staff tended to score lower on Social Restrictiveness (r=-0.44) and higher on Social-Learning Ideology (r=0.42), reflecting the significant differences between junior and senior staff on these scores. There was a slight tendency (r=0.39) for black staff to score higher on Benevolence. Thus, as staff gained more experience—the only staff characteristic to change over the next two years—OMI scores became even less clustered and less predictable from individual characteristics than they were at the first anniversary assessment.

In summary, the attitudes, opinions, and beliefs about mental patients held by the psychosocial staff showed significant change only over the first six months of the current two-year period. There were decreases in Mental Hygiene Ideology and increases in Social Restrictiveness, which moved the pattern and level of OMI scores even closer to the ideals underlying the psychosocial programs. The attitudes to which residents were exposed did not vary appreciably over the period and had no differential effect on resident behavior; however, the changes in OMI scores that did occur appeared to reflect staff responses to differential change in resident behavior during the first six months of the period. Even with the high turnover during the current period, the staff group as a whole remained remarkably consistent in reflecting the ideal assumptions underlying the psychosocial programs.

## ATTITUDES TOWARD AND INTERPRETATIONS OF TREATMENT PROGRAMS

Between 96% and 100% of clinical staff expressed differential opinions to the preliminary questions on the Therapist Orientation Sheet (TOS) at each anniversary assessment during the next two years. These questions asked staff to indicate which of the two psychosocial programs they believed was more effective and which was more enjoyable. While all of the opinions were obtained well in advance of any comparative data analyses, the proportion of staff believing the social-learning program was more effective accurately reflected the differential improvements that had occurred during the time preceding each judgment. By the first anniversary assessment, following a rapid and differential improvement by the residents, 96% of staff expressing opinions believed the social-learning program was more effective (up from an even division before the introduction of the programs). Following the reduction in functioning of both groups over the next six months and the first resident releases in both groups, more staff than before believed the milieu program was the more effective, but 80% still favored the social-learning program. The proportion of staff believing the social-learning program was the more effective over the three remaining assessments of the current period followed the gradual differential increase in resident functioning in the social-learning program: 88% at the third assessment, 93% at the fourth assessment, and a full 100% at the fifth. Thus, staff beliefs about the effectiveness of programs appeared to reflect accurately the objective results but provided no evidence that staff beliefs affected the ensuing responses of residents.

Changes were also apparent in the proportion of staff who found the respective programs to be the more enjoyable in which to work. By the first anniversary assessment staff had reversed an earlier preference for the milieu program, to the extent that 69% indicated the social-learning program was the more enjoyable. Throughout the next two years, the social-learning program continued to be considered the more enjoyable by the majority of staff expressing opinions, but not by the wide margins reflected in their beliefs about comparative effectiveness. Over the second through fourth anniversary assessments, in fact, fewer staff than at the first "six-month" assessment indicated the social-learning program was the more enjoyable (56%, 60%, and 54%, respectively, over assessments 2, 3, & 4). However, at the fifth anniversary assessment, over 79% of staff indicating preferences reported the social-learning program was the more enjoyable. The shift away from a preference for the milieu program coincided with the staff concern for potential problems in controlling assaultiveness as a result of the change in expulsion time that occurred just before the assessment. Their concern was also reflected in the nature and content of community meetings during the fifth anniversary assessment.

Average pattern differentiation scores on the TOS for all clinical staff working from the first through fifth anniversary assessments are presented in figure 21.2.[6] Scores are plotted for responses obtained under each of three instructional orientations by the same staff within each assessment: one set for each of the psychosocial programs—reflecting staff interpretations of the nature of programs (attitude scores) and relative use of techniques (technique scores) inferred from their training and experience—and, one set for their own personal beliefs or preferences as change agents. Original scores at the end of academic training are also plotted for comparative purposes.

The preferred attitude scores in figure 21.2 reveal a remarkable consistency of the staff groups over the next two years in their personal preferences about the nature of treatment. In fact, no significant overall change over time or differential change among scores was obtained at any point during the period for either continuing staff or all staff employed ($p$'s > 0.20).[7] The TOS attitude scores at the fifth anniversary assessment showed a significant reduction in level of all scores combined from the original (0) posttraining assessment ($p < 0.05$). However, this change was attributable to a significant reduction in A-5 ($p < 0.01$), while none of the remaining preferred attitude scores changed significantly ($p$'s > 0.20), even though staff employed at the fifth anniversary assessment included only 17% who had been employed at the original assessment. The overall differences among scores were maintained at every assessment over the entire two years ($p$'s < 0.01), with all differences between preferred attitude scores shown in figure 21.2 being significant, except for A-1 and A-4.

Comparisons of staff means of preferred attitude scores to the ideal responses for the nature of each psychosocial program (indicated in the left margin for each attitude score in figure 21.2) show that the pattern of the five staff scores remained significantly related to the milieu ideal over all assessments, without change over time ($r$'s from 0.91 to 0.97). Although differences were not significant ($p$'s > 0.10), the pattern was less related to the social-learning ideal at each assessment ($r$'s from 0.63 to 0.75), with the degree of relationship between staff means and the social-learning ideal failing to achieve significance on any assessment during the period. Similarly, the overall level of preferred attitude scores was closer to the milieu ideal ($D^2$'s ranging from 1.24 to 1.53) than to the social-learning ideal ($D^2$'s ranging from 2.61 to 3.19) at every assessment during the period ($p$'s=0.063). While none of the overall level differences from ideals of either program changed significantly during the next two years, the level of deviation from the social-learning ideal was significantly greater at the fifth anniversary assessment than at the original posttraining assessment ($p < 0.01$). Thus, the nature of treatment characteristics preferred by staff remained closer to the ideal milieu program, primarily as a function of preferences for therapeutic relationships that were at the midpoint of the "structured-unstructured," "nonpermissive-permissive" dimension (A-2).

An examination of the intercorrelations among TOS preferred attitude scores at the fifth anniversary assessment found only three significant intercorrelations, forming a three-score cluster, which only partially replicated the interrelationships found earlier. Specifically, A-3 and A-4 were positively related ($r=0.50$) and both were negatively related to A-5 ($r=-0.51$ & -0.38, respectively). Less predictability of TOS preferred attitude scores from individual staff characteristics was also obtained at the fifth anniversary assessment, with little replication of previous findings. Of the scores in the three-score cluster, A-5 was related to race and Extroversion ($r$'s in the ± 0.30s), reflecting a tendency for more introverted and black staff to endorse a need for some client discomfort

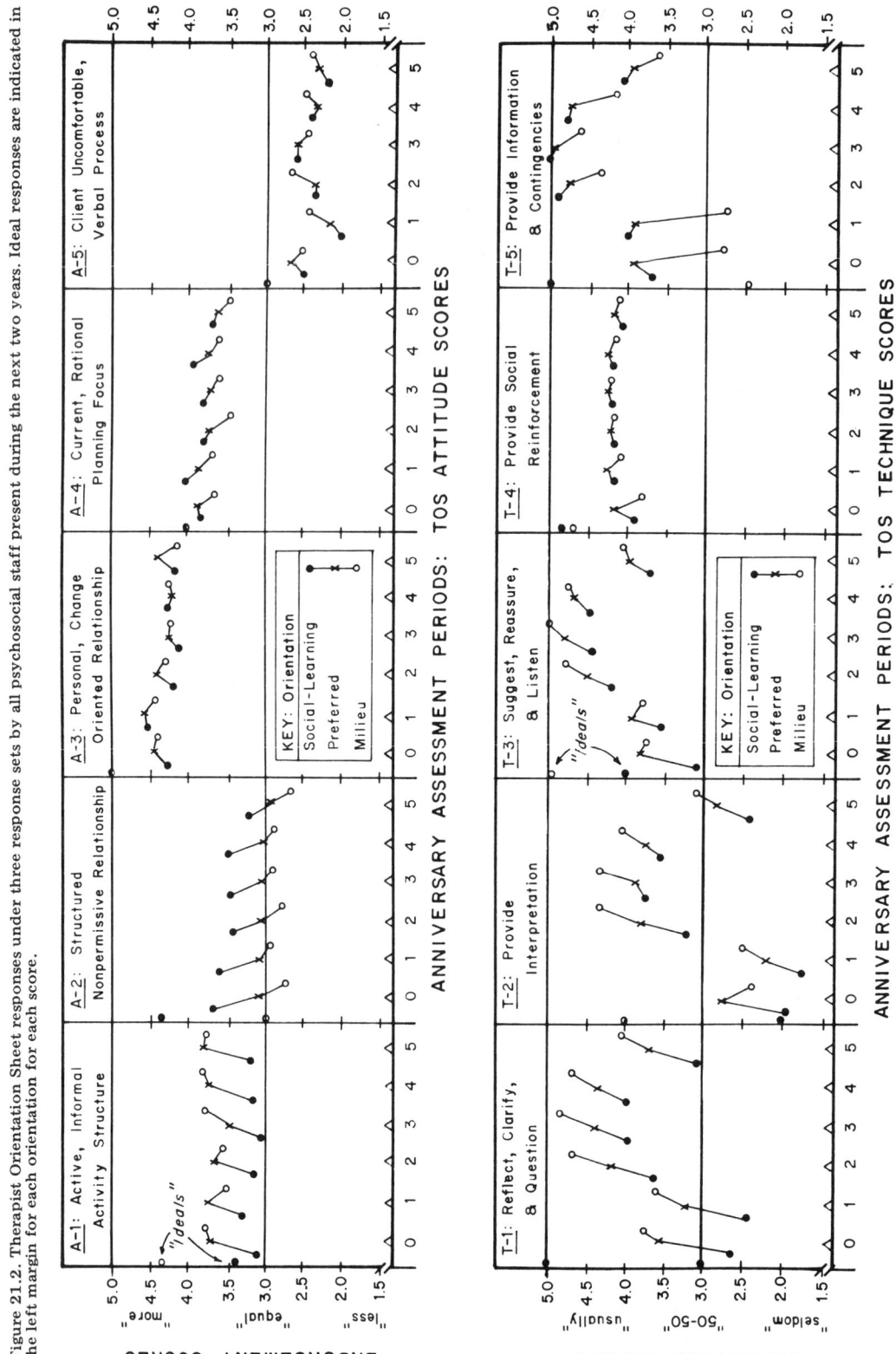

Figure 21.2. Therapist Orientation Sheet responses under three response sets by all psychosocial staff present during the next two years. Ideal responses are indicated in the left margin for each orientation for each score.

and verbal-conceptual learning at higher levels than more extroverted and white staff showed. A-3 and A-4 were both related to race and OMI-IV (r's in the -0.40s & -0.50s), reflecting a tendency for black staff and staff scoring higher on OMI Social Restrictiveness to prefer relatively less personal, change-oriented relationships with less focus on current, rational planning. The only other significant relationship between individual staff characteristics and preferred attitude scores was between A-2, education, and Extroversion (r's = ± 0.38), reflecting a tendency for staff who preferred relatively more structured, nonpermissive relationships to be less extroverted and more highly educated. Thus, at the end of the next two years, slightly different clustering occurred among TOS preferred attitude scores, and preferences for the nature of treatment were even less predictable from individual staff characteristics than before.

The attitude scores for each psychosocial orientation in figure 21.2 also reveals the essential parallelism of the staff groups over the next two years in their interpretation of the nature of each treatment program. Both continuing staff and total staff groups consistently produced different patterns of attitude scores in their interpretation of the nature of the milieu and social-learning programs at every assessment during the period ($p$'s < 0.01).[8] The only significant differential change occurring between orientations over successive anniversary assessments for attitude scores was between the third and fourth assessments for continuing staff ($p < 0.05$). There was a significant increase in the level of endorsement of scores in the social-learning orientation compared to an absence of change for the milieu orientation; however, the increase was largely a function of an increase in only A-4 for the social-learning orientation ($p < 0.05$), while the remaining four scores showed no significant change for either orientation ($p$'s > 0.10). The reduction in A-2 between the fourth and fifth anniversary assessments was significant over both orientations combined ($p < 0.05$). Although no differential change among the pattern of scores between orientations approached significance over any pair of successive anniversary assessments ($p$'s > 0.15), there was a significant differential change from the beginning (1) to the end (5) of the two-year period. Three of the TOS attitude scores in figure 21.2 (A-2, A-3, A-4) showed a significant decrease for both orientations combined ($p$'s < 0.05), while A-5 showed no significant change for either ($p > 0.20$). Only A-1 showed differential change between orientations from the beginning to the end of the next two years ($p < 0.05$), increasing for the milieu orientation and decreasing for the social-learning orientation.

By the end of the next two years, the only significant overall or differential change between orientations for any attitude score in figure 21.2 from the original posttraining assessment (0) was for A-2 ($p < 0.05$). The change reflects a reduction in the level of A-2 for both orientations but a significantly greater one for the social-learning than for the milieu orientation. However, even with the high turnover in the staff group, the pattern of differences within and between orientations remained constant in the staff interpretation of the nature of the treatment programs. Thus, at the fifth anniversary assessment, the same ordering of all TOS attitude scores in figure 21.2 within the social-learning orientation was maintained, with all differences between scores, except A-1 versus A-2, being significant. Within the milieu orientation, the same ordering was maintained, with all differences between scores being significant, except A-1 versus A-4 and A-2 versus A-5. At the fifth anniversary assessment, differences between orientations were not significant for A-3, A-4, and A-5 ($p$'s > 0.20), while social-learning scores were significantly lower than milieu scores on A-1 and significantly higher on A-2 ($p$'s < 0.01).

A comparison of the pattern of staff attitude scores under each psychosocial orientation to the ideal response for the nature of each program in figure 21.2 shows the directionality of these differences to be parallel to those desired, but with further deviations in the absolute level of endorsement. The extent to which staff interpretations of the nature of the milieu program maintained the same pattern as the ideal was apparent in the level of relationships over the five TOS attitude scores for the entire two-year period (r's from 0.95 to 0.99), without significant change at any assessment. Similarly, the extent to which staff interpretations of the nature of the social-learning program approached the ideal did not change significantly over the next two years (r's from 0.85 to 0.94), although the pattern at the fifth anniversary assessment was significantly less related to the social-learning ideal than that at the original posttraining assessment ($r = 0.96$ & $0.85$, respectively, for 0 & 5, $p < 0.05$). While the degree of relationship to the social-learning ideal was somewhat lower than that to the milieu ideal, the differences were not significant ($p$'s > 0.10), reflecting strong relationships within both orientations for the pattern of attitude scores.

Similarly the overall level of staff responses under the two orientations compared to their respective ideals did not differ significantly from one another at any time during the period ($p$'s > 0.10). The slight changes between the fourth and fifth anniversary assessments resulted in greater deviations from ideal levels of endorsement for both milieu ($D^2$'s=1.29 &

1.90, respectively, p < 0.01) and social-learning ($D^2$'s=1.54 & 2.70, respectively, p=0.063) orientations. However, even with the slight changes, the nature of the programs was interpreted differentially, with staff interpretations remaining quite close to the ideals underlying each program throughout the two-years.

The preferred technique scores in figure 21.2, in marked contrast to the consistency of attitude scores, show considerable change among treatment procedures that staff preferred to use over the next two years. Also of note is the extent to which the technique scores for both orientations also changed, parallel to changes in preferred technique scores. However, a detailed examination and analyses of these changes in preferred technique scores reveal that the only significant overall and differential changes occurred between the first and second anniversary assessments and between the fourth and fifth anniversary assessments (p's < 0.01)—each change in TOS technique scores following a major change in functioning of both resident groups: a decline over the first time and an increase over the second. No overall or differential change in preferred technique scores approached significance over the second, third, and fourth anniversary assessments (p's > 0.20), although significant differences between scores were maintained (p's < 0.01).

The nature of the changes in preferred technique scores from the first to the second anniversary assessment all involved increases in preferred utilization rates. The greatest increase occurred for T-2 (p < 0.01), reflecting a shift in preference for use of interpretation from "seldom" to "usually," while increases in T-1 and T-5 were also significant (p's < 0.05), and the increase in T-3 approached significance (p < 0.10). T-4 was the only preferred technique score failing to show an increase between the first and second anniversary assessments (p > 0.20). Although the changes resulted in higher reported preferences for utilization of most techniques, the resulting pattern during the middle of the period was not that different from that at the first anniversary assessment: T-3, T-4, and T-5 were still high and did not differ from one another, and T-2 was still lower than the remaining scores. The primary difference in relationships among preferred technique scores during the middle of the period was that T-1 had increased sufficiently so that it no longer differed significantly from T-3 and T-4.

The differential changes in preferred technique scores from the fourth to the fifth anniversary assessment involved significant decreases in all four scores that had increased earlier (p < 0.01), while T-4 again remained constant (p > 0.20). Even with the significant decreases during the last six months of the period, differential change among scores did occur from the beginning (1) to the end (5) of the next two years (p < 0.01), reflecting significant increases for both T-1 and T-2 (p < 0.05) and no significant change in T-3, T-4, and T-5 (F's < 1). While clearly several events had led to such changes in staff scores during the middle of the period, the overall effect of changes had essentially cancelled each other out by the fifth anniversary assessment, where neither overall nor differential change was apparent in the level or pattern of preferred technique scores from those existing at the original posttraining assessment (F's < 1). At the fifth anniversary assessment, T-2 was still the least-preferred technique, being significantly below all other scores; T-1 was significantly below T-4; and no other differences among preferred technique scores were significant.

The changes in preferred technique during the next two years resulted in a pattern of staff preferences that was more closely related to the social-learning ideal than to the milieu ideal, but with greater deviations from both ideal patterns during the middle of the period. At the beginning and the end of the current period, preferred technique scores were very close to the social-learning ideal (r's=0.94 & 0.91, respectively) and remained unrelated to the milieu ideal at both assessments (r's=0.02 & 0.05, respectively). During the middle of the period, the increases in preferred technique scores were such that no significant relationships existed to either ideal, becoming less closely related to the social-learning ideal (r's in the 0.70s), with nonsignificant negative relationships to the milieu ideal (r's in the -0.30s). Similarly the overall level of preferred technique scores deviated more from the milieu ideal than from the social-learning ideal at both the first anniversary assessment ($D^2$'s=9.60 & 1.66, respectively, p=0.063) and the fifth anniversary assessment ($D^2$'s=6.49 & 2.79, respectively, p=0.063), without significant change in either from the beginning to the end of the period. During the middle of the period, increases in preferred technique scores were such that deviations from ideals tended to balance one another so that no differences (p's > 0.10) were obtained between the deviations from milieu ideals ($D^2$'s=6.10, 6.47, & 5.84, respectively, for assessments 2, 3, & 4) or from social-learning ideals ($D^2$'s=5.45, 6.42, & 5.59, respectively for assessments 2, 3, & 4). As previously found following the introduction of the programs, the closer relationships of both pattern and level of preferred technique scores to the social-learning ideal at the beginning and end of the next two years paralleled the earlier findings about the greater proportion of staff reporting the social-learning program to be more enjoyable at the same assessments.

An examination of the intercorrelations

among TOS preferred technique scores at the fifth anniversary assessment found the same significant correlations that had been obtained at the first anniversary assessment, specifically, positive correlations between T-1 and both T-2 (r=0.58) and T-3 (r=0.60). Additionally, T-5 was positively correlated with both T-3 (r=0.63) and T-4 (r=0.37)—relationships that had occurred among preferred technique scores at the original posttraining assessment but that had dropped out at the end of the first six months. However, there was even less predictability of preferred technique scores from individual staff characteristics at the end of the next two years than at earlier assessments. T-1 was related only to age (r=-0.43) and Extroversion (r=0.39), reflecting a tendency for staff preferring relatively higher use of reflection, clarification, and questioning to be younger and more extroverted. T-2 was also related to Extroversion (r=0.37) and to OMI-III (r=-0.45), reflecting a tendency for staff preferring relatively greater use of interpretation to be more extroverted and to score relatively lower on Mental Hygiene Ideology. T-3, T-4, and T-5 were not related to any individual staff characteristics, and only T-5 was related to any other OMI score. This relationship reflected a tendency for staff preferring relatively greater use of advice and contingency management to score lower on OMI Social Restrictiveness (r=-0.49). Thus, while more clustering was apparent at the end of the period, preference for use of specific therapeutic techniques was almost totally unrelated to individual staff characteristics.

The technique scores for each psychosocial orientation in figure 21.2 show the major changes noted earlier in conjunction with preferred technique scores during the middle of the next two years. Both continuing staff and total staff groups consistently produced different patterns in their interpretations of the appropriateness of the relative use of different techniques between programs at every assessment over the two-year period (p's < 0.01). However, like preferred technique scores, differential changes among the level of scores within orientations were obtained between the first and second anniversary assessments and between the fourth and fifth ones (p's < 0.01), without significant overall or differential change over the second through fourth assessments.

The nature of all changes in technique scores from the first to the second anniversary assessment involved increases in utilization rates that staff interpreted as appropriate within each program. All technique scores, except T-4, showed significant increases for both orientations over those assessments, with only T-5 changing differentially between orientations—reflecting a greater increase for the milieu than for the social-learning orientation on T-5. The increases over the first six months of the period resulted in only one reversal in the relative pattern of technique scores within the social-learning orientation because of the increase in T-5, while T-4 remained constant. Following the second anniversary assessment increase, the pattern of scores within the social-learning orientation remained similar to the earlier pattern, with all differences among scores, except T-3 versus T-4, being significant. In contrast, the pattern of scores within the milieu orientation following the increase resulted in a total lack of discrimination, with none of the technique scores being significantly different from one another—as if the staff group interpreted appropriate technique utilization within the milieu program to be "everything at a high rate." However, the pattern of differentiation between orientations actually improved, with all technique scores at the second anniversary assessment being significantly different, except T-4. Thus, although staff lost differentiation in their interpretation of appropriate levels of utilization within the milieu program, they discriminated the relative levels of techniques between milieu and social-learning programs even better than before.

The differential changes in technique scores from the fourth to the fifth anniversary assessment encompassed significant decreases in all four scores that had increased earlier (p's < 0.01), without differential change between orientations except on T-1—reflecting a greater decrease for the social-learning orientation than for the milieu orientation on T-1. T-4, again, remained constant with neither change nor differences between orientations. Even with the significant decreases in scores within both orientations over the last six months, there was a significant differential change from the beginning to the end of the two-year period. Three of the TOS technique scores in figure 21.2 (T-1, T-2, T-3) showed a significant increase over the two years for both orientations (p's < 0.05), while T-4 showed no significant change for either (p > 0.20). Only T-5 showed differential change between orientations from the beginning to the end of the next two years (p < 0.01), increasing for the milieu but not for the social-learning orientation.

By the end of the next two years, the only technique score in figure 21.2 that had not shown overall or differential change within orientations from the original posttraining assessment was T-4 (F's < 1). All remaining technique scores showed increases in the interpretation of appropriate levels of utilization for both psychosocial programs (p's < 0.05), with only T-5 showing significant differential change between orientations—reflecting a significantly greater increase for the milieu orientation than for the social-learning orientation for T-5. The majority of these changes simply reflected movement over the two-year period, since few changes had occurred by the first anniversary assessment. At the end of the current period, technique scores within the milieu orientation were again differentiated by staff in a manner identical to the differentiation at the beginning of the period: T-1, T-3, and T-4 did not differ among themselves but were significantly higher than T-5, and T-2, once again, was significantly lower than all other scores. Within the social-learning orientation, T-3, T-4, and T-5 did not differ among themselves but were significantly higher than T-1, and T-2 remained significantly lower than all others. At the end of the period, staff continued their earlier differentiation between treatment programs with all technique score differences between milieu and social-learning orientations plotted in figure 21.2 being significant, except for T-4.

The differences between orientations for technique scores show relative staff interpretations in the direction of the ideal response for utilization of each group of techniques in figure 21.2. The extent to which the staff interpretations of the appropriate pattern of technique utilization approached the ideal for the social-learning program was apparent in significant relationships over the five TOS technique scores at the beginning and the end of the current period (r's > 0.99). Even with the increase in scores at the second anniversary assessment, the pattern of technique scores was still significantly related to the social-learning ideal (r=0.92); however, significant decreases in the degree of relationship were apparent at the third and fourth anniversary assessments (r's=0.80 & 0.87, respectively), followed by the significant increase, returning to earlier levels at the end of the current period. The pattern of endorsement of technique utilization had been less related to the milieu ideal (p < 0.10) even at the first anniversary assessment (r=0.73). The relationship of milieu technique scores to the milieu ideal became even lower during the middle of the next two years (r's=0.44, 0.27, & 0.56, respectively, for assessments 2, 3, & 4), and remained significantly lower at the fifth anniversary assessment (r=0.58, p < 0.05).

The overall level of staff technique responses under the two orientations compared to their respective ideals became closer, but not significantly, from the beginning to the end of the next two years for both social-learning ($D^2$'s= 1.96 & 1.79, respectively, for assessments 1 & 5) and milieu ($D^2$'s=5.88 & 4.20, respectively, for assessments 1 & 5). At the end of the period, the level of social-learning scores was closer to the ideal than it had been at the original posttraining assessment and closer than the level of milieu scores to the milieu ideal (p's=0.063). However, during the middle of the two-year period, the overall shift in the level of endorsement for technique scores resulted in nonsignificant increases in deviations from ideal levels for the social-learning orientation ($D^2$'s=2.47, 4.61, & 4.05, respectively, for assessments 2, 3, & 4). The middle-period deviations from the milieu ideal resulted in nonsignificant decreases from earlier assessments ($D^2$'s=3.97, 4.78, & 3.53, respectively, for assessments 2, 3, & 4), reflecting the too low levels of technique endorsement that had existed before. Thus, although staff interpretations of the appropriateness of the relative use of different techniques were differentiated in desired directions between programs throughout the next two years, the overall level of endorsement varied and the pattern became less related to the ideal for both programs during the middle of the period. However, the pattern of endorsement was closer to the ideal within the social-learning program throughout the entire two years, with both level and pattern of TOS technique scores becoming closer to the ideal within the social-learning program at the end of the period.

In summary, the attitudes and interpretations held by psychosocial staff regarding the treatment programs showed both complex changes and some remarkable consistencies over the next two years. Staff beliefs on the comparative effectiveness of the psychosocial programs accurately reflected the differential improvements that had occurred during the time preceding each judgment, with all staff expressing opinions favoring the social-learning program at the end of the current period. The social-learning program was also judged the more enjoyable by the majority of staff although the margin of preference became very slim during the middle three assessments. In general, it appeared that staff opinions and beliefs on the comparative effectiveness and enjoyability of the psychosocial programs were responsive to prior changes in resident behavior and other events but had no notable effect on the ensuing response of residents to the programs.

Preferred TOS attitude scores, reflecting staff preferences for the nature of the treatment programs, remained well differentiated and remarkably constant over the entire two-year period. The nature of treatment characteristics they preferred tended to be closer to the ideal milieu program than to the ideal social-learning program over the period, moving even further from the ideal social-learning program by the fifth anniversary assessment. At the end of the next two years, slightly different clustering occurred among TOS preferred attitude scores, and preferences for the nature of treatment were even less predictable from individual staff characteristics than before. While some differential changes occurred in the level of endorsement of TOS attitude scores for each program orientation from the beginning to the end of the current period, few changes occurred at points during the period, and only one score showed differential change from original posttraining to the fifth anniversary assessment. However, even with the high staff turnover and significant changes in some scores, the pattern of TOS attitude differences within and between orientations remained constant. The nature of the programs was interpreted differentially, with staff interpretations remaining quite close to the ideals underlying each program throughout the two-year period.

In marked contrast to the consistency of attitude scores, four of the five TOS technique scores under all response orientations showed increases over the first six months and decreases over the last six months of the current period. Only T-4 ("provide social reinforcement") remained constant under all assessment conditions. The changes in preferred TOS technique scores, reflecting staff preferences for the use of different treatment procedures, had essentially cancelled one another by the end of the period, to the extent that both level and pattern were functionally identical to those existing for the original staff group nearly two and a half years earlier. Also, in contrast to the closer approximation of staff preferences to the milieu ideal for the nature of treatment, preferred techniques were closely related to the social-learning ideal at the beginning and the end of the current period. However, during the middle of the period, when the endorsement of unusually high utilization rates occurred, preferred techniques were less related to the ideal pattern of both programs. By the fifth anniversary assessment, preferred technique scores again showed greater clustering in intercorrelations, but preference for the use of specific therapeutic techniques had become almost totally unrelated to individual staff characteristics.

Even with the large increases in endorsed utilization rates during the middle of the period, TOS technique scores—reflecting staff interpretations of the appropriateness of the relative use of different techniques—continued to differentiate between the milieu and social-learning programs in desired directions throughout the entire two years. While technique scores remained at significantly higher levels for both orientations during the middle of the period, scores within the social-learning orientation were still discriminated from one another. The increases within the milieu orientation were such that all techniques were interpreted as being appropriate at high utilization rates, with discrimination among technique scores returning only at the end of the period. Throughout the entire two years, the pattern of interpretation of appropriate techniques was closer to the ideal within the social-learning orientation than within the milieu orientation, but became further removed from the ideals of both programs during the middle of the period. Although changes were not significant, the overall level of TOS technique scores deviated less from the milieu ideal and more from the social-learning ideal during the middle of the period, reflecting changes from overall endorsement rates, which had been too low for the milieu orientation earlier. The decreases during the last six months, however, resulted in a closer approximation of technique scores to the ideal in both level and pattern within the social-learning program. Even with these decreases, the level of technique utilization endorsed by staff remained significantly above those at the beginning of the period for four of the five groups of techniques within the milieu orientation and for three of the five within the social-learning orientation.

All of the above changes, both in interpretation of appropriate levels of technique utilization within orientations and in preferred techniques, occurred at the same points in time, without changes in the nature of differentiation among the responses to the three different instructional orientations. The parallelism suggests that whatever happened between the first and second anniversary assessments to contribute to the increase in scores and whatever happened between the fourth and fifth anniversary assessments to contribute to the decrease influenced the staff group as a whole, without involving differential experiences within the two treatment programs. The composition of the staff group remained constant in all relatively stable personal-social characteristics over the entire period. In fact, the highest proportion of continuing staff between successive assessments of the current period occurred over the first and last six-month intervals (77%), while the middle period had fewer continuing staff at each assessment (56% at 3, 66% at 4). These data, combined with the fact that changes occurred for both continuing staff and total staff groups, argue against any subtle changes in the composition of treatment staff as the basis for TOS technique changes during the period.

Both assessment periods that showed changes in TOS technique scores were associated with major changes in overall resident functioning in both psychosocial programs in the six-month intervals preceding the TOS changes. During the first six months of the period, decreases in resident functioning occurred following the accidental death of a resident. An examination of notable events from the research log, the content of community meetings, and senior staff supervisory notes suggests a possible basis for the increases in TOS technique scores at the end of the first six months. Senior staff feedback on staff performance had already emphasized the need to increase the absolute level of interpretation, reflection, and clarification, and positive staff behavior, in general, in the milieu program, even before the resident's death. Following the death, positive programmatic procedures were given even more emphasis in both programs in an attempt to counter the grief, felt loss, and decline in functioning of residents. Concurrently, attempts were made to remove positive aspects of time out in the social-learning program to provide more effective negative consequences for inappropriate resident behavior. These programmatic changes occurred at the same time as increases in resident assaultiveness in the milieu program and the resulting concern with the protection of staff and other residents. Since these events naturally required increases in negative staff-resident interactions, the focus of in-service staff meetings and increased senior staff coverage of off-hours emphasized the need not only for increasing the control of inappropriate resident behavior but particularly focused on the need to emphasize genuine positive social interactions so that staff did not become aversive to residents. Thus, the focus on these characteristics of staff behavior within in-service training sessions, combined with increased senior staff coverage of off-hours, seems the probable basis for the increased endorsement of appropriateness and preference for higher levels of technique utilization at the second anniversary assessment.

During the last six months of the current period, major increases in resident functioning occurred in both groups. They were associated with the long-delayed availability of a number of materials and supplies, after improved procedures for controlling assaultive behavior and protecting staff and residents had been in effect. Weekend activity schedules were also changed during this period to ease the burden of junior staff by keeping off-unit activities scheduled at the same time for all residents within the programs. These events also resulted in greater senior staff coverage of off-hours to ensure appropriate implementation of the changed schedules and newly available consumables and grooming supplies. Thus, for the majority of the period, the focus of in-service training meetings, community meetings, and increased off-hour coverage by senior staff all shifted away from the earlier emphasis to appropriate means of implementing use of the material goods, consumables and supplies, and changed schedules. Of course, at the very end of the period, major discussions in all of the meetings focused upon the statewide policy directive that required a drastic reduction in length of time for time out and expulsion as a consequence for assaultive behavior. The discussions resulted in a review of procedures for all staff to ensure that other programmatic procedures for dealing with assaultiveness were clearly understood. Thus, the probable basis for endorsement of decreased levels of appropriateness and preferences for technique utilization and closer approximation to ideal levels of TOS technique scores at the fifth anniversary assessment appears to be the deemphasis of these characteristics within in-service training sessions and the renewed emphasis on overall coverage of appropriate programmatic procedures.

Staff opinions were responsive to the differential resident improvement during the next two years with regard to which program was the more effective and the more enjoyable, but interpretations of and preferences for the nature of treatment programs remained remarkably constant in their major characteristics. Staff interpretations of the appropriate levels of utilization of specific treatment techniques were responsive to the content emphasized during in-service training sessions, resulting in major level changes at the end of the first and last six-month intervals of the two-year period. However, staff interpretations of both nature and techniques were well differentiated in appropriate directions between psychosocial orientations over the entire two years, with staff preferences still remaining much closer to either psychosocial orientation than those of mental hospital staff.

## PERFORMANCE IN PSYCHOSOCIAL PROGRAMS

In view of the above changes in TOS technique scores, the objective data from the Staff-Resident Interaction Chronograph (SRIC) on the reliability and differentiation of the psychosocial programs as they actually operated become even more important.[9] How staff spent their time during the next two years is shown in figure 21.3, where total instances of activity and percentages of staff activity relative to the class of resident behavior in each program are plotted from the first through the fifth anniversary assessment.

In contrast to the stability of the rate of total staff activity up to the first anniversary assessment, staff dramatically increased their activity over the next two years. The greatest increase for both programs occurred over the first six months of the period, during the time

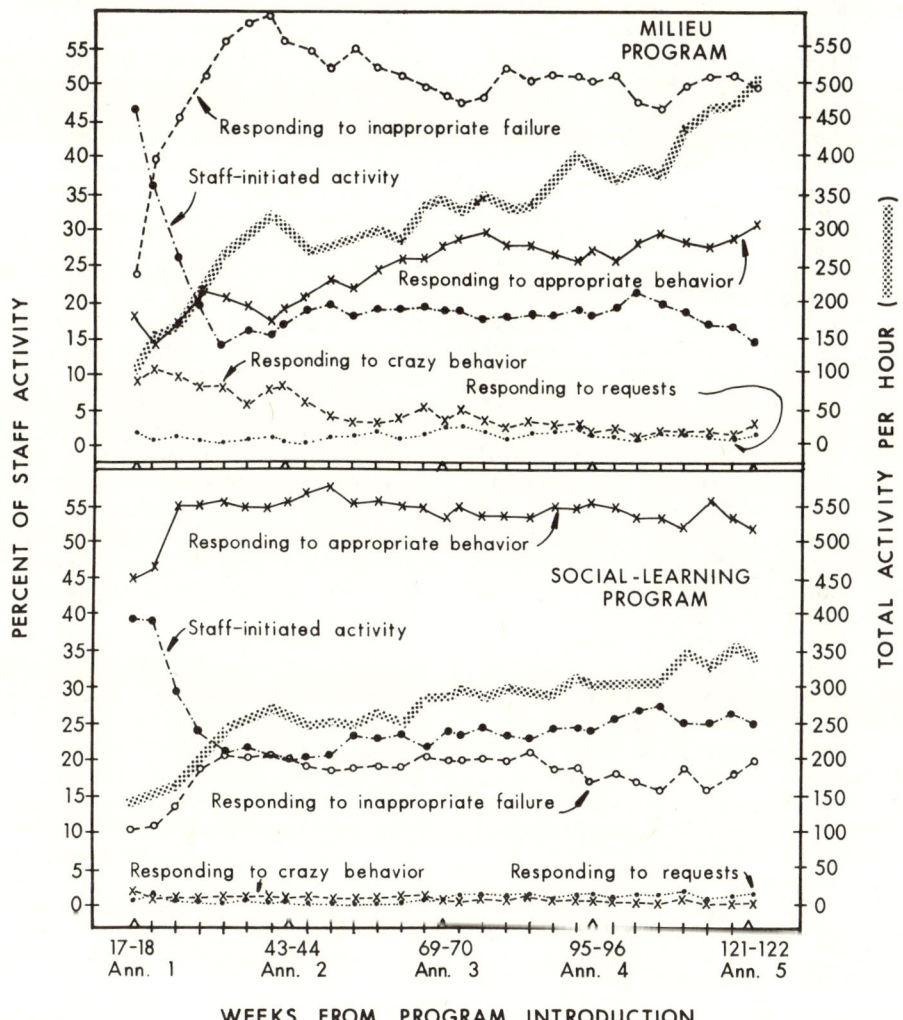

Figure 21.3. How staff spent their time during the next two years. Average total activity per hour is indicated by the shaded line and the scale in the right margin.

in which emphasis was upon counteracting the effects of the accidental death through tightening up on inappropriate behavior and increasing genuine positive social interactions. Total activity stabilized over the second six months when exceptionally long times for expulsion and time out were in effect. Gradual increases in total activity in both programs occurred again over the third six-month period, with the first notable increase in rate corresponding to the introduction of male student workers and transceivers to contact security officers for assistance with resident assaults. Another increase was notable just before the fourth anniversary assessment when the special sampling-exposure procedures for off-unit facilities and services were introduced. The major increase in staff activity over the last few months of the period corresponded to the change in weekend activity schedules and the introduction of the long-delayed material goods, consumables, and supplies. Common to all of these periods of increases in total staff activity were emphasis upon particular component procedures common to both psychosocial programs and an increased coverage of evening and weekend shifts by senior staff.

Although figure 21.3 shows parallel increases in total activity in both programs, the increase in the milieu program resulted in significantly higher levels of total activity than in the social-learning program over the entire two years ($p < 0.01$).[10] The average staff member had increased to the point of performing nearly 349 instances of activity per hour in the social-learning program during the fifth anniversary assessment—nearly two and a half times the level of activity performed before the current period. However, in the milieu program, the same staff had increased to the point of performing an average of over 508 instances of activity per hour—more than three and a half times the level performed earlier. Also, although the major increases in total staff activity in both programs corresponded to the time periods in which the resident groups showed both the greatest losses and greatest improvements in functioning, the relationship between resident functioning and total staff activity over the two years was significantly different between programs ($p < 0.05$)—showing a slight tendency for higher levels of staff activity to be associated with higher levels of resident functioning in the social-learning program ($r=0.35$) and with lower levels of resident functioning in the milieu program ($r=-0.41$).

An inspection of the focus of staff activities in figure 21.3 shows that the increases in total activity involved even greater differentiation between programs, in the same directions that had been established upon the original introduction of programmatic procedures. Figure 21.3 also shows that the major additional changes in focus of staff activity in both programs occurred over the first six months of the period, with relative stability thereafter. Thus, the increases in staff focus on appropriate components of resident behavior in the social-learning program increased to a stable rate of about 55% of all activity, while the focus upon resident failures increased to a stable rate of 25%. The only reduction in the proportion of staff focus in the social-learning program was in staff-initiated activity, which resulted in a stable level of 25% of staff activity not being in response to resident behavior over the last six months of the period. However, over the last eighteen months of the two-year period, only 15% of staff activity in the social-learning program did not involve interactions with residents, and irrelevant activity occurred at a rate too low even to appear in analyses (i.e., less than one occurrence every two weeks).

The changes in staff focus in the milieu program similarly led to further differentiation in the same direction that occurred after the initial introduction of the program, with the major change in focus involving the increased response to resident failures and the decreased focus on staff-initiated activity. The focus on resident failures in the milieu program stabilized at about 50% of all activity over the last half of the two-year period, remaining significantly above that of the social-learning program over the entire period ($p < 0.01$). The proportion of staff activities in response to crazy resident behavior gradually reduced to about 3% over the last half of the period, while responding to requests remained stable at just over 1% during the entire period. Although both of these areas of focus were low, they remained significantly above those of the social-learning program ($p < 0.01$). Focus on appropriate resident behavior in the milieu program gradually increased to a stable level of about 28% of staff activity over the last half of the period, but remained significantly below that of the social-learning program over the entire period ($p < 0.01$). Staff-initiated activities in the milieu program also remained below those for the social-learning program ($p < 0.05$) after the shift in focus during the first six months—varying between 15% and 20% over the remainder of the period. However, over the last eighteen months of the two-year period, only 10% of staff activity in the milieu program did not involve interactions with residents, and irrelevant activity occurred with an average incidence of less than two instances every hundred hours—too low to appear as a fraction of a percentage of total activity. Thus, staff increased their activity in both programs—more in the milieu than in the social-learning program, with additional changes in focus that further differentiated programs and increased the proportion of activities involving resident interaction.

The attention an individual resident received within both psychosocial programs dramatically increased over the next two years as a result of the increased activity of staff—even though the average number of residents for whom each staff member was responsible had increased from 17.3 to 18.5 in the milieu program and from 13.9 to 15.9 in the social-learning program from before the first anniversary assessment to the last six months of the next two years. The net effect of the change in focus and increased levels of staff activity over the next two years for the average individual resident is shown in table 21.1. The "average contacts per hour" columns show that the increased staff activity resulted in higher levels of resident contact immediately over the first six months of the period, without much change in the number of contacts through the end of the period. Compared to the average resident contacts during the first eighteen weeks of program operation (table 16.1), the first six months of the current period reflects a 52% increase for the average milieu resident and a 23% increase for the average social-learning resident.

Residents in both groups continued to receive the greatest proportion of contacts from staff as personalized, individual contacts. In fact, the "probability of contact" figures in table 21.1 show that each resident on the milieu unit during an average ten-minute period during waking hours was more likely to receive a personal, individualized contact from a staff member than not; the chances for such a contact in the social-learning program were about two out of three.

While the number of contacts a resident

Table 21.1. Amount of staff attention residents received during the next two years.

| Focus of attention resident received | Probability of contact in 10 min. | | | | Average contacts per hour | | | | Average interactions per contact | | | |
|---|---|---|---|---|---|---|---|---|---|---|---|---|
| | Milieu | | Social-learning | | Milieu | | Social-learning | | Milieu | | Social-learning | |
| | First 6 mos. | Last 6 mos. | First 6 mos. | Last 6 mos. | First 6 mos. | Last 6 mos. | First 6 mos. | Last 6 mos. | First 6 mos. | Last 6 mos. | First 6 mos. | Last 6 mos. |
| As individual | 0.562 | 0.570 | 0.681 | 0.658 | 3.37 | 3.42 | 4.08 | 3.95 | 3.19 | 4.71 | 2.92 | 4.01 |
| As part of group | .072 | .071 | .016 | .039 | .43 | .43 | .10 | .23 | .41 | .59 | .07 | .24 |
| Total | .634 | .641 | .697 | .697 | 3.80 | 3.85 | 4.18 | 4.18 | 3.60 | 5.30 | 2.99 | 4.25 |

received increased during the first six months of the period and remained relatively stable thereafter, table 21.1 reveals that the average interactions within contacts increased over the period. Thus, the number of contacts increased immediately, and the continued increase in staff activity resulted in the amount of interaction within each contact—instances of discrete verbal content or other staff behavior directed to the resident—continuing to increase over the two-year period for residents in both programs. The net effect on the total amount of attention received from staff (contacts x interactions) by the last six months of the period was a 300% increase for milieu residents and a 126% increase for social-learning residents compared to the eighteen weeks immediately following the introduction of programmatic procedures. These changes reversed the earlier advantage of the social-learning group; the average milieu resident at the end of the next two years was receiving about 14% more staff attention than the average social-learning resident was.

The nature of changes in staff behavior over the next two years is shown in figure 21.4, where the highest-frequency behaviors for both programs are plotted from the first through the fifth anniversary assessment.[11] Figure 21.4 reveals that the increases in staff-resident interaction over the next two years did not occur equally in all classes of staff behavior. The most dramatic changes within both programs involved increases in Positive Nonverbals, which directly paralleled the overall increases in staff activity, with the incidence of positively intonated utterances, smiles, etc., being higher in the social-learning program over the first eight months and higher in the milieu program over the remainder of the period. Positive Verbals also showed major increases over the first six months of the period in both programs, with further increases during the last few months, although total instances remained significantly higher in the social-learning program over the entire two years. Changes in Positive Nonsocials in the social-learning program directly paralleled changes in Positive Verbals, while remaining essentially absent in the milieu program. A similar parallelism is evident in the milieu program for Negative Verbals, which changed in parallel to Positive Verbals, while remaining at a constant, near-absent incidence rate in the social-learning program.

Of the staff behavior plotted in the top section of figure 21.4, only Negative Nonverbals deviated from the overall pattern of increased incidence of programmatic interactions during the first and last six months of the period. Although the incidence of Negative Nonverbals remained significantly higher in the milieu program than in the social-learning program, a major increase in the milieu program occurred over the first four months of the period, followed by a decrease to low absolute levels. The decrease corresponded to the release and replacement of residents and heavier senior staff coverage of evenings and weekends concurrent with the increased assaultiveness in the milieu program and attempts to remove positive aspects of time out in the social-learning program. The low absolute levels of Negative Nonverbals in the milieu program during the second six months corresponded to the period in which extended expulsion time was in effect.

The high-frequency behaviors plotted in the middle section of figure 21.4 show the greatest changes for Positive Statements and Positive Group References in the milieu program. Both classes of behavior showed major increases over the first six months in the milieu program, followed by a decrease upon the introduction of the extended expulsion time for assaultive behavior, with stability until the increased incidence during the last few months. These milieu-specific procedures remained at a stable, near-absent level within the social-learning program. Negative Group References in the milieu program showed a similar pattern, but at lower absolute levels of occurrence and with less marked changes. In contrast, Positive Prompts and Negative Prompts show a parallel pattern in the social-learning program, while remaining nearly absent in the milieu program.

Of the high-frequency staff behaviors plotted in the bottom section of figure 21.4, only Reflect/Clarify in the milieu program followed the pattern of major increases over the first six months and slight increases during the last few months. Reflect/Clarify in the social-learning program showed a gradual increase over the entire period, remaining significantly below the level in the milieu program throughout. Instruct/Demonstrate similarly showed a gradual and slight increase in incidence over the entire two years in both programs, without significant differences between them. Doing With also showed slight, gradual increases over the period for both programs, but the absolute incidence remained significantly higher in the social-learning program throughout.

These changes in specific classes of staff behavior directly paralleled the periods of change in TOS technique scores. The major increases in frequency of actual staff-resident interaction occurred over the first six months of the period. Additionally the major classes of behavior that staff actually increased reflected those areas of emphasis on positive programmatic procedures and genuine metacommunications in staff-resident interaction that had been the focus of the daily in-service

Staff Attitudes and Performance 231

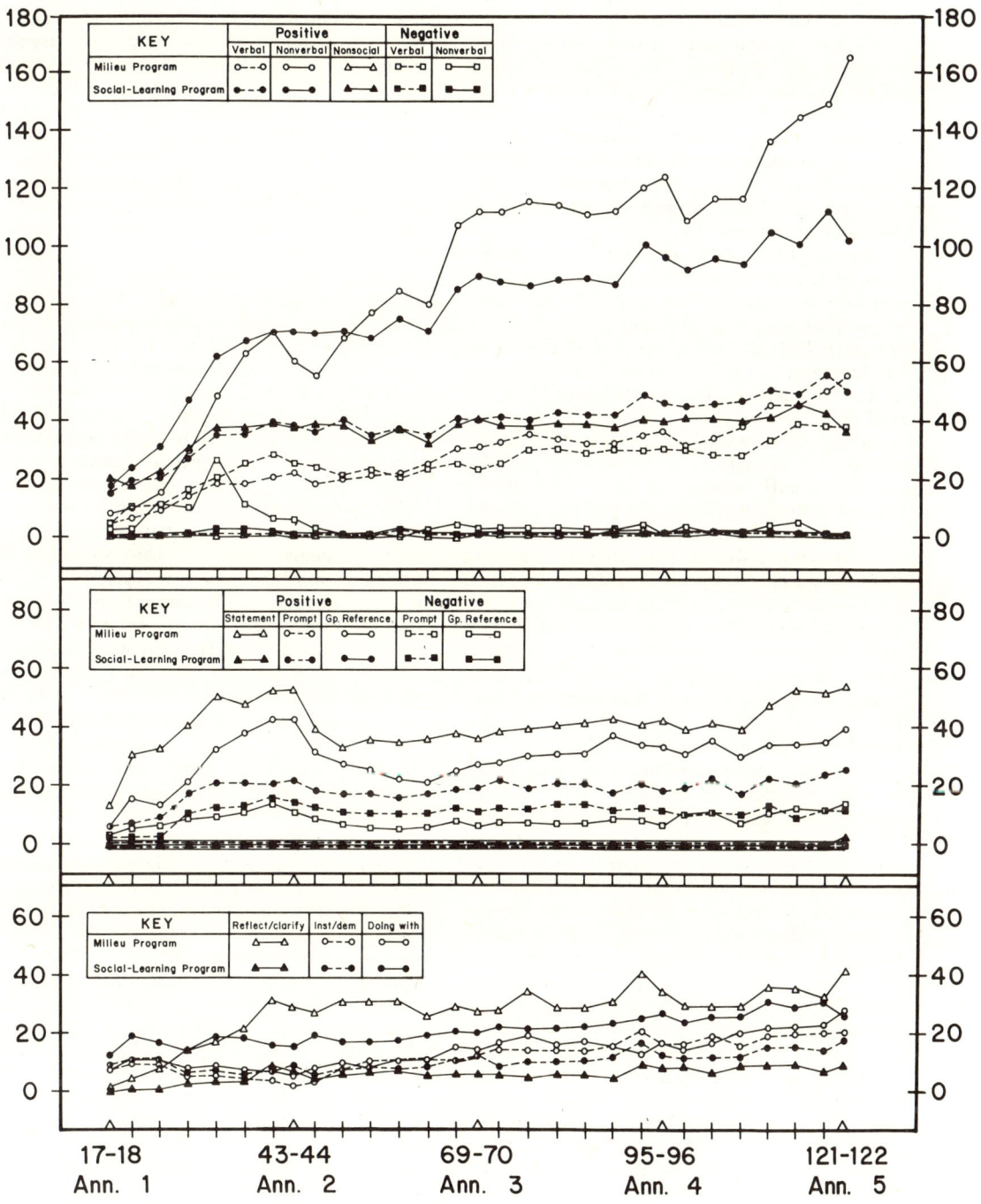

Figure 21.4. Average hourly instances of the highest-frequency staff interactions during the next two years.

WEEKS FROM PROGRAM INTRODUCTION

training sessions and senior staff feedback to junior staff. Similarly the increases during the last few months of the period continued to reflect increases in program-specific staff behavior and positive interactions associated with the introduction of the long-delayed materials and supplies. The major difference between actual changes in staff behavior and the changes in interpretations reported on TOS technique scores is that the actual staff performance of program-specific behaviors increased during the last six months, while the endorsed level of technique utilization on the TOS decreased at the same time.

How well staff differentiated their performance of the psychosocial programs during the period is indicated by the average hourly rates of staff activity over the next two years, presented in table 21.2.[12] Even with the differential increases in staff behavior shown in figure 21.4, the nature of the differentiation of staff performance within and between programs remained relatively constant over the entire period. The average total incidence of specific classes of staff behavior in table 21.2 shows that all of the changes in staff activity over the next two years resulted in higher frequencies of programmatic staff behavior, with even greater differentiation between programs. In fact, differences in average hourly rate between programs were significant over the entire two years for seventeen of the twenty-one classes of staff behavior. Negative Statements were totally inappropriate for staff in both programs, and did not differ—occurring at most on two occasions every hundred hours. Doing For was differentially allowable but did not differ between programs, remaining at a low rate of less than one instance per hour over the entire two years. Instruct/Demonstrate was differentially allowable between programs but did not differ. As a percentage of total interactions, Instruct/Demonstrate was lower than at the earlier period, although the total instances remained relatively constant—still reflecting too great a use of instructions in the milieu program—again accounting for the great majority of errors that occurred in the milieu program. Parallel differences were obtained between programs on an evaluation of the relative percentage of interactions accounted for by each class of staff behavior. Only Positive Nonverbals yielded different results; as shown earlier (figure 21.4), the marked increase in total incidence of Positive Nonverbals had resulted in higher levels in the milieu program over about the last three-quarters of the current period. However, the relative percentage of total interactions accounted for by Positive Nonverbals increased equally between programs, so no differences were apparent over the two years.

Three classes of staff behavior that had failed to show differences during the first eighteen weeks following program introduction did occur at significantly different rates over the next two years, even though differentiation was not required by the respective program manuals. Physical Force was used at an exceptionally low rate in both programs but was consistently more frequent in the social-learning program, reflecting an increase in physical contact required for the application of time out after the positive aspects of it were removed. However, even in the most frequent use, Physical Force required less than 0.1% of all staff-resident interactions—occurring at a maximum rate of only twenty instances every hundred hours. Announce and Attend/Record/Observe were totally appropriate in both programs but differed in rate over the next two years. Announce increased in the milieu program to a level significantly above that of the social-learning program, reflecting more of a tendency for staff to make separate and sequential announcements for separate living groups over the current period. In contrast, staff decreased the instances of Attend/Record/Observe in the milieu program to a level significantly below that of the social-learning program over the next two years, reflecting the higher rates of interaction that left little time for instances of observation without interacting in the milieu program.

All remaining differences in staff performance between programs during the next two years largely followed the differential requirements specified in the respective treatment manuals. Six of the eight classes of staff behavior that were performed at significantly higher rates in the milieu program were those that were differentially specified in the Milieu Manual and previously differentiated immediately upon the introduction of the programs. The six classes included milieu procedures that were to be applied at all times across all classes of resident behavior (Positive Statement, Positive Group Reference, Reflect/Clarify, Suggest Alternatives) and procedures that specified the nature of content for responding to inappropriate resident behavior (Negative Verbal and Negative Group Reference). While Positive Verbals were still performed at a lower rate in the milieu program than in the social-learning program, the increase in the milieu program for Positive Verbals and for Positive Nonverbals—the latter to a level above that for the social-learning program—followed requirements of the Milieu Manual and reflected the more positive nature of the entire program by the end of the period. When all of the above behaviors are taken into account, table 21.2 shows that nearly 88% of all staff-resident interactions in the milieu program over the

Table 21.2. Average hourly rate of staff activity on psychosocial units during the next two years.

| | Resident behavior to which staff responded | | | | | | | | | | | | Total staff behavior | | % of interactions | | % of all staff error | |
|---|---|---|---|---|---|---|---|---|---|---|---|---|---|---|---|---|---|---|
| | Appropriate | | Inappropriate Failure | | Inappropriate Crazy | | Request | | Neutral | | | | | | | | | |
| Staff behavior | Milieu | S.Lrng | Milieu | S.Lrng | Milieu | S.Lrng | Milieu | S.Lrng | Milieu | S.Lrng | | | Milieu | S.Lrng | Milieu | S.Lrng | Milieu | S.Lrng |
| Positive Verbal | 28.73+ | 40.71+ | 0.03- | | 0.02- | | | 0.01° | 0.01° | | | ° | 28.78 | 40.72 | 9.8% | 17.3% | 0.4% | 0.6% |
| Negative Verbal | 0.12- | 0.01- | 21.86+ | 0.73° | 4.66+ | 0.03° | 0.01- | | | | | - | 26.65 | 0.77 | 9.1% | 0.3% | 1.2% | 2.2% |
| Positive Nonverbal | 37.01+ | 54.32+ | 41.85° | 14.35° | 2.92° | 0.04- | 1.63° | 0.51° | 8.77° | 10.66° | | | 92.17 | 79.88 | 31.4% | 34.0% | 1.6% | 5.2% |
| Negative Nonverbal | 0.15- | 0.07- | 3.74° | 0.32° | 1.44° | 0.02° | 0.01° | | 0.03- | 0.06- | | | 5.36 | 0.48 | 1.8% | 0.2% | 0.8% | 15.6% |
| Positive Nonsocial | 0.09+ | 37.38+ | | 0.03- | | | 1.38° | 0.01° | 0.01° | 0.03° | | | 1.48 | 37.45 | 0.5% | 15.9% | | 3.8% |
| Negative Nonsocial | | 0.09- | 0.21- | 1.40+ | 0.08° | 0.03+ | 0.03- | | | - | | | 0.32 | 1.53 | 0.1% | 0.7% | 2.1% | 11.3% |
| Positive Statement | 0.86+ | 0.03° | 38.39+ | 0.19- | 1.43+ | | 0.02+ | ° | 0.80+ | 0.27° | | | 41.49 | 0.49 | 14.1% | 0.2% | | 21.6% |
| Negative Statement | - | 0.02- | - | | - | | - | | - | | | | | 0.02 | | | | 2.6% |
| Positive Prompt | 0.02+ | 5.29+ | 0.01- | 12.97+ | | 0.01+ | - | 0.01+ | - | 0.91+ | | | 0.03 | 19.18 | | 8.2% | 0.2% | 8.0% |
| Negative Prompt | - | 0.02- | 0.03- | 11.68+ | | 0.03+ | - | ° | - | 0.05- | | | 0.04 | 11.78 | | | 0.3% | |
| Positive Gp. Reference | 4.23+ | ° | 22.26+ | 0.03- | 0.54+ | - | 0.03+ | - | 3.17+ | 0.21° | | | 30.22 | 0.24 | 10.3% | 5.0% | | 8.0% |
| Negative Gp. Reference | 0.01- | - | 7.89+ | 0.01° | 1.19+ | ° | + | ° | 0.01° | - | | | 9.09 | 0.01 | 3.1% | 0.1% | 0.1% | 3.8% |
| Reflect/Clarify | 2.49+ | 1.84+ | 20.50+ | 2.52+ | 1.36+ | 0.01° | 0.18+ | 0.09° | 2.60+ | 1.35° | | | 27.13 | 5.81 | 9.2% | 2.5% | | |
| Suggest Alternatives | 0.13+ | 0.24° | 1.84- | 0.25° | 0.04° | - | 0.01+ | ° | 0.32+ | 0.02° | | | 2.34 | 0.50 | 0.8% | 0.2% | | |
| Instruct/Demonstrate | 0.76° | 1.07+ | 9.51+ | 6.95° | 0.12° | 0.03° | 0.06° | 0.05° | 2.15° | 2.68° | | | 12.60 | 10.78 | 4.3% | 4.6% | 83.5% | |
| Doing With | 8.81+ | 13.69+ | 0.01- | 0.02° | 0.01- | - | 0.17° | 0.17° | 5.35+ | 7.84+ | | | 14.35 | 21.71 | 4.9% | 9.2% | 0.2% | 2.3% |
| Doing For | 0.52- | 0.25° | 0.05- | 0.10- | - | - | 0.28° | 0.35° | 0.08- | 0.10° | | | 0.92 | 0.80 | 0.3% | 0.3% | 5.7% | 12.4% |
| Physical Force | - | - | 0.06° | 0.19- | 0.02° | 0.01° | 0.06- | - | - | - | | | 0.13 | 0.20 | | 0.1% | 0.5% | |
| Ignore/No Response | 0.13- | 0.06- | 0.19- | 1.62+ | 0.04- | 0.76+ | - | - | 0.04- | 0.03- | | | 0.40 | 2.47 | 0.1%[a] | 1.1%[a] | 3.5% | 10.7% |
| Announce | b | b | b | b | b | b | b | b | 2.98+ | 1.87+ | | | 2.98 | 1.87 | (0.9%) | (0.7%) | b | b |
| Attend/Record/Observe | b | b | b | b | b | b | b | b | 33.76 | 42.83+ | | | 33.76 | 42.83 | (10.2%) | (15.3%) | b | b |
| Total interactions | 84.05 | 155.09 | 168.42 | 53.37 | 13.86 | 0.98 | 3.85 | 1.19 | 23.30 | 24.18 | | | 293.46 | 234.80 | 100%[a] | 100%[a] | 3.9% | 0.4% |
| % correct interactions | 98.8% | 99.8% | 94.0% | 99.3% | 99.5% | 94.9% | 97.6% | 99.7% | 99.3%[a] | 99.4%[a] | | | 96.1% | 99.6% | b | b | 0.0% | 0.0% |
| Total activity | b | b | b | b | b | b | b | b | 60.08 | 68.91 | | | 330.24 | 279.53 | (113%) | (119%) | b | b |

Note. + = specifically programmed staff behavior; o = allowable staff choice; - = programmatic error. Empty cells signify less than 0.0045 instances per hour.
a. "Ignore-neutral" included in percentage figures, but not in total interactions.
b. Irrelevant cells.

next two years used procedures detailed for milieu therapy.

Negative Nonverbals continued to be performed at a significantly higher rate in the milieu program than in the social-learning program over the next two years, even though no differential requirements were specified. Analyses of SRIC sequences found even greater evidence that negative affect for staff was likely to have been generated and communicated in the milieu program than that apparent before the current period. Over the next two years, staff averaged over fifty instances of positive statements and negative feedback per hour in response to inappropriate resident behavior in the milieu program, but the procedures were effective in terminating inappropriate behavior only 68% of the time. On the average, the same resident inappropriate behavior continued to occur on 16.13 occasions per hour after having received positive statements and negative feedback, and staff appropriately continued to provide additional positive statements and negative feedback on 16.05 occasions. Thus, staff were quite reliable in staying with continued programmatic interactions for inappropriate resident behavior, but the latter rates of interaction clearly seem to have resulted in genuine communication of higher levels of negative affect experienced by staff. The highest rates of such continuing focus on inappropriate resident behavior also corresponded to the increase in Negative Nonverbals during the first six months of the period (figure 21.4). In fact, with such high-intensity focus on continuing inappropriate behavior, it is surprising that such negative affects accounted for only 1.8% of staff-resident interactions in the milieu program.

As during the first eighteen weeks of program operation, the three classes of staff behavior that accounted for the highest proportion of interactions in the social-learning program over the next two years consisted of positive social and nonsocial behaviors (Positive Verbal, Positive Nonverbal, Positive Nonsocial) while the fourth highest rate consisted of shared social activity (Doing With) (see table 21.2). Although all of these classes of behavior except Positive Nonverbals were performed at a significantly higher rate in the social-learning program than in the milieu program, differences were apparent for Positive Nonverbals as well. Only 40% of Positive Nonverbals in the milieu program were contingent on appropriate resident behavior, while 68% were contingent upon appropriate behavior in the social-learning program. Similarly 63% of Doing With was contingent upon appropriate resident behavior rather than being staff-initiated in the social-learning program. Thus, on an absolute level, the within-cell distribution of these behaviors in table 21.2 shows that over 62% of all staff-resident interactions in the social-learning program over the next two years was accounted for by positive social and material reinforcement contingent upon appropriate resident behavior.

The four remaining classes of staff behavior that were performed at significantly higher rates in the social-learning program than in the milieu program over the next two years were differentially specified by the respective manuals for dealing with inappropriate resident behavior and/or initiating new or different resident behaviors (Negative Nonsocial, Positive Prompt, Negative Prompt, Ignore/No Response). The absolute level of Negative Nonsocial and Ignore/No Response was notable in the low frequency with which these staff behaviors occurred, even when they were programmatically appropriate. Analyses of SRIC sequences on instances in which active ignoring was a required staff response also found that a basis for low rates of Ignore/No Response was in the success of prompts in changing resident behavior. Specifically staff averaged over twenty-four prompts per hour for inappropriate resident behavior over the next two years, and the prompts were effective in changing behavior more than 98% of the time. A prompted inappropriate behavior continued, on the average, on only forty-six occasions every hundred hours, and staff properly ignored that behavior on forty-three of those occasions. Thus, staff were quite reliable in application of active ignoring when it was required, but the success of other procedures continued to result in a restricted number of instances in which Ignore/No Response was the only appropriate staff behavior.

These differences between programs document that staff performance over the next two years clearly differentiated between programs on the basis of requirements specified in the respective treatment manuals. Table 21.2 also shows that the within-program accuracy in staff performance continued to improve over the exceptional levels that had been in evidence during the first eighteen weeks. Over 96% of staff-resident interactions in the milieu program followed specified procedures, with the increased accuracy beginning immediately after the beginning of the period (corresponding to the intensive emphasis on increasing utilization of specific milieu techniques). The accuracy of execution of social-learning procedures during the next two years was remarkable, with 99.6% of all staff-resident interactions following specified procedures.

The distribution of staff errors in table 21.2 reveals that the majority in the social-learning program were spread over inappropriate Positive Statements, Negative Nonverbals, and Doing

For. However, the exceptionally low total instances of errors in the social-learning program—averaging only eighty-seven instances of error in every hundred hours of working time—were such that the highest-rate error occurred only nineteen times in a hundred hours of staff activity. Only 29.9% of social-learning errors consisted of misapplication of milieu therapy procedures; the majority were Positive Statements for resident failures. Only 5.7% of the social-learning errors consisted of activities that were inappropriate at any time, while the remainder (64.4%) consisted of a misapplication of social-learning procedures; however, even these occurred at a remarkably low rate of 0.2% of all staff-resident interactions. Although the error rate in the milieu program improved considerably from that at the earlier period, milieu errors still occurred at a higher rate than social-learning errors did, with 3.9% of all interactions (11.40 instances per hour) being incorrect by milieu standards. As before, the majority of milieu errors (95.3%) consisted of the misapplication of social-learning procedures in the milieu program, while only 0.4% and 4.3% of milieu errors, respectively, consisted of activities that were inappropriate at any time and misapplication of milieu procedures. The majority of milieu errors still continued to consist of inappropriate Instruct/Demonstrate for resident failures (table 21.2).

Actual staff performance, thus, continued to be well differentiated between programs over the next two years, with the absolute accuracy of performance even improving over the exceptional levels achieved earlier. The accuracy of application of programmatic procedures still continued to be better in the social-learning program than in the milieu program, with the distribution of relative proportions of staff-resident interactions clearly following the specified procedures from the social-learning manual and reflecting the ideal distribution of technique utilization from the TOS (figure 21.2). Although the actual staff performance in the milieu program was well differentiated in appropriate classes of behavior from that in the social-learning program and was accurate on an absolute level, Instruct/Demonstrate still occurred at a level higher than desired, reflecting the only notable spillover of procedures from one program to the other.

The increased emphasis on genuine positive social interactions during the first six months of the period resulted in large differential increases in all milieu-specific behaviors except Suggest Alternatives. Although this class of behavior increased within the milieu program and remained higher than performance within the social-learning program, it still remained below desired levels specified for the ideal distribution of techniques in the milieu therapy manual and on the TOS (figure 21.2). The distribution of techniques staff utilized maintained a better differentiation within programs, as well as between programs, than the middle-of-the-period TOS technique interpretations would have suggested. In fact, the actual staff performance during the next two years—especially after the introduction of improved methods for handling assaultive behavior—was about as close to being perfect in both programs as anyone could desire.

The majority of changes in staff behavior over the next two years consisted of increases in appropriate programmatic interactions during periods in which the resident groups showed both overall decreases and increases in functioning. Therefore, within-program correlations between the average instances of each class of staff behavior and unitwide levels of resident functioning over standard time blocks of the present period yielded few relationships. The stable differentiation between programs and comparative effectiveness was apparent in parallel correlations over programs, which found every class of staff behavior that differed between programs also to yield significant correlations with changes in resident functioning. The latter correlations simply reflected higher levels of resident functioning to covary with all staff behaviors that occurred at higher rates in the social-learning program (mdn. r= 0.84, range 0.40 to 0.89) and to be related negatively to all staff behaviors that occurred at high rates in the milieu program (mdn. r= -0.85, range -0.43 to -0.90).

In summary, the objective data from the SRIC show considerable changes in actual staff behavior over the next two years. In contrast to the stability of total staff activity immediately after the programs began, staff increased their total activity level over the current period to over two and a half times the initial rate in the social-learning program and over three and a half times in the milieu program. The increases were most dramatic over the first six months of the period when the emphasis was upon counteracting the effects of the accidental death of a resident by being stricter about inappropriate behavior and increasing genuine positive social interactions. The second major increase occurred during the last few months of the next two years, concurrent with the introduction of materials, commodities, and a changed weekend activity schedule—all of which entailed greater senior staff coverage of evening and weekend shifts. Concurrent with the increase in staff activity during the first six months of the period were additional changes in focus that further differentiated programs in the directions established over the first eighteen weeks, with relative stability over the last three-quarters of the period. The changes in focus and increased activities resulted in major increases in the proportion of staff activities involving staff-resident interactions in both programs, with proportionally less staff activities devoted to announcements, relevant paperwork, and observing residents without interacting.

The additional increases in staff activity and shifts in focus resulted in residents in both programs receiving more individual, personalized contacts within the first six months of the period, with further increases in the amount of interactions within contacts over the remainder of the next two years. By the last six months of the period, the total staff attention received by an individual social-learning resident had increased 126%, and the total attention received by an individual milieu resident had increased 300% from the levels over the first eighteen weeks after program introduction. Thus, at the end of the period, the average milieu resident was receiving more staff attention than the average social-learning resident was—even though the social-learning program was clearly more effective.

The increases in staff activity reflected areas of emphasis on positive programmatic procedures and genuine metacommunications in staff-resident interactions that had been the focus of in-service training. The increases in actual staff behavior over the first six months in both programs directly paralleled the changes in TOS technique scores. The changes in staff activity toward the end of the period showed additional increases in the level of program-specific staff behavior, and the TOS technique scores showed decreased levels of endorsement at the same time but increased differentiation within programs. Thus, actual performance of staff differentiated between programs better than their self-recorded endorsement on the TOS on the absolute levels of technique utilization.

The differentiation of staff performance in the psychosocial programs over the next two years was remarkable. All of the changes in staff behavior resulted in higher frequencies of programmatic interaction, with even greater differentiation between programs. Both the focus of staff activity and the rate of performance of specific classes of staff behavior were in keeping with the differential requirements specified in the respective treatment manuals, with accuracy improving even over the exceptional levels achieved earlier.

Staff performed all milieu-specific interactions in the milieu program at a significantly higher rate than they did when working in the social-learning program, with 96.1% of all staff-resident interactions being appropriate on an absolute level. The distribution of relative proportions of staff-resident interactions in the milieu program more closely approached the ideal distributions specified in the Milieu Manual and on the TOS as a result of the differentiated increases in milieu-specific behaviors. Only two classes of staff behavior deviated significantly from milieu ideals, involving utilization of suggesting alternatives at a level lower than desired and providing specific instruction at a level higher than desired. The high level of instruction was primarily responsible for the majority of staff errors within the milieu program that consisted of an inappropriate spillover of techniques from the social-learning program.

When working in the social-learning program, staff not only performed social-learning procedures at a significantly higher rate than they did when working in the milieu program, but 99.6% of all staff-resident interactions in the program were appropriate on an absolute level. Additionally the distribution of relative proportions of staff-resident interactions in the social-learning program clearly followed those specified in the treatment manual and the ideal distribution of technique utilization from the TOS, with errors being nearly nonexistent. Thus, while staff continued to do a better job of reproducing all aspects of the ideal social-learning program, the improvement of performance in the milieu program resulted in absolute levels of accuracy, with clear and reliable differentiation between programs, that even exceeded the exceptional levels obtained earlier.

## SUMMARY

Staff attitudes, opinions, and beliefs about mental patients remained remarkably consistent over the entire period of the next two years. The only changes at all occurred during the first six months, with changes in two OMI scores moving the pattern and level even closer to the ideals underlying the psychosocial programs. By the end of the next two years, OMI scores were even less clustered and less predictable from individual staff characteristics than before. Even with the high staff turnover during the current period, the attitudes to which residents were exposed did not vary appreciably and had no differential effect on resident behavior. The few changes there were appeared to reflect staff responses to the differential change in resident behavior over the first six months of the period. However, the staff group as a whole remained consistent in reflecting the ideal assumptions underlying the psychosocial programs, with continued differences from typical mental hospital staff.

Opinions and interpretations of the psychosocial programs showed both complex changes and remarkable consistencies over the next two years. Staff beliefs on the comparative effectiveness of the programs reflected the relative improvements between programs that occurred during the six-month intervals preceding each judgment. By the end of the period all staff expressing opinions accurately believed that the social-learning program was more effective. The majority also reported that the social-learning program was the more enjoyable; however, the margin of preference became very slim at the end of the first six months, returning to a strong majority only at the fifth anniversary assessment. In general, staff opinions and beliefs on the comparative effectiveness and enjoyability of the psychosocial programs over the next two years reflected changes in resident behavior and other events immediately preceding the judgments, but the opinions and beliefs themselves had no notable effect on the resident responses that followed.

Preferred TOS attitude scores—reflecting staff preference for the nature of treatment programs—remained well differentiated and remarkably constant over the two-year period. By the fifth anniversary assessment, slightly different clustering occurred between preferred attitude scores, and such preferences were even less predictable from individual staff characteristics than before. The nature of treatment characteristics preferred by staff remained closer to the ideal milieu program than to the ideal social-learning program over the period. Although some differential changes occurred in the level of endorsement of TOS attitude scores for each orientation—reflecting staff interpretation of the nature of each psychosocial program—the pattern of scores showed few changes at points during the period, and only one score showed differential change from the original posttraining assessment to the fifth anniversary assessment. Even with the high staff turnover and changes on some scores, the pattern within and between psychosocial orientations remained constant, such that the nature of the programs continued to be interpreted differentially with staff interpretations remaining quite close to the ideals of each program over the entire two years.

TOS technique scores, in contrast to attitude scores, showed increases over the first six months and decreases over the last six months of the current period for four of the five scores under all response orientations. Preferred technique scores—reflecting staff preferences for use of different treatment procedures—showed changes that essentially cancelled out over time, so that both level and pattern at the end of the period were functionally identical to those of the original staff group nearly two and a half years earlier. At the beginning and end of the current period, preferred technique scores remained closely related to the social-learning ideal; however, the pattern of preferred techniques was less related to the ideal pattern of both programs during the middle of the period when endorsement of unusually high utilization rates occurred. By the fifth anniversary assessment greater clustering among preferred techniques was once again in evidence, but the preference for use of specific techniques had become almost totally unrelated to individual staff characteristics.

TOS technique scores for each program orientation—reflecting staff interpretation of appropriate technique utilization within each program—continued to show differentiation in desired directions between programs throughout the entire two years, even with the large increases in endorsed utilization rates during the middle of the period. However, during the middle of the period, scores within the social-learning orientation remained well differentiated, while the increased levels of technique utilization that were interpreted as appropriate for the milieu orientation lost discrimination—as if staff viewed appropriate use of techniques to be "everything at a high rate" in the milieu program. Discrimination among milieu techniques on the TOS returned only at the end of the period. The pattern of interpretation of appropriate techniques remained closer to the ideal within the social-learning orientation throughout the current period but became further removed from both ideals during the three middle assessments.

Even with the decreases during the last six months, the level of technique utilization endorsed by staff remained significantly above those at the beginning of the period for four of the five groups of techniques within the milieu orientation and for three of the five within the social-learning orientation—partially correcting interpretations that had been lower than desired at the beginning of the period. The changes in staff interpretations of the appropriate levels of utilization of specific techniques appeared to be the result of the content emphasized during in-service training and supervision. However, in spite of the changes during the middle of the period, technique interpretations remained well differentiated in appropriate directions between psychosocial orientations, with staff preferences still remaining much closer to either psychosocial orientation than those of mental hospital staff.

More important for determining the actual operation and differentiation of treatment conditions within and between programs are the objective data from the SRIC. In contrast to the stability of the amount of staff activity upon the introduction of treatment programs, during the current period total staff activity increased dramatically in both programs, with the major increases corresponding to the same time intervals in which TOS technique changes were observed. By the last six months, staff activity in the social-learning program had increased to two and a half times the level existing before the current period, while staff activity in the milieu program had increased to a level over three and a half times from earlier. Concurrently the focus of activities shifted during the first six months to provide additional differentiation between programs in the same direction that had occurred upon the initial introduction of the programs. Although the same staff continued to equate time and focus of work over psychosocial programs, the differentially greater increase in staff-resident interactions resulted in social-learning residents receiving a 126% increase in individual attention from staff by the end of the period, while milieu residents received an increase in individual staff attention of over 300% from the levels existing over the first eighteen weeks of program operation. Thus, by the end of the next two years, residents in both psychosocial programs were receiving considerably more attention from staff than that received in either baseline or traditional hospital programs, without changing staffing ratios; however, the average milieu resident was receiving more staff attention than the average social-learning resident—even though the social-learning program was clearly more effective.

The actual differentiation of staff performance in the two psychosocial programs over the next two years was remarkable. The specific increases in activity occurred in the areas of emphasis on positive programmatic procedures and genuine metacommunications that were the focus of in-service training and supervision, such that higher frequencies of programmatic interactions with even greater differentiation between programs occurred. Not only the focus of staff activity, but the rate of specific classes of staff behavior, and the resident behavior x staff behavior match became even closer to the differential requirements specified in the respective treatment manuals. Milieu procedures continued to be performed at differentially higher rates when staff worked in the milieu program, and social-learning procedures continued to be performed at differentially higher rates when they worked in the social-learning program. On an absolute level, 96.1% of all staff-resident interactions in the milieu program were correct over the next two years and the majority of errors still resulted from inappropriate spillover of social-learning procedures. On an absolute level, 99.6% of all staff-resident interactions in the social-learning program were correct, with errors being nearly nonexistent.

The distribution of relative proportions of specific staff behaviors actually performed in each program paralleled the utilization endorsements for TOS technique scores at the end of the period. However, during the middle of the period, when exceptionally high endorsement rates occurred on the TOS, staff performance was better differentiated within and between programs than were the staff interpretations of appropriate levels of utilization on the TOS. The increases in both interpretation and actual performance over the first six months appeared consistent and to be the result of increased emphasis upon counteracting the effects of the resident's accidental death by becoming stricter about inappropriate behavior and increasing genuine positive social interactions. The changes in both interpretations and actual performance over the last six months appeared to be the result of an increased emphasis upon in-service review of programmatic procedures resulting from the long-delayed arrival of materials and commodities, as well as changes in weekend activity schedules and preparations for changes in time out and expulsion time. These changes in TOS showed decreased levels of endorsement but better differentiation within programs once again, while actual staff behavior maintained differentiation but increased rates over the last six months of the period. While staff still did a better job of reproducing all aspects of the ideal social-learning program, the improvement of performance in the milieu program resulted in absolute levels of accuracy, with clear and reliable differentiation between programs that even exceeded the exceptional levels obtained over the first eighteen weeks.

The analyses of staff attitudes and performance over the next two years provides interesting information on staff and the nature of events to which they responded. More important, however, is the clear documentation of the differentiation of treatment programs according to prescribed procedures over the next two years, since actual staff performance—especially after the introduction of improved methods for controlling assaultive behavior—was about as close to being correct in both programs as could be required or desired. The documentation, combined with the overall equivalency of all other possible sources of influence, including psychotropic drugs, clearly established the differential outcome over this period to be a consequence of the differential treatment procedures applied within the two programs, with primary moderating effects involving the accidental death at the beginning of the period and the introduction of necessary commodities and materials at the end of the period.

## 22. Summary of Findings for the Next Two Years

The programs continued to be carried out according to the procedures of the respective manuals over the next two years, with all required assessments being maintained. The majority of the remaining administrative delays resulting from the original late notification of funding and decentralization of center operations were completed during the period. The original shortages in consumables and material goods were overcome by the last six months of the period. Through the introduction of volunteers and further administrative negotiations, downtown and off-unit facilities became available. The only notable procedural changes during the period were the length of time of expulsion and time out as a consequence for assaults and the addition of male student workers and transceivers to provide assistance to and protection of staff and residents. Several notable events occurred over the two-year period, the most important of which were the accidental death of a resident at the very beginning of the period and the first releases and replacements of improved residents. Staffing remained short, and both staff and residents experienced continuing morale problems until the improved procedures for dealing with assaults were worked out. By the last six months of the period, in spite of continuing shortages of staff and funds, all operations were functioning exactly as prescribed, with good morale and communication networks continuing on a day-to-day basis.

The outcome data reported in chapter 19 reveal the complexity of resident response to unitwide programs and the sensitivity of resident functioning—especially concurrent appropriate behavior—to a variety of environmental and psychological events. The continuous objective assessments of hour-by-hour behavior found overall resident functioning to decline during the first six months of the period following the resident's death. Overall resident functioning stabilized, or improved slightly, following improved procedures for controlling assaults and dramatically increased again over the last six months of the period, following the long-delayed availability of a number of commodities, materials, and supplies. The overall functioning of milieu residents at the end of the next two years showed essentially the same degree of improvement that had been obtained by the first anniversary assessment, with three-quarters of the residents showing significant improvement. Milieu procedures still obtained better response by females and residents with relatively shorter lengths of prior hospitalization. The overall level of functioning of social-learning residents showed continued additional improvement over the next two years, without regard to any individual resident characteristics; over 90% of these residents showed major and significant improvement by the end of the period. The social-learning program, thus demonstrated a clear overall superiority to the milieu program, without differential response to prior level of functioning, nature of problem behavior, or any resident demographic characteristic. Drug status was unrelated to resident improvement, although drugs had been withdrawn for the majority of residents during the next two years.

Nearly all components of maladaptive and adaptive behavior showed greater differentiation in effectiveness between programs over the next two years. The social-learning program showed even greater superiority than before in the reduction or elimination of extreme bizarre behaviors—one of the crucial target areas for rehabilitation of the severely disabled chronic population. The only class of maladaptive behavior in which milieu therapy obtained further reductions over the next two years was dysfunctional cognitive behavior. Both programs produced significant additional reductions in these clinically bizarre verbal and facial expressions indicative of thought disorder with equal effectiveness. Both programs maintained the earlier dramatic reductions in grossly inappropriate resident responses to minimal expectations, with the social-learning program remaining more effective with this class of inappropriate behavior. Similarly the highest-frequency, clinically bizarre motoric behaviors continued to show significant reductions in both programs, but the social-learning program was differentially more effective in maintaining or furthering the reduction of these crazy actions. Even with the improved consequences for assaultiveness, therapeutic community procedures were largely ineffective in controlling dangerous and aggressive acts, with the milieu group showing a significant increase over the next two years. Social-learning procedures, in contrast, maintained the reduced levels of dangerous and aggressive acts, both from pretreatment levels and in comparison to milieu therapy procedures.

Although residents in both programs demonstrated continued significant improvements in adaptive behavior, the social-learning program was differentially more effective with every class of adaptive behavior over the next two years. Components of the resocialization target of rehabilitation—resident self-care and interpersonal skills—were maintained at earlier levels of improvement by the milieu program, but the social-learning program continued to produce further differential and dramatic improvement in these areas of deficient resident functioning. The dramatic improvement in instrumental role performance that had been produced by social-learning procedures was maintained without waiver over the entire two years, while milieu therapy procedures failed to maintained without waver over the entire two next two years, milieu therapy procedures had been found totally ineffective in controlling dangerous and aggressive acts and totally ineffective in improving instrumental role performance. All other areas of resident functioning were improved by milieu therapy procedures, but only dysfunctional cognitive behaviors were as effectively treated by milieu therapy as by the social-learning program. All other classes of behavior and all other identified targets that are crucial for the rehabilitation of the severely disabled chronic mental patient were effectively treated by the social-learning program, and more so than by the milieu therapy program.

The characteristics of other ongoing resident activity over the next two years, reported in chapter 20, also showed a further differentiation of programs. Unitwide community meetings continued to reflect the differing purposes of meetings within each program, with specific characteristics being most related to program structure and focal topics of meetings. The comparative use of resources reflected differing program structures, with responsiveness to changes in the availability of resources during the period and evidence that how resources were used was more important than how many were obtained. Resident time spent awake was maintained at the high levels established upon the introduction of programs, but time spent with others increased and decreased during the period, parallel to other improvements in resident functioning. Additional changes in the variability of ongoing resident activity were related to the introduction of volunteers and differential improvements in functioning, with further differentiation in day-to-day processes emerging between programs. Although the differences continue to be interesting in their own right, as a whole, the characteristics of resident activities reported in chapter 20 support the differing program structures and procedures as the basis for the differential improvements reported in chapter 19, with additional support for the influence of identified notable events.

The details of staff attitudes and performance, reported in chapter 21, found remarkable consistencies in the attitudes, beliefs, and interpretations concerning mental patients and the nature of treatment programs over the period. Psychosocial staff remained as close to the ideals underlying the psychosocial programs as had the original staff group at the end of training. The few changes that did occur reflected response to prior changes in resident behavior, without even suggestive evidence that changes in staff beliefs or opinions had any effect on the resident responsiveness that followed. Interpretations of the nature of programs continued to be differentiated in desired directions, with interpretations remaining close to the ideals underlying each program at every assessment over the period. Staff preferences for the nature of treatment programs continued to be closer to the ideal milieu program over the entire period, and preferred techniques remained closer to the ideal social-learning program at the beginning and end of the period. However, during the middle of the next two years, there were changes in preferred techniques and in the interpretation of appropriate technique utilization in both programs, showing large increases in endorsed utilization rates over all orientations. The staff changes occurred following periods of major changes in functioning of both resident groups and appeared to be the result of the content emphasized during in-service training and supervision. Even with the changes at the beginning and end of the period, technique interpretations remained well differentiated in appropriate directions between psychosocial programs, with all staff preferences still remaining much closer to either psychosocial orientation than those of mental hospital staff.

The moment-to-moment continuous objective assessments of staff behavior, also reported in chapter 21, provided documentation of the continued differentiation of actual treatment conditions and evidence for the basis of the changes over the next two years. In contrast to the stability of total staff activity during the first eighteen weeks of operation, staff activity increased dramatically over the next two years, with the major increases occurring over the same time intervals as major decreases and increases in resident functioning. The specific increases in staff activity developed in those areas of emphasis on positive programmatic interactions that were the focus of in-service training and additional off-hour coverage by senior staff. There were higher frequencies of programmatic interactions with even greater differentiation between programs occurring in the same directions as those of the first eighteen weeks of operation. Even though the same staff continued to equate time and focus of work on each unit, clear and stable differences in focus and content of staff activities were maintained, with the level of activity increasing by over two and a half and three and a half times the initial levels, respectively, in the social-learning and milieu programs. These increases and the continued differentiation of procedures resulted in dramatic increases in the amount of attention individual residents in both programs received, with milieu residents receiving considerably more attention from staff than social-learning residents did—again providing evidence that how is more important than how much.

The rate of performance of specific staff behaviors and resident behavior-by-staff behavior match followed the differential requirements of the respective treatment manuals even more closely than before. The relative distribution of staff-resident interactions also approached the ideal patterns of technique utilization even more clearly for each program. Although staff still did a better job carrying out the ideal social-learning program, the two programs remained exceptionally well differentiated over the next two years, even with the major increases in total activity levels. In fact, performance of milieu procedures had improved to the point where 96.1% of all staff-resident interactions were correct on an absolute level over the entire two years, while prescribed procedures in the social-learning program were carried out at the incredibly high level of 99.6% of all staff-resident interactions.

Chapter 21 presents information on staff and the nature of events to which they responded. The clear documentation of appropriate differentiation of programs establishes that the differential outcome over the next two years was a function of the specified procedures. Primary moderating effects involving the accidental death, changes in consequences for assaults, and the introduction of necessary commodities and materials with which to operate were also documented. By the fifth anniversary assessment, both psychosocial programs had shown significant continuing impact on the most severely debilitated groups of chronically institutionalized adults ever subjected to systematic study. The social-learning program was differentially more effective with all targets of rehabilitation—in fact, with all classes of behavior, except dysfunctional cognitive behavior, which was equally responsive to both psychosocial programs.

The absolute level of improvement was striking. By the end of the period 11% and 25% of the severely debilitated groups, respectively, for the milieu and social-learning programs, were functionally indistinguishable from the normal population. One resident from each program had successfully remained in the community, and two more social-learning residents were ready for release to independent functioning as soon as jobs could be located. Even with such significant improvements, however, the group as a whole was still functioning only slightly above minimum levels, with 7% of social-learning residents and 25% of milieu residents still demonstrating levels of disturbance and deficiencies that required their continued institutional control. However, the smooth functioning of the psychosocial programs over the last six months of the period and the obvious clinical improvements that were observed after necessary facilities, commodities, and materials had been obtained —well in advance of any data analysis—offered hope that the remaining year of the original planned comparative operation would yield even more significant improvement for these residents.

PART 5

# The Next Year and a Half on the Psychosocial Units: Decline of Effectiveness and Search for Cause

## 23. Notable Events and Overview of the Next Year and a Half

In retrospect, the most notable event of the next year and a half was not only the maintenance of prescribed programs and all required assessments, but simple survival of all the numerous extraneous and unpredicted events of the period. As in previous periods, negotiations of bureaucratic red-tape to maintain operations remained a continuous undertaking. The alternation between statewide hiring freezes and increases in salary structure and/or fringe benefits still resulted in staff shortages, as well as a need for additional funding or sources of employee salaries. Some of these problems were covered through supplemental grant funds, some through participation in several federal programs for aiding the unemployed (Work INcentive; Model Cities; Emergency Employment Act), and some were circumvented by the assistance of university students in research but not in clinical work. Additionally several changes in state and federal review procedures required new review committees, reports, and agreements—all of which were eventually completed. In spite of continuing shortages of staff and funds, however, all other operations, commodities, facilities, and services, were maintained as described earlier, with administrative and communication networks remaining intact. Multiple changes in plans were nevertheless required over the period of the next year and a half.

The original design, as modified following the delay in initial notification of funding, called for one more year of operation of the psychosocial programs on a closed basis. Following the seventh anniversary assessment, the status of all residents was to be evaluated, with acceptable residents being placed in private extended-care facilities, to be followed up by project staff for the minimum six-month declining contact schedule. Regular Department of Mental Health follow-up was to take place thereafter, with six-month assessments on project instruments being obtained, for a total follow-up of two years on residents achieving successful community placement. Independent-release criteria, requiring work and significant others, were to be maintained up to that point. The original design also called for a planned transfer of all clinical staff from grant funds to regular state operating funds as each research phase was completed. The programs were to continue operating under prescribed procedures until sufficient analyses of intramural and extramural data were complete to determine what programs and procedures were the most effective overall or with particular classes of chronically institutionalized patients or problem behaviors. Following these analyses, the psychosocial units were to be converted to research-service-demonstration-training units, in which procedures found effective could be taught to other mental health staff, thereby shortening the lag between discovery, application, and diffusion of findings while maintaining treatment services. This plan had not only survived but had received support and encouragement through two state governors and three separate changes in the top administration of the Department of Mental Health, with the entire demonstration-training function to be supported by regular state operating funds.

By the beginning of this period, the problem of the "revolving-door" mental patient had become of major concern in the state, as well as nationally. Since readmissions were increasing dramatically as short stays in state and community psychiatric units became the usual practice and the proportion of long-stay patients continued to increase as greater numbers of readmissions occurred, the "revolving-door" acute mental patient was becoming the pre-chronic patient of the future.

Other than maintaining reliability checks and monitoring staff data to ensure proper operation of psychosocial programs, the data had purposely been filed and not systematically analyzed for residents up to this point to prevent possible staff reactivity to ongoing changes and to protect the integrity of the hospital comparison group. Nevertheless, the programs were working so smoothly and the clinical response of the residents was so obvious by the fifth anniversary assessment that considerably greater improvements were anticipated over the remaining year of the originally planned intramural period. The psychosocial programs that were doing so well with the hard-core population that had remained untouched by previous treatment procedures seemed ideal for effectively treating the revolving-door, prechronic patients.

An expanded design was, therefore, proposed to the State Department of Mental Health, to be undertaken totally on state operating funds. The additions made no change in the original design for evaluation of the chronic population but added treatment and controlled evaluation of the prechronic population during the last eighteen months of the planned community follow-up of the original chronic groups. Specifically at the end of the current year and a half, after psychosocial staff had completed the first six-month declining-contact follow-up of chronic residents, half of the beds on each psychosocial unit would be allocated to prechronic patients (the final plan called for two-thirds prechronic, one-third chronic). A three-way comparison of equated groups of prechronic mental patients, exactly parallel to the original design with chronic patients, could then be made, plus a test of the comparative speed of response of chronic patients in the presence of higher-functioning and, presumably, more rapidly responding prechronic patients. Concurrently private extended-care facilities would be monitored, with attempts to introduce minimum components of procedures found effective as ongoing programs in community facilities for continued long-term rehabilitation of the chronic population, after intramural programs had improved behavior to a point allowing community placement. During the period in which the evaluations were taking place, staff training, materials development, and institutional liaisons would be undertaken to prepare the psychosocial units for demonstration-training operations upon completion of the evaluations.

The expanded design would require considerable increases in operating funds, a large expansion of staff to work with families and extramural contacts of prechronic patients, training, research, assessment, and data analyses, as well as increased intramural staffing—which by now was less than that of public mental hospitals. Senior clinical and research staff met regularly on their own time to work out details of operations, staffing, and necessary liaison work, and the proposal and staffing plan was accepted by the Department of Mental Health. Throughout the remainder of the next year and a half, senior clinical and research staff continued to meet weekly on their own time to prepare details of the expanded operations—except during those periods when other events required coverage of off-hours on a regular rather than an intermittent schedule.

Changes in all of the time plans were required when it was discovered, just before the seventh anniversary assessment, that not enough beds were available in community extended-care facilities to accept sufficient numbers of residents from the intramural treatment groups to allow a controlled comparison of community stay. In fact, the locations of the beds were so scattered that the required declining-contact aftercare was impossible by the limited psychosocial staff, since travel time alone precluded any useful contact with large numbers of ex-residents. By this time, the community staff of the Department of Mental Health were no longer working on aftercare (see illustrative cases, chapter 19); therefore, psychosocial staff undertook negotiations with several local extended-care facilities to see if, in the course of occasional releases and frequent transfers, targeted facilities could gradually make available sufficient beds to accept improved residents from all three intramural groups. The negotiations relied upon the commitment of follow-up contact and consultation from psychosocial staff, which was readily given. Cooperation was also obtained from community staff of the Department of Mental Health and from local community clinics in the region to assist in placing other mental patients in ways that would eventually provide the needed centralized beds.

Concurrent with the discovery of the absence of necessary community beds, the data were examined for the first time to begin preliminary screening for resident evaluations by extended-care facilities. The data first examined included resident functioning through the sixth anniversary assessment, which indicated—to the dismay of all—that functioning on both psychosocial units had declined over the first six months of the current period. Before this time, all staff had been acutely aware that some residents in each program had increased assaultiveness to an excessively disturbing level. In fact, staff concern with increases in assaultiveness over the first few weeks of the current period—following the implementation of the statewide policy directive that placed a two-hour maximum on the length of time out or expulsion—had been considerable, and they had taken several actions.

For two and a half months at the beginning of the current period, attempts to control violent residents by psychotropic drugs had been continued in the usual manner. When no clear control was established clinically by drugs, a reemphasis of regular rather than intermittent coverage of off-hours had been undertaken by senior staff. Additionally two of the most effective change agents were temporarily transferred to the evening shift to help enforce procedures for dealing with assaults. The rate of increase in assaults was stopped for about three months following this focus until senior staff attempted to fade their off-hour coverage back to the usual intermittent schedule, and the top change agents returned to their regular shifts. The rate of assaults again increased; once again, senior staff coverage of off-hours was reemphasized, leading to another stabilization in the rate of increase in assaultiveness.

Thus staff had clearly been aware of increases in assaultiveness and had taken action to attempt to control assaults and to protect both staff and residents. They were successful in stabilizing the rates of assaultiveness for periods of eight to twelve weeks at a time. The intermittent stability in assaultiveness rates and the gradual deterioration of other areas of resident functioning were apparently such that staff habituated to day-to-day changes. Without regular monitoring of resident data over longer time periods, clinical and administrative staff believed a few specific residents had become severe problems for assaultiveness, and they had little notion of the extent to which assaults had increased on an absolute level and no idea of the gradual spread of effects—which had occurred steadily on a week-to-week basis—with a deterioration in the overall level of functioning of the residents.

A decision to extend the intramural period was then made, on the basis of the combined discovery of the absence of centralized community beds and the decline in functioning following the reduced consequences for assaultive behavior. Since procedures were already underway for processing positions and contacts for the expanded operation with prechronic patients and for obtaining available beds in community extended-care facilities, external contingencies established the length of the extension of intramural operation at one additional year beyond the original plan. During that year, it was hoped, sufficient analyses could be undertaken to identify the basis for the reversal of effectiveness, and attempts at correction could be made. Release criteria for all three groups were therefore maintained without change for the current year and a half, through the eighth anniversary assessment.

Research staff then undertook a detailed analysis of resident functioning, staff functioning, and other notable events from the data on file for the periods covering good and poor clinical response in a search for hypotheses. Concurrently senior research and clinical staff began regular weekly monitoring of incoming resident data to identify exactly where problems were occurring for resident groups, and they made systematic substudies to test alternative procedures. These data were still not shared with junior staff to prevent their reactivity. This approach was a reversal of the earlier one to resident data, which had seemed to be a good research strategy in principle but was obviously a mistake, since the existing data could have shown the nature of the problem within two weeks if it had been monitored.

Other notable events during the next year and a half may have potentially contributed to staff's lack of awareness of the extent of decline in resident functioning before data were examined. Over the first six months of the period, additional releases of improved residents occurred in both programs, with replacements again made at pretreatment levels of functioning of the released residents. The releases served both to strengthen existing staff beliefs concerning the continued effectiveness of programs and took additional senior staff time for the declining-contact follow-up. Concurrently the replacement with low-functioning residents could easily have been interpreted as contributing to lower levels of performance and more intolerable behavior on the units, independent of the current effectiveness of programs. Kate G. (see chapter 19) also achieved release again, but after the data had been examined.

A statewide reclassification of positions through the implementation of a Mental Health Career Series occurred just before the sixth anniversary assessment. It had been in preparation since the month before original psychosocial staff had been hired, over three years earlier, with numerous promises of implementation, followed by disheartening delays. Since the career series included increases in salaries for most staff, as well as providing opportunity for upward mobility within the system, staff were obviously pleased with this turn of events—possibly to the extent that selective perception occurred regarding resident functioning. Additionally the hiring of auxiliary staff and approval of the expanded plan for treating prechronics, as well as planning for demonstration-training operations, clearly contributed to positive affects and a general aura of excitement among all staff over the first six months of the period.

There were additional notable events just before the first examination of data, with some continuing for longer periods of time. They did not contribute to positive staff affect, but the effect on staff may have been sufficient to cloud a clear perception of the changes that were occurring in resident functioning at the beginning of the period. Even greater shortages of senior staff were imposed when an intern psychologist broke his contract to begin employment just before the sixth anniversary assessment, with nearly three months being required to find a replacement. Concurrently the unit supervisor was ill for over six months between the sixth and eighth anniversary assessments. In addition, just after the sixth anniversary assessment, lengthy meetings were called by central office staff to begin preparations to accredit the center as a hospital so that it could qualify for benefits under a number of federal programs. The preparations were disruptive both on philosophical grounds and because of the increased load of paperwork. Continuing meetings and other work were required of all clinical staff to convert psychosocial programs and resident records into a parallel set of medical records for patients in formats with no obvious utility beyond hospital accreditation. These preparations continued throughout the remainder of the intramural period—and beyond.

The last series of events began with intensity just after the sixth anniversary assessment, with continuing repercussions for about four months They revolved around accusations and attacks by a local state representative, through radio and newspaper articles, on the Department of Mental Health, "mental health" people in general, and the center and center staff in particular. The accusations affected both staff and resident morale throughout the center, to the extent that an investigation was requested and conducted by the appropriate legislative committee. The hearings and investigation of the institution and its programs were disruptive, simply because of the presence of investigators and the staff time required for participation. After the conclusion of the investigation, with public praise for the institution and programs by the committee, the local representative continued his accusations to the extent that public rebuttals were finally called for from the center administration. This exchange was still disturbing to residents but soothed staff to some degree, since no further accusations were forthcoming.

Changes in structure or procedure of psychosocial programs over the next year and a half were primarily a function of statewide policy directives or of temporary experimental evaluations of hypotheses resulting from the examination of data. There were occasional changes in the evening or hour of meetings on each unit to accommodate access to off-unit facilities. Also, appearance and meal behavior criteria were reordered on recording forms on the basis of empirically determined difficulty for residents, to the order presented in the manuals. These changes were all equated and inconsequential. Holiday schedules, the special Christmas programs, and the manner of dealing with all inappropriate and intolerable behaviors, except assaults, remained identical in both programs to those that had been in effect since the introduction of the programs.

While a two-day period of time out or expulsion had been in effect as a consequence for physical assaults on other residents or staff during the most effective treatment period, the statewide policy directive placed a maximum time of two hours on such procedures; the change was implemented immediately before the fifth anniversary assessment. It limited time out or expulsion as a consequence for assaults to the remainder of the functional period in which the assault occurred, and the next functional period (sixty-five minutes minimum), with return requiring an absence of inappropriate behavior for the last fifteen minutes before release. Analyses of resident data during the next year and a half found that this change was the primary basis for the decline in the effectiveness of both programs; however, no changes in that procedure were negotiated during the current time period.

An analysis of resident responsiveness also suggested that the availability of consumable items during the informal interaction periods had been associated with additional improvements and that cigarettes appeared to be one of the most favored choices of canteen items. Therefore, arrangements were made to make cigarettes and snacks available during all weekend coffee breaks for residents for token purchase in the social-learning program and on request in the milieu program. Inspection of the data also revealed that the group trips with staff and volunteers were not serving their intended purpose. Since trained-staff time was at a premium and the trips were time-consuming, they were terminated midway between the seventh and eighth anniversary assessments.

Even though off-unit facilities continued to be available through volunteer staffing, social-learning residents still failed to use them, and milieu residents had slipped back to lower levels of utilization than before. Since the earlier study of special sampling-exposure procedures had already generated several hypotheses about the failure of social-learning residents to use these resources, an eighteen-week replication of the earlier substudy, with modifications to evaluate those hypotheses, was begun just before the seventh anniversary assessment—ensuring that normal conditions existed during the assessment weeks. Living group composition was changed on the milieu unit just before the substudy to remove any preestablished negative interaction patterns. The substudy (published in McInnis et al., 1974), found the same results as had the earlier sampling-exposure study when identical procedures were reinstituted; milieu residents again increased their utilization of off-unit facilities and services under sampling-exposure conditions and generalized to usual announce-only conditions, while the social-learning group remained unaffected. However, when a special purchase-eligibility condition allowed social-learning residents on restriction because of standing fines to purchase passes by making an additional payment on the fine, they responded equally well to sampling-exposure procedures. A modeling effect was also apparent in which less-active residents tended to either use or not use off-unit facilities and services dependent upon the behavior of more active residents.

This substudy pointed out an extremely serious negative side effect of the high rates of accumulated token fines, and consequent restriction from use of other positive resources for social-learning residents over this period of declining functioning and increasing fines. The data further showed that social-learning residents were not making fine payments, to the extent that 75% of them possessed standing fines for a full week and could not, functionally, fully participate in the program. Therefore, the purchase-eligibility procedure, combined with a proportional-payoff schedule—which increased the reduction in fines per token payment as a function of the length of time without a new fine—was evaluated over the last eighteen weeks of the period. This procedure left all aspects of token earning and token costs intact but allowed access to all resources through an additional payment on the standing fine, in addition to the usual token cost. This substudy (published in Doty et al., 1974) found that the purchase eligibility, contingent proportional payoff procedures successfully returned residents to active participation in the overall program and increased the rate of payment on standing fines, without weakening the overall response-cost procedure for controlling inappropriate behavior. However, the incidence of assaults was not influenced by these procedural changes.

One final substudy of programmatic procedures was carried out during the last six months of the current period to determine if videotaped feedback might be a more effective group-training procedure than the verbal feedback with concrete examples that had been employed. To examine the question with minimal disruption to other procedures, equated subgroups were formed within the social-learning program for the regular twice-per-week small group meetings. Half of each meeting was then focused on a single target problem—appropriate meal behavior—with two groups receiving the usual verbal feedback procedures and two groups videotaped feedback of their own meal behavior for twelve weeks. Detailed analyses of this substudy (see Paden et al., 1974) found that neither group procedure produced significant improvement in meal behavior. Higher-functioning residents responded to the specific focus of training, whether videotape or verbal, while lower-functioning residents improved most by the usual programmatic procedures with direct feedback in the actual meal situation.

None of the procedural modifications changed the overall structure of programs or the specific nature of programmatic interactions. The substudies were all relatively brief in duration, allowing tests of hypotheses for future implementation rather than major changes during the current year and a half.

The use of psychotropic drugs was increased early in the attempts to control violent behavior—after the previous increase by staff during the fifth anniversary assessment. Over the first two and a half months of the period, as many as 56% of residents were receiving psychotropic drugs. However, even a maximum dosage of intramuscular phenothiazines failed to control the most assaultive residents of this population. After senior staff coverage of off-hours was increased, drugs were gradually reduced to 29% and 25%, respectively, for milieu and social-learning residents by the sixth anniversary assessment, to 21% and 14% by the seventh anniversary assessment and to 18% and 11% immediately after the seventh anniversary assessment through the end of the period.

The staffing of the psychosocial programs continued to remain below the necessary clinical complement over the entire year and a half. Only through participation in the several special federal programs was clinical staffing maintained at a reasonable level, while research staff was supplemented through university students' enrolling in individual studies. Although 97%, 94%, and 91% of the clinical complement were working, respectively, at anniversary assessments 6, 7, and 8, the figures are somewhat misleading because of a staff reorganization midway between the fifth and sixth anniversary assessment. Specifically when the two auxiliary rehabilitation counselors were finally hired, staff were reorganized to include the professional auxiliary staff as senior staff with full training on the floor and participation in policy decisions—thus increasing the number of senior staff but maintaining the full-time equivalent positions on the floor without change. This was accomplished by scheduling each of the new senior staff positions to work in programs two days per week to free interns for additional off-hour coverage and the multiple demands for paperwork. However, a net loss still occurred during the period as a result of the absence of the unit supervisor, who was ill, and the unanticipated failure of a new intern psychologist to enter employment, resulting in an open senior staff position for nearly three months. Supplemental staff, for eventual work in the extramural and training divisions of the expanded design, were processed to begin training just before the eighth anniversary assessment. However, they had no independent contact or interactions with residents in either psychosocial program during the current period.

The proportion of continuing clinical staff over the first and last six months of the period was comparable to that at earlier times (75% and 73%, respectively); however, the initial positive impact of the implementation of the career series was apparent in a 90% continuation of staff between the sixth and seventh anniversary assessments, even though another top change agent was promoted into an auxiliary educator position upon the retirement of the original educator. Of the staff working at the eighth anniversary assessment, 60% were continuous from the fifth anniversary assessment and 13% from the original staff group. With the higher proportion of continuing staff, both average age (28.9 years) and experience (1.85 years) of the staff group at the eighth anniversary assessment had increased over that existing at the beginning of the period and over that of the original staff group present before the arrival of the residents ($p$'s $< 0.05$). Also as a result of lower scores of new staff hired during the period, the average Extroversion score of the staff group at the eighth anniversary assessment was significantly lower than that of the original staff group ($p < 0.05$), falling just below the midpoint of the extroversion-introversion scale (18.1). None of the other characteristics of the staff group (education, sex, race, marital or parental status, or Emotionality) changed significantly from those of previous assessments ($p$'s $> 0.20$) or from those of the original group of staff (see chapter 9).

The remaining chapters of part 5 report the results of the operation of the psychosocial units over the next year and a half for both staff and residents, with changes in behavior related to the other notable events. As in parts 3 and 4, the objective outcome data on resident functioning, reported in chapter 24, present details of statistical analyses for the interested research worker; however, the professional clinician or program director can obtain details of results—including the analyses of the specific effects of changing consequences for assaults—by skipping these sections. Preprofessional staff and others without much time can obtain an understanding and clinical interpretation of the outcome over this period by inspecting the tables and figures and reading the summary and individual improvement rates section.

Changes in the characteristics of large group meetings, use of available resources, time spent awake and with others, and the relative variability of several classes of resident behavior within each psychosocial program are compared in chapter 25 along with relationships to notable events and changes in resident functioning. All staff data are reported in chapter 26, including attitudes, opinions, preferences, and interpretations, as well as objective data on the reliability and differentiation of actual staff performance and the nature of attention residents received over the next year and a half. As in parts 3 and 4, details of statistical analyses in chapters 25 and 26 are presented in the chapter notes, with results incorporated in the text. Each section of these two chapters ends with a detailed content summary and each chapter ends with a summary section, from which preprofessional staff and others short on time should be able to obtain a good understanding of findings, combined with study of the tables and figures. The major conclusions and results at the end of the next year and a half are briefly summarized in chapter 27.

# 24. Differential Effectiveness of the Milieu and Social-Learning Programs During the Next Year and a Half

## CHANGES IN GLOBAL FUNCTIONING [1]

Raw changes in total appropriate and inappropriate functioning from the fifth through eighth anniversary assessment periods—plotted relative to functioning before program introduction—are presented in figure 24.1. In sharp contrast to resident improvement before this period, there was a relatively consistent trend toward increases in inappropriate behavior and decreases in appropriate behavior over the entire year and a half for both programs. Appropriate concurrent behavior (TSBC) in particular showed a dramatic decrease during the first six months of the period following the change in time-out and expulsion times, with the milieu program actually falling below levels existing before the introduction of specific program procedures. In fact, with the exception of clinically inappropriate bizarre behavior (TSBC), the overall decreases in functioning for those in the milieu program returned to a level at or below that existing before the program introduction. Although residents in the social-learning program also showed overall decreases during the period, improvement appears to have been maintained above levels existing before the program introduction and above the level of functioning of the milieu program.

*Statistical evaluation.* Overall changes during this year and a half period were evaluated by a two-way repeated measures ANOVA on the standardized Global Functioning Factor Score (milieu vs. social-learning programs; anniversary assessments 5, 6, 7, 8). This analysis found significant main effects for programs ($F=5.84$, $df=1/54$, $p < 0.05$) and for time ($F=15.99$, $df=3/162$, $p < 0.01$), without a significant program x time interaction ($F < 1$). Additional two-way ANOVAs with partitioning of simple effects were carried out on successive pairs of anniversary assessment periods to clarify these findings. The significant time main effect was found to reflect consistent decreases in Global Functioning over both programs throughout the entire period, with decreases achieving statistical significance from anniversary assessments 5 to 6 ($F=20.38$, $df=1/54$, $p < 0.01$) and anniversary assessments 7 to 8 ($F=4.06$, $df=1/54$, $p < 0.05$). The decrease approached significance between anniversary assessments 6 and 7 ($F=3.39$, $df=1/54$, $p < 0.08$). Over the entire period from anniversary assessment 5 to 8, Global Functioning over both programs showed a significant decline from 53.24 to 47.94 ($F=24.55$, $df=1/54$, $p < 0.01$), without program x time interactions approaching significance at any point during the period (all $F$'s $< 1$). The significant program main effect was found to occur consistently over all assessment periods (all $F$'s $> 4.64$, $df=1/54$, $p < 0.05$), indicating that the significantly greater absolute level of Global Functioning of residents in the social-learning program was maintained throughout the entire period.

Comparisons of change from baseline to successive anniversary assessment periods found the decline of the current period for milieu residents to be of such an extent that overall improvement in Global Functioning from before the program introduction was no longer significant by the time of the seventh and eighth anniversary assessments ($F=2.18$ and $< 1$, respectively; $df=1/54$, $p > 0.10$). In contrast, while the social-learning program also showed declines, significant within-group improvement in Global Functioning from pretreatment was maintained at each assessment period (all $F$'s $> 20.93$, $df=1/54$, $p < 0.01$). Additionally differentially greater improvement of the social-learning program over the milieu program was also maintained at every anniversary assessment during the current period (all $F$'s $> 8.05$, $df=1/54$, $p < 0.01$). During the eighth anniversary assessment, the Global Functioning of social-learning residents was down to a mean of 50.95—still significantly higher than at pretreatment—and that of milieu residents was down to 44.93—only 1.03 above their pretreatment level.

## CHANGES IN MALADAPTIVE BEHAVIOR

The changes in Global Functioning clearly show that significant declines took place in both programs over the current period. Those

Figure 24.1. Overall changes in concurrent behavior (TSBC) and responsiveness within programs (Clinical Frequencies) during the next year and a half.

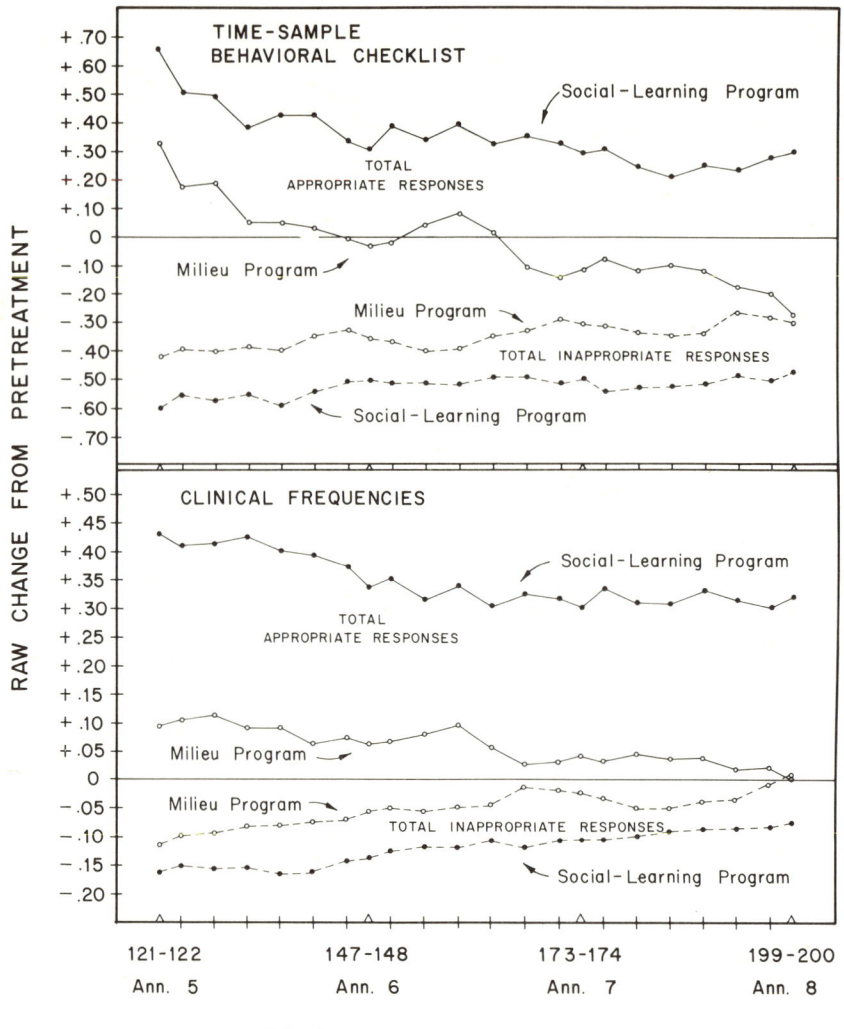

for milieu residents were so extensive that improvement from before program entry was no longer significant by the time of the seventh anniversary assessment. Although social-learning residents also showed decreases in Global Functioning over the next year and a half, they maintained significant improvement from before program entry and a significantly better absolute level of functioning than did milieu residents throughout the entire period.

The increase in Total Inappropriate Clinical Frequencies (figure 24.1) reflects a return to original levels of grossly inappropriate response to minimal expectations for appropriate behavior for milieu residents—entering the period with an average incidence of less than 8% with a steady increase to 20%. The parallel increase for social-learning residents reflects a change from less than 3% occurrence at the beginning of the period to over 11% at the end—still less than the 19% average incidence before the program introduction but an increase nevertheless. Perhaps more notable are the changes in concurrent, clinically inappropriate crazy behavior reflected in TSBC Total Inappropriate Behavior (figure 24.1), since this class constitutes one of the most important target areas for rehabilitation of the chronically institutionalized population. Although both programs also showed increases in the incidence of performance of clinically inappropriate behavior over the next year and a half (from 43% to 55% for milieu residents and from 33% to 45% for social-learning residents), both maintained levels well below the 90% incidence rate that had occurred before the program introduction.

However the changes in components of TSBC Total Inappropriate Behavior (plotted in figure 24.2) show considerable variability in response over the period, with only Cognitive Distortion reflecting a relatively smooth progression for both programs.

*Statistical evaluation.* To statistically evaluate changes in maladaptive behavior over this eighteen-month period, standardized scores for Total Inappropriate Clinical Frequencies and TSBC Schizophrenic Disorganization, Cognitive Distortion, and Hostile-Belligerence Indexes were entered into a three-way repeated measures ANOVA (milieu vs. social-learning programs; anniversary assessments 5, 6, 7, 8; scores). As expected from the primary analysis on Global Functioning, there were significant main effects in the overall analysis of maladaptive behavior for programs ($F=4.34$, $df=1/54$, $p < 0.05$) and time ($F=6.44$, $df=3/162$, $p < 0.01$). The time x scores interaction was also significant ($F=4.16$, $df=9/486$, $p < 0.01$), while no other main effects or interactions approached significance in the overall analysis (all $p > 0.10$).

Additional three-way ANOVAs with partitioning of simple effects and a priori tests of individual components were carried out on successive anniversary assessment periods to clarify the findings.[2] Significant program main effects were found to reflect the same superiority of the social-learning program to the milieu program in overall performance of maladaptive behavior at lower levels for the entire period. Even with increases in maladaptive behavior, the social-learning program residents were

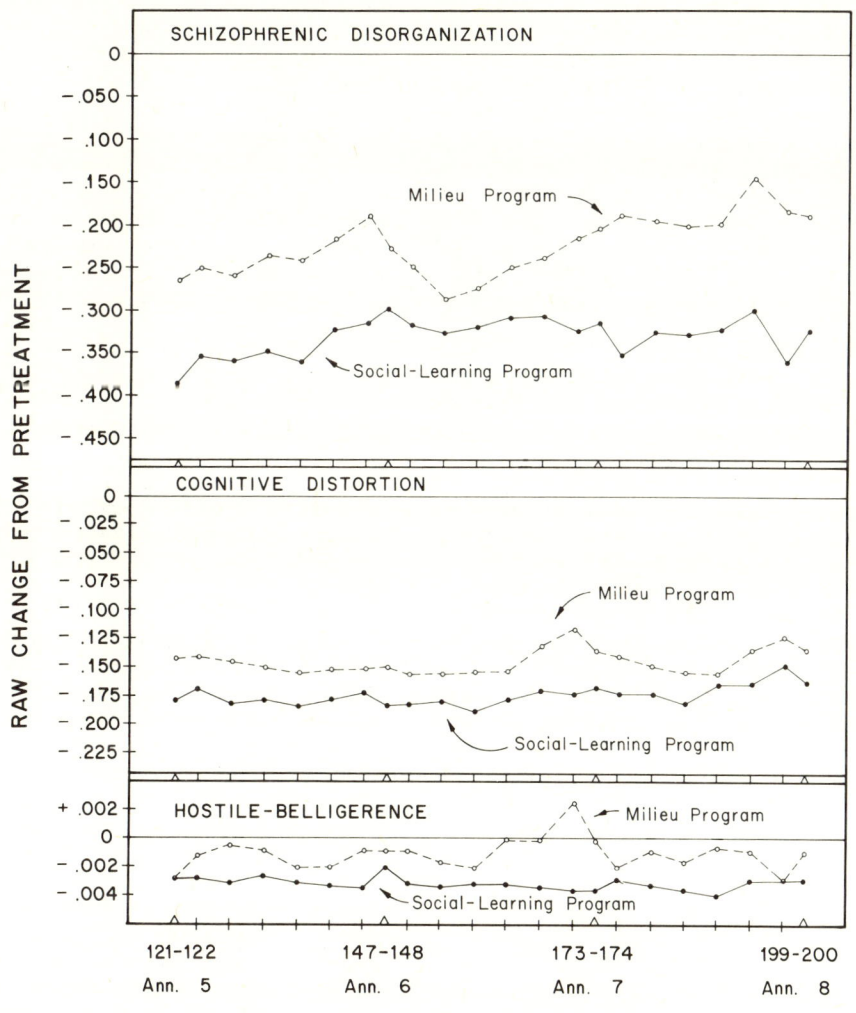

Figure 24.2. Changes in component clinically maladaptive behaviors from the TSBC during the next year and a half.

still significantly lower in overall maladaptive behavior during the eighth anniversary assessment ($F=17.88$, $df=1/54$, $p < 0.01$). As had previously been found for superiority in Global Functioning, not a single overall program x time interaction approached significance (F's < 1). However, in contrast to Global Functioning, the significant time main effect was largely attributable to significant increases in overall levels of maladaptive behavior during the first six months of the period over both programs ($F=11.39$, $df=1/54$, $p < 0.01$). These increases were maintained to the eighth anniversary assessment ($F=11.17$, $df=1/54$, $p < 0.01$) without additional significant increases over the last two six-month periods (all $p > 0.20$). Significant interactions involving scores were also obtained during the first six months and from the beginning to the end of the period, indicating that not all classes of maladaptive behavior were equally affected.

The one class of maladaptive behavior that closely paralleled the nature of change in Global Functioning throughout the eighteen-month period was Total Inappropriate Clinical Frequencies (figure 24.1). The only simple program x time interaction on any maladaptive behavior score during the entire period occurred for Inappropriate Clinical Frequencies between anniversary assessments 5 and 6 ($F=4.03$, $df=1/54$, $p < 0.05$); it reflects a significantly greater increase in Inappropriate Clinical Frequencies during the first six months of the period for milieu residents than for social-learning residents. The increase for milieu residents achieved significance ($F=13.39$, $df=1/54$, $p < 0.01$). Thereafter, Total Inappropriate Clinical Frequencies showed significant increases over the last two six-month periods (F's > 8.41, $df=1/54$, $p < 0.01$), without significant differential change between programs (F's < 1). The within-groups change from the beginning of the period to the eighth anniversary assessment was significant for both milieu ($F=25.29$, $df=1/54$, $p < 0.01$) and social-learning programs ($F=12.96$, $df=1/54$, $p < 0.01$), without significant differential change between them ($F=2.04$, $df=1/54$, $p > 0.10$). However, the absolute level of Total Inappropriate Clinical Frequencies remained significantly lower for social-learning residents than for milieu residents at every point during the period (all F's > 5.31, $df=1/54$, $p < 0.05$).

No other changes between milieu and social-learning programs approached significant differential effects over successive anniversary assessments of the current period, but Schizophrenic Disorganization (figure 24.2) did show a significant increase during the first six months for both programs combined ($F=10.54$, $df=1/54$, $p < 0.01$). Although a few point-to-point trends within the time period spanned a significant range, no additional significant increases occurred over anniversary assessments for either program after the increase obtained by anniversary assessment 6 (p's > 0.10). The overall increase in Schizophrenic Disorganization from the beginning to the end of the one and a half year period was significant ($F=5.88$, $df=1/54$, $p < 0.05$), without differential change between programs (F < 1). The increase in Hostile-Belligerence (figure 24.2) from anniversary assessment 5 to 6 approached significance ($F=3.24$, $df=1/54$, $p < 0.10$). However, outside of the peak occurring for the milieu program just before anniversary assessment 7, no further overall or differential changes even approached significance for Hostile-Belligerence (all $p > 0.20$). Both programs ended the period without significant change from the low levels at which the period began (F's < 1). Similarly, except for the peak just before anniversary assessment 7 for the milieu program, no within- or between-groups changes approached significance for Cognitive Distortion (figure 24.2). Rather, both programs essentially maintained the earlier reductions in dysfunctional cognitive behavior from the beginning to the end of the period, with neither significant gains nor losses (F's < 1).

Tests of the within-groups change from pretreatment baseline on each score found Schizophrenic Disorganization and Cognitive Distortion still to show significant reductions to each assessment period for both milieu (F's > 4.29, $df=1/54$, $p < 0.05$) and social-learning programs (F's > 12.23, $df=1/54$, $p < 0.01$). However, only the differentially greater reduction of the social-learning program was significant by the end of the period for Inappropriate Clinical Frequencies ($F=4.65$, $df=1/54$, $p < 0.05$), with the milieu program not differing significantly from the status before the programs began (F < 1). The reduction in Hostile-Belligerence by the end of the period was not significant for either program (p's > 0.10).

*Descriptive interpretation.* Thus, in contrast to the major reductions and/or maintenance of reduced levels of maladaptive behavior that had been achieved through the fifth anniversary assessment, the next year and a half was largely characterized by increases in maladaptive behavior. These increases occurred equally for both programs, with the social-learning program consistently maintaining lower levels than the milieu program did.

Both programs had produced significant reductions in gross inappropriate response to minimal expectations by the fifth anniversary assessment, with the social-learning program being differentially even more effective with this class of maladaptive behavior (Inappropriate Clinical Frequencies, figure 24.1). Both programs showed significant increases over the entire period of the current year and a half. Those for the milieu program were sufficient that the average incidence of Inappropriate Clinical Frequencies during the eighth anniversary assessment was essentially the same as that occurring before the program introduction over three and a half years earlier. The social-learning program maintained a significantly lower level of Inappropriate Clinical Frequencies than did the milieu program for the entire period. Additionally while Inappropriate Clinical Frequencies increased significantly for the social-learning program, the highest incidence occurring at the end of the period—11% of opportunities—was still a significant reduction from the 19% average occurrence obtained before the program introduction. Although both programs showed significant increases, the only significant differential change within the period occurred over the first six months, in which the milieu program increased Inappropriate Clinical Frequencies even more than did the social-learning program.

The possible association of notable events recorded in the research log to trends in resident behavior was examined. The start of the only significant trend for the entire period in Inappropriate Clinical Frequencies for both programs coincided with the beginning of the current time period. The only notable event associated with the beginning of the trend was the drastic reduction in length of time for time out and expulsion as a consequence for assaultive behavior. The change in procedure—the result of a statewide policy directive—appears to be responsible for the increase in Inappropriate Clinical Frequencies. The reduction had direct effects on Intolerable Behavior and clearly affected all other areas of functioning. Further support for the causal relationship of this procedural change lies in earlier findings that changes in the nature of dealing with assaultive behavior were related to increases and decreases in Inappropriate Clinical Frequencies—particularly changes in the length of time out and expulsion. Overall, then, the major outcome for the next year and a half for Inappropriate Clinical Frequencies was an increase in both programs to the extent that the milieu program failed to show improvement from pretreatment, but with the social-learning program still showing differentially greater effectiveness for this class of maladaptive behavior.

Both programs had also maintained significant improvement in Schizophrenic Disorganization by the fifth anniversary assessment, with the social-learning program once again demonstrating its greater effectiveness. While both programs maintained significant improvement from pretreatment over the entire eighteen months of the current period, they both showed significant increases in Schizophrenic Disorganization from the beginning to the end of the period, without differential change between them (figure 24.2). On an absolute level, the behaviors entering the Schizophrenic Disorganization Index—primarily bizarre motor behaviors (e.g., rocking, repetitive movements, blank staring, etc.)—had been the highest-frequency inappropriate clinical behaviors occurring before the introduction of the treatment programs. By the end of the year and a half period, the average milieu resident had increased the rate of performance of one of these bizarre behaviors from just over 32% at the beginning of the period to over 40% during the eighth anniversary assessment. Similarly the average social-learning resident had increased from about 24% to nearly 30% by the end of the period. Residents in both programs still showed considerable reductions from the 61% occurrence of Schizophrenic Disorganization before the program introduction, however.

The major significant increase in Schizophrenic Disorganization for both programs occurred during the first six months of the period—immediately following the change in time for expulsion and time out. There were two additional trends for milieu residents (figure 24.2), which span a sufficient range to indicate significant changes over some time points within the period—a reduction from the peak during the four-week block preceding anniversary assessment 6 to the low during the second block following assessment 6, and an increase from that low point to the peak during the four-week block following anniversary assessment 7. The only notable specific event associated with the beginning of the decreasing trend was a reemphasis on obtaining heavier senior staff coverage on evenings and weekends to help deal with assaultive behavior. A similar, and stronger, emphasis also occurred during the third and fourth four-week blocks after anniversary assessment 5. The additional coverage during this period was not associated with a decrease in Schizophrenic Disorganization, but when such coverage again began to fade, residents in both programs did show immediate increases in Schizophrenic Disorganization.

The start of the second upward trend in Schizophrenic Disorganization for the milieu program coincided with two notable events. The first was a series of newspaper articles by a local state representative in which previous accusations and attacks on the Department of Mental Health and the local institution were reiterated in detail. The nature of the accusations (e.g., that mental health workers were "wolves in charge of the sheep" and involved in a "conspiracy to take over state government," etc.) was such that staff and resident morale were notably affected. During the period of the increase, additional repercussions occurred, including an investigation of the institution and its programs by a legislative committee (which discounted all accusations and highly praised the institution) and newspaper responses to the representative when he continued accusations even after the investigation. The other notable event was the beginning of lengthy procedures to prepare the institution for hospital accreditation. They may have indirectly affected resident behavior because senior staff were heavily loaded with additional paperwork and committee meetings and were thus less available for direct on-the-floor contact with residents. The only notable event particularly associated with the end of the last upward trend in Schizophrenic Disorganization was the reintroduction of special sampling-exposure procedures to expose residents of both programs to off-unit facilities of the institution. These procedures began immediately before the seventh anniversary assessment. Overall, however, the major outcome for Schizophrenic Disorganization for the eighteen-month period was an increase in both programs, with both still maintaining significant reductions over the level existing before the program introduction and the social-learning program maintaining its differentially greater effectiveness for this class of clinically bizarre motoric behaviors.

Cognitive Distortion had shown continued significant reductions for both programs, without differential effectiveness between them by the fifth anniversary assessment. Over the current year and a half period, both programs essentially maintained the reductions in dysfunctional cognitive behavior that had been achieved earlier (figure 24.2). On an absolute level, the behaviors entering into the Cognitive Distortion Index—primarily bizarre verbal and facial behaviors indicative of thought disorder (e.g., delusions, hallucinations, incoherent speech, smiling without a stimulus, etc.)—had been reduced by over two-thirds, from the 24% average occurrence before the program introduction to between 7% and 8% average occurrence for both programs by the start of the current period. Both programs ended this period at about 9% average occurrence, showing neither additional gains nor losses and without differential effectiveness between them.

Figure 24.2 reveals only one particularly notable trend within the period for Cognitive Distortion—an increase for the milieu program that peaked immediately before the seventh anniversary assessment. The same increase and peak was also present for Hostile-Belligerence. The start of both of the increases coincided with the hearings of the legislative investigation as a follow-up on the accusations of the state representative. The upward trend termination coincided with a change in composition of living groups and the introduction of the special sampling-exposure procedures. While not significant, the slight upward trend in Cognitive Distortion just before anniversary assessment 8 coincided with the hiring of additional staff in preparation for expanded programs. While staffing levels in the treatment programs were not changed, it is possible that the presence of additional personnel for training may have been mildly disruptive. Overall, however, the major outcome for Cognitive Distortion over the entire period was the maintenance of earlier reductions of this class of clinically bizarre verbal and facial expressions, without differential effectiveness of the two programs.

By the fifth anniversary assessment, both programs averaged only about 0.1% incidence of Hostile-Belligerence—down from a low average incidence of 0.3% before the program introduction. At the end of the current period, neither program had shown overall or differential change; the social-learning program maintained an average incidence of less than 0.1%, and the milieu program showed a nonsignificant increase to just over 0.2%. The nature of behaviors entering into the Hostile-Belligerence Index—high-intensity aggressive behaviors (e.g., screaming, cursing, verbal intrusion, etc.)—are less adequately assessed by time sampling, since any occurrence of such behavior is clinically disruptive. Even with these restrictions, there was an increase in Hostile-Belligerence for the milieu program immediately after the change in time for expulsion and a major increase just before anniversary assessment 7 (figure 24.2). The second increase paralleled that for Cognitive Distortion and was associated with additional activities surrounding the accusations of the state representative. The termination of the increase was similarly associated with the change in living group composition and the beginning of the second special program of sampling-exposure. Except for the specific increments, however, Hostile-Belligerence varied nonsignificantly below the original low absolute level.

Because of the apparent importance of the change in time for expulsion and time out as a consequence for assaultive behavior in the overall poorer showing during this period—especially for the milieu program—the incidence of Intolerable Behavior takes on particular meaning. By the time of the fifth anniversary assessment, the data had already shown that therapeutic community procedures were inadequate to handle dangerous and aggressive acts such as physical assault, to the extent that those in the milieu program had shown an increase in average

## Differential Effectiveness of the Programs  255

weekly total incidence of Intolerable Behavior from 21 to 60.5. During the same period social-learning program residents had significantly reduced their Intolerable Behavior by nearly two-thirds the original level to a total weekly incidence of 11.25. Analyses of earlier data on Intolerable Behavior had suggested that the length of time for expulsion was particularly important for the milieu program, probably because group expulsion was the only consequence available for assaultive behavior in the therapeutic community. The social-learning program, on the other hand, employed token response costs resulting in other behavioral restrictions, as well as contingent time out, as a consequence for assaultive behavior. Thus, if the reduction in allowable time for expulsion and time out were the major basis for the failure of both programs to show additional improvements over the current period, increases in Intolerable Behavior would be expected following that change.

The changes in the average total weekly incidence of Intolerable Behavior in figure 24.3—plotted relative to incidence before program introduction—leaves little question of the effect. The first full four-week block immediately following the change in time showed increases that were significant for the milieu program (chi-square=4.40, df=1, $p < 0.05$) and approached significance for the social-learning program (chi-square=3.37, df=1, $p < 0.10$).[3] These immediate increases were to high levels of Intolerable Behavior that had not been even approached by the respective programs during the entire two-year period

Figure 24.3. Changes in incidence of aggressive and assaultive Intolerable Behavior during the next year and a half.

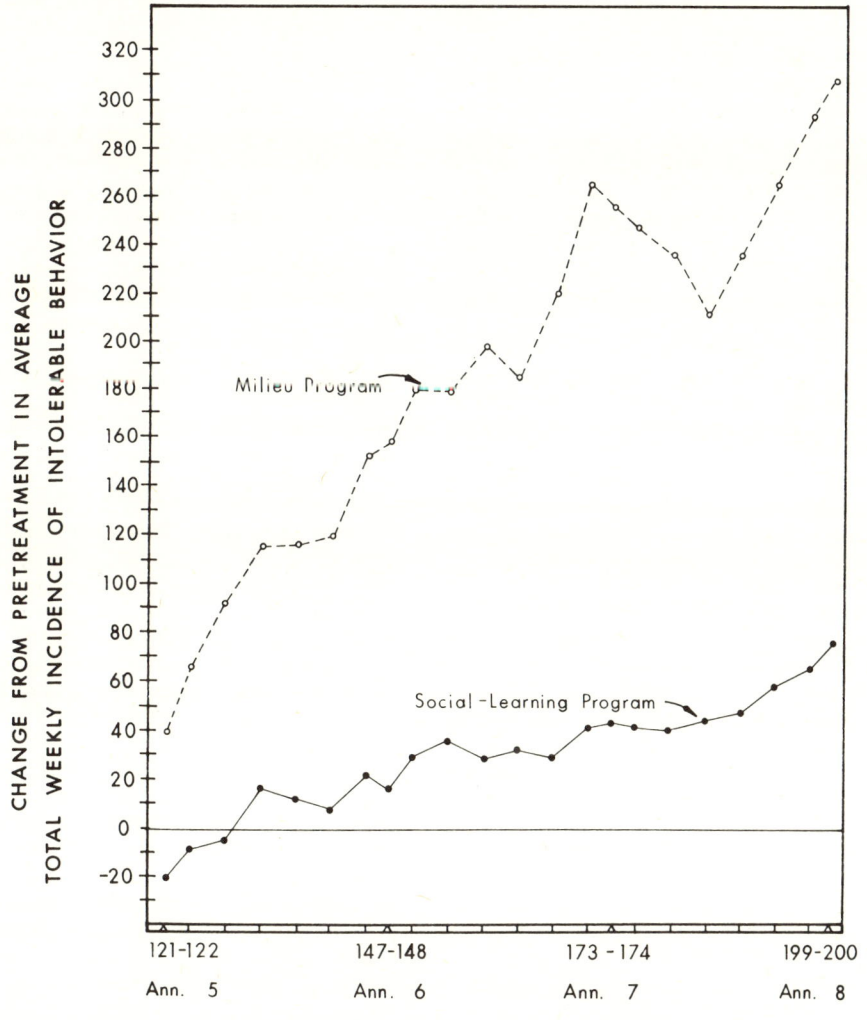

preceding the change in time out and expulsion. Figure 24.3 clearly shows that the effects of this change were continuing and cumulative, with the increases between each successive anniversary assessment being significant for both milieu (chi-squares > 4.37, df=1, p < 0.05) and social-learning programs (chi-squares > 5.49, df=1, p < 0.05). Although increases occurred in both programs, the social-learning program still maintained its relative superiority in controlling dangerous and aggressive acts at all points during the period (chi-squares > 74.57, df=1, p < 0.01). However, by the end of the period, both programs showed significant increases over levels of Intolerable Behavior existing even before the program introduction (chi-square=270.27 and 41.55, respectively, for milieu and social-learning, df=1, p < 0.01). At the high points, the average week on the social-learning units found nearly 110 separate incidents of dangerous and aggressive acts, while on the milieu unit, 330 incidents occurred —on the average, more than one every half-hour during waking hours.

Additional analyses of the day-to-day and week-to-week data surrounding the change in time-out and expulsion rules were carried out to determine if the effects might have been a function of specific residents having more opportunity to commit assaultive acts rather than the change reflecting a loss of the effectiveness of negative consequences. Before the time change, 64% of milieu residents and 25% of social-learning residents had committed at least one Intolerable Behavior during a two-week period. From one to three weeks after the change, all of the prior violators essentially maintained the same level of Intolerable Behavior that had occurred before the change; only 25% showed any increase at all on the milieu unit, and an equal number showed decreases. Similarly on the social-learning unit, fewer than 11% showed an increase during the weeks immediately following the change in the length of time out for assault. Thus, the increased incidence of Intolerable Behavior could not be attributed to more opportunity for a limited number of people.

Gradual increases in Intolerable Behavior started to occur in both programs in the fourth week following the change in consequences for assaultive behavior—first in the incidence among previous violators and later in other residents, some of whom had never before engaged in assault. In the milieu program, the most aggressive resident during the eighth anniversary assessment had increased from one incident during the two weeks before the change in expulsion time to 141 during the two-week period of the eighth anniversary assessment. The number of milieu residents committing at least one Intolerable Behavior during a two-week period increased from 64% to 82%. The social-learning program similarly found the most extreme resident to have changed from a zero incidence of Intolerable Behavior during the two weeks before the change to 36 during the two-week period of the eighth anniversary assessment. Concurrently the number of social-learning residents committing at least one Intolerable Behavior during a two-week period increased from 25% to 79%.

Although the overall change in Intolerable Behavior during the period reflected steady increases across each anniversary assessment period, there were several periods of relative stability in both programs and one reversal in the milieu program (figure 24.3). The trends, particularly for the milieu program appeared to be related to notable events from the research log. The immediate staff response to the increase in assaultiveness following the change in time-out and expulsion time was to increase the administration of psychotropic drugs—at least doubling the number of residents on drugs in both programs from the low during the previous two years (25% to 50% for milieu residents, 21% to 57% for social-learning residents). After two and a half months on this latter regime, assaultiveness was still increasing, and drugs were gradually reduced again— immediately to 29% and 25%, respectively, for milieu and social-learning residents (ultimately, to 18% and 11%). Concurrent with the reduction, senior staff made exceptional efforts to provide regular, rather than intermittent, coverage of evenings and weekends. They started during the third four-week block after anniversary assessment 5 and continued for the period reflected in figure 24.3 during which Intolerable Behavior was held at a constant level in both programs. However, when attempts were made to fade senior staff coverage of off-hours back to an intermittent schedule, increases noted immediately before anniversary assessment 6 again occurred. Senior staff coverage again was reemphasized immediately following anniversary assessment 6 and was once again associated with a relative stability of Intolerable Behavior.

The increases in Intolerable Behavior just before anniversary assessment 7 were coincident with the legislative investigation and newspaper responses to the accusations of the state representative. Both activities were potentially disruptive from the content of the accusations' providing distress to staff and residents. Additionally the demands on senior staff time for involvement in these activities, combined with the committee and paperwork entailed in the preparation for hospital accreditation, more heavily taxed their ability to be on the floor in direct contact with residents.

The stability in Intolerable Behavior for the social-learning program and the decrease for the milieu program occurring from the peak before to the third block following anniversary assessment 7 corresponds to the period during which special sampling-exposure procedures were instituted. The decrease in Intolerable Behavior during this time (figure 24.3) also parallels similar decreases in Cognitive Distortion and Hostile-Belligerence (figure 24.2). The total pattern thus suggests that the effects may have been a result of the increased coverage of off-hours by senior staff necessitated by the special procedures. The continuing increases in Intolerable Behavior occurred when senior staff coverage was once more reduced to an intermittent basis on completion of the sampling-exposure substudy. That the increase was considerably greater for the milieu residents than for the social-learning residents is further evidence that the special response-cost procedures of the social-learning program still provided some control of assaultive behavior, even with the ineffectiveness of the short time period for time out.

Overall the major outcome for the entire year and a half was an increase in Intolerable Behavior in both programs that was clearly a result of the reduction in the length of time of expulsion and time out as a consequence for assaultive behavior. Social-learning procedures were differentially more effective in controlling Intolerable Behavior than were therapeutic community procedures, but both programs showed increases above pretreatment levels that were clearly disruptive to other areas of functioning within the programs.

## CHANGES IN ADAPTIVE BEHAVIOR

The changes in components of maladaptive behavior clearly show a decline in effectiveness of both programs, with the social-learning program still maintaining superiority to the milieu program overall. Both programs showed increases in grossly inappropriate responses to minimal behavioral expectations. The increase for the milieu program was such that it not only remained inferior to the social-learning program but failed to show gains even over pretreatment levels by the end of the period. Both programs also showed significant increases in Schizophrenic Disorganization, although they both maintained significant improvement from pretreatment levels, and the social-learning program maintained its differentially greater effectiveness. The earlier improvements in Cognitive Distortion emerged from the current period relatively unscathed. Although no further improvement was obtained, both programs did maintain the significant gains made earlier for dysfunctional cognitive behaviors. Similarly, with two exceptions, the frequency of observed instances of time-sampled Hostile Belligerence remained low, without differential effectiveness between programs. The most dramatic changes during the period were the increases in aggressive Intolerable Behavior that occurred in both programs. They were largely a function of the change in consequences for assaultive behavior and appeared to moderate the failure of both programs to produce additional gains during the current period. Even though the social-learning program showed increases in dangerous and aggressive acts, it maintained significantly lower levels and increased less than the milieu program did. Overall, while both programs lost ground during the year and a half, the social-learning program still demonstrated its clear superiority in one of the critical target areas essential for rehabilitation of the chronically institutionalized population: elimination or reduction of extreme bizarre maladaptive behaviors.

The detrimental effects of the change in consequences for assaultive behavior and the resulting increases in aggressive acts are further apparent upon an examination of adaptive components of functioning. Both concurrent appropriate behavior (TSBC) and adaptive responsiveness within programs (Clinical Frequencies) showed declines over the year and a half (figure 24.1). The TSBC Total Appropriate Index appears to mirror changes in Intolerable Behavior. On an absolute level, social-learning residents decreased from an average performance of 3.11 concurrent appropriate behaviors during a two-second observation at the beginning of the period to an average of 2.74 appropriate behaviors during anniversary assessment 8 (up 0.30 from pretreatment baseline). Milieu residents entered the period performing about 2.86 appropriate behaviors on the average observation, showed a rapid drop to levels at or below pretreatment baseline, and ended the period with only 2.25 appropriate behaviors on the average observation (0.27 below pretreatment baseline).

Total Appropriate Clinical Frequencies similarly showed a steady reduction for both programs over the entire period, albeit less sharp than concurrent appropriate behavior (figure 24.1). The decrease reflects an average change for social-learning residents from over 61% terminal-level performance of social and instrumental behaviors during the fifth anniversary assessment to nearly 50% during the eighth assessment—still well over double the initial level before the program introduction. The decrease for milieu residents reflects an average change from about 35% normal performance of social and instrumental behaviors during anniversary assessment 5 to less than 26% during anniversary assessment 8—barely above the initial level existing before program introduction.

Of greater clinical interest are the changes in components of adaptive Clinical Frequencies that directly reflect the other identified target areas for rehabilitation of the chronically institutionalized population. These indexes, presented in figure 24.4, suggest that differential declines occurred over the components of adaptive behavior.

*Statistical evaluation.* To statistically evaluate changes in adaptive behavior over this time period, standardized scores for TSBC Total Appropriate Behavior and Clinical Frequencies for Instrumental Role Performance, Interpersonal Skills, and Self-Care Indexes were entered into a three-way repeated measures ANOVA (milieu vs. social-learning programs; anniversary assessments 5, 6, 7, 8; scores). Parallel to the findings for Global Functioning and maladaptive behavior, the overall analysis of adaptive behavior found significant main effects for programs ($F=7.30$, $df=1/54$, $p < 0.01$) and time ($F=13.85$, $df=3/162$, $p < 0.01$) without a program x time interaction ($F < 1$). However, the scores' main effect approached significance ($F=2.55$, $df=3/162$, $p < 0.06$), and all three interactions involving scores were significant: programs x scores ($F=3.49$, $df=3/162$, $p < 0.05$), time x scores and programs x time x scores ($F=6.21$ and $2.18$, respectively, $df=9/486$, $p < 0.05$).

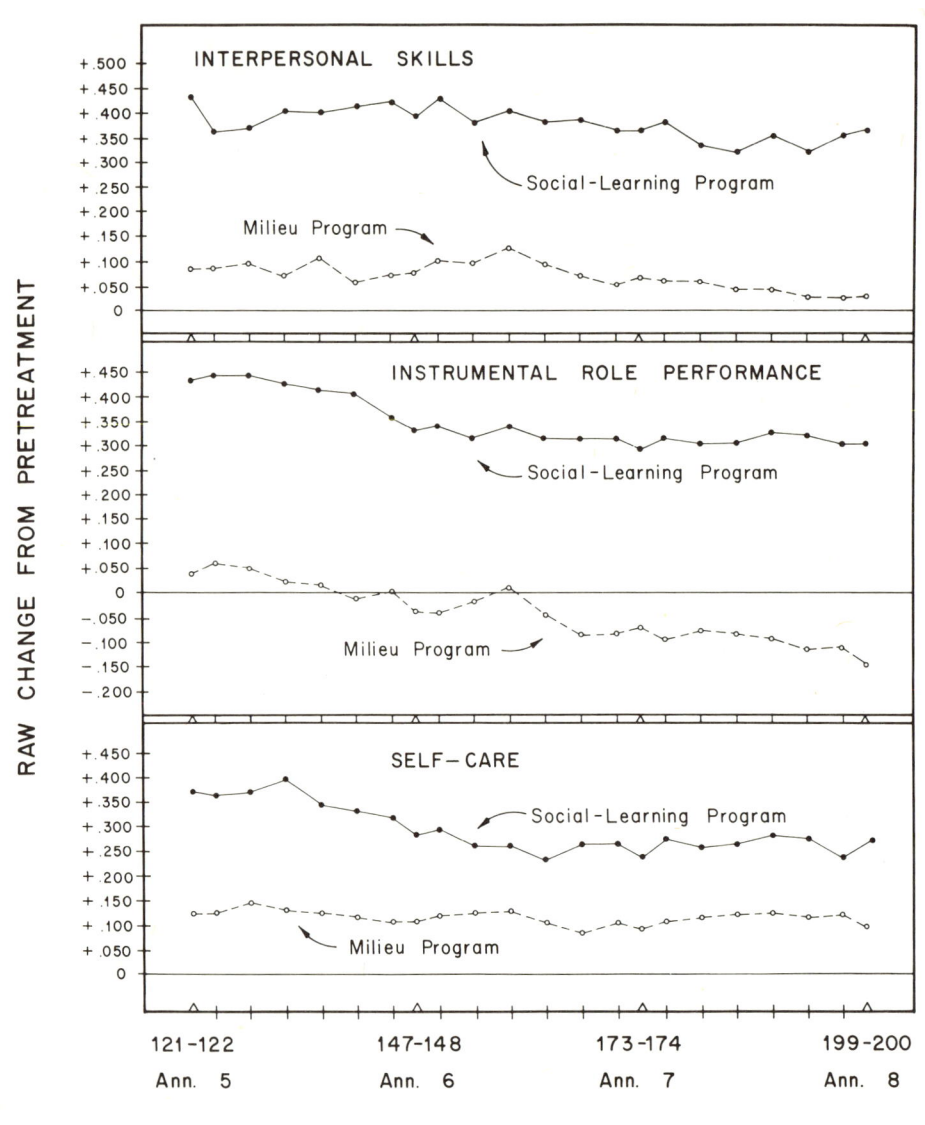

Figure 24.4. Changes in component adaptive behavior from Clinical Frequencies during the next year and a half.

Additional three-way ANOVAs with partitioning of simple effects and a priori tests of individual components were carried out on successive anniversary assessment periods to clarify the findings.[2] As previously found for maladaptive behavior, significant program main effects were found to reflect the superiority of the social-learning program to the milieu program in overall adaptive behavior for the entire period (all $F > 5.54$, df=1/54, $p < 0.05$). Also similar to maladaptive behavior, not a single overall program x time interaction approached significance for adaptive behavior (all $p > 0.15$), and the significant time main effect was largely attributable to decreases in overall level of adaptive behavior over both programs during the first six months of the period ($F=16.30$, df=1/54, $p < 0.01$). The decreases were maintained to the eighth anniversary assessment ($F=20.97$, df=1/54, $p < 0.01$) without additional significant changes over the last two six-month periods ($p > 0.10$). Significant interactions involving scores were also obtained during the first six months and from the beginning to the end of the period, indicating that not all classes of adaptive behavior were equally affected.

The overall reduction in concurrent appropriate behavior between anniversary assessments 5 and 6 (TSBC Total Appropriate Index, figure 24.1) was significant within groups for both milieu ($F=24.13$, df=1/54, $p < 0.01$) and social-learning programs ($F=20.08$, df=1/54, $p < 0.01$), without differential change between them ($F < 1$). The social-learning program showed no further significant changes in concurrent appropriate behavior after anniversary assessment 6 ($F$'s $< 1$), ending the period at a significantly lower level than that achieved by assessment 5 ($F=13.88$, df=1/54, $p < 0.01$). The milieu program, in contrast, showed continued decreases after anniversary assessment 6 that approached significance (p's $< 0.10$), ending the period not only at a significantly lower level than that achieved by assessment 5 ($F=35.72$, df=1/54, $p < 0.01$) but also showing significantly greater reductions over the entire period than that of the social-learning program ($F=5.07$, df=1/54, $p < 0.05$). On an absolute basis, social-learning residents maintained significantly higher levels of concurrent appropriate behavior than milieu residents did throughout the period (F's $> 4.27$, df=1/54, $p < 0.05$).

The decline in Instrumental Role Performance (figure 24.4) between anniversary assessments 5 and 6 was also significant over both programs combined ($F=6.58$, df=1/54, $p < 0.05$), without differential change between them ($F < 1$). Thereafter, the Instrumental Role Performance of social-learning residents remained stable for the rest of the period (F's $< 1$), while milieu residents showed further reductions, which approached significance between anniversary assessments 7 and 8 ($F=3.03$, df=1/54, $p < 0.10$). The overall reduction in Instrumental Role Performance from the beginning to the end of the period was significant over both programs ($F=10.18$, df=1/54, $p < 0.01$), without differential change between them ($F < 1$). On an absolute level, social-learning residents ended the period as they had begun it, with significantly higher levels of Instrumental Role Performance than milieu residents ($F=4.37$, df=1/54, $p < 0.05$).

The only class of behavior in which the social-learning program showed greater losses than the milieu program at any time during the period was Self-Care (figure 24.4). During the first six months of the period they had a significantly greater reduction in performance of Self-Care than those in the milieu program ($F=5.02$, df=1/54, $p < 0.05$). Thereafter, residents in both programs showed gradual, nonsignificant reductions for the remainder of the period ($p > 0.10$)—ending the year and a half at significantly lower levels than they had achieved by anniversary assessment 5 ($F=5.29$, df=1/54, $p < 0.05$), without significant differential change between them ($F=2.57$, df=1/54, $p > 0.10$). However, even with the decreases, the Self-Care performance of social-learning residents was maintained at a significantly higher level than that of milieu residents at every assessment during the period (all F's $> 4.16$, df=1/54, $p < 0.05$).

Interpersonal Skills (figure 24.4) also showed a significant decline over both programs from the beginning to the end of the period ($F=6.00$, df=1/54, $p < 0.05$), without differential change between them ($F < 1$). The simple program x time interactions for Interpersonal Skills approached significance between anniversary assessments 5 and 6 ($F=3.54$, df=1/54, $p < 0.10$) and between assessments 7 and 8 ($F=3.62$, df=1/54, $p < 0.10$)—reflecting relatively greater losses for the social-learning program during the first six months and for the milieu program during the last six months. However, as with other classes of adaptive behavior, the social-learning program consistently maintained the significantly higher levels of Interpersonal Skills performance over that of the milieu program at every assessment point during the entire period (all F's $> 8.68$, df=1/54, $p < 0.01$).

Those in both programs, then, showed losses in all four classes of adaptive behavior during the period. The extent of the losses for the milieu program were such that the within-groups change from the pretreatment baseline was no longer significant for Interpersonal Skills or Instrumental Role Performance from the point of the sixth anniversary assessment through the end of the period (all $p > 0.10$).

Additionally the within-groups improvement from pretreatment baseline in Self-Care only approached significance (F=3.27, df=1/54, p < 0.10) for the milieu program by the time of anniversary assessment 8, and the loss in TSBC Total Appropriate Behavior approached statistical significance by that assessment (F=3.81, df=1/54, p < 0.10). In contrast, even with the losses of the current period, the social-learning program maintained its significant improvement from pretreatment baseline on all four classes of adaptive behavior (F's > 4.55, df=1/54, p < 0.05) and differentially greater improvement than the milieu program did on every score at every point during the period (F's > 7.97, df=1/54, p < 0.01).

*Descriptive interpretation.* Thus, in contrast to the major improvements and maintenance of increased levels of adaptive behavior that had been achieved through the fifth anniversary assessment, the next year and a half was largely characterized by losses. For the most part, the losses occurred in both programs, with the social-learning program still maintaining its superiority. Both programs had produced significant improvements in concurrent appropriate behavior by the time of the fifth anniversary assessment with the social-learning program showing significantly greater improvements. During the current year and a half residents of both programs showed significant losses, with milieu residents showing significantly greater ones, to the extent that they ended the period at a level below that existing before the introduction of the programs (figure 24.1, TSBC). While social-learning residents also suffered losses, they maintained a significant improvement in concurrent appropriate behavior from the level existing before the program introduction and significantly greater improvement than milieu residents at every assessment point.

Both programs showed significant reductions in concurrent appropriate behavior during the six months immediately following the change in the length of time of expulsion and time out as a consequence for assaultive behavior. Thereafter, the social-learning program largely maintained stability for this class of appropriate behavior, while the milieu program showed additional variability and further losses over the remainder of the period. The point-to-point plots of TSBC Total Appropriate Behavior in figure 24.1 reveal that the reversal of the first downward trend in both programs occurred immediately following the third four-week block after anniversary assessment 5. It was coincident with the increased coverage of evenings and weekends by senior staff and parallels the temporary stability of Intolerable Behavior (figure 24.3). Similarly the temporary increase in concurrent appropriate behavior immediately after anniversary assessment 6 also parallels the relative stability in rates of Intolerable Behavior following a renewed emphasis of senior staff coverage of off-hours. The decline in concurrent appropriate behavior for milieu residents between anniversary assessments 6 and 7 also parallels increases in rates of Intolerable Behavior. These changes were associated with the legislative committee investigations and newspaper responses to the attacks of the state representative. The period of relative stability and later decrease in TSBC Appropriate Behavior during the last six months of the period also coincided with the special sampling-exposure procedures and ensuing reductions and increases of Intolerable Behavior for the milieu program.

The TSBC Appropriate Behavior Index appears to be exceptionally sensitive to environmental and psychological influences, with the primary mediating variable during the current period being the increases in assaultive behavior. Thus, the major outcome for the period for milieu residents was the decline in levels of concurrent appropriate behavior, paralleling increases in Intolerable Behavior—to the extent that they ended the period at a lower level of functioning than had existed even before the program introduction. Although the change in time-out procedures affected social-learning residents, their losses in concurrent appropriate behavior were not as drastic; they ended the period at levels of concurrent appropriate behavior that were still significantly higher than those existing before the program introduction.

Much less sensitivity to moment-to-moment influences was apparent in components of adaptive responsiveness within treatment programs (figure 24.4). There were reductions in both programs over the current period, with the only notable temporary increases in point-to-point plots occurring between anniversary assessments 6 and 7 for Interpersonal Skills and Instrumental Role Performance. Both of these increases paralleled those of TSBC Appropriate Behavior and were similarly concurrent with increased senior staff coverage of off-hours and parallel relative stability of Intolerable Behavior. Similarly both of the decreases paralleled other losses in functioning associated with repercussions of accusations by the state representative and concurrent increases in Intolerable Behavior—again stabilizing upon changing the composition of milieu living groups, the start of special sampling-exposure procedures, and temporary stability or reductions in Intolerable Behavior.

On an absolute level, the behaviors entering the Interpersonal Skills Index—relative frequencies of interpersonal interaction and communication skills—had originally been the most deficient of all areas of functioning. By the fifth anniversary assessment, the average milieu resident had approximately doubled the initial rate of terminal-level performance of these social skills but was still performing normal ones on only about 19% of available opportunities. By the end of the current year and a half, losses for milieu residents were sufficient that they no longer showed significant improvement; their normal Interpersonal Skills had increased only 3% from their initial level. While social-learning residents had shown dramatic improvements to nearly 48% normal performance of Interpersonal Skills by the fifth anniversary assessment, they also showed losses over the current period—to less than 40% normal performance on the average. Nevertheless, they still reflected a major improvement over their initial level and an end-of-period rate over three times that of milieu residents. Thus, while both programs showed overall losses in Interpersonal Skills during the period as a function of the change in procedures for controlling assaultive behavior, the social-learning program still showed differentially greater and major improvement in one of the components of the resocialization target for rehabilitation.

The behaviors entering the Self-Care Index—relative frequencies of terminal-level performance of self-maintenance activities (e.g., personal appearance, meal behavior, bathing, maintenance of personal living area, etc.)—reflect the other component of the resocialization target for rehabilitation. By the fifth anniversary assessment, both programs had also produced significant increases in the exceptionally low levels of Self-Care that had existed before the program introduction, with the social-learning program showing differentially greater effectiveness. During the current year and a half (figure 24.4), milieu residents showed a slight loss, from an average of over 25% normal performance of Self-Care activities at the beginning of the period to 22% during anniversary assessment 8—still above their initial rate of less than 13%. Social-learning residents had shown a marked improvement in Self-Care by the beginning of the period—to nearly 50% normal performance. By the end of the period, they had decreased to nearly 39% normal performance of Self-Care—a significant loss, but still three times their initial rate and significantly better than that of milieu residents.

Although Instrumental Role Performance had been initially less deficient than other areas of functioning, milieu residents had previously shown an increase, followed by a decrease, in this class of behavior—to the extent that they failed to show a significant improvement by the time of the fifth anniversary assessment. In contrast, the social-learning program had maintained its earlier improvements at a rate of over 81% normal performance during the fifth anniversary assessment. Both programs also showed losses in this class of adaptive behavior over the current year and a half. The losses for the milieu program were such that the average resident was performing normal Instrumental Role behavior 14% less than before introduction of programs—not a significant loss but below initial levels nevertheless. Social-learning residents also showed significant declines over the period but still ended the year and a half with a significant improvement from pretreatment, performing normal Instrumental Role behavior on over 67% of opportunities. The behaviors entering the Instrumental Role Index—primarily "on task" in classes and job training and "on time" at scheduled work, activities, and meetings—were still clearly more responsive to social-learning procedures and unresponsive to therapeutic community procedures. Thus, even with the losses of the current period, the superiority of the social-learning program was still maintained in this third major target area.

## SUMMARY AND INDIVIDUAL IMPROVEMENT RATES

The group analyses clearly show overall losses in both programs over the next year and a half, although the social-learning program still maintained its superiority. Residents in both programs showed decreases in Global Functioning, without differential loss between them. However, the extent of the losses in Global Functioning were such that the milieu residents as a group failed to maintain significant improvement from before the introduction of the programs by the end of the period. The social-learning residents, in contrast, not only maintained significant improvement in Global Functioning from before program introduction but continued with significantly greater improvement than milieu residents did throughout the period. Similar losses in previous effectiveness occurred in both maladaptive and adaptive components of functioning. The most dramatic changes during the period were increases in aggressive Intolerable Behavior, which were largely a result of procedural changes in dealing with assaultiveness. Dangerous and aggressive acts increased dramatically in both programs, with those in the milieu program reaching severely disruptive levels. Largely as a result of these unfortunate circumstances, both programs showed significant increases in grossly inappropriate responses to minimal behavioral expectations and in Schizophrenic Disorganization. While the social-learning program also maintained significant improvements from pretreatment and superiority to the milieu program in these classes of maladaptive behavior, the milieu program ended the period with significant reductions only in Schizophrenic Disorganization. No significant losses occurred by the end of the period for either program in time-sampled Hostile-Belligerence, which remained low, without significant differences. The earlier reductions in Cognitive Distortion were maintained without loss for both programs. Thus, by the end of the period, the social-learning program was still demonstrating clear superiority to the milieu program in the reduction or elimination of some classes of extreme bizarre behaviors—one of the crucial target areas for rehabilitation of the severely disabled chronic population.

The similar superiority of the social-learning program was maintained for adaptive behavioral targets as well. The detrimental effects of the changes in consequences for assaultive behavior were reflected in the losses of previous gains for adaptive behavior in both programs. Concurrent appropriate behavior again showed exceptional sensitivity to environmental and psychological influences, with milieu residents showing differentially greater losses than social-learning residents did during the period—to a level below that existing before program introduction. The classes of adaptive-behavior assessing components of the resocialization and instrumental role targets of rehabilitation also showed losses during the period. In adaptive behavior the losses were sufficient for the milieu program that neither Interpersonal Skills nor Instrumental Role Performance improved over the level existing before the programs began. While the social-learning program also lost ground during the current year and a half, all classes of adaptive behavior still showed significant gains from before the introduction of the program and significantly greater gains than the milieu program did. Thus, even with the losses following the procedural changes for handling assaultive behavior, the group analyses found a clear effectiveness of the social-learning program and clear superiority over the milieu program on all targets of rehabilitation of the chronically institutionalized population.

Since clinical workers are more often concerned with percentage improvement of individual cases than with parametric group differences, the Global Functioning Factor Scores were further evaluated to provide an indication of the extent of individual resident response during the period. Improvement rates presented in table 24.1 disclose that a full half of the residents in both programs showed significant decreases in functioning during the next year and a half, without differences occurring between programs. A few residents in both showed additional significant gains; however, the losses reflected in the group analyses following the change in procedures for handling assaultive behavior clearly appear in individual resident data as well.

Possible differential predictability of responsiveness over the period from demographic and level of functioning variables was examined by correlational analyses.[4] Only two significant correlations with change over the year and a half were obtained for the two programs combined, without a single significant difference occurring between programs on any variable. The two significant correlations found residents who declined in functioning over the period to tend toward lower levels of functioning at original program entry (r=0.30) and toward more gradual onset of initial symptomatology (r=0.31). Neither overall nor differential predictability was obtained from any of the remaining demographic variables (age, sex, race, socioeconomic status, process-reactive status, marital status, identified precipitants on initial hospitalization, current or total length of hospitalization, prior electroconvulsive or insulin shock, or other medical treatments) or from level of functioning or drug status at the beginning of the period.

An examination of possible predictability of individual resident change within the period found only two significant correlations with the decreases during the first six months (decreasing residents tended to be lower in socioeconomic

Table 24.1. Objective rates of change in overall functioning from the fifth to eighth anniversary assessments for original equated groups (N=28 each).

| Treatment program | Change from condition on fifth six-month assessment | | |
|---|---|---|---|
| | Worse[a] | No change | Improved[a] |
| Social-learning | 57.1% | 28.6% | 14.3% |
| Milieu therapy | 50.0% | 39.3% | 10.7% |

a. "Improved" and "worse" classification based upon individual change from assessment 5 to 8 exceeding 1.96 times the standard error of measurement on the standardized Global Functioning Factor Score. Chi-square "worse" versus "no change" and "improved" < 1.

level with longer total hospitalization, r's=-0.29 & -0.28, respectively), without significant differences between groups on any variable. Similarly no overall or differential predictability was obtained for resident change during the second six months of the period. No predictability of change over the last six months of the period was found over the combined groups; however, declining social-learning residents during the last six months tended to be older (r=-0.47) with relative longer periods of both current and total hospitalization (r's=-0.46 & -0.48, respectively), while declines of residents in the milieu program were unrelated to age and length of hospitalization (r's < 0.30).

In general, the correlational analyses reflect an absence of consistent overall or differential predictability of change within the period from demographic, level of functioning, and drug variables. The only other notable relationships with individual change during the year and a half involved correlations with Intolerable Behavior, none of which differed between programs. Although the prior frequency of dangerous and aggressive acts did not predict change during the period, change from anniversary assessment 5 to 6 was associated with the frequency of Intolerable Behavior at anniversary assessment 6 (r=-0.45) and change from anniversary assessment 6 to 7 was significantly associated with the frequency of Intolerable Behavior at anniversary assessment 7 (r=-0.29). By the end of the current year and a half, the incidence of Intolerable Behavior was negatively correlated with change (r=-0.40). All of these correlations indicated a tendency for residents who changed for the worse to be performing higher rates of dangerous and aggressive acts.

The relative greater influence of assaultive behavior to absolute levels of functioning following the change in time out and expulsion time was also clearly apparent in a significant increase in the relationship of individual Intolerable Behavior to Global Functioning from the fifth (r=-0.41) to the sixth anniversary assessment (r=-0.64). This increase in contribution of Intolerable Behavior to Global Functioning from the fifth anniversary assessment was even stronger by the end of the period (r=-0.70). However, as with other changes during the previous two years, with the exception of Intolerable Behavior, resident characteristics contributed relatively little to changes in functioning during the current year and a half.

The extent to which the losses during the year and a half affected comparative status is shown in table 24.2 where the individual improvement rates from program entry are presented. Although the percentage of residents showing significant improvement in both programs was still impressive, the cost of increased assaultiveness was apparent in the number of residents in both programs who were actually functioning at a lower level than before program entry by the end of the period. The superiority of the social-learning program was still clearly in evidence, but both programs showed the net effect of the circumstances prevailing during the next year and a half in lower rates of improvement than had been attained previously. Differential predictability of improvement from demographic, drug, and level of functioning data found milieu residents showing improvement at the end of the period to be more likely female than male (r=0.40); sex did not relate to improvement for social-learning residents (r=-0.05). The only other significant predictor of improvement was a tendency for shorter periods of current hospitalization to be related to improvement over combined groups (r=-0.30), without any other significant overall or differential relationships. Thus, with the exception of slight relationships for length of hospitalization in both programs and sex in the milieu program, overall improvement was not related to resident characteristics or behavior.

Two significant releases to independent living were achieved in each program during this period—largely attributable to the availability of jobs for residents who had previously improved and maintained functioning at normal levels. One of the milieu releases was the resident who had previously achieved significant

Table 24.2. Objective improvement rates in overall functioning from program entry to the eighth anniversary assessment for original equated groups (N=28 each).

| Treatment program | Condition at eighth six-month assessment | | |
| --- | --- | --- | --- |
| | Worse[a] | No change | Improved[a] |
| Social-learning | 14.3% | 3.6% | 82.1% |
| Milieu therapy | 25.0% | 32.1% | 42.9% |

a. "Improved" and "worse" classification based upon individual change from entry exceeding 1.96 times the standard error of measurement on the standardized Global Functioning Factor Score. Chi-square "improved" versus "no change" and "worse"=5.58, $p < 0.05$.

release and then had failed at community adjustment. She improved sufficiently to achieve significant release again. An additional release occurred from the social-learning program for a man who was diagnosed as having sufficient heart trouble that he could no longer participate in the active program. Although he did not meet criteria for independent functioning (requiring work), he had improved sufficiently to be released to a community placement at the time the physical problem was identified.

The decline in the effectiveness of both programs following the reduction of time for expulsion and time out for assaultive behavior was further reflected in the absence of movement within programs. Only one additional milieu resident achieved any promotions at all during the period, and none maintained higher step-level status. Similarly although an additional 25% of social-learning residents improved sufficiently to achieve promotions during the period, none maintained functioning at a level sufficient to remain on higher step levels. Thus, after a year and a half without effective negative consequences for dangerous and aggressive acts, not only were such acts occurring at a very high level, but few of the remaining residents in either treatment program were showing regular improvement. Some were even worse.

*A Few Illustrations.* Both programs still demonstrated remarkable improvements in functioning for significant numbers of the severely debilitated chronic population, with the social-learning program maintaining clear superiority to the milieu program. However, the most notable feature of the current period was the relative loss of effectiveness of both programs that occurred after the change in consequences for assaultive behavior. Brief case descriptions of residents who declined in functioning may help to illustrate the problems of the current period.

*Vera D. (milieu program)* showed responses over the year and a half following the reduction in expulsion time for assaultiveness that were typical of residents who had previously shown high rates of Intolerable Behavior. Upon entry to the milieu program, Vera was a forty-eight-year-old divorcee who had been hospitalized for over sixteen years. According to hospital records, she had completed the ninth grade and had worked at a variety of unskilled jobs—laundry, cannery, Works Progress Administration, etc.—until her admission with hallucinations and persecutory delusions. Before the introduction of the milieu procedures the only apparent vestige of clinical problems that had led to her initial hospitalization were frowning and grimacing without apparent stimuli on 26% of TSBC observations; the remainder of her clinically bizarre behaviors, at least one of which occurred on 74% of observations, consisted of social withdrawal, isolation, and blank staring. Normal social interactions occurred on only 2% of opportunities and her Self-Care Index of 0.16 reflected a total failure to maintain her appearance or her personal living area. In general, Vera displayed deficits at about the average level for the project group, with active clinically bizarre behaviors being below the average for the group as a whole. Vera's active withdrawal and inappropriate social interaction resulted in her being an unpleasant person to be around, but she did not display any assaultive behavior before the program began.

Vera's response to the milieu program up to the beginning of the current period had been dotted with sporadic outbursts of Hostile-Belligerence, largely in response to pressures from her living group to attend and participate in scheduled classes and activities rather than isolating herself or lying down. During one twelve-week period, Vera had resorted to physical assaults at a rate of over 2.5 per week, but they had been brought under control with the improved procedures for dealing with such acts, to the extent that she was performing an Intolerable Behavior, on the average, only once every other week by the time of the fifth anniversary assessment. Concurrent with the reductions in Intolerable Behavior, Vera had gradually improved in functioning, showing moderate, but significant, improvement. Her clinically bizarre behavior had been reduced from 74% of observations to 43% of them, and dysfunctional cognitive behavior was nearly absent. She was demonstrating normal social skills on only 10% of opportunities, which nevertheless represented a fourfold increase over her initial level. Although Vera was still functioning at an overall level that still required institutional control for her survival, she had shown improvements in nearly all areas, with the trend clearly being toward more rapid improvement after the revised procedures for dealing with dangerous and aggressive acts had been instituted.

Within three weeks after the reduction in the length of expulsion time for assaultiveness was imposed, Vera began increasing her verbal attacks, followed shortly by physical assaults at a level as high as any observed in the previous years of treatment. By the twelfth week she was performing an Intolerable Behavior at a rate greater than once per day—over four times as many incidents as in her worst earlier period. For Vera, the increase in Intolerable Behavior was paralleled by increases in the rate and number of clinically bizarre behaviors (grimacing without apparent stimulus, rocking, talking to herself, blank staring, repetitive movements, pacing, posturing) and decreases in adaptive behaviors over all areas of functioning. Variations in her functioning over the remainder of the current year and a half followed the notable events described earlier, showing decreases in Intolerable Behavior and other clinically bizarre acts with concurrent increases in adaptive functioning on every occasion in which senior staff coverage of off-hours was increased. Thus, Vera—and several other milieu residents with a prior history of assaultiveness—appeared to be particularly dependent upon external contingencies for controlling dangerous and aggressive acts. Such acts had become a high-frequency reaction to the pressures of the therapeutic community for her to change her preferred pattern of active withdrawal.

Her clinically bizarre behaviors were gradually reduced in frequency after peaking just before the sixth anniversary assessment—suggesting that milieu procedures were able to assist her in controlling such crazy behavior again. Vera's Intolerable Behavior, however, continued to increase over the remainder of the year and a half without effective consequences. She ended the period performing over twenty-five instances per week. Concurrently Vera also gradually decreased her performance of all adaptive behaviors to the point that previous therapeutic gains were not only lost, but her adaptive functioning in all areas was at or below initial entry levels. Thus, although milieu procedures had been able to reinstitute improvements in crazy behaviors after the initial disruption, the lack of effective consequences for dangerous and aggressive acts had resulted in Vera's active increases in such acts, with concurrent decreases in adaptive behaviors.

*Gary K. (milieu program)* showed responses over the year and a half following the reduction in expulsion time for assaultiveness that reflect the most debilitating effects of that procedural change for milieu residents who had never before engaged in aggressive behavior. At the time of entry to the milieu program Gary was a forty-three-year-old male who had never married. Although he had been hospitalized only about eight years at entry, his prehospital status had been one of minimal independence. He had continued to live in his parents' home except for brief periods of roaming around the country. Gary was reported to have dropped out of school in the eighth grade and had several nonviolent encounters with the law, including convictions for auto theft, vagrancy, and voyeurism. Before the introduction of the specific milieu therapy procedures Gary's functioning was low in absolute terms but among the higher levels for residents in the project. He performed clinically maladaptive behaviors on 63% of objective observations, primarily reflecting withdrawal and bizarre facial expressions. His Self-Care and Interpersonal Skills were above the original group average, but still showed deficits on about 85% of opportunities to perform. However, Gary's Instrumental Role Performance was among the highest of all project residents before the specific treatment procedures were introduced, reflecting attendance at all scheduled classes and activities and participation in 80% of them.

Gary had shown rapid improvement from the start of the program. Except for a brief period during the previous two years when some other milieu residents had increased assaultiveness, Gary had maintained decreased levels of clinically maladaptive behaviors, showing bizarre behaviors on less than 28% of observations during the fifth anniversary assessment. His improvements in adaptive behaviors had been maintained over the entire period, with his Self-Care and Interpersonal Skills doubling pretreatment levels, while his concurrent appropriate behavior had increased performance to an average of over three adaptive behaviors on every observation (the second highest level for males within the milieu program). On no occasion during the entire period of nearly two and a half years in residence in the milieu program had Gary shown a single instance of assaultive behavior. He had, in fact, achieved promotion to higher step levels and was a good model for other members of his living group and the community in general.

In contrast to Vera D., the change in expulsion time at the beginning of the current period had no direct affect on Gary, since he was not engaging in any dangerous and aggressive acts. He did show some increases in clinically bizarre behaviors suggestive of a stress response (rocking, pacing, shaking, posturing, talking to self) following the increase in assaultiveness of other residents and some decrease in concurrent appropriate behaviors (TSBC), which were particularly sensitive to external social and psychological conditions. However, he maintained his improved levels of functioning in all other areas for about eight months after the change in expulsion time. Indicants of stress reactions were even decreased, nearly to previous levels, during the periods in which senior staff coverage of off-hours and resulting stability in rate of assaults occurred. However, concurrent with the radio and newspaper attacks on the center by the local state representative, Gary's stress reactions began to steadily climb again, as well as nearly doubling the amount of time he spent alone. Steady increases in these behaviors continued over a period of sixteen weeks before his adaptive behaviors began to deteriorate. Eventually Gary showed a dramatic increase in clinically bizarre behaviors to a level nearly six times that which he had demonstrated at the fifth anniversary assessment. His adaptive behavior deteriorated to a third of the level he had demonstrated even before entry to the program. For the first time Gary began to perform assaultive behaviors—averaging four instances of Intolerable Behavior per week by the time of the seventh anniversary assessment.

The change in group composition and special sampling-exposure procedures seemed to have provided Gary with an adaptive means of avoiding the assaultiveness of other residents as his own clinically maladaptive behaviors and adaptive components of functioning almost immediately returned to earlier levels, and Intolerable Behavior dropped out altogether. However, after a period of twelve weeks, following the increased rate of assaultiveness by other residents, Gary's stress response returned, accompanied by a gradual deterioration in all aspects of adaptive functioning. By the eighth anniversary assessment he was actively avoiding contact with other residents on 75% of waking hours and had not only lost all previous gains from milieu treatment, but was functioning at an overall level significantly below that at entry to the program. From a man who had not shown a single instance of assaultive behavior before the change in expulsion time, a year and a half in the presence of other residents without effective controls on assaultiveness had resulted in Gary's performing nearly four instances of dangerous and aggressive Intolerable Behaviors per day. The effects on Gary clearly show how the externally imposed change in the single procedure for assaultiveness had far-reaching effects on all other components of program operation, with the result that the milieu had become distinctly nontherapeutic.

*Bobbi F. (social-learning)* showed responses fairly typical of those of other social-learning residents who had demonstrated assaultive behaviors before the reduction in the length of time out. Bobbi's previous response (see chapter 14) had been representative of agitated and aggressive residents in the social-learning program, having reduced aggressive Intolerable Behaviors from twenty-three per week to one every other week by the time of the first anniversary assessment. Concurrently significant improvements in adaptive behavior and decreases in bizarre behavior had occurred by the first anniversary assessment, although she had still clearly required institutional control for her survival. Over the two years between the first anniversary assessment and the start of the present period, Bobbi had shown a decline in functioning following the death of another resident that was similar to that of many other social-learning residents. The pattern at that time had first been a decrease in concurrent appropriate behavior, followed by an increase in bizarre motoric behaviors and social withdrawal, and finally an increase in assaultiveness.

Within four weeks of the institution of the longer time out periods, Bobbi had regained her earlier levels of improvement in all areas, and continuing objective improvement was in evidence at the fifth anniversary assessment. At that time her clinically bizarre behaviors had been reduced to less than 18% of her initial levels, and her concurrent appropriate behaviors had nearly doubled. All areas of adaptive functioning had increased from the nearly complete deficits existing before entry to the program to performance of self-maintenance and social skills indistinguishable from normal ones on nearly 60% of opportunities. Bobbi had performed only one instance of Intolerable Behavior in the four weeks before the change in time out was imposed. Overall, as with many other social-learning residents, Bobbi had literally changed from functioning as a savage animal to a pleasant human being, with quite a sense of humor.

The sequence of deterioration of the current period for Bobbi, and other similar social-learning residents, was considerably different from that described for Vera D. in the milieu program. Bobbi did not show any increase in assaultiveness until some ten weeks after the change in time-out procedures. Rather, her previous upward trend in concurrent adaptive behavior immediately leveled upon the introduction of the change and began a gradual decline over a period of weeks. Self-maintenance and social skills were also maintained, but a gradual increase in bizarre motoric behaviors started almost immediately. All of these changes are suggestive of stress reactions, more similar to that described for Gary K. rather than for Vera D. Once she performed an assaultive act and experienced the shortened time-out consequence, Bobbi rapidly accelerated to a level of nearly one Intolerable Behavior per day, accompanied by rapid deterioration in the performance of all adaptive behaviors and increases in bizarre motoric behaviors—actively avoiding other residents on over 87% of waking hours. Her dysfunctional cognitive behaviors, however, did not increase at all during this period—even though her past history had contained documented occurrences of blatant delusions and hallucinations.

By the seventh anniversary assessment, Bobbi was performing nearly two intolerable acts per day, with the result that her accumulated token fines had reached an astronomical figure, with the secondary negative side effect of removing access to backup reinforcers within the program. Bobbi was responsive to the special sampling-exposure procedures and the proportional-payoff substudy that were conducted in hope of overcoming these problems over the last six months of the current period. She immediately began to increase adaptive behavior and decrease maladaptive behaviors and gradually reduced her incidence of dangerous and aggressive acts. By the eighth anniversary assessment, her overall functioning was well above that achieved by the first anniversary assessment but still below the level achieved before the change in time-out procedures. She was, however, still performing Intolerable Behaviors at an average rate of once per week. Thus, although the reduced consequences for assaultiveness had clear negative effects, the alternative response-cost procedures, combined with more stable functioning as a result of earlier treatment, did not result in the complete devastation for Bobbi or other social-learning residents that was seen for milieu residents.

*Olivia J. (social-learning)* showed responses to the events of the next year and a half that were typical of those of several other social-learning residents who had never engaged in assaultive behavior. Upon entry to the social-learning program Olivia was a thirty-nine-year-old mother of two who had been separated from her common-law husband. She had been repeatedly institutionalized in at least six different hospitals over the previous eighteen years, most recently for five years. Hospital staff described her as "refusing to work, remaining socially isolated and occasionally hostile, but with no record of physical assault." Olivia's clinical picture before the introduction of social-learning procedures reflected the occurrence of bizarre behaviors on 64% of objective observations. Her most frequent bizarre behavior was blank staring, but she also showed inappropriate facial expressions, repetitive movements, posturing, rocking, and social withdrawal. Her Interpersonal Skills and Self-Care were particularly deficient, occurring at normal levels on fewer than 7% of opportunities. Although she attended scheduled classes, she participated in fewer than 7% and failed to participate at all in work. Olivia's initial response to the social-learning program was remarkable. She progressed steadily through the step levels, achieving promotion to step 4 at the same time as Thelma N. (illustrative cases, chapter 19)—performing social and self-maintenance behaviors indistinguishable from normal ones on over 88% of opportunities after only eleven weeks in the program.

Unfortunately Olivia was returned from her first overnight accompanied pass with her ex-common-law husband in a nearly stuporous state, apparently the result of a traumatic sexual incident with him. Olivia refused to specify exactly what had happened and her mate refused all further attempts at contact by psychosocial staff. Her functioning at the time of her return was at or below entry levels on all classes of behavior. Unlike her rapid initial progress, Olivia showed slow and steady improvements over the remainder of the two years before the change in the length of time out. By the fifth anniversary assessment she was again performing self-maintenance and social skills at a normal level on nearly 63% of opportunities, and clinically maladaptive behaviors were occurring on less than 39% of observations. Throughout the entire period before the imposed change in time out, Olivia had not performed an aggressive Intolerable Behavior.

Within two weeks of the reduction in the length of time out, Olivia had performed an Intolerable Behavior and gradually increased the rate to one incident every other week. Through the seventh anniversary assessment, Olivia varied between no instances of aggressive intolerable acts and biweekly incidents—largely as a result of the presence or absence of senior staff coverage of off-hours. Concurrently her adaptive behavior decreased slightly, and her maladaptive behavior increased somewhat with each period in which Intolerable Behaviors occurred at all, until the last three months of the period. Her housekeeping performance then decreased dramatically, but her concurrent appropriate behavior and Interpersonal Skills increased to levels even above those of her previous highest levels of performance—at the same time that her aggressive Intolerable Behavior increased to a new high of over ten incidents per week. Thus, for Olivia, and several other social-learning residents who had not previously engaged in assaults, the reduction of consequences for assaults, combined with the increase in assaultiveness from other residents, appears to have established conditions for observational learning of assaultive behavior. Before the last three months of the period, Olivia's rare assaultive incidents appeared to covary with the stress experienced in the program as a whole—occasionally striking out in frustration, as she had seen others do. However, her performance over the last three months suggested the increase in assaultiveness was goal directed, since the consequences of using such an approach were not costly. Thus, even in the instances in which the procedural change resulted in major increases in aggressive behavior for many social-learning residents, the additional components of the program appeared to provide a different functional process for such increases than the milieu program did. Nevertheless, the externally imposed change in a single procedure had dramatically reduced the effectiveness of the overall program.

# 25. Other Ongoing Resident Activity During the Next Year and a Half

## COMPARATIVE CHARACTERISTICS OF LARGE COMMUNITY MEETINGS

Productive characteristics of the large community meetings from the fifth through eighth anniversary assessments—obtained from the Group Activity Index (GAI) on Friday meetings—are plotted in figure 25.1.[1] The average straight speeches (i.e., appropriate initiation, response, or continuing normal conversation on a single topic) per meeting in figure 25.1 shows considerable variability, particularly for milieu meetings. The straight speeches within milieu community meetings ranged from a low of 78 instances per 45-minute meeting during the sixth anniversary assessment to a peak of 203 before the seventh assessment—ending the period with an average of 189 instances per meeting. Within social-learning community meetings, average straight speeches never again approached the 177 instances obtained during the fifth anniversary assessment. Rather, they showed a steady decline over the first six months, to a low of 81 instances, followed by a gradual increase to a peak of 130—ending the period with an average of 124 instances per meeting. As in the previous two years, residents at milieu community meetings averaged significantly more straight speech than those at social-learning community meetings over the entire period ($p < 0.01$).[2] Both peaks and low points during the next year and half were considerably lower than those of the previous two years. However, the amount of normal task-oriented talk in both sets of community meetings still remained at a level greater than three times that existing before the introduction of programmatic procedures.

The relationships between average straight speeches and unitwide measures of functioning not only differed from those of the previous two years but showed additional differential relationships between programs. The straight speeches during social-learning community meetings showed a steady decline during the first six months of the period—following the reduced length of time out for assaultiveness—with relative stability thereafter, paralleling changes over time in unitwide concurrent appropriate behavior ($r=0.51$) and changing in opposite directions to unitwide Schizophrenic Disorganization ($r=-0.55$). In contrast, average straight speeches in milieu community meetings covaried over time only with Hostile-Belligerence and Intolerable Behavior ($r$'s in the 0.40s). Thus, the total straight speeches in community meetings showed opposite relationships with functioning in other areas over the two programs—more straight speech in social-learning community meetings indicating better concurrent functioning in other areas, and more straight speech in milieu community meetings covaried with greater amounts of aggressive and assaultive behavior in other areas—reflecting the extent to which these behaviors constituted the focus of milieu community meetings.

The majority of major changes in straight speech within milieu community meetings were related to other events recorded in the research and community meeting logs. The lower rates of straight speech that occurred immediately after the reduction in expulsion time during the fifth anniversary assessment continued over the next two four-week blocks. The increase that then occurred in milieu community meetings was a joint function of increased activity of a new resident group leader (Kate G. was again elected when the previous group leader was released) and a large effort by staff, concurrent with senior staff's also providing regular rather than intermittent coverage of off-hours. The effort was reflected in the staff's doubling the amount of talk during community meetings. The major reduction in instances of straight speech in milieu meetings during the sixth anniversary assessment was totally a function of staff decreases. After nearly three months of senior staff coverage of evenings and weekends, attempts were made to fade such coverage back to an intermittent basis during the block before the sixth anniversary assessment. Concurrent with these attempts, some reduction in staff participation occurred within community meetings. However, partially because of fatigue and morale problems resulting from the increase

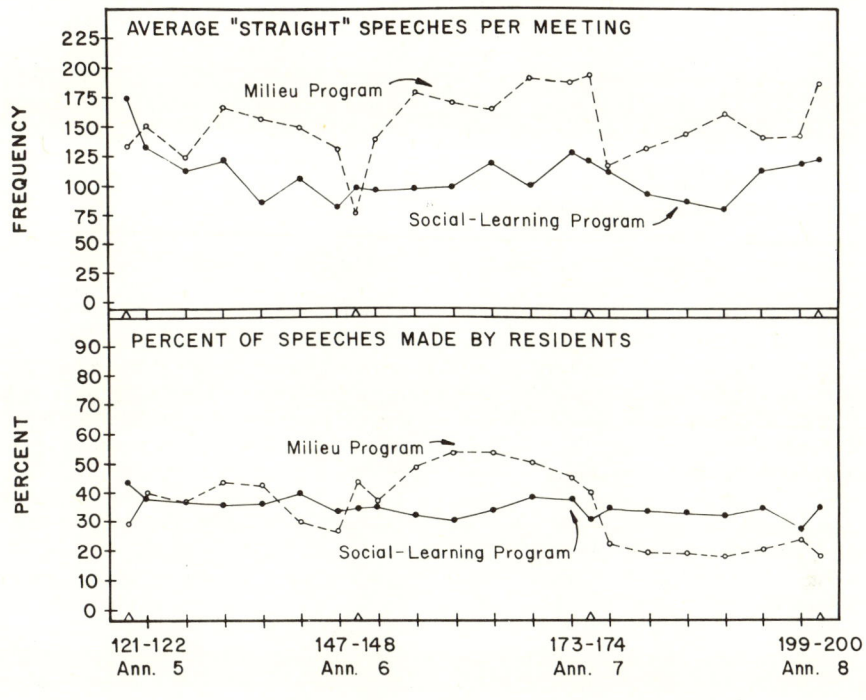

Figure 25.1. Productive characteristics of large community meetings during the next year and a half.

in assaultiveness that occurred when fading of off-hour coverage was attempted, staff initiation of interactions during community meetings for the two-week period of the sixth anniversary assessment dropped to half that of the earlier levels.

A reemphasis of senior staff effort to cover off-hours was paralleled by the increase in straight talk during milieu community meetings, reflected in the block immediately after the sixth anniversary assessment. Continuing increases in the amount of straight talk were apparent through the seventh anniversary assessment. The content of these meetings was concerned with the increases in assaultiveness during the period, the continuing newspaper and radio accusations, and the legislative investigations resulting from the activities of the local state representative. Although the focus of community concerns on increased assaultiveness continued through the end of the period, a dramatic reduction occurred in the amount of straight talk in milieu community meetings immediately after the seventh anniversary assessment. This reduction was totally a result of the election of a new resident group leader, since the former leader (Kate G.) was once again preparing for release.

Parallel differences in the structure and use of community meetings are also apparent from an examination of the proportion of straight speeches made by residents rather than staff in figure 25.1. As with earlier time periods, social-learning residents varied nonsignificantly around a 40% contribution of total straight speeches, ending the next year and a half at 35%. Once again, milieu residents showed considerable variability, remaining well below the levels that existed over the previous two and a half years, except for the period between the sixth and seventh anniversary assessments.

The trends in the proportion of speeches contributed by milieu residents were clearly affected by the same events that contributed to the variation in total straight speeches. Thus, the lower rates of resident participation evident immediately after the reduction of expulsion time for assaultiveness continued until a new resident group leader and staff increased contributions. The increase in the proportion of resident contribution at the sixth anniversary assessment reflected the large reduction in staff-initiated activity during meetings of that assessment period. Higher proportions of resident contribution again occurred between the sixth and seventh anniversary assessments, reflecting the combined effects of the active group leader, active staff, and the topics concerned with assaultiveness and with the state representative's accusations and the ensuing events. These increased levels of the proportion of resident speeches continued until the resident group leader was changed. The new group leader was much less active and effective, and milieu residents immediately reduced their proportion of contribution, which remained below that of social-learning residents—ending the next year and a half at a new low of only 18% contribution.

The differences in the target of resident speeches during community meetings that were apparent during the previous two years were still in existence. Straight resident speeches within social-learning community meetings were still regularly directed to staff (90%), with few to individual residents (9%) and even fewer to the group as a whole (1%). The proportions of resident speech were quite consistent over the entire period. Although the proportions of targets of resident speeches were significantly different for milieu residents compared to those of social-learning residents over the entire period ($p < 0.05$), milieu residents showed considerable variability in the proportion of their speeches directed to staff versus other residents. Speeches directed to the group as a whole remained relatively stable (6%). However, the proportion of speeches directed to other residents paralleled the total proportion of speeches made by residents. Only during the period between the sixth and seventh anniversary assessments were resident speeches regularly directed more to other residents (66%) than to staff (28%). At both the beginning and the end of the current period, the relationships were reversed, reflecting the attempts of less-skilled resident group leaders and the milieu resident group to seek guidance from the staff.

Thus, while there was considerable variability in productive characteristics over the period, especially for the milieu program, the community meetings in both groups still maintained higher levels of normal task-oriented conversations than those that had existed before the program introduction. The differing structure of community meetings was still apparent; the milieu community meetings continued to show higher amounts of straight speech and more resident-resident than resident-staff interactions. However, they no longer showed greater proportions of resident speech than in the social-learning program. Rather, the productive characteristics of milieu community meetings were particularly subject to the specific resident group leader in office and to the content of topics in community meetings. Productive characteristics of social-learning community meetings, in contrast, were stable and reflected the level of resident functioning outside of the meetings.

Figure 25.2. Nonproductive characteristics of large community meetings during the next year and a half.

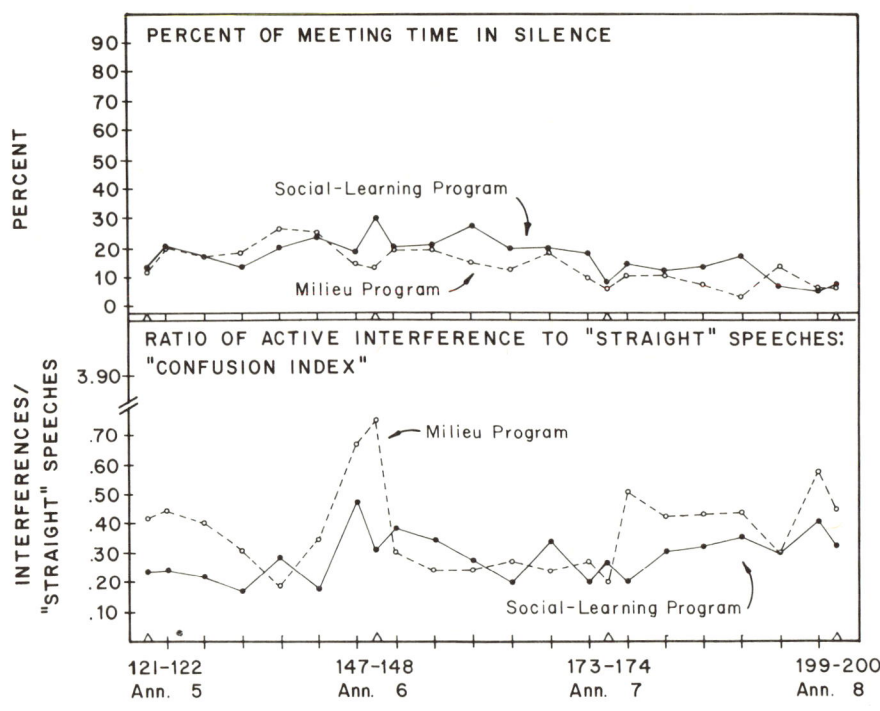

Nonproductive characteristics of community meetings over the next year and a half are presented in figure 25.2. The time spent in total silence continued to vary nonsignificantly around 20% of meeting time for both programs, without significant differences between them (p > 0.10). The last half of the period suggested a downward trend in the amount of time in silence, with both groups ending the period at about 7%. While both sets of community meetings remained well below the level of complete silence that had existed before the introduction of the programmatic procedures, the proportion of meeting time spent in silence by both groups during the current period varied in opposite directions to the number of interferences over time (r=-0.48), without significant relationships to straight speeches. Although these correlations were not significantly different, they suggest that the slight additional decrease in the amount of meeting time in silence was the result of more time being accounted for by active interferences.

Active interferences with ongoing community meeting functions (disrupting discussions, whispering or crazy talk, walking about, entering late or leaving early) increased over the period. The ratio of active interferences to straight speeches, presented in figure 25.2, showed considerable variability, with the relative amount of nonproductive confusion in community meetings increasing over that of the previous two years. Both the absolute number of interferences and the amount of confusion during meetings were significantly higher within milieu community meetings than within social-learning community meetings over the eighteen-month period (p < 0.01). Within-program changes in interferences covaried with unitwide Cognitive Distortion within the social-learning program (r=0.68). Within the milieu program, interferences in community meetings changed in opposite directions over time with unitwide Interpersonal Skills (r= -0.58 However, the differences between units in other areas of functioning during this period were reflected in significant correlations between community meeting interferences and unitwide means over time (r's in the ± 0.60s & ± 0.70s). These relationships showed that interferences in community meetings covaried over time with unitwide differences in inappropriate and intolerable behaviors and changed in opposite directions to appropriate behavior in other settings.

Both community groups showed major increases in interferences during the block before the sixth anniversary assessment, corresponding with attempts to fade senior staff coverage of evenings and weekends to an intermittent schedule and the resulting unitwide increases in Intolerable Behavior at that time.

The interferences in milieu community meetings then peaked during the sixth anniversary assessment, at the same time that staff participation was reduced, and unitwide Intolerable Behavior continued to increase. However, the reemphasis on senior staff coverage immediately after the sixth anniversary assessment again corresponded to reductions in confusion during community meetings. The lower levels of confusion were maintained until the milieu resident group leader was replaced.

Thus, over the entire year and a half, community meetings in both programs showed lower levels of normal task-oriented talk and higher levels of confusion than during the previous two years. The proportion of time spent silent was reduced slightly but reflected increases over time in the amount of active interference during meetings. The differing structure and function of community meetings in the two programs continued to be apparent, with milieu meetings showing more activity—both in straight speeches and in interferences and confusion—and more resident-resident rather than resident-staff interactions than in social-learning meetings. However, milieu meetings no longer showed greater proportions of resident speech than the social-learning program did, and the amount of meeting time spent in silence did not differ between programs. In fact, both productive and nonproductive characteristics of milieu community meetings were particularly subject to influence by the resident group leader in office and to the content of topics in community meetings, as well as to the amount of Intolerable Behavior occurring on the unit at other times. In contrast, the characteristics of social-learning community meetings were relatively stable, changing only with the levels of resident functioning outside the meetings.

## DIFFERENTIAL UTILIZATION OF RESOURCES

The relative use of facilities and services and of consumables from the fifth through eighth anniversary assessments are presented in figure 25.3.[3] Although there was equal access to resources for residents in both programs, the differing programmatic structures had produced differences in resource utilization that had been maintained through the previous two years. The utilization rates in figure 25.3 reveal that social-learning residents continued the use of facilities and services and of consumables at significantly lower rates than before program introduction (F's > 25.63, df=1/54, p < 0.01); their use of consumables remained at a higher level than that of facilities and services throughout the period (F's > 5.69, df=1/54,

Figure 25.3. Comparative rates of resource utilization during the next year and a half.

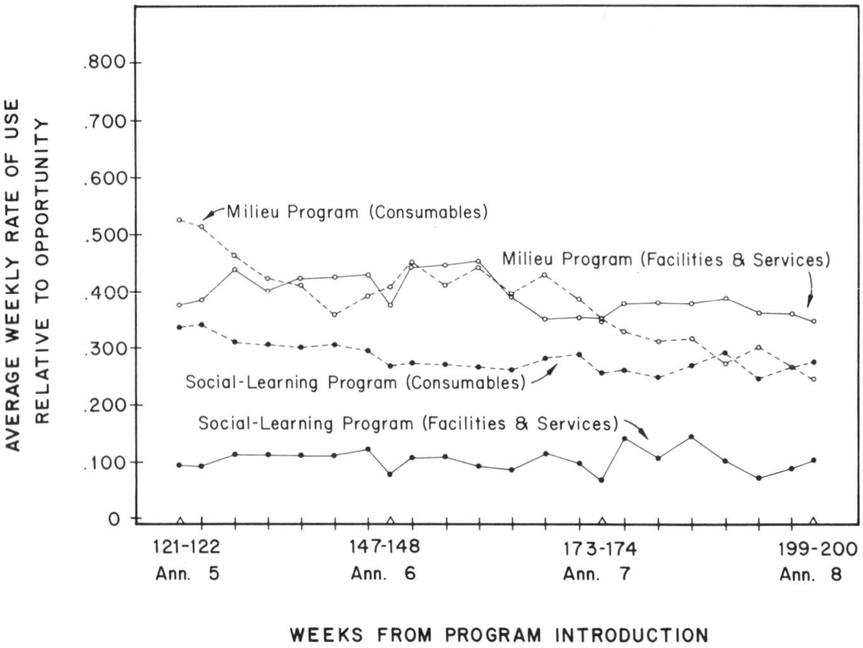

$p < 0.05$). As in the previous two years, milieu residents did not show significant differences between the rate of use of consumables versus facilities and services ($p > 0.20$) and continued to use facilities and services at a significantly lower rate than they had before the introduction of the program (F's $> 7.74$, df=1/54, $p < 0.01$). Throughout the next year and a half, neither group showed significant changes over time in the amount of facilities and services they used ($p > 0.15$), with utilization rates of the milieu group remaining significantly higher than those of the social-learning group at every point during the period (F's $> 32.97$, df=1/54, $p < 0.01$).

In contrast to previous time periods, the consumables' utilization rates presented in figure 25.3 reflect significant changes over time for both groups. By the time of the fifth anniversary assessment, milieu residents had not previously deviated from the level of consumables used before the program introduction, while social-learning residents had remained stable after a reduction immediately upon the introduction of programmatic procedures. During the next year and a half, however, residents in both programs showed significant reductions in their use of consumables over the first six months of the period (F=22.22, df= 1/54, $p < 0.01$), and those in the milieu program continued to show additional significant reductions over the remaining two six-month intervals (F's $> 6.28$, df=1/54, $p < 0.05$). Over the entire eighteen months, the reduction of consumables utilization by the milieu group was significantly greater than that of the social-learning group (F=29.92, df=1/54, $p < 0.01$), to the extent that both groups showed significant reductions from before the program introduction to the eighth anniversary assessment (F=105.10, df=1/54, $p < 0.01$), without differences between them (F $< 1$).

Also, in contrast to previous time periods, unitwide change in consumables' utilization over time within both programs were correlated positively with most unitwide levels of appropriate behavior and negatively with most unitwide meaasures of maladaptive behaviors (r's in the $\pm 0.70$s to $\pm 0.90$s), without differences between groups. Thus, even though more consumables were available during the current period, the overall increasing disruptions and lowered levels of functioning resulting from the change in time for expulsion and time out were paralleled by reductions in both groups' use of consumables. The basis for such a reduction within the social-learning group is easily seen in the increasing token response costs, and standing restrictions for residents who performed high levels of Intolerable Behavior. Until the end of the current year and a half, when the special purchase-eligibility procedure was experimentally evaluated, residents with standing token fines were restricted from purchasing all but minimum consumables. Thus, those who were performing higher rates of dangerous and aggressive acts were prevented by the program structure from utilizing all available consumable items.

The reduction in consumables' utilization by milieu residents during the current period reflects a different process, since they were not restricted from access to any consumables as a consequence of their behavior. The reduction reflects the lower levels of group functioning that resulted from the increased assaultiveness during the period. Since the living groups were responsible for serving the majority of consumables, the reduction in consumables' utilization reflects the failure of the living groups to work together enough to make consumables available to other residents, since the majority of their time was spent trying to deal with troublesome group members. However, even though residents of both programs ended the period at the same utilization rate for consumable items, the overall correlations of mean consumables' utilization with unitwide adaptive Clinical Frequencies over time (r's in the -0.40s) still reflected the higher levels of functioning of social-learning residents concurrent with lower rates of consumables' utilization relative to milieu residents. Thus, even during the period of declined functioning and declining utilization rates, the fact that the manner in which resources were obtained was more important than the amount obtained was still in evidence.

Although neither group showed significant changes in facilities' and services' utilization over the next year and a half, there was a significant tendency for mean facilities' and services' utilization within units to covary with average unitwide adaptive behaviors and to change in opposite directions to unitwide maladaptive behaviors over time (r's in the ± 0.40s & ± 0.50s). The major variance in facilities' and services' utilization for both programs occurred just after the seventh anniversary assessment, reflecting the increase in use of off-unit facilities as a result of special sampling-exposure procedures that were evaluated at that time. Slight improvements in functioning also occurred at that time, partially because of the more frequent presence of senior staff during evening and weekend hours, which affected the incidence of Intolerable Behavior. However, the overall correlation of mean facilities' and services' utilization with unitwide measures of functioning over time (r's from ± 0.60s to ± 0.80s) still reflected the higher levels of functioning of social-learning residents concurrent with the lower rates of resource utilization relative to milieu residents. As with consumables' utilization, these relationships indicate that how many resources were used was not as important as how they were obtained.

An examination of individual resident characteristics associated with utilization rates during the eighth anniversary assessment found several changes from relationships that had existed earlier, before the incidence of dangerous and aggressive acts became of such high intensity. Residents using more consumables within both programs tended to be performing higher levels of all adaptive behaviors (r's in the 0.80s & 0.90s) and lower levels of most maladaptive behaviors (r's from the -0.40s to -0.70s) and to be those showing significant improvement (r=0.46). In contrast to earlier periods in which these kinds of relationships were stronger within the social-learning group, there were no differences in the strength of these relationships between programs by the eighth anniversary assessment. Differences were still apparent in facilities' and services' utilization, which was significantly correlated with most adaptive and maladaptive behaviors within the social-learning group (r's from the ± 0.40s to ± 0.70s) more than within the milieu group. However, utilization was negatively correlated with the incidence of Intolerable Behavior (r=-0.50) within the milieu group at the eighth anniversary assessment, whereas no measures of functioning had been correlated with milieu facilities' and services' utilization earlier.

In summary, the overall pattern of resource utilization established upon the introduction of programmatic procedures for social-learning residents was maintained throughout the next year and a half. All resources within the program were used at lower rates than before program introduction, and consumables continued to be used at a higher rate than facilities and services—reflecting the greater value of consumable items as backup reinforcers for this population. As in the previous two years, milieu residents did not differ in the rate of their use of consumables versus facilities and services. Neither group showed significant changes in the utilization rates for facilities and services during the entire year and a half. Both continued to use them at lower rates than before program introduction, with milieu residents using significantly more than social-learning residents did at every point during the period. The minimal changes in utilization within both programs, however, tended to covary with other changes in resident functioning, primarily reflecting minor changes resulting from special-sampling exposure to off-unit facilities.

In contrast to facilities' and services' utilization, both groups showed significant reductions in consumables' utilization during the next year and a half, paralleling reductions in level of functioning over the period resulting from reduced consequences for assaultiveness. The reduction in the use of consumables by social-learning residents reflected the greater restrictions on token spending following increases in response costs for Intolerable Behavior. Milieu residents showed significantly greater reductions in consumables' utilization than social-learning residents did, ending the period with both groups using consumables at the same level for the first time since the introduction of the programs. While consumables were still free in the milieu program, the reduced rates of utilization followed lowering levels of living group functioning—from increases in assaultiveness—resulting in increasing failures of the living groups to provide the services that made consumables accessible to other residents.

By the time of the eighth anniversary assessment, higher-functioning and more improved residents in both programs were still using relatively more consumables than lower-functioning residents were, but without differences in the strength of the relationships between programs. As at earlier times similar relationships were also apparent within the social-learning group for utilization of facilities and services. However, the increased importance of the high rates of dangerous and aggressive acts within the milieu program was apparent in a negative correlation between Intolerable Behavior and utilization of facilities and services—the first time that any measure of functioning had been related to their use within the milieu program. Throughout the entire period, however, the higher levels of functioning concurrent with lower levels of resource utilization by social-learning residents relative to milieu residents still provide clear evidence that how resources were used was more important than how many were obtained.

## TIME SPENT IN PROGRAMS AND WITH OTHER PEOPLE

Differences between programs in the amount of time in which residents were awake and in contact with other people during the next year and a half were examined via TSBC indexes for "eyes open" and "with others."[4] By the time of the fifth anniversary assessment, the average resident had maintained time awake at 91% of observations—up significantly from 80% before the introduction of programs, without differences between groups. Over the next year and a half, average time awake remained quite stable; both groups remained at significantly higher levels than before the program introduction throughout the period ($F=28.14$, $df=1/54$, $p < 0.01$), without significant changes over time for either group ($F < 1$). However, by the time of the eighth anniversary assessment, gradual increases for social-learning residents (to 96%) and gradual decreases for milieu residents (to 88%) resulted in end-of-period proportions of time awake that were significantly different ($F=4.23$, $df=1/54$, $p < 0.05$).

The amount of time spent with other people had also increased significantly upon the introduction of the programs. By the fifth anniversary assessment, both groups had maintained 83% of time with others—up significantly from 66% before the program introduction—without differences between groups. Over the current year and a half, both groups showed steady declines in the amount of time spent with other people through the seventh anniversary assessment ($F$'s $> 4.96$, $df=1/54$, $p < 0.05$) without differences between groups ($F$'s $< 1$). Over the last six months of the period, social-learning residents remained relatively stable, without further declines in time with others ($p > 0.15$), while milieu residents continued to show further significant decreases ($F=8.65$, $df=1/54$, $p < 0.01$). Over both groups, unit-wide changes in time spent with others tended to covary with changes in Global Functioning and most adaptive components of resident behavior and to vary in opposite directions to mean changes in most maladaptive behaviors ($r$'s in the $\pm 0.40$s to $\pm 0.70$s), without significant differences between programs. The declines over the next year and a half were so extensive that by the eighth anniversary assessment, the average time with others no longer differed significantly ($p > 0.20$) from that at pretreatment levels for either social-learning (69%) or milieu (61%) residents. Thus, although both programs maintained increases in "time in" during the current period, the increased assaultiveness resulting from reductions in consequences for assaultive behavior reduced the amount of time spent with other people, as well as overall levels of functioning.

An examination of the relationship of individual resident characteristics to "awake" and "with others" status found that no significant differential relationships existed by the eighth anniversary assessment, except that milieu residents receiving psychotropic drugs were asleep more during waking hours ($r=-0.63$); no relationship with drugs existed for social-learning residents. Rather, overall correlations found a weak but significant tendency for residents of both programs who had "eyes open" a greater proportion of the time to be performing higher levels of adaptive behavior and lower levels of maladaptive behavior ($r$'s in the $\pm 0.30$s & $\pm 0.40$s). These tendencies were much stronger for time with others ($r$'s in the $\pm 0.60$s to $\pm 0.80$s), with the correlation of "with others" and improvement status ($r=0.63$) indicating that improved and higher-functioning residents at the end of the period were those spending greater proportions of time with other people—perhaps avoiding residents who were performing high rates of dangerous and aggressive acts.

Summarizing "time awake" and "with others," residents in both programs maintained the increased proportion of time awake that had been established upon the introduction of programs. While no significant changes in time awake occurred in either program over the current period, gradual increases by social-learning residents and gradual decreases by milieu residents resulted in social-learning residents showing significantly greater proportions of time awake by the eighth anniversary assessment. The increased assaultiveness reduced the amount of time spent with other people in both programs, parallel to changes in levels of functioning. The reductions were such that by the eighth anniversary assessment residents in both programs showed no differences from pretreatment levels in the amount of time spent with others. Milieu residents receiving psychotropic drugs still tended to spend more time asleep during waking hours, even after reductions in drug use during the period, while drug status was unrelated to other behaviors for social-learning residents. Higher-functioning residents in both programs showed a slight tendency to spend more time awake, and a stronger tendency to spend more time with other people. Residents in both programs who showed significant improvement were spending more time with others during the eighth anniversary assessment. Overall, while both programs had maintained higher levels of "time in" the access to procedures of respective programs was unrelated to improvement by the end of the current period. However, the analyses of time with others suggest that increased assaultiveness had resulted in avoidance of other intolerable residents by higher-functioning and more-improved residents in both programs.

## VARIABILITY OF RESIDENT ACTIVITY

The last group of descriptive characteristics of ongoing resident behavior to be examined is the individual variability within specific classes of activity—as distinct from the amount and level of behavior. The average Stereotypy/Variability scores for five classes of activity during the next year and a half are presented in table 25.1, providing a descriptive picture of the individual range of activity within each class, independent of amount.[5] While none of these scores differed between groups before program introduction, several differences had occurred through the fifth anniversary assessment.

The variability of concurrent clinically bizarre, crazy behaviors (from the TSBC) had shown significant reductions from pretreatment ranges within both programs by the fifth anniversary assessment, without differences between groups. Both groups showed increases that approached significance in the range of specific crazy behaviors during the first six months of the current period, immediately after the change in time of expulsion and time out as a consequence for assaultive behavior ($F=2.92$, $df=1/54$, $p < 0.10$). The reduction in the variability of crazy behaviors for both groups between the sixth and seventh anniversary assessments was significant ($F=11.50$, $df=1/54$, $p < 0.01$); it occurred in both programs at the end of the six-month period concurrent with the start of special sampling-exposure procedures for off-unit facilities. No changes in the variability of crazy behavior occurred over the last six months of the period, and none of the changes differed between programs at any time ($p > 0.20$). The slight increases and decreases during the period were such that neither group showed significant change from the beginning to the end of the period ($F < 1$). Although the variability of crazy behavior of milieu residents was higher than that of social-learning residents at nearly every point during the period ($r=0.50$), none of the differences between groups were significant ($F < 1$). Rather, by the eighth anniversary assessment, both groups still showed significant reductions in the variability of crazy behavior from that existing before introduction of programs ($F=25.87$, $df=1/54$, $p < 0.01$), without differential change between them ($p > 0.15$).

The variability of crazy behavior for social-learning residents did not covary with a single unitwide measure of functioning during the next year and a half. In contrast, the variability of crazy behavior for milieu residents tended to covary with unitwide changes in Instrumental Role Performance ($r=0.51$) and to change in opposite directions to unitwide levels of Intolerable Behavior ($r=-0.53$) and Cognitive Distortion ($r=-0.42$). Thus, while the social-learning program had maintained significantly greater reductions in clinically bizarre behavior during the current period, both programs had maintained a reduced range of specific crazy behaviors that individual residents were performing. However, the increase in the amount of crazy behavior during the next year and a half in the absence of increased range, particularly for the milieu group, reflects large increases in specific classes of bizarre behavior associated with assaultiveness.

The variability of concurrent appropriate behaviors (from the TSBC) had shown differential change between programs by the fifth anniversary assessment, with social-learning residents increasing the range of specific appropriate behaviors performed, while milieu

Table 25.1. Relative Stereotypy/Variability of resident activity.

| Treatment program | Assessment period | Crazy behaviors | | Appropriate behaviors | | Social contacts | | Resource utilization | | Physical location | |
|---|---|---|---|---|---|---|---|---|---|---|---|
| | | Mean | S.D. | Mean | S.D. | Mean | S.D. | Mean | S.D. | Mean | S.D. |
| Social-learning | Baseline | 4.41 | 1.631 | 3.85 | 1.390 | 1.89 | 0.217 | 2.86 | 0.635 | 3.02 | 1.507 |
| | Anniversary 5 | 3.01 | 1.775 | 4.72 | 1.540 | 2.43 | .321 | 1.93 | .702 | 4.93 | 1.189 |
| | Anniversary 6 | 3.20 | 1.120 | 4.74 | 1.882 | 2.50 | .323 | 1.78 | .691 | 5.32 | 1.334 |
| | Anniversary 7 | 2.87 | .974 | 4.89 | 1.962 | 2.67 | .433 | 1.53 | .723 | 4.48 | 1.092 |
| | Anniversary 8 | 3.10 | 1.024 | 5.13 | 1.509 | 2.54 | .386 | 1.96 | .736 | 4.51 | 1.258 |
| Milieu therapy | Baseline | 4.04 | 1.478 | 3.61 | 1.015 | 1.90 | .245 | 2.68 | .462 | 3.51 | 1.044 |
| | Anniversary 5 | 3.28 | 1.375 | 3.14 | 1.169 | 2.46 | .361 | 2.77 | .474 | 5.95 | 1.425 |
| | Anniversary 6 | 3.72 | 1.400 | 3.45 | 1.356 | 2.62 | .296 | 2.75 | .476 | 5.71 | 1.207 |
| | Anniversary 7 | 3.03 | 1.351 | 3.47 | 1.527 | 2.83 | .405 | 2.84 | .485 | 5.26 | 1.382 |
| | Anniversary 8 | 2.94 | 1.246 | 3.30 | 1.498 | 2.64 | .378 | 2.79 | .417 | 5.02 | 1.403 |
| Total | Baseline | 4.23 | 1.567 | 3.73 | 1.223 | 1.90 | .231 | 2.78 | .563 | 3.26 | 1.320 |
| | Anniversary 5 | 3.15 | 1.594 | 3.93 | 1.580 | 2.45 | .342 | 2.35 | .731 | 5.44 | 1.407 |
| | Anniversary 6 | 3.46 | 1.305 | 4.10 | 1.779 | 2.56 | .317 | 2.27 | .767 | 5.52 | 1.300 |
| | Anniversary 7 | 2.95 | 1.191 | 4.18 | 1.912 | 2.75 | .430 | 2.19 | .902 | 4.87 | 1.318 |
| | Anniversary 8 | 3.02 | 1.142 | 4.21 | 1.765 | 2.59 | .386 | 2.38 | .728 | 4.77 | 1.356 |

Note. Table entries are Stereotypy/Variability scores. A score of 1 represents complete stereotypy (all incidence of activity of a single type); higher scores reflect greater variability, with maximum possible scores (crazy behavior=17, appropriate behavior=17, social contact=3, resource utilization=19, physical location=17) indicating equal incidence of all types of activity.

residents remained at the same range that existed before the program introduction. Over the next year and a half, the social-learning group continued to show gradual increases in the range of appropriate behaviors performed, which approached significance from the beginning to the end of the period ($F=3.38$, $df=1/54$, $p < 0.10$). However, during the period, neither group showed significant differences over time or significant differential change between them ($p > 0.20$). Rather, social-learning residents continued to show significantly higher variability in the specific appropriate behaviors performed than milieu residents did at every point during the period ($F$'s $> 9.33$, $df=1/54$, $p < 0.01$).

The minimal changes in the variability of appropriate behavior were unrelated to unitwide changes in measures of functioning for social-learning residents but tended to covary for milieu residents with unitwide levels of Interpersonal Skills ($r=0.63$) and to change in opposite directions to clinically bizarre behavior ($r=-0.44$). By the eighth anniversary assessment, social-learning residents were still showing significant change in the variability of appropriate behavior, which differed from their own pretreatment level and from changes of milieu residents ($F$'s $> 11.90$, $df=1/54$, $p < 0.01$), while milieu residents showed no change from pretreatment ($F < 1$). Thus, both groups reduced the amount of concurrent appropriate behavior over the next year and a half, but the social-learning group still showed increases in both amount and range of appropriate behaviors from pretreatment. By the time of the eighth anniversary assessment, the milieu group showed no significant differences from pretreatment in either amount or range of concurrent appropriate behaviors performed.

The Stereotypy/Variability scores for social contacts had maintained increases in both programs by the fifth anniversary assessment. The level of variability did not differ at that time, but differential relationships had been found between programs and change in the range of people (i.e., other residents, staff, outsiders) with whom residents spent time. Additional significant increases in the variability of social contacts over both programs occurred through a peak during the seventh anniversary assessment, followed by a significant reduction to the eighth assessment; the overall change during the period reflected significant increases, without differences between the groups ($F$'s $> 4.68$, $df=1/54$, $p < 0.05$). The changes in the range of people with whom residents spent time were relatively smooth and parallel between programs at all points.

In contrast to the differential relationships over time during the previous two years, the variability of social contacts during the next year and a half tended to covary with the unitwide performance of most maladaptive behaviors and to change in opposite directions to most adaptive behaviors ($r$'s in the $\pm 0.50$s & $\pm 0.60$s) over both programs, without differences between the groups. Except for the peak variability around the seventh anniversary assessment—which reflected the increased range of social contacts during sampling-exposure to off-unit facilities—these relationships reflect two main processes: the tendency for visiting relatives and community volunteers to inappropriately initiate more contact with lower-functioning residents and the greater need for staff to be in the presence of assaultive residents to control their behavior. Thus, while the amount of time spent with other people had decreased in both programs over the next year and a half, the range of classes of people had increased for both groups but reflected more initiation by others than by the residents themselves.

The variability of resource utilization had maintained stable differences between programs by the fifth anniversary assessment, with social-learning residents continuing with significantly reduced ranges of facilities and services used, while milieu residents maintained the same range of use of facilities and services as they had before the program introduction. During the period, the greater variability in the use of facilities and services by milieu residents continued ($F=37.62$, $df=1/54$, $p < 0.01$). The level of variability of resource utilization was quite stable for both programs at every point in time, with the milieu group exhibiting no significant changes at all ($p > 0.20$). The social-learning group was also stable, except for a significant reduction in the variability of facilities and services used during the seventh anniversary assessment ($F$'s $> 4.25$, $df=1/54$, $p < 0.05$), reflecting a reduction of range during the time that off-unit facilities utilization increased as a result of the special sampling-exposure procedures. However, from the beginning to the end of the next year and a half, neither group showed significant change ($F < 1$). Rather, milieu residents continued to exhibit the same variability in facilities and services used as before the program introduction ($F < 1$), and social-learning residents continued to demonstrate significantly lower variability of resource utilization than they had during the pretreatment baseline throughout the period ($F$'s $> 35.84$, $df=1/54$, $p < 0.01$).

The Stereotypy/Variability scores for physical location had shown increases within both groups following the introduction of programs, with milieu residents increasing more than social-learning residents did and maintaining higher levels of location variability through the fifth anniversary assessment. Over the next year and a half, these scores—which provide an index of the relative amount of movement of individual residents within geographical areas of the units (e.g., corridors, lounge, dining area, common living area, etc.)—showed significant decreases for both programs (F=17.19, df=1/54, p < 0.01), without differential change between them (p > 0.10). However, the pattern of change in location variability over time was different between programs. The social-learning group showed increases in location variability that approached significance over the first six months following the reduction of time out for assaultive behavior (F=2.85, df=1/54, p < 0.10). This increase was followed by a significant decrease during the seventh anniversary assessment (F=13.23, df=1/54, p < 0.01), when the sampling exposure to off-unit facilities was in effect, with stability thereafter. None of the changes over time in location variability covaried with unitwide measures of functioning for the social-learning group. In contrast, the location variability of milieu residents showed steady decreases over the entire period, paralleling unitwide decreases in adaptive behavior and increases in most maladaptive behaviors (r's in the ± 0.60s to ± 0.80s). Throughout the entire year and a half, milieu residents continued to show greater individual variability than social-learning residents did in locations used (F's > 5.76, df=1/54, p < 0.05), but both groups still maintained higher location variability than had existed before the introduction of programmatic procedures (F=30.38, df=1/54, p < 0.01).

An examination of intercorrelations among all five Stereotypy/Variability scores during the eighth anniversary assessment found that only one significant relationship replicated over programs. The variabilities of social contacts and concurrent bizarre behavior were significantly correlated (r=0.40) without differences between programs. Unlike previous relationships, this correlation shows a tendency for residents who performed a greater range of crazy behaviors to be in contact with a greater range of other people (i.e., staff, residents, and outsiders). No other significant relationships among Stereotypy/Variability scores were obtained within the social-learning program; within the milieu program, location variability was again related to the variability of crazy behavior (r=0.50) and the variability of facilities and services used (r=0.44). Thus, milieu residents who were observed in wider ranges of physical locations on the unit also tended to perform a greater number of different types of bizarre behaviors and use a wider range of facilities and services. However, the stereotypy or variability of activities was still not a consistent attribute of residents in either program.

By the eighth anniversary assessment, only two sets of relationships between Stereotypy/Variability scores and measures of functioning remained similar to those found earlier. Residents showing greater variability in the range of concurrent appropriate behaviors still tended to be those with higher levels of functioning and less maladaptive behavior (r's in the ± 0.40s & ± 0.50s), without differences between groups. Similarly, social-learning residents using a greater range of facilities and services tended to be those performing higher levels of all adaptive behaviors and lower levels of most inappropriate behaviors (r's in the ± 0.30s to ± 0.50s), while the variability of resource utilization was completely unrelated to functioning for milieu residents. Unlike earlier findings, by the eighth anniversary assessment, the variability of clinically bizarre behavior was unrelated to other measures of functioning within both programs, and the variability of social contacts and of locations was related to functioning only within the milieu group. Within the milieu group, residents spending time with wider ranges of other people tended to be performing more concurrent appropriate behavior (r=0.46) and showing less Hostile-Belligerence (r=-0.37) and less Intolerable Behavior (r=-0.69). Milieu residents who used a wider range of locations during the eighth anniversary assessment tended to be those performing lower levels of Interpersonal Skills (r=-0.50) and Self-Care (r=-0.39) and higher levels of Cognitive Distortion (r=0.39).

To summarize, the relative variability of individual resident activity continued to reflect differential patterns of within-program processes over the next year and a half, as well as additional changes resulting from the problems involving assaultiveness over the period. Slight increases in the variability of crazy behavior followed immediately upon the change in expulsion and time-out procedures, and slight decreases were concurrent with sampling exposure to off-unit facilities. These changes in the variability of crazy behavior tended to covary with changes in the level of functioning for the milieu group but were unrelated to the level of functioning for the social-learning group. While both groups had increased the amount of clinically bizarre behavior during the current period, residents within both programs maintained significant reductions in the range of specific crazy behaviors performed, without differences between them. Changes in the variability of concurrent appropriate behavior were similarly unrelated to the level of functioning for the social-learning group but tended to covary with some unitwide changes in the level of functioning for the milieu group. However, while both groups had shown decreases in the amount of concurrent appropriate behavior over the current period, no significant change occurred within either program in the variability of appropriate behavior performed by individual residents. Rather, social-learning residents maintained higher levels of variability than milieu residents did throughout the next year and a half, such that increases in both amount and range of appropriate behaviors were continued above pretreatment levels. By the eighth anniversary assessment, the milieu group showed no significant differences from pretreatment in either amount or range of appropriate behaviors performed.

Residents in both programs continued to increase the range of class of people with whom they spent time during the period, peaking at the seventh anniversary assessment during sampling-exposure to off-unit facilities. While the variability of social contacts dropped significantly after this peak, the overall increase during the period was significant within both programs, without differences between groups. However, the variability of social contacts during this period tended to change in opposite directions to unitwide levels of functioning in both programs, reflecting the tendency for relatives and volunteers to initiate more contact with lower-functioning residents and the need for staff to be in more contact with assaultive residents to control their behavior. Thus, although the amount of time spent with other people had decreased in both programs over the next year and a half, the range of people contacted had increased but reflected more initiation by others than by residents themselves.

The variability of resource utilization continued to indicate stable differences between programs. The only significant change during the entire period was a reduction by social-learning residents during the time when off-unit facilities' utilization had increased. Otherwise, milieu residents continued to show the same variability in facilities and services used as before the introduction of the program, and social-learning residents continued to show significantly lower variability of resource utilization. Finally, both groups maintained higher variability of physical locations frequented than that which existed before the introduction of programs, but exhibited significant decreases in location variability over the current period. Milieu residents still showed higher location variability than social-learning residents did throughout the period, and the pattern of change over time was also different between programs. The change in location variability of social-learning residents was unrelated to other unitwide measures of functioning, increasing during the first six months of the period following the reduction of time out for assaultiveness and decreasing during sampling exposure to off-unit facilities. Milieu residents, in contrast, showed steady decreases in location variability, paralleling unitwide changes in level of functioning.

By the end of the period, the stereotypy/variability of activities was still not a consistent personal attribute, and differential patterning was apparent within programs. However, over both programs, residents functioning at relatively higher levels still tended to show greater variability in the range of concurrent appropriate behaviors performed. Differential relationships were obtained between levels of functioning and the remaining Stereotypy/Variability scores. Higher-functioning social-learning residents still tended to show greater variability in resource utilization, while no relationships existed for milieu residents. Unlike earlier findings, the individual variability of clinically bizarre behavior was unrelated to measures of functioning within either program, and the variability of social contacts and of locations frequented was related to functioning only within the milieu program.

## SUMMARY

In addition to the data on comparative effectiveness described in chapter 24, there were further differences in the characteristics of other ongoing activity during the next year and a half. The community meetings in both programs showed lower levels of normal task-oriented talk and higher levels of confusion than during the previous two years. The amount of time spent silent during community meetings did not differ between programs and was reduced slightly, but it reflected increases over time in the amount of interferences rather than increases in productive work. The differing structure and function of community meetings in the two programs continued to be apparent. Milieu meetings still showed more activity than social-learning meetings did, with greater amounts of confusion as well as greater amounts of straight speech being present. Milieu meetings also continued to show greater proportions of resident-resident rather than resident-staff interaction than social-learning meetings did. However, the influence of increasing problems with the handling of assaultive behavior was reflected in a continued reduction of the proportion of resident speech during milieu community meetings, which no longer differed from that during social-learning meetings. In fact, both productive and nonproductive characteristics of milieu community meetings were particularly subject to influence by the resident group leader in office and the content of topics of focus, in addition to the amount of intolerable behavior on the unit. In contrast, the characteristics of social-learning community meetings continued to be relatively stable over the next year and a half, changing only with the unitwide levels of functioning of the resident group outside of the meetings themselves.

Comparative utilization of resources also continued to show differences resulting from program structures and from the problems of assaultiveness over the next year and a half. All resources within the social-learning program continued to be used at lower rates than before program introduction. The greater value of consumable items as backup reinforcers for this population was still apparent in greater utilization of consumables than of facilities and services by the social-learning group. As during the previous two years, milieu residents—for whom resource utilization required only decision making—showed no differences between utilization of consumables versus that of facilities and services. Facilities' and services' utilization showed no significant change over time or between groups over the next year and a half. Rather, both groups continued to use facilities and services at lower rates than before the program introduction, with milieu residents using significantly more than social-learning residents did. However, both groups showed significant reductions in consumables' utilization, paralleling reductions in the level of functioning resulting from reduced consequences for assaultiveness. Milieu residents reduced their use of consumables during the period even more than social-learning residents did, to the extent that both groups were using consumables at the same rate by the end of the period for the first time since the introduction of the programs.

While consumables were more available during the current period and were free in the milieu program, the increases in assaultiveness over the next year and a half were at the basis of the reduced use of consumables in both groups. Consumables were functionally less accessible for milieu residents, since the living groups responsible for service provided increasingly less service as their members increased intolerable behavior. Similarly, as individual social-learning residents increased intolerable behavior, increases in token response costs placed greater restrictions on token spending required for access to most consumables. By the end of the period, higher-functioning and more improved residents in both programs were still using more consumables than lower-functioning residents were, but without differences in the strength of the relationship between programs. As in earlier periods, similar relationships were also apparent within the social-learning group for facilities' and services' utilization. For the first time that any measure of functioning had been related to the use of facilities and services within the milieu group, residents performing higher levels of intolerable behavior were found to use fewer facilities and services, again reflecting the increased importance assumed by the high rates of dangerous and aggressive acts. Throughout the entire period, however, the higher levels of functioning concurrent with lower levels of resource utilization by social-learning residents relative to milieu residents still provided continuing evidence that how resources were used was more important than how many were obtained.

Over the next year and a half, residents in both programs maintained the increased proportion of time awake that had been established upon the introduction of programs and continued over the previous two years. Although no significant changes in time awake occurred in either program over the current period, gradual increases by social-learning residents and decreases by milieu residents were such that significant differences existed between programs by the eighth anniversary assessment. The amount of time spent with other people was reduced in both programs, paralleling changes in the level of functioning after the reductions in consequences for assaultive behavior. The reductions were such that neither program showed differences from pretreatment in the amount of time residents spent with others by the end of the period. Even after psychotropic drugs had been reduced, milieu residents receiving them still tended to spend more time asleep during waking hours than those not receiving drugs; drug status was unrelated to other behaviors for social-learning residents. Higher-functioning residents in both programs still showed a slight tendency to spend more time awake, and higher-functioning and more improved residents were spending more time with others during the eighth anniversary assessment. Thus, while both programs had maintained high levels of "time in," the access to the procedures of respective programs was unrelated to improvement by the end of the current period. However, time with others had been influenced by the increased assaultiveness during the period, leading to overall reductions of the amount of time spent in social contact in both programs, with suggestive evidence that more improved and higher-functioning residents were avoiding their more intolerable colleagues.

Changes in the individual variability of ongoing resident activity also continued to show differences in the day-to-day processes within the psychosocial programs, but with several differences from earlier periods, reflecting the difficulties of this year and a half. Residents in both programs continued to increase the range of people (i.e., staff, other residents, outsiders) with whom they spent time, peaking at the seventh anniversary assessment during sampling-exposure to off-unit facilities. Although the variability of social contacts dropped after this peak, the overall increase during the next year and a half was significant, without differences between groups. However, the variability of social contacts tended to change in opposite directions to unitwide levels of functioning in both programs, reflecting a tendency for relatives and volunteers to initiate contact with lower-functioning residents and for staff to have more frequent contact of shorter durations with intolerable residents to control their behavior. Thus, while the amount of time spent with other people decreased in both programs, the range of people in contact with residents increased, but more as a function of initiation by others than by residents themselves.

None of the remaining Stereotypy/Variability scores covaried over time with unitwide measures of functioning for the social-learning group, but most did covary with other changes for the milieu group. Both groups showed slight increases in the variability of crazy behavior immediately after the change in expulsion and time-out procedures and slight decreases concurrent with sampling-exposure to off-unit facilities. Overall changes in the range of crazy behaviors performed covaried over time with the level of functioning only within the milieu program. However, while both groups had increased the amount of clinically bizarre behavior during the next year and a half, residents in both programs maintained significant reductions in the range of specific crazy behaviors performed, without differences between them. No significant change occurred within either program in the variability of concurrent appropriate behavior performed by individual residents, although minor variations over time tended to covary with some measures of functioning within the milieu group. Social-learning residents maintained higher levels of individual variability than milieu residents did throughout the next year and a half, such that increases in both amount and range of appropriate behaviors were continued above pretreatment levels. At the end of the period, the milieu group was significantly lower than the social-learning group was in both amount and range of appropriate concurrent behavior and did not differ from pretreatment levels in either aspect.

Stable differences between programs continued to be reflected in the variability of resource utilization. The only significant change during the period was a further reduction by social-learning residents during the increase in the use of off-unit facilities following special sampling-exposure procedures. Otherwise, social-learning residents were quite stable in showing significantly lower levels of variability of resource utilization throughout the period, while milieu residents maintained the same individual range of facilities and services used as before the introduction of the programs. Both groups maintained a higher variability of physical locations frequented than that existing before the introduction of programs, but a significantly decreased location variability during the next year and a half. Parallel to changes in the variability of crazy behavior, social-learning residents showed increases in location variability during the first six months of the period and decreases during sampling exposure to off-unit facilities. Milieu residents, in contrast, showed steady decreases in location variability over the entire period, parallel to unitwide changes in level of functioning. However, they continued to show significantly greater location variability than social-learning residents did throughout the next year and a half.

By the end of the period, higher-functioning residents in both programs still tended to show greater variability in the range of concurrent appropriate behaviors performed. As in earlier periods, higher-functioning social-learning residents also tended to show greater variability in resource utilization, while no relationship existed for milieu residents. Unlike earlier findings, the individual variability of clinically bizarre behavior was unrelated to measures of functioning within either program. The variability of social contacts and of locations frequented was related to functioning only within the milieu group. Differential patterning of interrelationships among Stereotypy/Variability scores was also apparent between programs, with only one significant relationship existing within the social-learning group. However, the stereotypy/variability of resident activities was still not a consistent individual attribute within either program.

Thus, the analyses of the characteristics of other ongoing resident activity during the next year and a half provide a descriptive picture that continues to be in keeping with the differential program structures. Additionally the influence of previously recorded notable events on ongoing processes provided additional support that the outcome data were primarily a function of the defined programmatic procedures and other identified events.

# 26. Staff Attitudes and Performance During the Next Year and a Half

OPINIONS ABOUT MENTAL PATIENTS

Average sten scores on the Opinions About Mental Illness Scale (OMI) for junior staff alone and all clinical staff combined from the fifth through eighth anniversary assessments are presented in figure 26.1.[1] Original scores at the end of academic training are also plotted for comparative purposes. Although Mental Hygiene Ideology had shown a significant decrease for continuing staff during the previous two years, none of the OMI changes had been significant from the original posttraining assessment to the fifth anniversary assessment. Over the next year and a half, the only significant overall or differential change among OMI scores at any time during the period occurred between the fifth and sixth anniversary assessments for continuing staff.[2] The significant differential change among scores ($p < 0.05$) during this period reflected a significant decrease in Benevolence ($p < 0.01$) and a significant increase in Social Restrictiveness ($p < 0.05$). Although items reflecting the potential dangerousness of mental patients resulted in a reduction in Mental Hygiene Ideology over this period of major increases in assaultiveness, the reduction was not significant; nor were changes in the remaining OMI scores over the first six months (p's > 0.20).

Over the entire eighteen month period, Social-Learning Ideology continued to show the exceptionally high levels of endorsement that had been obtained at the end of the original staff training. Although figure 26.1 suggests slight increases in Authoritarianism and Social Restrictiveness and decreases in Mental Hygiene Ideology over the last six months of the period, no overall or differential change on any score approached significance (p's > 0.20). However, the additional reduction in Mental Hygiene Ideology over the last six months of the period was sufficient that the change from the beginning of the period (anniversary assessment 5) to the end (anniversary assessment 8) was significant ($p < 0.05$). In fact, after a year and a half with ineffective procedures for handling assaultive behavior and the resulting increases in assaultiveness, staff did show significant differential change in OMI scores from those that had existed before the residents had arrived ($p < 0.05$). These changes included a significant reduction in Mental Hygiene Ideology ($p < 0.01$) and significant differential change ($p < 0.05$) between the decrease in Benevolence and the increase in Social Restrictiveness. At the eighth anniversary assessment, the reduction in Mental Hygiene Ideology was sufficient that Authoritarianism, Mental Hygiene Ideology, and Interpersonal Etiology no longer differed significantly but all were significantly higher than Benevolence and Social Restrictiveness.[3] Although the ordering of Benevolence and Social Restrictiveness was reversed over the period, these two scores still did not differ significantly from one another at the end of the period, except for junior staff alone.

Comparisons of the staff means with the ideal responses indicated in the margins of figure 26.1 for each score show that the pattern of the six staff scores remained parallel to the ideal assumptions underlying both psychosocial programs over the entire year and a half. In fact, although not significant, the changes that did occur resulted in the pattern moving closer to the ideal from the fifth (r=0.94) to the sixth anniversary assessment (r=0.97), without additional change through the eighth assessment (r=0.97).[4] The level of endorsement over all six staff scores combined tended to move closer to ideal assumptions from the fifth ($D^2=6.63$) through seventh ($D^2=5.83$) anniversary assessments and further from ideal assumptions at the eighth anniversary assessment ($D^2=6.96$), but none of these changes were significant (p's > 0.10).[5] Both Benevolence and Mental Hygiene Ideology moved closer to ideal assumptions, primarily through additional changes in more desirable (realistic) levels of endorsement of items reflecting potential dangerousness of residents and a reduction of "welfare" attitudes. However, the slightly greater deviation from ideal assumptions over the last six months was the result of small increases in Social Restrictiveness and

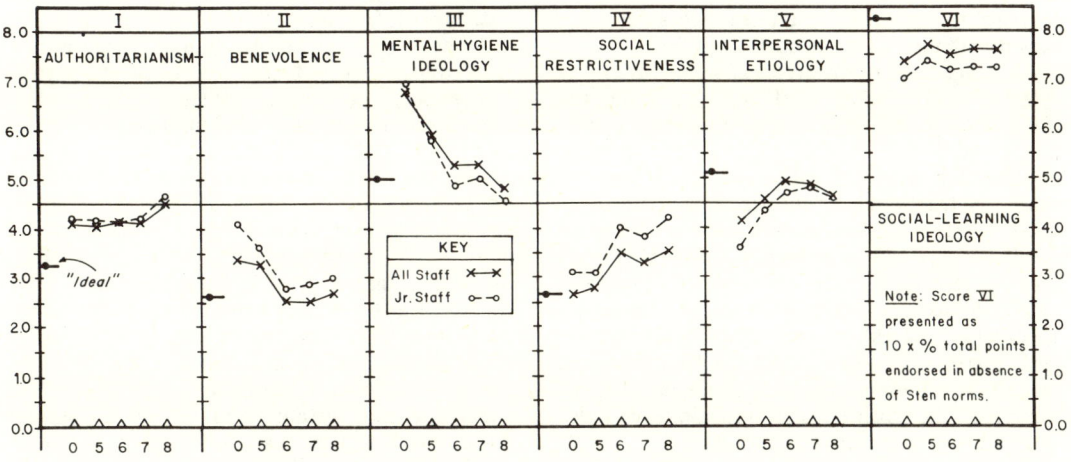

Figure 26.1. Opinions About Mental Illness Scale responses by all psychosocial staff present during the next year and a half. The ideal response is indicated in the left margin for each score.

Authoritarianism to higher levels than desired. All of these changes in staff attitudes on the OMI clearly reflect staff response to the increases in assaultiveness over this period, without any suggestion that staff attitudes affected ensuing resident behavior.

An examination of the intercorrelations among OMI scores at the eighth anniversary assessment found a new pattern of relationships. The only relationship replicating those of previous assessments was a positive correlation between Authoritarianism and Social Restrictiveness ($r=0.69$). However, both scores were negatively related (r's in the -0.40s) to Social-Learning Ideology, while Mental Hygiene Ideology had become positively related to Social-Learning Ideology ($r=0.44$) by the end of the period. None of these relationships had existed at the fifth anniversary assessment. The only predictability of OMI scores from individual staff characteristics involved education and experience, both of which simply reflected differences between junior and senior staff. Thus, senior staff (with more education and experience) still tended to score lower on Social Restrictiveness (r's in the -0.50s) and higher on Social-Learning Ideology (r's in the 0.40s) than junior staff did. Although the staff group became less extroverted over the current period, Extroversion scores were not related to OMI scores. Thus, after the year and a half of increasing assaultiveness from residents, staff attitudes tended to cluster differently, with Social-Learning Ideology becoming more central to other OMI scores, but the predictability from individual staff characteristics remained essentially constant.

In summary, the attitudes, opinions, and beliefs about mental patients held by psychosocial staff showed significant change over the period, even though less staff turnover occurred than at previous assessments. These changes included decreases in Benevolence and Mental Hygiene Ideology to levels more in keeping with the ideals underlying the psychosocial programs and increases in Social Restrictiveness to levels above those desired. They appeared to reflect staff responses to the increased assaultiveness of residents over the period, without even suggestive evidence that changes in staff attitudes had any effect on resident behavior. Even with the changes during the period, the staff group as a whole continued to reflect the ideal assumptions underlying the psychosocial programs and remained much closer to psychosocial ideals than to those of typical mental hospital staff.

## ATTITUDES TOWARD AND INTERPRETATIONS OF TREATMENT PROGRAMS

Between 96% and 100% of clinical staff expressed differential opinions to the preliminary questions on the Therapist Orientation Sheet (TOS) at each anniversary assessment during the next year and a half. The proportion of staff who believed the social-learning program was the more effective dropped slightly from 100% at the fifth anniversary assessment but remained in the clear majority over the rest of the period (94% at the sixth and seventh assessments, 97% at the eighth assessment). Similarly the proportion of staff who reported that the social-learning program was the more enjoyable in which to work remained in the majority throughout the period (79%, 72%, 84%, 76%, respectively, over assessments 5, 6,

7, and 8). Thus, staff beliefs of the effectiveness of programs continued to reflect the objective results, and the preference pattern established by the fifth anniversary assessment was maintained over the current period.

Average pattern differentiation scores on the TOS for all clinical staff working from the fifth through eighth anniversary assessments are presented in figure 26.2.[6] As before scores are plotted for responses obtained under each of three instructional orientations by the same staff within each assessment: one set for each of the psychosocial programs—reflecting staff interpretations of the nature of programs (attitude scores) and relative use of techniques (technique scores) inferred from their training and experience—and one set for their personal beliefs or preferences as change agents. Original scores at the end of academic training are also plotted for comparative purposes.

The preferred attitude scores in figure 26.2 reveal a considerable consistency of the staff group over the next year and a half in their personal preferences on the nature of treatment. In fact, no significant overall or differential change among scores was obtained between any pair of successive assessments ($p$'s $> 0.10$); however, there was a significant differential change from the beginning (anniversary assessment 5) to the end (anniversary assessment 8) of the period ($p < 0.01$), attributable to a reduction in A-1 and an increase in A-2 ($p$'s $< 0.01$), while the remaining three scores did not change significantly ($p$'s $> 0.20$).[7] However, the preferred TOS attitude scores at the eighth anniversary assessment showed no significant overall or differential change from the level and pattern of scores obtained from the original (anniversary assessment 0) posttraining assessment ($p$'s $> 0.10$), even though the staff employed at the end of the period included only 13% of those who had been employed at the original assessment. Differences among scores were maintained at every assessment over the next year and a half ($p$'s $< 0.01$). The order changed, however; all differences between preferred attitude scores shown in figure 26.2, except A-1 versus A-4, were significant through the seventh anniversary assessment. At the eighth anniversary assessment, the differential changes over the period for A-1 and A-2 were such that the only TOS preferred attitude scores failing to differ significantly were A-1 versus A-2.

Comparisons of staff means of preferred attitude scores to the ideal responses for the nature of each psychosocial program (indicated in the left margin for each score in figure 26.2) show that the pattern of the five staff scores remained significantly related to the milieu ideal through the seventh anniversary assessment ($r$'s of 0.96 to 0.97). While none of the differences were significant ($p$'s $> 0.10$), the pattern remained less related to the social-learning ideal through the seventh anniversary assessment ($r$'s from 0.63 to 0.69). However, the changes in preferred A-1 and A-2 were such that the pattern of staff scores at the eighth anniversary assessment became slightly less related to the milieu ideal and slightly more related to the social-learning ideal, with the result that staff means were equally related to both ideals ($r$'s=0.83). The overall level of preferred attitude scores remained closer to the milieu ($D^2$'s ranging from 1.24 to 1.78) than to the social-learning ideal ($D^2$'s ranging from 1.95 to 3.19) at every assessment during the period ($p=0.064$). However, the change over the entire year and a half was such that the level of deviation became more distant from the milieu ideal and less distant from the social-learning ideal by the last assessment of the period ($p=0.064$). Thus, although the nature of treatment characteristics staff preferred remained closer to the ideal milieu program over the next year and a half, changes were in the direction of the ideal social-learning program—perhaps as a result of the much greater assaultiveness that occurred in the milieu program.

An examination of the intercorrelations among TOS preferred attitude scores at the eighth anniversary assessment found only two significant correlations, both of which replicated relationships found earlier. A-5 was negatively related to both A-3 and A-4 ($r$'s= -0.39 & -0.55, respectively). The only descriptive characteristics of staff that were correlated with any preferred attitude scores were race and Emotionality; both were negatively related to A-2 ($r$=-0.57 & -0.40, respectively). These relationships reflect a tendency for black staff and more emotional staff to prefer relatively less structured, more permissive therapeutic relationships. A few significant relationships were obtained with OMI scores. Staff scoring higher on Interpersonal Etiology and Mental Hygiene Ideology tended to see less need ($r$'s in the -0.40s) for client discomfort and verbal learning process (A-5), while staff scoring higher on Mental Hygiene Ideology also tended to prefer ($r$=0.59) a more current, rational planning focus in treatment (A-4). Staff scoring lower on Social-Learning Ideology tended to prefer ($r$=-0.49) relatively more active, informal activity structure (A-1). Thus, at the end of the next year and a half, less clustering occurred among TOS preferred attitude scores, and preferences for the nature of treatment showed little predictability from individual staff characteristics, none of which replicated earlier relationships.

An inspection of the attitude scores for each psychosocial orientation in figure 26.2 also reveals the essential parallelism of the staff

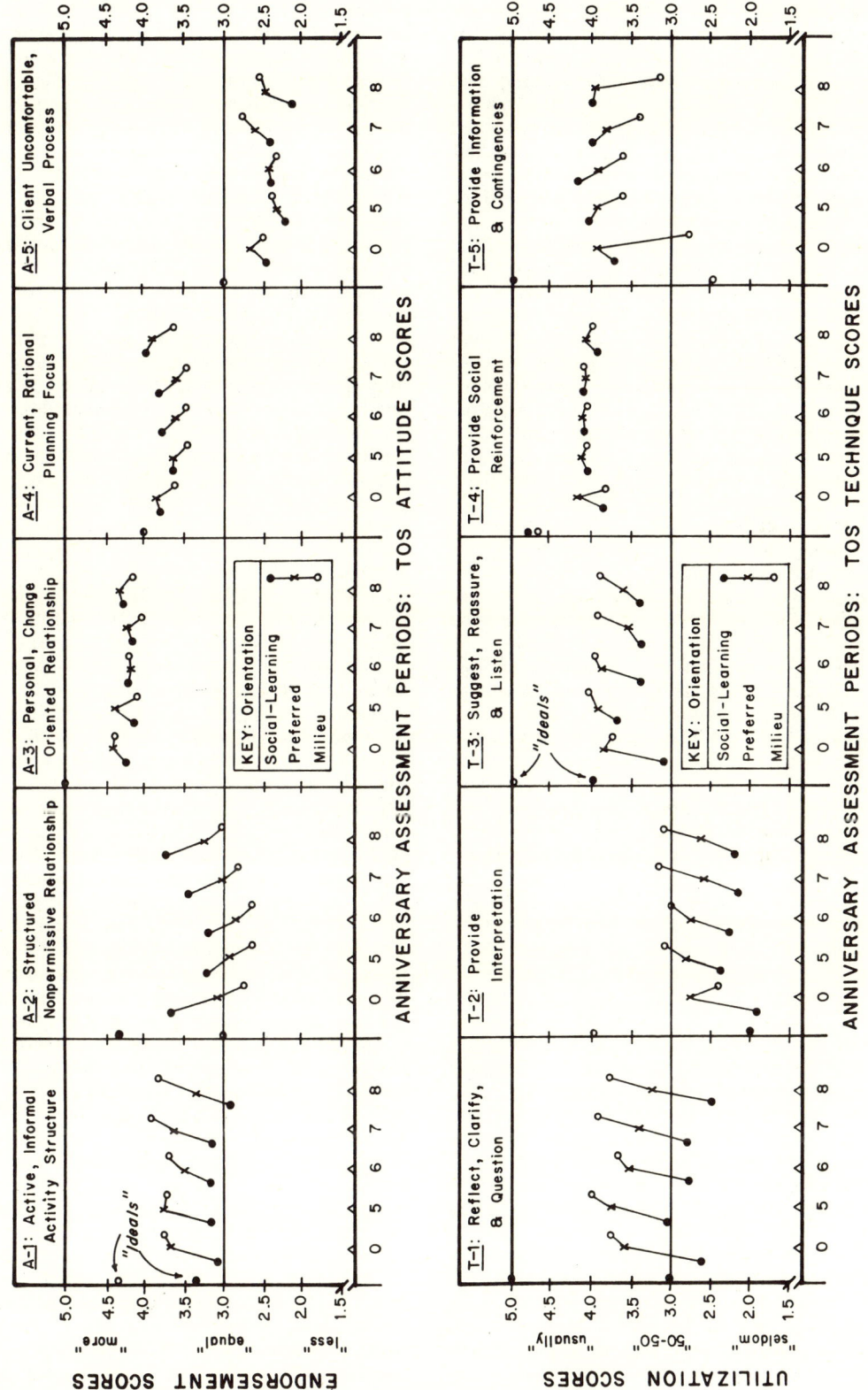

Figure 26.2 Therapist Orientation Sheet responses under three response sets by all psychosocial staff present during the next year and a half. Ideal responses are indicated in the left margin for each score.

over the next year and a half in their interpretation of the nature of each treatment program. Both continuing staff and total staff groups consistently produced different patterns of attitude scores in their interpretation of the nature of the milieu and social-learning programs at every assessment ($p$'s $< 0.01$).[8] No overall or differential change among scores or between orientations occurred over the first six months of the period, but the differential change among scores between orientations approached significance ($p < 0.07$) from the sixth to seventh anniversary assessments. Over that period, the increase in A-2 over both orientations combined was significant ($p < 0.05$), while differential change between orientations occurred for A-1 ($p < 0.05$) and A-5 ($p < 0.01$). Both differential changes reflected increases in the level of endorsement of scores for the milieu orientation without change for the social-learning orientation. Over the last six months of the period scores changed differentially over both orientations combined ($p < 0.05$); three of the attitude scores in figure 26.2 increased (A-2, A-3, A-4) and two decreased (A-1, A-5). The only differential change between orientations over the last six months was for A-5; there was a greater decrease for the social-learning than for the milieu orientation ($p < 0.05$).

There was a significant differential change from the beginning (anniversary assessment 5) to the end (anniversary assessment 8) of the current period for TOS attitude scores ($p < 0.05$); however, only A-1 showed differential change between orientations ($p < 0.05$), with the level of endorsement increasing for the milieu orientation and decreasing for the social-learning orientation. A-2 showed a significant increase for both orientations ($p < 0.05$). The remaining three scores did not change. By the end of the next year and a half, TOS attitude scores had changed in a manner that functionally cancelled out changes of the prior two years; scores at the last assessment of the period showed no significant overall or differential change ($p$'s $> 0.20$) from the level and pattern of scores at the original posttraining assessment nearly four years earlier.

Even with some changes during the period, the pattern of differences within and between orientations remained constant in the staff interpretation of the nature of treatment programs, with greater differentiation occurring by the eighth anniversary assessment. Thus, at the eighth anniversary assessment, the same ordering of all TOS attitude scores in figure 26.2 was maintained within the social-learning orientation, but all differences between scores were significant except A-2 versus A-4. Within the milieu orientation, the same ordering was maintained, with all differences between scores being significant except A-1 versus A-4. As at the original posttraining assessment, the last assessment of the period found social-learning scores significantly higher than milieu scores on A-2 and A-4 and significantly lower on A-1 ($p$'s $< 0.05$), with the difference on A-5 approaching significance ($p < 0.10$). A-3 did not differ significantly between orientations at any time ($p$'s $> 0.20$).

A comparison of the pattern of staff attitude scores under each psychosocial orientation to the ideal response for the nature of each program in figure 26.2 shows the directionality of the above differences to be parallel to those desired, with smaller deviations in the absolute level of endorsement over time. The extent to which staff interpretations of the nature of the milieu program maintained the same pattern as the ideal was apparent in the level of relationships over the five TOS attitude scores for the entire period ($r$'s from 0.95 to 0.99). Similarly the extent to which staff interpretations of the nature of the social-learning program approached the ideal did not change significantly over the period ($r$'s from 0.85 to 0.93), but the highest relationship was obtained at the last assessment. None of these differences were significant ($p$'s $> 0.10$), reflecting strong relationships to the ideal within both orientations for the pattern of attitude scores.

Similarly the overall level of staff responses under the two orientations compared to their respective ideals did not differ significantly from one another at any time during the next year and a half ($p$'s $> 0.10$). The slight changes that did occur over the period resulted in lesser deviations from ideal levels of endorsement for both social-learning ($D^2$'s from 2.70 to 1.68) and milieu orientations ($D^2$'s from 1.90 to 1.29), although only the change within the milieu orientation was statistically significant ($p < 0.01$). These slight changes tended to increase the approximation of staff interpretations to the ideals underlying each program, with the nature of programs continuing to be differentially interpreted throughout the period.

The preferred technique scores in figure 26.2 also show a considerable consistency of the treatment procedures that staff preferred to use over the next year and a half. In fact, no differential change among TOS preferred technique scores approached significance at any time during the period ($p$'s $> 0.20$). The only overall change even to approach significance was the slight reduction over all scores from the sixth to seventh anniversary assessment ($p < 0.10$). At the end of the period neither overall ($p$'s $> 0.10$) nor differential change ($p$'s $> 0.20$) was apparent in the level or pattern of preferred technique scores from those existing at the beginning of the period or at the original posttraining assessment. At the eighth anniversary assessment, as at earlier periods, T-3, T-4, and T-5 were still high and did not differ from one another, and T-2 was still significantly lower than all other scores. The only difference from earlier assessments in the order of scores was that the slight reduction in T-1 over the period resulted in a significantly lower level of endorsement for T-1 than for T-3, T-4, or T-5.

Comparisons of staff means of preferred technique scores to the ideals for each psychosocial program found that the pattern of the five staff scores remained quite close to the social-learning ideal over the entire eighteen months (r's from 0.91 to 0.98) but not to the milieu ideal throughout the period (r's from 0.05 to -0.17). Similarly, the overall level of preferred technique scores deviated more from the milieu ideal ($D^2$'s from 6.49 to 9.16) than from the social-learning ideal ($D^2$'s from 2.79 to 2.13) at every assessment during the period (p=0.064), becoming even more distant from the milieu ideal by the eighth anniversary assessment (p=0.064). Thus, both the pattern and level of preferred technique scores continued to approximate more closely the ideal social-learning program over the entire period, with the slight changes that did occur resulting in further deviations of staff preferences for technique utilization from the ideal milieu program.

An examination of the intercorrelations among TOS preferred technique scores at the eighth anniversary assessment found only two significant relationships: T-1 was positively related to T-2 (as at earlier assessments) and to T-5 (r's=0.49 & 0.37, respectively). Even less predictability of preferred technique scores was obtained from individual staff characteristics than at earlier assessments. None of the staff descriptive characteristics were related to preferred technique scores, and only three significant correlations were obtained with OMI scores: T-5 was correlated with OMI-III (r=0.46), reflecting a tendency for staff preferring relatively greater use of advice and contingency management to score higher on OMI Mental Hygiene Ideology, and T-4 was correlated with OMI-IV (r=-0.39) and OMI-VI (r=0.42), reflecting a tendency for staff preferring relatively greater use of social reinforcement to score lower on OMI Social Restrictiveness and higher on OMI Social-Learning Ideology. Thus, at the end of the next year and a half, less clustering occurred, and a preference for the use of specific therapeutic techniques continued to be almost totally unrelated to individual staff characteristics.

The technique scores for each psychosocial orientation in figure 26.2 also reveal the essential parallelism over the next year and a half in the staff interpretations of the appropriateness of the relative use of different techniques within each treatment program. Both continuing staff and total staff groups consistently produced different patterns of technique scores within and between orientations at every assessment during the period (p's < 0.01). The only overall or differential change that approached significance during the period occurred over the last six months (p < 0.10) and was totally attributable to a significant differential change in T-5 (p < 0.05), which was constant for the social-learning orientation and decreased for the milieu orientation. From the beginning to the end of the period, the slight decrease in the endorsed level of technique utilization over scores for both orientations approached significance (p < 0.10); the only differential change between orientations was that of T-5. By the end of the next year and a half, differential change from the original posttraining assessment approached significance (p < 0.10), reflecting no change for either orientation on T-1 and T-4 (p's > 0.20) and parallel increases for both on T-3 (p < 0.10) and T-5 (p < 0.05). Both orientations showed significant increases on T-2, with a greater increase for the milieu orientation than for the social-learning orientation (p < 0.05).

At the end of the current period, technique scores within the milieu orientation continued to show differentiation; T-1, T-3, and T-4 remained at significantly higher levels than T-2 and T-5, without differing among themselves, while T-2 and T-5 no longer differed significantly. Within the social-learning orientation, all differences between TOS technique scores were significant, except T-1 versus T-2 and T-4 versus T-5. Staff continued their earlier differentiation between treatment programs throughout the next year and a half; all technique score differences between milieu and social-learning orientations plotted in figure 26.2 were significant, except for T-4.

The differences between orientations for technique scores show relative staff interpretations in the direction of the ideal response for utilization of each group of techniques in figure 26.2. The extent to which staff interpretations of the appropriate pattern of technique utilization approached the ideal for the social-learning program was once again apparent in the exceptionally high relationships over the five TOS technique scores at every assessment during the period (r's > 0.99). The pattern of endorsement of technique utilization was significantly less related to the milieu ideal (p's < 0.05) through the seventh anniversary assessment (r's from 0.44 to 0.70) but increased to a level that did not differ from that of the relationship to the social-learning ideal at the eighth assessment (r=0.81, p > 0.10).

The overall level of staff technique responses under the two orientations compared to their respective ideals still found that the level of social-learning scores was closer to the ideal but deviated more from the beginning to the end of the period ($D^2$'s=1.79 & 2.42, respectively, p=0.064). The level of deviation of milieu scores from the milieu ideal, in contrast, did not change significantly during the period ($D^2$'s=4.20 & 4.39, respectively, at assessments 5 & 8, $p > 0.10$). By the eighth anniversary assessment, the slight changes in TOS technique scores were such that no significant differences in level or pattern of scores existed to their respective ideals between orientations or for the relationships that had been found at the original posttraining assessment nearly four years earlier (p's > 0.10). Thus, staff interpretations of the appropriateness of the relative use of different techniques were differentiated in desired directions between programs throughout the entire period. The slight changes resulted in the interpretation of technique utilization no longer being significantly closer to the ideal within the social-learning program than that within the milieu program by the last assessment.

In summary, the attitudes and interpretations held by psychosocial staff on the treatment programs showed remarkable consistency over the next year and a half. Staff beliefs of the comparative effectiveness of the psychosocial programs continued to reflect the objective results, with the great majority judging the social-learning program to be the more effective. The social-learning program continued to be judged the more enjoyable by the majority of staff, maintaining the preference pattern established by the fifth anniversary assessment. As at earlier time periods, it appeared that staff opinions and beliefs of the comparative effectiveness and enjoyability of psychosocial programs were responsive to prior changes in resident behavior, but had no notable effect on the ensuing response of residents to the programs.

Preferred TOS attitude scores, reflecting staff preferences for the nature of treatment programs, remained well differentiated and quite constant over the eighteen-month period, showing a slight differential change between two scores. While the nature of treatment characteristics staff preferred remained closer to the ideal milieu program than to the ideal social-learning program during the period, the slight changes there were moved in the direction of the ideal social-learning program. By the end of the next year and a half, less clustering occurred among TOS preferred attitude scores, and preferences for the nature of treatment still showed little predictability from individual staff characteristics, none of which replicated earlier relationships. Some differential changes came about in the level of endorsement of TOS attitude scores for each program orientation. The nature of these changes functionally cancelled out those of the previous two years so that the pattern and level of scores at the end of the current period no longer differed from those at the original posttraining assessment nearly four years earlier. Even with some changes during the period, the pattern of TOS attitude differences within and between orientations remained constant. The nature of programs was interpreted differentially, with staff interpretations remaining quite close, and moving closer, to the ideals underlying each psychosocial program throughout the year and a half.

Preferred TOS technique scores, reflecting staff preferences for the use of different treatment procedures, also remained well differentiated and remarkably constant over the period, showing no change over time and no differences from scores at the beginning of it, or at the original posttraining assessment. As at earlier assessments, in contrast to the closer approximation of staff preferences to the milieu ideal for the nature of treatment, preferred techniques remained more closely related to the social-learning ideal, with the slight changes moving even further from the ideal milieu program. By the eighth anniversary assessment, there was again less clustering among preferred technique scores, and preference for the use of specific therapeutic techniques remained almost totally unrelated to individual staff characteristics.

TOS technique scores, reflecting staff interpretations of the appropriateness of the relative use of different techniques, continued to differentiate between milieu and social-learning programs in desired directions throughout the entire year and a half; only one score showed differential change at any time. By the eighth anniversary assessment, both orientations showed significantly higher endorsed rates of utilization for two groups of techniques and differential change on one, as compared to the staff scores on the original posttraining assessment. While the level and pattern of appropriate technique endorsement was closer to the ideal within the social-learning program throughout the entire period, the slight changes there were resulted in staff interpretations moving closer to the ideal within the milieu orientation and further from the ideal within the social-learning orientation. By the end of the period, staff interpretations of the appropriateness of the relative use of different techniques were not only well differentiated between programs but did not differ significantly in the extent to which interpretations approached the ideals of the respective psychosocial programs. Thus, staff interpretations of both nature and techniques continued to be well differentiated in appropriate directions between psychosocial orientations over the entire year and a half, with staff preferences continuing to be much closer to either psychosocial orientation than those of mental hospital staff.

## PERFORMANCE IN PSYCHOSOCIAL PROGRAMS

The above TOS data indicate that staff continued to differentiate between programs over this period of decline in resident functioning. The objective data from the Staff-Resident Interaction Chronograph (SRIC) on the reliability and differentiation of the psychosocial programs as they actually operated become especially important during the current period.[9] SRIC data provide information to determine if changes other than the externally imposed reduction in time of expulsion and time out contributed to the decline in resident functioning.

How staff spent their time during the next year and a half is shown in figure 26.3, where total instances of activity and percentages of staff activity relative to the class of resident behavior in each program are plotted from the fifth through the eighth anniversary assessments. The most impressive feature of figure 26.3 is the remarkable stability of total staff activity and area of focus of staff behavior in both programs at levels achieved by the end of the previous two years. The rate of total staff activity remained at nearly two and a half times the original baseline level in the social-learning program and more than three and a

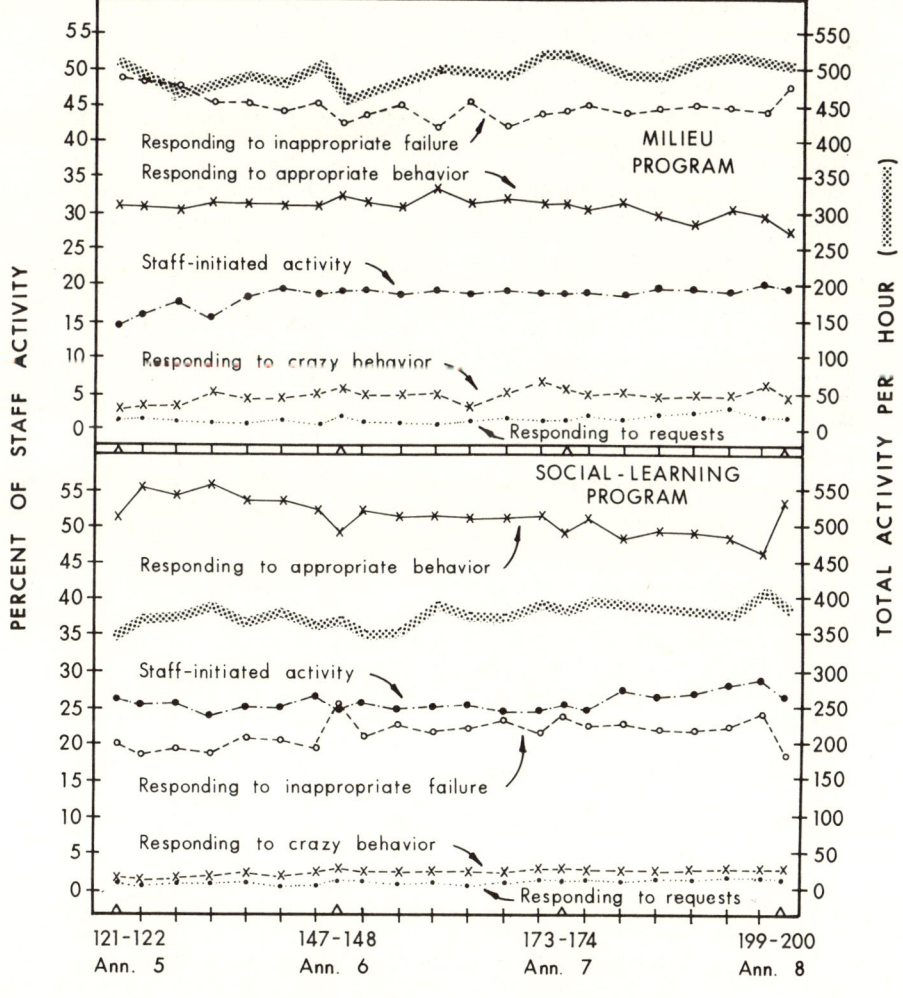

Figure 26.3. How staff spent their time during the next year and a half. Average total activity per hour is indicated by the shaded line and scale in the right margin.

half times the original level in the milieu program, without notable change at any time. Similarly, over half of all staff activity in the social-learning program continued to focus on appropriate components of resident behavior, while the focus of staff activity in the milieu program continued to be primarily on resident failures.

Although there were few changes in the focus of staff activity over the current period, those that did occur were systematically related to changes in resident functioning. The most notable change in this area in either program was the slight reduction in focus on resident failures in the milieu program over the first six months of the period, with a concurrent increase in staff-initiated activity. The proportion of staff activities focused on resident failures in the milieu program tended to covary with unitwide resident Global Functioning over the entire period ($r=0.55$), while the proportion of staff activity in response to resident failures in the social-learning program was negatively related to unitwide resident functioning over time ($r=-0.58$). In contrast, the proportion of staff activity focused upon appropriate behavior tended to covary with resident functioning in the social-learning program ($r=0.78$) and was unrelated to resident functioning in the milieu program. Although the proportion of staff activity focused upon crazy behavior remained exceptionally low in both programs, the slight increases directly reflected the increases in dangerous and aggressive Intolerable Behavior in both milieu ($r=0.71$) and social-learning ($r=0.80$) programs.

The proportion of activity and total instances of activity focused upon appropriate resident behavior continued to be significantly higher when staff worked in the social-learning program ($p < 0.01$).[10] Similarly the focus on resident failures, crazy behavior, and requests remained significantly higher in the milieu program (p's $< 0.01$). The proportion of staff-initiated activity was significantly higher when staff worked in the social-learning program, although total instances of staff-initiated activity were higher in the milieu program. However, over the entire period, only 14% of all staff activity in the social-learning program and 10% in the milieu program did not involve interactions with residents, and irrelevant behavior in both programs continued to occur at a rate too low even to appear as a fraction of a percentage. Thus, staff maintained the high activity levels and the differential focus that had been established previously. There were few changes in the focus of staff activity during the period, but those that did occur reflected the changes in resident behavior.

The attention received by an individual resident within both psychosocial programs was maintained at exceptionally high levels, without change over the period, with the average number of residents for whom each staff member was responsible being 17.2 in the milieu program and 16.2 in the social-learning program. The "average contacts per hour" column in table 26.1 shows that residents in both programs actually received more contacts from staff over the entire period of the next year and a half than they had during the last six months of the previous two years, when major improvements in functioning had occurred. Residents in both groups continued to receive the greatest proportion of contacts from staff as personalized, individual contacts. In fact, the "probability of contact" figures in table 26.1 show that an individual resident on either unit during an average ten-minute period during waking hours was likely to receive a personal, individualized contact from a staff member on about seven out of ten occasions.

Residents in the social-learning program continued to receive slightly more contacts from staff than those in the milieu program. However, table 26.1 shows that the greater activity level of staff in the milieu program maintained higher levels of interactions—instances of discrete verbal content or other staff behavior directed to the resident—within each contact. Thus, the total amount of attention received from staff (contacts x interactions) over the next year and a half was actually 37% greater for milieu residents and 11% greater for social-learning residents than that received during the six months immediately preceding the fifth anniversary assessment. In fact, over the next year and a half, the average milieu resident received nearly 41% more staff attention than the average social-learning resident did.

The nature of changes in staff behavior over the next year and a half is shown in figure 26.4, where the highest-frequency behaviors for either program are plotted from the fifth through the eighth anniversary assessment.[11] The staff behavior plotted in the top section of figure 26.4 shows exceptional consistency in the hourly frequency in both programs. Only Positive Nonverbals showed a notable change over the entire year and a half. The incidence of such positively intonated utterances, smiles, etc., did tend to covary slightly over time with the unitwide level of resident Intolerable Behavior in both milieu ($r=0.42$) and social-learning programs ($r=0.57$). However, the specific points of change, especially in the milieu program, suggest that the emphasis on genuine communications in in-service training, combined with senior staff coverage of evenings and weekends were the major influences on the changing rates of Positive Nonverbals as well as in imposing controls on aggressive resident

Table 26.1. Amount of staff attention, residents received over the next year and a half.

| Focus of attention resident received | Probability of contact in 10 min. | | Average contacts per hour | | Average interactions per contact | |
|---|---|---|---|---|---|---|
| | Milieu | Social-learning | Milieu | Social-learning | Milieu | Social-learning |
| As individual | 0.653 | 0.702 | 3.92 | 4.21 | 5.59 | 4.10 |
| As part of group | .083 | .050 | .50 | .30 | .71 | .29 |
| Total | .736 | .752 | 4.42 | 4.51 | 6.30 | 4.39 |

Figure 26.4. Average hourly instances of the highest-frequency staff interactions during the next year and a half.

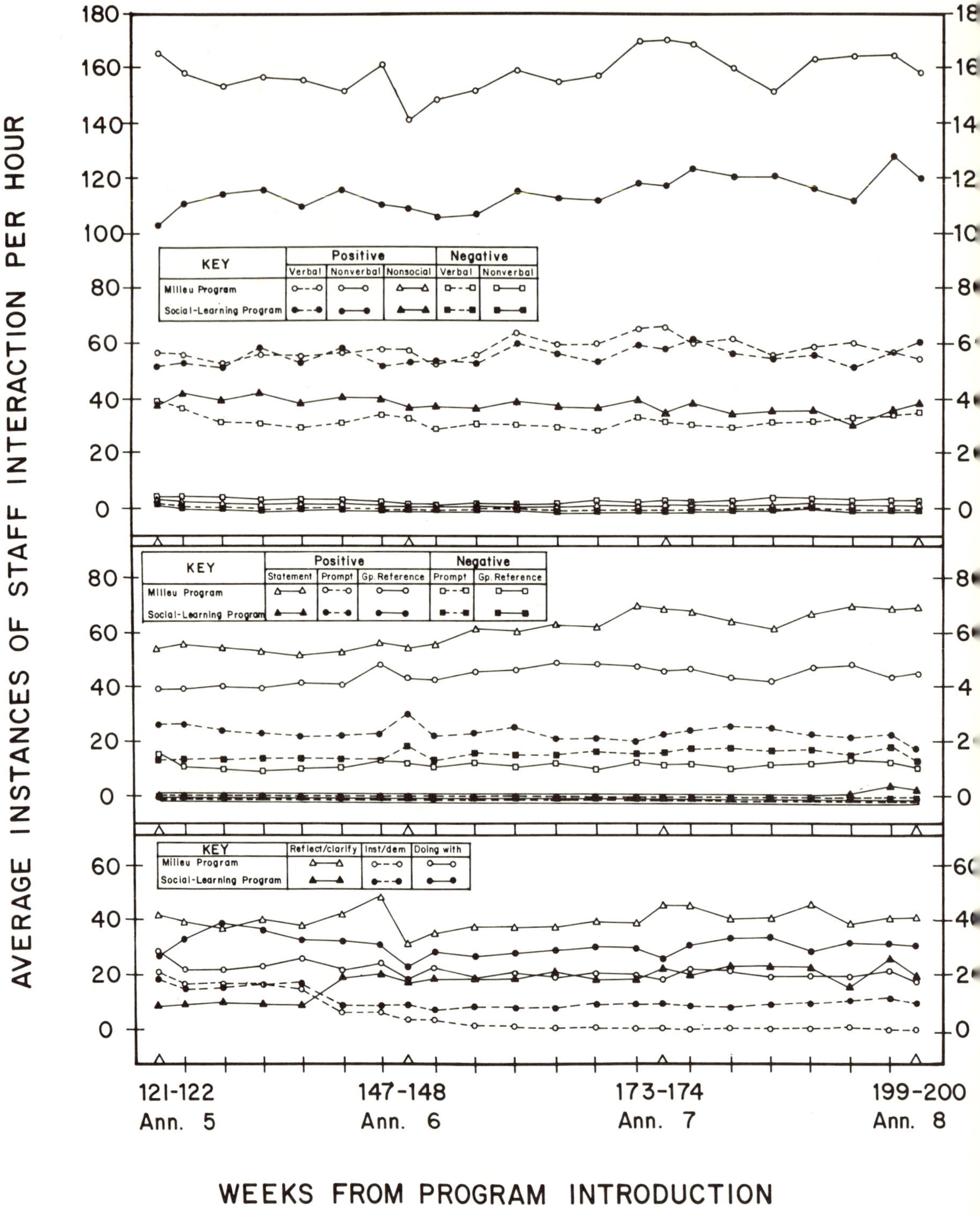

behavior. Positive Verbals, as well as Positive Nonverbals, showed a slight increase in frequency between the sixth and seventh anniversary assessments, corresponding in time with the legislative investigation of the institution and newspaper responses to the accusations of the state representative against the institution. Since these events were quite distressing to both staff and residents, emphasis was increased at that time on positive interpersonal communications between staff and residents.

Of the high-frequency staff behaviors plotted in the middle section of figure 26.4, only Positive Statements and Positive Group References in the milieu program showed any notable trends. Both classes of behavior showed gradual increases over the period, corresponding to declines in unitwide resident functioning (r=-0.83 & -0.72, respectively). These increases reflect the appropriate application of two of the highest-frequency milieu-specific procedures for dealing with resident failures, as the milieu residents declined in functioning over the period. The most notable changes in high-frequency staff behaviors plotted in the bottom section of figure 26.4 were in Reflect/Clarify and Instruct/Demonstrate. In both treatment programs, increases in Reflect/Clarify and decreases in Instruct/Demonstrate occurred during the first six months of the period, when extra effort of senior staff was made for off-hour coverage and the emphasis in in-service training sessions was not only to control assaultive behavior but to maintain appropriate interactions. Since the primary staff errors in the milieu program up to that time had continued to be inappropriate use of instruction, rather than reflection, clarification, and interpretation, feedback to junior staff had emphasized the need to reduce the use of instruction in the milieu program. The data in figure 26.4 indicate that staff responded with lower rates of instruction in both programs, only gradually increasing the appropriate use of instruction in the social-learning program over the last year of the period.

Two additional classes of staff behavior are worthy of mention, even though the low frequency of their total incidence precludes plotting them in figure 26.4. Physical Force and Negative Nonsocial staff behaviors reflect the primary means of dealing with resident assaults after an actual physical altercation had occurred: restraint and time out or expulsion. While these two classes of staff behavior still accounted for only a fraction of a percentage of all staff-resident interactions in either program, the change over the current period was notable. Specifically Physical Force and Negative Nonsocials within both programs increased over time parallel to changes in dangerous and aggressive acts (r's in the 0.40s & 0.50s). By the end of the current period, after a year and a half without effective consequences for assaultive behavior, the total incidences of Physical Force and Negative Nonsocials had increased 226% in the social-learning program and 344% in the milieu program over the levels from those of the two years before the current period.

An even clearer picture of the effect of reducing the time of expulsion and time out on staff, as well as resident, behavior may be seen by comparing the actual incidence of Physical Force and Negative Nonsocials as a consequence for assaultiveness for the four weeks before that change and for the last four-week block of the current time period. Before the change, the average staff member was required to use Physical Force to deal with assaultiveness less than once in 222 working hours in either program. Similarly the average staff member was required to expel a milieu resident for assaultiveness on only 15 occasions every 100 working hours and to place a social-learning resident in time out for assaultiveness on only 3 occasions every 100 working hours. After a year and a half of operating without an effective length of time for expulsion and time out and the resulting increase in assaultiveness, the average staff member working in the social-learning program was applying time out for assaults slightly over 4 times every 10 working hours (a fourteenfold increase). Physical force had to be applied by the average staff member in the social-learning program to control an assaultive resident nearly once every 10 working hours. The changes for staff working in the social-learning program were mild compared to those for them in the milieu program. By the end of the current period, the average staff member in the milieu program found it necessary to expel a resident for assaultiveness more than once every hour and to apply physical force to control an assaultive resident 3 times every 10 working hours. By the end of the period, each staff member was confronting an assaultive resident nearly three times as frequently in the milieu program as in the social-learning program—providing a clear basis for the higher proportion of staff who reported the social-learning program to be the more enjoyable in which to work.

How well staff differentiated their performance of the psychosocial programs during this period may be seen on an examination of the average hourly rates of staff activity over the next year and a half, presented in table 26.2.[12] Although a few changes in the total frequency of staff behavior occurred, the nature of differentiation of staff performance within and between programs remained quite constant over the entire period. The average total percentage of interactions of specific classes of

Table 26.2. Average hourly rate of staff activity on psychosocial units over the next year and a half.

| | Resident behavior to which staff responded | | | | | | | | | | | | Total staff behavior | | % of interactions | | % of all staff error | |
|---|---|---|---|---|---|---|---|---|---|---|---|---|---|---|---|---|---|---|
| | Appropriate | | Inappropriate Failure | | Inappropriate Crazy | | Request | | Neutral | | | | | | | | | |
| Staff behavior | Milieu | S.Lrng | Milieu | S.Lrng | Milieu | S.Lrng | Milieu | S.Lrng | Milieu | S.Lrng | | | Milieu | S.Lrng | Milieu | S.Lrng | Milieu | S.Lrng |
| Positive Verbal | 58.52+ | 56.38+ | 0.03- | 0.04- | - | - | 0.06o | 0.04o | o | o | | | 58.62 | 56.46 | 12.3% | 17.6% | 0.6% | 2.8% |
| Negative Verbal | 0.06- | 0.04- | 25.20+ | 0.87o | 7.03+ | 0.03o | - | - | 0.02- | - | | | 32.31 | 0.94 | 6.8% | 0.3% | 1.6% | 2.4% |
| Positive Nonverbal | 66.95+ | 69.80+ | 64.24o | 24.63o | 7.73o | 0.73- | 2.34o | 1.03o | 52.52o | 19.47o | | | 193.78 | 115.66 | 40.5% | 36.0% | 0.3% | 47.2% |
| Negative Nonverbal | - | 0.01- | 1.40o | 0.21o | 0.72o | 0.01o | o | - | 0.01- | - | | | 2.13 | 0.25 | 0.4% | 0.1% | 0.3% | 1.0% |
| Positive Nonsocial | 0.03- | 38.04+ | - | 0.04- | - | - | 1.42o | 0.02o | 0.05o | 0.21o | | | 1.50 | 38.30 | 0.3% | 11.9% | 0.6% | 2.6% |
| Negative Nonsocial | - | 0.02- | 0.02- | 1.75+ | 0.71o | 0.27+ | - | - | - | 0.01o | | | 0.73 | 2.05 | 0.2% | 0.6% | 0.3% | 2.3% |
| Positive Statement | 2.43+ | 0.06o | 51.52+ | 0.28- | 2.22+ | - | 0.03+ | - | 4.80+ | 0.73o | | | 61.00 | 1.07 | 12.8% | 0.3% | 0.3% | 18.2% |
| Negative Statement | - | 0.03- | 0.01- | - | - | - | - | - | - | - | | | 0.02 | 0.03 | | | 0.3% | 1.8% |
| Positive Prompt | - | 5.42+ | 0.02- | 16.39+ | - | 0.01+ | - | + | - | 0.87+ | | | 0.02 | 22.69 | | 7.1% | 0.3% | 2.8% |
| Negative Prompt | - | 0.02- | 0.03- | 14.79+ | 0.10- | 0.61+ | - | o | - | 0.02- | | | 0.12 | 15.44 | | 4.8% | 2.4% | |
| Positive Gp. Reference | 5.85+ | 0.03o | 31.89+ | 0.01- | 0.22+ | - | 0.01+ | o | 6.58+ | 0.49o | | | 44.55 | 0.54 | 9.3% | 0.2% | 0.3% | 0.8% |
| Negative Gp. Reference | 0.01- | - | 10.03+ | o | 1.99+ | o | + | o | 0.01o | - | | | 12.04 | | 2.5% | | | |
| Reflect/Clarify | 3.52+ | 3.05o | 30.48+ | 10.92+ | 1.51+ | 0.03o | 0.21+ | 0.14o | 4.39+ | 4.23+ | | | 40.11 | 18.36 | 8.4% | 5.7% | | |
| Suggest Alternatives | 0.18+ | 0.19o | 1.94+ | 0.33o | 0.03+ | - | + | - | 0.01+ | 0.01o | | | 2.16 | 0.53 | 0.5% | 0.2% | | |
| Instruct/Demonstrate | 0.35o | 1.13+ | 3.06+ | 6.36o | 0.03o | 0.10o | o | 0.02o | 1.76+ | 3.43o | | | 5.21 | 11.03 | 1.1% | 3.4% | | |
| Doing With | 12.45+ | 18.90+ | 0.02- | 0.01- | - | - | 0.29o | 0.35o | 8.94+ | 12.06+ | | | 21.70 | 31.32 | 4.5% | 9.8% | 0.5% | 0.8% |
| Doing For | 0.91- | 0.26o | 0.05- | 0.04- | 0.01- | - | 0.43o | 0.56o | 0.03- | o | | | 1.43 | 0.86 | 0.3% | 0.3% | 19.5% | 2.4% |
| Physical Force | - | - | 0.01o | 0.32o | 0.16o | 0.10o | - | - | - | - | | | 0.17 | 0.42 | | 0.1% | | |
| Ignore/No Response | 0.37- | 0.22- | 0.23- | 3.16+ | 0.01- | 1.90+ | 0.03- | - | 0.03- | 0.01- | | | 0.67 | 5.28 | 0.1%[a] | 1.6%[a] | 13.1% | 14.7% |
| Announce | b | b | b | b | b | b | b | b | 3.22+ | 1.88+ | | | 3.22 | 1.88 | (0.6%) | (0.5%) | b | b |
| Attend/Record/Observe | b | b | b | b | b | b | b | b | 45.66+ | 51.74+ | | | 45.66 | 51.74 | (8.7%) | (13.8%) | b | b |
| Total interactions | 151.62 | 193.60 | 220.18 | 80.16 | 22.48 | 3.77 | 4.82 | 2.17 | 79.12 | 41.53 | | | 478.24 | 321.22 | 100%[a] | 100%[a] | 1.1% | 0.5% |
| %correct interactions | 99.1% | 99.8% | 98.4% | 99.5% | 99.5% | 80.7% | 99.4% | 99.9% | 99.9%[a] | 99.9%[a] | | | 98.9% | 99.5% | b | b | 0.0% | 0.0% |
| Total activity | b | b | b | b | b | b | b | b | 128.03 | 95.15 | | | 527.13 | 374.84 | (110%) | (117%) | b | b |

Note. + = specifically programmed staff behavior; o = allowable staff choice; - = programmatic error. Empty cells signify less than 0.0045 instances per hour.
a. "Ignore-neutral" included in percentage figures, but not in total interactions.
b. Irrelevant cells.

staff behavior in table 26.2 reveals a remarkable consistency of differentiation within each program, with the distribution being nearly identical to that of the previous two years (table 21.2). Differentiation between programs was even greater than before. In fact, differences in the average hourly rate between programs were significant over the entire year and a half for twenty of the twenty-one classes of staff behavior. Negative Statements were totally inappropriate for staff in both programs and did not differ—occurring at most on three occasions every hundred hours.

Three classes of staff behavior showed significant differences between programs, where equality had occurred before. Doing For was differentially allowable between programs and did not differ in the relative percentage of total interactions; however, the average frequency was higher in the milieu program, with the majority being errors—doing things for residents that residents should have done themselves. Instruct/Demonstrate was differentially allowable and had consistently accounted for the majority of errors in the milieu program. Although Instruct/Demonstrate still accounted for the majority of milieu errors, the changes during the period appropriately reduced the frequency of this class of staff behavior to the extent that performance was significantly higher in the social-learning program—as required by the respective treatment manuals. The high rates of Positive Nonverbals over the current period were sufficiently differentiated that the milieu program was significantly higher in both frequency and percentage than the social-learning program.

Three classes of staff behavior that had occurred at significantly different rates over the previous two years continued to differ significantly between programs, even though differentiation was not required by the respective manuals. Physical Force continued to occur at a higher average rate in the social-learning program. However, the within-cell distribution shows that the higher rate for the social-learning program occurred only when dealing with resident failures. More Physical Force was required in the milieu program to deal with assaults, reflected as "inappropriate-crazy" behavior. But even with the increase in Physical Force during the period, such behavior still accounted for fewer than 0.1% of staff-resident interactions. While Announce and Attend/Record/Observe were totally appropriate in both programs, the differences in rate that were established over the previous two years continued. The significantly higher level of Announce in the milieu program continued to reflect the staff practice of making separate and sequential announcements for separate living groups, while general announcements were made in the social-learning program. Similarly the significantly lower levels of Attend/Record/Observe in the milieu program reflected the higher overall rates of interaction, which left little time for instances of observation without interacting in the milieu program. The higher total instances of this class of behavior in both programs also reflects the greater paperwork required by preparations for hospital accreditation of the institution during this period.

All remaining differences in staff performance during the next year and a half, as before, largely followed the differential requirements specified in the respective treatment manuals. Seven of the eight classes of staff behavior that continued to be performed at significantly higher rates in the milieu program than in the social-learning program were differentially specified in the milieu manual. These seven classes included milieu procedures that were to be applied at all times across all classes of resident behavior (Positive Statement, Positive Nonverbal, Positive Group Reference, Reflect/Clarify, Suggest Alternatives) and procedures that specified the nature of content for responding to inappropriate resident behavior (Negative Verbal, Negative Group Reference). Positive Verbals were not differentially specified in the respective treatment manuals as to rate but were required in both programs. Over the current period, the absolute frequency of Positive Verbals was slightly higher in the milieu program but remained as a significantly lower proportion of total interactions (the only class of staff behavior to show such a reversal between rate and percentage). When all of the above behaviors are taken into account, table 26.2 shows that over 93% of all staff-resident interactions in the milieu program over the next year and a half entailed procedures detailed for milieu therapy.

Negative Nonverbals decreased in total frequency but continued to be performed at a significantly higher rate in the milieu program than in the social-learning program over the next year and a half, even though no differential requirements were specified. Analyses of SRIC sequences continued to provide supportive evidence that negative affect for staff was likely to have been generated and communicated as a result of intense focus on inappropriate resident behavior in the milieu program. Over the next year and a half, staff averaged over 58 instances of positive statements and negative feedback per hour in response to inappropriate resident behavior in the milieu program, but these procedures were effective in terminating inappropriate behavior only 52% of the time. On the average, residents continued to perform the same inappropriate behavior on 27.72 occasions per hour after having received positive statements and negative feedback, and staff appropriately continued to provide additional positive statements and negative feedback on 27.70 occasions. Thus, staff were exceptionally reliable in staying with continued programmatic interactions. With such high-intensity focus on continuing inappropriate behavior, plus the increase in assaultiveness, it is remarkable that negative affects accounted for only 0.4% of staff-resident interactions in the milieu program over the period.

Table 26.2 shows that the three classes of staff behavior that continued to account for the highest proportion of interactions in the social-learning program over the next year and a half consisted of positive social and nonsocial behaviors (Positive Verbal, Positive Nonverbal, Positive Nonsocial), and the fourth highest-rate staff behavior still consisted of shared social activity (Doing With). While all of these classes of behavior except Positive Nonverbals regularly accounted for a significantly greater proportion of staff-resident interactions in the social-learning program than in the milieu program, differences continued to be apparent for Positive Nonverbals as well. Specifically fewer than 35% of Positive Nonverbals in the milieu program were contingent upon appropriate resident behavior, while over 60% were contingent in the social-learning program. Similarly, over 60% of Doing With was contingent upon appropriate resident behavior in the social-learning program rather than being staff initiated. Thus, the within-cell distribution of these behaviors in table 26.2 shows that over 57% of all staff-resident interactions in the social-learning program over the next year and a half were still accounted for by positive social and material reinforcement contingent upon appropriate resident behavior—even with the decrease in overall levels of resident functioning during the period.

The five remaining classes of staff behavior that were performed at significantly higher rates in the social-learning program than in the milieu program over the next year and a half continued to be those that were differentially specified by the respective manuals for dealing with inappropriate resident behavior and/or initiating new or different resident behaviors (Negative Nonsocial, Positive Prompt, Negative Prompt, Instruct/Demonstrate, Ignore/No Response). Even though the absolute level of all these classes of staff behavior was higher during this period of increased inappropriate behavior, the low frequency of Negative Nonsocial and Ignore/No Response was still notable. Analyses of SRIC sequences on instances in which active ignoring was a required staff response again found a basis for low rates of Ignore/No Response to be the success of prompts in changing resident behavior. Staff averaged nearly thirty-two prompts per hour for inappropriate resident behavior over the next year and a half, and the prompts were effective in changing behavior more than 98% of the time. A prompted inappropriate behavior continued, on the average, on only forty-seven occasions every hundred hours, and staff properly ignored that behavior on forty-four of those occasions. Thus, staff continued to be quite reliable in application of active ignoring when it was required, but the success of other procedures—even during this period of increasing inappropriateness of resident behavior—continued to result in a restricted number of instances in which Ignore/No Response was the only appropriate staff behavior.

The differences between programs document that actual staff performance over the next year and a half clearly differentiated between programs on the basis of requirements specified in the respective treatment manuals. Table 26.2 also shows that the remarkable within-program accuracy in staff performance of the social-learning program continued, with 99.5% of all staff-resident interactions following specified procedures. Additionally the few changes in the milieu program continued to increase the accuracy of staff performance to the extent that 98.9% of all staff-resident interactions in the milieu program over the entire period followed specified procedures.

An examination of the distribution of staff errors in table 26.2 reveals that by far the greatest proportion of staff errors in the social-learning program were accounted for by inappropriate Positive Nonverbals—suggesting that staff overcorrected for the increased incidence of negative interactions during the period. However, the exceptionally low total instances of error in the social-learning program were such that the highest rate of error occurred only seventy-one times per hundred hours of staff activity. Unlike previous periods, however, 66.7% of social-learning errors consisted of misapplication of milieu therapy procedures: Positive Statements for resident failures and Positive Nonverbals in response to crazy behavior. Only 2.6% of social-learning errors consisted of activities that were inappropriate at any time, while 30.7% showed a misapplication of social-learning procedures; however, the total error rate itself remained at a remarkably low level of only 0.5% of all staff-resident interactions.

Although the error rate in the milieu program showed considerable improvement, errors still occurred at a significantly higher level than in the social-learning program. As before, the majority of milieu errors (94.5%) still consisted of the misapplication of social-learning procedures, while only 1.4% and 4.1% of milieu errors, respectively consisted of activities that were inappropriate at any time or were a misapplication of milieu procedures. Although the level of inappropriate application of Instruct/Demonstrate was significantly reduced over the current period, this class of staff behavior was still the major spillover of social-learning procedures in the milieu program. Nevertheless, the total error rate for the milieu program over the entire period was an exceptionally low level of only 1.1% of all staff-resident interactions.

Actual staff performance thus continued to be well differentiated between programs over the next year and a half, with the absolute accuracy of performance maintaining or improving upon the exceptional levels achieved earlier. The accuracy of application of programmatic procedures still continued to be better in the social-learning program, with the distribution of relative proportions of staff-resident interactions continuing to follow the procedures from the social-learning manual and to reflect the ideal distribution of technique utilization from the TOS (figure 26.2). The accuracy of application of programmatic procedures in the milieu program was maintained at improved levels over prior periods, with the distribution of relative proportions of staff-resident interactions following the procedures in the milieu manual and the ideal distribution of technique utilization from the TOS (figure 26.2) even better than before. Only Suggest Alternatives remained below desired levels of performance, while Instruct/Demonstrate improved but remained higher than desired in the milieu program. The high levels of performance of all positive social interactions and nonverbal responses in both programs reflect a continuation of a genuine rather than a mechanical application of treatment procedures. Overall, in spite of the dramatic increases in assaultiveness, staff maintained their performance of both programs at a remarkably consistent level, remaining about as close to being perfect as possible over the entire period.

Several significant within-program correlations between average instances of each class of staff behavior and unitwide levels of resident functioning over standard time blocks were described earlier. In addition, the stable differentiation between programs and comparative effectiveness found over the previous two years was again apparent in parallel correlations over programs. Every class of staff behavior that differed between programs—except classes dealing with assaults (Physical Force, Negative Nonsocial)—also yielded significant correlations with changes in resident functioning. These correlations continued to reflect higher levels of resident functioning to covary with all staff behaviors that occurred at higher rates in the social-learning program (mdn. r=0.64, range 0.43 to 0.69) and to be negatively related to all staff behaviors that occurred at higher rates in the milieu program (mdn. r=-0.69, range -0.49 to -0.81). The two classes of staff behavior that were required for handling assaults did not yield significant relationships over programs but varied positively (r's in the 0.40s & 0.50s) with the unitwide incidence of Intolerable Behavior within each program. Thus, actual staff performance was in keeping with prescribed programmatic procedures and continued to be differentially related to resident functioning over the current period.

In summary, objective data from the SRIC show remarkable stability in the reliability and differentiation of actual staff behavior over the next year and a half. The total activity level of staff remained at nearly two and a half times the initial rate in the social-learning program and over three and a half times the initial rate in the milieu program, without notable change at any time over the period. Clear and stable differences in the focus of staff activities were maintained throughout, with differentiation between programs being identical to those in earlier periods. The slight changes in focus that did occur reflected changes in response to resident behavior, with an exceptionally high proportion of staff activities continuing to involve staff-resident interactions, with correspondingly low amounts of staff activities devoted to announcements, relevant paperwork, and observing residents without interacting.

Residents in both programs continued to receive very high levels of individual, personalized contacts from staff. In fact, the total staff attention an individual social-learning resident received over the year and a half was 11% higher and the total attention an individual milieu resident received was 37% higher than the levels existing over the last six months before the current period. The average milieu resident also received nearly 41% more staff attention than the average social-learning resident did—even though the social-learning procedures were clearly more effective. These differences provide clear evidence that how much attention was received was not as important as how the attention received came about.

Relatively few classes of staff behavior showed changes in frequency of utilization in either program over the next year and a half. As with the interpretation of appropriate techniques on the TOS, staff remained remarkably consistent in their performance of specific interactions. The few changes that did occur reflected the continued emphasis on positive programmatic procedures and genuine metacommunications in staff-resident interactions as a function of continuing in-service training and were highlighted when senior staff increased their coverage of evenings and weekends. Paralleling later changes on the TOS, staff more closely approached the ideal milieu program by increasing their use of reflection and clarification and decreasing their use of instruction immediately after the increase in senior staff emphasis after the staff reorganization during the first six months of the period.

The effects of the externally imposed reduction in consequences for resident assaults on staff behavior were clearly in evidence over the entire period. Paralleling increases in resident assaultiveness, staff activities involving physical restraint and expulsion or time out increased 226% in the social-learning program and 344% in the milieu program over levels existing during the entire two years before the change in consequences. The activities related to assaults still accounted for less than 0.2% of all staff-resident interactions in either program. However, after a year and a half without effective consequences for assaultiveness, the average staff member was required to confront an assaultive resident about once every two hours of work in the social-learning program and nearly three times as frequently in the milieu program. Although these activities were of low frequency on an absolute level and reliably applied in both programs, the intensity of such activity appears to provide a clear basis for the higher proportion of staff who reported that the social-learning program was the more enjoyable in which to work.

The actual differentiation of staff performance in the psychosocial programs over the next year and a half was remarkable. Both the focus of staff activity and the rate of performance of specific classes of staff behavior continued to be in keeping with the differential requirements specified in the respective treatment manuals, with the absolute accuracy maintaining or improving on the exceptional levels achieved earlier. Staff working in the milieu program performed all milieu-specific interactions at a significantly higher rate than they did when working in the social-learning program, with 98.9% of all staff-resident interactions being appropriate on an absolute level. The distribution of relative proportions of staff-resident interactions in the milieu program approached the ideal distributions specified in the milieu manual and on the TOS even more closely as a result of differential decreases in the use of instructions and increases in the use of reflection and clarification. The only classes of staff behavior that deviated at all from the ideal milieu program were an underutilization of suggesting alternatives and an overutilization of instructions. This overuse still accounted for the majority of staff errors in the milieu program and the primary instance of inappropriate spillover of techniques from one program to the other. However, even this error occurred on fewer than 0.1% of all staff-resident interactions, indicating how well the milieu program was actually carried out.

Staff working in the social-learning program not only performed social-learning specific procedures at a significantly higher rate than they did when working in the milieu program, but 99.5% of all staff-resident interactions in the program were appropriate on an absolute level. As before, the distribution of relative proportions of staff-resident interactions in the social-learning program clearly followed those specified in the treatment manual and the ideal distribution of technique utilization from the TOS; errors were nearly nonexistent. Thus, in spite of the dramatic increases in assaultiveness, staff maintained their performance of both programs with remarkable consistency, with clear and reliable differentiation of programs and levels of absolute accuracy that left little room for improvement.

## SUMMARY

Staff attitudes, opinions, and beliefs about mental patients changed significantly over the next year and a half, even though less staff turnover occurred than at earlier assessments. Two OMI scores decreased, moving closer to the ideals underlying the psychosocial programs, and one increased moving closer to that of the traditional mental hospital staff. The changes appeared to reflect staff response to increases in assaultiveness of residents preceding assessments, without even suggestive evidence that changes in staff attitude had any effect on resident behavior following each assessment. By the end of the next year and a half, OMI scores clustered differently than at earlier assessments, but predictability from individual staff characteristics remained low and, essentially, constant. Even with changes over the eighteen months, the staff group as a whole continued to reflect the ideal assumptions underlying the psychosocial programs, with continued differences from the typical mental hospital staff.

In contrast to the changes in opinions about patients, opinions and interpretations of the treatment programs showed remarkable consistency over the next year and a half. Staff beliefs of the comparative effectiveness of the psychosocial programs continued to reflect the objective differences between programs that occurred during the intervals preceding each assessment, with the great majority judging the social-learning program as the more effective. The majority of staff continued to judge the social-learning program as the more enjoyable as well, probably as a result of the differential levels of assaultiveness with which they had to cope. As at earlier time periods and with the

OMI, staff judgments of the comparative effectiveness and enjoyability of psychosocial programs appeared to be responsive to prior changes in resident behavior but had no notable effect on the ensuing response of residents to the programs.

Preferred TOS attitude scores—reflecting staff preference for the nature of treatment programs—remained well differentiated and quite consistent over the period. Slight differential change occurred on two scores, moving more in the direction of the ideal social-learning program; however, the nature of treatment characteristics preferred by staff remained closer to the ideal milieu program. By the eighth anniversary assessment, less clustering occurred between preferred attitude scores, and such preferences still showed little predictability from individual staff characteristics. There were some differential changes in the level of endorsement of TOS attitude scores for each orientation—reflecting staff interpretation of the nature of each psychosocial program. However, the changes were such that differences from the previous two years were cancelled out, with the pattern and level of scores at the end of the current period no longer differing from the original posttraining assessment nearly four years earlier. Even with some changes during the period, the pattern within and between psychosocial orientations remained constant; the nature of programs continued to be interpreted differentially, with staff interpretations remaining quite close—and moving closer—to the ideals of each program over the entire year and a half.

Preferred TOS technique scores—reflecting staff preferences for the use of different treatment procedures—also remained well differentiated and remarkably constant over the entire year and a half, showing no significant change. Preferred techniques still remained more closely related to the ideal social-learning program, with slight changes over the period moving even further from the ideal milieu program. By the eighth anniversary assessment there was less clustering among preferred techniques, but preference for the use of specific techniques remained almost totally unrelated to individual staff characteristics. Although one differential change occurred in the level of endorsement of TOS technique scores for program orientations —reflecting staff interpretation of appropriate technique utilization within each psychosocial program—milieu and social-learning programs continued to be differentiated in desired directions. The slight changes resulted in staff interpretations moving closer to the ideal within the milieu orientation and further from the ideal within the social-learning orientation. By the eighth anniversary assessment, staff interpretations of the appropriateness of the relative use of techniques were not only well differentiated between programs but no longer differed in the extent to which interpretations approached the ideals of the respective psychosocial programs. Thus, staff interpretations of both nature and techniques continued to differentiate between programs in desired directions, with staff preferences remaining much closer to either psychosocial orientation than those of the mental hospital staff.

More important for determining the actual operation and differentiation of treatment conditions within and between programs is the objective data from the SRIC. Total staff activity remained at nearly two and a half times the initial level that existed after program introduction in the social-learning program, and over three and a half times that in the milieu program, without notable change over the entire period. Clear and stable differences in the focus of activities were similarly maintained, and the differentiation of programs was identical to that of earlier periods. Although the same staff continued to equate time and activity focus over psychosocial programs, the differentially high rates of individual attention from staff were maintained at even higher levels throughout the next year and a half. Thus, residents in both psychosocial programs continued to receive exceptionally high levels of attention from staff; the average milieu resident received significantly more staff attention than the average social-learning resident over the entire period—even though the social-learning program was clearly more effective. The differences continue to provide clear evidence that how attention was applied was more important than how much was received.

The actual differentiation of staff performance in the two psychosocial programs over the next year and a half was remarkable. The few changes in specific staff activities reflected continuing emphasis on positive programmatic procedures and genuine metacommunications, which were the focus of in-service training and supervision, such that even greater differentiation between programs occurred. The focus of staff activity, the rate of specific classes of staff behavior, and the resident behavior x staff behavior match all remained in keeping with the differential requirements specified in the respective treatment manuals, with the conduct of the milieu program even improving over that of earlier levels. Specified milieu procedures continued to be performed at differentially higher rates when staff worked in the milieu program, and specified social-learning procedures continued to be performed at differentially higher rates when staff worked in that program. On an absolute level, 98.9% of all staff-resident interactions in the milieu program and 99.5% of all staff-resident interactions in the social-learning program were correct over the next year and a half, with errors being nearly nonexistent.

The distribution of relative proportions of specific staff behaviors actually performed in each program paralleled the ideals in the respective treatment manuals and on the TOS. The improvement in actual performance of the milieu program preceded the parallel endorsement on the TOS, with actual performance in both programs continuing to show closer approximations to ideal programs than the self-reported endorsement levels. While SRIC data clearly reflected the increase in assaultiveness during the next year and a half, what was found was a reliable application of existing procedures for dealing with assaultiveness rather than any change in staff activity that might have contributed to the increases in assaultive behavior. In fact, after a year and a half without access to effective consequences for assaultive behavior, each staff member was required to deal with an assaultive resident in the social-learning program about once every two hours on the average and nearly three times that rate in the milieu program.

The analyses of staff attitudes and performance over the next year and a half provide information on staff and the nature of the events to which they responded. More important, however, is the clear documentation of the differentiation of treatment programs according to prescribed procedures, with an absolute level of continuing accuracy in the application of both programs being exceptionally good. The documentation, combined with the overall equivalency of other sources of influence, including psychotropic drugs, clearly established that the overall decline in functioning during this period was caused by the externally imposed reduction in procedures for handling assaultive behavior, and the differential effectiveness of the two programs was clearly a function of the differential treatment procedures applied.

# 27. Summary of Findings for the Next Year and a Half

The programs continued to be carried out according to the procedures of the respective manuals over the next year and a half, with all required assessments being maintained. Volunteers, facilities and services, consumables, and material goods continued to be available at the levels established earlier, but shortages of staff and funds remained. Based upon the obvious clinical success achieved before the current period, an expanded design and staffing plan were approved by the State Department of Mental Health. The expansion involved a comparative evaluation of treatment of the prechronic mental patient during the analyses and follow up of the hard-core chronic groups, plus preparation for the conversion of the psychosocial units for demonstration-training functions in addition to research and service. Senior research and clinical staff worked on their own time throughout the period to develop operational details and staffing for the expansions.

Both the original time plan for releasing improved residents to private extended-care facilities on completion of the seventh anniversary assessment and the timing of the expansion required change. The combined discovery of the absence of centralized community beds to accept current residents and a decline in functioning over the first six months of the period—detected when resident data were examined for the first time—resulted in a decision to extend the intramural period of operation with the hard-core chronic groups. External contingencies set the length of extension at one additional year beyond the seventh anniversary assessment. Therefore, the entire period of the next year and a half continued operation of psychosocial programs as before, but with analysis and monitoring of resident data, including several substudies described in chapter 23, to identify possible bases for the decline in functioning. Several additional notable events occurred during the next year and a half, which placed added burdens on staff and affected the functioning of residents.

The outcome data reported in chapter 24 detail not only the absence of continued resident improvements, which had been occurring at the end of the previous period, but a decline in overall functioning for residents in both psychosocial programs over the next year and a half. While several extraneous events had occasional influence on resident behavior, the clear basis for the decline in functioning for both groups was found to lie in the reduction in the length of time out and expulsion as a consequence for resident assaults, which had been externally imposed by a statewide policy directive just before the current period began. Dangerous and aggressive acts increased dramatically over the period, without effective procedures for handling them. The problem was greater for the milieu group than for the social-learning group; the absolute incidence of assaults in the milieu program reached severely disruptive levels by the end of the period.

Although both psychosocial programs declined in effectiveness, with aggressive intolerable behavior exerting influence over nearly every other area of functioning, the social-learning program continued to maintain improvements from pretreatment levels and superiority to the milieu program at all times. However, by the end of the period, the continuous objective assessments of hour-by-hour behavior found that milieu residents as a group no longer showed improvement in overall functioning from the levels that had existed before the original introduction of programmatic procedures. Losses over the current period tended to occur for residents in both programs who were initially most debilitated; improvement tended to be associated with shorter lengths of hospitalization in both groups and with sex in the milieu group. As at earlier assessments, other demographic characteristics, prior level of functioning, and drug status were unrelated to improvement in either program.

Nearly all components of maladaptive and adaptive behavior showed continuing differentiation between programs, but with losses in effectiveness because of the reduction in consequences for assaults. The only areas of maladaptive behavior in which earlier improvements were maintained without loss in both programs were dysfunctional cognitive behaviors and hostile-belligerence. While the social-learning program maintained significant improvement and superiority to the milieu program, both psychosocial groups showed increased levels of grossly inappropriate resident responses to minimal expectations and clinically bizarre motoric behaviors. By the end of the period, the increases in the milieu program were of such an extent that grossly inappropriate responses to minimal expectations no longer showed significant improvement from pretreatment levels.

The detrimental effects of reduced consequences for assaultive behavior were even stronger on adaptive behavior in the milieu program. Losses in concurrent appropriate behavior, interpersonal skills, and instrumental role performance of milieu residents were to such low levels that the milieu group no longer showed significant improvement; only self-care remained at higher levels than those from before the introduction of therapeutic community procedures. Although residents in the social-learning program also lost ground over the next year and a half, all classes of adaptive behavior continued to show significant improvement for the group as a whole and significantly greater gains than those of the milieu program. Thus, even with the losses following procedural changes for controlling assaultive behavior, the social-learning program continued to show effectiveness and superiority over the milieu program on all targets of rehabilitation of the chronically institutionalized population. However, current procedures were obviously not effective in controlling resident assaultiveness in either program.

The characteristics of other ongoing resident activity, reported in chapter 25, also showed additional differentiation of programs and changes related to the increases in assaults resulting from the externally imposed changes for control of assaultive behavior. Unitwide community meetings continued to reflect the differing purposes within programs, with specific characteristics being most related to program structure. Therapeutic community meetings especially reflected the amount of assaultiveness on the unit, with the topics of focus and the specific resident group leader in office having major effects. Comparative use of resources continued to show differences resulting from program structures and problems resulting from increases in assaultiveness over the next year and a half, with significant reductions in the use of consumables, even though availability had not changed. The fact that how resources were used was more important than how many were obtained continued to be in evidence.

Resident time spent awake was maintained at the high levels established upon the introduction of the programs, but social-learning residents averaged more time awake than milieu residents did by the end of the period—partially because more milieu residents were still receiving psychotropic drugs. Time spent with others decreased to original levels over the period, paralleling changes in assaultiveness in both programs, with improved residents avoiding their more intolerable colleagues. Numerous changes in the variability of ongoing resident activity occurred over the period, with clear influence by notable events and changes in assaultiveness and even greater differentiation in day-to-day processes occurring between programs. While all of the differences continue to be interesting in their own right, the characteristics of resident activities reported in chapter 25 again support the differing program structures and procedures as the basis for between-program effects reported in chapter 24, while further confirming the influence of the reduction in consequences for assaults and other identified events.

The details of staff attitudes and performance, reported in chapter 26, found that attitudes, opinions, and beliefs about mental patients changed in response to the increases in assaultiveness of residents preceding each assessment, without resident behavior being affected by changes in staff attitudes. Even with changes over the period, the staff group continued to reflect the ideal assumptions underlying the psychosocial programs, with continued differences from those of typical mental hospital staff. Opinions and interpretations of treatment programs showed remarkable consistency over the next year and a half. Beliefs of the comparative effectiveness continued to reflect objective results, and preferences for working conditions continued to reflect the comparative level of assaultiveness with which staff were required to cope. Few changes occurred over the period in staff interpretations of either nature or techniques appropriate to each psychosocial program, with programs continuing to be differentiated in desired directions. Although staff preferences for the nature of treatment programs continued to be closer to the ideal milieu program, and those for technique utilization continued to be closer to the ideal social-learning program, all staff preferences remained much closer to either psychosocial orientation than those of the mental hospital staff.

The moment-to-moment continuous objective assessment of staff behavior, also reported in chapter 26, found remarkable stability and continued differentiation of staff performance over the entire eighteen months. Total staff activity remained at the exceptionally high levels establsihed over the previous six months without notable change during the next year and a half. Clear and stable differences in the focus of activities were similarly maintained, with differentiation of programs being identical to that at earlier periods. Even though the social-learning program continued to be the more effective, higher activity levels and more individual staff attention to residents continued in the milieu program over the next year and a half—again documenting that how attention is applied is more important than how much attention is received.

The rate of performance of specific staff behaviors and resident behavior-by-staff behavior match remained in keeping with the differential requirements specified in the respective treatment manuals, with the distribution of staff-resident interactions paralleling the ideal distribution for each program. The increase in resident assaultiveness was clearly reflected in the reliable application of existing procedures for dealing with assaultiveness, without any change in staff activity that might have contributed to increases in assaultive behavior. In fact, performance of milieu procedures had even improved to the extent that 98.9% of all staff-resident interactions were correct on an absolute level over the entire year and a half, and prescribed procedures in the social-learning program continued to be carried out at the very high level of 99.5% of all staff-resident interactions.

Chapter 26 presents information on staff and the nature of events to which they responded. The clear continuing differentiation of treatment programs in the same manner as previous periods, combined with the other identified changes and relationships, documents the differential effectiveness of the two programs to be a function of the differential treatment procedures applied. The decline in functioning during this period was further documented to be the result of the externally imposed reduction in procedures for controlling assaultive behavior.

Thus, by the eighth anniversary assessment, only the social-learning program had maintained a significant continuing impact on all classes of resident functioning, with continued superiority to the milieu program on all identified targets of rehabilitation for the severely debilitated chronic groups. Both psychosocial programs had released a significant number of residents to relatively independent functioning in the community, and both continued to show a significant number of residents with objective improvement. However, after a year and a half without effective consequences for assaultiveness, not only were assaults occurring at an incredibly high level, but few residents in either program were continuing to show improvement; some were even worse. By the end of the period, only slight hope existed that the remaining six months would be sufficient time to regain the level of improvements attained earlier, even if the procedural changes required by the problems identified during the current period could be implemented immediately.

# PART 6
# The Last Six Months on the Psychosocial Units: Attempts to Regain the Peak

## 28. Notable Events and Overview of the Last Six Months

The most notable event of the last six months of the intramural period was the accomplishment of all the multiple activities required within the remaining time allowed by external contingencies that had set the limits on the one-year extension. Both psychosocial programs operated without change from earlier procedures for the first two weeks of the current period, after which baseline conditions were reintroduced. After four weeks of operation under baseline conditions, the psychosocial programs were reintroduced with procedural changes based upon the data analyses and substudies of the previous year and a half. All required assessments were maintained throughout the period, with all other operations, commodities, facilities, and services being available at the same level as had existed during previous periods.

For the first time in the history of the project, the full complement of clinical staff was employed and trained by the start of the second baseline. This resulted partially from continued participation in the several federal programs for aiding the unemployed and partially from the reorganization of staff in preparation for the planned expansion to the treatment of prechronic mental patients. The reorganization, plus the supplemental staff who were in training for future work in the extramural and training divisions of the expanded design, provided additional help for community contacts and extra paperwork required during the period. Clinical staff were therefore actually maintained at the specified complement for all on-the-floor work and supervision, with only slightly more than the usual amount of negotiation of bureaucratic procedures, institutional meetings, and administrative duties detracting from work with the residents.

The burgeoning paperwork required by continuing preparations to accredit the center as a hospital did take additional clinical staff time to maintain the ongoing progress notes in the parallel medical record for each resident over the entire period; however, the research and clerical staff largely handled the large task of converting the detailed data on the actual changes in each resident's behavior from entry to the psychosocial programs to nonutilitarian progress notes in the format prescribed for hospital accreditation of medical records. The extra staff also made possible the community contacts necessary to continue negotiations with community clinics and psychiatric wards to gather population information on prechronic patients and to begin detailing procedures for handling assessments and patient flow for the expanded design. Concurrently work with private extended-care facilities continued, and sufficient centralized beds were finally available to accept improved residents from all three intramural groups to allow a controlled comparison of community stay.

Throughout the last six months, senior research staff continued weekly monitoring of incoming resident, as well as staff, data to propose psychosocial residents for community placement immediately after the completion of the ninth anniversary assessment. Until that time, earlier release criteria were maintained for psychosocial units; however, to allow the hospital adequate time for processing, staff in charge of the hospital comparison group were told that hospital patients who were acceptable for extended-care placement could be so placed starting at the eighth anniversary assessment.

The operation of psychosocial programs over the first two weeks of the period, thus exactly continued all procedures from the earlier period, including the last two weeks of the purchase-eligibility substudy. During this time, senior clinical and research staff met regularly to work out details of procedures and resident and staff schedules for the second baseline condition. Junior staff were informed of the forthcoming change in procedure four days before the reinstitution of baseline conditions, with the regular in-service training sessions devoted to training in baseline procedures. Full senior staff supervisory coverage of all shifts was instituted over the remaining four days to ensure that original programs were maintained up to the time of change.

Baseline conditions were then established for four weeks on both psychosocial units to provide a common base for assessing both generalized improvement from old programs and change that might occur from the reintroduction of programs with changed procedures. A statewide policy directive prohibiting institutionalized residents from serving food was also implemented concurrent with baseline procedures. Thus, dietary staff, who had functioned only in a supervisory capacity previously, took over all direct food service. This change, concurrent with the removal of programmatic procedures, modified resident schedules by doing away with dietary living groups on the milieu unit and dietary assistants on the social-learning unit. The morning schedule was therefore changed from that indicated in the treatment manuals by scheduling all residents in both programs to arise at 6:00 A.M. Otherwise, scheduled classes, activities, and existing group compositions were retained as in the previous operation of programs.

Instructions to staff and residents followed those detailed for original baseline conditions, with senior staff providing intensive coverage of all shifts over the first week of return to baseline to ensure appropriate staff behavior; they maintained regular intermittent coverage thereafter. Additionally the regular monitoring and feedback to staff from objective observational data was maintained during the second baseline, but had not yet been instituted in the first. The only other differences existing between the first and second baseline conditions concerned the availability of resources and use of psychotropic drugs. Because of the existence of volunteers and the higher levels of consumables that had been available for the previous two years, both off-unit facilities and services and on-unit consumables were more available during the second baseline than the first—remaining at the same level of availability that existed during prior operation of programs. During the first baseline, the great majority of residents had been receiving psychotropic drugs; few residents were receiving them during the last six months. Active drugs were held constant over the last six months—one of five coded placebos being prescribed if staff or residents wished to increase psychotropic drugs. Thus, the traditional means of dealing with assaults—restraints, tepid baths, physical separation, and instruction—were employed during both baseline conditions, but only placebos were administered during the second one.

During the operation of baseline conditions "quick and dirty" data analyses were completed on earlier program operations and substudies to identify specific problems that had been associated with the decline in functioning over the previous year and a half. Senior research and clinical staff then defined procedural changes to overcome the problems within the existing structure of both psychosocial programs and revised procedures and schedules. During the last four days of baseline, in-service training sessions were devoted to retraining junior staff in the revised psychosocial programs, with senior staff supervisory coverage of all shifts ensuring that changes in procedure did not occur until the scheduled time.

The reintroduction of the psychosocial programs with procedural changes followed immediately after the completion of the fourth week of baseline. The full revised programs began immediately, with required exposure procedures being followed for the first week to ensure some familiarity with new procedures for residents in each program. Senior staff also continued full coverage of all shifts over the first week to ensure that new procedures were being appropriately applied. Their supervision faded to intermittent coverage for the nineteen weeks remaining before disposition decisions were required for all residents.

The primary procedural change at this time concerned the length of time for time out and expulsion as a consequence for assaultive behavior. Since the reduction from two days to two hours had been clearly responsible for the increase in assaultiveness over the previous year and a half, approval was finally obtained from appropriate administrative and review groups to increase the length of time once again as an experiment. The length of expulsion or time out was from the instance of the assault until 5:30 A.M. the following morning. Although the time was less than half the period that had previously been effective, staff hoped that it would be sufficiently long to control assaults and would allow residents a new start through exposure to the respective programs at the beginning of the following day. As in previous time periods, nonassaultive intolerable behaviors continued to receive time out or expulsion for the remainder of the (forty-five minute) functional period, for a minimum stay of twenty minutes in both programs, as did other applications of time out in the social-learning program.

Differences in structure or procedure from program manuals did occur as a result of the procedural changes. The rate of fines was changed from those specified in the social-learning manual to provide further contrast between assaults (twenty-five tokens) and other intolerable behaviors (ten tokens) and minor infractions, such as the use of goods or facilities without paying required tokens (two tokens). All restrictions on token spending remained for social-learning residents with standing fines; however, the purchase-eligibility, proportional-payoff procedure was implemented as a regular practice on the basis of the results of the earlier substudy. Thus, residents with standing fines could still obtain access to all available resources in the program (except exclusion from scheduled activities) by making an additional payment on the standing fine before token purchases. Similarly proportional payoff on fines was regularly introduced as a function of the length of time without having received a new fine.

In addition to the statewide policy directive requiring paid dietary workers to serve food, analyses of earlier data found a high incidence of assaultiveness around meal times. Therefore, upon the reintroduction of the programs, the meal procedures were changed in each program from those in the manuals. Dietary living groups in the milieu program and dietary assistants in the social-learning program were not reinstituted; rather, paid dietary workers took care of all food service. As a result the morning schedule was changed, and the order of bed and area and appearance checks was then reversed, with appearance checks being moved from sleeping areas to the hallway mirrors, as the last check before breakfast. Meals on the social-learning unit were changed so that the early meal required token payments (three at breakfast, five at lunch, four at dinner), for which residents entered twenty minutes early and received a special meal, which included extra coffee, cigarettes, desserts, flowers, and tablecloths. Regular meals were available without token charge but required a twenty-minute wait while early meal customers and staff were eating; they consisted of the basic nutritious but less-appetizing meal, without extra portions except for token payment. Cigarettes and snacks were also made available at all coffee breaks.

The nights for evening meetings were also changed from those specified in the manuals to accommodate another change in access to off-unit facilities and to ease processing of papers in the business office. Also, the bed and area criteria were reordered on recording forms on the basis of empirically determined difficulty for residents, to the order listed in the manuals, for ease in staff recording. These changes were all equated and inconsequential. Holiday schedules, the special schedule for Christmas Day, and all other procedures remained identical to those that had been in effect since the original introduction of programs. Thus, for the last twenty weeks of the intramural period, the programs were reintroduced and continued in accordance with all details specified in the treatment manuals, with changes related to food service, the purchase-eligibility procedure, and the length of time for controlling assaultiveness.

The use of psychotropic drugs during the last six months was held constant to evaluate the changed procedures for dealing with assaults. Active psychotropic drugs remained constant at less than 18% for milieu residents and less than 11% for social-learning residents from just after the seventh anniversary assessment through the ninth assessment. If staff or residents wished to increase psychotropic drug administration or dosage for any reason, one of five coded placebos was prescribed.

The staffing of the psychosocial programs was finally at 100% of the clinical complement by the beginning of the second baseline procedure. Junior staff were increased to the full complement of twenty-five positions through continued participation in the several federal programs for aiding the unemployed. The reorganization of staff in preparation for the expanded work with prechronic patients and demonstration-training functions also allowed the full complement of full-time-equivalent senior staff positions for administration, training, and on-the-floor clinical work also to be filled (i.e., 4.5 full-time-equivalent positions) in spite of additional activities to be accomplished.

The reorganization involved the continuation of professional auxiliary staff and intern psychologists in new positions as division directors and assistant directors of the expanded staffing plan, and new intern psychologists and auxiliary staff were hired and trained. The research supervisor became the director of the expanded research division and was removed from clinical work over the last six months so that he could direct the preliminary data analyses for the current programs and assist in assessment and survey plans for the expanded design. The eleven total senior clinical staff were scheduled at one to two days per week to cover the 4½ positions for administration, training, supervision, and on-the-floor clinical work, equating time and focus over milieu and social-learning programs to maintain a constant staffing level for the ongoing intramural programs. The remainder of their time was devoted to processing and training the new and incoming staff for the expanded extramural and training division, hospital accreditation paperwork and meetings, further detailed planning and community contacts for the prechronic population, and developing accessibility of extended-care community beds for placing the improved residents in the original three intramural programs.

Thus, while staff data were analyzed for eleven senior clinical staff at the ninth anniversary assessment, since all eleven had regular contact with residents, only 4.5 senior staff positions were actually being filled at both the eighth and ninth anniversary assessments.

The increase in total complement filled, from 91% at the eighth anniversary assessment to 100% at the second baseline through the ninth anniversary assessment, was a function of increasing the junior staff positions filled from twenty-two to twenty-five. Auxiliary staff remained constant, with all three educator positions being filled. Including turnover and replacements of junior staff during the period, 72% of all staff working at the ninth anniversary assessment were continuous from the eighth assessment, and 11% were continuous from the original staff group. No significant changes occurred in the characteristics of the total staff group over the last six months. As at the eighth anniversary assessment, the staff group working at the end of the intramural period showed mean changes from the original staff group working before the initial arrival of residents, being older (29.2 yrs.), more experienced (2.01 yrs.), and with a lower average Extroversion score (18.2). None of the other characteristics of the staff group (education, sex, race, marital or parental status, or Emotionality) changed significantly ($p$'s $> 0.20$).

The remaining chapters of part 6 report the results of the operation of the psychosocial units over the last six months for both staff and residents, with changes in behavior related to the procedural changes. As in earlier parts, the objective outcome data on resident functioning, reported in chapter 29, present details of statistical analyses for the interested research worker; the professional clinician or program director can obtain details of results—including the analyses of the specific effects of changed consequences for assaults—by skipping these sections. Preprofessional staff and others short on time can obtain an understanding and clinical appreciation of the outcome over this period and the problems remaining at the end of the period, by inspecting the tables and figures and reading the summary and individual improvement rates section.

Changes in characteristics of large group meetings, the use of available resources, time spent awake and with others, and the relative variability of several classes of resident behavior within each psychosocial program are compared in chapter 30. Relationships of these characteristics to procedural changes and resident functioning over the last six months are also included, as well as an examination of the relationships between them and unitwide resident functioning over the entire intramural period of nearly four and a half years. All staff data are reported in chapter 31, including attitudes, opinions, preferences, and interpretations. Objective data on the reliability and differentiation of actual staff performance under baseline conditions and the reintroduction of both psychosocial programs, as well as the nature of attention received by residents, are also presented. Relationships of staff behavior to unitwide resident functioning over the entire intramural period are described as well.

The details of the statistical analyses in chapters 30 and 31 are provided in chapter notes, with the results incorporated in the text. Each section of these two chapters ends with a detailed content summary, and each chapter ends with a summary. The chapter summaries should provide a good understanding of the findings for preprofessional staff and others short on time combined with study of the tables and figures. Chapter 32 briefly summarizes the major conclusions and results at the end of the six-month period.

# 29. Differential Effectiveness of the Milieu and Social-Learning Programs During the Last Six Months

## CHANGES IN GLOBAL FUNCTIONING[1]

Raw changes in total appropriate and inappropriate functioning during the last six months—plotted relative to functioning before program introduction—are presented in figure 29.1, which shows differential response to the return to baseline procedures in both treatment programs, followed by a reversal of the trend of the previous year and a half upon the reintroduction of programs with procedural changes. Although the reintroduction of programs covered only a twenty-week period, the overall trends suggest that the declining effectiveness of the previous year and a half was not only stopped, but that increases in the level of functioning were again occurring. The overall superiority of the social-learning program appears to have been maintained throughout the period; however, changes upon return to baseline conditions suggest that the residents of the two programs responded in opposite directions to the removal of specific programmatic procedures.

*Statistical evaluation.* Changes during this period were evaluated by a two-way repeated measures ANOVA on the standardized Global Functioning score (milieu vs. social-learning programs; anniversary assessment 8, baseline 2, anniversary assessment 9). The overall analysis found effects approaching significance for programs ($F=3.87$, $df=1/54$, $p < 0.06$), time ($F=2.89$, $df=2/108$, $p < 0.06$), and for the program x time interaction ($F=2.83$, $df=2/108$, $p < 0.07$). Partitioning of these effects found that a significant simple interaction of programs x time occurred between anniversary assessment 8 and baseline 2 ($F=4.81$, $df=1/54$, $p < 0.05$), and the simple interaction of programs x time approached statistical significance between baseline 2 and anniversary assessment 9 ($F=3.54$, $df=1/54$, $p < 0.07$). The simple interactions reflected differential changes between points in time and programs. The change from anniversary assessment 8 to baseline 2 reflects a significant within-groups increase in Global Functioning for milieu residents when the pressure of the program was removed (mean change from 44.93 to 46.93, $F=4.77$, $df=1/54$, $p < 0.05$), while social-learning residents showed a slight, nonsignificant decrease in Global Functioning upon the removal of programmatic contingencies (mean change from 50.95 to 50.11, $F < 1$). In contrast, the change in Global Functioning from baseline 2 to assessment 9 reflects a significant increase for social-learning residents after programmatic contingencies were reintroduced (mean change from 50.11 to 52.04, $F=6.17$, $df=1/54$, $p < 0.05$), and milieu residents showed a slight, nonsignificant decrease at the same time (mean change from 46.93 to 46.79, $F < 1$).

From the beginning to the end of the six-month period, significant increases in Global Functioning were obtained over both programs ($F=5.19$, $df=1/54$, $p < 0.05$), without significant differential change between them ($F < 1$). Rather, the social-learning program maintained significantly higher levels of Global Functioning over both anniversary assessments ($F=4.66$, $df=1/54$, $p < 0.05$). The increases achieved by milieu residents during this time were sufficient that the within-groups increase in Global Functioning from before the program introduction to the last anniversary assessment again approached significance ($F=3.65$, $df=1/54$, $p < 0.07$). However, the increase in Global Functioning for social-learning residents from before the program introduction was not only significant itself ($F=38.94$, $df=1/54$, $p < 0.01$), but significantly greater than that of milieu residents ($F=9.38$, $df=1/54$, $p < 0.01$). Thus, as on previous anniversary assessments, social-learning residents were functioning at a significantly higher absolute level than milieu residents were on the last anniversary assessment ($F=5.57$, $df=1/54$, $p < 0.05$).

## CHANGES IN MALADAPTIVE BEHAVIOR

The changes in Global Functioning show that significant increases took place in both programs over the last six months. The major improvement for milieu residents first occurred during the second baseline, with programmatic

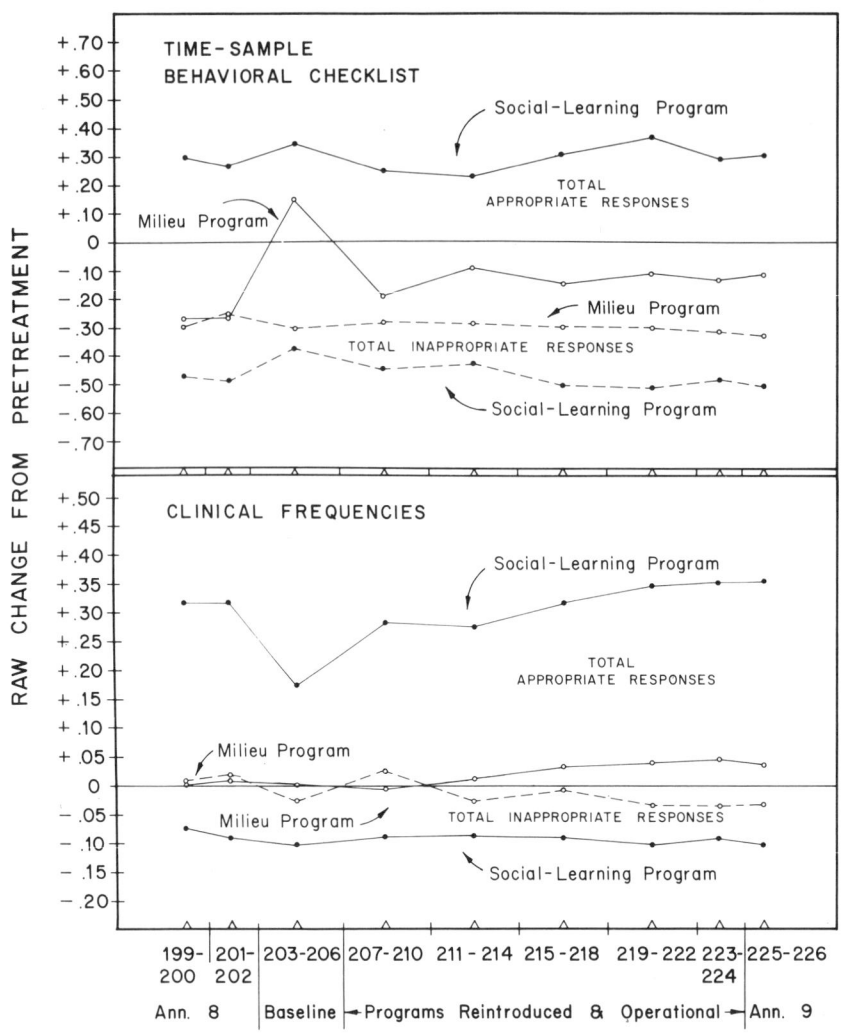

Figure 29.1. Overall changes in concurrent behavior (TSBC) and responsiveness within programs (Clinical Frequencies) during the last six months.

procedural changes maintaining the improvement, thereby reversing the trend of the prior year and a half. In contrast, social-learning residents sustained their earlier improvements in Global Functioning through the return to baseline procedures and showed additional improvements after the reintroduction of the program with procedural changes. By the last assessment period, milieu residents once again showed overall improvement in Global Functioning, which approached statistical significance, and social-learning residents showed significant gains in Global Functioning, which were significantly better than those of milieu residents.

Figure 29.1 suggests, however, that fewer changes occurred in maladaptive behavioral components of functioning than in adaptive components during the current period. Total Inappropriate Clinical Frequencies for milieu residents had returned to original levels of grossly inappropriate response to minimal expectations for appropriate behavior by the eighth anniversary assessment. From the 20% occurrence of Inappropriate Frequencies at the start of the period, milieu residents dropped to less than 17% occurrence upon the return to baseline procedures. A slight increase then occurred when programmatic procedures were first introduced, followed by a slow downward trend, ending the period with an average incidence of less than 16%. Total Inappropriate Frequencies for social-learning residents, in contrast, remained well below the original 19%

*Differential Effectiveness of the Programs* 311

incidence level during the entire six months—entering the period at over 11% with slight reductions during baseline and the reintroduction of programmatic procedures, ending the period at less than 9% occurrence.

There were relatively few changes during the last six months in concurrent, clinically inappropriate (crazy) behavior reflected in TSBC Total Inappropriate Behavior (figure 29.1). Rather, the procedural changes during the last six months appeared to have ended the upward trend of the previous year and a half for this important target area of rehabilitation. Both programs essentially maintained the major reductions obtained earlier, with slight additional improvements. Milieu residents entered the period with an average incidence of one clinically inappropriate behavior on 55% of opportunities, showed no change upon the return to baseline, and ended the period with an average incidence of 52%. Social-learning residents showed an increase in clinically inappropriate behavior upon the return to baseline, followed by additional reductions upon the reintroduction of programmatic procedures, and ended the period with an average incidence of less than 43%. Residents in both programs show considerable reductions from the 90% average occurrence before the original program introduction. However, changes in components of TSBC Inappropriate Behavior (figure 29.2) again suggest differential effectiveness.

Figure 29.2. Changes in component clinically maladaptive behaviors from the TSBC during the last six months.

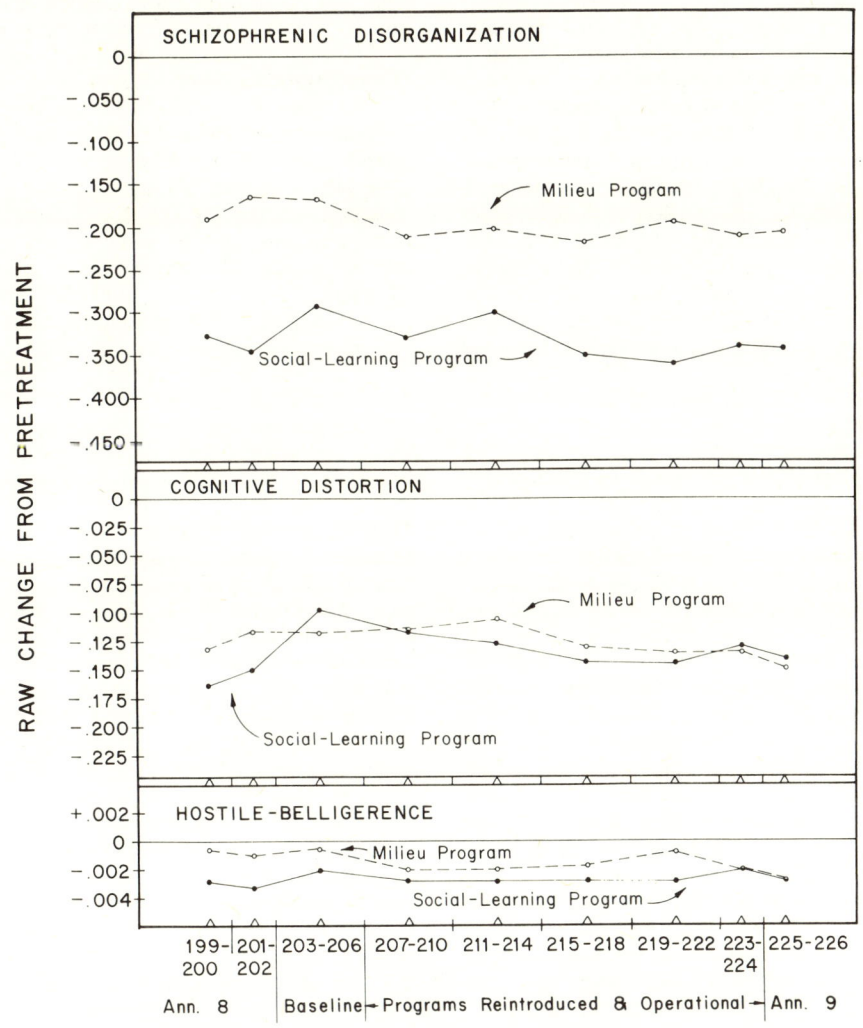

WEEKS FROM ORIGINAL PROGRAM INTRODUCTION

*Statistical evaluation.* To statistically evaluate changes in maladaptive behavior over the last six months, standardized scores for Total Inappropriate Clinical Frequencies and TSBC Schizophrenic Disorganization, Cognitive Distortion, and Hostile-Belligerence Indexes were entered into a three-way repeated measures ANOVA (milieu vs. social-learning programs; anniversary assessment 8, baseline 2, anniversary assessment 9; scores).[2] The overall analysis of maladaptive behavior during the last six months yielded a significant time x scores interaction (F=2.59, df=6/324, p < 0.05), and effects approaching significance for time (F=2.44, df=2/108, p < 0.10) and for the program x scores interaction (F=2.28, df=3/162, p < 0.10). No other main effects or interactions approached significance in the overall analysis (p > 0.10). Partitioning of simple effects found that the time x scores interaction was primarily attributable to differential changes in classes of maladaptive behavior upon return to baseline procedures. Over both programs combined, Total Inappropriate Clinical Frequencies showed a significant decrease from anniversary assessment 8 to baseline 2 (figure 29.1), and all three classes of concurrent, clinically inappropriate behavior (figure 29.2) increased at baseline 2 (F=3.91, df=3/162, p < 0.01). The only significant differential change between programs during the entire period occurred for Cognitive Distortion between anniversary assessment 8 and baseline 2 (F=5.48, df=1/54, p < 0.05), reflecting a significantly greater increase for social-learning residents than for milieu residents when the programmatic procedures were discontinued.

By anniversary assessment 9, after the reintroduction of programmatic treatment with procedural changes in controlling assaultive behavior, all four classes of maladaptive behavior were significantly reduced for both programs (F=7.63, df=1/54, p < 0.01), without differential change among scores or between programs (F's < 1). Over the reintroduction period, however, there were differences between programs and classes of maladaptive behavior (F=2.69, df=3/162, p < 0.05). Cognitive Distortion and Hostile-Belligerence did not differ between programs (F < 1), and social-learning residents maintained significantly lower levels of Schizophrenic Disorganization and Inappropriate Clinical Frequencies through the period (F=5.42, df=1/54, p < 0.05).

By the end of the final six months, both programs had shown significant reductions in maladaptive behavior as a function of the reintroduction of treatments and the new procedures for handling assaultive behavior. Tests of the overall status of maladaptive behavior from before the original introduction of programs to the last anniversary assessment found the social-learning program to produce significantly greater reductions than the milieu program did (F=9.12, df=1/54, p < 0.01). However, within classes of maladaptive behavior, both programs showed significant decreases in the absolute level of Hostile-Belligerence (F=4.14, df=1/54, p < 0.05) and Cognitive Distortion (F=27.40, df=1/54, p < 0.05), without differential effectiveness between them (F's < 1). On the other hand, the social-learning program showed significantly greater reductions than the milieu program did from before the original introduction of programs to the last anniversary assessment in Schizophrenic Disorganization and Inappropriate Clinical Frequencies (F=5.65, df=1/54, p < 0.05). The within-groups change in both of these two classes of maladaptive behavior were significant for the social-learning program (F's > 8.43, df=1/54, p < 0.01). The within-groups reduction for the milieu program was also significant for Schizophrenic Disorganization (F=5.94, df=1/54, p < 0.05) but not for Inappropriate Clinical Frequencies (p > 0.20).

*Descriptive interpretation.* Thus, the increases in maladaptive behavior that had been in process over the prior year and a half were effectively reversed by the procedural changes instituted during the last six months. Overall, both programs showed a slight but significant increase across all components of concurrent, clinically inappropriate behavior upon the termination of programmatic procedures during the return to baseline (figure 29.2), with the social-learning program showing a differentially greater change in Cognitive Distortion. In contrast to clinically inappropriate behaviors, slight reductions in Inappropriate Clinical Frequencies were obtained in both programs during the return to baseline (figure 29.1). This differential change in classes of maladaptive behavior suggests that even with the loss of effectiveness over the prior year and a half, the procedures of both treatment programs had maintained some continuing effectiveness for bizarre, clinically inappropriate behaviors. The slight decrease in Inappropriate Clinical Frequencies upon the return to baseline, on the other hand, is suggestive of some positive effects from removal of stress to perform. However, upon the reintroduction of programmatic procedures with changes in the consequences for assaultive behavior, both programs showed reductions over all classes of maladaptive behavior.

Even with the reductions in Total Inappropriate Clinical Frequencies (figure 29.1) during the last six months, the gross inappropriate response to minimal expectations of milieu residents was still occurring, on the average, on over 16% of opportunities. This rate was more than twice as great as the low that had been achieved by anniversary assessment 5 and did not differ significantly from the average rate of occurrence before the original introduction of the programmatic procedures. Thus, while the procedural changes begun upon the reintroduction of the milieu program during the last six months effectively reversed the previous trend, the twenty-week period remaining was not sufficient for there to be overall improvement in this class of maladaptive behavior for the milieu group. In contrast, the social-learning program had still maintained significant improvement in this class of maladaptive behavior even before procedural changes were introduced. Although the additional improvement to less than a 9% occurrence of Inappropriate Frequencies by the end of the last six months resulted in a rate that was still considerably higher than that of less than 1% previously achieved, it was a major and significant reduction from the 19% level at which the social-learning group had started. Overall, then, the major outcome for the last six months for Inappropriate Clinical Frequencies was a reversal of the earlier trend. However, the milieu program was unable to gain sufficiently to show improvement from pretreatment, while the social-learning program continued to show improvement from pretreatment and differentially greater effectiveness for this class of maladaptive behavior.

Even with increases in Schizophrenic Disorganization during the previous year and a half, both programs had still maintained significant improvement from before the original program introduction, with the social-learning program maintaining differentially greater improvement than the milieu program did. On an absolute level, the behaviors entering the Schizophrenic Disorganization Index—primarily bizarre motor behaviors (e.g., rocking, repetitive movements, blank staring, etc.)—had been the highest frequency inappropriate clinical behaviors occurring before the original treatment programs had begun. The reductions achieved following the reintroduction of the programs with the changed consequences for assaultive behavior during the last six months (figure 29.2) reflect renewed effectiveness of both programs for this class of behavior. Although neither program achieved the low levels of Schizophrenic Disorganization attained previously, the average incidence on the last anniversary assessment (39% for milieu, 28% for social-learning) reflected major and significant reductions from the 61% rate occurring before the introduction of the programs. Overall, then, the major outcome for Schizophrenic Disorganization was a reversal of the earlier trend, with residents in both programs sustaining significant improvement from pretreatment and the social-learning program maintaining its differentially greater effectiveness for this class of clinically bizarre motoric behaviors.

Both programs had maintained significant reductions in Cognitive Distortion, without increases during the previous year and a half, when most other classes of behavior reflected a loss of effectiveness. On an absolute level, the behaviors entering the Cognitive Distortion Index—primarily bizarre verbal and facial behaviors indicative of thought disorder (e.g., delusions, hallucinations, incoherent speech, smiling without a stimulus, etc.)—had been reduced from the 24% average occurrence before the original program introduction to about 9% for both programs at anniversary assessment 8. While Cognitive Distortion showed a relatively greater increase for social-learning residents upon the return to baseline (figure 29.2), both programs again reduced this class of clinically inappropriate behavior when the programs, with the procedural changes, started again. By the last anniversary assessment, both programs had reduced Cognitive Distortion to levels not significantly different from the lowest ones achieved earlier—ending the period with major and significant reductions to about a third of initial levels, without differential effectiveness between programs.

The nature of behaviors entering into the Hostile-Belligerence Index—high-intensity aggressive behaviors (e.g., screaming, cursing, verbal intrusion, etc.)—are less adequately assessed by time sampling, since any occurrence of such behavior is clinically disruptive. During the last six months, the absolute level of Hostile-Belligerence remained low but showed the same trends as other classes of maladaptive behavior. By the last anniversary assessment, however, the reintroduction of programs with the changed procedures for handling assaultive behavior had reduced the incidence of Hostile-Belligerence essentially to zero. The change was a significant reduction from the low 0.3% incidence existing before the original introduction of treatment procedures over both programs, without differential effectiveness between them.

The decline in effectiveness of both treatment programs over the previous year and a half was clearly tied with increases in Intolerable Behavior resulting from the reduced length of time for expulsion and time out as a consequence for assaultive behavior. Therefore, the incidence of Intolerable Behavior during the last six months takes on particular importance—specifically whether the renewed effectivenss of the treatment programs upon the reintroduction of greater time for expulsion and time out had parallel effects in reducing the incidence of dangerous and aggressive acts.

The changes in the average total weekly

incidence of Intolerable Behavior shown in figure 29.3—plotted relative to incidence before program introduction—leave little question of the effect. Both groups showed significant decreases from the exceptionally high peaks of Intolerable Behavior that had been evident during anniversary assessment 8 to the baseline condition (chi-squares=33.44 and 6.89, respectively, df=1, $p < 0.01$).[3] However, the social-learning program had already shown some decline before baseline procedures were introduced (chi-square=2.96, df=1, $p < 0.10$), such that the reduction from the rate of Intolerable Behavior during the last two weeks under previous social-learning procedures to baseline conditions was not significant (chi-square < 1). However, the reduction in this behavior from the last two weeks under previous milieu procedures to baseline conditions was dramatic and significant (chi-square=31.27, df=1, $p < 0.01$). Thus, the combination of removing pressure for performance under active treatment conditions, plus the substitution of traditional modes of dealing with assaultive behavior (restraints, tepid baths, physical separation, and instruction), significantly reduced the incidence of dangerous and aggressive acts from that which occurred following only therapeutic community procedures with an ineffective expulsion time. Although the social-learning group also showed some reduction under baseline conditions, the reduction was not significantly greater than that obtained under the old treatment conditions, even with an ineffective length of time out.

Upon the reintroduction of active treatment

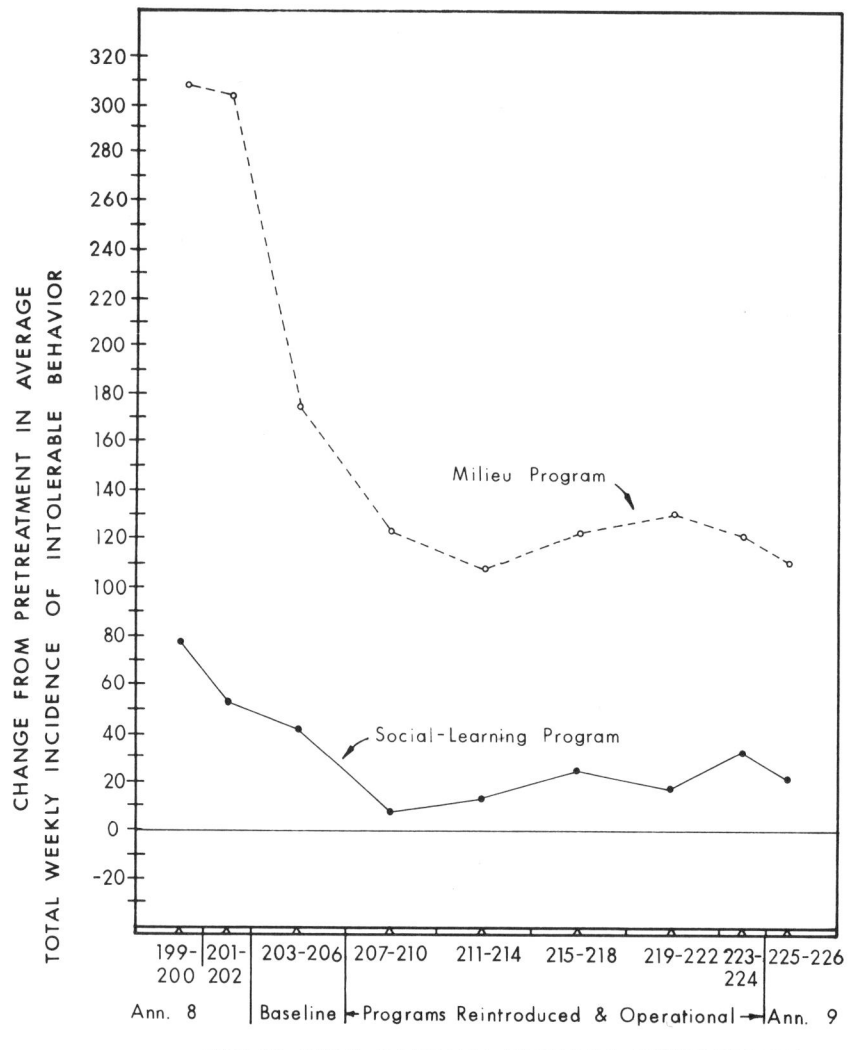

Figure 29.3. Changes in incidence of aggressive and assaultive Intolerable Behavior during the last six months.

procedures with the lengthened time of expulsion and time out as a consequence for assaultive behavior (and without traditional consequences), both treatment groups further significantly reduced the incidence of Intolerable Behavior from baseline conditions (chi-squares > 7.19, df=1, p < 0.01), and did not increase significantly again through the end of the period (p's > 0.20). Of residents committing intolerable acts under active treatment programs, 73.9% and 72.7%, respectively, for milieu and social-learning procedures, had reduced the incidence of such acts from anniversary assessment 8 to 9. The data are thus quite clear in implicating the previous procedures for controlling assaultive behavior not only as the basis for the prior decline in effectiveness but for the reinstatement of effectiveness during the last six months. As on all previous occasions since the first anniversary assessment, the total incidence of Intolerable Behavior was significantly lower in the social-learning program than in the milieu program at every point (chi-squares > 31.20, df=1, p < 0.01), further documenting the greater effectiveness of social-learning procedures in dealing with dangerous and aggressive acts. Even with the significant reductions, both groups were still showing higher rates of Intolerable Behavior than had existed before the original program introduction (chi-squares=85.78, and 7.67, respectively, for milieu and social-learning, df=1, p < 0.01). However, in each group, four residents alone accounted for over 61% of all instances of Intolerable Behavior during the last anniversary assessment.

## CHANGES IN ADAPTIVE BEHAVIOR

The changes in maladaptive behavior clearly show a return of prior effectiveness for both programs, with the social-learning program still maintaining its superiority to the milieu program overall. Residents in both showed additional reductions in all classes of maladaptive behavior upon the reintroduction of programmatic procedures following the change in consequences for assaultive behavior. The most dramatic change occurred in the reduction of aggressive Intolerable Behavior in both programs. Both, however, still showed a higher total incidence of Intolerable Behavior during the last anniversary assessment than had occurred before the original introduction of programs—but it was largely accounted for by a few residents. The social-learning program was significantly more effective in controlling dangerous and aggressive acts than the milieu program was throughout. Although there were slight decreases in grossly inappropriate responses to minimal behavioral expectations, the milieu program failed to show significant improvement from pretreatment for this class of maladaptive behavior on the last anniversary assessment. By the last anniversary assessment, both programs showed significant reductions from pretreatment levels in Schizophrenic Disorganization, Cognitive Distortion, and Hostile-Belligerence, and the social-learning program had also shown significant reductions in Inappropriate Clinical Frequencies. While both programs were equally effective in reducing Cognitive Distortion and Hostile-Belligerence, the social-learning program was differentially more effective in reducing Inappropriate Clinical Frequencies and Schizophrenic Disorganization. Thus, social-learning procedures were clearly superior to milieu procedures in one critical target area essential for rehabilitating the chronically institutionalized population.

Turning to an examination of adaptive components of functioning, both concurrent appropriate behavior (TSBC) and adaptive responsiveness within programs (Clinical Frequencies) showed differential responsiveness between programs upon the return to baseline and a reversal of the trend of the prior year and a half (figure 29.1). The TSBC Total Appropriate Index for milieu residents showed a sharp increase upon the return to baseline, largely accounting for the significant increase in Global Functioning found earlier. On an absolute level, milieu residents had decreased over the prior year and a half to the point where only 2.25 concurrent appropriate behaviors were occurring on the average observation during anniversary assessment 8. Upon return to baseline, they increased their concurrent appropriate behavior to an average of 2.68 (0.16 above pretreatment baseline) and then reduced it when the programmatic procedures were reintroduced. However, in contrast to the trend over the prior year and a half, milieu residents showed a gradual increase in concurrent appropriate behavior over the last twenty weeks, ending the period with a performance of 2.41 appropriate behaviors on the average observation. Social-learning residents had also shown a decline in performance of concurrent appropriate behavior over the prior year and a half but still performed an average of 2.74 appropriate behaviors during anniversary assessment 8 (up 0.30 from pretreatment baseline). During the current period, they also showed a slight increase in concurrent appropriate behavior during the return to baseline (to 2.80) and a slight reduction when the procedures started again. Similar to milieu residents and in contrast to the trend over the prior year and a half, the last twenty weeks following the reintroduction of social-learning procedures were characterized by gradual increases in concurrent appropriate behavior, ending the period with a performance of 2.75 appropriate behaviors on the average observation.

Total Appropriate Clinical Frequencies similarly showed increases during the last twenty weeks after the reintroduction of programs for both treatment groups (figure 29.1). However, clearly different responses were obtained upon the return to baseline. The milieu program had shown decreases during the prior year and a half to the point where terminal-level performance of social and instrumental behavior during anniversary assessment 8 occurred on an average of less than 26% of opportunities—barely above the initial level existing before the program introduction. During the last six months, the return to baseline had no effect at all on their social and instrumental behavior. With the reintroduction of the milieu program and the modified procedures for handling assaultive behavior, increases once again started to occur, and the residents ended the period with normal performance of social and instrumental behavior on 29% of opportunities. Although social-learning residents had also decreased the level of performance of this class of behavior during the previous period, they were still performing at a normal level on over 50% of opportunities during anniversary assessment 8. In contrast to the negligible effects of return to baseline for milieu residents, social-learning residents dropped to nearly 37% normal performance of social and instrumental behaviors when programmatic procedures were temporarily removed. The reintroduction of the social-learning program with changed procedures during the last twenty weeks was followed by a regular improvement in Total Clinical Frequencies. On the last anniversary assessment, they had improved to the point that they were performing normal social and instrumental behavior on an average of 55% of opportunities—nearly triple the rate existing before the original program introduction. Changes in the components of adaptive Clinical Frequencies (figure 29.4) suggest that this pattern held over both of the remaining target areas for rehabilitation of the chronically institutionalized population.

*Statistical evaluation.* To statistically evaluate changes in adaptive behavior over the last six months, standardized scores for TSBC Total Appropriate Behavior and Clinical Frequencies for Instrumental Role Performance, Interpersonal Skills, and Self-Care Indexes were entered into a three-way repeated measures ANOVA (milieu vs. social-learning programs; anniversary assessment 8, baseline 2, anniversary assessment 9; scores).[2] The overall analysis of adaptive behavior found that all main effects and interactions were significant, except for the program x score interaction ($F=1.78$, $df=3/162$, $p > 0.15$). Thus, effects were significant for programs ($F=5.08$, $df=1/54$, $p < 0.05$), time and the programs x time interaction (F's > 13.37, $df=2/108$, $p < 0.01$), scores ($F=2.92$, $df=3/162$, $p < 0.05$), and both time x scores and programs x time x scores interactions (F's > 7.72, $df=6/324$, $p < 0.01$).

Partitioning of simple effects found significant three-way interactions between programs, scores, and time over anniversary assessment 8 to baseline 2 and baseline 2 to anniversary assessment 9 (F's > 7.13, $df=3/162$, $p < 0.01$). All three components of adaptive Clinical Frequencies (figure 29.4) showed significant decreases for the social-learning group when the programmatic procedures were terminated during baseline 2 (F's > 5.03, $df=1/54$, $p < 0.05$), while none of these changes were significant for the milieu group (F's < 1.31, $df=1/54$, $p > 0.20$). The decrease in the adaptive behavior of the social-learning group upon the return to baseline was significantly greater than parallel changes for the milieu group for both Self-Care and Interpersonal Skills (F's > 22.57, $df=1/54$, $p < 0.01$). In contrast, concurrent appropriate behavior (TSBC, figure 29.1) showed increases for both groups after the return to baseline, with a significantly greater increase for the milieu group ($F=25.14$, $df=1/54$, $p < 0.01$).

When the programmatic treatment was reintroduced with the procedural changes for controlling assaultive behavior, Instrumental Role Performance (figure 29.4) was significantly increased for both programs ($F=15.35$, $df=1/54$, $p < 0.01$), without differential change between them ($p > 0.10$). Although the downward trend of the previous year and a half in Self-Care and Interpersonal Skills stopped for the milieu program, there were no further significant increases in these classes of adaptive behavior when the program started again ($p > 0.20$). The social-learning residents, in contrast, showed significant absolute increases in Self-Care and Interpersonal Skills upon the reintroduction of the program (F's > 33.18, $df=1/54$, $p < 0.01$) and differentially greater increases than those in the milieu program did (F's > 18.89, $df=1/54$, $p < 0.01$). Changes in concurrent appropriate behavior (TSBC, figure 29.1) from baseline 2 to anniversary assessment 9 found no change for social-learning residents ($F < 1$) and a significant loss for milieu residents ($F=9.16$, $df=1/54$, $p < 0.01$). However, the overall increase from the reintroduction of programs through the last anniversary assessment approached significance over both programs ($F=3.99$, $df=1/54$, $p < 0.06$), with the milieu program showing a significantly greater increase in concurrent appropriate behavior during the last twenty weeks than the

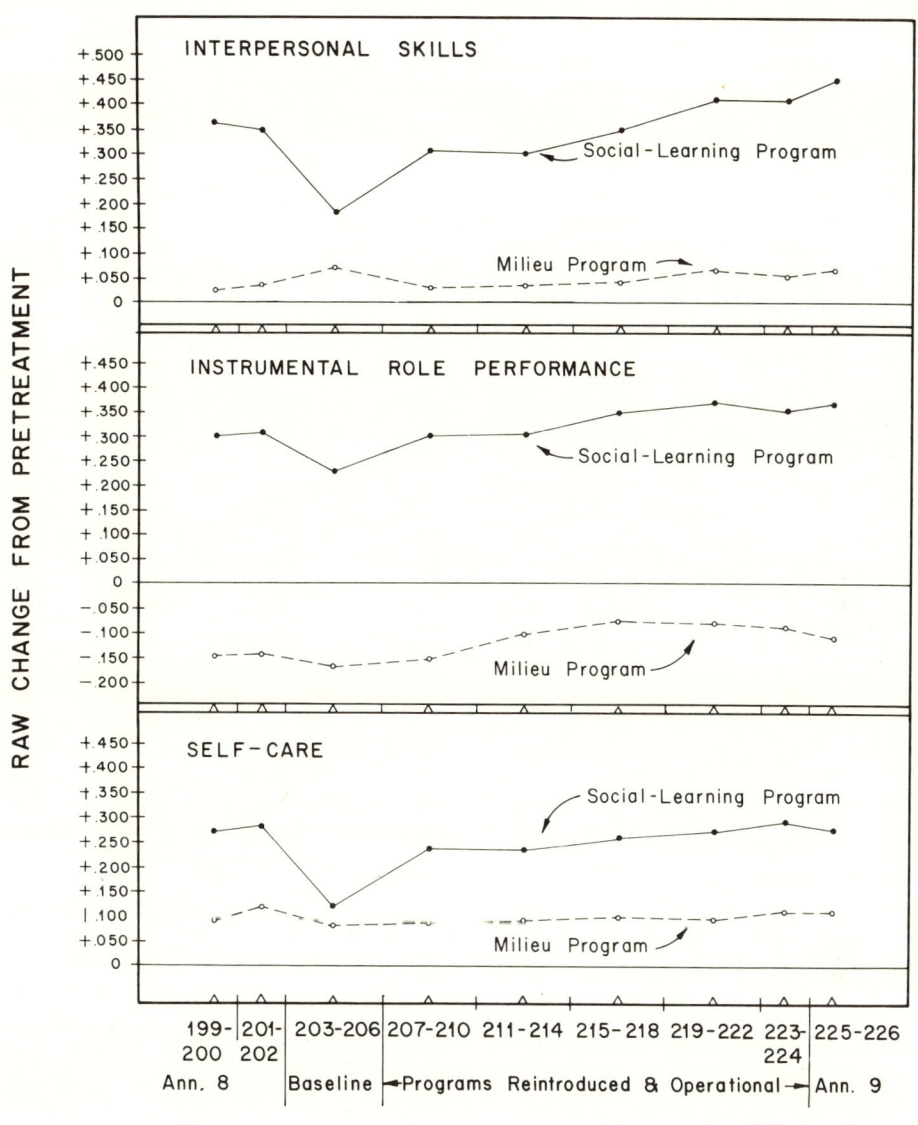

Figure 29.4 Changes in component adaptive behavior from Clinical Frequencies during the last six months.

social-learning program did (F=5.13, df=1/54, p < 0.05). Even with the complex interactions, the social-learning program still maintained higher levels of functioning over all adaptive behavior scores and all points in time during the last six months (F=5.08, df=1/54, p < 0.05).

By the end of the final six months, both programs had thus reversed the trend of the prior year and a half. Tests of the status of adaptive behavior from before the original introduction of programs to the last anniversary assessment found that the social-learning program produced differentially greater increases in all four components of adaptive behavior than the milieu program did (F's > 10.38, df=1/54, p < 0.01). Although the milieu program had shown increases over the last twenty weeks, the within-group change from the original pretreatment baseline was significant only for Self-Care (F=5.18, df=1/54, p < 0.05). The remaining components of adaptive behavior for the milieu program showed no significant change from the level of functioning that had existed before the original programs had begun (F's < 2.00, df=1/54, p > 0.10). In contrast, the social-learning program showed significant within-group increases in concurrent adaptive behavior (F=5.70, df=1/54, p < 0.05) and in each of the adaptive components of Clinical Frequencies

($F$'s > 17.72, df=1/54, p < 0.01), from pretreatment to the last anniversary assessment. The absolute level of performance during the last anniversary assessment found social-learning residents functioning at a significantly higher level than milieu residents were on every class of adaptive behavior ($F$'s > 4.57, df=1/54, p < 0.05).

*Descriptive interpretation.* Thus, the decreases in adaptive behavior that had been in process over the prior year and a half were effectively terminated or reversed by the procedural changes instituted during the last six months. For the milieu program, none of the components of appropriate Clinical Frequencies (figure 29.4) were significantly affected by the return to baseline procedures. Although slight increases were obtained in Interpersonal Skills and Self-Care over the last twenty weeks following the reintroduction of milieu procedures, the increases were not significant. Thus, the changed milieu procedures terminated the earlier downward trend but failed to show renewed effectiveness for these components of resocialization. While the lack of effectiveness of old milieu conditions on Instrumental Role Performance was also apparent upon the return to baseline, there was a renewed effectiveness upon the reintroduction of the milieu program with the changed consequences for assaultive behavior. In contrast to the milieu group, social-learning residents showed significant losses in all three components of appropriate Clinical Frequencies upon the return to baseline and significant increases in all three components upon the reintroduction of programmatic procedures. Thus, even with the decreased effectiveness resulting from changed time-out procedures during the prior year and a half, the social-learning program was still maintaining its improved performance of instrumental roles and resocialization. The reintroduction of programmatic contingencies with the changes in consequences for assaultive behavior thus reversed the previous trend and was again producing continued improvement across all three classes of adaptive behavior within the program.

In contrast to adaptive responsiveness within programs, both groups showed increases in concurrent appropriate behavior (TSBC, figure 29.1) upon the return to baseline and initial decreases after the reintroduction of the programs. The increase during baseline 2 for milieu residents was significantly greater than that for social-learning residents. Considering the parallel changes that occurred in the total incidence of Intolerable Behavior (figure 29.3), the increase in concurrent appropriate behavior during the return to baseline procedures was likely the result of the reduction in stress from both assaults and the pressure to perform. Although both groups again showed reductions in concurrent appropriate behavior when the programs were reintroduced, significant increases were obtained thereafter, thus indicating the renewed effectiveness of both treatments and reversing the prior trend.

Even with the increases over the last twenty weeks, milieu residents were performing only 2.41 concurrent appropriate behaviors on the average observation during the last anniversary assessment. This level was significantly below the peak that had been achieved by anniversary assessment 5 and did not differ significantly from that existing before the original introduction of the milieu program. Thus, while the procedural changes instituted when the milieu program started up again during the last six months effectively reversed the prior trend, the time remaining was not sufficient for milieu residents to achieve the improvement in concurrent appropriate behavior they had once made. The increases in concurrent appropriate behavior for social-learning residents over the last six months resulted in the performance of over 2.75 appropriate behaviors on the average observation during the last anniversary assessment. Although this level was also significantly lower than that they had achieved before the initial reduction in time out for assaultive behavior, it was a major and significant improvement over their original levels before the introduction of the social-learning program. Overall, then, the major outcome for the last six months for concurrent appropriate behavior was a reversal of the earlier trend, with renewed effectiveness for both programs. However, the milieu program did not gain sufficiently to show improvement from pretreatment, and the social-learning program continued to show improvement from pretreatment and differentially greater improvement for this class of appropriate behavior.

On an absolute level, the behaviors entering the Interpersonal Skills Index—relative frequencies of normal interpersonal interaction and communications skills—had originally been the most deficient of all areas of functioning. By the end of the previous year and a half, both programs had shown losses in earlier improvements. On the average, social-learning residents were still showing nearly 40% normal performance during anniversary assessment 8— still a major and significant improvement from pretreatment levels. Milieu residents, however, had lost sufficient ground by anniversary assessment 8 that they averaged only a nonsignificant 3% increase over pretreatment levels (figure 29.4). Although milieu residents gained an additional 4% in normal performance of Interpersonal Skills by the last anniversary assessment, they were still performing at a level significantly lower than that attained earlier and not significantly higher than the one existing before the original introduction of programs. In contrast, the increases in Interpersonal Skills for social-learning residents upon the reintroduction of programs during the last six months resulted in normal interpersonal interaction and communication on nearly 50% of opportunities —a major and significant improvement from pretreatment to a level even higher than that achieved previously and an absolute improvement of over six times that of milieu residents. Overall, then, the major outcome for the last six months for Interpersonal Skills was a reversal of the earlier trend for both programs, with particularly impressive renewal of effectiveness for social-learning procedures. Although milieu residents, as a group, did not gain sufficiently again to show significant improvement from pretreatment, social-learning residents gained even further, showing absolute and differentially greater effectiveness in the Interpersonal Skills component of the resocialization target for rehabilitation.

The behaviors entering the Self-Care Index— relative frequencies of terminal level peformance of self-maintenance activities (e.g., personal appearance, meal behavior, bathing, etc.)— reflect the other components of the resocialization target for rehabilitation. Although both programs had lost part of their earlier gains over the previous year and a half, at anniversary assessment 8 both still showed improvement from the low 13% normal performance existing before the introduction of programs; social-learning procedures still were more effective. During the last six months (figure 29.4), milieu residents showed a slight, nonsignificant increase in Self-Care—reversing the earlier trend. The average 24% normal Self-Care activities for milieu residents during the last anniversary assessment was lower than they had previously attained but still reflected a significant improvement over pretreatment levels. The social-learning program again reflected renewed effectiveness for Self-Care upon the reintroduction of programmatic procedures during the last six months—with residents attaining normal self-maintenance on nearly 41% of opportunities during the last anniversary assessment. Although the level was not as high as that they had achieved by anniversary assessment 5, it was still a major and significant improvement from pretreatment and over two and a half times the absolute improvement achieved by the milieu program. Overall, then, the major outcome for the last six months for Self-Care was a reversal of the earlier trend, with additional effectiveness for the social-learning program. Both programs showed significant improvement from pretreatment, with the social-learning program obtaining differentially greater improvement in the second component of the resocialization target for rehabilitation.

Although Instrumental Role Performance had initially been the least deficient of all areas of functioning, milieu procedures had failed to maintain earlier improvements in this rehabilitation target, even before the changes in procedures for controlling assaultive behavior. The behaviors entering the Instrumental Role Index—primarily "on task" in classes and job training and "on time" at scheduled work, activities, and meetings—were still being performed at a normal level by social-learning residents on over 67% of opportunities during anniversary assessment 8, even with losses of the previous year and a half. In contrast, the declines of the previous year and a half had resulted in an average performance of milieu residents that was below original levels. Both programs showed significant increases during the reintroduction of programs during the last six months (figure 29.4). However, the final level of normal Instrumental Role Performance of the milieu group was still not significantly different from that of their pretreatment performance. Social-learning residents improved to an absolute level of normal Instrumental Role Performance on over 74% of opportunities —still lower than that they had achieved on anniversary assessment 5 but a major and significant improvement, nearly twice the absolute level existing before the program introduction. Overall the major outcome for the last six months for Instrumental Role Performance was a reversal of the earlier trend for both programs. However, milieu procedures remained relatively ineffective, with residents showing no improvement from pretreatment; social-learning procedures showed absolute and differentially greater effectiveness for this target of rehabilitation.

## SUMMARY AND INDIVIDUAL IMPROVEMENT RATES

The group analyses clearly show that the procedural changes for controlling assaultive behavior during the last six months reversed the trends of the previous year and a half, leading to a renewal of effectiveness for both treatment programs. The social-learning program clearly emerged as the more effective. Neither group achieved the level of Global Functioning they had attained previously, but both improved over the last six months, to the extent that the milieu group once again approached significant improvement from pretreatment. Social-learning residents not only maintained significant improvement in Global Functioning from before the program introduction but maintained significantly greater improvement than milieu residents did throughout the period.

Although the trends of the previous year and a half were reversed for all classes of behavior in both programs, further differentiation of effectiveness did occur. The most dramatic changes in both programs during the period were the decreases in aggressive Intolerable Behavior as a function of changes in consequences for assaultiveness. By the last anniversary assessment, the total incidence of such dangerous and aggressive acts was still higher than that existing before the original program introduction but had been reduced to about a third of the disruptive levels occurring at the beginning of the period. By the end of the period, four residents in each program were accounting for the majority of incidents of Intolerable Behavior. As on all prior anniversary assessments, the social-learning procedures maintained a significantly lower incidence of Intolerable Behavior than milieu therapy procedures did at every point during the last six months. Milieu therapy procedures were largely ineffective in controlling dangerous and aggressive acts.

Although the group analyses found that both programs produced additional reductions in all classes of maladaptive behavior when the programmatic procedures were reintroduced with the changes in consequences for assaultive behavior, the overall outcome at the end of the period found further differential effectiveness between programs. By the last anniversary assessment, both programs had produced significant reductions from pretreatment levels in Schizophrenic Disorganization, Cognitive Distortion, and Hostile-Belligerence. The social-learning program had also produced significant reductions in Total Inappropriate Clinical Frequencies; the milieu program had not. Overall both programs were effective, and equally so, in reducing dysfunctional cognitive behavior and hostile-belligerence. Both programs were effective in reducing clinically inappropriate, bizarre motoric behavior; the social-learning program was differentially more so than the milieu program was. The milieu program was ineffective in reducing grossly inappropriate response to minimal expectations, and the social-learning program was effective and differentially more so with this class of maladaptive behavior. Thus, although milieu procedures were as effective as social-learning procedures with two classes of maladaptive behavior, the overall outcome for the crucial target area of reducing or eliminating extreme bizarre behavior clearly found the social-learning program to be differentially more effective.

The group analyses also found that the reintroduction of programmatic procedures with the changes in consequences for assaultive behavior reversed the trends of the prior year and a half for all classes of adaptive behavior. However, significant increases were obtained only by the milieu program in concurrent appropriate behavior and Instrumental Role Performance, whereas the social-learning program produced increases in all four classes of adaptive behavior. Even greater differential effectiveness was apparent between programs in adaptive behavior than in maladaptive behavior. By the last anniversary assessment, the milieu program had maintained effective increases from pretreatment in only one component of the resocialization target—Self-Care. In all other areas of adaptive functioning, including the remaining component of the resocialization target—Interpersonal Skills—and the instrumental role target, the milieu program was not effective. In contrast, by the last anniversary assessment the social-learning program had demonstrated significant effectiveness from pretreatment levels in increasing all four components of adaptive behavior—concurrent appropriate behavior, Interpersonal Skills, Self-Care, and Instrumental Role Performance—and differentially greater effectiveness than the milieu program did in all classes. Thus, for the crucial target areas of resocialization and improvement of instrumental role performance, as well as concurrent appropriate behavior, the social-learning program was clearly differentially more effective.

Since clinical workers are more often concerned with percentage improvement of individual cases than with parametric group differences, the Global Functioning Factor Scores were further evaluated to provide an indication of the extent of individual resident response during the period. The individual resident changes upon return to baseline conditions reflected the same differentiation of treatment programs as the group analyses. When old programmatic procedures were terminated, some residents in both programs showed improvement (25% in milieu, 17.9% in social-learning) as a result of the removal of pressure to perform and the concurrent reduction in assaultive behavior. However, the removal of programmatic contingencies resulted in a significant loss in level of functioning for 35.7% of social-learning residents; none of the milieu residents declined in functioning upon the return to baseline (Fisher exact probability $< 0.01$). Thus, the change rates for individual residents add further documentation that milieu procedures with ineffective consequences for controlling assaultive behavior did not maintain resident functioning, while social-learning procedures—even with an ineffective length of time out as a consequence for assaultive behavior—were still maintaining higher levels of functioning for a significant group of residents before return to baseline conditions.

Even with the decline in functioning upon the removal of programmatic contingencies for social-learning residents, however, significant

Table 29.1. Objective rates of change in overall functioning from program entry to the second baseline for original equated groups (N=28 each).

| Treatment program | Condition at second baseline | | |
|---|---|---|---|
| | Worse[a] | No change | Improved[a] |
| Social-learning | 3.6% | 14.3% | 82.1% |
| Milieu therapy | 21.4% | 25.0% | 53.6% |

a. "Improved" and "worse" classification based upon individual change from entry exceeding 1.96 times the standard error of measurement on the standardized Global Functioning Factor Score. Chi-square "improved" versus "no change" and "worse"=4.01, $p < 0.05$

generalized improvement was still in evidence. The improvement rates presented in table 29.1 show that both programs yielded an impressive proportion of residents demonstrating generalized improvement from the level of functioning that had existed before program entry under similar environmental conditions. In fact, the proportion of residents in each improvement category during the second baseline indicates a slightly better condition overall for both groups than had been obtained during the eighth anniversary assessment (see table 24.2). Additionally table 29.1 shows that the social-learning program produced significantly greater improvement rates than the milieu program did, even under conditions in which programmatic contingencies were removed.

Possible differential predictability of improvement from program entry to the second baseline from demographic and level of functioning variables found no significant relationships for the social-learning program.[4] The only significant prediction over both groups combined was attributable to a significant correlation within the milieu group, reflecting a tendency for improved milieu residents to have been functioning at a relatively lower level upon entry to the program ($r=-0.44$); initial level of functioning was not significantly related to improvement for social-learning residents ($r=-0.13$). Improvement of milieu residents also reflected a significantly greater tendency for females rather than males to have improved ($r=0.40$) than within the social-learning group, where improvement was unrelated to sex ($r=-0.15$). Thus, neither overall nor differential predictability of improvement during baseline was obtained for drug status or any of the remaining demographic variables (age, race, socioeconomic status, process-reactive status, marital status, nature of symptom onset, identifiable precipitants on initial hospitalization, current or total length of hospitalization, prior electroconvulsive or insulin shock, or other medical treatments).

The improvement rates obtained upon the reintroduction of treatment programs with changed procedures for controlling assaultive behavior are presented in table 29.2. In contrast to the losses obtained over the previous year and a half, there were additional gains for significant numbers of residents following the reintroduction of programs, with the social-learning procedures producing significantly more gains than the milieu program did. In fact, the rate of change over the last twenty weeks with the reintroduction of programmatic procedures was slightly better than the rates of change that had been accomplished during the second two years for both programs (see table 19.1). Correlational analyses found that improvement from the eighth to ninth anniversary assessments, following the reintroduction of the active programs, had no significant relationship to drug status, prior level of functioning, or Intolerable Behavior. Only one

Table 29.2. Objective rates of additional change in overall functioning from the second baseline to the last anniversary assessment for original equated groups (N=28 each).

| Treatment program | Change from condition on second baseline | | |
|---|---|---|---|
| | Worse[a] | No change | Improved[a] |
| Social-learning | 7.1% | 39.3% | 53.6% |
| Milieu therapy | 21.4% | 46.4% | 32.1% |

a. "Improved" and "worse" classification based upon individual change from baseline 2 to assessment 9 exceeding 1.96 times the standard error of measurement on the standardized Global Functioning Factor Score. Fisher exact probability, "improved" versus "worse"= 0.019.

significant correlation among demographic variables and improvement was obtained over both groups combined, reflecting a slight tendency for younger residents to improve more over both programs (r=0.29). The only significant differential predictors of improvement over the last six months were lengths of hospitalization. Milieu group improvement was significantly related to relatively shorter lengths of current and total hospitalization (r's=-0.54 & -0.47, respectively); the improvement of social-learning residents was not (r's=0.30). Thus, analysis of individual data further documents the renewed effectiveness of both programs and the superiority of social-learning procedures for the chronically institutionalized population without regard to individual resident characteristics or behavior.

The final status of residents' response to the overall programs after the procedural changes of the last twenty weeks is shown in table 29.3, where the individual improvement rates from program entry are presented. The percentage of residents showing significant improvement in both programs was still impressive—particularly the near-90% improvement rate for social-learning residents, which was significantly greater than the rate for milieu residents. No differential predictability of final improvement status was obtained from drug status, level of functioning, or demographic variables. However, the only significant correlation obtained over the combined groups was primarily caused by a significant tendency for improved milieu residents to have a relatively shorter length of current hospitalization (r=-0.44); such a relationship was not significant for social-learning residents (r=-0.19).

Even with the renewed effectiveness of programs over the last twenty weeks, during that period of time neither was able to regain the level of overall effectiveness that had previously been obtained before the changes in consequences for assaultive behavior (see table 19.1). Although the social-learning program still showed approximately the same exceptionally high percentage of residents who had objectively improved, in both programs some residents were still functioning at a lower level on the last anniversary assessment than before program entry.

The data for the individual residents again implicated assaultive behavior. All of the social-learning residents and the majority of the milieu residents who were functioning at worse levels during the last anniversary assessment had shown improvement in several areas of functioning. However, all of these social-learning residents and all but one of these milieu residents were accounted for by those who were still showing a high rate of aggressive Intolerable Behavior during the last anniversary assessment. Additionally, all but one of the milieu residents who showed no significant change at the last anniversary assessment had improved in some other areas of functioning but still showed some incidence of Intolerable Behavior. These individual data were also reflected in correlational analyses that found the rate of Intolerable Behavior during the last anniversary assessment to be highly and differentially related to Global Functioning for both social-learning (r=-0.81) and milieu residents (r=-0.56). Similarly the rate of Intolerable Behavior during the last anniversary assessment differentially (and negatively) related to improvement from program entry, more for the social-learning group (r=-0.79) than for the milieu group (r=-0.30). Thus, all social-learning residents and the majority of milieu residents who failed to demonstrate significant overall improvement by the last anniversary assessment were largely characterized by an excess of performance in a single class of inappropriate behavior. That class of critical behavior, therefore, became the primary focus of treatment for each resident before consideration of possible release.

Movement within step levels during the last six months also reflected renewed effectiveness. Continued declines during the prior year and a half had resulted in no residents within either intramural program maintaining status at higher step levels. The same lack of movement continued through the end of the second baseline. However, following the reintroduction of

Table 29.3. Objective improvement rates in overall functioning from program entry to the last anniversary assessment for original equated groups (N=28 each).

| Treatment program | Condition at last six-month assessment | | |
|---|---|---|---|
| | Worse[a] | No change | Improved[a] |
| Social-learning | 10.7% | 0% | 89.3% |
| Milieu therapy | 32.1% | 21.4% | 46.4% |

a. "Improved" and "worse" classification based upon individual change from entry exceeding 1.96 times the standard error of measurement on the standardized Global Functioning Factor Score. Chi-square "improved" versus "no change" and "worse"=9.91, $p < 0.01$.

programs with the procedural changes for controlling assaultive behavior, residents achieved promotions, even though only twenty weeks remained. One milieu resident improved sufficiently to be promoted and maintain status at higher step levels. There was considerable movement within the social-learning program; 18% of the residents achieved promotions, and 11% maintained stable improvement to remain at higher step levels.

Thus, by the time of the last anniversary assessment, the overall programs without individual focus on specific critical behaviors resulted in significant gains for the most severely debilitated groups of chronically institutionalized mental patients ever subjected to systematic study. Some of the gains were impressive, and both programs produced improvements to the point that some residents (and ex-residents) were functionally indistinguishable from the normal population: 25% from the social-learning program and 14% from the milieu program. Nevertheless, with the marked individual gains and overall improvements, even the superior level of functioning of the social-learning residents was still only slightly above minimum survival levels for the total group. While clinically bizarre behaviors had been reduced to nearly one-third the initial level on the average, bizarre motoric behaviors were still occurring about 28% of the time and bizarre cognitive behaviors about 9% of the time. Similarly while the severe deficits in social and instrumental behavior had been overcome to the extent that initial levels of functioning were nearly tripled, social and instrumental skills indistinguishable from normal ones were occurring only on 55% of opportunities for the social-learning group. Finally, even though the procedural changes of the last twenty weeks had reversed the trend for assaultive behavior and reinstituted effectiveness for both programs, some residents in both programs had not again reduced their incidence of Intolerable Behavior to a level where it no longer interfered with functioning.

*A Few Illustrations.* During the last six months, both programs gave evidence of renewed effectiveness. Improvements in functioning were obtained for significant numbers of the severely debilitated chronic population in both programs, with those produced by the social-learning program being superior to those of the milieu program and remarkable on an absolute level. However, a notable carry-over of the previous year and a half was the residents in both programs who had shown improvement in some areas but for whom aggressive Intolerable Behavior was still interfering to the extent that their overall functioning was worse than before program entry. Therefore, brief case descriptions of a few of these residents may help illustrate the nature of that problem.

*Vera D. (milieu program)* had increased her aggressive Intolerable Behavior over the previous year and a half when there were no effective consequences for such acts; she was typical of other milieu residents who had shown high rates of dangerous and aggressive acts at some time before the change in expulsion time (see illustrative cases, chapter 24). By the eighth anniversary assessment Vera was performing over twenty-five aggressive Intolerable Behaviors per week, and previous therapeutic gains she had made had declined to the point that her adaptive functioning in all areas was at or below initial entry levels. She continued to increase her rate of aggressive behavior through the return to baseline conditions, averaging nearly thirty instances per week, even after programmatic demands were removed. Concurrently her dysfunctional cognitive behaviors increased slightly, and her bizarre motoric behaviors quadrupled to a level even above that at original entry. Her adaptive responsiveness showed considerable variability upon the return to baseline conditions, with social and instrumental skills generally declining, while concurrent appropriate behaviors nearly doubled.

The reintroduction of the milieu program with improved procedures for controlling physical assaults immediately resulted in a reduction of her dangerous and aggressive acts to a stable level of about four per week through the last anniversary assessment. All of her maladaptive crazy behaviors similarly improved over the last twenty weeks, to the extent that both dysfunctional cognitive behaviors and bizarre motoric behaviors were occurring at less than a third the rate existing before original program entry. Her Self-Care, Interpersonal Skills, and Instrumental Role Performance showed slight increases over the twenty weeks after the reintroduction of programmatic procedures but were still significantly below original entry levels. However, some of her behaviors drastically declined from earlier levels (e.g., bathing from 92% to 0%, housekeeping from 33% to 0%), clearly reflecting a failure to perform rather than a skills deficit. These changes in performance, combined with the continuing occurrence of dangerous and aggressive acts in the absence of concurrent indications of stress, suggested that the carry-over of the negative effects from the prior year and a half for Vera, and other residents similar to her, was the result of active resistance to change that milieu procedures and expectancies alone, without consequences, were inadequate to overcome. This hypothesis was further strengthened by the fact that three weeks of intensive focus on Vera's intolerable acts after the last anniversary assessment were insufficient to bring them under control to the extent that she could achieve a significant community placement. After she failed to be accepted in a community placement from the milieu program, she spent six weeks receiving social-learning procedures, including overcorrection/restitution of her aggressive behavior; she then improved significantly and was successfully placed in the community (see chapter 33).

*Gary K. (milieu program)* had shown the most debilitating effects of the change in controlling assaultiveness over the previous year and a half for milieu residents who had not engaged in assaultive behavior before the procedural change (see illustrative cases, chapter 24). As noted in chapter 24, after Gary had improved in nearly all areas of functioning, he had then deteriorated in all areas and showed clear evidence of stress reactions in both clinically maladaptive and adaptive behavior during the year and a half without effective means of controlling assaultive behavior. By the eighth anniversary assessment, he was performing nearly four instances of dangerous and aggressive Intolerable Behaviors per day and was functioning at a level significantly below that at entry to the program.

In contrast to Vera D., after the return to baseline conditions during the last six months and the resulting reduction in pressure to perform, Gary immediately doubled his concurrent appropriate behavior, and his performance of dangerous and aggressive acts dropped from over twenty-six per week to seven per week. Concurrently nearly every Clinical Frequency Index showed slight improvement in performance of adaptive behaviors upon return to baseline conditions, and TSBC observations showed reductions in nearly every class of clinically maladaptive behavior. The reintroduction of the milieu program with the improved expulsion procedures for assaultive acts led to further gradual improvements in Gary's functioning, with clinically maladaptive behaviors being systematically reduced to less than half the rate existing during the second baseline. His adaptive social and instrumental skills showed over a fourfold increase by the last anniversary assessment. His dangerous and aggressive Intolerable Behaviors were further reduced after the reintroduction of revised milieu procedures, although he still committed them at rates of two to four per week by the end of the period.

Thus, the improvements in Gary's behavior after the reintroduction of the program with the improved expulsion procedures showed a renewed effectiveness of the procedures, particularly in overcoming previous deterioration based upon stress. However, the carryover of the prior year and a half was still in evidence in his continued performance of some aggressive acts. At the last anniversary assessment, Gary had shown significant improvement from pretreatment in the frequency of occurrence of bizarre motoric behaviors (from 51% 37%), but all other areas of functioning had not yet recovered his initial levels, let alone the high levels of performance achieved before the original change in expulsion time. Some continuing indications of stress reactions were still apparent, in that pacing, talking to self, repetitive movements, and rocking still occurred during the last anniversary assessment; none of these latter behaviors had been present at all before the original program introduction. Unlike Vera D., Gary responded well to the three weeks of focused milieu therapy after the last anniversary assessment, in which efforts were directly placed upon his intolerable acts (see chapter 33). He regained his prior improvements and ultimately achieved successful community placement.

*Nancy D. (social-learning)* was one of only three social-learning residents whose overall performance at the last anniversary assessment showed lower levels of functioning than at original entry. Upon entry to the program Nancy was a forty-seven-year-old housewife and mother of two who, in at least five admissions, had been committed to mental institutions for over twenty-one years and had a history of heavy sedation and restraints. Her clinical picture before the introduction of social-learning procedures showed normal social and instrumental behaviors on fewer than 28% of opportunities, presenting a bizarre, disheveled appearance over 95% of the time. Talking to herself was the most prominent crazy behavior, although she also showed significant rates of verbalized hallucinations, incoherent speech, repetitive movements, and blank staring, at least one of which occurred on 56% of objective observations. Although Nancy's history was replete with assaultive incidents, social-learning procedures had contained such behavior between zero and 2.5 per week before the change in length of time out. By the fifth anniversary assessment she had tripled her level of performance of normal social and instrumental skills and significantly reduced bizarre crazy behaviors—nearly halving the rate of talking to herself—and showed no aggressive behaviors at all.

Nancy was still showing evidence of responding to hallucinations over 18% of the time, one component of which was acting as if she were disciplining her imaginary children by striking them. After the change in length of time out as a consequence for assaults, she gradually increased such indications of hallucinatory behavior, including an occasional aggressive attack on other residents or staff in the midst of her ritual. Her dangerous and aggressive acts had reached an average incidence of between five and fifteen per week by the end of the year and a half without effective time-out procedures. Concurrently her bizarre behavior had increased almost 70%, nearly a third of which were accounted for by her hallucinatory behaviors. Similar to other social-learning residents who continued Intolerable Behavior over the previous year and a half, accumulated token fines functionally removed access to backup reinforcers within the program. Her performance of normal social and instrumental behavior under these circumstances gradually deteriorated to levels well below those existing even before the original introduction of programmatic procedures. These trends continued to escalate through return to baseline conditions, with her dangerous and aggressive acts reaching an average of twenty per week, while hallucinatory behavior increased to performance on over 58% of objective observations.

When social-learning procedures were reintroduced with extended time out for assaults, Nancy gradually reduced the frequency of both hallucinatory behavior and dangerous and aggressive acts to half their earlier levels, but they remained at levels higher than those from before the original change in time out. Similarly even though she was again demonstrating improvements in social and instrumental skills, only components of Self-Care showed significant improvement from initial entry levels; all of her remaining behaviors had not yet achieved even the initial levels of performance. Thus, Nancy's poorer showing at the last anniversary assessment reflected a clear carry-over from the year and a half without effective consequences for controlling assaults and appeared to reflect an ongoing spiral in which bizarre cognitive behaviors and aggressive acts interacted with each other. Three weeks of focused social-learning procedures with overcorrection/restitution for the critical hallucinatory and aggressive behaviors (see chapter 33) were sufficient to overcome these problems to the extent that Nancy once again showed significant improvement and achieved a successful community placement.

*Howard G (social-learning)* had shown the lowest level of continuing performance of any social-learning resident, even before the change in time out procedures. Upon entry to the social-learning program Howard was fifty-four years old and had been hospitalized for nearly twenty-seven years. Although he had finished high school, he had worked only intermittently at unskilled jobs and had never married. He had been a voluntary admission but had only one brief period of release, remaining continuously hospitalized for nearly twenty-six years; he had been mute and incontinent for the last several years. His clinical picture upon entry to the program revealed a total absence of social, communication, or other instrumental behavior, except for arising on request 28% of the time. More than one clinically bizarre behavior occurred on every objective observation, with high rates of withdrawal, blank staring, and smiling or grimacing without apparent stimulus predominating. By the fifth anniversary assessment, Howard had shown continuous improvement, but was still functioning only slightly above minimum survival levels. He had increased his Interpersonal Skills to normal performance on over 11% of opportunities and Instrumental Role Performance to normal levels on nearly 47% of opportunities. Similarly his bizarre maladaptive behaviors had been reduced to approximately one incident per observation on 28% of observations. He was showing slow but steady continuing improvement and was not performing any dangerous and aggressive acts.

Following the change in the length of time out, Howard gradually increased the rate of aggressive Intolerable Behaviors until he reached a stable level of about eight incidents per week after ten months. Concurrently his earlier gains in Self-Care and Interpersonal Skills deteriorated to the complete deficit level by the eighth anniversary assessment, and his Instrumental Role Performance declined to normal levels of performance on only 4% of opportunities. His bizarre, clinically crazy acts remained below original levels but nearly tripled the previous low rates that he had achieved before the change in time-out procedures. As with Nancy D., Howard did not reduce the incidence of either bizarre behavior or aggressive acts after the return to baseline conditions and the consequent removal of any pressure to perform within the program. Rather, his dangerous and aggressive acts continued at an average of nearly nine per week, and his bizarre motoric behaviors nearly doubled during the baseline period.

Upon the reintroduction of the social-learning program with extended time out for assaults, Howard reduced his dangerous and aggressive acts, but only to a level averaging five per week. He slightly increased his Interpersonal Skills and Instrumental Role Performance to levels above those at initial entry, but nowhere approaching earlier improvements. He showed no additional reductions over the last twenty weeks in the incidence of bizarre behavior, and his concurrent appropriate behavior still remained at less than half original levels. For severely debilitated residents such as Howard, the carry-over of the previous year and a half's losses may have been further confounded by the change in meal procedure in which meals were no longer available as backup reinforcers, since the delay period and difference in the quality of food were simply not potent enough to motivate someone who was still functioning at such a low level. Ultimately before Howard's aggressive intolerable acts were eliminated, focused overcorrection/restitution was necessary for eight weeks (see chapter 33), following which he regained significant improvement in other areas sufficient to achieve a successful community placement.

# 30. Other Ongoing Resident Activity During the Last Six Months

## COMPARATIVE CHARACTERISTICS OF LARGE COMMUNITY MEETINGS

Productive characteristics of the large community meetings during the last six months—obtained from the Group Activity Index (GAI) in Friday meetings—are plotted in figure 30.1.[1] An inspection of the average straight speeches (i.e., appropriate initiation, response, or continuing normal conversation on a single topic) per meeting in figure 30.1 shows a reduction for both groups upon the return to baseline conditions, with relative stability for the remainder of the period after programmatic procedures were reintroduced. These changes tended to parallel unitwide reductions in Intolerable Behavior over both programs (r=0.50); there were no differences between groups. The only notable difference between programs during the last six months was the increase in instances of straight speech during social-learning community meetings just before the return to baseline conditions. The increase was attributable to greater amounts of speech by both staff and residents during the meeting in which the ensuing program changes were announced. However, unlike the previous three and a half years, the average number of straight speeches during each forty-five-minute meeting did not differ between groups ($p > 0.20$).[2] Both community meetings averaged about the same level of straight speeches as the social-learning meetings had for the previous year, with the amount of normal task-oriented talk remaining at a level greater than three times that existing during the original baseline.

The proportion of straight speeches made by residents rather than staff in figure 30.1 shows a continuation of the pattern established during the previous six months, with stability through the return to baseline conditions. As in previous time periods, social-learning residents continued to contribute less straight speech than staff during community meetings, varying nonsignificantly around a 33% contribution. The low proportion of speeches contributed by milieu residents during the last six months was not at all similar to earlier, more active periods. In fact, they contributed a significantly lower proportion of speeches during community meetings than social-learning residents did ($p < 0.01$)—varying nonsignificantly around 18% until the last point, where only 5% of total straight speeches were by milieu residents. The individual GAIs indicated that the low rate of resident contribution to milieu community meetings continued to be a function of the less active and less effective resident group leader, as in the previous six months.

The differences in the target of resident speeches during community meetings were more in keeping with previous findings. Straight resident speeches within social-learning community meetings were still regularly directed to staff (92%); few were directed to individual residents (6%) and even fewer to the group as a whole (2%). These proportions were consistent over the last six months, without differences during baseline conditions. The proportion of resident speeches directed to the group as a whole by milieu residents (5%) was also relatively stable and did not differ from that of the social-learning group ($p > 0.10$). However, the proportion of resident speeches directed to other residents or to staff in milieu community meetings showed significant differences from that in social-learning community meetings and significant variability during the period ($p < 0.01$).

Before and after the return to baseline conditions, milieu residents regularly directed about 50% of speeches to other residents and about 45% of them to staff—similar to earlier milieu community meetings when active resident group leaders were in office. During the return to baseline conditions, when no therapeutic community structure was in operation, 80% of resident speeches were directed to staff. Upon the reintroduction of milieu therapy procedures and the election of a resident group leader (actually, reelection of the previous, ineffective resident group leader), resident speeches were again directed to other residents at a stable 50%. These proportions continued without variance until the next-to-last meeting

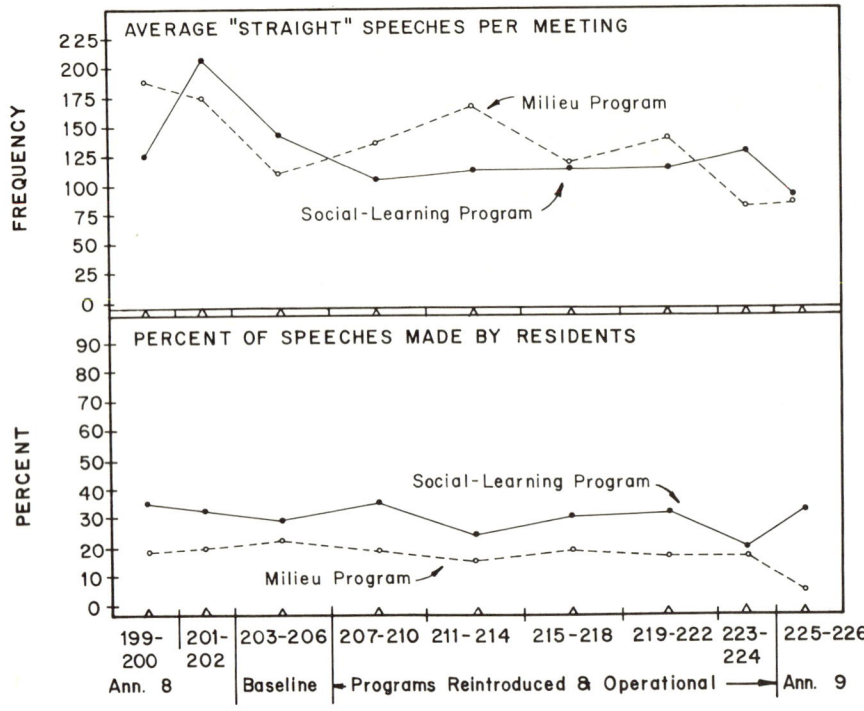

Figure 30.1. Productive characteristics of large community meetings during the last six months.

before the ninth anniversary assessment, when 83% of speeches were again directed to staff—largely reflecting attempts to get staff, rather than the ineffective group leader, to take responsibility for action. The last milieu meetings of the period then showed a complete reversal; 100% of resident speeches were directed to other residents after it became clear that staff were not going to take over the group leader's functions. However, 95% of all speeches during the last meeting of the period were contributed by staff, largely consisting of prodding residents to take action.

Nonproductive characteristics of community meetings over the last six months—presented in figure 30.2—also show differences from previous periods. The time spent in total silence during the meetings continued at even lower rates than at previous periods, without differences between groups ($p > 0.20$). Time silent for both groups was unrelated to other unit-wide changes in behavior, with the only notable changes at all occurring in milieu community meetings. A slight increase in time spent silent occurred during the return to baseline conditions, and the last two blocks of the period reflect no time silent at all within milieu community meetings.

Significant differences in active interferences with ongoing community meeting functions (disrupting discussions, whispering, or crazy talk, walking about, entering late or leaving early) were obtained over the last six months, with the number of interferences within both programs tending to parallel changes in Intolerable Behavior ($r=0.78$). The ratio of active interferences to straight speeches, presented in figure 30.2, shows considerable variability, with the relative amount of nonproductive confusion varying within the same range as during the previous year and a half. As in all previous time periods, both the absolute number of interferences and the amount of confusion during meetings were significantly higher within milieu community meetings than within social-learning community meetings over the entire period ($p < 0.01$). The absolute number of interferences decreased in both programs during the return to baseline, but the confusion index increased as a result of the lower amount of straight speech. During the remainder of the last six months, confusion and absolute interferences reflected similar patterns—most notable of which were the differences apparent when the programmatic procedures were reintroduced.

Thus, the community meetings during the last six months continued to reflect some stable structural differences between programs—specifically in the relatively greater proportions of

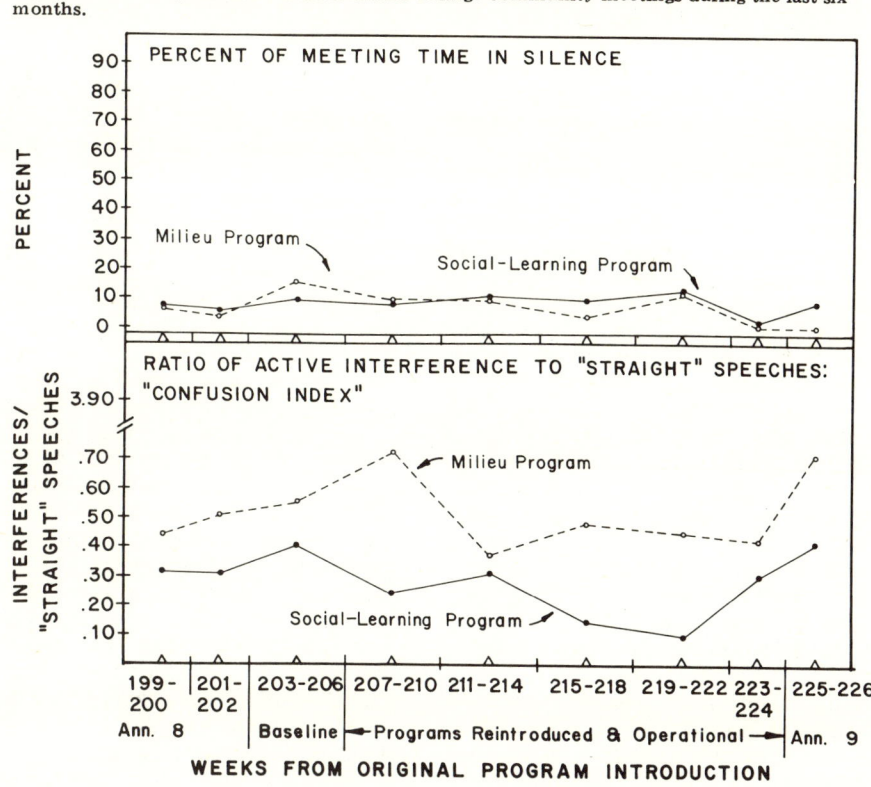

Figure 30.2. Nonproductive characteristics of large community meetings during the last six months.

resident speech directed to staff rather than other residents in the social-learning program, and overall meetings with less confusion and more on-task behavior within social-learning meetings than within milieu meetings. The amount of time spent in total silence continued at even lower levels than at earlier times during the intramural period, without differences between groups. However, paralleling the decrease in Intolerable Behavior over the last six months, the total amount of speeches decreased during the return to baseline conditions and remained at lower levels upon the reintroduction of programmatic procedures. Other than this change, characteristics of community meetings in the social-learning program did not vary during the return to baseline—continuing to reflect the essential commonality of both baseline and social-learning procedures in using the large community meeting for the communication of information. Milieu community meetings showed considerable changes when the therapeutic community structure was removed, thus changing the primary focus from resident problem solving to staff-resident communication of information. However, the sensitivity of milieu community meetings to the resident group leader in office was clear in the reversal of the proportion of speeches contributed by residents as compared to earlier periods and the attempts of residents to obtain leadership from staff after continuing frustration with an ineffective group leader. The relatively lower levels of total straight speech and of time silent in both groups during the last twenty weeks after the introduction of programs reflects a less-pressured pace during the period, following the obvious reductions in the amount of assaultiveness in both groups. Even so, both community meetings still reflected a proportion of time spent in complete silence of less than a fifth of that during pretreatment baseline and normal task-oriented talk at a level greater than three times that before the original introduction of programmatic procedures.

Over the entire intramural period of nearly four and a half years, milieu community meetings thus regularly showed significantly more interferences than social-learning community meetings did ($r=0.64$) and tended to have higher levels of straight speech ($r=0.32$), although straight speeches were particularly dependent upon the resident group leader in office and the topic of community meetings for the milieu group. Neither the proportion of speeches by residents ($r=0.05$) nor the proportion of time spent silent in meetings ($r=-0.06$) differed between programs over the total intramural period; however, stable structural differences were apparent in the target of speeches by residents. Milieu residents regularly directed more speeches to other residents (r=0.86) and less to staff (r=-0.87) than social-learning residents did and tended to address more speeches to the group as a whole as well (r=0.45).

To clarify further the nature of community meeting characteristics between the psychosocial programs, the four major GAI indexes were correlated with unitwide means of all objective measures of functioning over the sixty-three standard time blocks from the pretreatment baseline through the last anniversary assessment within each program. Within milieu community meetings, the total number of straight speeches tended to covary only with Interpersonal Skills (r=0.27) and to vary in opposite directions to the unitwide level of clinically bizarre behavior (r=-0.42). In contrast, the total number of straight speeches within social-learning community meetings tended to covary significantly with nearly all unitwide means for adaptive behavior (r's in the 0.30s to 0.60s) and to vary in opposite directions to most unitwide means for maladaptive behavior (r's in the -0.40s), with several of these correlations being significantly greater than those within the milieu program.

Nearly opposite relationships were obtained between groups for the proportion of community meeting straight speeches by residents rather than by staff. Within both programs, the proportion of speeches by residents tended to vary in opposite directions to the unitwide level of Intolerable Behavior (r's in the -0.50s), indicating greater proportions of talk by staff during community meetings when there were higher levels of Intolerable Behavior on the units. However, all remaining correlations involving the proportion of speeches contributed by residents differed significantly between groups. Nearly every correlation within the milieu program found the proportion of speech by residents in community meetings to covary with unitwide adaptive behavior and to change in opposite directions to unitwide maladaptive behavior (r's in the ± 0.50s to ± 0.70s). Relationships within the social-learning program were not only weaker, but occasionally in opposite directions. The only significant relationships within the social-learning program, beyond those with Intolerable Behavior, found that the proportion of speeches by residents covaried with unitwide means of both concurrent clinically bizarre behavior and concurrent adaptive behavior and changed in opposite directions to Interpersonal Skills (r's in the ± 0.20s & ± 0.30s).

Similar differences in patterning were also found for time spent silent and interferences. Within the social-learning program, the proportion of community meetings spent in total silence covaried slightly with the level of unitwide clinically bizarre behavior (r's in the 0.30s) and varied in opposite directions to both Inappropriate Clinical Frequencies and Interpersonal Skills (r's in the -0.20s). Within the milieu program, time silent tended to covary with the majority of unitwide levels of adaptive behavior (r's in the 0.30s to 0.50s) and with Cognitive Distortion (r=0.57). The majority of these correlations were significantly different between groups, with the only correlations including time silent, without significant differences being Intolerable Behavior and Inappropriate Clinical Frequencies (r's in the -0.20s & -0.30s). Interferences within social-learning community meetings were related to only one unitwide measure of functioning over time: Intolerable Behavior (r=0.30). Within both programs, the number of interferences during community meetings tended to reflect the amount of Intolerable Behavior occurring on the unit, without differences between groups in the strength of the relationship. However, interferences with milieu community meetings also tended to covary with unitwide levels of Inappropriate Clinical Frequencies (r=0.35) and Schizophrenic Disorganization (r=0.27) and to change in opposite directions to all measures of adaptive behavior (r's in the -0.30s & -0.40s).

Thus, over the entire intramural period of nearly four and a half years, the characteristics of large community meetings reflected both differences in structure and purpose within the two psychosocial programs and showed differential relationships to levels of functioning. The largest and most consistent difference in major characteristics between community meetings was in the relative amount of active interference and confusion, which was regularly higher within the resident-led milieu community meetings. Interferences remained relatively low and stable within social-learning meetings, with a slight tendency to vary only with the unitwide level of Intolerable Behavior. Interferences within milieu community meetings were not only higher but varied considerably, tending to reflect the unitwide level of other adaptive and maladaptive behavior, as well as Intolerable Behavior. The total amount of straight speech of staff and residents combined tended to be slightly higher in milieu meetings over the entire period after the introduction of programs. However, straight speeches in social-learning community meetings were more consistent and reflected the unitwide level of functioning of residents to a considerably greater extent than those of milieu meetings, which were particularly subject to influence by the resident group leader in office and external events that became the focus of resident or staff concern.

While the proportion of speeches made by

residents did not differ significantly over the total intramural period, the social-learning group remained relatively stable in this regard, with staff talking more than residents. Milieu residents, in contrast, varied widely in the relative amount of speech contributed by residents, reflecting both the level of functioning existing on a unitwide basis and the effectiveness of the resident group leader in office. The proportion of resident speeches in community meetings within the social-learning program tended to vary slightly with the amount of activity on the unit—both positive and negative —and to decrease with increases in Intolerable Behavior. The amount of community meeting time spent in complete silence decreased over time for both groups, without differences between programs. There were tendencies for time silent to vary with unitwide levels of both adaptive and maladaptive behaviors, depending upon the dominant activity at the time—more for milieu meetings than for social-learning meetings; however, time silent was one of the more stable characteristics of large group meetings over time.

Clear structural differences were maintained throughout with regard to the target of resident speeches, with social-learning residents regularly directing speech to staff the great majority of the time, while the speech of milieu residents was regularly directed to other residents more than to staff. Social-learning residents were stable throughout the intramural period in this area, reflecting the primary purpose of communication of information in social-learning community meetings. The resident-resident target of milieu speeches, in contrast, reflected the community responsibility for decision making. However, changes in the target of resident speeches from other residents to staff regularly occurred when an ineffective or inactive resident group leader was in office or when serious unitwide crises occurred, for which residents could not find resolutions, even with the controlled guidance of staff. Because of the level of functioning of this severely debilitated population and the resulting level of talent for prospective group leaders, therapeutic community meetings within the milieu program did not show the hoped-for stable change in positive functioning and decrease in confusion during meetings, which were more easily attainable under staff leadership in the social-learning program.

## DIFFERENTIAL UTILIZATION OF RESOURCES

The program structures had produced continuing differences in the rate of use of facilities and services (e.g., TV, lounge, radio, time with staff, off-unit facilities, etc.), while the declines in functioning over the past year and a half had resulted in significant reductions in the use of consumables (e.g., meals, coffee, snacks, canteen items) in both groups. In addition to changes in consequences for assaultiveness upon the reintroduction of treatment programs, it was hoped that the remaining procedural changes in food service and nature of token exchange would increase morale by removing a potential cause of frustration in both programs and provide greater access to backup reinforcers for social-learning residents. The change in food service (by the regular paid dietary staff rather than residents) was the result of a statewide central office directive and began upon the return to baseline conditions. The changes in the nature of token exchange, the result of the findings of earlier substudies, consisted of allowing residents on restricted status to purchase eligibility to obtain resources by making an additional token payment on any standing fines and charging tokens only for early special meals and desserts; regular meals were available without token charge but required a twenty-minute wait for less-appetizing (though still nutritious) meals.

The relative use of facilities and services and of consumables from the eighth through the ninth anniversary assessment—presented in figure 30.3—showed clear differences as a result of procedural changes during the last six months.[3] Residents in both groups showed significant increases in consumables' utilization immediately upon the return to baseline conditions ($F=235.67$, $df=1/54$, $p < 0.01$). The increases upon the reduced levels of Intolerable Behavior and the removal of token charges and the requirement that residents provide services were to levels of consumables' utilization even higher than the 51% of opportunities that existed before the original introduction of programs, suggesting a contrast effect following the functional deprivation conditions of the previous time period. Upon the reintroduction of programs and the changed procedures, residents in both groups showed even further significant increases in use of consumables ($F=23.49$, $df=1/54$, $p < 0.01$). For the first time in four years, the rate of consumables' utilization was maintained at significantly higher levels than those existing before original introduction for both groups ($F=41.33$, $df= 1/54$, $p < 0.01$), without differences between groups at any time during the period ($F$'s < 1). Over the entire period, the increase in consumables' utilization for both groups tended to vary only with unitwide decreases in Intolerable Behavior ($r=-0.54$). The greater value of consumables versus facilities and services for this population continued to be apparent for social-learning residents ($F$'s > 5.69, $df=1/54$, $p < 0.05$). Additionally the effects of the earlier functional deprivation were also apparent for

Figure 30.3. Comparative rates of resource utilization during the last six months.

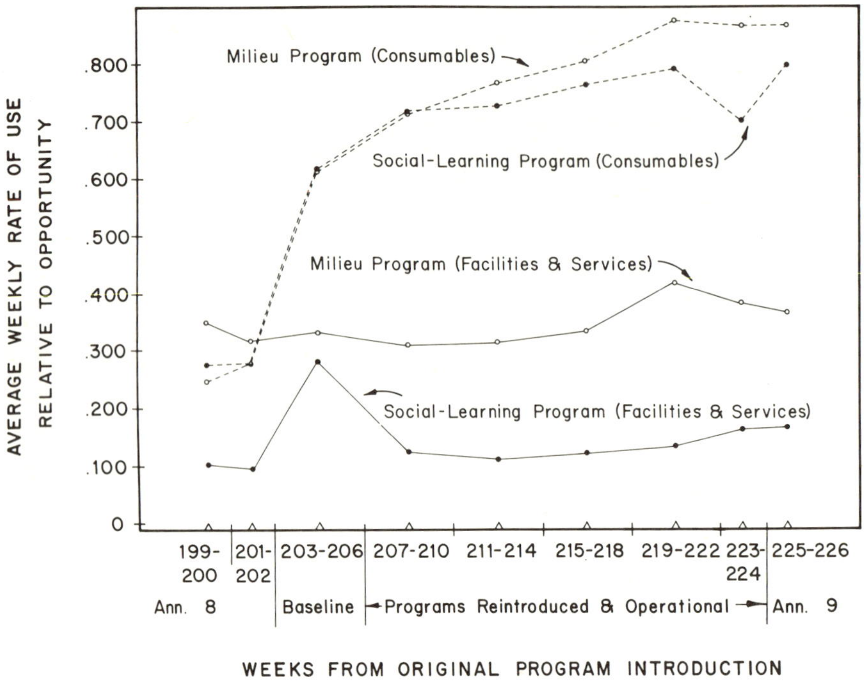

milieu residents, who, for the first time in over four years, used consumables at a higher rate than they used facilities and services from the second baseline on (F's > 23.18, df=1/54, p < 0.01), even though both were equally accessible and required only decision making.

In contrast to the consistent changes in the use of consumables, the use of facilities and services during the last six months showed differential change between groups. As shown in figure 30.3, the return to baseline conditions resulted in a significant differential change between groups (F=10.84, df=1/54, p < 0.01), with the milieu group continuing to use facilities and services at the same rate that they had under previous milieu procedures (F < 1), and social-learning residents significantly increased facilities' and services' utilization (F=18.90, df=1/54, p < 0.01) when token costs were removed, to the extent that the groups no longer differed during baseline conditions (F < 1).

Upon the reintroduction of the programs, social-learning residents again reduced their rate of facilities' and services' utilization (F=9.01, df=1/54, p < 0.01). Both groups showed increases over the last twenty weeks under new programmatic conditions (F=4.78, df=1/54, p < 0.05) without differential rates of change (p > 0.20). Changes in facilities' and services' utilization by milieu residents tended to be in opposite directions to unitwide levels of Cognitive Distortion and Inappropriate Clinical Frequencies over the entire period (r's in the -0.70s), while social-learning increases after the reintroduction of the program paralleled all adaptive behaviors (r's in the 0.70s & 0.80s). As in all previous time periods, the use of facilities and services by milieu residents was significantly greater than that of social-learning residents (F's > 10.33, df=1/54, p < 0.01). By the last anniversary assessment, facilities and services were still used at a significantly lower rate than that existing before the original introduction of programs for both milieu (F=6.61, df=1/54, p < 0.05) and social-learning groups (F=42.01, df=1/54, p < 0.01). Overall correlations of mean facilities' and services' utilization with unitwide measures of functioning over time (r's from ± 0.50s to ± 0.90s) still reflected the higher levels of functioning of social-learning residents concurrent with lower rates of utilization relative to milieu residents.

An examination of individual resident characteristics associated with utilization rates during the last anniversary assessment found considerably different relationships than those existing during the eighth anniversary assessment, with more similarity to earlier periods. The only measure of individual resident functioning that was associated with utilization rates for milieu residents during the last anniversary assessment was Intolerable Behavior. The relationships showed a tendency for those few milieu residents still showing high rates of Intolerable Behavior to use fewer consumables (r=-0.45) and fewer facilities and services (r=-0.47). In contrast, social-learning residents using relatively more resources tended to be those performing higher levels of all adaptive behaviors (r's in the 0.40s to 0.70s) and lower levels of most maladaptive behaviors (r's in the -0.50s & -0.60s). All of these correlations were significantly stronger within the social-learning program than within the milieu program, except for relationships with Intolerable Behavior. Additionally social-learning residents who used more consumables tended to be those showing significant improvement (r=0.53) at the last anniversary assessment.

In summary, the procedural changes during the last six months had dramatic and differential effects on resource utilization. Both groups showed significant increases in their utilization of consumables upon the return to baseline conditions, with further significant increases after the reintroduction of programmatic procedures. These increases were to significantly higher levels than those from before the original program introduction and did not differ between groups—suggesting that the value of consumable items had been strengthened as a result of the functional deprivation during the earlier period. Consumables were clearly of more value than facilities and services for residents in both psychosocial programs during the last six months. Thus, the reduction in Intolerable Behavior, combined with changes in food service and the nature of token exchange, clearly resulted in increases in the use of consumables for both milieu and social-learning residents.

In contrast to consumables' utilization, facilities and services continued to be used at lower rates than before the original program introduction by residents of both groups. Social-learning residents increased facilities' and services' utilization to the same level as milieu residents did during baseline conditions. Otherwise, milieu residents continued to use more facilities and services throughout the period than social-learning residents did. Both groups showed gradual and significant increases in the amount they used after the reintroduction of programs, however. Although both groups showed increases in resource utilization after the reintroduction of programmatic procedures, by the last anniversary assessment earlier differences in the characteristics of residents using resources within programs were again apparent. As at earlier times, higher-functioning residents within the social-learning program tended to use more facilities and services than lower-functioning residents did, and higher-functioning and more improved social-learning residents tended to be those using more consumables. In contrast, the level of functioning was totally unrelated to individual levels of resource utilization for milieu residents, except that the few residents who still showed extreme levels of Intolerable Behavior still tended to use fewer resources.

Over the entire intramural period of nearly four and a half years, milieu residents consistently used more facilities and services than social-learning residents did (r=0.91). Although procedural changes during the last six months had removed differences between programs for consumables' utilization rates, over the entire intramural period milieu residents had still used more consumables than social-learning residents had (r=0.42). Even with the equalized increases during the last six months, overall correlations of mean consumables' utilization with unitwide measures of functioning over standard time blocks for the entire intramural period (r's in the ± 0.20s to ± 0.40s) still reflected the greater improvement of social-learning residents concurrent with lower rates of consumables' utilization relative to milieu residents. Similar but stronger relationships were obtained for facilities' and services' utilization over the entire intramural period (r's in the ± 0.40s to ± 0.80s). These relationships over the intramural period, combined with the differential relationships between individual resident characteristics and resource utilization during the last anniversary assessment, provide clear evidence that how resources were used was more important than how many resources were obtained.

TIME SPENT IN PROGRAMS AND WITH OTHER PEOPLE

Differences between programs in the amount of time in which residents were awake and in contact with other people during the last six months were examined via TSBC indexes for "eyes open" and "with others."[4] By the time of the eighth anniversary assessment residents in both programs had maintained increases in the amount of time awake, from 80% of observations before the introduction of programs to 96% for social-learning residents and 88% for milieu residents. Over the last six months, the average time awake remained quite stable; there were no significant changes for either group at any point during the period, including the return to baseline (F < 1). Both groups maintained significantly higher levels than before the original program introduction (F=19.98, df=1/54, p < 0.01). Social-learning residents maintained slight but significantly higher levels of time awake throughout the period than milieu residents did (F=6.50, df=1/54, p < 0.05), with the last anniversary assessment showing essentially the same proportion of time awake as the earlier periods for both social-learning (95%) and milieu residents (87%).

The amount of time spent with other people had declined over the previous year and a half to the extent that, by the eighth anniversary assessment, the average time with others for social-learning residents (69%) and milieu residents (61%) no longer differed from the 66% rate that had existed before the original introduction of programs. Both groups showed significant increases upon the return to baseline conditions (F=14.37, df=1/54, p < 0.01)—to 75% for social-learning residents and 70% for milieu residents. However, both groups showed significant decreases to earlier levels upon the reintroduction of programs (F=10.13, df=1/54, p < 0.01), with gradual increases approaching significance over the twenty weeks when programs were again operational (F=3.33, df=1/54, p < 0.10). The pattern of change covaried only with unitwide levels of concurrent appropriate behavior (r's in the 0.70s), without differences between programs. However, the amount of time spent with others by the last anniversary assessment for both social-learning (71%) and milieu residents (65%) still did not differ from pretreatment levels (F < 1). Neither absolute proportion of time with others nor changes differed between groups at any point during the last six months (p's > 0.10).

An examination of the relationship of individual resident characteristics to "awake" and "with others" status during the last anniversary assessment again found consistent relationships, without differences between programs. Overall correlations found residents in both programs who spent more time with other people to be those who were performing higher levels of adaptive behavior and lower levels of maladaptive behavior (r's in the ± 0.50s to ± 0.80s) and to have improved more during the treatment period (r=0.56). Although the few residents in both programs who were still using psychotropic drugs still tended to be asleep more during waking hours (r=-0.45), differential relationships were obtained with "eyes open" status for other variables. The only measure of functioning that was related to the amount of time residents spent awake within both programs was concurrent appropriate behavior (r's in the 0.40s). Milieu residents spending relatively more time awake tended to be those showing higher levels of most adaptive behaviors and lower levels of most maladaptive behaviors (r's in the ± 0.30s to ± 0.70s); no further significant relationships existed for social-learning residents.

Over the entire period of nearly four and a half years, there was a significant tendency for residents of the milieu group to average less time awake (r=-0.59) and less time with others (r=-0.26) than residents of the social-learning group did. However, correlations over the sixty-three standard time blocks of the entire intramural period found remarkably consistent changes for the milieu group (r's in the ± 0.60s to ± 0.90s) indicating that the amount of time with others regularly covaried with the unitwide level of functioning to an even greater extent than for the social-learning group (r's in the ± 0.30s to ± 0.80s). Time with others regularly covaried with resident level of functioning within both programs. Although average time awake was exceptionally stable during the entire intramural period, the minor variations that did occur reflected differential patterns of relationships to measures of unitwide functioning between programs. Average time awake for milieu residents tended to covary over time with all adaptive behaviors (r's in the 0.40s & 0.50s) and to change in opposite directions to unitwide levels of Schizophrenic Disorganization (r=-0.70) and Inappropriate Clinical Frequencies (r=-0.46). In contrast, average time awake for social-learning residents did not covary significantly with any unitwide measure of adaptive behavior except Interpersonal Skills (r=0.70). Although average time awake for social-learning residents tended to change in opposite directions to all concurrent crazy behaviors, the relationship was weaker than that of milieu residents for Schizophrenic Disorganization (r=-0.45) and stronger for Cognitive Distortion (r=-0.45) and Hostile-Belligerence (r=-0.59).

Summarizing "time awake" and "with others," residents in both programs maintained the increased proportion of time awake that had been established upon the introduction of programs, with social-learning residents remaining awake more than milieu residents were. Neither group showed significant changes in the proportion of time spent awake during the last six months, even during the return to baseline conditions. Parallel to changes in concurrent appropriate behavior, both groups showed increases in the amount of time spent with others upon the return to baseline conditions and decreases immediately upon the reintroduction of programs. During the last twenty weeks with operational programs, both groups again showed increases in time with others, parallel to increases in concurrent appropriate behavior; there were no differences between groups. However, by the last anniversary assessment, the amount of time spent with others did not differ significantly from that existing before the original introduction of programs for either group.

The low proportion of residents who received psychotropic drugs still tended to spend more time asleep during waking hours at the last anniversary assessment. Although most residents in both programs were always awake during waking hours, changes over the intramural period tended to covary more with unitwide adaptive behaviors and in opposite directions to Schizophrenic Disorganization for the milieu group and to covary more with Interpersonal Skills and in opposite directions to Cognitive Distortion and Hostile-Belligerence for the social-learning group. By the last anniversary assessment, milieu residents who spent more time awake tended to be those performing higher levels of most adaptive behaviors and lower levels of most maladaptive behaviors. Since nearly all social-learning residents were awake during all waking hours, the only individual relationship existing during the last anniversary assessment showed a tendency for residents spending more time awake to perform more concurrent appropriate behaviors. Time spent with others regularly covaried with unitwide levels of functioning over the entire intramural period; relationships were stronger within the milieu program than within the social-learning program. By the last anniversary assessment, higher-functioning and more improved residents in both programs were spending more time with other people, without differences between groups.

## VARIABILITY OF RESIDENT ACTIVITY

The individual variability of ongoing resident activity—as distinct from the individual amount and level of behavior—is the last group of descriptive characteristics to be examined. The average Stereotypy/Variability scores for five classes of activity during the last six months are presented in table 30.1, which provides a descriptive picture of the individual range of activity within each class, independent of amount.[5] While none of the scores differed between groups before program introduction, there were several differences through the eighth anniversary assessment.

The variability of concurrent clinically bizarre, crazy behavior (from the TSBC) had been maintained at levels significantly below pretreatment within both programs by the eighth anniversary assessment, without differences between groups. The means presented in table 30.1 show that both groups increased the variability of crazy behavior upon the return to baseline conditions ($F=11.46$, $df=1/54$, $p < 0.01$) and reduced it upon the reintroduction of programs ($F=7.42$, $df=1/54$, $p < 0.01$). Although that of social-learning residents increased to a slightly less extent than that of milieu residents did upon the return to baseline conditions, the differences were not significant ($p > 0.10$). Neither group showed significant changes from the eighth to the ninth anniversary assessment ($F < 1$). Rather, residents of both programs ended the intramural period still showing significant reductions in the variability of crazy behavior from that existing before the original introduction of programs ($F=22.56$, $df=1/54$, $p < 0.01$), without differential change between them ($F < 1$).

The variability of crazy behavior did not differ between groups or change with unitwide measures of functioning during the last six months, but there was a significant tendency for milieu residents to show greater individual variability over the entire intramural period ($r=0.48$). Additionally correlations over the sixty-three standard time blocks of the intramural period found significantly different patterns of relationships within the two programs. Over the four and a half years, the average level of individual variability of crazy behavior for the social-learning group tended to covary with most unitwide levels of maladaptive behavior and to change in opposite directions to all unitwide levels of adaptive behavior (r's in the ± 0.30s to ± 0.60s). With the exception of unitwide levels of Cognitive Distortion ($r=0.50$), the variability of crazy behavior for milieu residents was related to changes in unitwide functioning in exactly opposite directions, varying positively with most adaptive behaviors (r's in the 0.20s & 0.30s) and negatively with most maladaptive behaviors (r's in the -0.30s & -0.40s).

These relationships indicate that, over the intramural period, improved levels of functioning within the social-learning program tended to be accompanied by reductions in both the amount and range of clinically bizarre behaviors. Within the milieu program, improved levels of functioning tended to be accompanied by reduced amounts but an increased range of clinically bizarre behaviors. However, by the last anniversary assessment, both programs had shown significant reductions in the amount of clinically bizarre behavior, with the social-learning program producing greater reductions than the milieu program did. Both programs had equally reduced the range of specific crazy behavior that individual residents were performing.

The variability of concurrent appropriate behaviors (from the TSBC) had shown differential change between programs. Social-learning residents maintained an increased range of specific appropriate behaviors performed through the eighth anniversary assessment, and milieu residents maintained the same range that had existed before program introduction. The means presented in table 30.1 reflect stability in the range of concurrent appropriate behaviors for social-learning residents throughout the last six months, including the return to baseline conditions (F's < 1), with higher individual variability than that existing at pretreatment

Table 30.1. Relative Stereotypy/Variability of resident activity.

| Treatment program | Assessment period | Crazy behaviors | | Appropriate behaviors | | Social contacts | | Resource utilization | | Physical location | |
|---|---|---|---|---|---|---|---|---|---|---|---|
| | | Mean | S.D. | Mean | S.D. | Mean | S.D. | Mean | S.D. | Mean | S.D. |
| Social-learning | Baseline 1 | 4.41 | 1.631 | 3.85 | 1.390 | 1.89 | 0.217 | 2.86 | 0.635 | 3.02 | 1.507 |
| | Anniversary 8 | 3.10 | 1.024 | 5.13 | 1.509 | 2.54 | .386 | 1.96 | .736 | 4.51 | 1.258 |
| | Baseline 2 | 3.46 | 1.274 | 5.08 | 1.730 | 2.29 | .345 | 2.89 | .916 | 4.31 | 1.459 |
| | Anniversary 9 | 3.14 | 1.142 | 5.24 | 1.696 | 2.65 | .362 | 2.41 | .752 | 4.29 | 1.267 |
| Milieu therapy | Baseline 1 | 4.04 | 1.478 | 3.61 | 1.015 | 1.90 | .245 | 2.68 | .462 | 3.51 | 1.044 |
| | Anniversary 8 | 2.94 | 1.246 | 3.30 | 1.498 | 2.64 | .378 | 2.79 | .417 | 5.02 | 1.403 |
| | Baseline 2 | 3.90 | 1.729 | 4.62 | 1.754 | 2.34 | .357 | 2.94 | .633 | 4.73 | 1.776 |
| | Anniversary 9 | 3.10 | 1.452 | 4.08 | 1.662 | 2.91 | .271 | 3.02 | .464 | 4.99 | 1.496 |
| Total | Baseline 1 | 4.23 | 1.567 | 3.73 | 1.223 | 1.90 | .231 | 2.78 | .563 | 3.26 | 1.320 |
| | Anniversary 8 | 3.02 | 1.142 | 4.21 | 1.765 | 2.59 | .386 | 2.38 | .728 | 4.77 | 1.356 |
| | Baseline 2 | 3.68 | 1.535 | 4.85 | 1.757 | 2.31 | .352 | 2.91 | .785 | 4.52 | 1.639 |
| | Anniversary 9 | 3.12 | 1.306 | 4.66 | 1.777 | 2.78 | .346 | 2.71 | .693 | 4.64 | 1.430 |

Note. Table entries are Stereotypy/Variability scores. A score of 1 represents complete stereotypy (all incidence of activity of a single type); higher scores reflect greater variability, with maximum possible scores (crazy behavior=17, appropriate behavior=17, social contact=3, resource utilization=19, physical location=17) indicating equal incidence of all types of activity.

being maintained at every point (F's > 14.25, df=1/54, p < 0.01). In contrast, milieu residents significantly increased the variability of concurrent appropriate behavior during the return to baseline conditions (F=48.79, df=1/54, p < 0.01) to the extent that they did not differ from social-learning residents at this time (p > 0.25). They again decreased the variability of concurrent appropriate behavior when programmatic procedures started again (F=7.53, df=1/54, p < 0.01) and then gradually increased it during the last twenty weeks of the program. Changes in the variability of concurrent appropriate behavior for the milieu group during this period paralleled those in unitwide appropriate behavior (r=0.89) and Interpersonal Skills (r=0.79). The increase over the last twenty weeks was significant (F=15.05, df=1/54, p < 0.01) and significantly greater than that of social-learning residents (F=5.54, df=1/54, p < 0.05). However, the level of individual variability of concurrent appropriate behavior achieved by milieu residents by the time of the last anniversary assessment was still significantly lower than that of social-learning residents (F=7.21, df=1/54, p < 0.01) and did not differ significantly from that existing before the original introduction of the program (p > 0.20).

Over the entire intramural period, there was a significant tendency for milieu residents to show significantly lower levels of individual variability in concurrent appropriate behavior than social-learning residents did (r=-0.76). Correlations over the sixty-three standard time blocks found that changes in variability of concurrent appropriate behavior over both programs tended to covary with unitwide changes over time for all appropriate Clinical Frequencies (r's in the 0.40s to 0.70s) and to change in opposite directions to the level of most maladaptive behaviors (r's in the -0.20s & -0.30s), without differences between groups. Thus, by the time of the last anniversary assessment, social-learning residents had maintained significant increases in the amount of concurrent appropriate behaviors over both pretreatment levels and over the level of milieu residents and increases in the range of specific appropriate behaviors performed as well. Although milieu residents were showing gradual increases after the program introduction, by the time of the last anniversary assessment they showed no significant differences from pretreatment level in either amount or range of concurrent appropriate behaviors performed.

The Stereotypy/Variability scores for social contacts had continued to show increases in both programs in the range of people with whom residents spent time (i.e., other residents, staff, outsiders) through the eighth anniversary assessment, without differences between groups. During the current period, both groups showed significant reductions in the variability of social contacts upon the return to baseline conditions (F=31.72, df=1/54, p < 0.01), followed by significant increases immediately upon program reintroduction (F's > 34.36, df=1/54, p < 0.01). These changes primarily reflected differences in staff activity, in which staff were less active and less available during baseline conditions. While residents within both programs remained stable in the variability of social contacts over the remainder of the period in which programs were again operational, the increase by milieu residents immediately when programs were reintroduced was significantly greater than that of social-learning residents (F=5.93, df=1/54, p < 0.05). This increase was so great that the milieu group was significantly higher than the social-learning group for the twenty weeks after programs were reintroduced (F=8.09, df=1/54, p < 0.01). At the time of the last anniversary assessment, both groups still showed significantly greater variability in social contacts than that existing before the original introduction of programs (F's > 146.76, df=1/54, p < 0.01).

Although mean differences in the variability of social contacts did not differ significantly between groups until the reintroduction of programs during the last six months, there was a slight tendency for milieu residents to show greater variability in social contacts over the entire intramural period (r=0.28). However, differential patterns of relationships over time were again found between programs for variability of social contacts over the intramural period. Correlations over the sixty-three standard time blocks within the milieu program found that mean changes in the range of social contacts covaried with unitwide levels of most maladaptive behaviors (r's in the 0.30s to 0.50s) except Cognitive Distortion (r=-0.59). The variability of social contacts within the milieu program changed in opposite directions to the unitwide level of Cognitive Distortion and to the unitwide level of all adaptive behaviors (r's in the -0.40s to -0.70s). These relationships were significantly different from those within the social-learning program except for unitwide variations involving Cognitive Distortion (r=-0.55), Intolerable Behavior (r=0.45), and Inappropriate Clinical Frequencies (r=0.41). In fact, the variability of social contacts within the social-learning program covaried significantly with unitwide levels of Interpersonal Skills (r=0.50) and tended to change in opposite directions to concurrent appropriate behavior (r=-0.38), concurrent bizarre behavior (r=-0.34), and Hostile-Belligerence (r=-0.50).

These correlations show that increased ranges of social contacts in both programs tended to reflect greater contacts by staff to control Intolerable Behavior and inappropriate interactions by visiting relatives and community volunteers to lower-functioning residents; these tendencies were stronger within the milieu program. The negative relationship of Hostile-Belligerence and other concurrent bizarre behaviors with the variability of social contacts over time within the social-learning program reflects the programmed active ignoring of such behavior by staff and volunteers, thus reducing the range of people with whom time was spent. Only within the social-learning program was there evidence that increased ranges of people contacted resulted from resident initiations and reflected increases in the range of social contacts as residents improved the unitwide level of Interpersonal Skills. Thus, although neither group showed changes from pretreatment in the amount of time spent with other people by the last anniversary assessment, the range of class of people contacted had increased within both programs, more for milieu residents than for social-learning residents. The increased range of contacts for milieu residents was largely the result of initiations by staff and volunteers, while that for social-learning residents also reflected initiations by higher-functioning residents with a broader range of people.

The variability of resource utilization had maintained stable differences between programs through the eighth anniversary assessment. Social-learning residents continued with significantly reduced ranges of facilities and services used, and milieu residents maintained the same range of use of facilities and services as before the program introduction. Means presented in table 30.1 reflect differential changes in the variability of facilities and services used, parallel to the changes reported earlier in utilization rates. The return to baseline conditions resulted in significant differential change between groups ($F=19.44$, $df=1/54$, $p < 0.01$), with the milieu group continuing to use the same range of facilities and services that they had earlier ($p > 0.20$), and social-learning residents significantly increasing the range of facilities and services used ($F=100.62$, $df=1/54$, $p < 0.01$), to the extent that the groups no longer differed during baseline conditions ($F < 1$). When the programs began again, social-learning residents again used a restricted range of facilities and services ($F=20.54$, $df=1/54$, $p < 0.01$), but both groups showed increases over the last twenty weeks under new programmatic conditions ($F$'s $> 6.21$, $df=1/54$, $p < 0.05$), with the social-learning group approaching a significantly greater increase than the milieu group did ($F=3.00$, $df=1/54$, $p < 0.10$). However, the variability of facilities and services used by milieu residents was significantly greater than that of social-learning residents at every point during the last six months when programs were operational ($F$'s $> 10.20$, $df=1/54$, $p < 0.01$). Thus, over the entire intramural period, the milieu group consistently used a greater range of resources than the social-learning group did ($r=0.91$). By the last anniversary assessment the two groups showed significant differential change from pretreatment ($F=11.92$, $df=1/54$, $p < 0.01$); social-learning residents had reduced the range of facilities and services they used from pretreatment ($F=7.89$, $df=1/54$, $p < 0.01$), and milieu residents increased theirs ($F=4.51$, $df=1/54$, $p < 0.05$).

The Stereotypy/Variability scores for physical location had shown increases from pretreatment levels in both groups, with milieu residents maintaining even higher levels than social-learning residents did through the eighth anniversary assessment. Over the last six months, these scores—providing an index of the relative amount of movement of individual residents across geographical areas of the unit (e.g., corridors, lounge, dining area, common living area, etc.)—showed no significant change over time within or between groups ($p$'s $> 0.10$). Rather, milieu residents approached significance in the greater individual variability in locations frequented over social-learning residents throughout this time ($F=3.16$, $df=1/54$, $p < 0.10$), but both groups still maintained higher location variability than they had before the introduction of programmatic procedures ($F=29.14$, $df=1/54$, $p < 0.01$).

Over the entire intramural period, milieu residents consistently showed greater location variability than social-learning residents did ($r=0.69$). Correlations between average location variability and unitwide measures of functioning over the sixty-three standard time blocks within each program found that location variability changed in opposite directions to clinically bizarre behaviors for both groups ($r$'s$=-0.58$). However, higher levels of location variability were more strongly associated with higher levels of unitwide Interpersonal Skills within the social-learning program ($r=0.69$) than in the milieu program ($r=0.34$). Location variability also tended to vary in opposite directions to unitwide levels of gross inappropriate response to minimal expectations within the milieu program ($r=-0.33$) but not within the social-learning program ($r=0.08$).

An examination of intercorrelations among all five Stereotypy/Variability scores during the last anniversary assessment found two significant relationships replicated over both programs. Location variability was positively related to both variability of social contacts and variability of concurrent behavior in both groups, without differences between them ($r$'s in the 0.30s & 0.40s). The only other significant correlation within the social-learning group found that residents who used a greater range of facilities and services were also performing a greater range of concurrent appropriate behaviors (r=0.63), while the variability of resource utilization was unrelated to other Stereotypy/Variability scores within the milieu group. Within the milieu group there was a tendency for residents who showed a greater range of social contact to show greater ranges of both concurrent appropriate and concurrent crazy behaviors (r's in the 0.40s). Greater ranges of crazy behaviors were also associated with greater location variability for milieu residents (r=0.46). Thus, by the last anniversary assessment, social-learning residents performing a wider range of concurrent appropriate behaviors tended to use a wider range of facilities and services and to frequent a greater number of different locations on the unit. Social-learning residents in contact with a greater range of people frequented a wider range of physical locations; however, the stereotypy/variability of activities was still not a consistent personal attribute for social-learning residents. In contrast, by the ninth anniversary assessment, the variability/stereotypy of milieu residents' activity all tended to cluster significantly, excluding the variability of resource utilization.

By the last anniversary assessment, relationships between individual Stereotypy/Variability scores and measures of functioning showed further differences from those existing at earlier periods. Social-learning residents showing greater variability in the range of concurrent appropriate behaviors still tended to be those functioning at higher levels, but only three classes of behavior showed significant correlations: Instrumental Role Performance (r=0.42), Interpersonal Skills (r=0.41), and Schizophrenic Disorganization (r=-0.52). While none of the latter correlations were significantly different from those within the milieu group, the only significant relationship within the milieu group found a tendency for lower ranges of concurrent appropriate behavior to be performed by residents still showing higher levels of Intolerable Behavior (r=-0.40). Also in contrast to earlier periods, the variability of social contacts was totally unrelated to functioning in either program, and only one significant relationship existed within each program with the variability of crazy behavior. This relationship found a tendency for residents performing a greater range of bizarre behaviors to be performing lower levels of Self-Care (r=-0.41), without differences between groups.

Social-learning residents using a wider range of facilities and services still tended to be those performing higher levels of most adaptive behaviors and lower levels of most maladaptive behaviors (r's in the ± 0.30s to ± 0.50s). The only significant relationship with the variability of resource utilization for milieu residents was opposite to that of social-learning residents. Milieu residents using a wider range of facilities and services tended to be those performing lower levels of Interpersonal Skills (r=-0.44). Although correlations did not differ significantly between groups, location variability was significantly related to different measures of functioning during the last anniversary assessment. Social-learning residents frequenting wider ranges of locations tended to be those still showing some Cognitive Distortion (r=0.43); milieu residents tended to be those performing lower levels of Interpersonal Skills (r=-0.44).

To summarize, the relative variability of individual resident activity continued to reflect differential patterns of within-program processes. The variability of crazy behavior did not change differentially between groups during the last six months. Rather, that of both groups increased significantly upon the return to baseline conditions and decreased significantly when the programs were reintroduced. Although the variability did not differ between groups over the last six months, there was a significant tendency for milieu residents to show a greater range of crazy behaviors than social-learning residents did over the total intramural period. However, over the entire intramural period, improved levels of unitwide functioning within the social-learning program tended to be accompanied by reductions in both amount and range of clinically bizarre behaviors. Within the milieu program, improved unitwide levels of adaptive behaviors tended to be accompanied by reduced amounts but an increased range of clinically bizarre behaviors. By the last anniversary assessment, both programs had shown significant reductions in the amount of crazy behavior in evidence, with greater reductions by social-learning residents than by milieu residents. However, both programs had equally reduced the range of specific crazy behaviors that individual residents were performing.

The variability of concurrent appropriate behavior for social-learning residents remained at stable, high levels throughout the last six months. In contrast, that of milieu residents paralleled changes in the level of concurrent appropriate behavior and Interpersonal Skills— increasing upon return to baseline, decreasing upon reintroduction of the program, and gradually increasing throughout the last twenty weeks. During the entire intramural period, the individual variability of concurrent appropriate behavior tended to covary with the unitwide level of functioning over time within both groups. By the last anniversary assessment, the milieu group showed no significant differences from pretreatment in either amount or range of concurrent appropriate behaviors performed, while social-learning residents were performing significantly greater amounts of concurrent appropriate behavior and a greater range as well.

Residents in both programs showed significant decreases in the range of class of people contacted during the return to baseline conditions, reflecting the lowered activity and availability of staff. Upon the reintroduction of programs, both groups showed significant increases in the variability of social contacts; the milieu group increased more and remained at higher levels throughout the last twenty weeks. There was a slight tendency for milieu residents to show greater individual variability in social contacts throughout the entire intramural period. However, the relationship of changes over time to levels of functioning suggested that higher-functioning social-learning residents tended to seek out a broader range of contact with staff and outsiders. Lower-functioning residents of both programs were inclined to receive more attention from relatives and volunteers, and residents performing Intolerable Behaviors tended to receive more contact from staff, which was needed to control their behavior. By the time of the last anniversary assessment, neither group showed changes from pretreatment in the amount of time spent with other people, but the range of social contacts had increased within both programs, more so for milieu residents than for social-learning residents. However, the increased range for milieu residents was largely caused by initiation by staff and volunteers, while that for social-learning residents also reflected initiations with a broader range of people by higher-functioning residents.

The variability of resource utilization showed gradual increases over the last six months for milieu residents. Social-learning residents increased the range of facilities and services they used during the return to baseline, reduced it upon the reintroduction of the program, and gradually increased it over the last twenty weeks. The variability of resource utilization remained consistently higher for the milieu group than for the social-learning group over the entire intramural period, including the times when active programs were in operation during the last six months. By the last anniversary assessment, milieu residents were showing significantly greater individual variability in resources used than that which had existed during pretreatment, and social-learning residents still used a significantly lower range of resources. Thus, although both groups were using fewer facilities and services than they had before the program introduction, social-learning residents had reduced both the amount and the range of resources used, and milieu residents had reduced the amount but increased the range. Milieu residents were still consistently using greater amounts and broader ranges of facilities and services than social-learning residents did.

Location variability showed no change over time or between groups during the last six months. Rather, as at all previous times during the intramural period, milieu residents maintained greater variability in the range of locations frequented than social-learning residents did. The relationship of changes over time to unitwide measures of functioning showed that location variability tended to change in opposite directions to the level of bizarre behaviors in both groups, but higher levels of location variability were more strongly associated with higher levels of Interpersonal Skills within the social-learning program. By the time of the last anniversary assessment, residents in both groups were still frequenting wider ranges of geographic locations than they had before the original introduction of programs.

By the end of the period, differential patterning was apparent within programs, with the stereotypy/variability of activities tending to reflect consistency for milieu residents across all activities except the variability of resource utilization. The stereotypy/variability of activities still failed to reflect a consistent personal attribute for social-learning residents. Differential relationships between levels of functioning and Stereotypy/Variability scores continued to be in evidence, but with further differences from earlier time periods. Relatively higher-functioning residents in both programs still tended to show greater variability in the range of concurrent appropriate behaviors performed, but relationships were weaker than at earlier periods, especially within the milieu group. Unlike earlier periods, the variability of social contacts was unrelated to functioning in either program, and only one significant relationship existed within each program for the variability of bizarre behavior and for the variability of locations frequented—each reflecting different patterns. Higher-functioning social-learning residents still tended to exhibit greater variability in resource utilization; the only significant relationship for milieu residents showed more variability in resources used by residents performing lower levels of Interpersonal Skills. In general, the stereotypy/variability of resident activities had become less related to the level of functioning in both groups by the last anniversary assessment—still appearing to be more differentiated by individual and situational characteristics within the social-learning group and becoming more of a consistent personal attribute within the milieu group.

## SUMMARY

There were thus further differences in the characteristics of other ongoing activity during the last six months, in addition to the data on comparative effectiveness described in chapter

29. The unitwide community meetings during the last six months continued to show relatively greater proportions of resident speech directed to staff rather than other residents in the social-learning program, and overall meetings with less confusion and more on-task behavior within social-learning meetings than within milieu meetings. The amount of time silent continued at even lower levels than before, without differences between groups. The total amount of straight speech by staff and residents decreased during the return to baseline conditions and remained at lower levels upon the reintroduction of programmatic procedures. The relatively lower levels of both straight speech and time silent in meetings of both groups during the last twenty weeks reflect a less pressured pace during the period, corresponding to the reductions in assaultiveness. Other characteristics of social-learning meetings did not vary during the return to baseline conditions, but milieu community meetings showed considerable change when the therapeutic community structure was temporarily removed. The sensitivity of milieu community meetings to the resident group leader in office was evident from a reversal of the proportion of speeches contributed by residents as compared to earlier periods and in attempts by residents to obtain leadership from staff after frustration with an ineffective group leader.

Over the entire intramural period of nearly four and a half years, the largest and most consistent differences in major characteristics between community meetings were the relatively greater amounts of active interference and confusion within the resident-led milieu community meetings. Interferences remained relatively low and stable within social-learning community meetings, with a slight tendency to vary over time only with the unitwide incidence of Intolerable Behavior. Interferences within milieu meetings were higher and tended to reflect the unitwide level of other adaptive and maladaptive behaviors, as well as the incidence of Intolerable Behavior. Although the total amount of straight speech tended to be slightly higher in milieu meetings over the intramural period, straight speeches in social-learning meetings were more consistent and reflected the unitwide level of functioning to a considerably greater extent than those of milieu meetings. Milieu meeting straight speeches were particularly subject to influence by the resident group leader in office and external events that became the focus of resident or staff concern.

Over the entire intramural period, the proportion of speeches by residents during community meetings did not differ significantly between groups. That of the social-learning group remained stable, with staff talking more than residents, and that of the milieu group varied widely, reflecting both the current level of functioning of the resident group and the effectiveness of the resident group leader. The amount of meeting time spent in silence decreased over time for both groups, with slight tendencies to vary with unitwide extremes of either adaptive or maladaptive behaviors—more for milieu meetings than for social-learning meetings. However, time silent was one of the more stable characteristics and did not differ between groups at any time. The target of resident speeches reflected clear structural differences between groups throughout the intramural period. Social-learning residents regularly directed most speech to staff, reflecting the primary purpose of communication of information in social-learning community meetings. Milieu resident speeches were directed to other residents more than to staff, indicating the community responsibility for decision making. However, milieu residents frequently shifted their speech to staff when an inactive resident leader was in office or when there were serious unitwide crises and solutions did not come readily.

Because of the level of functioning of this severely debilitated population and the available pool of talent for prospective group leaders, therapeutic community meetings within the milieu program did not show the hoped-for stable increases in positive functioning or a decrease in confusion during meetings. These characteristics were more easily attainable under staff leadership in the social-learning program. However, even with the slower pace of the last twenty weeks, both community meetings still reflected a proportion of time spent in silence of less than a fifth of that which occurred during pretreatment meetings and normal task-oriented talk at a level greater than three times that existing before the original introduction of programmatic procedures.

The comparative utilization of resources during the last six months showed dramatic effects of procedural changes on consumables' utilization, with continuing differential effects of program structures on the use of facilities and services. Significant increases in consumables' utilization occurred upon the return to baseline conditions and again after the reintroduction of programmatic procedures. Consumables were used at higher rates than those existing even before the original introduction of programs—suggesting that the value of consumable items had been strengthened by the functional deprivation during the earlier period. Consumables were of more value than facilities and services for residents in both programs during the last six months, without differences between groups at any time. The reduction of Intolerable Behavior, combined with changes in food service and the nature of token exchange, clearly resulted in increases in the use of consumables for both milieu and social-learning residents.

Facilities' and services' utilization, in contrast, continued at lower rates than before original program introduction for both groups. Except for an increase by social-learning residents during the return to baseline conditions, milieu residents continued to use more facilities and services throughout the last six months. Although both groups showed increases in the use of facilities and services after programs were reintroduced, earlier differences in the characteristics of residents who used resources were again in evidence by the last anniversary assessment. The level of functioning was totally unrelated to the individual rate of resource utilization for milieu residents, except that the few residents still showing high levels of Intolerable Behavior were using relatively fewer resources. Higher-functioning residents within the social-learning program still tended to be using more resources than the relatively lower-functioning residents within the program were.

Even though the procedural changes of the last six months removed earlier differences between programs in consumables' utilization rates, over the entire intramural period milieu residents had consistently used more facilities, services, and consumables than social-learning residents had. The overall relationships over time continued to reflect higher levels of functioning and improvement for social-learning residents concurrent with lower rates of resource utilization than for milieu residents—continuing to provide clear evidence that how resources were used was more important than how many were obtained.

The increased proportion of time awake, which had been established upon the introduction of programs, was maintained throughout the last six months, with social-learning residents remaining awake more than milieu residents, without changes over time. Changes in time spent with others paralleled other changes in concurrent appropriate behavior during the last six months, without differences between groups. Both groups increased time with others upon the return to baseline conditions, decreased it when the programs were reintroduced, and gradually increased it during the last twenty weeks. However, by the last anniversary assessment, time with others did not differ significantly from pretreatment levels for either group.

Over the entire intramural period there was a tendency for social-learning residents to average more time awake and more time with others than milieu residents did. Time spent with others regularly covaried with unitwide levels of functioning within programs over time during the intramural period, with relationships being stronger within the milieu program than within the social-learning program. Although the great majority of residents in both programs were always awake during waking hours, the minimal changes over time tended to vary with some measures of unitwide functioning but with different measures between programs. By the last anniversary assessment, the few residents receiving psychotropic drugs in both programs tended to be asleep more during waking hours. Milieu residents spending greater proportions of time awake tended to be those performing higher levels of most adaptive behaviors and lower levels of most maladaptive behaviors. Social-learning residents spending more time awake also tended to perform more concurrent appropriate behaviors, but nearly all were awake during all waking hours on the last anniversary assessment. By the last anniversary assessment, higher-functioning and more improved residents within both programs tended to spend more time with other people, without differences in the strength of the relationship between groups. Overall, both programs had increased "time in" and social-learning residents maintained higher levels than milieu residents did. Time with others tended to parallel the unitwide level of functioning and did not differ between groups by the last anniversary assessment, although it was related to the individual level of improvement within programs.

Changes in the individual variability of ongoing resident activity continued to show differences in the day-to-day processes within programs. The variability of bizarre behavior increased significantly upon the return to baseline conditions and decreased again when the treatment programs started again, without differences between groups. Over the total intramural period, milieu residents showed a higher range of crazy behaviors performed than social-learning residents did. However, within the milieu program, improved levels of unitwide adaptive behaviors tended to be accompanied by reduced amounts, but increased ranges of clinically bizarre behavior over time. Improved levels of adaptive behavior within the social-learning program tended to be accompanied by reductions in both the amount and range of bizarre behaviors. By the last anniversary assessment, social-learning residents had reduced bizarre behavior more than milieu residents had, but both programs had significantly reduced the amount of crazy behavior and equally reduced the range of specific crazy behaviors that individual residents were performing.

The variability of concurrent appropriate behavior during the last six months increased for milieu residents upon return to baseline conditions, decreased upon reintroduction of the program, and gradually increased again over the last twenty weeks in which the milieu program was operational. During the last six months, social-learning residents remained at stable levels of individual variability of concurrent appropriate behavior, remaining significantly above that of milieu residents during all times that programs were in operation. Over the entire intramural period the individual variability of concurrent appropriate behavior tended to vary with the average level of functioning over time within both programs. By the last anniversary assessment, the milieu group did not differ from pretreatment levels in either amount or range of concurrent appropriate behaviors. Social-learning residents, in contrast, were performing significantly greater amounts and signficantly greater individual ranges of concurrent appropriate behaviors than either milieu residents or their own pretreatment level.

The return to baseline conditions resulted in significant decreases in the variability of social contacts in both programs, reflecting the lowered activity and availability of staff. Upon the reintroduction of programs, both groups increased the variability of social contacts, with that of the milieu group increasing more and remaining higher than that of the social-learning group throughout the last twenty weeks. The milieu group showed slightly higher levels of individual variability in social contacts over the entire intramural period; however, the relationship of changes over time to levels of functioning suggested different processes were operating. Lower-functioning residents within both programs tended to receive more attention from relatives and volunteers, and residents performing Intolerable Behavior in both programs tended to receive more contact with staff to control their behavior. Higher-functioning social-learning residents also produced greater variability in social contacts by seeking out more staff and other outsiders. By the last anniversary assessment, neither group had shown changes from pretreatment in the amount of time spent with other people, but both had shown increases in the range of people with whom time was spent. Although the milieu program had resulted in greater increases in the range of social contacts than the social-learning program had, the increased range was largely the result of initiations by staff and volunteers; the increase of social-learning residents also reflected initiations by higher-functioning residents.

The variability of resource utilization over the last six months showed increases for social-learning residents during the return to baseline conditions, reductions upon the reintroduction of the program, and gradual increases over the last twenty weeks. Milieu residents gradually increased the variability of resources used over the last six months, which remained higher than that of social-learning residents at all times except during the return to baseline conditions. The milieu group, in fact, remained consistently higher in the variability of resources used relative to the social-learning group over the entire intramural period. By the last anniversary assessment, both groups were using fewer facilities and services than they had before the program introduction, but social-learning residents had reduced both the amount and range, and milieu residents had reduced the amount but increased the range. Milieu residents were still consistently using greater amounts and broader ranges of facilities and services than social-learning residents were during the last anniversary assessment.

Location variability did not change over time or between groups during the last six months. Rather, as at all previous times during the intramural period, milieu residents continued to frequent a wider range of locations than social-learning residents did. Over the entire intramural period, location variability tended to change in opposite directions to the level of bizarre behaviors in both groups over time, but higher levels of location variability were more strongly associated with higher levels of Interpersonal Skills within the social-learning program. By the time of the last anniversary assessment, residents in both groups were still frequenting wider ranges of geographical locations than they had before program introduction.

By the last anniversary assessment, higher-functioning residents within both programs still tended to show greater variability in the range of appropriate behaviors performed, but relationships were weaker than at earlier periods, especially within the milieu group. Higher-functioning social-learning residents still tended to show greater variability in resource utilization; the only significant relationship within the milieu group found greater variability in resource utilization for residents performing lower levels of Interpersonal Skills. Unlike earlier periods, the individual variability of social contacts was unrelated to functioning within either program, and only one significant relationship existed within each program for the variability of crazy behavior and for location variability—each reflecting different patterns between groups. Differential patterning of interrelationships among Stereotypy/Variability scores was also apparent between programs, tending to be consistent for milieu residents across all activities except the variability of resource utilization. In general, the stereotypy/ variability of resident activities had become less related to level of functioning in both groups by the last anniversary assessment—still appearing to be more differentiated by individual activities and structural characteristics within the social-learning group and becoming more of a consistent personal attribute within the milieu group.

The analyses of the characteristics of other ongoing resident activity during the last six months provide a descriptive picture in keeping with differential program structures and baseline conditions, and additional support that outcome data were influenced only by defined procedures.

# 31. Staff Attitudes and Performance During the Last Six Months

## OPINIONS ABOUT MENTAL PATIENTS

Average sten scores on the Opinions About Mental Illness Scale (OMI) for junior staff alone and all clinical staff combined from the eighth to ninth anniversary assessments are presented in figure 31.1.[1] Original scores at the end of academic training nearly four and a half years earlier are also plotted for comparative purposes. After the previous year and a half with increases in resident assaultiveness, the staff group had shown differential decreases in Benevolence and Mental Hygiene Ideology and increases in Social Restrictiveness. Although Authoritarianism had also increased during that period, the change had not been significant.

Over the last six months of the intramural period, both continuing staff and total staff groups showed significant differential change among OMI scores ($p < 0.05$).[2] Although figure 31.1 suggested decreases in Authoritarianism and Social Restrictiveness over this period of significant improvement in resident functioning, the only OMI score to show significant change was Mental Hygiene Ideology ($p < 0.05$). By the last anniversary assessment, significant differential change was still apparent from the OMI scores that had existed before the original arrival of residents ($p < 0.05$). Like those at the beginning of the present period, the changes included a significant reduction in Mental Hygiene Ideology and a significant differential change between the decrease in Benevolence and the increase in Social Restrictiveness ($p$'s $< 0.05$); the remaining three scores showed no change at all ($F$'s $< 1$).

As at all previous assessments, Social-Learning Ideology continued to show the exceptionally high levels of endorsement that had been obtained from the original staff group at the end of training. The changes over the last six months were such that Mental Hygiene Ideology, once again, was significantly higher than the remaining four scores at the ninth anniversary assessment.[3] Authoritarianism and Interpersonal Etiology still did not differ significantly but were higher than Benevolence and Social Restrictiveness for the total staff group; none of these scores differed for junior staff alone.

Comparisons of the staff means with the ideal responses indicated in the margins of figure 31.1 for each score show that the pattern of the six staff scores remained significantly parallel to the ideal assumptions underlying both psychosocial programs, without change over the last six months ($r$'s=0.97).[4] The level of endorsement over all six scores combined moved nonsignificantly closer to ideal levels ($D^2$'s=6.96 & 6.66, respectively, at assessments 8 & 9),[5] as a result of the slight changes in Authoritarianism and Social Restrictiveness. The changes were such that the pattern ($p < 0.05$) and level ($p=0.064$) of OMI scores on the last anniversary assessment were even closer to the ideal than at the original posttraining assessment.

An examination of the intercorrelations among OMI scores at the ninth anniversary assessment found a nearly identical pattern of relationships to that obtained on the eighth anniversary assessment. Specifically Authoritarianism and Social Restrictiveness were still positively correlated ($r=0.58$), while remaining negatively correlated to Mental Hygiene Ideology ($r$'s in the -0.40s) and to Social-Learning Ideology ($r=-0.37$ and $-0.65$, respectively, for Authoritarianism and Social Restrictiveness). Similarly the only predictability of OMI scores from individual staff characteristics continued to involve education and experience, reflecting differences between junior and senior staff. Senior staff (with more education and experience) still tended to score lower on Benevolence and Social Restrictiveness ($r$'s in the -0.30s) and higher on Social-Learning Ideology ($r$'s in the 0.40s) than junior staff did. Thus, the same clustering of OMI scores—with Social-Learning Ideology playing a more central role—and similar predictability from individual staff characteristics was maintained over the final intramural period.

In summary, the attitudes, opinions, and beliefs about mental patients held by psychosocial staff showed significant change over the last six months. As at previous time periods, the changes appeared to reflect staff responses to changes in resident behavior—in this instance, decreases in assaultiveness and improvements in

Figure 31.1. Opinions About Mental Illness Scale responses by all psychosocial staff present during the last six months. The ideal response is indicated in the left margin for each score.

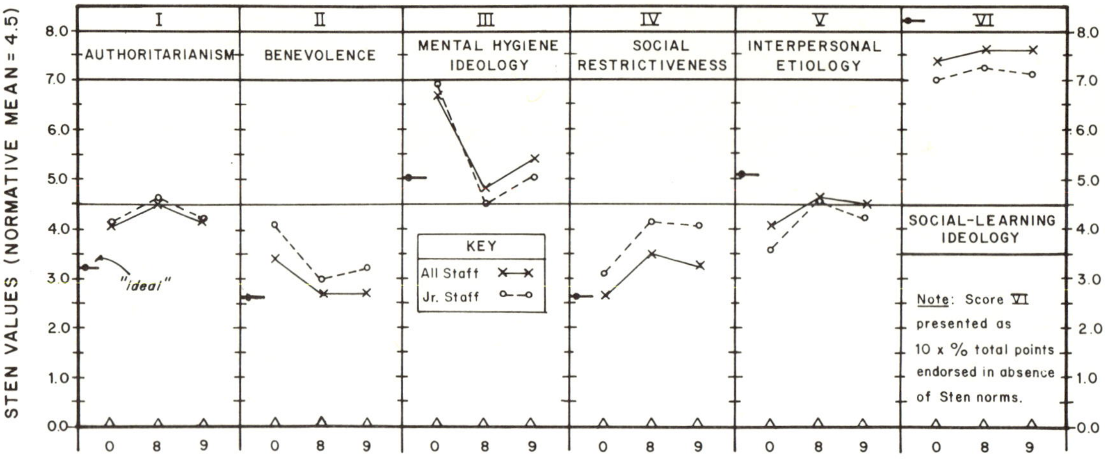

functioning following the reintroduction of treatment programs—without even suggestive evidence that their prior attitudes had any effect on the resident behavior that followed. Over the entire four and a half years of the intramural period, Mental Hygiene Ideology and, to a lesser extent, Benevolence and Social Restrictiveness, appeared to be particularly responsive to staff experience with increases and decreases in resident functioning. Interpersonal Etiology and Authoritarianism remained relatively stable, and there was evidence that Authoritarianism was slightly responsive to staff experience with assaultiveness. Social-Learning Ideology remained exceptionally stable throughout the entire intramural period, consistently being endorsed at high levels. Over the last six months, as well as during the entire intramural period, the staff group as a whole continued to reflect the ideal assumptions underlying the psychosocial programs—moving even closer over time—and remained much closer to psychosocial ideals than to those of typical mental hospital staff.

## ATTITUDES TOWARD AND INTERPRETATIONS OF TREATMENT PROGRAMS

Differential opinions were expressed by 97% and 100% of clinical staff, respectively, at the eighth and ninth anniversary assessments in response to the preliminary questions on the Therapist Orientation Sheet (TOS). The proportion of staff believing that the social-learning program was more effective at the last anniversary assessment (86%) still accurately reflected the objective results. At the same time more staff believed the milieu program was the more effective than had been the case at the eighth anniversary assessment, where the social-learning program was favored by 97% of staff expressing opinions. Similarly, although the social-learning program was still judged the more enjoyable in which to work by 69% of staff at the last assessment, the majority was less than the 76% preference for the social-learning program before the reduction in assaultiveness over the last six months. Thus, staff beliefs of the effectiveness of programs continued to reflect objective results, showing a change from the even division before the original introduction of programs, while the initial preference for the milieu program was reversed as a function of actual experience in the operating programs. Throughout the entire intramural period, staff opinions were responsive to changes in resident behavior preceding each judgment, but staff beliefs continued to have no effect on the ensuing response of residents to either program.

Average pattern differentiation scores on the TOS for all clinical staff working at the original posttraining assessment and at the eighth and ninth anniversary assessments are presented in figure 31.2.[6] Scores are plotted for responses obtained under each of three instructional orientations by the same staff within each assessment: one set for each of the psychosocial programs—reflecting staff interpretations of the nature of programs (attitude scores) and relative use of techniques (technique scores) inferred from the training and experience—and one for their personal beliefs or preferences as change agents.

The preferred attitude scores in figure 31.2 show an absence of change from the beginning to the end of the last six months in staff

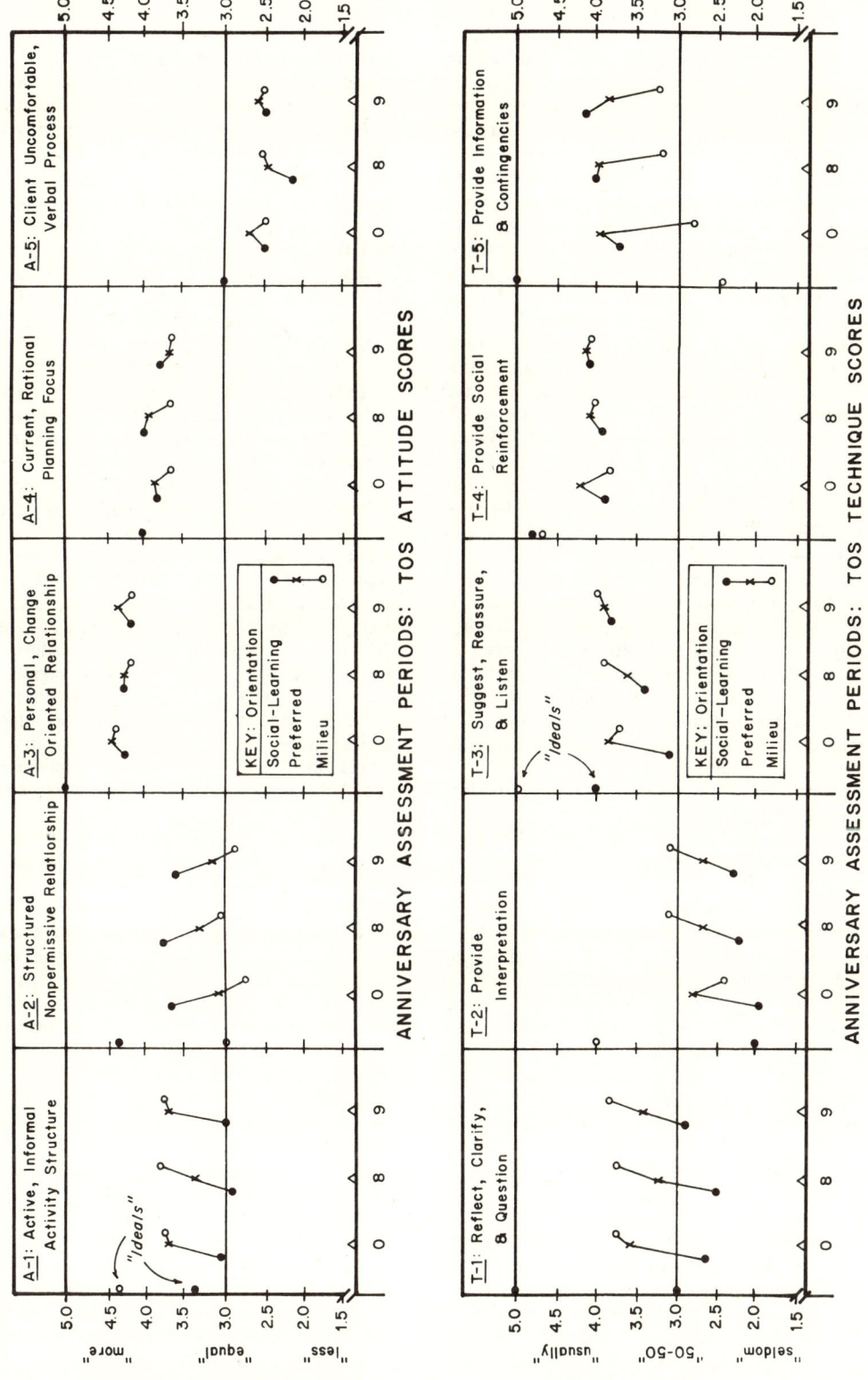

Figure 31.2. Therapist Orientation Sheet responses under three response sets by all psychosocial staff present during the last six months. Ideal responses are indicated in the left margin for each score.

personal preferences for the nature of treatment. In fact, no overall or differential change among scores even approached significance over the last six months or from the original posttraining assessment nearly four and a half years earlier (p's > 0.15).[7]—even though only 11% of the staff working at the last assessment had been employed at the original assessment. Differences among preferred attitude scores continued to be significant (p < 0.01), with all differences between scores, except A-1 versus A-4, being significant on the last anniversary assessment—an identical pattern to the original assessment.

Comparisons of staff means of preferred attitudes scores to the ideal responses for the nature of each psychosocial program (indicated in the left margin for each attitude score in figure 31.2) show that the slight changes that did occur moved the pattern of the five staff scores more closely to the milieu ideal (r=0.95) than to the social-learning ideal (r=0.72) once again (p < 0.10). The overall level of preferred attitude scores remained closer to the milieu ideal ($D^2$=1.07) than to the social-learning ideal ($D^2$=2.05) at the ninth anniversary assessment (p=0.064). In contrast to changes over the previous year and a half, the slight changes over the last six months moved closer in level to the milieu ideal, but not significantly so (p > 0.10). Thus, as at previous assessments, the nature of treatment characteristics preferred by staff continued to be closer to the ideal milieu program, primarily as a function of a preference for therapeutic relationships that were at the midpoint of the "structured-unstructured," "permissive-nonpermissive" dimension (A-2).

An examination of the intercorrelations among TOS preferred attitude scores at the last anniversary assessment found only two significant correlations, only one of which replicated relationships found at the eighth anniversary assessment. A-5 was once again negatively related to A-4 (r=-0.39), and A-4 was also positively related to A-2 (r=0.35). None of the individual staff characteristics were significantly related to preferred attitude scores, but a few significant relationships did occur with OMI scores. Staff preferring relatively more personal, change-oriented relationships (A-3) tended to score higher on OMI Mental Hygiene Ideology (r=0.42) and lower on Authoritarianism (r=-0.41). Staff preferring a relatively more active, informal activity structure (A-1) tended to score lower on OMI Social-Learning Ideology (r=-0.45) and higher on Social Restrictiveness (r=0.35) and staff scoring higher on Social-Learning Ideology tended to prefer (r=0.41) a more current, rational planning focus in treatment (A-4). Thus, at the last anniversary assessment, TOS preferred attitude scores continued to show little clustering and little predictability from individual staff characteristics but did show increased relationships to OMI scores.

An inspection of the attitude scores for each psychosocial orientation in figure 31.2 also reveals the essential parallelism of the staff group over the last six months. Significant differential change between orientations was obtained for continuing junior staff (p < 0.05), which was totally attributable to a significant increase in A-5 for the social-learning orientation (p < 0.01); no change occurred for the milieu orientation on A-5 (F < 1).[8] No other changes approached significance over the last six months (p's > 0.15). Scores at the last anniversary assessment showed no significant overall or differential change (p's > 0.20) from the level and pattern of attitude scores at the original posttraining assessment (0) nearly four and a half years earlier. Both continuing staff and total staff groups continued to produce consistently different patterns of attitude scores in their interpretation of the nature of milieu and social-learning programs (p's < 0.01). At the last anniversary assessment, the same ordering was maintained as at the original posttraining assessment for the social-learning orientation, with all differences between scores being significant except A-2 versus A-4. Within the milieu orientation, the same ordering was kept, with all scores differing significantly except A-1 versus A-4 and A-2 versus A-5. At the ninth anniversary assessment, social-learning scores were significantly lower than milieu scores on A-1 and significantly higher on A-2, but A-3, A-4, and A-5 did not differ between orientations.

A comparison of the pattern of staff attitude scores under each psychosocial orientation to the ideal response for the nature of each program in figure 31.2 shows that the directionality of the above differences were exactly parallel to those desired. As at the original posttraining assessment, the extent to which the staff interpretation of the nature of each program approached the ideal was apparent in significant relationships over the five TOS attitude scores for both milieu (r=0.98) and social-learning (r=0.96) orientations. Similarly the overall level of staff responses under the two orientations compared to their respective ideals did not change significantly over the last six months for either milieu ($D^2$=1.37) or social-learning ($D^2$=1.55) orientations, and they did not differ from each other (p's >0.10). Thus, the nature of programs not only continued to be differentially interpreted in an identical manner to the original posttraining assessment, but staff interpretations continued to be quite close to the ideals underlying each program.

The preferred technique scores in figure 31.2

also reveal the complete consistency of treatment procedures that staff preferred to use over the last six months. In fact, no overall or differential change among preferred technique scores approached significance over the last six months nor from the original posttraining assessment (p's > 0.20). Rather, scores continued to be regularly differentiated in the same manner as at earlier assessments (p < 0.01), with T-3, T-4, and T-5 remaining high and significantly greater than T-1 and T-2, while T-2 remained significantly lower than all other scores.

Comparisons of staff means of preferred technique scores to the ideals for each psychosocial program continued to show that the pattern of the five staff scores remained significantly closer (p < 0.01) to the the social-learning ideal (r=0.93) and unrelated to the milieu ideal (r=0.06) at the last anniversary assessment. Similarly the overall level of preferred technique scores continued to deviate more from the milieu ideal ($D^2=7.59$) than from the social-learning ideal ($D^2=2.34$) at the ninth anniversary assessment (p=0.064), without significant change over the last six months (p > 0.10). Thus, both pattern and level of preferred technique scores continued to approximate more closely the ideal social-learning program at the end of the intramural period.

An examination of the intercorrelations among TOS preferred technique scores at the ninth anniversary assessment once again found greater clustering, similar to findings at the fifth anniversary assessment. Significant correlations (r's in the ± 0.30s & ± 0.40s) found T-1 again to be positively related to T-2 and T-3; T-3 was negatively related to T-4 and T-5. T-4 and T-5 were also positively related. Sex was the only staff characteristic related to preferred techniques (r=-0.43), showing a tendency for females to prefer relatively less use of interpretation than males did.

Several significant relationships were obtained between preferred techniques and OMI scores. Negative correlations were obtained between OMI-I and both T-1 (r=-0.37) and T-3 (r=-0.44), and T-3 was also negatively related to OMI-IV (r=-0.42). These relationships show a tendency for staff preferring greater use of reflection, clarification, and questioning to score lower on Authoritarianism, while greater use of suggestion, reassurance, and listening tended to be preferred by staff scoring lower on Authoritarianism and Social Restrictiveness. T-4 was positively related to OMI-III (r=0.52) and OMI-V (r=0.38) and negatively related to OMI-IV (r=-0.50), reflecting a tendency for staff who preferred a relatively greater use of social reinforcement to score higher on Mental Hygiene Ideology and Interpersonal Etiology and lower on Social Restrictiveness. Mental Hygiene Ideology was also related to T-2 (r=-0.34) and T-5 (r=0.33), indicating that staff scoring higher on Mental Hygiene Ideology tended to prefer less use of interpretation and relatively greater use of advice and contingency management. Thus, at the end of the intramural period, greater clustering was again obtained among preferred technique scores, and several significant relationships were apparent between OMI scores and preference for use of specific therapeutic techniques, although both continued to be almost totally unrelated to individual staff characteristics.

The technique scores for each psychosocial orientation in figure 31.2 reveal the essential parallelism over the last six months in the staff interpretations of the appropriateness of relative use of different techniques within each treatment program. Both continuing staff and total staff groups continued to produce different patterns of technique scores between orientations (p < 0.01), without differential change (p > 0.15); however, the overall change over the last six months was significant (p < 0.05). There was a slight increase in the level of endorsement over all techniques for both orientations. At the ninth anniversary assessment, differential change from the original posttraining assessment had occurred (p < 0.05), showing no change for either orientation on T-1 and T-4 (p's > 0.20) and parallel increases in endorsed utilization rates for both orientations on T-2 and T-5 (p's < 0.05). Both orientations showed increases on T-3, but the increase was significantly greater for the social-learning orientation than it was for the milieu orientation (p < 0.05).

At the last anniversary assessment, technique scores within the milieu orientation continued to show differentiation, with T-1, T-3, and T-4 remaining at significantly higher levels than T-2 and T-5, without differing among themselves; T-2 and T-5 did not differ. Within the social-learning orientation, all differences between TOS technique scores were significant at the ninth anniversary assessment, except T-3, T-4, and T-5. Staff continued to differentiate between treatment programs in desired directions on T-1, T-2, and T-5; there were no differences between orientations on T-3 and T-4. The differences between orientations for technique scores show that relative staff interpretations moved in the direction of the ideal response for utilization of each group of techniques in figure 31.2. The extent to which staff interpretations of the appropriate pattern of technique utilization approached the ideal for the social-learning program at the last anniversary assessment was apparent in the exceptionally high relationship over the five TOS technique scores (r=0.99). The pattern of endorsement of technque utilization within the milieu orientation continued to be less related to the milieu ideal (r=0.75), but the level of relationship did not differ significantly from that of the social-learning orientation (p > 0.10).

The slight increase in endorsed utilization rates over the last six months resulted in the overall level of staff technique responses under the two orientations to move closer to their respective ideals. At the last anniversary assessment, the level of social-learning scores was significantly closer to the ideal ($D^2$=1.26) than at either the eighth anniversary assessment or the original posttraining assessment (p's=0.064). Although the level of milieu scores also moved closer to the milieu ideal, deviations continued to be greater than those of the social-learning orientation ($D^2$=3.98). Thus, staff interpretations of the appropriateness of the relative use of different techniques continued to be differentiated in desired directions between programs over the last six months. The level and pattern of endorsement remained closer to the ideal within the social-learning program, as it had at all previous assessments, but without significant differences over the last six months.

In summary, the attitudes and interpretations held by psychosocial staff of the treatment programs continued to show exceptional consistency over the last six months of the intramural period. Staff beliefs concerning the comparative effectiveness continued to reflect the objective results, with the great majority judging the social-learning program to be the better one in this respect. The social-learning program continued to be judged the more enjoyable by the majority of staff; however, the margin of those who thought the social-learning program was the more effective and the more enjoyable decreased over this period of renewed effectiveness of both programs. Throughout the entire intramural period of nearly four and a half years, staff opinions in this area were thus responsive to prior changes in resident behavior, but staff beliefs continued to have no effect on the ensuing response of residents to either program.

Preferred TOS attitude scores, reflecting staff preferences for the nature of treatment programs, remained well differentiated and quite constant over the last six months, without change from the original posttraining assessment nearly four and a half years earlier. As at all earlier assessments, the nature of treatment characteristics staff preferred remained closer to the ideal milieu program than to the ideal social-learning program, without significant change over the last six months. By the last anniversary assessment, these scores continued to show little clustering and little predictability from individual staff characteristics, but they did show significant relationships to three OMI scores. Only one slight differential change occurred over the last six months in the level of endorsement of TOS attitude scores for each program orientation. This change returned staff attitude scores to a pattern and level identical to that existing at the original posttraining assessment. Overall, the pattern of TOS attitude scores within and between orientations remained constant; the nature of programs continued to be differentially interpreted in a manner identical to that at the original posttraining assessment and continued to be quite close to the ideals underlying each program.

Preferred TOS technique scores, reflecting staff preferences for the use of different treatment procedures, also remained well differentiated and remarkably constant, showing no change over the last six months and no change from the original posttraining assessment. In contrast to the closer approximation of staff preferences for the nature of treatment to the milieu ideal, as at earlier assessments, preferred techniques remained closer to the social-learning ideal over the last six months. At the end of the intramural period, there was once again greater clustering among preferred technique scores and several significant relationships between OMI scores and preference for the use of specific therapeutic techniques. However, both continued to be almost totally unrelated to individual staff characteristics.

TOS technique scores, reflecting staff interpretations of the appropriateness of the relative use of different techniques, showed a slight increase in endorsed levels of utilization of all techniques over both programs during the last six months. However, no differential changes occurred, and staff continued to differentiate between milieu and social-learning programs in desired directions. The slight increases over the last period moved the level of appropriate technique endorsement even closer to the ideals of both treatment programs. By the last anniversary assessment, the level and pattern of endorsement remained closer to the ideal within the social-learning program, as it had at all previous assessments, but without significant differences over the last six months. Thus, staff interpretations of both nature and techniques continued to be well differentiated in appropriate directions between psychosocial orientations over the last six months of the intramural period, with staff preferences continuing to be much closer to either psychosocial orientation than those of mental hospital staff.

## PERFORMANCE IN PSYCHOSOCIAL PROGRAMS

The TOS data indicate that staff continued to differentiate between programs over the last six months. The objective data from the Staff-Resident Interaction Chronograph (SRIC) provide information on the reliability and differentiation of the psychosocial programs as they actually operated, including return to baseline conditions and the reintroduction of programs with procedural changes.[9] Given the renewed effectiveness of both programs over the last twenty weeks, SRIC data are particularly important for determining if changes other than those specified might have contributed to the reversal of previous trends in resident functioning.

How staff spent their time over the last six months is shown in figure 31.3, where total instances of activity and percentages of staff activity relative to the class of resident behavior in each program are plotted from the eighth through ninth anniversary assessment. There were clear differences in total instances of activity and focus of staff activity during the four-week return to baseline conditions, with nearly identical patterns of staff behavior occurring on both units. Upon the reintroduction of programmatic procedures, both total instances of activity and differential focus of staff activities returned to earlier levels and remained parallel to those existing over the previous two years.

An inspection of total staff activity during baseline conditions in figure 31.3 showed that the average staff member reduced his or her total instances of activity per hour to about 244 from the high rates existing when programmatic procedures were in effect. Although this level of activity represents a considerable reduction from that during the active psychosocial programs, it still represents an increase

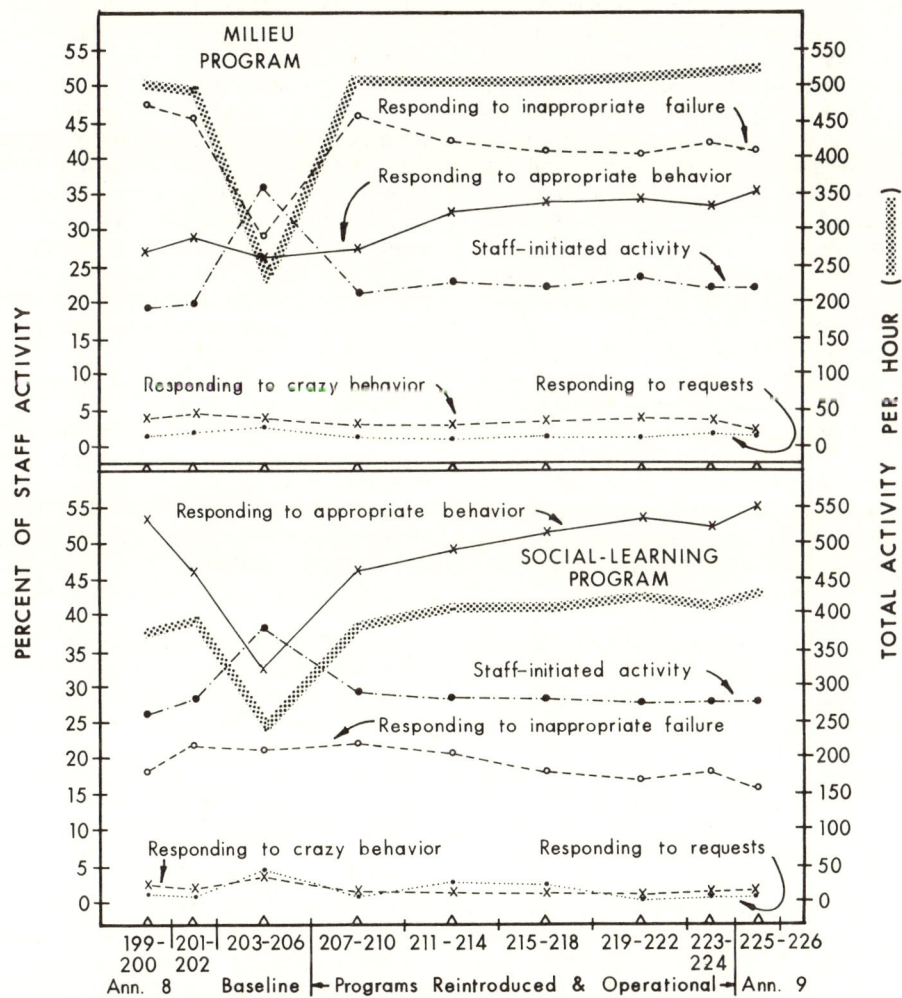

Figure 31.3. How staff spent their time during the last six months. Average total activity per hour is indicated by the shaded line and scale in the right margin.

of over 68% compared to original baseline conditions and a level of activity about 48% higher than that observed in the traditional hospital programs. However, like the traditional hospital programs and original baseline conditions, the greatest proportion of staff activity during baseline (37%) was not in response to resident behavior but was staff initiated. Over 24% of staff activity during baseline conditions did not involve interactions with residents at all; over 4% consisted of "ignore-neutral" job-irrelevant activity, and about 20% consisted of announcements, relevant paperwork, and observing residents without interacting. Although the relative focus on appropriate resident behaviors and resident failures still differed as much as 8% on psychosocial units during baseline conditions, the overall distribution of focus of staff activities on both units was closer to traditional hospital programs than to the respective psychosocial programs.

Over the last twenty weeks following the reintroduction of programmatic procedures, as during previous periods, the proportion of activity and total instances of activity focused upon appropriate resident behavior continued to be significantly higher when staff worked in the social-learning program ($p < 0.01$).[10] Similarly the total level of activity and the focus on resident failures and crazy behavior again remained significantly higher when staff worked in the milieu program ($p$'s $< 0.01$). Although total instances of activity in response to resident requests were significantly higher in the milieu program ($p < 0.05$), the proportion of focus on resident requests did not differ over the last twenty weeks. Both total instances and proportion of staff-initiated activity after the reintroduction of programmatic procedures were higher when staff worked in the social-learning program; however less than 14% of all staff activity in the social-learning program and less than 11% in the milieu program did not involve interactions with residents, and irrelevant behaviors in both programs occurred at a rate too low to appear even as a fraction of a percentage. The rate as well as the focus of staff activity over the last twenty weeks thus remained nearly identical to those at earlier periods; total activity in the social-learning program continued at over two and a half times the initial level, and that in the milieu program was over three and a half times the initial level.

The only significant relationships that existed between total instances or focus of staff activity and change in resident Global Functioning over the last six months occurred within the social-learning program, where both total activity ($r=0.71$), and instances of activity that focused on appropriate resident behavior ($r=0.77$) covaried with resident functioning. Although the proportion of staff activity focused upon crazy behavior remained exceptionally low, the slight decreases there were reflected the decreases in dangerous and aggressive Intolerable Behavior over the last six months in both programs ($r=0.86$). The stable differentiations between programs and comparative effectiveness found over every previous period were still apparent in parallel correlations over programs. Both areas of staff activity that occurred at higher levels in the social-learning program (responding to appropriate behavior and staff-initiated activity) continued to show covariation with higher levels of resident functioning ($r$'s$=0.92$ & $0.58$, respectively), while the two areas of focus that were higher in the milieu program were negatively related to levels of resident functioning ($r$'s$= -0.96$ & $-0.92$, respectively, for responding to inappropriate failures and inappropriate crazies). Similarly, in both programs, there was a significant negative correlation with total activity level ($r=-0.50$) and resident functioning, indicating the greater improvement of social-learning residents, concurrent with lower levels of total staff activity during the last six months. These correlations were representative of those that were obtained over the entire intramural period of nearly four and a half years between the focus of staff activity and unitwide levels of resident functioning ($r$'s in the $\pm 0.30$s to $\pm 0.80$s). Thus, during the last six months, staff maintained the high activity levels and the differential focus within programs at a stable rate before and after return to baseline conditions, with changes in resident functioning continuing to reflect parallel relationships to the focus of staff activity to those that had existed previously.

The attention received by an individual resident within the psychosocial units was reduced considerably upon the return to baseline conditions in both programs and returned to previous levels when the programs were reintroduced. Although the total staff and resident population remained constant over the period, the average number of residents for whom each staff member was responsible decreased slightly when baseline conditions began again on the milieu unit (to 16.4) and increased again upon the reintroduction of programmatic procedures (to 18.4). Opposite changes occurred on the social-learning unit; the average number of residents increased slightly during baseline 2 (to 17.3) and decreased again when the programs were reintroduced (to 16.2). The effect of the changes in focus of staff activity and the changes in activity level upon the return to baseline conditions and the reintroduction of programs for the average resident is shown in table 31.1.

The return to baseline procedures resulted in major decreases in both the number of

Table 31.1. Amount of staff attention residents received during return to baseline conditions and after reintroduction of programs.

| Focus of attention resident received | Probability of contact in 10 min. | | | | Average contacts per hour | | | | Average interactions per contact | | | |
|---|---|---|---|---|---|---|---|---|---|---|---|---|
| | Milieu | | Social-learning | | Milieu | | Social-learning | | Milieu | | Social-learning | |
| | Baseline | Program | Baseline | Program | Baseline | Program | Baseline | Program | Baseline | Program | Baseline | Program |
| As individual | 0.416 | 0.653 | 0.392 | 0.716 | 2.50 | 3.92 | 2.35 | 4.30 | 3.00 | 4.93 | 2.84 | 4.46 |
| As part of group | .095 | .088 | .103 | .047 | .57 | .53 | .62 | .28 | .68 | .67 | .75 | .29 |
| Total | .511 | .741 | .495 | .763 | 3.07 | 4.45 | 2.97 | 4.58 | 3.68 | 5.60 | 3.59 | 4.75 |

contacts and the amount of interaction residents received in both programs, with the majority of reductions occurring in individual, personalized contacts (compare to table 26.1). The reductions were to approximately equal levels on both units. However, the "probability of contact" figures in table 31.1 show that an individual resident on both units still had about a 40% chance of receiving a personalized, individual contact from a staff member during the average ten-minute-period during waking hours under baseline conditions—about double the amount provided in either the original operation of psychosocial programs or in the traditional hospital programs. The net effect on the total amount of "attention received" from staff (contacts x interactions) was a decrease during baseline to less than 41% of the prior level for milieu residents and to less than 54% of the prior level for social-learning residents; milieu residents continued to receive 6% more attention than social-learning residents did during baseline. The program reintroduction again increased the amount of attention an individual resident received to levels parallel to earlier ones, with the average milieu resident continuing to receive nearly 15% more staff attention than the average social-learning resident did over the last twenty weeks.

The nature of changes in staff behavior over the last six months are shown in figure 31.4, where the highest-frequency behaviors for both programs are plotted from the eighth through ninth anniversary assessment.[11] The staff behaviors plotted in the top section reveal that all highest-frequency behaviors were reduced upon the return to baseline conditions; there were increases in the lowest-frequency behaviors plotted, except for Positive Nonsocials in the milieu program, which remained nonexistent. The program reintroduction resulted in an immediate return of all staff behaviors in both programs to the levels existing before baseline conditions, with gradual increases continuing to occur in Positive Nonverbals and Positive Verbals in both programs and in Positive Nonsocials in the social-learning program, paralleling increases in resident functioning (r's in the 0.70s). Similarly, all of the high-frequency staff behaviors plotted in the middle section of figure 31.4 were reduced in frequency or remained nearly nonexistent upon the return to baseline conditions and immediately returned to stable performance at earlier levels upon the reintroduction of programmatic procedures.

Of the high-frequency staff behaviors plotted in the bottom section of figure 31.4, only Doing With in the milieu program and Reflect/Clarify in the social-learning program failed to change when baseline conditions began. Instruct/Demonstrate increased in both programs during baseline conditions and then returned to the stable performance of earlier levels when the programs were reintroduced. Reflect/Clarify in the milieu program and Doing With in the social-learning program decreased in frequency during baseline conditions, but Doing With took slightly longer to return to preexisting levels after reintroduction of programs, paralleling improvements in resident functioning (r's in the 0.70s & 0.80s).

Five additional classes of staff behavior showed notable change upon return to baseline conditions, but they are not plotted in figure 31.4 because of their overall low frequency. Negative Nonsocials and Suggest Alternatives functionally dropped out during baseline and then returned, and Negative Nonsocials returned to lower levels than before as a result of the decrease in assaultiveness. Ignore/No Response and Doing For both increased during baseline conditions and decreased upon the reintroduction of programs. Physical Force continued to account for only a fraction of a percentage of total staff-resident interaction in either program; it increased during baseline conditions on the milieu unit and remained stable on the social-learning unit. Even though the incidence of assault decreased during baseline conditions, the slightly greater use of Physical Force reflects the traditional modes of dealing with assaultive behavior (physical restraints, tepid baths, physical separation, and instruction) when time out and expulsion (Negative Nonsocials) were not used.

The success of the extended time of expulsion and time out as a consequence for assaultiveness over the last twenty weeks after the reintroduction of the programs had clear benefits for staff. During the last four weeks of the current period, Physical Force and Negative Nonsocials as a consequence for assaults revealed that the average staff member confronted an assaultive resident on twenty-eight occasions every hundred working hours in the social-learning program and on forty-nine occasions every hundred working hours in the milieu program. These rates of dealing with assaults were still high on an absolute level and considerably higher than the levels from before the original reduction in time of expulsion and time out two years earlier. However, they represent a reduction in the frequency with which an individual staff member had to deal with assaults to about half the level at the end of the previous year and a half in the social-learning program and about a third that in the milieu program, even though improved procedures had been in effect for only four months.

How well staff equated their performance during baseline conditions is shown in the average hourly rates of staff activity presented in table 31.2.[12] The changes in staff activity

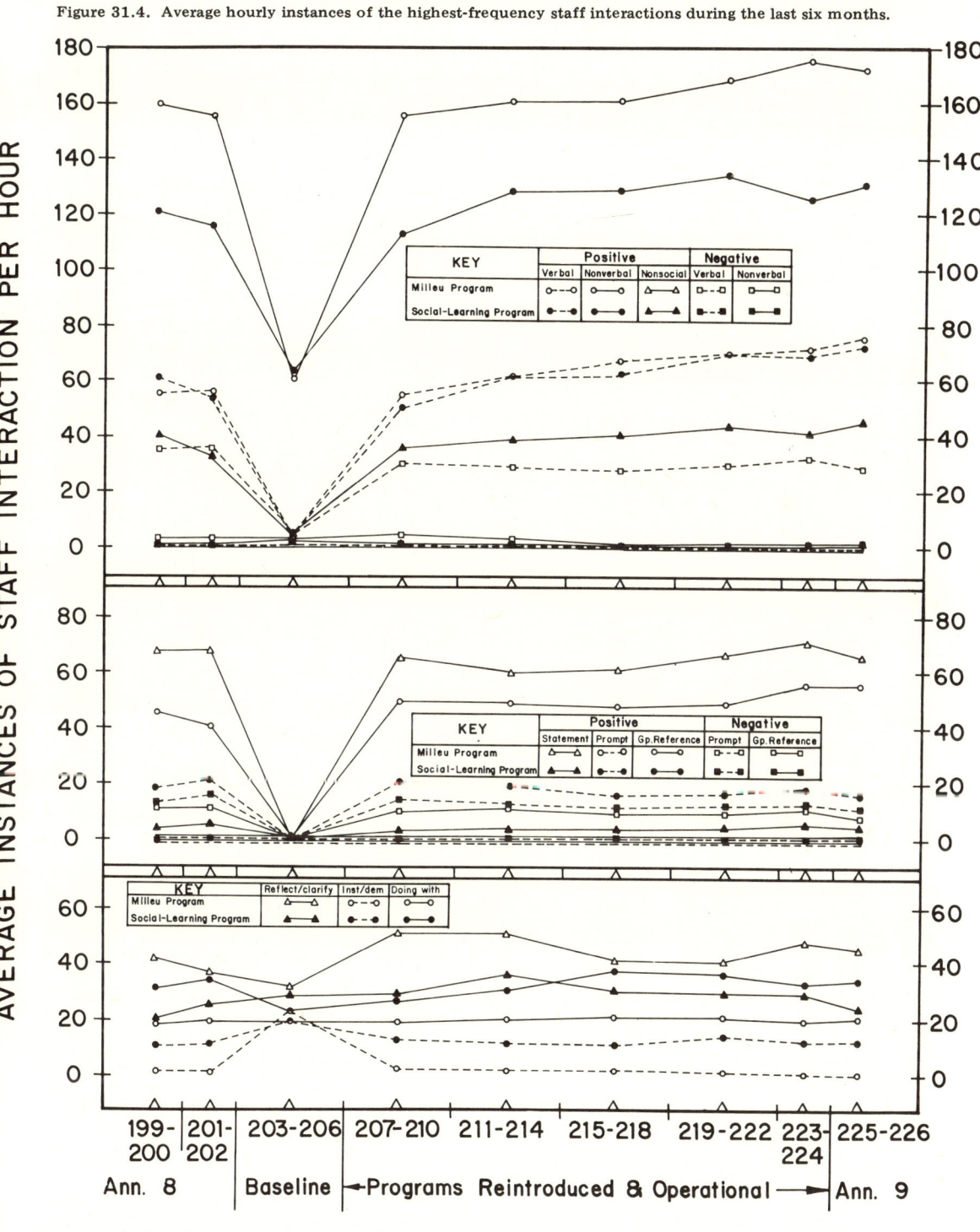

Figure 31.4. Average hourly instances of the highest-frequency staff interactions during the last six months.

Table 31.2. Average hourly rate of staff activity on psychosocial units during return to baseline conditions.

| | Resident behavior to which staff responded | | | | | | | | | | | | Total staff behavior | | % of interactions | | % of all staff error[c] | |
|---|---|---|---|---|---|---|---|---|---|---|---|---|---|---|---|---|---|---|
| | Appropriate | | Inappropriate Failure | | Inappropriate Crazy | | Request | | Neutral | | S.Lrng | | | | | | | |
| Staff behavior | Milieu | S.Lrng | Milieu | S.Lrng | Milieu | S.Lrng | Milieu | S.Lrng | Milieu | S.Lrng | Milieu | S.Lrng | Milieu | S.Lrng | Milieu | S.Lrng | Milieu | S.Lrng |
| Positive Verbal | 3.99+ | 5.08+ | - | - | 0.02- | - | - | o | o | o | | | 4.01 | 5.08 | 2.2% | 2.8% | | |
| Negative Verbal | - | 0.02- | 3.72+ | 2.50o | 1.66o | 0.94o | - | - | - | - | | | 5.38 | 3.46 | 2.9% | 1.9% | | 0.1% |
| Positive Nonverbal | 21.49+ | 25.95+ | 18.58o | 14.22o | 3.36o | 2.85- | 4.48o | 5.21o | 12.74o | 15.10o | | | 60.65 | 63.33 | 32.7% | 34.3% | 8.0% | 8.0% |
| Negative Nonverbal | 0.02- | 0.02- | 3.34o | 1.95o | 0.96o | 0.70o | o | o | 0.07- | - | | | 4.39 | 2.67 | 2.4% | 1.4% | 0.2% | 0.1% |
| Positive Nonsocial | 0.05- | + | - | - | - | - | 3.45o | 3.66o | 0.27o | 0.81o | | | 3.77 | 4.47 | 2.0% | 2.4% | 0.1% | |
| Negative Nonsocial | - | - | - | + | o | 0.04+ | + | - | - | - | | | | 0.04 | | | | |
| Positive Statement | 0.20o | 0.13o | 0.72+ | 0.41- | 0.07+ | 0.07- | + | o | 1.52+ | 1.98o | | | 2.51 | 2.59 | 1.4% | 1.4% | 0.2% | 0.2% |
| Negative Statement | - | - | - | - | - | - | - | - | 0.13- | 0.13- | | | 0.13 | 0.13 | | | 0.2% | 0.4% |
| Positive Prompt | 0.02- | 0.02+ | - | + | 0.02- | + | - | + | - | + | | | 0.04 | 0.02 | 0.1% | | | |
| Negative Prompt | - | - | - | - | 0.02- | o | - | o | - | o | | | 0.02 | 0.02 | | | | |
| Positive Gp. Reference | + | o | + | 0.04o | + | - | + | o | 0.02+ | 0.04o | | | 0.02 | 0.04 | | | | 0.1% |
| Negative Gp. Reference | - | - | - | - | + | o | + | - | o | - | | | | | | | | |
| Reflect/Clarify | 7.27+ | 7.46o | 19.52o | 16.27o | 0.80+ | 0.72o | 0.18+ | 0.13o | 4.30+ | 4.04+ | | | 32.07 | 28.62 | 17.3% | 15.5% | | |
| Suggest Alternatives | + | o | + | o | + | - | + | + | + | o | | | | 0.02 | | | | |
| Instruct/Demonstrate | 3.76o | 4.72+ | 13.81o | 10.18o | 1.55o | 1.19o | 0.09o | 0.05o | 4.54o | 5.60o | | | 23.75 | 21.74 | 12.8% | 11.8% | 26.1% | 19.3% |
| Doing With | 12.51+ | 15.03+ | 0.07- | 0.04- | 0.83- | 0.86- | 0.69o | 1.03o | 5.62+ | 6.77+ | | | 19.72 | 23.73 | 10.6% | 12.9% | 1.7% | 2.5% |
| Doing For | 0.09- | 0.13o | 1.27- | 0.76- | - | 0.04- | 0.78- | 0.63o | 0.25- | 0.13o | | | 2.39 | 1.69 | 1.3% | 0.9% | 3.0% | 2.1% |
| Physical Force | - | - | 0.51o | 0.27o | 0.22o | 0.27o | - | - | - | - | | | 0.73 | 0.54 | 0.4% | 0.3% | | |
| Ignore/No Response | 14.91- | 19.28- | 10.59- | 6.41+ | 0.40- | 0.59+ | 0.05- | 0.02- | 10.39- | 11.14- | | | 36.34 | 37.44 | 19.6%[a] | 20.3%[a] | 68.6% | 85.3% |
| Announce | b | b | b | b | b | b | b | b | 1.99+ | 2.07+ | | | 1.99 | 2.07 | (0.8%) | (0.9%) | b | b |
| Attend/Record/Observe | b | b | b | b | b | b | b | b | 46.52+ | 45.35+ | | | 46.52 | 45.35 | (19.0%) | (18.7%) | b | b |
| Total interactions | 64.31 | 77.84 | 72.13 | 53.05 | 9.91 | 8.29 | 9.72 | 10.75 | 29.46 | 34.56 | | | 185.53 | 184.49 | 106%[a] | 106%[a] | 28.6% | 0.0% |
| % correct interactions[c] | 76.5% | 75.2% | 64.3% | 97.6% | 87.0% | 53.9% | 99.5% | 99.8% | 63.2%[a] | 67.4%[a] | | | 71.4% | 80.7% | b | b | 0.0% | 0.0% |
| Total activity | b | b | b | b | b | b | b | b | 88.36 | 93.12 | | | 244.43 | 243.05 | (132%) | (132%) | b | b |

Note. If programmatic procedures had been in effect: + = specifically programmed staff behavior; o = allowable staff choice; - = programmatic error. Empty cells signify less than 0.0045 instances per hour.
a. "Ignore-neutral" included in percentage figures, but not in total interactions.
b. Irrelevant cells.
c. If programmatic procedures had been in effect.

Table 31.3. Average hourly rate of staff activity on psychosocial units after reintroduction of programs.

| | Resident behavior to which staff responded | | | | | | | | | | | | | | | | |
|---|---|---|---|---|---|---|---|---|---|---|---|---|---|---|---|---|---|
| | Appropriate | | Inappropriate Failure | | Inappropriate Crazy | | Request | | Neutral | | Total staff behavior | | % of interactions | | % of all staff error | | |
| Staff behavior | Milieu | S.Lrng | Milieu | S.Lrng | Milieu | S.Lrng | Milieu | S.Lrng | Milieu | S.Lrng | Milieu | S.Lrng | Milieu | S.Lrng | Milieu | S.Lrng | |
| Positive Verbal | 66.15+ | 63.11+ | 0.10- | 0.04- | - | - | 0.06o | 0.01o | o | o | 66.32 | 63.16 | 14.4% | 17.9% | 4.5% | 3.2% | |
| Negative Verbal | 0.05- | 0.01- | 23.38+ | 0.71o | 5.74+ | 0.02o | - | - | - | - | 29.17 | 0.75 | 6.4% | 0.2% | 2.3% | 1.0% | |
| Positive Nonverbal | 73.59+ | 75.81+ | 60.74o | 23.00o | 6.38+ | 0.49- | 2.61o | 1.58o | 21.07o | 25.28o | 164.39 | 126.16 | 35.8% | 35.9% | 2.3% | 36.2% | |
| Negative Nonverbal | - | - | 1.69- | 0.39o | 0.39- | 0.03o | o | o | 0.01- | - | 2.09 | 0.42 | 0.5% | 0.1% | 0.5% | 0.2% | |
| Positive Nonsocial | 0.05+ | 40.80+ | - | 0.04- | 0.48o | - | 1.26o | 0.02o | 0.10o | 0.03o | 1.41 | 40.89 | 0.3% | 11.6% | 2.3% | 2.9% | |
| Negative Nonsocial | - | - | 0.04+ | 1.84+ | 0.13+ | 0.13+ | 0.03+ | o | - | - | 0.55 | 1.98 | 0.1% | 0.6% | 3.2% | 0.4% | |
| Positive Statement | 3.38+ | 0.19o | 50.66+ | 0.18- | 2.11+ | - | 0.13+ | o | 7.82+ | 3.65o | 64.10 | 4.02 | 14.0% | 1.1% | 13.0% | |
| Negative Statement | - | - | - | - | - | - | - | - | - | - | | | | | 0.1% | 0.5% | |
| Positive Prompt | - | 2.64+ | - | 13.83+ | - | 0.01+ | - | + | - | 1.29+ | 0.02 | 17.78 | | 5.1% | 0.9% | 5.1% | |
| Negative Prompt | 0.04- | 0.04- | 0.01+ | 12.10+ | 0.01- | 0.34+ | o | o | - | 0.03- | 49.68 | 12.51 | 10.8% | 3.6% | | | |
| Positive Gp. Reference | 6.10+ | - | 35.05+ | 0.06o | 0.13+ | - | 0.05+ | o | 8.35+ | 0.22o | | 0.22 | | 0.1% | | | |
| Negative Gp. Reference | - | - | 8.41+ | - | 1.65+ | o | + | o | o | - | 10.07 | 0.06 | 2.2% | | | | |
| Reflect/Clarify | 5.86+ | 6.54o | 31.05+ | 14.91o | 0.80+ | 0.03o | 0.28+ | 0.24o | 7.23+ | 8.06o | 45.22 | 29.78 | 9.8% | 8.5% | | | |
| Suggest Alternatives | 0.08+ | 0.06o | 1.95+ | 0.27o | + | - | + | o | 0.01+ | o | 2.04 | 0.33 | 0.4% | 0.1% | | | |
| Instruct/Demonstrate | 0.41o | 2.11- | 0.43- | 5.76o | 0.04o | 0.19o | 0.02o | 0.06o | 0.92+ | 4.69o | 1.82 | 12.81 | 0.4% | 3.6% | 19.5% | 0.4% | |
| Doing With | 10.07+ | 17.80+ | - | - | - | - | 0.81o | 0.93o | 9.69+ | 14.71+ | 20.57 | 33.45 | 4.5% | 9.5% | 10.4% | 4.5% | |
| Doing For | 0.15- | 0.15o | 0.07- | 0.06- | - | - | 0.34o | 0.52o | 0.01- | 0.03o | 0.57 | 0.77 | 0.1% | 0.2% | | | |
| Physical Force | - | - | 0.02o | 0.49o | 0.08o | 0.05o | - | - | - | - | 0.10 | 0.55 | | 0.2% | | | |
| Ignore/No Response | 0.71- | 0.30- | 0.30- | 4.02+ | 0.08- | 1.93+ | - | - | 0.15- | 0.14- | 1.24 | 6.39 | 0.3%[a] | 1.8%[a] | 56.1% | 32.4% | |
| Announce | b | b | b | b | b | b | b | b | 4.30+ | 2.16+ | 4.30 | 2.16 | (0.8%) | (0.5%) | b | b | |
| Attend/Record/Observe | b | b | b | b | b | b | b | b | 49.96+ | 54.13+ | 49.96 | 54.13 | (9.7%) | (13.3%) | b | b | |
| Total interactions | 166.60 | 209.56 | 213.91 | 77.70 | 17.91 | 3.24 | 5.60 | 3.38 | 55.21 | 57.99 | 459.23 | 351.87 | 100%[a] | 100%[a] | 0.5% | 0.4% | |
| % correct interactions | 99.4% | 99.8% | 99.6% | 99.6% | 99.4% | 84.9% | 99.4% | 100% | 99.7%[a] | 99.7%[a] | 99.5% | 99.6% | b | b | 0.0% | 0.0% | |
| Total activity | b | b | b | b | b | b | b | b | 109.62 | 114.43 | 513.64 | 408.31 | (112%) | (116%) | b | b | |

Note. + = specifically programmed staff behavior; o = allowable staff choice; - = programmatic error. Empty cells signify less than 0.0045 instances per hour.
a. "Ignore-neutral" included in percentage figures, but not in total interactions.
b. Irrelevant cells.

upon the return to baseline resulted in staff's doing an excellent job of equating their performance over the two units. Both total interactions and total staff activivy were functionally identical, with the instances of specific staff behavior being distributed in parallel order for both level and proportion over units. Compared to staff performance under original baseline conditions, the proportions of each class of staff behavior were distributed similarly, except that Ignore/No Response was lower during the second baseline, with corresponding increases in Positive Nonverbals and Reflect/Clarify. The continuing high rates of these two classes of staff behavior during the second baseline suggest some carry-over of the previous intense focus upon increasing those components of interaction.

Compared to the distribution of staff behavior during the sample of the traditional hospital programs, the second psychosocial baseline was even closer to the actual performance of traditional programs than the first had been. The highest incidence of staff behavior in both traditional programs and the second psychosocial baseline condition were Positive Nonverbals and Attend/Record/Observe. Instruct/Demonstrate and Doing With similarly accounted for a significant proportion of staff interactions. Ignore/No Response and Reflect/Clarify were relatively high-frequency staff behaviors in both the second psychosocial baseline and the traditional hospital programs; however, traditional hospital staff showed relatively lower proportions of these two and a correspondingly higher incidence of Doing For. Thus, the actual staff behavior on psychosocial units during the return to baseline was exceptionally well equated and was much closer to traditional hospital procedures than to either of the psychosocial programs.

How well staff differentiated their performance of the psychosocial programs during the twenty weeks after the reintroduction of programmatic procedures is indicated by the average hourly rates of staff activity presented in table 31.3. As suggested earlier, comparisons of these rates of staff interactions during baseline (table 31.2) with the average hourly rates during the last twenty weeks of program operation (table 31.3) show that every program-specific interaction changed in desired directions when the programmatic procedures were reintroduced. An inspection of table 31.3 shows that staff not only changed behavior drastically from baseline conditions but returned to differentiation of performance within and between programs nearly identical to that of the previous year and a half (table 26.2).

Differences in the average hourly rates between programs were significant over the last twenty weeks on nineteen of the twenty-one classes of staff behavior, with all of the differences being like those of earlier periods. As before, Negative Statements were totally inappropriate in both programs and occurred with an equal frequency of less than one instance every two weeks during all staff working hours. Doing For was differentially allowable between programs and had not differed previously in the relative percentage of total interactions. During the last twenty weeks, Doing For also did not differ between programs in average frequency of occurrence, as a result of decreasing the incidence of inappropriately doing things for residents that they should do themselves in the milieu program. The only other difference between programs during this period that was not an identical relationship to those of the previous year and a half involved Positive Nonverbals. As before, their average incidence continued to be higher when staff worked in the milieu program; however, the slight decrease in total interactions in the milieu program and the slight increase in the social-learning program resulted in an equal proportion of Positive Nonverbals between programs over the last twenty weeks. As before, the total interaction rate and total activity level remained significantly higher in the milieu program than in the social-learning program over the entire period.

Physical Force, Announce, and Attend/Record/Observe continued to occur at significantly different rates, as they had over the previous three and a half years, even though differentiation was not required by the respective treatment manuals. Physical Force occurred at exceptionally low rates in both programs but was consistently more frequent in the social-learning program. The within-cell distribution in table 31.3 shows that the overall incidence of Physical Force required to deal with assaults (shown as "inappropriate-crazy") was considerably reduced in both programs, reflecting the success of the more effective procedures in reducing the frequency of assaultiveness. The relatively higher incidence of Physical Force in the social-learning program for "inappropriate-failures" reflected the occasional need for physical contact in the application of brief time out as a consequence of resident failures. However, even in its most frequent use, Physical Force still accounted for fewer than 0.2% of staff-resident interactions. Announce continued to occur at significantly higher rates in the milieu program, again reflecting the staff practice of making separate and sequential announcements for each living group, while general announcements were made in the social-learning program. Similarly the significantly lower levels of Attend/Record/Observe in the milieu program continued to indicate the higher rates of interaction, which left little time for observation without interaction in the milieu program. The slightly higher total instances of this class of behavior in both programs over the last twenty weeks also reflects the paperwork required by continuing preparations for hospital accreditation of the institution and by the purchase-eligibility procedure for payments on standing fines in the social-learning program and for the longer periods of time out and expulsion.

As before, all remaining differences in staff performance over the last twenty weeks followed the differential requirements specified in the respective treatment manuals. Thus, seven of the eight classes of staff behavior that continued to be performed at higher rates in the milieu program than in the social-learning program were differentially specified in the Milieu Manual. The seven classes included milieu procedures that were to be applied at all times across all classes of resident behavior (Positive Statement, Positive Nonverbal, Positive Group Reference, Reflect/Clarify, Suggest Alternatives), and those specifying the nature of contact for responding to inappropriate resident behavior (Negative Verbal, Negative Group Reference). Positive Verbals were not differentially noted in respective treatment manuals as to rate but were required in both programs. As before, the absolute frequency of Positive Verbals was slightly higher in the milieu program but remained as a lower proportion of total interactions (again, the only class of staff behavior to show a reversal between rate and percentage). When all of the above behaviors are taken into account, nearly 94% of all staff-resident interactions on the milieu unit after the reintroduction of programs involved specific procedures detailed for milieu therapy.

Negative Nonverbals decreased in frequency from the incidence during baseline and continued to be performed at a significantly higher rate in the milieu program than in the social-learning program over the last twenty weeks, even though no differential requirements were specified. Analyses of SRIC sequences again provided evidence that negative affect for staff was likely to have been generated and communicated as a result of intense focus on inappropriate resident behavior in the milieu program. Over the last twenty weeks, staff averaged over fifty-six instances of positive statements and negative feedback per hour in response to inappropriate resident behavior in the milieu program, but these procedures were effective in terminating inappropriate behavior only 55% of the time. On the average, the same inappropriate resident behavior continued to occur on 25.58 occasions per hour, and staff appropriately continued to provide additional positive statements and negative feedback on 25.42 occasions. Thus, staff were exceptionally reliable in staying with programmatic interactions, and it is remarkable that negative affects accounted for only 0.5% of staff-resident interactions, given such high-intensity focus on continuing inappropriate behavior.

As on all previous occasions over nearly four years of prior operation, the three classes of staff behavior that continued to account for the highest proportion of interactions on the social-learning unit after the reintroduction of the program consisted of positive social and nonsocial behaviors (Positive Verbal, Positive Nonverbal, Positive Nonsocial); the fourth highest rate consisted of shared social activity (Doing With). (See table 31.3.) While all of these classes of behavior except Positive Nonverbals regularly accounted for a significantly greater proportion of staff-resident interactions in the social-learning program than in the milieu program, differences in application continued to be apparent for Positive Nonverbals as well. Fewer than 45% of Positive Nonverbals in the milieu program were contingent upon appropriate resident behavior, but over 60% continued to be so in the social-learning program. Similarly, over 53% of Doing With continued to be contingent upon appropriate resident behavior in the social-learning program rather than being staff initiated. Thus, the within-cell distribution of these behaviors in table 31.3 shows that over 56% of all staff-resident interactions in the social-learning program over the last twenty weeks were accounted for by positive social and material reinforcement contingent upon appropriate resident behavior.

The five remaining classes of staff behavior in table 31.3 were performed at significantly higher rates in the social-learning program than in the milieu program over the last twenty weeks. These behaviors continued to be those that were differentially specified by the Social-Learning Manual for dealing with inappropriate resident behavior and/or initiating new or different resident behaviors (Negative Nonsocial, Positive Prompt, Negative Prompt, Instruct/Demonstrate, Ignore/No Response). Even though the levels of Negative Nonsocials, Positive Prompts, and Negative Prompts were somewhat reduced during this period of improved resident functioning, the low absolute frequency of Ignore/No Response was notable. Analyses of SRIC sequences on instances in which active ignoring was a required staff response found that the basis for low rates of Ignore/No Response was, once again, the success of prompts in changing resident behavior. Staff averaged over twenty-six prompts per hour for inappropriate resident behavior over the last twenty weeks, and the prompts were effective in changing behavior more than 98%

of the time. A prompted inappropriate behavior continued, on the average, on only thirty-five occasions every hundred hours, and staff properly ignored that behavior on thirty-two of thirty-five occasions. Thus, staff continued to be quite reliable in applying active ignoring when it was required, but the success of other social-learning procedures resulted in an even more restricted number of instances in which Ignore/No Response was the only appropriate staff behavior.

These differences between programs demonstrate that actual staff performance after the reintroduction of programmatic procedures clearly differentiated between programs on the basis of requirements specified in the respective program manuals in the same manner as during the previous year and a half. Table 31.3 also shows that the remarkable within-program accuracy in staff performance of the social-learning program was once again maintained over the last twenty weeks, with 99.6% of all staff-resident interactions following specified procedures. Additionally the slight changes in the milieu program improved the accuracy of staff performance to the extent that 99.5% of all staff-resident interactions in the program followed specified procedures—no longer differing significantly from the accuracy of performance of the social-learning program.

Such low rates of error in both programs nearly preclude meaningful analyses of sources of error. However, the distribution of staff errors in table 31.3 shows that inappropriate Ignore/No Response once again accounted for a considerable proportion of error in both programs, and inappropriate Positive Nonverbals in the social-learning program and inappropriate Instruct/Demonstrate in the milieu program still continued to be major contributors to error. Of social-learning errors, 49.3% consisted of misapplication of milieu therapy procedures in the social-learning program, and 82.3% of milieu errors continued to involve misapplication of social-learning procedures in the milieu program. Overall, however, these errors resulted in fewer than 0.4% of all staff-resident interactions in the milieu program and fewer than 0.2% in the social-learning program involving spillover of procedures from one program to the other.

Thus, actual staff performance not only continued to differentiate between programs in the same manner as during the previous year and a half, but the absolute accuracy of performance maintained the exceptional levels achieved earlier, without differences between programs over the last twenty weeks. The procedures and distribution of both programs followed the specifications from the respective program manuals and continued to reflect the ideal distribution of technique utilization from the TOS. The high levels of performance of all positive social interactions and nonverbal responses in both programs continued to reflect the genuine rather than mechanical application of treatment procedures, with both programs remaining correctly applied after the reintroduction of programmatic procedures. The consistency in actual performance of programs over the last twenty weeks with that of the prior two years clearly implicates the specific structural changes as the basis for the decline in functioning over the previous year and a half and the renewed effectiveness upon the reintroduction of programmatic procedures during the last six months.

Several significant within-program correlations between average instances of each class of staff behavior and unitwide levels of resident functioning over standard time blocks were described earlier. In addition, the stable differentiation between programs and comparative effectiveness found over the previous three and a half years was again apparent in parallel correlations over programs during the last six months. All but three classes of staff behavior that differed between programs also yielded significant correlations with changes in unitwide resident Global Functioning. Positive Verbals, Positive Nonverbals (r's in the 0.70s$_1$, and Ignore/No Response (r=-0.64) were significantly correlated only within the social-learning program. Otherwise the correlations continued to reflect higher levels of resident functioning to covary with all staff behaviors that occurred at higher rates in the social-learning program (mdn. r=0.82, range 0.63 to 0.94) and to be negatively related to all staff behaviors that occurred at higher rates in the milieu program (mdn. r=-0.84, range -0.66 to -0.89). The correlations over the last six months were representative of those that had been obtained over the entire intramural period of nearly four and a half years between unitwide levels of resident functioning and the relative proportion of specific classes of staff behaviors performed (r's in the ± 0.20s to ± 0.70s). Thus, actual staff performance was in keeping with prescribed programmatic procedures and continued to be differentially related to resident functioning over the last six months in the same manner as at previous time periods.

In summary, objective data from the SRIC show remarkable stability in the reliability and differentiation of actual staff behavior over the last six months, with clear changes occurring during the return to baseline conditions. At that time reductions in the rate of staff-resident interactions and total staff activity occurred with changes in the focus of staff activities and the distribution of specific staff behavior. The changes involved virtually every program-specific class of staff behavior, to the extent that actual staff behavior on the psychosocial units was exceptionally well equated during the second baseline. In fact, the approximation to the traditional hospital programs was even better than under original baseline conditions, although both baseline conditions were much closer to traditional hospital procedures than to either psychosocial program. When programmatic procedures were reintroduced, the total instances of activity, staff-resident interactions, and differential focus of staff activities returned to earlier levels and remained nearly identical to those existing over the previous two years. Over the last six months, then, staff maintained the high activity levels and differential focus at a stable rate before and after the return to equated baseline conditions, with changes in resident functioning continuing to reflect relationships to the focus of staff activity parallel to previous ones.

Even though the number of residents and staffing ratios remained constant over baseline conditions—with the same staff equated in time spent on each unit—the return to baseline resulted in a major decrease in the attention residents received to equal levels over the two units. However, even under baseline, psychosocial residents were still receiving considerably more attention from staff than they had during the original eighteen weeks of program operation nearly four years earlier. Upon the reintroduction of psychosocial programs the attention individual residents received increased to levels parallel to those existing earlier. Over the last twenty weeks, the average milieu resident continued to receive about 15% more staff attention than the average social-learning resident did—even though the social-learning procedures clearly continued to be more effective. As before, these differences continue to document that how much attention was received was not as important as how the attention received came about.

The actual differentiation of staff performance in the psychosocial programs during the twenty weeks following the reintroduction of programmatic procedures continued to be remarkable. Every program-specific interaction changed in desired directions, and changes in staff behavior continued to be differentially related to resident functioning over the last six months in the same manner as during previous time periods. The greater effectiveness of consequences for assaultiveness were evident in the frequency with which a staff member was required to confront an assaultive resident, which was reduced by about a half and a third, respectively, in the social-learning and milieu programs by the last anniversary assessment. Over the last twenty weeks, all other staff behaviors were essentially identical to those of the previous two years; both the focus and the rate of performance of specific classes of staff behavior continued to be in keeping with the differential requirements specified in the respective treatment manuals.

When working in the milieu program over the last twenty weeks, staff performed all milieu-specific interactions at a significantly higher rate than they did when working in the social-learning program. The accuracy of performance continued to be exceptional; 99.5% of all staff-resident interactions in the milieu program were correct. When working in the social-learning program at this time, staff not only performed social-learning-specific procedures at a significantly higher rate than they did when working in the milieu program, but 99.6% of all staff-resident interactions were appropriate on an absolute level. Staff errors in both programs were nearly nonexistent, with the inappropriate spillover of techniques from one program to the other occurring on fewer than 0.4% and 0.2% of all staff-resident interactions, respectively, in the milieu and social-learning programs. The distribution of relative proportions of staff-resident interactions in both programs were not only accurate in absolute terms but followed the procedures from the respective program manuals and continued to reflect the ideal distributions of technique utilization from the TOS. Thus, staff maintained their performance of both programs with remarkable consistency upon the reintroduction of programmatic procedures, with clear and reliable differentiation of programs and levels of accuracy that left little room for improvement.

## SUMMARY

Staff attitudes, opinions, and beliefs about mental patients again changed over the last six months. As on previous assessments, changes in OMI scores appeared to reflect staff response to changes in resident behavior—decreases in assaultiveness and improvements in functioning following the reintroduction of treatment programs—without staff attitudes having any notable reciprocal effect on residents. Some OMI scores were more responsive to differential experience than others. At the last anniversary assessment, OMI scores continued to cluster in the same way as at the previous assessment, with similar predictability from individual staff characteristics. Over the last six months, as well as the entire intramural period, the staff group as a whole continued to reflect the ideal assumptions underlying the psychosocial programs and remained much closer to psychosocial ideals than to those of typical mental hospital staff.

Opinions and interpretations of the treatment programs again showed remarkable consistency over the last six months. Staff beliefs of the comparative effectiveness of the psychosocial programs continued to reflect the objective results accurately. The great majority of staff continued to judge the social-learning program to be both more effective and more enjoyable, although the margin of preference declined slightly over the last six months, following the renewed effectiveness of both programs. Throughout the entire intramural period of nearly four and a half years, staff opinions thus appeared to be responsive to prior changes in resident behavior but had no notable effect on the ensuing response of residents to the programs.

Preferred TOS attitude scores—reflecting staff preference for the nature of treatment programs—remained constant and well differentiated over the last six months. As at all earlier assessments, staff preferences for the nature of treatment programs remained closer to the ideal milieu program than to the ideal social-learning program. Preferred attitude scores continued to show little clustering and little predictability from individual staff characteristics but indicated significant relationships to some OMI scores at the last anniversary assessment. The level of endorsement of TOS attitude scores for each program orientation—reflecting staff interpretation of the nature of each psychosocial program—showed only one slight differential change over the last six months. Overall the pattern and level of TOS attitude scores remained essentially constant, with the nature of programs continuing to be differentially interpreted and quite close to the ideals underlying each program.

Preferred TOS technique scores—indicating staff preferences for the use of different treatment procedures—also remained constant and well differentiated over the last six months. As at all earlier assessments, staff preferences for specific treatment techniques remained closer to those of the ideal social-learning program than to those of the ideal milieu program. Preferred technique scores once again showed greater clustering at the last anniversary assessment than at the previous assessment, with several significant relationships to OMI scores. Preferred techniques remained almost totally unrelated to individual staff characteristics. TOS technique scores for each program orientation—reflecting staff interpretation of appropriate technique utilization within each psychosocial program—showed no differential change over the last six months, although the endorsed level of utilization of all techniques in both programs increased slightly. Staff continued to differentiate between milieu and social-learning programs in the desired directions, with the slight increases over the last six months moving the level of technique endorsement even closer to the ideals of both treatment programs. As at all previous assessments, the level and pattern of technique interpretation remained closer to the ideal within the social-learning orientation, but differences in the approximation to respective ideals were not significant over the last six months. Thus, staff interpretations of both the nature and techniques continued to differentiate psychosocial orientations in desired directions without notable change over the last six months, with staff preferences continuing to be much closer to either psychosocial orientation than to those of mental hospital staff.

More important for determining actual operation and differentiation of treatment conditions within and between programs are the objective data from the SRIC. Virtually every program-specific class of staff behavior, as well as total activity and total staff-resident interactions, changed upon the return to baseline conditions, when residents on the two units again received essentially identical programs. The approximation to traditional hospital programs was even better during the second baseline than under original baseline conditions, although both baseline conditions were much closer to traditional hospital procedures than to either psychosocial program. Although the number of residents and staffing ratios remained constant, the return resulted in a major decrease in the amount of attention individual residents received. Even so, the attention received by individual residents remained considerably greater than that received during the original eighteen weeks of program operation, when rapid improvements were first obtained.

Upon the reintroduction of programs after the second baseline, every program-specific class of staff behavior changed in desired directions, with changes in staff behavior continuing to be differentially related to resident functioning over the last six months in the same manner as at previous time periods. Total instances of activity, level of staff-resident interactions, and differential focus and distribution of all classes of staff behavior returned to earlier levels for the last twenty weeks of the intramural period, remaining nearly identical to those existing over the previous two years. The greater effectiveness of procedures for controlling assaultiveness was apparent in the frequency with which individual staff were required to confront an assaultive resident, which was reduced by a half and a third, respectively, in the social-learning and milieu programs by the end of the period. Both the focus and rate of performance of all other staff behaviors reflected the same differentiations as at previous time periods. The attention individual residents received in each program returned to earlier levels when programmatic procedures were reintroduced. While the same staff continued to equate time and activity focus over psychosocial programs, the higher interaction rates in the milieu program continued to provide the average milieu resident with more staff attention than the average social-learning resident received. As before, the higher levels of attention concurrent with lower levels of improvement in groups which were once equated, continued to document that how attention was applied was more important than how much was received.

The differentiation of staff performance in the two psychosocial programs over the last twenty weeks continued to be remarkable. The focus of staff activity, the rate of specific classes of staff behavior, and the resident behavior x staff behavior match were once again in keeping with the differential requirements specified in the respective treatment manuals, with the exceptional levels of accuracy in execution being maintained. Milieu procedures continued to be performed at differentially higher rates when staff worked in the milieu program, and social-learning procedures continued to be performed at differentially higher rates when staff worked in the social-learning program. On an absolute level, 99.5% of all staff-resident interactions in the milieu program and 99.6% of all staff-resident interactions in the social-learning program were correct over the twenty weeks following the reintroduction of programmatic procedures. Errors were nearly nonexistent in both programs, and the inappropriate spillover of techniques from one program to the other was less than 0.4% in the worst instance. The distributions of relative proportions of staff-resident interactions in both programs paralleled the ideals in the respective treatment manuals and on the TOS. Overall, staff maintained their performance of both programs with remarkable consistency after the reintroduction of programmatic procedures, with clear and reliable differentiation and exceptionally high levels of accuracy.

Analyses of staff attitudes and performance over the last six months again provide interesting information on staff and the nature of events to which they responded. More important, however, is the clear documentation of the equivalency of conditions upon the return to baseline, and the continued differentiation of treatment programs according to prescribed procedures when the programs were reintroduced and the changes made. The consistency of actual performance over the last twenty weeks with that of the prior two years, combined with the equivalency of other sources of influence, including psychotropic drugs, establishes the specific structural changes introduced during this period as the basis for renewed effectiveness of the programs, while the differential effectiveness of the two programs remained a clear function of the differential treatment procedures applied.

## 32. Summary of Findings for the Last Six Months

The programs continued to be carried out without change for the first two weeks of the current period; then baseline conditions were reintroduced for four weeks, followed by a reintroduction of programs with procedural changes for the last twenty weeks. All required assessments were maintained, with volunteers, facilities and services, consumables, and material goods available at levels established earlier. The full clinical complement of staff was working from the introduction of baseline procedures through the end of the period. The reorganization of senior staff and the supplementary staff for the planned expansion to prechronic populations and demonstration-training functions allowed extra paperwork required for hospital accreditation to be accomplished without weakening the staffing of the ongoing programs. Additionally community contacts for the expanded operation and final location and arrangements for centralized beds in extended-care facilities to accept improved residents were carried out by these staff during this time.

Baseline conditions introduced were like those of the original baseline, except more resources were available and psychotropic drugs were administered to very few residents, with drug utilization being held constant over the last six months. The reintroduction of programs involved procedural changes based upon an analysis of problems and substudies from the previous year and a half. For the last twenty weeks of the period, psychosocial programs were continued in accordance with all details specified in the treatment manuals, but with changes related to food service and meals in both programs, implementation of the purchase-eligibility procedure for accumulated token fines in the social-learning program, and the changes in the consequences for assaults in both programs. The change to a longer period of time out or expulsion as a consequence for assaultiveness was the primary procedural change, since the earlier reduction in these consequences had been largely responsible for the decline in effectiveness of both psychosocial programs over the previous year and a half.

The outcome data reported in chapter 29 clearly show that the corrective procedural changes included upon the reintroduction of programs reversed the trends of the previous year and a half, leading to a renewal of effectiveness for both psychosocial programs. Although the twenty weeks remaining after the reintroduction was not enough time for either program to achieve the levels of overall functioning that had been attained before the original reduction in assaultive-behavior consequences, improvements were occurring to the extent that the milieu group once again approached significant overall improvement from original pretreatment levels. The continuous objective assessments found that the social-learning program continued to show major improvement on an absolute level, and significantly greater improvement than the milieu program over the entire period—including greater generalized improvement during the second baseline and greater numbers of residents improving after the reintroduction of programmatic procedures.

At the last anniversary assessment, the improvement of social-learning residents was totally unrelated to any individual resident characteristic, initial level of disturbance or level of functioning, or drug status at any time during the intramural period. The only significant relationship with improvement for milieu residents still showed a tendency for improved residents to be those with relatively shorter lengths of hospitalization. Thus, both programs showed renewed effectiveness, but the social-learning program was clearly superior to the milieu program in improving overall functioning of the severely debilitated chronic groups, without regard to any differential characteristics of residents or problems.

Although the trends of the previous year and a half were reversed for all classes of behavior, further differentiation of effectiveness did occur. Both programs produced additional reductions in all classes of maladaptive behavior after the reintroduction of programs. The most dramatic changes occurred in the reduction of dangerous and aggressive acts, which remained higher than the level from before the original program introduction but had been reduced to about a third that existing at the beginning of the current period. Only four residents in each program accounted for the majority of incidents of aggressive intolerable behavior, and those residents had shown improvement in other areas. As at all prior assessments, social-learning procedures were significantly more effective in controlling dangerous and aggressive acts; the milieu program—even with the longer expulsion time—remained largely ineffective in controlling assaultive behavior on an absolute level.

By the last anniversary assessment, both programs produced significant reductions, with equal effectiveness, in dysfunctional cognitive behaviors and hostile-belligerence. Residents in the milieu program also showed significant reductions in the highest-frequency bizarre motoric, clinically crazy behaviors, and the social-learning program showed even greater effectiveness with this class of maladaptive behavior. The social-learning program produced significant reductions in grossly inappropriate responses to minimal expectations, with differentially greater effectiveness than the milieu program. Thus, milieu procedures were as effective as social-learning procedures on only two of five classes of maladaptive behavior. The overall outcome for the crucial target area for rehabilitation of the chronically institutionalized population—reduction or elimination of extreme bizarre behavior—clearly found the social-learning program to be differentially more effective.

Even greater differential effectiveness was apparent between programs with regard to classes of adaptive behavior. Although the reintroduction of programs with corrective procedural changes had reversed the earlier trends for all classes of adaptive behavior, by the last anniversary assessment the milieu program had produced and maintained significant increases from pretreatment in only one class of adaptive behavior—resident self-care. Although improvements were again occurring in the milieu program in other areas of adaptive functioning over the last twenty weeks, none were significantly higher than original levels by the last anniversary assessment. In contrast, by the last anniversary assessment, the social-learning program had effected significant and dramatic increases in all four components of adaptive behavior—concurrent appropriate behavior, interpersonal skills, self-care, and instrumental role performance—with differentially greater effectiveness than the milieu program in all classes. Thus, the crucial target areas of resocialization and improvement of instrumental role performance, as well as concurrent appropriate behavior, were effectively treated by the social-learning program, and more so than by the milieu program.

The characteristics of other ongoing resident activity over the last six months, reported in chapter 30, continued to show further differentiation between programs, with changes upon return to baseline conditions. Unitwide community meetings continued to reflect the differing purposes within programs, with specific characteristics being related to program structure. The milieu community meetings showed considerable change upon the return to baseline and continued sensitivity to the specific resident group leader in office, and meetings in both programs reflected the reduction in assaultiveness and less-pressured pace after the reintroduction of programs with procedural changes. Clear differences in the characteristics and relationships of community meetings between programs were obtained over the entire intramural period. The comparative use of resources during the last six months showed dramatic effects of procedural changes on consumables' utilization, with continuing differential effects of program structures on use of facilities and services. Differential relationships were found between programs on analyses of resource utilization over the entire intramural period, with clear and significant documentation that how many resources were used was not as important as how available resources were employed.

Resident time spent awake over the last six months was maintained at the high levels established upon the introduction of programs, with social-learning residents averaging more time awake than milieu residents did—again, partially because relatively more milieu residents still received psychotropic drugs. Time spent with others over the last six months paralleled changes in concurrent appropriate behavior but did not differ between groups by the last anniversary assessment. Several interesting relationships were obtained between both time awake and time with others and changes in resident functioning over the entire intramural period. Changes in the individual variability of ongoing resident activity over the last six months continued to show differences in day-to-day processes within programs. Several changes were apparent upon the return to baseline and the reintroduction of programs, with differential relationships occurring over the last six months and over the entire intramural period. The characteristics of resident activities described in chapter 30 again supported the differing program structures and procedures as the basis for the between-program effects reported in chapter 29.

The details of staff attitudes and performance, reported in chapter 31, again found staff attitudes, opinions, and beliefs about mental patients to change in response to changes in resident behavior—specifically decreases in assaultiveness and improvements in functioning —without staff attitudes having reciprocal effects on residents. Even with changes over the last six months, as with those over the entire intramural period, the staff group as a whole continued to reflect the ideal assumptions underlying the psychosocial programs and remained much closer to psychosocial ideals than to typical mental hospital staff. In contrast to opinions about patients, opinions and interpretations of treatment programs continued to show remarkable consistency over the last six months. Beliefs of the comparative effectiveness continued to reflect accurately objective findings, and preferences for working conditions continued to show the relative level of assaultiveness to which staff were exposed. Over the last six months, as well as the entire intramural period, staff opinions of the effectiveness and enjoyability of psychosocial programs were responsive to prior changes in resident behavior, without having notable effects on the ensuing response of residents to the programs. Very few changes occurred over the last six months in staff interpretations of either nature or techniques appropriate to each psychosocial program. Programs continued to be differentiated in desired directions. As at all previous assessments, staff preferences for the nature of treatment programs continued to be closer to the ideal milieu program, and preferences for technique utilization continued to be closer to the ideal social-learning program. However, all staff preferences continued to be much closer to either psychosocial orientation than to those of mental hospital staff.

The moment-to-moment continuous objective assessment of staff behavior, also reported in chapter 31, provided documentation that both groups of psychosocial residents received essentially identical experiences upon return to baseline conditions. Actual staff performance at this time even more closely approximated traditional hospital programs than during the original baseline, although both conditions were equated between units and were much closer to traditional programs than to either psychosocial program. Upon the reintroduction of programs, every program-specific class of staff behavior once again changed in desired directions, with changes in staff behavior continuing to be differentially related to resident functioning over the last six months in the same manner as during previous time periods. Total staff activity, the level of staff-resident interactions, and the differential focus and distribution of all classes of staff behavior returned to earlier levels over the last twenty weeks after the reintroduction of programs, remaining nearly identical to those existing over the previous two years. The greater effectiveness of improved procedures for controlling assaults was also apparent. Although the same staff continued to equate time and activity focus over psychosocial programs, the higher interaction rates in the milieu program continued to provide the average milieu resident with more individual staff attention than the average social-learning resident received—once again documenting that how attention is applied is more important than how much attention is received.

The rate of performance of staff behaviors and resident behavior-by-staff behavior match after the reintroduction of programs remained in keeping with the differential requirements specified in the respective treatment manuals, with the distribution of staff-resident interactions continuing to parallel the ideal distribution for each program. In fact, performance of milieu procedures was even more accurate than before; programmatic errors occurred at a rate of less than one-half of one percent of all staff-resident interactions in both treatment programs. Thus, 99.5% of all staff-resident interactions in the milieu program and 99.6% in the social-learning program were correct on an absolute level over the twenty weeks after reintroduction of programs, leaving little room for improvement.

The clear documentation of the equivalency of baseline conditions and appropriate differentiation of programs in the same manner as at earlier time periods clearly established the differential outcome to be a function of the specified procedures and structural changes introduced. Thus, by the last anniversary assessment, both programs showed renewed effectiveness as a result of the corrective procedural changes introduced only twenty weeks earlier, with significant continuing impact on the most severely debilitated groups of chronically institutionalized adults ever subjected to systematic study. The social-learning program continued to have a significant impact, with even greater renewed effectiveness, on all identified targets of rehabilitation for the population and was differentially more effective than the milieu therapy program.

Even though the social-learning program was clearly more effective, both overall programs had resulted in objective gains, including the release of significant numbers of residents to relatively independent functioning with continued community stay. With the initial level of disability of the resident groups, the gains by the last anniversary assessment were remarkable. Both programs had produced improvements to the level that some residents (and ex-residents) were functionally at a level indistinguishable from that of other "normal" people: 25% for the social-learning program and 14% for the milieu program. An additional 67% of the original social-learning residents and 32% of the original milieu residents showed objective improvement to a level of functioning that would clearly allow release and survival outside a controlled institutional setting.

Even after reducing crazy behavior to less than a third of original levels and increasing social and instrumental behavior by over three times original levels, the absolute functioning of most residents was still marginal and not as high as it had been earlier. About half the milieu residents and a few social-learning residents still showed an excess of a single critical intolerable behavior—continuing from the earlier period when controls for assaults were ineffective, to the extent that other improvements were practically overshadowed. These critical behaviors became the primary focus for each of these residents in both psychosocial programs with regard to practical decisions regarding community placement.

Thus, the objective assessment data for the programs at the last anniversary assessment clearly established that the social-learning program was effective on an absolute level and differentially more so than the milieu program with these severely debilitated groups. There was considerable promise that the improved levels of functioning would result in the successful release and community stay for the majority of these residents who had spent, on the average, about two-thirds of their adult years in the confines of mental institutions.

# PART 7
# Psychosocial Versus Hospital Groups: Intramural Functioning and Community Placement

## 33. An Overview of Hospital Comparisons, Community Placement, and Termination of the Psychosocial Units

The state hospital comparison group remained exceptionally stable over the entire project period. The hospital was assigned to a different administrative region and was scheduled to become a facility for the developmentally disabled rather than the mentally ill toward the end of the intramural treatment period. Additionally, the continuing focus of the Department of Mental Health on the use of community psychiatric facilities and regional centers for acute and multiple-admission prechronic patients had resulted in a further decline in patient population. These changes had not yet affected the operation of the traditional treatment programs for long-stay patients, in which the hospital comparison group participated. The same hiring freezes, salary increases, and reclassifications that affected the psychosocial staff also occurred at the comparison hospital. However, other than changing the name of the administration and operation of chronic wards from Continued Treatment Service to Residential Unit Division and back again, no notable changes occurred in the organization, number of staff, or programs of the state hospital comparison over the four and a half years from the original pre-transfer assessment through the end of the intramural period.

Cooperative arrangements were maintained between research staff and the liaison worker and major administrative staff at the state hospital throughout the intramural period and beyond. The hospital superintendent did immediately require the liaison worker to identify the patients included in the equated comparison group. However, the exceptional cooperation of the liaison worker and assistant superintendent and clinical director allowed project staff access to necessary records and completion of all scheduled assessments on the Inpatient Assessment Battery over the entire period without difficulty. After the original pre-post transfer assessments with equation of all three groups, regular six-month anniversary assessments were obtained during the same week for residents in both psychosocial groups and the hospital comparison group, equating interviewers' contact over the three groups, as well as the time of assessment.

Monitoring of patient movement and release criteria was continued by the hospital liaison and regional computer monitoring to ensure appropriate assessments in the event of release of a hospital patient. None of the hospital comparison group was proposed for release to independent functioning during the entire period, and only two releases were attempted to nonindependent settings before release criteria allowed board and care placements without work. In one instance, a nursing home transfer by subregion community staff was held up for a patient who later achieved such community placement when the criteria allowed. In the other instance, a patient was released to her parents' care without responsibilities or work. Since subregion community staff had pressured the parents for such placement, albeit inappropriately, this patient was counted as a premature community placement, and a replacement was added to the hospital comparison group. The original patient soon failed in the home placement and was rehospitalized to the original comparison group. Other than an occasional AWOL patient during anniversary assessment weeks—who had to be assessed upon return a week or two later—all hospital assessments and monitoring went smoothly. There were no interventions in the ongoing hospital programs beyond the increased motivation of hospital staff to obtain improvement for comparison patients once they were identified by the superintendent.

Community placement facilities had been identified by the ninth anniversary assessment, and beds were made available over eight different targeted extended-care facilities in the region to allow initial placements for improved residents from all three intramural programs. Extramural psychosocial staff had negotiated the availability of these beds and were committed to providing the minimum declining contact aftercare consultation, as well as consultation as needed for the planned twenty-four month follow-up for released residents from all three intramural groups since community staff of the Department of Mental Health were no longer providing direct services. Two local extended-care facilities had made enough beds available that equal placement of residents from the original intramural groups—equating prerelease resident functioning between facilities—would allow a controlled comparison of two different modes of follow-up. Since preliminary analyses had already determined that social-learning procedures were clearly superior to any alternative for the population involved, all follow-up consultation was to follow social-learning procedures. If any resident failed at community placement over the follow-up period, reinstitutionalization would be to the social-learning program, which was to be in operation in accordance with the expanded design, with the two-thirds/one-third division between prechronic and chronic residents.

Although patients of the hospital comparison group could have been placed in extended-care facilities at any time over the previous six months, none had been released by the ninth anniversary assessment. Rather, hospital staff had been screening patients for prospective release and processing necessary legal aspects of discharge papers, medical records, etc. During the week following the ninth anniversary assessment, the processing and necessary informed consent from residents, relatives, and guardians were completed for all three groups. Over the next three weeks, screening of residents in all three intramural programs for acceptability was completed by staff of the extended-care facilities—either by extended-care staff visiting the institutions, or by institutional staff taking residents to extended-care facilities—and original transfers were completed.

The transfer and orientation to community facilities for releases from all three groups followed the therapeutic transfer procedures suggested by the earlier transfer substudy (chapter 13). All to-be-released residents or patients were informed in advance of the date of transfer by the same staff who were to accompany them. The location and physical plant of community facilities were described, and attempts were made to relate the location and surrounding community activities and resources to previous experiences. The pending releases were first described to psychosocial residents in unitwide meetings to explain the gradual departure of residents, since people were moved out in groups of two or three by automobile every other day.

Two local extended-care facilities, providing the great majority of community beds for all three intramural programs, made possible the transfer of released residents from the psychosocial programs in a manner that allowed a controlled evaluation of potentially more therapeutic transfer procedures. Equated subgroups from each psychosocial program received verbal orientation and actually visited the facilities. The results of this substudy (Lentz et al., in press) found losses in the level of functioning as a result of transfer to the new community living environments; less loss for residents who had visited the new facilities, regardless of prior treatment conditions or transfer to a large or small facility. As in the previous transfer study, residents who were most negatively affected by the transfer adapted to the new environment, and no differences existed between transfer groups after a few weeks.

Since the staffing of the extended-care facilities was not adequate to handle the transfer operations, the expanded psychosocial staff conducted all orientation and transfer procedures for releases from all three groups. To reduce the ambiguity of such a total change in environment and to provide the continuity of contact suggested by the first substudy of transfer procedures, psychosocial staff also provided orientation and coverage in the extended-care facilities for four to five days after each person arrived. During this period, each new arrival was introduced to staff and other residents of the extended-care facility and familiarized with schedules and the geography of the building, grounds, and nearby community resources. Attempts were made to reduce any stress reactions by providing information and applying appropriate social-learning procedures by psychosocial staff, who faded to a consultative role to facility staff by the end of the orientation period.

Concurrent with preparations for community placements, the focus of both psychosocial programs was shifted during the week following the ninth anniversary assessment. From the general focus on improving all areas of functioning, staff concentrated on the critical intolerable behaviors still existing for a few residents in each program that alone might preclude successful community placement. Analysis of the continuing objective resident data had identified two primary situations in which assaults were still occurring for residents who had not eliminated assaultiveness during the twenty weeks after the reintroduction of programs and the longer periods of time out or expulsion. Both situations involved attempted prevention of some single class of habitual inappropriate behavior—either a habitual annoying or destructive behavior (e.g., stool stuffing) or a habitual aggressive act (e.g., grabbing another resident's food tray).

After the ninth anniversary assessment through the completion of initial community placement decisions three weeks later, the psychosocial programs continued, and the respective treatment principles focused on these specific habitual behaviors. In both programs, the settings that were likely to elicit the habitual inappropriate behavior were repeatedly presented to each resident, and relevant programmatic interactions were applied to eliminate the inappropriate behavior and teach more adaptive ones. Other than this change in focus for a few residents, the primary procedural change in the milieu program was that brief expulsion to areas that were still in view of other community members—and still allowed positive statements, negative feedback, etc., from both staff and residents—was substituted for the expulsion room for dealing with habitual behaviors. Similarly time out with active overcorrection/restitution procedures (e.g. Foxx & Azrin, 1972, 1973) was substituted for the time-out room in the social-learning program to provide more intensive focal treatment of the critical habitual behaviors. The only notable changes in actual staff performance from that existing over the last twenty weeks of the intramural period for overall programs (table 31.3) were the slight increases in focus on "inappropriate-crazy" behaviors (0.62 per hour for the milieu program, 0.20 per hour for the social-learning program), with the distribution and accuracy of staff-resident interactions otherwise remaining constant.

Upon the completion of initial community placement decisions, the social-learning program was continued for an additional eight weeks, and the milieu residents who failed to be acceptable for community placement were transferred to the program for special treatment of their remaining intolerable behaviors. All residents who were still performing an intolerable behavior at the end of the overall programs or after the failure of focused milieu therapy thus received the focused social-learning program with overcorrection/restitution procedures directed to the critical behaviors—with two exceptions. One resident from each of the original psychosocial programs was still performing an aggressive intolerable behavior, but suffered from sufficient medical problems that staff were hesitant to involve them in the more active physical requirements of overcorrection procedures.

During the period of focused treatment, staffing in the intramural social-learning program was maintained at the same level as previously. The remainder of original and expanded psychosocial staff then set about renovating the empty unit and completing paperwork and community contacts in preparation for reopening the units for continued service and comparative evaluation of the expanded design with prechronic patients. Hospital accreditation paperwork also continued. Presidential impoundment of federal research funds required some rapid emergency requests for an extension and supplemental funds to support research staff until the impoundment was overcome. By this time, all but one clinical staff member had been transferred to regular state operating funds, so federal funding problems were of concern only to a small group of research staff. The supplement was eventually obtained, but notification came, once again, after the starting date for the extension.

All details within the center had been arranged for the expanded design and treatment of prechronic patients, including the addition of regular assessments of another ongoing unit in the center for comparative purposes, since the state hospital was no longer in the region. The initial at-risk population of prechronic patients in the region had been identified, and working relationships were established with the major community clinics and inpatient psychiatric units for assessments and referrals, with details established for all aspects of operations. The majority of staff needed for the expanded operation were in training, and recruitment was underway for completion of the supplemental staff. The plan at this point had been to treat the failures from the original milieu program with social-learning procedures. Then, when the psychosocial units were reopened with the two-thirds/one-third distribution of prechronic to chronic patients, the failures from the original hospital comparison group, and the two remaining failures from the original psychosocial programs, and any released residents who failed to maintain community placement would be treated during the follow-up period.

Instead the psychosocial units were terminated as a result of political decisions which were communicated on the very day that the next-to-last resident in continuing focused social-learning treatment had been accepted for community placement.

After having received encouragement through two state governors and three changes in the top administration of the Department of Mental Health, psychosocial staff had not been concerned when the newly elected governor of the state replaced the top administrative positions in the department. The pre-election platform chastised the previous governor for the lack of funds spent in mental health and the budget message had specifically targeted "... improving provision of institutional service to those requiring long-term treatment and rehabilitation ..."; prospects for the expanded design seemed quite promising. Even though only 97% of the previous year's apportions was requested for treatment of the mentally ill, the lead item in the narrative statement of budgetary activity was, "By focusing attention on chronically mentally ill adults, the department can return many patients in this group to the community." Further, the factors to be involved in the department's new emphasis were "... improved direct care staff/patient ratios ...", and "... emphasis on active treatment instead of custodial care ...". The current and proposed work of the psychosocial units had seemingly anticipated the needs of the state and the mentally ill population so well that the budget message led to much excitement among psychosocial staff. Mutual compliments were exchanged on the wisdom of proceeding with the expansion of operations on regular state operating funds, rather than dealing with the additional red-tape of another federal grant request.

The excitement and "delusions of wisdom" were short-lived when the manner of implementing the new emphasis in the Department of Mental Health was presented *fait accompli* in the center budget hearings. Specifically, the way of "improving" direct care staff/patient ratios was to be through layoffs of staff who did anything other than spend time with patients or medical and nursing staff needed for hospital accreditation—thereby increasing the proportion of remaining staff who did spend time with patients. Further, training, research, and evaluation were no longer to be activities supported by regular operating funds, as distinct from special research funds or centralized operations. Possibly because of employee unions who were already contesting layoffs of dietary workers elsewhere, over 2,000 current mental health staff at higher pay grades were to be laid off within six weeks. This included thirty-eight positions at the center, eight of which were the top-level professional and program staff across all divisions of the current psychosocial operation. In addition, a freeze was placed on remaining nonmedical or nonnursing positions above the technician (aide) level, of which nine were already vacant, and future layoffs were promised if normal attrition did not remove remaining staff who were not in patient direct care in a few months.

After futile attempts to gain reconsideration, the decision to terminate the psychosocial units was reluctantly faced. Over the six weeks between their closing and the termination of staff who were laid off, the majority of time was spent in finding jobs for people who had committed themselves to future work with the expanded project. In addition, assistance was also provided in finding new placements for an additional 39% of nonnursing professional and preprofessional staff who were not receiving support from the federal grant. The remainder of the time before the layoff was devoted to familiarizing the remaining staff who were to take over the coordination and conduct of the follow-up with the nature of contacts and agreements since all of the old extramural professional staff were to be laid off, and other extramural staff who did not find placements elsewhere were assigned to new intramural programs. Also, all of the detailed arrangements with community clinics and psychiatric units had to be disengaged, since the prechronic service was defunct.

Fortunately this catastrophe had come after the original comparative project had completed intramural treatments, so the integrity of evaluations with the hard-core chronic group was not jeopardized. The remaining research and clinical staff still on federal grant support were sufficient to complete commitments to clinical follow-up of released residents and collection of data—but the follow-up necessarily would be limited to a year and a half rather than two years. With the closing of the psychosocial units, the failures of the hospital comparison group could not be treated, but continued monitoring was maintained to determine if additional significant releases occurred from the original group. Neither could the two failures from original psychosocial programs be retreated. They were transferred to the comparison hospital, and the one psychosocial resident who was still improving under focal social-learning treatment was transferred to another unit in the center, where treatment was continued under the supervision of remaining psychosocial staff until significant release was achieved. Two additional releases from the hospital comparison group were also accomplished during this period, with required assessments obtained on significant releases.

The remaining chapters of part 7 report all comparative findings between psychosocial and hospital groups for the severely debilitated, chronically institutionalized population. Comparisons of the original equated groups over the entire intramural period, reported in chapter 34, include details of statistical analyses for the interested research worker; however, the professional clinician or program director can obtain details of results—including analyses of possible problems with rating scales, and differential predictability of improvement—by skipping the "statistical evaluation" section. Preprofessional staff and others short on time can obtain a good understanding of the outcome of intramural assessments of functioning by reading the program-by-program summary at the end of chapter 34. All comparative results on the success of the three intramural programs in achieving significant release for patients in mental institutions and the relative efficiency and predictability of such releases at the termination of the psychosocial units are presented in chapter 35, which is relatively short and incorporates statistical analyses in the text. A clear understanding of comparative release rates is provided in the tables and the summary at the end of the chapter. Chapter 36 briefly summarizes the major conclusions of the three-way comparison upon the termination of the intramural programs.

# 34. Comparative Intramural Change of the Psychosocial and Hospital Groups

THE INPATIENT ASSESSMENT BATTERY (IAB)[1]

Changes in the standardized IAB Functioning Score during the entire intramural treatment period—plotted relative to functioning before introduction of psychosocial programs—are presented in figure 34.1, which shows considerable variability among groups over the four and a half year period, with a general superiority of social-learning residents over both the milieu and hospital groups. IAB Functioning for the psychosocial groups also appears to reflect the overall trends found on continuous objective assessment. Improvements in functioning are suggested over the first half of the period, followed by declines during the time in which ineffective procedures for controlling assaultive behavior were operating. Sharp increases in functioning for both psychosocial groups are clearly apparent during the last six months, when more effective procedures for handling assaultiveness were reintroduced. In contrast, no major changes in IAB Functioning are apparent for the hospital group between any two successive anniversary assessments.

*Statistical evaluation.* Overall changes during the intramural period were first evaluated by a two-way repeated measures ANOVA on the standardized IAB Functioning Score (social-learning vs. milieu vs. hospital groups; anniversary assessments 0 through 9). This analysis found a significant main effect for time ($F=2.64$, $df=9/729$, $p < 0.01$) and a significant group x time interaction ($F=2.75$, $df=18/729$, $p < 0.01$), without a group main effect ($F=1.62$, $df=2/82$, $p > 0.10$). Additional two-way ANOVAs with partitioning of simple effects were carried out on scores from the equated pretreatment assessment (anniversary assessment 0) to each anniversary assessment and between successive pairs of assessments to determine the nature of within-group and between-group changes.[2]

The most important intramural test of comparative effectiveness between the psychosocial and hospital groups is the extent to which the changes in IAB Functioning from equated levels at entry to successive anniversary assessments differed between groups.

These multiple comparisons are summarized in table 34.1, which reveals that the mean increases in IAB Functioning achieved by the social-learning group were significantly better than the changes of the milieu therapy group at every anniversary assessment throughout the entire period. Similarly, the mean increase of the social-learning group were also significantly better than the changes of the hospital group at every anniversary assessment except 7 and 8, where the groups did not differ significantly. In contrast, there were only two significant differences between the milieu and hospital groups: the milieu group showing significantly greater mean increases at anniversary assessment 4 and significantly greater mean decreases at assessment 8.

An inspection of the differences in mean IAB Functioning Scores over anniversary assessments—rather than change—found parallel results for absolute level differences. Mean IAB Functioning of the hospital group approached a significantly higher level in comparison to the milieu group at anniversary assessment 8 ($F=3.47$, $df=1/81$, $p < 0.10$), without other differences approaching significance ($F$'s $< 1.92$, $df=1/81$, $p > 0.10$). Mean IAB Functioning of the social-learning group was significantly greater than that of the milieu group over all anniversary assessments after the first ($F$'s $> 4.38$, $df=1/81$, $p < 0.05$) and greater than that of the hospital group through assessment 6 ($F$'s $> 4.05$, $df=1/81$, $p < 0.05$). Since both psychosocial groups produced significantly greater variances than the hospital group did on the last three anniversary assessments, nonparametric analyses were also performed (see note 2). Mann-Whitney U tests yielded the same results as parametric tests in all instances except for the absolute level difference in ranked IAB Functioning Scores at anniversary assessment 9, where the social-learning group was significantly higher than the hospital group when tested nonparametrically ($Z=2.33$, $p < 0.01$).

An examination of changes within each group from the level of IAB Functioning at entry to the project found only one anniversary assessment even to approach significant change for the hospital group. The decrease from entry to

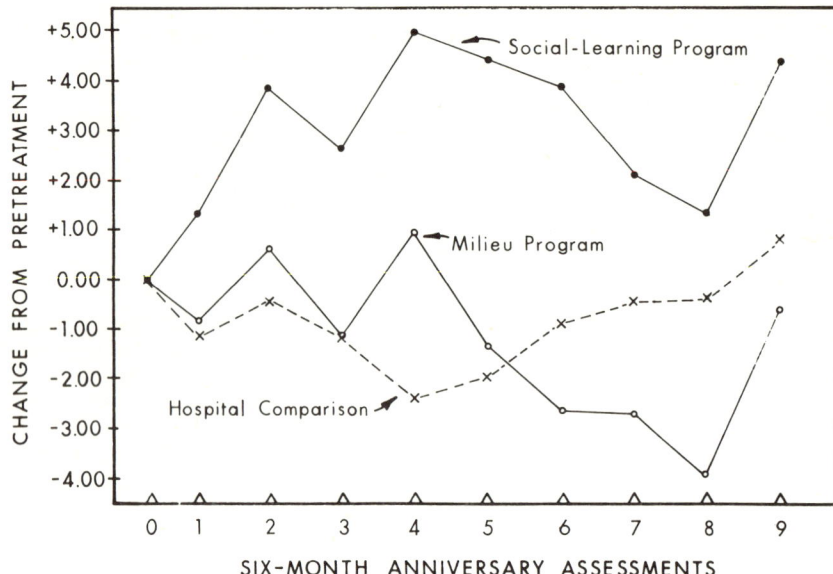

Figure 34.1. Changes in overall functioning from the Inpatient Assessment Battery during the intramural treatment period for the original equated groups (N=28 each).

the low point at assessment 4 for the hospital group approached significance (F=3.19, df= 1/81, p < 0.10). Otherwise, none of the anniversary assessments for the hospital group reflected changes in IAB Functioning that approached significant differences from the level at which the group began (F's <2.31, df=1/81, p > 0.20). Although the milieu group showed changes within the intramural period, only one anniversary assessment reflected an IAB Functioning level differing significantly from that before the milieu program began: assessment 8, at the end of a year and a half with ineffective procedures for dealing with dangerous and aggressive acts, when the group showed significantly lower IAB Functioning that it had upon original entry (F=5.39, df=1/81, p < 0.05). The average IAB Functioning at anniversary assessments 6 (F=3.79) and 7 (F=3.15) for the milieu group approached significant loss in comparison to the level at point of entry (df=1/81, p < 0.10), while none of the remaining anniversary assessments approached significance (F's < 1.18, df=1/81, p > 0.20). In contrast, the social-learning group failed to show a significant increase from the level before the program

Table 34.1. Significance of comparative change from entry among original groups on the Inpatient Assessment Battery (N=28 each).

| Anniversary assessment | Comparison of mean change from original level at entry | | |
| --- | --- | --- | --- |
| | Social-learning vs. milieu therapy | Social-learning vs. hospital comparison | Milieu therapy vs. hospital comparison |
| 1 | 3.592 [a] | 4.098 [a] | <1 |
| 2 | 4.157 [a] | 5.574 [a] | 1.417 |
| 3 | 4.112 [a] | 4.148 [a] | <1 |
| 4 | 4.042 [a] | 7.570 [a] | 3.528 [a] |
| 5 | 6.384 [a] | 7.010 [a] | <1 |
| 6 | 6.715 [a] | 4.803 [a] | 1.923 |
| 7 | 4.385 [a] | 2.318 | 2.080 |
| 8 | 4.318 [a] | 1.381 | 2.937 [a] |
| 9 | 4.555 [a] | 3.064 [a] | 1.494 |

Note. Table entries are Newman-Keuls $q$'s for changes plotted in figure 34.1.
a. $p < 0.05$ with critical value=2.817 for two-step comparisons and 3.386 for three-step comparisons (see Weiner, 1962).

introduction only at anniversary assessments 1, 7, and 8 (F's < 2.28, df=1/81, p > 0.10). Its increase in IAB Functioning achieved significance at p < 0.05 at anniversary assessment 3 (F=4.00, df=1/81) and at p < 0.01 at all remaining assessments (F's > 7.64, df=1/81).

An examination of changes from one anniversary assessment to the next within the intramural period similarly found a complete absence of significant within-group change for the hospital group. With the exception of the increase during the last six months (F=2.90, df=1/81, p < 0.10), none of these changes approached significance (F's < 1.97, df=1/81, p > 0.20). In fact, the only significant difference among levels of IAB Functioning for the hospital group over all assessments was between the low at assessment 4 and the high on the last anniversary assessment (F=6.99, df=1/81, p < 0.01). Thus the IAB Functioning of the hospital group plotted in figure 34.1 could be considered a flat horizontal line reflecting no significant change.

In contrast to the absence of change within the hospital group, changes within the psychosocial groups reflected considerable movement (see figure 34.1). Although several changes from one assessment to the next were significant within each psychosocial program and significantly different from those of the hospital group, few significant differential changes occurred between psychosocial groups from one assessment to the next. Of these, the increase in IAB Functioning of the social-learning group from anniversary assessment 0 to 1 was significantly greater than the parallel change for the milieu group (F=6.45, df=1/81, p < 0.05). Additionally the decrease of the milieu group from assessment 4 to 5 approached significance relative to the social-learning group (F=3.76, df=1/81, p < 0.10). The comparative change from assessment 1 to 5 was also tested, reflecting significantly greater increases for the social-learning group than for the milieu group over that two-year period (F=8.05, df=1/81, p < 0.01), paralleling the results of continuous objective assessments. However, none of the remaining simple interactions between psychosocial groups and successive pairs of anniversary assessments approached significance (F's < 2.72, df=1/81, p > 0.10), indicating the basic parallelism of the direction of psychosocial changes shown in figure 34.1.

Comparative changes between the psychosocial and hospital groups between successive anniversary assessments (see figure 34.1) found that the increase in IAB Functioning during the first six months for the social-learning group was significantly greater than that of the hospital group (F=8.40, df=1/81, p < 0.01), while milieu and hospital groups did not differ (F < 1). Changes over the next two years (anniversary assessments 1 to 5) similarly reflected a significant increase in IAB Functioning for social-learning residents (F=5.86, df=1/81, p < 0.05) that was significantly greater than that of hospital residents (F=9.23, df=1/81, p < 0.01), while milieu and hospital residents did not differ (F < 1). However, within this period, the increase in IAB Functioning from anniversary assessment 1 to 2 was significant for social-learning residents (F=6.79, df=1/81, p < 0.05) and approached significantly greater change than that of hospital residents (F=3.64, df=1/81, p < 0.10). None of the changes within or between groups approached significance between anniversary assessment 2 and 3 (all p's > 0.10); however, the increase from assessment 3 to 4 was significant for both psychosocial groups (F's > 5.73, df=1/81, p < 0.05) and significantly greater in comparison to the change of the hospital group (F's > 15.97, df=1/81, p < 0.05). The decline in IAB Functioning for milieu residents from anniversary assessment 4 to 5 was significant itself (F=6.02, df=1/81, p < 0.05) and in comparison to the change for hospital residents (F=8.76, df=1/81, p < 0.01). Neither within- nor between-group changes approached significance for social-learning and hospital groups over this six-month period (all p's > 0.20).

During the next year and a half (anniversary assessments 5 to 8) when shortened lengths of expulsion time and time out for assaultive behavior were in effect in the psychosocial programs, both showed significant decreases in IAB Functioning (F's > 4.13, df=1/81, p < 0.05), which were also significantly different from the parallel change for the hospital group (F's > 10.53, df=1/81, p < 0.05). Within this period, only the simple interaction between the milieu and hospital groups and the change from anniversary assessment 5 to 6 (F=6.00, df=1/81, p < 0.05) and between social-learning and hospital groups and the change from anniversary assessment 6 to 7 (F=4.08, df=1/81, p < 0.05) were significant. None of the remaining simple interactions approached significance (all p's > 0.10), and only one within-group change approached significance: the decrease for the social-learning group between anniversary assessments 6 and 7 (F=2.88, df=1/81, p < 0.10). During the last six months of the intramural period, following the reintroduction of procedures and the changes for controlling assaultive behavior, both psychosocial programs showed sharp increases in IAB Functioning (see figure 34.1). The increases were significant not only within social-learning and milieu groups (F's > 14.61, df=1/81, p < 0.01) but were significantly greater for each psychosocial program than the parallel increase was for the hospital group (F's > 4.49, df=1/81, p < 0.05).

*Descriptive interpretation.* The social-learning

program was differentially more effective than either the milieu program or the traditional hospital programs, which generally did not differ significantly. Parallel to findings with continuous objective assessments reported in previous chapters, the IAB Functioning of social-learning residents (figure 34.1) improved significantly more from pretreatment levels than that of milieu residents at every anniversary assessment. The improvement of social-learning residents was also significantly better than hospital residents at every anniversary assessment, except the seventh and eighth. In contrast, the milieu program showed significantly greater improvement than the hospital programs did only at the fourth anniversary assessment. These two groups showed no significant differential change from pretreatment at any other anniversary assessment except the eighth, where the loss of the milieu group was significantly greater than that of the hospital group.

The major overall trends in IAB Functioning also reflect changes for the psychosocial groups that parallel continuous objective assessments, both in comparison to each other and to the hospital group. Although none of the changes within groups was significant in IAB Functioning immediately following program introduction, the increase of the social-learning group was significantly greater than that of the milieu group (figure 34.1), paralleling earlier findings (chapter 14). The increase in IAB Functioning of the social-learning group by the first anniversary assessment was also significantly better than the change of the hospital group; milieu and hospital groups did not differ. From the beginning to the end of the next two years (anniversary assessments 1 to 5), as with continuous objective assessments, IAB Functioning showed a significant increase for the social-learning group, which was also significantly better than that of the milieu group, which showed no such change. The improvement of the social-learning group over the next two years was also significantly better than that of the hospital group, which showed no significant change and did not differ from the milieu group.

The IAB Functioning of the psychosocial groups over the next year and a half (anniversary assessments 5 to 8) reflected the same significant decline that was apparent in the continuous objective assessments during the period when the ineffective procedures for controlling assaults were operating. Over that period, the IAB Functioning of the hospital group did not change significantly. However, both psychosocial groups, although they did not change differentially between one another, reflected significant losses over the period in relation to the hospital group. Finally, changes in IAB Functioning for the psychosocial groups during the last six months—following procedural changes for handling assaults—clearly showed the same reversal of the downward trends of the previous year and a half and the renewed effectiveness of both programs that was reflected in continuous objective assessments. The increase in IAB Functioning of the hospital group approached significance over the last six months; both psychosocial groups not only increased significantly over the period but increased significantly more than the hospital group did. In fact, the increase in IAB Functioning over the last six months reflects a larger absolute change for both psychosocial programs than for any previous six-month period, even though the programs had been reintroduced with procedural changes for only twenty weeks by the time of the last anniversary assessment.

On an absolute level, the average standardized IAB Functioning Score for the social-learning group showed significant increases from pretreatment to all anniversary assessments, except 1, 7, and 8. Although not significant, even the low IAB Functioning Score of the social-learning group at anniversary assessment 8 (50.41) was above the pretreatment level (49.15), and the highest level achieved—at assessment 4 (54.06)—and the level on the last anniversary assessment (53.46) reflected major and significant gains for the group as a whole. In contrast, the average standardized IAB Functioning Score for the milieu group was significantly different from the pretreatment level (49.65) only at the low point at anniversary assessment 8 (45.65), with neither the highest level achieved—at anniversary assessment 4 (50.63)—nor the level on the last anniversary assessment (48.95) differing significantly from the level at which they started. Similarly the average standardized IAB Functioning Score for the hospital group did not differ significantly from the pretreatment level (50.44) on any anniversary assessment, including the low at anniversary assessment 4 (47.98) or the high on the last anniversary assessment (51.38).

The components of the IAB Functioning Score (see chapter 11) showed parallel comparative changes throughout the intramural period. At the last anniversary assessment, the increase from the pretreatment level of the social-learning group was significant on the NOSIE-30 (131.7 to 145.6) and significantly better than the changes of either the milieu group (127.1 to 126.7) or the hospital group (136.6 to 135.5), both of which declined slightly. Similarly the increase of the social-learning group was significant on the ISMF (48.41 to 54.25) and significantly better than the increases of either the milieu (49.11 to 51.11) or the hospital group (48.84 to 51.86).

The increase of the social-learning group on the MSBS was not significant on the last anniversary assessment (22.95 to 23.64) or significantly different from the change for the hospital group (24.16 to 23.54), but it was a significant gain relative to a loss for the milieu group (24.05 to 21.36). None of these changes in IAB components were significantly different between the milieu and hospital groups. Thus, both overall IAB Functioning and components reflected the differential superiority of the social-learning program in treating the severely disabled chronic population.

## SOME MINOR PARADOXES ON THE IAB

The comparative changes between residents of the social-learning and milieu programs on IAB Functioning from the original levels to each anniversary assessment and major trends over the intramural time periods are thus clearly parallel to the findings of the data from continuous objective assessments. However, three aspects of IAB Functioning, apparent upon an inspection of figure 34.1, do not reflect the findings from continuous objective assessments: the level of functioning within psychosocial groups relative to their absolute level of functioning prior to program introduction, the directionality of change between successive anniversary assessments through assessment 5, and the parallelism in directionality of change of the psychosocial groups.

Continuous objective assessment of resident behavior found that the social-learning group showed significant improvement in overall Global Functioning at every anniversary assessment. Additionally the milieu therapy group showed significant improvement at every anniversary assessment through the sixth and improvement approaching significance on the last anniversary assessment, with none showing Global Functioning even nonsignificantly below the level at which the group started. In contrast, the improvement reflected in IAB assessments failed to achieve statistical significance on three occasions for the social-learning group. More importantly, the IAB Functioning of the milieu group not only failed to show significant absolute improvement on seven of nine anniversary assessments but showed a significant loss in absolute level on assessment 8. Thus, although the overall comparisons show the same differential effectiveness of the programs, the level of functioning obtained on the IAB did not reflect the absolute level of improvement known to have been obtained from continuous objective assessments.

The directionality of change between IAB Functioning and objectively assessed Global Functioning was uniform from the fifth anniversary assessment through the end of the intramural period; both psychosocial programs showed significant decreases over the year and a half in which the ineffective procedures for controlling assaultive behavior were in effect, and significant increases on both sets of assessments during the last six months, following the reintroduction of programs with improved procedures. However, during the initial period following the introduction of programs, both psychosocial groups showed significant increases in objectively assessed Global Functioning, with a greater increase for the social-learning group. IAB Functioning during the same period also showed significantly greater improvement for the social-learning program but a nonsignificant loss for the milieu program (figure 34.1).

Similarly, although the overall changes in IAB Functioning over the next two years (anniversary assessments 1 to 5) yielded parallel results between groups, the directionality of changes from one assessment to the next were not in agreement with objectively assessed Global Functioning. Rather, Global Functioning showed significant decreases for both psychosocial programs from anniversary assessment 1 to 2 and significant increases for both from anniversary assessment 4 to 5, without other significant changes during the two-year period. In contrast, IAB Functioning showed a nearly opposite directionality of change (figure 34.1): Both programs increased IAB Functioning from anniversary assessment 1 to 2, the social-learning group significantly so; both programs reduced IAB Functioning from anniversary assessment 4 to 5, with the decline of the milieu group being significant and approaching a significantly greater loss than that of the social-learning group. Additionally, although the decline in IAB Functioning for both psychosocial groups from anniversary assessment 2 to 3 was not significant, the directionality of change was different for the social-learning group, and the significant increase in IAB Functioning for both psychosocial groups from anniversary assessment 3 to 4 contrasted with an absence of change in objective Global Functioning over that period.

*Related events.* The essential parallelism of the directionality of change in IAB Functioning for the psychosocial groups not only suggests a lack of sensitivity to known changes in objectively assessed behavior, but the probable influence of some other environmental events held in common. Detailed inspection of notable events from the research log, changes in components of objectively assessed functioning, and correlational analyses within psychosocial groups were undertaken in an attempt to determine the source of these paradoxes in the level and directionality of change in IAB Functioning. The two factor scores—overall

IAB Functioning and objective Global Functioning—were found to correlate significantly at each anniversary assessment (mdn. r=0.84, range 0.77 to 0.90), without significant or suggestive differences between successive assessments.[3] Only one significant difference in these correlations occurred between psychosocial programs. On anniversary assessment 7, the correlation within the social-learning program (r=0.95) was significantly higher than the correlation within the milieu program (r=0.80). Similarly the intercorrelation of residual change scores for IAB Functioning and objective Global Functioning—providing an indication of the extent of base-free parallel change (see chapter 11)—found significant correlations at each assessment (mdn. r=0.69, range 0.58 to 0.80), without significant or suggestive differences between successive anniversary assessments or between milieu and social-learning groups. Drug status was not significantly correlated with either level of functioning or change over groups or within groups. Thus, the correlational analyses indicate that both IAB and continuous objective assessments ordered individual residents in the same way; that the same residents tended to show relative improvements or declines on both sets of measurements on any given anniversary assessment; and that drug status was not predictive, overall or differentially, of level of functioning or of change.

The individual components of objectively assessed behavior revealed four indexes that provided suggestive data on the differences in the level and directionality of change in IAB Functioning. The one component of resident behavior that had previously been found to differ in directionality of change over both psychosocial programs from anniversary assessments 1 to 5 was the Interpersonal Skills Index. During this time (figure 19.3) this index—which measures relative frequencies of normal interpersonal interaction and communications skills—revealed a pattern of change on successive anniversary assessments almost directly parallel to that of IAB Functioning during the same period (figure 34.1).

Two other indexes suggested possible contributions to the low absolute level of IAB Functioning of the milieu group toward the end of the intramural period: TSBC Total Appropriate concurrent behavior and Instrumental Role Performance. The loss was not statistically significant, but both indexes reflected an absolute level of functioning for milieu residents on anniversary assessments 6, 7, 8, and 9 that, on the average, was below levels at initial entry to the project. The only component of objectively assessed behavior that showed significantly worse performance for the milieu group, paralleling changes on IAB Functioning, was Intolerable Behavior. The potential influence of the dangerous and aggressive acts reflected in the incidence of Intolerable Behavior on IAB Functioning was further suggested by the concordance of increases in Intolerable Behavior and decreases below original entry levels on IAB Functioning. Although the great majority of decreases in IAB Functioning and several of the increases in Intolerable Behavior were not statistically significant, every anniversary assessment that showed a level of IAB Functioning below the original entry level for the milieu program also showed a level of Intolerable Behavior above that existing before the introduction of the milieu program.

An examination of the intercorrelations among objectively assessed components of adaptive behavior and IAB Functioning did not suggest differential contribution of the above indexes. Rather, all adaptive components were equally related to IAB Functioning (mdn. r's from 0.75 to 0.84), without significant or suggestive differences between psychosocial programs or over successive anniversary assessments. Intercorrelations between Intolerable Behavior and IAB Functioning, however, added further supportive evidence to the influence of assaultive behavior to the paradoxical differences on IAB assessments. Although the differences in the level of correlations were not significant between milieu and social-learning groups during the first two and a half years, the relative levels are suggestive. None of the correlations between IAB Functioning and Intolerable Behavior were significant within the social-learning group through the fifth anniversary assessment (mdn. r=-0.25, range -0.11 to -0.33). Following the increase in Intolerable Behavior at anniversary assessment 6, all remaining correlations were significant for the social-learning group (mdn. r=-0.55, range -0.49 to -0.82).

In contrast, correlations within the milieu group between IAB Functioning and Intolerable Behavior were significant at every anniversary assessment from 2 to 9 (mdn. r=-0.53, range -0.37 to -0.58). Additionally, over both psychosocial groups combined, improvement in IAB Functioning was significantly negatively related to the incidence of Intolerable Behavior at every anniversary assessment (mdn. r=-0.44, range -0.36 to -0.54), indicating that residents failing to show IAB improvement tended to be performing dangerous and aggressive acts on each anniversary assessment. Although differences between groups were not statistically significant, the differential correlations of Intolerable Behavior with IAB improvement at anniversary assessment 5 are notable; no such relationship existed for the social-learning group (r=0.08), but there was a significant negative relationship for the milieu group (r=-0.37).

*Probable cause.* These analyses suggest that the incidence of Intolerable Behavior might underlie the differences in absolute level of IAB Functioning and the differential directionality of change over the first two and a half years compared to known changes in continuous objective assessments. Although all components of continuous objectively assessed classes of behavior were significantly related to IAB Functioning in expected directions at all anniversary assessments, Intolerable Behavior was the only one to show consistently both parallel directionality and parallel absolute level differences from pretreatment for the milieu group. The notable events recorded in the research log implicated changes in the length of time for expulsion and time out. Both of the paradoxical decreases in IAB Functioning (see figure 34.1, anniversary assessments 3 & 5) occurred immediately following reductions in the length of time of expulsion and time out as a consequence for assaultive behavior. The major change in procedure, which occurred just before anniversary assessment 5, had resulted in a slight increase in Intolerable Behavior during the assessment but did not show major increases in Intolerable Behavior or begin to have additional influences on other areas of functioning until a few weeks later.

The differences in directionality, combined with correlational and absolute level differences involving Intolerable Behavior, further suggested that the basis for the paradoxical relationships and parallelism on IAB assessments might be found in reactivity of measurement. The component instruments of the IAB consist of a time-limited structured interview and two standardized rating scales completed by technician-level staff. Although the reliability between raters was more than adequate for all three instruments, the time-limited interview—by its very nature—is more subject to error arising from temporary disturbances of residents than are the continuous observational assessments that cover more representative periods of time and situations. Rating scales, on the other hand, are more subject to staff reactivity. Clinical Frequency data were also recorded by the same staff who provided ratings, but little opportunity exists for judgmental biases to enter since the presence or absence of discrete behaviors are recorded immediately upon their occurrence. In contrast, the rating scales require intervening judgments of degree (rather than simple presence or absence) and recollection of broader classes of behavior over a period of several days—all of which allow for more reactive effects to enter from the staff who make the ratings. Thus, it seems probable that staff perceptions (and resident ratings) were somewhat negatively biased when staff were exposed to increases in physical assaults or to conditions that—based upon past experience—they anticipated might lead to increases in physical assaults. Such perceptual influences could result in residents' being accurately and reliably ordered relative to one another but with reactive ratings that shifted a few items by only one point, resulting in absolute level relationships similar to those obtained.

Further support for temporary reactivity in IAB assessments as the basis for paradoxical relationships comes from notable events occurring just before the paradoxical and parallel increases in IAB Functioning (see figure 34.1, anniversary assessments 2 & 4). Specifically, both paradoxical increases in IAB Functioning were preceded by events that led to increases in staff and resident morale but had little other immediate effects on resident functioning, except the performance of Interpersonal Skills. Thus, anniversary assessment 2 was preceded by the first resident releases and replacements, and anniversary assessment 4 was preceded by the introduction of long-delayed materials and commodities, changes in weekend schedules that made staff work easier, more frequent presence of senior staff during off-hours, and a special program to control an especially disruptive milieu resident. Staff reactivity as a contributor to the paradoxical change between anniversary assessments 4 and 5 is also supported by the increase in drug administration, which occurred immediately after the reduction in consequences for assault just before anniversary assessment 5 and by the changes in relative staff preference ratings between the two psychosocial programs. Thus, although IAB Functioning accurately and reliably reflected between-group differences in level, relative change, and major trends, the absolute level of functioning on IAB assessments appears to have been suppressed for the psychosocial programs by reactivity to the incidence of dangerous and aggressive acts.

## A COMMENT ON PSYCHOTROPIC DRUGS

By the end of the intramural period another notable difference between programs was the relative use of psychotropic drugs.[4] Drug status was not a significant predictor of treatment responsiveness on any measure at any time during the intramural period. Especially in view of the primacy with which maintenance chemotherapy is used with the chronically institutionalized population, the absence of significant relationships with the level of functioning throughout the four and a half year period for any of the three groups is particularly important. Drug status in the psychosocial programs had been purposively held constant during the

Table 34.2. Utilization of psychotropic drugs during the last six months of the intramural period for original groups (N=28 each).

| Treatment program | High dosage [a] | Low dosage | None |
|---|---|---|---|
| Social-learning | | 10.7% | 89.3% |
| Milieu therapy | 3.6% | 14.3% | 82.1% |
| Hospital comparison | 57.1% | 42.9% | |

a. >400 mg/day chlorpromazine or equivalent for a single drug. Chi-square=56.28, $df=2$, $p < 0.01$, drugs versus no drugs.

last six months through anniversary assessment 9 to evaluate the effectiveness of changed environmental procedures for handling assaultive behavior.

As shown in table 34.2, differences in the utilization of psychotropic drugs had indeed occurred. From the 91.7% of patients receiving psychotropic drugs at project entry, hospital use had increased to 100%, and psychosocial programs had reduced to 17.9% and 10.7%, respectively, for milieu and social-learning groups. The significant increase in functioning for pscychosocial groups over the last six months—with low drug status held constant—adds further evidence to the correlational data and the earlier controlled study of drug effects that seriously question the reliance on chemotherapy for the chronic population.

## SUMMARY AND PREDICTABILITY OF IAB IMPROVEMENT

The analyses presented here show the same differential effectiveness between the two psychosocial programs as had been found with continuous objective assessments. The social-learning program was differentially more effective than either the milieu therapy or the traditional hospital programs. For the most part, the milieu and hospital programs did not differ. The major overall trends in IAB Functioning reflected changes for the psychosocial groups that paralleled continuous objective assessments. The increase in the IAB Functioning of the social-learning group immediately following the program introduction was significantly greater than that of either the milieu or hospital groups, neither of which showed significant change. Over the next two years, the social-learning group kept showing additional significant improvement better than that of the other groups. A significant improvement of residents in the milieu program over patients in the hospital programs occurred at the fourth anniversary assessment, but neither group showed significant or differential change from the beginning to the end of the two-year period ending at the fifth anniversary assessment.

The negative effects of reducing the length of time for expulsion and time out for assaultive behavior just before the fifth anniversary assessment in psychosocial programs had been evident over the following year and a half in continuous objective assessments. IAB Functioning similarly reflected significant declines over this period for both psychosocial groups, while the hospital group did not change significantly. The renewed effectiveness of both psychosocial programs during the last six months, following the reintroduction of longer periods of expulsion and time out was apparent on IAB Functioning as well. Residents in both psychosocial programs showed significant improvement over the last six months, and they improved more than those in the hospital group did.

The IAB Functioning of social-learning residents reflected not only significant improvements over the other two groups at nearly every point during the intramural period but significant improvements in absolute level as well. In contrast, the IAB Functioning of the hospital group could essentially be presented as a flat horizontal line, since the absolute level did not differ significantly from that at project entry on a single anniversary assessment. The milieu group differed from pretreatment in absolute level of IAB Functioning only at the eighth anniversary assessment. However, the incidence of dangerous and aggressive acts appeared to have reactive effects on measurement, which reduced sensitivity to other improvements and suppressed the absolute level of functioning reflected on IAB assessments for the psychosocial groups.

The reactive effects were also apparent from the individual improvement rates on the IAB.[5] Even though individual improvement from entry to each anniversary assessment on the IAB ordered psychosocial residents in the same way as objective improvement data (mdn. r=0.60, range 0.52 to 0.71), IAB improvement never quite reflected the absolute number of residents who had objectively improved. On the last anniversary assessment, for example, objective improvement rates found that 89.3% of social-learning residents and 46.4% of milieu residents had improved significantly over all classes of behavior (table 29.3). Significant individual change in IAB Functioning at the same time found approximately a third of milieu and hospital residents improved and a third worse, without significant differences between them (chi-square < 1). While the social-learning group showed 71.4% residents improved on the IAB—significantly better than those in either the milieu or hospital groups (chi-squares > 8.95, p < 0.01)—the IAB assessments were still not including some improved residents. Not only was the incidence of Intolerable Behavior significantly negatively correlated with IAB Functioning on the last anniversary assessment for both social-learning ($r=-0.82$) and milieu residents ($r=-0.58$), but it was negatively correlated with IAB improvement scores as well. This correlation of Intolerable Behavior and IAB improvement (r's=-0.72 & -0.43, respectively, for social-learning and milieu groups) again reflected the extent to which residents failing to show improvement were those who were also performing dangerous and aggressive acts.

Possible differential predictability of IAB improvement from demographic variables was examined to see if personal characteristics other than assaultiveness were related to change over the three treatment programs (see note 3). The only consistent predictor of individual improvement on the IAB from entry to each successive anniversary assessment over all three groups combined was treatment group membership (mdn. $r=0.31$, range 0.26 to 0.51), indicating a significant tendency for improved residents to be first in the social-learning program, second in the milieu program, and last in the hospital programs. Within treatment groups, only one variable showed a greater than chance consistency for the social-learning group: on six of nine assessments social-learning residents showing significant improvement tended not to have received prior medical treatments (r's in the -0.30s & -0.40s). These correlations were not significantly different from zero-level correlations existing in the other two groups. There was a significant tendency for milieu residents showing IAB improvement to have relatively shorter periods of current hospitalization through the sixth anniversary assessment (mdn. $r=-0.51$, range -0.41 to -0.53). However, this relationship did not differ significantly from the zero-level correlations in the other two groups and dropped out for the milieu group thereafter, including the last anniversary assessment. Sex and socioeconomic status were both consistently correlated with IAB improvement for milieu residents (r's in the 0.30s & 0.40s). The correlations including socioeconomic status, however, dropped below significance when sex was partialled out of the relationship.

The correlation between sex and IAB improvement for the milieu group was not only significant but significantly different from the parallel relationship for the hospital group. On the last anniversary assessment, which was characteristic of previous points, milieu residents who showed IAB improvement tended to be female ($r=0.42$), and hospital residents tended to be male ($r=-0.34$). Sex was completely unrelated to improvement for social-learning residents ($r=0.00$). The only other significant correlation appearing more than once existed within the hospital group, where IAB improvements during the last half of the intramural period were negatively related to IAB Functioning at entry. On the last anniversary assessment, the negative relationship between initial IAB Functioning and change for the hospital group ($r=-0.62$) was significantly different from the zero-level correlations of both social-learning ($r=0.17$) and milieu groups ($r=0.08$). Other than an occasional significant negative relationship between prior IAB Functioning and change within milieu and hospital groups (r's in the -0.30s & -0.40s), only a chance number of significant correlations were found with IAB change from one anniversary assessment to the next, without significant differences between groups.

Summarizing correlational analyses, there was no regular overall or differential prediction of IAB improvement for the majority of demographic variables (age, race, socioeconomic status, process-reactive status, marital status, nature of symptom onset, identifiable precipitants on initial hospitalization, current or total length of hospitalization, prior electroconvulsive or insulin shock, or other medical treatments). In fact, none of the identified variables, including sex and prior level of functioning, significantly predicted improvement for residents in the social-learning program. Sex was a differential predictor between the milieu and hospital programs; females tended to do better than males in the milieu program, and males tended to do better than females in the hospital programs. The only consistent relationships that predicted improvement on continuous objective assessments were sex and length of current hospitalization for milieu residents. Shorter current hospitalization was also a significant predictor for milieu residents on IAB improvement, but only during the first half of the intramural period.

Other than sex, the only differential predictor between programs was the initial level of IAB Functioning, which was unrelated to change for psychosocial groups but was negatively related to it for the hospital group. About equal numbers of hospital residents showed "worse," "no change," and "improved" status at the last anniversary assessment, with the group data for hospitalized patients showing no mean change and a smaller variance than that of the psychosocial groups. Therefore, the negative relationship between initial level of functioning and change—indicating that higher-functioning residents became worse and lower-functioning residents improved—suggests that about 38% of the improvement variance on the IAB for the hospital group was the result of error of measurement (regression toward the mean). However, the major outcome of the correlational analyses overall is the relative absence of predictability of resident responsiveness by any variable other than treatment assignment.

In summary, as a group, patients in the traditional hospital programs failed to show significant change over the four and a half year intramural period, although at the time of the last anniversary assessment, approximately a third had improved and a third were worse in intramural functioning. These changes were unrelated to the level of drug dosage (although all were receiving psychotropic drugs) and showed a tendency for males and relatively lower-functioning patients on project entry to be among the improved subgroup, while females and relatively higher-functioning patients on project entry tended to be among the worse subgroup. Based upon intramural functioning, there is no evidence that traditional hospital procedures, including maintenance chemotherapy, made any significant impact on the chronically institutionalized population.

Comparative results of the overall milieu therapy program were less clear. On IAB assessments, milieu residents showed significant improvement in intramural functioning relative to the hospital group at the fourth anniversary assessment and significant loss at the eighth anniversary assessment, following a year and a half with ineffective procedures for dealing with assaultive behavior. Significant improvement relative to traditional hospital programs was obtained over the last six months, following the reintroduction of longer expulsion periods for assaultive behavior. However, on an absolute level, the milieu group did not show significant improvement on IAB assessments and did not differ from the hospital group on the last anniversary assessment. On the last anniversary assessment approximately a third of the milieu residents had improved and a third were worse on the IAB—as with the hospital group; the only significant predictor showed a tendency for females to be among the "improved" subgroup and males among the "worse" subgroup. These relationships were opposite to those in the hospital group. The IAB change for milieu residents was not related to other individual resident characteristics, initial level of functioning, or the use of psychotropic drugs.

Thus, based only upon intramural functioning as assessed on the IAB, results at the last anniversary assessment led to the conclusion not only that the social-learning program was better than the other two, but that the hospital and milieu programs were equally ineffective, with neither producing improvement. However, the reactivity of the IAB assessments to the incidence of dangerous and aggressive acts raises some question on the overall ineffectiveness of the milieu therapy program. On continuous objective assessments, the milieu program had produced improvement in Global Functioning that approached significance and improvements in several classes of behavior that were clearly significant. By the last anniversary assessment, the milieu program had effectively produced reductions in dysfunctional cognitive behavior and hostile-belligerence that were as great as those produced by the social-learning program. While not as effective as the social-learning program, the milieu program had also significantly reduced clinically inappropriate bizarre motoric behavior and had increased adaptive self-care behaviors. Although the social-learning program also showed significantly greater improvement on all remaining classes of behavior, the milieu program did not show any change on inappropriate response to minimal expectations, concurrent appropriate behavior, interpersonal skills, or instrumental role performance.

The milieu program showed significant change for the worse on only one class of behavior: the performance of the dangerous and aggressive acts reflected in Intolerable Behavior. Although the lengthened period for expulsion that was reintroduced during the last twenty weeks significantly reduced the incidence of Intolerable Behavior, overall milieu therapy procedures were still largely ineffective in controlling such acts. Thus, although the milieu program was clearly less effective than the social-learning program across all targets for rehabilitation of the chronically institutionalized population, the reactivity of IAB assessments to a single class of inappropriate behavior may have suppressed scores enough to mask real improvements of the milieu program relative to those of the hospital programs.

Residents failing to demonstrate significant overall improvement on IAB assessments as well as on continuous objective assessments in both psychosocial programs were largely accounted for by those still showing an excess of performance in that single class of inappropriate behavior. Although the relative effectiveness of the overall programs without focus on specific critical behaviors could not be clearer on intramural functioning, the practical effectiveness in achieving significant release might well be altered. That is, residents showing significant improvement in other areas of functioning sufficient to achieve community placement could potentially be precluded from release solely by the excess in that single class of inappropriate behavior. That class of critical behavior became the primary focus of milieu and social-learning procedures before consideration of release for residents still showing intolerable behavior.

However, unquestionable results on the effectiveness of the social-learning program on intramural functioning were yielded by the data at the last anniversary assessment, as well as at earlier periods. The overall social-learning program had produced significant gains for the most severely debilitated group of chronically institutionalized mental patients ever subjected to systematic study. The improvement occurred without regard to differences in individual resident characteristics, prior treatment history, or initial level of functioning and in the relative absence of psychotropic drugs. The incidence of dangerous and aggressive acts was the only factor that systematically influenced other resident behavior outside of program characteristics, and these acts could be controlled by social-learning procedures when adequate consequences for assaultiveness were possible. The improvements in intramural functioning and humanness produced by the overall social-learning program were clearly superior to both the milieu therapy and the traditional hospital programs. Based upon intramural functioning, the social-learning program is clearly the treatment of choice for the severely debilitated, adult, chronically institutionalized mental patient.

# 35. Comparative Release Rates

The comparative changes in intramural functioning left little question about the superiority of the social-learning program over both the milieu and the hospital programs. Although no significant differences were obtained between the milieu and hospital programs by the last anniversary assessment, the milieu program had produced some significant improvement on continuous objective assessments, which may not have been reflected on the Inpatient Assessment Battery (IAB) because of the reactivity to the incidence of Intolerable Behavior. By the time of the last anniversary assessment, significant releases to independent functioning, without reinstitutionalization, had already occurred for 10.7% of the original social-learning group and 7.1% of the original milieu therapy group. None of the original hospital group had achieved release to independent functioning.

Although the criteria for release were not reduced from independent functioning (requiring self-support and independent living arrangements) to community placement (allowing board and care living arrangements without work) until six months before the last anniversary assessment, two such releases had occurred. One early community placement was a social-learning resident whose heart trouble precluded his continued participation in the active treatment program but who had improved sufficiently for community placement. The other early community placement was a hospital resident who was placed by hospital staff in her parents' home, without individual responsibilities or self-support. The social-learning resident remained out of the institution, but the hospital patient had been reinstitutionalized.

## EFFECTIVENESS IN ACHIEVING SIGNIFICANT RELEASE

The overall effectiveness of the three treatment approaches in achieving significant release at termination of the psychosocial programs is presented in table 35.1, which shows the same superiority of the social-learning program to the other two groups in achieving significant release as had been found on intramural functioning (p's < 0.01).[1] Additionally the milieu therapy program was found to achieve more significant releases than the hospital program had, with additional releases approaching statistical significance for all residents treated (chi-square=3.21, df=1, p < 0.10).

The majority of significant releases were to private board and care homes (88.9%, 84.2%, and 100%, respectively, for the original social-learning, milieu, and hospital groups) rather than to independent living. Although the relatively high release rate for the hospital group suggests that community standards for acceptable functioning may have lowered over the project period, the comparative release rates between groups would not be affected. Given the level of initial disability and the fact that all residents had been rejected for such community placement four and a half years earlier, these release rates are indeed remarkable.

Although the release rates for all residents treated follow essentially the same pattern as for those for the original equated groups, the composition of the "ever treated" groups provides even more evidence of the practical superiority of the social-learning program. In addition to replacements for original patients who achieved early releases to independent living or early community placements (four, three, and one, respectively, for social-learning, milieu, and hospital groups)—in which original group equation was maintained—the "ever treated" group for the social-learning program also includes eight failures from the milieu program. Thus, every resident who received the social-learning program with specific focus on critical intolerable behaviors achieved release to community placement with a minimum of ninety days' stay, including residents who had failed to respond to focused milieu therapy. In fact, the only social-learning resident who failed to achieve significant release was one who had improved but was still performing an Intolerable Behavior that could

Table 35.1. Comparative rates of significant release at termination of intramural programs.

| Treatment program | % achieving significant release | | | |
|---|---|---|---|---|
| | No. | Original equated groups | No. | All residents treated |
| Social-learning | 28 | 96.4% | 40 | 97.5% |
| Milieu therapy | 28 | 67.9% | 31 | 71.0% |
| Hospital comparison | 28 | 46.4% | 29 | 44.8% |

Note. Significant release required a minimum continuous community stay of ninety days. Chi-square =16.90, $df=2, p < 0.01$ for original groups; Chi-square=24.46, $df=2, p < 0.01$ for ever-treated groups.

not be treated by focused overcorrection/restitution procedures because of his physical condition. Similarly, the only milieu failure who was not treated by social-learning procedures was one whose physical condition precluded the focused social-learning procedures. Functionally, all residents whose physical condition allowed active treatment participation in social-learning procedures improved and achieved significant release from the institution.

## EFFICIENCY IN ACHIEVING SIGNIFICANT RELEASE

The social-learning procedures were significantly more effective than those of either the milieu therapy or traditional hospital procedures in improving resident behavior and in achieving release from mental institutions with minimum stay in the community. Milieu therapy procedures approached significantly greater effectiveness compared to hospital procedures with regard to release criteria. The average project weeks in the institution at the termination of the psychosocial programs—presented in table 35.2—show that the psychosocial programs also involved significantly less time than the hospital programs did.[2]

The absolute time in programs presented in table 35.2 does not accurately reflect the minimum time required to produce significant release to community placement, since the minimum periods were largely a function of the previously established design. However, the comparisons between programs can indicate the relative efficiency of the three. For the original equated groups, both psychosocial programs showed significantly greater variance (F's > 3.81, df=27/27, p < 0.01) and significantly less time in institution (Z's > 3.88, p < 0.01, Mann-Whitney U test) than the hospital group did, without differences between the milieu and social-learning groups (p > 0.25). These differences primarily reflect the relatively early releases to independent functioning of the psychosocial groups.

When all residents treated are considered, significant differences were obtained between all groups in variance (F's > 3.29, p < 0.01) and in time spent in programs (Z's > 2.05, p < 0.05, Mann-Whitney U test). These differences reflect the shorter lengths of time in treatment for replacements and the remarkably short lengths of time required for focused social-learning procedures to eliminate intolerable behavior (usually eight weeks or less). The more effective procedures were also the more efficient. In fact, based upon the last six months of the intramural period and the speed with which focused social-learning procedures

Table 35.2. Comparative efficiency in achieving successful community placement at termination of intramural programs.

| Treatment program | Project weeks in institution | | | | | |
|---|---|---|---|---|---|---|
| | Original equated groups [a] | | | All residents ever treated [b] | | |
| | No. | Mean | S.D. | No. | Mean | S.D. |
| Social-learning | 28 | 213.3 | 47.12 | 40 | 161.2 | 94.78 |
| Milieu therapy | 28 | 215.1 | 43.32 | 31 | 207.5 | 53.85 |
| Hospital comparison | 28 | 231.1 | 22.18 | 29 | 231.4 | 21.83 |

a. Kruskal-Wallis $H=23.50, df=2, p < 0.01$.
b. $H=34.50, df=2, p < 0.01$.

were able to eliminate intolerable behavior, board and care placement as an ultimate target could reasonably be expected in twenty-six to thirty weeks of social-learning treatment for chronic mental patients without physical problems.

## RELATIONSHIP TO INTRAMURAL FUNCTIONING AND PREDICTABILITY OF SIGNIFICANT RELEASE

Although release rates paralleled the results of intramural assessments, the relationship of IAB Functioning to significant release was examined. Since IAB assessments had shown lower reliability for the hospital group and probable reactivity to Intolerable Behavior for psychosocial groups, differences in absolute level were of interest. A comparison of mean IAB Functioning Scores for all released residents (53.19) versus the mean for all residents not released (46.70) found that released residents scored significantly higher on the last IAB assessment than did those who did not achieve significant release (t=3.11, df=82, p < 0.01). Among released residents, the three groups did not differ significantly in average IAB Functioning (F < 1), and psychosocial residents who achieved release were no longer showing high rates of Intolerable Behavior. Thus, the equality of scores among released residents indicates that community placements were employing the same criteria across treatment groups for accepting and retaining residents.

Psychosocial residents who did not achieve significant release had a significantly larger variance (F=3.76, df=9/14, p < 0.05) and a significantly lower average IAB Functioning Score than hospital residents did (42.44 & 49.54, respectively, for psychosocial and hospital failures, t=2.90, df=9 & 14, p < 0.01). All psychosocial residents failing to achieve release were those who were still performing intolerable behaviors at a high rate (before transfer to focused social-learning procedures); therefore, the analyses further supported the reactivity of IAB assessments to dangerous and aggressive acts. Correlational analyses added supportive evidence to these findings.[3] The last objective Global Functioning Score significantly predicted release versus no release for milieu residents (r=0.53), with all components of continuous objectively assessed behavior contributing in expected directions (r's in the ± 0.30s & ± 0.40s). However, the two highest predictors of release for milieu residents were Total Inappropriate Clinical Frequencies (r=-0.60) and Intolerable Behavior (r=-0.49), reflecting the extent to which the dangerous and aggressive acts they represented affected not only IAB assessments but acceptability for release as well.

The release of social-learning residents could not be entered into correlational analyses, since all showed significant improvement after the focused treatment for those performing intolerable behavior on the last anniversary assessment, and all but one achieved significant release—thereby leaving no variance. The correlations between final scores on IAB assessments and release status for milieu and hospital groups showed that overall IAB Functioning was significantly related to release (r=0.55 & 0.40, respectively, for milieu and hospital groups), as were each of the individual components, without significant differences between groups. Final IMPS Total Morbidity scores were also significantly related to release, although at a lower level than IAB scores (r's=-0.37 & -0.38).[4] While differences between groups were not statistically significant, IAB improvement scores were significantly related to release for the milieu group (r=0.40) but not for the hospital group (r=0.17). The absence of a relationship between improvement and release for the hospital group adds further support to the intramural data, indicating the lack of impact of traditional hospital programs on the chronically institutionalized mental patient.

The correlations between demographic variables, drug status, and release showed only one significant predictor over milieu and hospital groups combined and only one significant differential relationship. The social-learning group could not be entered into correlational analyses since all but one resident achieved significant release. The significant differential relationship involved sex—the same differential predictor that had been found on intramural improvement. As with improvement in intramural functioning, releases from the milieu program tended to involve more females than males (r=0.38) to a significantly greater extent than in the hospital programs, where a slight tendency existed for more males than females to be released (r=-0.21). The one significant predictor over combined groups was drug status before release, in which patients receiving higher dosages of psychotropic drugs tended not to be released (r=-0.42). Although the differences between groups were not statistically significant, the relationship between drug status and release was primarily the function of a significant correlation within the hospital group (r=-0.38), while the correlation within the milieu group was not significant (r=-0.10). None of the remaining demographic variables (age, race, socioeconomic status, process-reactive status, marital history, nature of symptom onset, identifiable precipitants on initial hospitalization, current or total length of hospitalization, prior electroconvulsive or insulin shock, or other medical treatments) predicted release overall or differentially for milieu and hospital groups.

## SUMMARY OF COMPARATIVE RELEASE

Of the original equated groups, 10.7% of social-learning residents, 7.1% of milieu residents, and none of the hospital residents achieved release to independent functioning and self-support without reinstitutionalization. Given the severe debility of these patients at project entry, the fact that any of the patients achieved such release is remarkable. The remainder of all releases were to community placements in private extended-care board and room facilities. The level of functioning required for such living arrangements is marginal, but it does require an absence of extreme bizarre behaviors and acceptable levels of self-maintenance and social behavior to function not only within the home but with the local community. Since all patients had previously been rejected for such community placements before project entry, the release rates (table 35.1) provide clear, independent social-action criteria of relative effectiveness.

The comparative release rates show the superiority of the social-learning program to the other two groups in bringing residents to the point of achieving release from the institution with a minimum successful stay of at least ninety days in the community. Additionally, while yielding significantly fewer releases than the social-learning program did, the milieu program achieved more releases than the traditional hospital programs did, with the number approaching statistical significance. The more effective programs were also the more efficient; patients achieved release in less time than they did from the hospital programs.

The only significant differential predictor of release between groups was sex; females tended to be released more than males from the milieu program, and the opposite relationship was obtained for the hospital group. Patients receiving higher dosages of psychotropic drugs tended not to be released from the hospital. Drug status was unrelated to release in the psychosocial programs, where relatively few residents were receiving any drugs at all. Measures of intramural functioning were significant predictors of release, with higher-functioning residents being those who were successfully released. Improvement during the intramural period was also significantly related to release for psychosocial groups but not for the hospital group—further indicating that the treatment received by the hospital group had little to do with their ultimate status. However, the ineffectiveness of milieu therapy procedures in dealing with dangerous and aggressive acts was in evidence in relationship to release, since the strongest individual predictors of no release for the milieu group were indicators of such acts.

The release rates for the social-learning program are even more impressive since all but one milieu failure was successfully treated by social-learning procedures. The only social-learning resident failing to achieve significant release and the only milieu failure not treated by social-learning procedures were people whose physical condition precluded active participation in overcorrection/restitution for eliminating intolerable behavior. Thus, every resident whose physical condition allowed active treatment participation in social-learning procedures improved significantly and achieved significant release from the institution. The improvement and release occurred without regard to differences in individual resident characteristics, prior treatment history, or initial level of functioning and in the relative absence of psychotropic drugs. The social-learning procedures clearly emerge as the best treatment for the severely debilitated chronically institutionalized mental patient, based not only upon intramural functioning but the remarkable absolute effectiveness in achieving release with community stay as well.

# 36. Summary of Findings From Programs and Placement

The state hospital comparison remained exceptionally stable over the entire intramural period. Cooperative arrangements were maintained after the original equation of hospital and psychosocial groups, and all six-month anniversary assessments were made on schedule. Extended-care community facilities had been located by the last anniversary assessment, and negotiations were completed for psychosocial staff to carry out aftercare consultation and follow-up. During processing for release, both psychosocial programs focused treatment upon individual intolerable behaviors that still remained from the year and a half without effective consequences for assaults. Acceptable residents from all three intramural programs were released, with extended-care facilities determining acceptability, and psychosocial staff providing transfer and orientation to community placements. Failures from the milieu program were transferred to the social-learning program to receive continued focal treatment of critical intolerable behaviors.

Work had continued on the expanded design to include prechronic patients, with the majority of community arrangements and all intramural details completed, but future intramural operations were suddenly halted by new administrative policies in the Department of Mental Health, which resulted in layoff of over 2,000 employees in the department, including the top professional staff of the psychosocial units. The psychosocial units and all future expansions were immediately terminated. However, an extension and supplemental federal grant funds allowed the continued aftercare consultation and follow-up of releases from all three original intramural programs. Fortunately, the integrity of the evaluation of the comparative treatment of the hard-core chronic groups was not violated by these events, since the intramural treatment and community placements from the original programs had been completed on the very day that the layoffs were announced.

The comparisons between the original psychosocial and hospital groups on intramural functioning as assessed by the Inpatient Assessment Battery (IAB), reported in chapter 34, found the social-learning program to be differentially more effective than either the milieu therapy or the traditional hospital programs at nearly every anniversary assessment. The major overall trends in IAB Functioning reflected changes for psychosocial groups that paralleled continuous objective assessments. Over the first two and a half years, the social-learning program showed major and significant improvement, which was greater than that of either milieu or traditional hospital programs, and the milieu program produced slight gains compared to those of the hospital programs. The negative effects of reduced consequences for assaults were apparent in significant declines over the next year and a half in both psychosocial groups; the hospital group showed no significant change.

IAB Functioning, as well as continuous objective assessments, showed significant improvement for both psychosocial programs over the last six months, following the reintroduction of effective procedures for controlling assaultiveness. This increase of both milieu and social-learning groups was significantly greater than that of the hospital group. None of the assessed individual characteristics (age, sex, race, socioeconomic status, process-reactive status, marital status, nature of symptom onset, identifiable precipitants on initial hospitalization, current or total length of hospitalization, electroconvulsive or insulin shock, or other medical treatments) or initial level of functioning, or previous or current drug status predicted improvement in IAB Functioning for the social-learning group. Sex was a differential predictor of improvement between milieu and hospital programs, and initial level of IAB Functioning was a significant predictor of improvement in the hospital group but not in either psychosocial program.

Patients in the traditional hospital programs failed, as a group, to show significant change over the intramural period of nearly four and a half years; there was thus no evidence that traditional hospital procedures, including chemotherapy, made any significant impact on the chronically institutionalized population. The IAB Functioning of the milieu group showed significant differences from that of the hospital group on only two assessments over the entire period, without significant differences on the last anniversary assessment. However, the reactivity of IAB assessments to the incidence of dangerous and aggressive acts may have masked improvements known to have occurred from continuous objective assessments for the psychosocial groups. Although the milieu and hospital programs were less effective than the social-learning program was the reactivity of IAB assessments may have suppressed scores enough for the milieu program to mask real differences relative to hospital programs. Even with this reactivity, the improvements obtained in intramural functioning by the social-learning program were not only significant on an absolute level but were clearly superior to both the milieu therapy program and the traditional hospital programs.

The superiority of the social-learning program to the other two groups in intramural functioning was also apparent in the extent to which residents achieved release from the institution with a minimum successful stay of at least ninety days in the community. As detailed in chapter 35, of the original equated groups, 10.7% of social-learning residents, 7.1% of milieu residents, and 0.0% of hospital patients achieved significant release to relatively independent functioning and self-support without reinstitutionalization—any such release being remarkable, given the severe levels of disability at project entry. The remainder of all releases were to community placements in private extended-care board and room facilities.

The success of the social-learning program in bringing about sufficient improvement in residents for them to achieve significant release from the institution with successful community stay was impressive. Every resident whose physical condition allowed active treatment participation in social-learning procedures—including replacements and previous failures from the milieu program—improved significantly and achieved significant release from the institution. The improvements and releases were unrelated to individual resident characteristics, prior treatment history, or initial level of functioning and occurred in the relative absence of psychotropic drugs. Although it yielded significantly fewer releases than the social-learning program did, the milieu program did achieve more releases than traditional hospital programs did. The more effective programs were also the more efficient. Measures of intramural functioning were significant predictors of release, with the only significant differential predictor between groups being sex between milieu and hospital groups. Patients receiving higher dosages of psychotropic drugs tended not to be released from the hospital; drugs were unrelated to release in psychosocial programs, where few residents were still receiving them. The strongest individual predictors of no release in the milieu program reflected the continued presence of dangerous and aggressive acts.

Thus, although the level of functioning required for the majority of community placements was still marginal, the overall results upon the termination of the psychosocial units could not be clearer. After having spent about two-thirds of their adult lives in the confines of mental institutions, all of the most debilitated people ever subjected to systematic study whose physical condition allowed active participation in social-learning procedures achieved improvement and release with community stay. Based upon both objective and rated improvements in intramural functioning, and the remarkable absolute effectiveness in achieving release with community stay, social-learning procedures clearly emerge as the treatment of choice for the severely debilitated chronically institutionalized mental patient.

PART 8
# A Year and a Half After: Community Follow-up with Social-Learning Principles

## 37. Notable Events and Overview of the Follow-up Period

The most notable event affecting the overall project operation during the follow-up period was the sudden unanticipated statewide layoff of staff, which led to the decision to terminate psychosocial programs. These events, as detailed in chapter 33, fortunately did not violate the integrity of comparative evaluations of the intramural programs as notification came after intramural work and community placements of the original comparative project had been completed. The layoff of all original psychosocial aftercare staff resulted in a period of considerable confusion in the extended-care facilities because many prior agreements became invalidated, resulting in loss of credibility of all staff associated with the Department of Mental Health. The loss of support also restricted the formal follow-up to eighteen months rather than two years, and it restricted follow-up assessments of all released residents to components of the Inpatient Assessment Battery that could be obtained without professional staff on site (see chapter 11), although objective observational assessments were obtained in two extended-care facilities in which different modes of follow-up consultation occurred.

The confusion among extended-care facilities and community clinics was further aggravated by a period in which new aftercare staff had not yet been identified. Before the departure of the zone director and acting superintendent of the center, agreements were negotiated with the new administration of the Department of Mental Health to provide support for the minimum clinical staff judged necessary to complete the year and a half declining-contact aftercare consultation and support of previously obligated research personnel needed to complete data analyses to meet contractual obligations of the center to the federal government. Even with such agreements, any remaining professional staff who had not been laid off were understandably reluctant to remain in the system when job opportunities in other states appeared much more stable. Eventually three psychologists agreed to take on the job and risk the unknown support conditions and the known hostility existing in the community as a result of broken commitments by the department. Psychosocial aftercare consultation was, therefore, undertaken by one M.A.-level psychologist (Dale E. Theobald) assigned to the project and two part-time psychologists—one M.A.-level (William Kohen) and one B.A.-level (Christopher T. Power)—who had previously been trained on the project and were negotiated as temporary part-time workers on loan from their new intramural assignments. For a period of three months, the new aftercare consultants (working as two full-time equivalents) attempted to familiarize themselves with the problems existing with extended-care facilities and other community liaisons and to carry out the prescribed aftercare consultations.

Unfortunately, additional problems were imposed when a new superintendent came on the center payroll. Although he used human services terminology, "The Superintendent" (as he referred to himself) attempted a total restructuring of center operations along traditional hospital administrative lines (see chapter 4), with weekly "general rounds," multiple centralized services, and administration by fiat in written memos. He believed that "schizophrenia is a reliably diagnosed condition unquestionably caused by an enzyme deficit, resulting in a need for life-long phenothiazines and an exaggerated need-affiliation." He thus attempted to establish medical authority over all aspects of the center, including local community affiliations, with a stated lack of concern for agreements established before his arrival.

The new zone director, who replaced the original zone director and acting superintendent, appeared to take a true laissez-faire approach to administration. The superintendent's aggressive administration within a model completely contrary to prior center operations thus seemed to drive away the majority of talented staff who remained after the layoffs and disheartened those who remained. The superintendent arbitrarily negated previous agreements, which caused considerable difficulty for project staff during the follow-up period (e.g., terminating the project director's consultant status; refusing to pay salaries of research personnel upon termination of special federal assistance programs for the unemployed; demanding that research psychologists supported by the federal research grant for purposes of completing data analyses serve time "doing psychologicals" for center patients through the new Psychology Division); however, only two of his actions had direct impact on the follow-up of community placements: a further reduction of the part-time follow-up staff on-loan to a total of nine months rather than a year and an order on channels of admission to the center that caused another broken commitment to community clinics and extended-care facilities.

While the reduction of staff did not ultimately cause difficulty for follow-up, both the nature and the manner in which the superintendent established new policies on admissions caused additional problems in an environment already questioning the credibility of any agreements. New procedures were communicated by memo, prohibiting direct admissions to the center and requiring a long series of community assessments, reports, etc., following which—several days later—an admission could occur. Psychosocial aftercare staff had previous arrangements to admit any released resident directly for brief assessment and treatment should crisis intervention be necessary. Unfortunately one of the two instances in which such an admission was required over the follow-up period occurred immediately after the superintendent's directive on admissions, and the resident was denied admittance. A series of meetings were quickly held among intramural clinical directors, the center assistant superintendent, subzone community staff, and psychosocial aftercare staff in which new arrangements were agreed upon that appeared to meet the requirements of the superintendent's admission procedures and allowed reasonable fulfillment of prior agreements with community agencies and facilities; however, the superintendent was not available for the latter meetings. Upon his return he vetoed the new agreements, which was the final blow for many community agency staff and at least one extended-care operator, necessitating multiple meetings to again salvage tenuous community relations.

Ultimately, cooperative agreements were established with community facilities and agencies, completely excluding relationships with the center. Aftercare consultation then proceeded smoothly through declining contact, ultimate fading out of psychosocial consultants, and transfer of monitoring and aftercare consultation to usual community agencies. Details of the effects of the changes at the center, additional problems encountered in the extended-care facilities themselves, and the actual follow-up procedures and staffing that finally occurred are described in chapter 38.

Several other uncontrolled crises occurred over the follow-up period, which caused additional stress for remaining psychosocial research staff but did not affect the follow-up of released residents. As noted in chapter 33, presidential impoundment of federal research funds had required rapid emergency requests for an extension and supplenental funds to support research staff until the impoundment was overcome. The supplement was eventually obtained, but notification was made after the starting date for the extension once again. Ultimately the trained observer staff had to be reduced as a result of the superintendent's redistribution of funds to the extent that planned multi-institutional validity studies had to be delayed, and a new grant application was submitted to fund that effort later.

Meanwhile, the discovery of keypunch errors in some data, described in chapter 11, delayed data analysis beyond the time when the center computer had been removed. These delays, combined with the absence of one of the psychosocial research analysts for a required period of training in the army, followed by the graduation of the only two research analysts who were familiar with the computer programs and the massive amounts of data (Marco J. Mariotto and Joel P. Redfield), resulted in the need for another emergency request for a supplement and extension of federal funds. Through the continuing assistance of staff of the National Institute of Mental Health (James T. Cumisky and Howard R. Davis), the additional funds were again obtained. Two more extensions and supplements were finally required to complete data analysis because of the absence of federal funds to begin the new grant, but the latter crises occurred after completion of the final follow-up..

The remaining chapters of part 8 report the procedures and findings of the formal period of follow-up assessments and psychosocial aftercare consultation over the year and a half after community placements. The overall characteristics of psychosocial aftercare consultation are described in chapter 38, as well as details of timing and problems during this time. The procedures of two different modes of delivery of aftercare consultation are also presented in chapter 38, along with details of programs and staff behavior in two different extended-care facilities receiving the different modes of consultation. Readers not interested in the details can obtain an adequate orientation for understanding later chapters by reading the summary at the end of the chapter. Changes and predictability of the level of functioning in the community for significant releases from the original intramural programs and differences within community facilities receiving different modes of aftercare consultation are presented in chapter 39. It is relatively short, and statistical analyses are incorporated in text; preprofessional staff and others short on time can obtain a clear understanding of findings on the level of functioning in the community by reading the end-of-chapter summary. All data concerning the comparative results of the hospital, milieu, and social-learning programs in practical terms are presented in chapter 40. Statistical analyses are incorporated in text, but data concerning comparative release rates with continuing community stay, and relative efficiency of original treatment programs to the end of the formal follow-up period are straightforward and should be of interest to all readers. Details of cost-effectiveness may be less interesting to readers other than professional research workers, program directors, and legislators, thus the practical and economic outcomes are covered in the tables and the summary. Chapter 41 briefly summarizes the major conclusions of findings at the end of the formal project.

# 38. Follow-up Consultation to Community Facilities and Resulting Programs

## NONSPECIFIC CHARACTERISTICS OF PSYCHOSOCIAL AFTERCARE CONSULTATION

There were three different modes of aftercare consultation (independent functioning, case consultation to extended-care facilities, program consultation to extended-care facilities) in the community follow-up of releases from all three intramural treatment groups. Although the clients differed—ex-residents or significant others for independent releases versus extended-care facilities and staff for community placements—certain characteristics guided all psychosocial consultation and were thus nonspecific to any particular mode. A major guiding characteristic was that responsible aftercare consultants were to be identified, available, and predictable. Thus, consultation was to follow a declining-contact schedule, with additional contacts as needed before and after the initial six-months' intensive aftercare and twenty-four months of regularly scheduled assessments. The person and backup responsible for a client or facility for any time period was to be identified, and telephone numbers were available so that a knowledgeable consultant could be reached at any time. Necessary contacts initiated by a client were thus responded to immediately with telephone consultation and occasionally through on-site crisis intervention.

A second major nonspecific characteristic was that psychosocial aftercare consultation was geared toward the ultimate independence of the clients. In addition to the declining-contact schedule and preestablished dates for the termination of scheduled consultative contacts, the content of consultation was focused upon transfer of decision making and problem solving from the consultant to the client as rapidly as possible. Not only were consultant contacts faded, but within-contact interactions shifted from consultant-initiated solutions being applied and trained to eliciting solutions and implementation directly from the client. The last step in fading consultative contacts was when clients no longer relied upon consultants at all but merely informed the consultant of action and outcome.

A third nonspecific characteristic was that all psychosocial aftercare consultation followed an experimental-behavioral strategy with an educational focus (described in chapter 3). The content of consultation focused upon specific desirable or undesirable behaviors of ex-residents—descriptively defined as to the time, place, and circumstance in which behaviors were or were not occurring—and determined the focus of change efforts (the person's behavior, nature of environmental events, existing functional relationships, or the contingency of existing environmental events and the individual's behavior). Thus, assessment was always the first step of a consultative contact, including data collection when possible. A program of change was then designed and implemented, and assessment of the success of the procedures continued—again, with data collection when possible. When objective data could not be obtained, detailed descriptive reports of the frequency and/or intensity of behaviors in question were obtained. Experience with the first two releases to independent functioning from the milieu therapy program readily showed that milieu principles were infeasible for independent aftercare consultation (see the illustrative cases in chapter 19). Since preliminary analyses had already documented the clear superiority of the social-learning program for the chronically institutionalized mental patient, social-learning operational principles and procedures were adopted for all aftercare consultation.

Psychosocial residents who achieved release to relatively independent functioning all received individual aftercare consultation. The majority of significant releases from both psychosocial programs and all releases from the hospital comparison group were to private extended-care facilities. Original community placements for releases from all three intramural groups were arranged by psychosocial staff over eight separate facilities in five different communities within the region, ranging from the local community next to the center to communities up to eighty-five miles away. Following completion of the transfer and orientation procedures for all community placements, psychosocial staff established commitments to provide aftercare consultation to each extended-care facility on the declining-contact basis for the first six months, followed by six-month assessments for a total of two years, and consultation as needed in addition. The uncontrolled events described in chapters 33 and 37 resulted in a loss of psychosocial staff and reassignment of aftercare consultation to new psychosocial staff, changes in prior agreements, and a restriction of total follow-up to a year and a half rather than two years. The planned nonspecific characteristics for aftercare were implemented, nevertheless.

Prior agreements had been obtained from all extended-care facilities that no released project resident would be transferred without a four-day notice to aftercare staff, since private facilities in the region were notorious for shifting residents around. In the event that a transfer was to be considered on the basis of an undesirable behavior, that four-day period was to be allowed for consultation to change the undesirable behavior. In other instances, transfers were frequently initiated by a relative or the resident of the extended-care facility, usually based upon a desire to move to another location closer to the resident's original home. In these instances, the four-day period was to allow psychosocial aftercare staff time to investigate the alternative arrangements being considered, provide advice on which placement appeared to be in the ex-resident's best long-range interest, and make arrangements for follow-up assessment and consultation if a move was made. Extended-care staff were unreliable in following their part of the agreement, especially concerning moves initiated by residents or relatives and particularly during the first six months after placement when the commitments from psychosocial staff were changed. Of the original placements in extended-care facilities, 16.9% moved during the year and a half follow-up; about a quarter of the moves had been arranged before aftercare staff were notified. Generally, however, consultation was requested when problem behaviors occurred, and the relationship between extended-care facility staff and psychosocial staff ultimately became a positive one.

## TWO MODES OF FOLLOW-UP

Two local facilities made sufficient beds available to attempt a controlled comparison of two different modes of delivery of aftercare consultation: one focusing in the traditional manner upon the specific individual case and the other upon development of an ongoing program through which individual problems might be handled and, perhaps, residents further improved in functioning. Of the original community placements, 77.3% of significant releases to extended-care facilities from all three intramural groups were to these two facilities, with the prerelease level of functioning in the center or hospital being equated between them. The remainder of community placements were to the other six facilities, each of which received the traditional mode of case consultation but following the identified nonspecific characteristics of aftercare consultation. Except for the period of confusion during the first three months when original aftercare staff had been notified of their layoff and new aftercare staff had not yet been identified, consulting contacts with the other six facilities went largely according to schedule.[1] One full-time equivalent staff member handled these consultations, with one full-day travel needed to cover facilities in each of three geographic areas. By nine months after placement, regular consultations to facilities in other communities consisted largely of telephone checks, requiring fewer than four hours per month, with only an occasional request for consultation during the second six months of follow-up and none during the last six months.

*Community Facilities.* The two local extended-care facilities that were identified for a comparison of case consultation versus program consultation consisted of one 120-bed and one 65-bed facility, with staff-to-resident ratios of 0.22 to 0.25 over the follow-up period. The larger facility had previously been a monastic retreat, and the smaller one was a converted motel. Each facility was privately owned, and the operator had an office in the building but was not in contact with residents. An administrator was responsible for direct operations, assisted by an activities director and a program director (often B.A.-level), and all remaining staff were nonprofessional. Each facility was licensed for shelter-care service and was approved for activities and social rehabilitation programs, receiving licensing and approval from the State Departments of Public Health and Public Aid. Aftercare consultation for ex-mental patients was normally handled by the local community clinic, monitored by subzone staff of the Department of Mental Health. Nearly all residents of both facilities had previously been residents of state institutions and were supported through direct payments to the facility operator from public aid funds. Residents from the three original project groups constituted about 33% of the population of the smaller facility and about 26% of the population of the larger facility.

*Follow-up Contacts.* The larger facility was to receive usual case consultation from psychosocial staff following the nonspecific characteristics. The smaller one was to receive program consultation from psychosocial staff, through which a modified social-learning program would be instituted. Crisis intervention was provided in both facilities, and the same psychosocial aftercare staff handled all consultation to both facilities. Consultative contacts at both facilities were originally planned to start with full-day scheduled contacts for two weeks, following completion of the transfer and orientation of residents. Scheduled daily contacts at each facility were then to be systematically faded in two-week blocks to three per week, two per week, one per week, and finally a scheduled once per week walk-through for monitoring purposes, up to the last six months. For the last six months, the original plan called for fading to weekly, biweekly, and monthly telephone contacts, with no consultant-initiated contacts planned at all for the last three months.

During the initial period of intensive consultation, psychosocial aftercare consultants were to establish a modified social-learning program in the smaller facility, working out the details of scheduling, token costs, and record keeping with the administrator and the activities and program directors. A brief manual was prepared and distributed to all staff, and intensive consultation then focused on training staff following the same principles described for the integrated/technical mode of staff training that had been used in psychosocial programs but with consultants handling all modeling and training. Consultation was, therefore, geared toward assisting staff of the facility to carry out a program, with consultation for individual residents focused upon the activities director or program director, helping that person acquire skills in functional analysis to implement modifications of the overall program for dealing with unique problems.

Concurrently the same amount of scheduled consultant time at the large facility was to focus on individual residents, with the consultant first working out a specific program for any resident with whom facility staff wished assistance. Programs for treating particular resident behaviors were written and taught to the facility staff for treatment of individuals, and the consultant followed the procedures described in chapter 10 for on-the-job training but with a criterion of a single successful application. After the majority of questions had been raised for specific residents and several individual programs written, psychosocial aftercare consultants could fade direct problem solving by eliciting ideas from facility staff themselves, based upon the functional similarity of new questions and those for which programs had already been developed.

Although the essence of the above plans was eventually carried out, the planned schedule of contacts was drastically modified, and several unanticipated events required renegotiations (see chapter 37). Additionally, uncontrolled events within the facilities themselves resulted in fewer differences in procedure than had been originally established. Although a modified program was worked out and presented to staff in the smaller facility, a combination of rapid turnover of facility staff—particularly the activities director who changed four times during the first six months—and timing of the notification of layofffs of the original extramural psychosocial staff resulted in institution of a weak token-economy program, but without facility staff having completed training by the end of the first three months. There were further difficulties in program consultation when external personnel ordered facility residents who had not come from the project originally to be removed from any contingent consequences because contingent disbursement of either funds or goods was interpreted as being counter to public aid regulations. Thus, by the time new psychosocial aftercare staff were identified and introduced, the facility receiving program consultation was attempting to use social-learning principles in interpersonal interactions with all residents, but token consequences and backups could be used only with residents released from the original intramural project groups; furthermore, staff were not yet completely trained in either set of procedures. The facility receiving case consultation also had rapid staff turnover and it changed ownership, so that the individual programs that had been implemented were seldom retained or communicated beyond their first use. Additionally, the program instituted by the administrator of the facility receiving case consultation was a token-contingency one, but without staff training and with few effective backup reinforcers.

By the end of the first three months of aftercare consultation, none of the planned activities had been completed on schedule for either facility. There were numerous problems as a result of staff turnover in the facilities themselves, loss of credibility of psychosocial staff because of the layoff of all staff who had negotiated initial agreements, and lack of cooperation of facility operators to implement their part of agreements—perhaps as a result of the sudden termination of agreements by the Department of Mental Health. Over the next three months the new psychosocial aftercare staff (one full-time, two half-time on temporary loan from an intramural program) attempted to familiarize themselves with the people and problems and to carry out the planned aftercare consultation. Contacts during this period varied from two to five per week in each facility, and an equal number of contacts were spread over all other aftercare facilities. By the end of the second three months, the new psychosocial aftercare staff reported that little or no progress was being made in educational consultation because of staff turnover in each extended-care facility and failure of the operators to provide backing to consultants in staff training. Therefore, a meeting was held between the project director, small-facility operator, and psychosocial aftercare staff during which prior problems were identified and new agreements directly negotiated. The administrator of the large facility negotiated new agreements directly with psychosocial aftercare staff.

After clarification of the innocence of psychosocial staff in prior violations of agreements, a new schedule was negotiated and maintained for the remaining twelve months of follow-up. Over the third three-month period, intensive training and consultation occurred in both facilities, with three scheduled contacts per week during the first month of the period and two per week during the last two months. During the first month, a revised token-economy program was introduced at the facility receiving program consultation, with four two-hour academic training sessions for all staff preceding on-the-floor training in specific procedures. At the request of the administrator, the case consultation facility also received two two-hour academic training sessions at the beginning of the intensive consultation period.

At the end of the three months of intensive training and consultation, the part-time staff discontinued aftercare work, with one of them remaining available only as a backup to the remaining aftercare consultant. Over the next three months, scheduled contact with both facilities was systematically reduced to the once per week check, which continued for three additional months. Finally, scheduled psychosocial consultation was faded completely during the last three months of the follow-up period, with consultation being available at the initiation of the extended-care facilities. (None were made.) At the completion of the eighteen-month follow-up period, monitoring of significant project releases was transferred to usual community clinic sources, with the psychosocial staff member providing clinic staff with information on potential problems and effective modes of action for each resident.

*Community Facility Programs.* The administrator of the facility receiving case consultation had introduced a token economy but without staff training until the two sessions conducted by psychosocial staff during the seventh month of consultation. That training covered one two-hour session each on a social-learning model of deviancy (rather than illness) and a presentation of social-learning principles. Program content in the large facility was a day program: tokens could be earned for attendance and participation in scheduled activities and classes from 9 A.M. to 4 P.M. daily, to be exchanged for canteen items (clothing, cosmetics, candy, cigarettes, etc.) or money, at the rate of five cents per token, from 3 P.M. to 4 P.M. Classes and activities focused upon grooming, money management, job orientation, and maintenance of personal living area. While nearly 43% of weekday waking hours were devoted to scheduled activities, psychotropic drugs were heavily relied upon; over 80% of the residents were taking active drugs at every assessment in the facility over the follow-up period. Other than meals and morning and evening routines, the remainder of the time was unstructured; residents were free to use any recreational facilities, stores, etc., in the local neighborhood or downtown. Over the first three months of the aftercare period, student volunteers were available to provide transportation downtown. The requests for case consultation were almost totally focused on changing behavior that staff considered undesirable or that created management problems, rather than obtaining assistance with improving adaptive behaviors. Primary procedures employed were overcorrection/restitution and differential reinforcement of other, incompatible behaviors, through which more adaptive focus was attempted. Time out could not be used because of state regulations.

The facility receiving program consultation originally had developed a program similar in basic characteristics to the social-learning program that had been in operation at the center at the end of the period, except for the absence of time out, differential sleeping quarters, and controlled access to outside passes—all of which were against state regulations for the shelter-care level of services. Also, activities and classes were restricted to four per day rather than six, appearance checks to one per day rather than three, and no shaping chips were involved. Residents were free to use neighborhood recreational facilities and stores or to go downtown, and student volunteers were available to provide transportation during the first three months of aftercare consultation. Although the entire program was never quite fully implemented, most scheduled events did occur, providing nearly 63% of weekday waking hours devoted to scheduled rehabilitation activities. Psychotropic drugs were also used heavily in the facility as well, with over 80% of residents being on active drugs at each assessment over the last half of the period.

The program that was finally introduced into the facility receiving program consultation during the seventh month of aftercare consultation was even weaker than that originally planned. However, the program was implemented, did involve all residents in the facility, and continued after psychosocial consultation faded. Unfortunately, backup reinforcers for tokens were still limited, including only canteen items (clothing, cosmetics, candy, cigarettes, etc.) available four times per day, coffee and cookies, available after each meal and on two scheduled coffee breaks, money at the rate of five cents per token, and organized field trips, movies, and other outside activities. The morning routine was similar to that of the intramural social-learning program, but no other appearance checks were scheduled. A three-level step system was included. At the lowest step residents were scheduled for classes and activities for seven hours per day that focused on basic self-care skills, social-interactional skills, and reading and mathematics, with tokens for attendance and participation. Residents at the lowest step were excluded from eligibility for the outside backup reinforcers but could still arrange their own outside activities.

Residents were promoted to the second step after earning 90% of available tokens at the lowest level. At the second level, the schedule included a daily two-hour work-training job in the facility for which residents received immediate token payment and four hours of scheduled classes and activities. Residents were provided the opportunity to exchange tokens for money at the end of each day to encourage evening and weekend trips outside the facility. When 90% performance at the second level had occurred for two weeks, promotion to the third level was accompanied by five hours of scheduled work per day, with weekly payment in money rather than tokens, plus one hour of class a day (vocational planning and leisure-time planning). The top step used only social reinforcement and money, without token exchange. After three weeks of acceptable performance in the in-facility job, residents were eligible for recommendation to a sheltered workshop, which provided vocational training and cash reimbursement. Weekend schedules were functionally limited to odd jobs, since no classes, activities, or work were regularly scheduled.

This schedule thus still called for nearly 63% of weekday waking hours to be devoted to rehabilitation activities, and the staff received training in each functional activity. The training included an additional four hours of academic training, over that received by the case consultation facility, plus individual supervision and checkout of each staff once in each activity. However, the schedule and training were still light by original social-learning standards and only slightly more structured than that of the facility receiving case consultation. Additionally, the backup reinforcers in both extended-care facilities were exceptionally weak because of regulations of state agencies that precluded introduction of contingencies which were known to be effective.

## ACTUAL STAFF PERFORMANCE IN COMMUNITY FACILITIES

Although agreements with the operators of the two extended-care facilities precluded collection of any data on staff characteristics from staff themselves, full-week samples of staff performance in each facility were regularly obtained on the Staff-Resident Interaction Chronograph (SRIC) for examination at the end of each three months during the follow-up period.[2]

How staff spent their time in the two facilities is shown in figure 38.1, where total instances of activity and percentages of staff activity relative to the class of resident behavior in each facility are plotted over the entire follow-up period. An inspection of figure 38.1 shows that both community facilities had a relatively low level of staff activity by psychosocial standards. By the third month of aftercare consultation, even with the confusion and changes in staff, the facility receiving program consultation showed 28% higher rates of staff activity than the facility receiving case consultation. Over the last six months of the follow-up period, after psychosocial staff had faded intensive consultation, the facility receiving program consultation had increased total staff activity to a level over 63% higher than that of the facility receiving case consultation, remaining significantly higher over the entire follow-up period.[3] A comparison of activity levels with those of the intramural treatment programs of the project (table 5.4) reveals that the staff of the community facility receiving case consultation maintained activity just above the level observed for the sample of state hospital staff, and the facility receiving program consultation ranged from a low at about the average for psychosocial baselines (229 instances per hour) to a level midway between the psychosocial baseline average and the average for the social-learning program (278 instances per hour).

Even though the activity levels of staff in both extended-care facilities were considerably lower than that of the psychosocial programs, the focus of staff activity shown in figure 38.1 reveals an approximation to that of the social-learning program. Staff of both community facilities focused the majority of their activity on appropriate resident behavior, next most on staff-initiated activity, and next most on resident failures, with relatively little activity devoted to crazy behavior or resident requests. Comparisons with intramural project programs (table 5.4) reveal the focus of activity

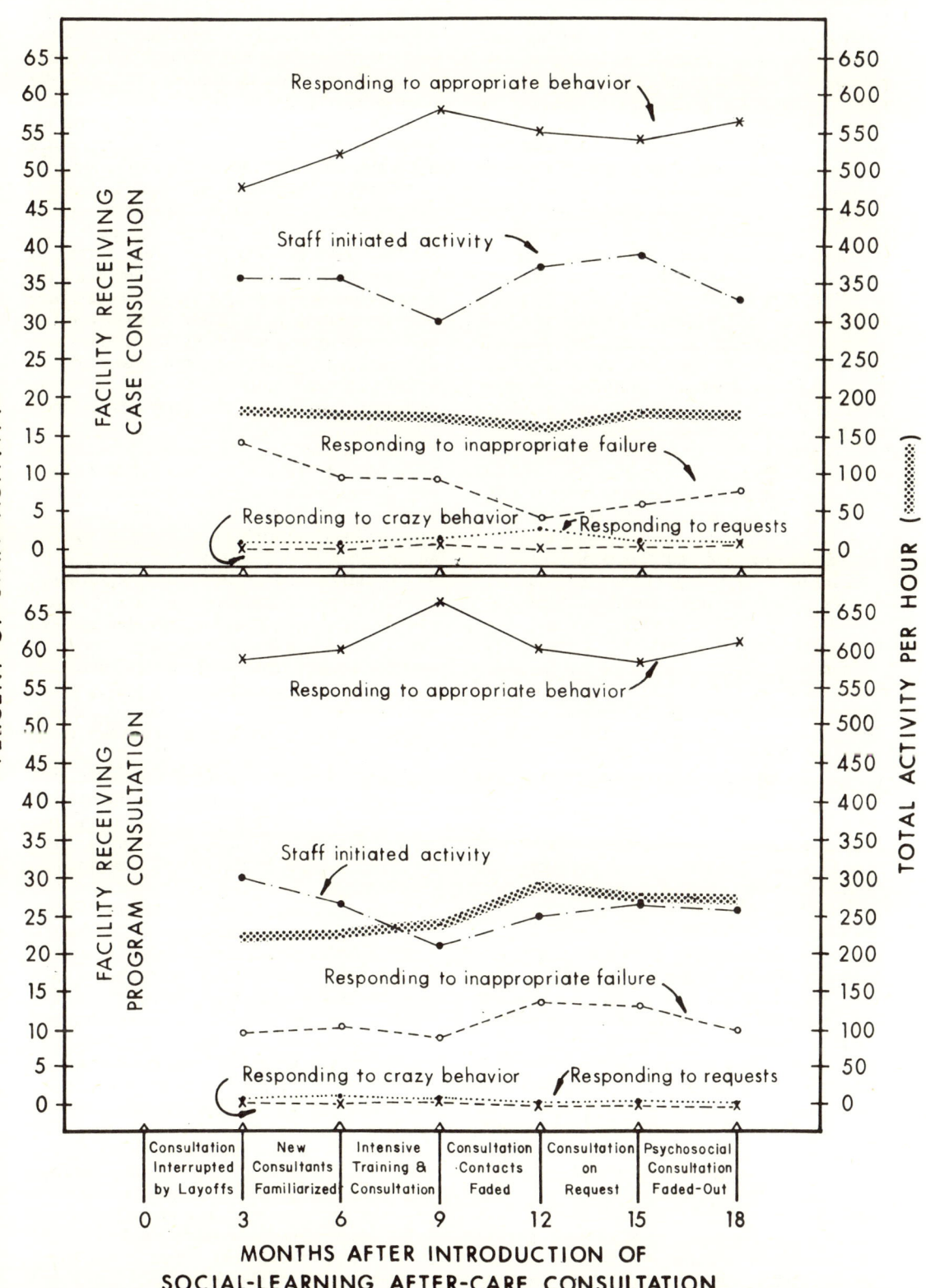

Figure 38.1. How staff of two community extended-care facilities spent their time while receiving social-learning consultation via different modes of delivery. Average total activity per hour is indicated by the shaded line and scale in the right margin.

was more similar to the social-learning program than to any other, and the community facility that received program consultation differed primarily in showing lower levels of focus on resident failures. The facility receiving case consultation showed significantly higher proportions of staff-initiated activity and lower rates of focus on either resident failures or appropriate behavior than the facility receiving program consultation—falling midway between the social-learning and hospital programs of the intramural treatment period.

Figure 38.1 also shows the primary effect of the intensive training and consultation between the sixth and ninth months of the follow-up period to have been an increased focus on appropriate resident behavior and a decrease in staff-initiated activity in both facilities. However, as consultative contacts were faded over the next three months, staff in both facilities gradually returned to their previous relative focus, although staff receiving program consultation also increased their total activity level at the same time. The proportion of staff activities focused upon resident failures changed differentially during the three months in which psychosocial consultative contacts were faded, with staff receiving case consultation decreasing and staff receiving program consultation increasing focus on resident failures. Staff in both facilities maintained consistency in both total activity and nature of focus over the last six months during which minimal consultation was faded to telephone consultation at the initiation of the facilities themselves. Although staff of both community facilities were spending from 21% to 25% of activities not in interaction with residents before the intensive intervention, fewer than 2% of activities were job irrelevant. However, over the last six months of the follow-up period, staff who received case consultation had increased the proportion of activities not involving resident interaction to nearly 29% of all activities, and staff who received program consultation had reduced noninteractive activities to fewer than 15% of the total and job-irrelevant activities to fewer than 0.1%.

Thus, the focus of the activities of staff of both extended-care facilities receiving psychosocial consultation was more closely related to the social-learning program than to the milieu program. The facility receiving program consultation was more closely related to the social-learning program than the other one was, although both had weak token economies. Intensive intervention was noticeable in staff performance but relatively short-lived, with staff largely returning to the activity focus that was already in effect after three months of consultation. The major difference between the two facilities was the total level of activity, which was low in both but higher in the facility receiving program consultation.

The attention received by an individual resident in the extended-care facilities also differed considerably. Following the intervention of psychosocial aftercare consultants, additional residents in each facility gradually became more active in the respective programs, with the result that the number of residents for whom facility staff were directly responsible increased. Staff in the facility receiving case consultation were responsible for more residents during every assessment, but the increase in the number of residents present for each staff member from the first six months to the last six months (25.2 to 26.4) was less than the corresponding increase for the facility receiving program consultation (21.9 to 24.9). The effect on the attention received by the average resident in each facility on the differences in activity level and number of residents for whom each staff member was responsible is shown in table 38.1.

The "average contacts per hour" column in table 38.1 shows that the number of contacts the average resident in both facilities received increased from the first six months to the last six months of the follow-up period, in spite of an increase in the number of residents for whom staff members were responsible. Although the staff receiving program consultation always provided more contacts, the increased contacts over the follow-up period were relatively greater for residents in a group, and case consultation was associated with a proportionately greater increase in individualized, personal contacts. The "probability of contact" figures show the average resident in either facility was less likely to receive a personalized contact than not during an average ten-minute observation, although the probability of contact was considerably greater in the facility receiving program consultation than in the facility receiving case consultation.

Table 38.1 shows that the amount of interaction within contacts—instances of discrete verbal content or other staff behavior directed to the individual—actually decreased in both facilities as the number of contacts increased. However, the net effect on the total amount of attention received from staff (contacts x interactions) by an individual resident was a slight decrease from the first six months to the last six months in the facility receiving case consultation but a slight increase in the other facility. The average resident in the facility that received program consultation obtained over twice the amount of staff attention over the last six months when consultation was faded than did the average resident in the facility that had received case consultation.

Comparisons of the data in table 38.1 with

Table 38.1. Amount of staff attention residents received in extended-care facilities with different modes of consultation.

| Focus of attention resident received | Probability of contact in 10 min. | | | | Average contacts per hour | | | | Average interactions per contact | | | |
|---|---|---|---|---|---|---|---|---|---|---|---|---|
| | Case consultation | | Program consultation | | Case consultation | | Program consultation | | Case consultation | | Program consultation | |
| | First 6 mos. | Last 6 mos. | First 6 mos. | Last 6 mos. | First 6 mos. | Last 6 mos. | First 6 mos. | Last 6 mos. | First 6 mos. | Last 6 mos. | First 6 mos. | Last 6 mos. |
| As individual | 0.227 | 0.330 | 0.404 | 0.470 | 1.36 | 1.98 | 2.43 | 2.82 | 1.83 | 1.75 | 2.79 | 1.99 |
| As part of group | .103 | .052 | .044 | .143 | .62 | .31 | .26 | .86 | .83 | .26 | .30 | .61 |
| Total | .330 | .382 | .448 | .613 | 1.98 | 2.29 | 2.69 | 3.68 | 2.66 | 2.01 | 3.09 | 2.60 |

parallel figures for the intramural programs of the project (table 5.5) reveal that the total amount of attention residents received in the facility receiving case consultation was at about the same level or slightly above that patients received in the sample of hospital programs. The attention residents received in the community facility receiving program consultation was about the same level as that received by psychosocial residents under baseline conditions. Neither facility approached the amount of attention provided in the psychosocial programs, which was 78% to 340% greater than that in the community facilities.

Thus, there were clear differences in the amount of attention residents received in the extended-care facilities, with the facility receiving program consultation providing more attention to individual residents than the one that received case consultation. The absolute amount of attention in both was far below that received by residents in either psychosocial program before release but at or above the levels of attention hospital patients had received.

The nature of changes in staff behavior in the two extended-care facilities are shown in figure 38.2, where the highest-frequency interactions for both facilities are plotted over the follow-up period. The staff behaviors plotted in the top section of figure 38.2 show Positive Nonverbals remained the highest-frequency behavior in both facilities but changed in opposite directions during intensive training and consultation by psychosocial staff. Positive Nonsocials are notable for the lack of change during and after intensive consultation in the facility receiving program consultation and for their relative absence in the facility receiving case consultation. Both programs had weak token economies, which should have provided relatively high rates of Positive Nonsocial if active implementation were carried out (see figure 31.4 for comparison). The other notable change over time in the top of figure 38.2 was

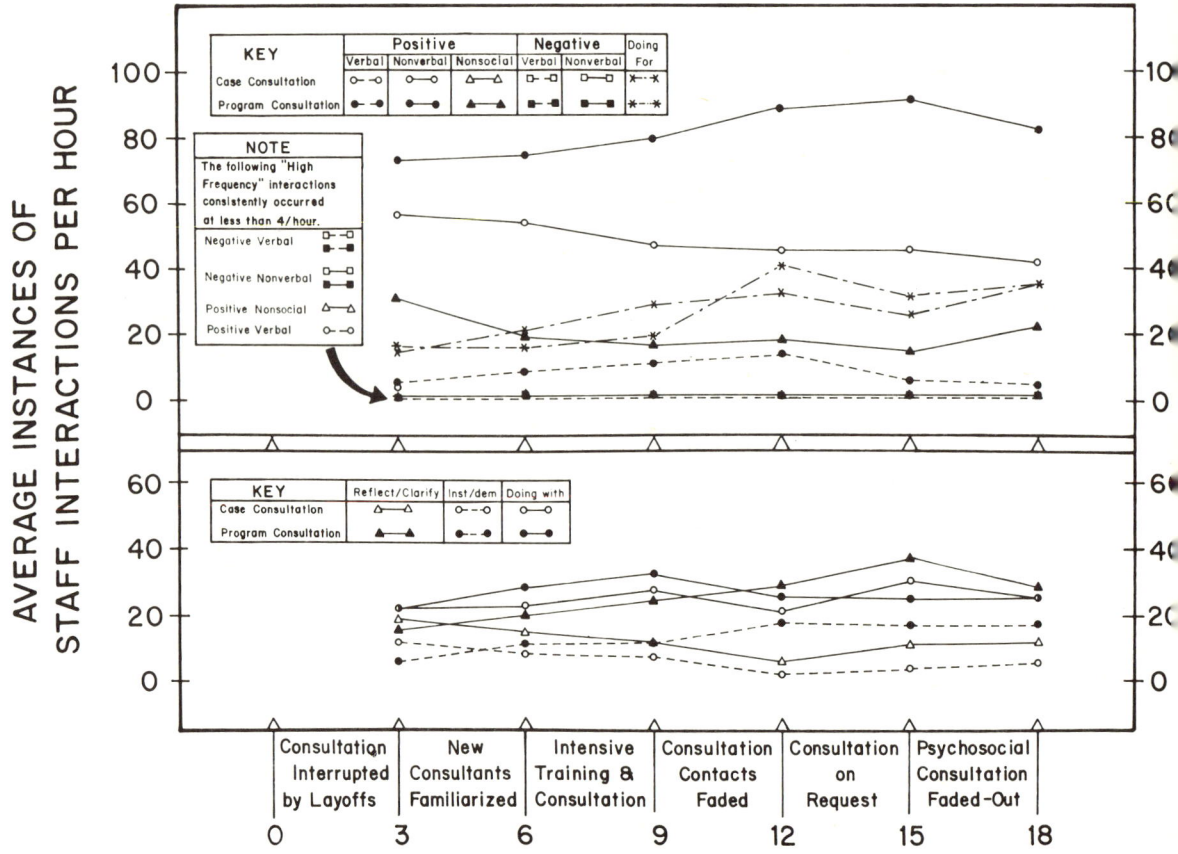

Figure 38.2. Average hourly instances of the highest-frequency staff interactions in two extended-care facilities receiving social-learning consultation via different modes of delivery.

Doing For which gradually increased in the facility receiving case consultation and did so dramatically in the other facility when consultation was faded. Doing For is a hallmark of the aide culture, with the increase over the period in which program consultation was faded suggesting that staff of the facility were aware of the preference of psychosocial consultants for other modes of interaction.

Notable changes in the lower part of figure 38.2 show Doing With increased slightly in both facilities during the period of intensive training and consultation and decreased slightly when consultation was faded. However, both Reflect/Clarify and Instruct/Demonstrate changed in opposite directions during or immediately after the intensive intervention period, with the facility receiving program consultation increasing both classes of staff behavior while the facility receiving case consultation decreased both. The only other class of staff behavior that changed over the period of intensive intervention is not plotted in figure 38.2 because of its low overall frequency. However, Ignore/No Response was reduced in both facilities over the period of intensive training and consultation and then remained at stable levels of about half the original rate. The absolute error rate was also reduced by approximately a quarter in the facility receiving case consultation and a half in the facility receiving program consultation. Although the error rates in both facilities were less than 5% at the end of the first six months of consultation—indicating exceptionally good discrimination of specific staff-resident interactions in both facilities—the distribution of staff behavior left much to be desired on the basis of social-learning principles.

The overall differentiation of staff performance in community facilities is shown in table 38.2. Since the only notable changes in staff behavior are discussed above, only average hourly rates of staff activity over the last six months of stable performance are presented to show the extent to which the extended-care staff approximated desirable performance after consultation was faded. The table reveals an interesting phenomenon: although staff in both facilities were performing specific staff-resident interactions with few discrete errors from social-learning principles with regard to each interaction (only 3.5% and 2.2%, respectively, for case consultation and program consultation) the overall distribution of staff-resident interactions was considerably removed from desirable performance when considered as total programs.

Comparisons with the distribution of staff behaviors in the intramural social-learning program and in the sample of traditional hospital programs (table 5.6) show that Doing For in both community facilities occurred at twice the rate of even the traditional hospital programs. From the social-learning perspective, a limited amount of Doing For is acceptable. However, these exceptionally high rates far exceed the limits allowed. Combined with the near absence of Positive Prompts and Negative Prompts in both facilities, the high rates of Doing For and the relatively high rates of Instruct/Demonstrate in "failure" and "neutral" columns in the facility receiving program consultation provide a picture of staff-resident interactions that behaviorally communicates a custodial-caretaking philosophy rather than behavioral indications that residents can do things for themselves. That the great majority of instances of Doing For were contingent upon appropriate resident behavior suggests that facility staff may have interpreted this class of behavior as a reward.

The highest rates of interactional errors in both community facilities occurred in response to crazy resident behavior, which was a low-frequency event in both facilities. Although Ignore/No Response occurred at a low absolute rate in both facilities, the highest error rates for any class of staff activity occurred with this class of behavior. In fact, in both community facilities, the instances in which staff failed to respond to resident behavior were more often incorrect than correct. With the exception of Reflect/Clarify, staff behaviors specific to milieu therapy were either low frequency, or nonexistent in community facilities. However, staff of the facility receiving program consultation used Reflect/Clarify at about as high a rate as the average for the intramural milieu program, while the rate at the facility receiving case consultation was about at the level of traditional hospital programs and the intramural social-learning program.

Positive Nonverbals and Doing With did occur at relatively high rates in both facilities, with the average hourly rate of Positive Nonverbals in the facility receiving program consultation approaching the average level of the intramural social-learning program. As with the intramural social-learning program, these classes of behavior were more often contingent upon appropriate resident behavior than not. Staff of the facility receiving program consultation also performed higher rates of Positive Verbals and Positive Nonsocials contingent upon appropriate resident behavior than did staff of the other facility. These behaviors are crucial to the implementation of social-learning procedures and show that staff of both community facilities performed at higher rates than staff of the traditional hospital programs but at far lower levels than those of the intramural social-learning program. Perhaps most reflective of the relative quality of staff performance in community facilities is the extent to which these four classes of staff behavior were contingent

Table 38.2. Average hourly rate of staff activity in extended-care facilities with different modes of consultation during the last six months of follow-up.

| | Class of resident behavior to which staff responded | | | | | | | | | | | | | | | | | |
|---|---|---|---|---|---|---|---|---|---|---|---|---|---|---|---|---|---|---|
| | Appropriate | | Inappropriate Failure | | Inappropriate Crazy | | Request | | Neutral | | Total staff behavior | | % of interactions | | % of all staff error | |
| Staff behavior | Case | Program | Case | Program | Case | Program | Case | Program | Case | Program | Case | Program | Case | Program | Case | Program |
| Positive Verbal | 1.73+ | 7.89+ | 0.03- | 0.06- | 0.03- | - | - | o | o | o | 1.79 | 7.95 | 1.5% | 3.3% | 0.7% | 1.2% |
| Negative Verbal | 0.15- | 0.19o | 1.18o | 3.02o | 0.06o | 0.22o | - | 0.13o | - | 0.03- | 1.39 | 3.59 | 1.1% | 1.5% | 3.6% | 6.8% |
| Positive Nonverbal | 33.75+ | 60.68+ | 3.52o | 12.95o | 0.30- | 0.40- | 1.73o | 0.89o | 4.92o | 12.92o | 44.22 | 87.84 | 36.4% | 36.9% | 7.1% | 7.7% |
| Negative Nonverbal | 0.15- | 0.67- | 0.59o | 1.41o | 0.03o | 0.09o | o | 0.06o | 0.12- | 0.15- | 0.89 | 2.38 | 0.7% | 1.0% | 6.4% | 15.9% |
| Positive Nonsocial | 0.06+ | 18.76+ | - | 0.06- | - | - | 0.06o | 0.03o | 0.03o | 0.03o | 0.15 | 18.88 | 0.1% | 7.9% | 9.2% | 1.2% |
| Negative Nonsocial | - | - | + | + | + | - | - | - | - | 0.03- | | 0.03 | | | | 0.6% |
| Positive Statement | 0.59o | 0.77o | 0.36- | 0.86- | 0.03- | - | o | o | 0.09o | 0.76o | 1.07 | 2.39 | 0.9% | 1.0% | 9.2% | 16.6% |
| Negative Statement | - | 0.03- | - | - | - | - | - | - | 0.18- | 0.27- | 0.18 | 0.30 | 0.1% | 0.1% | 4.3% | 5.8% |
| Positive Prompt | 0.03+ | 0.24+ | 0.06+ | 0.15+ | + | + | + | + | - | 0.12+ | 0.09 | 0.51 | 0.1% | 0.2% | | |
| Negative Prompt | 0.03- | - | 0.12+ | 0.28+ | + | 0.03+ | o | 0.49+ | - | 0.03- | 0.15 | 0.34 | 0.1% | 0.2% | 0.7% | 0.6% |
| Positive Gp. Reference | o | o | - | 0.09o | - | - | o | o | o | o | | 0.09 | | | | 1.7% |
| Negative Gp. Reference | - | - | o | o | o | o | o | o | - | - | | | | | | |
| Reflect/Clarify | 4.75o | 13.98o | 1.93o | 7.56o | 0.15o | 0.15o | 0.44o | 0.19o | 2.23o | 10.36o | 9.50 | 32.24 | 7.8% | 13.6% | | |
| Suggest Alternatives | o | 0.18o | o | 0.03o | - | - | o | o | 0.03o | 0.03o | 0.03 | 0.24 | | 0.1% | | |
| Instruct/Demonstrate | 1.53+ | 5.46+ | 1.82o | 7.44o | 0.06o | 0.19o | 0.09o | 0.09o | 0.89o | 4.60o | 4.39 | 17.78 | 3.6% | 7.5% | 2.8% | 0.6% |
| Doing With | 20.38+ | 22.09+ | 0.03- | - | 0.09- | 0.03- | 0.85o | 0.49+ | 4.63+ | 3.02+ | 25.98 | 25.63 | 21.4% | 10.8% | 10.7% | 6.6% |
| Doing For | 29.95o | 35.18o | 0.45- | 0.34- | - | - | 0.56o | 0.27q | 0.06o | 0.06o | 31.02 | 35.85 | 25.5% | 15.0% | | |
| Physical Force | - | - | o | o | o | o | - | - | - | - | | | | | | |
| Ignore/No Response | 0.45- | 1.59- | 0.06+ | 0.22+ | 0.12+ | 0.22+ | 0.03- | 0.21- | 1.79- | 0.21- | 2.45 | 2.24 | 2.0%[a] | 0.9%[a] | 53.8% | 34.8% |
| Announce | b | b | b | b | b | b | b | b | 0.24+ | 0.98+ | 0.24 | 0.98 | (0.1%) | (0.4%) | b | b |
| Attend/Record/Observe | b | b | b | b | b | b | b | b | 46.37+ | 39.05+ | 46.37 | 39.05 | (27.3%) | (14.0%) | b | b |
| Total interactions | 93.55 | 167.71 | 10.15 | 34.47 | 0.87 | 1.33 | 3.76 | 2.15 | 13.18 | 32.41 | 121.51 | 238.07 | 101%[a] | 100%[a] | 3.5% | 2.2% |
| % correct interactions | 99.2% | 98.5% | 91.4% | 95.9% | 48.3% | 67.7% | 99.2% | 94.0% | 84.1%[a] | 97.8%[a] | 96.5% | 97.8% | b | b | 0.0% | 0.0% |
| Total activity | b | b | b | b | b | b | b | b | 61.58 | 72.65 | 169.91 | 278.31 | (140%) | (117%) | b | b |

Note. + = specifically programmed staff behavior; o = allowable staff choice; - = programmatic error. Empty cells signify less than 0.0045 instances per hour.
a. "Ignore-neutral" included in percentage figures, but not in total interactions.
b. Irrelevant cells.

upon appropriate resident behavior. For both community facilities, 46% of all staff-resident interactions were accounted for by positive social or material reinforcement contingent upon appropriate resident behavior. This percentage compares to over 60% over the entire intramural treatment period for the social-learning program and less than 28% for the milieu program, psychosocial baselines, and traditional hospital programs. Thus, staff in community facilities were performing some crucial behaviors more in keeping with social-learning procedures than with traditional procedures, but at a level that was distinctly inferior to that of the intramural social-learning program.

## SUMMARY

The psychosocial aftercare consultation to community extended-care facilities was actually implemented, in spite of the numerous uncontrolled crises imposed by external events over the follow-up period. The nonspecific characteristics guiding all modes of aftercare consultation were implemented, ensuring that specific consultants were identified, available, and predictable; consultation moved toward ultimate independence of clients; and consultation followed an experimental-behavioral strategy with an educational focus. Since earlier analyses had already documented the superiority of social-learning procedures and principles for the population, this model was adopted for all aftercare consultation.

In spite of the confusion resulting from the layoff of original aftercare staff during the first three months and the difficulties encountered by new psychosocial aftercare staff over the next three months, some aftercare consultation was successfully faded by the end of the ninth month after original community placements. It included facilities that had each accepted only a few significant releases from the intramural programs, each of which received individual case consultation from psychosocial staff on a declining-contact schedule. Since all but one of the latter extended-care facilities were out of town, fewer agreements were influenced by the actions of the new center superintendent, regular consultation had faded to telephone checks on progress by the ninth month, without requests for consultation over the last six months of the follow-up period.

The two local extended-care facilities that had made sufficient beds available to accept the majority of community placements received different modes of aftercare consultation. One used the traditional mode of delivery, focusing upon individual cases, and the other received consultation that concentrated on program development. Although the uncontrolled external events resulted in less clear differentiation of procedures than had been originally planned, both modes of consultation were implemented, with weak token-economy programs in both facilities. By the end of the sixth month of consultation—after changes in psychosocial staff and initial agreements—psychosocial staff were convinced that the educational purpose of consultation was not being accomplished and thus fading of consultation could not yet occur. Therefore, active intervention and retraining were undertaken with intensive consultation for one month, followed by two months of consultation with a twice per week schedule. Consultation to both facilities was then faded over a three-month period to a once-per-week check, which continued for an additional three months before scheduled psychosocial contacts were terminated. Consultation could be initiated by the facilities themselves over the last three months of the follow-up period, even though no contacts were scheduled.

Three-month assessments of staff behavior in the community facilities found differences between them and differences associated with the period of active intervention by psychosocial staff and later fading of consultation. The staff of both facilities receiving consultation according to social-learning principles did show the focus of activities to be more closely related to the intramural social-learning program than to others, with the facility receiving program consultation being more closely related than the facility receiving case consultation. The facility receiving program consultation also showed much higher levels of staff activity and attention provided to residents; however, both facilities were exceptionally low compared to either psychosocial program, while falling at or above the levels that existed in the traditional hospital programs.

The classes of staff activity in both community extended-care facilities showed an interesting paradox. While discrete staff-resident interactions revealed high levels of accuracy in performing specific behaviors, the overall distribution of staff behaviors in both facilities was far removed from a desirable social-learning program. In fact, the distribution, plus an exceptionally high utilization of psychotropic drugs, suggested a basic approach more similar to the custodial-caretaking philosophy of the traditional state hospital rather than the re-educative, change-oriented philosophy desired by a social-learning approach. However, the remainder of staff behaviors in both community facilities fell midway between desirable social-learning activities and observed hospital activities, with a slightly better stable performance being achieved by the facility receiving program rather than case consultation.

# 39. Postrelease Levels of Functioning in the Community

Earlier analyses clearly established that the social-learning program was more effective in improving resident behavior and in achieving more significant releases to the community with a minimum ninety-day stay than either the milieu or the traditional hospital programs. Although the comparative effects between the milieu and hospital programs on intramural improvement were less clear because of the potential reactivity of measurement, the milieu program was successful in achieving significant release for more residents than the hospital programs did. These findings thus establish the social-learning program as the best treatment for the severely debilitated chronic mental patient.

## CHANGES IN FUNCTIONING FOR RELEASED RESIDENTS

Once a resident improves to the point of obtaining a significant release with a minimum stay in the community, the level of functioning observed in community placements is more likely to be the result of factors in the postrelease environment—in interaction with prior treatment history and prior level of functioning—than of the treatment procedures that may have been originally responsible for improvement. The extent to which significant releases from the original intramural groups may have differed in their functioning over the follow-up period was thus of interest. The practices of the community extended-care facilities that received the majority of the psychosocial releases and all of the hospital releases provided environments that were potentially interactive with prior treatment histories. Specifically the heavy use of psychotropic drugs in extended-care facilities represented a drastic change for those released from the psychosocial programs and a continuation of prior practices for released hospital patients. Additionally the programs within the private extended-care facilities represented an increase in activity and attention for releases from the hospital and a major decrease for releases from both psychosocial programs. Finally, the focus and approach engendered by the nonspecific characteristics of psychosocial aftercare consultation represented moderate change for releases from the social-learning program, more change for those from the milieu program, and considerable change for those from the hospital programs.

The level of functioning in the community for significant releases from the original equated intramural groups of twenty-eight residents each was first evaluated by analysis of partial IAB Functioning Scores from the prerelease assessments obtained for each individual through successive six-month follow-up assessments in the community for a year and a half.[1] The prerelease means for those achieving release with continuing community stay reflected nearly identical levels of functioning in the institution just before release for all three subgroups (54.43, 53.72, and 53.93, respectively, for social-learning, milieu, and hospital releases), even though the number of those treated by the social-learning program achieving significant release (twenty-seven) was considerably greater than that of either the milieu (nineteen) or hospital (thirteen) programs. The changes for all three groups combined over follow-up assessments were significant ($p < 0.01$), as was a curvature showing a mean decrease in IAB Functioning from prerelease assessments to the first six-month follow-up assessments (-3.71) followed by a linear increase over the remainder of the follow-up period (+0.89, p's $< 0.05$).

Over the entire follow-up period of eighteen months after release, none of the differences in level of IAB Functioning approached significance among the subgroups originally treated by the hospital, milieu, and social-learning programs (p's $> 0.20$); however, the differential change between groups approached statistical significance ($p < 0.10$). The mean decline in functioning of released residents from both psychosocial programs over the first six months in the community (-4.61) was significant (p's $< 0.01$), and both showed significantly greater average losses than the loss of hospital releases over the first six months out (-0.51, p's $< 0.05$). Even with the greater decline in average IAB Functioning over the first six months in the community, the absolute level of functioning did not differ between the groups released from the three different programs, and there were no further significant differences within or between groups through the year and a half follow-up (p's > 0.20).

The proportion of releases showing significant individual change did not differ among subgroups released from the original intramural treatment programs at any time over the follow-up period (p's > 0.20).[2] Overall, 32% of releases showed significant losses over the first six months in the community, and only 8% showed significant improvement. Over the last year of the follow-up, when average functioning was increasing, only 12% of those residing in the community showed significant improvement, and 7% showed a significant loss—ending the formal follow-up period with 7% functioning at higher levels and 29% functioning at lower levels than they had at the time of release. Even though the groups who achieved significant release showed no significant loss from prerelease to the end of the follow-up period and still showed significant improvement from pretreatment levels, one aspect of the change over the follow-up period was particularly notable. Those who declined in functioning—an equal proportion for all subgroups—had losses such that nearly 21% of all significant releases were functioning at a lower level in the extended-care facilities during the last follow-up than they were at the time of initial rejection for community placement six years earlier. These figures indicate that about a fifth of all releases were not maintained at the higher levels of functioning achieved before release, irrespective of the manner in which those higher levels of functioning came about; furthermore, the standards for acceptable functioning in extended-care facilities had lowered over the project period.

Overall, the only differential change for releases from the original intramural groups during the follow-up period was the greater loss of average levels of functioning over the first six months in the community for residents originally treated by either psychosocial program, without differences between the social-learning group and the milieu group. Even though the absolute level of functioning of releases from the psychosocial programs did not differ from that of releases from the traditional hospital programs at any assessment over the eighteen-month follow-up period, the differential change over the first six months is suggestive.

The relative environmental changes in common for releases from both psychosocial programs upon entering the community were increases in the numbers receiving psychotropic drugs and decreases in attention and activity. Concurrently releases from hospital programs experienced no change in the high numbers who continued to receive psychotropic drugs, but some increases in attention and activity were in evidence from the levels experienced in the hospital. The comparative differences suggest an interaction between postrelease environmental factors and prior treatment history, in which the change from nondrug to drug state may have interfered with prior learning to some degree for psychosocial releases. The relative changes in attention and activity may have served to support new behavior for the hospital releases but not for previously acquired behavior for the psychosocial releases. Since there were no differences between the milieu and social-learning releases at any time over the follow-up period, the differential focus of psychosocial aftercare consultation does not appear to have had interactive effects with prior treatment history. Rather, the gradual increase in IAB Functioning for all three groups after the first six months in the community coincides with resolutions of consulting problems for the majority of releases, suggesting that the active psychosocial aftercare consultation had beneficial effects regardless of prior treatment conditions.

The differential predictability of functioning over the follow-up period lends some support to the interpretation that the postrelease environments failed to support the performance of some previously acquired adaptive behavior for those released from the psychosocial treatment programs while differentially supporting new behavior for those released from the hospital treatment programs.[3] Specifically, partial IAB Functioning at each six-month follow-up over all significant releases combined was predictable from the prerelease IAB Functioning Scores, both total and partial (r's in the 0.70s), as well as from each component instrument (r's in the 0.50s to 0.70s). However, the predictability of functioning at follow-up assessments from prerelease assessments differed between releases from the psychosocial and hospital groups. The level of functioning of psychosocial releases at each follow-up assessment was predictable from the level of IAB Functioning in the center before release, without differences over time or between milieu and social-learning releases (all r's in the high 0.70s & low 0.80s). In contrast, the level of functioning of hospital releases was not predictable from that of IAB Functioning in the hospital before release at either the first (r=0.25) or second (r=0.34) six-month follow-up, but it became marginally predictable at the eighteen-month follow-up (r=0.58). The differences in predictability between releases from the hospital and the psychosocial programs were statistically significant over the first two follow-up assessments.

Partial IAB Functioning of psychosocial releases at each follow-up assessment was also predictable from objectively assessed levels of functioning immediately before release. The objective Global Functioning Factor Score before release predicted level of functioning at every follow-up assessment without differences over time or between milieu and social-learning releases (r's in the 0.70s & 0.80s), as did the indexes of adaptive behavior: TSBC Total Appropriate Behavior, Clinical Frequencies Total Appropriate Behavior, Self-Care, Interpersonal Skills, and Instrumental Role Performance (r's in the 0.60s & 0.70s). TSBC Total Inappropriate Behavior also predicted functioning during follow-up assessments (r's in the -0.70s), but the predictability of functioning in the community from clinically bizarre behavior was almost totally a function of the degree of Schizophrenic Disorganization observed before release (r's in the -0.60s to -0.80s), while neither Cognitive Distortion nor Hostile-Belligerence at prerelease were related to functioning in the community (r's < 0.15). Total Inappropriate Clinical Frequencies at prerelease was the only component behavior that approached differential prediction of functioning at follow-up between milieu and social-learning releases. Although differences between groups were not statistically significant, prerelease Inappropriate Clinical Frequencies did not significantly predict follow-up functioning for milieu releases (r's in the -0.20s) but did for social-learning releases (r's in the -0.60s & -0.70s). These differential relationships were the only suggestive evidence of an interaction between the aftercare approach and psychosocial treatment histories.

In contrast to the predictability of functioning at follow-up from the level of functioning before release, no significant predictability overall or within groups was obtained for any demographic characteristic (age, sex, race, socioeconomic status, process-reactive status, marital status, nature of symptom onset, duration of hospitalization, previous somatic treatments) or drug status before or during the follow-up period. Individual change in functioning over the first six months following release and over the last year of the follow-up period were totally unrelated to demographic characteristics, drug status before or during the follow-up period, prerelease level of functioning, or prerelease treatment group membership. Thus, change in functioning during the follow-up period was not predictable from any of the assessed variables, but the level of functioning in the community was differentially predictable from the prerelease level of functioning.

## CHANGES IN FUNCTIONING IN DIFFERENT COMMUNITY FACILITIES

Although these analyses suggest that some benefits accrued from the psychosocial aftercare consultation over the last year of the follow-up period, more detailed assessments were obtained in the extended-care facilities for which comparisons of case consultation versus program consultation were made. Although the uncontrolled movement of released residents during the follow-up period, the uncontrolled events described in chapters 37 and 38, and the small number of releases from the hospital group precluded the factorial design originally planned, partial IAB assessments and full-week TSBC observations were made in both facilities every three months after initial community placements.[4] By selecting sequential subgroups of residents who were continuous in each facility over full six-month intervals—equating subgroups between facilities at the beginning of each interval (mean and SD $p > 0.20$) on level of functioning, sex, and program of release—analyses could be made of possible overall or differential effects associated with the notable changes in aftercare consultation detailed in chapter 38.

The partial IAB Functioning Scores and the TSBC Total Appropriate and Total Inappropriate Indexes for the sequentially equated subgroups in both facilities over the follow-up period are presented in figure 39.1. The "0" months after transfer figure reflects the prerelease assessment before community placement for IAB Functioning. No prerelease assessment is plotted for TSBC data, since none were available for community placements who originated in the regional hospital. The overall trend of IAB Functioning for sequential subgroups in the two facilities reflects the same pattern of decline over the first six months, followed by increases over the last year, that was obtained for all original releases. The overall trend for TSBC Appropriate Behavior similarly indicates a general upward movement, and TSBC Inappropriate Behavior decreased slightly over the last year of consultation and follow-up.

An analysis of changes in resident behavior over the first six months after community placement in the facilities found that the overall decrease in IAB Functioning shown in figure 39.1 was significant for both facilities ($p < 0.01$).[5] Also the differential change between facilities from prerelease to the six-month follow-up approached significance ($p < 0.09$). More detailed analyses found that community placements in both facilities declined significantly over the first three months during which original psychosocial consultants were laid off ($p$'s $< 0.05$), but residents of the facility receiving program consultation showed a continued differential decline during the second three months ($p < 0.01$).

Thus, the problems of staff turnover and the lack of cooperation in the facility receiving program consultation were accompanied by a differential decrease in rated resident functioning, and the introduction and familiarization of new psychosocial consultants appeared to have stopped the earlier downward trend in IAB Functioning in the facility receiving case consultation. The only particularly notable changes in observed behavior of the facility staff over this three-month period was a slight increase in focus on appropriate resident behavior in the case consultation facility and a decrease in application of positive nonsocial goods and services in the program consultation facility. None of the changes in objectively assessed behavior (TSBC) were significant overall or between facilities from the three-month to the six-month follow-up assessments —raising the possibility that the significant decrease in IAB Functioning in the program consultation facility may have reflected staff reactivity to the turmoil of the period.[6]

The second six-month block of the follow-up

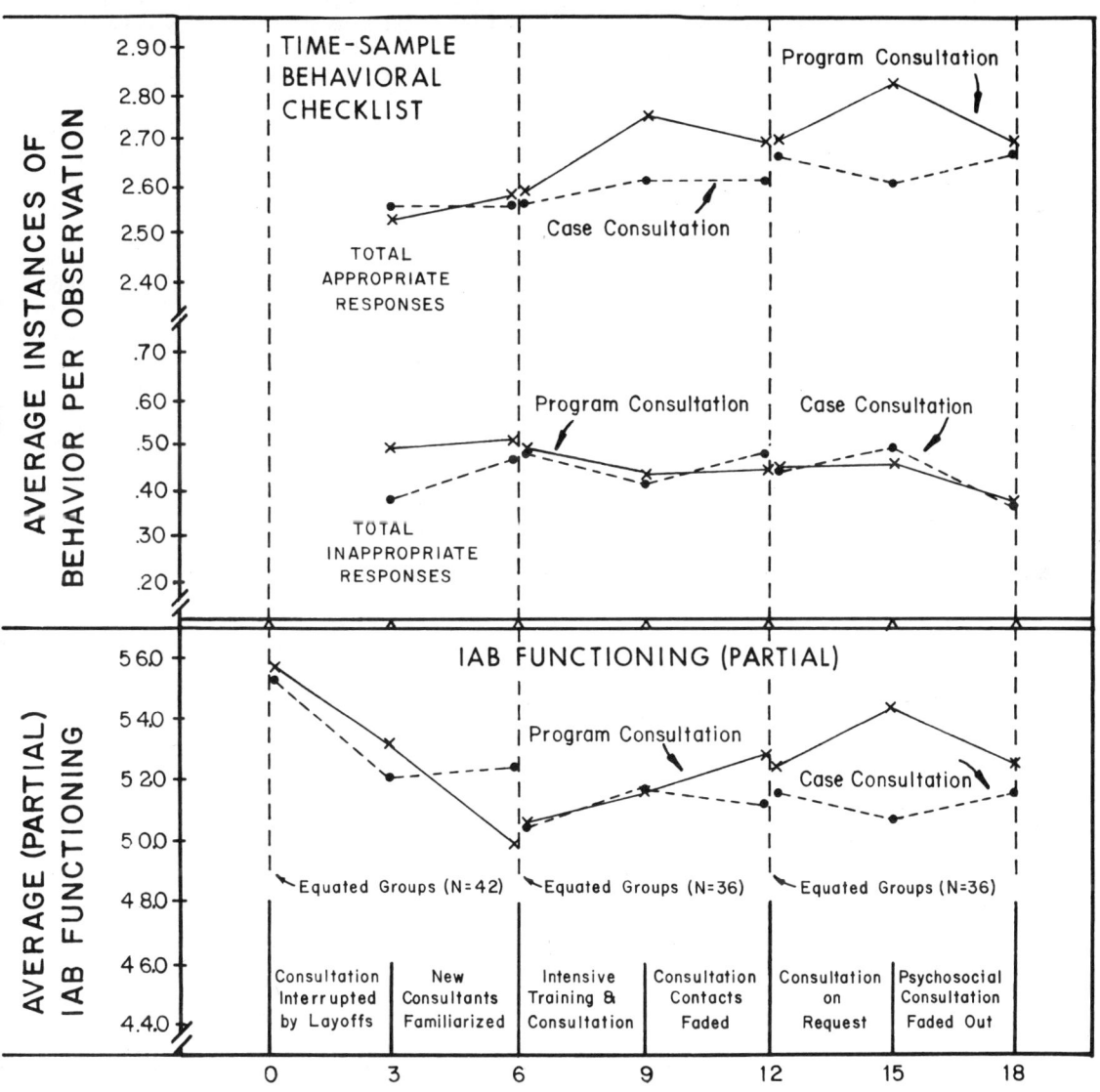

Figure 39.1. Level of functioning of sequentially equated resident subgroups in two community extended-care facilities receiving social-learning aftercare consultation via different modes of delivery.

period in figure 39.1 shows that the introduction of intensive training and consultation by psychosocial aftercare staff clearly reversed the earlier downward trend in IAB Functioning, with corresponding increases in objectively assessed TSBC Appropriate Behavior and decreases in TSBC Inappropriate Behavior. The pattern of change in resident behavior over the sixth to ninth month of follow-up, during intensive consultation, and the ninth to twelfth month of follow-up, when consultation was faded, corresponds with changes in the focus of facility staff on appropriate behavior and staff-initiated activity in both facilities. However, although the increases in IAB Functioning and TSBC Appropriate Behavior of residents in both facilities approached significance over the period of intensive training and consultation ($p$'s $< 0.10$), the overall change during the second six months of follow-up consultation was not significant ($p$'s $> 0.10$), and the differential changes between facilities at this time did not approach significance ($p$'s $> 0.20$). The only significant difference in resident functioning between the two facilities was that residents of the case consultation facility showed significantly greater variance in TSBC Appropriate Behavior during the last assessment of the period.

During the last six months of the follow-up period, the changes in rated IAB Functioning and changes in objectively assessed resident behavior corresponded (figure 39.1). Both IAB Functioning and TSBC Appropriate Behavior showed significant differential change between residents of the two community facilities. The increases in resident functioning in the program consultation facility over the first three months during which brief weekly monitoring was maintained by the psychosocial aftercare consultant, were significant ($p$'s $< 0.05$) as were the decreases in resident functioning over the last three months when no on-site consultation occurred ($p$'s $< 0.05$). These changes were significantly greater than those of residents in the case consultation facility over the same intervals ($p$'s $< 0.01$), who showed no significant change ($p$'s $> 0.20$). From the time that psychosocial aftercare consultation contacts were faded to weekly checks to the end of the follow-up period after three months without on-site consultations, both IAB Functioning and TSBC Appropriate Behavior showed the same levels of functioning, without differences between facilities. However, the decrease in TSBC Inappropriate Behavior for residents in both facilities was significant over this period ($p$'s $< 0.05$); there were no differences between facilities. The only notable differential changes in staff behavior over that six-month period were slight increases followed by decreases in positive nonverbal responses and reflection and clarification, with slight decreases followed by increases in doing things for residents by staff in the program consultation facility.

Overall, residents in the facility receiving program consultation appeared to have maintained slightly better functioning than those in the facility receiving case consultation; however, the major impact appears to have come from the introduction of active psychosocial aftercare consultation, no matter what the mode of delivery. Even with the comparability of staff-to-resident ratios and initial level of functioning of placements, with the same psychosocial aftercare consultants for both facilities, no cause-effect conclusions can be drawn on the comparative effectiveness of case consultation versus program consultation. Possible differences in personal-social characteristics of staff and operators remain as major uncontrolled variables, and there is suggestive evidence that staff of the program consultation facility were less discriminative in their judgments. Additionally the uncontrolled movement in and out of aftercare facilities, plus the indiscriminant use of psychotropic drugs, severely limits any other conclusions.

Nearly 40% of residents in the program consultation facility had progressed to higher step levels by the end of the follow-up period, and nearly 20% had been accepted for vocational training in a sheltered-workshop, compared to 3% in the case-consultation facility. However, these differences could have resulted from differential activity of staff in seeking placements. While IAB ratings were still potentially subject to bias, the TSBC data provide confirmatory evidence that psychosocial consultation reversed the prior trends toward declining functioning immediately after community placement. Additionally TSBC data obtained at the end of the follow-up period on thirty-five nonretarded residents in the program consultation facility—who were not project subjects—found them to show nonsignificantly lower levels of appropriate behavior and nonsignificantly higher levels of inappropriate behavior compared to project placements in either facility. Thus, objective assessments show that the level of functioning of project placements was at least as good as those of extended-care residents placed through usual channels who had also experienced the weak token economy of the program consultation facility. Firm conclusions about the empirical utility of case consultation versus program consultation cannot be drawn, but the findings indicate that psychosocial aftercare consultation made some impact on the operations and functioning of residents in community facilities, with continued impact after consultation was terminated.

## SUMMARY

Earlier data had already established the effectiveness of the social-learning program with the chronically institutionalized mental patient. The extent to which significant releases from the original intramural programs might have differentially changed in functioning over the follow-up period was of interest because of the potentially interactive effects between postrelease environmental factors and prior treatment conditions. The level of functioning in the community showed initial losses over the first six months, followed by slight increases over the last year for releases from all three original intramural treatment programs, suggesting that the psychosocial aftercare consultation had some beneficial effects over the last year of the follow-up period. On an absolute level, all released groups continued to show improved functioning from original levels before intramural treatment. However, about a fifth of all releases had declined in functioning after community placement to levels that were lower than those that existed when they were previously rejected for community placement.

Neither the number of residents showing significant change nor the absolute level of functioning at any assessment indicated significant differences among releases from the intramural milieu, social-learning, or hospital programs. However, a differentially greater loss in average level of functioning over the first six months out for psychosocial releases compared to hospital releases suggested that the postrelease environments interacted to some degree with previous treatment history. These factors most likely involved relative differences in the level of attention and activity experienced in the pre- and postrelease environment and relative differences in drug utilization. The level of functioning in the community was highly predictable from prerelease levels of functioning for psychosocial releases and less predictable for hospital releases, further supporting the potential interactive influence of postrelease environmental factors and prior intramural experiences. The change in functioning during the follow-up period was not predictable at all. Thus, the level of functioning in the community for releases from the original treatment groups indicated that ultimate beneficial effects were associated with psychosocial aftercare consultation, and there was some evidence of interactive effects between prior treatment history and postrelease environmental factors.

The extent to which the differing environments in the two extended-care facilities receiving case consultation or program consultation affected the level of community functioning was examined over sequential subgroups of residents in each facility, because external factors precluded a tight experimental design. Active intervention by psychosocial aftercare consultants, following social-learning principles, reversed the early trend of declining functioning for residents in the private extended-care facilities. Although both facilities had instituted weak token-economy programs, the program consultation facility showed higher levels of staff-resident interaction and slightly better implementation of social-learning procedures than the other facility. A slight edge in improved resident functioning also appeared for the program consultation facility; however, differences in resident functioning between the two facilities over the follow-up period were relatively minor and largely nonsignificant —suggesting that the provision of active psychosocial consultation, alone, was the primary factor, no matter what the mode of delivery. Some lasting educational benefit appeared to have resulted from psychosocial consultation because both staff and residents of the community facilities maintained relatively stable levels of performance after consultation ended, and released project residents continued to function at or above the level observed for other residents in the extended-care facility with the highest overall level of functioning.

# 40. Practical Outcome of the Psychosocial and Hospital Programs With Social-Learning Follow-up

The unexpected termination of the psychosocial programs precluded the original plan to treat all patients who had failed to improve sufficiently to achieve significant release from the less effective programs by the most effective program. Although all but one milieu failure had been successfully treated by social-learning procedures when the psychosocial programs ended, none of the hospital failures had been so treated, and two psychosocial failures were necessarily transferred to the hospital group. The layoff of staff had restricted the planned aftercare and follow-up of releases from all three intramural treatment groups to a year and a half rather than two years because of funding limitations. However, aftercare consultation following social-learning principles and procedures was carried out, with six-month assessments of all significant releases residing in the community, as well as monitoring the community stay of earlier releases.

Since hospital failures could not be treated with the program known to be most effective, the remaining patients of the hospital comparison group received an additional year and a half of treatment, during which significant releases could still occur. Both milieu and social-learning programs had terminated, so the only opportunity to produce significant releases had been accomplished by the time original comparisons of release rates were made. Thus, the data on overall practical outcomes presented below are based upon unequal conditions in which the hospital comparison group had additional opportunity to gain significant releases, while psychosocial groups could only be at risk to terminate previous significant releases. However, continuing community stay for any significant release reflects as much on postrelease environmental factors as on intramural treatment procedures, when the same criteria had been used for establishing the initial releases.

## COMPARATIVE RELEASE RATES WITH CONTINUING COMMUNITY STAY

Of the significant releases to the community —all of whom received declining-contact aftercare consultation by psychosocial staff following social-learning principles and procedures—fewer than 3% failed in community adjustment and were returned to a correctional or mental institution by the end of the formal follow-up period. Because of the success of continuing community stay, there were few changes from the comparative release rates originally achieved at the time of termination of the intramural psychosocial programs (table 35.1). In fact, of all significant releases from the original equated groups, only one resident failed at community functioning and required reinstitutionalization. That one resident was a male from the social-learning program who had remained in the community for over a year at the time he was arrested for attempting to cash a forged check. The arrest ultimately resulted in his commitment to an institution for the "criminally insane" when the local judge learned of his prior history of institutionalization. Thus, of the original equated groups, successful community stay at the end of the last year and a half follow-up would be reduced to 92.9% for the social-learning program, from the significant release rates for original releases presented in table 35.1, while those for the milieu and hospital comparisons would remain unchanged.[1]

The only other significant release requiring reinstitutionalization was a male who had initially failed in the milieu program and then had achieved significant release after brief treatment in the social-learning program. After he had spent over a year in successful community placement, he was admitted to a state hospital at the request of the psychosocial aftercare consultant to obtain diagnostic work and treatment for suspected stomach cancer. A state hospital seemed the only alternative for obtaining needed medical attention for his physical problems, since private physicians in the community had avoided examination and treatment of this man, who was supported by public aid funds. No other movement occurred from the community to an institution over the follow-up period; however, just before the end of the period, two additional patients from the hospital comparison group were released to extended-care facilities and eventually achieved the ninety-day minimum stay required for significant release.

The status at the final follow-up of all residents ever treated in any of the intramural treatment programs of the project is presented in table 40.1. The condition in institution for returnees, or those not achieving significant release, is based upon IAB improvement from original project entry to the last assessment in the institution (see chapter 11). Thus, for the hospital comparison group, in-institution figures reflect the status at the end of the follow-up period, nearly six years after the original assessment for the majority of patients. For the milieu program, the in-institution figures show the status at the end of the milieu program at the time residents were transferred to other groups. In-institution figures for the social-learning program reflect the status of the one resident who was transferred on termination of the program (improved) and the status at the time of the final follow-up in respective institutions for the two releases who were reinstitutionalized. An inspection of the condition of residents still in institutions at termination (table 40.1) shows no significant differences between those failing to achieve releases from milieu and hospital programs (chi-square < 1),[2] although more failures over both of the programs had shown declines in functioning than either a failure to change or improvement during intramural treatment (chi-square=4.59, df=1, p < 0.05). In contrast, the only institutionalized resident who had been treated by the social-learning program who was in the institution at the final follow up and functioning at a lower level than upon original entry was a reinstitutionalized resident who had failed at community placement.

Table 40.1 also shows that the same superiority of the social-learning program over the other two programs, which had been found on intramural functioning and on initial production of significant releases, was still in evidence with regard to continuing community stay. Even with the increased releases from the hospital group and with the loss of two significant releases from the social-learning group, a significantly greater proportion of residents treated by the social-learning program was still in the community at the final follow-up than those treated by the milieu program (chi-square =4.33, df=1, p < 0.05) or by the hospital programs (chi-square=15.16, df=1, p < 0.01). Although the milieu program had released more residents than the hospital programs had, with the difference in community stay approaching statistical significance for the initial releases (chi-square=3.21, df=1, p < 0.10), the additional releases late in the follow-up period increased the hospital release rate sufficiently that the total community stay differences between the milieu and hospital groups were not significant on the last follow-up (chi-square =2.41, df=1, p > 0.10). Thus, the previous differences between the treatment programs remained essentially unchanged as a result of the exceptionally stable community-stay rates achieved by all significant releases.

## COMPARATIVE EFFECTIVENESS AND EFFICIENCY OF ACHIEVING CONTINUING COMMUNITY STAY

Because of the differential release rates and stable community stay, the usual measure of effectiveness of institutional treatment programs in terms of days in community has somewhat less meaning. All but three significant releases (two milieu and one hospital) with continued community stay at the final follow-up had remained in the community from the time of their original release, ranging from less than three months to over five years earlier. Similarly the usual measure of efficiency of institutional treatment programs in terms of time-in-program is not an accurate reflection of minimum times that would be required to produce significant releases to community placements for the psychosocial programs, since minimum times

Table 40.1. Status at final follow-up for all residents ever treated.

| Treatment program | No. | Condition in institution of returnees and residents not achieving significant release | | | Residents achieving significant release with continuing community stay |
| --- | --- | --- | --- | --- | --- |
| | | Worse | No change | Improved | |
| Social-learning | 40 | 2.5% | 2.5% | 2.5% | 92.5% |
| Milieu therapy | 31 | 16.1% | 9.7% | 3.2% | 71.0% |
| Hospital comparison | 31 | 29.0% | 9.7% | 12.9% | 48.4% |

Note. Chi-square=17.18, $df$=2, $p$< 0.01 for in institution versus out of institution.

were largely a function of the previously established design. Since the hospital group had nearly two years in which placements to private board and care facilities could be made, time-in-program is a more realistic measure of efficiency for the hospital group. Nevertheless, the usual measures provide comparative data on the relative effectiveness and efficiency of the community stay obtained among the three treatment programs within the project.

Average "days in community" and "project weeks in program" are presented in table 40.2 for the original equated groups and for all residents ever treated in each intramural program at the time of the final follow-up. As was the case at the time of original releases, average time-in-program differed significantly among groups for both original equated groups and all residents treated.[3] In each instance, the psychosocial groups spent significantly less time in programs than the hospital group did (Z's > 3.84, $p < 0.01$, Mann-Whitney U test), and the psychosocial programs did not differ for the original equated groups ($Z < 1$), but all ever-treated social-learning residents spent significantly less time-in-program than milieu residents did ($Z=2.05$, $p < 0.05$). Although these figures for time-in-program reflect the additional time available to the hospital group over the follow-up period, the results on comparative efficiency are identical to those obtained at the time of termination of the psychosocial programs, before additional time was available to the hospital group (see chapter 35). The greater efficiency of the psychosocial programs primarily reflects the relatively early releases to independent functioning for the original equated groups, and differences in efficiency for all residents ever treated reflect the shorter time involved in the treatment of replacements and the remarkably short time required for focused social-learning procedures to treat failures from the milieu program.

An inspection of average "days-in-community" in table 40.2 also shows significant differences among the three programs in the amount of time treated groups spent out of the institution during the entire project period. Although social-learning residents averaged 141.5 more days in the community than milieu residents did for the original equated groups and 98.6 more days in the community for the larger group of ever treated residents, these differences were not statistically significant between psychosocial programs (Z's < 1.07, $p > 0.20$, Mann-Whitney U test). Both psychosocial groups, however, spent significantly more days in the community than the hospital group did for the original equated groups (Z's > 2.58, $p < 0.01$) and all residents ever treated (Z's > 3.16, $p < 0.01$). Thus, from the original equated groups, the social-learning program achieved more significant releases with continuing community stay than either the milieu or hospital programs did, and both psychosocial programs produced more in-community days as a result of less time in programs than the hospital programs did. When all residents ever treated were considered, the same relationships were found, except that the time-in-program for those treated by social-learning procedures was significantly less than the time-in-program of the milieu group.

The practical implications of these data are that the most effective program was also the most efficient. As noted in chapter 35, board and care placement as an ultimate target can reasonably be expected in twenty-six to thirty weeks for chronic mental patients without physical problems who are treated in an ongoing social-learning program in the absence of the design restrictions of the present project. The data further suggest that such placements can be maintained in the community with minimal monitoring after initial intensive consultation following social-learning principles and procedures. Such conditions offer hope of treatment procedures that are effective in absolute terms and are cost-effective compared to competing alternatives.

Table 40.2. Comparative effectiveness and efficiency of community placements at final follow-up.

| Treatment program | Original equated groups | | | | | All residents ever treated | | | | |
| --- | --- | --- | --- | --- | --- | --- | --- | --- | --- | --- |
| | | Days in community[a] | | Weeks in program[b] | | | Days in community[a] | | Weeks in program[b] | |
| | No. | Mean | S.D. | Mean | S.D. | No. | Mean | S.D. | Mean | S.D. |
| Social-learning | 28 | 591.0 | 358.25 | 213.3 | 47.12 | 40 | 555.7 | 303.64 | 161.2 | 94.78 |
| Milieu therapy | 28 | 449.5 | 430.87 | 215.1 | 43.32 | 31 | 457.1 | 409.44 | 207.5 | 53.85 |
| Hospital comparison | 28 | 270.6 | 315.06 | 260.6 | 45.54 | 31 | 244.4 | 309.76 | 243.0 | 69.48 |

a. Kruskal-Wallis $H > 14.92$, $df=2$, $p$'s $< 0.01$ for days in community.
b. $H > 28.77$, $df=2$, $p$'s $< 0.01$ for weeks in program.

## COMPARATIVE COST-EFFECTIVENESS OF PROGRAMS

A full-scale cost-benefit analysis attempts to calculate current costs of treatment programs and relate them to future benefits, with dollar values estimated for tangible direct benefits (e.g., savings in institutional expenditures), tangible indirect benefits (e.g., increased earnings and returns on income tax), and intangible benefits (e.g., reduction in grief, increased well-being)—all corrected for inflation and discounted for interest on funds saved or spent on future costs and benefits (Klarman, 1969). Although this approach is praise-worthy in its attempt to account for all possible variables, nearly all of the components are necessarily based on estimates (e.g., Conley et al., 1967; Halpern & Binner, 1972). Even a minor change in assumptions on which estimates of the hardest data of a cost-benefit analysis (i.e., tangible direct benefits) are based can drastically change the outcome (e.g., Foreyt et al., 1975). Additionally a review of the cost-benefit literature verifies May's (1970) conclusion that many of the figures reported appear to be "little better than thoughtful guesses." Thus rather than fall prey to the temptations of a full-scale cost-benefit analysis with future predictions, cost-effectiveness analysis limited to the comparative differential costs of accomplishing a specified objective (Klarman, 1969) seemed a better method for determining the relative economic advantage or disadvantage of the milieu, social-learning, and hospital programs.

Since the social-learning program was most effective in improving resident behavior intramurally and in achieving releases to the community, the cost per unit relative to available alternatives should be the major concern for decision makers. This information requires a comparison of the relative costs of operating programs, the relative dollars saved by each program, and the relative relationship of differential operating costs to dollars saved—all expressed on a per-case basis (May, 1970). Since the comparisons are all relative between programs operating within the same time frame and within the same cost-system, identical calculations in constant dollars can be used, capitalizing upon the best data sources available.

Relative treatment costs for residents of each program were compared without taking into account food and shelter or administrative costs of the institutions as a whole, since the programs could be conducted in any institution, and food cost allocations should be identical. These institutional costs can make tremendous differences to total treatment costs (see Ullmann, 1967) but are irrelevant to differential program costs.[4] Four major cost areas could potentially vary as a function of the specific programs: costs of treatment staff, costs of psychotropic drugs, costs of consumables and supplies used as token backups in the social-learning program, and costs of support personnel differentially required by the mode of operation of the programs. Staff and psychotropic drugs provided the greatest difference among program costs.

Complete salary figures were available for hospital staff in fiscal year 1970; therefore, comparative staffing costs were calculated by determining the actual average salary of professional and nonprofessional staff, separately, for each program in 1970 dollars and applying those figures to the average staff composition and staff-to-patient ratios for the entire intramural treatment period (see chapter 4). These calculations thus provide comparable per diem costs per resident between the actual staffing costs of the three programs, but they do not provide accurate total costs, because no correction for inflation was applied. Research records provided information of actual administration and dosage levels of psychotropic drugs, from which averages were calculated for the entire intramural treatment period and costed by the pharmacist to provide a per-diem cost per resident.

The differential daily costs of staff and psychotropic drugs, presented in table 40.3, show that psychosocial staff were more expensive than hospital staff, even though staff-patient ratios were approximately equal. Although the method of calculating staffing costs may have slightly overestimated relative costs of psychosocial staff—because of higher turnover during the treatment period, resulting in fewer staff at higher step levels within the same pay grade over time—the primary basis for lower staffing costs in the hospital programs was the extensive use of unpaid professional trainees (see chapter 9) and the greater proportions of nurses to psychologists or physicians among professional personnel, while psychologists predominated in the professional staff of the psychosocial programs. However, when the actual lengths of time spent in programs are taken into account, the cost per case changes considerably for staff, with the result that psychosocial programs were cheaper than the hospital programs were.[5] Psychotropic drug costs, also shown in table 40.3, reflect the major differences in emphasis put upon chemotherapy. More hospital patients received psychotropic drugs at higher dosage levels and the total cost per case ran nearly six times that of the social-learning program for originally equated groups.

The other costs of program operation were either equal in per diem costs or were cheaper for the psychosocial programs. The cost of

Table 40.3. Average treatment costs of staff and psychotropic drugs over the project period (in constant 1970 dollars).

| Source | Daily cost per resident (patient) | | | Total cost per case | | | | | |
|---|---|---|---|---|---|---|---|---|---|
| | | | | Original equated groups | | | All residents ever treated | | |
| | Social-learning | Milieu | Hospital | Social-learning | Milieu | Hospital | Social-learning | Milieu | Hospital |
| Total staff (Salary & fringe benefits) | $10.32 | $10.32 | $ 9.66 | $15,405.18 | $15,536.76 | $17,617.43 | $11,646.89 | $14,990.97 | $16,433.84 |
| Psychotropic drugs | .13 | .18 | .63 | 194.06 | 270.99 | 1,148.96 | 146.71 | 261.47 | 1,071.77 |
| Total | 10.45 | 10.50 | 10.29 | 15,599.24 | 15,807.75 | 18,766.39 | 11,793.60 | 15,252.44 | 17,505.61 |

Note. Only comparative costs have meaning because neither inflation nor discounting were included in calculations. See table 40.5.

consumables and supplies over the entire intramural treatment period yields an average daily cost per resident of sixteen cents in the social-learning program and twenty-two cents in the milieu program (1970 dollars), as a result of the lower utilization of goods available only on a contingent basis in the social-learning program. Hospital records were not adequate to retrieve comparable costs; however, those available suggest that considerably higher costs were likely involved, since clothing disbursements alone cost thirteen cents per day for chronic patients at the hospital; in addition there were other costs for regularly disbursed tobacco, cigarettes, snacks, cosmetics, and grooming supplies. Differentially required nontreatment support personnel included the hourly student workers to provide assistance for female staff in the event of assaults for psychosocial programs and housekeeping personnel in the regional hospital who did the work performed by residents in the psychosocial programs. The differential cost of the hospital housekeeping staff (salary and fringe benefits) over the once-per-month housekeeping contracted to an outside firm for the psychosocial units averaged twenty cents per patient per day, which was identical to the cost of the hourly student workers (in 1970 dollars). Psychosocial costs were probably relatively less since the student workers always received $1.50 per hour and hospital housekeeping staff increased wages and benefits over time. Thus, per-diem costs of the most effective program (social-learning) were equal to or less than all other programs on all components except staff, and the per-case cost even of staff was below competing alternatives.[6]

Dollar effectiveness values for residents of each program were compared on the basis of the savings to taxpayers of having chronically institutionalized mental patients where they were after release rather than in the regional hospital—which is where all patients who were not released would have been in the absence of the project. At the time of the majority of the releases (1973), the actual daily direct cost of maintaining a release in private extended-care facilities was a $9.17 payment to the facility from public aid funds to cover all food, shelter, maintenance, administrative, and treatment costs, plus eighty-two cents personal allowance directly to the resident of an extended-care facility from supplementary social security income payments (Illinois Department of Public Aid, 1973). Additionally the costs of psychosocial aftercare staff over the entire follow-up period—travel, salaries and fringe benefits—amounted to forty-six cents per release per day. Follow-up costs before the termination of the psychosocial programs were already included in intramural treatment costs. Computed in constant 1973 dollars, each day spent in an extended-care facility cost taxpayers $10.45, while each day an independent release spent in the community cost taxpayers forty-six cents.

Total costs per patient per day at the regional hospital for fiscal year 1973 were reported to be $30.92, which itself was less than 81% of the average cost of other public mental hospitals in the state (Illinois Department of Mental Health, 1973). However, the costs of maintaining a chronically institutionalized mental patient in the regional hospital were estimated to be only $27.44 per day, rather than $30.92, because of the differential staffing and facilities distribution in the hospital.[7] Thus, in constant 1973 dollars, every day a significant release spent in a community placement saved taxpayers $16.99, while every day a significant release spent in independent functioning directly saved taxpayers $26.98, which would have been spent to maintain each person in the regional hospital.

The differential direct savings computed on the basis of actual in-community days to the time of the final follow-up are presented in table 40.4 in constant 1973 dollars. The comparative effectiveness expressed in direct dollar savings shows that the psychosocial programs, including the milieu program, had a considerable advantage over the traditional hospital programs. It should be noted that the dollar figures in table 40.4 are gross underestimates of the actual dollars saved. Even by the time of the final follow-up, state mental hospital costs had spiraled nearly 36%, such that daily savings for the middle twelve months of the follow-up period had already increased to over $23 per day—not to mention the future savings that should have continued to accrue after termination of the formal follow-up period.

The comparative dollar cost-effectiveness among the three programs during the project period, summarized in table 40.5, shows the psychosocial programs produced considerable economic benefit compared to the traditional hospital programs. Even with conservative figures, including only staff and drug costs, the per-case operational expenses cost less, rather than more, by over 15% in both psychosocial programs than in traditional hospital programs among the original equated groups. The dollar-effectiveness savings in table 40.5 show the social-learning program was over two and a half times as effective as the hospital programs and over 28% more effective than the milieu program for the original equated groups. Although the milieu program had not shown significant differences in the amount of improvement obtained compared to the hospital programs, it was still nearly twice as effective considering direct dollar savings.

Most important for decision making on how

Table 40.4. Direct costs saved over the cost of continued hospitalization to the time of project termination (in constant 1973 dollars).

| Treatment program | Dollars saved by project termination | | Average direct savings per case | |
|---|---|---|---|---|
| | Original equated groups | All residents ever treated | Original equated groups | All residents ever treated |
| Social-learning | $328,663 | $425,166 | $11,738 | $10,629 |
| Milieu therapy | 255,844 | 282,756 | 9,137 | 9,121 |
| Hospital comparison | 128,716 | 128,716 | 4,597 | 4,152 |

Note. Only comparative savings have meaning because inflation, discounting, and future savings were not included in calculations. See table 40.5.

limited mental health funds should be spent are the cost-effectiveness and effectiveness-cost ratios presented in table 40.5 The figures—only for original equated groups where no confounding factors are potentially involved—provide clear, unambiguous answers to the questions of comparative effectiveness from a purely economic point of view. The cost-effectiveness ratios indicate that for the same dollar savings produced by traditional hospital programs, less than a third the differential dollar costs would be spent by the social-learning program, with the remainder of the comparative figures showing the more effective programs to also be the more cost-effective in comparison to each other. The effectiveness-cost ratios are even more important economically, since costs are typically redistributed rather than cut off completely. According to the effectiveness-cost ratios, for the same dollars spent on differential treatment costs, the social-learning programs returned over three times the dollar savings compared to traditional hospital programs and over 30% more than the milieu program did. Although the milieu program had not been consistently superior to the hospital programs, on an economic basis alone, it provided well over twice the return in savings for each dollar spent on differential treatment cost as that obtained by the hospital programs. Since these figures are conservative—not taking any future benefits into account—the economics of treatment clearly support the implementation of the most effective treatment program for the severely disabled chronic mental patient.

## SUMMARY

Continuing community stay for any significant institutional release reflects as much on postrelease environmental factors as on intramural treatment procedures when the same criteria have been used for establishing the initial releases. Nevertheless, the ultimate practical outcome of the comparative effectiveness of institutional treatment programs must take into account the extent to which institutional releases are maintained in the community with reasonable effort and the comparative costs involved. Over the formal follow-up period of approximately a year and a half after the termination of the psychosocial programs, only two more significant releases occurred from the hospital group. Over 97% of all these releases remained in the community during that period, when psychosocial aftercare consultation was provided and contacts declined to zero over the last three months. Because of the high community-stay rates of all significant releases who received psychosocial aftercare consultation, the previous differences between

Table 40.5. Comparative cost-effectiveness of programs over the project period.

| Comparison | Staff & drug costs | | Dollar effectiveness | | Cost/ effectiveness | | Effectiveness/ costs | |
|---|---|---|---|---|---|---|---|---|
| Social-learning/Hospital | $0.831 | ($0.674) | $2.553 | ($2.560) | $0.325 | ($0.263) | $3.072 | ($3.798) |
| Milieu/Hospital | .842 | ( .871) | 1.988 | ( 2.197) | .424 | ( .396) | 2.361 | ( 2.522) |
| Social-learning/Milieu | .987 | ( .773) | 1.285 | ( 1.165) | .768 | ( .664) | 1.302 | ( 1.507) |
| Hospital | 1.000 | ( 1.000) | 1.000 | ( 1.000) | 1.000 | ( 1.000) | 1.000 | ( 1.000) |

Note. Figures in the body of the table are for original equated groups (N=28 each); figures in parentheses are for all residents (patients) ever treated.

programs remained essentially unchanged at the end of formal follow-up from those existing at the time of termination of the intramural psychosocial programs.

The social-learning program maintained its clear superiority over the other two groups, with well over 90% of treated residents remaining continuously in the community at the time of the year and a half final follow-up, with some having maintained community stay for over five years. Although over 70% of the residents treated by the milieu therapy program were still in the community at the final follow-up, compared to fewer than 50% of the patients from the hospital group, these differences were not statistically significant with regard to the numbers achieving significant release with continuing community stay. However, as before, the efficiency of both psychosocial programs was significantly greater than that of the hospital program.

Cost-effectiveness analyses found that the social-learning program was the most effective and the least expensive. Considered in economic terms, during the project period it returned over three times the dollar savings of the hospital programs and over 30% more dollar savings than the milieu program for the same dollars spent on treatment costs. In economic terms, the milieu program showed considerable superiority to hospital programs, returning over twice the amount of dollar savings for each dollar spent in treatment costs. Since the comparisons were conservative—without taking any future benefits into consideration—the economics of institutional treatment not only support the implementation of the most effective treatment program but argue strongly in its favor.

# 41. Summary of Findings From Community Follow-up

Following the sudden statewide layoffs of staff, including original psychosocial staff, there were several problems in community relations and an extended period of confusion for psychosocial aftercare consultation and follow-up. Although these events had no impact on the original evaluation of comparative effectiveness—the social-learning program had already been established as the most effective one for bringing about significant improvements in functioning and more significant releases than either the milieu or hospital programs did—they did delay the original schedule of declining contacts. New center administration also caused considerable problems through active interference and violations of prior agreements, both in the mode of operations of psychosocial staff, and with community facilities and agencies. The result was a need for multiple extensions and supplements in federal funding to complete the community follow-ups and data analyses.

The formal follow-up period was limited to a year and a half after the completion of the original community placements because of the layoffs and associated problems. The consultation that was actually implemented is described in chapter 38. Since earlier analyses had already documented the superiority of social-learning principles and procedures for the population, that model was adopted for all aftercare consultation. By the ninth month of the follow-up period, aftercare consultation to extended-care facilities that had accepted only a few significant releases from the three intramural programs had been faded to telephone checks on progress, without requests for consultation over the last six months of the period. The two local extended-care facilities that had accepted the majority of community placements were more reactive to external problems and events, to the extent that an intensive period of training and consultation was necessary after the sixth month of the follow-up period. The two different modes of delivery of aftercare consultation—case consultation and program consultation—were implemented in these facilities, but with less clear differentiation of procedures than had been planned originally. After the period of intensive intervention to overcome the problems resulting from the external events, consultation was systematically faded; by the last six months of the follow-up period, there was only a once-per-week brief check for three months, followed by three months without scheduled contact.

Assessments of staff behavior in the two extended-care facilities found differences between the case consultation and program consultation facilities, as well as differences associated with the period of active intervention and the later fading of psychosocial aftercare consultation. Both facilities showed some approximation to desirable social-learning procedures, and the facility that received program consultation showed much higher levels of staff activity and a better approximation to social-learning procedures than the other facility. However, the overall level of activity and distribution of staff behaviors in both was far removed from the desirable social-learning procedures on an absolute level. In fact, an exceptionally high indiscriminate use of psychotropic drugs, plus the distribution of several classes of staff behavior, was more aligned with the custodial-caretaking philosophy of the state hospital than with the social-learning approach. Overall, the extended-care facilities appeared to fall midway between traditional hospital programs and the social-learning program in the actual staff behaviors performed, with program content and staff activity providing more than hospital programs, but much less than the intramural social-learning program.

Since postrelease environmental conditions are likely to have as much to do with community stay and in-community functioning as the intramural programs that brought about initial improvements—when release criteria are identical as they were in the current project—potentially interactive effects were of interest because of the differential change in conditions for releases from the three intramural programs. As detailed in chapter 39, the level of functioning in the community decreased over the first six months out, followed by slight increases over the last year of follow-up for releases from all three original intramural programs, suggesting some beneficial effects from psychosocial aftercare consultation over the last year of the period. A differentially greater loss occurred for releases from both psychosocial programs over the first six months. This change suggested some interactive effects between prior treatment history and the postrelease environment, since both psychosocial groups experienced increases in the use of psychotropic drugs and decreases in attention and activity, and the hospital group experienced no change in the use of psychotropic drugs but did experience increases in activity. Level of functioning in the community was highly predictable from prerelease measures for releases from both the milieu and social-learning programs but less so for hospital releases, further supporting the interpretation that postrelease environmental factors were interactive with prior intramural experiences. While absolute level of functioning was predictable from both objective measures and ratings obtained before release, change in functioning was not predictable at all, nor were other individual characteristics or use of psychotropic drugs related to in-community functioning.

On an absolute level, releases from the original intramural programs did not differ in functioning over any of the six-month follow-up assessments. All released groups continued to show improved functioning overall from original levels before intramural treatment, but about a fifth of all releases had declined in functioning after community placement to levels that were lower than those from when they were previously rejected for community placement—indicating that community standards had changed. Although these severely debilitated groups had shown significant improvement and had retained higher levels of functioning in the community than those they had had before the intramural treatment, the absolute level of in-community functioning was still marginal; only about a third of the releases from all three groups were functioning at levels indistinguishable from those of the normal population at the final follow-up assessment.

The extent to which the differing environments in the two extended-care facilities receiving case consultation or program consultation affected the level of community functioning again indicated that active intervention of psychosocial aftercare consultants following social-learning principles did reverse the initial trend toward declining functioning in the community facilities. A slight edge in improved resident functioning appeared for the facility receiving program consultation, but differences in resident functioning between the two facilities over the follow-up period were relatively minor. Overall, the provision of active psychosocial consultation alone appeared to be the primary factor, no matter what the mode of delivery. Both staff and residents of community facilities maintained relatively stable levels of performance after consultation was terminated, indicating that some lasting educational benefits had been achieved through aftercare consultation. Although the absolute levels of functioning were still marginal for project releases as a group, an objective observational sample of other residents from the best-functioning extended-care facility found that project releases were functioning at levels nonsignificantly above those of community placements through usual channels. Thus, project releases were representative of others in the community, even though they had started out as more severely debilitated before receiving treatment through the intramural programs of the project.

The overall practical outcome of hospital, milieu, and social-learning programs at the end of the formal follow-up period was essentially identical to that obtained upon initial termination of intramural psychosocial programs, since over 97% of all releases remained in the community over the declining-contact follow-up period. As detailed in chapter 40, the high community stay rates of all significant releases pointed to the clear superiority of the social-learning program, with over 90% of treated residents remaining continuously in the community at the time of the year and a half follow-up, including some who had been in the community for over five years. The differences were not statistically significant between milieu and hospital releases at the end of the follow-up period, even though over 70% of the residents treated by milieu therapy had achieved significant release with continuing community stay, compared to fewer than 50% of hospital patients. The efficiency of the milieu program was significantly greater than that of the hospital programs, as was the absolute amount of time released residents spent in the community. The social-learning program was significantly more efficient as well as more effective than the other two approaches.

Cost-effectiveness analyses showed that the social-learning program was the cheapest to operate as well. During the project period alone, it returned over 30% more dollar savings for every dollar spent in differential treatment costs than the milieu program did. Compared to traditional hospital programs, the milieu program returned well over twice the dollar savings and the social-learning program returned over three times the dollar savings for the same treatment costs as the traditional programs. As detailed in chapter 40, these comparisons were exceptionally conservative and did not take into account any future benefits that could occur beyond the termination of formal follow-up or any intangible benefits.

Thus, the social-learning program emerged as effective on an absolute level and significantly more effective than either traditional hospital programs or the most promising alternative psychosocial program for treating the severely debilitated chronically institutionalized mental patient; it improved the level of functioning more, achieved greater numbers of significant institutional releases, maintained community stay, and, in economic terms, it was the most cost-effective program to operate as well.

# PART 9
# Conclusions and Recommendations

## 42. Current Status of the Milieu and Social-Learning Approaches

Given the amount of information generated over the six years of data collection of the comparative project, several large books could be written relating aspects of the empirical findings to those reported elsewhere and to a multitude of theoretical formulations in a variety of areas. This final section will not indulge in such an intellectual exercise, nor will an attempt be made to summarize major findings beyond those related to the specific aims of the project.[1] Rather, the focus of the current chapter will be on conclusions of direct relevance to the specific aims of the comparative project, as detailed in chapter 3. Comments and recommendations on practical contributions and potential obstacles to improving institutional research and treatment will be presented in chapter 43.

### COMPARATIVE EFFECTIVENESS

The overall comparative results on the relative effectiveness of the programs in the current project could not be clearer. The social-learning program was significantly more effective than either the milieu program or the traditional hospital programs. Its greater effectiveness was consistent across all classes of functioning in the intramural setting and in the production of institutional release, based upon the same criteria. Since neither postrelease functioning nor rehospitalization rates differed among those who achieved significant release and received the same aftercare services, the social-learning program also maintained greater effectiveness over milieu and hospital programs in community stay. The improvements and releases within the social-learning program occurred without regard to individual demographic characteristics, previous length or type of treatment, nature of initial level, or severity of deficits or bizarre behavior and in the relative absence of psychotropic drugs. It was also more efficient and cost-effective, obtaining the superior effects with similar staffing levels to the hospital programs and the same staff, physical plant, activity schedule, and behavioral focus as the milieu program had.

Thus, the social-learning program clearly emerged as the treatment of choice for the chronically institutionalized mental patient, whether showing severe deficits in functioning, extremes of psychotic and bizarre behavior, or both.

### DIFFERENTIAL AREAS OF SUCCESS

Two additional aims of the project also related directly to the future treatment of institutionalized patients: to identify the limits of change that can be accomplished with the overall programs within staffing restrictions characteristic of public mental hospitals and to explore the systematic effects of both programs with regard to differential areas of success. Questions on the limits of change under currently available staffing levels have practical implications for length of treatment and discharge targets. Differential areas of success for social-learning and milieu programs have practical implications for the effective ingredients presumed to be operating in each program, with further implications for the responsiveness of different classes of problem behaviors to different treatment procedures.

The milieu and social-learning programs were not only equated on all potentially relevant characteristics of the patient population, but were equally high prestige programs in identical physical settings with exact equation in the degree of operationalization, clarity, specificity, explicitness, and order provided for both staff and residents. Both programs also provided identical activity structure and focus upon specific classes of behavior, with the same staff not only conducting both programs, but equating time and focus within programs, with both running concurrently over the same time periods, subject to the same extraneous events. The equation of all these variables made the comparative cause-effect conclusions on the relative effectiveness of the treatment programs technically possible for the first time in the history of controlled evaluation for any institutional treatment program.

The equation of the variables, combined

with continuous objective assessments, also allowed a better exploration of the systematic effects of the overall treatment techniques within programs on specific classes of resident behavior that had been identified as crucial for the rehabilitation of the chronically institutionalized mental patient. Although many of the effects have been detailed within previous chapters, an examination of relative changes longitudinally, over the entire intramural period, proved to be particularly illuminating.

## Nonspecific Attention and Activity

One variable that has been particularly difficult in all previous attempts at institutional program evaluation is the matter of the sheer volume of staff activity or attention received by patients, irrespective of the specific procedures applied. It has been confounded in every previous attempt to evaluate any institutional program, leading reviewers to state, for example, "it is tempting to conclude that practically any reasonable innovation will lead to improvement" (Erickson, 1975, p. 528). Staff-resident interaction must obviously occur for any program to have impact, and increases in such activity over none at all are likely to have beneficial effects (Ellsworth, 1968; Ullmann, 1967). However, the results of the current project clearly show that once staff-to-resident interaction is established, how staff activity and attention are applied is much more important than how much occurs.

No specific class of resident behavior within either psychosocial program covaried with total staff activity or total attention received by residents, although specific classes of staff-resident interaction differentially covaried with specific resident behaviors within programs. Additionally, although total staff activity remained constant from the original baseline over the first twenty weeks of treatment, major changes in resident functioning occurred during the same time period. The amount of attention received by individual residents from staff was higher in the social-learning program than in the milieu program during the first six months, even though total staff activity remained comparable. Over the remaining four years, staff activity and the individual attention received by residents gradually increased in the milieu program to the extent that milieu residents received more attention than social-learning residents did. Thus, greater social-learning improvements occurred under conditions of both more attention and less attention than did parallel milieu changes, clearly ruling out the volume of activity or attention as the major influencing factor in differential effectiveness.

## Rehabilitation Goals

*Adaptive Behavior.* A review of differential changes in specific classes of resident functioning over the entire intramural period further clarified the probable bases of influence on areas crucial for the rehabilitation of the chronic mental patient: resocialization, instrumental role performance, and reduction or elimination of extreme bizarre behaviors. There were severe deficits in all components of socialization before the psychosocial programs began, with the average resident demonstrating normal self-care (e.g., appearance, meal behavior, bathing) only 13% of the time and normal interpersonal skills (social interaction and communication) only 7% of the time. There were immediate improvements in self-care in both programs, which were maintained throughout the entire intramural period. However, clear differences in the pattern of change were apparent between programs. Residents of the milieu program obtained their highest level of self-care by the eighth week after the introduction of programmatic procedures, with the average resident performing normal self-maintenance activities about 30% of the time. A slight decline occurred in the milieu program over the first period of disruption—following the death of a resident—but the improved levels were maintained at about twice the initial levels. Self-care was, in fact, the only area of adaptive functioning in which milieu residents maintained improvement over pretreatment levels for the entire intramural period.

Social-learning residents also showed immediate improvement in self-care when the programmatic procedures were introduced, and the level was greater than that of milieu residents within four weeks after the introduction of programmatic procedures; it remained significantly higher at all points thereafter. Additionally, in contrast to the maintenance of initial improvements in self-care within the milieu program, social-learning residents continued to show gradual increasing improvements over the next thirty months, reaching a level of normal functioning over four times that existing at pretreatment. Although social-learning residents showed declines in the level of self-care during the period of increased assaultiveness (resulting from the reduction in length of time out), the average resident continued to perform normal self-maintenance activities at triple the level existing before the introduction of the program. The return to baseline conditions had no effect on self-care in the milieu program, nor did the reintroduction of milieu procedures during the last twenty weeks.

In contrast, there was a significant reduction in self-care for social-learning residents upon the return to baseline conditions, followed by an immediate improvement with continuing gradual increases upon the reintroduction of social-learning procedures.

Immediate improvements in interpersonal skills were also obtained upon the introduction of both programs, without differences between programs over the first six months. Thereafter, normal social functioning was maintained in the milieu program at about twice the initial level over a period of thirty-seven months, with temporary increases during times of high stress associated with a single aggressive resident. From the thirty-seventh month on, concurrent with the major increases in assaultiveness, the interpersonal skills of milieu residents gradually deteriorated to a level no better than that existing before the program had begun. The return to baseline conditions and the reintroduction of milieu procedures stopped the declining trend but did not result in further significant improvement.

In contrast, social-learning residents continued to show gradual improvements in interpersonal skills to a level over ten times that of their beginning level after twenty-eight months, remaining superior to milieu residents at every point from the seventh month on. The interpersonal skills of social-learning residents were then maintained over the first six months following the change in time out and the resulting increases in assaultiveness, with only slight and gradual reductions over the last year in which assaultiveness increased. Decreases in interpersonal skills occurred during the return to baseline procedures with further immediate and gradual increases occurring over the last twenty weeks after the reintroduction of social-learning procedures.

These patterns of change in self-care, interpersonal and communications skills suggest that both programs produced initial improvements in performance simply as a function of the increased activity levels and pressure to perform after specificity of desired behaviors had already been introduced. However, the communication of expectancies, group pressure, and practice in group problem solving and crisis resolution in the milieu program led to no further improvements beyond activating the performance of skills already existing before entry to the treatment program. In fact, the differential loss of original improvements in social skills for milieu residents while improvements in self-care were maintained further suggests that milieu-specific treatment techniques were not particularly potent even in maintaining performance of previously existing skills. This differentiation is suggested by the fact that self-care behaviors were the primary class of resident response within the milieu program where feedback procedures resulted in individual response-contingent social reinforcement.

In contrast, the individual prompts, consistent response-contingent consequences, focus on associative learning, and material as well as social reinforcement provided in the social-learning program regularly produced consistent gradual increases in performance indicative of the acquisition of new skills. The increases continued through the disruption of operations as a result of the reduction in length of time out as a consequence for assaultiveness. Even though some decrements in performance occurred during this period, the response-contingent components of the program continued to maintain performance at a much improved level. The decrement upon the removal of social-learning procedures during the return to baseline conditions further indicates the extent to which performance of social and self-care skills was being maintained by response-contingent procedures, but also shows generalization of improvement to conditions of minimal and erratic social reinforcement. Increases during the last twenty weeks after the procedural changes in handling assaultiveness indicated that further improvements were forthcoming as a result of social-learning procedures.

Thus, with regard to self-care, interpersonal interaction, and communications skills, milieu procedures appeared to do little more than activate dormant skills that had been deficient in performance; in addition maintenance over the long run appeared to be dependent upon social reinforcement rather than on milieu principles. Given the severe debility levels of the population, even the social reinforcement did little more than maintain normal self-care activities about a quarter of the time. Social-learning procedures not only produced significantly greater effects on all areas of resocialization but demonstrated clear evidence of overcoming learning deficits as well as performance deficits. By the twenty-eighth month of treatment, the average social-learning resident had improved to the point of demonstrating normal self-care and interpersonal skills about half of the time, with the trend being toward continued improvements.

Unfortunately, the limits of improvement in resocialization from the social-learning program cannot be determined because the change in time out was imposed while further gains were in progress, halting additional improvements for the group as a whole. The rate at which self-care and interpersonal skills were again improving after the reintroduction of social-learning procedures, with better methods available once again for handling assaults, suggests that the program had not yet approached its limits on resocialization. The social-learning program and principles thus are exceptionally effective in resocialization of the severely desocialized chronic mental patient.

Immediate improvements in instrumental role performance were also obtained upon the introduction of both psychosocial programs. Although the amount and quality of housekeeping and vocational skills were included in the assessment of instrumental role performance, because of the level of disability of the population, the majority of instrumental behaviors assessed within the project consisted of prevocational skills—primarily being on task in classes and job training positions and on time at scheduled meetings, activities, and work. As such, instrumental role performance reflects as much on attentiveness and attention span as on vocational performance in the group data. Even with the severely debilitated population, residents were less deficient in instrumental role performance than in self-care and social skills. The immediate increase in instrumental role performance for milieu residents had reached its highest level of the entire intramural period by the eighth week after the introduction of programmatic procedures. However, unlike self-care, it immediately began to deteriorate to the point that no improvement from pretreatment was maintained by the end of ten months. The added problems of increased assaultiveness after the length of expulsion was reduced resulted in further deterioration to below pretreatment levels, which were not again regained even with a reversal upon the reintroduction of better procedures for controlling assaultiveness.

In contrast, the social-learning program not only produced the immediate increase in instrumental role performance upon the introduction of programmatic procedures but continued to bring about systematic and relatively rapid increases to the point that the average resident was performing at a level indistinguishable from normal over 81% of the time by the eighteenth week of treatment. That exceptionally high level of performance was maintained even beyond the disruptions resulting from the reduction in time out, with only a slight decrement thereafter. In addition to maintaining the high level of instrumental role performance, social-learning residents also systematically increased the complexity of performance through continuing promotions to higher step levels. The return to baseline conditions also showed a slight decrement, but still provided evidence of generalized improvement, and the reintroduction of social-learning procedures during the last twenty weeks again brought about steady improvement.

The patterns of change in instrumental role performance suggest that initial improvements in both programs occurred simply as a function of the increased activity levels and pressure to perform with continuing specificity of desired behavior. Milieu therapy procedures were totally inadequate to maintain that initial level of improvement—even with the increasing activity and pressure from staff on living groups and individual residents. Thus, group pressure, practice in problem solving, and communication of expectancies without explicit consequences had no continuing effect on instrumental role performance. Social-learning procedures, on the other hand, were particularly effective for this class of behavior, producing and maintaining higher levels of performance over the initial increase within an additional fourteen weeks of treatment. Although the 81% normal performance of instrumental roles for the average social-learning resident appeared to be asymptotic, without indications that further improvements in rate were likely for the group as a whole, the limits on complexity of performance had not yet been approached by the time the reduction in time out for assaultiveness brought intramural improvements to a halt. Thus, the individual prompts, successive approximation, and response-contingent material and social reinforcement of the social-learning program, combined with brief time out and token response costs for failures, are exceptionally effective in increasing and maintaining attentiveness, time-on-task, and other prevocational skills for the chronically institutionalized patient. Over time, housekeeping and semiskilled vocational performances were also responding to social-learning procedures, but possible limits on the level of performance potentially attainable by the severely disabled chronic patient are unknown.

In contrast to social and instrumental behaviors, which systematically received response-contingent reinforcement in the social-learning program and feedback and positive expectancies in the milieu program, concurrent clinically appropriate behavior (TSBC) reflected the rate of occurrence of a number of normal facial expressions, positions, and elective activities that were not all consistently and continuously a direct focus of staff. The majority of the variance in concurrent appropriate behavior was accounted for by the number of normal elective activities in which residents engaged and thus provides some indication of the generalization of adaptive functioning. Immediate improvements in concurrent appropriate behaviors were obtained within both programs, without differences between milieu and social-learning residents over the first ten months of program operation. However, similar to other areas of functioning, the highest overall level of concurrent appropriate behavior in the milieu program was reached by the eighth week after the introduction of programmatic procedures.

Concurrent appropriate behavior in both programs appeared to be especially sensitive to extraneous external events, particularly showing decreases in response to events that, clinically, indicated negative emotional reactions, both at the group level and on clinical examination of individual cases. Residents in both programs showed significant decreases following the death of a resident, with considerable variability in response to a number of identifiable incidents. The decline was reversed for social-learning residents, and gradual increases were made up to a new high at the time the change in time out was imposed. From the tenth month on, the concurrent appropriate behavior of social-learning residents was always higher than that of milieu residents. The major reduction for residents in both programs immediately following the increases in assaultiveness, after the time out and expulsion changes were imposed, was greater than the reduction in social and instrumental behaviors, and it occurred more rapidly. However, even after the reduction, social-learning residents maintained a significantly improved level of concurrent appropriate behavior, with a slight increase during the return to baseline conditions. Upon the reintroduction of social-learning procedures after the second baseline, a slight decrease occurred, but systematic improvements were again apparent thereafter. Milieu residents, in contrast, had shown a rapid increase to earlier levels of concurrent appropriate behavior just before the change in expulsion time. The increases in assaultiveness were directly paralleled by decreases in concurrent appropriate behavior to levels below pretreatment for milieu residents—returning to levels above those existing before the original introduction of programmatic procedures only upon the return to baseline conditions.

Thus, although concurrent appropriate behaviors were not a direct crucial target of rehabilitation for the chronically institutionalized population, their incidence also fails to show any positive impact of milieu therapy procedures over the initial response to greater specification of desired activities, increased activity levels, and pressure to perform. In fact, the increased aversiveness and emotionality within the milieu program as a result of the high rates of physical assault actually had a negative effect, suppressing concurrent appropriate behavior for the milieu group as a whole. Social-learning residents also showed the declines in concurrent appropriate behavior associated with negative emotional reactions, but the declines were neither as frequent nor as severe as those of milieu residents. Additionally recovery of higher levels of concurrent appropriate behavior for social-learning residents was more systematic, paralleling improvements in other areas of functioning, to higher levels than had been reached upon initial program introduction. Further indications of generalization of adaptive behaviors for social-learning residents were also apparent in the increase in range as well as the amount of concurrent appropriate behaviors. Since no firm limit exists for concurrent appropriate behaviors, interpretation of the absolute level achieved by social-learning residents will have to await the establishment of normative data in other populations (Paul, in press). However, as with social and instrumental skills, the high point achieved by the social-learning residents before the change in time out procedures was reflecting a systematic increase, indicative of probable additional improvement had the most effective procedures been maintained.

*Maladaptive Behavior.* In considering the final crucial target of rehabilitation for the chronically institutionalized mental patient—reduction or elimination of extreme bizarre behaviors—the social-learning program also was more effective than the milieu program was, but milieu procedures influenced some components. In contrast to the complete failure of milieu therapy procedures or principles to maintain adaptive behaviors, overall concurrent clinically bizarre, crazy behaviors were maintained at significantly reduced levels throughout the intramural period, with reductions in the range of behaviors performed as well.

Bizarre motoric behaviors (e.g., rocking, repetitive movements, blank staring) were the most frequent observable class of crazy behaviors in the population, with the average resident demonstrating such behavior 61% of the time before the introduction of the psychosocial programs. Immediate reductions of more than 60% of pretreatment levels were obtained within both programs, without differences between milieu and social-learning residents over the first ten months of program operation. The lowest overall level of bizarre motoric behavior in the milieu program was reached by the eighth week after the introduction of programmatic procedures, and this class of crazy behavior was maintained significantly below pretreatment levels throughout the intramural treatment period, although the social-learning program was significantly more effective from the tenth month on.

Bizarre motoric behaviors in both programs were sensitive to extraneous external events; increases at the group level and for individual cases partially reflected negative emotional states and stress reactions. Residents in both programs showed significant increases following the death of a resident, with considerable variability in response to a number of identifiable stressful events. However, the increase was reversed for social-learning residents with an overall trend toward further reductions in bizarre motoric behaviors after the tenth month of treatment through the time that the change in time out was imposed. From the tenth month on, milieu residents increased their bizarre motoric behaviors, except during periods with the more effective techniques for controlling assaultiveness. Social-learning residents increased bizarre motoric behaviors over the six months following the increases in assaultiveness, and residents of both programs were again decreasing them after the reintroduction of longer time-out and expulsion periods during the last twenty weeks of intramural treatment.

The patterns of change in bizarre motoric behaviors, combined with correlational analyses, indicate that initial improvements in both programs were rapidly achieved as a function of increased focus and participation in adaptive activities resulting from pressure to perform, with continuing specificity of desirable and undesirable behavior. Although milieu procedures were less effective than social-learning procedures were and gave no evidence of further reducing bizarre motoric behaviors as treatment continued, this class of behavior was maintained at significantly lower levels than at pretreatment, primarily as a function of continued higher levels of alternative activity. Interpretation of metacommunications and reflection and clarification had little continuing impact. Direct focus on the communication of alternative adaptive behaviors expected and negative feedback in the milieu program gradually lost effectiveness in terminating ongoing bizarre behavior over time; effectiveness fell from 75% over the first eighteen weeks to 68% over the next two years to less than 55% over the last two years. Social-learning procedures for dealing with bizarre motoric behaviors—primarily ignoring and differential reinforcement of incompatible adaptive behaviors—not only maintained the initial improvements but produced even greater reductions over time. In contrast to feedback and positive statements without specific consequences in the milieu program, prompts for termination of excessive bizarre motoric behavior and initiation of incompatible adaptive behavior—which included specifying the individual consequence for each course of action—increased effectiveness in terminating ongoing bizarre behavior from 94% effectiveness during the first eighteen weeks to over 98% for the remainder of the intramural period. Thus, although the sheer volume of alternative activities involved in both psychosocial programs formed the basis for major reduction in bizarre motoric behaviors, social-learning procedures contributed additional effectiveness through a greater ability to terminate ongoing maladaptive behaviors and increase incompatible behaviors and through removing inadvertent reinforcement.

Even with the greater documented effectiveness of social-learning procedures for reducing bizarre motoric behaviors, the average resident was still performing such acts about 18% of the time at the most effective point, without indications of continuing reductions. Although these levels were well below that required for community tolerance and reflected a functional absence of bizarre motoric behavior for over 30% of the residents, the limits of change for the program as a whole appeared to have been reached for the severely disturbed chronic population. The pattern of responses for both resident groups and the functional relationships existing among component bizarre behaviors for individuals suggest that neither program had much direct influence on bizarre behaviors that reflected a stress response (anxiety). The overall social-learning program effectively reduced or eliminated bizarre motoric behaviors that appeared to have been a function of stimulus deprivation, self-stimulation, learning or performance deficits and those maintained by external reinforcement, or bizarre actions in response to maladaptive cognitions (delusions and hallucinations). It also reduced bizarre motoric behaviors reflecting a stress response to the proximity of other people for the majority of residents through continued reinforced exposure, and to the world outside mental institutions through graduated exposure with direct skill training.

Stress reactions resulting from external uncontrolled events appeared to be only partially reduced by the direct provision of information, advice, reassurance, and alternative adaptive behaviors—requiring the removal of the source of stress and passage of time before such reactions returned to prestress levels. These procedures were more effective in the social-learning program, with its greater emphasis on the provision of active solutions, than in the milieu program, where residents were required to resolve such problems more independently. A few residents still appeared to retain severe conditioned anxiety reactions to specific classes of stimulus events—some of which did not become apparent until sufficient improvement had occurred for the person to be reexposed to situations that were not available within an institution. Additionally a few residents retained such severe conditioned anxiety responses to certain classes of activities and events within the institution that graduated reinforced exposure was only partially successful in overcoming extreme avoidance responses, with increased levels of bizarre motoric behavior still being elicited if escape or avoidance were not possible.

Bizarre motoric behaviors were sufficiently reduced in the social-learning program and maintained at low enough levels in the chronic population to be tolerated by the outside community. However, to reduce or eliminate bizarre motoric behaviors based upon severe conditioned anxiety reactions for the few long-stay patients still exhibiting such problems and for acute patients for whom such problems would occur much more frequently, the social-learning program would require expansion. There are social-learning procedures available that offer promise for treating such stress responses, and these procedures could easily be incorporated within the social-learning program (Paul & Bernstein, 1973); however, they require more individualized treatment time by professionally trained staff than was allowed by the staffing of the psychosocial programs.

Bizarre dysfunctional cognitive behaviors indicative of thought disorder (e.g., verbalized delusions & hallucinations, incoherent speech, smiling without apparent stimulus) were relatively less frequent than bizarre motoric behaviors in the severely debilitated population. Before the introduction of programmatic procedures, the average resident was performing such dysfunctional cognitive behaviors about 24% of the time. Although both psychosocial programs produced immediate reductions in overt indicants of cognitive dysfunction, social-learning procedures had produced more systematic reductions to lower levels by the fourth month of treatment. Dysfunctional cognitive behaviors were sensitive to extraneous external events in the same manner as bizarre motoric behaviors were, reflecting negative emotional states and stress reactions. However, they appeared to increase temporarily as much as bizarre motoric behaviors did only in response to events with clear psychological impact, and they were relatively unaffected by physical stress and discriminative stimuli that influenced concurrent appropriate behavior and bizarre motoric behavior.

Unlike any other class of behavior, bizarre dysfunctional cognitive behaviors showed gradual and significant continuing improvement in the milieu program to an extent equaling the improvements in the social-learning program by the nineteenth month of treatment. Further improvements were underway at the time the changes in time out and expulsion were imposed. Both programs maintained the significant reduction in cognitive dysfunction throughout the year and a half in which assaults were increasing, and both again showed further reductions over the last twenty weeks of the programs. Thus, both significantly reduced dysfunctional cognitive behaviors to about a third the pretreatment level, and the reductions achieved by the milieu procedures were as great and as systematic as those achieved by social-learning procedures.

The same clinical procedures were applied to dysfunctional cognitive behavior within each program as were applied to bizarre motoric behaviors. Additionally the content within class periods in each program tended to emphasize activities that were directly incompatible with cognitive dysfunction. Thus, some reduction in dysfunctional cognitive behaviors appeared to be a result of the increased levels of incompatible activity in both programs. However, this was the only class of behavior within the chronically institutionalized population in which continuous feedback, reflection and clarification, and stated expectancies without specific consequences in the milieu program provided evidence of continuing treatment effects at all, let alone doing so as effectively as the corresponding social-learning procedures. These effects are in keeping with a considerable literature indicating that cognitive functions in general tend to be more consistent within individuals, less variable across situations, and more modifiable through simple transmission of information (see Mariotto & Paul, 1975).

The limits of change in dysfunctional cognitive behavior within the chronically institutionalized population under either psychosocial program remain unknown, because further improvements were gradually occurring at the time the procedural changes in controlling assaults occurred and at the termination of treatments. The average resident in both programs had reduced his or her performance of overt indicants of thought disorder to a low point of only 7% to 8% of the time. A few continued to show increases in cognitive dysfunction as an overall reaction to stress, including those that appeared to be the result of severe conditioned anxiety reactions. Thus, patient populations showing higher levels of cognitive dysfunction—particularly acute populations—would likely require more individual treatment with expanded procedures beyond those feasible with the programs and staffing levels as evaluated. However, in the chronically institutionalized population, dysfunctional cognitive behaviors were reduced and maintained at a low level where they were tolerated in the community; this class of behavior was the only objectively assessed area of functioning that still occurred at prerelease assessment and did not predict rated functioning of released residents in the community.[2] Thus, the actual levels of reduction in cognitive dysfunction achieved through the programs may be below the critical distress point of discrimination, at least for the settings in which the released individuals resided.

In contrast to the significant reductions maintained in concurrent clinically bizarre maladaptive behavior in the milieu program, grossly inappropriate response to minimal behavioral expectations (Inappropriate Clinical Frequencies) showed an almost direct mirror image of change in adaptive social and instrumental behavior. Such grossly inappropriate responses only occurred about 19% of the time for the average resident before the introduction of programmatic procedures. Immediate reductions were obtained in both psychosocial programs; however, the milieu program achieved its maximum reduction, to about half the initial level, after only four weeks of treatment and essentially retained that level for over twenty-seven months without further significant changes. Following the change in expulsion time for assaults and the ensuing increase in intolerable behavior, milieu residents gradually increased the rate of grossly inappropriate response to minimal expectations back to pretreatment levels. Although this trend was reversed following the return to baseline conditions and the reintroduction of programmatic procedures with more effective techniques for controlling violent acts, milieu residents did not again show significant reductions in this class of bizarre behavior.

The social-learning program, in contrast, not only produced rapid initial reductions but continued to reduce grossly inappropriate responses to the point that the average resident was performing such a bizarre act less than 1% of the time after only twelve weeks of treatment. The low rates were maintained—always less than 3% of the time—for over two years, until the change in time out was imposed. Although social-learning residents also increased the rate of grossly inappropriate responses to minimal expectations over the next year and a half without meaningful consequences for assaults, they continued to maintain significantly lower levels than milieu residents did and significant improvement over pretreatment levels during the entire intramural period.

Thus, the increased activity levels and pressure to perform after desired behaviors had been specified also appeared to account for the entire reduction in grossly inappropriate response to minimal behavioral expectations in the milieu program. The continued communication of expectancies, group pressure, and practice in problem solving and crisis resolution in the milieu program led to no further improvements beyond the initial activation of performance, and the procedures were inadequate to maintain improved levels of performance after increases in dangerous and aggressive acts had begun. In contrast, the individual prompts and consistent response-contingent consequences in the social-learning program were remarkably effective and efficient in eliminating grossly inappropriate responses and maintaining reduced levels through a variety of extraneous, uncontrolled events. The response-contingent components of the social-learning procedures maintained reduced levels of such inappropriate behavior in spite of the disruptive influence of assaults. In fact, the return to baseline conditions resulted in a slight decrease in grossly inappropriate responses, suggesting some relationship to the stressful conditions involving the earlier assaultiveness. Although the reintroduction of more effective procedures for controlling violent acts reversed the increasing trend, social-learning residents did not regain the earlier low levels within the remaining twenty weeks of treatment. However, the initial rapid and systematic reduction, followed by maintenance for over two years, clearly documents the exceptional effectiveness of social-learning procedures in reducing the absolute level of grossly inappropriate responses to minimal expectations for appropriate behavior in the chronically institutionalized population.

The last component of extreme bizarre behavior to be summarized—dangerous and aggressive intolerable behaviors—is perhaps the most important for the rehabilitation of any institutionalized population. This class of behavior constituted the most obvious failure of milieu procedures for the severely disturbed chronic patient. None of the interactional milieu procedures were effective in preventing dangerous and aggressive acts, including the expulsion period for assaults. Under this condition, assaultiveness continued to increase from the beginning of the program until a seventy-two-hour expulsion period was introduced; however, it merely retained the level of dangerous and aggressive acts of milieu residents to that existing before the introduction of programmatic procedures. A reduction of the expulsion time to forty-eight hours in the milieu program also failed to control dangerous and aggressive acts, which nearly tripled in frequency—even with the presence of male student workers as reminders of the consequences.

When expulsion time was reduced to only two hours, the result of a state central office policy decision, dangerous and aggressive acts within the milieu unit systematically increased to severely disruptive levels over the next year and a half when that limit was in existence. The only actions that caused even temporary stability or decline in the rate of increase in such intolerable behavior in the milieu program involved continuous rather than intermittent coverage of evenings and weekends by senior staff. Since staff behavior did not change during those periods, and male student workers were also present to assist in imposing expulsion, the most probable basis for such effects appears to lie in the discriminative stimulus value of persons in authority for the residents—perhaps as a carry-over from prior hospital experience. The incidence of dangerous and aggressive acts was reduced on the return to baseline conditions with the traditional consequences for assaultiveness, and was further reduced upon the reintroduction of milieu procedures with longer periods of expulsion. However, even with the more effective length of expulsion, the incidence of dangerous and aggressive acts never returned to levels existing before the original reduction in expulsion time.

Although control of dangerous and aggressive acts for the severely disturbed population was also the most difficult treatment problem within the social-learning program, its procedures were sufficiently flexible that control of such acts was eventually achieved for every individual treated. Brief seclusion as time out from positive reinforcement, combined with heavy token response-costs, were initially effective in controlling the majority of offenders. However, a significant number of residents with such a long institutional history found that the escape from social contact and activity within the program was reinforcing. Removal of the positive characteristics of the time-out room brought the dangerous and aggressive acts of those residents under control; however, it was not until the longer seventy-two-hour time-out period was introduced, in combination with the earlier procedures, that severely assaultive residents were reasonably controlled. While slight increases in assaults occurred upon the reduction of time out to forty-eight hours, its length, combined with severe token response-costs and availability of mild aversive stimuli in time out rooms, was effectively managing assaultive behavior at reduced levels, even though some instances continued to occur.

The reduction in the length of time out to two hours resulted in an increased incidence of dangerous and aggressive acts, which, combined with the side effects of accumulated token fines, terminated the steady improvements in functioning that had been occurring before the change; however, the combination of earlier improvements and continuing response-costs still maintained higher levels of functioning and greater control over violent acts in the social-learning program than in the milieu program, where such acts nearly completely devastated the previous fragile improvements. The purchase eligibility to obtain backup goods and services by making an additional payment on standing fines, combined with the proportional-payoff schedule contingent upon time without intolerable behavior, effectively allowed residents to reenter the program and slightly reduced the incidence of dangerous and aggressive acts. However, it was not until the longer length of time out was reinstituted that dangerous and aggressive intolerable behaviors were again significantly reduced. Even then, the earlier low levels of violence, which had been attained before the original reduction in the length of time-out, were not achieved. The combination of time out from positive reinforcement, token response costs, and extended physical overcorrection/restitution was completely successful in terminating such intolerable behaviors for every resident who received the procedures, after having failed to respond to time-out procedures previously applied. Since eight failures from the milieu program were also successfully treated by social-learning procedures with this focus, clear evidence of its effectiveness is indicated, even for the most violent residents.

Thus, milieu procedures were inadequate to reduce or eliminate extreme intolerable behaviors, particularly violent acts. Given the severely disturbed population, with a long history of aversive controls through electroconvulsive shock, insulin shock, restraints, and hydrotherapy during prior hospitalization, even extended seclusion through group expulsion or time out was not adequate to control, let alone retrain, the more violent residents. While "chemical straightjackets" could control some if they were kept in a stuporous state, which then precluded further treatment, even maximum drug dosages failed to control the most violent. Social-learning procedures employing immediate and consistent consequences with aversive characteristics—albeit mildly aversive compared to prior medical treatments—were successful in controlling dangerous and aggressive acts. The combination of heavy token response costs along with extended time out in seclusion, with intermittent stimuli removing positive characteristics of seclusion was completely successful in eliminating intolerable behavior for three-quarters of the resident population. Those procedures alone were adequate to control violent acts of the remaining 25% at low enough levels that the overall program functioned smoothly, allowing all residents to continue to improve over a variety of areas. Direct focused treatment through intensive physical overcorrection/restitution procedures was necessary to eliminate completely intolerable behaviors and violent acts for the few who failed to respond to the general program procedures.

The limiting factors for the overcorrection/restitution procedures appear to be only the physical condition of the resident and the practicality for staff. Since physical exertion seems to have been a necessary component to eliminate intolerable and violent acts for residents whose behavior was as extreme as those in the project population, physical health that would preclude exertion also precluded focused treatment. Practicality is a potential limiting factor for staffing in two regards. First, the size and strength of violent residents sometimes requires two, and occasionally three, staff members to prevent attacks and maintain performance during the course of overcorrection/restitution. Second, since extreme instances may require several hours of focused treatment, the limited staff-to-resident ratios nearly preclude conduct of an overall program for the majority if more than two exceptionally violent residents require overcorrection/restitution at the same time. However, the importance of eliminating violent acts, not only for the further improvement of the offender but for the overall effectiveness of treatment programs for the remainder of residents and the humane protection of other residents and staff, cannot be overstated. Most desirable would be sufficient staffing to eliminate violent acts soon after a person's entry to a treatment program. Since this alternative is unlikely under most funding conditions, a more practical solution might be to employ the general response-cost and time-out procedures on a continuing basis, with overcorrection/restitution applied sequentially —one at a time—for those who fail to respond rapidly to the general procedures.

## REPRESENTATIVENESS OF INTRAMURAL PROCEDURES AND FINDINGS

Both psychosocial programs described and implemented in the comparative project attempted to incorporate principles and techniques of earlier promising milieu and social-learning approaches. In addition to using the principles and techniques of instrumental and associative learning extended from controlled research, the social-learning program adopted a number of basic features directly from the promising programs of Ayllon and Azrin (1965) and Atthowe and Krasner (1968). Beyond the availability of written descriptions for both of these programs, the project director had the benefit of on-site visits to Ayllon and Azrin's program and six months as a staff member in the Atthowe and Krasner program before developing the Social-Learning Manual. As a result of the relatively well-established underlying principles and detailed procedural specification of earlier workers, combined with direct personal experience with previous ongoing programs, the integrated social-learning program of the comparative project appears to have been reasonably representative of both principles and procedures in other programs. Additionally, the program implemented in the comparative project appears to have representatively included the majority of principles and procedures that have been recommended for chronic patients since its inception (Ayllon & Azrin, 1968; Bandura, 1969; Kazdin, 1976; Liberman et al., 1974a; Ullmann & Krasner, 1975)—the only notable exclusion being the failure to use automated devices because of a preference for continuous pairing of social and material reinforcers.

Since the general milieu therapy approach historically has focused upon attitudes and values rather than principles and procedures, the milieu therapy program developed for the comparative project had less firm guidance from prior work. However, its principles and procedures were based upon a thorough review of previous descriptive reports, drawing particularly on the earlier work of Cumming and Cumming (1962) and Kraft (1966). Beyond the deductions from earlier written works, the program director had spent a year on the staff at the Fort Logan Mental Health Center and the project director had spent six months on the staff at Palo Alto Veterans Administration hospital, in a building which had four variations of therapeutic communities in operation, and had made on-site visits to Fairweather's (1964) program. Additionally direct consultation on milieu principles and procedures was obtained from Elaine Cumming and Alan Kraft in an attempt to ensure the representativeness of the milieu therapy program for chronic patients from recognized and personally valued practitioners.

The integrated milieu therapy program representatively included the majority of the "rationale, values, axioms, strategies, tactics" and "characteristics" of the "therapeutic community" that have been described and/or recommended since its inception (Almond, 1974a; Abroms, 1969; Clark & Yeomans, 1969; Daniels, 1970; Filstead & Rossi, 1973; Jones, 1968; Jones & Bonn, 1973; White, 1972). The only notable exclusions were the absence of staff sensitivity groups focusing on latent content of staff or resident behavior and the presumption that all interactions and emotional expression were of value. Rather, the nature of interactions and value of emotional expression were specified with regard to those that appeared promising for the chronic patient needing concrete progression in rehabilitation, and staff meetings remained problem-and-solution oriented—even when dealing with interpersonal staff conflicts.

In the eight years since the review of the literature made for the comparative project, literally hundreds of reports have appeared. Although a tally of the number of citations might find roughly equal publication activity concerning both psychosocial approaches drastic differences are apparent in the nature of publications. Articles and books related to the social-learning approach—token-economy programs in particular—regularly present evaluative data on some aspect of treatment effectiveness, with at least a crude assessment of some relevant variables. In contrast, articles and books on the milieu therapy approach—therapeutic community programs in particular—continue to discuss abstract values and attitudes without specification, let alone assessment, of relevant variables, seldom presenting data at all.

These characteristics of the milieu therapy literature led Gripp and Magaro (1976) to subtitle their review of the evidence on milieu therapy "Death Due to Cultural Exposure." It would come as some surprise to the twenty-eight participants of the National Institute of Mental Health sponsored International Conference on the Psychiatric Milieu (Austin Riggs Center, Stockbridge, Massachusetts) in Ocotber 1974 to learn that "milieu therapy is rapidly disappearing" and that Gripp and Magaro (1976) were preparing "an autopsy of the milieu approach . . . in order to determine the cause of death . . ." Nevertheless, the absence of further empirical evaluation of the effectiveness of the milieu approach was evident in both of the major reviews commissioned for this conference (Almond, 1974b; Eldred, 1974) and a condition that continued to be decried by a significant number of the participants. Gripp and Magaro also predict that the absence of sound experimental design in the evaluation of token economy programs "may be responsible for the ultimate disappearance of the token economy from the psychiatric institution at which point it will take its place as an historical institutional treatment alongside moral treatment and milieu therapy."

Any researcher with serious concerns for the internal validity of an individual study cannot help but empathize with the frustration and disenchantment indicated in Gripp and Magaro's pronouncements. It is frustrating and depressing to spend hour after hour wading through reports of treatment evaluations so poorly designed that no solid evidence could possibly result. It is more frustrating—even angering—to wade through complex experimental designs that at first appear to be sophisticated, only to discover lethal errors and confounding that preclude the conclusions drawn. The fact of the matter is that adequate comparative evaluations of total treatment programs for any institutional approach are notably absent in the literature.

However, when viewed in historical perspective, the progress of knowledge on the treatment of the chronically institutionalized mental patient by either milieu or social-learning approaches has been rapid to phenomenal. Burning as witches constituted the dominant treatment approach for psychotics for well over two hundred years, and custodial warehousing remained the primary way for at least one hundred years (Ullmann & Krasner, 1975)—one hundred twenty-five years considering the current status of most chronically institutionalized patients. In contrast, it has been just twenty-five years since the first milieu programs were reported (Vitale, 1964a) and a remarkably brief ten years since the publication of Ayllon and Azrin's (1965) first report of a token-economy program. Although any individual report in the literature appearing since the earlier literature review falls short of adequate experimental design for establishing cause-effect conclusions for a total treatment program, the progression of findings over studies, combined with the results of the comparative project reported in this book, is compelling.

*Reviews of Other Empirical Findings*

Several recent reviews of empirical findings on both social-learning and milieu therapy approaches have appeared since the earlier literature review in chapter 2. Reviews of relevant findings with institutionalized adult psychotic patients have covered social-learning procedures in general, including unitwide programs (Bandura, 1969; Davison, 1969; Hagen, 1975; Kazdin, 1976; Liberman, 1974; Liberman et al., 1974a; Ullmann & Krasner, 1975), token-economy programs in particular (Carlson et al., 1972; Gripp & Magaro, 1974; Kazdin, 1975; Kazdin & Bootzin, 1972), and milieu therapy and therapeutic community programs (Almond, 1974a, 1974b, 1975; Daniels, 1970; Eldred, 1974; Ellsworth, 1968; Gripp & Magaro, 1976; Meyers & Clark, 1972; Wing & Brown, 1970). Because of the recency and comprehensiveness of the existing reviews, only four relevant investigations with even approximate controls, which had not been included in the existing reviews, were found in a search of the literature at the time of this writing. Three were published after the completion of the existing reviews (Greenburg et al., 1975; Schwartz & Bellack, 1975; Steer & Boger, 1975), and the fourth had not yet been published in widely circulated sources (Stoffelmayr et al., 1973).

Extreme caution should be used in generalizing results across programs with the same name. Psychosocial treatment programs are complex systems, as indicated by the dramatic effects of uncontrolled variables such as a death or change in a single procedure for controlling assaultiveness in the current project, even when all other procedures were documented to remain constant. Limitations on generalization are further imposed by the failure of investigators either to define or assess relevant classes and domains of variables, including specific characteristics or programs. Although the failure to specify details of treatment procedures is common in reports of milieu therapy, this caution is equally true for social-learning procedures, particularly token-economy programs, since the term merely indicates the likelihood that some tangible response-contingent consequence was implemented. Reports of so-called token-economy programs that do not articulate, let alone monitor, the specific classes of patient behavior of focus, the criteria for disbursing or withholding tokens and other social and tangible consequences, the range and control of backups, the nature of staff-patient interaction, etc., may be no more related to other token-economy programs than the action of heroin is related to that of penicillin, even though both are administered by injection.

The majority of such reports in the literature occur in conjunction with testimonials which do not involve any assessment, some demonstration studies which involve only pre-post assessments of change, and some group studies involving comparisons to traditional hospital procedures. These have no formal scientific value alone but may provide crude hypotheses on the extension of procedures over settings or patient populations. Particular care should be taken in interpreting reports that compare an active treatment program with traditional hospital conditions when equation of patient groups is not documented, when more staff are added to only one program, or when the transfer of patients is confounded with treatment condition without assessing effects of transfer, since such studies (e.g., Gripp & Magaro, 1971) have no more validity than uncontrolled single group demonstration studies.

The accumulated findings from studies of milieu therapy programs with long-stay mental patients included in the recent literature tend to be consistent with those of the comparative project, although the lack of specificity and control in the few additional studies allows a very weak level of product, not only for single studies but of accumulated findings as well. In fact, only one study of milieu therapy with long-stay patients even attempted to assess changes in component behaviors, and that study (Stoffelmayr et al., 1973) also represents the only other attempt in the literature to compare directly milieu and social-learning approaches. Although Stoffelmayr's study has some problems with internal validity, largely because treatment programs were run at different times and in different locations, the investigators are to be congratulated for their efforts to select severely disabled patients as well as attempting a comparative evaluation. Four groups of ten patients each took part in the study; they were selected from the most severely withdrawn male psychotic patients functioning on open wards in three different hospitals, with a minimum of twenty years of hospitalization. This patient population thus represents the only one in the milieu literature that approaches the severity of deficits of those in the current project, although selection from open wards excluded the extreme levels of bizarre behavior present in patients in the current project. One group continued in their usual hospital routines, while the remaining three received psychosocial treatment focused upon increasing general activity levels, social interaction, and self-care skills—all of which were severely deficient in those studied. All three psychosocial programs included vigorous activity programs. Two different milieu programs were followed, with one using more structure and group meetings, with patients being treated as a group twenty-four hours per day, while the other met as a total group only during daytime hours and were housed on separate rehabilitation wards. The third program was based upon a token economy, and staff were trained in the delivery of response-contingent social and material reinforcers. Each treatment group was assessed every three months over a one-year period via objective observations and nurses' ratings on standardized scales. The investigators attempted to assess staff behavior observationally; however, the categories employed were not functionally related to treatment techniques or patient behavior. The staff of the token-economy program were found to be more active over time.

Stoffelmayr et al. found that the token-economy program produced significantly greater improvements than the usual hospital program did in all adaptive areas of functioning assessed and also significantly better improvements than either milieu therapy program did in self-care, overall increases in activity, and decreases in apathy. Consistent with the findings of the current comparative project, the milieu programs tended to show initial improvements in these classes of behavior but failed to maintain them over time; there were no differences from those of usual hospital procedures at the end of a year. The only class of behavior in which both milieu programs maintained improvements over the usual hospital program and improvement equal to that of the token economy was for decreases in rated Seclusiveness. The observed amount of social interaction showed the greatest improvement for those in the token-economy program, but those in the most active milieu program also showed significantly higher levels of social interaction by the end of a year than either of the remaining two groups. Those in the less-structured milieu program showed initial improvements that were not maintained over time. While none of the groups showed significant change in bizarre behavior, as assessed by observed Manneristic Behavior and rated Psychoticism, patients in the token-economy program were showing systematic decreases over time, and those in the milieu programs showed decreases that were not maintained as the treatment programs progressed.

Therefore, in the only other comparative study to systematically assess milieu therapy with severely disabled chronic mental patients, remarkably consistent results were obtained, indicating that active activity schedules and staff attention may temporarily activate dormant skills, but in the absence of consistent response-contingent consequences, initial gains are not even maintained, let alone improved upon.

No additional controlled studies of severely desocialized chronic patients have appeared in the literature, although longitudinal assessments of the full range of hospitalized mental patients (distinct from groups selected for rehabilitation potential) have also failed to show continuing improvements as a function of changes in hospital practices toward therapeutic community procedures. Wing and Brown (1970), for example, monitored long-stay patients in three hospitals over an eight-year period during which differences in milieu approach were introduced. Greatest initial changes were found in decreasing social withdrawal (negative symptom ratings), and decreases were also obtained in bizarre behavior (florid symptom ratings) with delusional behavior being more consistently reduced than other bizarre behaviors. The improvements were most related to the introduction of work and occupational therapy programs; however, after the less severely disabled patients were released early in the assessment period, the remaining long-stay patients failed to maintain their initial improvements.

Thus, recent empirical data yield a consistently negative picture of the effectiveness of the milieu therapy approach as investigators have begun to examine the moderately to severely desocialized chronic patient rather than specially selected, less-debilitated patients. While no data were presented, Jones appears to have reached a similar conclusion after five years of experience at a hospital with a large long-stay complement; he stated, "Anyone who has attempted some form of community treatment in a long-stay ward . . . knows how difficult it is . . . A daily ward meeting in a long-stay ward may turn out to be largely unproductive because of the patients lack of spontaneity and disordered perception of the world. It is usually much more productive to have small, relatively intimate groups, with some simple task supervised by a staff member" (Jones, 1968, pp. 46-47).

The remainder of the literature on long-stay patients included in recent reviews and studies that had appeared before the inception of the present comparative project, dealt with populations that were less severely disabled, consisting of more active "revolving door" patients, patients prescreened to possess higher levels of functioning or rehabilitation potential, or Veterans Administration patients. Of these studies, Ellsworth (1968) included unselected chronic patients from VA closed wards who appeared more disabled than those in the remainder of studies but less severely disabled than patients typically found in state mental hospitals. In general, none of the remaining reports are sufficiently detailed or controlled to draw firm cause-effect conclusions about the effectiveness of specific therapeutic community procedures or total treatment programs on identified classes of behavior. Several reports indicate increases in social interaction and decreases in rated bizarre behavior, but none provide even suggestive evidence that the changes were related to milieu procedures beyond the effects of introducing full activity schedules and active staff attention. Although no study provided data on control of dangerous and aggressive acts, one negative report with acute patients attributed failure to the inability of milieu therapy procedures to handle violence.

The Ellsworth study was the only report in the milieu literature that showed systematic increasing levels of functioning over time compared to relative stability in a comparison group. However, in the full report of the study, he noted that the usual components of a therapeutic community—patient government, small group discussions, open ward meetings—had been briefly tried but then abandoned, and the highest step level had no group activities at all. Furthermore, although the primary emphasis in descriptions of aide performance was on the major increases in interaction and communication of expectancies, examples provided of aide-patient interaction and aide training suggest that a large proportion of interactions would be more aptly described as the use of prompts and social reinforcement for adaptive behavior and behavior incompatible with maladaptive behavior. Thus, even the most promising report of milieu treatment with less severely disabled long-stay patients fails to provide support for the principles and procedures characteristic of therapeutic communities.

Rather, on detailed examination, the psychosocial approach Ellsworth described appears more closely related to social-learning procedures than to milieu therapy as described by others.

Ludwig (1971) is one of several clinicians to assert recently that even mildly disabled chronic mental patients must receive clear and consistent response-contingent consequences if they are to improve at all. In fact, one of the recent trends in the literature is to combine the focus on group activity, group pressure, and practice in problem solving with response-contingent consequences rather than communication of expectancies without explicit consequences (e.g., Heap et al., 1970; Olson & Greenburg, 1972; Greenburg et al., 1975). None of these have yet provided more than suggestive hypotheses because of problems of internal validity and/or weaknesses in assessment procedures and data analysis. Olson and Greenburg (1972) reported that mildly disabled VA patients increased target behaviors (attendance at activities) for which group contingencies were established for receipt of trust funds and canteen coupons, and patients receiving only additional group interaction decreased the same activities—all in comparison to no change for additional patients undergoing the usual hospital milieu program. However, nurses' ratings of social adjustment decreased for the contingent group and increased for the interaction group. The study covered only a four-month period and was fraught with design confounds and internal conflicts with staff and administration; however, it along with several other studies covered in reviews, indicates that requiring a group of mildly disabled patients to share positive and negative consequences for the behavior of group members can affect instrumental performance.

Greenburg et al., (1975) reported a study comparing an individualized token economy with a group incentive program using a therapeutic community structure, but with token contingencies for group behavior. Patients were apparently mildly disabled and likely revolving-door patients; they were selected from open wards and were reported to have a little over three years' hospitalization during the previous five years. The study was potentially well controlled, but the nature of assessment criteria and data presentation restrict its utility. Data on intramural functioning were reported only as the average percentage of social and nonsocial behaviors performed during the first month of operation, without indications of pretreatment levels. The justification for this presentation was that performance in both programs "reached an asymptote very rapidly" and that patients began to leave the programs during the second month. Therefore, the intramural data are likely to indicate only the extent to which either program activated and/or maintained existing adaptive behaviors. Non-social behavior (self-care and instrumental role performance) did not differ between programs (80% and 78%) but was higher than social behavior (interpersonal interaction and recreation), where the performance of patients in the token economy (69%) was significantly better than that of the patients in the group incentive program (60%). The most likely interpretation of these results is that both programs were reasonably effective management systems, and group contingencies did about as well in maintaining performance as did individual contingencies—neither procedure contributing much information to the treatment of the more disabled long-stay patient.

Thus, the recent literature has still not reported an adequate test of a well-articulated milieu therapy program. However, the additional studies that have appeared since the initial review are consistent with the findings of the current comparative project in providing little support for the effectiveness of milieu therapy for the severely debilitated long-stay patient. Positive reports have continued to appear on resocialization and some reduction in bizarre behavior for less disabled long-stay populations exposed to the milieu approach. But no support has yet appeared to indicate that the group structure, group pressure, practice in problem-solving and crisis resolution, and communication of expectancies and feedback without explicit consequences added anything at all to the improvements beyond the initial reactivation of skills resulting from the specification of desired behavior and the provision of a full activity schedule.

In the absence of other positive alternatives, the improvements in behavior would be preferable to allowing patients to continue wasting away under usual custodial conditions. However, given the documented superiority of the social-learning program of the comparative project, combined with the failure of demonstrated effectiveness for milieu procedures, milieu therapy can no longer be recommended as a treatment for the severely disabled, chronically institutionalized patient. The absence of documented positive effects of milieu procedures in less-disabled or acute populations also does not argue strongly for continued application of this psychosocial approach, and the presence of violent behavior would clearly counterindicate it. However, since positive reports continue to appear in the literature and the findings of the comparative project indicated that the program can reduce dysfunctional cognitive behavior, the milieu program (in chapters 6 and 7) is recommended for further evaluation with mildly disabled long-stay or revolving-door patients.

Findings from studies of social-learning

programs, in contrast to the milieu literature, reveal the accumulation of knowledge to have more closely approximated "ideal tactics" (Paul, 1969b) for developing clinical programs as "applied science" than any other institutional treatment approach—albeit unsystematically and in spite of design limitations of any single study. Although it follows a jagged course, a clear historical thread is discernible from the laboratory derivation of basic principles, followed by the extension of principles to the clinical context and the development of rudimentary procedures in both controlled and uncontrolled single case studies. Controlled studies of the effectiveness of procedures and techniques on identified problem behaviors had, in fact, documented the ability of social-learning procedures in isolation to effect short-term change in specified bizarre behaviors and deficits in instrumental role performance of long-stay mental patients well before the inception of total treatment programs. Following Ayllon and Azrin's pioneering development and extension of principles and procedures to a systematic ward-wide treatment program (1965), modification and trial of total treatment programs appeared in ever-increasing numbers of uncontrolled demonstration reports and controlled within-group studies. While these studies continue to appear, largely reporting variations over patient populations with different characteristics and more complex behavior problems, the last five years have witnessed an increasing number of group studies comparing the effects of total programs to traditional hospital procedures. Recently a few comparative evaluations have been attempted among competing active treatment programs. Most of these have suffered from serious design errors, but the progression of focus from evaluation efforts to comparative evaluations with competing systems is a highly desirable movement and an indication of the increasing maturity of the approach.

The accumulated findings from studies with long-stay mental patients included in the recent literature reviews show considerable consistency with those of the comparative project. Because of the regularity with which chronic populations demonstrate deficits in social and instrumental skills, nearly all unitwide programs have focused directly on such behaviors. Quite consistently, instrumental social-learning procedures have been found to overcome deficits in self-care skills and instrumental role performance and to increase social responsivity. More recent studies have begun to center on the quality of social interaction and communication skills within unitwide programs, regularly reporting significant gains. Several within-subject designs have documented the importance of response-contingent consequences in overcoming deficits in adaptive social and instrumental role behavior in the desocialized long-stay patient but allowed intraclass confounding of procedures, including the specificity of desired performance and amount of staff attention and activity. The differential findings of the comparative project, gaining support from those of Stoffelmayr et al (1973), add further evidence for the specificity of the effects of social-learning procedures over and above such nonspecific factors.

The severity of deficits in self-care, interpersonal interaction, communications skills, and instrumental role performance of patients in the comparative project have been approached or equaled only in a few reports by other investigators. An examination of the nature and speed of response to increasing instrumental role performance and components of resocialization, as well as reports of unresponsive patients (i.e., the most severely withdrawn) in some studies, suggests that some aspects of overall social-learning programs are of differential necessity, depending upon the severity of deficits in adaptive skills of patients treated. Specifically, for the severely desocialized patient, not only are tangible token contingencies necessary, but so is a tight economy, which includes control of primary reinforcers (e.g., food, sleep) as backups. Even then, the most severely desocialized patient appears to require shaping with primary reinforcers in very small steps over a period of several months both to initiate behavior and teach the value of tangible tokens. Moderately desocialized patients, more typical of the usual back ward, also appear to require tangible token contingencies. However, backups seem reasonably effective even when limited to luxury items, such as privileges, canteen goods, use of facilities and services, trust funds, early versus late entry to meals, etc. For the moderately desocialized mental patient, the control of primary reinforcers seems necessary only to overcome performance deficits rather than skill or ability deficits. For mildly desocialized patients, more typical of the revolving-door group or open ward patients who already attend off-unit activities, particularly in VA hospitals, social-reinforcement contingencies alone appear adequate for actual training in resocialization. Tangible token consequences or point systems for patients with relatively mild levels of desocialization appear to function primarily as management systems, ensuring performance of existing skills and attendance at scheduled treatment activities.

On a practical level, the findings of other studies coincide with those of the comparative project to show that instrumental social-learning principles and procedures are exceptionally effective in resocialization and increasing instrumental role performance. Less severely debilitated long-stay populations may not require the tight economy and control of primary reinforcers included in the social-learning program of the comparative project. However, the program detailed in chapters 6 and 8 is recommended for implementation, nevertheless, because the step system allows rapid progress to social reinforcement alone for the less debilitated patient, and the management system to maintain performance where necessary, while providing the needed contingencies for severely debilitated patients.

Accumulated findings on the effectiveness in reducing or eliminating extreme bizarre behaviors by means of overall social-learning programs are based on a smaller number of studies, since few reports have involved entire groups of chronic patients as severely disturbed or as violent as those in the comparative project, and fewer have obtained as detailed assessment of maladaptive behavior as of adaptive behavior. Nevertheless, the findings of studies included in recent literature reviews tend to be consistent with those of the comparative project. Gross inappropriate response to minimal behavioral expectations appears to occur only in the most severely debilitated patient populations, and as such, results tend to follow those for adaptive behaviors. Specifically programs that have used primary reinforcers as backups, along with contingent token response costs and time out, appear to reduce or eliminate gross inappropriate response to minimal behavioral expectations; programs with less stringent negative consequences for such behavior do not.

Considerable consistency across studies is found on bizarre motoric behaviors, when such behavior has been assessed. Major reductions in bizarre motoric behaviors are regularly reported in nearly all programs as a result of concurrent increases in adaptive behavior while ignoring the bizarre behavior. Several within-subject studies have shown additional reductions in bizarre motoric behavior as a result of eliminating delusional beliefs and through attaching direct response costs to specific behaviors, over and above the functional displacement achieved through increasing adaptive behavior. However, just as consistently, no unitwide program relying primarily on response-contingent procedures has completely eliminated such behavior in all patients. Reports in the literature are still at a developmental, case-study level, and promise is indicated for more extensive effectiveness in eliminating bizarre motoric behaviors for psychotic patients through social-learning procedures focused upon the direct treatment of respondents with regard to conditioned anxiety and stress reactions.

Dysfunctional cognitive behaviors have not been regularly assessed or monitored in the majority of reports of unitwide programs. Where attention has been directed to cognitive dysfunction in overall programs, it has usually been through rating scales or separate assessments, without continuous monitoring. Consistent with the results of the comparative project, these studies have reported significant improvements in dysfunctional cognitive behavior, but details of findings or reported programmatic procedures have not been sufficient to draw any generalizations. Several within-subject studies of special procedures focused on the reduction or elimination of specific delusions or overt indications of hallucinations within programs, as well as separate controlled studies, have reported significant reductions in cognitive dysfunction. While these studies have entailed response-contingent procedures in some phase of treatment of cognitive dysfunction, none have been designed to test the necessity of response-contingent components of procedures and none have reported complete elimination of bizarre cognitive behaviors only with response-contingent procedures. Studies by Meichenbaum and his colleagues (e.g., Meichenbaum & Cameron, 1973) tend to support the findings of the comparative project on the primary importance of corrective information transmission, and a few case studies have supported the earlier recommendations for more intensive focus on anxiety and stress reactions for patients whose bizarre cognitive behaviors continued after the application of overall programmatic procedures.

Dangerous and aggressive acts approaching the severity of those in the patient population of the comparative project have appeared only in two reports of unitwide programs, although several individual within-subject studies have focused upon violent acts. A variety of procedures, including aversive conditioning with electric shock, have been reported in the literature, but consistent reductions in violent acts for the majority of patients have been reported only for combined contingent response-cost, time-out procedures when primary reinforcers are lost in the process. However, in accord with the findings of the comparative project, the only procedure that has consistently eliminated dangerous and aggressive acts for all patients treated has been the vigorous application of overcorrection/restitution. The parameters used in the above procedures have seldom been reported, except to note that brief periods of time out or overcorrection have led to increases rather than decreases in assaultiveness.

The extent to which other procedures may have been developed for dealing with assaultiveness and gone unreported cannot be estimated. Anyone who has spent time around assaultive patients is aware that institutional staff develop and apply aversive procedures for dealing with the assaults—frequently with procedures more severe than any of those reported in the literature. While many reports in the literature attempt euphemistic descriptions of procedures to imply that aversive conditions are not involved in the elimination of dangerous and aggressive acts, little reading between the lines is necessary for the experienced clinician to identify the probable effective ingredients. As noted by Ludwig (1971), the issue is not whether such procedures should be used but rather whether they will be administered "openly, unapologetically, and in a consistent, systematic, goal-oriented manner rather than on a disguised, apologetic, and haphazard basis" (p. 36).

On a practical level, the findings of other studies thus provide support for the effects found for the social-learning program on the reduction or elimination of extreme bizarre behaviors. However, the support is more piecemeal and isolated than that on adaptive behavior because of absence of precise assessment of maladaptive behaviors in other studies, less severely disturbed patient groups, and a tendency for procedures involving aversive conditions to be glossed over or not reported at all. Because of the existing supporting data, the absence of negative reports, and the strength of the evidence within the comparative project itself, the integrated social-learning program, detailed in chapters 6 and 8, with the most effective procedural parameters, detailed in chapters 18, 28, and 33, is therefore recommended for implementation with long-stay patient groups.[3]

Less severely disturbed patient populations would not require all components of the social-learning program, and those components would not be activated in the absence of such extreme behaviors on the part of an individual patient but would be available if more severely disturbed patients were included. The social-learning program and staffing levels evaluated appear adequate for reducing levels of extreme bizarre behavior of long-stay patients to a point of community tolerance. However, higher levels of bizarre behavior based upon continuing conditioned anxiety or stress, likely with more acute problems, or complete elimination of bizarre behavior in long-stay patients, would probably require more individual treatment with expanded procedures incorporated within the specified program. These procedures would require more trained professional staff than the number included in the program evaluated.

## FACTORS RELATED TO RELEASE AND COMMUNITY STAY

Although the findings resulted in clear recommendations for the nature of treatment based upon behavioral characteristics of the long-stay mental patient, one last aim of the project relates directly to the practical outcome of such treatment recommendations: to explore the prognostic value of patient characteristics and functioning for release and community stay, as well as postrelease environmental factors. Both the milieu and social-learning programs covered in the recent reviews referenced earlier have regularly reported higher rates of institutional release with equal or lower rates of rehospitalization than achieved for the same population before institution of their psychosocial program or for concurrent populations treated by usual hospital procedures. Only two reports—one each for milieu and token economy programs—did not find higher overall release rates compared to other programs, and both of those reported more releases for longer-stay patients within their respective populations (Birky et al., 1971; Magaro & Giardina, 1970).

Release rates, taken in isolation, have always been meaningless as a measure of treatment success because of the ease with which simple administrative decisions and a variety of other factors can influence the act of institutional release (see Erickson, 1975). Net release has historically been a better comparative criterion, since community tolerance would correct for differing levels of administrative release requirements but only when patient groups and the nature of placement and aftercare services were reasonably equated (see Ellsworth, 1968). Comparisons of differential release and community stay rates across studies or time for the long-stay patient population become essentially meaningless in view of recent trends in community placements. As a practical matter, the least effective psychosocial treatment program of the current comparative project produced a higher release rate than any others that have been reported in the literature for chronically institutionalized mental patients. Similarly, the rehospitalization rates for releases who received social-learning aftercare consultation on a declining-contact basis were lower than those reported anywhere for any type of community placement—including those to extended-care facilities or other sheltered environments. While equal criteria and level of functioning for release and community stay within the comparative project were documented across the three treatment programs—allowing firm conclusions on the comparative effectiveness among the milieu, social-learning and hospital programs—the only comparative statements that can justifiably be made about the release and community stay rates elsewhere is that evidence that has been reported supports the effectiveness of psychosocial programs and suggests no contradictory evidence.

The prognostic value of patient characteristics and functioning for release and community stay within programs of the current comparative project have no parallel in the literature because of the initial severe disability levels of the patient population and the absence of reliable assessments in other studies spanning both intramural and extramural environments. Only the less-effective milieu and hospital programs found patient demographic characteristics to have any consistent predictive value at all for either within-institution change or achievement of release. The social-learning program was equally effective in producing improved functioning and release from the institution for all residents treated, irrespective of age, sex, race, socioeconomic status, process-reactive status, marital history, nature of symptom onset, identifiable precipitants on initial hospitalization, current or total length of hospitalization, prior electroconvulsive shock, prior insulin shock, other prior medical treatments, initial level or nature of functioning, and prior or current psychotropic drugs. Level of functioning at termination was, in fact, the major prognostic variable for the achievement of release across all three programs, thus providing confirmatory evidence that acceptability for release was primarily a function of patient behavior under circumstances existing in the comparative project.

Every class of behavior that had been identified as crucial for rehabilitation of the long-stay mental patient was a significant predictor of release for psychosocial residents, with the strongest negative predictors being the continued presence of dangerous and aggressive bizarre behaviors or other behaviors that would cause a management problem. Thus, the crucial classes of patient behavior that had previously been identified as significant in maintaining community stay for released patients in other studies were significant in obtaining release in the present project. The practical implications of these findings not only result in the strengthened recommendations for focusing on the identified targets of rehabilitation in future work but strongly support a recommendation for implementation of the Clinical Frequencies Recording System and TSBC as clinical assessment procedures.

While the absence of rehospitalization over the follow-up period left nothing to predict, the extent to which level of functioning in the community was predictable from prerelease functioning in the institution for psychosocial releases is without precedent in the literature. Consistent with the findings of others, demographic variables were totally unrelated to level of functioning in the community. However, previous studies have so regularly reported an absence of relationship between intramural and extramural measures of adjustment that reviewers have taken the lack of predictability of postrelease functioning as an established fact as well (see Erickson, 1975). The majority of releases from all intramural programs were residing in private board and care homes in the community and thereby shared a more common environment than did those in prior prognostic studies and an environment more closely related to the intramural environment than in studies where large proportions of expatients were functioning independently. However, the environmental-similarity hypothesis does not account for the absence of predictability of functioning for releases from the hospital programs, while the level of functioning for releases from both milieu and social-learning programs was highly predictable, not only on the same rating scales in and out of the institution but from objectively observed behavior in it as well. That the observed environmental characteristics in assessed extended-care facilities were slightly closer to those of the hospital than of the psychosocial programs also detracts from environmental similarity as the major basis for the predictability of releases from the psychosocial programs. Rather, two possibilities appear more likely as the basis for the exceptionally high predictability of in-community functioning of psychosocial releases: the greater care with which assessments were completed by staff and the greater validity of intramural assessments within the psychosocial units as a function of both programs maintaining actual performance at a level close to that at which residents were capable (see Lentz, 1975). The practical recommendations emanating from these hypotheses are obvious.

Postrelease environmental factors have been determined empirically to influence both rehospitalization and level of functioning in the community in other studies. Typical of findings from these investigations, the decline in functioning for released residents during the first few months in the community further strengthens earlier recommendations for continuity of care and declining contact aftercare, with the most intensive follow-up assistance being offered immediately following release. While the earlier recommendations for bridging the gap from institution to community for releases to independent functioning were not implemented in the comparative project because of situational problems of practicality (see illustrative cases, chapter 19), those recommendations still appear warranted on the basis of the original analysis. The differential losses in level of functioning over the first six months in the community for psychosocial releases, possibly resulting in part from the decreased levels of interpersonal stimulation, further support the earlier recommendations on the establishment of active and supportive social relationships before release.

Additionally the possibility that the differential declines in functioning were in part a reflection of a loss in transfer of learning resulting from the change from no drugs to drug use for the majority of psychosocial releases further leads to a recommendation that state-dependent learning in adult mental patients receive intensive investigation. The majority of psychosocial programs reported in the literature also indicate that psychotropic drug utilization is drastically reduced or eliminated during intramural treatment for long-stay mental patients. The complete absence of any beneficial effects of maintenance levels of psychotropic drugs, combined with suggestive negative effects on transfer of learning from nondrug states to drug states in the comparative project and elsewhere (see Overton, 1971; Paul et al., 1972) additionally leads to the recommendation that psychotropic drugs not be instituted as an automatic procedure for released mental patients. Rather, current findings suggest that no change from the drug status existing before release should be instituted during the first few months after release—whether that status is the presence or absence of psychotropic drugs.

The reversal of early declines in functioning for released residents from all three intramural programs after the institution of active aftercare consultation following social-learning principles, with continuing effects after consultation was faded, has important practical implications. The only prior report in the literature to systematically assess the level of functioning of ex-mental patients over time after placement in sheltered environments was Ellsworth (1968). Ellsworth found exceptionally high rates of regression in functioning for patients released to sheltered placements from the third to the twelfth month after release—i.e., over the period in which early declines were reversed for releases from the comparative project. Additionally he found that, of supervised placements, the lowest rehospitalization rates but highest additional regression (67%) was obtained in facilities that benefited financially for retaining ex-patients.

In contrast, only 29% of the released residents in the comparative project were functioning at lower levels than at discharge after eighteen months in private facilities that benefited financially from having beds full, and the direction of change was toward further improvement rather than additional deterioration. The shift in direction of the change in level of functioning, combined with the remarkable absence of rehospitalization for releases from the programs of the comparative project, leads to a recommendation that the transfer and orientation procedures described in chapter 33 and the nonspecific characteristics of aftercare procedures following social-learning principles, described in chapter 38, be implemented for released long-stay patients. This recommendation is not based upon any presumption that the procedures have been demonstrated to be better than others. Rather, they appear to be the only ones to date with any degree of empirical support at all.

The extended-care facility that received program consultation rather than case consultation showed slightly improved staff functioning and a corresponding slight edge in improvement of their residents. However, the weak programs that were instituted in both facilities seem unlikely to result in any major rehabilitation impact on the residents. Since the movement toward emptying state hospitals appears to be expanding, such extended-care facilities may, by default, become the only facilities for rehabilitating the better-functioning, long-stay mental patient. Board and care placement as an ultimate target for institutional release could reasonably be achieved for the most severely debilitated chronic mental patient without physical problems in twenty-six to thirty weeks of focused treatment in an ongoing social-learning program with adequate supplies, trained staff, most effective procedures for eliminating dangerous and aggressive acts, and continuous monitoring through Clinical Frequencies, SRIC, and TSBC. Although such a community placement is clearly preferable to continual wasting away in a state hospital at a subhuman level of existence, continued functioning at a marginal level for such ex-patients—or those who were already functioning at higher levels and were administratively declared maximum-benefit discharges—seems much less than our current treatment technology could potentially offer.

At the very least, residents currently in such private extended-care facilities—both releases from the intramural programs of the comparative project and the higher-functioning non-retardates from usual placement sources—are already functioning at a level high enough to engage in a Fairweather-type lodge operation (Fairweather et al., 1969; Sanders, 1972). Such an operation, involving resident-conducted, income-producing business and self-maintained group living arrangements, would be cheaper to taxpayers than current support conditions in private extended-care facilities and might increase the resident's own satisfactions and perceptions of self-worth. However, given the indications of continuing improvement within the social-learning program after all materials and supplies became available and before the externally imposed procedural changes brought ongoing improvements to a halt, this level of functioning seems far short of that potentially available for the long-stay patient.

There is no way to know yet what limits of functioning might be achieved for long-stay mental patients given the opportunity to participate in the ongoing social-learning program with the components known to be most effective maintained in continuous operation or to what extent independent functioning might be reliably achieved for patients who start at the level that allows transfer to private community facilities. The data at hand clearly indicate that the limits have by no means been approached. Therefore, a primary recommendation is that the movement toward emptying state hospitals by releases to sheltered community environments be slowed until fully operating social-learning programs, with all components now known to be most effective—including the ongoing assessment systems—have the opportunity to test the limits of improvement over the two to three years or more that might be required to bring the majority of chronically institutionalized patients to a level of independent functioning. Additionally, since considerable changes in bureaucratic regulations and funding criteria would be required (Kohen & Paul, 1976), if private extended-care facilities are to become the public rehabilitation centers of the future, residents so placed should not be denied the benefits of the treatment program that offers promise of improving functioning to a level allowing a more independent and meaningful life. Therefore, another recommendation is that existing community extended-care facilities be supported and monitored in the implementation of fully operational social-learning programs.

# 43. Concluding Comments on Institutional Research and Treatment

Serious questions from several quarters are being raised about the desirability of maintaining mental institutions at all. Many question the reasonableness of attempting to change problems that appear to be largely interactional in nature in the artificial setting of an institution, with the attendant problems of generalization of change to the community environment where improved functioning must ultimately be maintained. Others question the dehumanization attendant upon residence in any total institution. Infringement upon patients' rights and the high probability of abuse emanating from differential power relationships are seen by many as unavoidable effects of total institutions. Finally, the documented lack of effectiveness of prolonged hospitalization with traditional treatment programs has led many professionals to agree with Mendel's statement: "Since the hospital as a place of treatment for the severely ill psychiatric patient is always expensive and inefficient, frequently antitherapeutic, and never the treatment of choice, we mental health professionals need to develop a strategy for our contribution to dismantling mental hospitals" (1974, p. 8).

Many of these points are both accurate and persuasive, although not without counterarguments (e.g., Brill, 1975). However, the question of dismantling mental institutions remains moot for chronically institutionalized patients already in them—particularly the severely disabled who remain after attempts to place them elsewhere. These recalcitrant patients have no place to go until adequate treatment can prepare them to enter and survive in less-restrictive environments. For them, institutional treatment must remain a reality for the foreseeable future.

## ETHICAL ISSUES AND LEGAL TRENDS RELATED TO THE RECOMMENDATIONS

We presume that the conclusions and recommendations presented in chapter 42 will be taken seriously, since they are based on the most solid empirical evidence yet available. Although we have concerns about their inappropriate implementation based solely on the absence of technical competence to carry them out elsewhere, our greatest ones are related to ethical issues and current legal trends. Unquestionably, there will be others whose value systems are such that our recommendations will be rejected, with full understanding of the issues and procedures involved. These represent honest disagreements in values that we would, of course, hope to persuade to our way of thinking. Such informed disagreements based upon differing value systems are not, however, of primary concern.

Our major concern lies with those who may misinterpret the ethical issues and recommended procedures in such a way as to cause harm. The nature of institutional research and treatment, particularly with patients as severely debilitated as those in the current project, is such that procedural descriptions, findings and recommendations will predictably be quoted out of context and misinterpreted to bolster some emotionally laden argument. Of even greater concern—in fact, our greatest fear—is the possible misuse of component procedures from the recommended program or a misinterpretation of findings to justify other procedures in ways that might harm institutionalized patients. This issue is a direct focus of emerging trends toward ethical and legal regulation of institutional research and treatment.

Although we applaud the activity of other people and groups who are also concerned about important ethical and legal issues relating to the institutionalized mental patient, we have misgivings that the current nature of the decision-making processes and recommended safeguards may inadvertently result in long-range contra humane effects. Therefore, we shall briefly consider the current trends toward regulation of institutional research and treatment for long-stay residents of mental institutions in general and attempt to clarify our position on ethical and legal issues related to the implementation of the social-learning program, in particular.

## Regulation of Work with the Chronically Institutionalized[1]

Regulation of either research or treatment is ultimately based on concepts of right and wrong. Value judgments of right and wrong preclude definitive definitions based upon either logic or science (Ullmann & Krasner, 1975, pp. 603-622). However, the differential power relationships existing between staff and residents in mental institutions—particularly for the chronically institutionalized—set conditions whereby those with lesser power, the residents, are more open to wrongdoing than those who are not subject to such total institutions (Mendel, 1974). Similarly, the existing state of affairs, in which large numbers of people remain as long-stay residents of mental institutions, whether by choice or incapacity, places burdens on productive members of society, which many view as wrong, particularly if effective treatment procedures might lessen this burden (Hagen, 1975). Further the release of chronically institutionalized patients under conditions in which their skills are insufficient to care for themselves or their habitual modes of behavior pose serious burdens or clear danger to others is seen by many as wrongs against both the ex-resident and larger society (Brill, 1975; Rachlin, 1974). These conditions of possible wrongdoing seem to be the basis for most ethical concerns and regulatory safeguards. Additionally, in our value system, each issue represents sufficient potential for wrongdoing—with or without malevolent intent—that reasonable safeguards should be incorporated into any mental institution.

However, as Humphreys has noted in another context (1975), determination of right and wrong on the above issues involves the complex balancing and optimization of several factors: means and ends, short- and long-range effects, and individual and societal welfare. Since each of these focuses may be in conflict, ethical guidelines—and the administrative and statutory requirements through which ethical concerns are given substance—appear as attempts to provide protection from possible wrongdoing before the fact, i.e., before alternative decisions or courses of action have been implemented. Judicial decisions are called for after the fact of some alleged wrongdoing. However, the interpretations and standards established by court rulings clearly function even more broadly than previously existing administrative and statutory requirements as substantive attempts to provide protection from possible future wrongdoing before the fact (McGarry & Kaplan, 1973).

Goldiamond (1975) has detailed the requirements for rational decision making where balancing of such potentially conflicting factors is necessary. What is required is information on gains and losses provided by each alternative course of action. Actual gains and losses from any course of action can, of course, be determined empirically only after the fact and are very likely to be dependent upon the time, place, and circumstances involved. Therefore, ethical guidelines or more formal administrative and legal regulations whose function is to provide protection from possible wrongdoing before the fact appear to require a particular form.

To provide for the complex balancing of conflicting factors before the fact, it appears that ethical guidelines and administrative and legal regulations should take the form only of specifying the consensually agreed upon principles to be considered in choosing between alternative courses of action and prescribing the structure for monitoring the decision-making process. The principles to be considered in choosing between alternative courses of action should include a requirement that known cause-effect relationships be taken into account; however, the prescription and proscription of specific procedures or courses of action beyond those involved with the decision-making process presume after-the-fact knowledge of gains and losses in all times, places, and circumstances. Such procedural prescription and proscription before the fact nearly ensure that balancing and optimization of conflicting factors will not occur.

Even if ethical guidelines and formal administrative and legal regulations focus upon principles to be considered and the structure of decision making, without prescription and proscription of specific procedures, the possible gains and losses of alternative courses of action selected on the basis of such principles and structure remain informed estimates until after the fact of implementation. It seems the only way of determining whether the decisions generated from such ethically guided decision making, in fact, produce the desired consequences is to implement the actions and assess their effects. This empirical evaluation of operational results—with feedback and change into the decision-making structure—has been a hallmark of the experimental-behavioral strategy of research and treatment. Recent commentators have proposed that such empirical evaluation of operational results should be ethically required. In fact, empirical evaluation is seen as necessary not only for any treatment approach (e.g., Davison & Stuart, 1975; Schwitzgebel, 1973, 1974) but as a means of evaluating ethical standards themselves, whether expressed as guidelines and administrative policy governing research and clinical practice (e.g., Ullmann & Krasner, 1975; "Ethics of Ethicists," 1975) or more formally in mental health law and judicially stipulated standards (e.g., Friedman, 1975; McGarry & Kaplan, 1973).

Mental health law and the use of judicial procedures on behalf of institutionalized mental patients have shown phenomenal activity in recent years.[2] Such activity is likely to reflect only the well-known "tip of the iceberg" with regard to actions in the future (Greenblatt, 1974). Chief Judge David Bazelon—one of the most active in judicial standard setting in the area of mental health and institutional treatment—appears to agree with our earlier formulation of the appropriate role of regulatory mechanisms, including the courts. He indicated his view of the court's role in his keynote address to a conference on mental health and the law: "As a judge of the United States Court of Appeals for the past 24 years, I have been exposed to many of the problems to be addressed at this conference. My involvement is not as an expert in the behavioral sciences, but simply as a monitor of the decision making process" (1974, p. 644). Bazelon reminded his audience that questions come up for judicial determination on petitions for redress of grievances. Thus, the court's role was defined as a monitor of the decision-making process, with judgments of right and wrong to be made for specific actions after the fact of occurrence where gains and losses could reasonably be determined. However, principles employed in reaching such a decision after the fact in a specific instance of abuse should, in Bazelon's opinion, clearly be designed to bring about reform in similar conditions elsewhere.

Meisel (1975) argues that court decrees and promulgations of legislatures cannot enforce morality but will be of greatest value as safeguards against future wrongdoing in their role as ethical guides or ideals. The operational bases employed in reaching judicial decisions to correct after-the-fact abuses should provide an excellent source of carefully reasoned principles to be considered in choosing between alternative courses of action before the fact in other times, places, and circumstances. Unfortunately, in practice the nature of the court process and legal decisions, which are focused upon correcting an instance of abuse, often do not appear to be well suited for providing the flexibility required for balancing issues before the fact elsewhere. Rather than functioning as a source of principles to be considered, such rulings often command obedience, frequently with prescription and proscription of specific procedures. Additionally the nature of court rulings on petitions for redress of grievances after the fact of occurrence call for dichotomous decisions (e.g., at fault, not at fault). Although these decisions and the prescription and proscription of specific procedures seem apt for correcting conditions of abuse after the fact in a specific instance, their adoption as fixed regulatory rules for future conduct presumes to forecast outcomes under conditions in which possible gains and losses of alternative courses of action are unknown. These seem to be the very conditions that ensure that balancing and optimization of conflicting factors will not occur.

Another feature of many administrative, statutory, and judicial decisions that are invoked to correct specific instances of abuse is that the prescriptive and proscriptive procedures tend to focus on only one set of possible conflicting factors—those where an instance of wrongdoing has already occurred—without including necessary assessment operations to determine whether overall gains or losses might result from future applications. Because of the blatant nature of some instances of wrongdoing and the clarity with which the public's sense of decency has been violated by some institutional abuses, the majority of corrective administrative and legal rulings have been weighted toward individual rather than group or societal welfare, means rather than ends, and short- rather than long-term effects. Unfortunately, when decisions based on short-term humanitarian concerns to correct an instance of abuse are implemented as prescriptive and proscriptive regulations for future conduct, the long-term empirical consequences may be considerably less humane.

Examples of unintended long-term negative effects resulting from prescriptive regulations meant to correct an abuse are becoming more abundant, concurrent with the increased attempts to legislate morality. One recent area in which judicial attempts to correct specific abuses has had far-reaching negative, as well as occasional positive, effects is that of "institutional peonage" (Bartlett, 1964). Several courts had attempted to correct the exploitation of institutionalized mental patients in which the maintenance of an institution was accomplished by requiring patients to work involuntarily, without normal compensation. Wexler (1973) anticipated possible long-term negative effects from the federal court decision relating to institutional peonage in *Wyatt v. Stickney*—a landmark case of extraordinary and elaborate specificity in all areas of patients' rights.[3] The court attempted to correct specific instances of exploitation by proscribing all involuntary patient labor involving hospital operation and maintenance—whether therapeutic or not—specifically prohibiting privileges or release from being contingent upon such labor. The court further prescribed that voluntary institutional work was to be compensated at the prevailing minimum wage.

Wexler (1973) recognized that widespread adoption of the *Wyatt* standards on institutional labor might potentially remove necessary therapeutic training opportunities for chronically institutionalized patients and result in greater expenditures for less-effective therapy.

Shortly after the *Wyatt* decision, another federal court ruled in *Souder v. Brennen* that institutionalized mental patients were covered by the federal Fair Labor Standards Act.[4] The *Souder* decision was a class-action suit requiring compliance in all state and private institutions, with the Department of Labor being responsible for enforcing the law. The department recognized the absurdity of paying severely disabled patients in training at the full minimum wage rate and established complex procedures for paying less to institutionalized persons with impaired productivity. Nevertheless, with a few notable exceptions (e.g., in Massachusetts and Tennessee), Wexler's concerns were fully verified. Within a year after the *Souder* decision, citing lack of funds, bureaucratic problems, or euphemisms, the majority of states had drastically reduced the opportunity for patient work or eliminated such vocational training opportunities within mental institutions altogether ("Peonage to Pay," 1974). Thus, in this area of litigation, there are negative long-term effects for both individual people and society resulting from the application of prescriptive and proscriptive dichotomous decisions developed to correct specific instances of abuse—to the particular detriment of the very group of persons in whose behalf the litigation was started.

The negative effects of decisions and regulations in the area of institutional peonage are sufficiently widespread and public that such empirical consequences are likely to be identified and eventually fed back into the regulatory system for correction.[5] Many other unintended negative effects of prescriptive and proscriptive regulations based upon short-term humanitarian concerns to correct a specific instance of abuse are unlikely to be identified because of the absence of ongoing assessment operations that would allow empirical evaluation of gains and losses. Several clear examples of these conditions were apparent in the comparative project where ongoing assessment allowed the identification of overall long-term effects of specific procedures. The statewide limitation of the use of seclusion to a maximum of two hours is the prime example. The particular proscriptive and prescriptive safeguards may very well have been an appropriate response to correct an abuse in one situation. In this case, the abuse involved physical restraint rather than seclusion. it reportedly concerned a highly publicized incident in which adolescent patients at one state hospital had allegedly been tied for two days as punishment for mutual masturbation—a clear instance of inhumane treatment, which obviously required correction. However, when the time limitation on seclusion as well as restraint—which was likely an appropriate corrective action for the responsible staff in that institution—became statewide policy, the long-term effects were disastrous. This change, which was intended to guard against the application of inhumane procedures, resulted in the long-range lack of control of assaultive behavior. Long-term contra humane effects then occurred, not only for residents who had been receiving longer seclusion contingent upon incidents of assault, but for other residents and staff as well. The concurrent relative loss of effectiveness of both psychosocial programs from this one change in regulatory procedures further restricted the benefits to society that might have been obtained under the demonstrably more effective conditions. Although the negative effects were the result of an administrative ruling, similar legal rulings have been made in the *Wyatt* decision and elsewhere (e.g., Lucero et al., 1968).

These examples reflect unintended negative effects that result when dichotomous prescriptive and proscriptive rulings developed to correct abuses after the fact are applied as regulatory safeguards before the fact in other times, places, and circumstances. The *Wyatt* decision in many respects epitomizes these problems. Its major ruling was that involuntarily committed mental patients had a constitutional right to adequate treatment—thus confirming a position that originally began as a moral proposal (Birnbaum, 1960) and was later strengthened by judicial argument (Bazelon, 1969). Paradoxically the conditions specified under *Wyatt* for correcting abuses would simultaneously prohibit the treatment empirically demonstrated to be most effective from the current project if the standards were rigidly applied (Berwick & Morris, 1974; Wexler, 1973). Schwitzgebel (1973, 1974) has elaborated a basic problem in such judicial standards that attempt to correct abuses by prescription of structure (e.g., type and number of staff) and process (e.g., specific treatment procedures or mode of delivery) rather than requiring assessment procedures for determining outcome. The dichotomous, prescriptive, and proscriptive nature of legal decisions developed to correct after-the-fact abuses fail to provide adequate balancing for future conduct, even when regulatory insurance of adequate treatment was the espoused purpose of the court (Stickney, 1974; "Wyatt Victory 'Tarnished'?" 1975).

Even when court rulings avoid severely limiting prescription and proscription of procedures, the fact that judicial decisions are called for after the fact in instances of alleged wrongdoing still appears to detract from necessary balancing when such decisions form the basis for regulating future conduct. Such differential focusing and consequent potential for long-term negative effects appears to be a necessary component of any decision whose primary purpose is to correct an alleged abuse; the possible gains and losses of alternative courses of action in the future are not relevant to the facts of the action in the past and are therefore not considered. In 1975 the Supreme Court handed down its decision on the first "right to treatment" case to reach that level of appeal (*O'Connor v. Donaldson*, No. 74-8). The Fifth Circuit Appellate Court had originally upheld the verdicts of district courts in both the *Wyatt* case and *Donaldson v. O'Connor* on the right to adequate treatment as the basis for involuntary confinement of mental patients.[6] The appellate court also upheld the district court's award of punitive and compensatory damages in the *Donaldson* case. The Court did not affirm the constitutional right to treatment part of the lower court ruling or the award of damages, throwing the whole status of these issues into legal limbo (Wolfe, 1975). However, the Court did rule in favor of *Donaldson* on the basis of a constitutional right to liberty. The ruling was carefully limited, without prescriptive or proscriptive statements, holding that: "A state cannot constitutionally confine, without more, a nondangerous individual who is capable of surviving safely in freedom by himself or with the help of willing and responsible family members or friends . . ." (Peck, 1975, p. 316).

The Supreme Court ruling in *Donaldson* establishes an important principle that requires consideration in future choices among alternatives for other institutionalized mental patients. However, even though the Court did not include prescriptive and proscriptive standards typical of other judicial rulings, many commentators predicted negative long-range effects of the decision in the form of inappropriate release of chronic mental patients into the community (Asch, 1975; "Mental Patients Win 'Right to Liberty,'" 1975; Wolfe, 1975). Other long-range effects are anticipated if the award of damages is eventually upheld, ranging from a total avoidance of institutional work by trained professionals to defensive treatment practices that could "make the revolving door policy a spinning success" (Stone, 1974). These long-range negative effects seem likely not because of inappropriate prescription and proscription of procedures but because of the differential focus on one set of factors in after-the-fact rulings that have no requirements for balancing other factors when such decisions are invoked for before-the-fact regulation of conduct elsewhere.

Such a lack of balance seems apparent in most attempts at regulation of institutional work, whether professional, administrative, or legal. Many instances of regulation are initiated to correct actual or presumed abuses, and thus they result in a one-sided focus, whether involving litigation or not. As the public concern has become aroused about the plight of the institutionalized mental patient, regulatory efforts have come to focus on classes of activity that are relatively novel or more public. In fact, deviation from the status quo has been stipulated as a defining feature in which regulation comes into play for both research ("activity which departs from the application of those established and accepted methods necessary to meet his needs," Department of Health, Education, and Welfare, 1974a, p. 18917) and treatment ("treatment which is not recognized as standard psychiatric treatment," Friedman, 1975, pp. 50-51). Particularly with regard to chronically institutionalized mental patients, this one-sided focus of regulatory activities seems to encourage a totally unacceptable state of affairs since the "standard, established, and accepted methods" have proven to be not only ineffective but potentially harmful (see chapter 1; chapter 34; Paul et al., 1972).[7]

Until recently, regulation of work in mental institutions was heavily focused on research or experimental procedures as distinguished from treatment. Unfortunately, the determination of activities called "research" often appear to be based simply upon the inclusion of assessment operations to evaluate the effects of the activity. The same procedures might be carried out under the rubric of "treatment" if no comparative assessments were specified, while measurement of effects results in the classification of the activity as "research" (Davison & Stuart, 1975; Schwitzgebel, 1974). To the extent that the classification of the activity as "experimental" or "research" rather than "treatment" differentially calls forth regulation—with attendant bureaucratic barriers of increased paperwork, committee meetings, reviews, and time lags—differential incentives clearly exist for the direction in which an institutional unit director will move (Goldiamond, 1975). The adverse consequences of these impediments to scientific research and development not only restrict the body of scientific information available to society but, by discouraging ongoing evaluations of treatment, the ineffective practices of the status quo are further encouraged to the detriment of the institutionalized patients these regulations are intended to protect. Schwitzgebel (1974) has eloquently summarized this state of affairs: "To protect a relatively small number of patients from these admittedly 'experimental' procedures while at the same time coercing many more patients to undergo less effective 'treatment' procedures currently in vogue in standard psychiatric practice is, in terms of the old adage, straining at the gnat while swallowing the elephant" (p. 956).[8]

In the last few years, professional, administrative, and legal concerns with the regulation of treatment practices as well as research have increased dramatically with regard to the institutionalized mental patient. Nearly all commentators note that the conditions of possible wrongdoing and the resulting ethical concerns relate equally to any treatment approach with institutionalized persons. Nevertheless, the amount of activity generated on the proposed regulation of psychosocial treatment procedures has been heavily weighted on behavioral technology, evidenced by recent detailed analyses (e.g., Braun, 1975; Davison & Stuart, 1975; Friedman, 1975; Goldiamond, 1975; Hagen, 1975; Perpich, 1975; Stolz et al., 1975: Wexler, 1975a, 1975b).

The bases for such extraordinary concern about one class of treatment activity or one approach to intervention to the relative exclusion of others appear to derive from several factors. Foremost is the inappropriate identification of behavioral treatment approaches with biomedical treatments such as psychosurgery, electroconvulsive shock, and chemotherapy. In fact, the majority of the legal principles underlying the potential regulation of institutional treatment procedures were developed on the basis of alleged abuses of biomedical rather than psychosocial or behavioral techniques (Friedman, 1975; Goldiamond, 1975). Such inappropriate linking of biomedical and behavioral approaches appears to have been largely promulgated through fiction in such works as *1984*, *The Manchurian Candidate*, and *A Clockwork Orange*, in which the fantasied potency of mind-controlling techniques has led to considerable public fears (Stolz et al., 1975). These fears and reactive attempts at prescriptive and proscriptive regulations have been further heightened by a few widely publicized reports of outrageous programs conducted by overzealous professionals who claimed to base procedures on behavioral principles but in fact used practices abhorred by trained behavioral scientists (for a discussion of some of the more blatant examples, see Miron, 1968, and May, 1975).

Some other factors have also been suggested to contribute to the particular emphasis on regulation of behavioral technology. Representatives of several concerned disciplines, including behavioral clinicians and scientists (e.g., Davison & Stuart, 1975; Hagen, 1975), attorneys (e.g., Friedman, 1975), and representatives of the National Institute of Mental Health (e.g., Stolz et al., 1975) agree on the majority of these factors. The apparent success of behavioral approaches to treatment of particular classes of problems when other approaches have failed seems to provide some exaggerated concerns and public fear of control. Additionally basic differences in the philosophy of the nature of man frequently appear to be polarized by the language that behavioral clinicians use. Principles and concepts derived from laboratory work and carried over into clinical practices in an attempt to maintain precision sound less humanistic and more manipulative than terms used to discuss less empirically based treatment approaches—even though there is no indication the clinicians employing behavioral approaches are any less sensitive or more manipulative than those employing any other approach. Finally, a major feature inherent in the experimental-behavioral approach in general and behavioral treatment procedures in particular seems to have especially encouraged overemphasis on regulation to the relative exclusion of other approaches. This feature is the high visibility of explicitly defined procedures and objectives, which allows procedures and goals of behavioral treatments to be more easily scrutinized than other treatment approaches that remain relatively nebulous.

Unfortunately proposed regulatory guidelines for the use of behavioral procedures with institutionalized mental patients have to date taken the same prescriptive and proscriptive format as many judicial rulings. Such a format is characteristic of some attempts at regulation that are based upon misguided emotional reactions (e.g., Lucero et al., 1968; Lucero & Vail, 1968; Ball, 1968; Bragg & Wagner, 1968; Cahoon, 1968; Miron, 1968) where the approach to regulation is akin to Schwitzgebel's (1975) analogy of regulating wiretapping by eliminating telephones. However, the same prescriptive and proscriptive format is also characteristic of concerned and carefully reasoned proposals for regulatory guidelines (e.g., Friedman, 1975; see also Hagen, 1975). This format precludes the optimization and balancing of conflicting factors within specific times, places, and circumstances. Even when the proposed guidelines include the desirable feature of requiring the consideration of empirically derived cause-effect relationships (Friedman, 1975), their prescriptive and proscriptive nature threatens to freeze treatment procedures at a static state (Goldiamond, 1975).

Behavioral treatment procedures and programs in mental institutions can be considerably more effective than competing alternatives. In that sense, the technology is empirically demonstrated to be powerful and therefore worthy of regulation to ensure appropriate positive application with safeguards and balancing of all factors—means and ends, short- and long-term effects, and individual and societal welfare. However, it should be clear that the need for regulation is not inherent in any particular behavioral approach, since any technology is "ethically neutral" (Skinner, 1971). Like any other technology or treatment approach, behavioral procedures can be used either positively or "ineptly or for ends considered immoral" (Stolz et al., 1975). The problem in the current trend toward regulation of behavioral approaches is not that regulatory safeguards for behavioral treatment are not desirable but that the lack of balance in their focus on behavioral approaches to the relative exclusion of others will produce long-term undesirable effects for institutionalized persons and society.

The effects of regulating only one system or approach to treatment are particularly detrimental to the chronically institutionalized. Since a decision not to intervene with a particular treatment is a decision to continue the status quo, the chronically institutionalized are thereby relegated to continued incarceration under conditions of ineffective treatment (see Ullmann & Krasner, 1975; Schwitzgebel, 1974). Goldiamond (1975) has detailed the predictable negative effects of regulating only behavioral orientations while allowing alternative procedures or treatment orientations to operate without scrutiny. As with the differential regulation of research rather than treatment, bureaucratic barriers involved in the regulation of only one approach to treatment will predictably provide an incentive for the regulated approach to be avoided. Such avoidance might come about through total rejection of treatment procedures or programs or by redefining procedures and practices in language that circumvents the regulations. In either case, the quality and effectiveness of treatment, and consequently the restoration of liberty and nonrecidivism of maladaptive behavior, are all imperiled by discriminant regulation. Given the need for effective and ethical institutional practices and the importance of explicit evaluation of effects for determining such outcomes, it seems ironic that any approach that enhances explicitness, specificity, and assessment should be the focus of such discriminant regulatory proposals.

In summary, the recent focus of professional, administrative, and legal regulation of work with long-stay residents of mental institutions is a welcome emphasis on ethical issues. However, the trends to date appear nearly to ensure long-range contra humane effects because of the conditions in which regulatory efforts are called forth, the nature of the decision-making processes involved, and the format of the regulatory decisions. The majority of administrative, statutory, and judicial decisions are called for to correct a specific instance of abuse. The decision-making process thus tends to focus only on the set of factors that appear to be responsible for wrongdoing after the fact, with the format of the decisions being dichotomous prescription and proscription of procedures deemed necessary to correct that instance of wrongdoing.

When the decisions are then invoked as fixed regulatory rules for governing future conduct in other times, places, and circumstances, the conditions for rational decision making are precluded since the possible gains and losses for each alternative course of action cannot be considered. Therefore, balancing and optimization of means and ends, short- and long-term effects, and individual and societal welfare cannot occur. Similarly the more recent trends toward the establishment of regulatory safeguards focusing upon only one class of activity—retention criteria, research, or one approach to treatment—precludes rational decision making to balance alternative courses of action. Potential negative effects from this absence of balance are nearly ensured as a result of the incentive provided for institutional workers to avoid bureaucratic barriers or other personal aversive consequences that might result from possible violations of rules that obtain only for the regulated class of activity. Thus, to approach adequate safeguards against wrongdoing in work with long-stay residents of mental institutions, a major change in the structure and mechanisms of regulation is required.

*A Proposal for Establishing Mechanisms for Ethical Regulation*[9]

Every agency that has proposed ethical guidelines and almost every commentator who has considered institutional regulation have emphasized the establishment of an institutional review committee. A local review committee at the site of each residential treatment center is the most likely mechanism for providing reasonable safeguards. However, for such a committee to possess the flexibility to balance and optimize the multitude of conflicting factors, its scope of activities, focus, manner of operation, and composition would necessarily differ in several respects from those proposed elsewhere (e.g., Department of Health, Education and Welfare, 1974b; Friedman, 1975; Stolz et al., 1975).

The major difference in scope is that all treatment and research activities in the institution should be equally subject to scrutiny and regulation to avoid the negative incentives attendant upon discriminative regulation (Goldiamond, 1975). Thus, a single committee should be charged with an external review of all institutional programs to safeguard the individual rights of residents, staff, and the public at large. The major difference in the focus of committee activities would be that the committee should not attempt to apply previously established prescriptive and proscriptive regulations for particular procedures. Rather, it should attempt to approve or disapprove available alternative courses of action by considering the balance of probable gains and losses from the broader perspective of means and ends, short- and long-term effects, and individual and societal welfare and monitor outcomes to provide corrective feedback.

Thus, the single committee should function to evaluate and approve, disapprove, or work for a collaborative modification of programmatic proposals prepared by each director of an institutional unit. The proposals should be evaluated for soundness of operational and methodological procedures based upon current scientific knowledge, adequacy of staff training, and adequacy of specification of intermediate and ultimate goals, ongoing assessment, and record keeping as well as for reasonable consideration of other ethical principles. Ongoing monitoring of programs would then focus upon compliance with the approved proposals. Continuation of procedures or components of programs should be empirically determined by monitoring of outcomes in each particular time, place, and circumstance. The development of structure and process would remain the primary responsibility of the professional treatment staff—with external assurance and support for ethical practices—but the outcome would provide the test for continuation or change (Schwitzgebel, 1974).

The principles to be considered and balanced by the review committee in determining the acceptability of proposed practices should be drawn from existing discussions of ethical codes and regulations (see Braun, 1975; Davison & Stuart, 1975; Department of Health, Education and Welfare, 1974a & b), legal principles and rulings (see Friedman, 1975; Schwitzgebel, 1974, 1975), and scientific principles and findings (for chronically institutionalized mental patients, see chapters 1, 3, & 42 above and the references in them). However, regulations, rulings, and findings are continually changing and will likely require at least some alteration to optimize conflicting factors in any particular application. The empirical test of the outcomes of specified programs and procedures and of the weighting of ethical principles employed by the committee in the circumstances of application must become the central component for ensuring ethical and effective practices with public accountability.

The proposed composition of the review committee would also differ from those suggested elsewhere. The head of an institution (by tradition the superintendent) is ultimately responsible for the activities in it and for the allocation of funds through which incentive for specific activities may be obtained. Therefore, the superintendent or his or her representative should be the chairman of the review committee. Additionally, since institutional staff are responsible for carrying out programs and are affected by their structure, an employee representative should be a regular member of the review committee, elected by the institutional staff and provided with compensatory time off from other duties. All other committee members should be paid consultants appointed to provide specific competencies and representation by persons not affiliated with the institution or department. Regular members could be a physician competent in physical medicine; a lawyer competent in mental health law and civil liberties; two clinically experienced behavioral scientists, at least one of whom is competent in research methodology and program evaluation; and a nonprofessional community representative. In addition to the regular seven-person committee, a paid consultant should be added if an area of expertise of a proposal is not represented among the regular committee membership—as determined by the committee itself or upon the request of an individual investigator or director of a clinical unit. Similarly, should any individual resident, resident group, or their representative believe that the regular committee membership was not adequately representing their interests, provision should be made to add a private legal representative to the committee to participate in decisions related to that resident or group.

The review committee should meet as necessary, but at least monthly for continuous monitoring of approved programs and consideration of changes from existing proposals, with a comprehensive review of each institutional program at least yearly. The comprehensive reviews of original proposals and yearly reviews of programs should occur on a staggered basis to ensure adequate consideration for all. The committee should receive and investigate complaints about institutional programs, procedures, staff or resident behavior, or committee actions at the first scheduled meeting after the receipt of a complaint from any source or at an emergency meeting in unusual circumstances. Ideally, cooperative resolution and correction of conditions leading to complaints could be handled within the committee itself; however, external mechanisms for arbitration should be provided, as well as formal mechanism for appeal and redress of actions of committee members.

For review committees to function as protagonists of individual and societal rights and welfare, they should be able to temporarily waive proscriptive and prescriptive administrative and legal regulations, under specified conditions, to allow the empirical test of reasoned alternatives. In this way, entire programs—which are demonstrably complex social systems with many interdependencies—would not rise or fall on the basis of a single ruling, nor would they become static entities. Rather, such empirical feedback might result in responsive rather than reactive treatment programs and review committees that could continuously improve effectiveness and ethical practices.

Special problems concerning the chronically institutionalized population will predictably arise for committee determination because they are already in the institution and have been refractory to previous attempts at treatment. It is precisely these conditions in which ethical and legal principles are likely to require careful balancing for protecting the rights of the institutionalized and of larger society. Since the chronic population is already institutionalized, therefore remaining unproductive with restrictions on individual liberties, both ethical considerations and existing legal principles argue strongly against the continuation of the custodial conditions existing in most institutions. Effective programs that hold promise for changing patient functioning in ways that will allow their safe transition to less-restrictive community environments and consequently greater individual freedom should clearly be heavily weighted in any choice among alternative actions. This emphasis seems essential whether viewed from the position of the public interest in the rehabilitation, independence, and productiveness of citizens, or from the position of individual patient rights to adequate treatment (Friedman, 1975; Schwitzgebel, 1974).

Potential conflicts of principles and interests are likely to arise from several factors. A large number of long-stay residents in mental institutions are so severely disabled or exhibit such bizarre behavior that they cannot be accepted or even survive outside the institution without dramatic changes in functioning. This group's severity of disability also precludes the rational decision making needed to choose among alternatives or to cooperate in rehabilitation programs (see chapters 1 & 12). Others, perhaps capable of rational decision making, behave in ways that are objectively dangerous and sufficiently so as to pose a serious threat to other people (see chapter 18; Bach-Y-Rita, 1974; Rachlin, 1973). Still others may be capable of decision making but prefer to remain in a custodial environment rather than make the additional effort required of participation in rehabilitation programs or to exist outside the institution (see Braginsky et al., 1969; Ludwig, 1971).

All of these patient characteristics result in the need for more stringent treatment procedures for effective psychosocial programs than those that might be required for less recalcitrant populations. The demonstrably effective social-learning treatment program and procedures involve not only a multitude of factors that most people would find both beneficial and pleasurable but some contingent restrictions in which most people would experience some temporary discomfort, in addition to requiring considerable effort. Those most in need of an effective treatment are the very people who are likely to be unable or unwilling to decide rationally to enter a rehabilitation program that would provide long-term benefits, even though they might have very positive feelings about participation after their functioning had improved. This is the exact situation in which conflicting principles and interests may be the strongest, since it involves the possible imposition of treatment programs upon people in the absence of their stated desires or perhaps even contrary to their stated desires.

It would then be the task of the review committee to balance the possible gains and losses of each course of action proposed and to monitor the implementation and outcomes of their decisions. The principles most in need of consideration are those involving the protection of both individual people and society as a whole from harmful acts, maximizing individual freedom of choice and ensuring effective treatment in the best interest of the institutionalized patient by the least restrictive means possible. These considerations require complex determinations of several factors.

The determination of competency has been unsatisfactorily dealt with legally because the concept of competency has been treated as something present or not present. Competence does not appear to be reasonably determined in the abstract but must be tied to specific acts or performance in specific situations. As Friedman notes, "The goal in choosing a standard of competency is, on the one hand, to enhance self-autonomy and guard against paternalism and, on the other, to provide for vicarious judgment in the best interest of patients when necessary" (1975, p. 76). The most important determination for the chronically institutionalized patient is whether he or she is competent to decide whether to enter a particular program or whether the review committee or treatment staff should make such a decision in that person's behalf. The determination of competency to make such a decision should be based on a combination of current functioning and the nature of the goals to be achieved through treatment.

Following Davison and Stuart's (1975) distinction of "minimal goals" and "optimal goals" minimal goals of effective institutional treatment should be those that allow the person to survive safely in a less-restrictive community environment without posing serious burdens or danger to others. The criteria of functioning required to meet minimal goals would need empirical determination in each setting that differed significantly in the nature of available community environments and social supports; however, they would probably be those targets previously determined to be empirically related to community tenure (see chapter 1) and successful release (see chapter 35). The documented performance of minimum levels of self-care, interpersonal interaction, communication skills, and on-task and on-time components of instrumental role skills needed to care for oneself in a sheltered community environment and freely interact with the local community should be considered minimal goals. Similarly the elimination or reduction of extreme bizarre cognitive and motoric behaviors to minimum levels required for community tolerance and safe community interactions, including the complete elimination of dangerous and aggressive acts that cause harm to oneself or others, should also be considered minimal goals of institutional treatment for the long-stay resident of mental institutions. Optimal goals of treatment should be those that would enhance social functioning and instrumental role skills above minimal levels and reduce disruptive maladaptive behavior further to allow the patient greater freedom of genuine choice and self-autonomy in the social and economic world to increase satisfactions and achieve maximum personal freedom and dignity.

These criteria for minimal and optimal goals should serve not only as principles toward which treatment programs should be directed but to define the operational performance criteria for determining the institutionalized patients' competence to make judgments about treatment procedures in their own best interest. Thus, objectively assessed performance below the criteria established for minimal goals would define the conditions in which treatment in the patient's best interest would be determined by others—the professional treatment staff with the approval of the review committee.[10] Objectively assessed performance at or above the criteria established for minimal goals would define the conditions in which the patient's own decision would determine the course of action to be followed. Since minimal goals are defined as the level of functioning that would allow survival in a less-restrictive environment, one alternative course of action open to a long-stay mental patient who achieved that level would always be to leave the institution for some range of specified community settings, such as rehabilitation programs in less-restrictive environments than the mental institution, where work on optimal goals could continue, or a sheltered boarding arrangement (see Kohen & Paul, 1976). Someone functioning at that level could also choose to remain at the institution to participate in a rehabilitation program directed toward optimal goals so long as clear conditions and criteria for the eventual termination of intramural treatment were established. Intramural work on optimal goals within publicly supported mental institutions should be limited to the achievement of a level of functioning that allows relatively independent functioning in the community (financial independence with social skills adequate to develop an independent supportive social network); further work on optimal goals could then be undertaken extramurally at considerably less expense should the ex-resident so desire.

Informed consent has been the traditional legal and ethical basis proposed for safeguarding the rights of participants in research or patients receiving treatment and for protecting the liability of investigators or clinical practitioners. Friedman (1975) and Stolz et al. (1975) cover in considerable detail the principles for determining whether consent is "compent, knowledgeable, and voluntary" if it is to be valid; whether the consent should be obtained from relatives or guardians for patients judicially determined incompetent; and whether provision should be made for consent to be withdrawn at any time during the course of participation in research or treatment, with consequent termination of the activity if consent is withdrawn. The underlying principle that patients, their relatives, and research participants should be informed of purposes, procedures, and expected risks and benefits is desirable; to the extent possible, so is cooperative engagement of all participants—including cooperation in determination of treatment goals and procedures—whether the individuals are classified as competent or not. However, there are several problems with the current prescriptive approach to the use of informed consent as a regulatory safeguard to protect institutionalized mental patients from wrongdoing.

Schwitzgebel (1975) has detailed the characteristics of the "consensual model," which is derived from determinations of tort liability in surgery or medical practice. Basically, the same long-term negative effects that were noted earlier in connection with any regulatory procedure developed to correct abuses after the fact of occurrence are present in the application of informed consent for before-the-fact regulation. He further notes the limitations of the dichotomous, prescriptive characteristics of the consensual approach in protecting the legitimate interests of institutionalized patients with regard to psychosocial treatment programs, which involve complex systems, as distinct from biomedical procedures, which more reasonably lend themselves to regulation-by-consent procedures. As an alternative Schwitzgebel (1975) proposes a "contractual model" as a mode of encouraging the protection and balancing of the legitimate interests among all affected parties in psychosocial treatment and research, without the negative connotations and limiting features inherent in the consensual model. By approaching psychosocial programs and procedures as contractual activities, the limits and obligations of both institutionalized patients and staff can be negotiated, specified, and renegotiated as new information becomes available. Contracts can make explicit the goals, possible risks and expected benefits, behaviorally contingent methods and procedures, and specified time limits and assessment criteria in such a way as to account for the complexity of psychosocial behavior and approaches to change. In addition, the explicitness of such contracts appear to offer much greater opportunity for self-determination by institutionalized patients than mere consent to undergo a particular procedure, while concurrently increasing the accountability of investigators and therapists.

The operation of the institutional review committee proposed above would be more within the contractual model than the consensual model for psychosocial principles and procedures. In approving specific psychosocial activities for long-stay residents of mental institutions whose level of functioning falls below minimal goals, the committee would not be giving blanket consent for the application of any and all procedures. Rather, it would be agreeing to explicitly proposed methods and procedures contingent upon particular classes of resident behavior to be assessed and evaluated in specified ways. Thus, it would function as the protagonist of society and of the institutionalized patients in negotiating contractual agreements with the staff of institutional units. This mode of operation seems particularly beneficial under conditions where vicarious judgment is substituted for the patient's own decision making, since it clarifies both the limits and the positive expectations of staff behavior as related to resident behavior. The position and safeguards for residents should be strengthened since any failure to carry through approved procedures could be considered a breach of contract, in contrast to safeguards against only negligence or malpractice under a consensual model (see Schwitzgebel, 1975).

Even greater responsibility seems desirable for the review committee in two areas that have caused considerable problems within the consensual model. Wexler (1975b) has drawn attention to a particular problem of most consent regulations, which allows a relative or guardian of an incompetent patient to give consent to participation in the patient's behalf. Relatives and guardians should be cooperatively engaged in the determination of necessary treatment plans and procedures. However, experience (see illustrative cases, chapter 19) verifies Wexler's concern that relatives and guardians may frequently wish to ensure the continued confinement of the incompetent patient to the extent that their decisions may be based upon convenience to themselves rather than the best interest of the institutionalized person. In the case of conflict between relatives and guardians and institutional staff on the activities of the institutionalized who are functioning below the level of minimal goals, the institutional review committee would be in the best position to negotiate and determine the activities that would be in the best interest of the patient.

The second feature of the consensual model that poses particular problems for recalcitrant populations is the requirement that consent be revocable at any time. In the case of institutionalized patients who continue in treatment on their own volition to work on optimal goals, the consent model would require the revocation of any particular component of a treatment program at any time during the patients' participation. Wexler (1975a, b) has also drawn attention to the negative effects of such free revocation with chronic populations. Specifically, the point at which an individual would be likely to revoke consent in a psychosocial program entailing extra effort or some discomfort is precisely at the time when such effort or discomfort would be therapeutically most required. Free revocation would thus predictably sap the motivational effects of a treatment program at the very point when it was needed.

These negative effects could be circumvented in the contractual model. The patient deciding to remain institutionalized to continue work on optimal goals could contract to participate in a specific program for a fixed period of time. Since the contractual approach specifies obligations and requirements for patients as well as for staff, the timing of decisions to continue or discontinue participation could allow a reasonable period for treatment procedures to bring about desired changes in functioning. Reasoned consideration under conditions in which the discomfort of any particular moment would not be overriding could allow both patients and staff to decide whether to continue work on the same or different optimal goals with the same or different treatment programs on the basis of effectiveness. Rather than the dichotomous decision to continue or discontinue participation, the contractual model would further provide for renegotiations of goals and programs or for community placement at such decison points to allow for truly informed decisions based upon empirical information.

Although this contractual approach for those working on optimal goals relies on the patient's decision, the review committee should continue to take more responsibility in the approval of institutional programs than is typical under the consensual model for such competent patients. Thus, even for institutional residents who are documented to be functioning above the criteria for minimal goals, the proposed programs and procedures offered for them to decide upon should be approved in advance and continuously monitored by the review committee to be in the patient's best interest. In this way, assurance of the most effective treatment with appropriate safeguards appears more likely for all patients, without inadvertent negative incentives slipping in because of the differential application of bureaucratic barriers. Additionally, by requiring committee review and approval of release planning and follow-up proposals, as well as intramural programs, safeguards against inappropriate release of patients meeting minimal goals might be more adequately provided.

The determination of activities in the patients' best interest is the desired outcome of the decision-making processes. According to Friedman, a balanced decision that a procedure is in the best interest of an institutionalized person requires "that the benefits of the contemplated procedure clearly outweigh both the known harms and the possible risks or side effects. Ideally, there should be assurance that the proposed procedure is in fact efficacious; and that where the procedure is either intrusive or hazardous, less intrusive or hazardous procedures have first been exhausted" (1975, p. 87). The extent to which a balancing and optimization of conflicting factors is particularly needed when procedures may mean discomfort or physically harmful side effects is further evident in Friedman's analysis of legal principles to the effect that "a relatively safe procedure may not be in a person's best interest if there are even safer or more efficacious procedures available to effect the same behavioral change; conversely, a highly risky procedure or intrusive procedure may be in a client's best interest if the available alternatives are even more risky, more intrusive, or less effective" (p. 88).

The use of "best interest" here appears to be broader than Friedman's, where the discussion was entirely within the framework for determining conditions for the use of hazardous or intrusive procedures. According to Friedman, the determination of best interest in this regard is the "functional equivalent of consent by a competent patient." As with the use of consent procedures, the proposed principles for determinations of best interest appear to be reasonable regulatory safeguards for biomedical procedures in which tissue violations are employed with the hope of bringing about permanent alteration of functioning, with attendant physical risks. However, because of the complex continuing interactional nature of psychosocial procedures—including the more intrusive or those with potentially hazardous side effects—such a dichotomous approach to application or restraint of a single psychosocial procedure does not appear to protect the legitimate interests of institutionalized patients.

Legal and ethical principles that call for therapeutic techniques to employ the least restrictive, intrusive, or hazardous means possible to accomplish treatment goals are best. These determinations for psychosocial procedures, in contrast to biomedical ones, do not appear to be reasonably made outside the context of the total treatment program with knowledge of complementary techniques to be employed. The more restrictive or intrusive psychosocial procedures that may cause temporary discomfort are those that would likely be proposed for elimination or control of excessive or dangerous maladaptive behavior or for increasing motivation to learn and perform adaptive behavior. The evidence indicates that such procedures can be quite effective in relatively mild form compared to those of traditional institutional practices when they are applied in the context of an overall reeducative program with major focus and time devoted to adaptive interactions (see chapter 42; Stolz et al., 1975; Ullmann & Krasner, 1975). However, the same procedures employed in a singular fashion without the complementary constructive techniques can be responsible for some of the most onerous abuses perpetrated upon institutionalized individuals (see Goldiamond, 1975; May, 1975).

Review committee determinations of best interest following the broader contractual model rather than the consensual one would provide much better safeguards against unnecessarily restrictive or intrusive psychosocial procedures. Proposed programs should be scrutinized for specification of the contingency rules in which intrusive procedures would be applied for any class of behavior and for the appropriate sequencing of more intrusive procedures based upon the documented failure of less intrusive ones. However, the ethical acceptability and effectiveness of intrusive procedures in the treatment of the chronically institutionalized mental patient can be determined only in the context of the total system, with knowledge of the positive constructive procedures and interactions to be employed as well. Therefore, no intrusive procedures should be approved for implementation without a full program proposal that also specifies the positive constructional procedures that will be employed and the assessment operations by which monitoring of progress will be accomplished.

To summarize, the major recommendation for attempting to regulate work with long-stay residents of mental institutions centers around an institutional review committee that would combine the features typical of professional review, peer review, human rights, and consent committees proposed elsewhere. The major differences from other proposals in the scope of activities, focus, manner of operation, and composition of the committee are necessary to balance and optimize conflicting factors in different times, places, and circumstances. Rather than attempting to apply existing prescriptive and proscriptive regulations, the major need is in the external review of total program proposals required for all institutional activities, with continuous monitoring of outcomes to provide corrective feedback. Effectiveness and accountability through empirical tests should be the primary components for evaluating the weighting of the ethical principles employed by the committee and for determining the form of continuing programs and procedures.

More specific recommendations proposed to aid in ethical decision making with recalcitrant populations who are unable or unwilling to decide rationally to enter rehabilitation programs relate to the determination of competency, consensual versus contractual models for decision making, and procedures for determining what activities are in the best interest of the patient. An empirical approach to determining the competency of institutionalized persons to negotiate treatment participation in their own behalf is offered on the basis of functioning that meets the minimal goals of institutional treatment—proposed to be a level of functioning that allows safe community placement in a less-restrictive environment. The contractual model with the negotiation and specification of explicit goals, behaviorally contingent methods and procedures, specified time limits, etc., appears to offer major advantages in safeguarding the interests of all affected parties in psychosocial treatment and research. While biomedical procedures lend themselves more to the consensual model, the contractual model is proposed as a superior approach for the operation of review committees as well as for institutionalized persons making decisions in their own behalf about psychosocial activities, since the ongoing interactional complexity of psychosocial programs can be better taken into account. These factors are particularly apparent in the more intrusive psychosocial procedures in which the best interest of institutionalized patients can reasonably be determined only within the context of total program proposals that specify positive constructional procedures and assessment operations, as well as the more intrusive procedures themselves.

All of these recommendations provide an outline of structure and mechanism for ethical regulation of all practices involving long-stay residents of mental institutions, which may provide the flexibility to balance and optimize means and ends, short- and long-term effects, and individual and societal welfare. Like all other proposals, the only way in which the advantages and disadvantages of these recommendations can be determined is to implement the selected actions and empirically evaluate the results in operation. We hope that this can be accomplished in selected institutions because the human and dollar cost of continuing the status quo is too great by any standard.

*Ethical and Legal Status of the Recommended Social-Learning Program*

The ethical and legal issues in the implementation of the social-learning program are of particular importance, since it is recommended for implementation with long-stay patient groups based on documented effectiveness on an absolute level and the comparative effectiveness with regard to alternative practices, which established cause-effect conclusions for the first time in the history of controlled evaluation for any institutional treatment program. Since the social-learning program was not only the most effective but the most cost-effective as well, it is clearly the best treatment from both the economic and right-to-adequate-treatment perspectives.

The social-learning program is also the current treatment of choice for chronically institutionalized mental patients on purely ethical grounds. At the time the comparative project was conducted, both milieu and social-learning programs were probably subject to more ethical and legal approvals, monitoring, and scrutiny than any previous institutional program. Because the project was supported in part by a grant from the National Institute of Mental Health, programs and procedures were approved and monitored not only by the usual departmental and institutional review groups but by outside peer review and human subjects committees at local, state, and federal levels. Further, state legislative investigation and approval occurred in conjunction with accusations of a state representative against the department and the institution, as well as multiple monitoring and approvals in conjunction with hospital accreditation preparations. In addition to compliance with existing statutory and administrative regulations, particular care was taken to ensure that practices and procedures followed the spirit as well as the letter of the ethical guidelines of the American Psychological Association. In short, at the time and place in which the program was conducted, programs and procedures were not only documented to be legal, but through external monitoring, formal and informal staff discussions, and consultations with external sources, the programs reflected the best judgments of ethical practices that could be obtained from a wide variety of broadly experienced persons.

Nevertheless, recent court decisions and legal interpretations raise the specter that major system components of the social-learning program might become so limited as to prevent the most effective treatment from being provided to institutionalized mental patients. As succinctly stated by Wexler, "Indeed, if the law's general direction in the patient rights area proceeds uninterrupted, token economies may well become legally unavailable even if they are therapeutically *superior* to other approaches" (1973, p. 108). The majority of severely limiting conditions, paradoxically, come from the same case that first established a constitutional right to adequate treatment (*Wyatt v. Stickney*) and as such compels compliance only within that jurisdiction. However, the *Wyatt* standards are being taken as a model for administrative and legislative regulations elsewhere ("Wyatt Victory 'Tarnished,'" 1975), and are being accepted as rigid guidelines by some legal writers (e.g., Martin, 1975) and mental health professionals (e.g., Ayllon, 1975).

The unfortunate aspect of these developments is that the interpretations for regulation of future conduct have not been limited to the carefully reasoned principles set out by Judge Frank Johnson in *Wyatt*. Rather, the specific principles and standards enumerated for correcting blatant abuses in particular Alabama institutions at a specific time have also been interpreted as absolutes for regulation elsewhere. The standards have even included the prescription and proscription of structure and process that were required by court order in the *Wyatt* case after the institutions failed to develop adequate plans on their own (see Prigmore & Davis, 1973; Toomey et al., 1975). Acting upon suggestions from a variety of experts who served as amicus curiae, Judge Johnson stated that there are three fundamental conditions necessary for adequate treatment: a humane psychological and physical environment and facilities, qualified staff in numbers sufficient to administer adqauate treatment, and individualized treatment plans (Toomey et al., 1975). These conditions are clearly desirable and should provide a positive focus for developing ethical and legal decisions, without unnecessarily restrictive prescription and proscription of procedure. However, to interpret the specific prescription and proscription of structure and process which Judge Johnson detailed to correct abuses of patient rights in the particular Alabama institutions as absolute standards in other times, places, and circumstances (e.g., Ayllon, 1975; Martin 1975; Wexler, 1973) would result in legal restrictions against the implementation of the social-learning program.

The *Wyatt* standards may have been necessary to correct outrageous conditions in the particular institutions at the time of the ruling. However, it hardly seems likely that the court or the amicus curiae intended to preclude new treatment programs that could provide more effective and adequate treatment than the minimal corrections attempted by the *Wyatt* court. Because of the importance of the ethical issues—whether given legal substance or not— the components and characteristics of the social-learning program that have been the subject of legal concerns elsewhere should be clarified. Such a focus runs the risk of overemphasizing the more controversial aspects of the program, but perhaps the frequent misinterpretations that have been typical of legal discussions of other programs can be prevented, thus reducing the possible misuse of findings and allowing implementation decisions to be made more rationally.

The potential impact of the *Wyatt* decision on the social-learning program has been most provocatively indicated in Wexler's analysis (1973). The *Wyatt* court proscribed "all involuntary patient labor involving hospital operation and maintenance—whether therapeutic or not" and specifically prohibited privileges or release from being contingent "upon the performance of labor involving hospital maintenance" (p. 93). Even voluntary institutional work would require compensation at the prevailing minimum wage. All prevocational and vocational training within the social-learning program associated with individual assignments and odd jobs, as well as aspects of training and performance of self-care related to housekeeping and some components of each resident's own bed and area, would therefore run afoul of the *Wyatt* standards. Even though all of these activities were selected for specific therapeutic purposes, and were voluntarily engaged in by each resident, they are cost saving and contribute to institutional operation and maintenance. Privileges were indirectly contingent upon performance by token earnings at step levels 1-3 and by maintaining status at step 4, and the only monetary compensation involved at all (fifty cents per hour for individual vocational training assignments at steps 3 & 4) was below the minimum wage. Thus, a rigid application of the *Wyatt* standards would presumably rule out these major prevocational and vocational training components of the recommended social-learning program.

The *Wyatt* court also reaffirmed the "least

restrictive conditions necessary to achieve the purposes of commitment" from earlier rulings—a principle that appears to provide a sound basis for developing ethical and legal decisions. However, it was interpreted by Wexler as "presumably including, if clinically acceptable, ground privileges and an open ward" (1973, p. 94). This interpretation seems characteristic of a legal approach to viewing activities dichotomously as fixed or static entities, rather than as interactive components that could reasonably vary with different conditions over time. Even more provocative, along the same line of reasoning, is the major thrust of Wexler's analysis of judicial decisions concerning patients' rights, particularly concerning the possible impact of what can be used as backup reinforcers in token systems: "But, perhaps most significant for token economies. *Wyatt* and related legal developments seem to have a great deal to say regarding the definition of legally acceptable reinforcers . . . The crux of the problem . . . is that the items and activities that are emerging as absolute rights are the very same items and activities that the behavioral psychologists would employ as reinforcers—that is, as 'contingent rights' . . . Thus, the usual target behaviors for token economies would be disallowed and the usual reinforcers will be legally unavailable" (pp. 93-94). In addition to the prohibition of the *Wyatt* court against privileges being contingent upon work related to institutional operation, Wexler's (1973, 1975a,b) interpretation of court-defined rights of institutionalized patients is that items and activities specified as rights must be provided on an absolute, noncontingent basis—i.e., not directly contingent upon other behavior or indirectly contingent upon other behavior as benefits available through token costs.[11]

Since usual token economies vary considerably in the definition of reinforcers and contingency rules, the impact of Wexler's interpretation of the absolute-rights issue on the recommended social-learning program can be determined only by examining the components of the particular program. Of the items and activities mentioned by Wexler (1973) as absolute rights, a closet or locker for personal belongings, personal possessions and clothing, laundry service, a comfortable bed, writing materials, and visitors are provided without token cost in the social-learning program. These items and activities, in fact indirectly provide the opportunity to earn tokens through training in self-care and social interaction, with higher-quality and -quantity items and activities being available for token costs—presumably meeting Wexler's definition of acceptable idiosyncratic backup reinforcers. Other activities mentioned by Wexler as absolute rights are token-earning activities in the first three step levels of the social-learning program, including scheduled physical exercise, interaction with members of the opposite sex, some scheduled recreational activities and instructional movies, and scheduled individual and group sessions and appointments with staff. Opportunity to engage in these activities is not only provided but individually scheduled, shaped, and reinforced by token payment contingent upon appropriate attendance and participation, with detailed monitoring of individualized subtargets.

Several other items and activities mentioned by Wexler as absolute rights are available only through token payment at step levels 1-3 in the recommended social-learning program and are indirectly contingent upon other appropriate behavior via maintaining status at step 4. They include screens or curtains to ensure privacy, a chair, a bedside table, television viewing, some recreational activities and noninstructional movies, religious services, and resident-initiated appointments with staff. All these are completely contingent upon token exchange or step 4 status, although considerable efforts using sampling-exposure procedures were necessary to encourage residents to utilize them in the comparative project. Television viewing and some recreational activities also provide the opportunity to earn tokens through social interaction, but admission to these activities is a token-cost event.

Passes and food are also token-cost events but use more complex operating rules (see chapters 8 & 13; appendix C).[12] Admission to regular meals requires token exchange; however, continuous monitoring of actual consumption and body weight provides an override of token contingencies when necessary to ensure adequate nutrition. Thus, whether because of an absence of tokens or a refusal to eat, the medical meal procedure (appendix C) ensures an appropriate minimum diet for any resident who is below 90% of ideal weight, has failed to maintain adequate nutrition through meals purchased with tokens, or has a physical condition requiring a special diet. Food is also used as a direct reinforcer in shaping class (appendix C) for the lowest-functioning residents. Except for these four conditions, food is available only upon payment of tokens or step 4 status. Early meals, extra portions of food, candies, cookies, etc., and special foods are all available as token-cost items, but these consumables would presumably meet Wexler's (1973) definition of "acceptable" idiosyncratic rather than "primitive" backup reinforcers. Entry to either regular or early meals also provides the opportunity to earn tokens through acquisition of appropriate meal behavior, but admission remains a token-cost event.

Passes are available only as token-cost activities, although downtown training classes are token-earning events. Freedom to come and go off the treatment unit (similar to grounds privileges or open ward status in traditional settings) and the nature of passes available—accompanied or unaccompanied, center, downtown, etc.—are also indirectly contingent upon other resident behavior qualifying for a defined step level status. Thus, before being eligible to purchase an unaccompanied center pass, a resident would have to demonstrate safe and acceptable performance on an accompanied center pass, an absence of dangerous and aggressive acts, and minimal adaptive behavior on the unit to indicate the ability to leave and return in safety. Similar requirements exist for each level of pass involving greater distances, time, and more complex environments, as well as assignment to training positions involving freedom of movement off the treatment unit. These determinations are continuously operationalized by monitoring actual performance that meets the requirements for the given step level status rather than being fixed or static. A specified number of successful performances on each type of pass is also required for advancement to higher step levels, which provide the opportunity for greater token earnings, but passes themselves remain token-cost events.

These items and activities constitute only a portion of those provided to all residents, as token-earning, or as token-cost events in the recommended social-learning program; however, they appear to cover all items and activities Wexler calls absolute (1973).[13] By his interpretation, all of the above token-cost items and activities would be automatically precluded for the social-learning program by rigid application of *Wyatt*-type standards, since "drastic deprivations" are inferred when "absolute" rights are available only on a contingent basis. Although the items and activities provided as givens or as token-earning events in the social-learning program would not automatically run afoul of the legal interpretations, the fact that time-out procedures are a regular component of the recommended program presumably would. The defining characteristic of time-out in the social-learning program is that the opportunity to earn or spend tokens or to use other facilities and services is temporarily removed contingent upon the performance of specified inappropriate behaviors. By definition, all token-earning, all token-cost, and some given items and activities that Wexler defines as "absolute" rights to be available noncontingently are temporarily unavailable as contingent consequences for certain inappropriate behaviors—becoming available once again after specified time periods with performance of appropriate behavior. Thus, by Wexler's interpretation, time-out procedures would be automatically precluded in the social-learning program.

The components of the program that use more intrusive procedures or aversive stimuli need consideration since the *Wyatt* standards could also have impact here. Although considerable legal attention has been directed to aversive, intrusive, or restrictive psychosocial procedures—generally based upon the "least drastic means" rationale (Friedman, 1975)—the *Wyatt* standards were proscriptive of specific activities as additional rights of patients. According to *Wyatt*, patients have a right not to be subjected to "aversive reinforcement conditioning" and to be "free from isolation" (Martin, 1975, p. 178). The court further prescribed that patients could be placed in isolation or physical restraints for a time limit of one hour in emergency situations, but only on the order of a qualified mental health professional (Martin, 1975; Prigmore & Davis, 1973). Thus, similar to other components of the *Wyatt* ruling, the attempt to correct blatant abuses in particular Alabama institutions resulted in the blanket proscription of an entire class of procedures considered "unusual or hazardous," as well as prescription of the specific process by which isolation could be used.

Presumably the procedures proscribed under *Wyatt* could extend to any "aversive," "restrictive," or "intrusive" procedure, as those terms have been used elsewhere (e.g., Friedman, 1975; Stolz et al., 1975). Friedman points out that the determination of intrusiveness or restrictiveness "is largely a matter of subjective opinion and theoretical disposition" (p. 90). Therefore, at the risk of overemphasizing aversive components that play an important but exceptionally limited role in the social-learning program, all programmatic procedures that might cause even temporary discomfort will be summarized. These components all involve procedures directed at the reduction, elimination, or control of excessive or dangerous maladaptive behavior or those intended to increase motivational states to learn and perform adaptive behavior.

The majority of procedures in the recommended social-learning program that are directed toward reducing maladaptive behavior and increasing motivation consist of contingent positive reinforcement for adaptive behavior through both social and material consequences. Probably the least intrusive of the active, possibly aversive programmatic procedures—procedures that can occasionally cause mild discomfort for some individuals—are the active ignoring of bizarre behavior and the verbal prompts for individual consequences that would ensue contingent upon alternative courses of action available to the resident who is behaving inappropriately. In either case, the termination of the ongoing inappropriate behavior and engagement in adaptive activity would receive a positive material and/or social consequence. If these procedures failed to terminate ongoing maladaptive activity and institute adaptive behavior, staff would use a more intrusive consequence, which varies according to the class and severity of maladaptive behavior. In the case of bizarre behavior that interferes with adaptive performance or a maladaptive failure to perform appropriate behavior to the individual's specified criterion, the consequences would be the failure to receive a token, plus additional verbal prompts. Since the next higher criterion for each behavior is maintained through two consecutive failures before lowering the individual's criterion, continued failure would reduce the range and amount of desired token-cost items and activities that the person could acquire. Thus, continued maladaptive behavior would automatically result in the next more intrusive consequence—withholding admittance to facilities and services or access to consumables for which token payments were not made. More extreme continuations of such maladaptive behavior would result in more instances of discomfort through access to fewer backup reinforcers until the combination of lowered criteria and improved functioning once again resulted in higher token-earnings.

Token response-costs (fines) and time out constitute the next more intrusive negative consequences for the more severe maladaptive behaviors that are not eliminated or controlled by reinforcement of incompatible appropriate activities and/or verbal prompts.[14] These procedures have mild aversive properties that are designed to terminate the more severe maladaptive behaviors (those that violate unit rules and would not be allowed in the outside community), thereby allowing the resident to participate in the positive, constructive activities of the program. Minor infractions (behavior that is so inappropriate and offensive that it would result in a person's being removed if it occurred in the lobby of a crowded theater) and major infractions (behavior that interferes with the rights of others and is so inappropriate that it would result in a person's being arrested if it occurred in the lobby of a crowded theater) both result in brief time out in seclusion and token response costs—with greater response costs for the more severe class of inappropriate behavior (see appendix B). Since payment on token fines reduces the purchasing power for backup reinforcers, additional instances of discomfort result from the fine. The length of contingent time out in seclusion for both minor and major infractions is for the remainder of the forty-five-minute functional period, with a minimum stay of twenty minutes. The actual length of time spent in time out in seclusion for performing an inappropriate behavior of the severity of minor and major infractions could range from twenty to sixty-five minutes, with release and reentry to constructive activities before the start of the next functional period being contingent upon fifteen minutes of quiet activity.

Since the immediacy and consistency of contingent application of response costs and time out in seclusion are the primary effective ingredients, any trained staff member can be responsible for applying these consequences upon the observed occurrence of a specified inappropriate behavior by a resident who is that staff member's responsibility. That staff member is then responsible for completing a written report form detailing the inappropriate behavior, the stimulus setting, and the consequence applied for daily review by professional staff; a form on the time-out room door indicating the time in and time of release; a fine sheet indicating the nature and amount of token response cost, the amount paid, and the total accumulated fine remaining, if any; and in the event that a fine remains to be paid, changes on all token payment forms to indicate that the resident must make a payment on the standing fine to be eligible to purchase any other backup reinforcer. A specified staff member is responsible for checking and recording the status of any resident in time out every fifteen minutes by observation through a door window and for releasing the resident at the appropriate time with prompts for adaptive behavior in the next scheduled activity.

Token response costs and brief time out in seclusion for minor and major infractions are intended to function as negative reinforcers to terminate more severe inappropriate behavior and allow positive reinforcement of adaptive behavior to remain dominant. The proportional-payoff feature of fine payments by which longer periods of time without new infractions result in a larger reduction on standing fines for each token payment, is also designed to provide a greater incentive for continued control of more severe maladaptive behavior. Failure of all of these procedures to eliminate severe inappropriate behavior and allow increased adaptive activities in their place gradually results in more-aversive consequences as a function of continuing performance of the severe inappropriate behaviors. Each successive instance of a minor or major infraction results in brief time out in seclusion and an application of the token response cost. Thus, continued performance of those classes of maladaptive behavior results in higher accumulated fines and less opportunity to earn tokens, so the primary backup reinforcers would eventually be affected. Access to regular meals would become affected at the point where available tokens were inadequate to pay for all meals, plus at least a one token payment on the fine. Additionally, for residents who continued severe maladaptive behavior without performance of adaptive behavior to the point of accumulating fines of thirty tokens or more (equivalent to fifteen consecutive minor infractions or three consecutive major infractions without a single payment on the accumulated fine), regular beds are lost as a function of spending the night in time out until adaptive behavior results in fine payments to reduce the total below thirty tokens.[15] Any reduction in the frequency of the severe maladaptive behaviors immediately reduces the negative consequences and results in positive social and/or material consequences for adaptive behavior.

These procedures for dealing with major and minor infractions are regular programmatic components to be automatically followed by any trained staff member, with daily review of the detailed recordings of staff and resident behavior by senior staff. If a resident fails to reduce his or her severe maladaptive behaviors or to increase adaptive behaviors through the regular programmatic procedures, more aversive stimuli may be added to remove possible positive features of time out (see chapter 18). These more aversive components can be applied only on the direction of a trained professional staff member after review by the senior staff in the weekly meeting. The intermittent and unpredictable tooting of an aerosol air horn or spray of water mist through a high window while a chronic offender is in the time-out room is the first level of more aversive stimuli applied. If the severe maladaptive behaviors still continue, a special order to provide aversive heat-humidity conditions in the room can be invoked. However, even these conditions, which are intended to have aversive properties, are considerably less aversive on an absolute level than those usually existing in state mental hospitals. All of these conditions are monitored and determined daily by a specified senior staff member, and aversive conditions are terminated as soon as the resident begins to reduce the incidence of the severe maladaptive behavior, with corresponding increases of adaptive behavior and positive reinforcement procedures.

Procedures intended to be the most intrusive or aversive of all the techniques in the recommended social-learning program are directed toward eliminating physical assaults. The regular programmatic procedures recommended for controlling physical attacks or direct attempts or threats to do bodily harm are the same as those employed for other severe maladaptive behaviors, but they start with stronger negative consequences. Thus, if a verbal prompt fails to prevent an impending attack, the offender is immediately placed in time out in seclusion from the time of the incident until 5:30 the following morning and is fined twenty-five tokens. The period of time out functionally runs from four to twenty-three and a half hours, with all other recording, observation, monitoring, and contingency procedures being identical to those of the briefer time-out procedures. Because of the longer time periods, a resident in extended time out is provided the opportunity to use a restroom at scheduled times (approximately every four hours) and a medical meal if the period results in such a nutritional requirement. The longer time-out period and larger token response cost thus provide conditions intended to be more severely taxing as a consequence for assault, while providing the resident a fresh start in the constructive activities of the program at the beginning of the next day. Continued assaultive behavior without increases in adaptive functioning would result in the same sequential additions in the aversive characteristics of the time-out room described above for severe nonassaultive maladaptive behavior.

Physical force or restraint is the most intrusive procedure of all in the recommended social-learning program, and these procedures are limited in application to the minimum required to prevent physical harm or to eliminate assaultive behavior.[16] Force is sometimes needed to separate residents involved in a physical altercation or to restrain an assaultive resident en route to the time-out room. One to two staff members or a staff member and a student worker would apply only enough physical force to prevent the residents from harming themselves or others if they refused to respond to verbal instructions to terminate the attack and enter the time-out room. Assaultive residents who still failed to eliminate such dangerous and aggressive acts after the sequential application of the more aversive procedures of response-costs and time out in seclusion would receive time out with overcorrection/ restitution on an individual basis. These procedures require physical prompts on occasion to maintain the extra resident effort required, as well as occasional physical restraint by staff to inhibit attacks and bodily harm during the presentation of critical stimuli and prevention of inappropriate habitual responses (see chapters 33 & 42). As with other aversive consequences, the overcorrection/restitution procedures stop when the resident no longer performs the inappropriate behavior and is once again engaging in adaptive behavior with the major emphasis on positive material and/or social consequences. The primary difference from the termination of other aversive procedures is that active adaptive behavior without inappropriate behavior is required continuously for a full half-hour before the time out with overcorrection/

restitution is terminated and the resident returns to the usual constructive activities of the program.

These procedures should cover all negative components of the recommended social-learning program that could be considered aversive, restrictive, or intrusive by nearly any standard—with consequent deemphasis of the far more frequent positive procedures. Rigid application of the *Wyatt* standards to specific components of the social-learning program, rather than consideration of the integrated constructive/ eliminative package of procedures, would result in most unusual decisions. All time-out procedures using seclusion would automatically be precluded, since emergency applications (assaults) are longer than one hour (documented to be an ineffective length of time), and other applications constitute neither emergencies nor applications individually ordered by professional staff. Depending upon the breadth of interpretation of the proscribed aversive reinforcement, all procedures with any intent to establish mildly aversive consequences could presumably be prohibited, including token responses costs. The absence of effective backup reinforcers resulting from the presumed restrictions on token-cost items and activities described earlier and the absence of nearly all negative consequences would of course remove the basis for verbal prompts, including the specification of consequences. Paradoxically, the most intrusive specific procedure of all, overcorrection/restitution, would presumably be allowed, since the physical restraint involved occurs in emergency situations, is ordered by professional staff, and lasts less than one hour in any particular application. Thus, only two social-learning procedures would apparently be legally available to reduce, eliminate, or control excessive and dangerous maladaptive behavior or to increase motivational states if rigid application of the detailed *Wyatt* standards were to occur: active ignoring and emergency overcorrection/restitution with physical restraint.

Clearly, the application of the specific structure and process of the *Wyatt* standards as absolute prescription and proscription of individual procedures following Wexler's (1973) interpretation and the assumptions of others (e.g., Ayllon, 1975; Martin, 1975) would eviscerate the social-learning program. Perhaps such a total proscription should be considered if the recommended program were in fact—as Wexler (1973, 1975b) apparently believes—a "drastic scheme" involving such "massive deprivations" that it would be difficult to contend it could ever be in the best interest of institutionalized mental patients. Drastic schemes with massive deprivations would very likely violate the fundamental "humane psychological and physical environment" condition proposed by the *Wyatt* court as necessary for adequate treatment, in addition to the standards set out to correct abuses in the Alabama institutions.

The onerous tone of legal discussions of the more intrusive procedures involved in the social-learning program typically results from the presentation and interpretation of specific techniques in isolation as fixed or static entities rather than as limited components of a complex interactive package that includes positive, constructive techniques as well. However, even with this inappropriate focus, compare the most intrusive of the recommended psychosocial procedures with the "alternative" active treatments proposed for the chronic mental patient: "If, after one to two years of combined drug, ECT, and milieu therapy, there is not a substantial response to treatment, IST, with or without ECT, should be seriously considered. By this time the patient would seem to be headed for a lifetime of chronic illness and hospitalization, and the risks of IST to interrupt this career are justified. Finally, if the patient has been continuously ill for several years . . . pyschosurgery should be considered. Without psychosurgery, the patient is virtually doomed to a lifetime of tragic disquietude; with it, there is a small chance of surcease" (Rosenbaum, 1970, pp. 293-294).[17] Given such alternative proposals for active treatment, even psychosocial programs that were drastic schemes with massive deprivations would deserve consideration if their effectiveness could avoid such permanent intrusions of tissue with attendant physical hazards.

Exactly how drastic the scheme and how massive the deprivations actually are in the social-learning program is an important question for consideration in making implementation decisions. The patients participating in the comparative project were the most severely disabled of those ever subjected to systematic study. Empirical data on their experience should thus provide the most extreme picture of the level of deprivation or intrusiveness likely to be encountered elsewhere with the full implementation of the recommended social-learning program and assessment systems. Residents in the social-learning program clearly used fewer facilities and services and obtained fewer consumables than those in the milieu program did where specific performance contingencies were not required. Consumable items (food, cigarettes, etc.) were also more potent as backup reinforcers than facilities and services in the social-learning program. However, contrary to the notion that the amount of material goods and services are in the best interest of the residents, the social-learning group showed significantly greater improvement with lower rates of utilization of all resources than the milieu group did. Additionally utilization rates were significantly related to improvement for social-learning residents but not for milieu residents. Thus, even with the relatively low levels of facilities, services, and consumables available, how they were obtained (contingent rather than noncontingent) was considerably more important than how much was available. These facts appear to verify a note of Wexler's that is not in keeping with the thrust of his article: "it may be far more therapeutic to provide patients with certain privileges absolutely than it is to deny them those privileges absolutely, but . . . it is better still to provide the privileges on a contingent basis" (1973, p. 101).

The continuous objective observations on the SRIC and Clinical Frequencies Recordings provide empirical data on the absolute level of deprivation or intrusion actually experienced in the total integrated program. Even with the larger token response-costs for the majority of the intramural period (see chapter 28) and the ineffective length of time out for eighteen months (see chapter 24), residents in the social-learning program averaged only 9.16 instances per week of active "deprivation" or "intrusion" involving material goods, facilities, or services over the entire intramural period. Put another way, the average social-learning resident was denied access to any items or activities he or she attempted to acquire, was placed in time out, or paid tokens for fines rather than backup reinforcers—in total—on fewer than ten occasions per week. Of these negative events, time out in seclusion averaged only 1.67 instances per resident per week over the entire intramural period, even for the severely disturbed population, reflecting the success of verbal prompts and positive reinforcement in terminating inappropriate behavior (always greater than 94%). Thus, the presence of consistent positive and negative consequences increased the effectiveness of purely verbal procedures so that negative consequences were applied very infrequently.

Meal consumption was analyzed separately, since residents who had not earned enough tokens to purchase meals might simply fail to appear rather than attempt to enter and be denied admission. Also, food was the major primary reinforcer employed in the program. The greatest number of missed meals for social-learning residents averaged 9.52 per week, which occurred at the beginning of the program when motivational effects had not yet produced major improvements in token-reinforced functioning. The fewest number of missed meals—an average of 4.68 per resident per week—occurred during the period of maximum rates of improvement, just before the externally imposed reduction in time out in seclusion for assaults.

The analyses also revealed that the second largest number of missed meals for social-learning residents for the entire intramural period occurred during the last twenty weeks of the intramural program ($\bar{X}=9.46$ per week) when regular meals were provided without token charge but required a twenty-minute wait. Thus, for the long-stay population involved in the comparative project—even after showing major improvements in functioning—special meals were worth extra token payments for only a few residents and the additional delay to receive a basic (and therefore free) meal resulted in more missed meals than had occurred when token payments were required for all meals. Over the entire intramural project period, social-learning residents actually missed an average of 6.21 meals per week for any reason whatsoever. This figure compares with an average of 5.10 missed per week for residents in the milieu program and an average of 7.00 missed per week for the project director over the same period.

The actual amount of deprivation or intrusion caused by the contingency requirements and the application of procedures with intentional aversive components appears neither especially drastic nor massive when the procedures are integrated into the total social-learning program, which emphasizes positive, constructive, reeducational procedures. In fact, if only the nonsocial items and activities are considered, the average social-learning resident actually received material goods, services, and consumables in a positive-to-negative ratio of over twenty-three to one (i.e., for every instance in which an item or activity was denied or taken away, more than twenty-three items or activities were actively provided, compared to less than three to one in the milieu program). If social activities and attention from staff are taken into account as well, only 7.5% of all staff-resident interactions within the social-learning program consisted of any negative components, including active ignoring, compared to 12.3% within the milieu program and 20.9% within the traditional hospital programs. When the greater freedom from psychotropic drugs is added to the emphasis on the positive aspects of resident experience, the social-learning program emerges as not only absent of massive deprivations but as the most humane psychological and physical environment of all those provided for the chronically institutionalized.

In fact the recommended social-learning program and assessment systems may systematize and protect human rights better than other alternatives currently available for the chronically institutionalized mental patient. The defined and assessed performance criteria and contingency rules ensure the least restrictive or intrusive means necessary within the treatment program itself. Rather than the impractical suggestion that total programs be graded for intrusiveness and patients entered after failing in other programs (e.g. Wexler, 1973), the social-learning program as recommended provides the least intrusive treatment for each resident, nearly automatically.[18] By carefully assessing each component behavior for each resident in a detailed and individualized manner by the Clinical Frequencies Recording System and the TSBC, the achievements, excesses, and deficits in each area of functioning can determine the goals to be focused upon and the level achieved. Deprivations or more aversive procedures are only used contingent upon specific resident behaviors; thus, none at all would occur for the resident who responded positively to idiosyncratic goods and services, social reinforcement, and instruction alone.

Since the step system does not determine available reinforcers or privileges beyond the nature of passes and training positions that would be allowed (with attendant increases in available tokens and money), possible restrictions greater than that needed would be limited to the two- to three-week period necessary for assessment and determination of functioning. The brief restriction to accompanied passes and supervised activities with observation—which reasonably protects both the resident and the community—seems preferable to making placement and privilege decisions on a single determination of what is clinically acceptable, based upon the usual five-minute interview by a professional or on the more frequent undocumented recommendation of an aide. Further, the performance qualifications for advancing to step 2 in the social-learning program parallel our earlier recommendations for determining minimal goals of effective institutional treatment. Thus, if suggestions for an empirical determination of competency for institutionalized individuals to negotiate contractual treatment agreements or release to less-restrictive community settings on their own behalf are followed, entry into a fully operative social-learning program as recommended would also ensure maximum individual determination and freedom of choice within a minimum period. Incorporation of these recommendations could possibly improve the likelihood of the least-restrictive-means principle being put into operation in an "optimized" fashion, not only within the institutional program itself but with regard to being in the institution as well.

The mechanisms for ethical regulation of all institutional practices would likely not only approve but encourage the recommended social-learning program and assessment procedures on the basis of the documentation in this book.

In fact, the data presented here clearly indicate that "a re-evaluation of the emerging law might very well be in order" (Wexler, 1973, p. 102). Even without changes in current law and mechanisms for ethical regulation, it appears that the recommended program could be legally implemented by "waiver" for "incompetent patients" and "consent" for "competent patients" (Friedman, 1975, p. 75). However, implementation of the social-learning program, with or without modification, is recommended only when continuing assessment procedures for monitoring both staff and residents are included. Without the mechanisms for ethical review and monitoring, the only program that is recommended is the social-learning program with all assessments, including the Clinical Frequencies Recording System, Time-Sample Behavioral Checklist, and Staff-Resident Interaction Chronograph (see chapters 5 & 11; Paul, in press).

## FURTHER CONSIDERATIONS FOR IMPROVING INSTITUTIONAL PRACTICES

The ethical issues and legal trends appear to be the most critical factors related to both the implementation of the earlier recommendations and to ultimate improvement of any future institutional treatment or evaluation effort. Several other important factors should be noted here, too.

Ongoing assessment operations are clearly a prerequisite to either adequate research or treatment with institutionalized patients (see chapters 3, 5, 11, & 42). Without such assessments of both staff and resident behavior, neither treatment staff, investigators, nor institutional review committees—nor, in some instances, even the institutionalized people themselves—have a sound basis for decision making. The observational assessment systems employed in the comparative project offer the most detailed, reliable, and valid procedures for ongoing assessments yet available. They have the unique advantage of providing objective data on particular behaviors of residents with time-place-circumstance specificity in enough detail to provide day-to-day treatment programming and evaluation of resident functioning and staff performance while concurrently providing higher level scores for overall comparative program descriptions and evaluations. These assessment systems are not only necessary to the social-learning program but are desirable for any other program for long-stay residents of mental institutions (see Paul, in press).

The institutional administrative structure and physical location of programs for the chronically institutionalized can be important determinants of the viability of any programmatic undertaking. The usual institutional settings available within the public mental health system—state mental hospitals and smaller community mental health centers—are capable of housing and supporting active treatment programs similar to that recommended. The crucial feature for effective program development and staff functioning in both settings appears to be decentralization to a goal-oriented unit system in which competency and accountability are the defining characteristics of authority rather than professional title or discipline (see chapters 4 & 5). The needed competencies for designing, implementing, and evaluating treatment programs to change psychosocial and behavioral problems are not ensured by degree credentials and are notably unrelated to medical training.[19] Thus, the usual hospital structure, which is appropriate for dealing with physical problems, not only seems contratherapeutic by communicating an illness model to the institutionalized individual but also carries with it an administrative organization that sets conditions that do not encourage efficient and effective psychosocial approaches (see chapters 4, 5, 9, & 28). These problems of public institutions, among others, have led some to recommend moderately sized, privately operated residential treatment facilities as a means of circumventing the entire hospital structure (see Saper, 1975). We have similarly recommended that community extended-care facilities currently housing higher-functioning ex-residents released from public mental institutions provide a base for implementation of effective rehabilitation programs (chapter 42; Kohen & Paul, 1976). However, these alternatives seem unlikely for the severely debilitated population who will be accounting for an increasingly larger proportion of those in residence in public mental institutions.

Although smaller community mental health centers are gradually replacing larger state hospitals, the staff of the newer centers have usually not been exposed to the chronic population. When they are, they may find themselves ill equipped to deal with these people in the usual program (e.g., Greenblatt, 1965; Kraft et al., 1967) and are unaware of the magnitude of the problems posed by such "uninteresting cases" (e.g., DiMascio & Evans, 1965). The inclusion of units for the chronically institutionalized within the newer community mental health centers to provide both treatment and staff training might have the added advantage of inducing a few of the more zealous professionals to expand effective services to the large residual population of state hospitals. Psychosocial treatment programs for the chronically institutionalized, including the recommended social-learning program, would seem to be most desirably located in small private residential facilities in the community for residents working on optimal goals and in smaller community mental health centers for those working on minimal goals and optimal goals, with location in public hospitals being least desirable.

More important than the physical location is the institutional administrative structure, which can encourage the competency and accountability of effective treatment operations, with continuity of responsibility in the extramural environment after institutional release (see illustrative cases, chapter 19; chapter 38). Goal-directed, decentralized, and unitized administrative organization, with permanent rather than rotating staff and competency-based authority and responsibility as implemented in the regional center and the psychosocial unit, are desirable—if not necessary—structures for implementing psychosocial programs in any location (see chapters 4 & 5).

Staffing levels, staff training, and staff utilization are crucial determinants of both costs and effectiveness of any institutional program. Staff functioning and morale cannot be taken for granted, and staff problems cannot be treated as isolated incidents. Rather, the ongoing functioning of the staff group must be recognized for the complex social system it is, with mechanisms built in for continuous communication and monitoring of staff problems as well as for implementation of programmatic procedures. These characteristics are even more important in work with the severely debilitated population in which observable change in resident behavior is slow and staff exposure to dangerous and distasteful conditions is high. In the conduct of the comparative project, the usual amount of such staff problems was encountered; however, the administrative structure, training techniques, monitoring procedures, and communication networks implemented not only led to exceptional levels of performance but to greater identification with the unit and more rapid resolution of morale problems. These effects were apparent in staff activity levels that exceeded those of other units by a ratio of over four to one, while demonstrating an accuracy of performance unequalled elsewhere and showing attitudinal and technique preferences in keeping with the desired psychosocial orientation (see chapters 5, 9, 16, 21, 26, & 31). Further indications of positive identification and morale were apparent in more subtle indicators, such as willingness to work at unscheduled times, refusal of the entire staff of the psychosocial unit to participate in a walkout to protest a delay in salary increases, and almost no enrollment in the employee's union (until the statewide layoffs that led to the termination of the psychosocial unit and the appointment of the new superintendent).

Similar positive attitudes, program identification, and improved performances have been reported elsewhere as a result of a genuine emphasis on the value of preprofessional staff, focused training in specific psychosocial procedures, and objective evaluation of actual staff behavior within a structured setting (see Allen et al., 1974; Ellsworth & Ellsworth, 1970; Harris et al., 1974; Milby et al., 1975; chapter 10). Characteristics of staff utilization within the psychosocial unit appear to have been particularly useful in maintaining such positive features, even with low staffing levels and the resultant desirable cost-effectiveness ratios. The involvement of all professional staff in decision making, with responsibility for on-the-floor clinical work, as well as supervision, administration, and all other other actions within the integrated unit, while maintaining cross-training and competency criteria, seems particularly important (see chapters 4, 5, 9, 10, & 23). In fact, the only serious problems among professional staff in the comparative project occurred before the complete involvement of auxiliary staff was implemented, with ensuing resolution when all professional staff (other than the consulting physician) were included in the senior staff group. The parallel focus for junior staff, plus scheduling of paperwork at times that did not interfere with resident contact, similarly contributed to the positive features.

In fact, the exceptionally positive results in the comparative project on staffing, staff training, and staff utilization were strong enough to recommend implementation of the entire structure elsewhere, with few changes. One recommended change is that some senior staff should be assigned to cover usual off-hours on a regular basis, rather than intermittently, by assignment to split shifts or revolving shifts. This change is based upon the empirical findings of greater resident improvement when full coverage of off hours occurred (see chapters 19, 24, & 42). Second, the use of volunteers should be limited to nonprogrammatic functions in the social-learning program, without any direct resident training responsibilities. Contrary to usual institutional settings, in which untrained volunteers are found to make positive contributions to patient functioning (see Rappaport et al., 1971), interactional requirements in the social-learning program are sufficiently detailed that volunteers tend to get in the way of trained staff. They are, however, exceptionally useful in providing access to off-unit facilities and services and in-community experiences at little cost, with positive educational and personal outcomes for the volunteers themselves. Finally, more trained professional staff would be necessary if the resident population required additional direct treatment of maladaptive behaviors based upon respondent problems. Otherwise, the intramural administrative structure, training techniques, monitoring procedures, communication network, staffing levels and mode of staff utilization employed for the psychosocial unit are recommended for adoption upon the implementation of the social-learning program, with the operating principles appearing desirable for any other psychosocial program as well (see chapters 4, 5, 10, & 42).

Politics, bureaucratic procedures, and sources of support provide endless frustrations and may be the ultimate deterrent to improving institutional practices. The recent literature has emphasized the difficulties of "institutional politics" that have led to problems in implementing token-economy programs (see Richards, 1975) and more general problems of instituting behavioral programs in any "natural" setting (Reppucci & Saunders, 1974). Although the focus has been on behavioral programs in particular, the problems are those that would require attention upon attempts to implement any program that differed from the status quo. In fact, the characteristics and tactics Richards described for the "successful program politician" are likely to be employed to some extent by any institutional unit director who successfully implements and maintains any program at all.

However, within the framework of the decentralized unit system the demonstrated competency and reliability of the professional staff who have administrative contact with others outside the unit, including centralized services and administrators, typically result in minimal intrainstitutional conflict of the type Richards described. In fact, a normal concern for the other individuals as people rather than as competitors or bureaucrats—including sufficient concern to learn the regulations and evaluative system in which they must operate—usually results in cooperative support in accomplishing reasonably explained and detailed goals to the limits the bureaucratic system will allow (chapters 4, 13, & 18). Similarly, all of the problems described by Reppucci and Saunders (1974) appear to be reasonably handled by the provision of clearly specified treatment programs with defined goals and responsibilities and the administrative structure, staff training and monitoring procedures recommended above—all the problems, that is, with the notable exception of those stemming from the state and federal bureaucratic systems themselves and external politically based actions.

Ullmann (1967) and Saper (1975) have detailed the characteristics of the government bureaucracies in federal (Veterans Administration) and state mental institutions, respectively, which tend to displace efforts from the primary function of effective treatment to maintenance of a smoothly running system. In these systems, authority is diffused over a specialized hierarchy of intermediate and central office groups or individual people who, because of their distance from performance sites and a lack of understanding of undertakings, tend to focus on generation and compliance with a detailed network of rules on which to base decisions. Each group generates some of its own rules, and staff at each level of review within the hierarchy come to be dominated by rigid application of the regulations to avoid reprimands for deviation. These conditions lead to rigid inflexible decisions, conflicting regulations, increased paperwork, and large time lags in accomplishing even routine acquisitions, let alone introducing changes from routine procedures. Further, funding criteria are seldom related to the effectiveness of institutions or programs; they are more frequently based upon easily counted criteria, such as size of physical plant, number of staff or staff contacts, or the number of resident beds filled.

In the comparative project, there was a reasonably successful cooperative effort of institutional and administrative personnel in identifying persons in intermediary and central office positions who could cut through regulations to accomplish changes and speed up some routine procedures (see chapters 4, 9, 13, 18, 23, & 28). However, even in instances in which successful acquisition of unusual items (e.g., bicycle locks for cabinets) or changes in conflicting regulations (e.g., to allow residents to accumulate funds before release) were accomplished, some processes required from twelve to thirty-six months to be approved. Even then, large amounts of time had to be devoted to the most mundane of routine changes (e.g., the project director and business manager on one occasion spent an hour and a half arranging changes in the usual state procedures for acquisition and distribution of toilet paper to ensure that residents' toilets had adequate supplies). In addition to the ongoing frustrations of changing or working around conflicting and restrictive regulations with long time lags, departmentwide directives, such as arbitrary hiring freezes and unexpected salary increases, certainly support Saper's (1975) observation that long-range planning is risky. In fact, the combination of yearly budget determinations based upon criteria unrelated to treatment effectiveness, combined with arbitrary changes in staffing and salaries and ongoing paperwork and time lags, provide conditions in which bureaucratic barriers to planning and implementation of effective institutional programs is likely to be so aversive that few institutional unit directors will be willing to put forth the effort required (see chapter 33).

A combination of changes following those recommended by Ullmann (1967) and Saper (1975) might reduce the bureaucratic barriers and shift incentives in a direction that encourages planning and implementation of effective institutional programs. A drastic change should be considered in usual bureaucratic practices and funding criteria to the extent that responsibility for all aspects of budgetary management, staffing, supplies, etc.—all program components except maintenance functions—be decentralized to the program subunits on a block-grant, performance-contracting basis. If the procedures recommended for establishing mechanisms for ethical regulation were to be extended to funding of program operations as well, many of the bureaucratic barriers in usual operations might be overcome. Program proposals could also include a planned budget for operations that could be approved as a fixed amount available as a block grant to unit directors to accomplish the approved program. Without unexpected reductions or forced increase in costs, unit directors might find much more efficient means of staffing (without being bound by civil service categories) and more rapid and less expensive means of obtaining needed equipment and supplies than through central purchasing departments. Ongoing monitoring could then focus upon compliance with approved proposals, with periodic audits. Future funding levels and continuation or discontinuation of specific program components could then be based upon the empirically monitored outcomes achieved. Similar criteria could be applied to total institutions, as well as subunits. Kohen and Paul (1976) provide more specific recommendations on the way such a block-grant, performance-contracting approach might be applied to private extended-care rehabilitation facilities to provide incentives for effective treatment without increases in costs to the taxpayers.

The recommendations for funding institutional treatment units on a block-grant, performance-contracting basis share obvious similarities to the procedures followed in submitting research proposals and making grant awards through the National Institute of Mental Health (NIMH). Although the procedural model for NIMH research grants is in fact the model recommended, NIMH operating procedures themselves are not, since the NIMH bureaucracy itself produces numerous problems. The bureaucratic barriers in NIMH research funding appear to operate as much to discourage applied research as institutional bureaucratic barriers operate to discourage implementation of effective treatment. While the peer review system seems to provide the best available means for judging proposals, the extensive committee review procedures at several hierarchical levels and resulting increases in time and paperwork before peer review cause long delays between the submission of proposals and notification of action. Particularly for applied research, such delays—which can be twelve to forty months from submission to the receipt of awards—nearly ensure that commitments of staff, agencies, facilities, and salaries will be different by the actual starting date than they were at the time the proposal was prepared. Even after initial approvals and awards, the yearly question of amount of funds to be available, combined with impoundments and vetos of budgets which lead to delays in notification of awards beyond necessary starting dates, not only results in a very wary staff—who risk unemployment on a yearly basis or less—but also affects the design and operation of the applied research project itself (see chapters 3, 13, 33, 37, & 41). If good applied research is to be encouraged, granting agencies must also find some means of reducing or eliminating unnecessary duplications in review procedures and resulting time and paper demands, shortening the delay between proposal submission and the notification of awards, and making firm block-grant commitments for full project periods, which would be subject to monitoring but would not be dependent upon yearly determination of budgets on anything other than performance grounds.

All of these problems of bureaucracies and sources of funding are discouraging, but they can be negotiated and reasonably overcome if unit directors and investigators are willing to make the effort required. However, there is little hope of good institutional practices surviving massive assaults by top-level politicians who have no regard for empirically based quality and effectiveness of treatment, given the lack of accountability to continuing commitments that exists in current mental health bureaucracies. Even if such a politician is only at the superintendent's level, a blatant disregard for prior individual or agency agreements can have disastrous effects (see chapters 33, 37, 38, & 41). While litigation might provide compensatory damages in such cases, the real damage to continued effective practices cannot be readily undone because of the loss of credibility of the entire institution or department in the eyes of staff and others with whom commitments have been broken.[20] Similarly, long-term planning and preparations are even more futile if a governor decides it is politically expedient to replace the top professional administration of entire departments and discriminatively lay off institutional staff on grounds other than program effectiveness and cost-efficiency (see chapters 33, 36, 37, 38, & 41). In such circumstances, even resort to active political tactics (e.g., Wagner et al., 1975) results, at best, in a brief delay in the destruction of ongoing programs. Litigation, such as occurred in *Wyatt*, might eventually restore staff positions to effective programs, but the damage to continuing staff performance and morale—not to mention the loss of trained staff who must work during a drawn-out court battle—is strong enough to have functionally terminated ongoing practices, even if the units continued to exist.

Fortunately, such massive political assaults with complete disregard for the quality and effectiveness of institutional practices are relatively rare. The only possibility for protecting good institutional programs from such events is to build in accountability within the bureaucratic system—perhaps through contractual obligation of institutions, departments, or governmental offices to treatment proposals with ongoing monitoring of outcomes. If such obligations were not subject to violation by political officeholders without legislative, or at least public review, empirically based decisions with appropriate balancing of conflicting factors might be more likely. Some scheme for protecting and balancing the rights of good institutional practices is desirable.

## PROVIDING THE BEST TREATMENT WHILE EXTENDING KNOWLEDGE

The long-term goal of the work reported in this book is to improve institutional treatment practices in general and to reduce significantly the number of chronic residents of mental institutions in particular. The design and observational instrumentation of the comparative project have been demonstrated to provide a feasible model for investigating institutional treatment outcome under actual clinical conditions with more rigor than has been attained elsewhere. We thus recommend the design, procedures, and observational instrumentation as a model for future outcome studies directed at the determination of comparative cause-effect relationships for treatment programs with specified problems and populations (see chapter 3). However, unless the results from such highly controlled, small-sample research find their way into clinical practice elsewhere, with continuous monitoring and analysis to document effectiveness and necessary changes in other circumstances, little long-term change is likely from the cultlike fadism that historically characterized intervention procedures (see Paul, 1969b; Tourney, 1970).

The results of the comparative project have produced a treatment program that can be recommended as a current treatment of choice for chronically institutionalized residents of mental institutions. Similarly, the assessment systems appear to remove the major technical barrier to transfer of research findings to day-to-day clinical application providing practical, individual monitoring of relevant variables in ongoing clinical work, while concurrently yielding objective research data (Paul, in press). These characteristics of the treatment program and assessment systems make possible a strategy for instituting the best currently documented treatment while continuing to accumulate scientific knowledge in ongoing clinical work. The recommended social-learning program and assessment systems could be implemented in two units at any institution, conducted by the same staff, with appropriate counterbalancing of staff time and focus. In this way, changes could be systematically introduced and evaluated one at a time on only one unit by within-subject designs while allowing for comparison with those in operation on the other. Continuous systems monitoring and analysis could not only ensure continued effectiveness of the previously established procedures but allow systematic extensions and tests of effectiveness over variations of intramural and aftercare procedures, resident group composition, and differing problems, settings, and structure.

Such a combination of process and outcome research with ongoing clinical work would provide continuously upgraded programs without the usual lag in application of research findings (Marquis & Allen, 1966), while concurrently extending and testing the limits of previously established results from more expensive and time-consuming controlled comparative studies.

Although the recommended program is the current treatment of choice for the chronically institutionalized, the absolute level of functioning achieved by residents who were able to move to the community was still sufficiently marginal that efforts to develop even more effective programs are clearly called for. Given the human and financial costs of psychotic problems (Gunderson & Mosher, 1975) and the failure of alternative approaches to affect the chronically institutionalized, we hope that the strategies reported here, as well as the specific procedures recommended will be implemented. In this way, long-term improvement in institutional practices for the benefit of those served may come to pass not as the often-sought and elusive breakthrough but as a result of a cumulative progress in knowledge and technology.

# Appendixes

## A. Instruments for Assessing Staff Attitudes and Orientation

THERAPIST ORIENTATION SHEET (adapted from Paul, 1966)

*THERAPIST ORIENTATION SHEET I*

(Cover sheet used in hospital and before training for psychosocial staff)

Name _____ No. _____ Test Code [_____]
Date _____

Position: 1____ treatment staff           Shift: 1____ day
          2____ behavioral change agent         2____ evening
          3____ observer                        3____ night
          4____ other _____

The following pages contain a number of areas in which psychotherapists have been found to differ. Please indicate your position with regard to each area by placing a checkmark on the scale accompanying each area.

For example: 1. Activity-frequency

If you feel that with *most* clients you are *usually* active (talkative); or *usually* passive, you would place the checkmark as follows:

Active  X  :____:____:____:____: Passive  or  Active ____:____:____:____: X : Passive

If you feel you are *more often* active than passive; or *more often* passive than active, you would check as follows:

Active ____: X :____:____:____: Passive  or  Active ____:____:____: X :____: Passive

If you feel you are about equally active and passive with most clients, or active with as many clients as passive, you would check the middle space.

Active ____:____: X :____:____ Passive

Appendix A 470

## THERAPIST ORIENTATION SHEET II

(Cover sheet used after training and at subsequent six-month assessments for psychosocial staff)

Name _____ No. _____ Test Code _____
                                                       Date _____

Position:  1____treatment staff              Shift:  1____day
           2____behavioral change agent              2____evening
           3____observer                             3____night
           4____other _____

The following pages contain a number of areas in which psychotherapists (change agents) have been found to differ. Please indicate your position with regard to each area by placing numbers on the scale accompanying each area. There are three numbers you should use:

Use "1" to indicate your own personal preference for how you should act.
Use "2" to indicate how you think you are supposed to act on the learning unit.
Use "3" to indicate how you think you are supposed to act on the milieu unit.

Use these numbers throughout to respond to all items. Use the *special instructions for each item* to clarify the items.

Examples: 1. Activity-frequency

If you personally prefer to be *usually* active (talkative) with residents and think that you are supposed to be *more often* active than passive on the learning unit and *usually* active on the milieu unit, you would answer as follows:

Active  1, 3 : 2 :___:___:___  Passive

If you personally prefer to be *usually* passive with residents and think that you are supposed to be *more often* active than passive on the learning unit and *about equally* active and passive on the milieu unit, you would answer as follows:

Active ___:___: 3 : 2 : 1  Passive

Notice that the middle of the line equals "about equally," the spaces next to the middle of the line equal "more often," and the spaces at the ends of the line equal "usually."

If you do not understand these directions and examples, please ask the examiner to explain further.

Before you go on to the Therapist Orientation Sheet, please answer the following two questions:

1. Right now which of the two units, the milieu or the learning unit, do you think will be the most effective in changing residents so that they can live and work independently outside the Meyer Center?

*Most Effective* (check one)

Milieu . . . . . . . . . . . . . ___
Learning . . . . . . . . . . ___

2. Right now which of the two units, the learning or the milieu unit, do you think you will most enjoy working on?

*Most Enjoy* (check one)

Milieu . . . . . . . . . . . . .___
Learning . . . . . . . . . . .___

(TOS items and scales)

1. Activity:frequency
   Active \_\_\_:\_\_\_:\_\_\_:\_\_\_:\_\_\_ Passive
   (Talkative)               (Nontalkative)

2. Activity:type
   Directive \_\_\_:\_\_\_:\_\_\_:\_\_\_:\_\_\_ Nondirective

3. Activity:structure
   Informal \_\_\_:\_\_\_:\_\_\_:\_\_\_:\_\_\_ Formal

4. Relationship:tenor
   Personal \_\_\_:\_\_\_:\_\_\_:\_\_\_:\_\_\_ Impersonal
   (Involved)                (Detached)

5. Relationship:structure
   Unstructured \_\_\_:\_\_\_:\_\_\_:\_\_\_:\_\_\_ Structured

6. Relationship:structure
   Permissive \_\_\_:\_\_\_:\_\_\_:\_\_\_:\_\_\_ Nonpermissive

7. Relationship:therapist actions
   Planned \_\_\_:\_\_\_:\_\_\_:\_\_\_:\_\_\_ Spontaneous

8. Relationship:client dynamics
   Nonconceptualized \_\_\_:\_\_\_:\_\_\_:\_\_\_:\_\_\_ Conceptualized

9. Goals:source
   Therapist \_\_\_:\_\_\_:\_\_\_:\_\_\_:\_\_\_ Client

10. Goals:formalization
    Planned \_\_\_:\_\_\_:\_\_\_:\_\_\_:\_\_\_ Unplanned
    (Formalized)            (Unformalized)

11. Therapist comfort and security
    Always secure \_\_\_:\_\_\_:\_\_\_:\_\_\_:\_\_\_ Never secure
    (Comfortable)                 (Uncomfortable)

12. Client comfort and security
    Never secure \_\_\_:\_\_\_:\_\_\_:\_\_\_:\_\_\_ Always secure
    (Uncomfortable)              (Comfortable)

13. Client personal growth
    Not inherent \_\_\_:\_\_\_:\_\_\_:\_\_\_:\_\_\_ Inherent

14. Therapeutic gains:self-understanding (cognitive insight)
    Important \_\_\_:\_\_\_:\_\_\_:\_\_\_:\_\_\_ Unimportant

15. Therapeutic gains:emotional understanding (affective awareness)
    Unimportant \_\_\_:\_\_\_:\_\_\_:\_\_\_:\_\_\_ Important

16. Therapeutic gains:"symptom" reduction
    Important \_\_\_:\_\_\_:\_\_\_:\_\_\_:\_\_\_ Unimportant

17. Therapeutic gains:social adjustment
    Unimportant \_\_\_:\_\_\_:\_\_\_:\_\_\_:\_\_\_ Important

18. Therapeutic gains:confidence in effecting change
    Confident \_\_\_:\_\_\_:\_\_\_:\_\_\_:\_\_\_ Unconfident

19. Learning process in therapy
    Verbal-conceptual \_\_\_:\_\_\_:\_\_\_:\_\_\_:\_\_\_ Nonverbal-affective

20. Therapeutically significant topics
    Client-centered \_\_\_:\_\_\_:\_\_\_:\_\_\_:\_\_\_ Theory-centered

21. Therapeutically significant topics
    Historical \_\_\_:\_\_\_:\_\_\_:\_\_\_:\_\_\_ Current

22. Therapeutically significant topics
    Ego functions \_\_\_:\_\_\_:\_\_\_:\_\_\_:\_\_\_ Superego, Id

23. Theory of motivation
    Unconscious \_\_\_:\_\_\_:\_\_\_:\_\_\_:\_\_\_ Conscious

24. Curative aspect of therapist
    Personality \_\_\_:\_\_\_:\_\_\_:\_\_\_:\_\_\_ Training

The following items refer to the use of *specific techniques* in psychotherapy. Please check to indicate whether you use each technique: almost always, usually, about half the time, only occasionally, never.

|  | Use of Technique | | |
|---|---|---|---|
|  | Almost Always | 50-50 | Never |
| 25. Reflection and clarification of feelings | \_\_\_:\_\_\_:\_\_\_:\_\_\_:\_\_\_ | | |
| 26. Reflection and clarification of content | \_\_\_:\_\_\_:\_\_\_:\_\_\_:\_\_\_ | | |
| 27. Reflection and clarification of behavior | \_\_\_:\_\_\_:\_\_\_:\_\_\_:\_\_\_ | | |
| 28. Questioning of feelings | \_\_\_:\_\_\_:\_\_\_:\_\_\_:\_\_\_ | | |
| 29. Questioning of content | \_\_\_:\_\_\_:\_\_\_:\_\_\_:\_\_\_ | | |
| 30. Questioning of behavior | \_\_\_:\_\_\_:\_\_\_:\_\_\_:\_\_\_ | | |
| 31. Interpretation of feelings | \_\_\_:\_\_\_:\_\_\_:\_\_\_:\_\_\_ | | |
| 32. Interpretation of content | \_\_\_:\_\_\_:\_\_\_:\_\_\_:\_\_\_ | | |
| 33. Interpretation of behavior | \_\_\_:\_\_\_:\_\_\_:\_\_\_:\_\_\_ | | |
| 34. Suggestion (*not* hypnosis) | \_\_\_:\_\_\_:\_\_\_:\_\_\_:\_\_\_ | | |
| 35. Reassurance | \_\_\_:\_\_\_:\_\_\_:\_\_\_:\_\_\_ | | |
| 36. Information and advice giving | \_\_\_:\_\_\_:\_\_\_:\_\_\_:\_\_\_ | | |
| 37. Attentive listening | \_\_\_:\_\_\_:\_\_\_:\_\_\_:\_\_\_ | | |
| 38. Modeling techniques (examples) | \_\_\_:\_\_\_:\_\_\_:\_\_\_:\_\_\_ | | |
| 39. Positive attitude, confidence | \_\_\_:\_\_\_:\_\_\_:\_\_\_:\_\_\_ | | |
| 40. Warmth and understanding | \_\_\_:\_\_\_:\_\_\_:\_\_\_:\_\_\_ | | |
| 41. Reinforcement (approval-disapproval) | \_\_\_:\_\_\_:\_\_\_:\_\_\_:\_\_\_ | | |
| 42. Conditioning, counterconditioning | \_\_\_:\_\_\_:\_\_\_:\_\_\_:\_\_\_ | | |
| 43. Free association | \_\_\_:\_\_\_:\_\_\_:\_\_\_:\_\_\_ | | |
| 44. Auxiliary techniques (hypnosis, medication) | \_\_\_:\_\_\_:\_\_\_:\_\_\_:\_\_\_ | | |
| 45. Other (please specify) | \_\_\_:\_\_\_:\_\_\_:\_\_\_:\_\_\_ | | |

## SPECIAL INSTRUCTIONS FOR EACH ITEM
(added for institutional staff)

1. The extent to which you tend to talk to residents *(active)* as opposed to the extent to which you remain relatively quiet while letting the residents take the initiative in talking *(passive)*.

2. The extent to which *you* decide what activity is to be engaged in (for example, swimming) *(directive)* as opposed to letting the residents decide on the activity *(nondirective)*.

3. The extent you tend to structure an activity for residents *(formal)* as opposed to letting the residents develop their own structure for an activity *(informal)*.

4. The extent to which you treat residents on an individual basis as individuals *(personal)* as opposed to being detached, treating them as another "case" *(impersonal)*.

5. The extent to which you allow your interaction with residents to be "free" and "spontaneous" *(unstructured)* as opposed to being planned *(structured)*.

6. The extent to which you communicate to residents that they may act as they wish *(permissive)* as opposed to communicating that they must follow specific rules *(nonpermissive)*.

7. The extent to which you plan how you will act with residents ahead of time *(planned)* as opposed to the extent you do not plan before hand *(spontaneous)*.

8. The extent to which you think about what is going on "inside" the residents' minds as you talk to them *(conceptualized)* as opposed to not making inferences about their inner "dynamics" *(nonconceptualized)*.

9. The extent to which you choose the goals of your therapy with residents *(therapist)* as opposed to the extent to which you allow the residents to choose the goals for their therapy *(client)*.

10. The extent to which you formally plan the goals of therapy (for example, write them down or think them out thoroughly) *(planned)* as opposed to letting the goals develop moment to moment *(unplanned)*.

11. The extent to which you feel comfortable and secure when with residents *(always secure)* as opposed to the extent to which you feel uncomfortable and insecure *(never secure)*.

12. The extent to which your clients (residents) feel comfortable and secure *(always secure)* as opposed to the extent they feel uncomfortable and insecure *(never secure)*.

13. The extent to which you assume that the personal growth (improvement) of residents results from an inner tendency to become mentally healthy (if the tendency is not blocked in some way) *(inherent)* as opposed to the extent you assume that personal growth does not depend on such an inner tendency but is dependent on other things *(not inherent)*.

14. The extent to which you place importance on the residents' coming to understand themselves and their problems *(important)* as opposed to the extent you do not feel that such "insight" is important *(unimportant)*.

15. The extent to which you place importance on the residents' becoming aware of their emotions *(important)* as opposed to the extent to which you do not feel that such "affective (emotional) awareness" is important *(unimportant)*.

16. The extent to which you place importance on the residents' crazy behaviors being "reduced" or changed *(important)* as opposed to the extent to which you do not feel that changing or removing crazy behaviors is important *(unimportant)*.

17. The extent to which you place importance on the residents' imporving their ability to get along in society *(important)* as opposed to the extent you feel that getting along in society is not important or relevant to treatment *(unimportant)*.

18. The extent you feel you are confident in getting residents to improve *(confident)* as opposed to the extent you do not feel confidence in helping residents change *(unconfident)*.

19. The extent to which you believe that the important thing that clients (residents) learn in therapy is to understand and conceptualize (verbally) their difficulties and the causes for their difficulties *(verbal-conceptual)* as opposed to the extent to which you believe that the important way that residents learn is through experience *(nonverbal-affective)*.

20. The extent to which you feel that therapeutic conversation (talking with a resident) should consist of topics centered around and important to the client as an individual *(client centered)* as opposed to the extent to which you feel that the conversation should be about topics relating to a therapeutic theory (for example, psychoanalytic theory) as it relates to the resident *(theory centered)*.

21. The extent to which you feel that therapeutic conversation with a resident should focus on the resident's past *(historical)* as opposed to the extent to which you feel that the conversation should be about current events in the resident's life *(current)*.

22. The extent to which you feel that therapeutic conversation with residents should be about their *conscious* strengths and weaknesses and their ability to work and deal effectively with people *(ego functions)* as opposed to the extent to which you feel that the conversation should be about the "unconscious" aspects of their personalities—those that they do not know about *(superego, id)*.

23. The extent to which you believe that the residents' behavior is motivated unconsciously (that is, they don't know why they do what they do) *(unconscious)* as opposed to the extent to which you believe that the residents' behavior is motivated consciously (that is, they know the reasons for their behavior) *(conscious)*.

24. The extent to which you feel that the most important thing which makes you a successful therapist (change agent) is your personality *(personality)* as opposed to the extent to which you feel that the most important is your training *(training)*.

25. The extent to which you tend to reflect or restate to a resident how he or she seems to be feeling.

26. The extent to which you tend to reflect or restate the meaning of what residents say.

27. The extent you tend to reflect or restate to residents *what* they are *doing*.

28. The extent you ask residents how they are feeling, or how they feel in specific situations.

29. The extent you ask residents to explain and elaborate on what they say.

30. The extent you ask residents about their recent behavior.

31. The extent you explain to residents what their feelings mean.

32. The extent you explain to residents what their statements mean.

33. The extent you explain to residents what their behavior means.

34. The extent you use suggestion, for example, telling a resident what might be the best thing to do.

35. The extent you use reassurance, for example, "You *can* do this," as a therapeutic technique.

36. The extent you give residents useful information and advice.

37. The extent you just listen attentively to what the residents are saying.

38. The extent you use yourself, others, films, or anecdotes to provide good examples for residents to imitate.

39. The extent you maintain a confident attitude that residents can improve as you interact with residents.

40. The extent you try to be warm and understanding in your interactions with residents.

41. The extent you actively express approval or disapproval of actions of residents.

42. The extent you use conditioning (for example, pairing social reinforcement with material rewards) or counterconditioning (for example, pairing incompatible stimuli).

43. The extent you ask residents to free associate (say anything that comes into their minds).

44. The extent you use hypnosis, drugs, or other special techniques with residents.

45. Other techniques you use (please specify).

## TOS SCORING FORMAT: PATTERN DIFFERENTIATION SCORES*

### Attitude Section

| | Score assigned left end of continuum | Score assigned right end of continuum | |
|---|---|---|---|
| | **I** | | |
| 1. | 5 | 1 | |
| 3. | 5 | 1 | A-1 Active/informal |
| 14. | 5 | 1 | |
| | **II** | | |
| 2. | 5 | 1 | |
| 5. | 1 | 5 | |
| 6. | 1 | 5 | A-2 Structured/nonpermissive |
| 7. | 5 | 1 | |
| 8. | 5 | 1 | |
| 13. | 5 | 1 | |
| | **III** | | |
| 4. | 5 | 1 | |
| 16. | 5 | 1 | |
| 17. | 1 | 5 | A-3 Personal/change oriented |
| 20. | 5 | 1 | |
| 22. | 5 | 1 | |
| | **IV** | | |
| 9. | 5 | 1 | |
| 10. | 5 | 1 | |
| 11. | 5 | 1 | |
| 15. | 1 | 5 | A-4 Rational planning |
| 18. | 5 | 1 | |
| 21. | 1 | 5 | |
| 23. | 1 | 5 | |
| 24. | 1 | 5 | |
| | **V** | | |
| 12. | 5 | 1 | A-5 Client discomfort/verbal process |
| 19. | 5 | 1 | |

## Technique Section

| | Score assigned left end of continuum | Score assigned right end of continuum | |
|---|---|---|---|

### I

| | | |
|---|---|---|
| 25. | 5 ............ 1 | |
| 26. | 5 ............ 1 | |
| 27. | 5 ............ 1 | T-1 Reflect, clarify, question |
| 28. | 5 ............ 1 | |
| 29. | 5 ............ 1 | |
| 30. | 5 ............ 1 | |

### II

| | | |
|---|---|---|
| 31. | 5 ............ 1 | |
| 32. | 5 ............ 1 | T-2 Interpretation |
| 33. | 5 ............ 1 | |

### III

| | | |
|---|---|---|
| 34. | 5 ............ 1 | |
| 35. | 5 ............ 1 | T-3 Suggest, reassure, listen |
| 37. | 5 ............ 1 | |

### IV

| | | |
|---|---|---|
| 38. | 5 ............ 1 | |
| 39. | 5 ............ 1 | |
| 40. | 5 ............ 1 | T-4 Interpersonal reinforcement |
| 41. | 5 ............ 1 | |
| 43. | 1 ............ 5 | |
| 44. | 1 ............ 5 | |

### V

| | | |
|---|---|---|
| 36. | 5 ............ 1 | T-5 Information & contingency |
| 42. | 5 ............ 1 | |

*Examples of scoring continuum

Item 1. Activity-frequency
        Active   5 : 4 : 3 : 2 : 1   Passive
      (Talkative)                   (Nontalkative)

Item 5. Relationship-structure
      Unstructured   1 : 2 : 3 : 4 : 5   Structured

## SOCIAL LEARNING IDEOLOGY ITEMS ADDED TO THE OMI (Cohen & Struening, 1962)

"Social Learning Ideology" = $13 + \Sigma(52, 54, 57, 58, 59, 60) - \Sigma(53, 55, 56)$

"Strongly agree" is assigned a value of 1, and "strongly disagree" a value of 6, with single-point increments of the four intermediate levels of agreement/disagreement.

(Added OMI items and scales)

52. Mental illness is inherited.

strongly _____ agree _____ not sure but _____ not sure but _____ disagree _____ strongly _____
agree                     probably agree    probably disagree              disagree

53. There is no such thing as mental illness.

strongly _____ agree _____ not sure but _____ not sure but _____ disagree _____ strongly _____
agree                     probably agree    probably disagree              disagree

54. The use of punishment is never justified in dealing with the mentally ill.

strongly _____ agree _____ not sure but _____ not sure but _____ disagree _____ strongly _____
agree                     probably agree    probably disagree              disagree

55. Calling someone mentally ill involves a value judgment.

strongly _____ agree _____ not sure but _____ not sure but _____ disagree _____ strongly _____
agree                     probably agree    probably disagree              disagree

56. Both abnormal behaviors (deviant behaviors) and normal behaviors (socially appropriate behaviors) are learned.

strongly _____ agree _____ not sure but _____ not sure but _____ disagree _____ strongly _____
agree                     probably agree    probably disagree              disagree

57. A person who is called mentally ill should never be held responsible for his or her behavior.

strongly _____ agree _____ not sure but _____ not sure but _____ disagree _____ strongly _____
agree                     probably agree    probably disagree              disagree

58. The staff of mental hospitals should not attempt to control behavior.

strongly _____ agree _____ not sure but _____ not sure but _____ disagree _____ strongly _____
agree                     probably agree    probably disagree              disagree

59. Abnormal behavior is often caused by unconscious motivation.

strongly _____ agree _____ not sure but _____ not sure but _____ disagree _____ strongly _____
agree                     probably agree    probably disagree              disagree

60. Mental illness is often caused by chemical imbalance in the body.

strongly _____ agree _____ not sure but _____ not sure but _____ disagree _____ strongly _____
agree                     probably agree    probably disagree              disagree

## B. Revised Fine Costs That Replace "Token Costs" in Chapter 8

XI Fines - A resident who has been fined can purchase nothing until the fine has been paid in full without first making a payment of at least one token on the fine. Time away from scheduled activities cannot be purchased at all until the fine has been paid in full. The reduction in standing fines per token payment increases proportionally as a function of the length of time without incurring a new fine on the following basis: < 2 days, 1:1; 2-4 days, 1:3; 5-7 days, 1:5; 8-10 days, 1:10; 11-14 days, 1:15; > 14 days, 1:20. A resident who has been fined will also be sent to time out to be released after a specified minimum period in which at least the last 15 minutes consists of quiet activity.

1. *Minor infractions* of unit rules that are so inappropriate or offensive that the resident would be "kicked out" of the lobby of a crowded theater if the behavior were performed there. Includes use of goods or facilities without paying required tokens, and off-unit absence without prior explanation or approval (AWOL). These infractions do *not* directly violate other peoples rights.

    *Consequence:* Time out in seclusion for one functional period (minimum time of 20 minutes) ............................... 2 token fine (per ½ hr. for AWOL)

2. *Major infractions* of unit rules that directly interfere with the rights of others and are so inappropriate that the resident would be arrested if the behavior were performed in the lobby of a crowded theater. Includes stealing, creating a fire hazard, damaging things, excessive swearing, etc.

    *Consequence:* Time out in seclusion for one functional period (minimum time of 20 minutes) ................................................. 10 token fine
    (Stealing tokens also results in placement on a unique color token system)

3. *Assaultive behaviors*, including direct physical attacks on others, attempts to cause physical harm and direct threats to cause physical harm.

    *Consequence:* Time out in seclusion until 0530 the following morning . . . . 25 token fine

# C. Examples of Detailed Procedural Memos Recommended

SUBJECT: APPEARANCE CHECK PROCEDURES

There are 11 appearance items. They have been ordered to run from 1 (easiest to change immediately) to 11 (most difficult to change immediately). Residents are to be prompted or persuaded to make the "easiest" change first (the lowest numbered item); this way appearance is more of a gradual approximation by degrees to a desired goal of acceptable appearance. There are specific meanings for each item. A list of these behavioral descriptions is to be kept on the clipboard with the recording forms so that staff can refer to them when needed for clarification. Also, the recording forms include the criteria numbers and a line on which to write the particular item prompted or persuaded.

The general rule in determining appropriate appearance is whether or not the particular appearance would draw attention in the streets of Decatur. The behavioral descriptions are pretty thorough, but in the event of borderline cases, ratings can be established through answering the following: would the appearance call critical attention in a public setting, and would you feel uncomfortable having the resident with you?

This memo will be in three parts: procedures specific to the milieu unit, procedures specific to the social-learning unit, and procedures common to both units. The third part includes the criteria list and recording example.

I.  *Appearance: Milieu Unit*

A.  *How to do appearance check:*

Milieu Unit: Change Agent 1 does the following:

1. Announces appearance check by living group from area around mirror in north hall. The living group rotation schedule for appearance check is to be decided during a community meeting and followed thereafter unless revoted in another community meeting.
2. Praises resident for coming to appearance check.
3. Gives positive statements for standing in front of mirror if necessary.
4. "Inspects" residents and marks criteria missed on recording form.
5. Asks resident what he or she needs to do to improve appearance and help the living group.
6. Persuades for "easiest" criterion missed.
7. Praises and marks "1" on recording form if all criteria met. Positive statement for drugs and positive statement to get rest of group up for appearance check (change agent 2 distributes drugs).
8. Gives positive statements/negative feedback if resident failed to meet criteria and marks "0" on recording forms.
9. If all members of a living group do not come to appearance check a second announcement is made—"the following members of living group X are expected to get their appearance checked"—change agent waits several minutes for remainder of group.

B.  *General guidelines:*

1. Give specific negative feedback for one criterion.
2. Give feedback for something that can be *immediately* corrected.
3. Do not refer to the next appearance check.

4. *Do* refer to the expectancies of the living group.
5. If a resident says he or she can't alter what was suggested, the change agent should offer alternatives for solving the problem. Three alternatives are: 1) use of items in grooming kit, 2) purchase of items at canteen, 3) referral of problem to the resident's living group.
6. Though residents are *expected* to come to appearance check, they are not forced.

II. *Appearance: Social-Learning Unit*

A. *How to do appearance check:*

Social-Learning Unit: Change Agent 1 does the following:

1. Announces appearance check from area of mirror on north wall.
2. Praises resident for coming up.
3. Instructs resident, when necessary, to stand in front of mirror.
4. "Inspects" resident and marks criteria missed on recording form.
5. If resident fails to meet previous prompt, he or she is given a negative prompt ("Maude, it's good that you came up to appearance check, but you won't earn a token because you haven't combed your hair"). Then a positive prompt for next appearance check: "Maude, if you comb your hair by the next appearance check and look as good as you do now, you may earn an appearance token at the next appearance check."
6. If residents meet prompted criteria, they are praised and given a token.
    a. Shaping tokens go to residents who have met their last prompt and haven't lost earlier gains and to those who have not come up for appearance for the last three appearance checks (last three recordings).
    b. A resident who earns a terminal token and consistently earns terminal tokens is to be praised, but it is not necessary to prompt for next appearance check. Say something like, "Keep up the good work, Margaret."
    c. If residents earn a terminal token but do not consistently earn terminal tokens, they are to be given a prompt for the next appearance check along with praise and a token for this appearance check.
7. Change agent indicates on the recording form criteria not met and circles criterion prompted (easiest to change before next appearance check—lowest number).
8. Refers resident to change agent distributing drugs.
9. Makes second announcement of appearance check and calls off names of those who haven't come up. Waits several minutes for remainder.

B. *General guidelines:*

The change agent should always:

1. Tell why a token has not been earned.
2. Give a specific prompt.
3. Refer to something that can be corrected *before* the next appearance check; however, if residents can correct a criterion immediately so that they would earn either a shaping or terminal token, they may be prompted to correct it and receive a token for appropriately doing so.
4. Refer to *token consequence*.

III. *Appearance: Both Units*

A. Miscellaneous re appearance

1. Residents should ask permission to enter their rooms if that is necessary to prepare for appearance check at times other than morning routine.
2. If a resident doesn't have other clothes or shoes, still count off; everyone has been adequately supplied at one time or another.
3. An appearance check, as every other contact, can and *should* be done with spontaneity and friendliness. The appearance check is a good situation for informal chatting, especially during the recording period. Just a friendly word or two can help humanize the scrutiny of an appearance check. Also, a positive approach helps make even routine matters less routine for all concerned.

B. Appearance check criteria:

   1. Proper use of makeup
   2. Clean fingernails
   3. Hair combed
   4. Teeth brushed
   5. All appropriate clothing on
   6. Clothing buttoned, zipped, tucked
   7. Clothing clean and neat
   8. Body clean
   9. No odor
   10. Shaven
   11. Hair cut appropriately (males)

1. *Proper use of makeup*

   a. not excessive (like no excessive rouge and misplaced)
   b. women don't have to wear makeup
   c. no makeup for men (including fingernail polish)

2. *Clean fingernails*

   a. no dirt or grease around or under nails
   b. nails not filed to a point or excessively long

3. *Hair combed*

   a. hair not tangled or ratty
   b. no rags, pincurls, or curlers
   c. no credit for effort
   d. black residents and others with curly hair: if the hair doesn't have tight little ringlets and lint or fuzz in it, then it's probably been combed (should be relatively smooth).

4. *Teeth brushed*

   a. no food on teeth
   b. no grit on teeth
   c. breath so that you can stand within a few feet
   d. nicotine stains acceptable
   e. dentures in

5. *All appropriate clothing on*

   a. for women: blouse and skirt or slacks, or dress
   b. for women: hose not necessary, anklets OK but not required with shoes; hose or anklets necessary with heels
   c. loafers, sandles, and tennis shoes without socks acceptable for males also
   d. men: shirt, pants (belt if pant loops and belt available), shoes & socks
   e. general: shoes, socks, and shoestrings (things in pairs) should match
   f. pants not stuffed with newspapers, etc.
   g. no excessive clothing, i.e., 2 dresses, an overcoat when inside, etc.
   h. underwear not necessary for either if not noticeable (bras should be worn if breasts are pendulous (more than 2" sag)
   i. correct sex wearing apparel, i.e., jeans and slacks OK for women but dresses and gowns not appropriate for men
   j. colored and white T-shirts acceptable (undershirts not acceptable for outer wear)
   k. nonclothes worn inappropriate, etc.

6. *Clothing buttoned, zipped, tucked*

   a. fly zipped or buttoned
   b. sleeves buttoned if down (both sleeves should be rolled or down & buttoned)
   c. dresses, shirts, and blouses buttoned or zipped

d. straight cut shirts acceptable with tails out
e. tailed shirts tucked
f. button-down collar shirts buttoned if there are buttons
g. pants are correct length (not rolled up)
h. shoes laced
i. belt buckles buckled

7. *Clothing clean and neat*

   a. not wrinkled
   b. not soiled
   c. not torn
   d. hem in; slip should not show
   e. clothing on frontwards
   f. clothing right side out
   g. pockets not ripped off or torn
   h. shoes not covered with debris; leather shoes not heavily scuffed
   i. clothes not wet
   j. holes that are old or which do not draw attention (small) are acceptable
   k. stains that will not wash out (old stains) are acceptable

8. *Body clean*

   a. body free of food
   b. body free of dirt
   c. body free of blood
   d. body free of excrement and urine
   e. body free of saliva and mucous
   f. whiskers free of dried food, dirt, excrement, saliva, and mucous
   g. hair clean: free of visible dirt, grease, dandruff and other particles

9. *No odor*

   a. no urine or fecal odor
   b. no other weird, offensive odors, except things like tincture of benzion
   c. sweat odor is acceptable if resident has *just* been working (job, gym, and the like) and has "worked up a sweat"

10. *Shaven*

    a. all whiskers off chin, face and neck
    b. moustaches trimmed
    c. 5 o'clock shadow OK
    d. for women: underarms shaven if wearing sleeveless garment
    e. for women: no visible hair on legs
    f. blood, shaving cream, toilet paper stuck on bloody spots, and the like: count off
    g. beards: if a resident declares intention to grow beard in writing, staff should not count off for grubby stubble of first few weeks. This note should be kept on the appearance clipboard
    h. if a resident doesn't declare his intention to grow a beard but does grow a beard and likes it, then, if it is trimmed, staff shouldn't count off for it—should count off during "stubble" if not declared in writing

11. *Hair cut appropriately*

    a. no baldness due to crazy behavior
    b. no razor paths due to crazy behavior
    c. length:
    The standard should be relevant to age and social class. We should make individual judgments for each resident as to the accepted hair length and style—these days, almost "anything" goes; "naturals" OK

## The Appearance Check Form and How to Record

The appearance criteria have been ordered to reflect a ranking from "easiest" to "hardest" to change immediately. The "criteria" column contains the 11 numbers of the items. Criteria failed should have a single diagonal line drawn through them; criterion prompted or persuaded should be circled. The circled criterion should be the easiest criteria failed. Also, each box across from resident's names (in the "Criteria Not Met" column) is divided by a horizontal dotted line. Below this line are the criteria code numbers; above the dotted line is space for the rater to briefly describe in writing what the resident actually did to receive the prompt or positive statement/negative feedback.

Example:

|  | CRITERIA NOT MET |
| --- | --- |
| Smith, Mary | Hair combed <br> ------------------------------------------------------------------------- <br> 1  2  ③  4  5̸  6̸  7  8̸  9  1̸0  1̸1 |

Notice that 3 is circled, and the act is described in writing. Notice, also, that 3, which was prompted, is the "easiest" of the criteria not met.

SUBJECT: SHAPING CLASS PROCEDURES (Social-Learning Program)

The success of a token economy in shaping the behavior of the residents participating in the treatment program depends upon each resident's learning to value the tokens available such that he or she will work to earn them and will spend them for available backup reinforcers. Several residents initially function at such low levels that they fail to attend to any stimulus, including tokens. These residents are assigned to "shaping classes" entirely until they can graduate to regular class participation.

As specified in the memo on the regular classes, standard class procedures call for direct contact between resident and CA (change agent) once every quarter of the class period, either in the form of praise for good work or as one prompt per class for failure to participate in class. In between these contacts residents are expected to work independently without repeated instructions to stay busy. Thus, the major goal of shaping class is to give problem residents training needed to work independently in class and profit (educationally) from the learning situation in regular classes.

Intermediate steps in this training process involve showing residents that tokens are valuable, increasing residents' attention span, giving them the basic educational skills (writing, reading, adding, etc.) so that they can then work more independently on more complex tasks and eliminate crazy behaviors with classroom participation. The procedures outlined below have been designed with these goals in mind.

*Attendance*

Just as in the regular classes, residents have two minutes after the announcement to get to class and earn their attendance token. The only difference is that residents in shaping class are more likely than others to have special programs having to do with shaping attendance.

*Procedures in class*

The standard procedure is for each resident to be assigned different tasks (by the educator), which are closely coordinated with the target the resident must meet to earn a participation token. Thus, in shaping class, residents' targets involve the completion of different tasks rather than increasing amounts of time of independent work, as they are in the regular classes. Change agents, obviously, need to know the residents' assigned task very well in order to clarify it for the resident, help with it, and then to judge performance.

One of the most powerful procedures in shaping class that is not included in the regular classes is to give residents small portions of food for completing tasks that have been assigned to them. Food is given in conjunction with shaping chips and also along with tokens at the end of class, in hopes that the residents will learn that tokens are "good" things. Remember the principle of "association by contiguity" from the Social-Learning Manual?

The strategy for carrying out the shaping class program follows: Once the resident has been given an assignment by the educator, the change agent should begin working with the resident by clarifying the task (if necessary) and then stepping back and letting the resident work independently. If the resident cannot or does not pay attention to the assignment or is doing the work incorrectly, the CA should break the task down into smaller segments, give instructions for each of these, correct resident's errors, and let the resident work independently on successive segments. Then, when the entire task has been completed this way, have the resident start over and do the entire task alone. It will probably be necessary to require that the resident gradually do more and more of the assignment independently rather than jumping from giving a lot of help to asking for the whole thing to be done alone. Remember the principle of shaping—that's the name of this class.

In shaping class it is necessary that residents both pay attention to assigned work and complete the work correctly. This may seem as if we are requiring more from shaping class residents than others. Actually, the educators see to it that residents are working on a task that is well within the range of their ability and current functioning. This way we can focus our efforts on teaching residents to pay close attention to the assigned task, whereas in the regular classes we assume the residents already know how to pay attention and we focus more on teaching them new and more complex academic and practical skills.

Some shaping class members may engage in behavior that is both disruptive and interferes with their working on their assignment. Examples are: G.W. repeatedly looking over his shoulder and muttering to someone who isn't there; N.C. scolding her "children"; P.A. rubbing his head and jaw and grinding his teeth together. In addition to interfering with task-oriented work, another common feature of these examples is that, whether or not the residents' assignments are in front of them, there is something clear-cut and objective that you could tell each one to stop doing. That is important, because the way we deal with such behaviors in shaping class is to remove the resident's assignment and food dish and tell the resident that because he or she is doing such-and-such (be descriptive) we are removing the above items, and the items will be returned when he or she stops doing whatever such-and-such is. Then, when the resident stops doing whatever it was that interfered with working on the assignment, the assignment and food dish are returned, and the resident is verbally reinforced with something like "Good, Art!! Since you stopped rubbing your head you can have your assignment back, and the food is available to you again for working on the assignment." Make sure that the residents know that the food is only available when the assignment is in front of them.

Notice that the statement, "If you stop such-and-such, then you can have your food and assignment back," is a prompt and that we are only to prompt a resident once within one activity period. That rule, however, applies only to prompts that involve token consequences, whether tokens to be earned or tokens to be fined. Repeat the above procedure with removal of food dish and assignment as many times as is necessary within a class, as long as the resident is ignored until each individual prompt is met. Then the food and assignment should be returned and the whole process could start over if the resident engages in the same disruptive behavior or another one we are trying to eliminate.

The educators fill out a card that is attached to each resident's assignment folder. This card indicates the various tasks each resident is to work on and all behaviors that we are currently trying to eliminate through removal of food and assignments. Remember: it is important that any behavior we deal with in this way must be one that residents can stop or continue on their own, whether or not the assignment is in front of them. If a resident is writing all wrong answers, for instance, we have to deal with that in a different way since he or she would automatically stop when the assignment was removed.

*Prompts*

In addition to the prompts described above concerning the removal and return of food and assignment, the only prompts to be used in shaping class concerning tokens are at the end of class, during the chip-token exchange when the residents are told why they either earned or failed to earn a token and what they must do in the next class in order to earn a token.

*Changing residents' task targets*

As residents progress in shaping class it is necessary to change the tasks on which they are working and the targets they must meet to earn their tokens. At such times, the educators experiment for one week with proposed new tasks for a few minutes each day to judge what the resident's new target should be when he or she begins working on the new task. This decision is made in conjunction with one of the psychologists. During this trial week the educators see to it that the residents have enough time remaining in class to work on their current task and meet their current target to earn their token. However, since the residents won't be working full period on the current task, and sometimes won't even have enough time to meet their target for a token, the educators are the ones primarily responsible during these trial weeks, for deciding whether the resident earned a token on a given day.

*"Hold" targets:* In order to avoid a resident's targets inappropriately rising too high because of a single good performance, and in order to maximize the "success" that the residents experience in shaping class, each resident is assigned a ceiling or "hold" level on the target. The target cannot rise above that "hold" until the educator and psychologists decide the resident is ready, but the target could lower according to usual rules if the resident fails to meet the target on two successive days. It is not necessary, however, to write "hold" next to each resident's target. The ceiling or "hold" target for each resident is indicated on the card that includes the identified tasks and the behavior to be eliminated.

*Graduation from shaping class*

One purpose of shaping class is to help residents progress to the point where they can successfully participate in regular classes, A four-week transition period for moving residents gradually from shaping to regular classes is specified below. During this period the resident can adapt to working in class without receiving food for participation and allow assessment of performance when food isn't immediately available. It is important to stress that the resident is progressing, rather than being punished by removing the availability of extra food.

TRANSITION PROCEDURE

*Week 1*
Day 1—food given twice during a 10-minute period if resident is working.
Day 2—food given only when shaping chip given along with praise for work done.
Days 3-5—less food given when shaping chips given.

*Week 2*
Days 6-8—food given only at end of class if token earned.
Days 9 & 10—only tokens given, no food.

*Week 3*
Days 11-13—attend two shaping classes and one regular class with only tokens given.
Days 14 & 15—attend one shaping class and two regular classes with only tokens given.

*Week 4*
Complete transfer to regular classes.

*Questions and Answers:*

1. When and how are productivity chips used in shaping class?
    Ans. They are not used. Instead each resident exchanges shaping chips for a token immediately after the educator gives the rating, before the educator and CA move on to the next resident.
2. Who carries the food tray to and from the shaping class?
    Ans. The educator selects one of the first residents to show up for class to go to the dining area with the educator to get the tray before class. After class, the resident that has done the best job will be the one to carry the tray back to the dining area. This person receives a free cup of coffee and some other goodie from the dietary workers for doing this job.
3. What should a CA do if he or she feels that a resident's assignment is beyond the capabilities for independent work?
    Ans. Talk to the educator about it. It is necessary for the residents to work independently so we don't want to reinforce them with too much help for failing to do the assignment on their own. The educator knows the resident's capabilities well since they are together every day. An easier assignment can be assigned if both educator and CA agree that the current one is too difficult.

4. Do residents continue to earn food and chips even after they've met their whole target for earning a shaping token?
   Ans. They continue to earn food each time they repeat one additional segment of their target, for instance, if the target is two rows of arithmetic done three times, they receive food each time they do two rows. But, they earn shaping chips only during the time before meeting their token target.
5. What if a resident works well with repeated instruction but stops work the instant you leave?
   Ans. This is touchy, because we don't want to reinforce the failure to work, but ignoring doesn't seem to lead to progress either. Remember the concept of "fading." Don't give a lot of attention and help one time and then expect the resident to do it completely alone the next. Gradually give less and less help. You might move from praising every number written, to praising complete answers, to praising every other correct answer, etc., until one or two whole rows are completed independently. If you're teaching residents to comb their hair, gradually move from doing almost all of it for them, to guiding their hand, to just touching their hand while they do it, to letting them do it alone.
6. A resident in shaping class is scribbling on the assignment. Should you take the food and assignment away?
   Ans. No; the resident needs to be able to stop the conflicting behavior whether or not the assignment is there. You need to be able to tell the resident what to do in order to get the food and assignment back. If you took it away for scribbling on it, the resident would automatically stop. How could he or she then earn it back?
7. If a resident's target is 1 RTR (Response to Request) does that resident earn a token for responding to your request for him or her to sit down?
   Ans. Yes.

SUBJECT: MEDICAL MEAL PROCEDURES

Residents are placed on the medical meal list to ensure adequate nourishment through balanced caloric intake. Placement on the medical meal list may be based upon order of the unit supervisor or consulting physician for residents with specific nutritional requirements who need special diets (e.g., diabetes) or those who are found to be less than 90% of their ideal weight for height and body build at the monthly check (weekly check for residents already on the list). Residents are also placed upon the medical meal list if they fail to consume an average of one full meal per day for the previous seven days on their own. A resident on the medical meal list *must* eat each meal until he or she is removed from the list by surpassing the criteria for being placed on the list or by order of the unit supervisor or consulting physician for those on special diets.

I. *Medical Meals: Milieu Unit*

Milieu residents on the medical meal list receive a regular tray—meal behavior is recorded as "0." Residents who fail to eat on their own consistently should be referred to the living group and community group as any other problem. For those on the medical meal list for any particular day, *change agent 1 does the following:*

1. Check the medical meal list before announcing the meal.
2. Contact residents on the medical meal list, remind them and members of their group that they must eat—attempt to persuade them to do so.
3. Announce the meal and record attendance.
4. Give positive feedback to those who attend and their group members; negative feedback to group members who have a "missing" member on the medical meal list.
5. If all residents on the medical meal list do not come to the regular meal, a second announcement is made by name, with positive statements regarding expected attendance.
6. Positive expectations for living group members to encourage missing group members to attend are given once again, with negative feedback for their absence—positive feedback to the group if they are successful.
7. Residents on the medical meal list *must* eat. Therefore, if they do not attend on their own or with the persuasion of their living group, at the end of the regular meal period:
   a. escort the missing resident to the dining area.
   b. seat the resident at a central table while the dietary worker brings a tray.

c. provide continuous positive statements for eating and negative feedback for failure to come to the meal of his or her own accord until the resident has completed the meal.
  d. if the resident has not completed the meal by the next scheduled activity, record resident's location on the next scheduled activity form so he or she may be persuaded to finish eating and join the living group for the next functional period.

II. *Medical Meals: Social-Learning Unit*

Social-learning residents on the medical meal list receive a "medical meal" rather than a regular tray if they fail to pay tokens for either regular or early meals on their own. The "medical meal" is nourishing but is *not* intended to be tasty or pleasant to encourage residents to eat regular meals and pay for them with tokens. Dietary workers prepare "medical meals" by combining the required food into a tasteless blend served in a single container; therefore, "0" is recorded for meal behavior. For residents on the medical meal list for any particular day, *change agent 1 does the following:*

1. Check the medical meal list before announcing the regular meal.
2. Contact residents on the medical meal list and prompt them for attendance.
3. Announce the regular meal, collect tokens, and record entrance.
4. If all residents on the medical meal list do not come to the regular meal, a second announcement is made by name.
5. Verbally reinforce residents who attend and pay tokens for the regular meal; prompt re availability of a token for appropriate meal behavior.

Residents on the medical meal list *must* eat. Therefore, if they respond to the announcements but have too few tokens or are unwilling to pay for the regular meal, or if residents on the medical meal list fail to respond to announcements, *change agent 2 does the following:*

1. Escort them to the table on the far side of the passageway, explaining (negative prompt), "Since you didn't buy a meal, you'll have to be satisfied with a medical meal instead of the good food."
2. Seat the resident while the dietary worker brings the medical meal.
3. Prompt the resident for remaining at the table until the medical meal is finished.
4. Totally ignore thereafter until the medical meal is consumed, except for one prompt for completion, 5 minutes before the next scheduled activity.
5. Prompt for attending the next regular meal upon completion of the medical meal.

# Notes

## 2. MILIEU AND SOCIAL-LEARNING APPROACHES TO TREATMENT

1. This chapter summarizes literature covered by Paul (1969a). More recent literature is covered in part 9, along with the findings of the comparative project.

2. Ayllon and Azrin's book on the principles of token economies (1968) had not yet appeared when the comparative project was initiated. However, the project director had visited the Anna State program prior to writing the Social-Learning Manual described in chapter 8. The social-learning program that was developed appeared to have incorporated all of Ayllon and Azrin's recommended procedural rules, except for the absence of automated devices for delivery and recording reinforcers (by choice).

3. E. A. Hallsten and H. Hughes to G. L. Paul, 1967.

## 3. DESIGN AND OVERVIEW OF THE COMPARATIVE PROJECT

1. While the rationale for the comparative evaluation of the treatment programs presented here is proposed to hold for any treatment program, both the strategy and concepts of experimental-behavioral science can also be adopted for ongoing clinical assessment and treatment (see Paul, 1974). In fact, that experimental-behavioral strategy was characteristic of all ongoing clinical operations of psychosocial staff within the current comparative project.

2. Bernard R. Wagner (research associate), Wesley C. Becker and Joseph R. Williams (co-investigators), and John Nolte (milieu trainer) also participated in the original planning and development work related to the comparative project.

## 4. THE TREATMENT SETTING, ORGANIZATION, AND STAFFING

1. During the intramural treatment period of the project, the zone was reorganized to coincide with other governmental regions. Zone VI became region 3-b, with the southernmost and northernmost counties being transferred to adjacent administrative regions, leaving a sixteen-county area with a population (1970) of about 800,000. The regional hospital was assigned to a different region and was scheduled to be changed from a facility for the mentally ill to one for the developmentally disabled. The changes had no detectable effects on the treatment of either psychosocial group or of the hospital comparison group during the intramural treatment period.

2. Because of conflicting data over numerous statistical reports of the state Department of Mental Health and the hospital, all patient and staff data were derived from records of the hospital research director (J. R. Williams) and the hospital census sheets and available monthly computer printouts. Appreciation is expressed to Peter Levison, John Wiehaus, Edna Menard, and Ross Muehling for making the sources available.

3. The following psychologists served as graduate research assistants: J. B. (Dean) Orris, Lester L. Tobias, George K. Montgomery, Marco J. Mariotto, Roger M. Knudson, Richard I. Edelson, Joel P. Redfield, Patrick Vogel, Constance Duncan-Johnson, Al L. Porterfield, Mark Licht, and Christopher Power. Typically one assistant had primary responsibility for data processing and another for observer training and monitoring.

4. The following psychologists served as interns: Richard L. Hagen, W. Ed Craighead, James F. Calhoun, James P. Curran, Alan J. Litrownik, David W. Doty, Howard C. Himelstein, William Kohen, and Dale E. Theobald.

5. Weekly research meetings and research staff functioned in similar fashion and served the same purpose.

6. Part-time student workers and volunteers, who had no treatment functions, were also supervised by change agents.

7. Dee Strack received the first such promotion. Barbara Garren was later promoted in a similar manner upon Leota Walker's retirement.

8. Auxiliary professional staff included Robert Paden, Margaret Maynard, and Carolyn Paden, and expanded professional staff included David W. Doty, Ralph Trimble, and Howard Himelstein.

9. The staff-to-resident ratios were calculated by taking the average of staff employed at the beginning and end of each six-month period divided by the average of residents present at the end of each month. This calculation underestimated the staff-to-resident ratio for psychosocial units over the ninth six-month period since the full staff complement was available for over half the period. Exact figures for the last six months are: on-the-floor staff-to-resident ratio=0.522, 84.6% nonprofessional; total staff-to-resident ratio=0.633, 78.2% nonprofessional. The overall average increased 0.002 for on-the-floor staff and 0.003 for total staff. While psychosocial data are exact, comparison hospital data are, at best, approximations because only monthly samples were available within each period, and labeling of the composition of assigned staff and patients was not consistent over time. Hospital staff data include all professional and nonprofessional staff specifically assigned to nongeriatric Continued Treatment Service or Residential Unit Division who covered the same functions as psychosocial treatment staff, plus a proportion of central auxiliary staff covering the same functions, estimated as the proportion of nongeriatric chronic patients to total patients.

## 5. THE TREATMENT PROGRAMS AND THEIR ASSESSMENT

1. The Orientation and Common Procedures Manual presented in chapter 6, contains all original material, plus minor editorial changes that were introduced later to broaden the focus to prechronic as well as chronic populations.

2. Both program manuals presented in chapters 7 and 8 contain all original material, plus editorial changes, specific schedules, and procedural memos representative of operations over the majority of the intramural period. Deviations from the procedures presented in chapters 7 and 8 are detailed for appropriate time periods in chapters 13, 18, 23, and 28. See appendix C for the nature of some recommended memos.

3. The SRIC sample of hospital programs included ten days on site during the eighth anniversary assessment. The first three days consisted of determination of ward schedules, establishment of interobserver reliability, and attempted habituation of staff to the presence of observers. Seven full days of data were then obtained for analyses, covering functional periods within sixteen-hour days from SRIC observations of the most active staff member, equally weighted for actual clock hours of activity from 162 SRICs. The sample included four wards housing hospital comparison patients, selected to be representative of all wards with regard to size, staffing ratios, and male-female, open-closed dimensions. Reliabilities for all hospital SRIC data used in analyses ranged from average intraclass coefficients of $r=0.83$ to $r=1.00$, with the overall reliability of the instrument exceeding $r=0.99$ based upon three observers, cross-sectionally overlapped on 20 SRICs per pair.

## 9. THE CLINICAL STAFF AND THEIR ASSESSMENT

1. On several occasions, the standard procedures of the Department of Personnel were followed, in which their tests and evaluations provided the eligible list of candidates. Professional staff were never found to meet the position needs, although junior staff often did after the project director assisted in doing away with original civil-service examinations, and new screening procedures were established on a statewide basis. While no information is available on the hiring practices at the regional hospital, the fact that the majority of physicians at the hospital were of East-European extraction and several had come from the same hometown as the superintendent suggests that more individualized selection and recruiting was carried out at the hospital as well.

2. Differences between groups were evaluated on standardized scores via two-way ANOVAs (groups x scores), partitioning of simple effects and tests of individual components. Throughout all analyses conservative estimates of error df were employed for pooled mean squares, and harmonic mean N's were used for testing effects between groups of differing size (see Winer, 1962).

3. Differences between sten scores were evaluated by one-way ANOVAs followed by Newman-Keul's multiple comparisons at $p < 0.05$ (Winer, 1962).

4. All correlational analyses employed $p < 0.05$ (two-sided) for significance level.

5. TOS preferred scores were evaluated via two-way ANOVAs (groups x scores), partitioning of simple effects, and tests of individual components. Throughout all analyses conservative estimates of error df were employed for pooled mean squares, and harmonic mean N's were used for testing effects between groups of differing size. Differences between scores were evaluated by Newman-Keul's multiple comparisons at $p < 0.05$ (Winer, 1962).

## 10. NONPROFESSIONAL CLINICAL STAFF TRAINING

1. New clinical senior staff were similarly trained in an abbreviated integrated/technical mode by both senior and junior staff. Because new senior staff studied manuals, schedules, and forms on their own before employment—sometimes supplemented with assigned theoretical readings—they were usually trained in fewer than four weeks.
2. An additional four days were included for the initial group after completion of regular training and testing for instruction in special procedures for habituation, exposure, and baseline conditions instituted upon initial transfer of the resident population.
3. Nonproject personnel, including the zone director, a department professional services' representative, personnel officer, pharmacist, supervisor of volunteer services, and fire chief assisted in orientation to the zone and the center and provision of job-related information on their areas of responsibility, but none was involved in active training for treatment programs and procedures.
4. In addition to the project director and clinical senior staff, the original group of trainees received lecture-discussions on the topics from a consulting psychologist (Leonard P. Ullmann) and a research assistant (Lester L. Tobias). Later change-agent trainees received all training from project treatment staff alone.
5. Civil-service ratings were also examined and found to provide little objective discrimination of performance because of halo effects, lack of specificity of behaviors and time frames, and artificial restrictions placed on scale utilization. Similar problems are apparent in other reports in the literature for global ratings (Coe et al., 1967; Cuadra & Reed, 1957; Giebink & Stover, 1969; Vaughn et al., 1962; McClelland & Rhodes, 1969).

## 11. METHODS OF ASSESSING PATIENT BEHAVIOR

1. The Biographical Data Sheet is available in Paul (in press).
2. The Inpatient Multidimensional Psychiatric Scale (IMPS) (Lorr et al., 1962), was added to the structured interview for anniversary assessments 1-9 in hopes that it could serve as an additional instrument to also be administered in the community. While concurrent reliability and ordinal rankings were excellent for the IMPS for regular project interviewers, method factors as a result of shifting rater standards inherent in the instrument preclude its use for assessing differential levels or change (see Mariotto & Paul, 1974). Regular subzone community staff of the Department of Mental Health were totally unreliable with the IMPS. The structured interview protocols for the MSBS-PRS and MSBS-IMPS are available in Paul (in press).
3. Honigfeld (1966) also provides scoring keys for six factor scores covering narrower classes of behavior. However, because of the amount of variance accounted for by the Total Assets Score (see Lentz et al., 1971), the lower-level factor scores were not used for comparative analyses.
4. Data for selection of original groups and previous substudies were originally hand scored; computer programs became available only later because of staff shortages. IAB data were regularly keypunched and verified by operators from the Center Management Information Service and placed on file for later analyses, while the project's own keypunch operator handled the more complex ongoing observational and frequency data. Prior to final analyses of IAB data, keypunch error rates as high as 10% were discovered in those data keypunched and verified by nonproject personnel. Therefore, all IAB data were hand scored, and each score was checked against computer scoring; disagreements were repunched and rescored by computer. All analyses were based upon scores that yielded perfect agreement between hand scoring and computer scoring, with zero error. A problem of validity in the first three MSBS ratings obtained in hospitals had been immediately identified because hospital staff had "cleaned and dressed" patients for the MSBS interview, thereby invalidating two items (30 and 31), which were based on patient appearance (see Lentz et al., 1971). Therefore, on those occasions, positive credit was allowed for MSBS items 30 and 31 for patients in all groups only if each item had an 80% probability of occurrence based upon multiple regression from three NOSIE-30 items (1, 8, and 30), which predicted MSBS 30 and 31 over later time points.
5. Several conventions were adopted for all intramural analyses involving original equated groups. Two deaths early in the intramural period were carried in analyses to the time of their departure, with their equated replacements being substituted in original groups thereafter. Other replacements maintained original group equation at anniversary assessment 0 and were therefore entered only into correlational analyses until termination of the intramural phase. Scores from the last intramural assessment before release were carried throughout the remainder of intramural analyses of original equated groups for original patients achieving release before anniversary assessment 9. Missing data because of illness or absent-without-leave status at any point of assessment

were replaced by an individual assessment within two weeks. The previous score was substituted in instances where reassessment could not be obtained on four occasions over the last half of the intramural period.

6. Residual change from a previous assessment to a later one (the difference between obtained scores on the later assessment and those predicted by linear regression from the earlier assessment) would provide better comparative data on individual improvement rates between groups, independent of initial level. However, such use of residual change scores requires group equation at the first point, thereby ruling out their use for assessing change from any assessment other than anniversary assessment 0. However, the correlations between residual change and the improvement classification from pretreatment to each successive assessment were sufficiently high (mdn. $r=0.88$, range 0.83 to 0.90) that the improvement classification accurately reflects comparative rates of individual change.

7. Complete instrumentation for the Clinical Frequencies Recording System, including forms, definitions, instructions for summarizing for both clinical and research use, and a computer scoring program providing twenty-five index scores for individuals and groups is available in Paul (in press).

8. Complete recording forms, detailed definitional manuals, observer training procedures, and reliability, validity, and normative data for clinical and research use of the TSBC are available in Paul (in press), along with a computer scoring program that provides relative proportion scores for each individual on sixty-nine behavioral categories, six higher-level index scores, and six stereotypy/variability scores, plus group means and standard deviations for whatever time period is entered for total performance, on twelve different activity-time combinations.

9. Several additional subclasses of activity listed by MacDonald were recorded on the GAI but were found to lack adequate interobserver reliability in early assessments ($r$'s < 0.80). Therefore, reliabilities were determined over the entire intramural period for each category on the GAI (twelve different observer pairs over twelve meetings with an average of 31.3 residents and staff present for frequency data; ten different observer pairs over ten meetings with an average of 31.8 residents and staff present for time data), retaining only those scores with adequate reliability for analyses. Average intraclass reliability coefficients over observers and meetings for retained scores yielded a mdn. $r=0.95$ (range 0.87 to 0.99).

10. The correlations between residual change and the improvement classification from the pretreatment baseline to each successive anniversary assessment for the objective Global Functioning Score were also sufficiently high (mdn. $r=0.78$, range 0.68 to 0.86) that the "improvement" classification adequately reflects comparative rates of individual change.

11. The same conventions noted in note 5 for IAB analyses were adopted for all analyses of Clinical Frequency and TSBC data. However, only one substitution of a previous score was necessary, since all continuing residents provided at least a one-week score for standard time blocks.

12. Level of functioning in the community for continued significant releases was assessed on components of the IAB (ISMF & NOSIE-30) obtained on six-month postrelease follow-ups. Continued significant releases to extended-care facilities had IAB components completed in the same manner as described for the intramural period, while "independent" continued significant releases had IAB components scored from structured interview protocols from the resident and significant other. Three-month postrelease assessments, including the SRIC and TSBC, were obtained in two extended-care facilities to evaluate different modes of aftercare consultation.

## 12. THE CHRONICALLY INSTITUTIONALIZED POPULATION

1. All correlational analyses employed $p < 0.05$ (two-sided) for significance level, with differences tested via Fisher's Z' transformation for independent $r$'s, and Hotelling's t for nonindependent $r$'s (Edwards, 1960). Excluding the significant relationships existing over all three groups combined, only six correlations achieved significance within groups—actually less than expected by chance. Significant between-group differences were found for only two relationships involving these correlations: the sex/process-reactive correlation within the hospital group ($r=-0.41$) showed a significantly greater tendency for males rather than females to receive more "process" scores than within the milieu program ($r=0.17$); the race/precipitating factors correlation within the hospital group ($r=0.49$) was significantly different from those within both social-learning ($r=-0.37$) and milieu ($r=-0.31$) groups, indicating a tendency for precipitating factors to have been identified on initial hospitalization more frequently for blacks within the hospital group and whites within the psychosocial groups.

2. All IAB scores in table 12.2 reflect the average of the original assessment on which equated groups were selected and the post-transfer assessment prior to introduction of

psychosocial programs to provide the most stable pretreatment measures possible.

3. To compare with other populations see: for the MSBS: Dinoff et al., 1962; Dinoff et al., 1969; Farina et al., 1957; Finch et al., 1970; Haney et al., 1970; Lentz et al., 1971; Wagner & Paul, 1970. For the ISMF (SBSGI, in original format): Gruenberg et al., 1966; Kasius, 1966; Lentz et al., 1971; Paul et al., 1976. For the NOSIE-30: Honigfeld, 1966; Lentz et al., 1971; Muzekari et al., 1973; Pattison & Rhodes, 1974; Philip, 1973.

4. A better clinical picture of project patients may be obtained from the illustrative cases at the end of chapters 14, 19, 24, & 29, where component scores are described for residents, along with brief histories and details of responsiveness.

## 14. DIFFERENTIAL EFFECTIVENESS OF THE MILIEU AND SOCIAL-LEARNING PROGRAMS AFTER PROGRAM INTRODUCTION

1. During the current time period, the average reliability coefficient for raw terminal Clinical Frequency recordings was $\phi=0.97$ over twenty change agent-senior staff pairs on an average sample of nineteen recordings per pair. Average intraclass reliability exceeded $r=0.98$ for all TSBC scores used in analyses, obtained over twelve observer pairs, cross-sectionally overlapped for full-day observations on fifty-six residents.

2. Throughout all analyses, conservative estimates of error df were employed for pooled mean squares (Winer, 1962).

3. Throughout all analyses with df=1, chi-square was reduced by Yates correction for continuity (Siegel, 1956).

4. Correlational analyses employed $p < 0.05$ (two-sided) for significance level.

## 15. OTHER ONGOING RESIDENT ACTIVITY AFTER PROGRAM INTRODUCTION

1. Reliability of GAI indexes ranged from $r=0.87$ to $0.99$ (see chapter 11).

2. Differences between programs on GAI data were evaluated by point-biseral correlations between programs and unit means over standard time blocks. All correlational analyses employed $p < 0.05$ (two-sided) for significance level, with differences tested via Fisher's Z' transformation (Edwards, 1960).

3. Utilization data were obtained from Clinical Frequency recordings for which continuous spot checks regularly yielded reliability coefficients of $\phi > 0.99$. All ANOVAs paralleled those in chapter 14.

4. Average intraclass reliability exceeded $r=0.99$ for both "eyes open" and "with others," obtained over twelve observer pairs, cross-sectionally overlapped for full-day observations on fifty-six residents. All ANOVAs paralleled those in chapter 14.

5. See chapter 11 for format of Stereotypy/Variability scores. All ANOVAs paralleled those in chapter 14.

## 16. STAFF ATTITUDES AND PERFORMANCE BEFORE AND AFTER PROGRAM INTRODUCTION

1. See chapter 9 for an explanation of sten transformation and OMI differences between junior and senior staff (consistent throughout). Numbers of staff were: 24 (19 junior staff) at posttraining, anniversary assessment 0, and 26 (20 junior staff) at anniversary assessment 1, with 18 (13 junior staff) continuing over the entire period.

2. Differences between groups or assessment periods were evaluated on standardized scores via appropriate two-way ANOVAs (independent or repeated measures with scores as the second factor), partitioning of simple effects, and tests of individual components. Throughout all analyses, conservative estimates of error df were employed for pooled mean squares (see Winer, 1962).

3. Differences between sten scores were evaluated by one-way ANOVAs followed by Newman-Keul's multiple comparisons at $p < 0.05$ (Winer, 1962).

4. All correlational analyses employed $p < 0.05$ (two-sided) for significance level, with differences tested via Fisher's Z' transformation for independent r's and Hotelling's t for nonindependent r's (see Edwards, 1960).

5. Level deviations were quantified via $D^2$'s (sums of squared deviations) between staff means and the ideal over scores, with differences evaluated by two-sided randomization tests on $D^2$ components (see Siegel, 1956).

6. No consistent differences were obtained between junior and senior staff at any time during the intramural period.

7. TOS preferred scores were evaluated by ANOVAs parallel to those used with OMI data (see note 2), with differences between scores evaluated by Newman-Keul's multiple comparisons at $p < 0.05$ (Winer, 1962).

8. TOS scores for psychosocial orientations were evaluated using three-way ANOVAs (orientation, scores, assessment periods—for independent or repeated measures), partitioning of simple effects, and tests of individual components, with differences between scores evaluated by Newman-Keul's multiple comparisons

at $p < 0.05$. Throughout all analyses, conservative estimates of error df were employed for pooled mean squares (see Winer, 1962).

9. During this time period, reliabilities for all SRIC data used in analyses ranged from average intraclass coefficients of $r=0.91$ to $r=1.00$, with the overall average reliability of the instrument exceeding $r=0.99$, based upon six observer pairs cross-sectionally overlapped on an average sample of 52.5 SRICs per pair.

10. Differences between programs on SRIC data were evaluated by point-biseral correlations between programs and unit means over standard time blocks.

11. Analysis of staff error is even more remarkable if note is taken of the fact that all within-cell data in SRIC summary tables are rounded from actual total frequencies. Thus, a frequency cell without an entry reflects an observed rate of less than 0.0045 per hour or an actual occurrence of less than one instance every two weeks.

## 18. NOTABLE EVENTS AND OVERVIEW OF THE NEXT TWO YEARS

1. The procedures for dealing with resident assaults may seem extreme or overreactive to the reader who has not had direct clinical experience with populations as severely disturbed as those in this study (e.g., assaults ranged from the ordinary bodily blow to biting a finger off, breaking a leg, and literally hurling a staff member over a counter a distance of some ten feet). Actually the procedures were relatively benign in comparison to the history of aversive stimulation this group had previously received through usual medical procedures (e.g., electroconvulsive shock, insulin shock, and the canvas-restrained tubs of hydrotherapy). The major feature of the procedures was the immediate and consistent application of known consequences, which were designed to be sufficiently unpleasant to the offender to control his or her assaultiveness.

2. Several individual-subject investigations of specific drug response were also started during this period but had to be abandoned because of the illness and extended absence of the unit supervisor, who was the only clinical staff member who had access to the drug code.

## 19. DIFFERENTIAL EFFECTIVENESS OF THE MILIEU AND SOCIAL-LEARNING PROGRAMS DURING THE NEXT TWO YEARS

1. During this time period, the average reliability coefficient for raw terminal Clinical Frequency recordings was $\phi=0.94$ over seventy-three change agent-senior staff pairs on an average sample of sixteen recordings per pair. Average intraclass reliability exceeded $r=0.97$ for all TSBC scores used in analyses, obtained over a total of eighteen observer pairs, cross-sectionally overlapped for full-day observations within six-month intervals on fifty-six residents.

2. Throughout all analyses, conservative estimates of error df were employed for pooled mean squares (Winer, 1962).

3. Throughout all analyses with df=1, chi-square was reduced by Yates correction for continuity (Siegel, 1956).

4. All correlational analyses employed $p < 0.05$ (two-sided) for significance level, with differences tested via Fisher's Z' transformation for independent r's and Hotelling's t for nonindependent r's (Edwards, 1960).

## 20. OTHER ONGOING RESIDENT ACTIVITY DURING THE NEXT TWO YEARS

1. Reliability of GAI indexes ranged from $r=0.87$ to 0.99 (see chapter 11).

2. Differences between programs on GAI data were evaluated by point-biseral correlations between programs and unit means over standard time blocks. All correlational analyses employed $p < 0.05$ (two-sided) for significance level, with differences tested via Fisher's Z' transformation (Edwards, 1960).

3. Utilization data were obtained from Clinical Frequency recordings for which continuous spot checks regularly yielded reliability coefficients of $\phi > 0.99$. All ANOVAs paralleled those in chapter 19.

4. Average intraclass reliability exceeded $r=0.99$ for both "eyes open" and "with others," obtained over eighteen observer pairs, cross-sectionally overlapped for full-day observations on fifty-six residents. All ANOVAs paralleled those in chapter 19.

5. See chapter 11 for format of Stereotypy/Variability scores. All ANOVAs paralleled those in chapter 19.

## 21. STAFF ATTITUDES AND PERFORMANCE DURING THE NEXT TWO YEARS

1. See chapter 9 for an explanation of sten transformation and OMI differences between junior and senior staff (consistent throughout). Numbers of staff were: 26 (21 junior staff) at anniversary assessment 2, and 25 (20 junior staff) at anniversary assessment 3, with 20 (15 junior staff) continuing from assessment 1 to 2 and 14 (11 junior staff) continuing from assessment 2 to 3; 29 (24 junior staff) at

anniversary assessment 4, and 30 (24 junior staff) at anniversary assessment 5, with 19 (15 junior staff) continuing from assessment 3 to 4 and 23 (16 junior staff) continuing from assessment 4 to 5; 7 (4 junior staff) were continuing from assessment 1 to 5. See chapter 16 for numbers at anniversary assessments 0 and 1.

2. Differences between groups or assessment periods were evaluated on standardized scores via appropriate two-way ANOVAs (independent or repeated measures with scores as the second factor), partitioning of simple effects, and tests of individual components. Throughout all analyses conservative estimates of error df were employed for pooled mean squares (see Winer, 1962).

3. Differences between sten scores were evaluated by one-way ANOVAs followed by Newman-Keul's multiple comparisons at $p < 0.05$ (Winer, 1962).

4. All correlational analyses employed $p < 0.05$ (two-sided) for significance level, with differences tested via Fisher's Z' transformation for independent r's and Hotelling's t for nonindependent r's (see Edwards, 1960).

5. Level deviations were quantified via $D^2$'s (sum of squared deviations) between staff means and the ideal over scores, with differences evaluated by two-sided randomization tests on $D^2$ components (see Siegel, 1956).

6. No consistent differences were obtained between junior and senior staff at any time during the intramural period.

7. TOS preferred scores were evaluated by ANOVAs parallel to those used with OMI data (see note 2), with differences between scores evaluated by Newman-Keul's multiple comparisons at $p < 0.05$ (Winer, 1962).

8. TOS scores for psychosocial orientations were evaluated via three-way ANOVAs (orientation; scores; assessment period—for independent or repeated measures), partitioning of simple effects, and tests of individual components, with differences between scores evaluated by Newman-Keul's multiple comparisons at $p < 0.05$. Throughout all analyses, conservative estimates of error df were employed for pooled mean squares (see Winer, 1962).

9. During the current time period, reliabilities for all SRIC data used in analyses ranged from average intraclass coefficients of $r=0.91$ to $r=1.00$, with the overall average reliability of the instrument exceeding $r=0.99$, based upon eighteen observer pairs cross-sectionally overlapped on an average sample of 28.9 SRICs per pair.

10. Differences between programs on SRIC data were evaluated by point-biseral correlations between programs and unit means over standard time blocks.

11. While figure 21.4 is complex, only relative change needs to be examined; overall levels and differentiation of staff behavior during the period are presented in table 21.2.

12. See chapter 16 for a detailed explanation of the layout of SRIC summary tables, such as table 21.2.

## 24. DIFFERENTIAL EFFECTIVENESS OF THE MILIEU AND SOCIAL-LEARNING PROGRAMS DURING THE NEXT YEAR AND A HALF

1. During the present time period, the average reliability coefficient for raw terminal Clinical Frequency recordings was $\phi=0.95$ over forty-five change agent-senior staff pairs on an average sample of fourteen recordings per pair. Average intraclass reliability exceeded $r=0.97$ for all TSBC scores used in analyses, obtained over a total of twelve observer pairs, cross-sectionally overlapped for full-day observations within six-month intervals on fifty-six residents.

2. Throughout all analyses, conservative estimates of error df were employed for pooled mean squares (Winer, 1962).

3. Throughout all analyses with df=1, chi-square was reduced by Yates correction for continuity (Siegel, 1956).

4. All correlational analyses employed $p < 0.05$ (two-sided) for significance level, with differences tested via Fisher's Z' transformation for independent r's and Hotelling's t for nonindependent r's (Edwards, 1960).

## 25. OTHER ONGOING RESIDENT ACTIVITY DURING THE NEXT YEAR AND A HALF

1. Reliability of GAI indexes ranged from $r=0.87$ to $0.99$ (see chapter 11).

2. Differences between programs on GAI data were evaluated by point-biseral correlations between programs and unit means over standard time blocks. All correlational analyses employed $p < 0.05$ (two-sided) for significance level, with differences tested via Fisher's Z' transformation (Edwards, 1960).

3. Utilization data were obtained from Clinical Frequency recordings for which continuous spot checks regularly yielded reliability coefficients of $\phi > 0.99$. All ANOVAs paralleled those in chapter 24.

4. Average intraclass reliability exceeded $r=0.99$ for both "eyes open" and "with others," obtained over twelve observer pairs, cross-sectionally overlapped for full day observations on fifty-six residents. All ANOVAs paralleled those in chapter 24.

5. See chapter 11 for format of Stereotypy/Variability scores. All ANOVAs paralleled those in chapter 24.

## 26. STAFF ATTITUDES AND PERFORMANCE DURING THE NEXT YEAR AND A HALF

1. See chapter 9 for an explanation of sten transformation and OMI differences between junior and senior staff (consistent throughout). Numbers of staff were: 32 (25 junior staff) at anniversary assessment 6, and 31 (24 junior staff) at anniversary assessment 7, with 24 (19 junior staff) continuing from assessment 5 to 6 and 28 (22 junior staff) continuing from assessment 6 to 7; 30 (22 junior staff) at anniversary assessment 8, with 22 (17 junior staff) continuing from assessment 7 to 8. See earlier chapters (16 & 21) for numbers at anniversary assessments 0 and 5. Numbers reflect reorganization of clinical staff described in chapter 23.

2. Differences between groups or assessment periods were evaluated on standardized scores via appropriate two-way ANOVAs (independent or repeated measures with scores as the second factor), partitioning of simple effects, and tests of individual components. Throughout all analyses conservative estimates of error df were employed for pooled mean squares (see Winer, 1962).

3. Differences between sten scores were evaluated by one-way ANOVAs followed by Newman-Keul's multiple comparisons at $p < 0.05$ (Winer, 1962).

4. All correlational analyses employed $p < 0.05$ (two-sided) for significance level, with differences tested via Fisher's Z' transformation for independent r's and Hotelling's t for nonindependent r's (see Edwards, 1960).

5. Level deviations were quantified via $D^2$'s (sum of squared deviations) between staff means and the ideal overscores, with differences evaluated by two-sided randomization tests on $D^2$ components (see Siegel, 1956).

6. No consistent differences were obtained between junior and senior staff at any time during the intramural period.

7. TOS preferred scores were evaluated by ANOVAs parallel to those used with OMI data (see note 2), with differences between scores evaluated by Newman-Keul's multiple comparisons at $p < 0.05$ (Winer, 1962).

8. TOS scores for psychosocial orientations were evaluated via three-way ANOVAs (orientation; scores; assessment period—for independent or repeated measures), partitioning of simple effects, and tests of individual components, with differences between scores evaluated by Newman-Keul's multiple comparisons at $p < 0.05$. Throughout all analyses, conservative estimates of error df were employed for pooled mean squares (see Winer, 1962).

9. During the present time period, reliabilities for all SRIC data used in analyses ranged from average intraclass coefficients of $r=0.87$ to $r=1.00$, with the overall reliability of the instrument exceeding $r=0.99$, based upon eighteen observer pairs cross-sectionally overlapped on an average sample of 17.1 SRICs per pair.

10. Differences between programs on SRIC data were evaluated by point-biseral correlations between programs and unit means over standard time blocks.

11. While figure 26.4 is complex, only relative change needs to be examined; overall levels and differentiation of staff behavior during the period are presented in table 26.2.

12. See chapter 16 for a detailed explanation of the layout of SRIC summary tables, such as table 26.2.

## 29. DIFFERENTIAL EFFECTIVENESS OF THE MILIEU AND SOCIAL-LEARNING PROGRAMS DURING THE LAST SIX MONTHS

1. During this period, the average reliability coefficient for raw terminal Clinical Frequency recordings was $\phi=0.94$ over nine change agent-senior staff pairs on an average sample of sixteen recordings per pair. Average intraclass reliability exceeded $r=0.97$ for all TSBC scores used in analyses, obtained over ten observer pairs, cross-sectionally overlapped for full-day observations on fifty-six residents.

2. Throughout all analyses, conservative estimates of error df were employed for pooled mean squares (Winer, 1962).

3. Throughout all analyses with df=1, chi-square was reduced by Yates correction for continuity (Siegel, 1956).

4. All correlational analyses employed $p < 0.05$ (two-sided) for significance level, with differences tested via Fisher's Z' transformation for independent r's and Hotelling's t for nonindependent r's (Edwards, 1960).

## 30. OTHER ONGOING RESIDENT ACTIVITY DURING THE LAST SIX MONTHS

1. Reliability of GAI indexes ranged from $r=0.87$ to $0.99$ (see chapter 11).

2. Differences between programs on GAI data were evaluated by point-biseral correlations between programs and unit means over standard time blocks. All correlational analyses employed $p < 0.05$ (two sided) for significance level, with differences tested via Fisher's Z' transformation (Edwards, 1960).

3. Utilization data were obtained from Clinical Frequency recordings for which continuous spot checks regularly yielded reliability coefficients of $\phi > 0.99$. All ANOVAs paralleled those in chapter 29.

4. Average intraclass reliability exceeded r=0.99 for both "eyes open" and "with others," obtained over ten observer pairs, cross-sectionally overlapped for full-day observations on fifty-six residents. All ANOVAs paralleled those in chapter 29.

5. See chapter 11 for format of Stereotypy/Variability scores. All ANOVAs paralleled those in chapter 29.

## 31. STAFF ATTITUDES AND PERFORMANCE DURING THE LAST SIX MONTHS

1. See chapter 9 for explanation of sten transformation and OMI differences between junior and senior staff (consistent throughout). Numbers of staff were: 30 (22 junior staff) at anniversary assessment 8, and 36 (25 junior staff) at anniversary assessment 9, with 26 (18 junior staff) continuing from assessment 8 to 9. Numbers at assessment 9 reflect the same full-time equivalent senior staff as at assessment 8, but with more people because of the reorganization described in chapter 28.

2. Differences between groups or assessment periods were evaluated on standardized scores by appropriate two-way ANOVAs (independent or repeated measures with scores as the second factor), partitioning of simple effects, and tests of individual components. Throughout all analyses conservative estimates of error df were employed for pooled mean squares (see Winer, 1962).

3. Differences between sten scores were evaluated by one-way ANOVAs followed by Newman-Keul's multiple comparisons at $p < 0.05$ (Winer, 1962).

4. All correlational analyses employed $p < 0.05$ (two-sided) for significance level, with differences tested via Fisher's Z' transformation for independent r's and Hotelling's t for nonindependent r's (see Edwards, 1960).

5. Level deviations were quantified via $D^2$'s (sum of squared deviations) between staff means and the ideal over scores, with differences evaluated by two-sided randomization tests on $D^2$ components (see Siegel, 1956).

6. No consistent differences were obtained between junior and senior staff at any time during the intramural period.

7. TOS preferred scores were evaluated by ANOVAs parallel to those used with OMI data (see note 2), with differences between scores evaluated by Newman-Keul's multiple comparisons at $p < 0.05$ (Winer, 1962).

8. TOS scores for psychosocial orientations were evaluated via three-way ANOVAs (orientation; scores; assessment period—for independent or repeated measures), partitioning of simple effects, and tests of individual components, with differences between scores evaluated by Newman-Keul's multiple comparisons at $p < 0.05$. Throughout all analyses, conservative estimates of error df were employed for pooled mean squares (see Winer, 1962).

9. During this period, reliabilities for all SRIC data used in analyses ranged from average intraclass coefficients of r=0.83 to r=1.00, with the overall reliability of the instrument exceeding r=0.99, based upon nine observer pairs cross-sectionally overlapped on an average sample of 17.1 SRICs per pair.

10. Differences between programs on SRIC data were evaluated by point-biseral correlations between programs and unit means over standard time blocks.

11. Although figure 31.4 is complex, only relative change needs to be examined; overall levels and differentiation of staff behavior during the period are presented in tables 31.2 and 31.3.

12. See chapter 16 for a detailed explanation of the layout of SRIC summary tables, such as tables 31.2 and 31.3.

## 34. COMPARATIVE INTRAMURAL CHANGE OF THE PSYCHOSOCIAL AND HOSPITAL GROUPS

1. Interrater reliabilities of component instruments of the IAB over anniversary assessments 1 to 9 were: NOSIE-30, psychosocial groups mdn. r=0.94 (range 0.88 to 0.96), hospital group mdn. r=0.76 (range 0.45 to 0.86); ISMF, psychosocial groups mdn. r=0.97 (range 0.92 to 0.98), hospital group mdn. r=0.64 (range 0.40 to 0.82); MSBS, all r's > 0.98. NOSIE-30 and ISMF reliabilities by hospital staff were significantly lower than those by psychosocial staff ($p < 0.05$).

2. Throughout all analyses, conservative estimates of df were employed for pooled error mean squares and tests of individual components (see Winer, 1962). Variances were homogeneous across groups ($p > 0.05$, F max.) at all points through anniversary assessment 6. The variance of psychosocial groups was significantly greater than the hospital group on anniversary assessments 7, 8, and 9 ($p < 0.01$). Differences at these points were also tested by Mann-Whitney U on ranked IAB Factor Scores and ranked differences, with results reported in text (see Siegel, 1956).

3. All correlational analyses employed $p < 0.05$ (two-sided) for significance level, with differences tested via Fisher's Z' transformation for independent r's and Hotelling's t for nonindependent r's (see Edwards, 1960).

4. Data were also available on the Inpatient Multidimensional Psychiatric Scale (IMPS). However, method factors preclude its use for

assessing differential level or change (see Mariotto & Paul, 1974). The IMPS Total Morbidity Score was regularly negatively related to IAB Functioning within anniversary assessments (mdn. r=-0.65, range -0.56 to -0.76), showed a similar ranking of treatment groups to the IAB at each assessment, and was not correlated with drug status at any time.

5. "Improved" and "worse" classifications based upon individual change from entry exceeding 1.96 times the standard error of measurement on the Inpatient Assessment Battery Factor Score (see chapter 11).

## 35. COMPARATIVE RELEASE RATES

1. Throughout all analyses with df=1, chi-square was reduced by Yates correction for continuity (see Siegel, 1956).

2. "Project weeks in institution" were computed from the week following the original psychosocial baseline for original groups or from the week of transfer for replacements through termination of psychosocial programs.

3. All correlational analyses employed $p < 0.05$ (two-sided) for significance level, with differences tested via Fisher's Z' transformation for independent r's and Hotelling's t for nonindependent r's (see Edwards, 1960).

4. Although method factors preclude the use of the Inpatient Multidimensional Psychiatric Scale (IMPS) for assessing level differences or change, its concurrent validity in ranking subjects allows correlational analyses (see Mariotto & Paul, 1974).

## 38. FOLLOW-UP CONSULTATION TO COMMUNITY FACILITIES AND RESULTING PROGRAMS

1. Staff records following notification of layoffs and determination of new psychosocial aftercare staff were sufficiently loose and uninterpretable that little information was retained regarding actual contacts during the latter period.

2. Each assessment consisted of three days of habituation and reliability checks and seven days of data collection. Over the entire follow-up period, reliabilities for all SRIC data presented exceeded r=0.96, based upon repeating samples of three observer pairs cross-sectionally overlapped on an average sample of fifteen SRICs per pair.

3. Differences between extended-care facilities on SRIC data were evaluated by point-biseral correlations between facilities and means over three-month assessments at $p < 0.05$ (two-sided).

## 39. POSTRELEASE LEVELS OF FUNCTIONING IN THE COMMUNITY

1. Interrater reliabilities of component instruments of the partial IAB Factor Score over the three six-month follow-up assessments were: NOSIE-30, r's=0.81, 0.92, & 0.88; ISMF, r's=0.84, 0.85, & 0.87. One score at the last follow-up was obtained in an institution for a resident who had been reinstitutionalized at that time, and one score was a carry-over for a resident who had died. Partial IAB follow-up data for releases from original equated groups were evaluated via a two-way repeated measures ANOVA (groups x trials), partitioning of simple effects, and tests of individual components. Conservative estimates of error df were employed for pooled mean squares, with harmonic mean N's for testing between group effects (see Winer, 1962). The variances of releases from the hospital group were frequently smaller than one or the other of the variances of releases from psychosocial programs ($p < 0.05$); therefore, Mann-Whitney U tests on ranked scores were also performed (see Siegel, 1956), with the results of parametric and non-parametric tests being identical.

2. "Improvement" or "worse" classification was based upon individual change exceeding 1.96 times the standard error of measurement for the partial IAB Factor Score, based upon reliabilities during the follow-up period.

3. All correlational analyses employed $p < 0.05$ (two-sided) for significance level, with differences tested via Fisher's Z' transformation for independent r's and Hotelling's t for nonindependent r's (Edwards, 1960).

4. Interrater reliabilities of component instruments of the partial IAB over the six three-month follow-up assessments in targeted facilities were: NOSIE-30, program consultation facility mdn. r=0.83 (range 0.44 to 0.94), case consultation facility, mdn. r=0.89 (range 0.88 to 0.93); ISMF, program consultation facility, mdn. r=0.70 (range 0.23 to 0.79), case consultation facility, mdn. r=0.90 (range 0.85 to 0.93). Reliabilities of staff receiving program consultation were significantly lower than staff receiving case consultation on all ISMF ratings and on the first two NOSIE-30 ratings. Average intraclass reliability exceeded r=0.98 for the two TSBC scores used in analyses, obtained on repeating samples of three observer pairs cross-sectionally overlapped for full-day observations on average samples of 22 and 31.3 residents, respectively, in the facility receiving program consultation and in the facility receiving case consultation.

5. Data in figure 39.1 were evaluated via two-way repeated measures ANOVAs (groups x trials) for each score on each set of sequentially equated subgroups, with partitioning of

simple effects and tests of individual components. Conservative estimates of error df were employed for pooled mean squares throughout (see Winer, 1962).

6. In addition to the lower reliabilities of staff in the program consultation facility on ratings of IAB components (see note 1), evidence for less valid, possibly reactive, staff ratings was obtained on an examination of intercorrelations between TSBC data and the partial IAB Functioning Score within facilities. Over the six three-month follow-up assessments in the program and case consultation facilities the following correlations were obtained: IAB/TSBC Appropriate, program consultation facility, mdn. r=0.50 (range 0.29 to 0.61), case consultation facility, mdn. r=0.61 (range 0.48 to 0.70); IAB/TSBC Inappropriate, program consultation facility, mdn. r=-0.29 (range -0.19 to -0.38), case consultation facility, mdn. r=-0.67 (range -0.58 to -0.73). While none of the differences between validity coefficients were statistically significant between facilities, all validity coefficients within the case consultation facility were significant; neither of the coefficients were significant within the program consultation facility over the first two assessments, nor was the correlation of IAB/TSBC Inappropriate significant at the third.

## 40. PRACTICAL OUTCOME OF THE PSYCHOSOCIAL AND HOSPITAL PROGRAMS

1. One release from the original milieu group was hospitalized for less than two weeks during the follow-up period, after which she again achieved significant release with continuing community stay. Also, one milieu release required so much attention at the end of her first six months out that the period was counted as a temporary hospitalization; later she again achieved significant release with continuing community stay. Two deaths occurred over the follow-up period. A female replacement to the social-learning program who had achieved and maintained successful community placement died of leukemia, and a male original patient, who was still in the regional hospital, died of unknown causes. In both cases, the deaths were classified on the basis of their last assessment before death.

2. Throughout all analyses with df=1, chi-square was reduced by Yates correction for continuity (see Siegel, 1956).

3. Nonparametric tests were employed since the majority of the variances were marginally significant and earlier data (chapter 35) had employed such tests (see Siegel, 1956).

4. The self-contained nature and heavy administrative structure of the multiple central departments of the regional hospital likely cost considerably more than the center intramural operations for psychosocial programs on food, shelter, and administration; however, institutional records preclude reliable recovery of this information by subgroups, even if it were relevant (see Lindley, 1975).

5. "Total cost per case" in table 40.3 is based upon the entire project period, including follow-up. Identical relative costs are obtained if costs are calculated only to the time of termination of the psychosocial programs.

6. Although assessment costs beyond those obtained by the clinical staff are not included in the treatment costs, the clinical utility of the TSBC and SRIC are of such potential importance that their cost is worthy of mention. The total direct costs of continuous collection, summarization and feedback of TSBC and SRIC data for clinical use (requiring 0.5 research assistant, 1 chief observer, and 4 additional observers) was $1.41 per resident per day (in 1970 dollars). How such assessments could be included in ongoing hospital programs without added expense is obvious: Center costs of staffing a central snack bar ran only eleven cents per resident per day for psychosocial programs because treatment staff handled the majority of these activities themselves and all activities involving the on-unit canteens. In contrast, hospital costs of staffing the central commissary snack bar, alone ran $1.52 per patient per day. Thus, the complete SRIC and TSBC systems could have been implemented for hospital programs without additional costs simply by changing the management of canteens and snack bar to that used by the center.

7. The $27.44 figure clearly involves estimates because detailed figures were not available from hospital records. Staffing positions were known, but costs were necessarily estimated on the basis of changes from known pay grades and step levels for FY1970 to FY1973 rates in salary schedules, rather than actual salaries. For purposes of comparisons between programs, the specific figure is essentially irrelevant, since any constant amount would yield the same comparative figures.

## 42. CURRENT STATUS OF THE MILIEU AND SOCIAL-LEARNING APPROACHES

1. The interested reader is referred to a "A Guide to the Remainder of the Volume" in chapter 3 for assistance in locating details of empirical findings and relevant summaries in other areas presented in this book.

2. TSBC Hostile-Belligerence also failed to predict in-community functioning, but all released residents obtained "zero" indexes before release. While both milieu and social-

learning programs showed equal and significant reductions in Hostile-Belligerence, that time-sample measure was inadequate to assess impact on high-intensity, low-frequency behaviors; Intolerable Clinical Frequencies was a superior measure.

3. See appendixes B and C and chapter 43 (notes 11, 13, & 15) for more details on parameters recommended.

## 43. CONCLUDING COMMENTS ON INSTITUTIONAL RESEARCH AND TREATMENT

1. Many of the issues and recommendations discussed in this section apply equally to other populations and settings. However, in the interest of saving space and preventing misinterpretations, our discussion is restricted to the adult long-stay population of mental institutions.

2. It seems likely that our interpretation of the literature on the emerging law, legal principles, and legal processes will suffer from as great a deficit in understanding as that which appears when lawyers without clinical experience or special training in psychological and behavioral principles, techniques, and methodology attempt to interpret the literature on treatment and evaluation. We offer our interpretations, concerns, and recommendations in the spirit of increasing dialogue, and, possibly, understanding, among people and disciplines who all share a common goal of improving the status of both individuals and society. Organized efforts such as those of the Behavioral Law Center of the Institute for Behavioral Research (see *Arizona Law Review*, 1975, *17*, pp. 1-2) will continue to bring about developments in understanding by bringing together representatives of disciplines engaged in the study of the ethics of treatment and research and the advocacy of mental health law (e.g., American Bar Association, American Psychiatric Association, American Psychological Association, Mental Health Law Project, National Institute of Mental Health).

3. *Wyatt v. Stickney*, 325 F. Supp. 781 (M.D. Ala. 1971); 334 F. Supp. 1341 (M.D. Ala. 1971); 344F. Supp. 373 (M.D. Ala. 1972), and 344 F. Supp. 387 (M.D. Ala. 1972). *Wyatt v. Anderholt* on appeal, 503 F.2d 1305 (5th Cir. 1974); now *Wyatt v. Hardin* (see "Wyatt Victory 'Tarnished'?" 1975).

4. *Souder v. Brenan*, 367 F. Supp. 808 (D.D.C. 1973).

5. The basis for the *Souder* decision was ruled unconstitutional in 1976.

6. *Donaldson v. O'Connor*, 493 F. 2d 507 (5th Cir., 1974).

7. The manner in which such differential focus of regulation could result in practices totally contrary to the protections intended was personally emphasized to us in the following incident. In our deliberations on ways in which the extremely violent behavior of a few residents might be brought under control for their own protection and that of other residents and staff, some consideration was given to the contingent use of mild electric shock for aversive conditioning (Rachman & Teasdale, 1969). However, early in the explorations of the necessary safeguards and review procedures to be followed before evaluating such methods, the department director telephoned to explain that aversive conditioning was a politically sensitive issue. Therefore, more than the usual proposal, preparation, documentation, and committee reviews would be required—to the extent that approval would probably take about eighteen months. Instead, it was suggested that convulsive shock (which can cause tissue damage) be employed since "ECT is an accepted medical treatment." With those alternatives, our choice was to abandon either use of shock in favor of evaluating other procedures.

8. At the time of this writing, proposed rulemaking for the regulation of research with the "institutionalized mentally disabled," which involves comparative evaluations of ongoing treatment programs, may not automatically require participants to be defined as subjects at risk (see Department of Health, Education, and Welfare, 1974b, p. 30649). We hope that when the final rules and regulations are established, the effects of differential regulation may be corrected, at least in part. Similar hopes for more reasonable and balanced guidelines are held for the forthcoming recommendations from the National Commission for the Protection of Human Subjects in Biomedical and Behavioral Research, established by the National Research Act (PL 93-343).

9. Our thoughts on the mechanisms for ethical regulation are not meant to cover all issues or to stipulate specific implementation. That detail is precluded both by space limitations and by our belief that differences in time, place, and circumstances require differences in the structure and mode of operation of regulatory mechanisms. Rather our proposal is an outline of suggestions that might partially counteract some of the negative trends we see in current approaches. We hope that these suggestions will be considered, along with others, by those responsible for establishing ethical practices for long-stay residents of mental institutions.

10. It should be noted that the determination of resident performance meeting minimal goals was empirically derived and objectively assessable by the Clinical Frequencies Recording

System and the TSBC. These empirically derived criteria appear to be totally in keeping with the recent Supreme Court ruling defining principles for determination of the "right to liberty" (see note 6) and principles proposed by several ethical commentators of varying philosophical bent for setting limits on the right to refuse treatment or the right to be different (e.g., Halleck, 1974; Kittrie, 1971; Robinson, 1974).

11. To those not versed in legal interpretation, the absolute versus contingent rights issue for institutionalized patients seems paradoxical in that the entire legal system appears to be based on the presumption that individual rights are contingent upon appropriate behavior—defined by laws—the violation of which results in the contingent revocation of many of those rights. Even more paradoxical is the legal concern on the inviability of rights for institutionalized mental patients contingent upon expected benefits when 90% of criminal convictions in state and federal courts are estimated to result from plea bargaining (Manak, 1973), in which a defendant waives a number of constitutional rights for the benefit of receiving the lesser of two aversive consequences.

12. The meal charges detailed in chapter 8 and the purchase-eligibility procedures (chapters 28 & 30) are recommended for incorporation in future application of the social-learning program rather than the meal charges described in chapter 28. The total program was effective under both conditions, but fewer meals were missed under the earlier arrangement, and other backup reinforcers were maintained with the purchase-eligibility procedure.

13. Additional items and activities specified by the *Wyatt* court would presumably also fit Wexler's analysis of absolute rights. Among these are additional givens (receive telephone calls, send sealed mail) and additional token-cost activities (make telephone calls, additional privacy in one's room) within the social-learning program (see Prigmore & Davis, 1973).

14. The revised response-cost charges and purchase-eligibility procedures detailed in chapter 28 and appendix B are recommended for implementation rather than the original procedures described in chapter 8. As described in chapters 29 & 30, the later procedures effectively controlled maladaptive behavior and maintained greater participation in the full program.

15. Regular sleeping arrangements are also disturbed for any resident who has been incontinent in the previous week by restroom trips that are scheduled approximately every two hours during the night. Since all incontinent residents sleep in the free dorm, other residents who have not rented more private bedrooms are also disturbed. However, the effectiveness of the program in training residents to be continent is such that these nighttime disturbances are very short-lived.

16. We still recommend consideration of the forty-eight-hour time-out period for assaultive residents who fail to respond to the four to twenty-three and a half hour time-out consequence for assaults because of its earlier effectiveness and our belief that time out in seclusion is both more manageable and less intrusive than overcorrection/restitution procedures. Current data suggest that massive doses of phenothiazines ("chemical straightjackets") or mechanical restraints (e.g., "wet sheeting") are necessary to control assaultive or self-abusive persons only in circumstances in which staffing precludes the individual attention demanded for direct restraint and overcorrection/restitution (see chapter 42; Webster & Azrin, 1973).

17. Lest these recommendations be considered unusual, see Lehmann (1974), who concludes a review of the literature with similar recommendations, except for insulin shock therapy, and Racy & Goldstein (1975), who found that psychiatric residents (not patients) from a progressive medical school shared similar beliefs at the beginning and end of their first six months on an acute inpatient unit. However, it should also be noted that the *Wyatt* standards proscribe ECT and psychosurgery (Wexler, 1973).

18. The social-learning program also appears to have ensured other rights specified by the *Wyatt* court more adequately than programs elsewhere, including the right to be free of excessive medication, the right to prompt and adequate medical treatment for physical ailments, the right to a written description of the treatment program, the right to receive suitable educational services, and individualized post-institutionalization plans with transitional assistance in the community (Prigmore & Davis, 1973). However, the staffing—while empirically documented as adequate and effective—would not meet distribution and numbers specified under *Wyatt* for the Alabama institutions as psychologists, licensed practical nurses, and rehabilitation counselors were above the numbers stipulated, and psychiatrists, physicians, nurses, social workers, activity therapists, and all preprofessional staff, as well as total numbers, were below those stipulated (see Prigmore & Davis, 1973; Stickney, 1974).

19. The entire focus on "schizophrenia" as an illness or disease process may continue to lead up blind alleys (see Wyatt et al., 1971) because of the failure of the nomenclature to provide a homogeneous set of phenomena for which a biological basis can reasonably be found (see Blashfield, 1973) and the notorious lack of reliability and validity of such a classification in

practice (see Shields & Gottesman, 1972; Ullmann & Krasner, 1975). Even if an interactive genetic component were found to underlie some characteristic psychotic phenomena—as it likely does in some cases—current medical approaches have little to show of promise to date as a strategy for remediation. As Cancro states, "The presence of such a genetic component is therapeutically unimportant. The origins of the specific response disposition do not matter. What matters is identifying which patient is likely to respond to which treatment in which way" (1974, p. 70).

20. A related problem is that destructive effects of high-ranking executive, judicial, and legislative officials arising from politically motivated actions cannot be corrected even by litigation, since such officials are typically granted immunity to liability (Friedman, 1975). For example, the state representative who caused such upheaval at the regional center just before elections was eventually unseated several years later, but only on the basis of a felony conviction for an act that had occurred some five years earlier. Legal immunity for such officials should not be absolute when harm is caused to others.

# References

Abroms, G. M. Defining milieu therapy. *Archives of General Psychiatry*, 1969, *21*, 553-560.

Allen, G. J.; Chinsky, J. M.; & Veit, S. W. Pressures toward institutionalization within the aide culture: A behavioral-analytic case study. *Journal of Community Psychology*, 1974, *2*, 67-70.

Almond, R. J. *The healing community.* New York: Jason Aronson, 1974a.

———. Current status and recent developments in milieu treatment. Paper presented to the international conference on the psychiatric milieu, Stockbridge, Mass., October 9-13, 1974b.

———Issues in milieu treatment. *Schizophrenia Bulletin*, 1975, *13*, 12-26.

Anthony, W. A., & Buell, G. J. Psychiatric aftercare clinic effectiveness as a function of patient demographic characteristics. *Journal of Consulting and Clinical Psychology*, 1973, *41*, 116-119.

Anthony, W. A.; Buell, G. J.; Sharrett, S.; & Althoff, M. E. Efficacy of psychiatric rehabilitation. *Psychological Bulletin*, 1972, *78*, 447-456.

Appleby, L.; Proano, A.; & Perry, R. Theoretical vs. empirical treatment models: An exploratory investigation. In L. Appleby, J. M. Scher, & J. Cumming, eds., *Chronic schizophrenia*. Glencoe: Free Press, 1960.

Arnhoff, F. N.; Rubinstein, E. A.; & Spersimon, J. C. *Manpower for mental health.* Chicago: Aldine, 1969.

Arthur, G.; Ellsworth, R. B.; & Kroeker, D. Readmission of released mental patients: A research study. *Social Work*, 1968, *13*, 78-84.

Artiss, K. L. *Milieu therapy in schizophrenia.* New York: Grune & Stratton, 1962.

Asch, S. H. Review of "The rights of mental patients." *The Journal of Psychiatry and Law*, 1975, *3*, 125-130.

Atthowe, J. M., & Krasner, L. A preliminary report on the application of contingent reinforcement procedures (token economy) on a "chronic" psychiatric ward. *Journal of Abnormal Psychology*, 1968, *73*, 37-43.

Aumack, L. The patient activity checklist: An instrument and an approach for measuring behavior. *Journal of Clinical Psychology*, 1969, *25*, 134-137.

Ayllon, T. Intensive treatment of psychotic behaviors by stimulus satiation and food reinforcement. *Behavior Research and Therapy*, 1963, *1*, 53-61.

———. Behavior modification in institutional settings. *Arizona Law Review*, 1975, *17*, 3-19.

Ayllon, T., & Azrin, N. H. The measurement and reinforcement of behavior of psychotics. *Journal of the Experimental Analysis of Behavior*, 1965, *8*, 357-383.

———. *The token economy.* New York: Appleton-Century-Crofts, 1968.

Ayllon, T., & Haughton, E. Modification of symptomatic verbal behavior of mental patients. *Behavior Research and Therapy*, 1964, *2*, 87-97.

Ayllon, T., & Michael, J. The psychiatric nurse as a behavioral engineer. *Journal of the Experimental Analysis of Behavior*, 1959, *2*, 323-334.

Bach-Y-Rita, G. Habitual violence and self-mutilation. *American Journal of Psychiatry*, 1974, *131*, 1018-1020.

Ball, T. S. The re-establishment of social behavior. *Hospital & Community Psychiatry*, 1968, *19*, 230-232.

Bandura, A. *Principles of behavior modification.* New York: Holt, Rinehart, & Winston, 1969.

Barrett, W. W.; Ellsworth, R. B.; Clark, L. D.; & Enniss, J. Study of the differential behavioral effects of reserpine, chlorpromazine and a combination of these drugs in chronic schizophrenia. *Diseases of the Nervous System*, 1957, *18*, 209-215.

Bartholow, G. W., & Tunakan, B. Role of the community mental health center in the rehabilitation of the long-hospitalized psychiatric patient. In J. H. Masserman, ed., *Current psychiatric therapies.* New York: Grune & Stratton, 1967.

Bartlett, F. L. Institutional peonage: on exploitation of mental patients. *Atlantic Monthly*, 1964, *214*, 116-119.

Batman, R. H. Consultation as an educational

technique in psychiatric nursing. *Mental Hygiene*, 1968, *52*, 617-621.

Bazelon, D. L. The right to treatment: The court's role. *Hospital & Community Psychiatry*, 1969, *20*, 129-135.

———. Institutional psychiatry—"The self inflicted wound." *Catholic University Law Review*, 1974, *23*, 643-648.

Becker, H. S. *Outsiders*. Glencoe: Free Press, 1963.

Becker, W. C. A genetic approach to the interpretation and evaluation of the process-reactive distinction in schizophrenia. *Journal of Abnormal and Social Psychology*, 1956, *53*, 229-236.

———. The process-reactive distinction—A key to the problem of schizophrenia? *Journal of Nervous and Mental Disease*, 1959, *129*, 442-449.

Bellak, L., ed. *Handbook of community psychiatry and community mental health*. New York: Grune & Stratton, 1964.

Bendig, A. W. Pittsburgh scale of social extroversion-introversion and emotionality. *Journal of Psychology*, 1962, *53*, 199-210.

Bennett, C. L. The Dutchess County Project. In E. M. Gruenberg, ed., *Evaluating the effectiveness of community mental health services*. New York: Milbank, 1966.

Bensberg, G. J.; Barnett, C. D.; & Hurder, W. P. Training of attendant personnel in residential facilities for the mentally retarded. *Mental Retardation*, June 1964, 144-151.

Berrington, W. P. Resocialization: Undoing the damage. *International Journal of Social Psychiatry*, 1966, *12*, 85-97.

Berwick, P. T., & Morris, L. A. Token economies: Are they doomed? *Professional Psychology*, 1974, *5*, 434-439.

Birky, H. J.; Chambliss, J. E.; & Wasden, R. A comparison of residents discharged from a token economy and two traditional psychiatric programs. *Behavior Therapy*, 1971, *2*, 46-51.

Birnbaum, M. The right to treatment. *American Bar Association Journal*, 1960, *46*, 499-505.

Blashfield, R. An evaluation of the DSM-II classification of schizophrenia as a nomenclature. *Journal of Abnormal Psychology*, 1973, *82*, 382-389.

Bockoven, J. S. *Moral treatment in American psychiatry*. New York: Springer, 1963.

Bragg, R. A., & Wagner, M. K. Can deprivation be justified? *Hospital & Community Psychiatry*, 1968, *19*, 229-230.

Braginsky, B. M.; Braginsky, D. D.; & Ring, K. *Methods of madness: The mental hospital as a last resort*. New York: Holt, Rinehart, & Winston, 1969.

Braun, S. H. Ethical issues in behavior modification. *Behavior Therapy*, 1975, *6*, 51-62.

Bricker, W. A.; Morgan, D. G.; & Grabowski, J. G. Development and maintenance of a behavior modification repertoire of cottage attendants through T.V. feedback. *American Journal of Mental Deficiency*, 1972, *77*, 128-136.

Brill, H. The future of the mental hospital and its patients. *Psychiatric Annals*, 1975, *5*, 352-359.

Bromet, E.; Harrow, M.; & Kasl, S. Premorbid functioning and outcome in schizophrenics and nonschizophrenics. *Archives of General Psychiatry*, 1974, *30*, 203-207.

Bromet, E.; Harrow, M.; & Tucker, G. J. Factors related to short-term prognosis in schizophrenia and depression. *Archives of General Psychiatry*, 1971, *25*, 148-154.

Brooks, G. W. Rehabilitation of hospitalized chronic schizophrenic patients. In L. Appleby, J. M. Scher, & J. Cumming, eds., *Chronic schizophrenia*. Glencoe: Free Press, 1960.

Brown, G. W.; Carstairs, G. M.; & Topping, G. Posthospital adjustment of chronic mental patients. *Lancet*, 1958, *7048*, 685-689.

Bruce, M. Tokens for recovery. *American Journal of Nursing*, 1966, *66*, 1799-1802.

Buell, G. J., & Anthony, W. A. Demographic characteristics as predictors of recidivism and posthospital employment. *Journal of Counseling Psychology*, 1973, *20*, 361-365.

Butterfield, E. C., & Warren, S. A. The use of the MMPI in the selection of hospital aides. *Journal of Applied Psychology*, 1962, *46*, 34-40.

Cahoon, D. D. Balancing procedures against outcomes. *Hospital & Community Psychiatry*, 1968, *19*, 228-229.

Cancro, R. The rehabilitation of chronic schizophrenics: Genetic and environmental considerations. *The International Journal of Social Psychiatry*, 1974, *20*, 68-71.

Carlson, C. G.; Hersen, M.; & Eisler, R. M. Token economy programs in the treatment of hospitalized adult psychiatric patients. *Journal of Nervous and Mental Disease*, 1972, *155*, 192-204.

Chu, F., & Trotter, S. *The madness establishment*. New York: Grossman Publishers, 1974.

Clark, A. W., & Yeomans, N. T. *Fraser House*. New York: Springer, 1969.

Clark, D. H. The ward therapeutic community and its effects on the hospital. In H. Freeman, ed., *Psychiatric hospital care*. London: Bailliere, 1965.

Clark, D. H., & Oram, E. G. Reform in the mental hospital: An eight year follow-up. *International Journal of Social Psychiatry*, 1966, *12*, 98-108.

Clum, G. A. Intrapsychic variables and the patient's environment as factors in prognosis. *Psychological Bulletin*, 1975a, *82*, 413-431.

———. Intrapsychic and environmental variables as predictors of length of hospitalization. *Journal of Consulting and Clinical Psychology*, 1975b, *43*, 276.

Cochran, B. Where is my home? The closing of state mental hospitals. *Hospital & Community Psychiatry*, 1974, *25*, 393-401.

Coe, W. C.; Huels, M. A.; Curry, A. E.; & Kessler, D. R. Prediction of job performance of psychiatric nursing personnel. *Nursing Research*, 1967, *16*, 282-285.

Cohen, J., & Struening, E. L. Opinions about mental illness in the personnel of two large mental hospitals. *Journal of Abnormal and Social Psychology*, 1962, *64*, 349-360.

———. Opinions about mental illness: Mental hospital occupational profiles and profile clusters. *Psychological Reports*, 1963, *12*, 111-124.

Conley, R. W.; Conwell, M.; & Arrill, M. B. An approach to measuring the cost of mental illness. *American Journal of Psychiatry*, 1967, *124*, 63-70.

Crisswell, J. H. Considerations on the permanence of rehabilitation. Paper presented at the meeting of the American Psychological Association, Washington, D.C., September, 1967.

Cronbach, L. J., & Gleser, G. C. *Psychological tests and personnel decisions*, 2d ed. Urbana: University of Illinois Press, 1965.

Cropley, A. J., & Gazan, A. Some data concerning readmission of discharged schizophrenic patients. *British Journal of Social and Clinical Psychology*, 1969, *8*, 286-289.

Cuadra, C. A., & Reed, C. F. Prediction of psychiatric aide performance. *Journal of Applied Psychology*, 1957, *41*, 195-197.

Cumming, J., & Cumming, E. *Ego and milieu*. New York: Atherton, 1962.

Cunningham, M. K.; Botwinik, W.; Dolson, J.; & Weickert, A. A. Community placement of released mental patients: A five year study. *Social Work*, 1969, *14*, 54-61.

Curran, J. P.; Lentz, R. J.; & Paul, G. L. Effectiveness of sampling-exposure procedures on facilities utilization by psychiatric hard-core chronic patients. *Journal of Behavior Therapy and Experimental Psychiatry*, 1973, *4*, 201-207.

Dailey, W. F.; Allen, G. J.; Chinsky, J. M.; & Veit, S. W. Attendant behavior and attitudes toward institutionalized retarded children. *American Journal of Mental Deficiency*, 1974, *78*, 586-591.

Daniels, D. N. Milieu therapy. In C. P. Rosenbaum, ed., *The meaning of madness*. New York: Science House, 1970.

Davis, A. E.; Dinitz, S.; & Pasamanick, B. The prevention of hospitalization in schizophrenia: Five years after an experimental program. *American Journal of Orthopsychiatry*, 1972, *42*, 375-388.

Davison, G. C. Appraisal of behavior modification techniques with adults in institutional settings. In C. M. Franks, ed., *Behavior therapy: Appraisal and status*. New York: McGraw-Hill, 1969.

Davison, G. C., & Stuart, R. B. Behavior therapy and civil liberties. *American Psychologist*, 1975, *30*, 755-763.

Denman, S. B., & Ryder, F. P. Occupational satisfaction and dissatisfaction among psychiatric aides. *Hospital & Community Psychiatry*, 1971, *22*, 123-125.

Depue, R. A., & Dubicki, M. D. Hospitalization and premorbid characteristics in withdrawn and active schizophrenics. *Journal of Consulting and Clinical Psychology*, 1974, *42*, 628-632.

DiMascio, A., & Evans, A. S. The attitudes of psychiatric resident physicians at the Massachusetts Mental Health Center toward chronic schizophrenic patients. In M. Greenblatt, M. H. Soloman, A. S. Evans, & G. W. Brooks, eds., *Drug and social therapy in chronic schizophrenia*. Springfield, Ill.: Charles C. Thomas, 1965.

Dinoff, M.; Finch, A. J.; Finch, K.; & Hobbs, T. Comparison of regressed patients on the Minimal Social Behavior Scale. *Psychological Reports*, 1969, *24*, 922.

Dinoff, M.; Raymaker, H.; & Morris, J. R. The reliability and validity of the Minimal Social Behavior Scale and its use as a selection device. *Journal of Clinical Psychology*, 1962, *18*, 441-444.

Distefano, M. K., Jr., & Pryer, M. W. Stability of attitudes in psychiatric attendants following training. *Mental Hygiene*, 1970, *54*, 433-435.

Doty, D. W.; McInnis, T.; & Paul, G. L. Remediation of negative side-effects of an on-going response-cost system with chronic mental patients. *Journal of Applied Behavior Analysis*, 1974, *7*, 191-198.

Dunham, H. W., & Weinberg, S. K. *The culture of the state mental hospital*. Detroit: Wayne State University Press, 1960.

Durell, J.; Arnson, A.; & Kellam, S. G. A community-oriented therapeutic milieu. *Medical Annals, D.C.*, 1965, *34*, 468-474.

Edelson, M. The sociotherapeutic function in a psychiatric hospital. *Journal of the Fort Logan Mental Health Center*, 1967, *4*, 1-45.

Edelson, R. I., & Paul, G. L. Some problems in use of "attitude" and "atmosphere" scores as indicators of staff effectiveness in institutional treatment. *Journal of Nervous and Mental Disease*, 1976, *162*, 248-277.

Edwards, A. L. *Experimental design in psychological research*. New York: Holt, Rinehart, & Winston, 1960.

Eisenthal, S.; Harford, T.; & Solomon, L. Premorbid adjustment, paranoid-nonparanoid status, and chronicity in schizophrenic patients. *The Journal of Nervous and Mental Disease*, 1972, *155*, 227-231.

Eldred S. Review of current research related to the psychiatric residential milieu. Paper presented to the international conference on the psychiatric milieu, Stockbridge, Mass., October 9-13, 1974.

Ellsworth, R. B. The psychiatric aide as rehabilitation therapist. *Rehabilitation Counseling Bulletin*, 1964, *7*, 81-86.

———. *Nonprofessionals in psychiatric rehabilitation: The psychiatric aide and the schizophrenic patient.* New York: Appleton-Century-Crofts, 1968.

———. Feedback: Asset or liability in improving treatment effectiveness? *Journal of Consulting and Clinical Psychology*, 1973, *40*, 383-393.

Ellsworth, R. B., & Ellsworth, J. J. The psychiatric aide: Therapeutic agent or lost potential? *Journal of Psychiatric Nursing*, 1970, *8*, 7-13.

Ellsworth, R. B.; Mead, B. T.; & Clayton, W. H. The rehabilitation and disposition of chronically hospitalized schizophrenic patients. *Mental Hygiene*, 1958, *42*, 343-348.

Ellsworth, R. B., & Stokes, H. A. Staff attitudes and patient release. *Psychiatric Studies and Projects*, 1963, *7*, 1-6.

Epstein, L. J., & Simon, A. Alternatives to state hospitalization for the geriatric mentally ill. *American Journal of Psychiatry*, 1968, *124*, 955-961.

Erickson, R. C. Outcome studies in mental hospitals: A review. *Psychological Bulletin*, 1975, *82*, 519-540.

The ethics of ethicists. *Behavior Today*, 1975, *6*, 573-574.

Fairweather, G. W. *Methods for experimental social innovation.* New York: Wiley, 1967.

———, ed. *Social psychology in treating mental illness: Experimental approach.* New York: Wiley, 1964.

Fairweather, G. W.; Sanders, D. H.; Maynard, H.; & Cressler, D. L. *Community life for the mentally ill: An alternative to institutional care.* New York: Aldine, 1969.

Fairweather, G. W., & Simon, R. A. A further follow-up of psychotherapeutic programs. *Journal of Consulting Psychology*, 1963, *27*, 186.

Farina, A.; Arenberg, D.; & Guskin, S. A scale for measuring minimal social behavior. *Journal of Consulting Psychology*, 1957, *21*, 265-268.

Ferster, C. B. Classification of behavioral pathology. In L. Krasner & L. P. Ullmann, eds., *Research in behavior modification.* New York: Holt, 1965.

Filstead, W. J., & Rossi, J. J. Therapeutic milieu, therapeutic community, and milieu therapy: Some conceptual and definitional distinctions. In J. J. Rossi & W. S. Filstead, eds., *The therapeutic community.* New York: Behavioral Publications, 1973.

Finch, A. J., Jr.; Welsh, D. K.; Haney, J. R.; & Dinoff, M. Comparison of two versions of a minimum social behavior scale. *Psychological Reports*, 1970, *26*, 985-986.

Fishbein, M., & Ajzen, I. *Belief, attitude, intention and behavior.* Reading, Mass.: Addison-Wesley, 1975.

Foreyt, J. P.; Rockwood, C. E.; Davis, J. D.; Desvousges, W. H.; & Hollingsworth, R. Benefit-cost analysis of a token economy program. *Professional Psychology*, 1975, *6*, 26-33.

Forsyth, R. P., & Fairweather, G. W. Psychotherapeutic and other hospital treatment criteria: The dilemma. *Journal of Abnormal and Social Psychology*, 1961, *62*, 598-604.

Fowlkes, M. R. Business as usual—at the state mental hospital. *Psychiatry*, 1975, *38*, 55-64.

Foxx, R. M., & Azrin, N. H. Restitution: A method of eliminating aggressive-disruptive behavior of retarded and brain damaged patients. *Behavior Research and Therapy*, 1972, *10*, 15-27.

———. The elimination of autistic self-stimulatory behavior by overcorrection. *Journal of Applied Behavior Analysis*, 1973, *6*, 1-14.

Franks, C. M., ed. *Behavior therapy: Appraisal and status.* New York: McGraw-Hill, 1969.

Freeman, H. E., & Simmons, O. G. *The mental patient comes home.* New York: Wiley, 1963.

Friedman, P. R. Legal regulations of applied behavior analysis in mental institutions and prisons. *Arizona Law Review*, 1975, *17*, 39-104.

Galioni, E. G. Evaluation of a treatment program for chronically ill schizophrenic patients—a six year program. In L. Appleby, J. M. Scher, & J. Cumming, eds., *Chronic schizophrenia.* Glencoe: Free Press, 1960.

Galioni, E. G.; Adams, F. H.; & Tallman, F. F. Intensive treatment of back-ward patients—a controlled pilot study. *American Journal of Psychiatry*, 1953, *109*, 576-583.

Gardner, J. M. Teaching behavior modification to nonprofessionals. *Journal of Applied Behavior Analysis*, 1972, *5*, 517-522.

Garmezy, N. Process and reactive schizophrenia: Some conceptions and issues. *Schizophrenia Bulletin*, 1970, *2*, 30-67.

Gelfand, S. A behavior modification training program for psychiatric residents. *Journal of Behavior Therapy and Experimental Psychiatry*, 1972, *3*, 141-151.

Gericke, O. L. Practical use of operant conditioning procedures in a mental hospital. *Psychiatric Studies and Projects*, 1965, *3*, 1-10.

Giebink, J. W., & Stover, D. O. Adjustment, mental health opinions, and proficiency of child care personnel. *Journal of Consulting and Clinical Psychology*, 1969, *33*, 532-535.

Gilligan, J. Review of the literature. In M. Greenblatt, M. H. Soloman, A. S. Evans, & G. W. Brooks, eds., *Drug and social therapy in chronic schizophrenia*. Springfield, Ill.: Charles C. Thomas, 1965.

Glass, A. J. The future of large public mental hospitals. *Mental Hospitals*, 1965, 9-22.

———. Legislative aspects of the care of the mentally ill. *Illinois Department of Mental Health and Developmental Disabilities Journal of Research and Training*, 1974, *2*, 18-23.

Glass, G. V.; Willson, V. L.; & Gottman, J. M. *Design and analysis of time series experiments*. Boulder: Colorado Associated University Press, 1975.

Gleser, G. C. Psychometric contributions in the assessment of patients. In D. H. Efron, ed., *Psychopharmacology, review of progress, 1957-1967*. Washington, D.C.: Government Printing Office, 1968.

Goffman, E. *Asylums*. Garden City, N.Y.: Doubleday, 1961.

Goldberg, L. R., & Hase, H. D. Strategies and tactics of personality inventory construction: An empirical investigation. *Oregon Research Institute Research Monograph*, 1967, *7*, (1).

Goldiamond, I. Singling out behavior modification for legal regulation: Some effects on patient care, psychotherapy, and research in general. *Arizona Law Review*, 1975, *17*, 105-126.

Goldstein, A. P.; Heller, K.; & Sechrest, L. B. *Psychotherapy and the psychology of behavior change*. New York: Wiley, 1966.

Greenblatt, M. Therapeutic and nontherapeutic features of the environment. In M. Greenblatt, M. H. Soloman, A. S. Evans, & G. W. Brooks, eds., *Drug and social therapy in chronic schizophrenics*. Springfield, Ill.: Charles C. Thomas, 1965.

———. Class action and the right to treatment. *Hospital & Community Psychiatry*, 1974, *25*, 449-452.

Greenblatt, M.; Soloman, M. H.; Evans, A. S.; & Brooks, G. W., eds. *Drug and social therapy in chronic schizophrenia*. Springfield, Ill.: Charles C. Thomas, 1965.

Greenburg, D. J.; Scott, S. B.; Pisa, A.; & Friesen, D. D. Beyond the token economy: A comparison of two contingency programs. *Journal of Consulting and Clinical Psychology*, 1975, *43*, 498-503.

Gripp, R. F., & Magaro, P. A. A token economy program evaluated with untreated control ward comparisons. *Behavior Research and Therapy*, 1971, *9*, 137-149.

———. The token economy program in the psychiatric hospital: A review and analysis. *Behavior Research and Therapy*, 1974, *12*, 205-228.

———. Milieu therapy in the psychiatric hospital: Death due to cultural exposure. In P. A. Magaro, ed., *The construction of madness*. London: Pergamon Press, 1976.

Gruenberg, E. M. The social breakdown syndrome—some origins. *American Journal of Psychiatry*, 1967, *123*, 12-20.

———. The social breakdown syndrome and its prevention. In S. Arieti, ed., *American handbook of psychiatry*, 2d ed. New York: Basic Books, 1974.

Gruenberg, E. M.; Brandon, S.; & Kasius, R. D. Identifying cases of the social breakdown syndrome. In E. M. Gruenberg, ed., *Evaluating the effectiveness of community mental health services*. New York: Milbank, 1966.

Gruenberg, E. M., & Huxley, J. Mental health services can be organized to prevent chronic disability. *Community Mental Health Journal*, 1970, *6*, 431-436.

Gruenberg, E. M.; Snow, H. B.; & Bennett, C. L. Preventing the social breakdown syndrome. In *Social Psychiatry*, 47, the Association for Research in Nervous and Mental Disease, 1969.

Guerney, B. G., Jr., ed. *Psychotherapeutic agents: New roles for nonprofessionals, parents and teachers*. New York: Holt, Rinehart, & Winston, 1969.

Gunderson, J. G., & Mosher, L. R. The cost of schizophrenia. *American Journal of Psychiatry*, 1975, *132*, 901-906.

Gurel, L. Release and community stay criteria in evaluating psychiatric treatment. In P. H. Hoch & J. Zubin, eds., *Psychopathology of schizophrenia*. New York: Grune & Stratton, 1966.

———. A ten year perspective on outcome in functional psychosis. In *Highlights of the 15th Annual Conference: VA Cooperative Studies in Psychiatry*. Washington, D.C.: Veterans Administration, 1970.

Guttentag, M. Evaluation of social intervention programs. *Annals of New York Academy of Sciences*, 1973, *218*, 313.

Hagen, R. L. Behavioral therapies and the treatment of schizophrenia. *Schizophrenia Bulletin*, 1975, *13*, 70-96.

Hagen, R. L.; Craighead, W. E.; & Paul, G. L. Staff reactivity to evaluative behavioral observations. *Behavior Therapy*, 1975, *6*, 201-205.

Halleck, S. L. Legal and ethical aspects of behavioral control. *American Journal of Psychiatry*, 1974, *131*, 381-385.

Hallsten, E. A., & Fletcher, S. *Toward the systematic use of rewards.* Galesburg, Ill.: Galesburg State Research Hospital, 1966.

Halpern, J., & Binner, P. R. A model for an output value analysis of mental health programs. *Administration in Mental Health*, 1972, *1*, 40-51.

Hamlin, R., & Ward, W. Schizophrenic intelligence, symptoms, and release from the hospital. *Journal of Clinical Psychology*, 1973, *81*, 11-16.

Haney, J. R.; Welsh, D. K.; Finch, A. J., Jr.; & Dinoff, M. Comparisons of age matched regressed patients on the Minimum Social Behavior Scale. *Psychological Reports*, 1970, *27*, 104.

Harmatz, M. G.; Mendelsohn, R.; & Glassman, M. L. Gathering naturalistic, objective data on the behavior of schizophrenic patients. *Hospital & Community Psychiatry*, 1975, *26*, 83-86.

Harris, J. M.; Veit, S. W.; Allen, G. J.; & Chinsky, J. M. Aide-resident ratio and ward population density as mediators of social interaction. *American Journal of Mental Deficiency*, 1974, *79*, 320-326.

Hassall, C.; Spencer, A. M.; & Cross, K. W. Some changes in the composition of a mental hospital population. *British Journal of Psychiatry*, 1965, *111*, 420-428.

Heap, R. F.; Boblitt, W. E.; Moore, C. H.; & Hord, J. E. Behavior-milieu therapy with chronic neuropsychiatric patients. *Journal of Abnormal Psychology*, 1970, *76*, 349-354.

Hogarty, G. E., & Gross, M. Preadmission symptom differences between first-admitted schizophrenics in the predrug and postdrug era. *Comprehensive Psychiatry*, 1966, *7*, 134-140.

Hollander, M.; Plutchik, R.; & Homer, V. Interaction of patient and attendant reinforcement programs: The "piggyback" effect. *Journal of Consulting and Clinical Psychology*, 1973, *41*, 43-47.

Hollingshead, A. B., & Redlich, F. C. *Social class and mental illness.* New York: Wiley, 1958.

Honigfeld, G. *Nurses observation scale for inpatient evaluation (NOSIE-30).* Glen Oaks, N.Y.: Honigfeld, 1966.

Honigfeld, G., & Gillis, R. The role of institutionalization in the natural history of schizophrenia. *Diseases of the Nervous System*, 1967, *28*, 660-663.

Hugues, H. B. *2-B's credit system.* Anna, Ill.: Anna State Hospital, 1965.

Humphreys, L. G. Corporal punishment. *American Psychologist*, 1975, *30*, 708-709.

Hunter, M.; Schooler, C.; & Spohn, H. E. Measurement of characteristic patterns of ward behavior in chronic schizophrenia. *Journal of Consulting Psychology*, 1962, *26*, 69-73.

Illinois. Department of Mental Health. *Fiscal Year 1970: Mental Health Statistics for Illinois.* Springfield, Ill.: Department of Mental Health, 1970.

———. *Fiscal Year 1973: Mental Health Statistics for Illinois.* Springfield, Ill.: Department of Mental Health, 1973.

———. Department of Public Aid. *Notice to providers of group care services (rate schedule).* Springfield, Ill.: State Bureau of Medical Services, 1973.

Johnson, G.; Fox, J.; Schaefer, H. H.; & Ishikawa, W. Predicting rehospitalization from community placement. *Psychological Reports*, 1971, *29*, 475-478.

Joint Commission on Mental Illness and Health. *Action for mental health.* New York: Basic Books, 1961.

Jones, K., & Sidebotham, R. *Mental hospitals at work.* London: Routledge & Kegan Paul, 1962.

Jones, M. *The therapeutic community.* New York: Basic Books, 1953.

———. *Beyond the therapeutic community: Social learning and social psychiatry.* New Haven, Conn.: Yale University Press, 1968.

Jones, M., & Bonn, E. M. From therapeutic community to self-sufficient community. *Hospital & Community Psychiatry*, 1973, *24*, 675-680.

Kahne, M. J. Bureaucratic structure and impersonal experience in mental hospitals. *Psychiatry*, 1959, *363*, 375.

Kasius, R. V. The social breakdown syndrome in a cohort of long-stay patients in the Dutchess County Unit, 1960-1963. In E. M. Gruenberg, ed., *Evaluating the effectiveness of community mental health services.* New York: Milbank, 1966.

Kazdin, A. E. Methodological and assessment considerations in evaluating reinforcement programs in applied settings. *Journal of Applied Behavior Analysis*, 1973, *6*, 517-531.

———. Recent advances in token economy research. In M. Hersen, R. M. Eisler, & P. M. Miller, eds., *Progress in behavior modification.* New York: Academic Press, 1975.

———. Behavior modification and the "treatment of schizophrenia." In P. A. Magaro, ed. *The construction of madness.* London: Pergamon Press, 1976.

Kazdin, A. E., & Bootzin, R. R. The token economy: An evaluative review. *Journal of Applied Behavior Analysis*, 1972, *5*, 1-30.

Kelman, H. C. Compliance identification and internalization: Three processes of attitude change. *Journal of Conflict Resolution*, 1958, *2*, 51-60.

Kiesler, C. A.; Collins, B. E.; & Miller, N. *Attitude change*. New York: Wiley, 1969.

King, G. F.; Armitage, S. G.; & Tilton, J. R. A therapeutic approach to schizophrenics of extreme pathology: An operant-interpersonal method. *Journal of Abnormal and Social Psychology*, 1960, *61*, 276-286.

Kittrie, N. *The right to be different*. Baltimore: Johns Hopkins Press, 1971.

Klarman, H. E. Economic aspects of mental health manpower. In F. N. Arnhoff, E. A. Rubinstein, & J. C. Speisman, eds., *Manpower for mental health*. Chicago, Aldine, 1969.

Kohen, W., & Paul, G. L. Current trends and recommended changes in extended care placement of mental patients: The Illinois system as a case in point. *Schizophrenia Bulletin*, 1976, *4*, 575-594.

Kraft, A. M. The therapeutic community. In S. Arieti, ed., *American handbook of psychiatry*. New York: Basic Books, 1966.

Kraft, A. M.; Binner, P. R.; & Dickey, B. A. The community mental health program and the longer-stay patient. *Archives of General Psychiatry*, 1967, *16*, 64-70.

Kramer, M.; Goldstein, H.; Israel, R. H.; & Johnson, N. A. Application of life table methodology to the study of mental hospital populations. *Psychiatric Research Reports*, 1956, *5*, 49-76.

Kramer, M.; Pollack, E. S.; & Rednick, R. W. Studies of the incidence and prevalence of hospitalized mental disorders in the United States: Current status and future goals. In P. H. Hock & J. Zubin, eds., *Comparative epidemiology of the mental disorders*. New York: Grune & Stratton, 1961.

Krasner, L., & Atthowe, J., Jr. Token economy bibliography (mimeo). State University of New York at Stony Brook, 1968.

Krasner, L., & Ullmann, L. P., eds. *Research in behavior modification*. New York: Holt, Rinehart & Winston, 1965.

Krieger, G. Training nursing assistants for subprofessional role. *Mental Hygiene*, 1970, *54*, 152-154.

Lamb, H. R. Release of chronic psychiatric patients into the community. *Archives of General Psychiatry*, 1968, *19*, 38-44.

Lamb, H. R., & Goertzel, V. Discharged mental patients—are they really in the community? *Archives of General Psychiatry*, 1971, *24*, 29-34.

———. The demise of the state hospital—a premature obituary? *Archives of General Psychiatry*, 1972, *26*, 489-495.

Lazarus, A. A. Behavior therapy in groups. In G. M. Gazda, ed., *Theories and methods of group psychotherapy and counseling*. Springfield, Ill.: Charles C. Thomas, 1969.

Lehmann, H. E. The somatic and pharmacologic treatments of schizophrenia. In R. Cancro, N. Fox, & L. Shapiro, eds., *Strategic intervention in schizophrenia*. New York: Behavioral Publications, 1974.

Lehrman, N. S. Do our hospitals help make acute schizophrenia chronic? *Diseases of the Nervous System*, 1961a, *22*, 489-493.

———Follow-up of brief and prolonged hospitalization. *Comprehensive Psychiatry*, 1961b, *4*, 227-240.

Lentz, R. J. Changes in chronic mental patients' interview behavior: Effects of differential treatment history and explicit impression management prompts. *Behavior Therapy and Experimental Psychiatry*, 1975, *6*, 192-199.

Lentz, R. J.; Doty, D. W.; & Paul, G. L. "Routine" vs. "therapeutic" interinstitutional transfer of chronic mental patients: A further investigation. In press.

Lentz, R. J., & Paul, G. L. "Routine" vs. "therapeutic" transfer of chronic mental patients. *Archives of General Psychiatry*, 1971, *25*, 187-191.

Lentz, R. J.; Paul, G. L.; & Calhoun, J. F. Reliability and validity of three measures of functioning with "hard-core" chronic mental patients. *Journal of Abnormal Psychology*, 1971, *78*, 69-76.

Liberman, R. A view of behavior modification projects in California. *Behavior Research and Therapy*, 1968, *6*, 331-341.

———. Behavior modification of schizophrenia: A review. In W. J. DiScipio, ed., *The behavioral treatment of psychotic illness*. New York: Behavioral Publications, 1974.

Liberman, R. P.; DeRisi, W. J.; King, L. W.; Eckman, T. A.; & Wood, D. D. Behavioral measurement in a community mental health center. In P. O. Davidson, F. W. Clark, & L. A. Hamerlynk, eds., *Evaluation of behavioral programs in community, residential and school settings: The Fifth Banff international conference on behavior modification*. Champaign, Ill.: Research Press, 1974.

Liberman, R. P.; Wallace, C.; Teigen, J.; & Davis, J. Interventions with psychotic behaviors. In K. S. Calhoun, H. E. Adams, & K. M. Mitchell, eds., *Innovative treatment methods in psychopathology*. New York: Wiley-Interscience, 1974.

Lindley, C. J. Determining differential costs of psychiatric care in a VA hospital. *Hospital & Community Psychiatry*, 1975, *26*, 213-218.

Little, L. K. Effects of the interpersonal interaction on abstract thinking performance in schizophrenics. *Journal of Consulting Psychology*, 1966, *30*, 158-164.

Loevinger, J. Person and population as psychometric concepts. *Psychological Review*, 1965, *72*, 143-155.

Lorei, T. W. Prediction of community stay and employment for released psychiatric patients. *Journal of Consulting Psychology*, 1967, *31*, 349-357.

Lorei, T. W., & Gurel, L. Demographic characteristics as predictors of posthospital and employment and readmission. *Journal of Consulting and Clinical Psychology*, 1973, *40*, 426-430.

Lorr, M.; Klett, C. J.; & Cave, R. Higher level psychotic syndromes. *Journal of Abnormal Psychology*, 1967, *72*, 74-77.

Lorr, M.; Klett, C. J.; McNair, D. M.; & Lasky, J. *Inpatient multidimensional psychiatric scale (IMPS) manual.* Veterans Administration, 1962.

Lucero, R. J., & Vail, D. J. Public policy and public responsibility. *Hospital & Community Psychiatry*, 1968, *19*, 232-233.

Lucero, R. J.; Vail, D. J.; & Scherher, J. Regulating operant conditioning programs. *Hospital & Community Psychiatry*, 1968, *19*, 53-54.

Ludwig, A. M. *Treating the treatment failures: The challenge of chronic schizophrenia.* New York: Grune & Stratton, 1971.

McClelland, J. N., & Rhodes, F. Prediction of job success for hospital aides and orderlies from MMPI scores and personal history data. *Journal of Applied Psychology*, 1969, *53*, 49-54.

McCloskey, J. Influence of rewards and incentives on staff nurse turnover rate. *Nursing Research*, 1974, *23*, 239-247.

MacDonald, W. S. The large-group meeting hour: An evaluation of behavior in a structured situation. In G. W. Fairweather, ed., *Social psychology in treating mental illness.* New York: Wiley, 1964.

McGarry, A. L., & Kaplan, H. A. Overview: Current trends in mental health law. *American Journal of Psychiatry*, 1973, *130*, 621-630.

McInnis, T.; Himelstein, H. C.; Doty, D. W.; & Paul, G. L. Modification of sampling-exposure procedures for increasing facilities utilization by chronic psychiatric patients. *Journal of Behavior Therapy and Experimental Psychiatry*, 1974, *5*, 119-127.

Magaro, P. A., & Giardina, P. Comparing custodial and democratic treatment programs. *Hospital & Community Psychiatry*, 1970, *21*, 118-119.

Malzberg, B. *Cohort studies of mental disease in New York State: 1943-1949.* New York: National Association for Mental Health, 1958.

Manak, J. P. *Plea bargaining: The prosecutors perspective.* Chicago: National District Attorneys Association, 1973.

Mariotto, M. J., & Paul, G. L. A multimethod validation of the Inpatient Multidimensional Psychiatric Scale with chronically institutionalized patients. *Journal of Consulting and Clinical Psychology*, 1974, *42*, 497-508.

———. Persons versus situations in the real-life functioning of chronically institutionalized mental patients. *Journal of Abnormal Psychology*, 1975, *84*, 483-493.

Marler, D. C. The nonprofessionalization of the war on mental illness. *Mental Hygiene*, 1971, *55*, 291-294.

Marquis, D. G., & Allen, T. J. Communication patterns in applied technology. *American Psychologist*, 1966, *21*, 1052-60.

Martin, G. L. Teaching operant technology to psychiatric nurses, aides, and attendants. In F. W. Clark, D. R. Evans, & L. A. Hamerlynk, eds., *Implementing behavior programs for schools and clinics.* Champaign, Ill.: Research Press, 1972.

Martin, M. A practical treatment program for a mental hospital "back" ward. *American Journal of Psychiatry*, 1950, *10*, 758-760.

Martin R. *Legal challenges to behavior modification.* Champaign, Ill.: Research Press, 1975.

May, J. G., Jr. Moral, ethical, and legal considerations in behavior modification. In W. D. Gentry, ed., *Applied behavior modification.* St. Louis: Mosby, 1975.

May, P. R. A. *Treatment of schizophrenia.* New York: Science House, 1968.

———. Cost-efficiency of mental health delivery systems: I. A review of the literature on hospital care. *American Journal of Public Health*, 1970, *60*, 2060-67.

Mednick, B. R. Breakdown in high-risk subjects: Familial and early environmental factors. *Journal of Abnormal Psychology*, 1973, *82*, 469-475.

Meichenbaum, D. H. The effects of instructions and reinforcement on thinking and language behaviors of schizophrenics. Ph.D. dissertation, University of Illinois, 1966a.

———. The effects of social reinforcement on the level of abstraction in schizophrenics. *Journal of Abnormal Psychology*, 1966b, *71*, 354-362.

Meichenbaum, D., & Cameron, R. Training schizophrenics to talk to themselves: A means of developing attentional controls. *Behavior Therapy*, 1973, *4*, 515-534.

Meisel, A. Rights of the mentally ill: The gulf between theory and reality. *Hospital & Community Psychiatry*, 1975, *26*, 349-353.

Mendel, W. M. Lepers, madmen—who's next? *Schizophrenia Bulletin*, 1974, *11*, 5-8.

Mendel, W. M., & Rapport, S. Determinants of the decision for psychiatric hospitalization. *Archives of General Psychiatry*, 1969, *20*, 321-328.

Mental patients win "right to liberty." *APA Monitor*, September-October, 1975, *6* (9 & 10), 8 & 15.

Meyer, N. G. Provisional patient movement and administrative data, state and county mental hospital inpatient services, July 1, 1973-June 30, 1974. *Statistical Note 114*, National Institute of Mental Health, Division of Biometry, Survey and Reports Branch, April 1975.

Michaux, W. W.; Katz, M. M.; Kurland, A. A.; & Gansereit, K. H. *The first year out*. Baltimore: Johns Hopkins Press, 1969.

Milby, J. B.; Pendergrass, P. E.; & Clarke, C. J. Token economy versus control ward: A comparison of staff and patient attitudes toward ward environment. *Behavior Therapy*, 1975, *6*, 22-29.

Miller, D. Worlds that fail: Part I. Retrospective analysis of mental patients' careers. *California Mental Health Research Monograph*, 1965, No. 6.

———. Retrospective analysis of posthospital mental patients' worlds. *Journal of Health & Social Behavior*, 1967, *8*, 136-140.

Miller, D. H. The rehabilitation of chronic open-ward neuro-psychiatric patients. *Psychiatry*, 1954, *17*, 347-358.

Miller, D. H., & Clancy, J. An approach to the social rehabilitation of chronic psychotic patients. *Psychiatry*, 1952, *15*, 435-443.

Miron, N. B. The primary ethical consideration. *Hospital & Community Psychiatry*, 1968, *19*, 226-228.

Montgomery, G. K.; Paul, G. L.; & Power, C. T. Influence of environmental contingency history on acquisition of new discriminations by chronic mental patients. *Journal of Abnormal Psychology*, 1974, *83*, 339-347.

Moore, F. I., & Stewart, J. C. Important variables influencing successful use of aides. *Health Services Reports*, 1972, *87*, 555-561.

Morgan, N. C., & Johnson, N. A. The chronic hospital patient. *American Journal of Psychiatry*, 1957, *113*, 824-830.

Muzekari, L. H.; Weiman, B.; & Kreiger, P. A. Self-experimental treatment in chronic schizophrenia. *Journal of Nervous and Mental Disease*, 1973, *157*, 420-427.

Myers, K., & Clark, D. H. Results in a therapeutic community. *British Journal of Psychiatry*, 1972, *120*, 51-58.

Nameche, L. F. Life histories of schizophrenics before and after hospitalization. Paper presented at the meeting of the American Psychological Association, Washington, D.C., September 1967.

Neff, W. S., & Koltuv, M. *Work and mental disorder*. New York: Institute for the Crippled and Disabled, 1967.

Odegard, O. Pattern of discharge and readmission in psychiatric hospitals in Norway, 1926 to 1955. *Mental Hygiene*, 1961, *45*, 185-193.

Olson, R. P., & Greenburg, D. J. Effects of contingency contracting and decision making groups with chronic mental patients. *Journal of Consulting and Clinical Psychology*, 1972, *38*, 376-383.

Overton, D. A. Commentary. In J. A. Harvey, ed., *Behavioral analysis of drug action*. Glenview, Ill.: Scott, Foresman & Co., 1971.

Paden, R. C.; Himelstein, H. C.; & Paul, G. L. Video-tape vs. verbal feedback in the modification of meal behavior of chronic mental patients. *Journal of Consulting and Clinical Psychology*, 1974, *42*, 623.

Panyan, M.; Boozer, H.; & Morris, N. Feedback to attendants as a reinforcer for applying operant techniques. *Journal of Applied Behavior Analysis*, 1970, *3*, 1-4.

Parsons, T. The mental hospital as a type of organization. In M. Greenblatt, D. J. Levinson, & R. H. Williams, eds., *The patient and the mental hospital*. Glencoe: Free Press, 1957.

Pasamanick, B.; Scarpitti, F. R.; & Dinitz, S. *Schizophrenics in the community*. New York: Appleton-Century-Crofts, 1967.

Pattison, E. M., & Rhodes, R. J. Clinical prediction with the NOSIE-30 scale. *Journal of Clinical Psychology*, 1974, *30*, 200-201.

Paul, G. L. *Insight vs. desensitization in psychotherapy: An experiment in anxiety reduction*. Stanford: Stanford University Press, 1966.

———. The strategy of outcome research in psychotherapy. *Journal of Consulting Psychology*, 1967a, *31*, 109-118.

———. Insight vs. desensitization in psychotherapy two years after termination. *Journal of Consulting Psychology*, 1967b, *31*, 333-348.

———. Chronic mental patient: Current status—future directions. *Psychological Bulletin*, 1969a, *71*, 81-94.

———. Behavior modification research: Design and tactics. In C. M. Franks, ed., *Behavior therapy: Appraisal and status*. New York: McGraw-Hill, 1969b.

———. Extroversion, emotionality, and physiological response to relaxation training and hypnotic suggestion. *International Journal of Clinical and Experimental Hypnosis*, 1969c, *17*, 89-98.

———. Experimental-behavioral approaches to schizophrenia. In R. Cancro, N. Fox, & L. Shapiro, eds., *Strategic intervention in schizophrenia: Current developments in treatment.* New York: Behavioral Publications, 1974.

——— ed. *Observational assessment instrumentation for institutional research and treatment.* Cambridge, Mass.: Harvard University Press (In press).

Paul, G. L., & Bernstein, D. A. *Anxiety and clinical problems: Treatment by systematic desensitization and related techniques.* New York: General Learning Press, 1973.

Paul, G. L.; Eriksen, C. W.; & Humphreys, L. G. Use of temperature stress with cool air reinforcement for human operant conditioning. *Journal of Experimental Psychology*, 1962, *64*, 329-335.

Paul, G. L., & McInnis, T. L. Attitudinal changes associated with two approaches to training mental health technicians in milieu and social-learning procedures. *Journal of Consulting and Clinical Psychology*, 1974, *42*, 21-31.

Paul, G. L.; McInnis, T. L.; & Mariotto, M. J. Objective performance outcomes associated with two approaches to training mental health technicians in milieu and social-learning programs. *Journal of Abnormal Psychology*, 1973, *82*, 523-532.

Paul, G. L.; Redfield, J. P.; & Lentz, R. J. The inpatient scale of minimal functioning: A revision of the social breakdown syndrome gradient index. *Journal of Consulting and Clinical Psychology*, 1976, *44*, 1021-22.

Paul, G. L., & Shannon, D. T. Treatment of anxiety through systematic desensitization in therapy groups. *Journal of Abnormal Psychology*, 1966, *71*, 124-135.

Paul, G. L.; Tobias, L. T.; & Holly, B. L. Maintenance psychotropic drugs in the presence of active treatment programs: A "triple blind" withdrawal study with long term mental patients. *Archives of General Psychiatry*, 1972, *27*, 106-115.

Peck, C. L. Current legislative issues concerning the right to refuse versus the right to choose hospitalization and treatment. *Psychiatry*, 1975, *38*, 303-317.

From peonage to pay. *Behavior Today*, 1974, *5*, 331-332 (part I), 337-339 (part II).

Peretz, D.; Alpert, M.; & Friedhoff, A. Prognostic factors in the evaluation of therapy: In P. H. Hoch & J. Zubin, eds., *Evaluation of psychiatric treatment.* New York: Grune & Stratton, 1964.

Perpich, J. G. Behavior modification in institutional settings: A critique. *Arizona Law Review*, 1975, *17*, 33-38.

Person, P. H., Jr. *The relationship between selected social and demographic characteristics of hospitalized mental patients and the outcome of hospitalization.* Washington, D.C.: United States Government Printing Office, 1965.

Peterson, D. R. Scope and generality of verbally defined personality factors. *Psychological Review*, 1965, *72*, 48-59.

———. *The clinical study of social behavior.* New York: Appleton-Century-Crofts, 1968.

Peterson, P. B., & Olsen, G. W. First admitted schizophrenics in the drug era. *Archives of General Psychiatry*, 1964, *11*, 137-144.

Philip, A. E. A note on the Nurses' Observational Scale for Inpatient Evaluation (NOSIE). *British Journal of Psychiatry*, 1973, *122*, 595-596.

Piotrowski, Z. A., & Efron, H. Y. Evaluation of outcome in schizophrenia. In P. H. Hoch & J. Zubin, eds., *Psychopathology of schizophrenia.* New York: Grune & Stratton, 1966.

Pommer, D., & Streedbeck, D. Motivating staff performance in an operant learning program for children. *Journal of Applied Behavior Analysis*, 1974, *7*, 217-221.

Porter, L. W., & Steers, R. M. Organizational, work, and personnel factors in employee turnover and absenteeism. *Psychological Bulletin*, 1973, *80*, 151-176.

Prigmore, C. S., & Davis, P. R. Wyatt v. Stickney: Rights of the committed. *Social Work*, 1973, *18*, 10-18.

Quilitch, H. R. A comparison of three staff management procedures. *Journal of Applied Behavior Analysis*, 1975, *8*, 59-66.

Rachlin, S. On the need for a closed ward in an open hospital: The psychiatric intensive-care unit. *Hospital & Community Psychiatry*, 1973, *24*, 829-833.

———. With liberty and psychosis for all. *Psychiatric Quarterly*, 1974, *48*, 410-420.

Rachman, S., & Teasdale, J. *Aversion therapy and behaviour disorders: An analysis.* Coral Gables: University of Miami Press, 1969.

Racy, J., & Goldstein, R. H. Residents' perceptions of inpatient psychiatric care. *Comprehensive Psychiatry*, 1975, *16*, 171-177.

Rapaport, R. N. *Community as doctor.* Springfield, Ill.: Charles C. Thomas, 1960.

Rappaport, J.; Chinsky, J. M.; & Cowen, E. L. *Innovations in helping chronic patients.* New York: Academic Press, 1971.

Rashkis, H. A., & Smarr, E. R. Drug and milieu effects with chronic schizophrenics. *Archives of Neurology and Psychiatry*, 1957, *78*, 89-94.

Rawls, J. R. Toward the identification of readmissions and non-readmissions to mental hospitals. *Social Psychiatry*, 1971, *6*, 58-61.

Redfield, J., & Paul, G. L. Bias in behavioral observation as a function of observer familiarity with subjects and typicality of behavior.

*Journal of Consulting and Clinical Psychology*, 1976, *44*, 156.

Reich, R. Care of the chronically mentally ill—a national disgrace. *American Journal of Psychiatry*, 1973, *130*, 911-912.

Reidy, J. P. *Zone mental health centers: The Illinois concept.* Springfield, Ill.: Charles C. Thomas, 1964.

Reppucci, N. D., & Saunders, J. T. Social psychology of behavior modification: Problems of implementation in natural settings. *American Psychologist*, 1974, *29*, 649-660.

Richards, C. S. The politics of a token economy. *Psychological Reports*, 1975, *36*, 615-621.

Rickard, H. C.; Digman, P. J.; & Horner, R. F. Verbal manipulation in a psychotherapeutic relationship. *Journal of Clinical Psychology*, 1960, *16*, 364-367.

Rickard, H. C., & Dinoff, M. A. A follow-up note on "verbal manipulation in a psychotherapeutic relationship." *Psychological Reports*, 1962, *11*, 506.

Rieder, R. O. Hospitals, patients, and politics. *Schizophrenia Bulletin*, 1974, *11*, 9-15.

Robinson, D. N. Harm, offense, and nuisance: Some first steps in the establishment of an ethics of treatment. *American Psychologist*, 1974, *29*, 233-238.

Rosenbaum, C. P. *The meaning of madness* New York: Science House, 1970.

Rosenblatt, A. Providing custodial care for mental patients: An affirmative view. *Psychiatric Quarterly*, 1974, *48*, 14-25.

Rosenblatt, A., & Mayer, J. E. Revolving-door patients at Bronx state hospital: A preliminary report. *Journal of the Bronx State Hospital*, 1973, *1*, 5-11.

———. The recidivism of mental patients: A review of past studies. *American Journal of Orthopsychiatry*, 1974, *44*, 697-706.

Rosenhan, D. L. On being sane in insane places. *Science*, 1973, *179*, 250-258.

Rutledge, L., & Binner, P. Readmissions to a community mental health center. *Community Mental Health Journal*, 1970, *6*, 136-143.

Salzinger, K., & Pisoni, S. Reinforcement of affect responses of schizophrenics during the clinical interview. *Journal of Abnormal and Social Psychology*, 1958, *57*, 84-90.

Sanders, D. H. Innovative environments in the community: A life for the chronic patient. *Schizophrenia Bulletin*, 1972, *6*, 49-59.

Sanders, R.; Smith, R. S.; & Weinman, B. S. *Chronic psychosis and recovery.* San Francisco: Jossey-Bass, 1967.

Saper, B. Requiescat for the state hospital? *Journal of Clinical Psychology*, 1975, *31*, 223-235.

Schaefer, H. H. Investigations on operant conditioning procedures in a mental hospital. *California Mental Health Research Monograph*, 1966, *8*, 25-39.

Schaefer, H. H., & Martin, P. L. Behavior therapy for "apathy" of hospitalized schizophrenics. *California Department of Mental Hygiene Research Report*, No. 379, August 1966.

Schulberg, H. C., & Baker, F. *The mental hospital in human services.* New York: Behavioral Publications, 1975.

Schwartz, J., & Bellack, A. S. A comparison of a token economy with standard inpatient treatment. *Journal of Consulting and Clinical Psychology*, 1975, *43*, 107-108.

Schwitzgebel, R. K. Right to treatment for the mentally disabled: The need for realistic standards and objective criteria. *Harvard Civil Rights-Civil Liberties Law Review*, 1973, *8*, 513-535.

———. The right to effective mental treatment. *California Law Review*, 1974, *62*, 936-956.

———. A contractual model for the protection of the rights of institutionalized mental patients. *American Psychologist*, 1975, *30*, 815-820.

Sherman, L. J.; Ging, R.; Moseley, E. C.; & Bookbinder, L. J. Prognosis in schizophrenia: A follow-up of 588 patients. *Archives of General Psychiatry*, 1964, *10*, 123-130.

Shields, J., & Gottesman, I. I. Cross-national diagnosis of schizophrenia in twins: The heritability and specificity of schizophrenia. *Archives of General Psychiatry*, 1972, *27*, 725-730.

Sidman, M. Normal sources of pathological behavior. *Science*, 1960, *132*, 61-68.

Siegel, S. *Nonparametric statistics for the behavioral sciences.* New York: McGraw-Hill, 1956.

Singh, M. M., & DiScipio, W. J. Changes in staff anxiety and attitudes during a double blind study of haloperidol in acute schizophrenics within a structured milieu. *Journal of Nervous and Mental Disease*, 1972, *155*, 245-256.

Skinner, B. F. *Beyond freedom and dignity.* New York: Knopf, 1971.

Smith, W. G.; Kaplan, J.; & Siker, D. Community mental health and the severely disturbed patient. *Archives of General Psychiatry*, 1974, *30*, 693-696.

Sobey, F. *The nonprofessional revolution in mental health.* New York: Columbia University Press, 1970.

Sommer, R., & Osmond, H. Symptoms of institutional care. *Social Problems*, 1961, *8*, 254-263.

Sommer, R.; Witney, G.; & Osmond, H. Teaching common associations to schizophrenics. *Journal of Abnormal and Social Psychology*, 1962, *65*, 58-61.

Steer, R. A., & Boger, W. P. Milieu therapy with psychiatric-medically infirm patients. *Gerontologist*, 1975, *15*, 138-141.

Steffy, R. A.; Torney, D.; Hart, J.; Craw, M.; & Martlett, N. An application of learning techniques to the management and rehabilitation of severely regressed chronically ill patients: Preliminary findings. Paper presented at the meeting of the Ontario Psychiatric Association, Ottawa, Canada, February 1966.

Stewart, A.; LaFave, H. G.; Grunberg, F.; & Herjanic, M. Problems in phasing out a large public psychiatric hospital. *American Journal of Psychiatry*, 1968, *125*, 82-88.

Stickney, S. B. Problems in implementing the right to treatment in Alabama: The Wyatt v. Stickney case. *Hospital & Community Psychiatry*, 1974, *25*, 453-460.

Stoffelmayr, B. E.; Faulkner, G. E.; & Mitchell, W. S. *The rehabilitation of chronic hospitalized patients—A comparative study of operant conditioning methods and social therapy techniques.* Final report to the Scottish Home and Health Department, August 1973.

Stolz, S. B.; Wienckowski, L. A.; & Brown, B. S. Behavior modification: A perspective on critical issues. *American Psychologist*, 1975, *30*, 1027-48.

Stone, A. A. The right to treatment and the psychiatric establishment. *Psychiatric Annals*, 1974, *4*, 21-42.

Strauss, J. S., & Carpenter, W. T. The prediction of outcome in schizophrenia. II. Relationships between predictor and outcome variables: A report from the WHO international pilot study of schizophrenia. *Archives of General Psychiatry*, 1974, *31*, 37-42.

Struening, E. L., & Cohen, J. Factorial invariance and other psychometric characteristics of five opinions about mental illness factors. *Educational and Psychological Measurement*, 1963, *23*, 289-297.

Supreme Court strikes patient wage standards. *APA Monitor*, September-October, 1976, 16.

Szasz, T. S. *Law, liberty, and psychiatry.* New York: Macmillan, 1963.

Taube, C. A. Readmissions to inpatient services of state and county mental hospitals 1972. *Statistical Note 110*, National Institute of Mental Health, Division of Biometry, Survey and Reports Branch, November 1974.

———. State trends in resident patients—state and county mental hospitals inpatient service 1967-1973. *Statistical Note 113*, National Institute of Mental Health, Division of Biometry, Survey and Reports Branch, February 1975.

Taube, C. A., & Meyer, N. G. Children and state mental hospitals. *Statistical Note 115*, National Institute of Mental Health, Division of Biometry, Survey and Reports Branch, April 1975.

Theobald, D. T., & Paul, G. L. Reinforcing value of praise for chronic mental patients as a function of historical pairing with tangible reinforcers. *Behavior Therapy*, 1976, *7*, 192-197.

Toomey, B. G.; Simonsen, C. E.; & Allen, H. E. Rights to treatment: Issues and prospects. Paper presented at the 20th Annual Conference on Corrections, Tallahassee, Florida, February 1975.

Tourney, G. Psychiatric therapies: 1800-1968. In T. Rothman, ed., *Changing patterns in psychiatric care.* New York: Crown, 1970.

Tuchi, B. J., & Carr, B. E. Labor turnover. *Hospitals, J.A.H.A.*, 1971, *45*, 88-92.

Tyce, F. A., & Rynearsen, R. R. Preparing the hospital. *Hospital & Community Psychiatry*, 1966, *17*, 33-44.

Ullmann, L. P. *Institution and outcome: A comparative study of psychiatric hospitals.* New York: Pergamon Press, 1967.

Ullmann, L. P.; Forsman, R. G.; Kenney, J. W.; McInnis, T. L.; Unikel, I.P.; & Zeisset, R. M. Selective reinforcement of schizophrenics' interview responses. *Behavior Research and Therapy*, 1965, *2*, 205-212.

Ullmann, L. P., & Giovannoni, J. M. The development of a self-report measure of the process-reactive continuum. *Journal of Nervous and Mental Disease*, 1964, *138*, 38-42.

Ullmann, L. P., & Krasner, L. *A psychological approach to abnormal behavior*, 2d ed. Englewood Cliffs, N.J.: Prentice-Hall, 1975.

———, eds. *Case studies in behavior modification.* New York: Holt, Rinehart, & Winston, 1965.

Ullmann, L. P.; Krasner, L.; & Collins, B. J. Modification of behavior through verbal conditioning: Effects in group therapy. *Journal of Abnormal and Social Psychology*, 1961, *62*, 128-132.

Ullmann, L. P.; Krasner, L.; & Edinger, R. L. Verbal conditioning of common associations in long-term schizophrenic patients. *Behavior Research and Therapy*, 1964, *2*, 15-18.

Ullmann, L. P.; Weiss, R. L.; & Krasner, L. The effect of verbal conditioning of emotional words on recognition of threatening stimuli. *Journal of Clinical Psychology*, 1963, *19*, 182-183.

U.S. Department of Health, Education, and Welfare. Protection of human subjects: Rules and regulations. *Federal Register*, 1974a, *39*, 30648-57.

———. Protection of human subjects: Proposed rules. *Federal Register*, 1974b, *39*, 30648-57.

Vaillant, G. E. The prediction of recovery in schizophrenia. *International Journal of Psychiatry*, 1966, *2*, 617-627.

Vaughn, R.; Teitelbaum, S.; & Kumpan, H. A research project in psychiatric aide training. *American Journal of Psychiatry*, 1962, *119*, 555-559.

Vitale, J. H. The emergence of mental hospital field research. In G. W. Fairweather, ed., *Social psychology in treating mental illness*. New York: Wiley, 1964a.

———. The therapeutic community: A review article. In A. F. Wessen, ed., *The psychiatric hospital as a social system*. Springfield, Ill.: Charles C. Thomas, 1964b.

Vitale, J. H., & Steinbach, M. The prevention of relapse of chronic mental patients. *International Journal of Social Psychiatry*, 1965, *11*, 85-95.

Wagner, B. R.; Breitmeyer, R. G.; & Bottum, G. Administrative problem solving and the mental health professional. *Professional Psychology*, 1975, *6*, 55-60.

Wagner, B. R., & Paul, G. L. Reduction of incontinence in chronic mental patients: A pilot project. *Behavior Therapy and Experimental Psychiatry*, 1970, *1*, 29-38.

Wallace, C. J.; Davis, J. R.; Liberman, R. P.; & Baker, V. Modeling and staff behavior. *Journal of Consulting and Clinical Psychology*, 1973, *41*, 422-425.

Wanklin, J. M.; Fleming, D. F.; Buck, C.; & Hobbs, G. E. Discharge and readmissions among mental hospital patients. *Archives of Neurology and Psychiatry*, 1956, *76*, 660-669.

Webster, D. R., & Azrin, N. H. Required relaxation: A method of inhibiting agitative-disruptive behaviors of retardates. *Behavior Research and Therapy*, 1973, *11*, 67-78.

Weiss, R. L.; Krasner, L.; & Ullmann, L. P. Responsivity of psychiatric patients to verbal conditioning: "Success" and "failure" conditions and pattern of reinforced trials. *Psychological Reports*, 1963, *12*, 423-426.

Wexler, D. B. Token and taboo: Behavior modification, token economies, and the law. *California Law Review*, 1973, *61*, 81-109.

———. Behavior modification and legal developments. *American Behavioral Scientist*, 1975a, *18*, 679-684.

———. Reflections on the legal regulation of behavior modification in institutional settings. *Arizona Law Review*, 1975b, *17*, 132-143.

White, N. F. The descent of milieu therapy. *Canadian Psychiatric Association Journal*, 1972, *17*, 41-49.

Wilensky, H., & Herz, M. I. Problem areas in the development of a therapeutic community. *International Journal of Social Psychiatry*, 1966, *12*, 299-308.

Wilmer, H. A. Toward a definition of the therapeutic community. *American Journal of Psychiatry*, 1958, *114*, 824-834.

Winer, B. J. *Statistical principles in experimental design*. New York: McGraw-Hill, 1962.

Wing, J. K. Long-stay schizophrenic patients and results of rehabilitation. In H. Freeman, ed., *Psychiatric hospital care*. London: Bailliere, 1965.

Wing, J. K., & Brown, G. W. *Institutionalism and schizophrenia: A comparative study of three mental hospitals*. Cambridge: Cambridge University Press, 1970.

Witkin, M. J. Staffing of state and county mental hospitals: United States, 1973. *Statistical Note 109*, National Institute of Mental Health, Division of Biometry, August 1974.

Wohl, S. A. Follow-up community adjustment. In G. W. Fairweather, ed., *Social psychology in treating mental illness*. New York: Wiley, 1964.

Wolfe, B. E. The Donaldson decision. *Schizophrenia Bulletin*, 1975, *13*, 4-6.

Wyatt, R. J.; Termini, B. A.; & Davis, J. Biochemical and sleep studies of schizophrenia: A review of the literature 1960-1970. *Schizophrenia Bulletin*, 1971, *4*, 10-66.

Wyatt victory 'tarnished'?" *APA Monitor*, 1975, *6*, (9 & 10) 8.

Zolik, E. S.; Levin, I.; & Tito, J. Characteristics of schizophrenics responding to coordinated community care. *Proceedings of the 79th Annual Convention of the American Psychological Association*, 1971.

Zubin, J.; Sutton, S.; Salzinger, K.; Salzinger, S.; Burdock, E. I.; & Peretz, D. A. A biometric approach to prognosis in schizophrenia. In P. H. Hoch & J. Zubin, eds., *Comparative epidemiology of the mental disorders*. New York: Grune & Stratton, 1961.

Zusman, J. Some explanations of the changing appearance of psychotic patients. In E. M. Gruenberg, ed., *Evaluating the effectiveness of community mental health services*. New York: Milbank, 1966.

# Author Index

Abroms, G. M., 432
Adams, F. H., 8
Ajzen, I., 102
Allen, G. J., 117, 465
Allen, H. E., 456
Allen, T. J., 468
Almond, R. J., 432, 433
Alpert, M., 2
Althoff, M. E., 1, 2, 5, 6
Anthony, W. A., 1, 2, 3, 5, 6
Appleby, L., 8
Arenberg, D., 120, 492
Armitage, S. G., 9
Arnhoff, F. N., 113
Arnson, A., 8
Arrill, M. B., 415
Arthur, G., 4
Artiss, K. L., 7
Asch, S. H., 447
Atthowe, J., Jr., 10
Atthowe, J. M., 10, 11, 12, 432
Aumack, L., 132
Ayllon, T., 9, 134, 197, 432, 433, 437, 456, 461, 488
Azrin, N. H., 10, 134, 197, 371, 432, 433, 437, 488, 500

Bach-Y-Rita, G., 451
Baker, F., 21, 24
Baker, V., 117
Ball, T. S., 448
Bandura, A., 432, 433
Barnett, C. D., 117
Barrett, W. W., 7
Bartholow, G. W., 8
Bartlett, F. L., 445
Batman, R. H., 117
Bazelon, D. L., 445, 446
Becker, H. S., 3
Becker, W. C., 2
Bellack, A. S., 433
Bellak, L., 1
Bendig, A. W., 102
Bennett, C. L., 3, 8
Bensberg, G. J., 117
Bernstein, D. A., 191, 429
Berrington, W. P., 11
Berwick, P. T., 446

Binner, P., 1
Binner, P. R., 2, 8, 415, 464
Birky, H. J., 439
Birnbaum, M., 446
Blashfield, R., 500
Boblitt, W. E., 436
Bockoven, J. S., 3, 22
Boger, W. P., 433
Bonn, E. M., 432
Bookbinder, L. J., 2, 4
Bootzin, R. R., 433
Boozer, H., 113
Bottum, G., 467
Botwinik, W., 4, 6
Bragg, R. A., 448
Braginsky, B. M., 451
Braginsky, D. D., 451
Brandon, S., 120, 492
Braun, S. H., 448, 450
Breitmeyer, R. G., 467
Bricker, W. A., 117
Brill, H., 443
Bromet, E., 2
Brooks, G. W., 8
Brown, B. S., 448, 449, 452, 454, 457
Brown, G. W., 3, 4, 6, 433, 435
Bruce, M., 10
Buck, C., 3
Buell, G. J., 1, 2, 3, 5, 6
Burdock, E. I., 2
Butterfield, E. C., 117

Cahoon, D. D., 448
Calhoun, J. F., 119, 120, 128, 130, 132, 490, 492
Cameron, R., 438
Cancro, R., 501
Carlson, C. G., 433
Carpenter, W. T., 4
Carr, B. E., 105
Carstairs, G. M., 4, 6
Cave, R., 125
Chambliss, J. E., 439
Chinsky, J. M., 21, 113, 117, 465
Chu, F., 2
Clancy, J., 7
Clark, A. W., 432
Clark, D. H., 8, 433

Clark, L. D., 7
Clarke, C. J., 29, 465
Clayton, W. H., 8
Clum, G. A., 3
Cochran, B., 1
Coe, W. C., 490
Cohen, J., 102, 103, 107
Collins, B. E., 116
Collins, B. J., 9
Conley, R. W., 415
Conwell, M., 415
Cowen, E. L., 21, 113, 465
Craighead, W. E., 124
Craw, M., 10
Cressler, D. L., 6, 11, 441
Crisswell, J. H., 7
Cronbach, L. J., 119
Cropley, A. J., 4
Cross, K. W., 1
Cuadra, C. A., 113, 117, 490
Cumming, E., 7, 8, 9, 12, 432
Cumming, J., 7, 8, 9, 12, 432
Cunningham, M. K., 4, 6
Curran, J. P., 179
Curry, A. E., 490

Dailey, W. F., 117
Daniels, D. N., 432, 433
Davis, A. E., 1, 4
Davis, J., 432, 433, 500
Davis, J. D., 415
Davis, J. R., 117
Davis, P. R., 456, 458, 500
Davison, G. C., 10, 433, 444, 447, 448, 450, 451
Denman, S. B., 105, 106
Depue, R. A., 2
DeRisi, W. J., 117, 132
Desvousges, W. H., 415
Dickey, B. A., 2, 8, 464
Digman, P. J., 9
DiMascio, A., 464
Dinitz, S., 1, 4, 11
Dinoff, M., 9, 492
DiScipio, W. J., 29
Distefano, M. K., Jr., 113
Dolson, J., 4, 6
Doty, D. W., 246, 247, 370
Dubicki, M. D., 2
Dunham, H. W., 3
Durrell, J., 8

Eckman, T. A., 117, 132
Edelson, M., 7
Edelson, R. I., 102, 108, 116
Edinger, R. L., 9
Edwards, A. L., 490, 492, 493, 494, 495, 496, 497
Efron, H. Y., 1
Eisenthal, S., 2
Eisler, R. M., 433
Eldred, S., 433
Ellsworth, J. J., 113, 465

Ellsworth, R. B., 3, 4, 5, 7, 8, 12, 113, 117, 424, 433, 435, 439, 441, 465
Enniss, J., 7
Epstein, L. J., 5
Ericksen, C. W., 179
Erickson, R. C., 1, 2, 424, 439, 440
Evans, A. S., 4, 8, 464

Fairweather, G. W., 1, 4, 6, 10, 11, 12, 13, 441
Farina, A., 120, 492
Faulkner, G. E., 433, 434, 437
Ferster, C. B., 3
Fillstead, W. J., 432
Finch, A. J., 492
Finch, A. J., Jr., 492
Finch, K., 492
Fishbein, M., 102
Fleming, D. F., 3
Fletcher, S., 10
Foreyt, J. P., 415
Forsman, R. G., 9
Forsyth, R. P., 4
Fowlkes, M. R., 3
Fox, J., 4
Foxx, R. M., 371
Franks, C. M., 9
Freeman, H. E., 4
Friedhoff, A., 2
Friedman, P. R., 444, 447, 448, 449, 450, 451, 452, 454, 458, 462, 501
Friesen, D. C., 433, 436

Galioni, E. G., 8
Gansereit, K. H., 4
Gardner, J. M., 116
Garmezy, N., 120
Gazan, A., 4
Gelfand, S., 29
Gericke, O. L., 10
Giardina, P., 439
Giebink, J. W., 490
Gilligan, J., 1, 7
Gillis, R., 3
Ging, R., 2, 4
Giovannoni, J. M., 120
Glass, A. J., 1, 19
Glass, G. V., 15
Glassman, M. L., 132
Gleser, G. C., 119
Goertzel, V., 2, 5, 13
Goffman, E., 3
Goldberg, L. R., 34, 124
Goldiamond, I., 444, 447, 448, 449, 454
Goldstein, A. P., 9
Goldstein, H., 3
Goldstein, R. H., 500
Gottesman, I. I., 501
Gottman, J. M., 15
Grabowski, J. G., 117
Greenblatt, M., 4, 8, 445, 464
Greenburg, D. J., 433, 436
Gripp, R. F., 433, 434

Gross, M., 1
Gruenberg, E. M., 3, 120, 492
Grunberg, F., 2
Guerney, B. G., Jr., 113
Gunderson, J. G., 468
Gurel, L., 1, 3, 4, 13, 126
Guskin, S., 120, 492
Guttentag, M., 14

Hagen, R. L., 124, 433, 444, 448
Halleck, S. L., 500
Hallsten, E. A., 10
Halpern, J., 415
Hamlin, R., 2
Haney, J. R., 492
Harford, T., 2
Harmatz, M. G., 132
Harris, J. M., 465
Harrow, M., 2
Hart, J., 10
Hase, H. D., 34, 124
Hassell, C., 1
Haughton, E., 9
Heap, R. F., 436
Heller, K., 9
Herjanic, M., 2
Hersen, M., 433
Herz, M. I., 8
Himelstein, H. C., 124, 246, 247
Hobbs, G. E., 3
Hobbs, T., 492
Hogarty, G. E., 1
Hollander, M., 29
Hollingshead, A. B., 120
Hollingsworth, R., 415
Holly, B. L., 124, 136, 180, 441, 447
Homer, V., 29
Honigfeld, G., 3, 121, 490, 492
Hord, J. E., 436
Horner, R. F., 9
Huels, M. A., 490
Hughes, H. B., 10
Humphreys, L. G., 179, 444
Hunter, M., 132
Hurder, W. P., 117
Huxley, J., 3

Illinois Department of Mental Health, 417
Illinois Department of Public Aid, 417
Ishikawa, W., 4
Israel, R. H., 3

Johnson, G., 4
Johnson, N. A., 1, 3
Joint Commission on Mental Health and
   Illness, 19
Jones, K., 1
Jones, M., 7, 432, 435

Kahne, R. V., 3
Kaplan, H. A., 444
Kaplan, J., 2

Kasius, R. V., 8, 120, 492
Kasl, S., 2
Katz, M. M., 4
Kazdin, A. E., 15, 432, 433
Kellam, S. G., 8
Kelman, H. C., 117
Kenny, J. W., 9
Kessler, D. R., 490
Kiesler, C. A., 116
King, G. F., 9
King, L. W., 117, 132
Kittrie, N., 500
Klarman, H. E., 415
Klett, C. J., 125, 490
Kohen, W., 442, 452, 464, 466
Koltuv, M., 7, 8
Kraft, A. M., 1, 7, 8, 432, 464
Kramer, M., 1, 3
Krasner, L., 3, 9, 10, 11, 12, 432, 433, 444,
   449, 454, 501
Kreiger, P. A., 492
Krieger, G., 117
Kroeker, D., 4
Kumpan, H., 490
Kurland, A. A., 4

LaFave, H. G., 2
Lamb, H. R., 2, 5, 13
Lasky, J., 490
Lazarus, A. A., 83
Lehmann, H. E., 500
Lehrman, N. S., 3, 4
Lentz, R. J., 119, 120, 124, 128, 130, 132,
   179, 370, 440, 490, 492
Levin, I., 4
Liberman, R., 113
Liberman, R. P., 117, 132, 432, 433
Lindley, C. J., 498
Little, L. K., 9
Loevinger, J., 34, 124
Lorei, T. W., 3, 4
Lorr, M., 125, 490
Lucero, R. J., 446, 448
Ludwig, A. M., 3, 436, 439, 451

MacDonald, W. S., 125
McClelland, J. N., 117, 490
McCloskey, J., 105
McGarry, A. L., 444
McInnis, T. L., 9, 115, 116, 117, 246, 247
McNair, D. M., 490
Magaro, P. A., 433, 434, 439
Malzberg, B., 3
Manak, J. P., 500
Mariotto, M. J., 116, 117, 124, 429, 490, 497
Marler, D. C., 113
Marquis, D. G., 468
Martin, G. L., 116
Martin, M., 7
Martin, P. L., 10, 124
Martin, R., 456, 458, 461
Martlett, N., 10

May, J. G., Jr., 448, 454
May, P. R. A., 13, 415
Mayer, J. E., 3, 4
Maynard, H., 6, 11, 441
Mead, B. T., 8
Mednick, B. R., 2
Meichenbaum, D., 438
Meichenbaum, D. H., 9
Meisel, A., 445
Mendel, W. M., 2, 4, 444
Mendelsohn, R., 132
Meyer, N. G., 1, 29
Michael, J., 9
Michaux, W. W., 4
Milby, J. B., 29, 465
Miller, D., 4, 5
Miller, D. H., 7, 8
Miller, N., 116
Miron, N. B., 448
Mitchell, W. S., 433, 434, 437
Montgomery, G. T., 124
Moore, C. H., 436
Moore, F. I., 113
Morgan, D. G., 117
Morgan, N. C., 1
Morris, J. R., 492
Morris, L. A., 446
Morris, N., 113
Moseley, E. C., 2, 4
Mosher, L. R., 468
Muzekari, L. H., 492
Myers, K., 433

Nameche, L. F., 4
Neff, W. S., 7, 8

Odegard, O., 3
Olsen, G. W., 1
Olson, R. P., 436
Oram, E. G., 8
Osmond, H., 3, 9
Overton, D. A., 441

Paden, R. C., 124, 247
Panyon, M., 113
Parsons, T., 3
Pasamanick, B., 1, 4, 11
Pattison, E. M., 492
Paul, G. L., 1, 2, 3, 4, 5, 6, 9, 13, 14, 15, 16, 32,
    62, 83, 86, 102, 103, 105, 108, 115, 116,
    117, 119, 120, 124, 128, 130, 132, 136, 179,
    180, 191, 246, 247, 370, 429, 437, 441, 442,
    447, 452, 463, 464, 466, 467, 468, 488, 490,
    491, 492, 497
Peck, C. L., 447
Pendergrass, P. E., 29, 465
Peretz, D., 2
Peretz, D. A., 2
Perpich, J. G., 448
Perry, R., 8
Person, P. H., Jr., 1
Peterson, D. R., 3, 20, 21, 32, 102

Peterson, P. B., 1
Philip, A. E., 492
Piotrowski, Z. A., 1
Pisa, A., 433, 436
Pisoni, S., 9
Plutchik, R., 29
Pollack, E. S., 1
Pommer, D., 117
Porter, L. W., 105, 106
Power, C. T., 124
Prigmore, C. S., 456, 458, 500
Proano, A., 8
Pryer, M. W., 113

Quilitch, H. R., 117

Rachlin, S., 444, 451
Rachman, S., 499
Racy, J., 500
Rapaport, R. N., 8
Rappaport, J., 21, 113, 465
Rapport, S., 4
Rashkis, H. A., 7
Rawls, J. R., 4
Raymaker, H., 492
Redfield, J. P., 120, 124, 130, 492
Redlich, F. C., 120
Rednick, R. W., 1
Reed, C. F., 113, 117, 490
Reich, R., 2
Reidy, J. P., 19, 21, 22
Reppucci, N. D., 465
Rhodes, F., 117, 490
Rhodes, R. J., 492
Richards, C. S., 465
Rickard, H. C., 9
Rieder, R. O., 2, 5
Ring, K., 451
Robinson, D. N., 500
Rockwood, C. E., 415
Rosenbaum, C. P., 461
Rosenblatt, A., 2, 3, 4
Rosenhan, D. L., 3
Rossi, J. J., 432
Rubinstein, E. A., 113
Rutledge, L., 1
Ryder, F. P., 105, 106
Rynearsen, R. R., 1

Salzinger, K., 2, 9
Salzinger, S., 2
Sanders, D. H., 6, 11, 441
Sanders, R., 1, 3, 4, 8
Saper, B., 464, 465, 466
Saunders, J. T., 465
Scarpitti, F. R., 1, 4, 11
Schaefer, H. H., 4, 10, 124
Scherher, J., 446, 448
Schooler, C., 132
Schulberg, H. C., 21, 24
Schwartz, J., 433

Schwitzgebel, R. K., 444, 446, 447, 448, 449, 450, 451, 452, 453
Scott, S. B., 433, 436
Sechrest, L. B., 9
Shannon, D. T., 83
Sharrett, S., 1, 2, 5, 6
Sherman, L. J., 2, 4
Shields, J., 501
Sidebotham, R., 1
Sidman, M., 14
Siegel, S., 492, 493, 494, 495, 496, 497, 498
Siker, D., 2
Simmons, O. G., 4
Simon, A., 5
Simon, R. A., 1
Simonsen, C. E., 456
Singh, M. M., 29
Skinner, B. F., 448
Smarr, E. R., 7
Smith, R. S., 1, 3, 4, 8
Smith, W. G., 2
Snow, H. B., 3
Sobey, F., 113
Soloman, M. H., 4, 8
Solomon, L., 2
Sommer, R., 3, 9
Spencer, A. M., 1
Spersimon, J. C., 113
Spohn, H. E., 132
Steer, R. A., 433
Steers, R. M., 105, 106
Steffy, R. A., 10, 12
Steinbach, M., 4, 6, 11
Stewart, A., 2
Stewart, J. C., 113
Stickney, S. B., 446, 500
Stoffelmayr, B. E., 433, 434, 437
Stokes, H. A., 8
Stolz, S. B., 448, 449, 452, 454, 458
Stone, A. A., 447
Stover, D. O., 490
Strauss, J. S., 4
Streedbeck, D., 117
Struening, E. L., 102, 103, 107
Stuart, R. B., 444, 447, 448, 450, 451
Sutton, S., 2
Szasz, T. S., 3

Tallman, F. F., 8
Taube, C. A., 1, 2
Teasdale, J., 499
Teigen, J., 432, 433
Teitelbaum, S., 490
Termini, B. A., 500
Theobald, D. T., 124
Tilton, J. R., 9
Tito, J., 4
Tobias, L. T., 124, 136, 180, 441, 447
Toomey, B. G., 456

Topping, G., 4, 6
Torney, D., 10, 12
Tourney, G., 467
Trotter, S., 2
Tuchi, B. J., 105
Tucker, G. J., 2
Tunakan, B., 8
Tyce, F. A., 1

Ullmann, L. P., 1, 3, 5, 9, 13, 21, 33, 120, 126, 415, 424, 432, 433, 444, 449, 454, 465, 466, 501
Unikel, I. P., 9
U. S. Department of Health, Education, and Welfare, 447, 449, 450, 499

Vail, D. J., 446, 448
Vaillant, G. E., 2
Vaughn, R., 490
Veit, S. W., 117, 465
Vitale, J. H., 1, 4, 6, 11, 433

Wagner, B. R., 9, 32, 467, 492
Wagner, M. K., 448
Wallace, C., 432, 433
Wallace, C. J., 117
Wanklin, J. M., 3
Ward, W., 2
Warren, S. A., 117
Wasden, R. A., 439
Webster, D. R., 500
Weickert, A. A., 4, 6
Weiman, B., 492
Weinberg, S. K., 3
Weinman, B. S., 1, 3, 4, 8
Weiss, R. L., 9
Welsh, D. K., 492
Wexler, D. B., 445, 446, 448, 453, 456, 457, 458, 461, 462, 463, 500
White, N. F., 432
Wienckowski, L. A., 448, 449, 452, 454, 457
Wilensky, H., 8
Willson, V. L., 15
Wilmer, H. A., 7
Winer, B. J., 489, 492, 493, 494, 495, 496, 497, 498
Wing, J. K., 3, 4, 8, 11, 433, 435
Witkin, M. J., 29, 113
Witney, G., 9
Wohl, S. A., 4, 6
Wolfe, B. E., 447
Wood, D. D., 117, 132
Wyatt, R. J., 500

Yeomans, N. T., 432

Zeisset, R. M., 9
Zolik, E. S., 4
Zubin, J., 2
Zusman, J., 3

# Subject Index

*References to tables and figures are preceded by T and F*

Academic training, 58, 81-82, 387, 398; staff, 114-115, 116, 117, 118. *See also* Educators
Accountability, 450, 453, 455, 464, 467
Acquired (secondary) reinforcers, 75
Active ignoring, 170, 458
Activity periods, 57-58, 83-84
Adaptive behavior, T131, 132; first six months of project, 141-143, F142; next two years, 188-194, F189, 214, 240; next year and a half, 257-261, F258, 262; last six months, 315-319, F317, 365; goal of improving, 424-427, 459, 460. *See also* Communication skills; Instrumental role performance; Interpersonal skills; Self-care
Administrative structure, 24; competency and accountability in, 464
Aftercare, 46; problems of, 198-200, 201, 202-203. *See also* Community placement; Follow-up period
Aftercare consultation, 15-16, 18, 370, 372, 388, 394-395, 406, 412, 420; case and program, 395-398, F399, 400, T401, 402, F402, 403, T404, 405, 408-410, F409, 411, 421; educational, 397, 411, 421; vocational, 398
Age factor, 129, T129, 132, 223. *See also* Demographic variables
Aggressive behavior, 123, 125, 132, 141, 240, 301, 306, 430-432. *See also* Assaultiveness; Maladaptive behavior
Aide culture, 3, 40, 113, 135, 403, 435
American Psychological Association, 455
Anna State Hospital, token economy in, 10
Announce component, *see* Staff-Resident Interaction Chronograph (SRIC)
ANOVA, *see* Evaluation, statistical
Anxiety, *see* Stress reaction
Appearance check procedures, 80, 479-483
Appropriate behavior, T34, F139, F183, F250, F310, F409; response to, T37, F163, 164, T168, T169, F227, 228, T233, F289, 290, T294, F351, 352, T356, T357, 398, F399, T404; variability of, T153, 154, 155, 211, T212, 275-277, T276, 281, 335-337, T336, 342-343. *See also* Total Appropriate Behavior Index

Archival data, 119, 120
Assaultiveness, 123, 134, 141; changes in, 178, 179, 187, 195, 240, 244-245, 253, 256, 264-265, 293, 298, 301, 302, 303, 306, 307, 322, 370; dealing with, 185-186, 191, 206, 314-315, 320, 321, 354, 431, 432, 438-439, 460, 493n1
Assessment plan, 16-18, F17, 135, 175. *See also* Evaluation
Association by contiguity, 74-75
Attend/Record/Observe, *see* Staff-Resident Interaction Chronograph (SRIC)
Attention to residents, 37-39, T38, 424; first six months, 164-172, T165, T168, T169; next two years, 228-230, T229, 238, 241; next year and a half, 290, T291; last six months, 352-354, T353, F355, T356, T357; aftercare 400-402, T401, F402, 407. *See also* Interactions
Attitudes, staff: methods of assessing, 102-103, 106-108, F109, 110, 115-116, 117, 118; toward mental patients: first six months, 157, F158, 160, 161, 172, 176; next two years, 217-218, F218, 236, 240; next year and a half, 282-283, F283, 298; last six months, 345-346, F346, 348, 349, 361, 365-366; toward treatment programs: first six months, 157-162, F159, 172-174; next two years, 218-226, F220, 237; next year and a half, 283-289, F285, 298-299, 300, 302-303; last six months, 346-350, F347, 361-362, 363. *See also* Opinions About Mental Illness Scale (OMI); Preferred attitude scores; Therapist Orientation Sheet (TOS)
Authoritarianism scores, *see* Opinions About Mental Illness Scale (OMI)
Aversion, 74
Aversive controls, 431, 438-439, 458-463, 493n1, 499n7, 500n16. *See also* Psychotropic drugs

Backup reinforcers, 75, 77, 151, 209, 398, 437, 438, 457, 461
Baseline conditions, 134-135; reinstitution of, 305-306, 364
Bathing, 60, 65, 84-85

Bedtime routine, 60, 84-85
Behavioral approach, *see* Experimental-behavioral approach
Benevolence scores, *see* Opinions About Mental Illness Scale (OMI)
"Best interest" approach, 454, 455
Biographical data, 102, 120
Bizarre behavior, 5, 9, T34, T37, 43, 125, 128, 132; first six months, 145, 146, 164; next two years, 198, 200, 202, 211, 239-240; next year and a half, 249, 264, 265, 266, 267; last six months, 323, 324, 325, 365; responses to, T37, F163, 164, T168, T169, F227, 228, T233, F289, 290, T294, F351, 352, T356, T357, 371, 398, F399, 403, T404; variability of, 152-154, T153, 155, 156, 211, T212, 214, 216, 275, T276, 278, 281, 335, T336, 339, 342; overall reduction of, 382, 427-432, 438-439, 458-459
Bomb threat, 178
Bureaucratic factors, 465-467

Canteen time, 59, 84
Caretaking role, 3, 113
Case consultation, 395, 396, 397, 398, F399, 400, T401, 402, 403, T404, 405, 408-410, F409, 411, 420, 421, 441
Case descriptions, 144-147, 196-203, 264-267, 323-326
Certification checks, 115
Chaining, 76, 80
Challenge (crisis), 50, 51
Change agents, 27-28. *See also* Staff, junior
Change areas, individual, 46
Chemotherapy, *see* Psychotropic drugs
Chicago State Hospital, milieu therapy in, 8
Christmas program, 135-136
Civil-service ratings, 490n5
Class periods, 58, 81-82; staff, 114-115, 116, 117, 118; in community facilities, 397, 398
Clinical Frequencies Recording System, 33-34, 41, 115, 122-123, T131, 132, 440, 441, 462, 463; scores: first six months, 138, F139, 140, 141; next two years, 183, F183, 188, 204, 207, 211; next year and a half, F250, 257, 258, 273; last six months, 310-311, F310, 315, 316-319, 337. *See also* Total Appropriate Behavior Index; Total Inappropriate Behavior Index
Cliques, 51
Cognitive dysfunction; Cognitive Distortion Index, 125, T131, 132, 382, 408, 429-430, 438; scores: first six months, 138, 139, F140, 143, 154, 155; next two years, F184, 185, 187, 191, 194, 211, 239, 240; next year and a half, 251, F251, 252, 254, 257, 262, 271, 278, 302; last six months, F311, 312, 313, 315, 320, 332, 334, 335, 337, 339, 365. *See also* Time-Sample Behavioral Checklist (TSBC)
Communication, 43-44, 49; clarity of, 43-46, 52; of expectations, 49-50, 51, 52, 53, 134, 425; metacommunication, 50, 53, 236
Communication skills, 65, 90, 425
Community: exposure to, 46, 134, 135, 179, 186, 209, 246, 254; consideration of safety of, 452
Community groups, 52, 60. *See also* Community meetings
Community lodge, 11, 441
Community meetings, 55-56, 60, 83, 85, 125; first six months, 148-150, 156; next two years, 178, 204-208, 215, 240; next year and a half, 268-271, 279; last six months, 327-331, 341, 365. *See also* Confusion; "Confusion index"
Community mental health centers, 464
Community mental health ideology, 22
Community placement, 4-5, 43, 369-370, 384, 387, 394-395, 439-442; support in, 5-6, 11, 43, 46, 197-198; preparation for, 46, 58, 197, 83, 202, 370-371; evaluation of, 126, 241; transfer to 370, 395; staff performance in 398-405; differential changes in functioning in, 408-410, 411; and release rates, 412-413, T413; comparative effectiveness and efficiency of achieving, 413-414, T414, 419; cost of, 417. *See also* Aftercare consultation; Extended-care facilities; Follow-up period; Release to independent living
Community volunteers, 46, 179, 213, 216, 465
Competency in dealing with patients, 451, 464
Competition, group, 54, 55, 58
Concurrent appropriate behavior, 125, 191, 249, 257, 260, 315, 318, 320, 426-427; variability of, 154, 209, 211, 214-215, 216, 275-277, 278-279, 281, 335-337, T336, 339, 340, 342-343. *See also* Appropriate behavior
Concurrent inappropriate behavior, 125, T131, 132, 209, 278; variability of, 152-154. *See also* Inappropriate behavior
Confusion; "confusion index," F149, 150, 207, F207, F270, 271, 279, 328, 329, F329, 330, 341
Consensual approach, 452
Consent, informed, 452; revocation of, 453
Constitutional rights of patients, 446-447, 452, 456
Consultation, *see* Aftercare consultation
Consumables, *see* Resource utilization
Contiguity, association by, 74-75
Contingent rights, 457, 458, 500n11
Continuous systems monitoring, 14, 15, 41, 121-126, T131, 135, 441, 450, 466, 468
Contractual approach, 452-453, 454, 455
Convulsive shock treatment, 128, 499n7
Cooperation of all participants, 46, 58, 83, 452, 453, 465
Cost-effectiveness analysis, 415-418, T416, T418, 419, 421-422, 498
Counselor, rehabilitation, 28, 61, 85, 180
Crazy behavior, *see* Bizarre behavior

"Credit card," 78, 80
Credit system, canteen, 59
Crisis (challenge), 50, 51; resolution of, 425

Death: of a resident, 177-178, 186, 226, 239; discussion of, 204
Decentralization of authority, 464
Decision making, 50-51; by resident, 53; implementation of decisions, 56; by staff, 111; transferred from consultant to client, 394; ethical, 444; court's role in, 445
Dehumanization, institutional, 443
Delayed reinforcement, 78
Demographic variables, 129, T129, 132, 136, 262, 322; and IAB predictability, 381, 386; and functioning in community, 440
Design of comparative project, 13-18, F17; aims of, 15; planned expansion of, 305, 307, 371
Deviance: definition of, 3-4; tolerance for, 4, 5, 452
Directionality of changes, 377, 379
Discharge, see Release to independent living
Discriminative stimulus, 75, 76
Doing For; Doing With, see Staff-Resident Interaction Chronograph (SRIC)
*Donaldson v. O'Connor*, 447
Drugs, see Psychotropic drugs

Education, relation of, to OMI scores, 157
Educational aftercare consultation, 397, 411, 421
Educators, 28, 58, 81, 180
Effect, law of, 74
Effectiveness-cost ratios, 418, T418. See also Cost-effectiveness analysis
Employment: and community tenure, 5; training for, 28, 43, 46, 197, 398, 410, 456; skills needed for, 43; in sheltered environment, 398, 410. See also Job assignments
Environmental factors, postrelease, 398, 410, 418, 420-421, 439, 440, 441
Errors, staff, 124, 392, 490n4, 493n11; first six months, T169, 170-171; next two years, 232, T233, 234-235, 236; next year and a half, T294, 296-297, 298; last six months, T356, T357, 360, 366; aftercare, 403, T404
Ethical issues, 443-463; conflicts of, 451
Evaluation: methods of, 15, 33-36, 41, 102-103, 106-112, F106, F109, 115-117, 119-126; statistical, of patient behavior: first six months, 138-139, 141-142; next two years, 182, 184-185, 189-191; next year and a half, 249, 251-252, 258-260; last six months, 309, 312, 316-318; of community stay, 126, 241; of comparative intramural change, 373-375; empirical, of project findings, 433-439, 444; of ethical standards, 444. See also Monitoring, ongoing; Observation
Executive council, 58-59
Expectancy, law of, 49-50

Expectations of behavior, 64-65; communicating, 49-50, 51, 52, 53, 134, 425
Experimental-behavioral approach, 13-15, 394, 444, 448-449, 488n1
Exposure procedures, 46, 134, 135, 179, 186, 209, 246, 254
Expulsion time, 52, 136, 179, 191-192, 206, 293; required reduction of, 226, 244, 246, 253, 254-255, 256, 380; extension of, 306, 354; substitution for, 371. See also Time out
Extended-care facilities, 5, 11, 18, 127, 244, 370, 387, 391, 395, 464; changes in functioning of residents in, 406-410; cost of, 417. See also Aftercare consultation; Community placement
Extinction, 74
Extroversion score, 157, 308. See also Pittsburgh Scale of Social-Extroversion-Introversion and Emotionality
"Eyes open" (time awake), 125, 152, 210, 274, 275, 280, 333, 334, 342

Facilities' and Services' Utilization Index, 123. See also Resource utilization
Failures, inappropriate, responses to, T34, T37; first six months, F163, 164, T168, T169; next two years, F227, 228, T233; next year and a half, F289, 290, T294; last six months, F351, 352, T356, T357; in aftercare consultation, 398, F399, 400, T404
Family: help for, in handling problems, 46; included in prerelease group, 58, 83; responsibilities of, 453
Feedback, 51, 56; positive, 49, 50, 51, 53, 54, 55, 57, 60, 234; negative, 49-50, 52, 53, 54, 55, 60, 234; on staff performance, 115, 117, 232; verbal or videotaped, 247
Fines, 306-307. See also Response costs
Follow-up period, 45, 46, 388, 391-392, 440, 441; changes in functioning during, 4-5, 18, 406-411, 413, 420-421; summarized, 420-421. See also Aftercare; Aftercare consultation; Community placement
Food as reinforcer, 457, 461, 462. See also Meals
Fort Meade Veterans Administration hospital, milieu therapy in, 8
Free periods, 60, 84
Funding sources, 466-467

Galesburg State Research Hospital, 10
Gangs, delinquent, 51
Generalized reinforcers, 75, 77
Geographical zone of project, 19-20
Geriatric patients: in nursing homes, 2; in hospitals, 127
Global functioning; Global Functioning Factor Score, 126, T131, 132; first six months, 143-144, T144, 148, 151, 152, 164; next two years, 182, 183, 194-195, T195, 204, 210, 211; next year and a half, 249-250, 261,

Subject Index 523

262, T262, 263, T263, 301; last six months, 309-310, 315, 319, 320, 321, T321, 322, T322, 352; following release, 408, 440-441; differential changes in, 138, 377, 378, 382, 386
Goals: of psychosocial treatment, 5-6, 42-43, 46; of the comparative project, 423, 424-432, 458-460, 467-468; of effective institutional treatment, 451-452
Group Activity Index (GAI), 125-126, 148, 204, 268, 327
Group cohesiveness, 51, 53-54
Group competition, 54, 55, 58
Group contingencies, 436
Group living, rules of, 44, 47. *See also* Living groups
Group meetings, *see* Community meetings
Group planning for release, 46, 58, 83, 197, 202
Group pressure, 33, 51, 52, 425
Group problem solving, 11, 33, 46, 425
Group support, 5-6, 11, 43, 46, 197-198
Group therapy, 83
Group training for mutual support, 11
Group trips, 46, 192, 193; termination of, 246

Hospital: releases from, 1, 10, 369, 372, 384; community extension of, 11; comparison group in, 20-22, 29-30, 369; program content in, 31-33, T32; staff performance in, 36, 37, T37, T38, T39, 40, 41; chronic population of, 127, 128, 129; reduced population in, 127, 369; drug use in, 128, 380, 382, 389; failure of patient improvement in, 388-389
Hostile-Belligerence Index, 125, T131, 132, 382, 408; scores: first six months, 138, 139, 140-141, F140; next two years, F184, 185, 187, 188, 194; next year and a half, 251, F251, 252, 254, 257, 262, 268, 278, 302; last six months, F311, 312, 313, 315, 320, 334, 335, 337, 338. *See also* Assaultiveness; Intolerable behavior
Housekeeping jobs, 59-60, 84
Housekeeping skills, 46, 65
Hudson River State Hospital, milieu therapy in, 8
Hunger strike, 136

Ignore/No Response, *see* Staff-Resident Interaction Chronograph (SRIC)
Improvement of institutional facilities, 463-467
Improvement rates, 144-147, 196-203, 261-267, 319-326, T321, T322. *See also* Case descriptions
Inappropriate behavior, T34, 79, 132, F139, F183, F250, F310, F409. *See also* Bizarre behavior; Failures, inappropriate; Total Inappropriate Behavior Index
Inappropriate Clinical Frequencies, *see* Total Inappropriate Behavior
Incontinence, 500n15

Individual functional analysis, 14
Individual job assignments, 59-60, 61, 65, 85
Informed consent, 452; revoked, 453
Inpatient Assessment Battery (IAB) scores, 120-121, 128, 130, T130, 132, 135, 373-377, F374, T374, 384, 386, 388, 389, 391, 406-408, F409, 410, 413; paradoxes on, 377-379; predictability of, 380-383
Inpatient Multidimensional Psychiatric Scale (IMPS), 386, 490n2
Inpatient Scale of Minimal Functioning (ISMF), 120, T130, 376
In-service training, *see* On-the-job training
Institute for Behavioral Research, Behavioral Law Center of, 499n2
"Institutional peonage," 445-446
"Institutional politics," 465-467
"Institutional syndrome," 3
Instruct/Demonstrate, *see* Staff-Resident Interaction Chronograph (SRIC)
Instruction: academic, 58, 81-82, 387, 398; and reinforcement, 76; and shaping, 79; of staff, 114-115, 116, 117, 118
Instrumental role performance; Instrumental Role Index, 5, 7, 43, 123, T131, 132, 378, 408, 426; scores: first six months, 141, 142, F142, 143, 152; next two years, 189, F189, 190, 191, 193-194, 213, 240; next year and a half, 258, F258, 259, 261, 262; last six months, 316, F317, 318, 319, 320, 339. *See also* Adaptive behavior
Integrated/technical training, 117, 118
Interactional frame of reference, 2-6
Interactions: differential, among programs, 33, 34-40; social, after release, 45; social, among residents, 51, 56-57, 82-83; staff-resident, 34-40, 424. *See also* Social contacts; Staff-Resident Interaction Chronograph (SRIC)
Interference with community meetings: first six months, 149-150, F149; next two years, 206-207, F207; next year and a half, F270, 271, 279; last six months, 328, F329, 330, 341
Interpersonal Etiology scores, *see* Opinions About Mental Illness Scale (OMI)
Interpersonal skills; Interpersonal Skills Index, 65, 90, 123, T131, 132, 378, 408, 425; scores: first six months, 141, 142-143, F142, 155; next two years, 189, F189, 190, 191, 192-193, 194, 204-205, 209, 213; next year and a half, 258, F258, 259, 260-261, 262, 271; last six months, 316, F317, 318-319, 320, 334, 335, 337, 338, 339, 340. *See also* Adaptive behavior
Interpretation: of metacommunications, 50; descriptive, of behavioral changes: first six months, 139-141, 142-143; next two years, 185-188, 191-194; next year and a half, 252-257, 260-261; last six months, 312-315, 318-319; IAB Functioning, 375-377; staff, of treatment programs: first six months, 157-162, F159, 172-174; next two years,

218-226, F220, 237; next year and a half, 283-289, F285, 298-299; last six months, 346-350, F347, 361-362, 363
Intolerable behavior; Intolerable Behavior scores, 65, 123, 352, 367, 430-432; and staff sanctions, 52; and negative feedback, 53; means to control, 78; first six months, 141, 143, 152; next two years, 187-188, 194, 195, 204, 211; next year and a half, 253, 255-257, F255, 263, 265, 266, 267, 268, 271, 273, 274, 278; last six months, 313-315, F314, 318, 320, 322, 330, 331, 333, 337, 338, 341, 342, 343; special treatment for, 370-371; and IAB Functioning, 378, 379, 382, 384, 386. *See also* Aggressive behavior; Assaultiveness
Intrusive procedures, 454, 455, 458-463; level of, 461-463
Involvement, law of, 50-51

Job assignments, 46, 59-60, 61, 65, 84, 85; work-training, 398
Judicial decisions, 445-447, 456-457, 458, 500nn10,13

Kidnapping of a resident, 178

Lakeshore Psychiatric Hospital, token economy in, 10
Language, descriptive, in communication, 45-46
Learning, laws of, 74-75
Legal issues, 443-463, 499n2, 500nn10,11,13, 501n10; conflicts of, 451
Legislative investigation, 246, 253-254, 256
Liaison coordinator, 58, 83, 180
Living groups, 52, 58; responsibilities of, 54, 55, 56, 60; meetings of, 58, 60-63
Location variability: first six months, T153, 154, 155; next two years, T212, 213, 214, 215, 216; next year and a half, T276, 277-278, 279; last six months, T336, 338, 339, 340, 343

Maladaptive behavior, 125, T131, 132; first six months, 138-141, F139, F140; next two years, 182-188, F183, F184, 239-240; next year and a half, 249-257, F250, F251, F255, 301-302; last six months, 309-315, F310, F311, F314, 320, 321, 322, 364-365; goal of reducing or eliminating, 427-432, 458-460
Manneristic Behavior, 435
Mann-Whitney U tests, 373, 385, 414
Marital status, 128, T129. *See also* Demographic variables
Meals, 54-55, 64-65, 80-81, 500n12; medical, 136, 457, 486-487; missed, 461, 500n12; as reinforcers, 462
Measurement reactivity, 379, 380, 382, 389, 498n6
Menlo Park Veterans Administration Hospital, token economy in, 10

Mental Health Career Series, 245
Mental health center for psychosocial groups, 22-25, T23, 30; psychosocial units in, 25-29; legislative investigation of, 246, 253-254, 256; plans for accreditation of, 254, 305, 371; plans for expanding programs in, 305, 307, 371; treatment programs terminated in, 371-372, 388, 391, 412; new policies in, 391-392. *See also* Psychosocial programs
Mental health law, 455-447, 456-457, 458, 500nn10,13
Mental hospitals: resident population in, 1, 2; readmission to, 1; authority structure of, 3; milieu therapy in, 8; social-learning therapy in, 10. *See also* Hospital
Mental Hygiene Ideology scores, *see* Opinions About Mental Illness Scale (OMI)
Mental patients: assessing behavior of, 119-126, 130-132, T130, T131; characteristics of, 120, 128-130, T129; chronically institutionalized, 127-128; selection of, and group equation, 128-132; transfer of, 133-134; orientation of, 134; "revolving-door," 243; prechronic, 243, 244, 305, 371; historic treatment of, 433; literature on, 433-439; ethical and legal issues relating to, 443-463; regulation of work with, 444-455; exploitation of, 445-446; correcting abuse of, 445-447, 456-458; rights of, 446-447, 452, 456-458, 462, 499-500nn10,11,13,18; inappropriate release of, 447; consideration for improving institutional facilities for, 463-467
Metacommunication, 50, 53, 236
Milieu therapy, 7-9; setting and staffing for, 22-30, 57; program content, 31-36, T32, 54-62; resident schedule, T32, 52-53, 62-64; staff performance and assessment, 36-40, T37, T38, T39, 41; basic principles and concepts, 49-51; manual, 49-73, therapeutic community in, 51-53; rules for staff in, 53-54; resident behavior expectations, 64-65; change agent schedules, 65-73; clinical staff, 102-112; staff training, 113-118; medical meal procedure, 457, 486-487
Mind controlling techniques, 448
Minimum Social Behavior Scale (MSBS), 120, T130, 377
Minnesota Multiphasic Personality Inventory (MMPI), 102
Modeling, 76, 247
Money: as reinforcer, 75; spending allowance, 86
Monitoring, ongoing, 14, 15, 41, 121-126, T131, 135, 245, 305, 441, 450, 463, 466, 468
Morale problems, 106, 178, 179, 253-254, 391-392, 464, 467
Morning routine, 54, 64, 79-80
Movement, resident, *see* Location variability

National Institute of Mental Health (NIMH), 466

Negative feedback and statements, 49-50, 52, 53, 54, 55, 60, 234
Negative prompts, 76
Negative reinforcers, 74, 75, 459
Negative scores (Verbal, Nonverbal, Nonsocial, Statement, Prompt, Group Reference), *see* Staff-Resident Interaction Chronograph (SRIC)
Nonreactive observers, 124
Nurses Observational Scale for Inpatient Evaluation (NOSIE-30), 121, T130, 376

Observation, 36, 111, 115, 119, 124, 463
Off-hours coverage, 226, 244, 247, 256, 268-269, 465
Off-unit facilities, 179, 246
On-the-job training, staff, 115, 116, 117, 118, 135
Open-unit philosophy, 25
Opinions About Mental Illness Scale (OMI), 102-103, 106-108, F106, 115, 116, 117; scores: first six months, 157, F158, 160, 161, 172; next two years, 217-218, F218, 236; next year and a half, 282-283, F283, 284, 287, 298; last six months, 345-346, F346, 348, 349, 361; Social Learning Ideology items added to, 477-478
Orientation and Common Procedures Manual, 42-48, 489n1
Overall functioning, *see* Global functioning
Overcorrection/restitution procedures, 431-432, 460

Passes, 44, 47, 48, 61-62, 86, 91, 457-458
Patient costs, 417
Patton State Hospital, token economy in, 10
Peer group, 51
Personnel, *see* Staff
Performance, staff, in psychosocial programs: first six months, 162-172, F163, T165, T168, T169, 174, 176; next two years, 226-236, F227, T229, F231, T233, 237-238, 240-241; next year and a half, 289-298, F289, T291, T292, T294, 299-300, 302-303; last six months, 350-361, F351, T353, F355, T356, T357, 362-363, 366
Performance criteria, 78-79, 80
Personal-social characteristics: staff, 102, 104; resident, 120, 128-130, T129. *See also* Demographic variables
Philadelphia State Hospital, milieu programs in, 8
Physical Force score, *see* Staff-Resident Interaction Chronograph (SRIC)
Physical location, resident: first six months, T153, 154, 155; next two years, T212, 213, 214, 215, 216; next year and a half, T276, 277-278, 279; last six months, T336, 338, 339, 340, 343
Pittsburgh Scale of Social-Extroversion-Introversion and Emotionality, 102
Plea bargaining, 500n11

Political factors, 371-372, 465-467, 499n7, 501n20
Positive feedback and statements, 49, 50, 51, 53, 54, 55, 57, 60, 234
Positive prompts, 76
Positive reinforcers, 74, 75, 170, 178, 459
Positive scores (Verbal, Nonverbal, Nonsocial, Statement, Prompt, Group Reference), *see* Staff-Resident Interaction Chronograph (SRIC)
Power relationships, staff-resident, 444
Prechronic patients, 243; proposed program for 244, 305, 371
Predictability: of resident improvement, 143, 194-195, 262-263, 321, 380-383, 408; of significant release, 386, 389, 407-408, 411, 439, 440
Preferences, staff, on treatment and techniques, 108-111
Preferred attitude scores on TOS, 108, F109, 110, 116; first six months, 158, F159, 160, 162, 173; next two years, 219-222, F220, 224-225, 237; next year and a half, 284-286, F285, 288, 299; last six months, 346-348, F347, 350, 362. *See also* Therapist Orientation Sheet (TOS)
Preferred technique scores on TOS, F109, 110, 111-112, 116; first six months, 158, F159, 160-162, 173, 174, F220, 222-224, 225, 236, 237, 240; next year and a half, F285, 286-288, 299; last six months, F347, 348-350, 362. *See also* Therapist Orientation Sheet (TOS)
Premack principle, 75
Prerelease planning, 46, 58, 83, 197, 202, 370-371
Primary reinforcers, 75, 437, 438
Problem solving: group, 11, 33, 46, 425; practice in, 50, 51, 53; transferred from consultant to client, 394
Process-Reactive Scale, 120, 128, T129, 132, 195
Program consultation, 395-405, F399, T401, T404, 408-410, F409, 411, 420, 421, 441
Prompts, prompting, 76, 79, 80, 81, 84, 85, 136, 170, 234, 296, 425; negative and positive, 76; physical, 76, 460; verbal, 76, 458, 460
Proportional-payoff schedule, 247
Psychosocial programs: setting and staffing of, 22-30; content and assessment of, 31-36, T32; differential nature of interactions in, 33; differential staff performance in, 36-40, T37, T38, T39, 41; common assumptions of, 42; common objectives and areas of focus of, 42-43; common operational procedures and attitudes of, 43-46; introduction of, 135, 138; planned expansion of, 243, 244, 305, 307, 371; decline in effectiveness of, 244-245, 246-248; termination of, 371-372, 388, 391, 412; comparative effectiveness of, 423; differential areas of success of,

423-432; principles and techniques of, 432; representativeness of procedures and findings of, 432-439; and factors related to release, 439-442. *See also* Attitudes, staff, toward treatment programs; Interpretation, staff, of treatment programs; Milieu therapy; Performance, staff, in treatment programs; Social-learning therapy

Psychoticism, 435

Psychotropic drugs, 379-380, T380, 493n2; use of, in hospital, 128, 380, 382, 389; and withdrawal study, 136, 175; to control aggressive behavior, 180, 244; increased use of, 210, 247, 256; relation of, to time spent sleeping, 274, 275, 280; during last six months, 306, 307, 334, 342, T380; relation of, to release, 386, 387; cost of, 415, use of, after release, 397, 405, 406, 407, 441; as aversive control, 431

Purchase-eligibility procedure, 247, 500nn12,13

Race: of patient groups, 129, T129; relation of to attitudes and technique preferences, 110, 111, 219-221. *See also* Demographic variables

Rating scales, standardized, 119, 120, 121, 379

Reactivity of measurement, 379, 380, 382, 389, 498n6

Readmission to program, 178, 196, 201, 205, 243

Recidivism rates, 1, 2. *See also* Rehospitalization

Records, recordkeeping, 33-34, 45, 54, 79, 114, 459. *See also* Clinical Frequencies Recording System

Reflect/Clarify, *see* Staff-Resident Interaction Chronograph (SRIC)

Regional hospital, *see* Hospital

Regional management information service, 177

Regional mental health center, *see* Mental health center for psychosocial groups

Regional mental health system, 19-20

Regulation of work with chronic patients, 444-449; possible negative effects of, 445-447, 449; proposed mechanism for, 449-455

Rehabilitation counselor, 28, 61, 85, 180

Rehabilitation goals, 424-432

Rehospitalization, 1, 4, 5, 42, 412, 413, 439, 498n1; and vocational status, 7

Reinforcement, 74, 76; negative, 74, 75, 459; positive, 74, 75, 170, 178, 459; backup, 75, 77, 151, 209, 398, 437, 438, 457, 461; generalized, 75, 77; primary, 75, 437, 438; secondary, 75; in token economy, 76-78; social, 77, 78, 79, 80, 81, 82, 84, 85; avoidance of, 78; delayed, 78; immediate, 78, 82; paired with other stimuli, 78-79, 80; legal, 457; consumables as, 457, 461, 462

Release, to independent living, 178, 196-203, 239, 245, 263-264; from mental hospital, 1, 10, 369, 372, 384; from milieu therapy, 7-8; training for, 46, 58, 83, 197, 202, 370-371; evaluation of, 126, 241; effectiveness in achieving, 384-385, T385, 387, 413, T413; efficiency in achieving, 385-386, T385, 387; intramural functioning and predictability of, 386; changes in functioning after, 406-408, 411; factors related to, 439-442; inappropriate, 447. *See also* Aftercare; Community placement; Follow-up period

Replacement of residents, 178, 239, 245

Research grants, 466-467

Research meetings and staff, 26, 180, 371, 488n5

Resocialization, 42-43; as target of treatment, 5, 31, 123, 175, 240, 319, 320; with milieu therapy, 7-9; with social-learning therapy, 7, 9-10; need for, 132

Resources (consumables and supplies), cost of, 415, 417

Resource utilization: first six months, 150-152, F150, T153, 154, 155, 156; next two years, 208-210, F208, T212, 213, 214, 215, 240; next year and a half, 246, 271-274, F272, T276, 277, 279, 280, 281; last six months, 331-333, F332, T336, 338, 339, 340, 341-342, 343, 365; variability in: first six months, T153, 154, 155, 156; next two years, T212, 213, 214; next year and a half, T276, 277, 279, 281; last six months, T336, 338, 339, 340, 343; and improved behavior, 462

Response-contingent procedures, 425, 436, 438

Response costs, 74, 78, 79, 247, 257, 274, 459, 500n14

Review committee for ethical regulation, 449-455

"Revolving-door" patients, 243. *See also* Rehospitalization

Role playing, 114, 202

Roommates, 5-6, 11, 197-198

Rules of group living, 44, 47, 49, 56

Sampling-exposure procedures, 179, 186, 209, 246, 254

Scheduled activities: resident, T32, 52-53, 62-64, 77-78; change agent, 65-73

"Schizophrenia," 500n18

Schizophrenic Disorganization Index, 125, T131, 132, 408; scores: first six months, 138, 139, 140, F140, 141, 143; next two years, F184, 185, 186, 188, 194, 209, 211; next year and a half, 251, F251, 252, 253-254, 257, 261-262, 268; last six months, F311, 312, 313, 315, 320, 330, 334, 335, 339

Scoring of data, 490n4, 491n6; computer, 490n4, 491n8

Seclusion, limited, 446. *See also* Expulsion time

Secondary (acquired) reinforcers, 75

Seclusiveness, 434

Selection procedures: staff, 103-105; patient, 128-132

Self-care; Self-Care Index, 64-65, 89-90, 123,

T131, 132, 382, 408; scores: first six months, 141, 142, F142, 143; next two years, 189, F189, 190, 191, 193, 194, 209, 213; next year and a half, 258, F258, 259, 260, 261, 278; last six months, 316, 317, F317, 318, 320; as goal of treatment 424-425. *See also* Adaptive behavior

Self-report measures, 102

Sequential/professional training, 117, 118

Sex factor, 129, T129, 381, 382, 386, 388. *See also* Demographic variables

Shaping, 76, 77, 79, 80, 84

Shaping chips, 77, 78, 81, 82

Shaping class procedures, 483-486

Sheltered environment, 398, 410, 441

Shock treatment, 128, 499n7

Silence in community meetings, 148-149, F149, 156, 206, F207, F270, 271, 279, 328, 329, F329, 330, 341

Small group meetings, 58-59, 60-62, 83; re-educative, 83

"Social Breakdown Syndrome," 3

Social Breakdown Syndrome Gradient Index, 120

Social contacts, 45, 51, 56-57, 82-83; first six months, 152, T153, 154, 155, 156; next two years, 197, 210-211, T212, 213, 215-216, 240; next year and a half, 274-275, T276, 277, 278, 279, 280-281, 302; last six months, 333-335, T336, 337-338, 340, 343, 365; variability in: first six months, T153, 154, 155; next two years, T212, 213; next year and a half, T276, 277, 278, 280-281; last six months, T336, 337-338, 340, 343. *See also* Staff-Resident Interaction Chronograph (SRIC)

Social Learning Ideology items on OMI, 477-478

Social-learning therapy, 7, 9-10; setting and staffing for, 22-30; program content and assessment, 31-36, T32, 79-86; staff performance, 36-40, T37, T38, T39, 41; basic principles and concepts, 74-76; manual, 74-101; token economy in, 76-78, 89-92; procedural rules for staff, 78-79; resident schedule, T32, 77-78, 87-89; staff schedules, 92-101; clinical staff, 102-112; staff training, 113-118; superiority of, over other treatment modalities, 138, 382, 388, 389, 405, 406, 419, 420, 421, 422, 423; ethical and legal status of, 455-463; shaping class procedures in, 483-486; medical meal procedure in, 487

Social pressure, 33, 51, 52, 425

Social reinforcement, 77, 78, 80, 81, 82, 84, 85

Social Restrictiveness, *see* Opinions About Mental Illness Scale (OMI)

Socioeconomic status, 128, T129. *See also* Demographic variables

*Souder v. Brennen*, 446

Speeches, straight, in community meetings: first six months, 148, F149, 156; next two years, 204, 205, F205, F207; next year and a half, 268-270, F269, F270, 279; last six months, 327, F328, 329, 330, 341; target of 148, 206, 270, 327-328, 329, 330, 331, 341; task-oriented, 204, 206, 207, 270, 271, 279, 329. *See also* Interference with community meetings

Staff: ratio of, to residents, T23, 489n9; auxiliary, 25, 28-29, 308, 417, 490n3; research, 26, 180, 371, 488n5; clinical, 26-29, 30, 102-105, T104, 108-112, F109, 136, 180, 247-248; senior, 27, 30, 103, 105, 107, 108, 110, 113, 115, 116, 117, 122, 134, 226, 232, 244, 247, 256, 268-269, 305, 306, 307, 345, 465, 489n1, 490n1; junior, 27-28, 30, 103, 104, 105, 106, 107, 108, F109, 124, 135, 307-308, 345, 489n1, 490n4, 492n1, 493n1, 495n1, 496n1; interaction of, with residents, 34-40, 424; hospital, 36, 37, T37, T38, T39, 40, 41, T104, 105, 107, 108, F109, 110, 111, 112, 167; differential performance of, 36-40, T37, T38, T39, 41; procedural rules for, 53-54, 78-79; responsibilities of, by area, 57, 58, 59, 60, 82-83; schedules for, 65-73, 92-101; turnover in, 105-106, 114, 136, 180, 396, 409; morale problems of, 106, 178, 179, 253-254, 391-392, 464, 467; attitudes and preferences of, 106-112; training of, 113-118, 135, 396, 398, 400, 464, 490n1; errors by, T169, 170-171, 232, T233, 234-235, 236, T294, 296-297, 298, T356, T357, 360, 366, 493n11; reorganization of, 307, 364; and reactivity of measurement, 379, 380, 382, 389; aftercare, 394-405, 417, 420; salaries for, 415, 417, 498; need to reduce violent acts against, 432; relation of, to costs and effectiveness, 464-465; numbers of, 493-494n1, 495n1, 496n1. *See also* Attitudes, staff, toward mental patients; Attitudes, staff, toward treatment programs; Interpretation, staff, of treatment programs; Performance, staff, in psychosocial programs; Staff-Resident Interaction Chronograph (SRIC)

Staff-Resident Interaction Chronograph (SRIC), 34-36, T34, T35, 39, 41, 115, 116, 441, 462; scores: first six months, 163, 166-171, T168, T169, 173-174; next two years, 226-236, F227, T229, F231, T233, 237-238, 241; next year and a half, 289-298, F289, T291, F292, T294, 299-300; last six months, 351-352. F351, T353, F355, T356, T357, 360, 362-363; a year and a half later, 398-405, F399, T401, F402, T404, 411

State hospital, *see* Hospital

Step system, 44-45, 47-48, 52-53, 56, 58, 60-61, 77, 78, 85, 196, 264, 322-323, 458; in follow-up period, 398, 410

Stereotypy/Variability scores, 123, 125; first six months, 152-155, T153; next two years,

211-215, T212, 216; next year and a half, 275-279, T276, 281, 302; last six months, 335-340, T336, 342-344
Stimulus events, 74, 75; discriminative, 75
Straight speeches, *see* Speeches, straight
Stress response, 265, 266, 428-429
Student workers, 179, 397, 488n6
Suggest Alternatives, *see* Staff-Resident Interaction Chronograph (SRIC)
Supervision, 111, 115, 117
Support in community, 5-6, 11, 43, 46, 197-198, 465
Supreme Court decisions, 445-447, 456-457, 458, 500nn10,13

Tear gas, 179
Techniques, *see* Preferred technique scores on TOS
Therapeutic community, 33, 51-53, 329, 432. See also Milieu therapy
Therapist Orientation Sheet (TOS), 103, 108-111, F109, 112, 115, 116, 117, 469-476; scores: first six months, 158-162, F159, 171, 173, 174; next two years, 218, 219-226, F220, 237; next year and a half, 283-289, F285, 297, 299, 300; last six months, 346-350, F347, 362. *See also* Preferred attitude scores; Preferred technique scores
Therapy groups, 83
Time awake, 125, 152, 210, 240, 274, 275, 280, 302, 333, 334, 342, 365
Time out, 78, 79, 136, 178-179, 206, 293, 458, 459; positive aspects of, 226, 431; required reduction of, 226, 244, 246, 253, 254-255, 256, 380; extended, 306, 354, 431; substitution for, 371
Time-Sample Behavioral Checklist (TSBC), 36, 123-125, T131, 132, 378, 426-427, 440, 441, 463; scores: first six months, 138, F139, 141, 152, 154; next two years, 182, 183-184, F183, 188, 210; next year and a half, 249, 250, F250, 251, 257, 258, 260, 274, 275; last six months, F310, 311, 315, 333-335; in follow-up period, 408, F409, 410. *See also* Cognitive dysfunction; Hostile-Belligerence Index; Schizophrenic Disorganization Index; Total Appropriate Behavior Index; Total Inappropriate Behavior Index
Time spent with others, *see* Social contacts
Time spent in programs, 152, 210-211, 274-275, 333-335
Total Appropriate Behavior Index (TSBC and Clinical Frequencies), 123, 125, 126, T131, 378; first six months, F139, 141; next two years, F183, 188-189, 191, 204; next year and a half, F250, 257, 258, 260; last six months, F310, 315, 316; follow-up period, 408, F409, 410. *See also* Instrumental role performance; Interpersonal skills; Self-care
Total Assets Score, 490n3

Total Inappropriate Behavior Index (TSBC and Clinical Frequencies), 123, 125, 126, T131, 132, F409, 430; first six months, 138, 139, F139, 143, 155; next two years, 183, F183, 184, F184, 192, 213; next year and a half, 250, F250, 251, 252, 253; last six months, F310, 310-311, 312, 313, 315, 320, 330, 332, 334, 337; and predictability, 386, 408, 410
Token economy, 10, 33, 76-78, 79, 80, 81, 82, 83, 84, 85, 136, 306-307, 433, 434-435, 436, 437, 462; negative side effects of, 247; in community facility, 396, 397, 398, 405; and legal complications, 457-458, 459-460; shaping class procedures, 483-486
Training: vocational, 7, 28, 43, 46, 197, 398, 410, 456; academic, 58, 81-82, 114-115, 116, 117, 118; staff, 113-118, 396, 398, 400, 464; on-the-job, 115, 116, 117, 118, 135; hospital, 118; follow-up, 410
Transfer: to study locations, 133-134; to community facilities, 370, 395; of decision making and problem solving to client, 394
Trips, group, 46, 192, 193, 246
Turnover, staff, 105-106, 114, 136, 180, 396, 409

Utilization of Consumables Index, 123. *See also* Resource utilization

Value judgments, 444
Variability of resident activity, *see* Stereotypy/Variability scores
Variables, demographic, *see* Demographic variables
Veterans Administration patients, 435, 436
Veterans Administration Psychiatric Evaluation Project, 13
Visiting, 213
Vocational training, 7, 28, 43, 46, 197, 398, 410, 456
Volunteer workers, 46, 179, 213, 216, 397, 465

Weekend activities, 60, 84
Withdrawal study, 136, 175
"With others," 210, 274, 333, 334, 342. *See also* Social contacts
Work of patients: exploitation of, 445-446; payment for, 456; for therapeutic purposes, 456. *See also* Employment; Job assignments
Work with patients, regulation of, 444-449; proposals for, 449-455
Workshop, sheltered, 398, 410
Work skills, 46, 65
Work-training jobs, 398
*Wyatt v. Stickney*, 445, 446, 456-457, 458, 461, 500nn13,17,18

Zone system, 19-20, 22, 488n1